W9-BNV-070

PSYCHOLOGY:
An Introduction

PSYCHOLOGY:
An Introduction

Third Edition

JOSH R. GEROW
Indiana University—Purdue University at Fort Wayne

HarperCollins*Publishers*

Sponsoring Editor: *Anne Harvey*
Development Editor: *Bill Tucker*
Project Editor: *Melonie Parnes*
Text and Cover Design: *Dorothy Bungert*
Cover Photo: *Glen Hartjes, Image Studios, Inc.*
Photo Research: *Cheryl Kucharzak*
Production Manager: *Willie Lane*
Compositor: *Waldman Graphics, Inc.*
Printer and Binder: *R. R. Donnelley & Sons Company*
Cover Printer: *The Lehigh Press, Inc.*

For permission to use copyrighted material, grateful acknowledgment is made to the copyright holders on pp. C1—C3, which are hereby made part of this copyright page.

Psychology: An Introduction, Third Edition
Copyright © 1992 by HarperCollins Publishers Inc.

Library of Congress Cataloging-in-Publication Data

Gerow, Joshua R.
    Psychology : an introduction / Josh Gerow. — 3rd ed.
      p.   cm.
    Includes bibliographical references and indexes.
    ISBN 0-673-46447-4 (student ed.)—ISBN 0-673-46635-3 (teacher ed.)
     1. Psychology.   I. Title.
  BF121.G44   1992
  150—dc20   91-17861
                                                    CIP

91 92 93 94 9 8 7 6 5 4 3 2 1

To Nancy—
and all those who helped

Brief Contents

Detailed Contents

PREFACE

THE ORIGINAL VISION

I had been reviewing other people's books for years, so when I was first approached about writing an introductory psychology textbook, I had a reasonably clear vision of what I wanted that text to be like. What I find most encouraging about seeing *Psychology: An Introduction* evolve to a third edition is that so many psychology instructors seem to share that vision. Two general principles have remained constant throughout:

1. The text is written for the student who is unlikely to take more than one or two additional psychology classes. I have come to call these our "terminal introductory" students. By far, they comprise the majority of the students in my classes over the past 25 years. This may be our only opportunity to have an impact on these students.
2. The text puts into practice what we teach about making learning an effective, interesting, meaningful experience.

From these general principles, several guidelines flow naturally:

- Help beginning students understand the basic methods, concepts, and principles of psychology. Do not try to impress readers with how much you know. Cover the basics fully, but don't overwhelm them with details.

- Provide examples and applications. Then provide more examples. Show how psychology in all its aspects is relevant to the daily life experiences of the student.

- Help the student space or distribute his or her practice. Provide guidance within the text to help the student understand which points are central and which are less so.

- Avoid distracting features, such as built-in quizzes or "boxes" of tangentially related material. If it's interesting and relevant, put it in the text.

- As often as possible, show that today's psychology has emerged from a historical context. All of the "good stuff" of psychology has not been discovered within the last five years.

- Be as intellectually honest as possible. Avoid taking any one point of view when many are possible. Acknowledge that we have many important questions in psychology for which we do not have adequate answers.

- Without disrupting the flow of the text, include as many pedagogical aids as is reasonable. (See "Features of This Text" below.)

- Include illustrations, graphs, tables, and photos that are relevant as well as attractive.

- Assemble a package of ancillary materials that will allow the student to learn and the instructor to teach as easily and effectively as possible.

To remain true to these principles and guidelines and to put them into practice has been a struggle, but with each edition we are getting closer to that original vision.

What Is New in This Edition

Those of you who have used either of the first two editions of *Psychology: An Introduction* will see that the basic structure of the text has not changed. We still have 15 chapters in which each chapter is divided into two short, manageable topics. All of the previously used pedagogical aids have been retained and are described below in the section called "Features of This Text." What, then, is new?

Two changes are immediately noticeable: An entirely new art and design program has been incorporated throughout, and the order of Chapters 8–11 has been changed. All the remaining changes have been made within the 30 topics of the text.

A brief sampling of what is new in this edition includes the following:

Chapter 1—added a section on themes and threads to unite general principles and a section on meta-analysis.

Chapter 2—restructured the chapter and added a section on genetics.

Chapter 3—added sections on subliminal perception and visual pathways beyond the retina.

Chapter 4—added a section on geometric illusions.

Chapter 5—added a section on phobias and their treatment and expanded the section on reinforcement and punishment.

Chapter 6—added sections on biological bases of memory and implicit measures of memory.

Chapter 7—added a section on language acquisition.

Chapter 8—changed order of material, and expanded the section on racial/ethnic differences in IQ.

Chapter 9—expanded the section on moral development and added sections on adolescent sexuality and drug use.

Chapter 10—added a section on personality assessment and updated the section on STDs.

Chapter 11—added sections on eating disorders and theories of emotion.

Chapter 12—added sections on posttraumatic stress disorder and positive/negative symptoms of schizophrenia.

Chapter 13—expanded the section on ECT and updated the section on drug treatment.

Chapter 14—expanded sections on attitudes and bystander intervention.

Chapter 15—expanded sections on personnel selection and health psychology.

FEATURES OF THIS TEXT

There are several things that we have done in order to make the task of learning about psychology as easy and painless as we know how. For one thing, we've provided each instructor with a large assortment of supplementary materials and media to help in teaching the class. These are described below in the section called "Supplements to Accompany the Text." What I want to do here is describe briefly those features that are built-in to the text.

Topics.   Each of the 15 chapters is divided into two topics. Each topic is designed to be freestanding and comprehensible on its own. We see two advantages of this system. (1) It allows the instructor an added degree of flexibility, and (2) it provides material to the student in smaller, more manageable pieces that are coherent and meaningful.

Topic Outline.   Each of the 30 topics (and the Statistical Appendix) opens with a complete outline. This should be the first thing a student reads when beginning an assignment. The outline provides a general overview and shows how the material in the topic is interrelated.

Why We Care—A Topic Preview.   Following the topic outline is a prefatory section that attempts to do what its name suggests: To tell the reader why psychologists care about the material in the topic and, more importantly, why the reader should care. In addition, the section also serves to let the reader know in some detail precisely what will be covered.

Why We Care: A Topic Preview

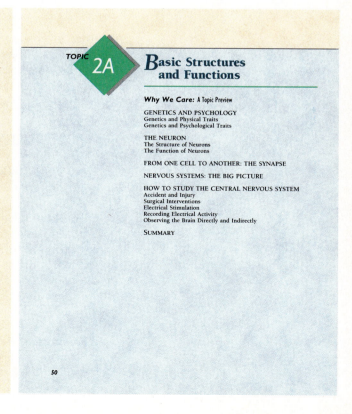

CHAPTER

2

THE BIOLOGICAL BASES OF BEHAVIOR

TOPIC 2A Basic Structures and Functions
TOPIC 2B The Central Nervous System

49

TOPIC

2A

Basic Structures and Functions

Why We Care: A Topic Preview

GENETICS AND PSYCHOLOGY
Genetics and Physical Traits
Genetics and Psychological Traits

THE NEURON
The Structure of Neurons
The Function of Neurons

FROM ONE CELL TO ANOTHER: THE SYNAPSE

NERVOUS SYSTEMS: THE BIG PICTURE

HOW TO STUDY THE CENTRAL NERVOUS SYSTEM
Accident and Injury
Surgical Interventions
Electrical Stimulation
Recording Electrical Activity
Observing the Brain Directly and Indirectly

SUMMARY

50

boldface *important key words and concepts are printed in boldface type in the text. Each term, along with its definition, appears in the margin.*

Why may we claim that psychology is a science?

Marginal, Boldface Glossary. In large measure, learning about psychology is a matter of developing the appropriate vocabulary. Important, key words and concepts are printed in the text in **boldface** type. Each term is defined in the text and the definition is repeated in the margin for ready reference. All definitions are collected in a complete, page-referenced glossary at the end of the text.

Before You Go On Questions. A series of questions labeled *Before you go on* appear throughout each topic. They typically occur after major content sections. This remains one of the most popular features of the text *from the students' point of view.* "Before you go on" questions can be answered easily if the reader has understood the previous material. They provide a quick and simple intermediate review.

Topic Summary. As its name suggests, this section provides a review of all the important material presented in each topic. Each *Topic Summary* is comprised of *Before you go on* questions and answers. You realize, of course that the brief answers to the *Before you go on* questions provided in the *Topic Summaries* are to be taken as suggestions only. Each item in the summary is page referenced.

Practice Test Items for *Psychology: An Introduction,* Third Edition come shrink-wrapped free with each new copy of the text. For each topic in the text, the student will find 15 multiple-choice and 5 true-false items—600 practice items in all. Two things make this feature unique. First, every item was written by the textbook's author. Second, answers are provided in annotated, paragraph form. A student cannot simply glance at a list of letters to see if he or she correctly answered an item. Reasons are provided to let the student know which alternatives are correct, which are incorrect, and *why*.

In order to prepare for a classroom exam, it should not be necessary to reread all of the assigned material. Students should only have to reexamine the *Topic Outline,* review the *Marginal Glossary* terms and the *Topic Summaries* for answers to the *Before you go on* questions, and then test themselves by attempting the questions in the *Practice Test Items* book.

SUPPLEMENTS TO ACCOMPANY THE TEXT

Two Test Banks. Over 3000 professionally reviewed multiple choice and essay questions. Each bank provides 100 test items per chapter.

TestMaster Computerized Test Bank. A powerful test-generation system. TestMaster allows the instructor to construct test files using multiple choice and essay questions from the Gerow test banks. Questions can be exchanged between the TestMaster program and the instructor's word processing software allowing instructors to modify questions and create entirely new questions. It is available for both IBM and Macintosh computers.

Instructor's Resource Kit. An extensive collection of demonstration ideas, teaching strategies, and supplementary lecture notes. The Resource Kit provides a rich source of ideas for experienced teachers as well as new instructors of introductory psychology.

PSYCHOLOGY ENCYCLOPEDIA Laser Disc. One of the most useful teaching aids to come along since the textbook. The laser disc contains both stills—material that would normally be found on slides and transparencies—and video materials. Each frame can be accessed by a hand-held remote control. The PSYCHOLOGY ENCYCLOPEDIA Laser Program does away with the clumsiness of slides and transparencies while simultaneously allowing for greater control over the visual display you give your class.

Video Briefs. A two volume series of video clips ranging in length from 50 seconds to 8 minutes. The briefs help instructors bring experiments, interviews, documentary footage, and dramatic examples into the classroom.

Videos. HarperCollins offers a wide variety of videos through a special media program. Please contact your representative or write to the publisher directly for details.

Transparencies. A set of 100 color transparencies. Many of the transparencies include overlays that permit precise labeling and detail.

Study Guide. Designed to help students get the most from the Gerow introductory text. Each chapter concludes with study tips especially developed for college students.

SuperShell: Computerized Tutorial. Features diagnostic and feedback capabilities. SuperShell provides immediate correct answers and the text page reference on which the topic is presented. When students miss a question, the question begins to appear more frequently. A "flash cards" feature provides a drill to help students learn important terms and concepts. Available for IBM computers.

JOURNEY Interactive Software. Full-color, graphic learning modules in experimental research, the nervous system, learning, development, and psychological assessment. Available for IBM and Macintosh computers.

THE INTEGRATOR. A chapter-by-chapter cross-reference to all software, media, and print materials accompanying *Psychology: An Introduction*, Third Edition. Under each major chapter heading, corresponding references to the appropriate ancillaries are listed (test items, transparencies, videos, films, laser disc and other resources).

For further information on how to obtain any of the package components, please contact your local representative or HarperCollins, College Marketing Group, 10 East 53rd Street, New York, NY 10022-5299.

ACKNOWLEDGMENTS

Although I realize that it sounds cliché, I must first mention my wife, Nancy. She has read all of this manuscript in all of its various forms and has provided me with sound advice throughout. Perhaps more importantly, she remained supportive and encouraging in the face of all of my aggravating behaviors during the process of putting this project together. Once again, my colleagues at IPFW have proven to be a source of support and information. I have "borrowed" their expertise freely and I appreciate their generosity: Bruce Abbott, Ken Bordens, Lenore DeFonso, Dennis Cannon, Nancy Kelley, Carol Lawton, and W. Jeffry Wilson. I also wish to thank Bill Buskist at Auburn University for his contribution to this edition.

Many of the people with whom I worked at HarperCollins were unknown to me before this revision began. They have all done a super job. Bill Tucker served as developmental editor, and it was with Bill that I maintained almost daily contact. From the very first day and very first page, he had made this project his own and has, I suspect, lost as much sleep over it as I have. To the extent that the prose is literate and concepts are explained clearly, we have Bill Tucker to thank. Anne Harvey provided support as psychology editor at HarperCollins. Other "company people" who deserve special mention for their role in putting this text together are: Otis Taylor for his role as Marketing Manager; Leslie Hawke for her help with the supplements; Dorothy Bungert who designed this edition; Cheryl Woike Kucharzak for providing illustrations; and Melonie Parnes in Project Editorial. Finally, a special thanks to Joanne M. Tinsley and Susan Driscoll for their continued support and creativity throughout this project.

Right from the start it was obvious to me that—these days—no one person can write a complete survey of general psychology, even at the introductory level. Previous editions have benefited from the advice and suggestions of scores of fine reviewers. The friends and colleagues who took so much time from their busy schedules to contribute to this revision as supplement authors, test bank reviewers, and manuscript reviewers were enormously helpful. Simply listing names here seems a woefully inadequate acknowledgment of their contribution.

Supplement Authors:

Nancy Kelley, Indiana University-Purdue University/Fort Wayne
Glenda S. Smith, North Harris County College
Sarah Rundle
Eva Conrad, San Bernardino Valley College
Mark Rafter, Chaffey College

Test Bank Reviewers:

Walter Bobkiewicz, Oakton Community College
Grace Galliano, Kennesaw State College
Mary Jo Litten, Kansas State University
Thomas Brothen, University of Minnesota
Bill Buskist, Auburn University

Reviewers:

Michael Aamodt, Radford University; Sharon Akimoto, University of Utah; Mark Alcorn, University of Northern Colorado; Gary Bothe, Pensacola Junior College; Thomas Brothen, University of Minnesota; Robert Brown, Georgia State University; Bill Buskist, Auburn University; Roy Cain, Pan American University; Charlotte Callens, Prince George Community College; James Calhoun, University of Georgia; Karen Christoff, University of Mississippi; Philip Compton, Ohio Northern University; Richard T. Comstock, Monroe Community College; Alfrieda Daly, Rutgers University; Marc

DesLauriers, Kansas City Community College; George Diekhoff, Midwestern State University; David Donovan, Northwestern University; Sherry Ellis, Virginia Commonwealth University; Warren Fass, University of Pittsburg/Bradford; William Filbert, Dodge City Community College; John Flanagan, Eastern Kentucky University; Donald Foshee, Valdosta State University; Margaret Fulton, Edison Community College; David Geary, University of Missouri; Judy Gentry, Columbus State Community College; Robert Gentry, College of Charleston; Fredrich Gibbons, Iowa State University; Bryan Gibson, University of Utah; William Gibson, Northern Arizona State; John Goodwyn, School of the Ozarks; Susan Goodwyn, University of California/Davis; Paula Goolkasian, University of North Carolina; William Gray, University of Toledo; Larry Gregory, New Mexico State University; Bruce Hill, Triton College; Wendy James-Alderidge, Pan American University; Philip Langer, University of Colorado; Robert MacAleese, Spring Hill College; Marian Miller, Psychological Service Association; Daniel D. Moriarty, University of San Diego; Arthur Mueller, Community College of Baltimore; Dennis Nagi, Hudson Valley Community College; James Pate, Georgia State University; Carrol S. Perrino, Morgan State University; Virginia Philo, State University of New York/Albany; John Pinto, Morningside College; Lillian Range, University of Southern Mississippi; Robert Riesenberg, Raymond Walters College; Ernst E. Roberts, El Paso Community College; Aaron Roy, Ashland College; Robert Seibel, Pennsylvania State University; Paul Sheldon, Villanova University; Frank Sjursen, Shoreline Community College; Randall Smith, Ouachita Baptist University; Roy Smith, Mary Washington College; Leo Spindel, Centennial College; Dalmus A. Taylor, Wayne State University; Laura Thompson, New Mexico State; Roscoe Thornthwaite, Pembroke State University; Ann Weber, University of North Carolina; Lisa Whitten, State University of New York/Old Westbury; Clair Wiederholt, Madison Area Technical College; Robert Wiley, Montgomery College; Cynthia Willis, Kansas State University; Richard Willis, University of Pittsburg; Randall Wright, Ouachita Baptist University; Cecilia K. Yoder, Oklahoma City Community College.

I would also like to thank reviewers of the First and Second Editions: Robert Ahlering, Central Missouri State University; Roger Allen, North Central Michigan College; Lou Banderet, Northeastern University; Alan Benton, University of Illinois, Circle Campus; Linda Berg-Cross, Howard University; John Best, Eastern Illinois University; Elaine Blakemore, Indiana University—Purdue University at Fort Wayne; Tom Blakemore, Indiana University—Purdue University at Fort Wayne; Walter Bobkiewicz, Oakton Community College; Cynthia Brandau, Belleville Area Community College; Lynn Brokow, Portland Community College; Gary Brown, Kellogg Community College; William Calhoun, University of Tennessee, Knoxville; Edward Clemmer, Emerson College; Donald Cusumano, St. Louis Community College; William O. Dwyer, Memphis State University; Sandra Edwards, Auburn University; Barbara Engler, Union County College; Jody Esper, Valparaiso University; Terence Fetterman, West Valley College; Linda Flickinger, St. Clair County Community College; Cynthia Ford, Jackson State University; James Frost, Cuyahoga Community College; E. Scott Geller, Virginia Polytechnic Institute; David Griese, SUNY Farmingdale; Ernest Gurman, University of Southern Mississippi; Donald Hall, Radford University; Al Heldt, Grand Rapids Junior College; Sandra Holmes, University of Wisconsin, Stevens Point; Christine Jazwinski, St. Cloud State

University; Carl Johnson, Central Michigan University; Leon Keys, Ferris State College; Linda Leal, Eastern Illinois University; Paulette Leonard, University of Central Arkansas; Ken LeSure, Cuyahoga Community College; Earl Magidson, Kennedy King College; Willie Manning, Clayton State College; Cynthia Marshall, Skyline College; Sue Martel, Cleveland State Community College, Cleveland, Tennessee; Terry Maul, San Bernardino Valley College; Rick McNeese, Sam Houston State University; Karla Miley, Black Hawk College, Quad-Cities Campus; Hal Miller, Brigham Young University; James Nelson, Parkland College; Steve Nida, Franklin University; Faye Tyler M. Norton, Charlottesville, VA; Radha Parker, University of Central Arkansas; Martin Pearlman, Middlesex County Community College; Donald Ragusa, Bowling Green State University; Daniel W. Richards III, Houston Community College; Joel Rivers, Indiana University—Purdue University at Fort Wayne; Joan Rosen, Miami-Dade Community College, South; Steve Rosengarten, Middlesex County Community College; Connie Sanders, University of Tennessee; Michael Scoles, University of Central Arkansas; Fred Shaffer, Northeast Missouri State University; Freddie Shannon, Wayne County Community College; Raymond Shrader, University of Tennessee; W. S. Terry, University of North Carolina, Charlotte; Thomas Tighe, Moraine Community College; Kathy Trabue, Ohio State University; Walter Vernon (deceased), Illinois State University; Wayne Von Bargen, Psychological Service Associates—Fort Wayne, IN; Phyllis Walrad, Macomb Community College; Paul Watson, University of Tennessee; Don Welti, Northern Kentucky University; Ursula White, El Paso Community College; Linda Wickstra, St. Louis Community College; Jeffrey Wilson, Indiana University—Purdue University at Fort Wayne; Paul Wilson, Park Center—Fort Wayne, IN; Mike Zeller, Mankato State University.

Josh R. Gerow

THE NATURE OF PSYCHOLOGY

TOPIC IA   Toward a Definition

TOPIC IB   The Goals and Methods of Psychology

TOPIC

1A

Toward a Definition

Why We Care: A Topic Preview

"Why do I feel this way?" "Why did he do that?" "How can she possibly believe anything so strange?" Questions such as these are fundamental to the human species. Questions about feelings, thoughts, and behaviors have challenged theologians and philosophers for thousands of years. Since late in the nineteenth century, these issues have been at the center of the science of psychology. In this introductory topic, our intent is to define the essential nature of psychology.

We care about the material in this topic because it sets the stage. It introduces, in very general terms, many of the issues, concerns, approaches, and methods that we will be discussing in greater detail throughout the rest of this book. In later chapters we'll explore in detail questions about our emotions, our motivations, our sexuality, and our psychological development. We'll examine the nature and causes of psychological disorders and see how they can be treated. We'll see psychology applied in the classroom, business settings, athletics, and other social situations. We'll examine the relationships between our brain and our behaviors. We'll look at how we process information about the world in which we live through sensation, perception, learning, and memory. But we should start at the beginning and generate a working definition of psychology. Doing so will enable us to focus on psycholgy's subject matter and its general approach to that subject matter (Henley et al., 1989).

Once we have defined psychology, we'll take a very brief look at some of the major events and contributors to its past. As a scientific discipline, psychology did not just spring forth, full-blown, only a few years ago. Of particular interest will be the observation that throughout its history, the very definition of psychology has changed a number of times. By examining its history, we can more fully appreciate the nature of psychology as we know it now, at the close of the twentieth century. Indeed, once we have reviewed some history, we'll summarize some of the approaches that can be found in modern psychology today.

This topic ends with a discussion of some of the abiding themes and threads that have been central to psychology throughout the years. These themes are overarching areas of concern and interest within psychology. What makes them "threads" is that we will find them interwoven throughout the rest of our discussion. In fact, we often will be reminded of many of the points raised in this topic as we progress through subsequent chapters.

DEFINING PSYCHOLOGY

psychology *the scientific study of behavior and mental processes*

Psychology is the science of behavior and mental processes. This is a standard and fairly common definition—one that millions of psychology students before you have commited to memory. If there is a problem with this definition, it's that it is somewhat sterile; it doesn't tell us very much about what psychologists actually study or how they go about it. We'll take the rest of this chapter, and in fact the rest of this book, to fill in the details in an attempt to make this definition more meaningful. First, let's see what it means to say that psychology is a science; then we'll consider the subject matter of psychology.

Psychology Is a Science

There are many ways to find out about ourselves and the world in which we live. Some of what we have come to believe we have taken as a matter of faith ("There is a God—or there isn't"). Some of our understanding has come through tradition, passed on from previous generations, accepted simply because "they said it is so." Some of what we believe we credit to "common sense" ("You beat a dog often enough and sooner or later it will get mean"). Some of the insights that we have about ourselves and the human condition we have taken from works of art, from literature, poetry, and drama. Psychology, however, claims that there is a better way to come to an understanding of its subject matter: by applying the values and methods of science.

Given that psychology is a science, we should have some appreciation of what it is that qualifies a discipline to be a science. Most simply put, we can say that a **science** is an organized body of knowledge gained through application of scientific methods. So to qualify as a science, a discipline has to demonstrate two things: (1) the existence of an organized body of knowledge and (2) the use of scientific methodology.

science *an organized body of knowledge gained through application of scientific methods*

1. **An organized body of knowledge:** Over the years, psychologists have accumulated a great deal of information about their subject matter. We have learned much about the behaviors and mental processes of organisms, both human and nonhuman. We are coming to understand how feelings, behaviors, and thoughts affect our nervous systems and vice versa. We have developed a reasonably clear vision of how we learn about the world in which we live and how we remember what we have learned. We can now identify many of the determinants of individual growth and development. We have isolated many of the factors that influence the adjustments organisms make to their environments and to each other, and we at least have a sense of how such adjustments can become maladaptive.

   To be sure, we can still ask many interesting and important questions for which we have no good answers. Not having all the answers can be frustrating at times, but that is part of the excitement of psychology; there are still so many questions to be answered. The truth is, however, that psychologists *have* learned much about their subject matter. What is known is reasonably well organized. You have in your hands one version of the organized collection of knowledge that is psychology. In terms of our first requirement, then, psychology is a science.

2. Gained through scientific methods: What we know in psychology we have learned through the application of **scientific methods**, which we may define as systematic procedures of observation, description, control, and replication. To explain something scientifically is often a matter of ruling out, or eliminating, alternative explanations. It is important to realize that the "scientific method" is as much an attitude or an approach to problem solving as it is a carefully delineated set of procedures that must be followed rigorously. There is no one way to do science.

There are, however, some guidelines. The basic process goes something like this: The scientist (psychologist) makes observations about his or her subject matter (behavior and/or mental processes). On the basis of these observations, a **hypothesis** is developed. A hypothesis is a tentative explanation of some phenomenon that can be tested and then either supported or rejected. In a way, a hypothesis is an educated guess about one's subject matter.

After formulating a hypothesis, the scientist again observes and describes relevant events, which are analyzed to see if the hypothesis was well founded. Alternative hypotheses or explanations are examined also. The results of one's investigation are then communicated to others who may test them further. In science, one's hypothesis may be rejected or it may be supported, but it cannot be "proven" as true. This is because, no matter how much support one finds for one's hypothesis, there still may be other, alternative hypotheses, as yet unthought of, that will do a better job of explaining the observed phenomenon.

And so it is with all sciences. Specific techniques and procedures vary considerably from one science to another. But then the scientific status of psychology does not depend on the extent to which it resembles chemistry, or physics, or biology, but on how well it explains behavior and mental processes (Simon, 1990). For that matter, the specific procedures that psychologists use vary considerably. We'll review some of the more commonly used methods of psychologists in Topic 1B, where we'll consider a number of examples. For now what is important is the realization that through its reliance on scientific methods, psychology fulfills our second requirement for qualifying as a science.

scientific methods *systematic procedures of discovery that include observation, description, control, and replication*

hypothesis *a tentative proposition or explanantion that can be tested and confirmed or rejected*

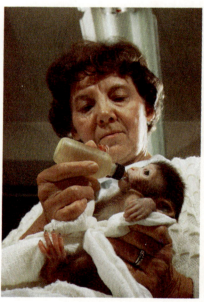

When studying behavior and mental processes, psychologists often find it convenient, if not necessary, to use nonhuman animals in their research.

BEFORE
YOU GO
ON

Why may we claim that psychology is a science?

The Subject Matter of Psychology

Simply skimming through the pages of this book should quickly convince you that trying to list everything that psychologists study would not be very instructive. Our list would be altogether too long to be useful. However, it would be fair to suggest, as our definition does, that the subject matter of psychology is behavior and mental processes. We've already noted that psychologists are interested in studying both human and nonhuman organisms. Now let's explore a bit more fully what it is about organisms that psychologists seek to understand.

behavior *what an organism does; an action of an organism that can be observed and measured*

Psychologists Study Behavior. By **behavior** we mean what organisms *do*; how they act, react, and respond. Some of the behaviors of organisms are observable and—at least potentially—can be measured. If I am concerned with whether a rat will press a lever under some circumstance, I can observe its behavior directly. If I wonder about Susan's ability to draw a circle, I can ask her to do so and observe her efforts. Observable, measurable behaviors such as lever pressing and circle drawing have an advantage as a subject matter of a science because they are **publicly verifiable**. That is, a number of observers (public) can agree on (verify) the behavior of the organism being studied. We can all agree that the rat did or did not press the lever or that Susan drew a circle, not a triangle. Events, including behaviors, that can be publicly verified have greater credibility in science. Susan may believe that she can draw a circle (and that belief may be of some interest), but if she cannot or will not actually do so, why should we believe her own self-report?

publicly verifiable *the agreement (verifiability) of observers (public) that an event did or did not take place*

Psychologists Study Mental Processes. When psychology first emerged as a separate discipline late in the nineteenth century, it was defined as the science of **mental processes**, or the science of consciousness. Eventually, it became clear that mental processes were not easy to study, particularly for a discipline struggling to demonstrate that it was a science. The problem was (and still is) that mental processes are private and personal, and thus are difficult to verify publically. After all, your mental activity goes on in *your mind*, and I can't get into your mind to share those activities with you. For nearly 50 years in this century (from the 1920s to the 1970s), mental processes were virtually ignored by psychology, which focused instead on the study of observable behaviors. Now no one ever denied that mental processes existed, or claimed that they were unimportant or uninteresting. The issue was that psychology simply was not prepared to study mental processes in a scientific manner.

mental processes *internal activities of consciousness, including cognitions and affect*

Mental processes can be divided into two major types: cognitions and affect. **Cognitions** include one's perceptions, beliefs, thoughts, ideas, and the like. *Cognitive* processes include such activities as perceiving, thinking, knowing, understanding, and remembering. On the other hand, **affect** refers to one's feelings, mood, or emotional state. Here we have a scheme that we will encounter repeatedly: the *ABCs* that comprise the subject matter of psychology. That is, the subject matter of psychology may be taken to be *a*ffect, *b*ehavior, and *c*ognition. To understand a person at any given time, or to be able to predict what one will do next, we have to understand what he or she is feeling (*A*), doing (*B*), and thinking (*C*).

cognitions *the mental processes of knowing, perceiving, thinking, remembering, and the like*

affect *the feelings or mood that accompany an emotional reaction*

The study of mental processes is now clearly entrenched in mainstream psychology. We'll see throughout this book many examples of how psychologists have managed to learn about internal, private, and personal mental events and at the same time maintain scientific respectibility. After all, a psychology silent on such topics as thinking, planning, problem solving, and feeling would be barren indeed (Kimble, 1989).

Psychologists Use Operational Definitions. In general terms we say that psychologists study what organisms do, how they feel, and what they think. Psychologists find it useful, and occasionally imperative, to define their subject matter in terms of the operations they use to measure it. When they do so, they are using **operational definitions**. Operational definitions define concepts in terms of the procedures used to measure them. Let's look at a few examples.

Let's say we are interested in the conditions under which a rat turns left, rather than right, in a maze (Figure 1.1). Now it seems like a relatively simple matter to determine the direction that a rat turns in a maze. But what will constitute *a turn*? How will you *measure* the turn of a rat in a maze? Will sticking its nose around the corner be taken as a turn? What if it gets most of its body around the corner and then scoots back? Does the rat's tail have to make it all the way round? As silly as it may sound, you may have to operationally define *a turn in the maze* by specifying just how you intend to measure it.

What if we wanted to compare the behaviors of hungry and nonhungry rats in the same maze? How do we know when a rat is hungry? How will we define *hungry rat*? What we can do is offer an operational definition, specifying that—at least for our study—a hungry rat is one that has been deprived of food for 24 hours. (Alternatively we may operationally define a hungry rat as one that has lost 15 percent, or 20 percent, of its normal body weight.)

Operational definitions become particularly useful when we consider mental processes. How shall we define *anxiety* in a study comparing the performance of students who experience either high or low anxiety during test taking? How shall we define *intelligence* if we want to compare the intelligence of students who have had access to a preschool program with students who have not? Terms like anxiety and intelligence are difficult to define precisely or in ways with which all psychologists would agree. Sometimes our only recourse is to use operational definitions and specify how we intend to measure these concepts during the course of our study. We

operational definition *a definition of a concept given in terms of the methods (or operations) used to measure that concept*

Figure **1.1**

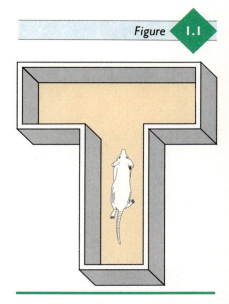

A rat in a T-maze. Determining whether a rat turns left or right may necessitate operationally defining what we mean by "turn."

Because we cannot observe a person's intelligence directly, we may choose to operationally define intelligence as "that which an IQ test measures."

might operationally define *anxiety* in terms of measurable changes in some physiological processes such as blood pressure, heart rate, and sweat gland activity. We might operationally define *intelligence* as the score on a certain psychological test.

There are some limitations with operational definitions. They may *over*simplify truly complex concepts (surely, there is more to what we mean by intelligence than a few numbers from a test). On the other hand, they *do* allow us to specify exactly how we are going to measure the behavior or mental process we are studying, and as a result, they help us communicate accurately with others. Operational definitions also can be used to side step lengthy philosophical discussions. Rather than agonizing over the "true" nature of intelligence, we operationally define intelligence as "that which an IQ test measures." Rather than considering all of the factors that affect the aging process, we may operationally define old age as "living for 65 years or more." Notice that someone else may choose to define old age as "living for 75 years or more." Such a definition would be no more right or wrong than the first. It is simply different. Have you noticed that medical science has had to resort to an operational definition of what it means to be dead? With increases in organ transplant surgery, one must be quite certain what one means when declaring a patient "dead." We will see many examples of operational definitions throughout this text.

BEFORE YOU GO ON

What is the subject matter of psychology?

What are operational definitions, why do we use them, and what are their limitations?

PSYCHOLOGICAL APPROACHES PAST AND PRESENT

No two psychologists approach their subject matter in exactly the same way. As individuals, psychologists bring their own experiences, expertise, values, and prejudices to the study of behavior and mental processes. This is true today, and it always has been the case. In this section we can add to our definition of psychology by considering some of the major perspectives or approaches that have evolved throughout psychology's history. Let's begin by considering the origins of the independent discipline of psychology.

Psychology's Roots in Philosophy and Science

Psychology did not simply appear full-blown as the productive, scientific enterprise that we know today. We already have made the point that most of the questions that engage psychologists (and you and me) today can be traced to the beginnings of our species on the planet. But seeking answers to one's questions about behavior and mental processes in a casual way is quite different from looking for such answers in a systematic, formal way. The formal roots of psychology can be found in both philosophy and science.

We first credit the philosophers for suggesting that it is a reasonable and potentially profitable endeavor to seek explanations of human behaviors at a human level. After all, most of the earliest explanations tended to be largely at the level of God—or the gods. If someone were smarter than you, well, it was because God willed it that way. If someone suffered from fits of terrible depression that could not be attributed to any obvious cause, it was because that someone had offended the gods. What philosophers did was to convince us that we might be able to explain why people did what they did and felt and thought as they did without constant reference to God's intentions in the matter.

Take the French philosopher René Descartes (1596–1650) for example. Descartes liked to think about the nature of thinking. As he "lay abed of a morning thinking" (something that even his schoolmaster allowed given that Descartes was so good at it), he pondered how the human body and mind functioned to produce the very process he was then engaged in—thinking. For us, Descartes's main contribution was that he envisioned the human body to be rather like a piece of machinery—intricate, complicated machinery to be sure, but machinery nonetheless. If the body was composed essentially of tubes and gears and valves and fluids, then its operation must be subject to natural, physical laws, and those laws could be, and should be, discovered. Descartes went a bit further. Humans possess more than just a body. They have "souls" or minds. It is likely that the mind also functions through the actions of knowable laws, but getting at these laws is likely to be a bit more difficult. Here's where Descartes had a truly important insight. We *can* learn about the mind, and the laws under which it operates, because the mind and the body *interact* with each other. That interaction takes place in the head, probably the brain (actually, in the pineal gland, thought Descartes). We call Descartes's position in these matters **interactive dualism**. *Dualism* because the mind and the body are separate entities, and *interactive* because they influence each other. Thus we have with Descartes the real possibility that we might be able to understand the mind, how it works, and how it interacts with the body.

Nearly 100 years later, across the English Channel, a group of British thinkers moved philosophy—at least that part of philosophy concerned with the human mind and how it worked—very close to what was soon to become psychology. This group got their start from the writings of John Locke (1632–1704). Locke was sitting around with some friends after dinner one evening discussing philosophical issues when it became clear that no one in the group really understood how the human mind comes to understand anything, much less complex philosophical dilemmas. Locke thought that by their next meeting, he could provide the group with a short explanation of the nature of human understanding. What was to have been a simple exercise took Locke many years to complete and provided philosophers with a whole new set of ideas to deal with.

Locke, and those who followed his initiative, are known as **British empiricists**. Their major concern was how we come to represent the world "out there" in the internal world of the mind. Others (including Descartes) had asked this very question before, and many had assumed that we are born with certain basic ideas—notions about ourselves, the world, and, of

René Descartes

John Locke

interactive dualism *Descartes's position that a separate body and mind influence each other and are thus knowable*

British empiricists *philosophers (including Locke) who claimed, among other things, that the contents of mind come from experience*

course, God. Locke and the other empiricists thought otherwise. They believed that we are born into this world with our minds empty, essentially like blank slates. (The notion of the mind as a blank slate, or *tabula rasa*, was not new with Locke; it had been introduced as far back as Aristotle [384–322 B.C.]). So how does the mind come to be filled with all its ideas, thoughts, and memories? To this question Locke answered, "In one word, from *experience*."

Philosophy had gone nearly to the brink. Attention clearly was focused on the mind, how it worked, what contents it held, where those contents (ideas) came from, how those ideas could be manipulated, and how the mind and the body could influence each other. But philosophers are philosophers; they think about their subject matter. They are not scientists. Could the methods of science provide answers to some of the philosophers' questions?

Charles Darwin

During the nineteenth century, natural science was making progress on virtually every frontier. By the middle of the century, Charles Darwin (1809–1882) had returned from his lengthy sea voyage on the *Beagle*, and in 1859 published his revolutionary *The Origin of Species*, which reported his observations from his trip and also spelled out the details of evolution. Few nonpsychologists were ever to have as much influence on psychology as did Darwin. What Darwin did for psychology was to confirm that the human species as an object was part of the natural world of animals, special through no particular divine intervention. The methods of science could and should be turned to try to understand this creature of nature called human. Darwin also made it clear that the different species of this planet are, in a nearly infinite number of ways, related to one another. The impact of this reality, of course, is that something that we discover about the nature of the sloth or the ground squirrel or the rhesus monkey may enlighten us about ourselves.

Gustav Fechner

In 1860, a year after the debut of *The Origin of Species*, a German physicist, Gustav Fechner (1801–1887) published a volume that certainly was unique as a physics text. Fechner applied his training in the methods of physics to the psychological process of sensation. What, Fechner wondered, was the nature of the relationship between the physical characteristics of a stimulus and the psychological experience of sensing that stimulus? For example, if the intensity of a light source is doubled, will an observer see that light as being twice as bright as it was before? Fechner found that the answer was no. Using the precise scientific procedures of a physicist, Fechner went on to determine the mathematical relationship that exists between certain physical aspects of stimuli and a person's psychological experience of those stimuli. What Fechner did was to apply the methods of science to a fundamentally psychological question about the mind and experience.

The mid-1800s also found physiologists coming to a better understanding of how the human body functions. By then it was known that nerves carry electrical messages to and from different parts of the body, and that the nerves serving vision are different from those that serve hearing and the other senses and are different, too, from those that activate muscles and glands. Of all the great biologists/physiologists of the nineteenth century, the one whose work is most relevant to the beginning of psychology is Hermann von Helmholtz (1821–1894). Although a physician by trade, von Helmholtz's true love was pure science, the laboratory, and research. In the physiology laboratory, von Helmholtz developed an interest in matters that were clearly psychological. He performed experiments and wrote theories on how the nervous system is involved in reflex behaviors, on how long it takes to react to stimuli, on how we process information through our senses, on how we experience color, and on similar issues of a psychological nature. But in the mid-1800s there was no psychology—at least no formal, recognized science of psychology as we know it today.

By the late nineteenth century, psychology's time had come. Philosophy had become intrigued with mental processes, the nature and the sources of ideas, and the contents of the mind. Physiology and physics had begun to focus attention on the operation of the nervous system—on sensation and perception—and were doing so using scientific methodology. Biologists were raising questions about relationships between humankind and other species, and about how mental processes might help us to adapt and to survive. What was needed was someone with a clear vision to unite these interests and these methods to establish a separate discipline. Such a person was Wilhelm Wundt.

Hermann von Helmholtz

BEFORE YOU GO ON

In what way did the philosophy of Descartes and Locke prepare the way for psychology?

In what way did the science of Darwin, Fechner, and von Helmholtz influence the emergence of psychology?

Psychology Begins: The Early Years

It is generally claimed that psychology "began" in 1879 when Wilhelm Wundt (1832–1920) officially opened his laboratory at the University of Leipzig. Wundt had been educated to practice medicine, and he had studied physiology. At Heidleberg University he served as a laboratory assistant to the great von Helmholtz. He also held an academic position in philosophy. Wundt was a scientist/philosopher with an interest in such psychological processes as sensation, perception, attention, word associations, and emotions.

Wundt wanted to find out how the mind worked. He wanted to be able to carefully and systematically describe its contents. For Wundt, psychology was the scientific study of the mind, of consciousness. He was a scientist who left nothing to chance. All of his hypotheses were to be tested and then retested in his laboratory under carefully controlled conditions.

One of Wundt's most successful students was an Englishman, Edward B. Titchener (1867–1927), who left the laboratory in Leipzig to open his own at Cornell University in New York state; he remained there for 35 years. Titchener championed the cause of Wundt's psychology—his scientific study of the mind— and extended some of Wundt's methods. (It's also now clear that he distorted some of Wundt's ideas to suit his own purposes.) He continued to do experiments and he refined **introspection**, a method for studying consciousness first used in Wundt's laboratory. In-

Wilhelm Wundt (center) and students in the Leipzig laboratory.

introspection *a technique in which one examines one's own mental experiences and reports them in the most fundamental, basic way*

Edward B. Titchener

William James

functionalism *an approach to psychology emphasizing the study of the mind and consciousness as they help the organism adapt to the environment*

trospection literally means to look within, and Titchener trained many students to do just that—to look into the workings of their own mind and report what they saw. Titchener trained many students because he, like Wundt, did not believe that just anybody could introspect with accuracy and consistency—two hallmarks of good science. Introspectors were to avoid using common words or labels for the objects they observed. Thus a banana was not to be described as "a banana," but it was to be described as it was experienced in consciousness, in the most basic of terms, such as "yellowness" and "smoothness," for example. The technique was used in many experiments where introspective descriptions of experiences were recorded over and over again as stimulus characteristics were modified under different conditions. Introspection in the formal sense that Wundt and Titchener used it was eventually abandoned by psychology, but introspection in the sense of, "Try to describe to me how you feel, or what you're thinking about right now" is still a useful source of information.

About the same time that Wundt's and Titchener's laboratories were flourishing, an American philosopher at Harvard University, William James (1842–1910), began to take issue with the sort of psychology that was practiced there. James never thought of himself as a psychologist, although he taught classes in the subject, opened a demonstration laboratory (in 1875, even before Wundt's), and published a wonderful two-volume textbook in 1890, *Principles of Psychology*. William James did agree that psychology should rightfully study the mind and consciousness. He defined psychology as "the science of mental life," a definition very similar to Wundt's. He thought that the German-trained psychologists were off base trying to discover the contents and structure of the human mind. (Titchener had named his type of psychology "structuralism.") James argued that consciousness cannot be broken down and analyzed into elements or particles. Consciousness is dynamic, a stream of events, personal, changing, and continuous. Psychology should be concerned not with the structure of the mind, but with its function. The focus of study should be on the practical *uses* of the mind and mental life. In this regard, James was responding to the lead of Darwin. To survive requires that members of a species adapt to the environment. How does the mind function to help the organism adapt and survive in the world?

James's practical approach to psychology found favor in North America, and a new type of psychology emerged—largely at the University of Chicago. There, psychologists continued to focus their scientific study on the mind, but emphasized the utilitarian, adaptive functions of the mind. As a result, we refer to this approach to psychology as **functionalism**. It was well established by the 1920s. Functionalist psychologists relied heavily on experimental methods, continued to use introspection (although they were much less rigid than Titchener about how to do so), and introduced the study of animals to psychology. Accepting and fostering the study of animals in the psychology laboratory is a direct influence of Darwin. In fact, one of the characteristics of functionalism in general was its willingness to be open to a wide range of topics—so long as they were in some way related to mental life, adaptation, and practical application. As a result, we can trace the origin of child psychology, educational psychology, and social, industrial, and organizational psychology to this approach.

As more and more bright young scientists were drawn to the study of psychology, academic departments and laboratories began to prosper throughout the United States and Canada. Scientific psychology was well under way. Regardless of one's particular interest, psychology was the scientific study of the mind, its structures, and/or its functions.

BEFORE YOU GO ON

When and where did psychology "begin," and whom do we credit with formally establishing the discipline?

Briefly describe the first approaches that psychologists took toward their subject matter.

Behaviorism

John B. Watson (1878–1958) was born on a farm in South Carolina. In his last year at nearby Furman University, Watson's mother died, thus relieving one of the pressures he felt to enter the ministry. Instead, he enrolled as a graduate student in psychology at the University of Chicago. He had read about the new science of psychology as an undergraduate and thought that Chicago would be the best place to study. He was soon very disappointed. It turned out that he had little flair for introspection and developed little sympathy for attempts to study mental processes and consciousness with scientific methods. Even so, he stayed on as a psychology major, studying the behavior of animals, white rats in particular.

With his Ph.D. in hand, at the age of 29, Watson moved to Johns Hopkins University in Baltimore, where he nearly single-handedly changed the nature of psychology. Watson argued that if psychology were to become a mature, productive scientific enterprise, it had to give up its preoccupation with the mind and mental activity. Psychology should concentrate on something that can be observed and measured. It should give up the study of the mind and focus on *behavior*: hence the name of a new approach to psychology: **behaviorism**.

Neither Watson nor the behaviorists that followed him ever claimed that people do not think, have ideas, or form mental images. What he did say was that such processes were not the proper subjects of scientific investigation. Science must focus on those events that observers can measure and agree upon, and behaviors fit the bill. No one else, after all, can share your thoughts, your ideas, or your images. We have no way of seeing what you see in your mind's eye. Watson argued that we ought to leave all these private, mental events to the philosophers and theologians, and make psychology as rigorously scientific as possible. Watson once referred to behaviorism as "common sense grown articulate. Behaviorism is a study of what people *do*" (Watson, 1926, p. 724).

No one has epitomized the behaviorist approach to psychology more than B. F. Skinner (1904–1990). Skinner took Watson at his word and spent a long and productive professional career in psychology attempting to demonstrate that we can predict and even control the behaviors of organisms by studying relationships between their overt, observable responses and the circumstances under which those responses are made.

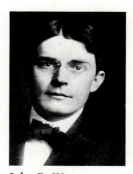

John B. Watson

behaviorism *an approach to psychology emphasizing the overt, observable, measurable behavior of organisms*

B. F. Skinner

Skinner simply has avoided any reference to the internal states of his subjects, be they rats, pigeons, or people. What matters for Skinner is how behaviors are modified by changes in the environment. Behaviorists would not address the question of "why" a rat turns left in a maze by talking about what the rat wanted or what the rat was thinking at the time. Rather, they would try to specify the environmental conditions (the presence of food, perhaps) under which a rat is likely to make left turns—we should focus on observable events and leave the internal affairs of the organism out of our explanations. For more than 50 years, Skinner consistently held to the argument that psychology should be defined as "the science of behavior" (Skinner, 1987, 1990).

In the 1990s we can find little left of the approach to psychology taken by Wundt and/or Titchener. We can see in the diversity of psychology today many of the ideas and the questions of functionalism, but functionalism *as a specific approach* to psychology is no longer with us. On the other hand, behaviorism—to varying degrees and in different varieties—is still with us. Indeed, many believe that it remains the dominant approach to psychology. What we'll do now is briefly take a look at some of the other approaches to psychology that are also still in evidence today.

Psychoanalysis

We will have ample opportunity to discuss the many and varied contributions of Sigmund Freud (1856–1939) in later chapters. We'll refer to Freud in our discussions of child psychology, memory, consciousness, personality theory, and psychotherapy. Freud was born in what is now Czechoslavakia, and he moved to Vienna with his family when he was 4 years old. He remained a resident of Vienna until the Nazi invasion in 1938 when he moved to England, where he died the next year.

Freud was trained in medicine, but his intellectual love was science and research. He practiced as a physician out of economic necessity and became intrigued with what were then called "nervous disorders." Freud

Sigmund Freud

was struck by how little was known about these disorders and chose to specialize in psychiatry.

In fact, Freud was not a laboratory scientist. He performed few experiments. Most of his insights concerning the nature of the mind came from his careful observations of his patients and himself. Freud's works were particularly perplexing to the behaviorists. They were arguing against a psychology that concerned itself with consciousness, and here was Freud declaring that one's mental processes and behaviors were subject to forces of which we were not aware. Our thoughts and actions are often under the influence of the *unconscious* mind, wrote Freud. Many of our behaviors are expressions of instinctive strivings, he claimed. Freud's views were clearly at odds with those of Watson.

Not only did Freud study and write about the nature of personality and its development, but he also put his thoughts into practice in the diagnosis and treatment of psychological disorders. We call the approach to psychology that traces its origins to Sigmund Freud **psychoanalysis**.

psychoanalysis *a Freudian approach to psychology emphasizing the influence of the unconscious and instincts*

BEFORE YOU GO ON

Briefly summarize behaviorism and psychoanalysis as approaches to psychology.

Humanistic Psychology

An approach we call **humanistic psychology** or, simply, humanism, arose in many respects as a reaction against behaviorism *and* psychoanalysis. Its original leaders were Carl Rogers (1902–1987) and Abraham Maslow (1908–1970). Humanistic psychologists take the position that the individual or the self should be the central concern of psychology. It is their argument that we need to focus on the "person" in psychology. If we only attend to stimuli in the environment and overt responses to those stimuli, we're leaving the person out of the middle—and that's dehumanizing. Such matters as caring, intention, concern, will, love, and hate are real phenomena and worthy of scientific investigation whether they can be directly observed or not. Any attempt to understand people without considering such processes will be doomed. Rogers and Maslow, and their intellectual heirs, also tend to emphasize the possibility of personal growth and achievement. To the humanists, Freudian reliance on instincts as even partially responsible for human action was too controlling. Our biology notwithstanding, we are—or can be—in control of our destinies. Taking this approach led Maslow to develop a theory of human motivation (see Topic 11A) and Rogers to develop a system of psychotherapy (see Topic 13B).

humanistic psychology *an approach to psychology emphasizing the person or self as a central matter of concern*

Carl Rogers

Abraham Maslow

Gestalt Psychology

In the first quarter of this century a group of German scientists was taking an approach to psychology that was decidedly different from that of Wundt, James, or Watson. Under the leadership of Max Wertheimer

gestalt *whole, totality, configuration; where the whole (gestalt) is seen as more than the sum of its parts*

(1880–1943), this approach became known as Gestalt psychology. Now, **gestalt** is one of those words that is very difficult to translate literally into English. It means "whole," or "configuration," or "totality." In general terms, if you can see the big picture, if you can focus on the forest and not the individual trees, you have formed a gestalt. Indeed, it was the big picture of perception and consciousness that intrigued the Gestalt psychologists.

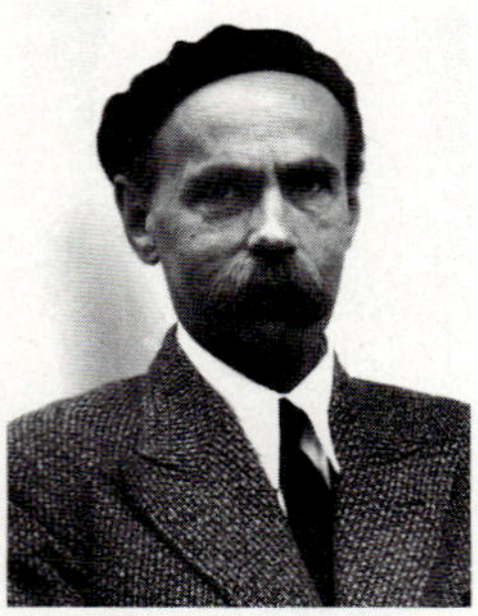

Max Wertheimer

Gestalt psychologists argued against trying to analyze perception, or awareness, or consciousness into discrete, separate entities. To do so would be to destroy the very essence of what was being studied. "The whole is *more* than the sum of its parts," they said. When we look at a drawing of a cube, we do not see individual lines and angles and surfaces. We naturally combine these elements to form a whole, a gestalt, which we recognize as a cube. When we look at a banana we see a banana and not yellowness or smoothness, no matter what Titchener's introspectionists might want to tell us.

As Locke would have wanted, Gestalt psychologists focused largely on perception. Among other things, they examined the factors that determine which of many stimuli we attend to. They developed principles to describe how we organize the world we perceive, how we form meaningful gestalts from the bits and pieces of our sensory experience. Gestalt psychologists recognized that one's perception and thus one's knowledge requires a context or frame of reference. It is often the context in which it occurs that gives a stimulus its meaning (see Figure 1.2). Unlike Locke, the Gestalt psychologists claimed that some basic, set ways of perceiving the world are innate and unlearned. That is, *everything* in the mind need not come through experience as Locke had argued. We see the world in three dimensions; we attend to contrasts between adjacent stimuli; stimuli in motion tend to grab our attention; large stimuli appear to us closer than small ones. Why? Gestalt psychologists would say, "because"—because that's the way we were born to see, and learning or experience has little to do with it.

Figure 1.2

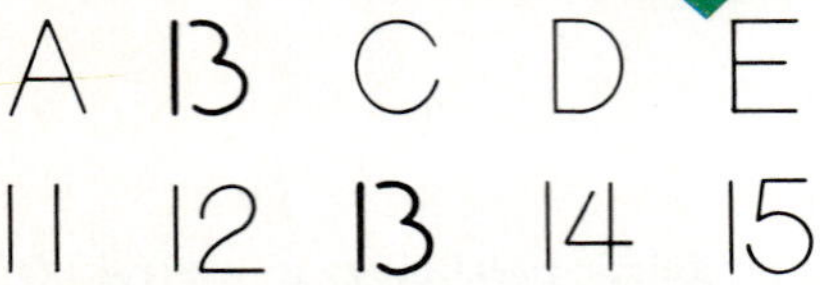

Gestalt psychologists believe that the meaning of events reflects an appreciation of the context in which they appear. Is the bold figure a B or a 13?

BEFORE YOU GO ON

What is the major thrust of the humanistic approach in psychology?

What does gestalt mean?

What area of psychology was of major concern to the Gestalt psychologists?

The Psychology of Individual Differences and Mental Measurement

Our review of history has thus far focused on rather formal approaches to psychology. Paralleling these developments, others were taking a more applied approach to behavior and mental processes. These pioneers directed their attention to the measurement of individual differences.

Sir Francis Galton (1822–1911) was a first cousin of Charles Darwin and was greatly influenced by him. Galton was intrigued by the theory of evolution and by the promise that it held for the possible improvement of the human race. Galton reasoned that if only the very best of the species were allowed to have children, in the long run only the very best of characteristics would survive, and humankind would be all that much better off. He reasoned further that before one could improve the human condition, one needed to measure and catalog the range of human abilities and aptitudes as they exist at the moment. Galton set out to do just that. He devised countless tests of individual differences—the ways in which persons are different from each other. The tradition in psychology that recognizes individual differences and attempts to measure them accurately and reliably comes from Galton's original efforts. In many ways it is fair to refer to Galton as the founder of psychological testing. Galton also devised many statistical procedures to help him deal with the vast amount of data (measurements) that his mental tests generated.

Sir Francis Galton

At the turn of the century, Alfred Binet (1857–1911) advanced Galton's work on testing. Binet was given a real, practical problem by the French Ministry of Education. Could he devise an instrument to assess the educational potential of young schoolchildren? Could "general intelligence" be measured? Binet thought that it could, and by 1900 he wrote a number of tests to do just that. Aided by Théophile Simon, he published a test of intelligence in 1905. The original Binet-Simon test has undergone a number of significant revisions, most recently in 1986. One of the most notable revisions was published in 1916 by Lewis Terman at Stanford University, at which time the test became known as the Stanford-Binet Intelligence Scale. This revision translated Binet's test into English and "Americanized" many of the items.

Psychological testing is obviously a major industry in North America. The psychological testing of mental or cognitive skills and aptitudes has become a political issue. Can tests be used to guide employment decisions? When? Under what conditions? Do the paper-and-pencil instruments that are being used as college entrance exams (such as the SAT or ACT) do what they are designed to do? We'll get to these questions, and other related issues, in Chapter 8. For now, we simply acknowledge that the concern for individual differences and for measuring those differences have been with us in psychology for nearly 100 years.

BEFORE YOU GO ON

What were the major contributions of Sir Francis Galton and Alfred Binet to the development of psychology?

Modern Approaches

So far in this topic, we have offered a definition of psychology and have taken a glance at psychology's past. In this section, let's follow some of our own advice. We've suggested that when scientists are faced with a concept that is difficult to define in abstract terms, they often rely on operational definitions. Well, here's a sort of operational definition of psychology: *Psy-*

Clinical and counseling psychologists occasionally find that having patients engage in purposeful activities, such as painting, can be therapeutic.

chology is what psychologists do. I'm sure that you recognize that this definition is tongue in cheek. I'm not proposing it as a serious definition of psychology, but there is something to be said for it. One of the things that you'll be learning about in this course is the wide range of things that psychologists do. In a sense, this course and this text provide a definition of psychology. If you were to ask me what psychology is, I might answer, "Everything in this book—and more."

The largest professional organization of psychologists, the American Psychological Association, or APA, lists over 40 divisions or specialty areas to which its members belong. For now, we need not be that detailed. The short list we have here combines many of the APA divisions into broader categories. A danger inherent in lists like this one is that someone may infer that it provides a ranking in some order of importance. Be assured; none is intended.

Physiological/biological psychology is concerned with the interactions between bodily activity, behavior, and mental processes. This is the subfield in psychology most concerned with the structures and functions of the brain and the role it plays in guiding our behavior. When we ask, "Why did I do (or feel, or think) that?" psychologists who favor this approach will look to physiological, genetic, or biochemical explanations.

Developmental psychology is concerned with the physical and psychological development of the individual from conception through death. Most developmental psychologists focus primarily on the childhood years, while some attend primarily to adolescence, adulthood, or old age, or take a broader life span approach. In many ways, developmental psychologists share common interests with those in many other areas because they deal with so many basic psychological functions: intellectual and cognitive development, emotional development, sensory and perceptual development, and social and moral development, to name just a few.

Educational/instructional psychology is devoted to the processes of learning and memory and to the application of what we know about these processes to real-life situations. In both academic and business settings, educational and instructional psychologists often serve as consultants to improve training and education programs.

Clinical psychology includes those psychologists whose concern is with the psychological well-being of the individual. The training of clinical psychologists provides them with the means to diagnose and treat persons with psychological disorders. Clinical psychologists usually have Ph.D.s in psychology (or the more recent Psy.D. degree). This distinguishes them from psychiatrists, who have earned a medical degree (M.D.) and, as a result, can prescribe drugs and use other forms of medical treatment. Clinical psychology is by far the largest subfield in psychology. When combined with counseling psychology (see below), this subfield accounts for nearly 60 percent of all psychologists.

Counseling psychology is another applied area of psychology and is very much like clinical. Counseling psychologists, however, tend to serve persons with less severe and less chronic (long-lasting) disorders. They are more likely to be involved in such processes as grief counseling for disaster victims, divorce counseling, or short-term counseling with college students who are having adjustment problems.

Health psychology is one of the newer subfields in psychology. In general, health psychologists are commited to the notion that one's physical health is (or can be) affected by psychological variables and vice versa. Finding ways to prevent or reduce behaviors that are known to have an adverse affect on one's health is typical of the activities of the health psychologist.

Cognitive psychology includes those psychologists who investigate the basic processes of the mind: perception, learning, memory, and thinking. There are specialty areas within cognitive psychology. Psycholinguists, for example, are interested in language—how it is acquired, how it is produced, how it is perceived and interpreted. Some cognitive psychologists are interested in artificial intelligence—using computers to increase our understanding of the human mind.

Psychometrics involves the development and use of psychological tests and the statistical interpretation of data. Psychological testing is still big business in our society, particularly in education and business settings.

Social psychology reflects the observation that most organisms do not and cannot live without the company of others. How the behaviors of an individual affect others, and vice versa, is the general concern of social psychology. Predictably, this area, too, has many subfields, with interests in sex roles, attitudes, prejudice, intergroup conflict, conformity, and the like.

Industrial/organizational (I/O) psychology is defined largely by the work setting of the psychologist. What he or she may do there covers a wide range of possibilities. Some I/O psychologists are concerned with marketing and advertising; some are concerned with group productivity or consumer satisfaction; some are concerned with the design of equipment; others are concerned with personnel decisions of hiring, firing, or training; still others focus on helping those who suffer from the stress of the workplace.

Of course, this list is incomplete and provides only an overview. No doubt, there are many psychologists who claim that they do not fit any of these categories. Others might claim that they fit two or more. Still, as you read through the rest of this text, you'll be introduced to many psychologists who follow the approaches outlined in this topic. The diversity of psychology is one of the things that makes it such an exciting field to study.

BEFORE YOU GO ON

What are some of the subfields of modern psychology, and what might we expect from a psychologist working in a particular subfield?

SOME IMPORTANT THEMES AND THREADS

We have already made the point that psychologists have learned a lot about the behaviors and mental processes of organisms. Some of the conclusions that we can now draw about psychology and its subject matter seem so important, so general in their application, that they deserve special mention. The "themes and threads" listed here are so well established that they are almost part of our definition of psychology. In every chapter that follows you will recognize a reflection of these important ideas. The intent here in this first topic is to give you a few things to think about and to look for in the topics that follow.

An Organism's Nature and Nurture Interact

How much of who we are—our affect, behavior, and cognition, again—is the result of our inheritance, our biological *nature*? And how much of who we are reflects the influences of our environment, our learning experiences, our *nurture*? Is intelligence inherited (nature) or due to experience (nurture)? Is aggressiveness inborn (part of our nature), or is it learned (resulting from our nurture)? Does alcoholism reflect one's innate, unchangeable nature, or is it a learned reaction to events in the environment?

Early in psychology's past it was realized that questions about one's nature and nurture were not either-or questions. Sometimes we may be able to determine the extent to which one's experiences or one's inheritance contribute to some psychologically relevant characteristic. This issue is far from trivial. At the moment, we do not have readily available means of altering our biological nature. There is some hope, however, that we may be able to alter one's experiences in such a way as to bring about significant changes. For example, think of the implications of discovering that some psychological disorder is totally genetic in origin—no matter what one did, if certain genes are present, the disorder will eventually appear. Now contrast that with the implications of the discovery that the disorder has no biological basis, but is totally a response to pressures of the environment.

What we will see repeatedly, and in many different contexts, is that one's behaviors and mental processes result from an *interaction* of inherited, genetic influences and environmental influences. In this context, interaction is a difficult concept. We'll extend our understanding as we go along. But for now, the logic is that any psychological characteristic is not going to be the result of *either* heredity *or* experience, but will reflect the extent to which these two forces have influenced each other. As one researcher put it, "most behavioral traits appear to be influenced by many genes, each with small effects, [and] behavior is substantially influenced by nongenetic factors" (Plomin, 1990). Here's another way to say basically the same thing: "For all psychological characteristics, inheritance sets limits on, or creates a range of potentials for development. Environment determines how near the individual comes to developing these potentials" (Kimble, 1989).

Taking intelligence as an example, what this means is that person A may be born with the inherited, genetic potential to be extremely bright. But what if person A is born in a ghetto or barrio of a large city and receives poor childhood care, poor nourishment, poor educational opportunities, and the like? That person probably will not turn out to be very intelligent—in an academic sense. On the other hand, if person B is born with genes that severely limit his or her intelligence, all the training, education, and experience the environment may provide probably will not raise that person's intelligence very far above those limits set by its nature. On the other hand, person B will probably be better off as a result of training than he or she would be without it. We'll see reference to the relative contributions of nature and nurture a number of times, most notably in the chapters on development, intelligence, personality, and psychological disorders.

BEFORE YOU GO ON

What does it mean to say that nature and nurture interact?

Things Are Not Always as They Seem

The deceptively simple and classic notion that we are introducing here has a name: **phenomenology**. Phenomenology has to do with the study of events *as they are experienced by the individual*, not as they actually occur "in reality." Now as you might imagine, we can easily get involved in some fairly deep philosophical discussions here, but we need not. What we need to appreciate now—and what we need to keep an eye out for as we go along—is the notion that as active agents in the world, we each select, attend to, interpret, and remember (i.e., experience) different aspects of the very same world.

Here's a very simple example of what we're talking about. (It is also a classic example, attributed to the philosopher John Locke, 1632–1704). Imagine that you have before you three pails of water. The water in the pail on your left is really quite hot; the water in the pail on your right is nearly ice cold, and the water in the center pail is nearly body temperature. You put your left hand into the hot water and your right hand into the cold. Then, after a minute or two, you place both hands in the center pail of water. What is its temperature? How does the water feel? To your left hand, the water seems quite cool, while to your right hand the very same water feels quite warm. Well, what *is* the temperature of the water in the center pail? Is it cool or is it warm? Now a physicist may come along and measure the temperature of the water in that center pail with astonishing accuracy. But we're not interested in the physics of the water. We're interested in the psychology of your *experience* of the water, and we may—with something of a smug smile—report that the water in the center pail is both warm *and* cool. What matters is, in fact, not the actual, physical temperature of the water, but rather your comparative experience of that water.

Here's another simple example (from Bruner & Goodman, 1947). Children are given the opportunity to change the size of a small circle. They are asked to make the circle exactly the same size as a quarter. Almost all of the children consistently overestimate the size of the coin. But what is more interesting is that poor children overestimate the size of the quarter to a significantly greater degree. To the poorer children, quarters seem *much* larger than they actually are.

phenomenology *the study of events as they are experienced by the individual; that experience is reality*

THE CAT SAT BY THE DOOR.

(A)

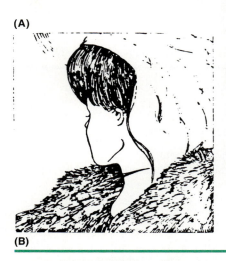

(B)

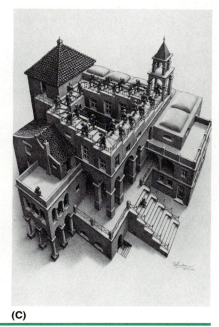

(C)

(A) The highlighted letter is neither an A or an H. It is interpreted to be one or the other based on our experience with the English language. (B) What do you see? This ambiguous drawing may be an old woman or a young Victorian lady depending on the context in which it is viewed. (C) Are the figures marching up or down the stairs? A careful inspection of these figures will reinforce the point that "things are not always as they seem."

This theme has practical relevance in many areas of psychology. It will show up most clearly in our discussion of sensation and perception, where we note that what we perceive often depends more on what we want to perceive or expect to perceive than what is "really there." A quick study of Figure 1.3 will give you an idea of what I mean.

BEFORE YOU GO ON

What does phenomenology mean in psychological terms?

For Many Questions in Psychology There Are No Simple Answers

There are many good questions in psychology for which there are, as yet, no good answers. For some questions we do have answers, answers with which almost all psychologists would agree. On the other hand, for some questions we don't even have reasonably acceptable hypotheses. What you are going to encounter in your study of psychology is that complex phenomena often have complex explanations.

As an example, let's briefly anticipate a discussion we'll have later when we cover psychological disorders. What causes schizophrenia? For the moment, let us simply acknowledge that schizophrenia is one of the most devastating and debilitating of all the psychological disorders, afflicting approximately 2.5 million people in the United States today. What causes the distortions in the way a person feels, thinks, and acts that is schizophrenia? The truth is that we just don't know. As it happens, we have several hypotheses, and each in its own right holds some promise, but the picture is complex. Part of the answer is genetic; schizophrenia does tend to run in families. Part of the answer is biochemical; the brains of persons with schizophrenia do not function in the same way as the brains of those who do not have schizophrenia. Part of the answer is environmental, or situational; stress and experience can bring on symptoms and/or at least make symptoms worse than they would be otherwise. So, what causes schizophrenia? Answer: a number of interacting factors, some genetic, some physiological, some environmental, perhaps all operating at the same time. And so it goes for virtually *all* of our behaviors and mental processes.

The main point of this theme or thread in psychology is that if you are looking for simple answers to explain your own behavior or the behavior of someone else, you're bound to be disappointed. Disappointed you may be, but please don't be discouraged. Behaviors and mental processes are complex, and explaining them is going to take a certain degree of complexity. Complexity in and of itself should not be worrisome. Behaviors and mental processes generally have multiple causes. Our challenge is to discover them.

Psychology Has Practical Application in the Real World

We might get an argument from biologists, chemists, physicists, geologists, and even some astronomers, but I am quite willing to make the claim that no science has more practical, utilitarian application in the real world than does the science of psychology. In everyday life, people *can* get by without thinking about physics or geology or biology; but they cannot get by without thinking *psychologically*. They must take into consideration a multitude of sensations, perceptions, memories, feelings, and consequences of their actions if they are going to survive, much less prosper. As you read about psychology on the following pages, you should always be on the lookout for how the topic you're reading about can be put to use in your own life.

Here's an example you can put to use right now. When we get into our discussion of learning and memory, we'll make the point that material is easier to learn and easier to remember if it is meaningful. So one of your jobs as a learner—as a student in a beginning psychology class—is to make the material about which you are learning as meaningful as possible. What that means, among other things, is that part of your job is to find ways in which you can personally relate to the issues you are reading about. In psychology, finding such relevance is relatively easy. After all, the subject

One application of psychology in the real world is the development of programs to change people's behavior in ways that benefit the physical environment.

matter of psychology is the behavior and mental processes of organisms—and that includes you and me.

Let's briefly consider two areas in which psychological principles can be usefully applied. One area is concerned with health issues, the other with the pollution of the environment. We'll return to both in more detail later. Getting old and dying are natural processes; they just happen naturally. But the truth is that many people never get old, they just die—unnaturally, and in many cases the cause of their death was preventable. It is possible to prevent some deadly or debilitating diseases, such as polio, smallpox, or measles, by being vaccinated against them. What we have come to appreciate in the last decade or so is the extent to which illness and even death can be attributed to dangerous life-styles (Matarazzo, 1980; Miller, 1983). Look at it this way: "7 of the 10 leading causes of death in the United States are in large part behaviorally determined. We believe these unhealthy behaviors can be significantly reduced with help from psychologists" (Heffernan & Albee, 1985, p. 202). We are coming to understand that it is not easy, but basic principles of psychology *can* be used to help people stop smoking, cut down on alcohol use, increase exercise, wear safety belts in automobiles, cope with life's stresses, decrease overeating, engage in safe(er) sexual practices, and many other behaviors where the end result is the application of psychology to improve the physical health of the individual.

As we approach the twenty-first century it is becoming increasingly obvious to many of us that the physical health of the planet Earth is also in jeopardy (e.g., Brown et al., 1990). Overpopulation, the greenhouse effect, the erosion of the ozone layer, overused landfills, acid rain, the pollution of groundwater, and the pollution of the air are just some of the issues with which psychologists are becoming involved. The problem for psychology is how to turn global issues, such as the loss of the tropical rain forests, into local actions that have real and immediate impact on individuals. Some of the problems that face the planet today just seem overwhelming—beyond the resources of individuals. They are not. Most of the problems our environment faces today have been caused by the actions (the behaviors, the feelings, and the cognitions) of individuals. Some of the problems have accumulated their effect over a long period of time, but each is ultimately the result of decisions made by individuals. Now the trick—the challenge—is to apply psychology to individuals in the real world to improve the lot of the real world (cf. Saegert & Winkel, 1990).

BEFORE YOU GO ON

Why do there tend to be few simple answers in psychology?
In what way can we claim psychology to be one of the most applied
of all the sciences?

In this topic we have defined psychology as the scientific study of behavior and mental processes. In other words, we have agreed that psychologists use scientific methods to study *affect*, *behavior*, and *cognitions*. We've also noted some very central ideas about psychology, which we've called themes: that who we are reflects the interaction of our biological inheritance and our psychological experiences; that one's perception or experience of the world is often more important psychologically than what really happens in the world; that behaviors and mental processes are complex and can seldom be explained simply; and that psychology has practical, relevant application in the real world. In this topic we have also taken a brief look at psychology's history, noting that although it emerged as a separate, scientific discipline only 100 years ago, many of its abiding issues and questions are ancient. We've also seen that the one discipline of psychology includes a number of different areas, approaches, or perspectives from which psychologists view their subject matter. Now it is time to consider in more detail just how psychologists go about doing what they do. What psychologists do—their goals and their methods—are issues to which we now turn.

SUMMARY

Why may we claim that psychology is a science?

We may claim scientific status for psychology because it meets two criteria: It has an organized body of knowledge and it uses scientific methods. / *page 5*

What is the subject matter of psychology? What are operational definitions, why do we use them, and what are their limitations?

The subject matter of psychology is behavior and mental processes, or affect, behavior, and cognitions. Operational definitions define concepts in terms of the techniques, or operations, used to measure those concepts. They allow us to communicate precisely how we are going to go about measuring a concept. At the same time, they may appear to oversimplify complex concepts. / *page 8*

In what way did the philosophy of Descartes and Locke prepare the way for psychology? In what way did the science of Darwin, Fechner, and von Helmholtz influence the emergence of psychology?

Both René Descartes and John Locke directed the attention of philosophy to the study of the mind—how it interacts with the body and how it acquires information. Charles Darwin (from biology), Gustav Fechner (from physics), and Hermann von Helmholtz (from physiology) each brought scientific and experimental methodology to bear on questions that were essentially psychological. / *page 11*

When and where did psychology "begin," and whom do we credit with formally establishing the discipline? Briefly describe the first approaches

that psychologists took toward their subject matter.

We credit Wilhelm Wundt for having founded psychology at the University in Leipzig in 1879. Wundt and Titchener used experiments and introspection to study the mind or consciousness, particularly its structure and its contents. Following the suggestions of James, the functionalists also were concerned with the mind and mental activity, but focused on the adaptive usefulness or function of consciousness. / *page 13*

Briefly summarize behaviorism and psychoanalysis as approaches to psychology.

Behaviorism (associated with Watson and Skinner) holds that the subject matter of the science of psychology should be measurable and observable—thus, behavior. Psychoanalysis, associated with Freud and his followers, asserts that one's behaviors and mental processes are often under the influence of basic instincts and unconscious forces. / *page 15*

What is the major thrust of the humanistic approach in psychology? What does gestalt mean? What area of psychology was the major concern of Gestalt psychologists?

Humanistic psychology (associated with Rogers and Maslow) focuses on the self or the person, emphasizing internal processes and the potential for growth and development. As such, this approach can be seen as a reaction against behaviorism and psychoanalysis. *Gestalt* means whole, totality, or configuration. Gestalt psychologists focus their study on factors that affect the selection and organization of perceptions. / *page 16*

What were the major contributions of Sir Francis Galton and Alfred Binet to the development of psychology?

Galton drew the attention of psychologists to the measurement of the ways in which people differ from one another. He may be considered the founder of psychological testing. Binet authored the first truly successful test of general intelligence, an oft-revised test that is still in common use. / *page 17*

What are some of the subfields of modern psychology, and what might we expect from a psychologist working in a particular subfield?

Physiological psychologists study the nervous system and how it affects behaviors and mental processes. Developmental psychologists study the growth and development of the individual throughout the life span. Educational psychologists study and try to improve the processes of learning and memory. Clinical psychologists have many subspecialties, but are generally involved in the diagnosis and treatment of behavioral and mental disorders. Counseling psychologists tend to focus on the treatment of persons with less severe problems. Cognitive psychologists study mental processes, such as memory, thinking, and problem solving. Health psychologists are involved with how psychological factors affect one's physical health and well-being. Psychometric psychologists are involved in the construction and evaluation of psychological tests. Social psychologists study how the behavior of an individual influences and is influenced by others. Industrial/organizational psychologists work in business and industry attempting to use psychological principles to solve the many problems that arise in those settings. / *page 19*

What does it mean to say that nature and nurture interact?

It means that who we are—our affect, behaviors, and cognitions—jointly reflect certain characteristics that we have inherited and experiences that we have had with our environments. Both our nature and our nurture are important, yet neither is sufficient to explain the source of an organism's behaviors or mental processes. / *page 21*

What does phenomenology mean in psychological terms?

The position of phenomenology asserts that in many cases what matters to an individual most is not so much what happens to that individual as what that individual has experienced. In other words, what is perceived is often more important than what was. / *page 22*

Why do there tend to be few simple answers in psychology? In what way can we claim psychology to be one of the most applied of all the sciences?

Because psychology studies the complex phenomena of behavior and mental processes of organisms, we find that there are few simple answers to our questions. Behaviors and mental processes are usually caused by a multitude of interacting physical, biological, and psychological factors. At the same time, psychology is a very relevant and applied field of study because the major focus of its study is people. / *page 25*

The Goals and Methods of Psychology

Why We Care: A Topic Preview

In Topic 1A, we explored some of the implications of a standard "textbook" definition of psychology—psychology is the science of behavior and mental processes. In this topic, we'll examine the nature of psychology from a different perspective. We'll deal with two related questions: (1) What are the goals of psychology? That is, what is it that psychologists are trying to do? (2) What are the methods that psychologists use to reach their goals? The logic here is that if we appreciate psychology's goals and methods, at least in general terms, we'll have a better understanding of what psychology is all about.

Throughout the rest of this book we'll be considering a great deal of information—and many conclusions drawn from that information. We have to have some appreciation of where that information came from. For example, I may say, "It was found in an experiment . . .", or, "A recent survey indicated that . . .", or, "The scores on both measures were highly correlated." The purpose of this topic is to review the basic procedures that are involved in doing experiments, conducting surveys, interpreting correlations, and the like.

We begin with a discussion of the goals of psychology. We'll find out that there is more than one opinion about psychology's goals. Which goal you adopt as a psychologist often depends on what kind of psychologist you are.

Once we have a general idea of the goals of psychology, we turn our attention to psychology's methods. We've already claimed that one reason why we can say that psychology is a science is that it employs scientific methods. Now we need to take a look at some of the techniques that psychologists use to study their subject matter. We will use this context to mention ethical considerations with which psychologists must deal in their attempts to reach their goals.

At this point, our characterization of psychology's goals and methods will be necessarily broad and general. We'll be filling in the details as we go along. For now, we care about goals and methods because they help us to understand the very nature of psychology, and because they provide a framework for all of the specific examples of psychology in action that follow.

THE GOALS OF PSYCHOLOGY

In the most general terms, we can say that psychology has two inter-related goals. One is the goal of the science of psychology; the other is the goal of the practice of psychology. The first is a goal held in common by all the sciences; the second is a goal of application. To put it a bit differently: One goal of psychology is to discover and understand the scientific laws that govern its subject matter, behavior and mental processes, while the other goal is to apply those laws in the real world.

If psychologists—at least some psychologists—are trying to discover scientific laws about behavior and mental processes while others are trying to apply those laws, we'd better ask, "What *is* a scientific law?" To put it simply, a **scientific law** is a statement about one's subject matter that one believes, *on the basis of evidence*, to be true. For example, there is a law in physics that states that a gas, when heated, expands. This law is a statement about their subject matter (gases) that physicists believe to be true. Their belief stems from evidence obtained in the process of doing research on gases. It describes the relationship that exists between gases and heat. In biology there is a scientific law that describes the relationship between the rate and depth of our breathing and the amount of carbon dioxide (not oxygen, curiously enough) that we inhale. In psychology we have a scientific law that tells us that when responses are rewarded, they are likely to be repeated. This law tells us about the relationship between rewards and the likelihood that responses will occur in the future.

Scientific laws, including those in psychology, have two important characteristics. (1) They describe *relationships*. How are carbon dioxide and breathing related, for instance? The greater the percentage of carbon dioxide in the air, the deeper and faster one's breathing will be. (2) They allow us to make *predictions* about our subject matter. What will happen to the size of a balloon if the temperature rises markedly? The balloon will get larger as the gases inside expand.

One goal of psychology, then, is to discover statements that describe relationships among behaviors and mental processes that we believe to be true. The bulk of this topic is devoted to a discussion of how psychologists go about discovering scientific laws in their discipline.

What about the second goal, applying those laws? As we noted in our first topic, most psychologists are *practitioners*, which means that they put into practice existing psychological laws and principles. Of those psychologists who are practitioners, most are clinical or counseling psychologists. Their goal is to apply what we know to help individuals deal with problems that are affecting their ability to cope with or adjust to the environment, which includes other people. We'll discuss the methods that these psychologists use in Chapter 13. Some practitioners have as their goal the application of psychological knowledge to human problems that occur in the workplace—the industrial/organizational psychologists we mentioned in Topic 1A (see also Topic 15A).

Psychological practitioners can be found in a variety of settings, dealing with a variety of issues. Some apply psychology in an attempt to improve the performance of athletes; some advise attorneys on how best to present legal arguments in the courtroom; some establish programs to increase the use of automobile safety belts; some help people train their pets; and, as we shall see again and again in the rest of this book, the list goes on.

scientific law *a statement about one's subject matter thought to be true, based on evidence*

I hope you recognize that the science of psychology and the practice of psychology are *not* necessarily mutually exclusive endeavors. For one thing, many of my colleagues who are practicing clinical, or counseling, or industrial psychologists are also active scientific researchers.

Notice too, the implication that when we add a practice element to the science of psychology, we add the notion of *control*. Science usually can demonstrate that it understands a scientific relationship by making certain predictions and then seeing if those predictions come true. For example, are we right about our observation about expanding gases and heat? Let's get a balloon, partially inflate it, and then see what happens when we increase the temperature. The "better," or more precise, a scientist's predictions, the more impressed we are with his or her science. Seldom do we ask the scientist to exercise control over her or his subject matter. It's one thing to predict when a volcano will erupt. We don't really expect geologists to do anything about it. We're impressed that astronomers can predict the next time we'll be able to observe a given comet or star, but hardly expect those astronomers to produce comets for viewing or to control the stars. But, the practitioners of psychology expect to do exactly that: They expect, on the basis of their knowledge of psychology, not only to predict behavior and mental processes, but to change them. It should go without saying that in this regard, prediction and control are related to the more general goal of improving the lives, or the "quality of life" of organisms.

Psychologists, then, have two goals, and they are not at all mutually exclusive. One is to discover psychological laws. The other is to apply those laws. The focus of the rest of this topic will be on the first of these goals, discovering the lawful relationships that exist among behaviors and mental processes. Our coverage of the second goal—application—will be scattered throughout the text in every topic, but most particularly in the chapter on psychotherapy and treatment interventions for psychological disorders.

BEFORE YOU GO ON

What are the two major goals of psychology?

OBSERVATIONAL METHODS IN PSYCHOLOGY

In this section, we begin our discussion of the methods psychologists use to study the relationships among factors that influence behavior and mental processes. Our discussion of research in psychology opens with comments about observational methods. Before we can explain what people do, we must first make valid observations of just what it is that people do. As it happens, many of our casual, commonsense observations about behaviors are simply not true. "You can spot a gay guy a mile away, they're so effeminate." (No, they're not.) "Most people older than 65 are unhappy complainers." (No, they're not.) "Mothers pay more attention to good babies than they do to bad babies." (No, they don't.) If many of our everyday observations lead to conclusions that are incorrect, how, then, can psychologists go about making valid observations? In the next few sections, we'll review some of the steps psychologists can take to do just that.

Naturalistic Observation

naturalistic observation *the method of observing and noting behaviors as they occur naturally*

As its name implies, the methodological approach called **naturalistic observation** involves carefully watching behaviors as they occur naturally, without any involvement from the observer. There is a strong logical appeal to the argument that if you are trying to understand what organisms do in real life, you should simply watch them while they are doing it, noting their behaviors and the conditions under which those behaviors occur.

As straightforward and logically appealing as naturalistic observation may sound, it does present a few difficulties. For one thing, if we truly do want to observe people (or any other organism, for that matter) *the way they naturally act*, then we must make sure that they do not realize we are watching them. As you know from your own experience, people may act very differently from "normal" if they think they are being watched. You may do all sorts of things in the privacy of your home that you would never do if you thought someone was watching you.

observer bias *when one's own motives, expectations, and past experiences interfere with the objectivity of one's observations*

A second problem of which we must be wary is **observer bias**. Observers should not let their own motives, expectations, and previous experiences interfere with the objectivity of their observations. It might be very difficult for a researcher to be objective in her observations of a group of children in a playschool setting if she constantly is comparing their behaviors to that of her own two children. One solution to the problem of observer bias is to have observers note behaviors as they occur without full knowledge of the particular relationships that are under investigation in the research study. Another protection against observer bias is to check the reliability (dependability) of observations by using several observers, and only relying on those that can be verified by a number of observers.

A third potential problem with naturalistic observation is a bit more difficult to deal with. The behaviors you want to observe may not be there when you are. For example, if you are interested in conformity and want to observe people conforming naturally, in the real world, just where would you go? Where are you likely to observe conformity happening naturally? Yes, there are some environments in which conformity behaviors are more likely to occur than others. But there surely is no guarantee that during any particular day, or week, or month, the people you are watching will provide any evidence of conformity at all. If you start manipulating a situation so that people are more likely to conform, you are no longer doing *naturalistic* observation. To use this method you often have to be lucky, and you almost certainly will have to be patient.

Although it has its problems, there are occasions when naturalistic observation is the most suitable method that psychologists have available. For example, studying chimpanzees in zoos and laboratories (even when we use observational methods to do so) will tell us little about the behaviors of chimpanzees in the wild. Many examples come from psychologists who have been frustrated in their attempts to study the language development of very young children. By the time they are 3 or 4 years old, children demonstrate all sorts of interesting language behaviors. However, these same

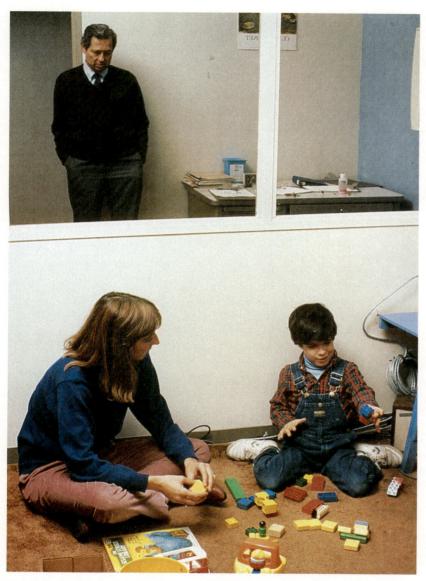

Naturalistic observation involves watching behaviors as they occur naturally— without any involvement by the observer. In this case, a doctor observes a child's behavior through a one-way mirror.

children may be too young to understand and properly follow the instructions that many experiments require. Almost certainly, they are unable to introspect and respond sensibly to questions about their own language usage. Perhaps all we *can* do is carefully watch and listen to young children as they use their language and try to determine what is going on by observing them as they interact naturally with their environments. A psychologist who studies language development with her husband reports that they often spend their summers "looking quite foolish" following behind toddlers, "recording their every utterance in dime-store notebooks" (Gelman et al., 1987).

BEFORE YOU GO ON

What is naturalistic observation?
List some of the potential problems that can arise with this method.

Surveys

When we want to make observations about a large number of subjects, we may use a **survey** method. Doing a survey amounts to asking many people the same question or set of questions. The questions may be asked in person or in a telephone interview, or they may be asked in the form of a written questionnaire. Survey studies yield data that would be difficult to gather otherwise.

If we wanted to know, for example, if there was a relationship between income level and the type of automobile one drives or television programs that one watches regularly, we could ask about these issues in a survey of a large number of people. Surveys can tell us what large portions of the population think and feel about and can provide insights about general preferences for products or services (or political candidates). If the staff of the cafeteria on your campus really wanted to know what students preferred to eat, they could survey a sample of the student population. Textbook publishers often survey psychology instructors to see what they would like to have included in the books that they use.

Perhaps the most critical aspect of observations made from survey data is the size and representativeness of the **sample** that is surveyed. A sample is a subset or portion of a larger population that is chosen to be studied. We would like to be able to generalize or extend our observations beyond those subjects we survey in our sample. Textbook publishers who only survey instructors at small liberal arts colleges, or cafeteria managers who only survey students attending morning classes, may very easily collect information (make observations) that do not generalize to the intended population—that is, the larger, complete pool of subjects from which the sample is drawn.

Case Histories

The **case history** method provides another sort of observational information. In the case history method, one person—or a small sample of persons—is studied in depth, often over a long period of time. Use of this method usually involves an intense and detailed examination of a wide range of variables. The method is usually retrospective, which means that we start with some given state of affairs (a situation that exists today) and go back in time to see if there is any relationship between this state of affairs and previous experiences and events. We may use interviews and/or psychological tests as a means of collecting our data.

As an example, let's say that we are interested in Mr. X, a known child abuser. Our suspicion (hypothesis) is that Mr. X's own childhood experiences might be related to his present status as a child abuser. We talk to Mr. X at length and interview his family and his friends—those who knew

survey *a means of collecting observations from a large number of subjects, usually by interview or questionnaire*

The data from surveys can tell us what a large number of people think about a limited number of issues.

sample *the portion of a larger population chosen for study*

case history *an intensive, retrospective, and detailed study of some aspects of one (or a few) individual(s)*

him as a child—trying to form some retrospective picture of Mr. X's childhood. If we find some clues—for example, Mr. X was punished with severe spankings, or he missed class at school significantly more often than other children—we may then explore the early childhood experiences of other known child abusers, looking to find common experiences that might be related to the fact that they abuse children now that they are adults.

I have always been intrigued by the choices college students make when they decide on a major course of study. Why do some students choose to major in psychology, while others choose mathematics or fine arts as a major? Perhaps the case history method could provide some insights about the factors related to one's choice of a college major. How would we proceed? We'd choose a sample of students, perhaps seniors, from each major, and ask them a number of (hopefully) penetrating questions about their experiences, listening for something that all students of one major had in common but that was different from the experiences of those who opted for other majors.

As we shall see, Freud based most of his theory of personality on his intensive examination of the case histories of his patients (and himself). The advantage of the case history method is that it tends to provide us with a wealth of detailed information about a few individual cases. The disadvantage is that we have to be particularly careful when we try to generalize our findings beyond those individuals we have chosen to study.

Now that we have briefly reviewed some of the ways in which psychologists make careful, reliable, observations, we need to see how these observations can be translated into psychological laws.

BEFORE YOU GO ON

How can surveys and case history studies be used to help us understand behavior and mental processes?

CORRELATIONAL METHODS IN PSYCHOLOGY

As you know, observations are often very important and/or useful in their own right. Observations about people's behaviors, thoughts, or feelings often provide interesting insights. How many people in the United States and Canada *do* smoke cigarettes? What *do* the majority of Americans really think about abortions performed during the first trimester of pregnancy? How do most people feel about Sylvester Stallone making yet another *Rambo* movie? They may be interesting, insightful, and informative, but observations take the form of scientific laws only when they can be related consistently to other observations. **Correlation** is a statistical procedure that we can use to assess the nature and degree to which sets of observations are lawfully related. In fact, to say that observations are correlated is to say that they are related to each other (co-related) in some way.

Let's work through an example to see how this method works. We'll say that we are interested in whether or not there is a relationship—a correlation—between reading ability and performance in introductory psychology. The only difficult part of this study is devising acceptable opera-

correlation *a largely statistical technique used to determine the nature and extent of the relationship between two measured responses*

tional definitions for the responses in which we are interested. That is, we need to decide on how we will actually measure *reading ability* and *performance in introductory psychology*. Once we've done that, we can make our measurements, which will provide us with two sets of numbers. Then we can determine if a relationship exists between our two observed responses. Let's look at this procedure step by step.

We need to come up with operational definitions for the responses we care about. *Performance in introductory psychology* isn't difficult to deal with at all. We'll take that to mean the total number of points earned by a student on classroom exams over the course of the semester. *Reading ability* is a little more difficult. What do we mean by *reading ability*? We could design a test of our own to measure those behaviors that we think reflect reading ability, but it turns out that we're in luck. There are many tests of reading ability already available, and after reviewing them, we decide to use the Nelson Denny Reading Test, the NDRT (Brown, 1973).

Now we're ready to collect some data (make our observations). We'll give a large group of students our reading test (the NDRT). Once the tests are scored, we have one large set of numbers. At the end of the semester, we add up all the points earned by each of our students and we have a second set of numbers. So for each student in our study we have a pair of numbers—one indicating reading ability and one indicating performance in the introductory psychology course. We want to know if these observations are correlated. From here on out, our method is much more statistical than it is psychological.

We enter our pairs of numbers into a calculator (or a computer if we have a large set of numbers). A series of arithmetic procedures is applied—there are prescribed formulae for these calculations that need not concern us here. The result of these calculations is a single number, called the **correlation coefficient**. The actual value of a correlation coefficient may be any number between -1.00 and $+1.00$. What does this number mean? How can it be the basis for a scientific law? It takes some experience to be truly comfortable with the interpretation of correlation coefficients, but we can make some general observations.

First, let's deal with the sign of the correlation coefficient, which can be positive ($+$) or negative ($-$). A positive coefficient tells us that our two measured responses are related to each other and that high scores on one of our responses are associated with high scores on the other. It also tells us that low scores on one measure are associated with low scores on the other. Most of the correlations with which we are familiar are of this positive type—the correlation between SAT scores and college grade point averages, for example. In our example, a student who does well on the reading test will probably do well in an introductory psychology course. Those students who do poorly on the reading test are likely to earn lower grades in the psychology course. We can only make these predictions, however, if our two measured responses are positively correlated. As it happens, there is ample evidence that such is the case (Gerow & Murphy, 1980). Figure 1.4A shows what a graph of the scores measured in our example might look like, showing a positive correlation. This example shows us the major use of correlations: If we determine that two responses are correlated, we can use our observation of one response to make predictions about the other.

What if our calculations result in a correlation coefficient that is a negative number? Here, too, we have a useful psychological law. We can

correlation coefficient *a number that indicates the nature ($+$ or $-$) and the strength (0.00 to $+1.00$ or -1.00) of the relationship between measured responses*

Figure **1.4**

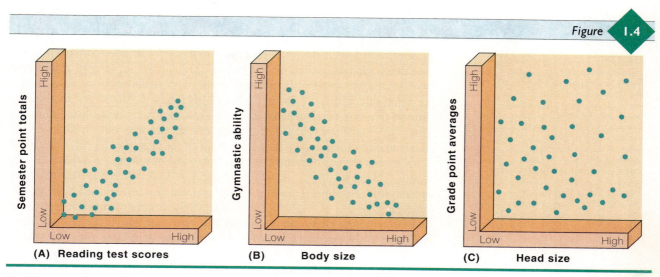

Positive, negative, and zero correlation. (A) A graph depicting the reading test scores and semester point totals earned by 40 students. These data indicate a positive (+) correlation between the two measured responses. As reading test scores increase, so do semester point totals. (B) A graph depicting the body size and gymnastic ability of 40 students. These data indicate a negative (−) correlation between the two measured responses. As body size increases, gymnastic ability decreases. (C) A graph depicting head size and grade point averages earned by 40 students. These data indicate a zero (0) correlation between the two measured responses. There is no relationship between head size and grade point averages.

still use scores on one response to predict scores on the other. But, when our correlation coefficient is negative, we know that the relationship between our two measured responses is inverse, or upside down. With negative correlation coefficients, high scores on one response predict low scores on the other. If we measured body size and looked to see if it were lawfully related to gymnastic ability, we might very well find a negative correlation: Large body size is associated with poor gymnastic ability (low scores), while small body sizes are associated with good gymnastic ability (high scores). Notice that if these two sets of observations are negatively correlated, we can still use body size to predict gymnastic ability. Figure 1.4B shows a set of data depicting the possible relationship between gymnastic ability and body size, a negative correlation.

What if our correlation coefficient turned out to be zero, or nearly so (say, 0.0003)? In this case, we would have to conclude that the two sets of observations that we have made are simply not related to each other in any consistent, lawful way. Let's say that I worked from the faulty notion that intelligence is a function of brain size, and that one's head size tells us how big a person's brain is. No doubt if I were to measure the head size of a large number of students and also measure grade point average (attempting to a show a lawful relationship between intelligence and grades), I would find that the calculations for the correlation coefficient would result in a number very close to zero. As correlations approach zero, predictability decreases. Figure 1.4C completes our set of examples by showing what a graph of data from two sets of unrelated measures would look like.

So much for the sign of the correlation coefficient. What about its actual numerical value? Again, it takes a little practice to get used to working with numbers such as $-.46$, $+.55$, and $+.002$. There are statistical tests that we can use to determine the usefulness (or significance) of a calculated correlation coefficient. Among other things, these tests can tell us the likelihood that our coefficient is or is not significantly different from zero. For now, let us just say that *the closer we get to the extremes of $+1.00$ or -1.00, the better or stronger the relationship between the responses we have measured.* This means that as our correlation coefficient approaches $+1.00$ or -1.00 (say, $+.84$, or $-.93$), we will have increased confidence in our ability to predict one response knowing the other. The closer our coefficient gets to zero (say, $-.12$, or $+.004$), the weaker the relationship and the less useful it is for making predictions. We should also mention that the confidence we have in the predictability of our correlations is in large part determined by the number of paired observations that are used in our calculations. In general, the larger the sample—the more observations we have made—the greater the confidence we can put in our correlation coefficient.

As you read through this text, you'll encounter a number of studies that use a correlational analysis of measured observations. It is important, then, that you keep in mind two important points about correlations. (1) *Cause-and-effect conclusions are inappropriate for correlational studies.* Even if two responses are very well correlated with each other, we cannot support the claim that one causes the other. For some reason, this point seems difficult to remember. Sometimes logic overwhelms us. It does make sense that an inability to read will actually cause some students to do poorly in an introductory psychology class where reading is so important. Yes, it does make sense. *But*, if all we have to guide us is the fact that reading ability and grades are correlated, we can make no statement at all about cause and effect—all we can say is that they are related. (2) *Even when two responses are well correlated with each other, we cannot make predictions for individual cases.* As I said, reading ability and introductory psychology grades *are* positively correlated. By and large, students who read well do well in the course, and by and large, students who do not read well tend to do poorly. So, *in general*, we can use reading test scores to predict grades, but we have to allow for exceptions. A few poor readers may do very well indeed, and a few excellent readers may still fail the course. Exceptions are to be expected. In fact, the further from $+1.00$ or -1.00 our correlation coefficient is, the more exceptions we can expect. Like most scientific laws, statements of correlation hold true only "by and large," "generally," "in the long run," or "more often than not."

BEFORE YOU GO ON

What data are needed to calculate a correlation coefficient?

How does a correlation coefficient tell us about the relationship between two measured responses?

EXPERIMENTAL METHODS IN PSYCHOLOGY

Most of what we know today in psychology we have learned by doing **experiments**. Experiments involve a set of operations used to investigate relationships between manipulated events and measured events, while other extraneous events are controlled or eliminated. Now in the abstract, that's quite a mouthful. The actual procedures are not that difficult. Like all other methods in psychology, experiments involve making observations.

In fact, before we go on, we should pause momentarily to reiterate some of the general comments made earlier about scientific research. All research begins with observations, in psychology we deal with observations about an organism's behaviors or mental processes. On the basis of our intitial observations we formulate a hypothesis, which, you will recall, is a statement about our subject matter that can be tested to determine whether it can be supported or must be rejected. Sometimes all we need to do to find support for our hypothesis is to make additional observations. If we believe that students would like the cafeteria to make pizza available every day, we need only survey students to find out. Sometimes we need to see if two or more responses are related to each other in some lawful way. If we hypothesize that performance in a course is related to the students' reading ability, we need to measure reading ability and performance and calculate a correlation coefficient. We need to put our hypothesis to the test.

One of the important things about experiments is they are intended to discover cause-and-effect relationships. With experiments we're no longer content to discover that two measured observations are simply related; now we want to be able to claim that, at least to some degree, one is caused by the other. To see if such a claim can be made, an experimenter manipulates one variable to see if that manipulation causes any measurable changes in another variable. In this context, a variable is simply something that can vary—a measurable event that can take on different values. Experimental methods are described in terms of variables.

The events or conditions that an experimenter manipulates are called **independent variables**. Those the experimenter measures are **dependent variables**—their value should *depend* on the experimenter's manipulation of independent variables. The hope is that the manipulation of the independent variable will cause predictable changes in the dependent variable—changes predicted by one's hypothesis. Now if there *are* changes in the measured dependent variable, the experimenter would like to claim that these changes are due *solely* to the influence of the manipulated independent variable. In order to make such a claim, it must be shown that all other variables that might have influenced what is being measured have been controlled or eliminated. These factors that need to be eliminated from consideration are often called **extraneous variables** (extraneous means "not essential" or "irrelevant"). So, to do an experiment, a researcher manipulates independent variables, measures dependent variables, and eliminates or controls the effects of extraneous variables. If you haven't encountered this before, don't be discouraged. It's not as confusing as it may sound on first reading. Going over a couple of examples will help considerably.

After a few quizzes in your biology class you notice that the student sitting right in front of you is consistently scoring higher than you are—not by much, but by enough to be aggravating. You ask this student how

experiment *a series of operations used to investigate relationships between manipulated events (independent variables) and measured events (dependent variables), while other events (extraneous variables) are eliminated*

independent variables *those events in an experiment that are manipulated by the experimenter and that are hypothesized to produce changes in responses*

dependent variables *those responses measured in an experiment whose values are hypothesized to depend upon manipulations of the independent variable*

extraneous variables *those factors in an experiment that need to be minimized or eliminated so as not to affect the dependent variable*

she does it, and she tells you that she has "a system" that she learned in high school. To help remember a series of otherwise unrelated concepts, she weaves the terms together to form some sort of story. Recalling the story is relatively easy and can be used to help her recall terms for her quizzes. This system sounds sensible to you, and you decide to do an experiment to test if there is a cause-and-effect relationship here. (This is a decision that was also made in 1969 by Gordon Bower and M. C. Clark.)

You get some volunteers from your introductory psychology class and divide them into two groups. One group (A) is asked to memorize a list of 10 unrelated nouns. They are left to their own resources to learn the list however they would like. The other group (B) is asked to memorize the very same list of nouns, but they are told about the scheme of tying the words together to form some sort of meaningful story, and they are told to try to use this strategy in learning the list.

Now let's get our terminology in here. It is your belief that how people go about memorizing will have an effect on the memorizing process. You have manipulated this process, so whether or not learners are told to use a certain strategy in memorizing is your *independent variable*. You believe that this variable will have an effect on memory. How will you measure this to see if it is so? In other words, what will be your *dependent variable*? You ask all the students to return three weeks later. At that time you ask them all to "write down as many of the words as you can recall from the list you learned three weeks ago." So you operationally define your dependent variable to be the average number of words from the list recalled three weeks later. When you look at your data, you discover that, on the average, group A recalls 3.5 words of the original 10, and group B (those that made up a story) recall 8.2 words correctly. It seems that a story-generating strategy is truly useful in memorizing words. That strategy seems to cause significantly better recall.

Before we get too carried away, we had better consider the possible *extraneous variables* that might have been operating in this experiment. These are factors that might have affected the average recall of our two groups of students over and above what was manipulated (memorization strategy). It should be clear that these factors should have been considered before you actually did the experiment. What extraneous variables might be involved in this experiment? For one thing, we need to be certain that the students in each of our groups are of essentially the same ability to begin with. It would not do if the students in group A were poor, struggling students while those in group B were honor students. It also is obviously the case that both groups of learners need to be presented with identical materials to be learned, and the list of words needs to be presented in the same way to both groups.

The short of it is—and this is a very important point—when we are done with our experiment and find differences in our dependent variable, we want to be able to claim that these differences are due to our manipulation of the independent variable, and to nothing else. In fact, it is the extent to which extraneous variables are anticipated and eliminated that determines the quality of an experiment. Figure 1.5 reviews the steps in our example experiment.

Let's take a quick look at another potential experimental question. Suppose you believe that a stimulating environment during early childhood improves intellectual functioning at adolescence. You propose to do an

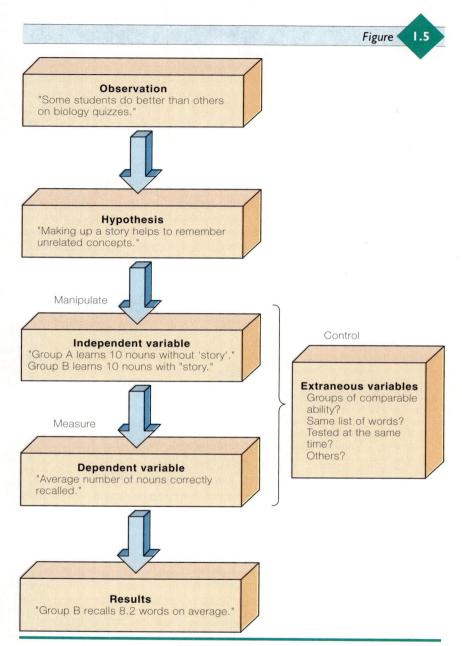

Figure 1.5

The stages involved in our example experiment illustrating the different types of variables.

experiment to support your observation. You have two groups of newborn children, with 20 in each group. One group will be reared for three years in a very stimulating environment filled with toys and games, bright wallpaper and pictures in the nursery, and many adults around every day. The other group of 20 children will be reared in isolation, in quiet, empty rooms, with only their basic biological needs attended to. *Wait a minute!* This sort of experimental manipulation is unethical and would be out of the question.

You wouldn't isolate and deprive a group of children this way—particularly if your very own hypothesis is that doing so would have negative consequences.

This problem provides a good example of an experiment that you might want to do with rats. Rats could be raised in cages that provide differing amounts of stimulation. When the rats approach maturity, you could test their ability to negotiate mazes and/or learn a variety of responses. Early exposure to stimulation would be your independent variable, and their scores on your tests of learning ability would be your dependent variables.

One advantage of using rats in experiments is that extraneous variables are usually easy to deal with. You seldom have to worry about previous experience, inherited differences, parental influences, and the like (all of your rats have a known and very similar genetic history, and all have been reared in very similar conditions). The problem with using rats is obvious. Even if you demonstrate your point with rats, you may then have to argue that the data you have collected for rats is, in some way, applicable to humans. As we shall see, in many cases this argument is not difficult to make, and with the advantage of ease of control, we can see why the use of nonhuman organisms in psychology is commonplace. Now that we have covered the essential procedures involved in doing experiments, we can examine some of the considerations that often determine the quality of an experimental method in a little more detail.

BEFORE YOU GO ON

What is the essence of doing an experiment?
Define independent, dependent, and extraneous variables in the context of an experiment.

Exercising Control

As I have said, the value of an experimental finding is related to the researcher's ability to eliminate or control the influence of extraneous variables. The most difficult extraneous variables to deal with are often those that involve the past experience of the subjects. Such was the case in our example experiment involving a memorizing strategy. In a typical experiment, the independent variable is manipulated by presenting one group of subjects with some treatment (such as a hint about how to memorize a list of words) while withholding that treatment from another group. Subjects in both groups are then measured to see if the treatment produced any effect in the chosen dependent variable. By definition, those subjects who receive some treatment or manipulation are said to constitute the **experimental group**. An experiment may have a number of experimental groups. Our example of memorizing lists used just one. If an additional group had been available, we might have given them a different hint to aid their recall, for instance. Subjects who do not receive our experimental treatment are said to be in the **control group**. Experiments usually have but one control

experimental group *those participants in an experiment who receive some treatment or manipulation—there may be more than one in an experiment*

control group *those participants in an experiment who do not receive any experimental treatment or manipulation*

group; in our example, this was group A, which received no hint about how to memorize the words.

To make sure that your control and experimental groups of subjects begin the experiment on an equal footing, you could do one of a number of things. You could try to match the groups on the characteristic of interest. In our example, you might have done this by giving all your subjects a recall test before the experiment began and then assigning them to either group A or group B so that the average scores on this test were equal, or nearly so.

A more common technique would be to place subjects in groups by **random assignment**, which means that each participant in your research has an equal chance of being assigned to any one of the groups that you are using in your experiment. If assignment is truly random, then those honor students would be equally likely to be in either of your two groups—the one that does or the one that doesn't get a hint about weaving the words into a story. And remember, this sort of consideration—matching or randomly assigning subjects—is something that must be made before the experiment is actually begun.

random assignment *the selection of members of a population in such a way that each has an equal opportunity to be assigned to any one group*

Another method for dealing with control variables that may arise from the differing past experiences of subjects is called a **baseline design**. Although there are several such designs, each amounts to arranging things so that each subject serves in both experimental and control group conditions. Imagine, for example, that you wished to see if a certain drug caused an increase in the running speed of white rats. Using a baseline design, you would first measure the running speed of rats without giving them the drug (a control, or baseline measure). Then you would check the running speed of the same rats after they were given the drug. Changes in their behavior (your dependent variable again) could then be attributed to the drug (your independent variable). You could then check the running speed of the rats again, after the effects of the drug wore off, to see if their behavior returned to its baseline rate.

baseline design *a method in which subjects' performance with an experimental treatment is compared with performance without that treatment (the baseline)*

Overcoming Bias

Human subjects in psychology experiments usually are helpful and well motivated to do whatever is asked of them. In their efforts to please, they may very well act in an experimental situation in ways they would never act otherwise. In other words, experimental subjects sometimes do what they think the experimenter wants them to do. When experimental subjects are reacting to their perception of the experimenter's wishes, they are not responding to the independent variables of the experiment. In order to overcome this difficulty, subjects are generally not told anything at all about how the experimenter expects them—or wants them—to act. This is called a **single-blind technique** because the subjects are not aware of (are blind to) the purpose or the hypothesis of the experiment.

single-blind technique *a protection against bias in which subjects are kept from knowing the hypothesis of an experiment*

For similar reasons, it is often helpful to keep the person measuring the dependent variable unaware of the goals or hypotheses of the experiment. Occasionally, it is very easy to misread a clock, misperceive a rat's reaction in a maze, misinterpret a subject's verbal response, or give unintentional cues to a subject. This is particularly true when one *wants* a clock to give a certain time or *expects* a rat to make a given response. You should recognize this problem as a version of one of the themes we listed in Topic

double-blind technique *a protection against bias in which both the subjects and the data collector/analyzer are kept from knowing the hypothesis of an experiment*

1A (see page 21) where we acknowledged that what we perceive is not always precisely what happened. Notice that we're not talking about downright dishonesty here; we're talking about the honest errors that can be made in analyzing data when one has a stake in the outcome of the analysis. To offset this possible source of bias, we use a **double-blind technique** in which neither the subject nor the person collecting the data knows what the hypothesis of the experiment is. Obviously, *somebody* has to know what is going on, and that somebody is the person who will analyze the data — but not collect it.

For example, in our experiment that involved memorizing a list of words with and without a hint to aid the process, we would not tell the students/subjects about our hypothesis, nor would we tell the people counting the number of words correctly recalled which group any subject belonged to. In our example of raising rats under different levels of stimulation, we would see to it that the experimenters rating the learning ability of the rats (our dependent variable) did not know the conditions under which the rats were raised (our independent variable). (And we don't have to worry about keeping anything from the rats, which is another good reason to consider using nonhuman subjects.)

Meta-analyses

Before we leave our discussion of research methods in psychology, there is one technique that has become quite popular of late that deserves at least a brief note here. Some experiments may be impossible or difficult (or too expensive) to do on a large scale with many subjects. For example, although ethics may prevent us from raising young children in isolation, deprived of stimulation from the environment, we may be able to identify a few adolescents who, as children, happened to have relatively isolated, deprived childhoods. We might now compare their learning abilities with adolescents whose childhood experiences were apparently normal and with adolescents who seem to have had particularly stimulating childhood experiences. Our findings, based on only a few dozen adolescents, with many variables not under careful control, would be tentative at best, no matter what those findings happened to be. But what if, over the years, many very similar studies were conducted by many different researchers in many different places. Each such study, in and of itself, would not be very convincing. But what if there were some way to combine — average, in a way — the results of all these studies, so that we could discern an overall, cumulative impact of stimulation on children as reflected in a number of different, independent experiments and/or correlational studies? Such is precisely the intent of a procedure called **meta-analysis**, which we may define as a statistical procedure of combining the results of many studies to see more clearly the relationship, if any, between independent and dependent variables. In a way, what a meta-analysis does is minimize the error or the confounding that can plague individual, smaller studies.

meta-analysis *a statistical procedure of combining the results of several studies to see more clearly any relationships among observations that may be present*

Meta-analysis research sometimes uncovers relationships that are not clearly delineated in individual studies, and sometimes produces results that even contradict some of the studies that are being analyzed. A recently reported meta-analysis (Hyde, Fennema & Lamon, 1990) examined an issue that we'll look at in some detail in Topic 10B: gender differences in mathematics performance. They analyzed 100 studies that involved the testing of 3,175,188 subjects! It's difficult to imagine any one research project that would involve over 3 million subjects. What these researchers found was that there really aren't many differences between males and females in mathematical performance. Girls showed a slight advantage in computational skills in elementary and middle school. Males did slightly better than females in mathematical problem solving in high school and college, particularly in tests of advanced mathematics. What differences that did exist were found to be very small, and in most comparisons—now across many subjects—there were no real differences at all. Clearly, this is the sort of finding that any one study, no matter how well conceived, is unlikely to give us.

There are many factors that researchers in psychology must attend to, whether they are doing correlational studies, collecting survey data, recording case histories, making naturalistic observations, or doing experiments. The major intent is to see to it that one's observations and descriptions of relationships are as free from bias, error, and extraneous variables as possible. Another factor that researchers consider is ethics. Ethical considerations are relevant to all of the methods that psychologists use in their efforts to understand behavior and mental processes. In our next section, we'll take a brief look at ethics in psychological research.

BEFORE YOU GO ON

How do random assignment, baseline designs, single- and double-blind techniques, and meta-analyses help to minimize error in psychological experiments?

ETHICAL CONSIDERATIONS IN PSYCHOLOGICAL RESEARCH

Ethical and moral concerns can be found in all the sciences. In most of the sciences, ethical issues usually center on the application of knowledge. We know how to split the atom; should we build a bomb? We can manufacture effective insecticides; should we use them? We can devise means to render people infertile; should we? We can use machinery to keep people alive indefinitely; should we? We can bury radioactive waste; where should we?

Psychology has something of a unique problem with regard to ethics. To be sure, ethical considerations are very important in the application of psychological knowledge, be it in diagnosis, therapy, counseling, training, or whatever. (These we'll deal with in later chapters.) A unique aspect of psychology is that ethical considerations are often central in the *gathering,* accumulation, or discovery of information. After all, the objects of study are living organisms. Their physical and psychological welfare need to be protected as we investigate their behaviors and mental processes. Psychologists have long been concerned with the ethical implications of their work. Since 1953, the American Psychological Association has regularly revised and published *Ethical Principles of Psychologists* for practitioners and researchers alike. The most recent version was amended in 1989 and published in 1990. We'll deal very briefly with a few of the issues these guidelines address with regard to research.

As one plans his or her research, the degree to which subjects will be put at risk should be assessed. What are the potential dangers, physical or psychological, that might accompany participation? Even if potential risks are deemed to be slight, they need to be considered and balanced in the light of what potential good might come from the experiment. Researcher Gregory Kimble put it this way, "Is it worth it? Do the potential benefits to science and eventually to animal and human lives justify the costs to be extracted here and now?" (Kimble, 1989, p. 499). Seldom will any one psychologist have to make the ultimate decisions about the potential benefits or risks of research. Advisory committees of researchers, familiar with the techniques and the problems of the proposed research, will have to approve it before the project begins.

What are some other ethical issues related to research in psychology? (1) The subject's confidentiality must be guaranteed. Often, the subject's name is not even used; it is replaced instead with an identification number. No matter what you are asked to do or say, you should be confident that no one will have access to your responses but the researchers. (2) Participation in research should be totally voluntary. There are no circumstances under which you should feel coerced or compelled to participate in psychological research. Volunteers should be allowed the option of dropping out of any research project, even after it has begun. For example, college students *cannot* be offered extra credit to participate in psychological research unless other options are available for earning the same amount of extra credit. (3) Subjects should participate in experiments only after they have given their advised consent. Subjects must know what the potential dangers of participation are going to be, why this project is being done, and what is going to be expected of them. For example, no one can have access to your college records (your GPA, your entrance exam scores, etc.) without your specific knowledge and approval. Obviously, some deception may be required when doing experiments. Even so, the amount of deception needs to be balanced with the promise of the outcome of the research. (4) Particularly if subjects have been deceived about the true nature of an

debrief *to fully inform a subject about the intent and/or hypotheses of one's research once data have been collected*

experiment, and even if they haven't been, all subjects should be **debriefed** after the experiment has been completed. That means, if nothing else, that the true nature of the project and its basic intent should be explained fully to all those who participated in it. Clearly, this becomes particularly relevant for studies using a single- or double-blind procedure. Subjects also should be provided with a copy of the results of the project when the results are available.

Published ethical guidelines for the use of animals in research also are quite stringent. Only experts trained and experienced in animal care and housing should have responsibility for laboratory animals. Those experts must then provide training to all others working with the animals in the proper, humane treatment of the animals under their care. Every effort must be made to minimize discomfort, illness, and pain of animals. Putting animals in a situation where they might experience injury, pain, or stress is acceptable *only* if no other procedure is available and the goal is justified by its prospective scientific, applied, or educational value. As with human subjects, there are usually review committees that must approve the design of any research using nonhuman animals, where the major concern is the ethical, humane protection of the animals.

BEFORE YOU GO ON

Cite four ethical issues that must be considered when doing psychological research.

The aim of this chapter was to describe the nature of psychology in very general terms, leaving many of the specifics and details to subsequent chapters. What have we learned? We have learned that psychology is a science that studies behavior and mental processes. It emerged as a separate discipline just over 100 years ago. Psychologists approach their subject from a number of different perspectives, but have just two broad goals: (1) to discover and understand the relationships that may exist among behaviors and/or mental processes and (2) to apply what is known about these relationships in real-world settings. In order to meet their first goal, psychologists use scientific methods that can be classified as methods of observation, of correlation, and of experimentation. It is only from doing experiments that cause-and-effect relationships can be inferred. Finally, we have learned that psychologists have ethical concerns about their work, be it with humans or nonhumans.

SUMMARY

What are the two major goals of psychology?

One goal of psychology is to discover and understand the scientific laws of behavior and mental processes. That is, psychologists aim to make statements about their subject matter that they believe to be true on the basis of evidence gained through scientific methods. These statements tell us about relationships that exist among behaviors and mental processes, and allow us to make predictions about them. A second, related goal is to apply that understanding in real-world settings. / *page 31*

What is naturalistic observation? List some of the potential problems that can arise with this method.

Naturalistic observation involves the careful, reliable observation of behaviors as they occur naturally. Use of this method requires that (1) the subjects not be aware of the fact that they are being observed, (2) the observer's biases not influence observations, and (3) patience be exercised for those behaviors that occur infrequently. / *page 34*

How can surveys and case history studies be used to help us understand behavior and mental processes?

Surveys provide a few responses (observations) from very large samples of respondents, whereas case histories tend to provide detailed and specific information (observations) about just a few subjects. In either case, one may discover relationships among the responses observed. / *page 35*

What data are needed to calculate a correlation coefficient? How does a correlation coefficient tell us about the relationship between two measured responses?

In order to calculate a correlation coefficient, one needs to measure two responses of the same group of subjects, yielding a set of paired observations. Positive correlation coefficients tell us that high scores on one response are associated with (predict) high scores on the other and that low scores on one response are associated with (predict) low scores on the other. Negative correlations tell us that the two responses are inversely related with high scores on one measure associated with low scores on the other. Correlation coefficients of or near zero tell us that our measured responses are not related in any lawful way. The closer the coefficient is to its possible extremes of $+1.00$ or -1.00, the stronger the relationship between the responses, but in no case can one infer a cause-and-effect relationship from correlational data. / *page 38*

What is the essence of doing an experiment? Define independent, dependent, and extraneous variables in the context of an experiment.

An experiment involves manipulating independent variables, measuring dependent variables, and minimizing the influence of extraneous variables. Independent variables are those hypothesized to have an effect on some mental process or behavior. To see if such is the case, one looks for changes in some measured dependent variable that are consistent with changes in the manipulated independent variable. In order to claim a cause-and-effect relationship between the independent and the dependent variable, all other events that could have affected the dependent variable must have been controlled or eliminated. / *page 42*

How do random assignment, baseline designs, single- and double-blind techniques, and meta-analyses help to minimize error in psychological experiments?

Random assignment of subjects to experimental or control conditions of an experiment assures that each subject has an equal opportunity to be in any experimental treatment. Any preexperimental differences among subjects should thus balance out over groups. With baseline designs, the same subjects serve in both experimental and control conditions, thus serving as their own control. Single- and double-blind techniques protect against bias by not informing the subject (single-blind) or both the subject and the experimenter (double-blind) about the hypothesis under investigation. A meta-analysis is a procedure of statistical control that essentially combines the results of a number of smaller studies in one large analysis. / *page 45*

Cite four ethical issues that must be considered when doing psychological research.

Subjects in research experiments must have their confidentiality maintained. They should provide their advised consent before voluntarily participating in the research and should be debriefed about the project when it is over. Above all, one should always consider whether any potential risks in the research are offset by the present or future value of the results that may come from the research. Similar considerations are given to the use of animals in research. / *page 47*

THE BIOLOGICAL BASES OF BEHAVIOR

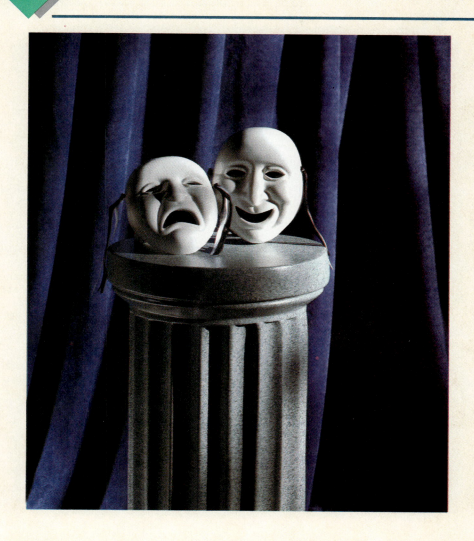

TOPIC 2A Basic Structures and Functions

TOPIC 2B The Central Nervous System

TOPIC

2A

*B*asic Structures and Functions

Why We Care: A Topic Preview

We've seen that psychologists attempt to discover and apply laws about the behavior and mental processes of organisms. We've seen that psychology is a discipline with many divergent subfields that uses a number of different scientific methods. This chapter reflects an observation that is becoming more clear every day, regardless of one's approach to psychology: In order to understand how people behave, think, and feel, we must understand at least the fundamentals of the biology and physiology of the organisms we are studying.

Our aim here is not to become amateur biologists or physiologists. We need not be experts in all areas of human anatomy. We need not be overly concerned with bones, blood, or muscle tissues, or how the lungs pass oxygen into the bloodstream, or how the stomach digests food. We have just two major concerns. One is with the nature of the genetic transmission of characteristics from one generation to the next. We've already alluded to the fact that this transmission is not a simple matter. But because so much of who we are reflects our genetic history, at least we ought to be aware of some of the important issues involved. Our second concern—once we've laid the proper foundation—is with the structure and functions of the central nervous system. It is the central nervous system, the brain and the spinal cord, and the nerve cells leading toward it and away from it that are most involved in behavior and mental processes. Ultimately, all of our behavior and mental processes— from the blink of an eye to profound and abstract thought—are no more, and no less, than the integrated actions and reactions of our nervous systems, and that is why we care.

Discovering just how our nervous systems work has become an exciting subfield of modern psychology. New data and new theories rush at us daily. And I'd like to let you in on a little secret (something your instructor knows from experience). Before the course begins, most introductory psychology students claim that they will be least interested in a chapter on biological-physiological bases (no matter who wrote the text). At the end of the term, however, it is this chapter that is most often chosen as "best" or "favorite" of them all.

In this topic, we'll start off with an overview of some of the general principles of genetics. We'll introduce some of the vocabulary and look at the relationship(s) between genetics and behavior. Then we'll begin our discussion of the nervous system. We'll take a building-block approach here. First, we'll describe the single, individual nerve cell. We'll see how these cells interact with each other and with other cells, and we'll discuss how the billions of nerve cells in our bodies work together to form the major nerve systems of the human body. Finally, we'll set the stage for our next topic by reviewing some of the methods that scientists use to discover the intricate workings of the spinal cord and the brain.

GENETICS AND PSYCHOLOGY

genetics *the science that studies the transmission of traits or characteristics from one generation to the next*

The science of **genetics** studies how traits and characteristics are passed from one generation to the next. Its focus is on heredity, on the *nature* side of the nature-nurture issue we introduced in Topic 1A. As is the case for psychology, questions about inheritance and an application of genetics often preceded an understanding of any underlying principles or genetic laws. For thousands of years, humans have engaged in the selective breeding of all sorts of plants and animals. Some dogs have been bred to be "lap dogs" and good pets, while others have been bred to retrieve or do field work with livestock. Ages ago, humankind discovered that when meaty bulls mated with meaty cows, the resulting calves tended to be meaty also. Rose growers have been creating new varieties of flowers for centuries through selective breeding (they call it hybridization). To some degree, it always has been appreciated that children tend to be more like their parents, and like each other, than anyone else; that many traits, both physical and psychological, seem to "run in families."

Genetics and Physical Traits

gene *the basic mechanism of hereditary transmission; that which gets passed from one generation to the next*

chromosome *literally, "colored body"; that tiny, threadlike structure found in 23 pairs in human cells that carry genes*

We can claim that the formal discipline of genetics began at about the time of the U.S. Civil War, when a monk, Gregor Mendel, discovered the nature of one of the mechanisms of heredity as he studied the selective breeding of the lowly pea. What Mendel discovered in his studies of peas was the **gene**, the basic mechanism of hereditary transmission. The genes that Mendel assumed to exist (at the time there was no way he could actually *see* a gene) can be found on microscopically tiny structures called **chromosomes**, which means "colored" (*chroma*) "body" (*some*). Chromosomes, in turn, live in the nucleus of every single cell in a living organism (even bacteria have them). And they live there in pairs.

So, exactly how does the process of genetic transmission work? No doubt you've heard this story before, and you recognize that the process is actually very complex and subtle, even though the basics are quite straightforward. Let's review. The nucleus of all human cells contains 23 pairs of chromosomes, *except* for the sex cells (the sperm in males, the ovum in females) which hold only half of each of the 23 possible pairs. At conception, the male and female sex cells unite to produce a new cell, producing a new mixture of 23 chromosome pairs (and, hence, genes), half from the father and half from the mother.

dominant gene *a gene that carries a trait that will be expressed regardless of the gene it is paired with*

recessive gene *a gene that carries a trait that will be expressed only if it is paired with another similar recessive gene*

If both parents contribute a gene that is ultimately responsible for some physical characteristic (say, blue eyes), then their child will be bound to have blue eyes. If both parents contribute a gene that results in brown eyes, their child will develop brown eyes. The story starts to get interesting when one parent contributes a gene that develops blue eyes while the other parent contributes a gene that develops brown eyes. Here's where the notion of dominant gene and recessive gene becomes relevant. A **dominant gene** is one whose characteristics will be expressed, or will show up, regardless of the gene paired with it. With eye color, the gene for brown pigmentation is dominant, so a child who inherits a "brown-eye" gene from either parent (who must be brown-eyed, of course), will also have brown eyes. A **recessive gene**, on the other hand, expresses its characteristic only when it is paired with another, similar recessive gene. With eye color, the gene for

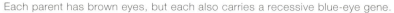

Figure **2.1**

Each parent has brown eyes, but each also carries a recessive blue-eye gene.

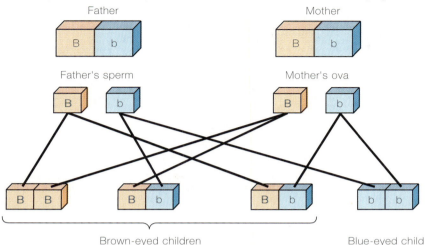

Father   Mother

Father's sperm   Mother's ova

Brown-eyed children   Blue-eyed child

Genetic transmission of dominant/recessive traits. Here, two brown-eyed (B) parents each carry a recessive blue-eyed gene (b). Only a child who receives the recessive gene (b) from both parents will, in fact, have blue eyes.

blue pigmentation is recessive, so a child who inheritis a "blue-eye" gene from either parent (who may appear to be either brown-eyed or blue-eyed) will have blue eyes only if another "blue-eye" gene is inherited from the other parent. It's really not all that complicated; perhaps Figure 2.1 will help.

When we talk about the genetic transmission of physical traits, we often use eye color as an example. This is because the pigmentation of the human eye is one of the few noticeable characteristics that can actually be accounted for, in most cases, by just a couple of known genes. But even eye color is often a complicated matter of gene interaction. Many genes will express their characteristic, or show their presence, only if *other genes* are present also. There are a few other complications that also deserve mention. One is that genes do not literally create any physical characteristic directly. For example, a gene for brown eyes does not "make brown eyes," but causes a certain chemical to be manufactured during the early stages of development which, in turn, *has the effect of* producing brown eyes. We do not inherit characteristics; we inherit genetic codes which, in turn, produce particular chemicals.

Another complication is the fact that the noticeable effects of some genes require time and development before they are expressed. For example, there is a type of baldness called male pattern baldness that is inherited in a straightforward fashion. Obviously, the observable consequences of this "gift" of heredity takes some time to be expressed. A third complication is that even physical characteristics that are primarily determined by genetic transmission require at least some minimal environmental interaction for those traits to be evidenced. As a simple example, consider why I happen

The genetic transmission of physical traits is often reflected in the extent to which children resemble their parents.

to be 6′4″ tall. A lot of it has to do with the fact that both of my parents were taller than average, and that on both sides of *their* families there were a number of relatives who were tall also. There happened to have been a good number of genes that promote tallness around, and I got some of them. But, that I am 6′4″ tall also reflects the fact that I was, and continue to be, well fed and cared for. My environment, in other words, allowed those genes to be expressed close to their full potential.

Before we go on, we had better address the issue of what in the world all this has to with psychology. The truth is, of course, that our inherited, physical characteristics have a great deal to do with how we think, feel, and behave. What we call self-image is in large measure determined by traits that are more physical than psychological. For example, in our chapter on social psychology, we'll see that physical attractiveness is correlated with many variables. Deciding to invest extracurricular time in the basketball team is an option that seldom occurs to people who happen to be considerably shorter than average. In a similar vein, we should point out that one's sex is determined by genes. Whether you are male or female is largely a genetic matter, and one of considerable importance to you, no doubt (this importance is reflected by the fact that we have devoted the entire Topic 10B to the matter). The impact of the genetic transmission of physical traits on one's psychological reactions becomes particularly obvious when we consider the number of diseases and disorders that are (at least in part) caused by genetic factors. When psychologists ask about who you are as a person, at least some of the answer must be in terms of genetically determined physical characteristics.

BEFORE YOU GO ON

What are some of the basic concepts involved in any discussion of the genetic transmission of physical characteristics?

Genetics and Psychological Traits

What we inherit are chromosomes and genes, which, in turn, produce certain chemicals. We do not inherit our mother's talent for music, our father's aggressiveness, or Aunt Tillie's mental illness. We do not inherit behaviors. We inherit chemicals. But such assertions may be overly literal. There is, in fact, considerable evidence that many of our behaviors, our cognitive skills, and our emotional reactions are influenced greatly by genetic factors.

Perhaps we should ask where all this considerable evidence comes from. In truth, most of the evidence is indirect—there is no one particular piece of research we can point to. What we have here is more a matter of the accumulated weight of data from a number of different types of studies. Three types of research have proven to be particularly useful.

1. **Inbreeding studies:** A typical inbreeding study might involve mating organisms with a certain trait, while also breeding organisms that do not

display that trait. If environmental conditions are held nearly constant over several generations, we may conclude that observed differences in the two strains of organisms are due to the genes they inherited through the inbreeding. Quite obviously, such studies are not done with humans, so we're faced with the task of arguing that whatever results we may find for rats or monkeys are relevant for humans as well.

2. **Family history studies:** This approach to determining the influence of heredity is the oldest, first employed systematically by Sir Francis Galton in the 1800s, when he concluded that "genius" tended to "run in families" and thus had a genetic basis (Galton, 1870). The logic here is that when a trait tends to show up more consistently within groups that are genetically related than it does otherwise, we may assume some genetic basis for that trait. For example, schizophrenia is a psychological disorder we will be discussing at length later on. It occurs in the general population at a rate of about one person in 100. But, if you have a sibling (brother or sister) with the disorder, your odds are 1 in 6. If that sibling happens to be an identical twin (which means with exactly the same set of genes), then your odds are 1 in 2. There are all sorts of problems with these studies, too. Obviously, persons from the same family share much in common above and beyond a set of genes. They are reared in very similar environments, and most of the time, the more closely related two people are, the more similar their environments. Family history research cannot tell us that environmental factors are irrelevant, but they can show us that genetic transmission is influential.

3. **Adoption studies:** This type of research is not without its problems and critics, but the logic is clear. Let's look at siblings who were adopted at an early age and see the extent to which they are now similar to their biological parents and to their adoptive parents. If we can locate identical twins who were separated at or near birth and raised in adoptive environments, we'd have an advantage; we'd have two identical genetic histories and two different environments (e.g., Farber, 1981). Such studies are rare and often troublesome (if twins are separated and reared in different homes, how can we begin to qualify *how* different the two environments really are). Nonetheless, some studies have shown us interesting data. For example, assume that a child with one schizophrenic parent is adopted by parents neither of whom is schizophrenic. That child will be significantly more likely to become schizophrenic than will a child of nonschizophrenic parents who is reared by parents of whom one is schizophrenic (Wender et al., 1974).

So what do studies of the effects of heredity on behavior and mental processes tell us? We seem to be approaching a point in time where we can see no human endeavors that are not to some degree influenced by that individual's genetic constitution. But remember that we do not inherit behaviors; we inherit genes. Some of those genes seem able to predispose us—in exceedingly complex ways—to be more or less susceptible to, more or less likely to do, think, or feel as we do. As it happens, we will be back over this ground many times in the following chapters as we cover different psychological characteristics.

When we get to the chapter on intelligence and cognitive aptitudes (Chapter 8), we'll review evidence that suggests that intellectual levels, including those we label as "retarded," are strongly influenced by heredity. Of late, considerable attention has been focused on the role of genetics in the development of a number of diseases and disorders, from Alzheimer's to alcoholism, epilepsy, depression, and schizophrenia. These data will be reviewed in Chapter 12. For now, however, let's look at a good example of how easy it is to overinterpret heredity/environment data.

For many years, research seemed to indicate that certain varieties of depression have a genetic basis. Much of these data was from family studies (for example, Allen, 1976). In 1987, a report was published that claimed to have located the specific gene (a dominant gene on chromosome 11) that produced a type of depression, at least in the population of Old Order Amish in Pennsylvania that were in the study (Egeland et al., 1987). Well, you can imagine the excitement that *that* caused! A pattern of behaviors as complex as depression, all from the action of one little gene. What a break-through! In fact, the researchers were very guarded in their statement of results, and for good reason. It turns out that there is no simple relationship between any one gene and any variety of depression, even for this special population of subjects (Kelsoe, et al., 1989; Merikangas, Spence & Kupfer, 1989; Plomin, 1990). Note that it is still almost certainly the case that there is a relationship between depression and as yet unknown genetic factors.

We will see other examples of the influence of genetics on behavior. In the developmental psychology chapter, we'll discuss heredity as it influences emotionality and intelligence. In the chapter on motivation, we'll see that there is considerable evidence that one's body weight and size is fairly well established by one's genes, and that there may be genes governing "impulse control" that may be useful in helping us understand phenomena such as gambling and/or alcoholism (e.g., Goodwin, 1985; Gabrielli & Plomin, 1985).

Of all the structures we inherit from our parents, none is more re-markable than the complexly interacting set of cells that comprise our nervous systems. It is to that aspect of our biological being that we now turn, focusing first on the single nerve cell, or neuron.

BEFORE YOU GO ON

What is it that we inherit from our parents?
What psychological traits are influenced by our genetic histories?
What are three ways of studying the influence of genes on behavior, cognition, and emotion?

THE NEURON

Our exploration of the nervous system begins at the level of the single nerve cell, which is called a **neuron**. Neurons are microscopically small. They were not recognized as separate structures until about the turn of the century. They exist throughout our nervous systems by the billions. Neu-

neuron *a nerve cell, the basic building block of the nervous system that transmits neural impulses*

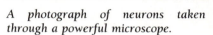

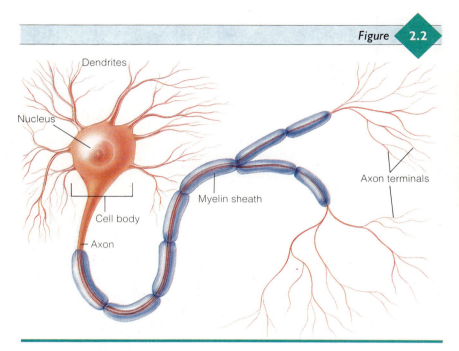

A typical neuron with its major structures.

A photograph of neurons taken through a powerful microscope.

rons are so tiny and so complex that estimating their number is very difficult, if not absurd. Just to give you an idea of the sizes and numbers we're talking about, there are approximately *125 million* specialized neurons that line the back, inside surface of each human eye, and about *100 billion* neurons can be found in the human brain (Hubel, 1979; Kolb, 1989).

The Structure of Neurons

We may not be sure about snowflakes, but it is a sure bet to claim that no two neurons are identical. There really is no such thing as a typical neuron, but most do have a number of structures in common. Figure 2.2 illustrates these common features, and Figure 2.3 illustrates what a few neurons actually look like.

One structure that all neurons are certain to have is a **cell body**. The cell body is the largest concentration of mass of the neuron. It contains the nucleus of the cell, which contains the genetic information that keeps the cell functioning.

Extending away from the cell body are a number of tentaclelike structures called **dendrites,** and one particularly long structure called the **axon**. Our drawing in Figure 2.2 is very much simplified, showing only a few dendrites, when in a mature neuron there may be thousands. Typically, the dendrites reach out to receive messages, called neural impulses, from other nearby neurons. These impulses are sent along to the cell body and then on down the axon toward other neurons or to muscles or glands. Some axons are quite long—as much as 2 to 3 feet long in the spinal cord. It is generally true, then, that within a neuron, impulses travel from dendrite to cell body to axon, and most of the trip will be made along the axon.

cell body *the largest mass of a neuron, containing the cell's nucleus, and which may receive neural impulses*

dendrites *branchlike extensions from a neuron's cell body where most neural impulses are received*

axon *the long, taillike extension of a neuron that carries an impulse away from the cell body toward the synapse*

myelin *a white, fatty covering found on some axons that serves to insulate and protect them, while increasing the speed of impulses*

The neuron illustrated in Figure 2.2 has a feature not found on all neurons. You can see that the axon of this neuron has a cover or sheath of **myelin**. Myelin is a white, fatty substance found on about half of the neurons in an adult's nervous system. It is the presence or absence of myelin that allows us to tell the difference between the gray matter (dendrites, cell bodies, and unmyelinated axons) and the white matter (myelinated axons) that we can see so clearly when we look at sections of nervous system tissue.

Myelin is a feature of neurons that is not yet developed at birth; it develops and adheres to axons as the nervous system matures. Myelin serves a number of useful functions. It protects the long, delicate axon. It acts as an insulator, keeping the activity of one neuron separate from those that happen to be nearby. Myelin speeds impulses along the length of the axon. Myelinated fibers carry impulses at rates nearly 10 times those that are unmyelinated (up to 120 meters per second). There are some diseases that attack the myelin on axons, which then slows and ultimately stops neural impulses that activate muscle fibers (multiple sclerosis is the most common). We tend to find myelin sheaths on axons that carry impulses relatively long distances throughout the body. Fibers that carry messages up and down the spinal cord, for instance, are myelinated fibers, while those that carry impulses back and forth across the spinal cord are not.

axon terminals *the series of branching end points of an axon where one neuron communicates with the next in a series*

Whether they are myelinated or not, axons end in a branching series of bare end points called **axon terminals**. It is at the axon terminals that each neuron communicates with other neurons (usually at their dendrites). The spreading axon terminals and the large number of dendrite extensions allow one tiny neuron to interact with hundreds, even thousands, of other neurons. To quickly review: Within a neuron, impulses typically travel from the dendrites, to the cell body, to the axon (which may be myelinated), and ultimately to the axon terminals.

Here's a far-reaching observation about neurons, particularly those in our brains: Virtually no neurons are generated after we are born. We are born with more neurons than we will ever have again. In fact, we are born with about twice as many neurons as we'll ever use. What happens to the rest? They just die off, or in some cases, we actively kill them (by a number of means, including physical damage, or more commonly with drugs such as alcohol). Bryan Kolb (1989), of the University of Lethbridge in Canada, gives us this analogy. During normal development, the brain is "constructed" in a manner rather like that in which a statue is chipped away from a block of granite. Rather than building up the finished product one small piece at a time, more material than what one needs is made available. Then, what is needed and/or used is retained, and the rest dies away. Here's a related reality: In order to have those billions of neurons in our brains at the time of birth, brain cells must be generating at a rate of approximately 250,000 per minute while the brain is being formed *before birth* (Cowan, 1979). There are obvious implications about prenatal care in this observation, which we'll explore in Chapter 9.

The fact that when neurons die they are not replaced with new ones makes neurons rather unique among cells. We're constantly making new blood cells to replace lost ones. If we didn't, we could never donate a pint of blood. Skin cells are constantly being replaced by new ones. You rinse away skin cells by the hundreds each time you wash your hands. Neurons are different; once they're gone, they're gone forever. As it happens, we are often in luck, however, because *the functions* of lost neurons can be taken over by other, surviving neurons.

Have you noticed that in this section we have tried to focus on the structure of the neuron and have found it nearly impossible to do so without reference to the function of the neuron: the transmission of neural impulses? We have seen that impulses are typically received by dendrites, passed on to cell bodies, and then to axons. We know that myelin insulates some axons and speeds neural impulses along, but we haven't really described what that neural impulse is. Let's do so now.

BEFORE YOU GO ON

What are the major structures of a neuron?

What is myelin, and what is its function?

The Function of Neurons

The function of a neuron is to transmit neural impulses from one place in the nervous system to another. The actual detailed story of how impulses are generated and transmitted is a very complex one, dealing with electrical and chemical changes that are extremely delicate and subtle. That the process is as well understood as it is is a wonder in itself. Let's start with a working definition: A **neural impulse** is a sudden and reversible change in the electrical charges within and outside a neuron that travels from the dendrites to the axon terminal when the neuron fires. Now let's see what all that means.

Neurons exist in a complex biological environment. As living cells, they are filled with and surrounded by fluids. Only a thin membrane (rather like a skin) separates the fluids inside a neuron from the fluids outside it. These fluids contain tiny dissolved chemical particles called **ions**. Chemical ions carry a very small, but measurable, electrical charge, either positive (+) or negative (−). These electrically charged ions float around in all the fluids of the body, but are heavily concentrated in and around the nervous system. And it's no great mystery where they come from: They come from the foods and liquids we eat and drink that are dissolved by our digestive system.

Neurons that are just lying around not doing anything are said to be neurons at rest, although "at rest" doesn't seem an accurate description. This is because a tension develops between the electrical charge of ions moved and trapped *inside* the neuron and the electrical charge of ions moved and trapped *outside* the neuron. A balanced state would exist if the positive and negative electrical charges on both sides of the neuron's membrane were equal. But this is not the case. When it is "at rest," the inside of the neuron has a negative (−) charge compared to the positive (+) charge of the fluids on the outside of the neuron. Hence the tension (and why "at

neural impulse *a sudden and reversible change in the electrical charges within and outside the membrane of a neuron, which travels from the dendrite to the axon end of a neuron*

ion *an electrically charged (either + or −) chemical particle*

resting potential *the difference in electrical charge between the inside of a neuron and the outside when it is at rest (− 70 mV)*

rest" is not very descriptive). The positive and negative ions, like the poles of a magnet, are drawn toward each other, but they cannot become balanced because of the neuron's membrane, which separates them. This imbalance of electrically charged chemical particles makes a neuron at rest like a tiny battery, holding a small electrical charge, called a **resting potential**. The electrical charge of a neuron at rest is about 70 millivolts (mV). To be more precise, we should say that the resting potential of a neuron is − 70 mV, because we measure the inside relative to the outside, and the inside of the neuron is where we have the concentration of negative ions. If this sounds at all mysterious to you, just think about a common D-cell battery of the sort you use in a flashlight. It, too, has two aspects (with batteries we call them poles), one positive and the other negative. The electrical charge that is possible with one of these batteries—its resting potential—is usually about 1500 mV, much greater, of course, than that of a tiny neuron.

When a neuron is stimulated to fire, or to produce an impulse of its own, the electrical tension of the resting potential is released. Suddenly and very quickly, the polarity of the nerve cell changes. For a very brief instant (about one-thousandth of a second) at one point along the length of the neuron, the electrical charge within the cell becomes more *positive* than the area outside the cell. The whole "charge" of the cell changes instantaneously. This new charge is called the **action potential**, or neural impulse. The measurable electric potential is now about + 40 mV, the positive sign indicating that the inside of the neuron is now more positive than the outside. There are more positive ions inside than outside. Now, for just a few thousandths of a second, there is a period (called the *refractory period*) during which the neuron cannot fire, because there is no tension there to release as an action potential. Then, very quickly, in a few thousandths of a second, the neuron returns to its original state, with the tension redeveloped. It is ready to fire again.

action potential *the short-lived burst of a change in the difference in electrical charge between the inside and the outside of a neuron when it fires (+ 40 mV)*

To repeat, what happens is something like this. When a neuron is at rest, there is a difference between the electrical charge inside and outside of it (the inside being slightly negative). When the neuron is stimulated, the difference suddenly reverses, so that the inside is slightly positive. Then the tension of the resting potential returns again. Figure 2.4 shows this process in the form of a graph.

We've already made the point that when a neuron is stimulated, an impulse travels from the dendrite to the cell body, and then down the axon to the axon terminal. Notice, though, that when an impulse "travels down a neuron," *nothing physically moves from one end of the neuron to the other*. The only movement of physical particles that takes place is the movement of the electrically charged ions *into and out of the neuron* through its membrane. What travels "down the neuron" is where this action potential takes place. What moves along the neuron is where the release of tension of the resting potential occurs.

all-or-none principle *the fact that a neuron will either fire and generate a full impulse (an action potential), or it will not fire at all*

When a neuron is stimulated, it either transmits an impulse or it doesn't. A neuron either fires or it doesn't. This fact is called the **all-or-none principle**. This principle is of particular interest to us because it relates directly to a psychological question: How does the nervous system react to differences in stimulus intensity? How do our neurons react to the differences between a bright light and a dim one, a soft sound and a loud one, a tap on the shoulder and a slap on the back? Here's where the all-

Figure **2.4**

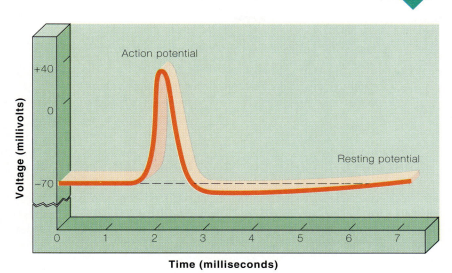

Time (milliseconds)

Changes in electrical potential that occur during the firing of a neuron. Note that voltage is negative (−70 millivolts) when the neuron is at rest, and positive (+40 millivolts) during the firing of the impulse. Note, too, that the entire process lasts but a few milliseconds.

or-none principle comes in. The electrical charge of the resting potential is either released or it isn't. There is no in-between or degree of firing. We cannot say, for example, that for a dim light a neuron fires softly, or slightly, or gently, releasing only some of the tension of the resting potential, while for brighter lights, more ions are exchanged, and the release of tension that becomes the action potential is greater.

It is also true that neurons do not necessarily generate impulses, or fire, every time they are stimulated. Each neuron has a level of stimulation that must be surpassed in order to get it to transmit an impulse. The minimum level of stimulation required to get a neuron to fire is called the **neural threshold**. When this concept is coupled with the all-or-none principle, we have some insight about how we process differences in stimulus intensity. High-intensity stimuli (bright lights, loud sounds, and so on) don't get neurons to fire more vigorously, but stimulate more neurons to fire and/or to fire more frequently. High-intensity stimuli are above the threshold of a greater number of neurons than are low-intensity stimuli. So the difference in your experience of a flashbulb going off in your face and a candle viewed at a distance is largely a matter of the number of neurons involved and the rate at which they fire, not the intensity with which they fire.

Now that we've examined the individual nerve cell in some detail, we had better see about how neurons communicate with each other: how neural impulses are transmitted from one cell to another. The story of how impulses travel *between* neurons is just as remarkable, but quite different from the story of how impulses travel *within* neurons.

neural threshold *the minimum amount of stimulation required to produce an impulse within a neuron*

BEFORE YOU GO ON

What is the basic process involved when a neuron fires?
What is the all-or-none principle?
What is meant by the concept of neural threshold?

FROM ONE CELL TO ANOTHER: THE SYNAPSE

We've seen enough about impulse transmission within neurons to appreciate that it is a very rapid and complicated electrochemical process. When an impulse is sent on to an adjoining neuron, the story changes completely. The general location where an impulse is relayed from one neuron to another is called the **synapse.** Here's what happens there.

As we've seen, at the very end of an axon there are many branches that are called axon terminals (refer back to Figure 2.2). Throughout the neuron, but concentrated in the axon terminals, are incredibly small containers called **vesicles**. The vesicles hold complex chemicals called **neurotransmitters**. When a neural impulse reaches the axon terminal, the vesicles there at the very end, near the membrane, burst open and release the neurotransmitter they have been holding. Released from the vesicles, the neurotransmitter floods out into the **synaptic cleft**, a tiny space between two neurons. It is important to note that the two neurons involved do not actually touch; they are separated by the synaptic cleft. Once in the synaptic cleft, some neurotransmitter molecules move to the membrane of the next neuron, where they may fit into "receptor sites" and enter the membrane. See Figure 2.5.

Then what happens? Actually, any number of things. Let's look at a few. The most reasonable scenario for synaptic activity is that in which the neurotransmitters flood across the synaptic cleft, enter into receptor sites in the next neuron in a chain of nerve cells, and by so doing, excite that next neuron to release the tension of its resting potential and fire a new impulse down to its axon terminals. There, neurotransmitter chemicals are released from vesicles, cross the synaptic cleft, and stimulate the next neuron in the sequence to fire. In fact, this *is* the case, when the neurotransmitter is an *excitatory* chemical. What it does, simply, is stimulate the next neuron in a sequence to fire.

But as it happens, there are many neurons throughout our nervous systems that contain neurotransmitters that have the opposite effect. When they are released, they flood across the synaptic cleft and actually work to prevent the next neuron from firing. We refer to these neurotransmitters as *inhibitory*. If you think back to our last section when we talked about neural thresholds, you can now see how that concept works in a new light. Imagine a neuron's dendrite, sitting there "at rest," with many axon terminals (of other neurons) just across the synaptic cleft. For this neuron to

synapse *the general location where an impulse is relayed from one neuron to another by means of neurotransmitters*

vesicles *the small containers, concentrated in axon terminals, that hold neurotransmitter molecules*

neurotransmitters *chemical molecules released at the synapse that will, in general, either excite or inhibit neural impulse transmission*

synaptic cleft *the space between the membrane of an axon terminal and the membrane of the next neuron in a sequence*

Figure   **2.5**

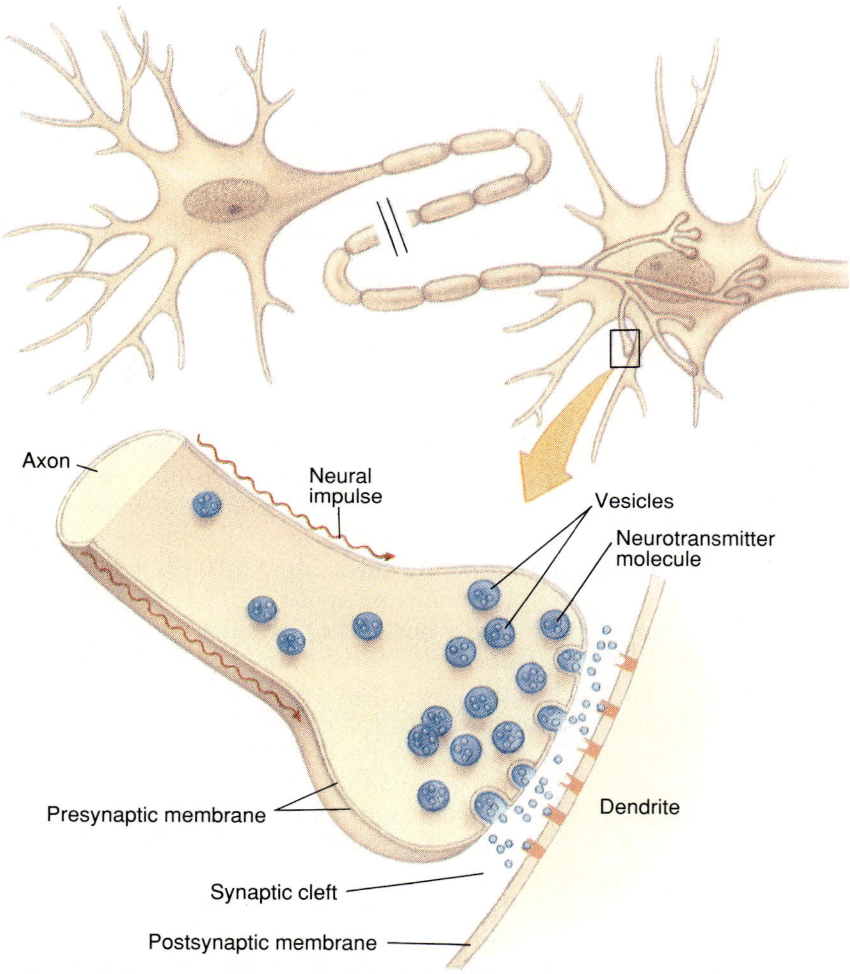

Axon

Neural
impulse

Vesicles

Neurotransmitter
molecule

Presynaptic membrane

Dendrite

Synaptic cleft

Postsynaptic membrane

A synapse, in which transmission is from upper left to lower right. As an impulse enters the axon terminal, vesicles release neurotransmitter chemicals through the presynaptic membrane into the synaptic cleft. The neurotransmitter then stimulates the postsynaptic membrane of the next dendrite.

begin a new impulse, it may require more excitatory chemical than just one axon terminal can provide, particularly if nearby terminals are releasing inhibitory neurotransmitters at about the same time. So that brings up another possibility. An impulse may race down a neuron, release an excitatory neurotransmitter into the synaptic cleft, which then may flood across to the membrane of the next neuron, and as a result, nothing may happen. And in fact, nothing *will* happen unless there is sufficient excitatory neurotransmitter chemical to activate an impulse in the next neuron.

Not long ago, it was believed that neurons produced and released one of just two neurotransmitters. There were excitatory neurons and there were inhibitory neurons. Now we realize that this view is much too simplistic. Although one neuron produces and releases just one neurotransmitter, we know of nearly 60 different neurotransmitters today, and it is virtually certain that there are many others that have yet to be discovered. We'll run into neurotransmitters again, in our discussion of the physiological basis of reward in the learning chapter, in our discussion of drugs, and in our discussion of the causes of certain psychological disorders, for instance. For now though, we ought to at least briefly note some of the better-known neurotransmitters.

Acetylcholine, or ACh, can be found throughout the nervous system. It is the most common of the excitatory transmitters. Not only is ACh found in the brain, but it commonly works in synapses between neurons and muscle tissue cells. Acetylcholine (usually pronounced "uh-**see'**-til-**koh'**-leen") is also implicated in normal memory function and is thus a prime candidate for research on memory problems, such as those found in Alzheimer's disease.

Norepinephrine and *dopamine* are two important inhibitory neurotransmitters. They are related in the sense that both seem to be involved in mood regulation. When there is too much norepinephrine in a person's brain and/or spinal cord, the result is often a feeling of arousal, anxiety, agitation, and the like. (One of the things that cocaine does is to increase the release of norepinephrine, leading to a state of agitation and a "high" mood state.) Too little norepinephrine in the brain and spinal cord has been linked to feelings of depression. Dopamine is one of the neurotransmitters that most intrigues psychologists. It seems to be involved in a very wide range of reactions. Either too much or too little dopamine within the nervous system seems to produce a number of different effects, depending primarily on which system of nerve fibers in the brain is involved. Dopamine has been associated with some of the thought and mood disturbances of some psychological disorders and with the impairment of movement responses (not enough dopamine and we find difficulty in voluntary movement; too much and we find involuntary tremors.) Some pathways in the brain in which we find dopamine have been the focus of research that is trying to determine the physiological basis of reinforcement.

Endorphins (plural, because there appear to be many of them) are our natural pain suppressors. By and large, what we call our pain threshold—our ability to tolerate different levels of pain—is a function of the production of endorphins (Watkins & Mayer, 1982). With excess endorphins, we feel little pain; a deficit in endorphins results in more experienced pain.

As you can imagine, we could continue this list through a number of different neurotransmitters, but for now it is the basic idea of what they do that matters: They excite or inhibit the transmission of neural impulses throughout the nervous system, and that excitation or inhibition can have a considerable effect on our thoughts, feelings, and behavior.

Finally, so that our simplified description does not leave a false impression, let me make one point clear: Neural impulse transmission is seldom a matter of one neuron simply stimulating one other neuron that in turn stimulates yet one more. Remember that any neuron may have hundreds or thousands of axon terminals and synapses. Any one neuron, then, has the potential for exciting or inhibiting (or being excited by or inhibited by) many other neurons.

Summarize neural impulse transmission at the synapse. Name four neurotransmitters and indicate some psychological reaction with which they are involved.

NERVOUS SYSTEMS: THE BIG PICTURE

Now that we have a sense of how neurons work, individually and in combination, let's step back for a moment to consider the broader context in which they do what they do. We've already made the point that little of any consequence gets accomplished by the actions of only a few individual neurons. Behavior and mental activity generally require large numbers of integrated neurons working together in complex, organized systems. Figure 2.6 depicts how these systems are related to each other.

The first major division of the nervous system is determined wholly on the basis of anatomy. The **central nervous system (CNS)** includes all of the neurons and nerve fibers found in the spinal cord and the brain. In many ways, this system of nerves is the most complex and intimately involved in the control of our behavior and mental processes. The **peripheral nervous system (PNS)** is simply composed of all the neurons in our body *not* in the CNS—that is, the nerve fibers in our arms, face, fingers, intestines, and so forth. In general, neurons in the peripheral nervous system carry impulses either *from* the central nervous system to the muscles and glands (on *motor neurons*, or *motor fibers*) or *to* the CNS from receptor cells (on *sensory neurons*, or *sensory fibers*).

The peripheral nervous system is itself divided into two parts, based largely on the part of the body being served. The **somatic nervous system** includes those neurons outside the CNS that serve the skeletal muscles and that pick up impulses from the major receptors—the eyes and ears, for example. The other component of the PNS is the **autonomic nervous system (ANS)**, where "autonomic" means essentially the same thing as "automatic." This implies that the activity of the ANS is in large measure (but not totally) independent of CNS control. The fibers of the ANS are involved in activating the smooth muscles, such as those of the stomach and intestines, and the glands. The ANS also provides feedback to the CNS on the activity of these internal processes.

Because the autonomic nervous system is so involved in emotional responding, we'll return to it again in that context. For now, we can note that the ANS is made up of two parts also, the **sympathetic division** and the **parasympathetic division**. These two divisions commonly work in opposition to each other, the former being active when we are in states of emotional excitement or under stress, and the latter becoming active when we are relaxed and quiet. An overview of the autonomic nervous system and the structures affected by it is presented in Figure 2.7. Here you can see that the sympathetic and the parasympathetic division each act on the same organs, but do so in opposite ways.

central nervous system (CNS) *those neurons in the brain and spinal cord*

peripheral nervous system (PNS) *those neurons not found in the brain or spinal cord, but in the periphery of the body*

somatic nervous system *sensory and motor neurons outside the CNS that serve the sense receptors and the skeletal muscles*

autonomic nervous system (ANS) *those neurons of the PNS that activate the smooth muscles and glands*

sympathetic division *(of the ANS) those neurons involved in states of emotionality*

parasympathetic division *(of the ANS) those neurons involved in the maintenance of states of calm and relaxation*

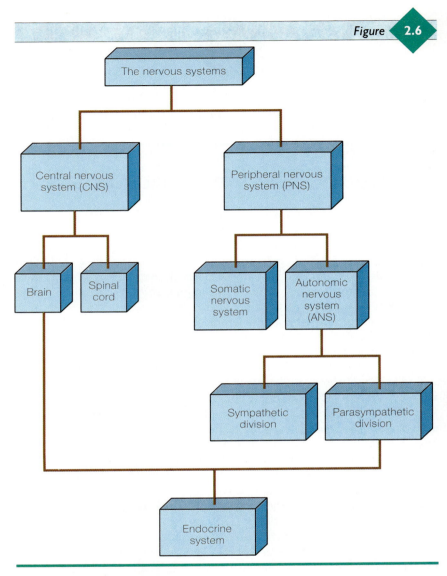

Figure **2.6**

The organization of the human nervous systems.

As you can see, there is one other system depicted in the overview of Figure 2.6: the **endocrine system**. The endocrine system is influenced by the central nervous system and can, in turn, influence nervous system activity, but *it is not a system of nerves*. It is an interconnected network of glands that has its effect behavior through the secretion of chemicals called **hormones** into the bloodstream. Curiously, many of the hormones produced by the endocrine system are chemically very similar to neurotransmitters and have many of the same overall effects. The endocrine system's glands and hormones are controlled both by the brain of the central nervous system and by the autonomic nervous system, which is why we have drawn it as we have in Figure 2.6. We've also included mention of the endocrine system here because its overall function is very similar to that of the nervous systems: to transmit information from one part of the body to another. The

Figure **2.7**

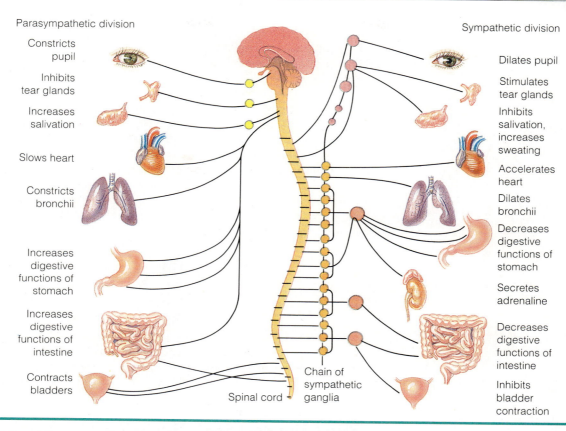

Parasympathetic division

Constricts pupil

Inhibits tear glands

Increases salivation

Slows heart

Constricts bronchii

Increases digestive functions of stomach

Increases digestive functions of intestine

Contracts bladders

Sympathetic division

Dilates pupil

Stimulates tear glands

Inhibits salivation, increases sweating

Accelerates heart

Dilates bronchii

Decreases digestive functions of stomach

Secretes adrenaline

Decreases digestive functions of intestine

Inhibits bladder contraction

Chain of sympathetic ganglia

Spinal cord

The division of the autonomic nervous system. The parasympathetic division becomes active when we are relaxed and quiet, while the sympathetic division is active when we are aroused or excited. (Adapted from Gardner, 1963.)

nervous systems do so through the transmission of neural impulses; the endocrine system employs hormones sent through the bloodstream. As it happens, the endocrine system is slower to react, but many of its effects are longer lasting. Most of the endocrine system's involvement in our behavior occurs in states of emotion and motivation. We'll return to a discussion of this system in the context of these topics.

There is good reason to separate out all of these different organizations of neurons. It's not just an academic exercise. It helps make a very complex system easier to deal with, and it reminds us that not all neurons in our body are there doing the same thing for the same purpose at the same time. But we have to keep in mind that the outline of Figure 2.6 is very simplified to this extent: All of the nerve fibers in each of the different systems have profound influences on each other. They are not at all as independent as our diagram might imply.

For example, let's trace some of the events that would occur if you were to step on a tack left on the kitchen floor. Receptor cells in your foot would respond to the tack and send impulses up your leg (on sensory neurons of the somatic division of the PNS) to your spinal cord (CNS).

There, some impulses would be sent back down your leg (on motor neurons of the somatic division of the PNS) to get it to jerk up off the floor. At the very same time, other impulses would be sent up the spinal cord to your brain, where you would become aware of what was happening (all in the CNS). At the same time, you would be angry that someone had left a tack on the floor (the anger involving the sympathetic division of your ANS). Perhaps in your excitement of hopping about the kitchen and planning revenge for whoever left the tack around, your endocrine system would become active, flooding extra doses of hormones into your bloodstream. Eventually, you'd settle down, the parasympathetic division of your autonomic nervous system taking over again. It is almost always the case that even when we can classify a certain response as being largely determined by some part of the nervous system, we need to recognize that no division of the nervous system operates independently from the others.

We're almost ready to begin our discussion of the structures and functions of the human central nervous system. Before we do, however, we'll address the question of how scientists have learned what they have about the intricate and complex structures of the spinal cord and brain.

BEFORE YOU GO ON

Name the different human nervous systems, and indicate how they are related to each other.

HOW TO STUDY THE CENTRAL NERVOUS SYSTEM

The complexity of the billions of neurons that make up the spinal cord and the brain is truly awesome. That we know as much as we do about their tiny and delicate structures is a credit to those scientists who have taken up the challenge of trying to understand this most important system of nerve fibers. In this section, we'll briefly review five of the approaches that have helped us learn about the central nervous system.

Accident and Injury

One way to find out how the central nervous system functions is to work backward. In this case, we ask what happens to an organism's behaviors or mental proceseses if a part of the spinal cord or brain is damaged by injury or disease. If, for example, a person is found to be blind after suffering a wound to the back of the head, we might reasonably hypothesize that vision is normally coded there, in the back of the brain. This was the method used by the neurologist Pierre-Paul Broca (1824–1880), who discovered that speech production is processed in a small area toward the front, and usually on the left side, of the brain. Broca's conclusions were based on observations he made of human brains during autopsies. People

Pierre-Paul Broca

with similar speech disorders commonly had noticeable damage in the very same area of the brain. Logic then led Broca to suspect that normal speech functions are controlled by this portion of the brain, which we now call Broca's area.

One of the strangest cases of brain injury that helped our understanding of brain function is the story of Phineas Gage. In 1848, Gage, a 25-year-old railroad construction foreman, had the misfortune of being too close to an explosion. The explosion, which he accidentally caused himself, drove an iron bar into his head through his left jaw and out through the top of his skull (Figure 2.8). Much to everyone's surprise, Gage survived this massive injury to his brain. He was declared recovered in just a few weeks. Although he survived until 1861, his behavior—in fact, his whole personality—changed completely. He became loud, profane, and irresponsible, and he seemed unable to plan and think ahead—an almost total reversal from the Phineas Gage his friends had known before the accident. The changes in his behavior were directly related to the damage to Gage's brain. Important pathways in the front, upper part of his brain, which would normally exert voluntary control over the emotional behaviors originating in his lower brain centers, had been severed. After the accident, his emotions were expressed directly, without the supervision and restrictions of the higher brain areas.

Figure **2.8**

A cast of the head and the actual skull of Phineas Gage. Note the places on the skull pierced by the iron rod.

Surgical Interventions

By definition, we cannot control the location or the extent of damage to the nervous system when it occurs by accident or disease. What we can do is surgically cut or remove some particular portion of the spinal cord or brain to see what effects might result. Quite obviously, we don't go around cutting into human brains motivated solely by the curiosity of what might happen as a result. The procedure is used sparingly and almost always with nonhuman subjects.

The logic of this method is the same as for naturally occurring CNS damage. A very small **lesion**, or cut, is made in a particular place in, say, a rat's brain. That rat then refuses to eat, even if food is readily available. The procedure is repeated with other rats and the results are the same. We may then reasonably conclude that the lesioned part of the brain plays some role in the feeding behaviors of rats.

lesion *a cut or incision that destroys specific areas of tissue*

Electrical Stimulation

One of the most significant advances in technology that has aided our study of the central nervous system was the development of the **electrode** for stimulating and/or recording the activity of very small areas of nervous system tissue. An electrode is a very fine wire (often made of platinum) that can be eased into a specific area of the brain. Once in position, the electrode can deliver a mild electric current, artificially stimulating that region of the brain to respond. This technique was first used successfully back in the early 1870s (Sheer, 1961).

By using a stimulating electrode, one can map out many of the functions of different parts of the spinal cord and brain (e.g., Penfield, 1975; Penfield & Rasmussen, 1950). Most of the time, when an electrode stimulates an

electrode *a fine wire used to either stimulate or record the electrical activity of neural tissue*

area of human brain, there is simply no discernible reaction at all. Sometimes, however, the artificial stimulation produces a noticeable reaction. For example, you may deliver a mild stimulus current to the tissues near the surface of the very back of the brain. When you do so, your subject reports a visual experience, a flash of lights not unlike fireworks—thus reinforcing your hypothesis that vision is processed in the back of the brain. A stimulus from an electrode in a particular location in the left side of the brain produces a muscle twitch in the patient's right arm, even though the patient claims not to have moved at all. Here's evidence that perhaps this area of the brain controls muscles in the right arm.

Recording Electrical Activity

Not only can electrodes be used to stimulate nervous system tissue, they also can be used to measure and record the electrical activity of the nervous system. Remember that nerve impulses are largely changes in electrical charges that sweep down nerve fibers. Some recording electrodes are so small and sensitive that they can be used to detect electrical changes in individual neurons. Most recordings of single nerve cell activity are made using nonhuman subjects, particularly those animals that have large neurons, such as the squid. These tiny recording electrodes have helped us learn about the true nature of the neural impulse and impulse transmission. Single-cell recordings also allowed David Hubel and Thornton Wiesel (1979) to discover individual cells in the brains of cats and monkeys that only respond to very specific types of visual stimulation. Their work (which earned them a Nobel Prize) also prompted them to propose that the entire visual field (what we see) is completely represented in the brain, although in somewhat distorted form. Their work also confirmed the insight that neural impulses from the eyes are processed at the back of the brain.

electroencephalograms (EEGs) *recordings of the general levels of electrical activity of the brain*

In 1929, Hans Berger, a German psychiatrist who had been using the technique for nearly 20 years, reported that electrodes attached to the scalp of an individual could pick up and record the general electrical activity of the brain. Recordings of such brain activity are called **electroencephalograms**, or **EEG**s for short. Electroencephalograms do not provide very much in the way of detailed information about the specific activity of small areas of the brain, but they do provide a wealth of information about overall brain activity (Figure 2.9). Electroencephalograms can be used to tell us about a person's level of arousal or what stage of sleep he or she is in (see Topic 4B). The technique is sensitive enough to reinforce impressions that we may have gotten from other sources. For example, when a person looks at a bright, colorful, detailed picture, EEG activity at the back of the brain increases. We should also mention that a relatively new technology (that goes by the tongue-twisting name of magnetoencephalogram, or MEG) may provide us with a more detailed description of the electrical activity of the brain. This procedure can record very slight and short-lived changes in electrical activity, but for now its usefulness as a research tool remains to be demonstrated (Adler, 1990a).

Observing the Brain Directly and Indirectly

Certainly one way to study regions of the central nervous system is simply to look at them. The development of the microscope helped a great

Figure **2.9**

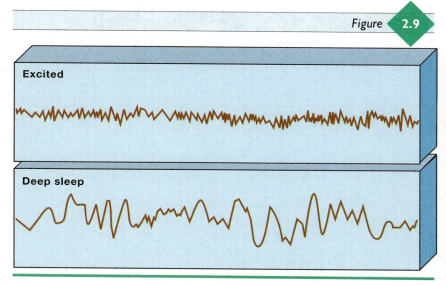

Excited

Deep sleep

EEG recordings of normal brain waves of a human adult at rest.

Figure **2.10**

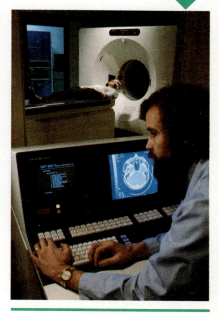

A CAT scan provides computer-enhanced images of the brain with a noninvasive procedure.

deal in this regard, making small anatomical details of structure visible. The more powerful electron microscope allows us to look even closer and to take the sort of photographs we've used in this topic. But normal microscopic examination restricts us to looking at dead tissue—cells removed from their usual surroundings. What a great advantage there would be in having a detailed look at the brain of a living, behaving organism. To a degree, X-ray technology allows us to do just that. Particularly when dyes or radioactive substances are entered into the brain, we can get a fairly good view of at least the major structures there. But the picture is not a clear one. Some important structures, such as tumors, may remain hidden behind less important ones.

Recently, computer technology has joined with X-ray technology to do what is called a **CAT scan** of the brain. The *CAT* is an acronym for *computerized axial tomography* (see Figure 2.10). This device takes a series of thousands of X-ray pictures of the brain from many different angles; the process is very brief and not dangerous. The images are fed into a computer that enhances their quality and combines them into a set of pictures of "slices" of the brain. The CAT scan can thus take a series of computer-enhanced pictures of the brain that together make what amounts to a three-dimensional view of the brain. Significantly, the CAT scan is noninvasive, which means that the pictures can be taken of a living subject without physically having to "invade" the brain with any sort of instrument.

Since the CAT scan became generally available in the early 1980s, newer and more powerful devices for imaging the brain have come into use. An even clearer picture of the structures of the living, intact, human brain are possible using **magnetic resonance imaging (MRI)**. This technique allows for very precise and detailed high-resolution pictures of the brain in cross-section. MRI is not a form of X-ray technology. Magnetic resonance images are constructed (by computers, again) from the detection of very small waves of energy that are produced by cells when the brain is placed

CAT scan *(computerized axial tomography) a method of imaging brain structures through the computer enhancement of X-ray pictures*

MRI *(magnetic resonance imaging) a process that provides clear, detailed pictures of the brain by recording energy from cells when the brain has been placed in a magnetic field*

PET scan *(positron emission transaxial tomography) a method of imaging the brain and its activity by locating small amounts of radioactive chemical injected into the brain*

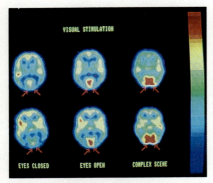

These PET scans show the increased activity that occurs in the brain in response to visual stimulus. Note that most activity results from a complex stimulus.

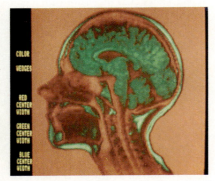

Pictured is an NMR scan of a normal brain.

in a strong magnetic field. This, too, is a noninvasive method of studying brain structure.

While CAT scans and MRIs can tell us about the structure of the brain, the **PET scan**, and its more recent derivatives, goes beyond structure: It not only gives us a picture of the inside of the living brain, but provides us with insights about brain function as well. PET scans (PET stands for positron emission tomography) involve injecting a radioactive substance into the brain. This chemical tends to concentrate in those areas of the brain that are being most active—areas where oxygen or glucose are being metabolized most rapidly. (In some forms of PET scans a different chemical is used that gravitates to areas of greatest blood flow.) The PET scan then provides a picture of those areas of the brain that are the most active. PET scans of subjects who are looking at a complex visual stimulus show increased activity in the back regions of the brain. When the same subject is listening to a story, for example, the PET scan shows increased brain activity on the right side, near the temple. The usefulness of this technique for studying the brain activity of persons with psychological disorders is obvious (Turkington, 1985). An even more recent development, with great potential, is the single-photon emission computed tomography (SPECT) brain scan. This procedure can also provide a picture of brain areas in action, and it has the advantage of being able to examine smaller areas that are deeper in the brain than can the standard PET scan (Holman & Tumeh, 1990).

BEFORE YOU GO ON

Briefly summarize five techniques used to study the central nervous system.

We simply cannot divorce who we are in this world from the biological bases of our behaviors and mental processes that we inherit from our parents and generations before them. Whatever else we may be, we are biological organisms, and it behooves us as students of psychology to appreciate the fundamentals of genetic transmission and the basic structures and functions of the nervous system. That living cells as tiny as neurons can provide the basis for all our actions, mental or behavioral, is a notion that takes some time to get used to. But neurons do not act alone. The complexity of the individual nerve cell multiplies geometrically with the activity of neurotransmitters at synapses. In this topic we have seen how the nerve cells of the human body are organized in large, complex systems. For us, the most relevant of those systems is the central nervous system, composed of the brain and the spinal cord. Now that we have reviewed how scientists go about studying these structures, it is time to review some of what they have learned.

What are some of the basic concepts involved in any discussion of the genetic transmission of physical characteristics?

Physical characteristics are inherited to the extent that genes, carried on chromosomes, are passed from the sex cells of both parents to the child. Each cell in the body contains 23 pairs of chromosomes in its nucleus (except the sex cells, which contain only 23 single chromosomes). Genes may be dominant, which means that the trait they carry will necessarily be expressed, or recessive, in which case they must be paired with another similar recessive gene in order to be expressed as a trait. / page 54

What is it that we inherit from our parents? What psychological traits are influenced by our genetic histories? What are three ways of studying the influence of genes on behavior, cognition, and emotion?

In discussing the inheritance of psychological traits, we need always to keep in mind that we directly inherit only genes, not behaviors or traits of any kind. Nonetheless, virtually all important human characteristics have some foundation in one's genetic history. In particular, there is evidence for a genetic factor in intellectual and emotional reactivity and in the development of a number of psychological disorders, including lack of impulse control. These results come from inbreeding studies, from the study of identical twins, and from the study of adopted individuals. / page 56

What are the major structures of a neuron? What is myelin, and what is its function?

Neurons are microscopically tiny living cells made up of a cell body, which contains the cell's nucleus; a number of dendrites that usually receive impulses; and an axon that carries an impulse away from the cell. The axons of some neurons are covered by a white, fatty myelin sheath that insulates and protects the delicate structure and speeds impulses along the axon. Even myelinated axons end with a set of branching axon terminals. / page 59

What is the basic process involved when a neuron fires? What is the all-or-none principle? What is meant by the concept of neural threshold?

When a neuron fires, a tension created by an imbalance of electrically charged chemical ions is quickly released. When a neuron is *not* firing, or is at rest, the inside of the neuron is more negatively charged than the outside (the resting potential of -70 mV). At the point where an impulse occurs, this polarity changes, and the inside of the neuron becomes momentarily positive compared to the outside (the action potential of $+40$ mV). The all-or-none principle claims that a neuron's firing either takes place totally or not at all; that is, there is no such thing as a partial firing of a neuron. The concept of neural threshold says that there is a minimal amount of stimulation required to get a neuron to fire in the first place. / page 62

Summarize neural impulse transmission at the synapse. Name four neurotransmitters and indicate some psychological reaction with which they are involved.

At the synapse, an impulse triggers the release of neurotransmitter chemicals from small vesicles in the axon terminal. These chemicals flood into the synaptic cleft, embed themselves in receptor sites in the membrane of adjacent neurons, and when sufficient amounts of the neurotransmitter are present, either excite or inhibit impulse transmission. Acetylcholine (ACh) is the most common excitatory neurotransmitter found throughout the central nervous system (CNS) and at synapses between the nervous system and muscle tissue. Norepinephrine and dopamine are inhibitory neurotransmitters, the former implicated in reactions of agitation, arousal, and depression; the latter implicated in cognitive and affective reactions and in movement responses. Endorphins are a class of neurotransmitter involved in the suppression of or reaction to pain. / page 65

Name the different human nervous systems, and indicate how they are related to each other.

See Figure 2.6. The major division is into CNS and PNS, where the CNS is divided into brain and spinal cord and the PNS is divided into the somatic and autonomic nervous systems. The ANS is further divided into sympathetic and parasympathetic divisions. The endocrine system is a network of glands that, under the influence of the brain and ANS, secrete hormones into the bloodstream, which, in turn, influence behavior and mental processes. / page 68

Briefly summarize five techniques used to study the central nervous system

We can study the central nervous system by (1) observing the effects of injury or accident on behavior; (2) lesioning parts of the CNS and noting the results; (3) electrically stimulating specific regions of the CNS; (4) recording the electrical activity of individual nerve cells or, with the EEG, larger areas of the brain; and (5) looking at the brain with X rays, CAT scans, MRI procedures, or PET scans. / page 72

The Central Nervous System

Why We Care: A Topic Preview

We're ready now to consider the hundreds of billions of neurons that together form the central nervous system: the spinal cord and the brain. Most clearly now we will see how physiological structures and functions impact regularly on our behaviors and our mental processes. With the spinal cord we see the first and simplest interactions between stimuli in the environment, cells in the nervous system, and responses of the organism—the spinal reflex.

Then there's the brain. The human brain. What is it like? A vast computer? The seat of understanding? The processor of information? A warehouse of memories of experiences past? A reservoir of emotion? The source of motivation? Yes, it is all of these, and more. We care about the structures and functions of the brain because it is in the brain that all our conscious, voluntary actions and reactions begin. It is in the brain that all our emotions are experienced, and it is here that all our cognitions are manipulated and stored—and that is why we care.

Our goal in this topic is to examine briefly some of the more important structures and functions of the central nervous system. Starting with the spinal cord, we'll work our way up to the base of the brain, through its midsection to the outer layers of the brain, the cerebal cortex. As we go, we'll look at a number of small areas of the central nervous system. We will describe their anatomical features and point out how they are involved in our everyday lives. Breaking the system down into small manageable areas and discussing them one at a time is about the only choice we have. But when we fragment our discussion of the spinal cord and brain this way, we can easily lose sight of the fact that they comprise a unified system in which all of the various parts work together and interact with other complex systems. Some of our normal functions can be localized in particular areas or structures of the CNS, but the adaptability and integration of its many different functions force us to consider the CNS as a whole, as more than simply the sum of its parts.

Discussions of the structures and functions of the central nervous system occasionally sound rather impersonal, as if we were talking about some strange mass of gooey tissue in a glass jar. What you'll need to do from time to time is remind yourself that we're talking about your brain and your spinal cord—and mine too. As you read these words, it is your spinal cord that carries the impulses to the muscles in your arm to turn the page, your brain that directs your eyes to move across the page, your brain that processes impulses from your eyes, your brain that seeks understanding, and your brain that monitors your heart rate and keeps you breathing while you read.

THE SPINAL CORD

As we have noted, the central nervous system consists of the brain and the spinal cord. In this section, we'll describe both the structure and the function of the spinal cord, reserving our discussion of the brain for later. As we examine the role of the spinal cord we can see clearly the role of the nervous system in behavior.

The Structure of the Spinal Cord

spinal cord *a mass of interconnected neurons within the spine that conveys impulses to and from the brain and is involved in some reflex behaviors*

The **spinal cord** is a massive collection of neurons within the spinal column that looks rather like a section of rope or thick twine. It is surrounded and protected by the hard bone and cartilage of the vertebrae. Sometimes it is difficult to remember that the spinal cord itself is made up of soft, delicate nerve fibers living just inside our backbone.

A cross-sectional view of the spinal column and the spinal cord is illustrated in Figure 2.11. There are only a few structural details that need mention. These details will become relevant shortly, when we talk about the function of the spinal cord. Note that the spinal cord itself—the neurons of the CNS—is located in the middle of the spinal column that reaches from your lower back to high in your neck, just below your brain. Then note that the nerve fibers that enter and leave the spinal cord do so from the side, not the front or back. Neurons, and the impulses they transmit, enter the spinal cord on what are called *dorsal roots* (where *dorsal* means "toward the back"). Impulses that leave the spinal cord do so on *ventral roots* (where ventral means "toward the front").

A cross-sectional view of the spinal cord showing dorsal and ventral roots and gray matter and white matter.

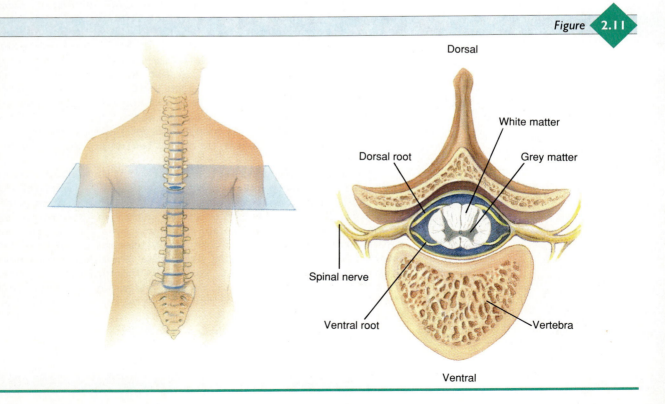

Figure **2.11**

Dorsal

White matter

Dorsal root

Grey matter

Spinal nerve

Ventral root

Vertebra

Ventral

Also notice that the center area of the spinal cord itself is made up of dark gray matter, rather in the shape of a butterfly, while the outside area is light, white matter. Remember, this means that the center portion is filled with cell bodies, dendrites, and unmyelinated axons, while the outer section is filled with myelinated axons. Both of these observations about the structure of the spinal cord provide keys to understanding its function.

The Functions of the Spinal Cord

The spinal cord has two major functions, one of which is to transmit neural impulses rapidly to and from the brain. Whenever sensory impulses originate below the neck and go to the brain, they do so through the spinal cord. When the brain transmits motor impulses to parts of the body below the neck, those impulses first travel down the spinal cord.

Impulses to and from different parts of the body leave and enter the spinal cord at different levels (impulses to and from the legs, for example, enter and leave at the very base of the spinal cord). If the spinal cord is cut or damaged, the consequences can be disastrous, resulting in a loss of feeling from the part of the body served and a loss of voluntary movement (paralysis) of the muscles in the region. Quite clearly, the higher in the spinal cord that damage takes place, the greater will be the resulting losses.

Once impulses get into the spinal cord, they race up and down the ascending and descending pathways found in the white matter areas (see again Figure 2.11). Remember that this area looks white because of the myelin covering on the axons found there. Remember, too, that one of the functions of myelin is to speed impulses along their way—as in the relatively long distances up and down the spinal cord.

The second major function of the spinal cord is its role in **spinal reflexes**. These are very simple automatic behaviors that occur without conscious, voluntary action of the brain. To understand how these reflexes work, follow along with the drawing in Figure 2.12. Here we have yet another drawing of the spinal cord, but we have added receptor cells in the skin, motor neurons to muscles in the hand, and have labeled the neurons within the spinal cord as interneurons (located, as they are, between sensory and motor neurons).

Let's trace your reaction to having your fingertip placed over the flame of a candle (we'll assume that you're blindfolded at the time). Receptor cells in your fingertip would respond to the flame, sending neural impulses racing along sensory (or afferent) neurons, through a dorsal root and into the spinal cord. Then, two things would happen at almost the same time. Impulses would rush up the ascending pathways of the spinal cord's white matter to your brain. But impulses would also travel through interneurons and go right back out of the spinal cord through a ventral root on motor (efferent) neurons to your arm and hand, where muscles would be stimulated to contract, and your hand would jerk back from the flame.

Here, then, we have a simple reflex. Impulses travel *in* on sensory neurons, *within* on interneurons, and *out* on motor neurons. Said just a bit differently, we have: in on afferent neurons, within on interneurons, and out on efferent neurons. We're now clearly involved with behavior. We have an environmental stimulus (here, a flame), activity in the central nervous system (neurons in the spinal cord), and an observable response (hand withdrawal).

spinal reflex *an automatic, involuntary response to a stimulus that involves sensory neurons carrying impulses to the spinal cord, interneurons within the spinal cord, and motor neurons carrying impulses to muscles*

Figure 2.12

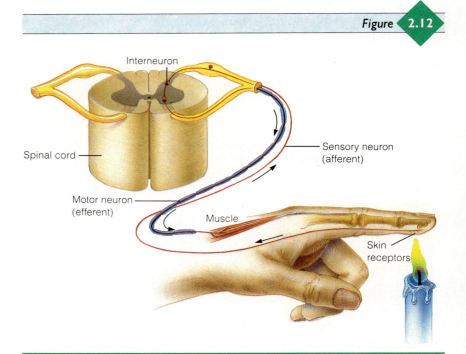

Interneuron

Spinal cord

Motor neuron
(efferent)

Muscle

Sensory neuron
(afferent)

Skin
receptors

A spinal reflex. Stimulation of the receptor in turn stimulates sensory neurons, interneurons, and motor neurons. Impulses also ascend to the brain through tracts in the white matter.

There are a couple of observations we must make about the reflex of the type depicted in Figure 2.12 before we go on. First, the fact that impulses enter the spinal cord and immediately race to the brain is not indicated in the drawing. As you know very well, in a situation like the one depicted, you may jerk your hand back "without thinking about it," but very soon thereafter you are well aware, indeed, of what has happened. That awareness occurs in the brain, not the spinal cord. The awareness that what happened was painful is a reaction of the brain, not the spinal cord. It is also the case that some reflexes are even more simple than the one in Figure 2.12 in that no interneurons are involved. That is, it is quite possible for sensory neurons to form synapses directly with motor neurons inside the spinal cord, which is what happens in the familiar knee-jerk reflex. On the other hand, you should realize that the total complex pattern of behaviors involved in having one's finger burned in a flame would actually involve many more than just three or four neurons.

BEFORE
YOU GO
ON

Why does spinal cord injury sometimes cause paralysis?
Describe the major features of a spinal reflex.

"LOWER" BRAIN CENTERS

There are many different ways in which we could organize our discussion of the brain. We'll choose a very simple one and divide the brain into two parts: the cerebral cortex, and everything else—which we're referring to as lower brain centers. Because the cerebral cortex plays so many important roles (such as initiating voluntary movements, storing memories, interpreting sensory inputs, and others we'll review shortly), this division is a reasonable one.

What we are calling lower brain centers are "lower" in two ways. First, they are physically located below, or under, the cerebral cortex. Second, they are the brain structures to develop first, both in an evolutionary sense and within the developing human brain. They are the brain structures we most clearly share with other animals. In no way should you think of these lower centers as being less important. As we will soon see, our very survival depends on them. You can use Figure 2.13 as a guide to locate the different structures as we discuss them.

The Brain Stem

As you look at the spinal cord and brain, you really can't tell where one ends and the other begins. There is no abrupt division line separating these two components of the central nervous system. Just above the spinal cord there is a slight widening of the cord that suggests that we're into brain tissue. Here are two important structures that together form what we call the **brain stem**—the medulla and the pons.

The very lowest structure in the brain is the **medulla**. In one sense, the medulla acts like the spinal cord in that its major functions involve

brain stem *the lowest part of the brain, just above the spinal cord, comprised of the medulla and the pons*

medulla *an area of the brain stem that monitors breathing and heart rate, and where most cross laterality occurs*

Figure ◆ **2.13**

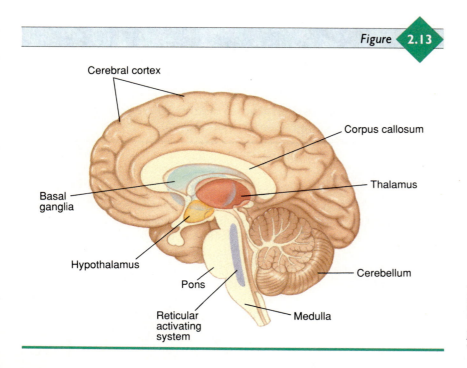

Cerebral cortex

Corpus callosum

Thalamus

Basal ganglia

Hypothalamus

Pons

Reticular activating system

Cerebellum

Medulla

The major structures of the human brain. Note the orientation of the "lower" brain centers—the medulla, pons, cerebellum, and reticular activating system.

nuclei *small collections or bundles of neural cell bodies*

involuntary reflexes. There are all sorts of little structures called **nuclei** (actually, collections of neural cell bodies) within the medulla. These nuclei control such functions as reflexive eye movements and tongue movements; you don't, for example, have to think about blinking your eye as something rushes toward it; your medulla will produce that eye blink reflexively.

The medulla also contains nuclei that control breathing reflexes and that monitor the muscles of the heart to see that it keeps beating rythmically. We *can* exercise some voluntary control over the nuclei of the medulla, of course, but only within certain limits. The medulla controls our level of respiration (breathing), but clearly we can override the medulla and hold our breath. We cannot, however, hold our breath until we die (as some children occasionally threaten). We can hold our breath until we lose consciousness, which is to say until we give up higher-level voluntary control, and then the medulla picks up where it left off and breathing continues.

It is at the level of the medulla that nerve fibers to and from the brain cross over from left to right and vice versa. By and large, centers in the left side of the brain receive impulses from and send impulses to the right side of the body. Similarly, the left side of the body sends impulses to and receives messages from the right side of the brain (which explains why electrically stimulating the correct area in the *left* side of the brain will produce a movement in the *right* arm). This process of fibers crossing from one side of the body to the opposite side of the brain is called **cross laterality**, and it takes place here in the brain stem.

cross laterality *the process of nerve fibers crossing over at the brain stem so that the left side of the body sends impulses to and receives impulses from the right side of the brain and vice versa*

pons *a brain stem structure forming a bridge between the brain and the spinal cord*

Just above the medulla is a structure called the **pons**. (The pons is one structure—there is no such thing as a "pon.") Primarily the pons serves as a relay station, a bridge (which is what *pons* means), sorting out and relaying sensory messages from the spinal cord and the face up to higher brain centers and reversing the relay for motor impulses coming down from higher centers. The cross laterality that begins in the medulla continues in the pons.

BEFORE YOU GO ON

Name the two brain stem structures, indicate where they are located, and describe what they do.

The Cerebellum

cerebellum *a spherical structure at the lower rear of the brain involved in the coordination of bodily movements*

Your **cerebellum** is just about the size of your closed fist. It is more or less spherical and sits right behind your pons, tucked up under the base of your skull. The cerebellum itself looks like a small brain. Its outer region (its cortex) is very convoluted, meaning that the tissue there is folded in upon itself, creating many deep crevices and lumps.

The major role of the cerebellum is in smoothing and coordinating rapid body movements. Most intentional, voluntary movements originate in higher brain centers (usually the motor area of the cerebral cortex) and are only coordinated by the cerebellum. Because of the close relationship between body movement and vision, many eye movements originate in the cerebellum.

Our ability to casually stoop, pick a dime off the floor, and slip it into our pocket involves a complex series of movements made smooth and regular by our cerebellum. When athletes train a movement, such as a golf swing or a gymnastic routine, we sometimes say that they are trying to get into a groove, so that their trained movement can be made simply and smoothly. In a sense, such athletes are training their cerebellum.

Few of our behaviors are as well coordinated or rapid as the movements required to make speech sounds. Next time you're talking to someone, try considering just how quickly and effortlessly your lips, mouth, and tongue are moving—thanks to your cerebellum. Damage to the cerebellum disrupts fine, coordinated movements. Speech becomes slurred; one may shake and stagger when walking. In fact, a person with cerebellum damage may appear to be quite drunk. (On what region of the brain do you suppose alcohol has a direct and noticeable effect? The cerebellum, of course.)

Damage to the cerebellum may disrupt motor activity in other ways as well. If the outer region of the cerebellum is damaged, persons suffer jerky **tremors**, or involuntary trembling movements, when they try to move (called intention tremors). Damage to inner, or deeper, areas of the cerebellum leads to "tremors at rest," where the limbs and/or head may shake or twitch rhythmically even when the person tries to remain still.

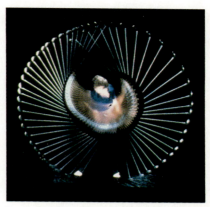

Learning to make a golf swing smooth and consistent may involve training the cerebellum.

tremors *involuntary, trembling, jerky movements*

BEFORE YOU GO ON

Where is the cerebellum located, and what is its major function?

The Reticular Activating System (RAS)

The **reticular activating system**, or **RAS**, is a different sort of brain structure. In fact, it is hardly a brain structure at all. It is a complex network of nerve fibers that begins down in the brain stem and works its way up through and around other structures all the way to the top portions of the brain.

Just exactly what the reticular activating system does, and how it does so, remain something of a mystery. As its name implies, however, the RAS is very much involved in determining our level of activation or arousal. It no doubt influences whether we're awake and attentive, drowsy, asleep, or at some level in between. Electrical stimulation of the RAS can produce EEG patterns of brain activity associated with being awake and alert. Lesions of the RAS cause a condition of constant sleep in laboratory animals (Lindsley et al., 1949; Moruzzi & Magoun, 1949). In a way, then, the reticular activating system acts like a valve that either allows sensory messages to pass from lower centers up to the cerebral cortex or shuts them off, partially or totally. What we really don't know yet is just how the RAS does what it does, and what stimulates it to produce the effects that it does.

reticular activating system (RAS) *a network of nerve fibers extending from the brain stem to the cerebrum that is involved in maintaining levels of arousal*

The Limbic System

limbic system *a collection of structures, including the amygdala and septum, which are involved in emotionality; and the hippocampus, involved forming long-term memories*

The **limbic system** is actually a collection of structures rather than a single, unified one. It is of utmost importance in controlling the behaviors of nonhuman animals, which do not have as large or well developed a cerebral cortex as humans do. The limbic system controls many of the complex behavioral patterns we usually think of as instinctive. The location of the limbic system and its constituent parts are presented in Figure 2.14.

Within the human brain, parts of the limbic system are intimately involved in the display of emotional reactions. One center in the system, the *amygdala*, produces reactions of rage and/or aggression when stimulated, while another area, the *septum*, seems to have the opposite effect, reducing the intensity of emotional responses when stimulated. The influence of the amygdala and the septum on emotional responding is quite immediate and direct in nonhumans. In humans, it is more subtle, reflecting the influence of other brain centers in addition to the limbic system.

Another center in the limbic system, called the *hippocampus*, is less involved in emotion and more involved with the forming of memories. People with a damaged hippocampus are often unable to "move" experiences into permanent memory storage. They may remember events for short periods of time. They also may be able to remember events from the distant past, but only if those events occurred before the hippocampus was damaged.

The Hypothalamus

hypothalamus *a small structure near the limbic system in the center of the brain, associated with feeding, drinking, sex, and aggression*

Perhaps the first thing to say about the **hypothalamus** is that it is often considered a part of the limbic system. It is located near the limbic system, and it too is involved in our motivational and emotional reactions. Among other things, it influences many of the functions of the endocrine system, which, as we have seen, is involved in emotional responding (see Topic 2A).

The major responsibility of the hypothalmus seems to be to monitor critical internal bodily functions. It has centers (nuclei again) that control feeding behaviors. It is sensitive to the amount of fluid in our bodies and indirectly gives rise to the feeling of being thirsty. The hypothalamus also acts something like a thermostat, triggering a number of automatic reactions should we become too warm or too cold. This small structure also is involved in aggressive and sexual behaviors. It acts as a regulator for many hormones. To be sure, we'll discuss the hypothalamus again in more detail when we study needs, motives, and emotions in later topics.

The Basal Ganglia

basal ganglia *a collection of structures in front of the limbic system that produce and depend on dopamine to control large, slow bodily movements*

A curious set of tissues is the **basal ganglia**. Like the limbic system, the basal ganglia are really a collection of loosely connected, smaller structures (whose names need not concern us). Like the cerebellum, the basal ganglia primarily work to control motor responding. Unlike the cerebellum, the role of the basal ganglia is more tied to large, slow movements—their initiation and their coordination. Although the basal ganglia are clearly related to the movements of some of our body's larger muscles, there are

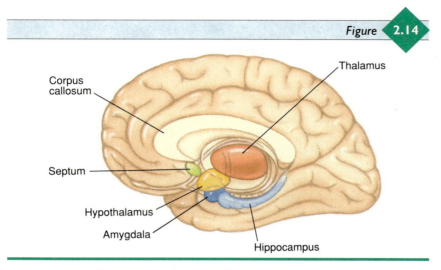

Figure 2.14

A number of small structures make up the limbic system, including the amygdala, septum, hypothalamus, thalamus, and hippocampus.

no pathways that lead directly from the ganglia, down the spinal cord, and off to those muscles.

Some of the functions of the basal ganglia have become clearer as we have come to understand the nature of **Parkinson's disease**. The most noticeable symptoms of this disease are some impairment of movement and involuntary tremors. At first there may be a tightness or stiffness in the fingers or limbs. As the disease progresses, the initiation of movement becomes very difficult, if not impossible. Walking, once begun, involves a stiff set of shuffling movements. In advanced cases, voluntary movement of the arms is nearly impossible. The disease is more common with increasing age, afflicting approximately 1 percent of the population.

It turns out that the neurotransmitter *dopamine* is usually found in great quantity in the basal ganglia. In fact, the basal ganglia provide the source of much of the brain's dopamine. In Parkinson's disease, the cells that produce dopamine die off, and as a result, levels of the neurotransmitter in the basal ganglia (and elsewhere) decline. As dopamine levels in the basal ganglia become insufficient, behavioral consequences are noted as symptoms of the disease. Treatment then, you might think, would be to simply inject lots of dopamine back into the basal ganglia. As it happens, that isn't possible—simply put, there's no way to get the chemical in there so it will stay. But another drug, called L-dopa, can be used (in pill form) to the same effect: L-dopa increases the availability of dopamine to the basal ganglia, and as a result the course of the disease can be slowed (reversing the course of Parkinson's disease is as yet not possible).

The Thalamus

The last structure to discuss as a lower brain center is the **thalamus**. It sits right below the covering of the cerbral cortex and is very involved

Parkinson's disease *a disorder of movement caused by damage to tissues in the basal ganglia*

thalamus *the last sensory relay station; it sends impulses to the appropriate area of the cerebral cortex*

with its functioning. It is a busy place. Like the pons, it acts as a relay station for impulses traveling to and from the cerebral cortex.

Many impulses from the cerebral cortex to lower brain structures, the spinal cord, and eventually out to the peripheral nervous system pass through the thalamus. Overcoming the normal function of the medulla (by voluntarily holding our breath, for example) involves messages that pass through the thalamus. The major role of the thalamus, however, involves the processing of information from the senses.

In handling incoming sensory impulses, the thalamus "integrates," or collects, organizes, and then directs sensory messages to the appropriate area of the cerebral cortex. Sensory messages from our lower body, our eyes, ears, and other senses (except for smell, which has its own special pathway) pass through the thalamus. For example, it is at the thalamus that nerve fibers from an eye are spread out and projected onto the back of the cerebral cortex.

Because of its role in monitoring impulses to and from the cerebral cortex, the thalamus has long been suspected to be involved in the control of our sleep-wake cycle (Moruzzi, 1975). Although this issue is not yet settled, some evidence (Lugaresi et al., 1986) suggests that nuclei in the thalamus (as well as some in the pons) do have a role in establishing a person's normal pattern of wakefulness and sleep.

BEFORE YOU GO ON

Indicate the location and briefly describe the major function of the RAS, the limbic system, the hypothalamus, the basal ganglia, and the thalamus.

THE CEREBRAL CORTEX

cerebral cortex *(or cerebrum) the large, convoluted outer covering of the brain that is the seat of cognitive functioning and voluntary action*

The human brain is a homely organ. There's just nothing very pretty about it. When we look at a human brain, the first thing we are likely to notice is the large, soft, lumpy, creviced outer covering of the **cerebral cortex** (in fact, *cortex* means "outer bark, or covering"). The cerebral cortex (also called the cerebrum, or just cortex) of the human brain is significantly larger than any other brain structure. Indeed, it is the complex and delicate development of the cerebral cortex that makes us uniquely human. It is our center for the processing and storage of information about the world in which we live. It is the starting place for virtually all of our voluntary action.

Lobes and Localization

Figure 2.15 presents two views of the cerebral cortex, one a top view, the other a side view. You can see from these illustrations that the deep

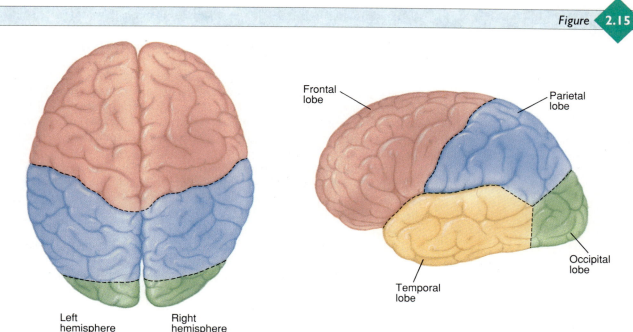

Frontal lobe

Parietal lobe

Occipital lobe

Temporal lobe

Left hemisphere

Right hemisphere

The human cerebral cortex is divided into the left and right hemispheres, which in turn are divided into four lobes that house various functional areas.

folds of tissue of the human cerebral cortex provide us with markers for dividing the cerebrum into major areas. The most noticeable division of the cortex can be seen in the top view. Here we clearly can see the very deep crevice that runs down the middle of the cerebral cortex from front to back, dividing it into the left and right **cerebral hemispheres**.

A side view of a hemisphere (Figure 2.15 shows us the left one) allows us to see the four major divisions of the cerebral cortex that are found in each hemisphere. These divisions are referred to as *lobes* of the brain. The **frontal lobes** are the largest and are defined by two large crevices called the central fissure and the lateral fissure. The **temporal lobes** are located at the temples, below the lateral fissure, again, with one on each side of the brain. The **occipital lobes**, at the very back of the brain, are defined somewhat arbitrarily, with no large fissures setting them off, and the **parietal lobes** are wedged in behind the frontal lobes and above the occipital and temporal lobes.

Using the methods we discussed in the last section of Topic 2A (see pages 68–72), we have learned much about what normally happens in the different regions of the cerebral cortex. Scientists have mapped out what goes on in most of the cortex, but many of the details of cerebral function are yet to be understood. Three major areas have been mapped: *sensory areas*, where impulses from our sense receptors are sent; *motor areas*, where many of our voluntary movements originate; and *association areas*, where sensory and motor functions are integrated and where higher mental

cerebral hemispheres *the two halves of the cerebral cortex, separated by a deep fissure running from front to back*

frontal lobes *the largest of the cerebral lobes, located in front of the central fissure and above the lateral fissure*

temporal lobes *the lobes of the cerebrum, located at the temples*

occipital lobes *the cerebral lobes at the very back of the brain*

parietal lobes *the lobes of the cerebrum found behind the frontal lobes, in front of the occipital lobes, and above the temporal lobes*

processes are thought to occur. We'll now review each of these areas in turn, referring to Figure 2.16, where general locations have been indicated.

Sensory Areas. Let's review for just a minute. Receptor cells (specialized neurons) in our sense organs respond to stimulus energy from the environment. These cells then pass neural impulses along sensory nerve fibers, eventually to the cerebral cortex. Senses in our body below our neck first send impulses to the spinal cord. Then, it's up the spinal cord, through the brain stem and thalamus, and beyond. After they leave the thalamus, those impulses from our senses go to a particular **sensory area**, depending on which sense is involved.

sensory areas *those areas of the cerebral cortex that receive impulses from our sense receptors*

Reflecting their relative importance to us, large areas of the cerebral cortex are involved with vision and hearing. Virtually the entire occipital lobe handles visual information (labeled "visual area" in Figure 2.16). Auditory (hearing) impulses end up in large centers ("auditory areas") in the temporal lobes.

Our body senses (touch, pressure, pain, and so on) from different parts of our body send impulses to a strip at the very front of the parietal lobe (labeled "body sense area" in Figure 2.16). Within this area of the parietal lobe we can map out specific regions that correspond to different parts of the body. When we do so, we find that some body parts—the face, lips, fingertips, for example—are overrepresented in the body sense area of the cerebral cortex, reflecting their high sensitivity. (In other words, some parts of the body, even some very small ones, are processed in larger areas of the cortex than are other parts.)

This is a good place to remind ourselves of the concept of *cross laterality* (page 80). Cross laterality refers to the fact that information from senses on the left side of the body crosses over to the right side of the brain, and vice versa, with this crossing occurring in the brain stem. When someone touches your right arm, that information ends up in your left parietal lobe. A tickle to your left foot is processed by the right side of your cerebral cortex.

Motor Areas. We have already seen that some of our actions, at least very simple and reflexive ones, originate in our central nervous system below the cerebral cortex. Although some lower brain centers such as the basal ganglia may be involved, it is still fair to say that most voluntary activity originates in the cerebral cortex—in strips at the very back of our frontal lobes. These **motor areas** (remember, there are two of them, left and right) are directly across the central fissure from the body sense areas in the parietal lobe (see Figure 2.16). As it happens, we need to make the disclaimer that the actual, thoughtful decision-making process of whether or not one *should* move probably occurs elsewhere, almost certainly further to the front of the frontal lobes.

motor areas *the strips at the back of the frontal lobes that control voluntary movement*

Electrical-stimulation techniques have allowed us to map out locations in the motor areas that correspond to, or control, specific muscles or muscle groups. As is the case for sensory processing, we find that some muscle groups (such as those that control movements of the hands and mouth) are represented by disproportionally larger areas of cerebral cortex.

As you know, we also find cross laterality at work with the motor area. It is your right hemisphere's motor area that controls the movements of the

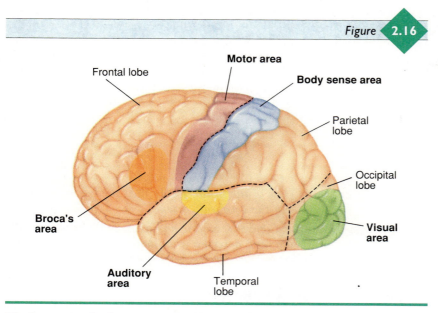

Figure **2.16**

Frontal lobe

Motor area

Body sense area

Parietal lobe

Occipital lobe

Visual area

Broca's area

Auditory area

Temporal lobe

The human cerebral cortex areas of localization.

left side of your body and vice versa. Someone who has suffered a cerebral stroke (a disruption of blood flow in the brain that results in the loss of neural tissue) in the left side of the brain will have impaired movement in the right side of the body.

Association Areas. Once we have located the areas of the cerebral cortex that process sensory information and originate motor responses, we find that we've still got a lot of cortex left over. The remaining areas of the cerebral cortex are called **association areas**. There are three of them in each hemisphere: frontal, parietal, and temporal. The occipital lobe is so "filled" with visual processing, there is no room left over for an occipital association area.

Exactly what happens in our association areas is not well understood. We assume that it is here that incoming sensory information is associated with outgoing motor responses—which is why we call them association areas.

There is considerable support for the idea that it is in our association areas that so-called higher mental processes occur. Frontal association areas are involved in a number of such processes. As Broca discovered more than a century ago, some language and speech behaviors are localized in the frontal association area. Damage to the frontal lobes often interrupts or destroys the ability to plan ahead, to think quickly, or to think things through.

In this context, we should remind ourselves not to get too carried away with cerebral localization of function. Let's not fall into the trap of coming to believe that separate little parts of the cerebral cortex operate inde-

association areas *those areas of the frontal, parietal, and temporal lobes in which higher mental processing occurs*

pendently and have the sole responsibility for any one function. This is a point that neurologist Marcel Kinsbourne makes this way: "There are no discontinuities in the brain. No independent channels traverse it; nor is its territory divisible into areas that house autonomous processors" (1982, p. 412). This will be particularly important to keep in mind as we now look at the division of the cerebral cortex into right and left hemispheres.

BEFORE YOU GO ON

Given a side view of the brain, locate the four lobes of the cerebral cortex.

Locate the primary sensory, motor, and association areas of the cerebrum, and describe what happens there.

The Two Cerebral Hemispheres

Even the ancient Greeks knew that the cerebral cortex was divided into two major sections or hemispheres. That there should be a division of the cerebral cortex into two halves seems quite natural. After all, we have two eyes, arms, legs, lungs, kidneys, and so forth. Why not two divisions of the brain? Within the last 30 years, interest in this division into two hemispheres has heightened as we have accumulated evidence that suggests that each half of the cerebral cortex may have primary responsibility for different functions—particularly different mental functions.

In most humans, the left hemisphere is usually the larger of the two halves, contains a higher proportion of gray matter, and is thought to be the dominant hemisphere (active to a greater degree in more tasks). We already noted that the language center is housed in the left cerebral hemisphere. At least this is true for virtually all right-handed people. For most, but not all, left-handers, language may be processed primarily by the right hemisphere. Because humans are so language oriented, not much attention was given to the "lowly" right hemisphere. Then, a remarkable surgical procedure, first performed in the 1960s, provided us with new insights about the two cerebral hemispheres (Sperry, 1968, 1982; Springer & Deutsch, 1981).

Normally, the two hemispheres of the cerebral cortex are richly interconnected by a series of fibers called the **corpus callosum** (which can be seen in Figure 2.14). Through the corpus callosum, one side of our cortex remains in constant and immediate contact with the other. Separating the functions of the two hemispheres is possible, however, through a surgical technique called a **split-brain procedure**, which is neither as complicated nor as dangerous as it may sound. The procedure amounts to destroying the corpus callosum's connections between the two hemispheres. The procedure was first tried on humans in 1961 by Joseph Brogan in an attempt to lessen the severity of the symptoms of epilepsy. As an irreversible treatment of last resort, the split-brain procedure was found to be very successful.

corpus callosum *a network of nerve fibers that interconnect the two hemispheres of the cerebrum*

split-brain procedure *a surgical technique of severing the corpus callosum, allowing the two hemispheres to operate independently*

Most of what we know about the activities of the cerebral hemispheres we have learned from split-brain subjects, both human and animal. One of the things that makes this procedure remarkable is that under normal circumstances, split-brain patients behave quite normally. Only in the laboratory, with specially designed tasks, can we clearly see the results of having made the hemispheres of the cerebral cortex function independently (e.g., Gazzaniga & LeDoux, 1978; Hellige, 1983). To be sure, all of the answers aren't in, but we can draw some tentative conclusions.

Experiments with split-brain patients confirm that speech production is a left-hemisphere function in a great majority of people (again, virtually all right-handers). Suppose you have your hands behind your back. I place a house key in your left hand, and ask you to tell me what it is. Your left hand feels the key. Impulses travel up your left arm and spinal cord and cross over to your *right* cerebral hemisphere—remember cross laterality. You can readily tell me that the object in your hand is a key because your brain is intact. Your right hemisphere passes information about the key to your left hemisphere, and your left hemisphere directs you to say, "It's a key." Now suppose that your corpus callosum is severed (that you are a split-brain subject). Now you cannot answer my question, even though you understand it perfectly. Why not? Your right brain knows that the object in your left hand is a key, but without the corpus callosum, it has no way to inform the left hemisphere, where your speech production apparatus is located. You *would* be able to point out the key from among other objects placed before you, under the direction of the right cerebral hemisphere. And once your eyes saw you do so, they would communicate that information to your left hemisphere, and now it too would know, and tell us, what your right hemisphere knew all along.

A major task of the left hemisphere, then, is the production of speech and the use of language. But before we go any further, we need to pause and caution against overinterpretation. When results from early split-brain studies were first made known, many people—nonpsychologists and psychologists alike—rushed to some premature conclusions. What we now appreciate is that virtually no behavior, virtually no mental process, is the simple and single product of just one hemisphere (e.g., Hellige, 1990). What is more reasonable to assert is that one hemisphere dominates the other or may be the primary processing area for certain actions and reactions. For example, the left hemisphere is clearly dominant in the perception and interpretation of speech. *But*, some language processing seems to be more the responsibility of the right hemisphere. The right hemisphere is more immediately involved in the processing of common phrases and clichés, such as "How do you do?" or "Have a nice day!" (e.g., Kempler & Van Lancker, 1987).

Granted that we have to be careful and shouldn't overinterpret, what are some of the activities that are processed *primarily* in one hemisphere or the other? We've seen that the left hemisphere can be given credit for processing most of our language skills, and given our heavy reliance on language, that's no small matter. Simple arithmetic tasks of calculation also seem to be primarily a left-brain function. Indeed, the left hemisphere has often been credited with the processing of information in an analytical, one-piece-at-a-time sort of way, although the data here are a bit tenuous (see Hellige, 1990, p. 59).

A major task of the left hemisphere of the cerebral cortex is the reception and production of language and speech.

There is evidence that creativity, particularly for drawing and spatial relations, is largely a function of the right hemisphere of the cerebral cortex.

What, then, of the right hemisphere? The clearest evidence is that the right hemisphere dominates in the processing of visually presented information (Bradshaw & Nettleton, 1983; Kosslyn, 1987). Putting together a jigsaw puzzle, for instance, uses the right hemisphere more than the left. Skill in the visual arts (painting and drawing, for example) is associated with the right hemisphere more than the left. The right hemisphere is also credited with being more involved in monitoring our levels of emotionality, both in interpreting emotional stimuli and in expressing emotional reactions. Consistent with the hypothesis that the left hemisphere tends to be analytic and sequential in dealing with information, the right is thought to be better able to grasp the big picture, see the overall view of things, and to be somewhat more creative.

These few possibilities are intriguing. There is no doubt that there are differences in the way the two sides of the cerebral cortex normally process information. But the differences are slight, and many remain controversial. If fact, we are finding that the more we study hemispheric differences, the more we tend to find similarities. It seems that any special programs or courses that claim to be designed to train or educate one side of our brains to the exclusion of the other are misguided, no matter how well intentioned they may be.

BEFORE YOU GO ON

What is a split-brain procedure, why is it done on humans, and what have we learned from it?

Briefly summarize the different functions of the left and right cerebral hemispheres of the human brain.

Although we have learned a great deal about the human nervous system, its structures, and how it affects our thoughts, feelings, and behaviors, there remain many mysteries to be solved. If nothing else, we have learned not to look for simple answers, a point we made back in Topic 1A. We have learned that areas of the brain and spinal cord do not function independently in producing even the simplest of human reactions. We also have learned that a true understanding of behavior and mental processes requires a working knowledge of the underlying anatomy and physiology. This observation will be reinforced in virtually every topic that follows.

Why does spinal cord injury sometimes cause paralysis? Describe the major features of a spinal reflex.

If the spinal cord is damaged, impulses originating in the brain to move parts of the body cannot get past the damaged area to activate the appropriate muscles, resulting in paralysis. In a spinal reflex, impulses enter the spinal cord on sensory fibers, may or may not form a synapse with interneurons, and then exit the spinal cord on motor fibers to activate a muscle response. At the same time, impulses are sent to the brain on fibers in the white matter. / *page 78*

Name the two brain stem structures, indicate where they are located, and describe what they do.

The brain stem is made up of the *medulla*, at the very base of the brain, which controls a number of very important reflexes, monitors heart rate and breathing, and is where most cross laterality occurs, and the *pons*, just above the medulla, which acts like a bridge, passing impulses between the spinal cord and the brain. / *page 80*

Where is the cerebellum located, and what is its major function?

The cerebellum is located at the rear and base of the brain and is most involved in the smoothing and coordinating of rapid muscular responses. / *page 81*

Indicate the location and briefly describe the function of the RAS, the limbic system, the hypothalamus, the basal ganglia, and the thalamus.

The RAS (or reticular activating system) extends from the brain stem through the middle of the brain to the cerebral cortex and is involved in maintaining levels of arousal. The limbic system, just above the brain stem, is involved in emotional expression (the amygdala and septum in particular) and the transfer of information into long-term memory (the hippocampus). The hypothalamus, which is near the limbic system, is involved in such reactions as feeding, drinking, sex, aggression, and temperature regulation. The basal ganglia, just in front of and above the limbic system, are a set of structures that control slow body movement and that produce much of the brain's dopamine. The thalamus, located just below the cerebral cortex, is a final relay station for sensory impulses that it projects up to the appropriate area of the cerebrum. / *page 84*

Given a side view of the brain, locate the four lobes of the cerebral cortex. Locate the primary sensory, motor, and association areas of the cerebrum, and describe what happens there.

See Figures 2.15 and 2.16 to review the locations of the frontal, temporal, parietal, and occipital lobes of the cerebral cortex and the primary sensory, motor, and association areas. The sensory areas of the cerebral cortex (visual, auditory, and body sense) receive impulses (through the thalamus) from all our senses. Voluntary motor activity is initiated in the motor areas of the cerebral cortex, and cognitive processing, such as memory, thinking, and problem solving, are thought to take place in the so-called association areas. / *page 88*

What is a split-brain procedure, why is it done on humans, and what have we learned from it? Briefly summarize the different functions of the left and right cerebral hemispheres of the human brain.

The split-brain procedure severs the fibers of the corpus callosum, the structure that sends impulses back and forth between the two cerebral hemispheres, thus allowing them to operate independently. It is used as a treatment of last resort for epilepsy. The split-brain procedure has allowed us to study the functions of the hemispheres of the cerebral cortex operating independently and to localize the features of each. Although one hemisphere may dominate another in some cases, seldom does one have total and complete control of any important brain function. However, it is safe to say that language and speech are usually processed in the left hemisphere, while visual, spatial information is usually processed in the right. Also possible, but less certain, is the left hemisphere's dominance in simple calculations and the sequential, analytical processing of information, while the right hemisphere is thought to be more involved with "the big picture," with the visual arts, and with emotionality. / *page 90*

CHAPTER 3

SENSORY PROCESSES

TOPIC 3A   Vision

TOPIC 3B   Hearing and the Other Senses

Why We Care: A Topic Preview

In this chapter, we begin our discussion of how we find out about the world, make judgments about it, learn from it, and remember what we have learned. This chapter is all about sensation—the first of a number of stages involved in the cognitive processing of information about the world in which we live. You may recall from Topic 1A the observation of the philosophers Aristotle and John Locke who claimed that we are born knowing nothing. As newborns, we do possess certain reflexes and our physiology is such that we are not totally unresponsive to the world around us, but our memories—our minds—are blank slates. By the time we are adults, our memories are packed with all sorts of information, some of it critically important (knowing the difference between things that are edible and things that are not), some of it comparatively trivial (knowing the difference between hard rock and punk rock music). As for Aristotle and Locke, a centrally important question for many psychologists is how all that information gets processed into our memories. In short, we are asking how it is that we find out about ourselves and the world in which we live. Answers to such questions necessarily begin here, with the consideration of how our senses work.

Everything we know, all of the information in our memories, got there originally through our senses as physical energy from the world around us. That energy normally takes one of many different forms: light, sound, heat, pressure, and so on. What our senses do, each in its own way, is to take that energy from our environments and convert it into neural impulses—the energy of the nervous system. We care about sensory processes because it is important for us to understand how our senses take that first step in converting the physical world of our environment into the psychological world we have stored away in our minds.

This topic has two major sections. The first deals with general issues that are relevant for each of our sensory processes. We'll define some basic terms, discuss how we measure the sensitivity of our senses, and introduce the concept of sensory adaptation.

The remainder of the topic covers vision. We begin our discussion of the senses with vision because of its importance—it provides us with a great deal of information about the world—and because we know more about visual processing than we do about our other senses. In our discussion of vision, as will be the case for the other senses as well, we'll first examine the nature of the relevant stimulus, in this case light, and then we'll discuss the relevant sense organ, in this case the eye.

SOME BASIC CONCEPTS

The plain truth of the matter is that we do not experience any breaks in the way we process information. The whole process seems quite continuous. We hear someone say something in class and discover some time later that we can remember what was said. Information from our environment somehow got stuck away in memory. If there were any subprocesses along the way, we were not aware of them. What we are going to do for the next few chapters, then, is a bit artificial, at least in terms of our everyday experience. We are going to break down information processing into separate subprocesses. We begin in this chapter with our discussion of sensory processes, or what we often just call sensation. **Sensation** may be defined as that process of converting the physical energy of the environment into the neural energy of our nervous system. It is the process of getting the world "out there" into the world of our experience. The psychology of sensation is concerned with how our different senses manage to do what they do.

To aid our discussion, let's now introduce just a few important terms. *Sense receptors* are the specialized neural cells located in our *sense organs* that actually change physical energy into neural impulses. That means that each of our sense receptors is a **transducer**, a mechanism that converts (transduces) energy from one form to another. A light bulb is a transducer: It converts electrical energy into light energy (and a little heat energy). Your eye is a sense organ that contains sense receptors that transduce light energy into neural energy. Your ear is a sense organ that contains sense receptors that transduce the mechanical energy of sound wave vibrations into neural energy.

Now, before we get into the story of how each of our sense organs goes about transducing physical energy from the environment, we're going to consider briefly a few concepts that apply to all of our senses. First, we'll examine one of the oldest topics in experimental psychology, psychophysics; then we'll consider the phenomenon of sensory adaptation.

sensation *the process of receiving information from the environment and changing that input into nervous system activity*

transducer *a mechanism that converts energy from one form to another—a basic process common to all our senses*

Sensory Thresholds

Psychophysics is the study of the relationships that exist between the physical attributes of stimuli and the psychological experiences that they produce. It is the oldest subfield in psychology. Many of the methods of psychophysics were developed long before Wundt opened his psychology laboratory in Leipzig in 1879. There are two ways to think about what psychophysics is all about.

At the simpler, more applied level, we can say that the techniques of psychophysics have been designed to assess the sensitivity of our senses, providing answers to such questions as: "Just how good *is* your hearing after all these years of playing bass in a rock band?" At a more theoretical level, we can think of psychophysics as providing a means of systematically relating the outside, *physical* world to the inner, *psychological* world. Now, the same question we just asked gets recast into a question that sounds like: "How much of a change in the physical intensity of this sound will it take for you to hear, or experience, a difference in loudness?" Most psychophysical methods are designed to measure sensory thresholds. There are

psychophysics *the study of the relationship between physical attributes of stimuli and the psychological experiences they produce*

two kinds of sensory thresholds: absolute thresholds and difference thresholds. We'll discuss absolute thresholds first.

Absolute Thresholds. Imagine the following simple experiment. You're seated in a dimly lighted room, staring at a small box. The side of the box facing you is covered by a sheet of cloudy plastic. Behind the plastic sheet is a light bulb. I can decrease the physical intensity of the light bulb to the point where you cannot see it at all. I can also increase the light's intensity to the point where you can see it very clearly. I also have many intensity settings available between these extremes. My basic question is: At what point of *physical* intensity will the light first become visible to you?

Common sense tells us that there should be some value of physical intensity below which you cannot see the light and above which you can. That point, for you, would be your absolute threshold. The term *threshold* here means the same thing that it means in other contexts—a point of crossing over. (You cross the threshold of a door as you move from outside to inside, or vice versa.) The notion of threshold is clearly related to that of *sensitivity*, but in an inverse sort of way. That is, as threshold levels decrease, we say that sensitivity increases. The lower the threshold of a sense receptor, the more sensitive it is.

Now let's return to our imaginary experiment in which I am trying to determine your absolute threshold for sensing a light. I repeatedly vary the light's intensity and ask you to respond "Yes, I see the light," or "No, I don't see the light," depending on your experience. (In this experiment, I'll not allow you the luxury of saying that you don't know or aren't sure.)

When this experiment is actually done, we discover something that at first seems strange. I can reduce the intensity of the light so low that you never report seeing it. And I can present light intensities so high that you always say you see the light. However, there are many intensities in between where your responses are inconsistent over a number of presentations of

Determining absolute threshold values. (A) The idealized case, in which there is a point before which the stimulus is never detected and after which it is always detected, and (B) the realistic case, where absolute threshold is the intensity of stimulation that is detected 50 percent of the time.

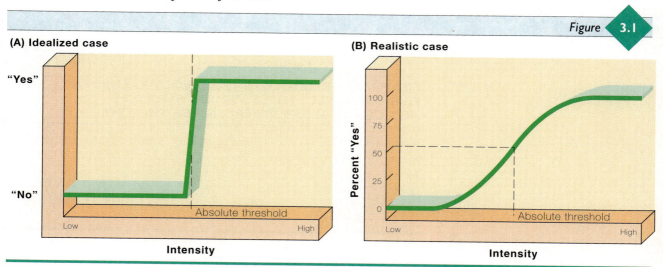

Figure 3.1

(A) Idealized case

"Yes"

"No"

Absolute threshold

Low   High

Intensity

(B) Realistic case

Percent "Yes"

100

75

50

25

0

Absolute threshold

Low   High

Intensity

the very same light intensity. That is, there are intensities of light to which you sometimes respond yes and sometimes respond no, even though the actual, physical intensity of the light is unchanged.

In reality, there just isn't very much that's absolute about our absolute thresholds at all. They keep changing from moment to moment, reflecting small, subtle changes in the sensitivity of our senses. (They also reflect such factors as momentary shifts in our ability to pay attention to the task at hand.) Figure 3.1 shows (A) what we might like to happen in an experiment like the one we've just described, and (B) what actually does happen in such an experiment.

absolute threshold *the physical intensity of a stimulus that one can detect 50 percent of the time*

Because there are no truly "absolute" measures of sensory sensitivity, psychologists resort to the following operational definition of **absolute threshold:** the physical intensity of a stimulus that a subject reports detecting 50 percent of the time. In other words, intensities below threshold are those detected less than 50 percent of the time, and intensities above threshold are detected more than 50 percent of the time. This complication occurs for all our senses, not just for vision. I would have the same general result if I tested your ability to detect sounds, smells, touches, or tastes.

So what good is the notion of an absolute threshold, and why should we care? Determining absolute thresholds is not just an academic exercise. For one thing, as a measure of sensitivity, absolute threshold levels can be used to discover if one's senses are operating properly and are detecting low levels of stimulation (which is exactly what happens when you have your hearing tested, for example). Engineers who design sound systems need to know about absolute thresholds—speakers that do not reproduce sounds above threshold levels aren't of much use. Warning lights must be designed to be well above absolute threshold if they are to be of any use to us. How much perfume is required for it to be noticed? How low must you whisper so as not to be overheard in a classroom? Do I really smell natural gas in the house, or is it my imagination? Can one basil leaf in the tomato sauce be detected, or will two be required? These are psychophysical questions about absolute thresholds as they pertain to everyday experiences outside the laboratory. Unless physical stimuli exceed absolute threshold levels, they may not be experienced (sensed) at all. As it happens, our sense receptors are remarkably sensitive, as the oft-quoted examples in Figure 3.2 attest.

Figure **3.2**

EXAMPLES OF ABSOLUTE THRESHOLD VALUES FOR FIVE SENSES (I.E., THESE STIMULI WOULD BE NOTICED AT LEAST 50 PERCENT OF THE TIME)

Vision	a candle flame seen from a distance of 30 miles on a clear, dark night
Hearing	the ticking of a watch under quiet conditions from a distance of 20 feet
Taste	1 teaspoon of sugar dissolved in 2 gallons of water
Smell	one drop of perfume in a three-room apartment
Touch	the wing of a bee dropped on your cheek from a height of one centimeter

(From Galanter, 1962.)

How is the process of sensation defined?
What is psychophysics?
What is an absolute threshold, and how is it related
to the sensitivity of our senses?

Subliminal Perception. The concept of **subliminal perception** has interested and frustrated psychologists for more than 40 years. The first thing to recognize is that *limen* is the Latin word for "threshold." Because *sub* means "below," *subliminal perception* literally means "below threshold perception." On the face of it, what we have here is a contradiction, referring to our ability to perceive something that is below our ability to perceive it. The idea is intriguing: Somehow we can be influenced by stimuli of which we are not consciously aware.

Picture this. You are sitting in a theater watching a movie. Bruce Willis is about to jump from a building just before it explodes. Suddenly, there on the screen, in great big letters, is a message: *BUY COKE,* followed shortly by another, *HOW ABOUT SOME POPCORN?* If this sort of interruption actually occurred, you'd probably be upset, leave the theater, and demand your money back. You paid to see a movie, not a series of commercial messages. But what if the messages embedded in the movie were *so* brief and/or *so* dim as to be below your absolute threshold for vision? You don't even realize they are there. Can they still influence your behavior?

When we ask the question this way, the answer is a clear and resounding *no.* Although the implications for misuse are clear, it's almost a shame that subliminal perception in this sense doesn't work. Wouldn't it be useful *if we could* reduce shoplifting by embedding antishoplifting messages into the background music in retail stores? Wouldn't it be wonderful *if we could* earn more money, or improve our study habits, or become more self-confident *with no effort* by simply listening to audiotapes or watching videotapes into which subliminal messages had been inserted? But, again, these tapes do not work—at least they do not work through anything like subliminal perception. Many people claim to have been helped by such tapes. Perhaps they have been. But the best explanation is that when people genuinely believe that the tapes will help, and have invested a good deal of time and money in them, they rather easily can convince themselves that the tapes are of value (Balay & Shevrin, 1988; Dixon, 1971; Duncan, 1985; Vokey & Read, 1985).

The possibility that subliminal messages can have direct and potentially devastating effects on behavior was a major issue in a Reno, Nevada, courtroom during the summer of 1990. CBS Records and the English heavy-metal band Judas Priest were charged with directly causing the deaths of two young men, Raymond Belnap, age 18, and James Vance, age 20. On December 23, 1985, these two men each turned a loaded shotgun to his face and pulled the trigger. Vance died immediately. Belnap destroyed his

subliminal perception *the process of responding to, or perceiving, stimuli that are presented at levels below one's absolute threshold*

face, but survived the blast. He died in 1988 due to complications following a drug overdose. The Nevada trial centered on the allegation that CBS and Judas Priest were responsible for the "wrongful" death of Vance and Belnap because they had "intentionally and recklessly" embedded subliminal messages on one of their records—a favorite of Belnap and Vance, one they were listening to that day in December 1985. The messages were suicidal in nature ("Let's be dead!" "Do it. Do it."), the prosecution claimed. As it happened, the judge found for the defendants. Both victims were described as very troubled young men who had a long history of drug use and abuse. Ironically, however, the judge in the case (Judge Jerry Whitehead) ruled that there *were* "subliminals" on the recording, but that they were not placed there intentionally. The judge did go on in his 68-page ruling to declare that he had heard no evidence that subliminal messages could have had the effect of causing anyone to commit suicide, or any act like it. (And Judas Priest decided to call their next concert tour "Subliminal Criminals.") In Topic 1A I made the point that psychology has practical application in the real world. Occasionally that application is somewhat bizarre.

Is it true, then, that stimuli presented at levels slightly below one's absolute threshold can have *no* effect? No, that's too strong a statement. Although subliminally presented messages are not going to get you to get up from your TV set and march down to the store to buy some new type of snack food, there *is* evidence that to some degree we may be sensitive to stimuli that are below absolute threshold levels. Here's one example of this sort of evidence.

A subject sits in front of a small screen. A word is flashed on the screen so dimly and briefly that the subject does not report seeing the word. Let's say the word is *EASTER.* Now two words are presented on the screen that the subject *can* see clearly. The task is to choose the word related in some way to the word that was not seen. Let's say the choice words in this example are *Bunny* and *Pencil.* Even when subjects claim they are just guessing, they choose *Bunny* significantly more frequently than chance would predict. If the subliminal prompt were *PEN,* not *EASTER,* then they would tend to choose *Pencil.* It is as if, somehow, the initial subliminally presented word influences their choice (e.g., Cheeseman & Merikle, 1984; Dixon, 1971, 1981; Fowler et al., 1981).

So there seems to be evidence that some stimuli below the levels of our absolute thresholds of detection can have some discernible impact on us. On the other hand, there is no evidence that subliminal messages can directly influence actual behaviors in any meaningful way.

Difference Thresholds. The truth is, we don't often encounter situations that test our abilities to detect the presence of very-low-intensity stimuli. We often *are* called upon to detect differences between or among stimuli that are above our absolute thresholds. The issue here is not if the stimuli can be detected, but whether or not they are in some way *different* from each other. So, a **difference threshold** is defined as the smallest difference between stimulus attributes that can be detected. As you may have anticipated, we do have the same complication here when we try to measure absolute thresholds. To very slight degrees, one's difference threshold for any stimulus attribute tends to vary from moment to moment. So again we operationalize our definition and say that to be above one's dif-

difference threshold *the minimal difference in some stimulus attribute, such as intensity, that one can detect 50 percent of the time*

ference threshold, differences between stimuli need to be detected more than 50 percent of the time.

For example, imagine that I have two cans of paint, both the exact same shade of red. You can easily see that they are the same color. I slowly add some white paint to one of the cans. At what point do the two cans of red paint no longer look the same to you? The point at which the difference between the paints is first barely detectable would be your difference threshold—for colors of paint, anyway.

Now let's go through another example. I present you with two tones. You claim to be able to hear them both (they're both above your absolute threshold), and you report that they are equally loud. If I gradually increase (or decrease) the intensity of one of the tones, I will eventually reach a point at which you can just notice a difference between the loudness of the two tones. As it happens, **just noticeable difference**, or **j.n.d.**, is a technical term that is actually defined as the amount of change in a stimulus that makes it just noticeably different from what it was. You recognize this as essentially the same thing as a difference threshold.

The concept of just noticeable difference is relevant in many contexts. A parent asks a teenager to "turn down that stereo!" The teenager reduces the volume, but not by a j.n.d. from the parent's perspective, and trouble may be brewing. Does the color of the belt match the color of the dress closely enough? Can anyone tell the difference between the expensive ingredients and the cheaper ones? Is this car so much cheaper than that one that the difference in price really makes a difference?

just noticeable difference (j.n.d.) *the minimal change in some stimulus attribute, such as intensity, that can be detected*

Signal Detection. We have made the point that sensory thresholds are not stable, fixed values. They vary from moment to moment and thus are defined in terms of probability—as a 50 percent point above which some attributes of stimuli, or their differences, can be detected.

To say that sensory thresholds change is to say that the sensitivity of our senses continuously changes. It changes because of momentary shifts in attention and because of the random electrical activity of the nerve cells in our sensory systems. Occasionally, nerve cells fire without any stimulation from the outside environment. Even if you were standing in a deep cave (or a closet, for that matter) where there was no light, with your eyes closed, you would still have something of a visual experience—you would sense small flashes of light. The firing of sensory nerve cells creates a background noise that varies randomly from moment to moment.

When we are asked to determine if a stimulus has been presented, what we really are being asked to do is to judge whether or not we can detect a signal against a background of other stimuli and randomly changing neural activity. When we think of threshold determination in this way, we are using the basics of what is called **signal detection theory**. Signal detection theory takes the position that stimulus detection is a decision-making process of deciding if a signal exists against a background of noise (Green & Swets, 1966).

According to this theory, one's absolute threshold may be influenced by many factors in addition to the actual sensitivity of one's senses. We've already seen that random nervous system activity needs to be accounted for. So do the individual's attention, expectations, and biases. For example, there is evidence that in an experiment to determine one's absolute thresh-

signal detection theory *the view that stimulus detection is a matter of decision making, of separating a signal from background noise*

The trading floor at the Chicago Board of Trade provides a challenging environment in which to test signal detection theory.

old, subjects are simply more likely to say that yes, they detect a stimulus, than they are to say that they don't (Block, 1965). Other subjects may be overly cautious, not saying yes until they are absolutely sure that the stimulus in question has been presented. And, of course, some subjects simply don't pay much attention to what they are doing throughout the experiment, saying yes or no virtually at random.

Without going into all the details of *how* it is done, let's just say that signal detection procedures take into account, and mathematically eliminate, a number of factors such as background noise, level of attention, and subject bias in the determination of sensory thresholds. The result is a clearer picture of sensory sensitivity.

Sensory Adaptation

Before we get on to our discussion of individual sense receptors and how they work, we need to introduce one more concept. This is a phenomenon with which you are quite familiar: sensory adaptation. **Sensory adaptation** is a condition in which our sensory experience tends to decrease with the continued exposure of a stimulus.

sensory adaptation (in most cases) the process in which our sensory experience tends to decrease or diminish with continued exposure to a stimulus

Many of our common experiences provide us with examples of sensory adaptation. When we first jump into the pool or the lake, the water feels very cold. But after only a few minutes, we adapt and are reassuring our friends to, "Come on in; the water's fine." When we first walk into a house where cabbage is cooking, the odor is nearly overwhelming, but soon we adapt and do not notice it at all. When the compressor motor of the refrigerator first turns on, it seems to make a terribly loud noise, one that we soon do not notice at all—until the compressor *stops* and silence returns to the kitchen. Sensory adaptation again.

There is an important psychological point hidden in these examples. It is that one's ability to detect the presence of a stimulus (one's threshold) depends in large measure on the extent to which our sense receptors are being newly stimulated or have to some degree already adapted. Another way of saying the same thing is to note that our sense receptors respond to *changes* in stimulation. The constant stimulation of a receptor leads to adaptation, and less of a chance that that stimulation will be detected.

There is an exception to this usage of the term *adaptation*. Have you thought of it? What happens when you move from a brightly lighted area to a dimly lighted area? Perhaps you enter a darkened movie theater on a sunny afternoon. At first you can barely see anything at all. But in a few minutes (usually no more than 15–20), you are seeing reasonably well. What do we say happened? We say that you have "adapted to the dark." Here we are using the term adaptation in quite a different way. **Dark adaptation** refers to the fact that with time spent in the dark, our visual receptors actually become *more* sensitive to what little light is available. In terms of threshold values, we say that our threshold for light intensity *decreases* because, as you'll recall, the lower our threshold, the more sensitive our sense receptors.

dark adaptation *the process by which our eyes become more sensitive to light as we spend time in the dark*

BEFORE YOU GO ON

Can subliminal messages affect our behaviors?
What is a difference threshold, or j.n.d.?
Briefly summarize the basic ideas of signal detection theory.
What is sensory adaptation?

THE STIMULUS FOR VISION: LIGHT

Light is the stimulus for vision. Now we don't have to become physicists to understand how vision works, but it will be helpful to have an appreciation of the physical nature of light so we can see how it gives rise to our visual experiences. **Light** is thought of as a *wave form of radiant energy*. What that means is that light *radiates* from its source in the form of *waves* (which we call light waves). Light waves have three important physical characteristics that are related to psychological experience: wave amplitude, wavelength, and wave purity.

light *a radiant energy that can be represented in wave form with wavelengths between 380 and 760 nanometers*

Wave Amplitude (Intensity)

One of the ways in which light energy may vary is in its intensity. When we think about light traveling in the form of waves of energy, differences in intensity correspond to differences in the **wave amplitude** of light. The amplitude of a wave is represented by its height. You can refer to Figure 3.3 and assume that the two waves in the drawing represent two different light waves. One of the physical differences between light (A) and light (B) is in the height of the waves, or wave amplitude.

wave amplitude *a characteristic of wave forms (the height of the wave) that indicates intensity*

The amplitude of a light wave represents a light's *physical* intensity. Our psychological experience of intensity is what we call **brightness**. The difference between a dim light and a bright light is due to the difference in

brightness *the psychological experience associated with a light's intensity or wave amplitude*

Figure **3.3**

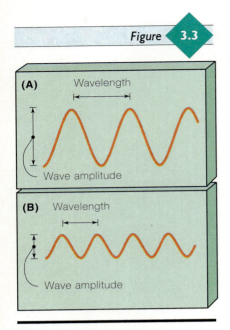

Representations of light waves differing in wavelengths and wave amplitude. See text for explanation of how these physical characteristics are related to our psychological experience of light.

wavelength *a characteristic of wave forms that indicates the distance between any point on a wave and the corresponding point on the next cycle of the wave*

nanometer (nm) *one millionth of a millimeter—the unit of measurement for the wavelength of light*

hue *the psychological experience associated with a light's wavelength*

wave amplitude. Of the two lights in Figure 3.3, (A) has the higher amplitude and thus would be seen as the brighter light. Dimmer switches that control the brightness of some light fixtures are in essence controlling the amplitude of light waves.

Wavelength

A second physical characteristic of waves of energy such as light waves is **wavelength**, which is the distance between any point in a wave and the corresponding point on the next cycle—from peak to peak, for example. In Figure 3.3, one difference between waves (A) and (B) is their wavelength, where (A) has the longer wavelength. Although it is difficult to imagine distances so tiny, we *can* measure the length of a light wave. Our unit of measurement is the **nanometer (nm)**, which is equal to one-billionth of a meter or one-millionth of a millimeter.

As it happens, there are many types of radiant energy that can be thought of as traveling in waves. However, the human eye only responds to radiant energy in wave form that has a wavelength between roughly 380 and 760 nm. This is the range of light waves that makes up what we call the visible spectrum. Wave forms of energy with wavelengths shorter than 380 nm (such as X rays and ultraviolet rays) are so short that they do not stimulate the receptors in our eyes, and they go unnoticed. Wave forms of energy with wavelengths in excess of 760 nm (microwaves and radar are two examples) do not stimulate the receptor cells in our eyes either.

We have seen that wave amplitude determines our experience of brightness. Wavelength is the attribute of light that determines the **hue**, or color, we perceive. As light waves increase in length from the short 380-nm wavelengths to the long 760-nm lengths, our experience of them changes—from violet to blue to green to yellow-green to yellow to orange to red along the color spectrum (see Figure 3.4, which also presents some of the invisible varieties of radiant energy in wave form).

A source of radiant energy with a 700-nm wavelength will be seen as a red light. In fact, that's precisely what a red light *is*. (A bright red light has a high amplitude, and a dim red light has a low amplitude, but both have 700-nm wavelengths.) As we can see from Figure 3.4, if a light generated waves 550 nm long, it would be seen as a yellow-green light, and so on. Note that yellow-green is a single hue produced by a given wavelength of light (550 nm). It is *not* some sort of combination of yellow and green. We simply have no other name for this hue, so we call it yellow-green.

Let me present you with an apparently simple problem: I have two lights, one red (700 nm) and the other yellow-green (550 nm). I've adjusted the *amplitudes* of these two light sources so that they are exactly *equal*. They are of different hues because their wavelengths are different. On the basis of what we've said so far, what about their brightness? With both amplitudes equal, will the lights appear equally bright?

As a matter of fact, they won't. The yellow-green light will appear much brighter than the red light. It will also appear much brighter than a blue light of equal amplitude. We say that wavelength and wave amplitude *interact* to produce apparent brightness. Wavelengths of light in the middle

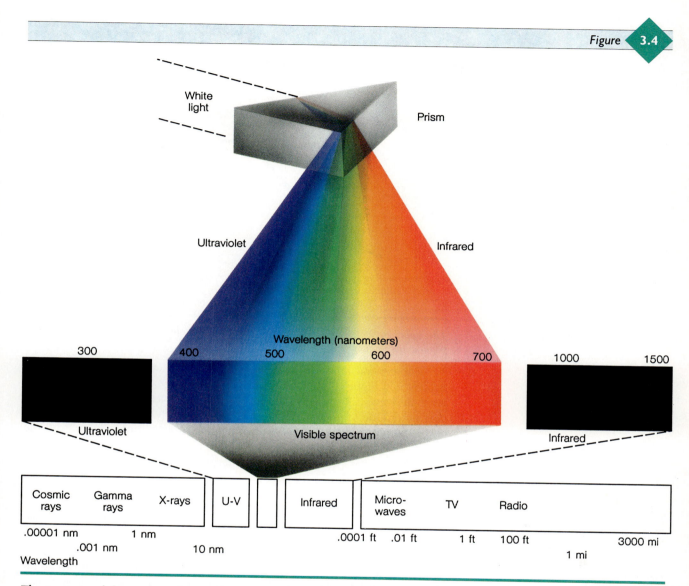

Figure **3.4**

The spectrum of electromagnetic energy in wave form of which light is but a small segment. Here we see that light is energy with a wavelength between 380nm and 760nm. As wavelength increases, our experience of light changes to produce a "rainbow."

of the range of visible spectrum (such as yellow-green) appear brighter than do wavelengths of light from the extremes—*if* their amplitudes are equal.

Now I can get a red light to appear as bright as a yellow-green one, of course, but to do so I'll have to increase its amplitude (or physical intensity, if you prefer). Doing so is a bit expensive, however. What we have here is a fairly good argument that the lights on emergency vehicles should not be red, but should be yellow-green. With *everything else being equal,* yellow-green lights will appear brighter than red ones.

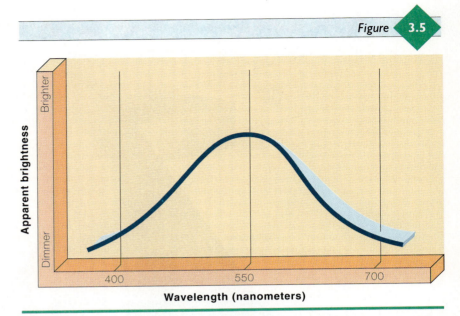

Figure 3.5

The apparent brightness of lights of different wavelength, assuming that all amplitudes are equal.

The general relationship between wavelength and apparent brightness is shown in Figure 3.5. Note that we have here an example of a point made back in Topic 1A—that everything is not always as it appears. Amplitude *does* determine brightness. If you have two red lights, one dim, one bright, the difference between them is a difference in amplitude. *But*, across the visible spectrum, apparent brightness—brightness as judged by a person, not a light meter—is determined by both amplitude *and* wavelength.

Wave Purity

Imagine a light of medium amplitude with all its wavelengths exactly 700 nm long. The light would appear to be of medium brightness. And because the wavelengths are all 700 nm, it would appear red. More than that, it would appear as a pure, rich red. We call such a light **monochromatic** because it is made up of light waves all of one (*mono*) length or hue (*chroma*). In truth, we seldom see such lights outside the laboratory because producing a pure, monochromatic light is an expensive thing to do.

Even the reddest of lights that you and I see in our everyday experience have other wavelengths of light mixed in along with the predominant 700-nm red. (If the 700-nm light wave did not predominate, the light wouldn't look red at all.) Even the red light on top of a police car has some violet, green, and yellow wavelengths of light in it.

The physical purity of a light source determines the psychological experience that we call **saturation**. Pure, monochromatic lights are the most highly saturated; their hue is rich and obvious. (I think of lights that are highly saturated as being so filled (saturated) with the one wavelength that there isn't room for any other.) As more and more different wavelengths get mixed into a light, it becomes lower and lower in saturation, and it starts to look pale and washed out.

monochromatic *literally one-colored; a pure light made up of light waves all of the same wavelength*

saturation *the psychological experience associated with the purity of a light wave, where the most saturated lights are monochromatic and the least saturated are white light*

| Figure | 3.6 |

THE PHYSICAL CHARACTERISTICS OF LIGHT WAVES INFLUENCE OUR PSYCHOLOGICAL EXPERIENCE OF LIGHT.

Physical Characteristic	Psychological Experience
Wave amplitude (intensity)	Brightness
	These two interact
Wavelength	Hue
Wave purity	Saturation

What do we call a light that is of the lowest possible saturation, a light that contains a random mixture of wavelengths of light? By definition, it is **white light**. It is something of a curiosity that white light is in fact as *impure* a light as possible. A pure light has but one wavelength; a white light contains many wavelengths.

True white light is as difficult (and as expensive) to produce as is a pure monochromatic light. Fluorescent light bulbs produce reasonable approximations, but their light contains too many wavelengths from the short, or blue-violet, end of the spectrum. Light from regular incandescent light bulbs contain too many light waves from the orange and red end of the spectrum, even if we paint the inside of the bulb with white paint. A prism can take a beam of white light—sunlight is a reasonable approximation—and break it down into its various parts, giving us the experience of a rainbow of hues. Where did all those hues come from? They were there all along, mixed together to form the white light.

We have seen that three physical characteristics of light influence the nature of our visual experience. Wave amplitude is the primary determinant of brightness; wavelength determines hue; and wave purity determines saturation. These relationships are summarized in Figure 3.6.

white light *a light of the lowest possible saturation, containing a mixture of all visible wavelengths*

BEFORE YOU GO ON

In what ways do the major physical characteristics of light waves of energy (amplitude, length, and purity) affect our psychological experience of light?

THE EYE

Vision involves changing light wave energy into the neural energy of the nervous system. This transformation of energy takes place in the eye. Yet most of the structures of the eye have little to do with the actual process of transducing light energy into neural energy. Instead, they are there to ensure that the light waves that enter the eye are well focused by the time they get back to the layer of cells that responds directly to light waves.

Figure   3.7

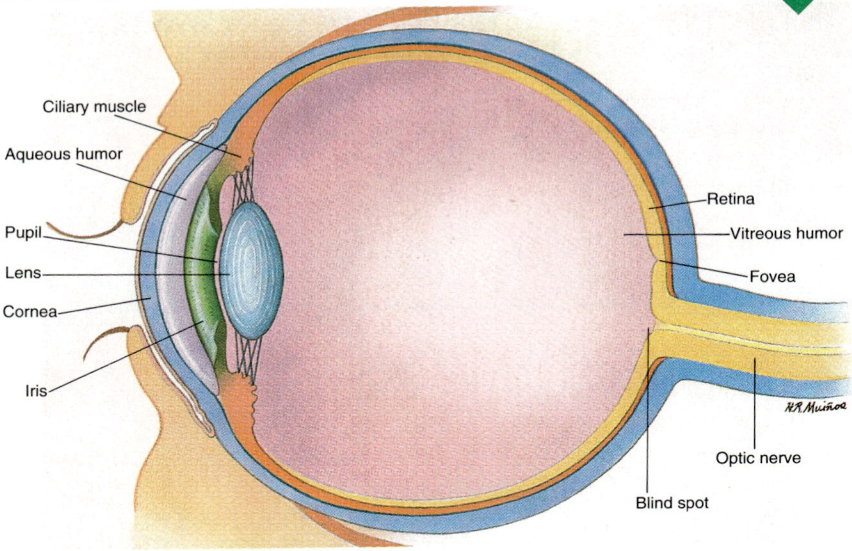

The major structures of the human eye.

Structures that Focus Visual Images

Using Figure 3.7 as a guide, let's trace the path of light as it passes through a number of structures, ultimately to produce a visual experience. Light first enters the eye through the **cornea**. The cornea is the tough, round, virtually transparent outer shell of the eye. Those of you who wear contact lenses float them on your corneas. The cornea has two major functions. One is to protect the delicate structures behind it. The other is to start bending the entering light waves in order to focus an image on the back surface of the eye.

Having passed through the cornea, light then travels through the **pupil**, which is an opening in the **iris**. The iris is the part of your eye that is pigmented, or colored. When we say that someone has blue, brown, or green eyes, we are really referring to the color of the iris. The iris expands or contracts, changing the size of the pupil. This is a reflexive reaction. It's not something you can control by conscious effort. Contractions of the iris that change pupil size are most commonly made in response to the level of light present, opening the pupil wide when only small amounts of light are present and reducing its size (protectively) in response to high-intensity lights. Increasing pupil size is also one of the automatic responses that occurs with heightened levels of emotionality—a very adaptive reaction to let in as much light as possible.

After the pupil, the next structure light encounters is the **lens**. As in a camera, the main function of the lens of the eye is to *focus* a visual image. The lens changes shape to bring an image into focus, becoming flatter when we try to focus on an object at a distance and becoming fatter, or rounder, when we try to view something up close. This, too, is largely a reflex. Obviously, lenses are not normally as hard as glass or they wouldn't be

cornea *the outermost structure of the eye that protects the eye and begins to focus light waves*

pupil *the opening in the iris that changes size in relation to the amount of light available and emotional factors*

iris *the colored structure of the eye that reflexively opens or constricts the pupils*

lens *the structure behind the iris that changes shape to focus visual images in the eye*

able to change their shape. (Sometimes, with age, our lenses tend to harden, making it difficult to focus and requiring that we use glasses to help out.)

Some very powerful little muscles control the lens. They are called **ciliary muscles**, and they push on the lens or relax in order to change its shape. The process in which the ciliary muscles change the shape of the lens is called **accommodation**. It is often the case that an image does not focus as it should, either because of the shape of the lens or a failure of accommodation. It is also sometimes the case that a healthy lens and functioning ciliary muscles still can't get an image to focus because of the shape of the eyeball itself. In any of these cases, the result is nearsightedness or farsightedness. Figure 3.8 shows examples of what happens in these cases.

There is a space between the cornea and the lens that is filled with a clear fluid called **aqueous humor**. This humor (which means "fluid") provides nourishment to the cornea and the other structures at the front of the eye. The aqueous humor is constantly being produced and supplied to the space behind the cornea, filtering out blood to keep the fluid clear. If the fluid cannot easily pass back out of this space, pressure builds within the eye, causing distortions in vision or, in extreme cases, blindness. This disorder is known as *glaucoma*.

There is another, larger space *behind* the lens that is also filled with a fluid or humor. This fluid is called **vitreous humor**. It is not nearly as watery as aqueous humor. It is thick and filled with tiny structures that give it substance. Its major function is to keep the eyeball rounded.

The Retina

So far we've mentioned a number of structures, each important in its own way, but none of them doing much more than allowing light waves back through the eye to other structures, usually in more focused form. It is at the **retina** of the eye that vision begins to take place. Here, light energy is transduced into neural energy.

The retina is really a series of layers of specialized cells at the back surface of the eye. These cells are nerve cells and in a true sense should be thought of as part of the brain. The location of the retina and its major landmarks are shown in Figure 3.7, while Figure 3.9 shows the retina in more detail.

To describe the retina, let's move from the back of the retina out toward the front. The layer of cells at the very back of the retina are the receptor cells for vision, the transducers, or **photoreceptors**, of the eye. It is here that light wave energy is changed into neural energy.

As it happens, there are two types of photoreceptor cells: **rods** *and* **cones**. They are very aptly named, because that's just what they look like: small rods and cones. Their ends or tips respond to light wave energy and begin a neural impulse. These impulses travel down the rods and cones and pass on to (form a synapse with) other cells, also arranged in layers.

At these layers of nerve cells there is considerable combination and integration of neural impulses. Each rod and each cone does not have a single direct pathway to the cerebral cortex of the brain. Impulses from many rods and cones are combined right in the eye (by *bipolar cells* and *ganglion cells*, among others). Fibers from ganglion cells gather together to

ciliary muscles *small muscles attached to the lens that control its shape and focusing capability*

accommodation *the process in which the ciliary muscles change the shape of the lens in order to focus a visual image*

aqueous humor *watery fluid found in the space between the cornea and the lens that nourishes the front of the eye*

vitreous humor *the thick fluid behind the lens of the eye that helps keep the eyeball spherical*

retina *layers of cells at the back of the eye that contain the photosensitive rod and cone cells*

photoreceptors *light-sensitive cells (cones and rods) of the retina that convert light energy into neural energy*

rods *photosensitive cells of the retina that are most active in low levels of illumination and do not respond differentially to different wavelengths of light*

cones *photosensitive cells of the retina that operate best at high levels of illumination and are responsible for color vision*

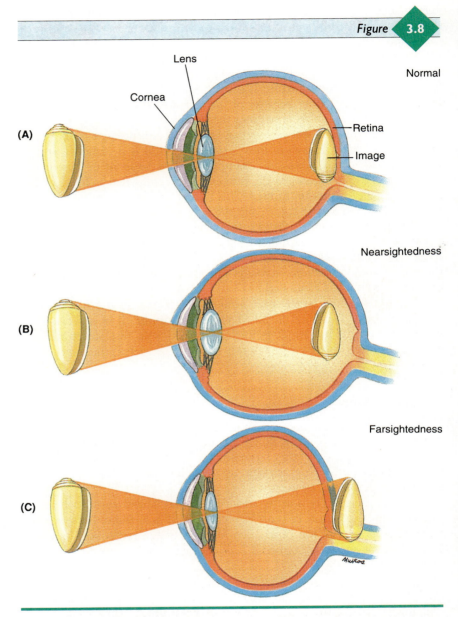

Lens

Cornea

Normal

(A)

Retina

Image

Nearsightedness

(B)

Farsightedness

(C)

Sightedness. (A) Normal vision, where the inverted image is focused by the cornea and lens in the retina. (B) Nearsightedness, where the focused image falls short of the retina because the eyeball is too rounded. (C) Farsightedness, where the focused image falls beyond the retina because the eyeball is too short or the lens too flattened.

optic nerve *the fiber composed of many neurons that leaves the eye and carries impulses to the occipital lobe of the brain*

form the **optic nerve**, the collection of neurons that leaves the eye and starts back toward other parts of the brain.

Notice again the arrow in Figure 3.9 that indicates the direction of the light entering the retina. It is drawn correctly. Yes, light waves first pass through all those layers of cells, past all those nerve cells, to reach the tips of the rods and cones, where they are transformed into neural impulses. The layering of cellular structures in the retina does seem to be somewhat

Figure **3.9**

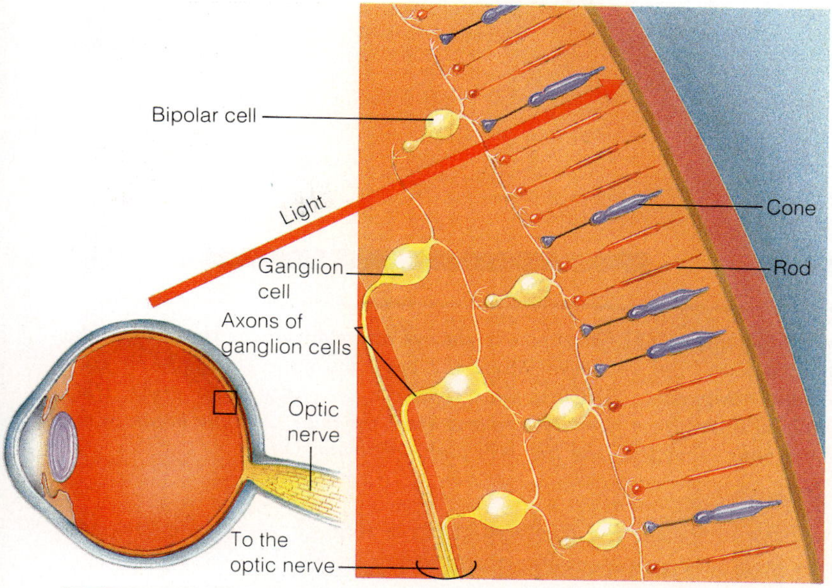

Bipolar cell

Light

Cone

Ganglion cell

Rod

Axons of ganglion cells

Optic nerve

To the optic nerve

The major features of the human retina.

inside out. It would seem to make more sense to point the light-sensitive tips of the rods and cones out toward the incoming light, yet virtually all mammalian retinas are constructed in the manner shown in Figure 3.9.

The two main features of the retina depicted in Figure 3.7 are the **fovea** and the **blind spot**. The fovea is a small area of the retina where there are very few layers of cells between the entering light and the cone cells that fill the area. There are no rods in the fovea, only cones, which are tightly packed together. It is here at the fovea that our vision is best, that our *acuity*, or ability to discern detail, is best—at least in daylight or in reasonably high levels of illumination. If you were to try to thread a needle, you would want to focus the image of the needle and thread directly on the fovea.

The blind spot of the retina is where the nerve impulses from the rods and cones, having passed through all those other layers of cells, exit the eye. At the blind spot, there are no rods and cones—there's nothing there but the optic nerve threading its way back deeper into the brain. Because there are no rods or cones, there is no vision here, which is why this area is called the blind spot. Figure 3.10 shows you how to locate your own blind spot.

The Visual Pathway After the Retina

To keep track of what happens to impulses once they have left the eyes at their respective blind spots, follow along with Figure 3.11. Considerable visual processing takes place within the layers of the retina; there are, after all, many more rods and cones in the retina than there are ganglion cell fibers leaving it. Visual information continues to be altered as it races back to the visual area of the occipital lobes of our cerebral cortexes. One chal-

fovea *the region at the center of the retina, comprised solely of cones, where acuity is best in daylight*

blind spot *the small region of the retina, containing no photoreceptors, where the optic nerve leaves the eye*

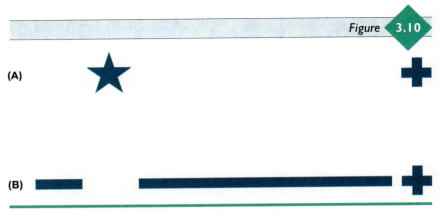

Finding your blindspot. (A) Close your right eye and stare at the cross. Hold the page about a foot from your eye. Move the page until the star falls on your blindspot and disappears. (B) Close your right eye and stare at the cross. Hold the page about a foot from your left eye and move the page until the break in the line falls on your blindspot. The line will look unbroken.

lenge we have in tracing the pathway of nerve fibers between the eyes and the cortex is simply a matter of sorting out left and right.

We know that everyone has a left and a right eye. Everyone also has a left and right occipital lobe. Now we need to introduce the concept of left and right *visual fields*. All this means is that when you look out at the world, everything off to your left is said to be in your left visual field, while everything you see off to your right is said to be in your right visual field. We have drawn Figure 3.11 so that the left visual field is blue and the right visual field is red. Looking at the big picture here, we see that all the stimuli located in our left visual field end up in our right occipital lobe, and all the stimuli from our right visual field end up in our left occipital lobe.

optic chiasma *the location in the brain where impulses from light in the left visual field cross to the right side of the brain and light from the right visual field cross to the left side of the brain*

The sorting out of which fibers in the optic nerve get directed where occurs largely in what is called the **optic chiasma**. Look at Figure 3.11 again and notice that, in fact, each of our eyes receives light energy from *both* visual fields. So what happens is this: Light that enters our left eye from the left initiates neural impulses that cross at the chiasma and go over to the right side of the brain, while light that enters our left eye from the right initiates neural impulses that go straight back to the left hemisphere. Now see if you can describe in words the same situation for the right eye.

From the optic chiasma, nerve fibers pass through other centers in the brain. For example, there is, for each side of the brain, a cluster of cells (a superior colliculus) through which nerve fibers pass that controls the movement of our eyes over a patterned stimulus, perhaps fixing our gaze on some aspect of the pattern. Beyond the superior colliculus, nerve cells form synapses with neurons in the thalamus, which as we saw in Topic 2B, project neural impulses to the layers of cells in the visual cortex of the occipital lobe.

Perhaps the most critical thing to realize about this brief description is that vision doesn't really happen in our eyes. Yes, the eye is the structure that contains the transducers that convert light energy into neural impulses. But the actual experience of "seeing" a stimulus is something that happens in our brains. Our brains reassemble in our awareness one complete visual

Figure **3.11**

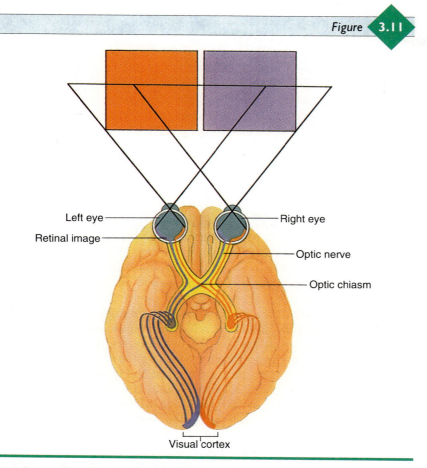

According to the principle of cross-laterality, stimuli entering our left visual field are sent to the right occipital lobe for processing, while stimuli in the right visual field are sent to the left occipital lobe.

field that we experience as continuous, not divided into right and left. To be sure, the detection, recognition, and interpretation of patterns of light, shade, color, and motion are functions of the cerebral cortex.

List the major structures of the eye, and describe the function of each.
Briefly trace the path of impulses from each eye to the cerebral cortex.

RODS AND CONES

Let's go back now and deal with the fact that the human eye contains two distinctly different photoreceptor cells: rods and cones. Not only are there two different kinds of receptor cells in our retinas, but they are not there in equal number. In one eye, there are about 120 million rods, but only 6 million cones, which means that rods outnumber cones approximately 20 to 1.

Not only are rods and cones found in unequal numbers, but they are not evenly distributed throughout the retina. We've already indicated that cones are concentrated in the center of the retina, at the fovea. On the other hand, rods are concentrated in a band or ring surrounding the fovea, out toward the periphery of the retina.

These observations have led psychologists to wonder if the rods and cones of our eyes have different functions. They don't look alike. They're not found in equal numbers. They're not evenly distributed throughout the retina. Maybe they function differently.

In fact, we claim that cones function best in medium to high levels of illumination (as in daylight) and are primarily responsible for our experience of color. On the other hand, our rods operate best under conditions of reduced illumination. They are more sensitive to low-intensity light. As it happens, however, our rods do not discriminate among wavelengths of light, which means that rods do not contribute to our appreciation of color.

Some of the evidence supporting these claims can be verified by our own experiences. Don't you find it difficult to distinguish among different colors at night or in the dark? The next time you are at the movies eating some pieces of candy that are of different colors, see if you can tell them apart without holding them up to the light of the projector. You probably won't be able to tell a green piece from a red one because they all appear black. You can't discriminate colors well in a dark movie theater because you are seeing them primarily with your rods, which are very good at seeing in the reduced illumination of the theater but which don't differentiate among different wavelengths of light.

If you are looking for something small outside at night, you'll probably not see it if you look directly at it. Imagine that you're changing a tire along the road at night. You're replacing the wheel and can't find one of the lug nuts that you know is there someplace in the gravel. If you were to look directly at it, the image of the nut would fall on your fovea. Remember, your fovea is made up almost entirely of cones. Cones do not operate well in relative darkness, and you'll not see the nut. To have the best chance of finding it, you'll have to get the image of the nut to fall on the periphery of your eye where your rods are concentrated.

One of the reasons why nocturnal animals (such as many varieties of owls) function so well at night is that they can see very well in the dark. They see so well because their retinas are packed with rods. Such animals usually have no fovea, or have fewer cones and are demonstrably color blind. (How you might test the color vision of an owl is discussed in Topic 5B.)

Let's mention just one other piece of evidence that supports the idea that our rods and our cones essentially provide us with two different types of vision. Let's take a closer look at what really happens during dark adaptation. Recall that dark adaptation is the name given to the process of our eyes becoming more sensitive (our thresholds lowering) as we spend time in the dark (page 103).

Figure 3.12 is a graphic representation of the dark-adaptation process. It shows us that with time spent in the dark, our sensitivity increases, or

Many nocturnal animals see well in the dark because of a high concentration of rods in their retinas.

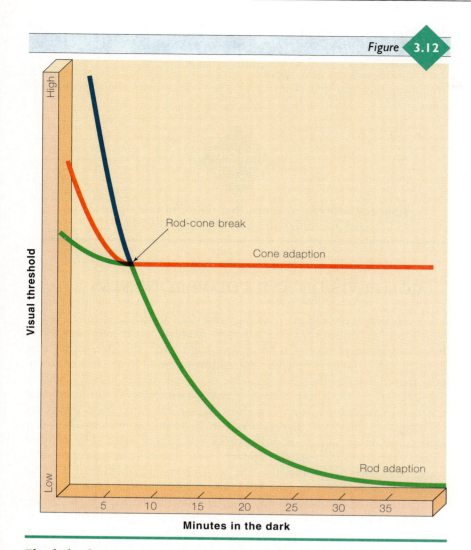

Figure 3.12

The dark adaption curve. At first, both rods and cones lower thresholds, or increase sensitivity. After 6–8 minutes, the cones have become as sensitive as possible; adaption then is due to the rods alone.

our threshold decreases. At first, we can only see very bright lights (say, the light reflected from the movie screen), then we can see dimmer lights (those reflected from people in the theater), and then still dimmer ones (those reflected from pieces of candy perhaps) are detected as our threshold drops. As Figure 3.12 indicates, the whole process takes about 20 to 30 minutes.

But there is something strange going on. The dark-adaptation curve is not a smooth, regular one. At about the 7-minute mark, there is a change in the shape of the curve. This break in the smoothness of the curve is called the *rod-cone break*. At first, for 6 or 7 minutes, both rods *and* cones increase their sensitivity (represented by the first part of the curve). But our cones are basically daylight receptors. They're just not cut out for seeing in the dark, and after that first few minutes, they have become as sensitive as they are ever going to get. The rods, on the other hand, keep on lowering their threshold, becoming more and more sensitive (represented by the part of the curve after the "break").

Now that we've reviewed the nature of light and the nature of the eye, the stimulus and receptor organ for vision, we'll finish this discussion by examining how our eyes—our cones—provide us with the experience of color.

BEFORE YOU GO ON

How and why can we claim that rods and cones provide us with two different kinds of visual experience?

COLOR VISION AND COLOR BLINDNESS

Explaining how the eye codes or responds to different intensities of light is not too difficult. Coding is largely handled by the frequency of the firing of the receptor cells in the retina. High-intensity lights cause more rapid firings of neural impulses than do low-intensity lights. It is also sensible that high-intensity lights stimulate more cells to fire than do lights of low intensity. How the eye codes different wavelengths of light to produce different experiences of color, however, is another story. Here things are not simple at all. To be honest about it, I should say that psychologists really don't know exactly how the process occurs. Two theories of color vision have received research support, even though both were proposed many years ago. As is often the case with competing theories that try to explain the same phenomenon, both are probably partially correct.

The older of the two theories of color vision is the *trichromatic theory*. It was first proposed by Thomas Young very early in the nineteenth century and was then revised by Hermann von Helmholtz, the noted physiologist, about 50 years later. As its name suggests, the *tri*chromatic theory proposes that the eye contains *three* separate and distinct receptors for color.

primary hues *red, green, and blue; those colors of light from which all others can be produced*

Although there is considerable overlap, each receptor responds best to one of three **primary hues** of light: red, green, and blue. These hues (or colors of light) are primary because by the careful combination of the three, all other colors can be produced. You see this in action every day on your television screen. The picture on your TV screen is made up of a pattern of very small dots, each one being either red, green, or blue. From these three wavelengths alone, all other colors are constructed, or integrated. (Don't get confused here with the primary colors of *pigment*, which are red, blue, and yellow. These are the three colors of paint, dye, pastel, etc., which can be mixed together to form all other pigment colors. Our eyes respond to light, not to pigment, and the three primary hues of light are red, blue, and green.)

Because the sensitivity of the three types of receptors in our eyes overlaps, when our eyes are stimulated by a nonprimary color, say orange, the orange-hued light will stimulate each receptor to varying degrees in such a way as to produce the sensation of orange. What gives this theory credibility

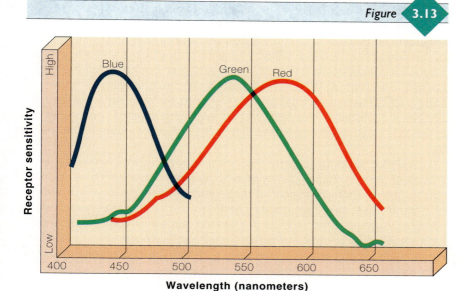

Figure 3.13

The relative sensitivities of three different kinds of cones to light of different wavelengths. Note that although there is considerable overlap, each cell is maximally sensitive to different wavelengths (or colors).

is that *there really are* such receptor cells in the human retina. Obviously, they are cones (which are responsible for color vision). The relative sensitivity of these three cone systems is shown in Figure 3.13.

Ewald Hering thought that the Young-Helmholtz theory left a good bit to be desired, and in 1870 he proposed a theory of his own. This theory has come to be called the *opponent-process theory*. Hering's position is that there are three *pairs* of visual mechanisms that respond to different wavelengths of light. One mechanism is a blue-yellow processor, one a red-green processor, and the third deals with black-white differences.

Each mechanism is capable of responding to *either* of the two hues that give it its name, but not to both. That is, the blue-yellow processor can respond to blue *or* to yellow, but can't handle both at the same time. The second mechanism responds to red *or* green, but not both. The third codes brightness. Thus, the members of each pair work to oppose each other, giving the theory its name. If blue is excited, then yellow is inhibited. If red is excited, then green is inhibited. A light may appear to be a mixture of red and yellow perhaps, but cannot be seen as a mixture of blue *and* yellow, because both blue and yellow cannot be excited at the same time. (It is rather difficult to imagine what a "reddish green" or a "bluish yellow" would look like, isn't it? Can you picture a light that is bright and dim at the same time?)

Although the opponent-process theory may at first appear overly complicated, there are some strong signs that Hering was on the right track. In the first place, excitatory-inhibitory mechanisms such as he proposed for red-green, blue-yellow, and black-white have been found. As it happens, they are not at the level of rods and cones in the retina (as Hering had thought), but at the layer of the ganglion cells (see again Figure 3.9) and also in a small portion of the thalamus.

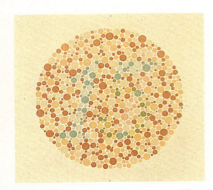

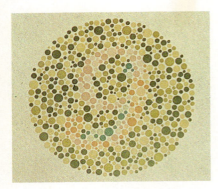

An illustration of the effect of red-green color-blindness. People with normal vision will be able to distinguish the images from the backgrounds, while people who are red-green color-blind will not.

Some support for Hering's theory comes from our experiences with *negative afterimages*. If you stare at a bright green figure for a few minutes and then shift your gaze to a white surface, you will notice an image of a red figure. Where did that come from? The explanation for the appearance of this image is as follows: While you were staring at the green figure, the green component of the red-green process fatigued because of all the stimulation it was getting. When you stared at the white surface, both the red and green components of the process were equally stimulated, but because the green component was fatigued, the red predominated, producing the experience of seeing a red figure. Figure 3.14 gives an example for you to try.

Evidence supporting both theories of normal vision has come from studies of persons with color vision defects. Defective color vision of some sort occurs in about 8 percent of males and slightly less than 0.5 percent of females. Most cases are clearly genetic in origin. It makes sense that if cones are our receptor cells for the discrimination of color, then people with some deficiency in color perception should have a problem with their cones. Such logic is certainly consistent with the Young-Helmoltz theory of color vision.

In fact, for the most common of the color vision deficiencies (*dichromatism*) there is a noticeable lack of one particular type of cone—which type depends upon the color that is "lost." Those people who are "red-green color blind," for instance, have trouble telling the difference between red and green. People with this sort of color blindness also have trouble distinguishing yellow from either red or green. The deficiency is not in actually seeing reds or greens. It is in distinguishing reds and greens from other colors. Put another way, someone who is red-green color blind can clearly see a bright red apple; it just looks no different from a bright green apple.

So we have some evidence that cones are central to our experience of color when we discover that color vision defects can be traced to defects in the cones of the retina. It is also the case that damage to cells higher in

Figure 3.14

To illustrate the experience of color fatigue, stare at the green figure for 30 seconds, and then shift your gaze to a completely white surface. You should see the same figure, but it will appear red because the green receptors are fatigued. Now try the same experiment with the blue figure. What color do you see when you shift your gaze?

the visual pathway—more toward the cerebral cortex—are also implicated in some (rather rare) cases of color vision problems. When these problems do occur, there tend to be losses for both red and green or losses for yellow and blue, color pairings predicted by the opponent-process theory (e.g., Schiffman, 1990, pp. 262–265).

Because cone cell systems have been found in the retina that respond differentially to red, blue, and green light, we cannot dismiss the trichromatic theory. Because there are cells that do operate the way the opponent-process theory predicts, we cannot dismiss this theory either. Well, which one is right? Probably both. Our experience of color likely depends upon the interaction of different cone cells *and* different opponent-process cells within our visual pathway—a marvelous system indeed.

BEFORE YOU GO ON

Briefly summarize the trichromatic and the opponent-process theories of color vision.

In this topic, we have begun our discussion of the process of sensation, the process by which information from the physical world around us is converted, or transduced, into the psychological world of our experience. We've defined a few basic terms, explored a few issues of psychophysics, summarized the physical characteristics of light, and examined how those characteristics affect our experience. We've seen how the minute and complex structures of our eyes pass a range of wave form energies in focused form to the photoreceptors of our retinas, where they are sent on to other levels of the brain where they are transformed into the visual representations of the world we live in. In our next topic, we'll go on to explore the other senses and see how they change other forms of physical energy into the energy of the nervous system.

SUMMARY

How is the process of sensation defined? What is psychophysics? What is an absolute threshold, and how is it related to the sensitivity of our senses?

Sensation is the first step in information processing. It involves the transduction of physical energy from the environment into the energy of the nervous system at our senses. Psychophysics is a subfield of psychology that attempts to specify the nature of the relationships between physical stimuli and psychological reactions and to assess the sensitivity of our senses. An absolute threshold is the intensity of a stimulus that can be detected 50 percent of the time. The lower one's threshold for any sense, the more sensitive it is; thus, sensitivity and threshold are inversely related. / *page 99*

Can subliminal messages affect our behaviors? What is a difference threshold, or j.n.d.? Briefly summarize the basic ideas of signal detection theory. What is sensory adaptation?

Subliminal means "below threshold," and there is evidence that some subliminal stimuli may have small effects on our behaviors and/or mental processes, but there is little evidence that our behaviors can be influenced in any significant ways by subliminal messages. A difference threshold is a difference between stimuli that can be detected 50 percent of the time. It is that point when stimuli are detected to be just noticeably different (j.n.d). Signal detection theory considers threshold in terms of detecting a signal against a back-ground of noise, where the subject's biases, motivation, and attention are also considered. Sensory adaptation is the name given to the phenomenon of our senses becoming less and less sensitive to stimuli that are constantly presented. An exception is dark adaptation, where our eyes actually become more sensitive to stimulation with increased time in the dark. / *page 103*

In what ways do the major physical characteristics of light waves of energy (amplitude, length, and purity) affect our psychological experience of light?

We can think of light as a wave form of radiant energy having three major characteristics: wave amplitude, which determines our experience of the light's brightness; wavelength, which determines our experience of hue; and wave purity, which determines a light's degree of saturation, from the extremes of pure, monochromatic light to the lowest-saturation white light. / *page 107*

List the major structures of the eye, and describe the function of each. Briefly trace the path of impulses from each eye to the cerebral cortex.

Before light reaches the retina, it passes through several structures whose major function is to focus an image on the retina. In order, light passes through the cornea, the pupil (or opening in the iris), aqueous humor, lens (whose shape is controlled by the ciliary muscles), and vitreous humor. Then, at the retina, after passing through layers of neural fibers that combine and integrate visual information (ganglion and bipolar cells, for example), light reaches the photosensitive rods and cones which are the actual transducers for vision. Neural impulses that originate at the rods and cones are collected at the optic nerve and exit the eyeball at the blind spot. From there, fibers go to the optic chiasma, where some are sent straight back and others cross to the opposite side of the brain. The process works so that images from the left visual field are ultimately processed in the right side of the brain, while images from the right visual field are processed in the left side of the brain. From the optic chiasma, impulses travel through the superior colliculi, the thalamus, and finally to the occipital lobes of the cerebral cortex, where visual experiences are actually processed. / *page 113*

How and why can we claim that rods and cones provide us with two different kinds of visual experience?

Cones, which are concentrated in the fovea, respond best to medium to high levels of illumination ("daylight") and respond differentially to light of different wavelength (or color). While rods, concentrated in the peripheral retina, do not discriminate among colors, they do respond to relatively low levels of light. Evidence for this point of view comes from common experience, the examination of the retinas of nocturnal animals, and data on dark adaptation. / *page 116*

Briefly summarize the trichromatic and opponent-process theories of color vision.

These theories attempt to explain how the visual system codes different wavelengths of light, the process that gives rise to our experience of color. The trichromatic theory (associated with Young and Helmholtz) claims there are three different kinds of cones, each maximally sensitive to just one of the three primary colors—red, green, or blue. The opponent-process theory (associated with Hering), claims that there are three pairs of mechanisms involved in our experience of color: a blue-yellow processor, a red-green processor, and a black-white processor. Each of these can respond to either of the characteristics that give it its name, but not to both. There is anatomical and physiological evidence that supports both these theories, some of which comes from our understanding of why some people have defects in color vision. / *page 119*

Why We Care: A Topic Preview

No one needs to convince us that vision is a very important sense. Try a little experiment on your own. Try to bypass your heavy reliance on vision and spend the better part of a day doing without it. Try to go about your normal everyday activities while blindfolded.

One thing you will realize almost immediately is just how heavily we normally rely on vision. But consider for a moment the quantity and quality of information that you do receive from your other senses. You soon may come to a new appreciation of your other senses as they inform you of the wonder of your environment: the aroma and taste of well-prepared barbecue, the sounds of birds and music, the touch and feel of textures and surfaces, the sense of where your body is and what it's doing, the feedback from your muscles as you move—all these and more, all through your nonvisual senses. An exercise such as this should soon convince you of why we care about the material covered in this topic.

In this topic, we'll briefly discuss a number of senses, noting, as we did for vision, the relevant stimulus for each and indicating in general how each sense receptor works. We'll start with hearing and then move to the chemical senses of taste and smell. We'll consider the skin senses of touch, pressure, and temperature. Then we'll cover those senses that help us maintain our balance and tell us where different parts of our bodies are positioned. Finally, we'll take a look at pain—a sense that is as mysterious as it is important.

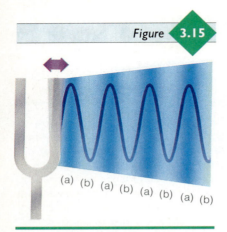

Figure **3.15**

Sound waves are produced as air pressure is spread by the tine of a tuning fork vibrating to the right (a) and left (b). The point of greatest pressure is the high point of the wave; least pressure is indicated by the low point of the wave.

loudness the psychological experience correlated with the intensity, or amplitude, of a sound wave

decibel scale a scale of our experience of loudness in which 0 represents the absolute threshold and 120 is sensed as pain

hertz (Hz) the standard measure of sound wave frequency that is the number of wave cycles per second

pitch the psychological experience that corresponds to sound wave frequency and gives rise to high (treble) or low (bass) sounds

Sound is a series of pressures of air that produce vibrations of the eardrum.

HEARING

Hearing (or more formally, *audition*) provides us with nearly as much useful information about our environment as vision. One of its main roles is its involvement in our development of language and speech. Without hearing, these uniquely human skills are difficult to acquire.

The Stimulus for Hearing: Sound

The stimulus for vision is light; for hearing, the stimulus is sound. Sound is made up of a series of pressures of air (or some other medium, such as water) that beat against our ear. We can represent these pressures as sound waves. As a source of sound vibrates, it pushes air against our ears. Figure 3.15 shows how we may depict sound as a wave form of energy.

As was the case for light waves, there are three major physical characteristics of sound waves—amplitude, frequency (the inverse of wavelength), and purity—and each of them is related to a different psychological experience. We'll briefly consider each in turn.

Wave Amplitude (Intensity). The amplitude of a sound wave depicts its intensity—the force with which the air strikes our ear. The physical intensity of a sound determines the psychological experience we call **loudness**. That is, the higher its amplitude, the louder we perceive the sound to be. Soft, quiet sounds have low amplitudes (see Figure 3.16).

Measurements of the physical intensity of sound are given in units of force per unit area (which is really pressure, of course). Loudness is a psychological characteristic. It is measured by people, not by instruments. The **decibel scale** of sound intensity has been constructed to reflect *perceived loudness*. Its zero point is the lowest intensity of sound that can be detected, or the absolute threshold. Our ears are very sensitive receptors and respond to very low levels of sound intensity. (In fact, if our ears were much more sensitive, we could hear molecules of air bouncing against our eardrums.) Sounds that are louder than those produced by jet aircraft engines or fast-moving subway trains (around 120 decibels) are experienced more as pain than as sound. Figure 3.17 shows decibel levels for some of the sounds we might find in our environment.

Wave Frequency. When we discussed light, we noted that wavelength was responsible for our perception of hue. With sound, we use *wave frequency*, the number of times a wave repeats itself within a given period of time, rather than wavelength. For sound, frequency is measured in terms of how many waves of pressure are exerted every second. The unit of sound frequency is the **hertz**, abbreviated **Hz**. If a sound wave repeats itself 50 times in one second, it is a 50-Hz sound; 500 repetitions is a 500-Hz sound, and so on. Waves of different frequency are shown in Figure 3.16, where you can see the relationship between wavelength and frequency.

The psychological experience corresponding to sound wave frequency is **pitch**. Pitch is our experience of how high or low a tone is. The musical scale represents differences in pitch to the human ear. Low frequencies correspond to low, bass sounds, such as those produced by foghorns or tubas. High-frequency vibrations give rise to the experience of high-pitched sounds, such as the musical tones produced by flutes or the squeals of smoke detectors.

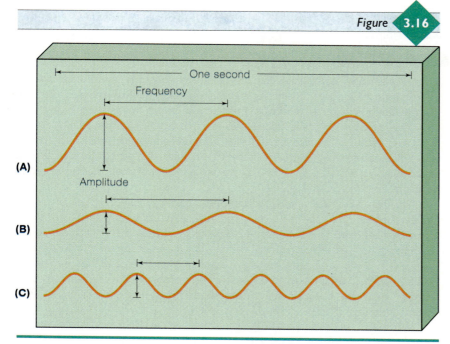

Figure 3.16

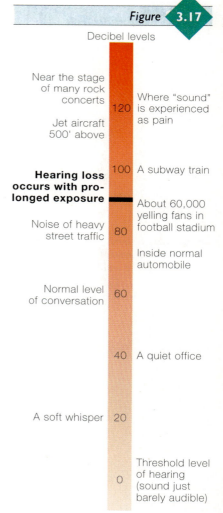

Figure 3.17

How the physical characteristics of sound waves influence our psychological experiences of sound. (1) Though waves (A) and (B) have the same frequency, wave (A) has a higher amplitude and would be experienced as a louder sound. (2) Though waves (B) and (C) have the amplitude, wave (C) would be experienced as having a higher pitch because of its greater frequency.

Just as the human eye cannot respond to all possible wavelengths of radiant energy, so the human ear cannot respond to all possible sound wave frequencies. A healthy human ear responds to sound wave frequencies between 20 Hz and 20,000 Hz. If air strikes our ears at a rate less than 20 times per second, we'll not hear a sound. Sound vibrations faster than 20,000 cycles per second usually cannot be heard either, at least by the human ear. Many animals, including dogs, *can* hear sounds with frequencies above 20,000 Hz, such as those produced by dog whistles.

You will recall that for light, wave amplitude and wavelength interact so that lights of different wavelengths do not appear to be equally bright, even if all their intensities are adjusted to be equal. Well, we have the same sort of interaction when we deal with sound and sound waves. Sound wave intensities and frequencies interact to produce our sensation of loudness.

What this means is that all wave frequencies of sound do not seem to be equally loud (a psychological experience) even if all their intensities are equal (a physical reality). Put another way, to have a high-frequency sound appear as loud as a medium-frequency sound, we would have to raise the amplitude of the high-frequency sound. Fortunately, most of the sounds that are relevant and important to us every day—speech sounds, for example—are usually of mid-range frequency and thus are easily heard.

Wave Purity. A third characteristic of sound waves is wave purity (its opposite is called complexity). You'll recall that we seldom experience pure,

Loudness values in decibel units for various sounds.

monochromatic lights. Pure sounds are also uncommon in our everyday experience. A pure sound would be one in which *all* of the waves from the sound source were vibrating at exactly the same frequency. Such sounds can be produced electronically, of course, and tuning forks produce reasonable approximations, but most of the sounds we hear every day are complex sounds, composed of many different sound wave frequencies.

A tone of middle C on the piano is a tone of 256 Hz. (Again, this means that the source of the sound, here a piano wire, is vibrating 256 times per second). A *pure* 256-Hz tone is composed of sound waves (vibrations) of only that frequency. As it happens, the middle C of the piano has many other wave frequencies mixed in with the predominant 256-Hz wave frequency. (If the 256-Hz wave did not predominate, the tone wouldn't sound like middle C.)

The psychological quality of a sound, reflecting its degree of purity, is called **timbre**. For example, each musical instrument produces a unique variety or mixture of overtones, so each type of musical instrument tends to sound a little different from all others. If a trumpet, a violin, and a piano were each to play the same note (say that middle C of 256 Hz), we could still tell the instruments apart because of our experience of timbre. (In fact, any one instrument may display different timbres, depending on how it is constructed and played.)

With light, we found that the opposite of a pure light was white light—a light made up of all the wavelengths of the visible spectrum. Again, the parallel between vision and hearing holds up. Suppose that I have a sound source that can produce all of the possible sound wave frequencies. I produce a random mixture of these frequencies from 20 Hz to 20,000 Hz. What would that sound like? Actually, it would sound rather like a buzzing noise. The best example would be the sound that one hears when a radio (as it happens, FM works better than AM) is tuned to a position in between stations. This soft, whispering, buzzing sound, containing a range of many audible sound frequencies, is useful in masking or covering other unwanted sounds. We call a random mixture of sound frequencies **white noise**, just as we called a random mixture of wavelengths of light *white light*.

The analogy between light and sound, between vision and hearing, is striking. Both types of stimulus energy can be represented as waves. In both cases, each of the *physical* characteristics of the waves (amplitude, length or frequency, and purity or complexity) is correlated with a *psychological* experience. All of these relationships are summarized in Figure 3.18.

timbre *the psychological experience related to wave purity by which we differentiate the sharpness, clearness, or quality of a tone*

white noise *a sound composed of a random assortment of all wave frequencies from the audible spectrum*

Figure **3.18**

THE PHYSICAL CHARACTERISTICS OF LIGHT AND SOUND WAVES AFFECT OUR PSYCHOLOGICAL EXPERIENCES OF VISION AND HEARING AS ILLUSTRATED IN THIS TABLE.

Physical Characteristic	Psychological Experience for Vision	Psychological Experience for Hearing
Wave amplitude	Brightness	Loudness
Wavelength or frequency	Hue	Pitch
Wave purity or mixture	Saturation	Timbre

BEFORE YOU GO ON

What are the three major physical characteristics of sound, and which psychological experiences do they produce?

The Ear

It is deep inside the ear that the energy of sound wave pressures is transduced into neural impulses. As with the eye, most of the structures of the ear simply transfer energy from without to within. Figure 3.19 is a drawing of the major structures of the human ear. We'll use it to follow the path of sound waves from the environment to the receptor cells for sound.

Figure **3.19**

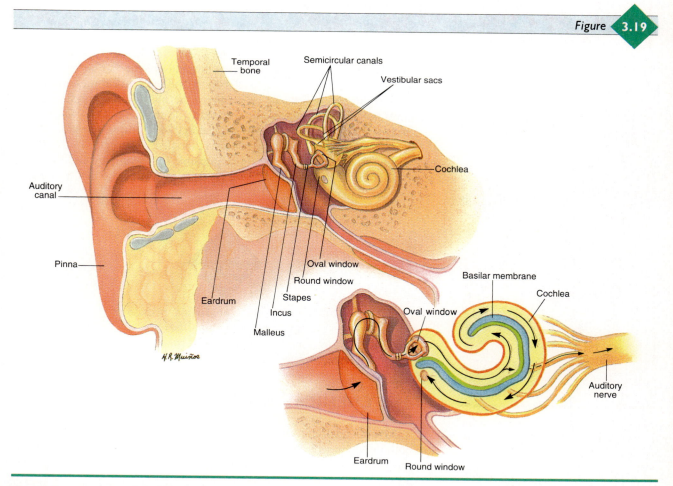

The major structures of the human ear.

pinna *the outer ear, which collects and funnels sound waves into the auditory canal toward the eardrum*

eardrum *the outermost membrane of the ear; is set in motion by the vibrations of a sound; transmits vibrations to the ossicles*

malleus, incus, and stapes *(collectively, ossicles) three small bones that transmit and intensify sound vibrations from the eardrum to the oval window*

cochlea *part of the inner ear where sound waves become neural impulses*

basilar membrane *a structure within the cochlea that vibrates and thus stimulates the hair cells of the inner ear*

hair cells *the receptor cells for hearing, located in the cochlea, stimulated by the vibrating basilar membrane; they send neural impulses to the temporal lobe of the brain*

The outer ear is called the **pinna**. Its main function is to collect sound waves from the air around it and funnel them through the auditory canal toward the **eardrum**. (Notice that when we are trying to hear soft sounds we sometimes cup our hand around our pinna to gather in as much sound as we can.) Air waves push against the eardrum (technically, the tympanic membrane), setting it in motion so that it vibrates at the same rate as the sound source. Once the eardrum is vibrating back and forth, the sound moves deeper inside the ear.

There are three very small bones (collectively called *ossicles*) in the middle ear. These bones are, in order, the **malleus, incus**, and **stapes** (pronounced *stape-ese*). Because of their unique shapes, these bones are sometimes referred to as the *hammer, anvil*, and *stirrup*. These bones pass the vibrations of the eardrum along to the *oval window*, another membrane like the eardrum, only smaller. As the ossicles pass the sound vibrations along to the oval window, they amplify them, increasing their force.

When sound is transmitted beyond the oval window, the vibrations are said to be in the inner ear. The main structure of the inner ear is the **cochlea**, a snaillike structure that contains the actual receptor cells—the transducers—for hearing. As the stapes vibrates against the oval window, a fluid inside the cochlea is set in motion at the same rate.

When the fluid within the cochlea moves, the **basilar membrane** is bent up and down. The basilar membrane is a small structure that runs just about the full length of the cochlea. Hearing takes place when very tiny **hair cells** are stimulated by the vibrations of the basilar membrane. Through a process not yet fully understood, the mechanical pressure of the basilar membrane on the hair cells starts a neural impulse that leaves the ear, traveling on the auditory nerve toward the temporal lobe.

So it is in the ear that the physical energy of sound is transduced into the neural energy that gives rise to a psychological experience in the brain. Most of the structures of the ear are responsible for amplifying and directing waves of pressure to the hair cells in the cochlea, where the neural impulse begins.

Figure 3.20

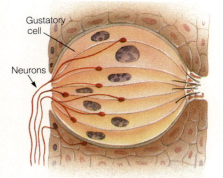

Gustatory cell

Neurons

Enlarged view of a taste bud, showing how the sensation of taste travels from the gustatory receptor cells to the brain.

BEFORE YOU GO ON

Summarize how sound wave pressures pass through the different structures of the ear.

THE CHEMICAL SENSES

Taste and smell are referred to as chemical senses because the stimuli for both of them are molecules of chemical compounds. For taste, the chemicals are dissolved in liquid (usually the saliva in our mouths). For smell, they are dissolved in the air that reaches the smell receptors high inside our noses. The technical term for taste is *gustation*; for smell, it is *olfaction*.

If you have ever eaten while suffering from a severe head cold that has blocked your nasal passages, you appreciate the extent to which our experiences of taste and smell are interrelated. Most foods seem to lose their taste when we cannot smell them. This is why we differentiate between the *flavor* of foods (which includes such qualities as odor and texture) and the *taste* of foods. A simple test demonstrates this point very nicely. While blindfolded, eat a small piece of peeled apple and a small piece of peeled potato, and see if you can tell the difference between the two. You shouldn't have any trouble making this discrimination. Now hold your nose very tightly and try again. Without your sense of smell to help you, such discrimination—on the basis of taste alone—is very difficult.

The tip of the tongue is most sensitive to sweet tastes.

Taste (Gustation)

Our experience of the flavors of foods depends so heavily on our sense of smell, texture, and temperature that we sometimes have to wonder if there is any sense of taste alone. Well, there is. Taste seems to have four basic psychological qualities—and many combinations of these four: sweet, salty, sour, and bitter. You should be able to generate a list of foods that produce each of these basic sensations. Most foods derive their special taste from a unique combination of the four basic taste sensations. Have you noticed that it is more difficult to think of examples of sour- and bitter-tasting foods then it is to think of sweet and salty ones? This reflects the fact that we usually don't like bitter and sour tastes and have learned to avoid them.

The receptor cells for taste are located on (*in* might be more precise) the tongue. These receptors are called **taste buds**. We all have about 10,000 taste buds, and each one is made up of a number of parts (see Figure 3.20). When parts of taste buds die (or are killed by foods that are too hot, for example) new segments are regenerated. Fortunately, we are always growing fresh new taste receptor cells. That observation in itself makes taste a unique sense: As receptor cells, taste buds are essentially nerve cells, and we've already noted that nerve cells are usually not replaced when they die.

Different taste buds respond primarily to chemicals that produce one of the four basic taste qualities. That is, some receptor cells respond best to salts, while others respond primarily to sweet-producing chemicals, like sugars. As it happens, these specialized cells are not evenly distributed on the surface of the tongue. Receptors for sweet are at the very tip of the tongue, receptors for salty tastes are toward the front, sour receptors are on the sides, and bitter receptors are at the back of the tongue. A sour vinegar solution dropped right at the tip of the tongue might very well go unnoticed until some of it gets washed over to the side of the tongue. To best savor a lollipop, children learned ages ago to lick it with the tip of the tongue. The locations of the primary taste receptors are shown in Figure 3.21.

taste buds *the receptors for taste located in the tongue*

Figure **3.21**

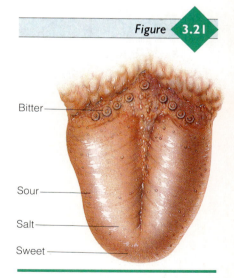

Bitter

Sour

Salt

Sweet

The four primary qualities of taste are experienced in specific areas of the tongue.

Smell (Olfaction)

Smell is a sense that is poorly understood. It is a sense that often gives us great pleasure—think of the aroma of bacon frying over a wood fire or of freshly picked flowers. It also can produce considerable displeasure—consider the smell of old garbage or rotten eggs.

The sense of smell originates in cells located high in the nasal cavity, very close to the brain itself. We know that the pathway from these receptors to the brain is the most direct and shortest of all the senses (see Figure 3.22). What we don't understand well is how molecules suspended in air, or some other gas, actually stimulate the small hair cells of the olfactory receptor to fire neural impulses.

We know that the sense of smell is very important for many nonhumans. The dog's sense of smell is legendary. In fact, many organisms emit chemicals, called **pheromones**, that produce distinctive odors. Sometimes pheromones are secreted by cells in the skin, sometimes in the urine, and occasionally from special glands (in some deer, this gland is located near the rear hoof). One purpose of pheromones is to mark or delineate one's territory. If you take a dog for a walk around the block and discover that the pooch wants to stop and deposit small amounts of urine on just about every front lawn, that dog is leaving behind a pheromone message that says essentially, "I have been here; this is my odor; this is my turf."

Most commonly, pheromones carry sexually related messages to members of the opposite sex of the same species. Most often that message is roughly translated into, "I am available for sexual activities." Of course, the result is that the odor of these pheromones tends to attract members of the opposite sex. Knowledge of this relationship can be useful. Japanese beetles are a common pest, particularly for people who grow roses. They are very difficult to kill safely with standard poisons. Traps are now available that contain a small amount of a pheromone attractive to Japanese beetles. The beetles smell the odor the trap gives off, come rushing to investigate, and slide off a slippery plastic platform to their doom in a disposable plastic bag.

It is likely that pheromone production is related to the sex hormones, even in humans. For example, there is evidence that women who live in close quarters (say in a college dormitory) for very long soon synchronize their menstrual cycles. This can be related to the fact that the same thing happens in rats when the only contact between groups of rats is that they share the same air supply and thus the same odors (McClintock, 1971; 1979). It also may be true that humans use pheromones to attract members of the opposite sex (Cutler et al., 1986; Wallace, 1977). If we do, the real effect is no doubt very small, although people who advertise perfumes and colognes would have us think otherwise (e.g., Doty, 1986).

For many years, psychologists have been trying to determine if there are primary odors, perhaps not unlike the primary tastes. A number of schemes have been proposed, and each seemed reasonable in its day. One scheme suggests that there are four basic odors from which all others may be constructed: fragrant, acid, burnt, and, of all things, goaty. Another scheme cites six primary odors. Yet another plan, called the stereochemical theory (Amoore, 1970), names seven primary qualities of smell and further suggests that each primary quality is stimulated by a unique type or shape

pheromones *chemicals that produce an odor used as a method of communication between organisms*

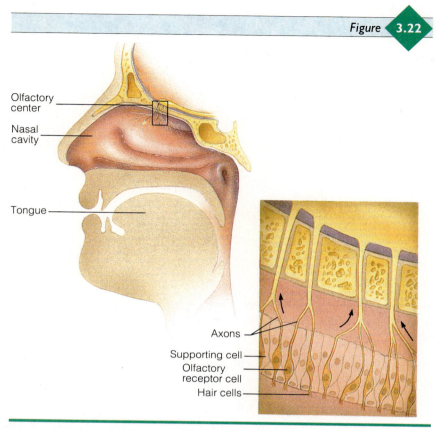

Figure **3.22**

Olfactory center

Nasal cavity

Tongue

Axons

Supporting cell

Olfactory receptor cell

Hair cells

The olfactory system showing its proximity to the brain and the relationship between the sensations of taste and smell.

of chemical molecule. For the moment, it is just impossible to be any more definite, since there seems to be evidence both for and against Amoore's theory—and any other that has been proposed.

BEFORE YOU GO ON

Discuss the chemical senses of taste and smell, noting the stimulus and sense receptor for each.

Do taste and smell each have primary qualities? If so, what are they?

THE SKIN (CUTANEOUS) SENSES

Most of us take our skin for granted—at least we seldom think about it very much. We frequently abuse our skin by overexposing it to the sun's

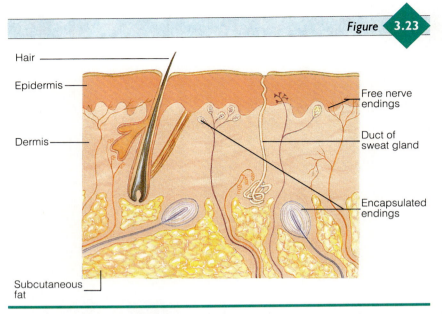

Figure **3.23**

Hair

Epidermis

Dermis

Free nerve
endings

Duct of
sweat gland

Encapsulated
endings

Subcutaneous
fat

A patch of hairy skin, showing the different layers of the skin and the various nerves.

rays in summer and to excess cold in winter. We scratch it, cut it, scrape it, and wash away millions of its cells every time we shower or bathe.

Figure 3.23 is a diagram of just some of the structures found in an area of skin from a hairy part of the human body. Each square inch of the layers that make up our skin contains nearly 20 million cells, including a large number of special sense receptors. Some of the skin receptors have *free nerve endings*, while others have some sort of small covering over them. We call these latter ones *encapsulated nerve endings*, and there are many different types. It is our skin that somehow gives rise to our psychological experience of touch or pressure and of warmth and cold. It would be very convenient if each of the different types of receptor cells within the layers of our skin independently gave rise to a different type of psychological sensation, but such is not the case.

Indeed, one of the problems in studying the skin senses, or *cutaneous* senses, is trying to determine just which cells in the skin give rise to the different sensations of pressure and temperature. We can discriminate clearly between a light touch and a strong jab in the arm and between vibrations, tickles, and itches. Again, a simple proposal is that there are different receptors in the skin responsible for each different sensation. Unfortunately, this proposal is not supported by the facts. Although *some* types of receptor cells are more sensitive to *some* types of stimuli, current thinking is that our ability to discriminate among different types of cutaneous sensation is due to the unique combination of responses that the many receptor cells have to different types of stimulation.

By carefully stimulating very small areas of the skin, we can locate areas that are particularly sensitive to temperature. We are convinced that warm and cold temperatures each stimulate different locations on the skin. Even so, there is no consistent pattern of receptor cells found at these locations, or temperature spots, as they are called. That is, we have not yet located

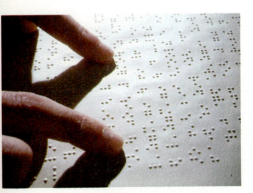

The tips of the fingers contain many cutaneous receptors for touch or pressure.

specific receptor cells for cold or hot. As a matter of fact, our experience of hot seems to come from the simultaneous stimulation of both warm and cold spots. A rather ingenious demonstration shows how this works. Cold water is run through one metal tube and warm water is run through another tube. The two tubes are coiled together (see Figure 3.24). If you were to grasp the coiled tubes, your experience would be one of *heat*—the tubes would feel hot even if you knew that they weren't.

BEFORE YOU GO ON

What are the cutaneous senses, and what are the transducers for each?

THE POSITION SENSES

Another sensory capacity we often take for granted is our ability to know how and where our bodies are positioned in space. Although we seldom worry about it, we can quickly become aware of how our bodies are positioned in regard to the pull of gravity. We also get sensory information about where different parts of our body are in relation to each other. We can tell if we are moving or standing still. And unless we are on a roller coaster, or racing across a field, we usually adapt to these sensory messages quickly and pay them little attention.

Most of the information about where we are in space comes to us through our sense of vision. If we ever want to know just how we are oriented in space, all we have to do is look around. But notice that we *can* do the same sort of thing even with our eyes closed. We have two systems of position sense over and above what vision can provide. One, the **vestibular sense**, tells us about balance, where we are in relation to gravity, and acceleration or deceleration. The other, the **kinesthetic sense**, tells us about the movement or position of our muscles and joints.

The receptors for the vestibular sense are located on either side of the head, near the inner ears. Five chambers are located there: three semicircular canals and two vestibular sacs. Their orientation is shown back in Figure 3.19. Each of these chambers is filled with fluid. When our head moves in any direction, the fluid in the semicircular canals moves, drawn by gravity or the force of our head accelerating in space. The vestibular sacs contain very small solid particles that float around in the fluid within the sacs. When these particles are forced against one side of the sacs, as happens when we move, they stimulate different hair cells that start neural impulses. Overstimulation of the receptor cells in the vestibular sacs or semicircular canals can lead to feelings of dizziness or nausea, reasonably enough called *motion sickness*.

Receptors for our kinesthetic sense are located primarily in our joints, but some information also comes from muscles and tendons. These receptors sense the position and movements of parts of the body—again, information to which we seldom attend. Impulses from these receptors travel to

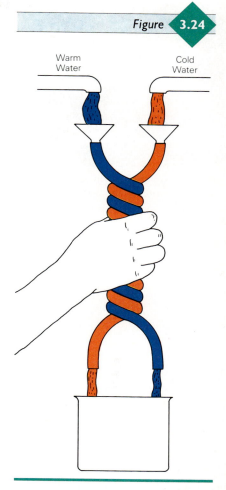

Figure **3.24**

Warm Water   Cold Water

A demonstration that our sensation of hot may be constructed from the sensations of warm and cold. Even if you know the coiled tubes contain only warm and cold water, when you grasp the tubes they will feel hot.

vestibular sense *the position sense that tells us about balance, where we are in relation to gravity, and acceleration or deceleration*

kinesthetic sense *the position sense that tells us the position of different parts of our bodies and what our muscles and joints are doing*

Rollercoaster rides provide considerable stimulation to the vestibular sense.

our brain through pathways in our spinal cord. They provide excellent examples of reflex actions. As muscles in the front of your upper arm (your biceps) contract, the corresponding muscles in the back of your arm (triceps) must relax if you are to successfully bend your arm at the elbow. How fortunate it is that our kinesthetic receptors, operating reflexively through the spinal cord, take care of these details without our having to manipulate consciously all the appropriate muscular activity. In fact, about the only time we even realize that our kinesthetic system is functioning is when it stops working well, such as when our leg "falls asleep" and we have trouble walking.

BEFORE YOU GO ON

What are our position senses, and how do they operate?

PAIN: A SPECIAL SENSE

Our sense of pain is a very curious and troublesome one for psychologists who are interested in sensory processes. Pain, or certainly the fear of it, can be a very strong motivator; we'll do all sorts of things to avoid it. Pain is certainly unpleasant, but at the same time, it is terribly useful. Feelings of pain alert us to problems occurring somewhere within our bodies, warning us that steps might need to be taken to remove the source of pain. Without a sense of pain, a person might very well die of a burst appendix. Our feelings of pain are particularly private sensations—they are difficult to share or describe to others (Verillo, 1975).

Just what *is* pain? What causes the sensation of pain? What are its sense receptors? At present, we really don't know. Many stimuli can cause pain. Very intense stimulation of virtually any sense receptor can produce pain. Too much light, very strong pressures on the skin, excessive temperatures, very loud sounds, and even too many "hot" spices can all result in our experiencing pain. But as we all know, the stimulus for pain need not be intense. Under the right circumstances, even a light pinprick can be very painful.

Our skin seems to have many receptors for pain, but pain receptors can also be found deep inside our bodies—consider stomachaches, lower back pain, and headaches. Pain is experienced in our brains, but pain is the only "sense" for which we can find no one specific center in the cerebral cortex.

Reactions to pain show great individual differences and reflect a number of psychological as well as physiological factors (Melzack, 1973). For relatively short-lived, stabbing pain, our first reaction often occurs at the level of a spinal reflex. You stop by to have your cholesterol checked and get the tip of your finger jabbed with a sharp blade to draw a bit of blood. Your very first reaction to the pain—which really doesn't last very long at all—is to quickly and reflexively pull back your hand and arm.

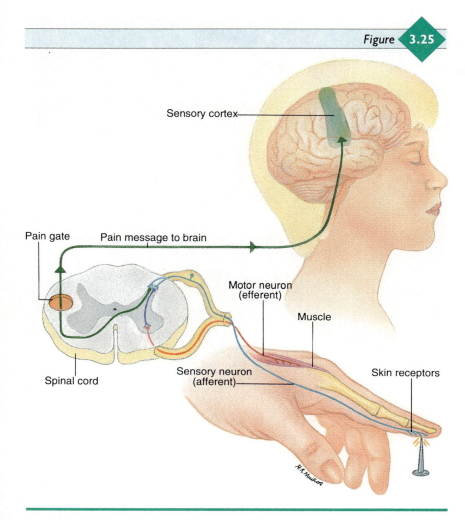

Figure **3.25**

How the gate-control theory of pain works. A stimulus on the skin initiates neural impulses that enter the spinal cord and rush through a "pain gate" to the brain. Many mechanisms (including the release of endorphins through acupuncture) can act to close the gate, at least to some degree, thus reducing the experience of pain by the brain.

A theory of pain still attracting attention from researchers (most of it supportive, some not) is that of Melzack and Wall's **gate-control theory** (1965; Melzack, 1973). It suggests that our experience of pain is something that happens not so much at the level of the receptor (say, in the skin), but within the central nervous system. The theory proposes that a gatelike structure in the spinal cord responds to stimulation from a particular type of nerve fiber—one that "opens the gate" and allows for the sensation of pain by letting impulses on up to the brain. Other nerve fibers can offset the activity of the pain-carrying fibers and "close the gate" so that pain messages are cut off and never make it to the brain. Figure 3.25 presents the basic idea of the gate-control theory.

There are several situations in which this notion of an opening and closing gate to pain seems reasonable. Let's look at some observations about

gate-control theory *the theory of pain sensation that argues that there are brain centers that regulate the passage of pain messages from different parts of the body to the brain*

The gate-control theory developed by Ronald Melzack (pictured here) and Patrick Wall proposes that pain centers in the brain are responsive to stimulation from nerve fibers that "open the gate" and allow for the sensation of pain.

pain that seem consistent with the idea of a mechanism that opens and closes, allowing pain sensations to pass to the brain or not.

One of the things that happens when we are exposed to persistent pain is that certain neurotransmitters—*endorphins*—are released in the brain (Hughes et al., 1975; Terenius, 1982). We've already noted that endorphins (plural because there may be a number of them) naturally reduce our sense of pain and generally make us feel good. When the effects of endorphins are blocked, pain seems unusually severe. It turns out that, whatever else endorphins do, they stimulate nerve fibers that go to the spinal cord and effectively "close" the gate that monitors the passage of impulses from pain receptors.

Think of some of the other mechanisms that often are useful in moderating the experience of pain. Hypnosis and cognitive self-control (just trying very hard to convince yourself that the pain you're experiencing is not that bad and will go away) *are* effective (Litt, 1988; Melzack, 1973). That pain can be controlled to some extent by cognitive training is clear from the success of many classes aimed at reducing the pain of childbirth. The idea is that psychological processes can influence the gate-control center in the spinal cord. We also have ample evidence that **placebos** can be effective in treating pain. A placebo is a substance (perhaps in pill form) that a person *believes* will be effective in treating some symptom—such as pain—when, in fact, there is no active pain-relieving ingredient in the substance. When subjects are given a placebo that they genuinely believe will alleviate pain, endorphins are released in the brain which, again, can help to close the gate to pain-carrying impulses (Levine et al., 1979).

Another process that works to ease the feeling of pain, particularly pain from or near the surface of the skin, is called counterirritation. The idea

placebo *an inactive substance that has its effect because a person has come to believe that it will be effective*

here is to stimulate forcefully (but not painfully, of course) an area of the body *near* the location of the pain. Dentists have discovered that rubbing on the gum near where a novacaine needle is to be inserted significantly reduces the patient's experience of the pain of the needle. Again, as you might have guessed, the logic is that all that stimulation from the nearby rubbing action serves to close the pain gate so the needle has little effect. And speaking of needles, the ancient oriental practice of acupuncture can also be tied in to the gate-control theory of pain. What we don't know yet is exactly why acupuncture works as well as it does when it is effective; there are cases where it doesn't work well at all, but these usually involve patients who are skeptics and "don't believe in" acupuncture. That sort of observation suggests that at least some of acupuncture's benefits derive from its function as a placebo. But the really important aspect may be its function as a counterirritant. There also is evidence that acupuncture releases endorphins in the brain. Perhaps each or all of these functions serve the major purpose of controlling pain by closing off impulses to the brain.

BEFORE YOU GO ON

What produces the sensation of pain, and how might that sensation be controlled or reduced?

What is the gate-control theory of pain?

In this topic, we have reviewed the structures and functions of a number of different human senses. We have seen that hearing, like vision, is stimulated by physical wave forms of energy and that the measurable characteristics of those waves (amplitude, frequency, and complexity) give rise to different psychological experiences of sounds (loudness, pitch, and timbre). We've noted the interrelationship between taste and smell. We've reviewed a number of our different skin senses, as well as those senses (vestibular and kinesthetic) that inform us about our body's position in space. Finally, we have introduced some of the current thinking about the sense of pain. It is clear that at any one time, our brains are receiving a remarkable amount of information from all of our sensory receptors. How we deal with all that information is the question we address in Chapter 4.

SUMMARY

What are the three major physical characteristics of sound, and which psychological experiences do they produce?

Like light, sound may be represented as a wave form of energy with three major physical characteristics: wave amplitude, frequency, and purity (or complexity). These in turn give rise to the psychological experiences of loudness, pitch, and timbre. / *page 127*

Summarize how sound wave pressures pass through the different structures of the ear.

Most of the structures of the ear (the pinna, auditory canal, eardrum, malleus, incus, stapes, and oval window) intensify and transmit sound wave pressures to the fluid in the cochlea, which then vibrates the basilar membrane, which in turn stimulates tiny hair cells to transmit neural impulses along the auditory nerve toward the temporal lobe of the brain. / *page 128*

Discuss the chemical senses of taste and smell, noting the stimulus and receptor for each. Do taste and smell each have primary qualities? If so, what are they?

The senses of taste (gustation) and smell (olfaction) are very interrelated. They

are referred to as the chemical senses because both respond to chemical molecules in solution. The receptors for smell are hair cells that line the upper regions of the nasal cavity; for taste, the receptors are cells in the taste buds located in the tongue. Taste appears to have four primary qualities (sweet, sour, bitter, and salty), but for smell, the issue of primary qualities and how many there may be is less certain. / *page 131*

What are the cutaneous senses, and what are the transducers for each?

The cutaneous senses are our skin senses: touch, pressure, warm, and cold. Specific receptor cells for each indentifiable skin sense have not yet been localized, although they no doubt include free nerve endings and encapsulated nerve endings, which most likely work in combination. / *page 133*

What are our position senses, and how do they operate?

One of our position senses is the vestibular sense, which, by responding to the movement of small particles suspended in a fluid within our vestibular sacs and semicircular canals, can inform us about orientation with regard to gravity or accelerated motion. Our other position sense is kinesthesis, which,

through receptors in our muscles and joints, informs us about the orientation of different parts of our body. / *page 134*

What produces the sensation of pain, and how might that sensation be controlled or reduced? What is the gate-control theory of pain?

A wide variety of environmental stimuli can give rise to our experience of pain, from high levels of stimulus intensity, to light pinpricks, to internal stimuli of the sort that produce headaches. There seems to be no one receptor for the pain sense. The central nervous system is clearly involved in our experience of pain, as a gate-control mechanism in the spinal cord that either blocks or sends impulses carrying information about pain to the brain. Given the gate-control theory of pain, anything that can block the passage of pain impulses—close the gate—will control our experience of pain. This is directly accomplished through endorphins and counterirritation. Closing the gate apparently can be controlled by pain-killing medication, hypnosis, self-persuasion, placebo effects, and acupuncture. / *page 137*

PERCEPTION AND CONSCIOUSNESS

TOPIC 4A   Perception

TOPIC 4B   Varieties of Consciousness

TOPIC 4A

Perception

Why We Care: A Topic Preview

Perception is a complex, active, occasionally creative process. It acts on stimulation received and recorded by the senses. **Perception** is a process that involves the selection, organization, and interpretation of stimuli. We may think of perception as a somewhat more cognitive and central process than sensation. One way in which you can think of the role of perception in our daily lives is to say that our senses present us with information about the world in which we live, while perception represents (re-presents) that information, often flavored by our motivational states, our expectations, and our past experiences.

In fact, as we go through the material in this topic, it will become clear to you that perception as a cognitive process is very much related to both sensation and memory. Perception is the active process that helps us make sense of the multitude of stimuli that bombard us every moment of every day. By giving meaning to sensory input, perception readies information for storage in memory. Perception may be thought of as bridging the gap between what our senses respond to and what we can later remember. This is why we care.

We also care about the processes of perception because there is no other content area in psychology that is more related to the observation we made in Topic 1A that "things are not always as they seem." Indeed, most of this topic is concerned with describing the ways in which our perceptions, and thus our memories, are influenced by factors above and beyond the actual stimuli that happen to be present in our environment at any time. In other words, what we perceive can be influenced by more than just what is there to be perceived, and in this topic, we'll examine those influences.

First, we'll deal with perceptual selection. This discussion is based on the premise that we cannot process fully, at any one time, all the stimuli that produce a response at our sensory receptors (that are above our sensory thresholds). You recognize this as a matter of paying attention. Somehow we manage to attend to some stimuli, but almost always at the expense of others. We'll consider some of the factors that determine which stimuli we will pay attention to.

Second, we'll discuss perceptual organization. Here the issue is how the bits and pieces of information relayed from our sense organs become organized and interpreted as meaningful objects or events. After all, we don't really "see" the dots of light and shade and color that our eyes respond to; we "see" people and horses and cars and things. We group and organize some stimulus events as belonging with others—How? On what basis do we do so? We'll end the topic with an examination of three perceptual processes that we often take for granted: our perception of depth and distance, our perception of motion, and the constancy of perception over different times and situations.

perception *the cognitive process of selecting, organizing, and interpreting stimuli*

PERCEPTUAL SELECTIVITY: PAYING ATTENTION

Imagine that you are at a party, engaged in a dreadfully boring conversation with someone you've just met. From time to time, it occurs to you that wearing your new shoes was not a good idea—your feet hurt. You are munching on an assortment of tasty appetizers. Music blares from a stereo at the other end of the room. Aromas of foods, smoke, and perfumes fill the air. There must be at least 50 people at this party, and you don't know any of them. Your senses are being bombarded simultaneously by all sorts of information: sights, sounds, tastes, smells, even pain. Suddenly, you hear someone mention your name. You redirect your attention, for the moment disregarding the person talking right in front of you.

What determines which of many competing stimuli attract and hold our attention? In fact, there are many variables that influence our selection of stimuli from the environment. In this section, we'll discuss some of the more important ones. These variables can be divided into two general types: stimulus factors and personal factors. By stimulus factors, I mean those characteristics of stimuli that make them more compelling (or attention-grabbing) than others, no matter who the perceiver is. By personal factors, I mean those characteristics of the person, the perceiver, that influence which stimuli get attended to or perceived. We'll start by considering stimulus factors.

Stimulus Factors in Selectivity

Some stimuli are simply more compelling than others; they are more likely to get our attention—more likely to be "selected in" for further processing and interpretation. They tend to operate regardless of who the perceiver is, and because individual differences seem to matter little here, they're called *stimulus factors.*

contrast *the extent to which a stimulus is in some physical way different from other surrounding stimuli*

The most common and important stimulus factor in perceptual selection is **contrast**, the extent to which a given stimulus is physically different from the other stimuli around it. One stimulus can contrast with other stimuli in a variety of ways. For example, we are more likely to attend to a stimulus if its *intensity* is different from the intensities of other stimuli. Generally, the more intense a stimulus, the more likely we are to select it for further processing. Simply put, a shout is more compelling than a whisper; a bright light is more attention-grabbing than a dim one; an extreme temperature is more likely to be noticed than a moderate one.

Notice that this isn't always the case, however. The context in which a particular stimulus occurs can make a difference. A shout may be more compelling than a whisper, unless everyone is shouting; then it may very well be the soft, quiet, reasoned tone that gets our attention. If we are faced with a barrage of bright lights, a dim one may, by contrast, be the one we process more fully.

The same argument holds for the stimulus characteristic of physical *size.* By and large, the bigger the stimulus, the more likely we are to attend to it. There is little point in building a small billboard to advertise your motel or restaurant. You'll want to construct the biggest billboard you can afford in hopes of attracting attention. Although it may not hold true for billboards, contrast effects are such that when we are faced with many large stimuli, one that is smaller may be the one to which we attend. It seems to me that the easiest player to spot on a football field is usually the place-kicker, who tends to be much smaller than the other players and tends not to wear as much protective padding.

A third physical dimension that may determine perceptual selectivity, and for which contrast is relevant, is *motion*. Motion is a powerful factor in determining visual attention. A bird in flight is much easier to see than a bird sitting in a bush. In the fall, walking through the woods, you may come close to stepping on a chipmunk before you notice it, so long as it stays still—an adaptive response of camouflage that chipmunks do well. But if that chipmunk makes a dash to escape, it is easily noticed scurrying across the leaves. Once again, the *contrast* created by movement is important. As you enter a nightclub, your attention is immediately drawn to the dance floor by the bright lights and the moving throng dancing to the loud music. How easy it is to spot the one person, right in the middle of the dance floor, who, for whatever reason, is motionless, frozen against the background of moving bodies, contrasting as an easily noticed stimulus.

We often attend to stimuli that are different, or that contrast with other nearby stimuli.

Although intensity, size, and motion are three physical characteristics of stimuli that readily come to mind, there are many others. Indeed, any way in which two stimuli may be different (contrast) may provide a dimension that determines which stimulus we attend to. (Even a very small grease spot can easily grab one's attention if it's strategically located in the middle of a solid yellow tie.) This is precisely why we have printed important terms in **boldface type** throughout this book—so that you will notice them, attend to them, and then recognize them as important stimuli.

Here's yet another dimension that sometimes influences the stimuli we attend to: novelty-familiarity. The basic issue is still contrast. When we are in an old, familiar setting or environment, what is likely to catch our attention? Something new, different, and unusual. On the other hand, when we are in a new and different environment—out of town, perhaps—we are likely to notice something familiar. We may, for example, hardly notice our neighbors around the neighborhood. But if we're off on vacation, surrounded by hundreds or thousands of strange, unfamiliar people at an amusement park, we'll notice those neighbors almost immediately as familiar stimuli in a novel situation. (Notice that which stimuli are novel and which are familiar depends, to some extent, on the experience of the individual. Thus, we could refer to this as a "personal factor" in perceptual selectivity. However, because the main issue here is contrast, we'll list novelty-familiarity as a stimulus factor in attention.)

There *is* another stimulus characteristic that can determine attention, but for which contrast is really not relevant, and that is *repetition*. Simply put, the more often a stimulus is presented, the more likely it is that it will be attended to—everything else being equal, of course. Note that we have to say "everything else being equal" or we start to develop contradictions. We just agreed that novel stimuli attract attention. But if stimuli are repeated over and over, then they're no longer going to be very novel. True; but there's nothing in this list of variables that suggests that each is independent from the others. Novelty may determine attention. In another situation, one's attention may be determined by repetition.

Instructors who want to get across an important point will seldom mention it just once, but rather will repeat it, perhaps more than once. (Most students recognize that generally there is a high correlation between the importance of a piece of information and how often it is mentioned in class.) This is why we have repeated the definitions of important terms in the text, in the margin, *and again* in the glossary at the end of the book. If the leaky faucet only dripped once or twice in the night, you might not notice it. What gets your attention is that it drips and drips and drips.

Think again of the billboard you're going to erect to advertise your motel or restaurant. No matter how large or bright it is, and even if you have managed to build motion into it, you will be well advised to construct as many billboards as your budget will allow if you want to get the attention of as many people as possible. The people who write and schedule television commercials want you to attend to their messages, and repetition is obviously one of their main techniques.

To summarize, there are many ways in which stimuli may differ— brightness, size, motion, color, pitch, and loudness, for example. The greater the contrast between any one stimulus and the others around it, the greater the likelihood that that stimulus will capture or draw our attention. And, everything else being equal, the more often a stimulus is presented (at least up to a point), the greater the likelihood that it will be perceived and selected for further consideration and processing.

BEFORE YOU GO ON

What stimulus factors determine the selection of perceptions?

Personal Factors in Selectivity

Sometimes, what we attend to is determined not so much by the physical characteristics of the stimuli present, but by personal characteristics of the perceiver. For example, imagine that two students are watching a football game on television. Both are being presented with identical stimulation from the same TV screen. One says, "Wow, did you see that tackle?" The other viewer responds, "No, I was watching the cheerleaders." The difference in perception here is hardly attributable to the nature of the stimuli since both students received the same sensory information from the same TV. The difference is due to characteristics of the perceivers, which we are calling *personal factors*. Although there are many personal factors that ultimately determine the selection of our perceptions, we can categorize them as being a function of motivation, expectation, and/or past experience.

Imagine that the two students watching the football game on TV are avid supporters of the two teams involved. One is a fan of the Chicago Bears; the other is a staunch backer of the Green Bay Packers. Our TV viewers may have a small wager on the outcome of this important game. Suppose that the Bears win the hard-fought contest with a last-second field goal. Now, both students have watched exactly the same game on the same TV, but which of the two is more likely to have perceived the officiating of the game as fair, honest, and above reproach? Which student is more likely to have seen the game as "one of the poorest refereed games ever"? The perception of the officiating may depend on who won, who lost, and the motivation of the perceiver. In large measure, the viewers, like all spectators, tended to see what they *wanted* to see. You might not be surprised to learn that research confirms this very scenario (Hastorf & Cantril, 1954).

One thing that most people are interested in is themselves, whether they like to admit it or not. Hence, when we are at a party, we are drawn to a nearby discussion when we hear our own name. Similarly, many instructors have learned the old lesson that to capture the drifting attention of a class, they need only say, "Now about your next exam . . . ," or "With regard to sex. . . ." It's rather impressive to see so many heads turn at the slightest mention of these key motivating terms.

It is true that we often perceive what we want to perceive, and it is equally true that we often perceive what we *expect* to perceive, whether it's really there or not. Similarly, we often do not notice stimuli when they *are* present simply because we did not "know" they were coming—we didn't expect them. When we are psychologically prepared to perceive something, we say that we have formed a **mental set**. Notice that we can also develop a mental set, or expectation, *not* to perceive something. Sometimes we fail to notice things simply because we did not expect them to be there.

Take just a second and quickly glance at the message in Figure 4.1. What did the message say? (If you've seen this demonstration before, you'll have to try it with someone who hasn't.) Many people claim that the message was *PARIS IN THE SPRING.* In fact, there are two *THE*s in the triangle—*PARIS IN THE THE SPRING.* Most people familiar with the English language and with this particular phrase do not expect there to be two *thes* right next to each other. Following their mental set, they report seeing only one. Other people may develop a different mental set or expectation. Their line of reasoning may go something like this: "This is a psychology text, so there's probably a trick here someplace, and I'm going to find it." In this particular instance, such skeptics get rewarded. There *is* a trick, and if their mental set was to find one, they did so. This example makes the point that sometimes our own expectations not only affect what we perceive, but also affect what we don't perceive. In other words, if you don't expect something to happen, if you're not "looking for it," you may miss it.

We will see later (Chapter 7) that our inability to change a mentally set way of perceiving a problem may interfere with our finding a solution to that problem. What we call "creative" problem solving often is a matter of perceiving aspects of a problem in new, unique, or unexpected ways. Thus, even as complex a cognitive process as problem solving often hinges on basic perceptual processes.

Have you noticed that when we say that paying attention is due to motivation and expectation, we are claiming that what we perceive is often influenced by our *past experiences*? Much of our motivation comes from our past experiences. For example, the two television viewers of the football game between Chicago and Green Bay were not born fans of those two teams. Their allegiances reflect their past experiences. Similarly, expectations develop from past experiences. We are likely to expect to perceive, or be set to perceive, what we have perceived in the past in similar circumstances. Perhaps two personal examples will make clear what I mean here.

I once took a course in comparative psychology that examined the behaviors of nonhuman organisms. One of the co-teachers of the course was an ornithologist (a scientist who studies birds). One of the requirements of the course was to participate in an early morning outing to go bird-watching. The memory is very vivid to this day: Cold, tired, clutching my

mental set *a predisposed (set) way to perceive something; an expectation*

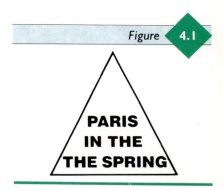

Figure 4.1

Our mental set affects our perception. How many "the"s did you see when you first glanced at this simple figure? Why?

thermos of warm coffee, I slopped through the marshland looking for birds, as the sun was just rising. After 20 minutes of this unpleasantness, our instructor had identified 10 or 11 different birds. I wasn't quite certain, but I thought I had spied a duck. I didn't know just what sort of duck it was, but I did think that I had seen a duck. Now the differences in perception between my instructor and me that cold, wet morning could be explained in terms of motivation (he *did* care much more than I); but mostly, I suspect, his ability to spot birds so quickly and surely reflected his experience. He knew where to look and what to look for.

One other experience having to do with the selection of perceptions is relevant here. Some years ago I accepted an invitation to ride along with a city police officer during a normal working day. Many things impressed me that day, not the least of which was the extent to which that police officer was seeing a totally different city from the one I was seeing. Because of his experience, motivation, and mental set, he was able to select and ultimately respond to stimulus cues that I didn't even notice. For example, he spotted a car that was parked in an alley. I didn't even notice a car there, but he saw it immediately and recognized it as one that had been reported as stolen.

Our selection of stimuli from our environment is usually automatic and accomplished without conscious effort. The process is influenced by a number of factors. Some of those influences depend on the nature of the stimuli themselves; we've called these "stimulus factors." The implication is that what we perceive is determined to some extent by the bits and pieces of information we receive from our senses. This sort of processing is called *bottom-up processing*. For example, we may attend to a particular stimulus because it is significantly larger, smaller, more colorful, louder, or slower than the other stimuli around it. Sometimes we attend to a stimulus simply because it is presented to us over and over again.

But as we have seen, whether stimuli are attended to, or perceived, can be influenced by the nature of the person. In this case, selection is a matter of applying concepts and information already processed. Selection depends on what the perceiver already knows. This selection is referred to as *top-down processing*. Examples include the use of motivation, mental set, and past experience to influence perceptual selectivity, whether it's a matter of looking for birds on a cold morning, spotting stolen cars, or solving problems.

BEFORE YOU GO ON

What personal factors are involved in perceptual selectivity?

PERCEPTUAL ORGANIZATION

As we have seen, one of our basic perceptual reactions to the environment is to select certain stimuli from among all those that strike our receptors so that they may be processed further. A related perceptual process involves organizing the bits and pieces of experience that are presented to

Figure   **4.2**

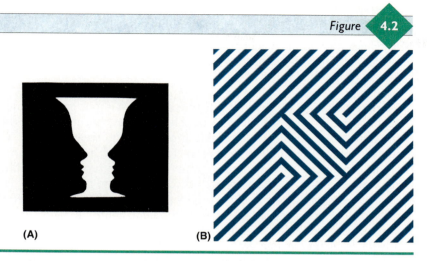

(A)   (B)

(A) A classic reversible figure-ground pattern. What do you see here? A white vase or a birdbath? Or do you see two black profiles facing each other? Can you clearly see both figures at the same time? (B) After a few moments' inspection, a small square should emerge as a figure against the ground of diagonal parallel lines.

our senses into meaningful, organized wholes. We do not really hear the individual sounds of speech; we organize them and perceive them as words, phrases, and sentences. Our visual experience is not one of tiny bits of color and light and dark, as recorded at the retina, but of identifiable objects and events. We don't perceive a warm pat on the back as responses from hundreds of individual receptors in our skin.

Perceptual organization or grouping was a perceptual process of considerable interest to the Gestalt psychologists. As you recall from Topic 1A, **gestalt** is a German word that, roughly translated, means something like "configuration" or "whole" or "totality." One forms a gestalt when one sees the overall scheme of things. If you have a general idea of how something works, or can appreciate the general nature of something without overly attending to details, you have formed a gestalt.

One of the most basic principles of Gestalt psychology is that of the **figure-ground relationship**. Of all the stimuli in your environment at any one time, those that you attend to and group together are said to be *figures*, while all the rest become the *ground*. As you focus your attention on the words on this page, they form figures against the ground (or background, if you prefer) formed by the rest of the page. When you hear your instructor's voice during a lecture, that voice is the figure against the ground of all the other sounds in the room. Figure 4.2 provides a couple of examples of the figure-ground relationship.

The Gestalt psychologists were interested in factors that influenced our attention to stimuli in the environment. They wrote about many of the issues we discussed in our last section. They were also intrigued by how the process of perception enabled us to group and organize stimuli together to form meaningful gestalts. As was the case for perceptual selection, several factors influence how we organize our perceptual worlds. Again it will be useful to consider stimulus factors (bottom-up processing) and personal factors (top-down processing) separately.

gestalt *whole, totality, configuration, or pattern; the whole (gestalt) being perceived as more than the sum of its parts*

figure-ground relationship *the Gestalt psychology principle that stimuli are selected and perceived as figures against a ground or background*

Stimulus Factors

By stimulus factors, we are referring to characteristics of stimuli that help us perceive them as being organized together in one figure or gestalt. We'll consider five of the most influential: proximity, similarity, continuity, common fate, and closure.

proximity *the Gestalt principle of organization claiming that stimuli will be perceived as belonging together if they occur together in space or time*

Proximity. Glance quickly at Figure 4.3(A). Without giving it much thought, what did you see there? A bunch of X's yes, but more than that, there were two separately identifiable groups of X's, weren't there? The group of eight X's on the left seems somehow separate from the group on the right, while the X's within each group seem to go together. This illustrates what the Gestalt psychologists called **proximity**, or *contiguity*. This means that events occurring close together in space or time are generally perceived as belonging together as part of the same figure. In Figure 4.3(A), it's difficult to see the X's as falling into four rows or four columns. They just belong together as two groups of eight X's each.

Proximity operates on more than just visual stimuli. For example, sounds that occur together (are contiguous) in speech are perceived as going together to form words or phrases. In written language there are physical spaces between words on the printed page; with spoken language there are (usually) very brief pauses between words. Thunder and lightning usually occur together, the sound of thunder following shortly after our experience of the lightning. And as a result of our experience of thunderstorms, it's rather difficult to even think about lightning without also thinking about thunder.

similarity *the Gestalt principle of organization claiming that stimuli will be perceived together if they share some common characteristic(s)*

Similarity. Now glance at Figure 4.3(B) and describe what you see there. We have a collection of X's and 0's that clearly are organized into a simple pattern. The usual way to organize these stimuli is to see them as two separate columns of X's and two of 0's. Perceiving rows of alternating X's and 0's is very difficult. This drawing demonstrates the Gestalt principle of **similarity**. Stimulus events that are in some way alike, or have properties

Figure 4.3

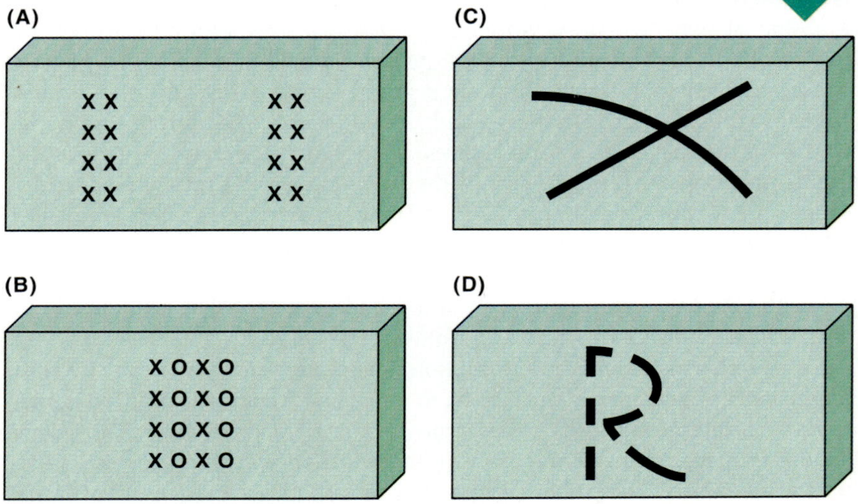

(A)

```
X X        X X
X X        X X
X X        X X
X X        X X
```

(C)

(B)

```
X O X O
X O X O
X O X O
X O X O
```

(D)

(A) These Xs are organized as two groups, not four rows or columns, because of proximity.
(B) Here we see two columns of Os and two of Xs because of similarity.
(C) We tend to see this figure as two intersecting lines, one straight and one curved, because of continuity.
(D) This figure is perceived as an R—which it is not—because of closure.

in common, tend to be grouped together in our perception—a "birds of a feather are perceived together" sort of thing. Australian koalas are perceived (and thought of) by most of us as bears, because to us, they look more like bears than anything else. As it happens, they're not. They are related more to kangaroos and wallabies than to bears.

Continuity. The Gestalt principle of **continuity** (or good continuation) suggests that we tend to see things as ending up consistent with the way they started off. Figure 4.3(C) illustrates this point with a simple line drawing. The clearest, easiest way to organize this drawing is as two separate but intersecting lines—one straight, the other curved. It's difficult to imagine seeing this figure any other way.

Very often our perceptions are guided by a logic that says, for example, "Lines that start out straight should continue as straight." The Gestalt principle of continuity also may account for some of the ways in which we organize our perceptions of people. Aren't we particularly surprised when a young man who was an award-winning honor student throughout high school suddenly does poorly at college and flunks out? That's not the way we like to view the world working. We wouldn't be nearly as surprised to find that another student, who barely made it through grade school and high school, failed to pass at college. This is a lot like continuity or good continuation: We want to see things continue as they started off—largely a matter of "as the twig is bent, so grows the tree."

Common Fate. Common fate describes our tendency to group together in the same figure those elements of a scene that appear to move together in the same direction and at the same speed. The truth is, common fate is not unlike continuity, but it applies to moving stimuli. The next time you get to look down on traffic from a tall building, notice how clear it is to see the lines of traffic moving—as if together—in opposite directions, up and down the street. Remember that chipmunk sitting motionless on the leaves in the woods? So long as both the chipmunk and the leaves stay still, the chipmunk won't be noticed. But when it moves, the moving parts of the chipmunk all move together—sharing a common fate—are organized together, and we see it clearly scurrying away.

Closure. Perhaps the most commonly encountered Gestalt principle of organization is called **closure**. This is our tendency to fill in gaps in our perceptual world. Closure provides an excellent example of what I mean when I say that perception is an *active* process. It underscores the notion that we constantly are seeking to make sense out of our environment, whether that environment presents us with sensible stimuli or not. This concept is illustrated by Figure 4.3(D). At a glance, anyone would tell you that this figure is the letter *R*, but of course it is not. That's not the way you make an *R*. However, it may be the way we *perceive* an *R* due to closure.

Closure occurs commonly during our everyday conversations. Just for fun some day, tape-record a casual conversation with a friend. Then try to write down exactly what was said during the conversation. A truly faithful transcription will reveal that many words and sounds were left out. Even though they were not actually there as stimuli, they were not missed by the listener because he or she filled in the gaps (closure) and understood what was being said.

continuity *the Gestalt principle of organization claiming that a stimulus or a movement will be perceived as continuing in the same smooth direction as first established*

common fate *the Gestalt principle of organization claiming that we group together into the same figure elements of a scene that move together in the same direction at the same speed*

closure *the Gestalt principle of organization claiming that we tend to perceive incomplete figures as whole and complete*

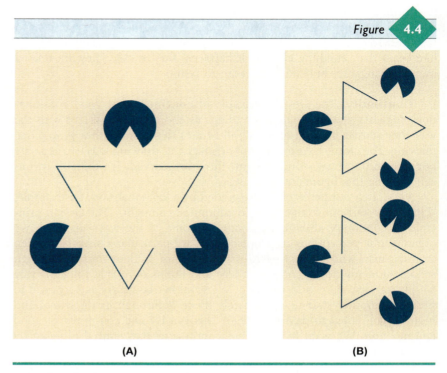

Figure   4.4

(A)   (B)

Examples of subjective contours.

subjective contours *the perception of a contour (a line or plane) that is not there, but is suggested by other aspects of a scene*

A phenomenon that many psychologists believe is a special case of closure is our perception of **subjective contours**, in which arrangements of lines and patterns enable us to see figures that are not actually there. Now if that sounds just a bit spooky, look at Figure 4.4, where we have two examples of subjective contour. In Figure 4.4(A) you can "see" a white triangle that is so clearly there it nearly jumps off the page. The triangle is in front of the other patterns on the page and seems even whiter than the page itself. There is no one accepted explanation for subjective contours (Bradley & Dumais, 1975; Coren, 1972; Kanizsa, 1976; Rock, 1986), but it does seem that the phenomenon is a good example of our perceptual processes filling in gaps in our perceptual world in order to provide us with sensible information.

Personal Factors

We can cover the personal factors that influence perceptual organization rather quickly because they are the same as those that influence selection: motivation, expectation, and past experience. We perceive stimuli as going together, as part of the same gestalt or figure, because we want to, because we expect to, and/or because we have perceived them together in the past.

When I was a graduate student, I had the opportunity to observe a now-classic demonstration that I've never had the nerve to try on my own. It was early in the term, so I easily could sit unnoticed in the large lecture hall. A few minutes after the lecture began, students quietly settled down, listening attentively, jotting down notes. Suddenly, a screaming student burst through the large doors at the rear of the lecture hall. I recognized this student as the professor's graduate assistant, but no one else in the class knew who he was or what he was doing. I felt that he overacted a bit as he stomped down the center aisle, yelling the foulest of obscenities at the professor, "Dr. XXXX, you failed me for the last time you #&*&@% so-and-so! You're going to pay for this you *%$*@%#!" Everyone gasped as the crazed student raced down the aisle, leaped over the lectern, and grabbed for the professor.

The professor and the student struggled briefly, and suddenly—in clear view of everyone—there was a bright, chrome-plated revolver! Down behind the lectern they fell. *Bang!* The sound of the loud, sharp gunshot filled the room. No one moved; the students seemed frozen to their seats. The graduate student raced out through the same side door that the professor had entered just minutes before. The professor lay sprawled on the floor, moaning loudly. Still, no one moved. At just the right dramatic moment, the professor drew himself up to the lectern and said, "Now I want everyone to take out a pencil or pen and write down exactly what you saw."

I'm sure that I need not describe the results of this demonstration for you; you can guess what happened. I never did read all of the nearly 600 descriptions that the students wrote, but I did help summarize many of the results. Of all the misperceptions that took place that day, perhaps the most striking had to do with how the students organized their perception of the gun. In fact, the professor brought the pistol to class and placed it on top of his notes before he began his lecture. When the "crazed student" crashed into the classroom, the professor reached down, grabbed the gun, and pointed it at the student as he came charging down the center aisle. The student *never* had the gun in his hand! The professor had it all along, and it was the professor who pulled the trigger, firing the shot that startled us all. Fewer than 20 students of all those in the room reported seeing this as it actually occurred. Virtually everyone "organized" that gun into the hands of the raging student. No one was *mentally set* for or expected the professor to have a gun in class. Certainly no one *wanted* to see their professor with a gun. And, hopefully, no one had ever *experienced* a professor bringing a gun to class. (Seeing crazed students with guns is not a common experience either, but with television and movies, it's certainly a more probable one.) Notice that paying attention, or stimulus *selection*, was not at issue here. Everyone saw the gun. The students' reports of their perceptions differed from reality in terms of how they *organized* the gun in the classroom scene. This demonstration will become relevant again when we discuss ways in which our memories may be distorted, reinforcing our earlier point that perception and memory are very much related.

How we perceive—judge, interpret, organize—a stimulus is often flavored by how we perceive other stimuli presented at about the same time. In other words, a very important factor in how we organize our perceptions is the *context* in which they are perceived. We are seldom asked to make perceptual judgments in a vacuum. Figures are usually presented in a given ground, or context. Context often affects what we expect to perceive or think we have perceived. We might be startled when we turn on our car radio and hear what sounds like a loud, piercing scream. In a moment, given a context, we realize that we have just tuned in to a fine arts station and have heard two notes from a soprano's rendition of an operatic aria, not a scream after all.

Figure 4.5 provides two examples of the effect of context on visual perception. In Figure 4.5(A), is the highlighted stimulus the letter *H* or the

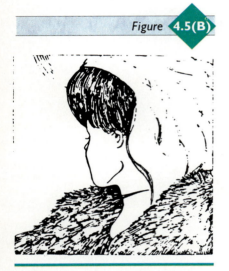

THE CAT SAT BY THE DOOR.

Is the highlighted letter an A or an H? In fact, it is neither and can be interpreted as one or the other only on the basis of context and our past experience with the English language.

Figure ◆ 4.5(B)

This perceptually ambiguous drawing can be interpreted in different ways depending on the context in which it is viewed. Do you see a young woman or an old woman? (After Boring, 1930).

letter *A*? In fact, by itself, it doesn't seem to be a very good example of either. But in the proper context—and given our past experience with the English language, and given the process called closure—that same stimulus may appear to be an *A* or an *H*.

Figure 4.5(B) presents Edwin Boring's (1930) classic *ambiguous figure*. Looked at one way, the drawing depicts a demure young lady, dressed in Victorian-style clothing, a large feather in her hat, looking away from the viewer. Looked at another way, the same picture shows an old woman, chin tucked down into her collar, hair down to her eyes, with a rather large wart on her nose. Now, if I had shown you a series of pictures of young men and women dressed in Victorian costume, as if they were at a grand ball, and *then* presented Figure 4.5(B), you almost certainly would have seen the young lady. In the context of a series of pictures of old, poorly dressed men and women, you probably would have organized the very same line drawing to depict the old woman. "Things are not always as they seem."

How we organize our experience of the world depends on a number of factors. Our perception that some stimuli in our environments "go together" with other stimuli to form coherent figures is a process influenced by the proximity or similarity of the events themselves, by our interpretations of closure and continuity, by the context in which those stimuli appear, and by our own personal motives, expectations, and past experiences.

BEFORE YOU GO ON

List stimulus and personal factors that determine how we organize stimuli in perception.

THE PERCEPTION OF DEPTH AND DISTANCE

We have noted that perception is a more complex cognitive process than the simple reception of information that we call sensation. Perception requires that we select and organize stimulus information. Perception also involves actively recognizing, identifying, and assigning meaning to stimulus events. For the remainder of this topic, we'll examine three perceptual processes that we often take for granted: the perception of depth and distance, the perception of motion (both real and apparent), and perceptual constancies.

One of the ways in which we interpret a visual stimulus is to note not only *what* it is that we are seeing, but *where* it happens to be. We perceive the world in which we live for what it is—three-dimensional. So long as we are paying attention (surely a required perceptual process), we don't run into buildings or fall off cliffs. We know with considerable accuracy just how far we are from objects in our environment. What is remarkable and strange about this ability is that the light reflected from objects and events in our environment falls on *two*-dimensional retinas. The depth and distance in our world is not something we directly *sense*; it is something we *perceive*.

The ability to judge depth and distance accurately is an adaptive skill that plays an important role in determining many of our actions. Our ability to make such judgments so well reflects the fact that we are simultaneously responding to a large number of clues or cues to depth and distance. Some of these cues are built into the way our visual systems work and are referred to as *ocular cues*, while others, called *physical cues*, have more to do with our appreciation of the physical environment itself.

Ocular Cues

Some of the cues we get about distance and depth reflect the way our eyes work. Cues that involve both eyes are called binocular cues (*bi* means "two"); those cues that only require one eye are called monocular cues (*mono* means "one").

Binocular cues for depth result from the fact that our eyes are separated. For example, when we look at a nearby three-dimensional object, each eye gets a somewhat different view of it. Hold a pen with a clip on it a few feet in front of your eyes. Rotate the pen until the clip can be viewed by the right eye, but not the left. (You check that by closing first one eye then the other as you rotate the pen.) Now each eye (retina) is getting a different (disparate) view of the same object. This phenomenon is called **retinal disparity**. It is a powerful cue that what we are looking at must be solid or three-dimensional. Otherwise, each eye would see the same image, not two disparate ones. See Figure 4.6.

Two applications of this phenomenon with which you may be familiar are in 3-D movies and stereoscopes. Stereoscopes are nineteenth-century devices that allow one to view two (slightly) different images of the same scene or object. When we try to justify the two versions of the same scene, we tend to see it as three-dimensional. Movies in 3-D work on a similar principle. One camera takes a picture of what a left eye would see, while another takes a picture of what a right eye would see. These images are then fused on one film and projected onto a screen (and appear very blurry), to be decoded with the use of a red lens for one eye and a green lens for the other.

Another binocular cue to depth and distance is called **convergence**. Convergence is the name we give to the action of our eyes turning inward, toward each other when we view something up close. Convergence reflects the fact that we "know" how our eyes are aligned in our heads, even if we seldom pay much attention to it. As we gaze off into the distance, our two eyes aim outward in almost parallel fashion. As we focus our view on objects that are close to us, our two eyes come together, or converge, and we simply interpret that convergence as an indication that what we are looking at is close to us. Convergence is also illustrated in Figure 4.6.

The rest of the cues we'll consider are monocular. (Even the physical cues listed below are often referred to as monocular cues because they can be appreciated by persons who can see with but one eye.) A unique monocular cue to distance, at least for relatively short distances, is **accommodation**. This process, you'll remember, is the changing of the shape of the lens, by the ciliary muscles, to focus images on the retina. When we focus on distant objects, accommodation flattens our lens, and when we focus on nearby objects, our lens gets rounder or fatter, thanks to the action of the ciliary muscles. Although the process is reflexive and occurs automat-

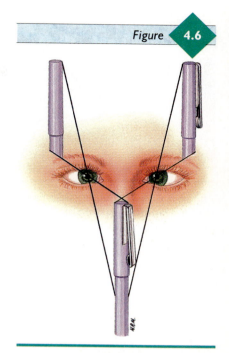

Figure **4.6**

When looking at one object, the right eye sees a different image than the left eye due to retinal disparity. This disparity gives us a cue that the object we are viewing is three-dimensional.

retinal disparity *the phenomenon in which each retina receives a different (disparate) view of the same three-dimensional object*

convergence *the tendency of the eyes to move toward each other as we focus on objects up close*

accommodation *the process in which the shape of the lens is changed by the ciliary muscles to focus an image on the retina*

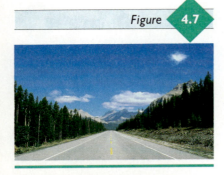

Figure 4.7

Although we know that the sides of the road are parallel, they appear to come together in the distance, an example of linear perspective.

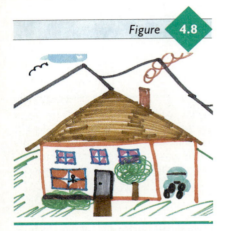

Figure 4.8

A house on a stick: the failure of linear perspective in a child's drawing.

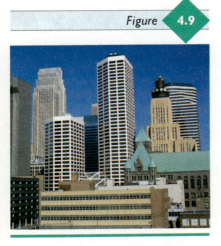

Figure 4.9

Interposition occurs when objects in the foreground partially cover objects that are farther away.

ically, our brain can react to the activity of our ciliary muscles in terms of the distance of an object from our eyes. That is, our brain "knows" what our ciliary muscles are doing to focus an image and interprets these actions in terms of distance. Accommodation does not function as an effective cue for distances beyond arm's length because the changes in the activity of the ciliary muscles in such cases are too slight to be noticed. But it is within arm's length that accurate decisions about distance are most critical.

Physical Cues

The physical cues to distance and depth are those we get from the structure of our environment. These cues are sometimes called *pictorial cues* because they are used by artists to create the impression of three-dimensionality on a two-dimensional canvas or paper. There are many pictorial cues. Here are some of the most important.

1. *Linear perspective* (see Figure 4.7): As you stand in the middle of a road, looking off into the distance, the sides of the road—which you know to be parallel—seem to come together in the distance. Using this pictorial cue in drawing obviously takes some time and experience to develop. Have you ever seen a child's drawing of a house that looked something like Figure 4.8? There are the roof, the chimney (with smoke, of course), the windows, the door, and the front sidewalk. Because the child *knows* that the sidewalk is as wide at the street as it is by the door, it is drawn as two parallel lines. The result looks like a house on a stick. Only later will the child come to appreciate the usefulness of linear perspective and will make the sidewalk appear wider in the foreground at the street.

2. *Interposition* (see Figure 4.9): This cue to distance reflects our appreciation that objects in the foreground tend to cover, or partially hide from view, objects in the background, and not vice versa. It seems like a silly thing to contemplate, but one of the reasons I know that people sitting in the back of a classroom are farther away from me than people sitting in the front row is the information that I get from interposition. People (and other objects) in the front partially block my view of the people sitting behind them.

3. *Relative size* (see Figure 4.10): This is a commonly used clue to our judgment of distance. As it happens, very few stimuli in this world change their size, but lots of things get nearer to or farther away from us. So, everything else being equal, we tend to judge the object that produces the larger retinal image as being closer to us. This may sound like a silly thing to do, but have a friend hold an object up very close to your closed eye. We'll imagine your friend is holding an apple. When you open your eye, all you see is "red." At first, you may not even experience the object in front of your eye as an apple. Now have your friend slowly move the apple away from you. As the apple is moved away, the image of that apple on your retina gets smaller and smaller. If your friend moves far enough, you eventually may lose sight of the apple altogether. Now you know that apples do not shrink, and you interpret the reduction in retinal size as a cue to distance—as retinal size gets smaller, the object is moving away.

4. *Texture gradient* (see Figure 4.11): Standing on a gravel road, looking down at your feet, you clearly can make out the details of the texture of the roadway. You can see individual pieces of gravel. But as you look on down

the road, the texture gradually changes, details giving way to a smooth blending of a textureless surface. We interpret this gradual change (which is what *gradient* means) in texture as indicating a gradual change in distance.

5. *Patterns of shading* (see Figure 4.12): Drawings that do not use shading look flat and two-dimensional. Children eventually learn that if they want their pictures to look lifelike, they should shade in tree trunks and apples and show them as casting shadows. Two-dimensional objects do not cast shadows, and how objects create patterns of light and shade can tell us a great deal about their shape and solidity.

6. *Motion parallax* (see Figure 4.13, p. 156): This rather technical-sounding label names something with which we are all familiar. The clearest example may occur when we are in a car, looking out a side window. Even if the car is going at a modest speed, the nearby utility poles and fence posts seem to race by. Objects farther away from the car seem to be moving more slowly, and mountains or trees way off in the distance seem not to be moving at all. This difference in apparent motion is known as motion parallax. The observation of this phenomenon during a train ride in 1910, by the way, was what first got Max Wertheimer interested in what evolved into Gestalt psychology.

There are many cues that let us know how near or far we are from objects in our environment and that many of those objects are solid and three-dimensional. Some of these cues depend on the workings of our visual system, while others depend on our appreciation of cues from the physical layout of objects in the world around us. Because we constantly get input from all of these factors at the same time, our judgments of distance and depth tend to be very accurate.

BEFORE YOU GO ON

Name and describe some of the cues that give us information about depth and/or distance.

THE PERCEPTION OF MOTION

As an object moves across our field of view, say from right to left, how do we *know* that the object is moving? At first you may feel like ignoring what appears to be such a simple question. If you think about it for a while, you'll come to realize that our perception of motion is a complex process.

Perceiving Real Motion

So long as our heads, bodies, and eyes are still, the answer to our question of how we know a stimulus is moving *is* fairly simple. Light reflected from the moving object produces an image on the retina that

Figure 4.10

Although all these hot air balloons are about the same size, those in the distance appear much smaller because the image that they cast on our retinas is smaller.

Figure 4.11

Gradients of texture provide cues to distance so we can see more details of objects that are closer to us.

Figure 4.12

Patterns of light and shadow provide us with information about the three-dimensionality of objects in our environment.

Figure   **4.13**

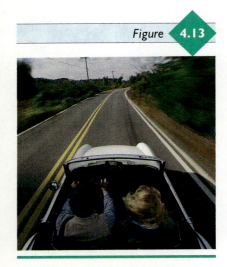

As we move through the environment, stationary objects near us seem to whiz by very quickly, while objects that are farther away seem to move by us more slowly. This cue to distance is called motion parallax.

illusion *a perception that is at odds with (different from) what we know as physical reality*

phi phenomenon *the visual illusion of the apparent motion of stationary lights flashing on and off in sequence*

autokinetic effect *the visual illusion of apparent motion in which a stationary pinpoint of light in an otherwise dark environment appears to move*

successively stimulates adjoining rods and cones, stimulation that we interpret (perceive) as motion.

The problem is, our eyes, heads, and bodies are seldom perfectly still. As we scan a room, for example, images of the objects in the room stimulate successive rods and cones on the retina. But we don't see everything in the room as moving. Our brain is able to compensate for the movements of our eyes, head, and body (Wallach, 1987). In fact, if we focus our attention on a flying moth, as an example, keeping its image at about the same place on our retina as it darts and dashes about the room, everything else in the room stimulates a series of different retinal areas. But because we *know* that we are moving our head and our eyes to focus on the moth, we perceive the moth as moving and the room as stationary. Of course, it is also true that if we keep our head relatively still and move our eyes to focus on that moth, we know that our eyes are moving to do so.

Our judgments of motion are influenced by details we seldom think about. Everything else being equal, we will tend to see small objects as moving faster than larger ones even if their actual speeds are the same. Objects that are seen moving against a plain, empty background are seen as moving more slowly than when they move against a patterned background (Gregory, 1977).

We already have discussed how factors such as personal motivation and expectations affect the organization of our perceptions. They may also affect our perception of motion. First we see a sleek, bright red sports car, driven by a teenager, traveling down the street. It is followed soon after by an old clunker, driven by a "little old lady." If both cars were, in fact, traveling at the same rate of speed, we'd be more likely to perceive the first car as going faster. Notice how these judgments are yet another example of top-down processing. That is, our judgment is not based solely on the information provided us by our senses. Our perception of speed is also influenced by our experiences with teenagers, little old ladies, sports cars, and clunkers.

The Perception of Apparent Motion

As interesting as our perception of real motion is, even more intriguing is our perception of motion when in fact there isn't any. When our perceptions (our psychological experiences) seem to be at odds with what we know as (physical) reality, we are experiencing an **illusion**. There are two classic illusions of motion: the phi phenomenon and the autokinetic effect.

The **phi phenomenon** can be illustrated with just two lights. If two equally bright lights of the same color flash on and off alternately, it is very easy to see them as one light moving back and forth. Look at Figure 4.14(A). Imagine that each small circle represents a stationary light bulb. One at a time, each light flashes on for a fraction of a second. The lights come on in order—light 1, then 2, then 3, and so on. If the lights flash on and off fast enough, an observer will perceive a single light traveling in a circular path. The phi phenomenon also accounts for our perception of the movement of lights in theater marquees or in large signs (see Figure 4.14(B)). The arrow may look like it is moving through space, even though we know that it is securely fastened to the wall. Perhaps you recognize this as a subset of the Gestalt principle of closure: We fill in the gaps between the flashing stimuli and see them as moving.

Our second illusion of motion is a powerful one. The **autokinetic effect** is the apparent movement of a pinpoint source of light in an otherwise darkened environment. You might want to construct the apparatus for demonstrating this illusion yourself. To do so, you'll first need to locate a rather large room that you can completely darken. Get a good flashlight and cover the lens with black paper or tape so that no light escapes. Poke a very small hole in the paper or tape covering so that only a small pinpoint of light can be seen. Secure the light at one end of the room, with the hole pointed out toward the center of the room. Turn off all the lights except for your flashlight. Within seconds a strange thing happens as you stare at that stationary point of light: It starts to move and float around. Even though you know very well that the light is stationary, it will appear to move.

As it happens, psychologists do not have a complete explanation for this phenomenon. The most commonly accepted view is that the apparent movement is produced by very small head and body movements (e.g., Pola & Martin, 1977; Post & Leibowitz, 1985). As you try to focus on the light, your eyes, head, and even your body move—drifting slowly—which causes the pinpoint of light to cast an image that moves across your retina. Because the image moves across your retina, and you do not feel your body moving, your brain perceives the light as moving.

The autokinetic illusion can be a problem for pilots or ships' captains, who must navigate at night with only a single distant beacon or light source as a guide. With no other frame of reference but that one light source, the light will appear to move, making it difficult to determine exactly where it is. For the same reason, military pilots in World War II had difficulty maintaining flight formations at night when the only way they could tell where they were in the formation was to make judgments based on small lights on the wingtips of adjacent aircraft. The solution to this problem was to replace the constant light with a flashing one. We also may experience the autokinetic effect when we try to stare at a single star or planet in the early evening sky. With no other context to provide a background, we may perceive the stationary star as moving.

BEFORE YOU GO ON

What are two illusions of motion?
How are they produced?

THE CONSTANCY OF PERCEPTIONS

A perceptual process that we usually take for granted is called *constancy*. Perceptual constancies help us organize and interpret the stimulus input

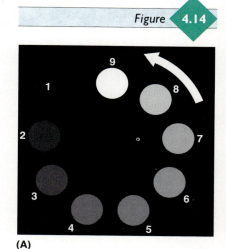

Figure **4.14**

(A)

(B)

(A) The rapid consecutive flashing of these stationary lights will appear to be a single light traveling in a circle due to the phi phenomenon.
(B) Though these lights are stationary, the rapid consecutive lighting of them creates an illusion of motion.

we get from our senses. It is because of the constancy of perception that we can recognize a familiar object as being the same regardless of how far away it is, the angle from which we view it, or the color or intensity of the light reflected from it. You can recognize your textbook whether you view it from a distance or close up, straight on or from an angle, in a dimly or brightly lighted room, or in blue, red, or white light—it will still be your textbook, and you will perceive it as such regardless of how your senses detect it. If it were not for perceptual constancy, every individual sensation might be perceived as a new experience and little would appear familiar to you.

Size Constancy

size constancy *the tendency to see objects as being of constant size regardless of the size of the retinal image*

We have already mentioned the role of **size constancy** in helping us know how far away we are from an object. A friend standing close to us may fill our visual field. At a distance, the image of the same person may take up only a fraction of our visual field. The size of the image on our retina may be significantly different, but we know very well that our friend hasn't shrunk but has simply moved farther away.

Our tendency to view objects as remaining the same size depends on a number of factors, most importantly the quality of the depth perception cues that are available to us and our familiarity with the stimulus object. To demonstrate the importance of depth cues, we can construct an environment in which they are virtually absent. Such an environment is created in a *ganzfeld*. Although there are many versions of ganzfelds, one of the most striking is a large, smooth, hollow sphere that is lighted indirectly. When you look inside the sphere, there are no visual cues to tell you about up and down or front and back (see Figure 4.15). You can approximate the experience of looking into a ganzfeld by cutting a Ping-Pong ball in half and placing one half over each eye. The experience is particularly eerie if you lie on your back and look up toward the sky on a sunny day.

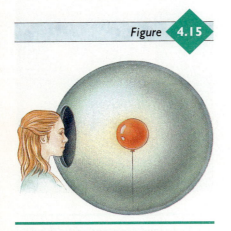

Viewing a partially inflated balloon inside a ganzfeld.

In a ganzfeld, a balloon may be inflated in full view of a subject who will claim, because of size constancy, that she is watching a colored circle or disk move closer and closer. As the air is released from the balloon, the subject reports that the circle is moving farther away. Once the stimulus is recognized as a balloon (a stimulus that *does* change its size), size constancy no longer dominates, and the subject's report of what is happening becomes more accurate. Notice that at first, the subject's perception was based solely on the information available to her senses. Her perception, then, was based on her best interpretation of the information her senses provided. She was constructing an experience using bottom-up processing. But, once she recognized the stimulus object as a balloon, a concept with which she was familiar, her perception of what was happening changed. Then she used her memory and experience with balloons to process the situation from the top down. In a ganzfeld, then, we may be forced to perceive directly what our senses detect, without the added cues from the environment that we usually use to interpret the world around us.

Shape Constancy

shape constancy *the tendency to see objects as being of constant shape regardless of the shape of the retinal image*

Shape constancy refers to our perception of objects as maintaining their shape even though the retinal image they cast may change. Shape

Figure **4.15**

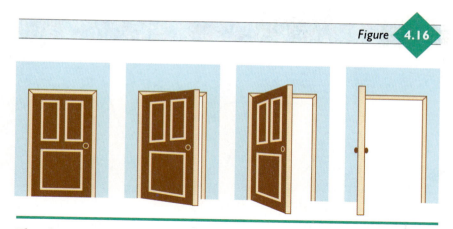

Figure 4.16

Though we see four different images, we know we are looking at a door because of shape constancy.

constancy may be simply demonstrated with any familiar object, say the nearest door in your field of view. As you look at that door from different angles, the shape of the image of the door on your retina changes radically. Straight on it appears to be a rectangle; partially open, the image is that of a trapezoid; from the edge, fully open, the retinal image is of a straight line. Regardless of the retinal image, because of shape constancy, you still see that object as a door. See Figure 4.16.

Lightness and Color Constancy

In discussing constancy, we use the term *lightness* rather than "brightness." This is to remind us of the difference between the intensity of a light source (brightness) and the intensity of light reflected from a surface (lightness). That is, lights may seem to have different brightnesses, but surfaces have different lightnesses. Due to **lightness constancy**, the apparent relative lightness of familiar objects is perceived as being the same regardless of the actual amount or type of light under which it is viewed. The white shirt that you put on this morning may be *sensed* as gray when you pass through a shadow, or as black when night falls, but it is still *perceived* as a white shirt—in no way darker than it was this morning.

The same is true for color perception. If you know that you put on a white shirt this morning, you would still perceive it as white even if I were to illuminate it with a red light. Now most of the light waves reflected by the shirt into your eyes would be associated with the experience of red (about 700 nm), but you will still know the shirt is white. Someone else, who didn't know any better, might perceive the shirt as red, but you'd perceive it as white because of color constancy.

Geometric Illusions and Impossible Figures

By now, you should fully appreciate that the relationship between the "real world" and our perception of that world is tenuous at best. What we come to perceive is often flavored by many factors above and beyond any physical reality that impinges on our sense receptors. We've seen a number

lightness constancy *the tendency to see objects as the same lightness regardless of the intensity of light reflected from them*

Figure 4.17

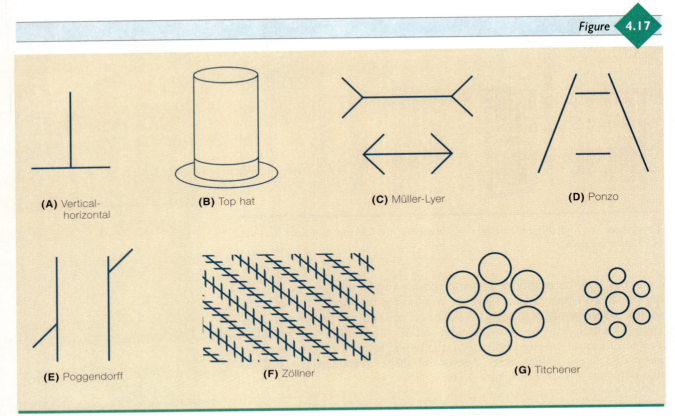

(A) Vertical-
horizontal

(B) Top hat

(C) Müller-Lyer

(D) Ponzo

(E) Poggendorff

(F) Zöllner

(G) Titchener

A few geometrical illusions. In each case you know the answer, but the relevant questions are: (A) Are the vertical and horizontal lines the same length? (B) Is the brim as wide as the hat is tall? (C) Are the two horizontal lines the same length? (D) Are the two horizontal lines the same length? (E) Are the two diagonals part of the same line? (F) Are the diagonal lines parallel? (G) Are the two center circles the same size?

of applications of this theme. The interaction between physical reality and our psychological experience can be appreciated clearly when we consider illusions and impossible figures. We have defined illusions as "experiences in which our perceptions are at odds with what we know as physical reality."

Several very simple and very compelling geometrical illusions are presented in Figure 4.17. Consider Figure 4.17(A). This drawing depicts the *vertical-horizontal illusion.* Figure 4.17(B) is the same illusion, of course, but in slightly more meaningful terms. Are the lines in Fig. 4.17(A) the same length? Yes, you know they are—we're talking about illusions here. But, do they *appear* to be the same length? No, they do not. The vertical line seems significantly longer than the horizontal one. The hat in Figure 4.17(B) seems to be considerably taller than it is wide. The illusion is inescapable.

Notice that the vertical-horizontal illusion works even after you have measured the two lines to confirm that they are the same length. They *still* don't look equal. This is one of three fundamental facts about illusions: They do not depend on our ignorance of the situation.

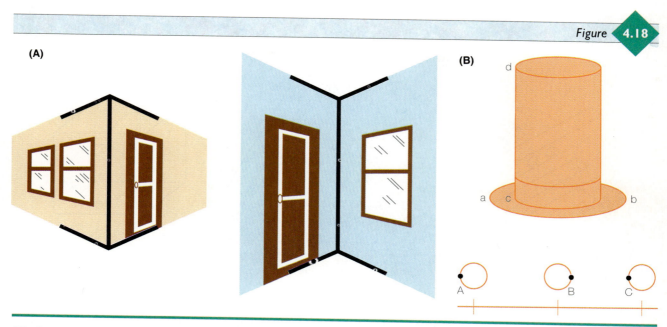

Figure 4.18

(A) One attempt to "explain" the Müller-Lyer illusion as the representation of edges and corners.
(B) A variant of the Müller-Lyer illusion. The distance from A to B is equal to the distance from C to D. The explanation in terms of edges and corners no longer seems reasonable.

A second fact about illusions is that they do not "occur" at the retina. Figure 4.17(C) is the well-known *Müller-Lyer illusion*, named after the man who first drew it. The top line would continue to appear longer than the bottom one even if the two (equal) lines were presented to one eye, and the arrowlike vanes were presented to the other. A third fact about illusions is that their effects do not depend on movements of the eye. Illusions appear vividly even when they are flashed before the eyes so quickly there is no opportunity to scan the presented image (Gillam, 1980).

Illusions of the sort presented in Figure 4.17 are not new. Psychologists have been searching for reasonable explanations for illusions for well over 100 years. How do geometrical illusions give rise to perceptions, to visual experiences that are at odds with the physical reality detected by the eyes? Frankly, we just can't say. A number of factors seem to be working together to create illusions. In general, perhaps the most reasonable observation we can make about illusions is that they provide evidence of our perceptual constancies being overapplied. The effects of illusions depend in large measure on how we perceive and interpret clues to the size of objects in a three-dimensional world and in accord with inferences we make about the world based on our experience with it (Coren & Girgus, 1978; Gillam, 1980; Gregory, 1977; Hoffman, 1983). Here's just one example. A reasonable-sounding explanation of the Müller-Lyer illusion is that the vanes of the arrows are taken to represent corners, as in a room. To see what I mean,

Figure   4.19

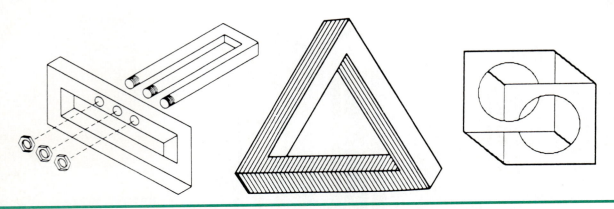

Impossible figures—examples of conflicting visual information.

refer to Figure 4.18(A). When corners are near to us or far away, we are presented with perspective cues to their distance. Hence, we "see" the "arrows" of the illusion as representing corners and edges (Gregory, 1977). Sounds pretty good, doesn't it? Then, why in Figure 4.18(B) do we see the distance between points *A* and *B* as shorter than the distance between points *B* and *C*—when they are, in fact, equal?

The main instructional point about illusions is that they remind us that perception is a higher-level process than simple sensation; that perception involves the organization and interpretation of the information we get from our senses, and that things are not always as they seem. This point is made even more dramatically with what are called impossible figures (see Figure 4.19).

BEFORE
YOU GO
ON

Name and give an example of four types of perceptual constancy.

Perception is a complex cognitive process that involves the selection and organization of the stimulation received by our senses. Many factors help determine which of the stimuli we sense become figures or are attended to for further processing. Some of those factors, such as contrast and repetition, involve characteristics of the stimuli themselves; others, such as expectation and motivation, involve characteristics of the perceiver. The organization of the bits and pieces of sensory experience into meaningful integrated gestalts is also influenced by stimulus and personal factors. The world that we have stored in our memories is the world as our perceptions present it to us. We often may take perception for granted, but without it, there would be no way we could interpret or give meaning to the world around us.

4A

SUMMARY

What stimulus factors determine the selection of perceptions?

Of all of the information that stimulates our receptors, only a small portion is attended to, or selected for further processing. One set of factors that affects which stimuli will be attended to concerns the characteristics of the available stimuli. We are more likely to attend to a stimulus if it *contrasts* with others around it (where contrast may be in terms of intensity, size, motion, or any other physical characteristic). The simple *repetition* of a stimulus also increases the likelihood that it will be attended to. / *page 144*

What personal factors are involved in perceptual selectivity?

The selection of stimuli is partly based on characteristics of the perceiver, such as motivation, expectation (or mental set), and past experience. In this case, we say that information is processed from the top down, rather than from the bottom up. / *page 146*

List stimulus and personal factors that determine how we organize stimuli in perception.

The perceptual organization of stimuli depends in part on the characteristics of the available stimuli, such as proximity, similarity, continuity, common fate, and closure. The personal factors that affect perceptual organization are the same as those that affect selection: motivation, mental set, and past experience. / *page 152*

Name and describe some of the cues that give us information about depth and/or distance.

We are able to perceive three-dimensionality and distance even though we sense the environment with a two-dimensional retina because of the many cues with which we are provided. Some have to do with the visual system itself and are called ocular cues, such as retinal disparity (each eye gets a different view of the same three-dimensional object), convergence (when we look at something up close, our eyes move inward, toward each other), and accommodation (our lenses change shape to focus images as objects move toward or away from us). Other cues come from the environment, including the physical cues of linear perspective (parallel lines seem to come together in the distance), interposition (near objects partially block our view of more distant objects), relative size (everything else being equal, the smaller a stimulus, the farther away we judge it to be), texture gradient (details of texture that we can see clearly up close are difficult to see at a distance), patterns of light and shade, and motion parallax (as we move by stationary objects, those close to us seem to move past us more rapidly than those objects in the distance). / *page 155*

What are two illusions of motion? How are they produced?

The perception of motion when there is none is an example of an illusion. The phi phenomenon is such an illusion and can be demonstrated by flashing lights on and off in sequence, giving the appearance of a light in motion. The autokinetic effect occurs when a stationary point of light is perceived as moving in an otherwise darkened environment. / *page 157*

Name and give an example of four types of perceptual constancy.

Perceptual constancies bring stability to our perceptual world. With size constancy, we perceive objects as remaining the same size even when the size of their retinal images changes. Similarly, shape constancy refers to the stability of our perception of an object's shape regardless of the shape of its retinal image. With lightness and color constancy, we are able to perceive an object's true color or brightness regardless of the intensity or wavelength of light that is actually reflected from it. / *page 162*

Varieties of Consciousness

Why We Care: A Topic Preview

Consciousness is such an integral part of our lives that we might argue that to be alive is to be conscious. You may remember that the earliest psychologists (including Wilhelm Wundt, E. B. Titchener, and William James) actually defined psychology as the science of consciousness or mental activity. But, dealing with consciousness scientifically proved to be a very tricky business. After decades of struggling, psychologists were more than happy to abandon consciousness and turn their attention to observable behavior, as John B. Watson (and behaviorism) suggested they should. But consciousness would not go away, and within the past 20 years, the study of consciousness has reemerged, resuming its place in mainstream psychology.

You may have wondered why I chose to position the discussion of consciousness here, in the same chapter as the discussion of perception. Although I might have placed this topic in a number of different chapters, I think it is sensible to consider the issues related to the psychology of consciousness here, in the context of our study of how we process information we receive from the environment. Consciousness refers to our awareness, our perception, of the environment and of our own mental processes. To be fully conscious is to be awake, aware, alert, and attentive. The extent to which we are conscious or aware of ourselves and our environment will necessarily influence the extent to which we can process information. This is why psychologists care about consciousness, and why it fits here in our discussion.

In this topic, we will find two things helpful. Let us first consider some matters of definition to gain a better appreciation of just what consciousness is. We'll then look at a number of "altered" states of consciousness. Perhaps we can better appreciate "normal" consciousness if we examine those conditions in which our consciousness, or awareness, is altered, changed, or distorted. We'll consider the changes that take place in our consciousness when it is affected by sleep, hypnosis, meditation, and drugs.

THE NATURE OF CONSCIOUSNESS

consciousness *our awareness or perception of the environment and of our own mental processes*

We shall define **consciousness** as the awareness, or perception, of the environment and of one's own mental processes. Consciousness, then, is a state of the mind. It is a state of awareness. Normal, waking, or immediate consciousness is the awareness of those thoughts, ideas, feelings, and perceptions that are active in our minds. With this as a working definition, we might ask how to best characterize the nature of consciousness. What are its aspects or dimensions?

When he addressed a group of psychologists at a national conference, Wilse Webb, a respected researcher in the field of sleep and dreaming, was faced with the task of describing the nature of consciousness. Webb (1981) claimed that we could do no better than to read what William James had to say about consciousness nearly 100 years ago. Indeed, James had a great deal to say about consciousness (1890, 1892, 1904).

For James, there were four basic realities that relate to what we are calling our normal, waking consciousness. We should try to keep these four observations in mind—in our own consciousness—as we read through this topic.

1. Consciousness is always *changing*. Consciousness doesn't hold still. It cannot be held before the mind for study. "No state once gone can recur and be identical with what was before," James wrote (1892, p. 152). He also wrote, "Consciousness, then, does not appear to itself chopped up in bits. Such words as 'chain' or 'train' do not describe it fitly as it presents itself in the first instance. It is nothing jointed; it flows. A 'river' or 'stream' is most naturally described. In talking of it hereafter, let us call it the stream of thought, of consciousness. . ." (James, 1890, p. 243).

2. Consciousness is a *personal* experience. Consciousness does not exist without an individual to have it. My consciousness and yours are separate and different. The consciousness I can experience with certainty is mine. You may try to tell me about yours, but I will never be able to fully appreciate your consciousness.

3. Consciousness is *continuous*. Our awareness of our environment and of ourselves cannot be broken into pieces. There are no gaps in our awareness. We really can't tell where one thought begins and another leaves off. Here again James's metaphor of the mind as a "stream of consciousness," sometimes flowing rapidly as ideas rush through the mind, sometimes moving more slowly as we pause and reflect, is appropriate.

4. Consciousness is *selective*. Awareness is often a matter of making choices, of selectively attending to or focusing on some aspect of experience while ignoring others. "We find it [consciousness] always doing one thing, choosing one out of several of the materials so presented to its notice, emphasizing and accentuating that and suppressing as far as possible all the rest" (James, 1890, p. 139). We had a good bit to say about the factors that influence the selective nature of consciousness in our last topic.

One way in which we may gain a better understanding of normal states of consciousness is to examine consciousness when its nature has been altered. By definition, if we are in an altered state of consciousness, our perception of ourselves and the environment will be in some way altered or changed. The nature of these changes and how they are produced is the focus of the remainder of this topic. We will first discuss a change in the state of our consciousness that is quite normal and common: sleep. (Altered states of consciousness need not be weird or bizarre.) Then we'll examine three means of altering one's consciousness that require some voluntary, deliberate action: hypnosis, meditation, and the use of drugs.

BEFORE YOU GO ON

What is normal, waking consciousness, and what, according to William James, are its four basic characteristics? What is an altered state of consciousness?

SLEEP AND DREAMS

Sleep alters our consciousness by reducing our alertness, awareness, and perception of events occuring around us. Sleep is a very normal process, yet it is one we do not understand well. We are seldom aware or conscious of our own sleeping, even though we may very well spend more than 200,000 hours of our lifetime asleep. Sleep can be considered a temporary loss of consciousness. We can know that we have been asleep. We can be certain that we will sleep again. We can suspect that we are dreaming, but we find it difficult to be sure.

Just as the level or degree of our awareness varies during the day, so does our sleep vary in its level or quality from night to night and throughout the night. The study of sleeping and dreaming, as variants of consciousness, has intrigued psychologists for many years. In this section, we'll examine some of what we know about this state of consciousness we call sleep.

Stages of Sleep

How do we know when someone is asleep? Self-reports of sleeping are notoriously unreliable. A person who claims that he or she "didn't sleep a wink last night" may have slept soundly for many hours. It may be that some people who claim they have **insomnia,** the chronic inability to get to sleep and to get an adequate amount of sleep, actually dream that they are awake and then remember their dreams (Dement, 1974).

Our best, most reliable indicators of sleep are physiological measurements, usually of brain activity and muscle tone. The **electroencephalogram (EEG)** is an instrument that measures and records (on an electroencephalo*graph*) the electrical activity of the brain. It does so through small electrodes that are pasted onto the scalp. The process is slightly messy, but it is in no way painful. The **electromyogram (EMG)** similarly produces a record of a muscle's activity, tone, or state of relaxation.

When you are in a calm, relaxed state, with your eyes closed, but not yet asleep, your EEG pattern shows a rhythmic cycle of brain wave activity called **alpha activity**. In this presleep stage, we find relatively smooth EEG waves cycling 8 to 12 times every second. If, as you sit or lie there, you start worrying about an event of the day or trying to solve a problem, the

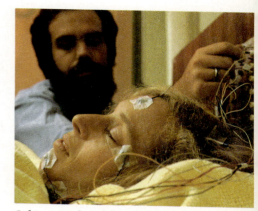

Subjects in sleep labs provide scientists with information about humans during sleep. By hooking the subjects to EEGs, scientists can study the activity of the brain during sleep.

insomnia *the chronic inability to get to sleep and to get an adequate amount of sleep*

electroencephalogram (EEG) *an instrument used to measure and record the electrical activity of the brain*

electromyogram (EMG) *an inst ument used to measure and record muscle tension/relaxation*

alpha activity *an EEG pattern associated with quiet relaxation and characterized by slow wave cycles of 8 to 12 per second*

Figure 4.20

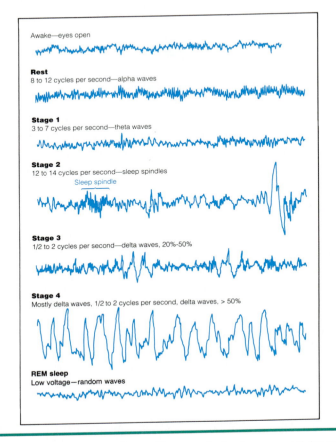

The EEG records of sleeping subjects illustrate the brain wave activity associated with the different stages of sleep.

smooth alpha waves become disrupted and are replaced by an apparently random pattern of heightened electrical activity typical of what we usually find in wakefulness.

As you drift from rest and relaxation into sleep, your brain waves change, as alpha waves give way to the stages of sleep. The EEG tracings of sleeping subjects reveal that sleep can be divided into four different stages (Borbely, 1986). As we describe these four stages, you can refer to Figure 4.20, which shows the EEGs of a subject in each of the stages of sleep. Remember that these tracings were chosen because they best illustrate each of the four stages. Actual EEG tracings are not always this clear.

Stage 1: This is a very light sleep from which you can be easily aroused. The smooth, cyclical alpha pattern disappears, replaced by the slower *theta waves* (3–7 cycles per second). The amplitude, or magnitude, of the electrical activity also lessens considerably. At the same time, your breathing is becoming more regular, and your heart rate is slowing and blood pressure is decreasing. This stage does not last very long—generally less than 10 minutes. Then, you start to slide into stage 2 sleep.

Stage 2: In this stage, the basic EEG pattern is similar to stage 1—low amplitude with no noticeable wavelike pattern. The difference is that we now see what are called *sleep spindles* in the EEG record. These are brief, high-amplitude bursts of electrical activity that occur with regularity (about every 15 seconds). You're really getting off to sleep now, but still can be easily awakened.

Stage 3: Now you're getting into deep sleep. There is a reduction in the brain's electrical activity. Now we can clearly make out *delta wave* activity in your EEG. Delta waves are high, slow waves (from 0.5 to 3 cycles every second). In stage 3 of sleep, delta waves constitute between 20 and 50 percent of your EEG pattern. Your internal functions (temperature, heart rate, breathing) are lowering and slowing. It's going to be difficult to wake you now.

Stage 4: Now you're in deep sleep. Your EEG record is virtually filled with slow delta waves, recurring over and over again (as opposed to stage 3 sleep, where delta waves comprised only a portion of your brain wave activity). At this point, readings from an electromyogram indicate that your muscles have become totally relaxed. About 15 percent of your night's sleep will be spent in this stage of deep sleep.

It usually takes about an hour to go from stage 1 to stage 4. How long it actually takes will, of course, depend somewhat on how tired you are and the physical conditions that surround you. We'll assume a nice, quiet, dark room, with a comfortable and familiar bed. After an hour's passage through these four stages, the sequence reverses itself. You go back through stage 3, then to stage 2, but before going through the cycle again, something truly remarkable happens. Your eyes start to move rapidly under closed eyelids.

BEFORE YOU GO ON

What are the EEG and the EMG?
Briefly describe the four stages of sleep.

REM and NREM Sleep

In the early 1950s, Nathaniel Kleitman and Eugene Aserinsky made quite a discovery. They noticed that as sleeping subjects began their second cycle into deeper levels of sleep, their eyes darted back and forth under their closed eyelids (Aserinsky & Kleitman, 1953). This period of **r**apid **e**ye **m**ovement is called **REM sleep**. The most noteworthy aspect of this discovery is that when sleeping subjects are awakened during REM sleep, they usually (about 85 percent of the time) report that they are having a vivid, storylike dream. When awakened during sleep periods that are not accompanied by rapid eye movements (NREM sleep), subjects report significantly fewer and much more fragmented dreams (Kleitman, 1963). At first it was believed that eye movements during REM sleep were being made as the dreamer literally viewed, or scanned, images produced by the dream. It turns out that a dreamer's eye movements are unrelated to the content of

REM sleep *rapid eye movement sleep during which vivid dreaming occurs, as do heightened levels of physiological functioning*

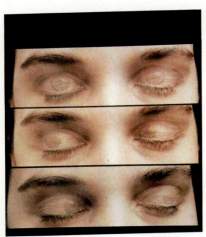

The rapid eye movements of REM sleep are captured in this double-exposure photograph.

his or her dream. Eye movements are produced instead by a cluster of cells in the brain stem that is very near other clusters of cells that have been implicated in moving us in and out of REM and NREM sleep cycles (Hobson, 1977; Kiester, 1980).

REM sleep patterns occur throughout the night, normally lasting from a few minutes to half an hour. About 90 to 120 minutes each night is spent "REMing." During these REM periods, we are probably dreaming. As one goes through a night's sleep, REM periods tend to become longer and dreams more vivid. Dream time seems very well correlated with real time. That is, if subjects are awakened after five minutes of REM sleep, they report that they had been dreaming for about five minutes. If they are left to REM for 20 minutes, they report that they have had a longer dream (Dement & Kleitman, 1957). So much for the notion that all our dreaming is jammed into just the last few seconds before we wake.

Everyone REMs. Everyone dreams. Some of us may have difficulty remembering what we have dreamed when we awake in the morning, but we can be sure that in the course of a normal night's sleep, we have dreamed several times. (There's no great mystery why we don't remember our dreams any better than we do. Most dreams are quite ordinary, boring, and forgettable. Unless we make some conscious effort to do so, we seldom try to store dream content in our memories so that they can be recalled later. That is, we are seldom motivated to remember our dreams.)

The normal pattern of REM occurrences is presented in Figure 4.21, from research by William Dement (1974). Notice in this figure that during the course of a night's sleep, one *does not necessarily pass through all the stages of sleep in an orderly fashion.* That is, in some cycles, stage 3 may be passed over completely; in another cycle, stage 4 may be absent. Indeed, toward the end of our sleeping, we tend not to return to the deep sleep of stage 4 between REM cycles. If you refer back to Figure 4.20, you will find an EEG tracing typical of the sort found during REM sleep. Note that it looks very much like the tracing indicating wakefulness.

Although we're sure that everyone does dream, we're not sure just *why* everyone dreams. Some theories have their basis in the writings of Sigmund

Dreams can be disruptive. Here, a five-year-old child suffering from nightmares followed by severe headaches is videotaped and studied by a psychiatrist.

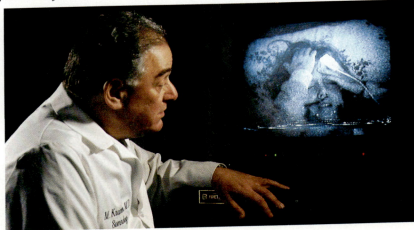

Figure **4.21**

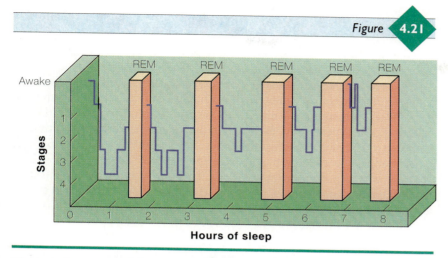

The typical sequence of sleep stages during a typical night of a young adult. Notice the recurring REM sleep throughout the night.

Freud (1900), who believed that dreaming allows us the opportunity to engage in fantasy and wish fulfillment of a sort that would probably cause us discomfort or embarrassment if we entertained such thoughts while we were awake. Freud saw dreams as a pathway (a *royal road*, as he called it) to the discovery of the content of our unconscious mind—content that might otherwise be kept from conscious awareness.

More modern theories of the function of REM sleep and dreaming tend to emphasize the physiological activity that occurs during this phase of sleep. One hypothesis argues that REM sleep helps the brain consolidate memories of events that occurred during the day. In one study, for example, subjects were less able to recall stories they read before they went to bed if their REM sleep was interrupted during the night (Tilley & Empson, 1978). Another intriguing notion is that dreams (and our recall of them) represent convenient cognitive "explanations" for what may be simply the random activity of our brains. That is, if the area of the brain associated with the movement of our legs becomes active while we are asleep, our brain will "manufacture" a reasonable story—a dream—that involves our running, kicking, or in some way using our leg muscles (Hobson & McCarley, 1977).

Dreaming isn't the only thing that happens during REM sleep. From the outside, a sleeper in REM sleep seems quiet and calm, except for those barely noticeable eye movements. On the inside, however, there is quite a different story. One noticeable change is a type of muscular immobility— called **atonia**. The paralysis of atonia is not caused by a tensing of one's muscles, but because centers in the brain stem are keeping the muscles from acting (Chase & Morales, 1990). It does seem adaptive to have the body lie still so that the dreamer does not react to the action of his or her dreams. This state of immobilization is occasionally interrupted by slight muscle "twitches" (which you may have observed if you've watched a sleeping dog that appears to be chasing an imaginary rabbit in its dreams). Some people do not demonstrate normal atonia but thrash about wildly during

atonia *muscular immobility, associated with REM sleep, caused by the total relaxation of the muscles*

REM sleep, a disorder reasonably called REM sleep disorder (Mahowald & Schenck, 1989).

In many ways, the REM sleeper is very active, even though he or she may be oblivious to, or not conscious of, most external stimulation. During REM sleep there is usually an excitement of the sex organs, males having a penile erection, females having a discharge of vaginal fluids (although this latter finding is not as common). Breathing usually becomes shallow and rapid. Blood pressure levels may skyrocket and heart rates increase, all while the subject lies "peacefully" asleep. Because all this physiological activity is going on, REM sleep is sometimes referred to as paradoxical sleep. There doesn't appear to be very much quiet and peaceful about it at all. These changes take place regardless of what the subject is dreaming about. It matters little whether one is dreaming about lying on the beach getting a tan, enjoying some sexual encounter, or engaging in hand-to-hand combat; physiologically, the reactions are the same.

BEFORE YOU GO ON

What are REM and NREM sleep?
What occurs during REM sleep?

The Function(s) of Sleep

Although there is a great deal we don't know yet, we have learned quite a bit about sleep. We can trace sleep through its various stages and cycles and note when dreams are likely to occur. We now know that everyone sleeps, although for varying lengths of time. Among other things, how long we sleep is related to our age—the older we get, the less we tend to sleep. We know that everyone REMs and dreams, although many people cannot remember many of their dreams. What we don't know yet is *why* we sleep. We have yet to agree on the *function* that sleep serves. "Perhaps sleep does not have a function. Perhaps, as some of my own students have argued with me, we should accept our failure to isolate a specific function of sleep as evidence for nonexistence of such a function" (Rechtschaffen, 1971, p. 87). We may not know why we sleep, but we have some hypotheses on the subject. Let's first examine what happens when we are deprived of sleep and then consider a couple of possible explanations for sleep's function.

Deprivation Studies. In 1960, William Dement reported the results of a sleep deprivation experiment that he had just completed. His report had quite an impact. Dement had systematically deprived college student volunteers of the opportunity to engage in REM sleep. Whenever EEG records indicated that his subjects were falling into REM patterns of sleep, they were awakened. The number of REM deprivations increased as dawn approached, as subjects tried unconsciously to get in their REMing. After five nights of interrupted REM sleep, Dement's subjects showed a variety of strange behavioral reactions. They were irritable, somewhat paranoid, noticeably anxious, and unable to concentrate. Subjects who were awakened just as frequently, but during NREM sleep, showed no such negative effects. Here seemed to be a major breakthrough! We sleep because we need to REM; we need to dream.

The catch is that even Dement has been unable to replicate these findings in later studies (Dement, 1974). *In fact, most sleep deprivation studies—on animals as well as humans—show remarkably few adverse side-effects of deprivation of any kind of sleep* (e.g., Martin, 1986; Webb & Cartwright, 1978). Even with lengthy deprivation, there are few lasting changes in the subjects' reactions, particularly if the subject is in good physical and psychological health to begin with. If the task at hand is interesting enough, there is little impairment of intellectual functioning after prolonged sleep deprivation (Dement, 1974; Webb, 1975). Apparently, we can adapt to deprivation, perhaps by taking little catnaps while we're awake. Very short episodes of sleep, called **microsleeps**, can be found in the EEG records of waking subjects, both animal and human. Microsleeps increase in number when normal sleep is disrupted.

That's not to say that there aren't *any* effects from being deprived of sleep. Subjects deprived of REM sleep for a few nights and then left alone will spend long periods REMing, as if to catch up on lost REMs. But this *REM rebound effect* is generally only found for the first night after deprivation, and then patterns return to normal. There is some evidence that NREM sleep (particularly stage 4 deep sleep) also rebounds (Agnew, Webb, & Williams, 1964). When, in 1965, 17-year-old Randy Gardner set the Guinness world record by going without sleep for nearly 266 hours, he slept for 14 hours the first night after deprivation, but by the second night returned to his normal 8 hours of sleep.

Sleep as a Restorative Process. One of the oldest and most intuitively appealing hypotheses of why we sleep proposes that during the course of a good, restful night's sleep, the body has an opportunity to restore the energy it expended during wakefulness. If sleep restores energy or repairs bodily damage, there should be a clear correlation between amount of daily exercise and the extent and nature of nightly sleep. Unfortunately, such relationships are next to impossible to find (Hartman, 1973; Horne & Minard, 1985). This position is also difficult to reconcile with data on the amount of sleep characteristic of different mammals. The giant sloth, for example, sleeps nearly 20 hours a day; a beaver about 11 hours (Pinel, 1990, p. 372). And it is difficult to think about activity in terms of "busy as a sloth" or "lazy as a beaver."

Nor is there any compelling evidence of significant changes taking place in blood chemistry as the result of sleeping (Schneider & Tarshis, 1986, p. 395). And we clearly do have evidence that sleep, particularly REM sleep, is far from restful and quiet, at least at a physiological level. Recall that during REM sleep, many internal physiological processes (blood pressure, gastric secretions, and the like) are as active as during wakefulness, if not more so.

All of this is *not* to say, however, that significant physiological and biochemical events don't take place during sleep. Indeed, a number of significant changes do take place when we sleep—at least some of the time. At least some of the time we may sleep precisely so that these changes *can* occur. For example, during sleep there *is* an increased production of growth hormone (GH) secretions. This hormone promotes the growth of bone

A study conducted at Loughborough University of Technology in England tested the effects of 72 hours of sleep deprivation on volunteers. Despite the weary looks of the four student volunteers in the "after" pictures they did not experience any adverse side-effects, which supports the findings of previous studies.

microsleeps *very brief episodes of sleep discernible only by examination of an EEG record*

tissue and increases the normal rate of cell division, two processes that are very important during childhood and adolescence (Oswald, 1980). The problem is, unfortunately, that the relationship between sleep and increased growth hormone production, although positive, is not very strong. Growth hormone production in infants and many older adults seems quite unrelated to sleep.

Recently, research has begun to focus on changes that occur in brain chemistry (as opposed to blood chemistry) during sleep. Here results have been more positive. There is evidence, for example, that the brain—at least in cats—increases its production of certain complex chemicals (proteins) during sleep, REM sleep in particular. As we noted earlier, the reasoning then is that this process in turn aids in the consolidation of long-term memories of events experienced during the day (McCarley & Hoffman, 1981).

As we have seen before, and as we will see again, the issue is not a simple one. (Remember our discussion of "For many questions in psychology there are no simple answers" back in Topic 1A?) If there are processes of a physiological or biochemical sort that restore the brain or body and require that we sleep in order to do so, these processes are very subtle and complex.

Sleep as an Evolutionary Process. Sleeping isn't a learned response. It just happens. That it happens is rooted in our biology. That it happens as it does is also rooted in our evolutionary history (Kleitman, 1963a; Webb, 1974, 1975). In this view, sleep is an evolved adaptation to our environment, not so much to restore energy as to conserve it.

Sleeping is simply a part of being alive—a process we share with many organisms. Some animals, given the way that they have evolved, sleep for only a few minutes or hours each day. Examples include those animals whose only defense against predators is to be vigilant and quick to run away, such as rabbits, sheep, and antelope. Other animals—lions, for example—sleep even more than humans because they are relatively unthreatened by their environment and are able to easily find food and shelter. They can sleep when and where they please without fear. Humans are diurnal (daytime) animals, and we are guided largely by our visual sense, which works best during daylight hours. At night, we are free to rest and relax, conserving energy and preparing ourselves to face the new day in the morning. From this perspective, the answer to the question "Why do we sleep?" is that in terms of survival and adapting to our environments, this system works well.

BEFORE YOU GO ON

What are the effects of depriving someone of sleep?
Briefly summarize the restorative and evolutionary approaches to the issue of the function of sleep.

HYPNOSIS

Now that we have reviewed some of the evidence and theories of the altered state of consciousness called sleep, we can turn to those states that require some effort to attain. **Hypnosis** is an altered state of consciousness that one enters voluntarily. Hypnosis is characterized by (1) a marked increase in suggestibility, (2) a focusing of one's attention, (3) an exaggerated use of imagination, (4) an inability or unwillingness to act on one's own, and (5) an unquestioning acceptance of distortions of reality (Hilgard & Hilgard, 1975). There is little truth to the belief that being hypnotized is like going to sleep. In fact, few of the characteristics of sleep are to be found in the hypnotized subject. EEG patterns, for example, are significantly different.

Hypnosis has been used, with varying degrees of success, for a number of different purposes. As you know, it is used as entertainment, as a show business routine where members of an audience are hypnotized usually to do silly things in public. Hypnosis has long been viewed as a method for gaining access to memories of events not in immediate awareness. Hypnosis has also been touted as a process of treatment for a wide range of psychological and physical disorders. In this section, we'll provide answers, as best we can at the moment, to some common questions about hypnosis.

Hypnosis is an altered state of consciousness that one enters voluntarily. It has been used for a variety of purposes, including treatment of some psychological and physical disorders.

hypnosis *an altered state of consciousness characterized by an increase in suggestibility, attention, and imagination*

1. Can everyone be hypnotized? No, probably not. The susceptibility to hypnosis varies widely from person to person. Some resist and cannot be hypnotized. Contrary to popular belief, you cannot be hypnotized against your will, which is why we say that one enters a hypnotic state voluntarily (although I must acknowledge that some hypnotists do claim that they can hypnotize anyone under the right conditions, which is why I hedged and said "probably" not).

2. What best predicts who can be easily hypnotized? Although not everyone can be easily hypnotized, some people are excellent subjects, can readily be put into deep hypnotic states, and easily learn to hypnotize themselves (Hilgard, 1975; 1978). A number of traits are correlated with one's hypnotizability. The most important factor seems to be the ability to engage easily in daydreaming and fantasy, to be able to "set ordinary reality aside for awhile" (Lynn & Rhue, 1986; Wilkes, 1986, p. 25). Other positively related traits include suggestibility and a certain degree of passivity or willingness to cooperate, at least during the hypnotic session. Another intriguing notion is that persons who were often punished in childhood, or are avid readers, runners, or actors, are good subjects for hypnosis. The logic is that these people have a history of self-induced trancelike states (to escape punishment, to focus on and become absorbed in the task at hand), which makes them more likely to be hypnotized (Hilgard, 1970).

3. Can I be made to do things under the influence of hypnosis that I would be embarrassed to do otherwise? Next to being unknowingly hypnotized, this seems to be the greatest fear associated with hypnosis. Again, the answer is *probably* no. Under the influence of a skilled hypnotist, you may very well do some pretty silly things and do them publicly. But under the right circumstances, you might do those very same things without being hypnotized. It is unlikely that you would do under hypnosis anything that you would not do otherwise. It is also the case that under certain (unusual)

circumstances, people can do outrageous—and dangerous—things, which is why hypnosis should be used with caution.

4. Are hypnotized subjects simply more open to the suggestions of the hypnotist, or is their consciousness really changed? This question does not get a clear yes or no answer either. The issue is in dispute. Some believe that hypnosis is really no more than a heightened level of suggestibility (Barber, 1972; Spanos & Barber, 1974). Others believe it to be a special state, separate from the compliance of a willing subject. When hypnotized subjects are left alone, they maintain the condition induced by their hypnosis. Subjects not hypnotized, but simply complying as best they can with an experimenter, revert quickly to normal behaviors when left alone (Hilgard, 1975; Orne, 1969).

5. Can hypnosis be used to alleviate pain—real, physical pain? Yes. It won't (can't) cure the underlying cause, but it can be used to control the feeling of pain. Hypnosis can be used to create **hallucinations** in the hypnotized subject. Hallucinations are perceptual experiences that occur without sensory input—that is, false experiences. Some hallucinations are termed positive because the subject is led to perceive something that is not there. Pain reduction uses negative hallucinations: that is, the failure to perceive something (pain in this case) that *is* there. If a subject is a good candidate for hypnosis in the first place, there is a good chance that at least a portion of perceived pain can be blocked from conscious awareness (Hilgard & Hilgard, 1975; Long, 1986).

6. Is a person in a hypnotic state in any sense aware of what she or he is doing? Yes, but in a very strange way. It seems that within the hypnotized subject is what Hilgard calls a hidden observer who may be quite aware of what is going on. In one study (Hilgard & Hilgard, 1975), a subject was hypnotized and told that he would feel no pain as his hand was held in a container of ice water (usually very painful indeed). When asked, the subject reported feeling very little pain, just as expected. The hypnotic suggestion was working. The Hilgards then asked the subject if "some part of him" was feeling any pain and to indicate the presence of such pain by using his free hand to press a lever (or even to write out a description of what he was feeling). Even though the subject continued to *report verbally* no feeling of pain, the free hand (on the behalf of the "hidden observer") indicated that it "knew" there was considerable pain in the immersed hand.

7. Can I remember things under hypnosis that I couldn't remember otherwise? Probably not, although there is no more hotly contested issue with regard to hypnosis than this. In the everyday sense of "Can you hypnotize me to remember my psychology material better for the test next Friday?" the answer is "Almost certainly not." (Sorry.) Now, I might be able to convince you under hypnosis that you had better remember your psychology and lead you to *want* to remember your psychology, but there is no evidence that hypnotic suggestion can *directly* improve your ability to learn and remember new material. In the more restrictive sense of "I don't remember all the details of the accident and the trauma that followed. Can hypnosis help me recall those events more clearly?" the answer is less definite. When we get to our discussion of memory (Chapter 6), we'll see that distortions of memory in recollection easily can occur in normal states. In hypnotic states, the subject is suggestible and susceptible to distortions in recall furnished by the hypnotist (even assuming that the hypnotist has no reason to cause distortions). To the extent that hypnosis can reduce feelings of

hallucinations *perceptual experiences without sensory input; that is, perceiving that which is not there or not perceiving that which is there*

anxiety and tension, it may help in the recollection of anxiety-producing memories. The evidence is neither clear nor convincing on this issue in either direction. What of the related question, "Can hypnosis make me go back in time (regress) and remember what it was like when I was only 3 or 4 years old?" Here, I'm afraid, we *do* have a clear-cut answer, and the answer is no. So-called age-regression hypnotic sessions have simply not proven to be valid (e.g., Nash, 1987).

Hypnosis does alter one's consciousness, does open one to suggestions of the hypnotist, can be used to treat symptoms (if not their underlying causes), and can distort one's view of reality. However, we are learning that it is neither mystical nor magical; there are limits to what hypnosis can do.

BEFORE YOU GO ON

What is hypnosis?

What changes in consciousness does it produce?

Who can be hypnotized?

MEDITATION

Meditation is a self-induced state of altered consciousness character-ized by a focusing of attention and relaxation. Meditation is usually asso-ciated with ancient or Eastern cultures and has been practiced for many centuries. We tend to think of meditation in a religious context. Meditation became quite popular in North America in the 1960s. It was then that psychologists began to study the process seriously. In this section, we'll first review the process of meditation, and then we'll look at the claims that have been made about its potential benefits.

There are a number of different kinds of meditation, but the most popular form requires mental focusing, or concentration. *Transcendental meditation (TM)* is a form of this variety (Maharishi, 1963). In TM, one begins meditating by assuming a comfortable position and becoming calm and relaxed. The meditator then directs his or her attention to one particular stimulus. This could be some simple bodily function, such as one's own breathing. Attention could be focused on some softly spoken or chanted word, or phrase, or *mantra*, such as "ummm," "one," or "calm." As attention becomes focused, other stimuli, either external (events in the environment) or internal (thoughts, feelings, or bodily processes), can be blocked from consciousness. The challenge is to stay relaxed, to remain peaceful and calm. By definition, a state of meditation cannot be forced; it just happens. Its practitioners claim that to reach an altered state of awareness through med-itation is not difficult (Benson, 1975).

Once a person is in a meditative state, there *are* measureable physio-logical changes that take place that allow us to claim meditation to be an altered state of consciousness. The most noticeable is a predominance of alpha waves in the EEG record (remember, such waves characterize a re-

meditation *the focusing of awareness in order to arrive at an altered state of consciousness and relaxation*

During meditation breathing usually slows and deepens, oxygen intake is reduced, and heart rate may decrease.

laxed state of the sort experienced just *before* one enters into sleep). Breathing usually slows and becomes deeper. Oxygen intake is reduced, and heart rate may decrease (Wallace & Benson, 1972).

There is no doubt that many people can enter meditative states of consciousness. Any doubts that have arisen concerning meditation center on the claims for its benefits. One of the major claims for meditation is that it is a reasonably simple, very effective, even superior way to enter into a state of relaxation. The reduction of bodily (somatic) arousal is taken to be one of the main advantages of meditation. The claim is that by meditating, one can slow bodily processes and enter into a state of physical as well as psychological calm.

Researcher David Holmes (1984, 1985) reviewed the evidence for somatic (bodily) relaxation through meditation. On a number of different measures of arousal and relaxation, including heart rate, respiration rate, muscle tension, and oxygen consumption, Holmes concluded that there were *no differences* between meditating subjects and subjects who were "simply" resting or relaxing. After reviewing the data of dozens of experiments, he concluded,

> . . . There is not a measure of arousal on which the meditating subjects were consistently found to have reliably lower arousal than resting subjects. Indeed, the most consistent finding was that there were not reliable differences between meditating and resting subjects. Furthermore, there appear to be about as many instances in which the meditating subjects showed reliably higher arousal as there are instances in which they showed reliably lower arousal than their resting counterparts (1984, p. 5).

Another claim often made for meditation is that people who practice meditation are better able to cope with stress, pressure, or threatening situations than are people who do not practice meditation. Once again, Holmes (1984, 1985) reports that he could find no evidence to support this claim. In fact, in four of the studies he reviewed, Holmes found that under mild threat, meditating subjects showed *greater* arousal than did nonmeditating subjects.

I must add two important notes here: (1) A number of psychologists have taken issue with Holmes's methods and conclusions, and argue that meditation *does* offer advantages over simply resting, suggesting also that "resting" is a difficult concept to define (see, e.g., Shapiro, 1985; Suler, 1985; West, 1985). (2) Notice that Holmes in no way argues that meditation isn't of any value. He just argues that with regard to somatic arousal, there is no evidence that it is any better than resting.

Some of the claims made for meditation techniques go beyond simple relaxation and somatic arousal reduction. Claims that meditation can raise one to transcendental heights of new awareness and thus make you a better person are viewed with considerable skepticism in psychology. Some people claim that they have an enormous "openness" to ideas and feelings, that they have hallucinatory experiences, and that they can divorce themselves from their bodies and minds when they meditate. Such experiences might, in some instances, be true. The idea that a meditator can exist apart from present experience and view life "as if from without" is not too far removed from Hilgard's notion of a "hidden observer" in hypnosis. Nonetheless, the majority of psychologists who have investigated meditation continue to question any claims for a heightened state of well-being that is achieved through such little effort and that relies more on testimonials of personal experience than on hard scientific evidence (Webb, 1981).

BEFORE YOU GO ON

What is meditation?
Is meditation an effective means of relaxation and reduction of somatic activity?

ALTERING CONSCIOUSNESS WITH DRUGS

In this section, we will discuss some of the chemicals that alter one's consciousness by inducing changes in our perception, mood, and/or behavior. Because of their ability to alter basic psychological processes, these chemicals are referred to as **psychoactive drugs**.

Drugs have been used for centuries to alter one's state of consciousness. No reasonable person would take a drug because he or she expected to have a bad, negative, or unpleasant experience. Psychoactive drugs are taken—at least initially—in order to achieve a state of consciousness that the user considers to be good, positive, pleasant, even euphoric. As we all know, however, the use of drugs that alter our mood, perceptions, and behaviors often has seriously negative outcomes. In this regard, there are a few terms that will be relevant for our discussion. Although there is not complete agreement on how these terms are used, for our purposes, we'll use the following definitions.

1. **Dependence:** (a) when continued use of a drug is required to maintain bodily functioning (called physical dependence), or (b) when continued use of a drug is believed to be necessary to maintain psychological functioning at some level (called psychological dependence). *"I just can't face the day without my three cups of coffee in the morning."*
2. **Tolerance:** a condition in which the use of a drug leads to a state in which more and more of it is needed to produce the same effect. *"I used to get high with just one of these; now I need three."*
3. **Withdrawal:** a (usually extreme) negative reaction, either physical or psychological, that results when one stops taking a drug.
4. **Addiction:** an extreme dependency, physical or psychological, in which signs of tolerance and painful withdrawal are usually found. *"No way I'm gonna give it up no matter what. It feels too good; and the pain is too great without it."*

One other distinction we should make is that between drug use and **drug abuse**. The dividing line here is not clear, of course, but we generally feel that we are dealing with abuse when we find (1) a lack of control as evidenced by daily intoxication and continued use, even knowing that one's condition will deteriorate; (2) a disruption of interpersonal relationships

psychoactive drug *a chemical that affects psychological processes and consciousness*

dependence *a state in which drug use is either necessary or believed to be necessary to maintain functioning at some desired level*

tolerance *in using a drug, a state in which more and more of the drug is required to produce the same desired effect*

withdrawal *a negative, painful reaction that may occur when one stops taking a drug*

addiction *an extreme dependency, usually accompanied by symptoms of tolerance and painful withdrawal*

drug abuse *a lack of control, a disruption of interpersonal relationships or difficulties at work, and a history of maladaptive use for at least one month* and/or difficulties at work that can be traced to drug usage, and (3) indications that maladaptive drug use has continued for at least one month (American Psychiatric Association, 1987). Hidden in this distinction is the observation that drug use may not have negative consequences; drug abuse will.

There are many psychoactive drugs. We'll focus on four different types: stimulants, depressants, hallucinogens, and (as a separate category) marijuana. Not only will we try to describe the effects of using these drugs, but we'll also briefly address the consequences of their abuse.

Stimulants

stimulants *drugs (such as caffeine, cocaine, and amphetamines) that increase nervous system activity*

Chemical **stimulants** do just that—they chemically stimulate, or activate, the nervous system. They produce a heightened sense of arousal, creating not only an increase in general activity, but also an elevation of mood.

Caffeine is one of the most widely used of all stimulants. It is found in many foods and drinks (coffee, tea, and chocolate) as well as many varieties of painkillers. It is also an ingredient in many soft drinks, notably colas, but it can be found in others. In moderate amounts, it seems to have no dangerous or life-threatening effects on the user. At some point, a mild dependence, at least of a psychological nature, may develop. Although it is not yet known precisely *how* caffeine does so, it temporarily increases cellular metabolism (the general process of converting food into energy), which then results in a burst of new-found energy. It also seems to block the effects of some inhibitory neurotransmitters in the brain (Julien, 1985).

After excessive or lengthy use, giving up sources of caffeine may result in the pain of withdrawal. If you tend to drink a lot of coffee and cola drinks during the week, but take a break from them during the weekend, you may experience the headaches of caffeine withdrawal. There is usually a rebound sort of effect when caffeine intake is stopped. For example, you may drink many cups of coffee to help stay awake enough to withstand an all-night study session, but within a few hours after you stop drinking the caffeine, you may rebound and experience a streak of mental and physical fatigue—perhaps right at exam time!

Nicotine is another very popular stimulant, usually taken by smoking and absorption by the lungs. Nicotine is carried from the lungs to the brain very quickly—in a matter of seconds. There is no doubt that nicotine is a stimulant of central nervous system activity, but it does relax muscle tone slightly, which perhaps explains in part the rationalization of smokers who claim that they can relax by having a cup of coffee and a cigarette. Nicotine seems to have its stimulant effect by activating excitatory synapses in both the central and peripheral nervous systems (McKim, 1986).

Many individuals develop a tolerance to nicotine, requiring more and more of it to reach the desired state of stimulation. Indeed, beginning smokers generally cannot smoke more than one or two cigarettes without becoming ill. The drug often leads to dependency. In 1989, then Surgeon General C. Everett Koop declared cigarette smoking an addiction, claiming it the single most preventable cause of death in our society, accounting for more than one-sixth of all the deaths reported in 1985 (DeAngelis, 1989). How ultimately addictive nicotine (or perhaps any other drug) becomes may depend primarily on how quickly it enters the brain. That is, people who take many quick deep puffs when smoking may become addicted more easily to nicotine than will people who take slow, shallow puffs (Bennett, 1980).

Cocaine is a naturally occurring stimulant derived from leaves of the coca shrub (native to the Andes mountains in South America). The allure of cocaine and its derivative "crack" is the rush of pleasure and energy it produces when it first enters the bloodstream, either through the mucous membranes when inhaled as smoke ("free basing"), inhaled through the nose as a powder ("snorting"), or directly through injection as a liquid. A cocaine "high" doesn't last very long—15 to 20 minutes is typical.

"Crack" cocaine is often ingested in smoke.

There are many physiological reactions that result from cocaine use. It elevates blood pressure and heart rate. Another reaction is that the drug blocks the reuptake of two important neurotransmitters. That means that once these neurotransmitters have entered a synapse, cocaine will prohibit their being taken back up into the neuron from which they have been released. The end result is that, for some period of time at least, excessive amounts of these neurotransmitters are available in the nervous system. The two neurotransmitters in question are *norepinephrine*, which acts in both the central and peripheral nervous system to provide arousal and the sense of extra energy, and *dopamine*, which acts in the brain to produce feelings of pleasure and euphoria.

It seems that some of the physiological effects of cocaine use are very long-lasting, if not permanent, even though the psychological effects last but a few minutes. Not only is the rush of the psychological reactions to cocaine or "crack" short-lived, but these reactions are followed by a period of letdown approaching depression. As the user knows, one way to combat letdown and depression is to take more of the drug. Such a vicious cycle invariably leads to dependency and addiction. Cocaine is such a powerfully addictive drug that many individuals can become both psychologically and physically dependent on its use after just one or two episodes. Cocaine addiction tends to run in families to such an extent that current research is exploring the hypothesis that there is a genetic basis for cocaine addiction. Cocaine is a drug that no one can handle safely.

Amphetamines are synthetically manufactured chemical stimulants that usually come in the form of capsules or pills under many "street names," such as bennies, uppers, wake-ups, cartwheels, dexies, or jellie babies. In addition to blocking reuptake, amphetamines actually cause the release of excess dopamine and norepinephrine. However, their action is considerably slower and somewhat less widespread than is that of cocaine. Once the amphetamine drug takes effect, users feel alert, awake, aroused, filled with energy, and ready to go. Unfortunately, such results are short-lived and illusory. The drug does not create alertness so much as it masks fatigue, which will ultimately overcome the user when the drug wears off. It now seems clear that these are not the only effects of amphetamine use; it has a direct effect on the heart and circulatory system, causing irregular heartbeat and increased blood pressure, for example (McKim 1986). Although it sounds trite, speed (yet another name for amphetamines) does kill. Once again, with the amphetamines, tolerance and dependency build quickly, and withdrawing from the use of amphetamines can be a long and painful process.

What are stimulant drugs, and what are their effects?

Depressants

depressants *drugs (such as alcohol, opiates, heroin, and barbiturates) that slow or reduce nervous system activity*

In terms of their effects on consciousness, **depressants** are the opposite of stimulants. They reduce one's awareness of external stimuli, slow bodily functioning, and decrease levels of overt behavior. Predictably, the reaction one gets to depressants depends largely on how much is taken. In small doses, they may produce relaxation, a sense of freedom from anxiety, and a loss of stifling inhibitions. In greater amounts, they may produce sedation, sleep, coma, or death.

Alcohol is doubtless the most commonly used of all the depressants. It has been in use for thousands of years. In many ways, alcohol is the most dangerous of all drugs, largely because of its popularity and widespread use. More than two-thirds of Americans drink alcohol on a regular basis, and more than $36 *billion* per year is spent on distilled spirits alone (Mayer, 1983). More than that, it is estimated that between 10 and 15 percent of the adult population of North America are alcohol *abusers* (Mayer, 1983; National Council on Alcoholism, 1979). Nearly $600 million in federal funds are spent each year in attempts to study, prevent, and/or treat alcohol abuse (Nathan, 1983). Over $30 *billion* of lost productivity in the United States alone is attributed to alcohol-related problems (Quayle, 1983). Alcohol is certainly the most deadly of drugs. In the summer of 1990, the Centers for Disease Control released a study that indicated that well over 100,000 deaths a year in the United States could be attributed directly to alcohol consumption. The potentially devastating effects of alcohol consumption by pregnant women is also well documented. Alcohol use has been associated with a myriad of problems of the newborn (see Topic 9A).

Perhaps the first thing to remember about alcohol is that it *is* a depressant. Some individuals may feel that they are quite entertaining and stimulating when they drink alcohol, but their nervous system activity is actually being depressed, or slowed. Alcohol increases urination, leading to an overall loss of fluids. It affects vision by raising thresholds, making it more difficult to detect dim lights. There is virtually no doubt that alcohol affects mood, leading to feelings of friendly elation as levels rise and of anger, depression, and fatigue as alcohol levels drop (Babor et al., 1983).

The specific effects of alcohol on the drinker usually reflect a number of interacting factors. Primary among them (again) is *amount*. What matters most is the amount of alcohol that gets into a person's bloodstream, usually through the stomach. The amount of alcohol in one's bloodstream (blood alcohol level, or BAL) at any one time is affected by how much one drinks and by how fast the alcohol can get into the bloodstream, which in turn is affected by what else happens to be in the stomach at the time. Indeed, drinking on an empty stomach may be more dangerous than drinking while or after eating, because the alcohol will be more quickly absorbed. In most states, one-tenth of 1 percent alcohol in the bloodstream is considered

The behavioral impact of many drugs often depends on dosage. With too much alcohol, one may lose consciousness altogether.

enough to declare someone legally drunk. At this level, brain activity is so affected that decision making becomes distorted and motor coordination is impaired (both are the sorts of skills usually required to drive safely).

The effect that alcohol has on a person may also be a function of the person's frame of mind. Sometimes a few drinks produces little apparent effect on a person. Sometimes a couple of beers can have that same person dancing around the room, lampshade on head, acting in a generally foolish way. At other times, the same two cans of beer may turn the same person into a crying, "sad drunk." That is, a person's reactions may reflect cognitive variables—one's frame of mind and one's perception of what is going on in the environment at the time.

Opiates, such as morphine and codeine, are also called analgesics, because they can be used to reduce or eliminate sensations of pain. It was for this purpose that they were first commonly used. In small doses, they create feelings of well-being and ease, relaxation, and a trancelike state. Unlike alcohol, they seem to have little effect on motor behavior. The catch, once again, is that they produce very strong dependence and addiction. Their removal results in extreme pain and depression.

Heroin is an opiate, originally (in the 1890s) derived from morphine, but thought not to be as addictive—a thought soon proven wrong. Strong dependency and addiction grow rapidly. As with other drugs, we find that the addictive nature of heroin may be related to its very rapid entry into the brain. (Methadone, used in some treatment programs for long-term heroin users, is a drug with many of the chemical properties of heroin and many of the same psychological effects. A major difference is that methadone is very slow to reach the brain and tends not to produce heroin's predictable "rush," which makes it somewhat less addictive.)

Those effects of heroin (above whatever painkilling use it may have) seem to be most related to one's emotional state and mood. Unlike alcohol, or the opiates like morphine, there are seldom hallucinations or thought disturbances associated with heroin use. But as increased amounts of heroin become needed to produce the desired emotional states of pleasant euphoria, tolerance builds—and the increased dosages of heroin can cause breathing to stop, often for long enough periods that death results.

Barbiturates are synthetically produced sedatives. Like the opiates, there are many types and varieties. All slow nervous system activity—in small amounts producing a sense of calm and tranquility, and in higher doses producing sleep or coma. They have this effect either by blocking receptor sites on the postsynaptic membrane of excitatory synapses or by enhancing the effects of inhibitory neurotransmitters. Some barbiturates are addictive, producing strong withdrawal symptoms when their use is discontinued. All will produce dependency if used with any regularity. As is generally the case, once addiction develops, getting off these drugs is very difficult.

BEFORE YOU GO ON

What are depressant drugs, and what are their effects?

Hallucinogens

The chemicals we call **hallucinogens** have the most unpredictable effects on consciousness. One of the main reactions to these drugs is the formation of hallucinations, usually visual. That is, users often report seeing things when there is nothing there to see, or they see things in ways that others do not. Hallucinations of hearing, smell, touch, and taste are possible, but much less common.

LSD, lysergic acid diethylamide, is a potent and popular hallucinogen. Psychologically, LSD raises levels of emotionality that can produce profound changes in perception, usually vivid visual hallucinations. One of the first steps in the discovery of how LSD works was finding that levels of a particular neurotransmitter, called serotonin, increased when LSD was given to animals (Jacobs & Trulson, 1979; Jacobs, 1987). In itself, this was not too surprising, because LSD (and similar hallucinogens, such as mescaline) has a chemical composition much like that of serotonin. Serotonin has its effects, both excitatory and inhibitory, on many areas of the brain. To quote neuroscientist Barry Jacobs, "Once a drug acts upon the brain serotonin system, it sets in motion a cascade of events involving much of the enormous complexity of the brain and many of its constituent neurochemical systems. Thus, the brain serotonin system acts as a trigger for a multitude of changes whose elaboration generates the hallucinatory experience" (1987, p. 387). We now know that levels of serotonin increase with LSD use because the LSD acts on serotonin receptor sites, acting just as if it was a neurotransmitter. And very small doses (measured in only millionths of a gram) can produce major behavioral effects.

The changes in mood that take place under LSD are usually extreme exaggerations of one's present mood. From the start, this has been viewed as one of the dangers of LSD. Many individuals are drawn to drugs like LSD because things are not going well for them. Among other things, they are depressed and becoming hopeless. They think that LSD might help cheer them up. In fact, it may worsen their mood, resulting in a "bad trip," by exaggerating the feelings they had when they took the drug.

hallucinogens *drugs (such as LSD) whose major effect is the alteration of perceptual experience and mood*

The hallucinations that occur under the influence of LSD usually involve an exaggeration of some actual perception. That is, colors seem much more vivid, stationary objects appear to move, dimly lit stimuli take on a glow, and otherwise unnoticed details become very apparent. On some occasions, LSD gives rise to an experience of *synesthesia*, in which a stimulus of one modality is perceived in a different modality. For example, the individual may "hear" colored lights, "see" sounds, "feel" odors, and so forth.

BEFORE YOU GO ON

What are hallucinogenic drugs, and what are their effects?

Marijuana—A Rather Special Case

Marijuana is a consciousness-altering drug that we'll consider as a special case because it doesn't fit neatly into any of the three categories we've used above. In some ways, marijuana acts as a depressant. In small dosages, its effects are similar to those of alcohol: decreased nervous system activity and depression of thought and action. In higher doses, however, marijuana acts very much as if it were a hallucinogen, producing hallucinations and alterations in mood.

Marijuana is produced from the cannabis plant. This plant was once the source of most of the rope manufactured for sailing ships in the eighteenth century and was an important crop in the American colonies, grown by George Washington, among other notables. As a source of raw materials for twine and rope, the plants were farmed in great numbers throughout the Midwest during World War II. Because the cannabis plant is hardy, many of the remnants of those farms of the early 1940s can still be found in Illinois and Indiana where every summer adventurers come in search of yet another profitable—albeit illegal—harvest.

The active ingredient in marijuana is the chemical compound tetrahydrocannabinol, commonly known as THC. THC is also the active ingredient in hashish, a similar but more potent drug also made from the cannabis plant. Although marijuana, in large doses, has been found to increase overall levels of some neurotransmitters, it is not known just how it produces this effect. There do not seem to be any specific receptor sites at synapses for THC, or at least none have been found yet.

Marijuana is one of the most difficult drugs for society to deal with. It is currently illegal to sell, possess, or use the drug, yet in many ways, it seems no worse than alcohol. There is evidence that marijuana tolerance may develop, but virtually none that it is addictive. Is marijuana dangerous? Certainly, if for no other reason than it is usually smoked, and smoking is clearly a danger to one's health. It is also dangerous in the sense that alcohol is dangerous. Excessive use leads to impaired judgment, impaired reflexes, unrealistic moods, and poor physical coordination (Bennett, 1982; Weil et al., 1968).

The most debatable aspect of marijuana use involves the results of moderate to heavy long-term use. People are tired of hearing this response (users in particular), but the evidence just isn't in yet. The data are more suggestive than definitive. Marijuana use seems to cause bronchitis and other lung ailments (usually associated with smoking, but with marijuana, even more so). It may have genetic implications (it seems to produce some chromosomal abnormalities in nonhumans, at least). It may adversely affect the body's immune system and white blood cells. Its use can impair memory function, affecting memories of recent events in particular. It seems to have predictably negative effects when taken during pregnancy, resulting in smaller babies, increased numbers of miscarriages, and so on (Grinspoon, 1977; Julien, 1985).

BEFORE YOU GO ON

What is the active ingredient in marijuana, and what effects does it produce?

To be conscious is to be aware of one's own mental processes and one's environment. Our conscious perceptions are personal, ever changing, continuous, and selective. Our states of consciousness change subtly as we move from alert wakefulness through the stages of sleep and dreaming. We can voluntarily induce changes in the state of consciousness by meditating, undergoing hypnosis, or using any one of a wide variety of psychoactive drugs.

What is normal, waking consciousness, and what, according to William James, are its four basic characteristics? What is an altered state of consciousness?

We define consciousness as the perception or awareness of our environment and of our own mental processes. According to William James, consciousness can be characterized as always (1) changing, (2) personal, (3) continuous, and (4) selective. By definition, we experience an altered state of consciousness whenever the nature of our awareness or perceptions is changed or altered. / *page 167*

What are the EEG and the EMG? Briefly describe the four stages of sleep.

The EEG (electroencephalogram) is an instrument that measures the general pattern of the electrical activity of the brain, the most common indicator of sleep stages. The EMG (electromyogram) measures muscle tone or tension, another indicator of sleep. In addition to a state of relaxed wakefulness, characterized by EEG alpha waves, we say there are four stages, or levels, of sleep: (1) light sleep with low-amplitude, slow theta waves; (2) sleep showing low-amplitude EEG waves with sleep spindles present; (3) a level where delta waves enter the EEG pattern; and (4) deep sleep, with more than 50 percent delta wave activity. / *page 169*

What are REM and NREM sleep? What occurs during REM sleep?

REM sleep is rapid eye movement sleep, and it occurs four to seven times per night. Several events occur during REM sleep, most noticeably vivid, storylike dreams. During REM sleep, we find loss of muscle tone (atonia); excitement of sexual organs; shallow, rapid breathing;

and increased heart rate and blood pressure. During NREM sleep, one progresses through the four stages of sleep, accompanied by little dream activity. / *page 172*

What are the effects of depriving someone of sleep? Briefly summarize the restorative and evolutionary approaches to the issue of the function of sleep.

People who have been deprived of sleep show a rebound effect by making up for lost sleep at the earliest possible time, usually in just one night. This is true for REM sleep more than for NREM sleep. In most cases, there are remarkably few adverse effects of sleep deprivation. The restorative view of sleep suggests that it is a time needed by the body to restore energy and repair damage. Little evidence supports this view directly. Alternative versions suggest that sleep does promote physical growth, the formation of long-term memories, and restoration of chemical depletion in the brain. The evolutionary perspective claims that sleep is an evolved, adaptive response that promotes conservation of energy at night when humans, being diurnal, don't function well anyway. / *page 174*

What is hypnosis? What changes in consciousness does it produce? Who can be hypnotized?

Hypnosis is an altered state of consciousness into which one enters voluntarily and is characterized by an increase in suggestibility, a strict focusing of attention, an exaggeration of imagination, a reduction of spontaneous activity, and an unquestioning acceptance of distortions in reality. Not everyone can be hypnotized. Those who can most readily be hypnotized are persons who easily

engage in fantasy and daydreaming and who show signs of suggestibility and a willingness to cooperate with the hypnotist. / *page 177*

What is meditation? Is meditation an effective means of relaxation and reduction of somatic activity?

Meditation is a self-induced altered state of consciousness characterized by an extreme focusing of attention and a distortion of perceptions. There are many claims for the benefits of meditation. It does seem to be an effective means of relaxing and reducing overall levels of somatic activity, but there is evidence that it is not significantly better in these regards than a number of other techniques. / *page 179*

What are stimulant drugs, and what are their effects?

Stimulants are psychoactive drugs such as caffeine, nicotine, cocaine, and amphetamines. Their basic effect is to increase the level of nervous system activity and to elevate mood, almost always by affecting the activity of the neural synapse, increasing levels of the neurotransmitters norepinephrine and dopamine. With heavy use, tolerance may develop, as may dependence and addiction. / *page 182*

What are depressant drugs, and what are their effects?

The depressants include such drugs as alcohol, the opiates (for example, morphine, codeine), heroin, and a variety of synthetic barbiturates. All depressants slow nervous system activity, reduce one's awareness of external stimuli, and in small doses, may alleviate feelings of nervousness and anxiety. In large doses, however, they produce sedation, sleep, coma, or death. Tolerance, dependency, and addiction may result from the use of these drugs. / *page 184*

What are hallucinogenic drugs, and what are their effects?

Hallucinogens are drugs that alter mood and perceptions. LSD is an example. They get their name from their ability to induce hallucinations, where a user may have an experience unrelated to what is going on in the user's environment. Synesthesia, a hallucinatory experience that crosses sensory modalities ("hearing" lights, for example), may occur under the influence of LSD. / *page 185*

What is the active ingredient in marijuana, and what effects does it produce?

The active ingredient in marijuana is the chemical compound THC. Listing its short- and long-term effects is difficult because of contradictory evidence. It is at least as dangerous as cigarette smoking, and it is illegal. Of more concern is long-term, heavy use. Here many of the negative side effects that we associate with long-term alcohol use seem present: impaired judgment and reflexes, unrealistic mood, and poor coordination. In addition, marijuana may have adverse effects on the body's immune system and has been implicated in producing a range of negative consequences when taken during pregnancy. / *page 186*

LEARNING

Classical Conditioning

Why We Care: A Topic Preview

Who we are, as unique individuals in this world, is ultimately determined by the interaction of just two influences: our inherited characteristics (or our nature) and our experiences with our environment (or our nurture). We first introduced this point in Topic 1A, and we will be reminded of it many times again. Our nature is established at the moment of conception. As yet, there isn't much that we can do about the genes we have inherited from our parents. On the other hand, there is at least some hope that we can influence who we are—what we feel, what we do, what we know—by attending to how we change as a function of our experiences. To examine changes in our affect, behaviors, or cognitions that take place as a function of experience is to be concerned with the process of learning, the focus of this chapter.

How we learn and adapt to our environments is clearly a major issue in psychology. In some way, directly or indirectly, learning has an impact on every issue we cover in psychology, and that is why we care. Learning affects how we perceive the world, how we find out about the world and ourselves as we grow and develop, how we form social relationships, how we change effectively during the course of psychotherapy. The human organism is poorly suited to survive in this world without learning. If we are to survive, much less prosper, we must profit from our experiences.

In this topic, we'll begin by defining learning. Then we'll concentrate on a simple form of learning: classical conditioning. At first, most of our descriptions of classical conditioning will be based on Ivan Pavlov's work with salivating dogs. Then, once we have the basic principles in hand, we'll consider why classical conditioning is so important to all of us and how the procedures of classical conditioning can be found regularly in our daily lives. We'll also review how psychologists today view classical conditioning, discovering as we do so that some of Pavlov's original assumptions may not have been valid ones. We'll close with an example of how the principles discussed in this topic can be applied to your learning about psychology.

A DEFINITION OF LEARNING

learning *demonstration of a relatively permanent change in behavior that occurs as the result of practice or experience*

Let's begin with a definition. We shall say that **learning** is demonstrated by a relatively permanent change in behavior that occurs as the result of practice or experience. This is a rather standard definition and it raises some important points that we should explore.

For one thing, we say that learning is *demonstrated by* changes in behavior. The issue here is that learning is a process (like many others in psychology) that cannot be observed directly. In a literal sense, there is no way that I can directly observe, or measure, what you have learned. All I can measure directly is your performance, or your behavior. To determine if you have learned something, I must ask you to perform and then make inferences about your learning on the basis of your performance. Sometimes I may be wrong.

For example, you may learn everything there is to know about the psychology of learning for your next exam. But just days before your exam, someone you care about becomes seriously ill. As a result, you don't get much sleep. With your resistance weakened, you develop a sinus headache and catch the flu. When you come to class to take your exam, you have a high fever, feel miserable, and can't concentrate. You fail the exam. Your instructor may infer (incorrectly in this case) that you haven't learned very much about learning. On the other hand, there may be someone else in class who hasn't studied at all and has actually learned very little. But the exam is of the multiple-choice type, and she correctly guesses the answers to 90 percent of the questions. Now your instructor might infer (incorrectly again) that this student has learned a great deal.

One way to express the point we're making here is to say that what is learned is some *potential*, or predisposition, to respond. Because what is learned is simply potential, we will not recognize that learning has taken place until that potential is realized in behavior. (This issue will reemerge in our discussion of memory. What gets graded on most exams, after all, is not so much what you have learned as what you appear to have remembered.)

We also say that the changes that take place in learning must be *relatively permanent*. They are not fleeting, short-lived, or cyclical changes, such as those due to fatigue or temporary shifts in motivation.

Imagine, for example, that you want to study the behavior of a skilled typist. You are going to observe Sharon, a secretary who reportedly types 87 words per minute without error, where typing 60 to 65 words per minute is generally considered a good rate.

Early Monday morning you go watch Sharon type. You find her typing only 54 words per minute and making an error every other line. Disappointed, you seek out another typist, but are told that there is none better than Sharon. Two hours later, after pausing for breakfast, you return to Sharon's desk and now find her typing away at 91 words a minute without error! You wouldn't want to claim that between 8:15 and 10:15 on that Monday morning Sharon "learned" how to type. There's a better explanation for the change in behavior that you have observed. It's called *warm-up*. Sharon will probably go through this short-term, cyclical change in her behavior every Monday morning, and to a lesser degree on every other morning of the week. And it is *fatigue*, not forgetting, that would best account for her decreased typing skills if you were to watch her again at the end of the day. These are important changes in behavior, but they are not due to learning. Learned changes are relatively permanent.

We have another phrase in our definition to remind us that there are other, occasionally important, changes in our behavior that do not result from learning. We say, by definition, that learned changes in behavior result from *practice* or *experience*. For one thing, this phrase reminds us that some changes may be due to maturation (that is, heredity). The fact that birds fly, that salamanders swim, or that humans walk probably has more to do with genes and physical development than with learning and experience. This phrase also reminds us that those changes in our behaviors due to automatic physiological reactions, such as sensory adaptation, are not learned. When we enter a darkened theater, we don't really "learn" to see in the dark. Our vision improves and our behaviors change as our eyes adapt to the lighting in the theater. Consider your own behavior when you sit in a tub of hot water. Your behavior changes as you settle down and relax, as you adapt to the hot water—more of a physiological change than a learned one.

One final point about the nature of learning is worth mentioning. As students, parents, and teachers, we often fall into the habit of thinking that learning is necessarily a good thing. Clearly, it isn't always so. We can learn bad, ineffective habits as readily as we learn good, adaptive ones. For example, no one I know ever honestly claimed to enjoy the first cigarette that he or she smoked. Yet many people have learned the habit, which is hardly an adaptive one.

If we put these ideas together, we come up with our definition of learning: Learning is demonstrated by (or inferred from) a relatively permanent change in behavior that occurs as the result of practice or experience. In this topic and the next one, we will discuss two varieties of learning that we call *conditioning*. Although conditioning and learning are not technically synonymous terms, they can be used interchangeably. For the sake of simplicity, we will follow common usage here and agree to call the most basic, fundamental types of learning "conditioning."

Changes in behavior that are due to learning can be traced to practice or experience. Tigers learn to sit and stand on stools. They learn behaviors that are at odds with what may come naturally for tigers.

**BEFORE
YOU GO
ON**

How do we define learning?

PAVLOV AND A CLASSIC DEMONSTRATION

When we think about learning, we generally think about such activities as memorizing the Bill of Rights, studying for an exam, or learning to *do* things, like ice skate. But our study of learning begins in the laboratory of a Russian physiologist who taught dogs to salivate in response to tones. How salivating dogs could be relevant to college students may be difficult to imagine at first, but the relevance soon will become apparent.

Psychology was just beginning to emerge as a science late in the nineteenth century. At this time, Ivan Pavlov, a physiologist, was studying the

Ivan Pavlov (seated) watches a dog in one of his laboratory's testing chambers.

basic processes of digestion—work for which he was awarded the Nobel Prize in 1904. Focusing on the salivation reflex in dogs, Pavlov knew that he could produce salivation in his subjects by forcing food powder into their mouths. A **reflex** is defined as an unlearned, automatic response that occurs in the presence of a specific stimulus. Every time Pavlov presented the food powder, his dogs salivated.

reflex *an unlearned, automatic response that occurs in the presence of specific stimuli*

Pavlov's reputation in psychology stems from the fact that he pursued something not so simple as reflexive responses. He noticed that occasionally, his dogs would salivate *before* the food was put in their mouths. They would salivate at the very sight of the food or even at the sight of the laboratory assistant who delivered the food. With this observation, Pavlov went off on a tangent that he pursued for the rest of his life (Pavlov, 1927; 1928). We now call the phenomenon he studied **classical conditioning**—a type of learning in which an originally neutral stimulus comes to elicit a new response after having been paired with another stimulus that reflexively elicits that same response. In his honor, we sometimes call this type of learning Pavlovian conditioning.

classical conditioning *learning in which an originally neutral stimulus comes to elicit a new response after having been paired with a stimulus that reflexively elicits that same response*

To demonstrate classical conditioning, we first need a stimulus that consistently produces a predictable response. The relationship between this stimulus and the response it evokes is usually a natural, unlearned, reflexive one. Given this stimulus, the same response always follows. Here is where Pavlov's food powder comes in. If we present the food powder, the salivation response reliably follows. There is no learning in this reflexive association, so we call the stimulus an **unconditioned stimulus (UCS)** and the response that it elicits an **unconditioned response (UCR)**. So now we have a UCS (food powder) producing a UCR (salivation).

unconditioned stimulus (UCS) *in classical conditioning, a stimulus (for example, food powder) that reflexively and reliably evokes a response (the UCR)*

To get classical conditioning under way, we need a second, *neutral stimulus* that, when presented, produces a minimal response or a response of no particular interest. For this neutral stimulus, Pavlov chose a tone.

unconditioned response (UCR) *in classical conditioning, a response (for example, salivation) reliably and reflexively evoked by a stimulus (the UCS)*

At first, when a tone is sounded a dog *will* respond. It will, among other things, perk up its ears and try to orient toward the source of the sound. We call this response an **orienting reflex**. After awhile, however, the dog will get used to the tone and essentially will ignore it. Technically, we call this process **habituation** and say that the dog habituates to the tone. *Habituation is itself a simple variety of learning*—essentially, the dog learns *not* to orient toward the tone.

orienting reflex *the simple, unlearned response of orienting toward, or attending to, a new or unusual stimulus*

habituation *in classical conditioning, a simple form of learning in which an organism comes to ignore a stimulus of no consequence*

Now we are ready to go. We have two stimuli—a tone that produces a minimal response of no particular interest and food powder (UCS) that reliably produces salivation (UCR).

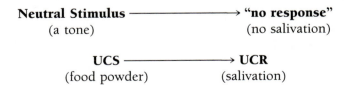

Neutral Stimulus ⟶ **"no response"**
(a tone)   (no salivation)

UCS ⟶ **UCR**
(food powder)   (salivation)

Once we get our stimuli and responses straight, the rest is easy. The two stimuli are paired. That is, they are presented at about the same time—the tone first, then the food powder. The salivation occurs automatically in response to the food powder. So we have a neutral stimulus, then a UCS, which is followed by UCR, or tone-food-salivation.

Neutral Stimulus   +   **UCS** ⟶ **UCR**
(a tone)   (food powder)   (salivation)

Each pairing of the two stimuli may be considered a conditioning *trial*. If we repeat this procedure a number of times—for a number of trials—conditioning, or learning, takes place. We find a relatively permanent change in behavior as a result of this experience. After a number of trials, when we present the tone by itself, the dog salivates, something it did not do before. Now the dog salivates not just in response to the food powder, but also in response to the tone. Clearly, the tone is no longer "neutral." Because of conditioning, it produces a response, so we now call the tone a **conditioned stimulus (CS)**. To keep the salivation response that it elicits separate from the salivation we get in response to the food powder, we call it a **conditioned response (CR)**, indicating that it has been conditioned, or learned.

CS ⟶ **CR**
(a tone)   (salivation)

conditioned stimulus (CS) *in classical conditioning, an originally neutral stimulus (for example, a tone) that, when paired with a UCS, comes to evoke a new response (a CR)*

conditioned response (CR) *in classical conditioning, the learned response (for example, salivation) evoked by the CS after conditioning*

Let's review this one more time: (1) We start with two stimuli—the neutral stimulus, which elicits no response, and the UCS, which elicits the UCR. (2) We repeatedly present the two stimuli together. (3) We find that when we present the CS alone, it now elicits a CR.

What you must realize is that the same type of stimulus—a tone, for example—can be either a neutral stimulus (before learning occurs), or a conditioned stimulus (when it elicits a learned response). Similarly, the same type of response—say, salivation—can be either an unconditioned response (if it is elicited without learning) or a conditioned response (if it is elicited as the result of learning).

If you have a pet at home, you've no doubt seen this very process in action. If you keep your pet's food in the same cabinet all the time, you may note a full range of excited, anticipatory behaviors by your pet every time you open that cabinet door. The open cabinet door (CS) has been repeatedly paired with the food within it (UCS), now producing the same sort of reaction (CR) that was originally reserved only for the food (UCR).

Shortly we'll look at how classical conditioning influences human reactions, but before we go on, let's make it clear that classical conditioning is not something that only occurs in dogs and cats. You, too, demonstrate a classically conditioned salivation response (particularly when you're hungry) when you see pictures or smell the aromas of your favorite foods. And, if you respond with anxiety at the sight of your instructor entering the classroom with a stack of exam papers, you are demonstrating a classically conditioned response.

Before we examine some of the procedures associated with classical conditioning, we need to consider two technical points. These two points remind us that even fundamental psychological processes are not quite as simple as they first appear. First, the CR seldom reaches the strength of the UCR no matter how many times the CS and the UCS are paired. For example, in Pavlov's demonstration, we never get as much saliva in response to the tone (salivation as a CR) as we originally got in response to the food powder (salivation as a UCR).

Second, *how* the conditioned stimulus and the unconditioned stimulus are paired does matter. If you think about it, you'll realize that there are many ways in which two stimuli can be presented at about the same time (e.g., simultaneously, or UCS then CS, or CS then UCS, with varying time intervals in between). Of the alternatives, one method consistently seems to work best: The CS comes first, followed shortly (within a second) by the UCS, or tone-food-salivation again. (I tell my classes that Pavlovian conditioning is basically a matter of "ding-food-slobber.")

BEFORE YOU GO ON

Summarize the essential procedures involved in classical conditioning.

CLASSICAL CONDITIONING PHENOMENA

Now that we have the basics of classical conditioning in mind, we can consider some of the details that go along with it—some of the procedures developed in Pavlov's laboratory. We'll first see how a classical conditioning experiment actually proceeds. Just to keep our terminology firmly in mind, we'll continue to refer to the original Pavlovian example of salivating dogs.

Acquisition

acquisition *the process in classical conditioning in which the strength of the CR increases with repeated pairings of the CS and UCS*

The stage of classical conditioning during which the strength of the CR increases—where a dog acquires the response of salivating to a tone—is called **acquisition**. When conditioning begins, the conditioned stimulus (CS) does not produce a conditioned response (CR), which is why we refer to it as a neutral stimulus at this point. After a few pairings of the CS and UCS together (conditioning trials), we can demonstrate the presence of a CR. To do that, of course, we'll have to present the conditioned stimulus (CS) by itself. Now we discover that there is some saliva produced in response to the tone presented alone. The more trials of the CS and UCS together, the more the dog will salivate in response to the tone when it is presented alone. Over repeated trials, the increase in CR strength (here, the amount of saliva in response to the tone) is rather rapid at first, but soon starts to slow and eventually levels off. The first part of Figure 5.1 illustrates this acquisition phase of a classical conditioning demonstration.

Extinction and Spontaneous Recovery

Assume that we now have a dog producing a good deal of saliva at the sound of a tone. Continuing to present the CS + UCS pair adds little to the amount of saliva we get when we present the tone alone. Now suppose that we go through a series of trials during which the CS (the tone) is presented but is *not* paired with the UCS (no more food powder). The result of this procedure is that the CR will weaken. As we continue to present the

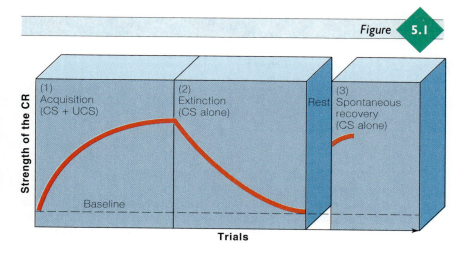

Figure 5.1

The stages of conditioning. (1) Acquisition is produced by repeated pairings of the CS and the UCS. The strength of the CR increases rapidly at first and then more slowly. (2) Extinction is produced by presenting the CS without the UCS. The strength of the CR decreases. (3) After a rest interval, spontaneous recovery produces a partial return of the CR.

tone alone, the dog provides less and less saliva. If we keep it up, the dog will eventually stop salivating to the tone. This process is called **extinction**, and we say that the CR has extinguished.

It would appear that we're right back where we started. Because the CR has extinguished, when we present the tone, our dog does nothing—at least it no longer salivates. Let's give our dog a rest and return it to the kennel for awhile. When the dog is returned to the laboratory and the tone is sounded, the dog salivates again! Not a lot, perhaps, but the salivation does return, or recover. Since it recovers automatically, or spontaneously, we call this phenomenon **spontaneous recovery**. Extinction and spontaneous recovery are also illustrated in Figure 5.1.

Spontaneous recovery takes place after extinction and following a rest interval, which indicates two things. First, one series of extinction trials may not be sufficient to eliminate a conditioned response. Because of the possibility of spontaneous recovery, to get our dog to stop salivating altogether, we may have to run a series of extinction trials. Second, what is happening during extinction is not literally "forgetting"—at least not in the usual sense. It seems that the response is not forgotten so much as it is *suppressed*. That is, the learned salivation response is still there, but it is not showing up in performance during extinction; which is why it can (and does) return later, in spontaneous recovery.

extinction *the process in classical conditioning in which the strength of the CR decreases with repeated presentations of the CS alone (without the UCS)*

spontaneous recovery *the phenomenon in classical conditioning in which a previously extinguished CR returns after a rest interval*

BEFORE YOU GO ON

In classical conditioning, what are acquisition, extinction, and spontaneous recovery?

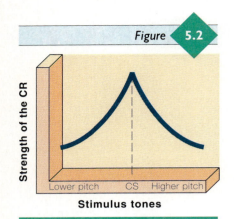

Figure ◄ 5.2

Strength of the CR

Lower pitch   CS   Higher pitch

Stimulus tones

Generalization. Presenting stimuli other than the CS may produce a CR. How much CR is produced depends on the similarity between the new stimulus and the original CS.

generalization *the phenomenon in classical conditioning in which a CR is elicited by stimuli different from, but similar to, the CS*

discrimination *the phenomenon in classical conditioning in which an organism learns to make a CR in response to only one CS but not to other stimuli*

Generalization and Discrimination

During the course of conditioning, assume that we consistently use a tone of a given pitch as the conditioned stimulus. After repeated pairings of this tone with food powder, a dog salivates when the tone is presented alone.

What will happen if we present a different tone, one that the dog has not heard before? Typically, the dog will salivate in response to it also. This response may not be as strong as the original CR (again, there may not be as much saliva). How strong it is depends on how similar the new tone is to the original CS. The more similar it is to the original, the more saliva will be produced. This process is called **generalization**, and we say that a conditioned response will generalize to other new, yet similar, stimuli.

This is a powerful process. It means that an unconditioned stimulus need not be paired with all possible conditioned stimuli. If you choose an average, or mid-range, CS, the conditioned response will automatically generalize to many other similar stimuli. Conditioning trials do not have to be applied over and over again for separate stimuli. A graph of this process is presented in Figure 5.2. Imagine that a young boy is bitten by a large black Labrador retriever. Originally, this dog was a neutral stimulus, but having been paired (associated) with the trauma and pain of a bite, the dog is now feared by the boy (a conditioned response). Is it not predictable that the boy's conditioned fear will generalize to other large black dogs—and, to a lesser extent, to small gray ones?

So if a dog is conditioned to salivate to a tone of middle pitch, it will also salivate to higher and lower tones through generalization. What if we do not want it to? What if we want our dog to salivate to the CS alone and *not* to other tones? We would use **discrimination** training, a process in which an organism learns to make a CR in response to only one CS but not to other stimuli. In a sense, discrimination is the opposite of generalization. To demonstrate discrimination training, we would present a dog with many tones, but would pair the UCS food powder with only one of them—the CS we want the dog to salivate to. We might, for example, pair the food powder with a tone of middle C. A lower tone, say A, would also be presented to the dog, but *would not* be followed by food powder. At first, there probably would be some saliva produced in response to the A tone (generalization). Eventually, however, our subject would learn to discriminate and would no longer salivate to the A tone.

Some discriminations may be too difficult to make. One of Pavlov's students conditioned a dog to salivate to a stimulus circle. The circle was paired with food powder, and after awhile the dog learned to salivate when the CS circle was presented. When the dog was then presented with a stimulus in the shape of an ellipse, the dog salivated—generalization again. The circle and the ellipse were then presented many times. Now the circle was always followed by food powder; the ellipse never was. Eventually, the dog learned to discriminate, salivating only to the circle and never to the ellipse. This procedure was repeated, gradually changing the shape of the oval to make it rounder and more similar to the conditioned stimulus circle. Still, the circle was always followed by food powder; the ellipses were not.

At one point, the dog could no longer discriminate between the two stimuli. The oval now looked too much like the circle. Because it was unable to discriminate between the two stimuli, we might predict that the dog would simply salivate to both of them. However, the behavior of the animal in this situation changed markedly. It stopped salivating altogether. It began to bark and whimper and tried to escape.

To Pavlov, the dog appeared very nervous and anxious. The dog was being asked to make a discrimination that it could not make. It was in a conflict. Pavlov referred to the dog's reactions as *experimental neurosis,* claiming that ". . . in short, it presented all the symptoms of acute neurosis" (Pavlov, 1927, p. 291). Whether or not the reaction of this laboratory animal gives us insight about neuroses in humans is open to debate. Do we develop anxiety and nervousness simply because we are unable to make the proper discriminations among stimuli? The situation is probably not that simple, but as Barry Schwartz (1984, p. 128) says, it is tempting to think of neurosis in such terms, and if nothing else, "What Pavlov's demonstration showed is that a very specific, isolated conditioning experience can transform the general behavior of an animal. It is not implausible that some human neuroses might stem from particular conditioning experiences of this sort."

BEFORE YOU GO ON

In classical conditioning, what are generalization and discrimination?

THE SIGNIFICANCE OF CLASSICAL CONDITIONING: WHAT ABOUT PEOPLE?

It is time to leave our discussion of dogs, tones, salivation and Pavlov's laboratory. We need to turn our attention to the practical application of all this. We can find examples of classically conditioned human behaviors all around us. Indeed, we can find here ample support for the observation made in Topic 1A that "psychology has practical application in the real world."

In the Laboratory

Of one thing we can be sure: We easily can bring the procedures of classical conditioning directly into the human learning laboratory. Here's a laboratory demonstration that you can do with a friend. Have your subject seated at a desk, relaxed, and staring straight ahead. Position a drinking straw just off to the side of your subject's face so that it cannot be seen. (Getting your subject to relax and stare ahead under these conditions is the only difficult part of this procedure.)

Your UCS (unconditioned stimulus) will be a strong puff of air through the straw into your subject's eye. The obvious UCR (unconditioned response) will be an involuntary, sudden blink of the eye. For a conditioned stimulus, just tap on the desk. After a brief habituation period, your subject will not respond to your tap, and you'll be ready to go. Remember the best sequence: CS-UCS-UCR, or tap-puff-blink. Repeat this procedure a dozen times or so and then present the CS alone. Tap on the desk and your subject will (should) respond with the CR (conditioned response) by blinking to the tap on the desk.

This *does* qualify as conditioning. There will be a relatively permanent change in your subject's behavior as a result of the experience of pairing together a tap and a puff of air to the eye. As it happens, this is not a particularly useful or significant sort of learning—the response here is rather trivial—but it is learning.

Conditioned Emotional Responses

One of the most significant aspects of classical conditioning is its role in affecting our emotional responses to stimuli in our environment. There are very few stimuli that naturally, or instinctively, produce an emotional response. Yet think of all those things that *do* directly influence how we feel.

For example, very young children seldom seem afraid of spiders, plane rides, or snakes. (Some children actually seem to enjoy each of these.) Now consider how many people you know who *are* afraid of these things. There are many stimuli in our environments that cause us to be afraid. There are stimuli that produce within us feelings of pleasure, calm, and ease.

What scares you? What makes you feel relaxed and at ease? Why? Might you not feel particularly upset or distressed in a certain store because you once had an unpleasant experience there? Might you fondly anticipate a vacation at the beach because of a very enjoyable vacation you had there as a child? Do you shudder at the sight of a police car? Do you smile at the thought of a payroll envelope? In each of these cases, we are talking about classical conditioning. (To be fair, we must say that not all of our learned emotional reactions are acquired through classical conditioning alone. As we shall see in Topic 5B, there are other possibilities.)

When I was a senior in high school, I agreed to have surgery on my nose. (A somewhat clumsy child, I had broken it a number of times.) I won't bore you with all the details of the operation. Suffice it to say that the surgery was done under local anesthetic and was painful, messy, and altogether unpleasant. That surgery was performed many years ago, but to this day, when I visit a hospital I get a slight ache in my nose. Now, I know better. I know that the pain is just "in my head," but my nose still hurts! What is happening here is that I am being reminded of some relatively permanent classical conditioning. The CS of hospital sights, sounds, and odors was paired with the UCS of an operative procedure that caused a UCR of pain and discomfort. This pairing, which lasted for a number of days, led to the establishment of a CR of discomfort associated with the CS of the hospital. Notice that this conditioned response *generalized* to many other hospitals, not just the one in which the surgery was performed. And the conditioned response has obviously lasted a long time.

Here's another example: Assume that I have before me two small boys, each 3 years old. I ask them to say quickly, out loud, everything they think of when I say a word. I say "dog." Boy 1 smiles broadly and responds, "Oh, doggie; my doggie; Spot; my friend; good dog; go fetch; friend; my dog; Spot." Boy 2 frowns and responds, "Oooo dog; bite; teeth; blood; bad dog; hurts me; bad dog." Now both of these boys know what a dog *is*. How

Until they are classically conditioned to feel otherwise, many children enjoy playing with spiders, snakes, bugs, and caterpillars.

Words mean different things to different people. For example, young children who have pleasant experiences with dogs will probably have pleasant thoughts and feelings about dogs as they grow older.

they feel about dogs is another matter and is quite obviously a function of their experience with dogs—a classically conditioned emotional reaction.

Advertising provides us with many examples of attempts to use classical conditioning to change the way we feel about products or services. How many times have you seen TV ads showing healthy, good-looking young people having a great time—at the beach playing volleyball, riding bicycles down mountain trails, swinging on ropes over cool streams, and so on—while drinking large amounts of brand X. All those attractive, "fun" stimuli are designed to make us "feel good." The intent of pairing "fun stimuli" (here the UCS) with brand X (the CS) is to have us acquire a "feel-good" response (CR) to the beverage being advertised. We can analyze television commercials in other ways as well, but claiming that the procedures of conditioning are at work here is quite reasonable.

BEFORE YOU GO ON

What sorts of responses are most readily influenced by classical conditioning? Give examples.

The Case of "Little Albert"

Let's take a somewhat detailed look at a famous example of the conditioning of an emotional response. In 1920, John B. Watson (yes, the founder of behaviorism) and his student assistant, Rosalie Rayner, published a summary article on a series of experiments they performed with "Little

Albert." Albert's experiences have become quite well known, and even though Watson and Rayner's summary of their own work tended to over-simplify matters (Samuelson, 1980), the story of Little Albert still provides a good model for the classical conditioning of emotional responses.

Eleven-month-old Albert was given many toys to play with. Among other things, he was allowed to play with a live white rat. Albert seemed to enjoy the rat; he certainly showed no signs of fearing it. Then conditioning began. One day, just as Albert reached for the rat, one of the experimenters (Rayner) made a sudden loud noise by striking a metal bar with a hammer. The loud noise was frightening—that much Watson and Rayner had established two months earlier during initial observations of Albert in the laboratory. At least Albert made responses that Watson and Rayner felt indicated fear.

After repeated pairings of the rat and the noise, Albert's reaction to the rat underwent a relatively permanent change. Now when presented with the rat, Albert would at first start to reach out toward it, then he would recoil and cry, often trying to bury his head in his blanket. He was clearly making emotional responses to a stimulus that did not elicit those responses before it was paired with sudden loud noises. This sounds like classical conditioning: The rat is the CS and the loud sudden noise is the UCS that elicits the UCR of an emotional fear response. After repeated pairings of the rat and the noise (the CS and UCS), the rat elicits the same sort of fear response (or CR). Figure 5.3 presents a diagram of the procedures used to condition Little Albert to be afraid of a white rat.

It seemed clear to Watson and Rayner that Little Albert's conditioned fear of a white rat had generalized to a brown rabbit.

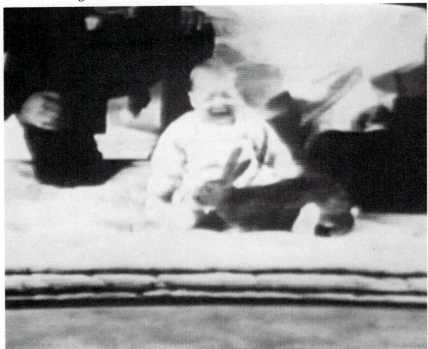

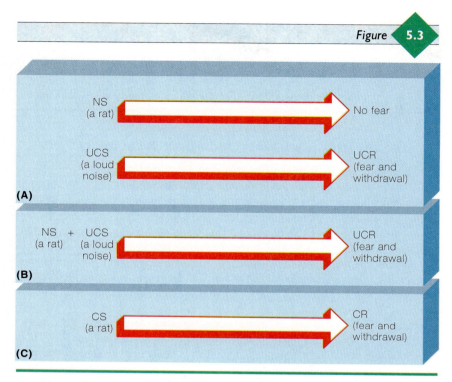

Figure 5.3

(A)

NS (a rat) → No fear

UCS (a loud noise) → UCR (fear and withdrawal)

(B)

NS (a rat) + UCS (a loud noise) → UCR (fear and withdrawal)

(C)

CS (a rat) → CR (fear and withdrawal)

Conditioned fear in "Little Albert" as an example of classical conditioning.

Watson and Rayner then went on to demonstrate that Albert's fear of the white rat *generalized* to all sorts of other stimuli: a dog, a ball of cotton, and even a mask with a white beard and mustache. In some instances, however, Watson and Rayner did not test for generalization as they should have. They occasionally paired the loud noise (UCS) with new stimuli before testing to see what the reaction might be (Harris, 1979).

Several issues have been raised concerning the Watson and Rayner demonstration of learned fear—not the least of which is the unethical treatment of poor little Albert. It is unlikely that anyone would even attempt such a project today. Watson had previously argued (1919) that emotional experiences of early childhood could affect an individual for a lifetime, yet here he was purposely frightening a young child (and without the advised consent of his mother). In fact, Albert's mother removed him from the hospital before Watson and Rayner had a chance to undo the conditioning. They were convinced that they could remove Little Albert's fear, but as fate would have it, they never got the chance. It should also be mentioned that a number of researchers who tried to replicate Watson and Rayner's experiment, despite ethical considerations, were not totally successful (Harris, 1979).

Even with all these technical disclaimers, it is easy to see how the Little Albert demonstration can be used as a model for describing how fear and other emotional responses can develop. When they began their project, Albert didn't respond fearfully to a rat, cotton, or a furry mask. After a few trials of pairing a neutral stimulus (the rat) with an emotion-producing stimulus (the loud noise), Albert appeared afraid of a number of white, furry, fuzzy objects.

Briefly summarize the Little Albert experimental demonstration.

Intense Irrational Fears and Their Treatment

There are many things in this world that are life-threatening and down-right frightening. Being afraid of certain stimuli is often a very wise, rational, and appropriate reaction. If, for example, you are walking in the downtown center of a large city late at night and you are approached by three huge thugs dragging motorcycle chains and holding knives, you are likely to feel a reaction of fear.

Occasionally, however, we find people who experience discomforting, distressing fears of stimuli that are *not* threatening in a real or rational sense. Some people are intensely afraid of flying on airplanes, of elevators, of heights, of small closed-in areas, of spiders, or of the dark. Psychologists say that these people are suffering from a **phobic disorder**—an intense, irrational fear of some object that leads a person to avoid contact with it. There are many possible explanations for how phobic disorders become established, but one clear possibility, of course, is classical conditioning.

This explanation suggests that an individual experiences an intense and natural emotional response to a powerful, emotion-producing stimulus—perhaps some traumatic event, such as a severe injury or an accident. When such an emotion-producing stimulus occurs in the presence of another, neutral stimulus, the pairing may result in the formation of a conditioned fear response to the originally neutral stimulus. As a working example, let's imagine a youngster at a local carnival becomes separated from his parents and gets swept away by a large crowd into a tent where clowns are performing. The child is (sensibly) very frightened by the separation from his parents, and after they are reunited, requires considerable reassurance before he settles down. Should we be terribly surprised if this child—even much later as an adolescent or an adult—appears to be irrationally afraid of carnivals, circuses, or clowns? Certainly not, if one believes that classical conditioning can account for the formation of phobic fears.

Sadly enough, phobic disorders are far from uncommon. Best-guess estimates place prevalence rates at between 7 and 20 percent of the population—that's tens of millions of people (Marks, 1986; Robins et al., 1984). Note that phobic reactions seldom extinguish on their own. Why not? There are a few reasons, but one is that someone with a phobia is usually successful at avoiding the conditioned stimulus that elicits the fear. Someone with a fear of flying simply may be able to get by driving or taking a bus or train. Although there are a number of different techniques that can be used to treat phobic disorders (see Topic 13B, p. 623), one of the most common is based directly on principles of Pavlovian conditioning. The procedure, called **systematic desensitization**, was introduced over 30 years ago by therapist Joseph Wolpe (1958; 1969; 1981). Let's review how this process works. You can easily see classical conditioning at work here.

phobic disorder *a psychological disorder in which a person suffers from an intense, irrational fear of an object or situation that leads the person to avoid it*

systematic desensitization *the application of classical conditioning procedures to alleviate anxiety in which anxiety-producing stimuli are paired with a state of relaxation*

In its standard form, there are three stages of systematic desensitization. First, the therapist instructs the subject to relax. There are many ways to go about such training. Some procedures use hypnosis, but most simply have the subject relax one foot, then both feet, then one leg, then both, and so on, until the whole body is relaxed. No matter what method is used, this phase generally doesn't take very long, and after a few hours of training at the most, the subject knows how to enter a relaxed state quickly.

The second step is to construct an "anxiety hierarchy"—a list of stimuli that gradually decrease in their ability to elicit anxiety. The most feared, most anxiety-producing stimulus is placed at the top of the list (for our example subject, that might be "clowns," followed by "carnival," "circus," "mimes," and so on). Each item that follows elicits less and less fear until, at the bottom of the list, we place stimuli that elicit no fear at all.

Now treatment is ready to begin. The subject relaxes completely and thinks about the stimulus lowest on the anxiety hierarchy. The subject is then instructed to think about the next highest stimulus, and the next, and so on, all the while remaining as relaxed as possible. As progress is made up the list toward the anxiety-producing stimuli at the top, the therapist constantly monitors the subject's tension/relaxation level. When anxiety seems to be overcoming relaxation, the subject is told to stop thinking about that item on the hierarchy and to think about an item lower on the list.

Systematic desensitization is more than just the simple extinction of a previously conditioned fear response. A new response (relaxation) is being acquired to "replace" an old one (fear). The process is called *counterconditioning*. The logic is quite obvious. A person cannot be relaxed and anxious at the same time—these are incompatible responses. So, if I pair a stimulus (the CS) with the feeling associated with being relaxed (the UCS), through classical conditioning it will come to produce a reaction of calm (a new CR), not the incompatible response of tension and anxiety (the old CR). For many people, this technique can be effective (e.g., Wilson, 1982). It works best for those anxieties or fears that are associated with easily identifiable, specific environmental stimuli; it works least well for a diffuse, generalized fear, for which hierarchies are difficult to generate.

A phobic fear of heights is one conditioned emotional response that can be lessened with systematic desensitization.

BEFORE YOU GO ON

What is a phobic disorder?
How is systematic desensitization used to treat phobic disorders?

RETHINKING WHAT HAPPENS IN CLASSICAL CONDITIONING

As you read this topic on classical conditioning, you may very well get the impression that what we are describing here is only of historical interest.

After all, most of our discussion has dealt with procedures and phenomena that we associate with Pavlov's laboratory soon after the turn of the century. Psychologists' interest in classical conditioning did not begin and end with Pavlov's lab, however. In fact, Pavlovian conditioning has been and continues to be a very active area of research in experimental psychology (Domjan, 1987; Rescorla 1987, 1988; Spear, Miller, & Jagielo, 1990).

Psychologists today are interested in understanding precisely what happens during classical conditioning. They want to understand the factors that influence the effectiveness or efficiency of the procedure. In this section, we'll review a few approaches to research in classical conditioning. If nothing else, the points raised in this section should remind you of two of the themes we mentioned back in Topic 1A: (1) Nothing is as simple as it may first appear; and (2) we should always keep in mind the fact of our animal nature.

Just What *Is* Learned in Classical Conditioning?

Pavlov believed, and so did generations of psychologists who followed him, that *any* stimulus paired with an unconditioned stimulus could effectively serve as a conditioned stimulus. It's easy to see how psychologists came to this conclusion. A wide variety of stimuli *can* be paired with food powder and as a result come to elicit a salivation response. It also seemed very reasonable to characterize Pavlovian conditioning as essentially a matter of "stimulus substitution" in which one stimulus (the CS), through conditioning, comes to substitute for another (the UCS). The long-standing belief was that any neutral stimulus that was paired with a UCS could become a CS, *and* it was further understood that the time interval between the CS and the UCS had to be very brief.

We now see conditioning in a much broader light. Conditioning is now viewed as the learning of relationships that exist among events in the world. Conditioning is seen as an active search for sensible ways to represent the environment, a search for information that one stimulus gives about another (Rescorla, 1988; Spear et al., 1990). Robert Rescorla puts it this way: "Pavlovian conditioning is not a stupid process by which the organism willynilly forms associations between any two stimuli that happen to co-occur. Rather, the organism is better seen as an information seeker using logical and perceptual relations among events, along with its own preconceptions, to form a sophisticated representation of its world" (1988, p. 154). What we need to do now is see just what this new thinking about classical conditioning really means, and where it came from. We'll look at two related issues: the nature of an effective CS, and the timing of the CS-UCS pairing.

Can *Any* Stimulus Serve as a CS?

At least two lines of research suggest that one cannot just present *any* stimulus with an unconditioned stimulus and expect conditioning to result. One research program is associated with Robert Rescorla, the other with Leon Kamin. Let's deal with Rescorla's data first (1968, 1987).

A rat can be conditioned to fear the sound of a tone by presenting that tone and consistently following it with a mild electric shock. It doesn't take many of the tone-shock pairings for the conditioned response (fear of tone) to develop. This is a straightforward example of classical conditioning. Assume that we present a second rat with a tone, occasionally following it with a mild shock. But for this rat, we also simply present the shock from time to time *without the preceding tone*. Now this rat might end up with quite a few shocks without a preceding tone, but it will have as many tone-shock pairings as our first rat. Will this second rat demonstrate any conditional response to the tone when the tone is presented alone? No, it won't. Even though this rat experienced the same number of tone-shock pairings, there will be no conditioning. A related phenomenon can be found in Kamin's research (1968, 1969).

In a demonstration of a phenomenon called *blocking*, rats are shocked (UCS) at the same time a noise (CS) is presented. Classically conditioned fear of the noise is readily established. The rats are then presented with a number of trials in which the noise *and* a light (a new "compound" CS) are paired with the UCS of a shock. Even though the light (now presented with the noise) is paired with the shock several times, no conditioned fear of the light can be found. That is, when the light is now presented to these rats *by itself*, no fear reaction can be detected. The light remains a neutral stimulus. The rats had already learned that noise was a good predictor of shock; the light was redundant.

In both these cases (and others; see, e.g., Miller & Spear, 1985; Pearce & Hall, 1980; Rescorla & Wagner, 1972), it seems that what matters most in determining whether a stimulus will act as a CS is *the extent to which that stimulus provides useful information or predicts (or signals) the occurrence of another stimulus*. In the basic Pavlovian demonstration, the tone was highly informative: Every time the tone was presented, food powder followed, and in this case the tone was an effective CS. In Rescorla's experiments, we see that if a tone does not reliably predict the onset of shock (if some shocks occur without a signaling tone), then that tone will not be an effective CS no matter how many times it is paired with the UCS. And in Kamin's experiments, we see that because the rats had already learned that the noise predicted the onset of shocks, adding the light as a potential CS provided no additional useful information and hence was ineffective.

Let's take just a bit longer to recast this discussion in human terms. If we can talk about rats representing their environment by learning which stimuli are likely to signal or predict others, isn't it reasonable to think about classical conditioning in humans in a similar vein? We experience a pleasant, warm feeling when we see a picture of a beach because it is the beach that is best associated with our favorite vacation—not the fact that we happened to have left on a Wednesday. Beaches predict fun and good times; Wednesdays don't. We have not learned to associate the fireplace with the pain of being burned, even though we may have first been burned when we placed our hand into the fire there. Although Little Albert's fear generalized to many stimuli, Albert developed no particular fear of blankets, even though he was sitting on a blanket each time Raynor created the unpleasant loud noise that Albert did associate with the rat.

Now, let's consider two additional complications that have arisen in our search to understand the basic process of classical conditioning: the fact that the CS and the UCS do not always have to be paired close together in time, and the fact that some responses seem easier to condition than others.

*Under what circumstances are stimuli
likely to serve effectively as CSs?*

Must the Time Interval Between the CS and UCS Always Be Brief?

Pavlov recognized that the time interval between the CS and the UCS was a critical variable in classical conditioning. For nearly 50 years, it was generally assumed that the best interval between the CS and UCS was a very brief one (about 4 seconds for salivary conditioning (Gormezano, 1972) and about 0.5 second for eye blink conditioning (Beecroft, 1966)). The claim found in most textbooks on learning was that the shorter the interval between the CS and UCS, the faster conditioning would be. It now appears that there is at least one excellent example of classical conditioning in which the CS-UCS interval may be much longer than just a few seconds—even hours long. This example also reinforces the point that some stimuli make more effective conditioned stimuli than others. The example is found in the research on the formation of aversions (very strong dislikes) to certain tastes.

Many experiments have confirmed that both rats and people can be classically conditioned to avoid particular foods (Garcia et al., 1966; Gemberling & Domjan, 1982; Revulsky & Garcia, 1970). In the experiments using rats, subjects eat or drink a food that has been given a distinctive taste. Then they are also poisoned, or treated with X rays, so that they will develop nausea. However, the feelings of nausea do not occur *until hours after the food has been eaten.* (In a few days, the rats are perfectly normal and healthy again.) Even though there has been a long delay between the flavored food (CS) and the feelings of nausea (UCS), the rats learn to avoid the food, often in just one trial. Similarly, children being treated for cancer may experience nausea as an unpleasant side effect of chemotherapy. Such children will often show a strong taste aversion for whatever they ate hours before their treatment—even if what they ate was something pleasant, like ice cream (Bernstein, 1978).

The time delay between the CS and the UCS here is obviously at odds with the standard belief that, to be effective, the CS and the UCS need to be paired together in time. Another difficulty centers on why the *taste* of previously eaten food should so commonly serve as the CS for nausea that occurs hours later. That is, why is the nausea associated with the taste of food instead of some other stimulus event that could be paired with the nausea? Think of this experience happening to you. You go to a restaurant and order a piece of pumpkin pie. Hours later, you suffer severe stomach cramps and nausea. Why should you associate these with the pie and not the type of chair you sat on, or the color of the car you drove to the restaurant, or the person you ate with? As it happens, we may have a predisposition or bias, rooted in our biology, for associating some things with others, particularly if they have a functional basis (Mackintosh, 1975,

1983; Revulsky, 1985). Food followed by nausea is an excellent example of just such a predisposed association.

BEFORE YOU GO ON

What do taste aversion studies tell us about the relationship between the CS and UCS in classical conditioning?

APPLYING CLASSICAL CONDITIONING TO YOUR STUDY OF PSYCHOLOGY

Every so often, it is a good idea to pause and reflect on the psychology you have been reading to see if you can find a practical application for what you have been learning about. As we come to the end of this topic, now might be just such a time. We've spent a lot of time discussing Pavlov and salivating dogs. By now you should be convinced that classical conditioning also applies to humans. Is there an example of how classical conditioning can be relevant for studying psychology?

One thing that many how-to-study books recommend is that students find one special place to do most of their studying. This place may be at home or somewhere on campus, but the suggestion is usually given that some location be reserved *only* for studying. Behind this idea is the logic of classical conditioning.

Recommending that students find a special place for studying is based on the observation that even common locations in our environment can act as conditioned stimuli and can come to elicit conditioned responses. It

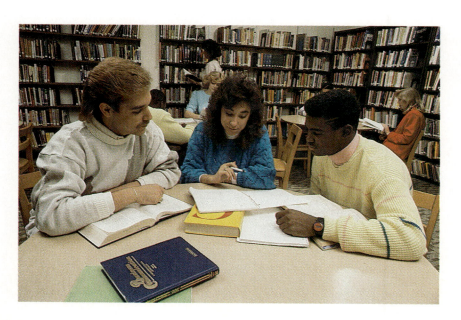

If at all possible, it is best to condition yourself to study in just a few locations, reserved only for that purpose. The campus library is one recommended location for studying.

wouldn't be a good idea to recommend studying in bed, for example. Being in bed has been associated with anything but studying—being sick perhaps, or just sleeping. Studying at the kitchen or dining room table is seldom a good idea either, for the same sort of reason: Those places have been conditioned to a different set of responses (eating) that are not compatible with effective studying.

You should try to study in the same place or, at most, two or three places. Try to do nothing there but study. For this purpose, college libraries serve very well. It makes excellent sense to slip into an unused classroom during the day to study. There is an advantage to studying and learning in the same physical environment in which you will be tested later. (We'll return to this point in Chapter 6.)

BEFORE YOU GO ON

Why is it recommended that only a few locations be used for studying?

Learning is a process that cannot be observed directly. It is inferred from our observation of relatively permanent changes in behavior (or performance) that occur as the result of practice or experience. In this topic, we have reviewed the procedures of classical, or Pavlovian, conditioning. We have seen that one of the major applications of Pavlovian conditioning is its role in eliciting emotional behaviors. Many of the stimuli to which we respond emotionally do not elicit those responses naturally or reflexively; they do so through classical conditioning. In other words, many of the stimuli in our environments that give rise to pleasant or unpleasant feelings do so because they have been previously paired with more inherently pleasant or unpleasant experiences or situations. We have looked at other ways in which classical conditioning can have an impact on our daily lives. In the next topic, we move on to consider other types of learning.

SUMMARY

How do we define learning?

Learning is demonstrated by a relatively permanent change in behavior that occurs as a result of practice or experience. We may define "conditioning" similarly, as it is a basic form of learning. / *page 193*

Summarize the essential procedures involved in classical conditioning.

In classical, or Pavlovian, conditioning, a neutral stimulus that originally does not elicit a response of interest is paired with an unconditioned stimulus (UCS), one that reflexively and reliably produces an unconditioned response (UCR). As a result of this pairing, the once-neutral stimulus becomes a conditioned stimulus (CS) and elicits a conditioned response (CR) that is the same kind of response as the original UCR. / *page 196*

In classical conditioning, what are acquisition, extinction, and spontaneous recovery?

In classical conditioning, acquisition is an increase in the strength of the CR that occurs as the CS and the UCS continue to be presented together, whereas extinction is a decrease in the strength of the CR that occurs when the CS is repeatedly presented without being paired with the UCS. Spontaneous recovery is demonstrated by the return of the CR after extinction and a rest interval. / *page 197*

In classical conditioning, what are generalization and discrimination?

In generalization, we find that a response (CR) conditioned to a specific stimulus (CS) will also be elicited by other, similar stimuli. The more similar the new stimuli are to the original CS, the greater the CR. In many ways, discrimination is the opposite of generalization. It is a matter of learning to make

a CR in response to a specific CS, which is paired with a UCS, while learning not to make a CR in response to other stimuli, which are not paired with a UCS. / *page 199*

What sorts of responses are most readily influenced by classical conditioning? Give examples.

Classical conditioning has its most noticeable effect on emotion and mood, or affect. Most of the stimuli to which we respond emotionally have probably been classically conditioned to elicit those responses, called conditioned emotional responses. / *page 201*

Briefly summarize the Little Albert experimental demonstration.

In the Watson and Rayner 1920 "Little Albert" demonstration, a sudden loud noise (the UCS) was paired with the neutral stimulus of a white rat. As a result, Albert came to display a learned fear response (a CR) to the originally neutral rat. The conditioned fear also generalized to other, similar stimuli. This demonstration has been used to explain learned emotional reactions to events in our environments. / *page 204*

What is a phobic disorder? How is systematic desensitization used to treat phobic disorders?

A person with a phobic disorder suffers from an unusually intense, irrational fear, which is assumed to have been learned, probably through classical conditioning. Systematic desensitization uses counterconditioning, training a person to relax and stay relaxed while thinking about a hierarchy of stimuli that are more and more likely to elicit anxiety or fear. If relaxation can be conditioned to thoughts of anxiety-producing stimuli, the sense of calm will replace the competing response of anxiety. / *page 205*

Under what circumstances are stimuli likely to serve effectively as CSs?

Pavlov, and many others, believed that any stimulus could serve effectively as a conditioned stimulus (CS) if it were repeatedly paired with an unconditioned stimulus (UCS). We now believe that this is an oversimplification. Those stimuli that are most effective as CSs are those that best or most reliably predict or signal the UCS. Stimuli are effective conditioned stimuli only if they provide useful information to the organism; for example, a shock *is* going to follow this tone. / *page 208*

What do taste aversion studies tell us about the relationship between the CS and UCS in classical conditioning?

Taste aversion studies, in which subjects develop a strong dislike and avoidance of a particular taste, tell us that the time interval between the CS and UCS may be very long, even hours. This result is in conflict with early conclusions that classical conditioning progressed most rapidly with very short CS-UCS intervals (seconds or fractions of a second). They also provide evidence for the observation that some behaviors are more easily, or more naturally, conditioned than others. Associating nausea with the taste of food is more "natural," for example, than associating it with other stimuli. / *page 209*

Why is it recommended that only a few locations be used for studying?

Environmental settings may be classically conditioned to produce predictable conditioned responses (sleeping in the bedroom, eating in the dining room, for example). These learned responses may be incompatible with studying and learning. If one designates a special place as a study area, responses conducive to good study should become associated with that area. / *page 210*

Operant Conditioning and Beyond

Why We Care: A Topic Preview

In Topic 5A, we discussed classical conditioning. Remember our original definition: Conditioning is demonstrated by a relatively permanent change in behavior that occurs as a result of practice or experience. In classical conditioning, we noted that relatively permanent changes in behavior can arise through the pairing of two stimuli, a CS and a UCS. As a result of this pairing, the CS comes to elicit a response that it did not elicit originally, called a CR. In this topic, we will examine other ways in which behaviors can be changed through learning. We care about these processes for the same reason we cared about classical conditioning: They help us understand how organisms come to feel, think, and behave as they do. Our behaviors may be rooted in our biology, but they are subject to modification. Our discussion of just how behaviors can be modified continues now as we consider operant conditioning and other, more cognitive approaches to learning.

In operant conditioning, the basic premise is that behaviors are influenced by the consequences they produce. Learning is a matter of increasing the rate of those responses that produce positive consequences and decreasing the rate of responses that produce negative consequences. We'll see in this topic that many human behaviors can be understood in terms of operant conditioning. We will begin by defining some of the terminology of operant conditioning. Because the concept of reinforcement is so important in operant conditioning, we'll spend a good deal of time examining some of the varieties and principles of reinforcement. Then we'll discuss a related process: punishment.

We can say that classical and operant conditioning are behavioristic in orientation. They focus on observable events (stimuli) in the environment and on observable behaviors (responses) of the learner. The data from many experiments, and from our own experiences, suggest that there can be more to learning than the formation of simple associations between stimuli (S-S) or between stimuli and responses (S-R). There are occasions when describing learning only in terms of observable stimuli and responses seems overly simplistic.

In a broad sense, it now is time for us to consider the nature of the learner in addition to considering the nature of stimuli and responses. Such approaches go by a variety of different labels, but we may refer to them all as being basically cognitive. That means that these approaches emphasize the mental processes (cognitions) of the organism involved in the learning task. These approaches focus on learning that involves the acquisition of information or knowledge, which then may or may not be reflected in behavioral changes. A good deal of your learning as a student can be thought of in this way. You have altered many of your cognitions on the basis of your

(continued)

SUMMARY

What is the essence of operant conditioning?

Operant conditioning is that type of learning in which the probability or rate of a response is changed as a result of its consequences. Reinforced responses increase in rate, while nonreinforced responses decrease in rate. / page 216

What is shaping, and how does it work? Describe acquisition, extinction, and spontaneous recovery as they occur in operant conditioning.

Shaping is a procedure used in operant conditioning to establish a response that can then be reinforced—that is, to get the response that we want to occur in the first place. We shape a response by reinforcing successive approximations to that response. In operant conditioning, acquisition is produced by reinforcing a desired response so that its rate will increase. Extinction is the phenomenon of decreasing the rate of a response (to return to baseline levels) by withholding reinforcement. After a rest interval, a previously extinguished response will return to a rate above baseline; that is, in the same situation, it will spontaneously return or recover. / page 218

Give an operational definition of a reinforcement. Distinguish between a positive and a negative reinforcer.

In general, reinforcement is a process that increases the rate or probability of the response that it follows. A positive reinforcer increases the rate of the response that precedes its presentation. Negative reinforcers increase the rate of the response that precedes their removal or termination. / page 221

Compare and contrast primary and secondary reinforcers, and give examples of each.

Primary reinforcers are stimuli that are in some way biologically important or related to an organism's survival, such as food for a hungry organism or a warm shelter for a cold organism. Secondary reinforcers increase the rate of a response because of the organism's previous learning experience. That is, secondary reinforcers, such as praise, money, letter grades, or promotions, are acquired reinforcers. / page 222

Define FR, FI, VR, and VI intermittent schedules of reinforcement.

Intermittent schedules of reinforcement provide a reinforcer for less than each and every response. The FR (fixed-ratio) schedule calls for a reinforcer after a set number of responses (for example, one reinforcer after every five responses). A VR (variable-ratio) schedule randomly changes the ratio of reinforcers to responses but maintains some given ratio as an average. The FI (fixed-interval) schedule calls for the administration of a reinforcer for the first response after a specified time interval. A VI (variable-interval) schedule calls for a reinforcer for the first response after a time interval, where the length of that time interval is randomly varied. In general, responses reinforced by fixed schedules are more resistant to extinction than responses that have been reinforced every time they occur (which is a CRF, or continuous schedule of reinforcement). Responses acquired under variable schedules of reinforcement are even more resistant to extinction than are those acquired by fixed schedules. / page 226

What is a punisher? How can punishers be used effectively?

A punisher is a stimulus that decreases the rate or probability of a response that it follows. Punishers can be effective in suppressing a response when they are strong enough and delivered immediately after the response to be punished. Fear, anxiety, aggression, and an overall suppression of behavior may accompany punishment, which in itself provides no information about what an organism should do in a given situation. Punishing one response should, thus, be paired with the reinforcement of another, more appropriate response. / page 227

In the context of operant conditioning, what are generalization and discrimination?

In operant conditioning, generalization occurs when a response reinforced in the presence of one stimulus also occurs in the presence of other, similar stimuli. Discrimination, on the other hand, is a matter of differential reinforcement: reinforcing responses to some stimuli while extinguishing responses to other (inappropriate) stimuli. / page 229

What is instinctive drift, and what does it tell us about the limits of conditioning?

Instinctive drift is the term used by the Brelands to note that some behaviors are more difficult to condition than others. That is, in spite of conditioning efforts, an organism will "drift" toward doing what comes naturally. / page 231

What is a learning set?

A learning set is an acquired strategy of how to go about learning in an effective manner. Harlow refers to the development of learning sets as "learning to learn." Through repeated experience with a particular learning task, one develops an effective (cognitive) strategy for dealing with similar tasks that are encountered in the future. / page 232

What is learned when one forms a cognitive map? What is latent learning?

According to Tolman, when one acquires a cognitive map, one develops a mental representation (or picture) of one's surroundings—an appreciation of general location and where objects are located. The formation of a cognitive map can be viewed as a type of latent learning. That is, latent learning is the acquisition of information (an internal, cognitive process) that may not be demonstrated in performance until later, if at all. / page 235

Summarize the basic concepts of social learning theory and modeling.

Bandura's social learning theory emphasizes the role of observation of others and imitation in the acquisition of cognitions and behaviors. We often learn by imitating models through vicarious reinforcement and punishment. / page 237

How can operant conditioning and cognitive approaches be used to improve your study skills?

Effective studying should be reinforced. Students can modify their own studying behaviors by also supplying reinforcers at appropriate times. Cognitive approaches suggest that one should imitate successful models (students who do well) and use each class as an opportunity to develop useful learning sets. / page 238

6

MEMORY: REMEMBERING AND FORGETTING

TOPIC 6A   The Nature of Memory

TOPIC 6B   Retrieval and Retrieval Failure

The Nature of Memory

Why We Care: A Topic Preview

It's nearly impossible to imagine what life would be like without memory. For one thing, this sentence in your textbook would make no sense. Without your memory, you'd have no idea of what a textbook is or why you had it open in front of you. The black patterns of print that you now recognize as words would appear to be no more than random marks. In fact, without memory, we would have no idea of who we are. As a student, your major concern with memory right now may be to do whatever you can to remember as much as possible for your next exam. Surely, we care about memory in an academic, study-learn-test, sense. But the importance of memory goes well beyond classroom exams. All of those things that define us as individuals—our feelings, beliefs, experiences, behaviors, moods, and attitudes—are stored away somehow in our memories. There are few psychological processes that are as central to our sense of self and to our perception of the world as memory, and that is why we care.

Over the past 30 years, there have been some significant changes in the way that psychologists think about memory. Psychologists are prepared to accept the notion that memory may not be just one unified structure or process; there may be a number of types or levels of memory. Contemporary views imply that all the information stored in memory does not necessarily get processed in the same way or get stored in the same place. There may very well be two or three (or more) memory processes or storehouses. This basic idea provides the centerpiece for our discussion in this topic.

A second significant change in thinking about memory reflects the idea that memory is not simply a passive receptacle of information. One's use of memory is now viewed as an active process, whereby information is actively processed into memory, stored there, and then actively retrieved.

This topic will focus on the process of getting information into one's memory and storing it there. First, we'll formulate a working definition of memory. Then we'll explore the possibility that there are different kinds of memory, what these types of memory might be, and how they function. Topic 6B will deal with the practical matter of retrieval, or getting that information out of our memory when we want it.

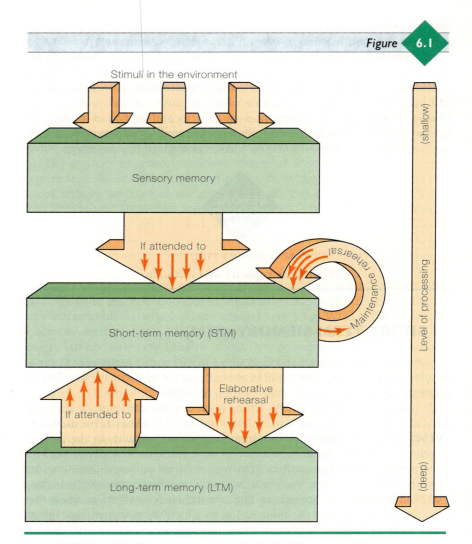

Figure ◆ **6.1**

A simplified model of human memory. See text for description.

The Duration of STM

Interest in short-term memory processing can be traced to two experiments reported independently in the late 1950s (Brown, 1958; Peterson & Peterson, 1959). We'll review the Petersons' experiment.

On a typical trial, a subject is shown three consonants, such as KRW, for 3 seconds. Presenting the letters for 3 seconds assures that they are attended to and, hence, encoded into STM. The subject is asked to recall the three letters after retention intervals ranging from 0 to 18 seconds. This doesn't sound like a very difficult task, and it isn't. Anyone can remember three letters for as long as 18 seconds. However, in this experiment, subjects are prohibited from rehearsing the letters during the retention interval. They are given a "distractor" task to perform right after they see the letters. They are asked to count backward, by threes, from a three-digit number supplied by the experimenter.

Figure **6.2**

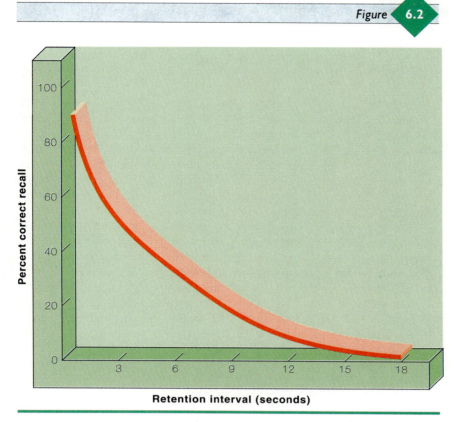

Retention interval (seconds)

Recall of letters as a function of retention interval when maintenance rehearsal is minimized. (Peterson & Peterson, 1959)

For example, if you were a subject, you would be shown a letter sequence, say KRW, and then you immediately would have to start counting backward from, say, 397 by threes, or "397, 394, 391, 388," and so forth. You'd be instructed to do your counting out loud and as rapidly as possible. The idea is that the counting task prohibits you from rehearsing the three letters you were just shown.

Under these conditions, your correct recall of the letters depends on the length of the retention interval. If you are asked to recall the letters after just a few seconds of counting, you won't do too badly. If you have to count for as long as 15 to 20 seconds, your recall of the letters drops to almost zero (see Figure 6.2). Because you cannot rehearse them and are distracted by the counting task, the letters are soon unavailable to you.

This experimental example is not as abstract as it may first appear. Consider this scenario. Having studied psychology for three hours, you decide to reward yourself and have a pizza. You decide to splurge and have the pizza delivered (having heard this afternoon that Pizza City offers free delivery). Never having called Pizza City before, you turn to the yellow pages to find the number: 555–5897. You repeat the number to yourself: 555–5897. You close the phone book and return it to the desk drawer. You dial the number without error. Buzzz- buzzz-buzzz-buzzz. Darn, the line's busy! Well, you'll call back in a minute.

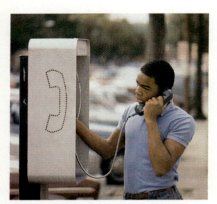

If we are not interrupted, we can easily hold a telephone number in STM long enough to dial it.

maintenance rehearsal *a process of rote repetition (reattending) to keep information in STM*

Many mathematical operations require that we use STM to hold information until we can use it in our calculations.

Just as you hang up the phone, the doorbell rings. It's the paper boy. You owe him $11.60 for the past two weeks' deliveries. Discovering that you don't have enough cash on hand to pay for the paper *and* a pizza, you write a personal check. "Let's see, today's date? What is today's date? 10–15–91. How much did you say I owed you? Oh yes, $11.60, plus a dollar tip, comes to $12.60. This is check number 1079; I'd better write that down: 1079. There you go. Thanks a lot."

The paper boy leaves, and you return to your studying. Then you recall that you were going to order a pizza. Only five or six minutes have passed since you got a busy signal from Pizza City. As you go to dial the phone, however, you cannot for the life of you remember the phone number. Back to the yellow pages. A number once attended to became active in your short-term memory long enough for you to use it. When you were kept from rehearsing it, and when other numbers entered STM as interfering information, that number was soon inaccessible.

One way in which we can increase or stretch the duration of short-term memory is to rehearse the information stored there. The type of rehearsal we use simply to keep material active in our short-term memory is called **maintenance rehearsal**, or rote rehearsal, which amounts to little more than simple repetition of the information already in our STM. To get material into STM (encoding), we have to attend to it. By repeating that material over and over (as we might if we wanted to remember a telephone number until we could dial it), we are essentially reattending to it with each repetition.

So one characteristic of STM is that it does not store information for very long. By attending to information, we *do* keep it available well beyond the limits of sensory memory. As a rule of thumb, we can say that, if left unrehearsed, material will stay in STM for about 15 to 20 seconds. Actually, what experiments like the Petersons' tell us is that once in short-term memory, some information may become unavailable almost immediately. Once encoded into STM, it may take 20 seconds for all of it to be lost. That's better than sensory memory, but short-term memory, by itself, still won't help much when it comes to taking an exam next week.

At least the duration of STM is long enough to allow us to use it occasionally in everyday activities. Again, the telephone number example is relevant. Usually all we want to do with a phone number is remember it long enough to dial it. Not too often do we feel the need to make a permanent record of a telephone number.

Using STM in mathematical computations is another good example, particularly when we do those computations "in our head." Multiply 28 by 6 without paper and pencil. "Let's see. Eight times 6 is 48. Now I have to keep the 8 and carry the 4." Stop right there. Where do you "keep the 8" and where do you store the 4 until it is needed? Right. In your STM. And, for that matter, where did the notion that 8 x 6 = 48 come from in the first place? Where did the notion of what "multiply" means come from? How did *this* information get into STM? Right, again. This is an example of information entering STM, not "from the outside," through our senses, but from long-term storage (see Figure 6.1 again).

Yet another example of STM in action is in the processing of language. As you read one of my longer sentences, such as this one, it is useful to have a short-term storage place to keep the beginning of the sentence that you are reading in mind until you finally get to the end of the sentence, so that you can figure out the basic idea of the sentence, before deciding whether or not anything in that sentence is worth remembering.

Having discussed the duration of short-term memory, let's deal now with its capacity. Just how much information can we hold in STM for that 15 to 20 seconds?

BEFORE YOU GO ON

For how long is information stored in STM?
What is required to get material into STM and then keep it there?

The Capacity of STM

In 1956, George Miller wrote a charming paper on "the magical number seven, plus or minus two." In it, he argued that the capacity of our short-term memories is very small—limited to just 5 to 9 (or 7 ± 2) bits or "chunks" of information.

In the context of short-term memory, the concept of chunk is a rather technical term. A **chunk** is the representation in memory of a meaningful unit of information. And the claim is that we can store approximately 7 ± 2 meaningful pieces of information in STM. You should also notice that adding the notion of chunking to our discussion significantly affects our ability to specify the capacity of STM with any precision. In other words, "chunk" is an imprecise measure of capacity (Anderson, 1980a).

We can easily attend to, encode, and store five or six letters in STM. Holding the letters YRDWIAADEFDNSYE in your short-term memory would be quite a challenge. Fifteen randomly presented letters exceed the capacity of STM for most of us. What if I asked you to remember the words *Friday* and *Wednesday*? Now keeping just these two simple *words* in STM is very easy—even though they contain (the same) 15 letters. Here, you would be storing just 2 chunks of (meaningful) information, not 15. In fact, you easily could store *50* letters in short-term memory if you recoded them into the one meaningful chunk: "days of the week."

As we all know, we can readily store a telephone number in our short-term memory. Adding an area code makes the task somewhat more difficult because the 10 digits now come fairly close to the upper limit of our STM capacity. Notice, though, how we tend to cluster the digits of a telephone number into a pattern. The digit series 2194935661 is more difficult to deal with as a simple string than when it is seen and encoded as a phone number: (219) 493-5661 (Bower & Springston, 1970). Regrouping the digits in this way lets us see them in a new, more meaningful way.

So, by chunking bits and pieces of information together, we can add meaningfulness to what we are attending to and thus extend the apparent capacity of short-term memory. Here's one last example. Can you hold this number in your STM: 49162536496481? The 14 digits here are beyond the capacity of most people's short-term memory. But if you recognize these as a series of numbers, each being the *square* of the digits 2 through 9 (4/9/16/25/36/49/64/81), the task is an easy one because you have chunked

chunk *a somewhat imprecise concept referring to a meaningful unit of information as represented in memory*

Chunking information together while listening to a lecture is an effective way to store it for later study.

(and recoded) the material in a meaningful way. Using a similar system of chunking digits into meaningful clusters, one student demonstrated an ability to recall more than 80 randomly presented digits (Ericsson & Chase, 1982).

In any event, short-term memory works something like a leaky bucket. From the vast storehouse of information available in our sensory memory, we scoop up some (and not much at that) by paying attention to it and hold it for a while until we either use it, maintain it with rehearsal, move it on to long-term storage, or lose it.

BEFORE
YOU GO
ON

How much information can be held in STM?
How can chunking affect the capacity of STM?

How Information Is Represented in STM

The material or information stored in our sensory memory is held there in virtually the same form in which it was presented. Visual stimuli are represented as visual memories or impressions, auditory stimuli form auditory memories, and so on.

We recognize that getting information into STM is not necessarily an automatic process. We first have to attend to the material to encode it into short-term memory. How, then, is information stored or represented in STM?

Conrad (1963, 1964) was one of the first to argue that information is stored in STM with an acoustic code. What that means is that material tends to be processed in terms of how it *sounds*. Conrad's conclusion was based on his interpretation of the errors that subjects make in short-term memory tasks.

For example, in one experiment, he presented a series of letters to his subjects. The letters were presented *visually*, one at a time, and then subjects were asked to recall the letters they had just seen. It was not surprising that the subjects made many errors over the course of the experiment. What *was* surprising was that when subjects responded with an incorrect letter, it was very frequently with a letter that *sounded* like the correct one. For example, if subjects were supposed to recall the letter E and failed to do so, they would commonly recall V, G, or T, or a letter that sounded like the E they were supposed to recall. They rarely responded F, which certainly looks more like the E they had just seen than does V, G, or T. (By the way, this is true whether the subjects gave their recall orally or in writing.)

Experiments by Baddeley (1966) made the same point, but with a different technique. In these experiments, subjects were asked to recall short lists of common words. Some lists were made up of words that all sounded alike (e.g., man, ban, pan, fan, can). Other lists contained words that had similar meanings; that is, they were semantically alike (e.g., large, huge, giant, big, enormous). A third type of list contained a random assortment of words. Lists were only five words long and, hence, were within the capacity of short-term memory. The lists that were the most difficult to recall were those that contained acoustically similar items (that is, the "man, ban" list). Baddeley's argument is that the acoustic similarity caused confusion within STM, whereas semantic similarity did not.

It seems, then, that using short-term memory is a matter of talking to ourselves. No matter how it is presented, we tend to encode and process information acoustically, the way it sounds. At least that's what most of the early evidence seemed to suggest. Subsequent research has not changed the view that acoustic coding is the most important method of coding for STM. However, it is possible that some material may be encoded in STM in other ways—being represented visually or semantically, for example (Cooper & Shepard, 1973; Martindale, 1981; Shulman, 1971, 1972; Wickens, 1973). Perhaps the most we can say at the moment is that there is a tendency to rely heavily on the acoustic coding of information in short-term memory, but other codes also may be used.

BEFORE YOU GO ON

What evidence do we have that information tends to be encoded acoustically in STM?

LONG-TERM MEMORY (LTM)

Long-term memory (LTM) is memory as you and I usually think of it—memory for large amounts of information held for long periods of time. As we did for sensory and short-term memory, we'll begin by considering two basic issues: capacity and duration.

Our own experiences tell us that the capacity of our long-term memories is huge—virtually limitless. At times we may even impress ourselves with the amount of material we have stashed away in LTM (for instance, when we play Trivial Pursuit or TV game shows). Just how much can be stored in human memory may never be measured, but we can rest assured that there is no way we will ever learn so much that there won't be room for more.

For an example of memory's huge capacity, consider an experiment by Standing, Conezio, and Haber (1970). Over the course of five days, they presented 2500 different pictures to subjects and asked them to remember them all. Even a day or so later, subjects correctly identified, from a new collection of pictures, 90 percent of the ones they had seen before. Standing (1973) increased the number of pictures that subjects viewed to 10,000. (As you can imagine, it took a long time simply to view 10,000 pictures.) Again, subjects later correctly recognized more than 90 percent of them.

There seems to be no practical limit to the amount of information we can process (or encode) into long-term memory. (Getting that information out again when we want it is another matter, which we'll get to in Topic 6B.) How long will information stay in LTM once it is there? Assuming that you remain free from disease or injury, you are likely never to forget in-

long-term memory (LTM) *a type of memory with virtually unlimited capacity and very long, if not limitless, duration*

The capacity of our long-term memories seems almost limitless, which is especially apparent when we use LTM to play games such as Trivial Pursuit®.

formation such as your own name, your parents' names, or the words to "Happy Birthday to You."

At the moment, it is impossible even to imagine an experiment that could tell us with any certainty how long our memories remain stored in LTM. One thing we know for a fact is that we often cannot remember things we know we once knew. We do tend to forget things. The issue is *why*. Do we forget because the information is no longer *available* to us in our long-term memories, just not there any more? Or do we forget because we are unable to get the information out of LTM, which implies that the information is still available, but now somehow not *accessible*? And the problem is, "How can we ever be sure that a memory failure is due to the relevant information being unavailable and hence inaccessible under all conceivable conditions rather than just merely being inaccessible under the prevailing conditions?" (Watkins, 1990, p. 330).

Most psychologists believe that once information is processed into LTM, it stays there until we die. In fact, in a survey published in 1980, 84 percent of the psychologists who were asked agreed with the statement that "everything we learn is permanently stored in the mind, although sometimes particular details are not accessible" (Loftus & Loftus, 1980, p. 410). In this view, forgetting is a failure of *retrieval* of stored information.

Have you ever handed in an exam paper, walked out of the classroom, and suddenly realized very clearly the answer to an exam question you could not think of minutes before while you were taking the exam? This sort of experience reinforces the notion that memories may be available but not always accessible. How pleasant (or, perhaps, unpleasant) it is to think that everything we ever knew, everything that ever happened to us, is still there someplace, ultimately retrievable if we only knew how to get it out.

As intriguing as this view may be, there is reason to believe that it is not totally accurate. A review article by Elizabeth and Geoffry Loftus (1980) raised again the issue of the relative permanence of long-term memories. The Loftuses reviewed the data supporting the argument for permanence and found that "the evidence in no way confirms the view that all memories are permanent and thus potentially recoverable" (p. 409). They claim that the bulk of such evidence is neither scientific nor reliable. They further claim that when we think we are recalling specific memories of the long-distant past, we are often reconstructing a reasonable facsimile of the original information from bits and pieces of our past. That is, when we do remember something that happened to us a long time ago, we don't recall the events as they actually happened. Instead, we recall a specific detail or two and then *actively reconstruct* a reasonable story, a process that in itself creates new memories. But even if we do reconstruct new recollections of past experiences, that would not necessarily mean that our original memory was no longer available. It might only suggest that we can maintain several versions of the same event in long-term memory (McCloskey & Zaragoza, 1985).

A number of implications of this line of research have practical importance. One of the most obvious is in the area of eyewitness testimony. If it is in fact true that long-term memories are not permanent and that they can be distorted or replaced by information processed later, we may be forced to reconsider the weight given to eyewitness testimony in courts of law (e.g., Buckhout, 1975; Clifford & Lloyd-Bostock, 1983; Loftus, 1984; MacLeod & Ellis, 1986; McCloskey & Egeth, 1983).

What do the "experts" say about eyewitness testimony? On what issues would psychologists be willing to go to court themselves and claim that valid, scientific evidence exists? Just this question was recently put to 113 researchers who had published data on eyewitness testimony (Kassin, Ellsworth, & Smith, 1989). Statements about eyewitness testimony that these experts claim are reliable and accurate are presented in Figure 6.3 (p. 258).

We have a sense of the nature of long-term memory's capacity and duration of storage. Now we need to address the issue of how long-term memories are formed. We'll also see that there may be several different types of LTM.

Inaccurate eyewitness testimony indicates that our long-term memories are not perfect and are subject to distortion. On the basis of eyewitness testimony the man on the bottom was imprisoned for 5 years for a crime committed by the man on the top.

BEFORE YOU GO ON

Are long-term memories necessarily permanent?

Encoding in LTM: A Matter of Repetition and Rehearsal

We already have seen how simple repetition (maintenance rehearsal) can be used to keep material active in short-term memory. This sort of rehearsal is also one way to move information from STM to LTM. Within limits, the more one repeats a bit of information, the more likely it will be remembered—beyond the limits of short-term memory. Although there *are* circumstances when this is true, in many cases the simple repetition

Figure **6.3**

STATEMENTS ABOUT EYEWITNESS TESTIMONY WITH WHICH THE "EXPERTS" AGREE.

1. An eyewitness's testimony about an event can be affected by how the questions put to the witness are worded.
2. Police instructions can affect an eyewitness's willingness to make an identification and/or the likelihood that he or she will identify a particular person.
3. Eyewitnesses' testimony about an event often reflects not only what they actually saw but information they obtained later on.
4. An eyewitness's confidence is not a good predictor of his or her identification accuracy.
5. An eyewitness's perception and memory for an event may be affected by his or her attitudes and expectations.
6. The less time an eyewitness has to observe an event, the less well he or she will remember it.
7. Eyewitnesses sometimes identify as a culprit someone they have seen in another situation or context.
8. The use of a one-person showup instead of a full lineup increases the risk of misidentification.
9. The rate of memory loss for an event is greatest right after the event, and then levels off with time.
10. White eyewitnesses are better at identifying other white people than they are at identifying black people.

From Kassin, Ellsworth, & Smith, 1989, pp. 1089–1098.

of information is not sufficient to process it into LTM. Simply attending to information—the essence of repetition—is an inefficient means of encoding information in long-term memory.

To get information into long-term memory usually requires more than simply repeating that information over and over. We need to think about it, reorganize it perhaps, form images of it, make it meaningful, or relate it to something already in our long-term memories. To get information into LTM we need to "elaborate" on it, to use the term proposed by Craik and Lockhart (1972). We need to process it more fully, using **elaborative rehearsal**.

Do you see how the distinction between maintenance and elaborative rehearsal can fit a model of memory that deals with levels of processing? When we do no more than attend to an item, our processing is fairly minimal, or shallow, and that item is likely to remain in memory for a relatively short time. The more we rehearse an item elaboratively, the deeper into memory it is processed. And indeed, the model claims, the more we can relate to new material, the more meaningful we can make it, and the more we can elaborate it (the deeper we can process it), the easier it will be to remember. Consider a hypothetical experiment in which subjects are asked to respond to a list of words in different ways. In one case, they are asked to count the number of letters in each word. In another they are asked to generate a word that rhymes with the one they are reading, and in a third case they are asked to use each word in a sentence. The logic is that in each case, the words were processed at an increasingly "deeper" level as subjects focused on (1) the simple, physical structure of the words,

elaborative rehearsal *a mechanism for processing information into LTM that involves the meaningful manipulation of the information to be remembered*

(2) the sounds of the words as they are said aloud, and (3) the meaning of the words and their role in sentence structure. In such an experiment, as processing increases, so does the recall of the subjects (Cermak & Craik, 1979; Craik & Tulving, 1975).

BEFORE YOU GO ON

Contrast elaborative rehearsal with maintenance rehearsal as a means of encoding information into long-term memory.

Are There Different Types of Long-term Memories?

Our own experiences tell us that the information we have stored away in LTM can be retrieved in many different forms. We can remember the definitions of words. We can picture or visualize people and events from the past. We can remember the melodies of songs. We can recall how our bodies moved when we first tried to ski or roller skate. It may be that information in our long-term memories is processed by different subsystems or types of LTM. Different kinds of information may be stored in different places by different processes. This notion of different LTM systems is a relatively new one in psychology, and as you might expect, there is no general agreement on just what all of the systems within LTM might be (Johnson & Hasher, 1987). Here, we'll briefly review four possible LTM systems.

Procedural Memory. Endel Tulving has suggested that the information we have stored in LTM is of three different types (1972, 1985, 1986). Although the three can and do interact with each other, he sees them as basically different. One type of long-term memory is called **procedural memory**. This is the lowest level of the three proposed by Tulving. Procedural memory enables "organisms to retain learned connections between stimuli and responses, including those involving complex stimulus patterns and response chains, and to respond adaptively to the environment" (Tulving, 1985, p. 387). In this memory, we have stored our recollections of learned responses, or chains of responses, to particular stimuli. Also stored here is our collection of patterned responses that we have learned well, such as how to balance and ride a bicycle, how to type, or how to swing a golf club. The memories we have stored here are generally put into use with virtually no effort. For example, at one time in your life, handwriting was difficult at best, as you strained to form letters and words correctly. But by now, your writing skills or "procedures" are so ingrained in procedural memory that you can retrieve the steps involved almost without thinking.

procedural memory *in LTM, where stimulus-response associations and skilled patterns of responses are stored*

Semantic Memory. A more complex type of memory is what Tulving calls **semantic memory**. In it we store all our vocabulary, simple concepts, and rules (including the rules that govern our use of language). Here we

semantic memory *in LTM, where vocabulary, facts, simple concepts, rules, and the like are stored*

Basic procedures or techniques, such as those required to ride a bicycle, are stored in procedural memory (top). The meanings and correct spellings of words are stored in semantic memory (middle). Life experiences, mundane and dramatic, are stored in episodic memory (bottom).

have stored our knowledge of ourselves and the world in which we live. In a way, our semantic memories are crammed with facts, both important and trivial, such as:

Who opened the first psychology laboratory in Leipzig in 1879?

How many stripes are there on the American flag?

Is "Colorless green ideas sleep furiously" a well-formed, grammatical sentence?

What do dogs eat?

If we can answer these questions, we have found those answers in our long-term semantic memories. The information, or answers, that we have stored in semantic memory seem to be stored there in an organized fashion. How semantic memory might be organized is an issue we'll explore in our next section.

Episodic Memory. The third type or system of memory proposed by Tulving is called **episodic memory**. It is here that we store the memories of our life events and experiences. It is a time-related memory, and in a sense, it is autobiographical. For example:

What were you doing the day the Challenger space shuttle exploded?

When and where did you learn how to ride a bike?

How did you spend last summer's vacation?

What did your dog eat yesterday?

The answers to these sorts of questions are stored in our episodic memories.

Metamemory. A fourth possibility for a long-term memory system is what John Flavell called **metamemory** (1971; Flavell & Wellman, 1977; Maki & Swett, 1987). Metamemory refers to our knowledge of how our own memory systems and subsystems work. If I were to ask you your mother's maiden name, you would know almost immediately whether or not you stood any chance of recalling that name. If I were to ask you to recall the maiden name of *my* mother, you probably wouldn't even begin to search your memory for that information. You just know that you don't know, and such is the function of one's metamemory. The concept of metamemory has become the focus of much research on the cognitive development of children. This research centers on how we come to appreciate the workings of our cognitive processes, including our memories, and how we learn new and more efficient strategies for using those processes (e.g., Flavell, 1979; Kail & Nippold, 1984).

BEFORE YOU GO ON

Name and briefly describe four possible systems or types of LTM.

The Organization of Semantic Long-term Memory

The capacity of our short-term memory is so small that if we wanted to retrieve an item from it, we easily could scan all the information stored there to find the item we were looking for. On the other hand, long-term memory has such a huge capacity that to engage in an exhaustive search of all the information we have stored there would be a very inefficient strategy for locating any particular piece. Fortunately, the information in semantic long-term memory tends to be stored in an organized fashion. On this point psychologists are in agreement. What is much less certain is just *how* the information in our semantic memories is organized. Although we cannot review all the possibilities here, we'll take a look at some of the hypotheses and data that have emerged concerning how we store information in our long-term memories.

Category Clustering. Just to give you an idea of what we mean when we talk about the organization of long-term memory, consider a classic study by W. A. Bousfield (1953). Bousfield showed that, in recall, we tend to group words together in conceptual categories, even if they were presented in a random order. He called this phenomenon **category clustering**. For example, subjects are presented with a list of words such as these: *Howard, spinach, zebra, plumber, Bernard, dentist, carrot, weasel, Edward,* and so on. There are 60 words on the list. After hearing the list, subjects are asked to write, in any order, as many of the words from the list as they can recall. Subjects are told nothing about the nature of the list of words, but it is in fact made up of 15 words from each of four different conceptual categories: animals, men's names, professions, and vegetables—which you may have noticed as you read the sample list.

When subjects recall such a list, they do a rather strange thing. They do not write down the words in a random order or in the order in which the words were presented, but they group them into categories. For example, a subject might write a number of men's names, then some animals, then a couple of professions, followed by a few vegetables. Then, at the end of the recall, the subject may just add a word or two from any category. Subjects recall many more words and form larger clusters when they are told about the organization in the list before it is presented. (This reinforces a point we alluded to earlier: Encoding influences retrieval.) Thus, one way in which words may be stored in long-term memory is by conceptual category. When we can sort and store information in categories, we do so.

Subjective Organization. What about words that do not fit so neatly into categories? How might they be organized? Research by Tulving shows just how powerful our tendency to organize verbal material is. He called the type of clustering that he studied **subjective organization**.

Tulving (1962) presented subjects with a list of 16 unrelated words to be learned and later recalled. He presented the same list to subjects over and over, each time in a different order until the list was learned. Because there was no organization in the list itself, any consistency at recall must reflect an organization imposed by the subject recalling the list. Tulving found a strong tendency for subjects to recall many words together, in the same sequence, on successive recall trials. Each subject tended to organize his or her own recall in his or her own way, consistently grouping clusters

episodic memory *in LTM, where life events and experiences are stored*

metamemory *in LTM, our stored knowledge of how our own memory systems work*

category clustering *at recall, grouping words together into categories even if they are presented in a random order*

subjective organization *the tendency of subjects to impose some order on their recall of randomly presented events or items*

of two or three words in the same order on different recall attempts, even though the items were always presented in a different order. Thus, it seems that even when categories are not readily available, we will still use some sort of organizational structure to guide our use of semantic memory.

Network Models. Collins and Quillian (1969) have proposed that semantic memories are organized in hierarchies of information. Approaches like that of Collins and Quillian are among what are called **network models** of memory. Figure 6.4 presents a very small segment of a possible network, or hierarchy, for a few of the words that you probably have in your semantic memory. At the top of this chart of semantic organization is the term *animal*. Associated with it are some of its defining characteristics: "has skin," "can breathe," "moves around." Below *animal* are found (among others) two concepts, *bird* and *fish*, each with its defining characteristics. Below this level we find even more specific examples, including *canary, robin, shark,* and *salmon*, each with its defining characteristics. It is possible, of course, to go even farther. That is, if you once had a canary named Pete, your semantic memory might include a level below *canary*, separating Pete and his (or her) characteristics from all other canaries. Or you might have a level above *animal* called *living things*.

This system looks quite complicated as presented in Figure 6.4, and in this figure we've left out many of the things that we know about animals, fish, birds, and canaries just to make it reasonably simple. Is there any evidence that memories are stored in this fashion? Yes, there is. Suppose I ask you the following questions and require that you respond yes or no.

1. Can canaries sing?
2. Do canaries have feathers?
3. Do canaries have skin?

I suspect that none of these questions gave you a hard time. But if we were to have measured how long it took you to answer each question, we might have found what Collins and Quillian found. The first was answered most quickly, the second took longer, and the third, longer yet. Each question required that you search a higher and higher level of memory to find the answer (singing is associated directly with canaries, feathers with birds in general, and skin with animals in general). An assumption of this model is that concepts can be clearly and neatly defined and then organized. Such is not always the case. (We'll look at this issue in some detail in Topic 7A.) The exercise we just went through for *canary* might yield different results if our example hadn't been such an obvious example of a bird (Rosch, 1973). How might you answer the same three questions if they dealt with an ostrich or a penguin?

Another network model is referred to as *spreading activation theory* and was introduced by Collins and Loftus in 1975. The basic idea is similar to that of Collins and Quillian, but it does not rely on a hierarchical, top-to-bottom sort of structure. Figure 6.5 shows a small segment of a spreading activation model for the concepts related to the target concept **fire engine**. Note that each concept in this structure can be related to several others. You'll also notice that the lines between items are not all the same length. The implication is that the shorter the line, the stronger the relationship between the two concepts. For example, the line between *Red* and *Sunsets* is much longer than that between *Red* and *Cherries*. The prediction is, then,

network models *organizational schemes that describe the relationships among meaningful units stored in semantic memory*

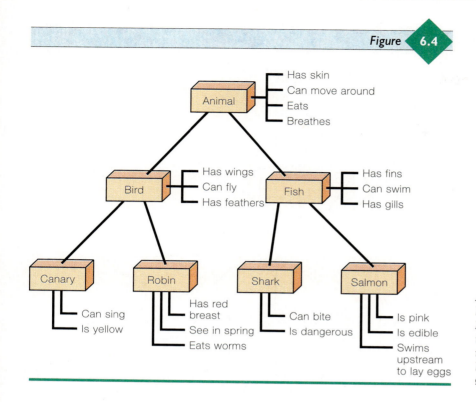

Figure 6.4

An illustration of how information may be organized in semantic memory. Members of a category are organized in a hierarchy. The information to be retrieved must be located within the hierarchy to be recalled. (Collins & Quillian, 1969.)

that if the concept *"Red"* becomes activated (if you think about red) then you are more likely to think about cherries than sunsets. Although there are problems with this model (McCloskey & Glucksberg, 1979), there is also research support suggesting that some concepts may be stored in this way (e.g., Kiger & Glass, 1983; Neely, 1977).

Yet another network model of semantic LTM is called **ACT theory** by its originator, John Anderson (1976, 1980b, 1983). (In this context, *ACT* stands for "adaptive control of thought.") According to this theory, what we have stored in long-term memory are interrelated *propositions*, not just words or simple concepts. In this theory, a proposition is an abstract notion indeed, but we can think of propositions as being short, simple sentences that can be judged as true or false. Examples include such propositions as "Canaries are birds." "Canaries can fly." "I have a canary." "My canary's name is Fred." "I bought Fred this morning." Anderson claims that we store these propositions in long-term memory. Notice how propositions can be typical of both semantic memory ("Canaries are birds") and episodic memory ("I bought Fred this morning").

ACT theory in its more recent form (called ACT★, read "ACT-star") goes a few steps further, suggesting that the propositions we have stored in memory are of two types: (1) *Declarative knowledge*, referred to as "knowing that." Declarative knowledge might include a proposition such as "My shoelaces are tied." This sort of information is stored in what Anderson calls declarative memory. (2) *Procedural knowledge*, referred to as "knowing how." Procedural knowledge might include the knowledge of how to go about tying one's shoes. This sort of information is stored in production

ACT theory *a network model of LTM (both episodic and semantic) that suggests that we store meaningful and related propositions that can be judged as true or false*

Figure 6.5

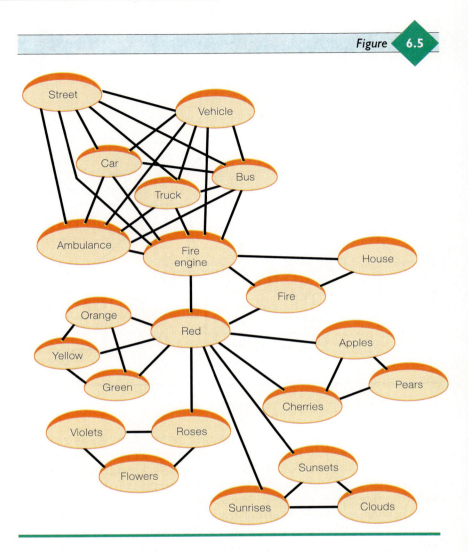

A spreading activation model representing reactions to the target concept "fire engine." The length of each line indicates the strength of the association between the concepts. (After Collins and Loftus, 1975.)

memory. Production memory stores propositions that relate a given condition to a specified action, such as "If red, then stop." "If green, then go." Or "If the nail still sticks up, then hit it again." This sort of information is usually quite difficult to put into words, which is one reason why Anderson believes that it is stored in a different kind of memory. Procedural knowledge is exactly the sort of information that Tulving claimed is stored in procedural memory, and Anderson's declarative knowledge is precisely what Tulving argues is stored in either our semantic or episodic memories (e.g., Anderson, 1983, 1986, 1987; Hunt, 1989).

It would be altogether improper to leave the impression that we know how words, concepts, and facts are organized in our semantic memories. We are quite sure that there *is* organization, but we have conflicting ideas about what that organization is. It may be categorical or hierarchical; it may be a series of interrelated networks of information. Perhaps the best description of how information is represented in long-term memory will reflect some combination of these approaches. On the other hand, our memories may be organized in ways not yet imagined.

BEFORE YOU GO ON

Briefly summarize ways in which information may be represented in long-term memory.

THE BIOLOGICAL BASES OF MEMORY

We may safely assume that memories of our experiences are stored in our brains. A very compelling logic suggests that as information is encoded, stored, and retrieved, there must be reliable changes in the structures or functions of the nervous system. The search for where and how memories are formed within the nervous system is not a new line of research, but within the last decade it has become one of the most exciting and most promising. We won't get into many of the details, but we will take a brief look at some of the research aimed at discovering the biological foundations of memory.

What We've Learned from the Study of Brain Damage

Karl Lashley (1890–1958), a student of John B. Watson, spent over 30 years trying to find the particular part of the brain in which memories are stored. Lashley taught rats, cats, and monkeys to negotiate all sorts of complex mazes. He then systematically removed or lesioned (cut) portions of the learner's cerebral cortex. Having destroyed a part of brain, he tested his subject's memory for the previously learned task. What Lashley found was quite unexpected (Lashley, 1950). It sparked a surge of research that still continues. Lashley discovered that specific memories have no specific location in the brain. When he went looking for a memory in the brain to lesion, he could not find one. What he did find was that, in general, the more brain tissue he destroyed, the more impaired the organism's performance, but *it seemed to matter very little where the damage occurred.*

We now recognize a few of the limitations of Lashley's studies. For one thing, he studied maze learning, a rather compex set of procedures that involves the interaction of many senses and many muscle groups. Lashley may have been correct about memories for mazes: They probably are not stored in any one particular location. But some types of memories do seem to be found in certain predictable locations. Individual experiences of sight, sound, or touch may very well be stored in—or near—the relevant sensory area of the cortex (Squire, 1986, 1987).

Another "problem" we see in Lashley's work is that it focused only on the cerebral cortex. More recent evidence suggests that many lower brain centers are intimately involved in encoding and storing information (e.g., McCormick et al., 1982; Mishkin & Appenzeller, 1987; Thompson, 1969, 1981, 1986). The lower brain center that has attracted the most attention is the *hippocampus.* Brain surgery on one individual, known to us only as H.M., stimulated this attention (Milner, 1959).

H.M. suffered from epilepsy. For almost 11 years, he experienced an average of one large convulsive attack and a number of partial seizures each day. Finally, it was decided that drastic treatment was needed. The parts of the temporal lobes would be severed, and the hippocampus would be removed from both sides of H.M.'s brain. The surgery was remarkably successful: Epileptic seizures became very rare. Sensory, perceptual, and intellectual functioning were very much intact. But there were disastrous effects on H.M.'s memory. He could not form new long-term memories. He could remember clearly what he had known before the surgery. Failure to recall events before the surgery would have meant a diagnosis of *retrograde* (backward-acting) *amnesia*—the loss of memory for events that occurred before the onset of the amnesia. No, this was not the problem. H.M. had *anterograde* (forward-acting) *amnesia*—the inability to form new long-term memories. H.M. could not form lasting memories for events that occurred after his surgery. (Amnesia need not result only from surgery, of course; any insult to the brain might cause amnesia.)

H.M. could read a magazine over and over, responding to it each time as if it were for the first time. When asked what year it was, he would answer "1953"—the year in which his surgery was performed. With great effort, he could memorize a three-digit number for a short time, but if he were distracted, the number would be lost, as would his memory of spending effort trying to learn it in the first place. After his surgery, H.M. had only a short-term memory. His experiences provide impressive evidence that the hippocampus is involved in the formation of long-term memories (Milner, 1965; Corkin, 1984; Milner, Corkin, & Teuber, 1968). Studies of other humans and with nonhumans reinforces the view that the hippocampus is involved in moving short-term experiences into long-term storage (Mishkin & Appenzeller, 1987; Squire, 1982).

Memory at the Level of the Neuron

When information is encoded as a memory, changes take place in the central nervous system. In humans, most of those changes take place in the brain, and many such changes occur in the cerebral cortex. Well, *that* sounds simple enough. But what sorts of changes take place as memories are stored? Exactly what is changed, and in what ways? You can anticipate my response: Answers to these questions are not yet available, and what hints we do have suggest that the processes involved are incredibly complex. If the nervous system is in some way altered as memories are formed, that alteration must be at the level of the neuron or the synapse. Given the recency of most of the research in this area, the story changes regularly, but here is some of what psychologists suspect.

First, let's make sure that we realize what *doesn't* happen. We do not grow or develop new neurons as a function of experience. Recall from our discussion in Chapter 2 that we are born with about as many neurons as we'll ever have. Learning and memory must take advantage of existing neurons. For one thing, there is evidence that experience does increase the number of axon endings, dendrites, and synapses in the brain (Greenough, 1984; Rosenzweig et al., 1972).

By the 1970s, the best guess was that evidence for memory formation could be found by examining changes that take place at the synapse (Bartus et al., 1982; Deutsch, 1973; Kandel & Schwartz, 1982; Matthies, 1989; McNaughton & Morris, 1987). The basic argument that emerges from the research—most of it done with simple, nonhuman animals—is that with repetition, with experience, the flow of impulses across synapses becomes easier and easier. It is as if synapses become more efficient with practice.

If memories are formed because experience or practice allows certain neurotransmitters to work more effectively at the synaptic level, then what would happen if something were done to disrupt or block the action of those neurotransmitters? You would predict that memories formed at synapses that used those neurotransmitters would be disrupted. This is essentially what happens. The neurotransmitters most often involved in studies like these are acetylcholine (ACh) and serotonin.

A slightly different line of research claims that experience does not increase, or alter in any way, the neurotransmitter released at synapses. What matters most, these scientists argue, are changes in the postsynaptic membrane. The most common changes are thought to be increases in the number of effective receptor sites (e.g., Lynch & Baudry, 1984). The point is that as synapses are used and used again, the number of receptor sites increases, and this makes more efficient use of the synapse.

What can we conclude as a sort of interim summary? We can be quite sure that the formation of memories involves making some synaptic transmissions easier than they once were. What remains to be determined is whether changes at the synapse involve increases or decreases in the amount of neurotransmitter present, or physical changes in the neuronal membranes involved to allow existing neurotransmitters to function more effectively.

BEFORE YOU GO ON

What has the study of amnesia told us about locating memory in the brain?

At the level of the neuron, what changes take place when memories are formed?

We have covered a lot of ground in this topic, much of it very technical. We have tried to show that memory is not a simple receptacle for information that passively enters our senses and gets dumped someplace where we can get it out whenever we wish. Multistore models of memory claim that to encode and store information requires a series of steps needed to move that information through distinct memory stores. A levels of processing model claims that there is but one memory store where information is processed at different levels. What I've tried to do in this topic is present a model of memory that borrows heavily from a multistore viewpoint, but that also acknowledges the usefulness of a levels of processing approach. This model includes a sensory, short-term, and long-term component.

We have also seen that there are different types of long-term memory and that information in long-term memory is clearly organized, although we may not yet fully appreciate the complex patterns of organization that best characterize our memory systems. It is still true, however, that on a practical level, what matters most to us, day in and day out, is whether or not we can get information out of our memory systems when we want to. We consider this process of retrieval in Topic 6B.

SUMMARY

How do we define memory? Compare multistore and levels of processing models of memory.

Memory is the cognitive process of actively representing information in memory (encoding), keeping it there (storage), and later bringing it out again (retrieval). There are many current theories about the nature of memory. One view, the multistore model, suggests that there are (usually three) different, distinct memories, or stores of information, each with its own mechanism for processing information. The levels of processing model contends that there is but one memory store, but different levels or depths to which information is processed into that memory. / *page 247*

What is sensory memory? What is its capacity and duration?

Sensory memory gives us the ability to store large amounts of information for very brief periods of time. In this memory, we cannot manipulate or encode information, which is assumed to be stored in the form in which it is received by our sense receptors. Visually presented material lasts in sensory memory for but a fraction of a second; auditorially processed material may last for as long as 10 seconds. / *page 249*

For how long is information stored in STM? What is required to get material into STM and then keep it there?

Once entered into short-term memory, information can be held there for ap-

proximately 15–20 seconds before all of it fades or is replaced by new information. Some information will be inaccessible soon after encoding. Processing information to this memory requires that we attend to it. Information can enter STM either from sensory memory or long-term memory. We can keep information in STM by reattending to it, a process called maintenance rehearsal. / *page 253*

How much information can be held in STM? How can chunking affect the capacity of STM?

It is reasonable to say that the capacity of STM is limited to approximately 7 ± 2 bits of information. This assumes that the information is unrelated and meaningless. By "chunking" information together into meaningful clusters or units, more can be processed in STM, but the limit remains about 7 ± 2 chunks. / *page 254*

What evidence do we have that information tends to be encoded acoustically in STM?

Information in our short-term memories may be encoded in any number of forms, but acoustic coding seems most common. When errors in recall from short-term memory are made, those items recalled in error are most likely to *sound* like the items that were to be recalled. Words that sound alike are more likely to cause STM confusion than do words that mean the same thing. / *page 255*

Are long-term memories necessarily permanent?

Although LTM may hold information for a very long time, we cannot claim LTM to be a permanent memory. The problem is that there is, at the moment, no scientific means of separating whether or not information is unavailable or inaccessible when retrieval fails. Once in long-term memory, information is subject to distortion and/or replacement. / *page 257*

Contrast elaborative rehearsal with maintenance rehearsal as a means of encoding information into long-term memory.

Although maintenance rehearsal may sometimes be sufficient to encode or move material from STM into LTM, there seems to be little doubt that the best mechanism for placing information into LTM is elaborative rehearsal—that is, to think about the material, forming associations or images to the material and relating it to something already stored in LTM. The more one can elaborate, or the "deeper" the elaboration, the better retrieval will be. / *page 259*

Name and briefly describe four possible systems or types of LTM.

Information may be stored in different ways in a variety of LTM systems. One of the most basic is our procedural memory, in which we retain learned connections between stimuli and re-sponses—in essence, how we perform simple, well-learned behaviors. Episodic memories are those that record one's life experiences and events. Thus, they are autobiographical. Semantic memories are those that store one's facts, knowledge, and vocabularies. Metamemory is the name for the memory system that provides us with the awareness of how our own memory systems work. / *page 260*

Briefly summarize ways in which information may be represented in long-term memory.

Psychologists believe that we store semantic, or meaningful, units in LTM, and further assume that these units are well organized, perhaps in a number of different ways. For example, there is evidence that we access words in LTM as if they were stored in conceptual categories (category clustering). In fact, even when structure is not imposed on a list of words to be memorized, subjects generally impose their own subjective organization onto the list. Recently, attention has focused on complex systems, called network models, such as spreading activation theory, which describes some of the complex interrelations that exist among stored concepts or, like ACT and ACT★, describe the organization among propositions that we have stored in LTM. / *page 265*

What has the study of amnesia told us about locating memory in the brain? At the level of the neuron, what changes take place when memories are formed?

Research by Karl Lashley, published in the 1950s, showed us that individual memories for complex phenomena were not stored in specific locations in the cerebral cortex. In fact, we now realize that many lower brain structures are involved in memory processes. From the study of amnesics, H.M. in particular, we realize that the hippocampus is crucial in moving information from STM into LTM. That is, persons with a damaged hippocampus suffer from anterograde amnesia, the inability to form long-term memories.

We are not yet sure what happens at the neuronal level when memories are formed, stored, or retrieved. Promising research suggests that synaptic pathways that are used repeatedly become more and more efficient in their ability to transmit impulses. This may be because more neurotransmitter chemical is available as memories are formed, or because new receptor sites are formed on the postsynaptic membrane as memories are formed. / *page 267*

Why We Care: A Topic Preview

As we have defined it, memory involves three related processes: encoding, storage, and retrieval. The first two processes were discussed in Topic 6A, where we saw how information is processed into memory (encoded) and kept there (storage). In this topic, our focus shifts to the practical matter of retrieval—the process of getting information out of memory.

Retrieval is an important memory process regardless of the type of information we have stored or where we have stored it. Whether we are talking about a simple, well-learned habit stored in procedural memory, a definition stored in semantic memory, a personal experience stored in episodic memory, or a telephone number temporarily stored in short-term memory, if retrieval fails at the critical time, that information will be of no use to us.

Consistent with the terminology we have been developing, we can say that remembering demonstrates successful retrieval and that forgetting demonstrates retrieval failure. I hope you recognize that this usage of retrieval and retrieval failure is both circular and trivial. To say that we forget something because we are unable to retrieve it explains nothing. The real issue, of course, is, why did retrieval fail? Was the information we were seeking simply not there—not available to us? Or was the information there, in memory, but inaccessible at the time? What factors influence the extent to which information can be retrieved on demand? What can be done to increase the likelihood that retrieval will succeed? These are the issues we explore in this topic.

The first issue we'll consider is how retrieval is measured. Whether someone can remember the answer to a question often hinges on just how the question is asked. As we consider measuring memory, we'll see that some evidence of retention can be found through indirect assessment. The bulk of our discussion will deal with the relation between the processes of encoding and retrieval. As it happens, getting information out of memory depends, perhaps more than anything else, on how (or if) it got into memory in the first place. We'll end this topic by examining factors that can inhibit our retrieval of memories. Successful retrieval may involve overcoming these inhibitory factors. As we have done before, we'll try to point out how you can apply what we know about memory retrieval in your everyday life.

MEASURING RETRIEVAL

One factor affecting the retrieval of information from long-term memory is how one is asked to go about retrieving it. This is a factor over which you and I seldom have much control. For instance, unless you have an unusually democratic instructor, you will not be allowed to vote on what kind of exams will be given in class. Students generally are asked to retrieve information in one of a number of standard exam formats chosen by their instructor.

In this section, we'll see how retrieval is influenced by our choice of measuring technique. First we'll consider direct, or explicit, measures of retrieval. With these techniques a subject consciously attempts to retrieve specified information from memory. Second, we'll consider indirect, or implicit, measures of retrieval. With these techniques subjects demonstrate memory when they can take advantage of previous experiences (in memory) without consciously trying to do so.

Direct, Explicit Measures of Memory

Let's design an experimental example to work with for a while. Imagine that we have subjects come to the laboratory on a given Tuesday to learn a list of 15 randomly chosen words. Some subjects take longer than others, but all eventually demonstrate that they have learned the list. The subjects report back to the laboratory two weeks later, when our basic question is: "How many of the words that you learned two weeks ago do you still remember?" How could we find out?

recall *a measure of retrieval in which an individual is given the fewest possible cues to aid retrieval*

One thing we might do is ask for simple **recall** of the list of words. To do so, we need only give the subjects a blank sheet of paper and ask them to write, in any order, as many of the words from the previously learned list as they can. (Technically, this is "free recall." If we asked the subjects to recall the list in the order in which it was presented, we would be asking for "serial recall.") This is a very difficult type of retrieval task. For recall, we provide the fewest possible cues to aid the retrieval. We merely specify the information we want and essentially say, "There, now go into your long-term memories, locate that information, get it out, and write it down." Let's assume that one subject correctly recalls six words.

recognition *a measure of retrieval in which an individual is required to identify material previously learned as being familiar*

Now suppose that we furnish our subject with a list of 50 words, including those on the previously learned list. Now we instruct her to "circle the words on this list that you *recognize* from the list you learned two weeks ago." In this case, we're not asking for recall, but for **recognition**, a retrieval task requiring a subject to identify material learned previously. Isn't it likely that our subject will do better on this task? She recalled 6 words of the original 15, so let's say she recognizes 11 words. Now, in a way, we have a small dilemma. Should we say that our subject remembered 6 words or 11 words? The answer is, both or either. Whether our subject remembered 6 words or 11 words depends on how we asked her to go about remembering.

In virtually all cases, retrieval by recognition is superior to retrieval by recall (e.g., Bahrick, 1984; Brown, 1976; Schacter, 1987). Figure 6.6 provides some clear-cut data in support of this point. It shows that over a two-

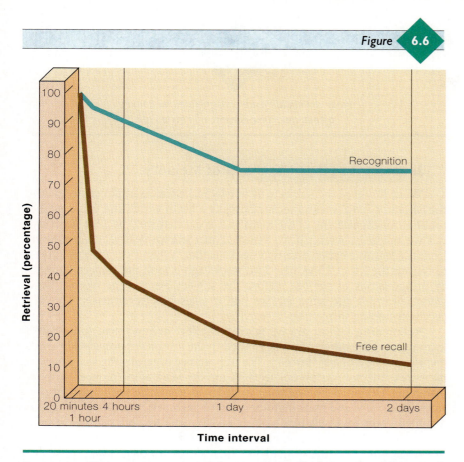

Figure 6.6

Two curves demonstrating retrieval for nonsense syllables over a 2-day period. In one case, retrieval is measured with a test for recognition, while the other tests for recall. (From Luh, 1922.)

day period, tests of retrieval by recognition are superior to tests of retrieval by recall. With recall, we provide minimal retrieval cues; with recognition, we provide maximum cues and ask the subject to identify a stimulus as being one that he or she has seen before (Mandler, 1980). Or, as Benton Underwood, a psychologist who studied memory processes for many years, described the difference: In recall we ask, "What is the item?" In a recognition task we ask, "Is this the item?" (cited in Houston, 1986, p. 280).

Most students I know would much rather take a multiple-choice exam, in which they only have to recognize the correct response from among a small number of alternatives, than a fill-in-the-blank test (or an essay test), which requires recall. Multiple-choice tests are easier than fill-in-the-blank tests. But, consistent with an argument we will develop below, there are situations in which just the opposite is true. For example, if students *expect* a fill-in-the-blank test and study for such a test, they may very well do better on it than they would on a multiple-choice test, even though the latter measures retrieval through recognition (Leonard & Whitten, 1983).

BEFORE YOU GO ON

*How do recall and recognition measures
affect our assessment of retrieval?*

Indirect, Implicit Measures of Memory

What if one of the subjects in our hypothetical example came back to the laboratory two weeks after memorizing a list of words and could neither recall nor recognize any of the items? I suspect that we'd be a bit surprised, but we might be wrong if we assumed that our subject retained nothing from the learning experience two weeks earlier. What if we ask this subject to relearn the list of 15 words? Two weeks ago it took the subject 10 trials, or presentations of the list, before the subject learned the words. Now, when relearning the same list, we find it takes only seven trials. This is a common finding in memory research.

relearning *a measure of memory in which one notes the improvement in performance when learning material for a second time*

Relearning almost always takes less effort or time than did original learning, and the difference is attributed to the advantage provided by one's memory of the original learning. The importance of relearning as a sensitive measure of memory dates back to 1885 and the work of the pioneer memory researcher Hermann Ebbinghaus. In order to minimize the impact of previous experience and meaningfulness on his memorizing tasks, Ebbinghaus designed "nonsense syllables"—such as *dax, wuj, lep, pib, loz*—as stimuli for his experiments. (As it happens, not all syllables are equally nonsensical—some *are* more meaningful (*tix, luv, bot*) than others (*wuj, xyg, keq*).) Ebbinghaus served as his own subject, memorizing list after list of nonsense syllables under various conditions of practice. Later, he would assess his memory for what he had learned. He noted that even when recall was poor, he could relearn a list of syllables in just a few presentations.

Because relearning does not require that a subject directly retrieve any information from memory, it is referred to as an indirect, or *implicit*, test of memory retention (Graf & Schacter, 1985). Implicit tests of memory have become an active area of research in cognitive psychology (Richardson-Klavehn & Bjork, 1988; Roediger, 1990; Schacter, 1987). Among other things, this research supports the hypothesis that information may be stored in different types of long-term memory.

Although we may think of the relearning of verbal materials, such as words or nonsense syllables, as an indirect measure of memory, most current implicit tests of retention focus on *procedural memories*, (see Topic 6A, p. 259) or what Anderson calls *procedural knowledge*. Procedural memories include the storage of "knowing how to go about doing things," such as tying a shoelace, typing, speaking, or riding a bicycle. Remembering how to do these things is virtually automatic, or unconscious. In fact, when we try to specifically recall how to do them, our performance may deteriorate; or "In some sense, these performances reflect prior learning, but seem to resist conscious remembering" (Roediger, 1990, p. 1043).

Let's look at one example of how implicit memory tests provide some intriguing data on amnesia. In our discussion of anterograde amnesia in

Topic 6A, we saw that some people with amnesia (such as H.M.) are unable to transfer information from STM to LTM. What is learned today will be forgotten tomorrow.

Warrington and Weiskrantz (1968, 1970) had amnesic and control subjects learn a list of words. Retention of the list was tested. In two direct, explicit measures, recall and recognition, the control subjects were superior to the amnesic subjects, who predictably scored poorly. Then the subjects were given two indirect or implicit tests. Neither was presented as a test of memory, but as a guessing game. In one, they were shown a few letters (such as tab . . .) and were asked to identify a word that began with those letters. In the other, they were to identify words that had been mutilated so that they were very difficult to read. The question was, how many words from the previously learned list would be identified in either task? It turned out that words from the list learned previously were easier to identify than "new" words (the advantage is attributed to a process called *priming*). What is significant is that there were no differences between the amnesic and nonamnesic subjects on the implicit tests of memory. This finding has been replicated many times (see Shimamura, 1986).

What this means, of course, is that even in the worst of amnesia cases, all of memory processing may not be lost. Some long-term memories—those in procedural memory—may be very resistant to destruction. Remember the last time you heard about a victim of retrograde amnesia. Typically, we hear about some adult found wandering about, totally unaware of who he is, where he came from, or how he got there. There seems to be no *direct* recollection of any long-term memories. But have you noticed that such amnesia patients *do* demonstrate all sorts of long-term memories? They remember how to talk. They remember how to eat. They remember how to get dressed. They remember, in short, all those procedures stored in their procedural memory.

BEFORE YOU GO ON

*What are implicit tests of retention,
and what do they tell us about long-term memory?*

ENCODING AND RETRIEVAL

We have repeatedly made the point that encoding, storage, and retrieval are interrelated memory processes. In this section, we'll explore the important relations that exist between retrieval and encoding. At one level, the issue is quite simple: If you do not encode information appropriately, you will have difficulty retrieving it. To repeat an example we used earlier, you cannot recall my mother's maiden name because you've never known it in the first place. You have never heard my mother's maiden name before, but you *have* had countless encounters with pennies. Can you draw a picture of a penny, properly locating each of its features? Can you recognize from

Figure   6.7

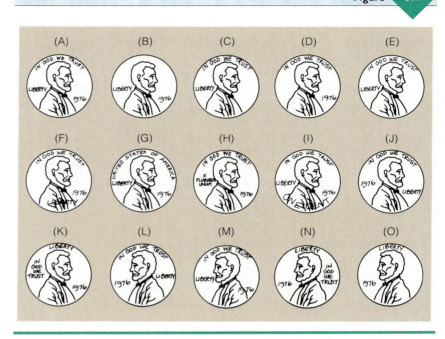

Fifteen drawings of the top side of a penny, testing encoding and retrieval. (Nickerson & Adams, 1979.)

a series of drawings which one accurately depicts a penny (see Figure 6.7)? In fact, very few of us can correctly recognize a drawing of a penny, and even fewer can recall all of its essential features, nearly 90 percent forgetting that the word *LIBERTY* appears right behind Lincoln's shoulder (Nickerson & Adams, 1979). These retrieval failures do not result from a lack of experience but from a lack of proper encoding. There are three general encoding issues that we'll discuss here: context effects, encoding strategies, and the amount and spacing of encoding practice.

The Effects of Context

Retrieval tends to be best when the situation, or context, in which retrieval takes place matches the context that was present at encoding. When cues that were present at encoding are also present at retrieval, retrieval is enhanced. This observation is called the **encoding specificity principle.** Essentially, it asserts that we can only retrieve what has been stored, and how we retrieve information depends on how it was encoded in the first place (Flexser & Tulving, 1982; Newby, 1987; Tulving & Thompson, 1973). The principle suggests that not only do we encode and store particular items of information, but we also note and store the context in which those items occur. The encoding specificity principle is just as valid for animals as it is for humans. "Ease of retrieval . . . is quite strongly influenced by the context in which the animal is asked to retrieve it. The closer the test context is to training conditions and the more unique the

encoding specificity principle *the hypothesis that we can only retrieve what we have stored and that retrieval is enhanced to the extent that retrieval cues match encoding cues*

context is for specific memories, the better the retrieval" (Spear, Miller, & Jagielo, 1990, pp. 190–191).

Here's a hypothetical experiment (based on Tulving & Thompson, 1973) that demonstrates encoding specificity. Subjects are asked to learn a list of 24 common words. Half of the subjects are also given cue words to help them remember each item on the list. For the stimulus word *wood*, the cue word is *tree*, for *cheese*, the cue word is *green*, and so on for each of the 24 words. The other half of the subjects receive no such cue during their memorization (that is, while encoding). Later, subjects are asked to recall as many words from the list as they can. What we discover at recall is that the cue helps those subjects who had seen it during learning, but it actually decreases the recall for those subjects who had not seen it during learning. If learning takes place without a cue, recall will be better without it.

We suggested in Topic 5A that you should choose one special place for studying and that your kitchen table, for example, would not be a good choice because that setting is already associated with eating experiences (and many others). In other words, the context of a kitchen is not a good one for encoding information unless you expect to be tested for retrieval in that same context—which seems highly unlikely. This advice was reaffirmed by a series of experiments by Steven Smith (1979). For example, he had subjects learn some material in one room, and then he tested their recall for that material in either the same room or a different one. When a different room—a different context, with different cues—was used for recall, retrieval performance dropped substantially. Simply instructing students to try to remember and think about the room in which learning took place helped recall considerably.

These context effects are clearly related to what has been called **state-dependent memory.** The idea here is that, to some degree, retrieval depends on the extent to which a person's state of mind at retrieval matches the person's state of mind at encoding (Leahy & Harris, 1989, p. 146). When learning takes place while a subject is under the influence of a drug, for example, being similarly under the influence of that drug at retrieval has beneficial effects (e.g., Eich et al., 1975; Goodwin et al., 1969; Parker et al., 1976). Some intriguing research by Gordon Bower (Bower et al., 1978; Bower, 1981) and others suggests that one's mood also may predict retrieval. Using moods (sad or happy) induced by posthypnotic suggestion, Bower found that retrieval was best when mood at retrieval *matched* mood at learning, regardless of whether that mood was happy or sad. This effect seems particularly true for female subjects (Clark & Teasdale, 1985).

There is also evidence that our memories for emotionally arousing experiences are likely to be easier to recall than emotionally neutral events (Thompson, 1982). This may be because emotional arousal increases the levels of certain hormones (adrenaline in particular) that, in turn (perhaps by increasing glucose levels), help to form vivid memories associated with the emotional arousal (Gold, 1987; McGaugh, 1983). That emotional arousal may help to form particularly vivid memories helps us understand what Brown and Kulik (1977) call **flashbulb memories.** These are memories of (usually important) events that are unusually clear and vivid. You probably have flashbulb memories of a number of events: your high school graduation; the funeral of a close friend; or what you were doing on January

state-dependent memory *the hypothesis that retrieval can be enhanced by the extent to which one's state of mind at retrieval matches one's state of mind at encoding*

flashbulb memories *particularly clear, and vivid memories that are easily retrieved but not necessarily accurate in all detail*

28, 1986, when the space shuttle *Challenger* exploded, killing all on board. Which flashbulb memories *you* have will depend on how old you are, of course. I also should mention that although flashbulb memories *are* particularly clear and vivid, there is little reason to believe that they are necessarily any more complete or any more accurate than any other memories (Mc-Closkey, Wible, & Cohen, 1988). Notice too, that flashbulb memories seem to be memories of events stored in what we have referred to as episodic memory.

In this section, we have seen that the retrieval of information from memory depends in large measure on the context and cues provided by events that occur at the time of encoding. Retrieval is enhanced to the extent that the situation, or one's state of mind, is the same at retrieval as it was at encoding. Emotional arousal at encoding seems to strengthen the encoded information.

BEFORE YOU GO ON

How does the situation in which one encodes information affect retrieval of that information?

Strategies that Guide Encoding

Once again using the term of Craik and Tulving (1975), we may say that to practice material in such a way as to maximize the chances of retrieving it when we want it, we need to use elaborative rehearsal. We need to develop strategies that will meaningfully encode information in our long-term memories in such a way that we can easily get it out again. In this section, we'll examine some effective elaboration strategies. We'll begin by considering meaningfulness in general, and then we'll briefly review some specific techniques, called mnemonic devices (after the Greek goddess of memory, Mnemosyne). These techniques involve using existing memories to make new information more meaningful. We'll end this section with a discussion of how schemas—complex cognitive representations of general knowledge—affect our elaboration of information at encoding and retrieval.

Meaningfulness. I have a hypothesis. I believe that I can determine the learning ability of students by noting where they sit in a classroom. The good, bright students tend to choose seats farthest from the door. The poor, dull students sit by the door, apparently interested in easily getting into and out of the room. (Although there may be some truth to this, I'm not serious.) To make my point, I propose an experiment. Students seated away from the door are asked to learn a list of words that I read aloud only once. I need a second list of words for those students seated by the door because they've already heard my first list.

The list that my "smart students" hear is made up of words such as *cat, dog, mother, father, black, white,* and so forth. As I predicted, they have no problem recalling this list after one presentation. The students huddled by the door get my second list: *insidious, tachistoscope, sophistry, flotsam,*

In order to learn new material students should do whatever they can to make what they are studying meaningful. Asking questions about a new subject and relating it to things that are already familiar add more meaning to the material.

episcotister, and so forth. Needless to say, my hypothesis will be confirmed.

This is obviously not a very fair experiment. Those students sitting by the door will yell foul. My second list of words is clearly more difficult to learn and recall than the first. The words on the first list are shorter, more familiar, and easier to pronounce. However, the major difference between these two lists is the **meaningfulness** of the items—the extent to which they elicit existing associations in one's memory. The *cat, dog, mother* list is easy to remember because each word in it is meaningful. Each word makes us think of many other things, or produces many associations. That is, these items are easy to elaborate. Words like *tachistoscope* are more difficult because they evoke few, if any, associations.

An important point to keep in mind is that meaningfulness is not a characteristic or a feature built into materials to be learned. *Meaningfulness resides in the memory of the learner. Tachistoscope* may be a meaningless collection of letters for many people, but for others, it may be a word rich in meaning, a word with which they can readily form many associations. That is, what is meaningful is a function of our individual experiences.

It then follows that one of your tasks as a learner is to do whatever you can to make the material you are learning meaningful. You need to seek out and establish associations between what you are learning and what you already know. You need to rehearse elaboratively what you are encoding so that you can retrieve it later. You need to be prepared to ask yourself a series of questions about what you are studying. What does this mean? What does it make me think of? Does this remind me of something I already know? Can I make this material more meaningful? If you cannot, there is little point in going on to more confusing material. Perhaps you now see a major reason for our including **"Before you go on"** questions within each topic.

meaningfulness *the extent to which information evokes associations with information already in memory*

BEFORE YOU GO ON

What is meaningfulness?
How does meaningfulness relate to retrieval?

Mnemonic Devices. Retrieval is enhanced if we can actively elaborate on the material we are learning—if we can make it meaningful and organize it in some way during the encoding process. Often this is simply a matter of reflecting on what we are learning and actively forming associations with previously stored memories. Now let's examine some specific encoding techniques, called **mnemonic devices,** that we can use to aid our retrieval by helping us organize and add meaningfulness to new material.

An experiment by Bower and Clark (1969) shows us that we can improve the retrieval of otherwise unorganized materials if we can weave that material into a meaningful story. This technique is called **narrative chaining.** One group of college students was asked to learn a list of 10 simple nouns in order. It is not a difficult task, and subjects had little trouble with it. Then they were given another list of 10 nouns to learn, and then an-

mnemonic devices *strategies for improving retrieval that take advantage of existing memories in order to make new material more meaningful*

narrative chaining *the mnemonic device of relating words together in a story, thus organizing them in a meaningful way*

Figure **6.8**

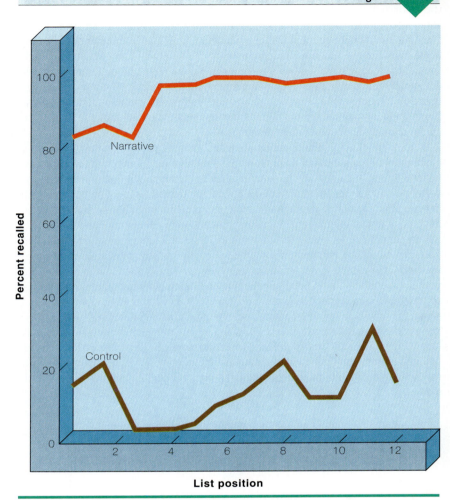

Percent correct recall for words from 12 lists learned under two conditions. In the narrative condition, subjects made up short stories to aid recall, while in the control condition, rote memorization—no mnemonic device—was used. (After Bower & Clark, 1969.)

other—12 lists in all. These subjects were given no instructions other than to remember each list of words in order.

A second group of subjects was given the same 12 lists of 10 nouns each to learn. It was suggested to them that they make up little stories that used each of the words on the list in turn. Immediately after each list was presented, both groups were asked to recall the list of words they had just heard. There was virtually no difference in the recall scores for the two groups. Then came a surprise. *After all 12 lists had been recalled,* subjects were tested again on their recall for each list. The experimenters provided one word from one of the 12 lists, and the subjects were to recall the other nine words from that list. The difference in recall between the two groups of subjects in this instance was striking (see Figure 6.8). Those who used a narrative-chaining technique recalled 93 percent of the words (on the average), whereas those who did not so organize the random words recalled only 13 percent of them.

The message seems clear and consistent with what we have said so far. A technique that adds organization and meaningfulness to otherwise meaningless material is a means of elaborative rehearsal that will improve retrieval. Organizing unrelated words into stories helps us remember them.

Forming *mental images*, or pictures in our minds, is another technique that improves memory. Using imagery at encoding to improve retrieval has proven to be very helpful in many different circumstances (Begg & Paivio, 1969; Marschark et al., 1987; Paivio, 1971, 1986). It is Paivio's contention that visual images provide a unique and useful way of encoding meaningful information; that is, we are at an advantage when we can encode not only what a word means, but also what it looks like. It is because imagery helps retrieval that words such as *horse*, *rainbow*, and *typewriter* can be recalled more readily than words such as *treason*, *session*, and *effort*—even when factors such as meaningfulness and frequency of occurrence are equated.

Assume, for example, that you have to memorize the meanings of a large number of Spanish words. You could use simple rote repetition, but this technique is tedious and not very efficient. Atkinson (1975) suggested that to improve your memory for foreign language vocabulary, it is useful to imagine some connection visually tying the two words together. He calls this the *key word* method of study. For example, the Spanish word for "horse" is *caballo*, pronounced *cab-eye-yo*. To remember this association, you might choose *eye* as the key word and picture a horse actually kicking someone in the eye. Or, if you are not prepared to be that gruesome, you might imagine a horse with a very large eye. The Spanish word for "duck" is *pato*. Here your key word might be *pot*, and you could picture a duck wearing a pot on its head (see Figure 6.9) or sitting in a large pot on the stove. This may sound strange, but research data suggest that it actually works very well (Pressley et al., 1982).

The same basic technique works whenever you need to remember any paired sort of information. Gordon Bower (1972), for example, asked students to learn lists of pairs of English words. Some subjects were instructed to form a mental image that showed some interaction between the two words. One pair, for instance, was *piano-cigar*. There are many ways to form an image of a piano and a cigar: The cigar could be balanced on the edge of the piano, for one. Recall for word pairs was much better for those subjects who formed mental images than it was for those who did not. It is also the case that more commonplace and interactive images are *more useful* than strange and bizarre ones (Bower, 1970; Wollen et al., 1972). That is, to remember the *piano-cigar* pair, it would be better to picture a cigar balanced on a piano than it would be to picture a piano actually smoking a cigar (see Figure 6.10). If you wanted to remember that it was Bower and Clark who did the experiment on narrative chaining, try to picture two *story-tellers chained* together, each holding a *Clark Bar* in their hands as they take a *bow* on a theater stage. Again, it sounds silly, but it works.

One of the better-known mnemonic devices that involves imagery is called the **peg word method** (Miller, Galanter, & Pribram, 1960). This strategy is most useful when we have to remember items in order. Using this device is a two-step process. The first step is to associate common

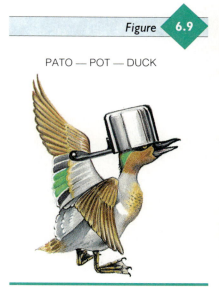

Figure 6.9

PATO — POT — DUCK

An illustration of how the key word method can help foreign vocabulary retention. (After Atkinson, 1975.)

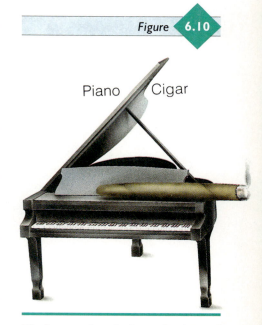

Figure 6.10

Piano   Cigar

The key word method can also be used to help remember pairs of English words. (After Wollen, Weber, & Lowry, 1972.)

peg word method *the mnemonic device of forming interactive visual images of materials to be learned and items previously associated with numbers*

THE PEG WORD MNEMONIC SCHEME

Figure 6.11

One is a Bun
Two is a Shoe
Three is a Tree
Four is a Door
Five is a Hive
Six are Sticks
Seven is Heaven
Eight is a Gate
Nine is a Line
Ten is a Hen

Proposed by Miller, Galanter, & Pribam (1960).

method of loci *the mnemonic device that mentally places information to be retrieved at a series of familiar locations (loci)*

nouns (peg words) that rhyme with the numbers from 1 to 10 (and beyond 10 if you're up to it). Figure 6.11 is the set of associations that Miller and his colleagues suggested. If you have a list of words to memorize, the second step is to form an interactive image of the word you're memorizing and the appropriate peg word.

To see how this might work, suppose that you have to remember the following words in order: *book, glass, ring, nose.* Having already memorized your peg word scheme, you make up an image associating each word on the list and its peg word, perhaps: (1) a *book* in the middle of a hamburger *bun,* (2) a *shoe* in a *glass,* (3) a wedding *ring* around the trunk of a *tree,* (4) a person's *nose* stuck in a *door,* and so on. At retrieval, you first recall the peg words in order (*bun, shoe, tree,* and *door*), and then recall the word from the list that you've associated with each peg word. This may sound like a lot of extra work to go through, but once you've mastered your peg word scheme, the rest is remarkably easy.

The last imagery-related mnemonic device we'll mention may be the oldest in recorded history. It is attributed to the Greek poet Simonides and is called the **method of loci** (Yates, 1966). The idea here is to get in your mind a well-known location (*loci* are locations), say the floor plan of your house or apartment. Visually place the material you are trying to recall in different places throughout your house in some sensible order. When the time comes for you to retrieve the material, mentally walk through your chosen locations, recalling (or retrieving) the information you have stored at each different place.

Some time ago, I was asked to present a short talk at a high school. There were several points I wanted to make, and I didn't want to use written notes as a memory aid. I also didn't want to appear as nervous as I knew I was going to be, so I decided to try the method of loci. I divided my talk into five or six major ideas, imagined my house, and walked through it in my mind. I stored my introduction at the front door, point 1 got me to the living room, point 2 to the dining room, and so on through the house until I got to my conclusion at the back door. Even though I have been telling others about the method of loci for many years, this was the first opportunity I had to use it, and I was very impressed with how easy it was to remember my little speech.

In this section, we've reviewed a number of specific techniques that we can use to improve the retrieval of information from memory. In each case, the basic message is that when we can organize otherwise unrelated material in a meaningful way, retrieval will be enhanced.

BEFORE YOU GO ON

Describe narrative chaining, mental imagery, the peg word method, and the method of loci as mnemonic devices.

Schemas. The encoding specificity hypothesis tells us that how we retrieve information will be affected by how we encoded that information. One of the processes that influences how we encode and retrieve infor-

Figure 6.12

THE BALLOONS PASSAGE (SEE FIGURE 6.17).

If the balloons popped, the sound would not be able to carry since everything would be too far away from the correct floor. A closed window would also prevent the sound from carrying since most buildings tend to be well insulated. Since the whole operation depends on a steady flow of electricity, a break in the middle of the wire would also cause problems. Of course the fellow could shout, but the human voice is not loud enough to carry that far. An additional problem is that a string could break on the instrument. Then there could be no accompaniment to the message. It is clear that the best situation would involve less distance. Then there would be fewer potential problems. With face-to-face contact, the least number of things could go wrong.

From Bransford & Johnson, 1972.

mation is our use of schemas (which are sometimes referred to as scripts). A **schema** is defined as an organized, general knowledge structure that we have stored in long-term memory (Mayer, 1983). Schemas provide a general framework that we may use to understand new information and also to remember or retrieve that information later (Alba & Hasher, 1983; Lord, 1980).

Let's take a look at a few examples of research that involve the use of schemas as encoding strategies. Before you go any further, stop and read the short passage in Figure 6.12. As it stands, the paragraph doesn't make much sense, does it? All the words are sensible. Even individual sentences seem reasonable. But as a story it seems virtually meaningless because without additional information, you have no way, no schema, available to comprehend the meaning of the passage (Bransford & Johnson, 1972). Now look at the drawing in Figure 6.17 at the very end of this topic. This drawing provides a schema that gives meaning to the paragraph. Subjects who were shown this picture *before* they read the passage recalled more than twice as much about it than did subjects who did not see the picture at all or who were shown the picture *after* they read the paragraph. The message here is that schemas seem to help retrieval only if the same schemas were available at or before encoding.

I've never learned to play chess. I know what a chessboard looks like and I can probably name most of the pieces. I realize that there are rules or restrictions on how pieces can be moved in a chess game, but I don't know what those restrictions are. In other words, I have a very sketchy schema for chess. If you were to show me a chessboard with the pieces positioned as if in the midst of a game and then later ask me to reconstruct what I had seen, I'm afraid that I would do very badly. When chess experts are shown the board and later are asked to reconstruct the positions of the pieces from memory, they do very well (DeGroot, 1965, 1966). Part of our explanation for their success is that they have very complete and detailed schemas for chess games, which helped them to encode and later retrieve the positions of the pieces on the board. On the other hand, if chess pieces are positioned randomly on a chessboard (not consistent with the rules of the game), the memory of chess experts for the location of the pieces will be no better than mine or that of other novices (Chase & Simon, 1973). This is because the randomly positioned pieces don't fit the experts' schemas

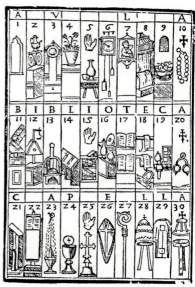

The method of loci is an ancient mnemonic device. This illustration was done by a Dominican monk in the sixteenth century. On the top are the abbey and the surrounding buildings through which the speaker will mentally walk, picking up the ideas (llustrated on the bottom) that he or she needs to recall.

schema *a system of organized, general knowledge, stored in long-term memory, that guides the encoding and retrieval of information*

Chess experts, such as Karpov and Kasparov, pictured here, have very detailed and elaborate schemas to aid them in the retrieval of information about the positioning of the pieces during a chess match.

for chess, taking away their advantage. The important point here is that a detailed schema is not necessarily going to help one's retrieval, unless the retrieval task takes advantage of the information stored in that schema (Brewer & Nakamura, 1984). This general result has been found for expertise in a number of very different areas such as computer programming (Adelson, 1984) and medicine (Norman, Brooks, & Allen, 1989).

The role of prior knowledge at encoding was also nicely demonstrated by an experiment by Anderson and Pichert (1978). All subjects read the same story about a couple of boys playing alone in a house. The story contained a number of details about the house and its contents. One group of subjects was asked to read the story from the perspective of a potential buyer of the home, while a second group of subjects was asked to read the story from the point of view of a burglar who is planning to rob the house. When recalling the story from the buyer's perspective, subjects remembered details like a leaky roof and a large living room. Subjects who took the burglar's point of view remembered where jewelry was kept and that the house contained a large television set. Then, once they felt that they had recalled all the details they could, subjects were asked to reconsider the story from the other perspective, using the other schema or script. For both groups, recall scores went up. In other words, bringing in a new schema at retrieval proved to be helpful, even though that schema was not actively used at encoding. Think in terms of your own memory. If I ask you to tell me all the details of your last trip to the dentist, won't you rely heavily on your overall knowledge of what it is like to go to the dentist in general? Then you'll supplement your recall of your last specific visit by adding whatever details you can recall.

So what is the bottom line? Whenever to-be-remembered information is consistent with prior, existing information (such as schemas) retrieval is enhanced. If to-be-remembered material is at odds with existing schema, those schemas may actually inhibit retrieval.

BEFORE YOU GO ON

What are schemas, and how do they affect retrieval?

Amount and Distribution of Encoding Practice

One point that I have made over and over again is that retrieval, no matter how it is measured, depends largely on how one goes about encoding or practicing that information. We'll end this section with the related observation that retrieval is also a function of the amount of practice and how that practice is spaced or distributed. One of the reasons why some students do not do as well on classroom exams as they would like is that they simply do not have (or make) enough time to study or practice the material covered on the exams. A related reason is that some students do not schedule wisely what time they have.

Overlearning. What you and I often do once we decide to learn something that we want to remember is read, practice, and study the material until we know it. In other words, we practice until we are satisfied that we have encoded and stored the required information in our memories, and then we quit. Another way of expressing this is to say that we often fail to engage in **overlearning,** the process of practicing or rehearsing material over and above what is needed to learn it. Consider this fictitious example, and see if you can extend this evidence to your study habits.

overlearning *the practice or rehearsal of material over and above what is needed to learn it*

A subject comes to the laboratory to learn a list of nonsense syllables, verbal items such as *dax, wuj, pib, and zuw.* There are 15 items on the list, and the material has to be presented repeatedly before our subject can recall all of the items correctly. Having correctly recalled the items once, our subject is dismissed with instructions to return two weeks later for a test of his recall of the nonsense syllables. Not surprisingly, he doesn't fare very well on the retrieval task.

What would have happened to our subject's recall if we had continued to present him with the list of syllables at the time of learning, well beyond the point where he first learned them? Say the list was learned in 12 trials. We have the subject practice the list for 6 more presentations (50 percent overlearning, or practice that is 50 percent over and above that required for learning). Or let's require an additional 12 trials of practice (100 percent overlearning). What if we required an additional 48 trials of practice (400 percent overlearning)?

The effects of such overlearning practice are well documented and very predictable. The recall data for this imaginary experiment might look like those presented in Figure 6.13. Notice three things about these data: (1) If we measure retrieval at different times after learning, forgetting is rather

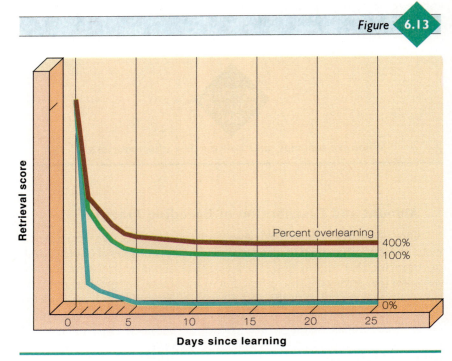

Figure **6.13**

Idealized data showing the effect of overlearning on retrieval. Note the "diminishing returns" with additional overlearning. (Krueger, 1929.)

impressive and quite sudden. (This is but one of the results of the work on memory that Ebbinghaus reported back in 1885, and that many other researchers have confirmed since then.) (2) Overlearning improves retrieval, having its greatest effects with longer retention intervals. (3) There is a "diminishing returns" phenomenon present; that is, 50 percent overlearning is much more useful than no overlearning; 100 percent overlearning is somewhat better than 50 percent; and 400 percent is better than 100 percent, but not by very much. For any task or individual, there is probably an optimum amount of overlearning. In summary, with everything else being equal, the more we practice what we are learning, the easier it will be to retrieve it. How one *schedules* one's practice or learning time is also an important factor in determining the likelihood of retrieval, and it is to this issue that we turn next.

Scheduling of Practice. Some of the oldest data in psychology support the notion that retrieval can be improved if practice (encoding) is spread out over time with rest intervals spaced in between. The data shown in Figure 6.14 are fairly standard. In fact, this 1946 experiment provides such reliable results that it is commonly used in psychology laboratory classes. The task is to write the letters of the alphabet, but upside down and from right to left. (If you think that sounds easy, you should give it a try.)

Subjects are given the opportunity to practice this task under four different conditions. The *massed-practice* group works on the task without a break between trials. The three *distributed-practice* groups receive the same

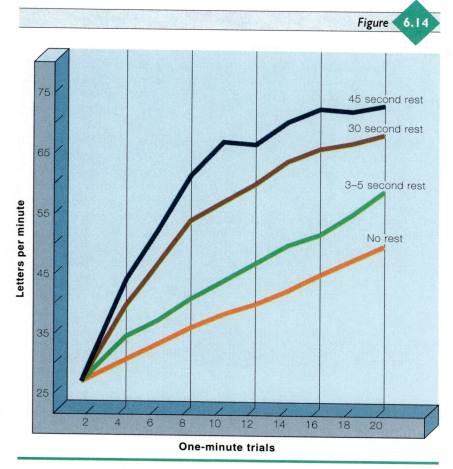

Figure 6.14

Improvement in performance as a function of distribution of practice time. The task was the printing of inverted capital letters, with twenty 1-minute trials separated by rest intervals of varying lengths. (After Kientzle, 1946.)

amount of actual practice, but get rest intervals interspersed between each 1-minute practice trial. One group gets a 3- to 5-second break between trials, a second group receives a 30-second rest, and a third group gets a 45-second break between practice trials.

As we can see in Figure 6.14, subjects in all four groups begin at about the same (poor) level of performance. After 20 minutes of practice, the performance of all the groups shows improvement. By far, however, the massed-practice (no rest) group does the poorest, and the 45-second-rest group does the best.

The conclusion to be drawn from years of research is that, almost without exception, distributed practice is superior to massed practice. There are exceptions, however. Some tasks might suffer from having rest intervals inserted in practice time. In general, whenever you must keep track of many things at the same time, you should mass your practice until you have finished whatever it is you are working on. If, for example, you are working on a complex math problem, you should work it through until you find a solution, whether it's time for a break or not. And, of course, you should not break up your practice in such a way as to disrupt the meaningfulness of the material you are studying.

Quite clearly, what we're talking about here is the scheduling of study time. Discussions of study schedules make up the major part of all how-to-study books. The message is always the same: Many short (and meaningful) study periods with rest periods interspersed are more efficient than a few study periods massed together. There *may* be occasions when cramming is better than not studying at all, but as a general strategy, cramming is inefficient.

Now let's assume that you're going to follow this advice to prepare for a test scheduled for next week. The test will cover two chapters of material in your text, and material covered in class. What this means, of course, is that you'll schedule a number of short (45-minute or so) study periods throughout the week. You'll not even try to study an entire chapter, but will break it into shorter, meaningful topics (as we've done with this text). And when studying any one topic, you'll break it up into even shorter, meaningful chunks (separated, perhaps, by "Before you go on" questions). Such a strategy of spreading out study sessions will be much more efficient than trying to get all your studying done in one or two sessions, say, over one weekend.

BEFORE YOU GO ON

What is overlearning, and how does it affect retrieval?
Compare and contrast massed and distributed practice, noting their effects on retrieval.

INTERFERENCE AND RETRIEVAL

Think back to when you were 15 years old. Can you remember all the gifts you got for your birthday that year? Can you remember *any* of them? I know I can't. Because I have schemas in long-term memory for teenagers' birthday parties, I suspect that I can guess what I might have gotten for my birthday that year and generate a fairly reasonable list. But there seems to be no way that I can directly retrieve that information from my long-term memory with any certainty. One possibility is that that information is no longer there. It may, in some literal sense, be lost forever. Perhaps I never encoded that information in a way that would allow me to retrieve it effectively. Another possibility is that that information is in fact available in memory, but inaccessible at the moment simply because I have had so many birthdays since my fifteenth one. So much has happened and entered my memory since then that the material I am looking for is covered up and being *interfered with* by information that entered later.

How about your most recent birthday? Can you recall the gifts you received for your last birthday? That's a little easier, but remembering with confidence is still not that easy. Here again, our basic retrieval problem may be one of interference. Assuming that what we are searching for is still there

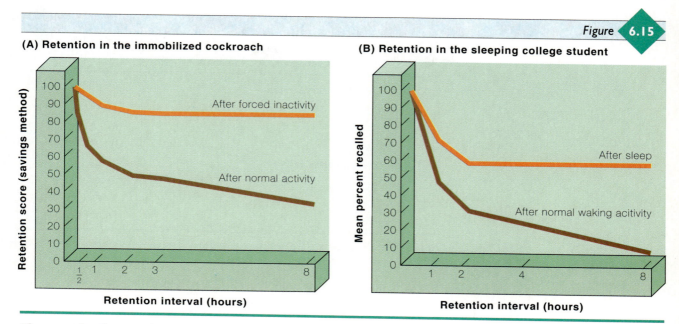

Figure **6.15**

(A) Retention in the immobilized cockroach

(B) Retention in the sleeping college student

These graphs illustrate how activity following learning can interfere with the retrieval of the learned material. In both cases, normal waking activity caused more interference with retrieval than did forced inactivity (for cockroaches) or sleeping (for students). (Minami & Dallenbach, 1946.)

(and that *is* an assumption), we may not be able to retrieve it because so many *previous* experiences (presents received earlier) are getting in the way, interfering with retrieval.

Retroactive Interference

The basic idea that interference can account for retrieval failure is an old one in psychology. Some early experiments, for example, demonstrated that subjects who were active for a period after learning remembered what they had learned less well than subjects who used the intervening period for sleep (Jenkins & Dallenbach, 1924). The graphs in Figure 6.15 show apparently comparable data from two experiments—one with college students who had learned a list of nonsense syllables, and the other with cockroaches that had learned to avoid an area of their cage. In either case, subjects who engaged in normal waking activity did worse on tests of retrieval over different retention intervals.

When interfering activities come *after* the learning of material to be remembered, we are dealing with **retroactive interference.** Let's go back into the laboratory. We'll need two groups of subjects randomly assigned to either an experimental group or a control group. The subjects in both groups are asked to learn something (almost anything will do; we'll assume a list of nonsense syllables). Having learned their lists, the groups are then treated differently. Subjects in the experimental group are now required to learn something else, perhaps a different list of nonsense syllables. At the same time, control group subjects are asked to do nothing (which is im-

retroactive interference *the inhibition of retrieval of previously learned material caused by material learned later*

Figure 6.16

DESIGNS OF EXPERIMENTS TO DEMONSTRATE RETROACTIVE AND PROACTIVE INTERFERENCE.

(A) Retroactive Interference

	Learn	Learn	Test
Experimental Group	Task A	Task B	Retrieval of Task A
Control Group	Task A	Nothing	Retrieval of Task A

(B) Proactive Interference

	Learn	Learn	Test
Experimental Group	Task A	Task B	Retrieval of Task B
Control Group	Nothing	Task B	Retrieval of Task B

Note: If interference is operating, the control group will demonstrate better retrieval than will the experimental group.

possible, of course, in a literal sense). These subjects might be asked to rest quietly or to play some simple game.

Now for the test. Both groups of subjects are asked to retrieve the material presented in the *first* learning task. Control group subjects will show a higher retrieval score than experimental group subjects. For the latter group, the second set of learned material interferes with the retrieval of the material learned first. Figure 6.16(A) summarizes this research design.

Most of us are familiar with retroactive interference from our own educational experiences. A student who studied French in high school takes a few courses in Spanish at college and now can't remember very much French. The Spanish keeps getting in the way. I have two students who are scheduled to take a psychology exam tomorrow morning at 9:00. Both are equally able and equally well motivated. One is taking only one class—mine. She studies psychology for two hours, watches TV for two hours, and goes to bed. She comes in the next morning to take the exam. The second student also studies psychology for two hours, but then must read a chapter and a half from her sociology text, just in case she is called on in class. After reading sociology, she goes to bed, comes to class, and takes the exam. Everything else being equal, this second student will be at a disadvantage. The sociology that she studied will retroactively interfere with her retrieval of the psychology she learned previously. What is this student to do? She has to study psychology, and she knows that she had better read her sociology, too. Perhaps all she can do is to set herself up for proactive interference.

Proactive Interference

proactive interference *the inhibition of retrieval of recently learned material caused by material learned earlier*

Proactive interference occurs when *previously* learned material interferes with the retrieval of material learned later. First follow along in Figure 6.16(B), then we'll get back to our student and her studying problem. We have two groups of subjects, experimental and control. The experimental group again starts off by learning something—that same list of syllables, perhaps. This time the control group subjects begin by resting quietly while the experimental group goes through the learning task. Both groups then learn a second list of syllables. We now test for retrieval, but this time we test for the retrieval of the more recently learned material. Once again, the control group subjects will be at an advantage. They have none of that first list in their memories to interfere with the retrieval task. But the advantage is not as great as it was in the case of retroactive interference. Proactive interference is seldom as detrimental as retroactive interference.

Although both retroactive and proactive interference effects are well documented, there are many factors that influence the *extent* of such interference (Underwood, 1957). For example, very meaningful, well-organized material is less susceptible to interference than is less meaningful material, such as nonsense syllables.

It should also strike you as reasonable that *the nature of the interfering task* matters a great deal. As a general rule of thumb, the more similar the interfering material is to the material being retrieved, the greater will be the interference. Think of my student who had to study for her psychology exam *and* read a sociology text. She will experience more interference (retroactive *or* proactive) than will a student who has to study for the psychology exam and work on calculus problems. In this context, I might even suggest that working on calculus is rather like doing nothing. I would make such a suggestion only in the sense that there is little about calculus to get in the way, or interfere, with the psychology lesson. Hence, I advise that if you're going to take more than one course at a time, those courses should be as different from each other as possible, to minimize possible interference effects.

BEFORE YOU GO ON

Briefly describe retroactive and proactive interference.
Which of these two generally has the greater impact on retrieval?

Retrieval often depends on how it is measured, as well as the number and quality of retrieval cues that are available to us. We have seen that the quality and quantity of one's learning, or encoding, have a definite influence on memory. To improve our chances of retrieving information from memory, we need to spend time with the material we are learning. We need to encode that information in a meaningful and well-organized way, whenever possible matching cues available at retrieval with those present at encoding. We need to do what we can to avoid the effects of interference.

We now need to add one final point to our discussion. Something else that we can do to improve our retrieval of information from memory is *practice retrieval* itself. Perhaps you'll recall from our discussion of the definition of learning that we cannot assess or measure learning directly. We only can measure performance and, on that basis, make inferences about what may have been learned. We say that classroom exams are designed to measure what you have learned. But they do so indirectly by measuring what you can remember or retrieve at the time of the test. Why don't we spend more time, then, practicing what is really going to matter—getting

Figure 6.17

A picture for the balloons passage. (From Bransford & Johnson, 1972.)

learned material out of our memories? In short: Retrieval is a skill that can be practiced. The more you practice it, the better you will be at it. Try to anticipate test questions. Work example problems at the end of textbook chapters or in accompanying study guides, if they are available. Ask yourself questions about the material you are studying. The time you spend doing so will pay off.

How do recall and recognition measures affect our assessment of retrieval?

One's retrieval of information from memory is often a function of how we ask for retrieval. When we ask for retrieval by recall, we provide the fewest possible retrieval cues. With recognition, we provide the information to be retrieved and ask that it be identified as familiar. Retrieval by recognition is generally superior to retrieval by recall. / page 274

What are implicit tests of retention, and what do they tell us about long-term memory?

As opposed to explicit tests of retrieval, implicit tests assess the extent to which previously experienced material is helpful in subsequent tasks. For example, relearning shows us that even when once-learned material cannot be recalled or recognized as familiar, that material will be easier to relearn than it was to learn in the first place. Other indirect tests of retention include such things as asking subjects to recognize physically mutilated or distorted words, where some words have been previously shown to the subjects and others have not. Subtle indirect tests of implicit memory also show us that even amnesic patients who demonstrate very poor recall and recognition skills (by definition) still demonstrate retention of some experiences, usually experiences of the sort stored in procedural memory. / page 275

How does the situation in which one encodes information affect the retrieval of that information?

The greater the extent to which the cues or context available at encoding match the cues or context available at retrieval, the better retrieval will be. The encoding specificity hypothesis asserts that how we

retrieve information depends in large part on how it was encoded. Psychologists have found that matching the individual's state of mind at encoding and at retrieval improves retrieval. Heightened emotionality at encoding may also produce memories that are more vivid, even if they are not more accurate. / page 278

What is meaningfulness? How does meaningfulness relate to retrieval?

Meaningfulness is the extent to which material is related to, or associated with, information already stored in memory. In general, meaningful material (or material that is made meaningful) is easier to retrieve than meaningless material. Meaningfulness resides in the individual, not in the material to be learned. / page 279

Describe narrative chaining, mental imagery, the peg word method, and the method of loci as mnemonic devices.

In general, mnemonic devices are strategies used at encoding to organize and add meaningfulness to material that will be retrieved. Narrative chaining involves making up a story that weaves together, in meaningful fashion, a list of otherwise unrelated words that need to be remembered in order. A number of mnemonic devices suggest forming visual images of the material to be learned, which may provide an additional code for that material. The peg word method requires first learning a word associated with each of the numbers 1 to 10 (if there are 10 items to be learned) and then forming an interactive image of these words and items that need to be recalled in order. The method of loci also uses mental imagery and involves mentally placing terms to be retrieved in a sequence of familiar locations. / page 282

What are schemas, and how do they affect retrieval?

Schemas, or scripts, are organized, general knowledge systems that we have stored in long-term memories. Based on one's past experiences, schemas summarize the essential features of common events or situations. They are used as a means of guiding the organization and giving meaning to new information. The more complete one's schema for to-be-remembered information, the better will be encoding and retrieval. / page 285

What is overlearning, and how does it affect retrieval? Compare and contrast massed and distributed practice, noting their effects on retrieval.

Overlearning involves the rehearsal of information above and beyond that needed for immediate recall. Within limits, the more one overlearns, the greater the likelihood of accurate retrieval. In massed practice, study or rehearsal occurs without intervening rest intervals. Distributed practice uses shorter segments of rehearsal interspersed with rest intervals. In almost all cases, distributed practice leads to better retrieval than does massed practice. / page 288

Briefly describe retroactive and proactive interference. Which of these two generally has the greater impact on retrieval?

Retroactive interference occurs when previously learned material cannot be retrieved because it is inhibited or blocked by material or information that is learned later. Proactive interference occurs when information cannot be retrieved because it is inhibited or blocked by material that was learned earlier. Retroactive interference is generally more detrimental to retrieval than is proactive interference. / page 291

HIGHER COGNITIVE PROCESSES

TOPIC 7A   Concepts and Language

TOPIC 7B   Problem Solving

Concepts and Language

Why We Care: A Topic Preview

Cognitions include one's ideas, beliefs, thoughts, and images. When we know, understand, or remember something, we use cognitions to do so. Cognitive processes, then, involve the formation, manipulation, and use of cognitions. Cognitive processes are many and varied. We already discussed a number of fundamental cognitive processes when we talked about the selective and organizing nature of perception, the relatively permanent changes in mental processes that take place with learning, and the encoding, storing, and retrieving of information in memory.

In this chapter, we will consider three complex cognitive tasks: concept formation, the use of language, and problem solving. Topic 7A deals with concepts, how they are formed, and how they are used to communicate through language. In Topic 7B, we will discuss problem solving. Because these cognitive tasks rely heavily on perception, learning, and memory, we can refer to them as "higher" cognitive processes.

In this topic, we will generate a working definition of what a concept is. As Howard Pollio expressed it, "Right at the beginning it is important to emphasize how difficult a concept is the concept of concept" (1974, p. 98). We'll see that there are several types of concepts and at least two ways to think about them: a classical view and a probabilistic view.

Once we have dealt with matters of definition, we will attend to how concepts are acquired or learned. Psychologists agree that most concepts are learned. How they are learned is the debatable issue.

The second higher cognitive process we'll examine in this topic is language. Our use of language reflects a remarkable set of mental processes. Again, our first step will be to define what language is. We'll review some research and theories that deal with our ability to produce and comprehend language. Finally, we'll take a brief look at language acquisition.

Although we may refer to the activities discussed in this chapter as higher cognitive processes, it should be clear to you that they are in no way rare or unusual. Particularly as a student, you encounter concept formation, communicating effectively with language, and problem solving as important, day-to-day activities. In your study of psychology alone, you already have formed many new concepts, some of them simple, some of them complex. Your ability to understand and use those concepts directly reflects your facility with language. Forming concepts and using language may be higher cognitive processes, but they are processes upon which we rely every day.

Our ability to form concepts allows us to mentally represent objects and events in categories or classes.

concept *a mental representation of a category or class of events or objects*

THE CONCEPT OF CONCEPT

Think about chairs. Really. Take a minute or two to think about chairs. As you do this, try to notice what is happening.

Images come to mind. You "see" a large variety of chairs in different contexts. You may have thought about high chairs, armchairs, dining room chairs, rocking chairs, chairs in a classroom, easy chairs, chairs with smooth leather seats, overstuffed chairs upholstered with flowery fabric, broken chairs, kitchen chairs, and so on. We all know what a chair is. We have all formed a concept or a category that we've agreed to label *chair*.

As you thought about chairs, did any one particular chair—a standard, definitional chair—come to mind? Were there any features or attributes that all, or most, had in common? What are the defining characteristics of chairs? Most have four legs, although beanbag chairs have no legs at all. Most chairs are used for sitting, although we do stand on chairs to reach high places. Many chairs are used in association with tables and some with desks. Most chairs have a back. However, if the back gets too low, you have a stool, not a chair. Chairs have limited widths: They usually accommodate only one person. If they are wider, they become love seats or sofas. Chairs are usually considered to be pieces of furniture.

Now try a different task. Consider the following statements:

A rogaritz is usually white.

A rogaritz is hard and dry.

Rogaritzen (the plural of rogaritz) can be of any color.

Rogaritzen can be used to write on a blackboard.

A rogaritz will fit comfortably in one hand.

You shouldn't put a rogaritz in your mouth.

Using rogaritzen usually creates messy dust.

Have you figured out what a *rogaritz* is? Have you ever used *rogaritzen*? Would you recognize a *rogaritz* if you saw one? How many uses for *rogaritzen* can you think of? If you can answer these questions—if you know what a *rogaritz* is—you have acquired a new concept: the concept of *rogaritz* (after Werner & Kaplan, 1950). You recognize it as a piece of chalk. Because we already have a perfectly good word with which to label this concept, I suppose there's no compelling reason to try to remember the new concept label *rogaritz*.

I've asked you to go through these mental gymnastics so that you can better appreciate the definition of concept. A **concept** is the *mental representation* of a category, or class, of events or objects. Note that concepts represent categories, classes, or groups of things, not just single individual cases.

A world without concepts would be unimaginable. If we had no way to organize or classify our experiences, our impressions of our environments (and of ourselves) would be chaotic. Because we have a *concept* of chair, for example, we do not have to treat each and every encounter with a chair as a new experience. We do not have to make up a new and different label or word for every single chair we see, nor do we have to decide what a chair is for every time we see one. We only have to recognize an object as having the characteristics appropriate for this category and refer to it as a chair. We may think of concepts as "building blocks for human thought and behavior" (Medin, 1989, p. 1469).

We can define a concept, then, in terms of attributes or features that are related according to some rule or rules. This *attribute-rule* approach works fairly well for a concept like chair. We've listed above some of the *attributes* associated with the category of objects called "chair." Perhaps you've thought of others. The *rule* that relates these features states that chairs share many, if not all, of these attributes at the same time. This is what we will call the classical view of concepts. According to this point of view, learning a new concept is a matter of learning the attributes that characterize it and the rule that relates those attributes (Bourne et al., 1983). (As we will soon see, there are some concepts for which this attribute-rule approach does not seem to work well.)

Before we examine an alternative point of view, we'll take a closer look at concepts in this classical, formal sense. Generally, this means we'll discuss concepts as they have been studied in the psychology laboratory. Then we'll look at concepts as they tend to be used in the world outside the laboratory.

Concepts in the Laboratory: The Classical View

Defining concepts in the psychology laboratory is fairly easy. Among other things, it's totally arbitrary—we can make up our own concepts and define them however we'd like. We can take the classical attribute-rule approach to concepts and apply it quite literally. First, we decide which attributes we'd like to deal with—perhaps color, shape, and size. Then we provide a limited number of values for each of our attributes. *Color*: Possible values of this attribute may be red, green, or blue. *Shape*: The possible values may be round, square, or triangular. *Size*: The values may be small, medium, or large. So we have chosen three attributes, each of which may have one of three values. All we need to do now is decide what rules we'll use to relate these values to form concepts.

Let's say that we want to define a new concept: the concept of *wug*. To do so, we now need a rule that tells us the relationships among the values of our attributes. Let's say a *wug* is square, blue, and small. We have thus assigned *wug* a value on each of the three attributes. Moreover, we have specified that to qualify as a *wug*, we must have all three values. To put it simply, *wugs* are small blue squares. We could use these same three attributes to define *luks* as large red triangles, and so on. Take a look at Figure 7.1. Given these items, can you find the *wugs* and the *luks*? Doing so demonstrates that you've learned a couple of new formal concepts. **Formal concepts**, then, are those in which the attribute values are relatively few in number, clearly defined, and clearly related by a rule.

There are several ways in which the values of attributes can be related by rules to define formal concepts. Let's briefly mention just four attribute-rule combinations: *conjunctive*, *disjunctive*, *affirmative*, and *relational*.

Rules specifying that concepts must have one of a number of values define conjunctive concepts. Thus, *wug* is a conjunctive concept because *wugs* must be small *and* blue *and* square. Blueness, or squareness, or small-ness alone does not define a *wug*. One value of each of our three attributes must be present for us to have a *wug*. Another example of a conjunctive concept might be short-term memory, which we discussed in Chapter 6. The defining characteristic of this memory is that it has a limited capacity

Membership in some categories or concepts is occasionally difficult to determine. These days, the concept of soldier must be broad enough to include females, although women are seldom thought of as prototypic.

formal concepts *concepts with relatively few, well-defined attribute values and clearly defined rules to relate them*

Figure 7.1

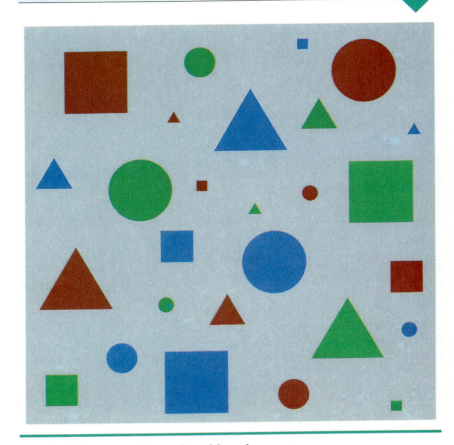

Stimuli of the sort used in studies of formal concepts.

and a limited duration. (Here we have only two defining attributes, whereas there were three for *wug*.)

Disjunctive concepts are defined by an either-or rule regarding attributes. For example, a *dax* is defined as being *either* red *or* large. Can you find a *dax* in Figure 7.1? There are many more *daxes* than *wugs*—15 in all. In baseball, the concept of a strike gives us an example of a disjunctive concept. A strike is defined as being *either* a "pitch that crosses home plate in a prescribed area" *or* "a ball batted into foul territory," *or* "a pitch swung at and missed."

Affirmation rules represent a third attribute-rule combination. They simply specify membership in a concept by stating or affirming just one attribute value, for instance, *all green objects*. In this case, size and shape do not matter at all. An item is a member of an affirmative concept if it has the affirmed value of one given attribute. In real life, there are not many examples of affirmative concepts—objects or events that can be categorized on the basis of one attribute alone (all living things, or anything that is red, would be examples).

A fourth attribute-rule combination involves a formal concept with which you are familiar: the relational concept. These concepts are defined in terms of comparisons of values on some dimension or attribute. The concepts of *larger than*, *nearer than*, and *smarter than* are relational. When we identify a concept as being "bigger than a bread basket" or "faster than a speeding bullet," we are using a relational rule (big*ger*, fas*ter*) to tell us about attributes (size and speed) that are relevant for that concept.

Formal concepts such as these we've just listed are very useful in the psychology laboratory, where we can carefully exercise control over the various features that define particular concepts. We'll see shortly that most of the early research on concept formation involved formal concepts. But as useful as this classical approach has been, it is not without problems (Medin, 1989). For one thing, there are any number of concepts—shared by many of us—for which we have great difficulty precisely specifying the defining attributes. "Birds fly." Well, not *all* birds fly. "Violins are made of wood." Well, not *all* violins are made of wood." In fact, even experts sometimes have difficulty naming defining attributes or features of concepts with which they are familiar.

A related problem with the attribute-rule approach to concepts in day-to-day life is that not all examples of concept membership are equally good examples (Barsalou, 1989). Some chairs we know about are simply better examples of chairs than others. And membership in a given category is often quite unclear. Is a lamp a piece of furniture? How about a rug? Or a radio? As we mentioned above, there is another approach that psychologists have found useful: the probabilistic view.

BEFORE YOU GO ON

How can we use attributes and rules to define concepts?

Concepts in the Real World: The Probabilistic View

Talking about attributes with values and the rules that combine them may be reasonable for the sorts of concepts we study in psychology laboratories, but what about concepts as they occur in real life; those referred to as **natural concepts**? Is it always possible to define concepts in terms of attributes and rules? Remember the problems we had when we tried this with *chairs*? Real or natural concepts are often not easily defined and may be referred to as "fuzzy" concepts (Labov, 1973; Oden, 1987; Zadeh, 1965).

How would you characterize the difference between a cup and a bowl? Somehow we know what a cup is, and we know what a bowl is, but there is no clear distinction between the two. Each is a fuzzy concept. If you think this distinction *is* clear, consider the drawings of cups in Figure 7.2. Do *any* of them look at least a little like a bowl? This is why we often find ourselves saying things like, "Technically speaking, a tomato is really a fruit, not a vegetable." "In a way, a bat is rather like a bird." "Actually, a spider is not an insect." We didn't have this problem with formal concepts, such as *wugs* and *daxes*, but we encounter it regularly when we use natural concepts (Rosch & Mervis, 1975).

natural concepts *the potentially "fuzzy" sorts of concepts that occur in real life, with ill-defined attributes and/or rules*

Figure **7.2**

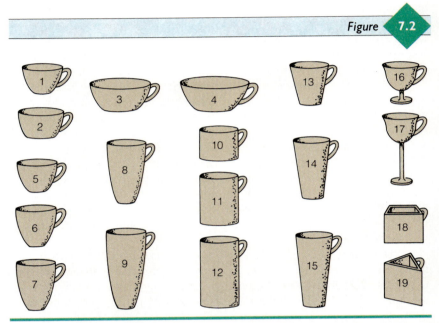

What is a cup? To some degree, each of these objects may be classified as members of the concept CUP, but some seem to be better examples than others, suggesting that CUP is a fuzzy concept.

prototype *the member of a concept or category that best typifies or represents that concept or category*

One way to deal with this complication is to follow the lead of Eleanor Rosch (1973, 1975, 1978). She has proposed that we think about naturally occurring concepts or categories in terms of **prototypes**. A prototype is a member of a category that best typifies or represents the category to which it belongs; it is the ideal or best member of the concept.

Rosch is suggesting that within our concept of chair, there are some instances that are more typical and better examples—more "chair-ish" than others. A robin may be a prototypic bird. Crows are less prototypic. Vultures are even less typical, and the fact that a penguin even *is* a bird is occasionally hard to remember. (For that matter, just who decides on category membership can be argued: "Penguins, of course, really are birds biologically

Using prototypes is one way to help us better define natural concepts. In this way, a robin may be a more likely prototype than a penguin for the concept of bird.

GOODNESS OF EXAMPLE RANKINGS FOR THE FURNITURE CATEGORY

Member	Goodness of Example Rank	Member	Goodness of Example Rank	Member	Goodness of Example Rank
Chair	1.5	Vanity	21	Mirror	41
Sofa	1.5	Bookcase	22	Television	42
Couch	3.5	Lounge	23	Bar	43
Table	3.5	Chaise lounge	24	Shelf	44
Easy chair	5	Ottoman	25	Rug	45
Dresser	6.5	Footstool	26	Pillow	46
Rocking chair	6.5	Cabinet	27	Wastebasket	47
Coffee table	8	China closet	28	Radio	48
Rocker	9	Bench	29	Sewing machine	49
Love seat	10	Buffet	30	Stove	50
Chest of drawers	11	Lamp	31	Counter	51
Desk	12	Stool	32	Clock	52
Bed	13	Hassock	33	Drapes	53
Bureau	14	Drawers	34	Refrigerator	54
Davenport	15.5	Piano	35	Picture	55
End table	15.5	Cushion	36	Closet	56
Divan	17	Magazine rack	37	Vase	57
Night table	18	Hi-fi	38	Ashtray	58
Chest	19	Cupboard	39	Fan	59
Cedar chest	20	Stereo	40	Telephone	60

From Rosch, 1975.

speaking, although it is not clear why we should be willing to give biologists the last word on the matter" (Oden, 1987, p. 215)).

Figure 7.3 lists members of a "furniture" category (Rosch, 1978). You can see which are the *best* examples of the concept of furniture. Within this category, *lamp* turns out be a poor example, and of the 60 items rated, *fan*, *ashtray,* and *telephone* ranked at the bottom of the list, barely qualifying as furniture.

Automobile manufacturers created something of a concept definition problem when they introduced a vehicle now generally called a mini-van. Mini-vans are not real vans, but they aren't cars either, nor are they station wagons. They certainly aren't trucks. Hence, a new label for a new concept was devised: mini-van.

In Rosch's view, then, some categories are rather poorly delineated and may very well spill over into others. This view argues that some instances of a concept provide good examples, while others provide poorer examples. Excellent examples (prototypes) share the largest number of attributes common to members of the category *and* have few attributes that cause them to be confused with others (Lasky & Kallio, 1978).

As it happens, the prototype approach to defining concepts is not without a few problems of its own. For one thing, what we've said so far about this view fails to take context or situational variables into account. What does that mean? Essentially the problem here is that what is most typical, or prototypical, of a given category depends on the situation (e.g., Roth &

Sometimes, new concepts with new labels—such as minivans—are developed.

Shoben, 1983). "Robin" may be a prototypical bird in some general, diffuse way, but not in the minds of hunters, out in the field with their bird dogs. Is there really such a thing as a most typical "chair?" Don't we have to ask, "In what context?" What is the best example of a beverage? Water? Coffee? Tea? Beer? Soda? For whom and in what context?

BEFORE YOU GO ON

How does the concept of prototype
help our understanding of what a concept is?

Forming Concepts

By the time we get to be college students, our minds are crammed with a huge variety of mental representations—both formal and natural concepts. How were those concepts acquired? Where did they come from? Philosopher John Locke (1690/1964) asked, "How comes it (the mind) to be furnished?" To his own question, Locke replied, "I answer in one word, from experience." Few psychologists today would argue with Locke's conclusion that concepts are learned—they are acquired through experience.

A Classic Demonstration. Figure 7.4 shows some of the stimulus materials that Edna Heidbreder used in her 1946 study of concept formation. Each item in a set (there are five sets here) was presented to a subject *one at a time*. As each picture was presented, Heidbreder would name it, using the nonsense label included in Figure 7.4 for the first three sets. The subjects in the experiment *did not* see these names.

Subjects were told to learn the name associated with each picture. Each set of pictures was presented over and over until the subject could supply the name associated with each picture. This wasn't too difficult to do, and soon subjects could provide a label for each item in set 1. Then the items in set 2 were presented one at a time. Subjects were asked to learn the label for each of *these* little pictures. As you can see, the names for the items of set 2 are the same as those used for set 1.

This procedure was repeated for 16 different sets of pictures. Each time, the subjects had to learn the label or name associated with a picture. The pattern behind what Heidbreder was doing is obvious to us as we look at all the pictures and their labels in Figure 7.4. It is clear that all drawings of people are labeled *relk*. Collections of six small things are named *mank*. Circular items are *fards*, and so on. *Ling* thus becomes a label for a concept—roughly, things appearing in pairs.

Heidbreder's subjects eventually formed the same concepts that you and I can see so clearly in Figure 7.4. Remember, though, that they were seeing these items one at a time, couldn't see the provided label, and didn't even realize that they were in a concept formation experiment. They thought that they were simply learning verbal labels for little pictures.

As subjects progressed through the sets of picture-label pairs, they required fewer and fewer presentations of the stimuli to form the picture-

We may experience flowers and form our concept of them at a very young age and carry that same idea throughout our lives.

Figure **7.4**

	Set 1		Set 2		Set 3		Set 4		Set 5

The sets of images Heidbreder used in her experiments on concept formation. As each image was presented, it was given a nonsense label (labels are shown in the first three sets). The subjects were presented with the images and the nonsense labels until they could supply the labels themselves. Thus, they came to label drawings of trees as "mul"—and a new concept had been formed.

label association. Toward the end, some subjects provided the correct response name for a pictured item even before Heidbreder had a chance to say it. Significantly, subjects often could not state what rule *or* attributes were underlying a particular concept, but they could identify new members of that concept. Among other things, this finding implies that we may form concepts that we can use, but that we really cannot describe or "talk about" to others. Heidbreder's study not only suggested how we form (at least some) concepts, but it also convinced psychologists that concept formation tasks could be brought into the laboratory and studied systematically.

Developing Strategies and Testing Hypotheses. Subjects in concept-learning experiments often go about forming concepts in systematic ways. To be sure, some people just guess at random whether or not a presented item belongs in a given category, particularly at first. Most subjects, however, develop some strategy to guide their responding (Bruner, Goodnow, & Austin, 1956; Johnson, 1978). In this context, a strategy is a systematic plan or procedure for identifying members of a category or concept.

One way to think about concept formation is to say that subjects go through a process of *hypothesis testing*. That is, they develop a hypothesis, or reasonable guess, about what is going on, and they test that hypothesis when presented with new stimuli. For example, saying to yourself, "I think that all members of this concept are green" is a hypothesis. You test it by finding another green stimulus and seeing if it fits within the category, too.

Notice that this approach to concept formation works whether we are dealing with formal concepts in terms of rules and attributes or with natural categories in terms of prototypes. In the former, classical case, hypotheses about specific attributes and rules are formed and tested. In the latter, probabilistic case, new stimuli are tested in terms of their similarity to a prototype (Posner & Keele, 1968, 1970).

In a sense, what we are suggesting here is that concepts are formed in accord with theories we have about the world. For example, "I think that a spider looks a lot like my idea of what an insect is. It may not be the best example of an insect, but it sure looks like one to me." When you test that hypothesis (perhaps in a biology class), you discover that you're wrong, because as much as a spider may appear similar to your prototypic insect, it happens to belong in a different category (that of *arachnid*).

This hypothesis-testing view of concept formation helps explain the presence of some concepts that are otherwise difficult to account for (Medin, 1989). Consider this list: *children*, *money*, *photo albums*, and *pets*. Are they in any way members of the same category, or concept? Once I tell you that I am thinking about "items to remove quickly if one's house is on fire" the list makes perfectly good sense, because it fits our view, our theory, of the way the world works, or should work (Barsalou, 1983).

Notice also that forming concepts requires the active involvement of one's memory. When presented with a new stimulus, we retrieve from memory other similar stimuli and make judgments concerning whether or not we can match the new stimulus with any already-existing category or concept. If the newly presented stimulus matches the prototypic example of a concept (stored in memory), then we will have little difficulty adding it to our preexisting concept. If the new stimulus does *not* match a prototype, we have to decide if we're faced with a poor example of a known concept or if we should devise a whole new category to include the new stimulus (Stern, 1985).

What many experiments since Heidbreder's in 1946 have demonstrated is that subjects form concepts in a very systematic way, based on what they know at the time, developing strategies and testing hypotheses. But even as Heidbreder's study suggests, people cannot always tell us what strategies, or theories, they are using. For example, young children (ages 6 to 8) have a very reasonable notion of the concept of *family*, but even much older children (ages 12 and 13) can seldom tell you the rule or the attributes or the prototype that defines *family* for them (Watson & Amgott-Kwan, 1984).

We have defined concepts and have seen some of the processes by which they are formed. Now we will see how the complex cognitive process of language use allows us to communicate to others our knowledge, concepts, or mental representations of the world.

BEFORE YOU GO ON

What does Edna Heidbreder's classic study of concept formation tell us about the process?

What does it mean to say that people use hypothesis testing in forming concepts?

LANGUAGE

Because we form concepts, we bring order and economy to our understanding of objects and events in the world. Because we use language, we are able to communicate that understanding to others. In this sense, using language is a social process. It is a social process that reflects a marvelously complex cognitive activity. The philosopher Suzanne Langer put it this way: "Language is, without a doubt, the most momentous and at the same time the most mysterious product of the human mind. Between the clearest animal call of love or warning or anger, and a man's least, trivial *word*, there lies a whole day of Creation—or in modern phrase, a whole chapter of evolution" (1951, p. 94).

In this section, we'll review some of the issues involved in the subfield of psychology called psycholinguistics. **Psycholinguistics** is a hybrid discipline, made up of scientists trained in psychology *and* linguistics. Psycholinguists "are interested in the underlying knowledge and abilities which people must have in order to use language and to learn language in childhood" (Slobin, 1979, p. 2). First, let's define the concept of language.

psycholinguistics *the science that studies the cognitive processes involved in the use and acquisition of language*

A Definition of Language

How shall we characterize this mysterious product of the human mind called language? **Language** is a large collection of arbitrary symbols that have significance for a language-using community and that follow certain rules of combination (after Morris, 1946). Now let's pull apart this definition and examine some of the points that it raises.

language *a large collection of arbitrary symbols that have significance for a language-using community and that follow certain rules of combination*

Language is the vehicle for communicating our understanding of events to others.

Although we say the symbols of language are arbitrary, a number of people need to agree on what the symbols are and how they will be used.

First, language is made up of a large number of *symbols*. The symbols that make up language are commonly referred to as words, labels that we have assigned to concepts. They are labels for our mental representations. When we use the word *chair* as a symbol, we don't use it to label one specific instance of a chair. We use the word as a symbol to represent our concept, our mental idea, of chairs. Notice that as symbols, words do not have to stand for real things in the real world. We have words to describe objects or events that cannot be perceived directly, such as *ghost* or, for that matter, *mind*. With language, we can communicate about owls and pussy-cats in teacups, four-dimensional, time-warped hyperspace, and a beagle that flies his doghouse into battle against the Red Baron. Words stand for our cognitions, our concepts, and we have a great number of them. They allow us to communicate what we know.

It is important that we define the symbols of language as being *arbitrary*. By doing so we imply that there is no requirement or reason for representing anything with the particular symbol we do. You call what you are reading a book (or a textbook, to use a more specific symbol). We have all agreed (in English) that *book* is the appropriate symbol for what you are reading. But we don't have to. We could all agree to call it a *fard*, if we'd like. Or a *relm*. The symbols of a language are arbitrary. They are not genetically determined. They can be whatever we like, but once established by common use or tradition, they become part of one's language and must be learned and applied consistently by each new language user.

To be part of a language, at least in a practical sense, our language symbols need to have *significance for a language-using community*. That is, a number of people need to agree on the symbols that are used in a language and need to agree on what those symbols mean. This is another way of saying that language use is a social enterprise. For example, there is a language-using community for which the utterance *"Kedinin üstünde halt var"* makes sense or has significance. I'm not part of that community, but many people are. To them—people who know Turkish—the statement reads roughly, "The cat is on the mat" (Slobin, 1979, p. 4). You and I might decide to call what you are now reading a *fard*, but then you and I would be in a terribly small language-using community. We're better off going along with the majority here and using the word *book*.

The final part of our definition tells us that the symbols of a language must *follow certain rules of combination*. What this means is that language is structured. Language is rule-governed. Language is used to communicate ideas, to share our thoughts and feelings with others. There are ways of communicating that do not involve language, of course. What makes language use a special form of communication is the fact that it is governed by rules of combination. For one thing, there are rules about how we can and cannot string symbols together in language. In English, we say, "The small boy slept late." We do not say, "Slept boy late small the." Well, we could say it, but no one will know for sure exactly what we mean by it, and everyone will recognize that the utterance violates the combinatorial rules of English. When the rules of language are violated, utterances lose their meaning, and the value of language as a means of communication is lost. We'll have much more to say about the structure of language in the next section.

Even with this complex definition of language, there are a few points we've left out. For one, using language is a remarkably *creative*, *generative* process; very few of the utterances we make are utterances we've ever made before or even encountered before. It's unlikely, for example, that you have ever before read a sentence just like this one. Virtually every time we use our language, we use it in a new and creative way, which emphasizes the importance of the underlying rules or structure of language. A second point: Language (symbol use) allows for *displacement*: the ability to communicate about the "not here and the not now." We can use language to discuss yesterday's lunch and tomorrow's class schedule. We can talk about things that are not here, never were, and never will be. Language is the only form of communication that allows us to do so.

One final observation: Language and speech are not synonymous terms. Speech is but one (common) way in which language is expressed as behavior. There are others, including writing, coding (as in Morse code), or signing (as in American Sign Language).

BEFORE YOU GO ON

What are some of the defining characteristics of language?

Describing the Structure in Language

When psycholinguists analyze a language, they usually do so at three levels. At all three levels, we can see rules and structure at work. The first level involves the system of sounds that are used when we express the language as speech. The second level deals with the meaning of words and sentences, and the third concerns the rules that are used for combining words and phrases to generate sentences. Let's briefly consider each of these levels of analysis.

phoneme *the smallest unit of sound in the spoken form of a language*

Speech Sounds and Structure. The individual speech sounds of a language are called **phonemes**. These are the sounds we make when we talk to each other. Phonemes themselves have no meaning, but when they are put together in the proper order, the result is a meaningful utterance. The word *cat*, for example, is made up of three phonemes: the initial consonant sound (actually a "k" sound here), the vowel sound of "a" in the middle, and another consonant sound, "t." How phonemes are combined to produce words and phrases is rule-governed, as we have said. If we were to interchange the two consonant sounds in *cat*, we would have an altogether different utterance, with an altogether different meaning: *tack*. There are approximately 45 different phonemes in English. (And because the correspondence between those 45 sounds and the 26 letters of our alphabet is often muddled at best, it is no wonder many of us have problems spelling.)

To use a language requires that one knows which speech sounds (phonemes) are part of that language and how they may be combined to form larger language units. For example, the difference between *time*, *climb*, *rhyme*, and *grime* is the initial phoneme or phonemes of each utterance. We recognize each of these as acceptable words in English. We also recognize that *blime* and *frime* are not English words, although we also know that they could be. The "bl" and "fr" sound combinations of *blime* and *frime* are acceptable in English: They follow the rules. You recognize that *gzlime* or *wbime* are not words. They violate the English rules for combining sounds into words.

BEFORE YOU GO ON

What are phonemes, and in what way are they rule-governed?

semantics *the study of the meaning of words and sentences*

morpheme *the smallest unit of meaning in a language*

Meaning and Structure. Describing a language's phonemes, noting which sounds are relevant and which combinations are possible, is only a small part of a complete description of a language. Another level of analysis involves *meaning* in the language. The study of the meaning is called **semantics**.

Researchers interested in semantics take the morpheme to be their unit of analysis. A **morpheme** is the smallest unit of meaning in a spoken language. A morpheme is a collection of phonemes that means something. In many cases, *morpheme* and *word* are synonymous terms. In addition to words, morphemes include all of the prefixes and suffixes of a language. For example, the utterance *write* is a morpheme and a word; it has meaning, and it is not possible to subdivide it into smaller, meaningful units. *Rewrite* is also a word and has meaning, but it is composed of two morphemes, *write* and *re*, which in this context does have meaning—roughly, "write it again." *Tablecloth* is another word composed of two morphemes, *table* and *cloth*. When we change a noun from singular to plural, *boy* to *boys* or *ox* to *oxen*, for example, we are adding a morpheme to the noun—a morpheme that indicates plurality—that changes our meaning.

Notice that the way we generate morphemes is governed by rules. For example, we cannot go around making nouns plural in any old way. The pural of ox is oxen, not oxes. The plural of mouse is mice, not mouses, mousen, or meese. If I want you to write something over again, I have to ask you to *rewrite* it, not *write-re* it. We all know what a *tablecloth* is, but the combination in *clothtable* is rather nonsensical. Notice too, how morphemes are verbal labels for acquired concepts (mental representations). Telling you to rewrite something would make no sense if we did not share a concept of "writing" and a concept of "doing things over again."

In English, meaning is related to word ordering. How morphemes are strung together to form longer utterances, such as phrases and sentences, has important implications for the meaning being expressed. There is all the difference in the world between "The girl hit John" and "John hit the girl." The rules that govern the ordering of elements to form phrases and sentences bring us to the third level of analysis.

BEFORE YOU GO ON

What is semantics?

What are morphemes?

Sentences and Structure. The aspect of our language that most obviously uses rules is reflected in our ability to generate sentences—to string words (or morphemes) together to create meaningful utterances. "Communication surely does not consist of an unordered pile of morphemes. How can morphemes be combined into sensible utterances in a certain language?" (Hörmann, 1986, p. 57). The rules that govern the way sentences are formed (or structured) in a language are referred to as the **syntax** of a language.

To know the syntax, or syntactic rules, of one's language involves a peculiar sort of knowledge or cognitive ability. We all know what the rules of English are in the sense that we can and do use them, but few of us know what the rules are in the sense that we can tell anyone else what they are. We say that people develop a *competence*—a cognitive ability that governs their language use. That ability allows us to judge the extent to which an utterance is a meaningful, well-formed sentence. Competence with the syntactic rules of English can be demonstrated with a few examples of what are called linguistic intuitions (Howard, 1983; Slobin, 1979). **Linguistic intuitions** are judgments or decisions that we can make about the extent to which utterances are acceptable in a language. What makes them intuitive is that we can make these judgments without being able to specify exactly how they are being made.

For example, we know that "The dog looks terrifying" fits the rules of English and that "The dog looks barking" does not. Somehow, we recognize that "The dog looks watermelon" is downright absurd. The first utterance means something. The second and third do not. At the same time, we can recognize that the utterance "Colorless green ideas sleep furiously" fits the rules of English even though it doesn't make any sense (Chomsky, 1957).

syntax *the rules that govern how the morphemes of a language may be combined to form meaningful utterances*

linguistic intuitions *judgments or decisions about the syntactic acceptability of utterances without the ability to specify why*

It may be a silly thing to say, but we realize intuitively that it is an acceptable thing to say.

We are also able to recognize that these two utterances communicate the same message, even though they look (and sound) quite different:

The student read the textbook.

The textbook was read by the student.

In either case, we know who is doing what. However, putting this basic idea into either of two forms does change the psychological focus of what is being said. In the first, we find out what the student did, and in the second, we focus on the notion that it was the textbook that was read. Again, we see that the way elements are structured in language affects the meaning of what is being communicated. Semantics and syntax cannot be separated.

Another linguistic intuition that demonstrates our competence with the rules of our language is in our ability to detect ambiguity. Consider these two sentences:

They are cooking apples.

They are cooking apples.

Now there's no doubt that they appear to be identical, but upon reflection we can see that they may be communicating very different (ambiguous) ideas. In one case, we may be talking about what some people are cooking (apples as opposed to spaghetti). In the other, we may be identifying a variety of apple (those best suited for cooking as opposed to those best suited for eating).

In part, this sentence about apples is ambiguous only when we are not aware of the context in which it was used. Is the sentence in response to a question about what some people are doing or in response to a question about different sorts of apples? This is not an isolated example of ambiguity in language. There are many, such as, "The shooting of the policemen was terrible," or "Flying airplanes can be dangerous." When we start referring to context, we again are reminded of the *social* nature of language use.

pragmatics *the study of how social context affects the meaning of linguistic events*

The Social Situation and Structure. Pragmatics is the study of how linguistic events are related to the social context in which they occur. Our understanding of sarcasm (as in "Well, it certainly is a beautiful day!" when in fact it is rainy, cold, and miserable); or simile (as in "Life is like a sewer. . ."), or metaphor (as in "That slam dunk certainly delivered the knockout blow"), or cliché (as in "It rained cats and dogs") depends on our appreciation of the context of the utterance and the intention of the speaker.

In fact, pragmatics deals with decisions made by language users (as producers or comprehenders) based on the social situation at the moment. Think how you modify your language use when you talk to your best friend, a preschool child, a professor in her office, or a poor driver who just cut you off at an intersection. Once again, how you use language to communicate depends on certain general rules you have acquired about matching one's style of speech— in terms of formality or complexity or content, intonation, intensity, and so on—to the social situation.

Psycholinguistics has some very high goals. To understand the cognitive competence people must have in order to use language requires understanding how we use the sounds (phonemes) of spoken language, how we assign meaning to morphemes, how we combine words and morphemes to form sentences, and how we alter our language to match the social situation. Our study of the psychology of language involves us with the most complex of cognitive tasks. In our next section, we'll look at some of the issues involved in developmental psychologuistics—the study of language acquisition.

BEFORE YOU GO ON

What is syntax?

What are linguistic intuitions?

What is pragmatics?

Language Acquisition

One of the most significant achievements of childhood is the acquisition of language. There are very few, if any, cognitive skills that can compare to language in complexity and usefulness. How children go about acquiring language skills has been a concern of many psycholinguists. The process seems nearly magical: gooing, cooing, babbling one day, then a word or two, then "Why is the sky blue, Daddy, why is the sky blue?"—and all in the span of just a few months time.

Let me tell you now that there simply is no answer to the question, "How do humans acquire language?" Steven Pinker, director of the Center for Cognitive Science at MIT calls language acquisition "the jewel in the crown of cognition—it is what everyone wants to explain" (deCuevas, 1990, p. 63). At best, we have tentative theories and hypotheses. We are only now getting reasonably close to adequately describing *what* happens. Describing *how* it happens will take longer.

What Happens in Language Acquisition. We've suggested that language can be described at different levels: sounds (phonemes), meanings (morphemes), and structure (syntax). Let's consider the development of each of these facets of language use in turn.

Infants create speech sounds spontaneously. They come into the world with a cry, and make noise with disturbing regularity forever after. At about the age of 6 months, random cries and noises are replaced by the more regular sounds of **babbling**. Babbling is the production of speech phonemes, often in repetitive, rhythmic patterns. A curiosity is that when children babble, they do so by producing virtually all the known phonemes of all known languages. (As we'll soon see, phonemes that are not part of one's language then drop out of the child's repertoire.) All babies babble in the same general way (Nakazima, 1962; Oller, 1981). An adult cannot distinguish the babbling of a Chinese infant from that of a Greek infant or an American infant. Even deaf infants produce babbling sounds that are indistinguishable from those of hearing children (Lenneberg, Rebelsky, & Nichols, 1965).

The acquisition of vocabulary follows soon after babbling begins. In all cases, comprehension, or understanding, comes before production. That is,

babbling *speech sounds produced in rhythmic, repetitive patterns*

children understand and respond appropriately to the meaning of utterances long before they are able to produce those utterances themselves. We usually notice the appearance of a child's first word or two at about the age of 1 year (parents often argue that the onset of meaningful speech is earlier, but independent observers often fail to confirm what may be parental wishful thinking). Once it begins, word and morpheme acquistion is truly remarkable. A 1-year-old may produce only two or three words (remember: he or she may very well understand dozens of words, but can produce only a few). By the age of 2 years, word production is up to about 50. In terms of comprehension, by age 2½, a child understands 200–300 words; by age 3 over 1000; by age 6, somewhere between 8000 and 14,000 words (Benedict, 1979; Brown, 1973; Carey, 1978).

Describing the development of syntactic rules in children has proven to be quite difficult. For one thing, as linguists began to understand the rules that govern adult language, it seemed reasonable to look for these same rules in the language of children. What soon became apparent was that the syntax of adult forms of language do not emerge until long after children have begun stringing words and morphemes together in utterances. Even though we do not find adult structure or rules in the language use of children, children still use language in a rule-governed way. That is, young children do not just speak adult language badly; instead, their language follows its own rules.

holophrastic speech *the use of one word to communicate a number of different meanings*

The first use of vocalization as language is called **holophrastic speech**. Holophrastic speech is the use of just one word to communicate a range of intentions and meanings dependent upon gestures, intonation, and so on. Before this stage is apparent, a child may produce a number of words, but will do so only as a naming exercise. Words are used as labels for concepts and nothing else. With holophrastic speech, individual words are used to communicate a range of possibilities. Imagine it yourself. Picture a young child sitting in a high chair. Can't you just see how the one-word utterance *milk* could be used to communicate such things as *"I want my milk!"* or "Uh-oh, I dropped my milk," or "Oh yea! here's my milk," or "Yuck, not milk again."

At about the age of 2 years, we can note the appearance of two-word utterances. When carefully analyzed, these two-word utterances are very regular, as if they were being put together according to some rather strict rules. Given an understanding of the words *big* and *little* and many nouns, a child may say, "big ball," "big plane," "big doggie," "little stick," "little cup," and so on. What is curious is that this child will never reverse this word order. He will not say "ball big" or "doggie little" (Braine, 1976).

From the point of the two-word utterance on, language development—syntax development—is so rapid that it is difficult even to note the stages through which the process passes. From the two-word utterance stage there is a period that is typified by "telegraphic speech" comprised of nouns, verbs, and adjectives, but hardly any "function words" such as articles or prepositions. We hear children say things such as: "Daddy go store now" or "Billy draw pictures." Then, at roughly age 2½ years, language use expands at an explosive rate. There really is no noticeable three-word or four-word stage of development. Phrases are lengthened, noun phrases first, so that "Billy's ball" becomes "Billy's red ball," which soon becomes "Billy's red ball that Mommy got at the store." By the time children are ready to begin school, at about age 5, they demonstrate both the understanding and the production of virtually every type of acceptable type of sentence structure in their language.

Now that we have a very basic idea of what happens when children acquire language, we'll briefly consider how we can account for the process.

BEFORE YOU GO ON

What are some of the landmark events that occur during language acquisition?

Theories of Acquisition. How does language acquistion happen? If you took a foreign language in high school or are taking one now, did it ever occur to you that there were little children somewhere in the world who were acquiring the same language that you were struggling with? And they were not having any problems with it at all. Acquiring one's language is a cognitive feat at which all (normal) humans succeed.

Have you noticed that throughout this section I have avoided the phrase *language learning*, referring instead to *language acquisition* or *language development*? This was intentional because I did not want to suggest that acquring language is simply a matter of learning. On the other hand, language is certainly not innate or instinctive in the usual sense, or everyone would speak the very same language. What we are going to end up with here is a reminder of an observation we made back in Topic 1A: "An organism's nature and nurture interact." Some of language acquisition can be accounted for by learning (in all the ways we discussed in Chapter 5), but some aspects of language acquisition defy explanation in terms of learning and suggest an inherited basis for language acquisition. We here cannot get into all the details of the debate over which aspects of language development are a function of learning (one's nurture) and which suggest a biological basis (one's nature), but we can review some of the issues.

Theories of language development in terms of learning (e.g., Skinner, 1957; Whitehurst, 1982) certainly have their place. No one will claim that language emerges free of the influence of learning, experience, conditioning, reinforcement, and the like. We can be most comfortable with learning approaches when we try to account for the acquisition of phonemes and morphemes. Indeed, acquiring the phonemes of one's language seems to be a relatively straightforward process, albeit slightly backward. The infant spontaneously produces phonemes from all languages, but learns, through imitation and reinforcement, which sounds need to be "saved" for use in his or her language. Those that are not appropriate for the child's language are simply not used and disappear from the child's repertoire (deVillers & deVillers, 1978).

Learning theories are not terribly strained when it comes to the acquisition of words and morphemes. What we're dealing with here is largely the development of labels for concepts—concepts that are clearly learned as we noted earlier in this topic. There are, no doubt, many varieties of learning involved in word acquisition. Some of the meaning of words comes from classical conditioning (Topic 5A, pp. 196–200). The use of some words and morphemes is reinforced and the use of others is not, as operant conditioning predicts. Some vocabulary growth results from observational learning—using words that others use. Some words develop through direct instruction. By and large, learning—one's nurture—seems to handle morpheme acquisition rather nicely. But there are a few problems.

For one thing, as children begin to acquire morphemes that change the meaning of a word (called bound morphemes), they do so with disturbing regularity. For no good reason that learning theory can account for, children learn to add *-ing* to words before they learn to form possessives (by adding *-'s*), which they learn before learning to form the past tense of verbs (by adding *-ed*). That is, when asked what he is doing, a child may be expected first to respond, "I draw." Later will come "I drawing." Only after the *-ing* morpheme is in place may we expect "That Billy's picture." Only later will we hear something like "I drawed it yesterday." In other words, there is a predictable sequence in which many morphemes seem to be acquired. This may reflect limits set by the child's genetic constitution or it may reflect limits set by the child's cognitive growth (i.e., he or she may not understand the basic concept of past tense until after the concept of possessive is acquired), but in either case, simple learning theory is strained.

Another example that provides a problem for learning theory is called **overregularization**. By definition, overregularization is the continued application of an acquired language rule (for forming plurals or past tense, for example) in a situation where it is not appropriate. A child might say, "I have two foots," or "four mans," or "I goed to the store," even *after* using the words *feet*, *men*, and *went* appropriately in similar contexts. What accounts for overregularization? Biologically oriented theories (e.g., Chomsky, 1965, 1975; Lenneberg, 1967; McNeil, 1970) suggest that there must be some innate, "prewired" biological mechanism that compels the child to seek out and apply rules during acquisition. This mechanism (called a language acquisition device or LAD), becomes particularly active and useful when we are about 1 year old, and effectively turns off by the time we are 5 or 6 years old. In this scenario, the child is so predisposed to find and use rules that she or he will do so with great consistency, even when a particular application of the rule is wrong. The truth of the matter is that "two foots" is a much more reasonable construction than "two feet," even though "two foots" is not likely to have been heard in adult speech (Anisfeld, 1984).

Reliance on some sort of LAD becomes even more sensible when we consider the acquisition rules of the sort that are reflected in the generation of sentences. (And I should add that nobody has the slightest idea of what a LAD would look like or how it would work.) The basic argument for an innate predisposition for the acquisition of language rules comes largely from the orderliness of language development. The ages of the children are not always the same, but with uncanny regularity, children everywhere go about acquiring their different languages in virtually the same pattern. The phenomenon of holophrastic speech, the stability of the two-word utterance, the expansion of noun phrases, and the ordered acquisition of bound morphemes has been noted over and over as a consistent pattern—a pattern much more consistent than we could ever expect of the learning histories of the children being observed (Slobin, 1979).

Another point that is often raised against the learning approach is that when it comes to the rules of syntax, most adults by far cannot tell us what

overregularization *the excessive application of an acquired language rule (e.g., for plurals or past tense) in a situation where it is not appropriate*

the rules of their language *are*. The argument then comes quickly: How can you begin to teach something to someone else, if you haven't got the slightest idea yourself of what it is that you're teaching? The argument is sensible. Yet, there is the logic that as adults we *do* have certain linguistic intuitions. We can tell when an utterance is correctly formed, even if we can't specify why. We can use this intuition to reinforce proper use and to correct improper use. The problem is, when we carefully watch adults interacting with young children, we find that they are much more likely to correct the *content* of what the child says than the *form* in which it is said. For example, if a child says, "Me no like oatmeal," a parent is likely to respond with a statement such as, "Sure you do; you eat it all the time" (Brown, 1973; Brown, Cazden, & Bellugi, 1969).

Here's the way Mabel Rice summarized some of these issues in a recent review (1989, p. 153): "There is a remarkable similarity in the general acquisition sequence for language skills across languages and cultures, although there is considerable individual variability in learning strategies and rate of acquisition. . . . Explicit language teaching from adults is not necessary. In fact, if adults try to structure and direct a child's language learning, the outcome may be interference. . . ."

So when it comes to explaining language acquisition, just where are we? Well, we're a long way from any final answers, but at the moment we seem to be where we commonly are when we are faced with two opposing theoretical positions—particularly when one position favors learning (or nurture) and the other favors innate factors (or nature). Some aspects of language are learned. For most language acquisition processes, learning, imitation, and reinforcement provide unsatisfactory explanations. A reasonably conservative position, for now, is an interactionist position: Humans are born with a predisposition to acquire certain aspects of language. Which language they acquire, and which aspects, will reflect their experiences in their language-using community.

BEFORE YOU GO ON

Briefly summarize the learning-oriented and biology-oriented theories of language acquisition.

In this topic, we have examined two related and complex cognitive processes: concept formation and language use. Concepts are our mental representations of the world, both real and imagined. Concepts represent classes or categories of objects and events, and in so doing, help us bring order and meaningfulness to our experiences. Most of our concepts can be symbolized by words—the meaningful, arbitrary units of language. Language use is an excellent example of structured, rule-governed behavior. All language users demonstrate a knowledge—a competence—of the rules of their language, whether or not they can state explicitly what those rules are. It is this competence, this implicit knowledge of the structure of one's language, that is most difficult to account for when one considers how language is acquired.

SUMMARY

How can we use attributes and rules to define concepts?

Concepts are mental representations of categories or classes of objects and events. They are often defined in terms of certain critical attributes that are related to each other by some rule. Formal concepts are those in which the number of attributes is relatively small, the values of attributes are well known, and the rules that relate them are clear. Concepts may be defined by conjunctive rules, disjunctive rules, affirmation rules, or relational rules. / *page 301*

How does the concept of prototype help our understanding of what a concept is?

A prototype is the best example or most typical member of a category or concept. It is the member of a concept class that has most of the attributes that define that concept and few attributes that cause it to be confused with other concepts. The notions of prototype and best fit allow us to deal with the fuzzy concepts that we often encounter in nature. The standard notion of prototype, however, fails to take context into account. / *page 304*

What does Edna Heidbreder's classic study of concept formation tell us about the process? What does it mean to say that people use hypothesis testing in forming concepts?

Heidbreder's 1946 study demonstrated that concept labels are learned, that concept formation can be meaningfully studied in the laboratory, and that con-

cepts may be acquired by strategies of which even the learner is unaware. Concepts usually are learned by developing a systematic plan or strategy for discovering the essential attributes of a concept and the rule that unites those attributes. In large measure, concept formation strategies involve generating and then testing hypotheses about potential membership in a class or concept. Forming and testing hypotheses about concept membership applies to natural as well as formal concepts. / *page 307*

What are some of the defining characteristics of language?

Language is a complex and creative cognitive skill used for communication. A language is made up of a large number of arbitrary symbols, usually words, that stand for or label our conceptualization of objects and events, that have meaning for users of that language, and that are combined in accordance with certain rules. The use of language is a generative process that, among other things, allows us to communicate about the not here and the not now. / *page 309*

What are phonemes, and in what way are they rule-governed?

A phoneme is the smallest unit of sound in the spoken form of a language—that is, a speech sound. Phonemes are rule-governed in the sense that each language is comprised of only a portion of all possible phonemes, and how they may be combined within a given language follows strict rules. / *page 310*

What is semantics? What are morphemes?

Semantics is the name we give to the study of meaning, in the context of this topic, the meaning of words and sentences. Morphemes are the smallest units or elements of meaning in a language. Morphemes include words, prefixes, and suffixes. Morphemes provide labels that allow us to communicate about concepts. The way in which morphemes are ordered, or structured, in language generally affects their meaning. / *page 311*

What is syntax? What are linguistic intuitions? What is pragmatics?

Syntax refers to the rules that govern the way morphemes in a language are structured to produce sentences. Language users demonstrate a competence with these rules even though they may not be able to state them explicitly. Our knowledge of syntax, or sentence structure, is reflected in linguistic intuitions, judgments that language users can make about the structure of utterances. For example, we can determine intuitively (without being able to explain why) when utterances are syntactically correct and when they are not. We can tell when two sentences that take different forms are communicating the same idea or message. We can identify ambiguous sentences and can often remove that ambiguity only when we are aware of a larger context in which the utterance occurred. A concern with how social context affects meaning is called *pragmatics*. / *page 313*

What are some of the landmark events that occur during language acquisition?

Although infants cry and babble, the first truly linguistic utterances are called holophrastic speech. This occurs when one word is used to communicate a range of feelings, intentions, and meanings. A two-word stage of development shows the presence of structure in word ordering: a syntax that is not merely a copy of adult language structure. From the two-word utterance on, language development is extremely rapid. By the time a child is 5 years old he or she will know thousands of words (will understand more than she or he will produce) and combine those words in virtually every acceptable sentence structure in the language. / *page 315*

Briefly summarize the learning-oriented and biology-oriented theories of language acquisition.

Neither learning-experiential nor instinctual-biological theories can totally account for language acquisition. Clearly, one's learning history has an impact on language development, particularly in the formation of words and morphemes (we do not all speak the same language in the same way). At the same time, learning theory is challenged by the cross-cultural regularities that seem to occur in language acquisition— by the fact that all children of all languages seem to develop their languages in the same general, patterned way. The complex process just seems too rapid and too regular not to have a strong biological basis. / *page 317*

Problem Solving

Why We Care: A Topic Preview

In their 1954 textbook, **Experimental Psychology**, Woodworth and Schlosberg began their chapter on problem solving with this observation: "If the experimentalist could show us how to think clearly, and how to solve our problems successfully and expeditiously, his social contribution would be very great" (p. 814). The study of problem solving is a classic one in psychology. You will notice that some of the references we cite in this topic are quite old, reflecting this long-standing interest. We have learned a lot about problem solving since Woodworth and Schlosberg published their text, but the hope implied in their introductory statement is still largely unfulfilled.

Our daily lives are filled with problems of various sorts. Some are simple, straightforward, and/or trivial; others are complex and very important to us. In this topic, we'll focus our attention on cognitive, or intellectual, problems: those that require the manipulation of cognitions for their solution. The first thing we'll do is define the nature of problems, and then we'll consider how we can go about solving them.

Solving problems requires a number of interrelated processes. We must first recognize that a problem exists. Then we must decide how to represent the problem in such a way as to maximize our chances of solving it. Then we have to devise some strategy to help us reach the goal of solving the problem. Finally, we must assess whether or not our proposed solution actually does solve the problem at hand.

As was the case for concept formation and language use, problem solving is clearly a "higher" cognitive process. It requires that we perceive the nature of the problem and learn the most efficient path toward a solution, using our memories as we go along.

WHAT IS A PROBLEM?

Sometimes our goals are obvious, our present situation is clear, and the way to get from where we are to where we want to be is obvious also. In such cases, we really don't have a problem, do we? Say you want to have a nice breakfast. You have eggs, bacon, and bread available. You also have the implements needed to prepare these foods, and you know how to use them. You know that, for you, a nice breakfast would be two eggs over easy, three strips of fried bacon, and a piece of buttered toast. With little hesitation, you can engage in the appropriate behaviors and reach your goal.

On the other hand, a **problem** exists when there is a discrepancy between one's present state and one's perceived goal state *and* there is no readily apparent way to get from one to the other. In situations where the path to goal attainment is not clear or obvious, a problem exists, and you need to engage in problem-solving behaviors—as might be the case if halfway through the preparation of breakfast, you discover that you have no butter or margarine.

A problem-solving situation can be thought of as having three major components: (1) an *initial state*, which is the situation as it exists, or is perceived to exist, at the moment; (2) a *goal state*, which is the situation as the problem solver would like it to be, or the end product; and (3) *possible routes or strategies* for getting from the initial state to the goal state.

In addition, psychologists make a distinction between well-defined and ill-defined problems. Well-defined problems are those in which both the initial state and the goal state are clearly defined. We know what the current situation is, know what the goal is, and may even know some of the possible ways to go about getting from one to the other. "What English word can be made from the letters *teralbay*?" We recognize this question as presenting a problem. We understand what the question is asking, have some ideas about how we might go about answering it, and surely we'll know when we have succeeded. "How do you get home from campus if you discover that your car, which is in the campus parking lot, won't start?" Again, we know our initial state (on campus with a car that won't start), and we'll know when we have reached our goal (when we're at home), but we have to undertake a new or different way to get there.

Most of the problems that you and I face every day, though, are of the ill-defined variety. In such cases, we do not have a clear idea of what we are starting with, nor are we able to clearly identify or define any one ideal solution. "What should my college major be?" Many high school seniors (and some college seniors) don't even know what their options are. They have few ideas about how to find out about possible college majors. And, once they have selected a major, they're not at all sure that their choice was the best one—which may explain why so many college students change their majors so often.

"Write the script for a movie that will be a smashing success." The screenwriter certainly knows what a script is and probably knows what the producers mean by "smashing success." Beyond that, however, this problem is certainly ill defined. This is the same sort of ill-defined problem you may face when assigned a term paper. All you may know is that the paper must be on some topic in psychology, at least 15 pages long, well-written, and original!

problem *a situation in which there is a discrepancy between one's current state and one's desired, or goal, state, with no clear way of getting from one to the other*

These students are faced with an ill-defined problem: "What should I choose as a college major?"

Because ill-defined problems usually involve many variables that are difficult to define (much less control) psychologists usually study problems that are at least reasonably well defined. In the setting of the psychology laboratory, we try to present subjects with a complete description of the initial state of the problem and specify what a solution or goal state would be.

BEFORE YOU GO ON

What are the three components of a problem?
Contrast well-defined and ill-defined problems.
Give an example of each.

PROBLEM REPRESENTATION

Once we realize that we're faced with a problem, the first thing we should do is put it in some form that allows us to think about it in familiar terms. We need to come up with a way to *represent* the problem in our own minds, interpreting the problem so that the initial state and the goal state are clear to us. We also need to note if there are restrictions on how we can go about seeking solutions. (For a crude example, if you were charged with determining whether dogs or cats swim better, you could hardly just throw one of each into a pool to see which survived the longest.) In short, we need to understand the nature of the problem. We should try to make the problem meaningful, relating it to information we have available in our memories.

By examining a few of the problems of the sort that have been used in the psychology laboratory, we can see that how we choose to represent a problem can be critical. Consider the problem presented in Figure 7.5. On first inspection, you might decide that this problem is just too difficult to even attempt, requiring an in-depth knowledge of trigonometry or geometry. But if you work with the representation of the problem for a moment, you may recognize that if you know the diameter of the circle is 10 inches, then any radius of the circle must be 5 inches long. That in itself doesn't help much until you see that line L is a diagonal of the rectangle, and that the other diagonal happens to be a radius of the circle. It then becomes obvious that line L must be 5 inches long (see Figure 7.6). If the problem's initial state is not restated, or represented, in this way, the problem is very difficult to solve.

Now refer to the problem presented in Figure 7.7. Thinking about this problem as it is presented—in words—can be maddening. You may picture yourself walking up and down a mountain on two different days, mentally visualizing a narrow path, trying to find a point on the path where you might be at precisely the same time on two different days.

As is often the case with real-life problems, this statement of the problem contains a good deal of irrelevant information. Useful problem representation often involves sorting out what matters and what doesn't. Cer-

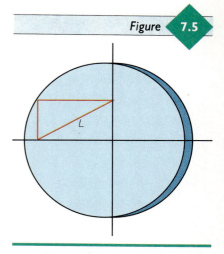

Figure 7.5

A problem in which representation is critical. The diameter of this circle is exactly 10 inches long. What is the length of line "L"? (From Köhler, 1969.)

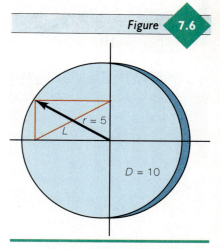

Figure 7.6

An example of a problem in which representation is critical. The diagonal of this circle is exactly 10 inches long. What is the length of Line "L"? (From Köhler, 1969.)

Figure 7.7

THE MOUNTAIN-CLIMBING MONK PROBLEM— ANOTHER EXAMPLE OF THE IMPORTANCE OF PROBLEM REPRESENTATION.

One morning, exactly at sunrise, a Buddhist monk began to climb a tall mountain. A narrow path, no more than a foot or two wide, spiraled around the mountain to a glittering temple at the summit. The monk ascended at varying rates of speed, stopping many times along the way to rest and eat dried fruit that he carried with him. He reached the temple shortly before sunset. After several days of fasting and meditation, he began his journey back along the same path, starting at sunrise again walking at variable speeds with many pauses along the way. His average speed descending was, of course, greater than his average climbing speed. Show that there is a spot along the path that the monk will occupy on both trips at precisely the same time of day.

From Duncker, 1945.

Problems come in a variety of forms, from the academic problems of physics to finding the right piece for a jigsaw puzzle. Often, the correct representation of a problem is the most difficult aspect of problem solving.

tainly the fact that we're dealing with a monk is not relevant and neither are the temple, the dried fruit, the fact that the path happens to be narrow, or that the trip was made on two different days.

You might think about or represent this problem in terms of just one climber making the trip in one day. Or, better still, imagine that there are two climbers: one starting from the top of the mountain, the other starting from the bottom. Because both take the same path, surely they will meet somewhere on that mountain trail sometime during the day (see Figure 7.8). When you represent the problem in this way, the solution becomes readily apparent.

So, it might help to represent the mountain-climbing problem visually, actually drawing out the ascending and descending pathways on a sheet of paper. As it happens, visually representing the problem presented in Figure 7.9 in this way would not be wise. One can readily imagine a subject working on this problem by drawing little train stations with trains moving toward each other, tracing the path of a bird racing back and forth between the trains. If you tried this, you discovered that it didn't help much.

Instead of visualizing this problem, think about the arithmetic and the logic involved. The stations are 50 miles apart. The trains travel at 25 miles per hour. At that rate, how long will it take for the trains to meet? Exactly one hour. You also know that the bird flies at a rate of 100 miles per hour. Now if the bird flies for just one hour (back and forth—or anyplace else, for that matter), how far will it have flown? Right! Exactly 100 miles. As in the previous example, the solution becomes obvious as soon as the problem is stripped to its essentials and is represented in such a way that a solution is possible.

Here's one final example of the importance of problem representation (Adams, 1974). "Imagine that you have a very large sheet of paper, 1/100 of an inch thick. Imagine folding it over onto itself so that now you have two layers of paper. Fold it again so that there are four layers. It is impossible to actually fold a sheet of paper 50 times, but imagine that you could. About how thick would the paper be if it were folded 50 times?" Picturing just what a piece of paper folded 50 times would look like is very difficult.

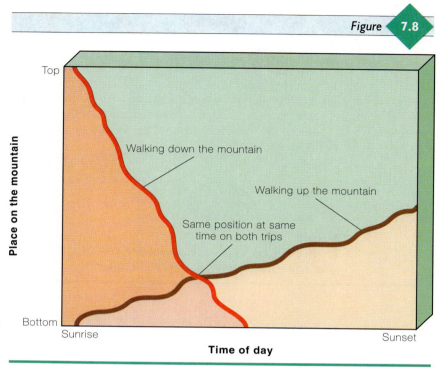

Figure **7.8**

Top

Walking down the mountain

Walking up the mountain

Same position at same
time on both trips

Place on the mountain

Bottom
Sunrise

Sunset

Time of day

A graphic representation that makes the solution easier to see.

Some subjects guess a few inches, while some imagine that the folded paper would be several feet thick. Many have no idea at all. So representing this problem in visual terms will be of little help. If one recognizes this as a problem of mathematics, involving exponents, then a correct solution is more likely. Actually, 50 folds would increase the paper's thickness by a factor of 2^{50}. That comes to 1,100,000,000,000,000 inches, and the resulting paper would be so high it would nearly reach from the earth to the sun!

Figure **7.9**

ANOTHER PROBLEM WHOSE SOLUTION MAY DEPEND MOST ON HOW IT IS REPRESENTED IN THE MIND OF THE PROBLEM SOLVER.

Two train stations are fifty miles apart. At 2:00 P.M. one Saturday afternoon two trains start toward each other, one from each station. Just as the trains pull out of the stations, a bird springs into the air in front of the first train and flies ahead to the front of the second train. When the bird reaches the second train it turns back and flies toward the first train. The bird continues to do this, flying back and forth between the two trains until the trains meet.

If both trains travel at the rate of twenty-five miles per hour and the bird flies at one hundred miles per hour, how many miles will the bird have flown before the two trains meet?

From Posner, 1973.

Choosing the best way to represent a problem is not a simple task. Very often problem representation provides *the* stumbling block to problem solution (Bourne et al., 1983). Once you realize that you are faced with a problem, your first step in solving it should be to represent it in a variety of ways. To the extent that you can, eliminate unessential information. Relate the problem to other problems of a similar type that you have solved before. Having done so, if the solution is still not obvious, you may choose to develop some strategy to move from your representation of the problem to the goal of its solution. We now turn to how one might go about generating possible problem solutions.

BEFORE YOU GO ON

*In the context of problem solving,
what is meant by problem representation?*

PROBLEM-SOLVING STRATEGIES

Once you have represented the initial state of a problem and have a clear idea of what an acceptable goal state might be, you still have to figure out how to get to your goal. Even after you have adequately represented a problem, how to go about solving it may not be readily apparent. You might spend a few minutes guessing wildly at a solution, but soon you'll have to settle on some strategy. In this context, a **strategy** is a systematic plan for generating possible solutions that can be tested to see if they are correct. The main advantage of cognitive strategies appears to be that they permit the learner or problem solver to exercise some degree of control over the task at hand. They allow learners to choose the skills and knowledge that they will bring to bear on any particular problem at any time (Gagné, 1984). There are quite a few possible strategies that one might choose to try. In this section, we'll consider two different types of strategies: algorithms and heuristics.

strategy *in problem solving, a systematic plan for generating possible solutions that can be tested to see if they are correct*

Algorithms

An **algorithm** is a problem-solving strategy that *guarantees* that you will eventually arrive at a solution if the strategy is correctly applied. Algorithms involve systematically exploring and evaluating all possible solutions until the correct one is found. It is sometimes referred to as a *generate-test* sort of strategy in which one generates hypotheses about potential solutions and then tests each one in turn. This sort of strategy is commonly encountered in concept formation tasks. To use an algorithmic strategy in concept formation, each attribute of a concept would be examined and tested one at a time to determine if the attribute is part of the concept's definition. Given their speed of computation, most computer programs designed to solve problems use algorithmic strategies.

algorithm *a problem-solving strategy in which all possible solutions are generated and tested and an acceptable solution is guaranteed*

Simple anagram problems (letters of a word presented in a scrambled fashion) *can* be solved using an algorithm. "What English word has been scrambled to make *uleb*?" With sufficient patience, you can systematically rearrange these four letters until you hit on a correct solution: *leub, lueb, elub, uleb, buel, beul, blue*. There it is, *blue*. With only four letters to deal with, finding a solution generally doesn't take very long—there are only 24 possible arrangements of four letters ($4 \times 3 \times 2 \times 1 = 24$).

On the other hand, consider the anagram composed of eight letters that we mentioned earlier: *teralbay*. In fact, there are 40,320 possible combinations of these eight letters—$8 \times 7 \times 6 \times 5 \times 4 \times 3 \times 2 \times 1 = 40,320$ (Reynolds & Flagg, 1983). Unless your system for moving letters around just happens to start in a good place, you could spend a lot of time trying to come up with a combination that produces an English word. If we were dealing with a 10-letter word, there would be 3,628,800 possible combinations to check.

Imagine that you go the supermarket to find just one item: a small jar of horseradish. You're quite sure the store has horseradish, but you have no idea where to find it. One plan would be to systematically go up and down every aisle of the store, checking first the top shelf, then the second, then the third, until you spied the horseradish. This strategy would work *if* the store carried horseradish *and if* you searched carefully. There must be a better way to solve such problems. We could use some heuristic strategy.

Heuristics

A **heuristic** strategy is an informal, rule-of-thumb method of generating and testing problem solutions. Heuristics are more economical techniques for solving problems than are algorithms. When one uses a heuristic, there is no guarantee of success. On the other hand, such strategies are usually much less time consuming than algorithm strategies and do lead searches for paths toward goals in a logical, sensible way.

A heuristic strategy for finding horseradish in a supermarket might take you to different sections in the store in the order you believed to be most reasonable. You might start with spices, and you'd be disappointed. Next, you might look among the fresh vegetables. Then, upon recalling that horseradish needs to be refrigerated, you go next to the dairy case, and there you'll find the horseradish. You would not have wasted your time searching the cereal aisle or the frozen food section—real possibilities if you tried an algorithmic strategy. Another, more reasonable, heuristic strategy would be to ask an employee where the horseradish is kept. Let's now take a look at three heuristic strategies: *means-ends analysis, working backward,* and *hill climbing.*

If you have tried the *teralbay* anagram problem, it is likely that you have employed a heuristic strategy. To do so, you rely on your experience with the English language (remember that basic cognitive processes such as the use of memory are required for problem solving). You seriously consider only those letter combinations that you know occur frequently. You generate and test the most common combinations first. You just don't worry much about the possibility that the solution may contain a combination like *brty*. Nor do you search for a word with an *aae* string in it. You

heuristic *a problem-solving strategy in which hypotheses about problem solutions are generated and tested in a time-saving and systematic way, but that does not guarantee an acceptable solution*

explore words that end in *able*, because you know these to be fairly common. But that doesn't work. What about *br* words? No, that doesn't work either. How about words with the combination *tray* in them? *Traybeal*? No. *Baletray*? No. "Oh! Now I see it: *betrayal*."

This type of heuristic strategy is called a *means-ends analysis* (Newell & Simon, 1972). In this strategy, one always keeps the final goal in mind, but first works toward the setting of subgoals. In the *teralbay* anagram example, subgoals are defined in terms of letter combinations that make sense or are commonly found. Once the subgoals are reached, they are manipulated in an attempt to reach the final goal. The example of the search for horseradish also involved a means-ends analysis—first find the proper section of the store, then search for the specific product.

Here's another example. If José has decided that it is his goal to be a family practice physician, he cannot simply rent an office and practice medicine. Getting to the ultimate goal of being a physician (or almost anything else) involves establishing a series of subgoals and procedures for reaching those subgoals before moving on to others. The final goal state (ends) may always be in José's mind, but right now he has to get a good grade in introductory psychology (the means, or a subgoal along the way) or he's going to have difficulty graduating (another subgoal), much less getting into medical school.

A related type of heuristic strategy that you have probably used involves the procedure of *working backward*. In this strategy, the goal state of a problem may be better defined than either the initial state *or* the means to get to the goal. Sometimes it is easier to trace a path from the goal of a maze to its starting point than it is to trace the same path in the other direction.

Suppose that you know what you want to have for supper tonight: a Chinese dinner of eggrolls, shrimp in lobster sauce, and fried rice. There's your goal state, now how do you get there? "What would I have to do to get that dinner on my table tonight? I'd have to fry rice. In order to fry rice, I'll need something to fry it in. No problem; I'll use my new wok. But I need the rice to fry. How *do* you fry rice, anyway?" When you check your Chinese cookbook, you discover that to fry rice, you need to first cook the rice then let it cool, or chill it, before frying. "I haven't got the time to buy rice, then boil it, then cool it, then fry it. How else could I get fried rice to the table?" It may be at this point that you decide that your problem has no reasonable solution, and you may decide to stop at your neighborhood Chinese restaurant on the way home for a carry-out.

Note how this "fried rice" example is different from a problem in which you want to try out a new wok and don't know what to do with it until you work through a series of decisions, finally settling on the goal of fried rice. The *working backward* example starts with the goal.

A problem-solving strategy called *hill climbing* requires that every action we take (real or imagined) moves us somehow closer to our ultimate goal state (Atwood & Polson, 1976). Problem solving is often a matter of, "Let's just forge ahead; we'll get there sooner or later, so long as we keep moving forward" (or upward to maintain the hill-climbing analogy). For example, as one stands on the tee of a golf course, the goal is to get the ball into the hole on the green while hitting it as few times as possible. A certain logic says that no matter how far we hit the ball, if it moves toward the green, we're at least going in the right direction. But in real life, as in golf, successful problem solving sometimes requires that we make a move *away from* our ultimate goal. If your ball lands behind a tree, your only course of action may be to hit it to the side or backward out onto the fairway so that your *next* shot can be successful. Sometimes it may be wiser to hit the ball around a sand trap rather than over it, even if the latter shot would be more directly aimed at the hole.

By now you should realize that these three heuristic strategies are *not* mutually exclusive. Mostly, they differ in emphasis. When we are faced with complex problems in real life, we may use all of these strategies. You want to do as well in this course as possible. How do you go about it? First, you make sure that you understand the nature of the ultimate goal— exactly what will it take (how many points) to get the grade of your choice? By what *means* can these *ends* be attained? Then *work backward*. How many points will you need at the end of the semester? How many points will you need just before the final? How many will you need after the next test to keep on track toward your goal? Then engage in a bit of *hill climbing*. Every point you earn on your next test, paper, or project is one more point that moves you closer to your ultimate goal.

BEFORE YOU GO ON

How are algorithmic and heuristic strategies used to solve problems?

BARRIERS TO EFFECTIVE PROBLEM SOLVING

By and large, it is difficult to solve problems without relying heavily on one's memory. If you failed to remember that the radius of a circle is equal to one-half its diameter, you couldn't solve the problem presented in Figure 7.5. If you forgot how fast the bird was flying, you couldn't deal with the problem in Figure 7.9. If you couldn't remember the recipe for something you wanted to have for supper, you would have a hard time buying the correct ingredients when you went to the grocery store. Regardless of the type of problem or the type of strategy employed to solve it, solving problems effectively requires that we use our memories.

There are times, however, when previous experiences (and memories of them) create difficulties in problem solving. We'll look at three such cases in this section.

Mental Set and Functional Fixedness

In Topic 4A, we claimed that our perceptions can be influenced by our expectations or mental set. We said that we often perceive what we are set to perceive. The concept of mental set is also very relevant in problem solving. A **mental set** is a tendency to perceive or respond to something in a given or set way. It is, in essence, a cognitive predisposition. We may have or develop expectations that interfere with effective problem solving.

mental set *a predisposed (set) way to perceive something; an expectation*

Figure **7.10**

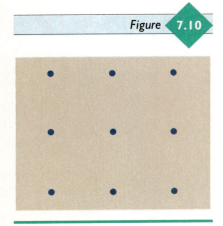

The classic "nine-dot problem." The task is to connect all nine dots with just four straight lines, without removing your pen or pencil from the paper. (From Scheerer, 1963.) (See Figure 7.14 at the end of the chapter for the solution.)

functional fixedness *the phenomenon in which one is unable to see a new use or function for an object because of experience using the object in some other function*

One clever (but unpleasant) demonstration of the negative consequences of mental set involves giving a class a lengthy surprise test, perhaps 50 true-false items. The instructions at the top of the first page state clearly: "Place all of your answers on the attached answer sheet. Do not write on this exam. *Read all the items on this test before making any marks on the answer sheet.*" Having taken so many true-false tests before, many students do not read any of the instructions. They just start into the test, working away. Some students read the instructions and choose to ignore the warning about reading all the items first. Only those students who do so get to read item 50 before they begin to answer the questions. Item 50 reads, "This is not really a test. I just wanted to see if you would follow directions. Please sit quietly until I collect the papers."

Figure 7.10 provides another example of how an inappropriate mental set can interfere with problem solving. Most subjects when first presented with this problem make an assumption (form a mental set). They assume the nine dots form a square and that their lines somehow must stay within that square. Only when this mental set is "broken" can the problem be solved. See Figure 7.14 at the end of the chapter (p. 337) for one solution to Figure 7.10.

Mental sets do not necessarily hinder problem solving. A proper or appropriate mental set can be facilitating. For example, if I were to have told you to look beyond the confines of any imagined square when attempting the problem in Figure 7.10, *that* mental set—which seems strange out of context—would have made the problem easier to solve.

The phenomenon of **functional fixedness** may be thought of as a type of mental set. The process was defined by Duncker (1945) as the inability to discover an appropriate new use for an object because of experience using the object in some other function. That is, the problem solver fails to see a solution to a problem because he or she has "fixed" some "function" to an object that makes it difficult to see how it could help with the problem at hand.

A standard example is one used by Maier (1931). Two strings dangle from the ceiling. The problem is that they are so far apart that a subject cannot reach both of them at the same time. The goal is to do just that: to hold on to both strings at once. If there were nothing else in the room, this problem might never get solved. However, there are other objects in the room that the subject can use, including a pair of pliers (see Figure 7.11). One solution to this problem is to tie the pliers to one string and start the pliers swinging like a pendulum. As the subject holds the other string, the string with the pliers attached can be grasped as it swings over to the subject. Because many subjects fail to see pliers as useful (functioning) for anything but turning nuts and bolts, they fail to see the pliers as a potential pendulum weight and thus may fail to solve the problem. They have "fixed" the "function" of the pliers in their mind.

Another famous example that demonstrates functional fixedness is one reported by Duncker (1945). Here, subjects are provided with a box of tacks, a candle, and some matches. The task is to use these materials to mount the candle on the wall and light it. Obviously, one cannot just tack a candle to the wall. The solution to this problem requires breaking the mental set of functional fixedness for the box in which the tacks are presented, seeing it as a potential candleholder, tacking *it* to the wall, and mounting the candle on it (see Figure 7.12).

Figure **7.11**

Maier's two-string problem. The subject is to manage to get both strings in his grasp. They are separated so that when one string is held, the other cannot be reached. See text for an explanation of the solution. (After Maier, 1931.)

A number of experiments (e.g., Glucksberg & Danks, 1968) have shown that some subtle changes in the way in which the materials are presented have an effect on solving this problem. For example, when the box of tacks is labeled *TACKS*, the problem is much more difficult to solve. Using an empty box and having the tacks scattered about increases the likelihood that subjects will overcome the functional fixedness of seeing the box as something that holds things.

BEFORE YOU GO ON

What is a mental set, and how might a mental set hinder problem solving?

What is functional fixedness, and how might it hinder problem solving?

Biased Heuristics and Decision Making

For some of the problems we encounter in real life, we are provided with a finite set of possibilities from which we must choose a correct or "best" alternative. Looked at this way, we see that some decision-making tasks are very much like the problems we have been considering in this topic. We've seen that problem solving requires us to use our past expe-

Figure **7.12**

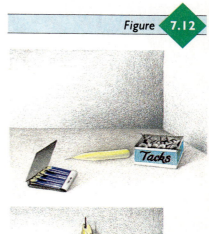

The materials provided in the candle problem, and how the problem can be solved. (After Duncker, 1945.)

availability heuristic *the rule of thumb that suggests that whatever is more available in our memory is also more common or probable*

representativeness heuristic *the rule of thumb that suggests that judgments made about a prototypic member of a category will hold for all members of the category*

positive test strategy *the heuristic of sticking with an acceptable decision or solution, even if a better one might exist*

rience—knowledge of common letter strings in English, for example—to devise strategies for reaching goal states. Occasionally, our heuristic strategies—rules of thumb used to guide problem solving—based on perceptions of past experience are biased. Such biases create a barrier to effective problem solving.

Some of the strategies that we use to make decisions require that we estimate the frequency or the probability of events, and as it happens, many of them are notoriously poor. Most of the research on judging probabilities and frequencies has been reported by Daniel Kahneman and Amos Tversky (1973, 1979, 1984) (cf. Tversky and Kahneman, 1974). We'll briefly summarize how certain biased heuristics can mislead us.

The **availability heuristic** is the assumption that things that come readily to mind are more common, or more frequently occurring, than things that are difficult to recall or think of. For example, I show you a list that includes the names of 19 famous women and 20 less famous men. Later, you will almost certainly overestimate the number of women on the list, because those famous names were more available to you. The media (newspapers, TV, radio, and so on) often draw our attention to events (make them available) in such a way that we tend to overestimate their frequency of occurrence. For example, when reports of terrorist bombings at foreign airports make the televison news, many Americans cancel their plans for European vacations, overestimating the risk of flying to Europe. Even without terrorists, most people will *over*estimate the number of airplane crashes that occur each year, compared to the number of automobile crashes that occur, simply because we tend to hear more about the airplane accidents.

The **representativeness heuristic** is the assumption that judgments made about the most prototypic member of a category will hold for all members of the category. You are told that a group of men is composed of 70 percent lawyers and 30 percent engineers. You are told that one of the men, chosen at random from the group, has hobbies that include carpentry, sailing, and mathematical puzzles. You are to decide if this man is an engineer or a lawyer. Because you believe these hobbies to be representative of engineers and not lawyers, you may say that the man is an engineer, even though (by chance) the likelihood that he is a lawyer is more than twice (7 to 3) the chance that he is an engineer.

Which group includes more tobacco chewers—professional baseball players or college students? The answer is college students (largely because there are so many of them, even though a smaller *percentage* uses chewing tobacco). Or let me ask you this: If I flip a coin (and you may assume that it's a fair coin) and it turns up heads five times in a row, what is the chance of getting tails on the next flip? Actually, the probability is no better than it's been all along, 50–50 (the fact that heads have appeared the previous five times is of absolutely no consequence to the coin).

There are other heuristic strategies that may bias our decision making and may interfere with problem solving. You probably recognize a multiple-choice test item as the sort of problem that requires you to decide which of a number of alternatives (usually four) best answers a question. A problem-solving heuristic that may cause you trouble is called the **positive test strategy**. This is the strategy that claims that if something works, don't drop it to try something else (e.g., Klayman & Ha, 1987). In many ways, this is the heuristic that suggests: "If it isn't broken, don't fix it." In many cases this approach is a sensible one, but there certainly are instances when even *better* solutions—more useful decisions—could be found if only one continued to look. Have you ever fallen into the "trap" of saying that alternative A was the correct answer to a multiple-choice item simply because it was correct, only to discover later that alternatives B and C were also correct, thus making alternative D, "all of the above," the *best* answer to the question?

Successful problem solving often requires that we break out of the restraints imposed by improper mental sets, functional fixedness, and some heuristic strategies. In large measure, to be able to overcome these barriers is to be able to solve problems creatively, and it is to this subject that we turn next.

BEFORE YOU GO ON

What are the availability and representativeness heuristics, and how might they hinder problem solving?

Overcoming Barriers with Creative Problem Solving

Creative solutions to problems are new, innovative, and useful. It is very important to note that in the context of problem solving, *creative* means more than unusual, rare, or different. Someone may generate a very original plan to solve a given problem, but unless that plan *works*, we shouldn't view it as creative (Newell et al., 1962; Vinacke, 1974). For example, if you were to think about how to keep warm on a cold winter's night, you might come up with the idea of popping bushels of warm popcorn for everyone to sit in. The popped corn would keep everyone warm, at least for a short while. Such a solution may border on the unique, unusual, and creative, but it certainly doesn't seem very workable, no matter how creative it may be. Creative solutions should be put to the same test as more ordinary solutions: Do they solve the problem at hand?

Creative solutions generally involve a new and different organization of elements of the problem. As mentioned earlier, it is often at the stage of problem representation that creativity is most noticeable. Seeing a problem in a new light, or combining elements of a problem in a new and different way, may lead to creative solutions. One observation has been made many times: There is virtually no correlation between what we are here calling creative problem solving and what is usually referred to as intelligence (Barron & Harrington, 1981; Horn, 1976; Kershner & Ledger, 1985). At least there are virtually no significant correlations between tests for creativity and tests for intelligence.

We say that creative problem solving often involves **divergent thinking**, that is, starting with one idea and generating from it a number of alternative possibilities and new ideas—the more the better (Dirkes, 1978; Guilford, 1959). When we engage in **convergent thinking**, we take many different ideas, or bits of information, and try to focus and reduce them to just one possible solution (See Figure 7.13). Obviously, convergent thinking has its place in problem solving. But for creative problem solving, divergent

divergent thinking *the creation of many ideas or potential problem solutions from one idea*

convergent thinking *the reduction or focusing of many different ideas into one possible problem solution*

No More Oversleeping

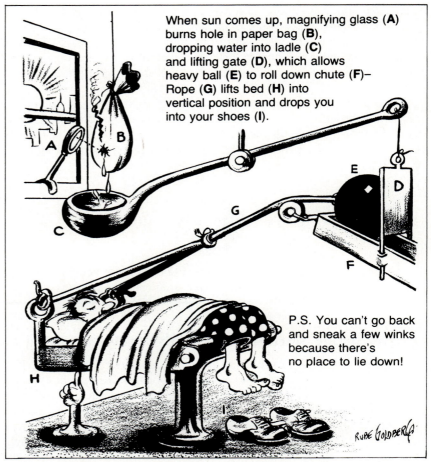

When sun comes up, magnifying glass (**A**) burns hole in paper bag (**B**), dropping water into ladle (**C**) and lifting gate (**D**), which allows heavy ball (**E**) to roll down chute (**F**)— Rope (**G**) lifts bed (**H**) into vertical position and drops you into your shoes (**I**).

P.S. You can't go back and sneak a few winks because there's no place to lie down!

Creative problem solutions must be more than different or unusual—they must provide a workable solution to the problem at hand.

thinking is generally more useful because many new and different possibilities are explored. We need to remember, however, that all these new and different possibilities for a problem's solution need to be judged ultimately in terms of whether or not they really solve the problem.

Creative problem solving can be divided into four interrelated stages. This view of the problem-solving process is another old one in psychology, but it has held up rather nicely over the years (Wallas, 1926).

1. *Preparation:* This is not unlike problem representation. The basic elements of the problem are considered. Past experience becomes relevant, but should not become restrictive. At this stage of problem solving, it is very important to overcome the negative effects of mental set and functional fixedness. Different ways of expressing the problem are considered, but a solution is not found.

2. *Incubation:* In this stage, the problem is put away for a while and not thought about. Perhaps fatigue that has developed during failed efforts can then dissipate. Perhaps inappropriate strategies can be forgotten. Perhaps unconscious processes can be brought to bear on the problem. Why setting

Figure **7.13**

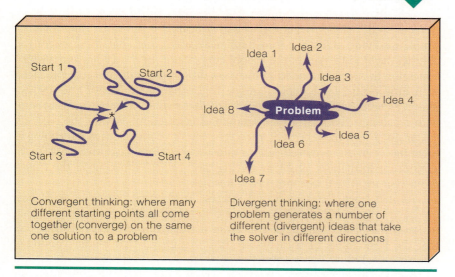

Convergent thinking: where many different starting points all come together (converge) on the same one solution to a problem

Divergent thinking: where one problem generates a number of different (divergent) ideas that take the solver in different directions

A schematic representation of the nature of convergent and divergent thinking in the context of problem solving.

aside a problem may lead to its creative solution we cannot say for sure. We do know, however, that it is often very useful (cf. Yaniv & Meyer, 1987).

3. *Illumination:* This is the most mysterious stage of the problem-solving process. Like insight, a potential solution to a problem seems to materialize as if from nowhere. Some critical analogy becomes apparent, as does a new path to the problem's solution (Glass et al., 1979; Metcalfe & Wiebe, 1987).

4. *Verification:* Now the proposed solution must be tested, or verified, to see if it does in fact provide an answer to the question posed by the problem.

You have probably noted that there is really nothing that extraordinary about Wallas's description of the creative problem-solving process. It sounds very much like the sort of thing that anyone should do when faced with a problem to solve. The truth is, however, that we often fail to go through these stages in any systematic fashion. To do so consciously often helps problem solving. It has long been recognized that good problem solvers show more conscious awareness of what they are doing during the course of problem solving than do poor problem solvers (Glaser, 1984).

BEFORE
YOU GO
ON

What is the difference between divergent and convergent thinking?
What are the four stages of creative problem solving,
according to Wallas?

An unresolved issue in psychology today is the extent to which problem-solving skills can be taught independently from content knowledge.

CAN WE TEACH PROBLEM-SOLVING SKILLS?

Have you ever heard someone say something like, "We do not want our schools to teach our children just the facts, but to teach them how to think as well?" Many psychologists and educators believe that thinking and problem-solving skills are somehow "teachable" and that these cognitive abilities *ought* to be part of the school curriculum. In the 1930s and 1940s, education in America tended to focus on drill, repetition, and rote practice, with little regard for higher cognitive functions. In the 1950s and 1960s, Skinner's behaviorism and reinforcement theory flooded into the classroom with teaching machines and programmed instruction. Within the past 25 years, along with the rebirth of interest in cognitive processes in psychology, there has been an increased call for educators to teach cognitive skills such as concept formation, problem solving, and critical thinking in the classroom (Glaser, 1984; Greeno, 1989; Resnick, 1987).

As it happens, this increased interest in teaching cognitive skills has not been reflected in the performance of schoolchildren. According to one major study of the impact of education in this country, there is evidence that the basic skills of students are improving, but that higher cognitive skills are declining. For example, in mathematics, "There appears to be an increase in the performance associated with basic skill and computation, but little improvement and even a reported decline in mathematical understanding and problem solving" (cited in Glaser, 1984).

What can be done to improve the problem-solving skills of students? This very question is one of the most actively researched issues in cognitive psychology today. It has a number of tentative answers. For one thing, it *is* helpful for students simply to know about the basic nature of problem solving. Teaching students about problem representation, algorithms, heuristics, mental sets, and functional fixedness is in itself a helpful thing to do (e.g., Adams, 1974; Greeno, 1978; Hayes, 1987; Newell & Simon, 1972). Most programs of this sort are "knowledge-free" in the sense that they do not require any particular expertise on the part of the student. ". . . In large part, abstract tasks, puzzle-like problems, and informal life situations are used as content" (Glaser, 1984, p. 96). In other words, most of the material used to teach students about thinking and problem solving has been similar to what we have used in this topic: anagrams, puzzles, and mountain-climbing monks.

It is the position of cognitive psychologist Robert Glaser (1984) that instruction in problem-solving strategies and techniques needs to rely on a sound knowledge base. Ability to solve problems requires, Glaser says, an interaction between general cognitive abilities to manipulate information (higher cognitive processes) *and* a base level of adequate information to manipulate (knowledge). The essence of this argument is this: if you don't *know* much about the particular elements of a given problem, you are going to have difficulty solving it regardless of how much you know about heuristics, strategies, and problem solving in general.

Consider an experiment conducted by Chi in 1978. Chi found that on a standard test of memory for digits, 10-year-old children did significantly less well than adults. The children in Chi's study were expert chess players, however, and the adults were not. When children and adults were tested on their memory of chess pieces arranged on a chess board, the children's memories were far superior to those of the adults. The adults may have had better, more efficient strategies for performing the memory task at hand, but the children simply knew more about chess, and that gave them the advantage.

One of Glaser's arguments, then, is that problem-solving skills can be taught, but they need to be taught in the context of a specific "domain" of knowledge and understanding (Chi & Glaser, 1985). On the one hand, it makes little sense to try to teach students the higher cognitive skills of concept formation and problem solving if they do not have an adequate base of knowledge or information with which to work. On the other hand, it makes little sense to do no more than drill students over and over again on basic facts without exploring theories, concepts, relationships, and how such facts can be used to solve problems. Or, as Glaser puts it, "As individuals acquire knowledge, they also should be empowered to think and reason" (1984, p. 103).

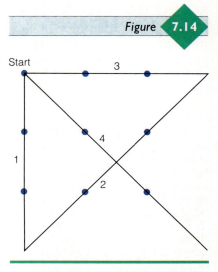

Figure **7.14**

A solution to the "nine-dot problem."

BEFORE YOU GO ON

Briefly summarize Glaser's position on teaching problem-solving skills.

Problem solving is obviously a higher cognitive process. To solve problems requires that we rely on our perceptions, learning, and memories. To solve a problem requires that we understand a situation as it exists, understand the situation as we would like it to be, and then discover some way to reach this desired goal state. To do so effectively and efficiently often requires that we represent the nature of the problem correctly, generate an appropriate problem-solving strategy, and overcome the inhibiting influence of mental set, functional fixedness, or the choice of misleading heuristic strategies. It is clear that an important goal of education is to teach effective and efficient problem-solving strategies. What is less clear is the extent to which problem-solving strategies—or thinking skills in general—can be taught outside the context of a knowledge base.

What are the three components of a problem? Contrast well-defined and ill-defined problems. Give an example of each.

We can say that a problem has three components: (1) an initial state—the situation as it exists at the moment; (2) a goal state—the situation as the problem solver would like it to be; and (3) routes or strategies for getting from the initial state to the goal state. Whether a problem is well defined or ill defined is a matter of the extent to which the elements of the initial state and goal state are well delineated and clearly understood by the problem solver. An example of a well-defined problem might be that which you face when a familiar route home from campus is blocked. An example of an ill-defined problem might be that which you face when you have to write a term paper on a topic of your choice. / *page 323*

In the context of problem solving, what is meant by problem representation?

Problem representation involves the mental activity of thinking about the nature of a problem so as to put it into a form with which we can deal effectively. In essence, representation involves putting a problem into familiar terms. / *page 326*

How are algorithmic and heuristic strategies used to solve problems?

Algorithms and heuristics are types of strategies, or systematic plans, we can use to solve problems. Algorithms involve a systematic search of all possible solutions until the goal is reached; with algorithms, a solution is guaranteed. A heuristic strategy—of which there are many—is a more informal, rule-of-thumb approach that involves generating and testing hypotheses that *may* lead to a problem solution in a sensible, organized way. / *page 329*

What is a mental set, and how might a mental set hinder problem solving? What is functional fixedness, and how might it hinder problem solving?

A mental set is a tendency or predisposition to perceive or respond in a particular way. Mental sets generally develop from past experience and involve the continued use of strategies that have been successful in the past. Because those ways of perceiving or solving a problem that have worked in the past may no longer be appropriate for the problem at hand, mental sets often hinder effective problem solving. Functional fixedness is a type of mental set in which an object is seen as serving only a few fixed functions. Because we may not see a familiar object as being able to serve different functions, fixedness often interferes with effective problem solving. / *page 331*

What are the availability and representativeness heuristics, and how might they hinder problem solving?

These two heuristic strategies, based on our past experience, often mislead us in problem solving. For example, we tend to judge as more likely or more probable those events that are more readily available to us in memory—the avail-ability heuristic. We also tend to over-generalize about events that are proto-typic representatives of a category or concept—the representativeness heuristic. / *page 333*

What is the difference between divergent and convergent thinking? What are the four stages of creative problem solving, according to Wallas?

Divergent thinking is seen as a useful technique in problem solving in which a large number of alternative possibilities of problem solution are generated to be tested later for usefulness. Convergent thinking involves taking a large number of ideas or possibilities for problem solution and reducing them to one or a few. Problem solving in general, and creative problem solving in particular, have four interrelated stages: preparation (in which the problem is represented mentally), incubation (in which the problem is put aside for a while), illumination (in which a potential solution becomes known), and verification (in which the potential solution is tested to see if it does solve the problem at hand). / *page 335*

Briefly summarize Glaser's position on teaching problem-solving skills.

Although there is evidence that students can profit from instruction in problem-solving strategies in general, it is Robert Glaser's view that problem solving first requires an extensive knowledge base or understanding of the content area that needs to be manipulated in the problem-solving process. / *page 337*

INTELLIGENCE AND PSYCHOLOGICAL TESTING

TOPIC 8A   Intelligence Testing

TOPIC 8B   Differences in Measured Intelligence

TOPIC

8A

Intelligence Testing

Why We Care: A Topic Preview

THE NATURE OF INTELLIGENCE
Defining Intelligence
Theoretical Models of Intelligence
> Spearman's "g"
> Thurstone's Primary Mental Abilities
> Guilford's Structure of Intellect
> Vernon's Hierarchical Model
> Sternberg's Triarchic Model

THE NATURE OF PSYCHOLOGICAL TESTS
A Working Definition
Criteria for a Good Test
> Reliability
> Validity
> Norms

PSYCHOLOGICAL TESTS OF INTELLIGENCE
The Stanford-Binet Intelligence Scale
The Wechsler Tests of Intelligence
Group Tests of Intelligence

SUMMARY

Why We Care: A Topic Preview

Our last few chapters have dealt with a number of cognitive processes. We have covered perception, consciousness, learning, memory, concept formation, language, and problem solving. In this topic, we turn our attention to intelligence. When we consider intelligence, we consider the essence of one's cognitive processing. All of the cognitive processes we've discussed are bound up in intelligence. The use of one's intelligence may be thought of as the most complex of cognitive processes. In our discussion of intelligence (which continues into Topic 8B), we will see first just how difficult it is to define the concept. We'll generate a definition that we can work with, but we'll also consider some of the theories that psychologists have put forth to describe intelligence. We'll consider an operational approach to intelligence and look at ways in which intelligence is measured. This discussion will require a consideration of the nature of psychological testing and measurement in general.

In a strict sense, measurement is the assignment of numbers to some characteristic of interest according to rules or according to an agreed-upon system. The rules for many physical measurements are well established and simple. We say that you are 5' 10'' tall because from head to toe your height equals 70 inches, where an inch is defined as a standard measure of length, and you have 70 of them. Most of the rules for psychological measurement are seldom as clear-cut. Are you of near average intelligence? Compared to whom, and measured how? Are you extroverted and outgoing, or are you introverted and shy? Just how extroverted are you? How do we know? What is the standard, the rule, or the system against which we can compare you and your behavior?

Much of the measurement in psychology involves psychological testing. If experience counts for anything, you are already something of an expert on such tests. At least you are an expert on taking tests. To have survived to this point in your education means that you have taken hundreds of tests, most of them designed to assess some cognitive ability or skill. Surely you will be faced with more of them in the future. As you know from your own experience, there is a wide range of instruments that we can label as tests. In this topic, we'll examine the nature of psychological tests in general and discuss the criteria by which tests can be judged and compared.

Once we have reviewed some general issues regarding testing and have dealt with the concept of intelligence theoretically, we can describe some of the more popular and useful attempts to measure intelligence. Psychological testing, intelligence testing in particular, is big business. We care about this topic because it helps us understand what intelligence is and what it is not, and because it helps us understand what psychological tests can and cannot do.

THE NATURE OF INTELLIGENCE

Intelligence is a troublesome concept in psychology. We all know what we mean when we use the word, but we have a terrible time trying to define intelligence concisely. We wonder if John's failure in school is due to his lack of intelligence or to some other factor, such as an emotional disorder. You may argue that locking my keys in my car was not a very intelligent thing to do. I may argue that anyone with any intelligence can see the difference between reinforcement and punishment.

In this section, we'll do two things. First, we'll develop a working definition of intelligence. Then, we'll review some of the ways in which psychologists have conceptualized the nature of intelligence. We'll see that about the only point of agreement among theorists is that intelligence is a reflection of one's cognitive reactions. From that point on, there is considerable disagreement about the concept.

Defining Intelligence

intelligence *the capacity to understand the world and the resourcefulness to cope with its challenges; that which an intelligence test measures*

Intelligence has been variously defined as the sum total of everything you know, as the ability to learn and profit from experience, or as one's ability to solve problems and to cope with the environment. Of course, there is nothing wrong with any of these definitions or uses of the term. The problem is that none seem to say it all. We have gotten into the habit of using intelligence as a general label for so many cognitive abilities that it virtually defies specific definition.

Nonetheless, we should settle on some definition to guide our study through the rest of this chapter. I propose that we accept two definitions, one academic and theoretical, the other operational and practical. For our theoretical definition of **intelligence**, we can do no better than the one offered by David Wechsler, who defines it as "the capacity of an individual to understand the world about him [her] and his [her] resourcefulness to cope with its challenges" (1975, p. 139).

Some people are born with the predisposition to become extremely intelligent. This inherited potential must be encouraged and nurtured in a stimulating environment to be fully realized.

This definition, and others like it, does present some ambiguities. Just what does one mean by "capacity"? What is meant by "understand the world"? What if the world never really challenges one's "resourcefulness"? Would such people be less intelligent? What at first reading may seem like a very sensible and inclusive definition of intelligence may, upon reflection, pose even more definitional problems.

Perhaps we ought to follow our advice from Topic 1A, where I suggested that defining concepts operationally often helps overcome such difficulties. We have to be somewhat careful here, but we may operationally define intelligence as "that which intelligence tests measure." Notice that using this definition simply sidesteps the thorny conceptual problem of coming to grips with the "true" nature of intelligence; it doesn't solve it. But it does what most operational definitions do—it gives us a definition we can work with for a while. To use this definition meaningfully, we need to understand how intelligence tests go about measuring intelligence. Before we get to a discussion of intelligence tests, however, it would be helpful if we did two things. We should spend a bit of time reviewing some of the more useful ways in which psychologists have described the nature of intelligence. We also need to discuss psychological tests in general, and see what it takes to develop a "good test," but first, more on the nature of intelligence.

BEFORE YOU GO ON

Provide a theoretical and an operational definition of intelligence.

Theoretical Models of Intelligence

Theoretical models of intelligence are attempts to categorize and organize the different aspects of intellectual (cognitive) abilities into sensible groupings. In a way, they are sophisticated attempts to provide a definition for what we mean when we talk about intelligence. In this section, we'll briefly review a few such models.

Spearman's "g." One of the first theories of intelligence was proposed by a British psychologist, Charles Spearman. Spearman was one of the pioneers of mental testing and the inventor of many statistical procedures that could be used to analyze test scores.

Spearman's image of intelligence came from his inspection of scores earned by subjects on a wide range of psychological tests designed to assess many different cognitive skills. His approach was correlational. He looked at the extent to which scores on these many different instruments were related to each other.

What impressed Spearman was that no matter what cognitive ability a specific test was designed to measure, some people always seemed to do a little better than others. In other words, those people who scored high on some tests tended to score high on all the tests (to varying degrees, of course). It seemed as if there were some raw intellectual power that facilitated performance in general, while variations in performance reflected relative strengths and weaknesses in specific tasks. Spearman (1904) concluded that intelligence is made up of two things: a general intelligence, called a **g-factor**, and a collection of specific intellectual skills, called **s-factors**. Furthermore, Spearman believed that "g" was independent of knowledge of content—it went beyond just knowing facts. It involved the ability to see, understand, and apply relationships in all content areas. In this view, everyone has a certain degree of "g," or general intelligence, which Spearman thought was probably inherited, *and* everyone has some specific skills that are useful in some tasks but not in others.

Looking at intelligence in terms of what a variety of different tests measure, and how such measures are related to each other, became a popular way to think about intelligence. Psychologists went about giving many types of tests to all sorts of people. They applied statistical techniques (many of them devised by Spearman) to their test scores and looked for areas of overlap and independence.

g-factor *in Spearman's model, a general, overall intellectual skill*

s-factors *in Spearman's model, those specific cognitive abilities that together with "g" constitute intelligence*

Figure 8.1

THURSTONE'S SEVEN PRIMARY MENTAL ABILITIES

Verbal comprehension (V)	The ability to understand ideas, concepts, and words, as in a vocabulary test.
Number (N)	The ability to use numbers to solve problems quickly and accurately.
Spatial relations (S)	The ability to visualize and manipulate patterns and forms in space, as in the ability to recognize an object viewed from a different prospective.
Perceptual speed (P)	The ability to determine quickly and accurately whether or not two complex stimuli are identical or in some way different.
Word fluency (W)	The ability to use words quickly and fluently, as in the ability to solve anagrams and produce rhymes.
Memory (M)	The ability to remember lists of materials, such as digits, letters, or words presented previously.
Inductive reasoning (I)	The ability to discover a general rule from presented information, to discover relationships, as in, "what number comes next? 2, 4, 6, 8, —."

After Thurstone, 1938.

Thurstone's Primary Mental Abilities. When L. L. Thurstone examined the correlations among the different tests of cognitive abilities that he had administered, he found something different from what Spearman had noted. Thurstone (1938) felt that there was no evidence to support the notion of a general g-factor of intellectual ability. Instead, he claimed that abilities fell into seven different categories or groupings, which he called the seven **primary mental abilities** (see Figure 8.1). Each of the factors in this model is taken to be separate and independently measurable. To know one's intelligence requires that you know how one fares on all seven factors.

Guilford's Structure of Intellect. From Spearman's view that intelligence is made up of two factors ("g" and "s"), we moved to Thurstone's theory that intelligence is made up of seven independent abilities. With the model of J. P. Guilford (1967), matters get much more complicated. He proposed that intelligence can be analyzed into three intersecting dimensions. Guilford claimed that any intellectual task can be described in terms of the mental *operations* that are used in the task, the *content* or type of material that is involved, and the *product* or outcome of the task. Each of these three main dimensions has a number of possible values. That is, there are five different operations, four possible contents, and six possible products. The three dimensions of this model, and their values are presented in Figure 8.2.

If you study Figure 8.2, you'll discover that there are 120 possible combinations of content, operations, and products in Guilford's model. (In 1988, Guilford increased the possible number of combinations to 150 by dividing the memory operation into "recording" and "retention" to separate memory into encoding and retrieval stages [see Topic 6A]. His basic logic remained the same, however.) Remembering that Guilford's model is the-

primary mental abilities *in Thurstone's model, the seven unique abilities taken to comprise intelligence*

Figure **8.2**

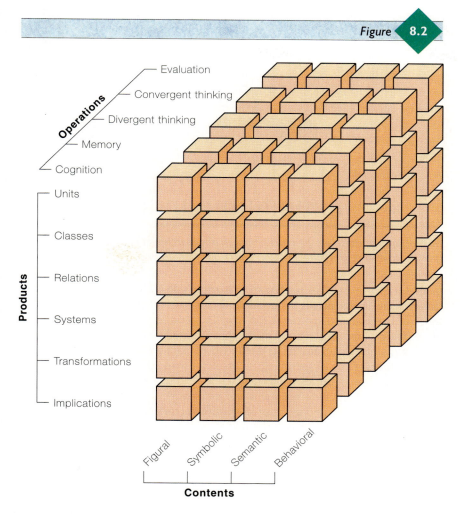

Guilford's model of intelligence. In this model, there are three major divisions (contents, products, and operations), each with its own subdivisions. Each subdivision may interact with all others, yielding 120 specific intellectual skills or abilities. (After Guilford, 1967.)

oretical, we still can ask, "What does this mean in real life?" Just to give you an idea of how this system works, let's choose one of the 120 "cells," or intersections, depicted in Figure 8.2—the one where *cognition, figural,* and *units* intersect (i.e., the little "block" in the uppermost left corner). What would this intellectual skill be like? Guilford says it's a matter of recognizing diagrams (cognitive) or pictures (figural) of simple, well-defined elements (units). To test this ability, one might be shown an incomplete drawing of a simple object and asked to identify it as quickly as possible. The intersection of *cognition, semantic,* and *units* values would be tested with a simple vocabulary test.

Vernon's Hierarchical Model. Philip Vernon (1960, 1979) has suggested that we think of intelligence as a number of skills and abilities that are arranged hierarchically (see Figure 8.3). At the very top is a general

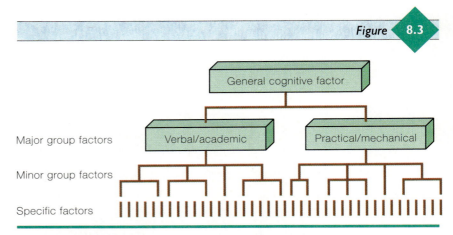

Intellectual abilities may be represented in a hierarchy from very general to very specific according to Philip Vernon. (After Vernon, 1960.)

mental, cognitive ability similar to Spearman's "g." Under it are two major factors: one is essentially a *verbal/academic* sort of intelligence, while the other is a *mechanical, practical* sort. Either of these in turn can be thought of as being comprised of yet more specific intellectual skills. The verbal/academic skill, for example, is made up of *numerical* and *verbal* abilities, among others. Each of these can be broken down still further (verbal skills may include such things as *vocabulary* and *word usage*); and further still (vocabulary may include *synonyms* and *antonyms*). Seeing cognitive abilities as including general and structured specific factors gives us a model that is something of a combination of the approaches of Spearman, Thurstone, and Guilford.

Sternberg's Triarchic Model. Robert Sternberg is a cognitive psychologist intrigued by the nature of intelligence. His concern reflects a more modern vision than the theories we've reviewed so far in that the focus of concern here is more on *how one uses intellectual abilities* than it is on *describing one's intellectual abilities.* Sternberg's approach is called triarchic, because he sees intelligent behavior as a reflection of the input of three different processes or components (1979, 1981, 1985, 1988). One set of components or processes of intelligent behavior involves what Sternberg calls *metacomponents*. These are the skills that we bring to bear when we set about to solve a problem. "Just what is the problem here?" "How shall I get started?" "What will I need to see this through?" "How will I know when I've succeeded?" The second set of abilities is called *performance components*. These are the actual skills we use in our attempt to solve problems. This component involves what we know about ourselves and the world. For example, when working on a math problem, once we realize that two numbers must be multiplied, it is the performance component of our cognitive abilities that gets that job done. Finally, Sternberg proposes that intelligence includes a set of abilities he calls *knowledge-acquisition* components. These are the techniques and strategies we have for collecting and assimilating new information. In some ways, this component is related to Harlow's concept of "learning-to-learn" (see pp. 231–232). Part of "being intelligent" is to demonstrate that one can profit from experience.

I am sure that you appreciate that what we have reviewed here so briefly is only a small sampling of the many theoretical approaches to intelligence that have been proposed over the years. Given the diversity of opinion about what intelligence *really means*, it is not surprising that psychologists often have resorted to the operational approach of defining intelligence in terms of the tests they have devised to measure it. Now that we have a general idea of the sorts of theoretical issues that psychologists have struggled with, we can turn our attention to psychological tests in general. Our discussion of tests of intelligence will then follow.

BEFORE YOU GO ON

Briefly summarize the approaches to intelligence taken by Spearman, Thurstone, Guilford, Vernon, and Sternberg.

THE NATURE OF PSYCHOLOGICAL TESTS

We have seen that there are several different ways to define the concept of intelligence. We'll soon see that there are a number of different ways of measuring it. Although the focus of our discussion in this chapter *is* intelligence, we recognize that psychological tests have been devised to measure the full range of human abilities and characteristics. For that reason, we'll examine psychological testing in general. Let's start with a definition and then consider the criteria by which we can evaluate the quality of a psychological test.

A Working Definition

We will define a **psychological test** as "an objective, standardized measure of a sample of behavior" (Anastasi, 1982). Let's take a look at the important terms within this definition.

A psychological test measures *behavior*. It measures behavior because that is all we *can* measure directly. We simply cannot measure those mental concepts that we call feelings, aptitudes, or abilities. All we can measure is overt, observable behavior. On the basis of our behavioral assessment, we may be willing to make inferences and assumptions about underlying internal processes. But behavior is all we can measure.

It should be clear that any one psychological test can measure only a *sample* of behavior. Let's say that I want to know about your tendency to be aggressive. I cannot very well ask you everything about you that relates to aggression in your life. ("List *all* of the situations in which you have ever acted aggressively," for instance.) What I have to do instead is sample (systematically identify a portion of) the behaviors in which I am interested. I then assume that responses to my sample of items can be used to predict responses to related questions that I have not asked. Even a classroom exam only asks you about a sample of the material you have learned in preparation for that exam.

psychological test *an objective, standardized measure of a sample of behavior*

Notice that psychological tests are twice removed from what we often think we are doing when we test someone. For instance, let's say that I am interested in how you feel about psychology. Perhaps I want to compare your feelings with those of someone who has never taken a psychology class. First, there is no way that I can get inside the two of you and assess your feelings directly. I have to assume that your responses (behaviors) to my test items accurately reflect your feelings (and that you're not just trying to be nice and make me feel good, for example). Second, because time prohibits me from asking everything that I might wish to ask, I have to assume that my questions and your answers provide an adequate sample of what I want to know. So, instead of measuring your feelings directly, I am forced to make *inferences* based on a *sample* of behavior.

There are two other definitional points to consider. If a psychological test is to have any value, its administration must be *standardized* and its scoring should be *objective*. Here is where your experience as a test taker may be relevant. Imagine taking a college placement test that will be used to determine which courses in English composition you will be required to take. You are given 45 minutes to answer 50 multiple-choice questions *and* write a short essay on a prescribed topic. Later, you discover that other students were given the same examination, but with instructions to "take as long as you like to finish the test." You also discover that those students could write their essay on any one of three suggested topics. You would be justified in complaining that something is wrong with the testing system. What it lacks is standardization. As much as possible, everyone taking a test—any kind of test—should take it under the same conditions, follow the same instructions, have the same time limits, and so on. What we want to know about are differences between individuals, not differences between testing situations.

A psychological test also should be objective. Objectivity in this context refers to the evaluation of the responses that exam takers make to test items—scoring the test, in other words. Different examiners (at least those of the same level of expertise) should be expected to give the same interpretation and evaluation to a test answer or response. If the same responses to a psychological test lead one psychologist to declare a person perfectly normal, a second psychologist to consider the person a mass of inner conflict, overridden with anxiety, and a third to wonder why this person is not now in a psychiatric institution, we have a problem. Assuming that the problem is with the test and not the three psychologists, the problem is one of objectivity. Although strict, literal objectivity is a goal seldom reached by psychological tests (particularly those designed to assess personality characteristics), it is a worthy goal. Note that I am *not* claiming here that a psychological test must yield exactly the same results every time it is scored. Testing situations that yield subjective impressions *can* be very useful. Still, the criteria for evaluating test responses must be objective enough to yield a degree of consistency in the interpretation of those responses.

So it appears that all we need for a psychological test is a series of items or questions for subjects to respond to that are administered in a standard fashion and scored objectively. That doesn't sound very difficult to do. It isn't. The world is full of "tests" that meet these definitional criteria. Weekly papers at the supermarket, scores of magazines, newspapers, and even television programs regularly include psychological tests. As a consumer of such tests as well as a student of psychology, you should be able to assess the usefulness of the measuring devices that we call psychological tests. It is to this matter that we turn next.

What is a psychological test?

Criteria for a Good Test

As easy as it may be to write a test, it is very difficult to write a good one. To qualify as a good, useful, psychological test, a technique needs to have three characteristics: reliability, validity, and adequate norms. To ensure that a test has these characteristics takes time and effort (and money). It is for this reason that many of the tests found in the popular press tend not to be good tests. In this section, we'll define and give examples of these three criteria for a good test.

Reliability. In the context of psychological testing, **reliability** means the same thing that it means in other contexts: consistency or dependability. For example, suppose that someone gives you an objective, standardized measure of a sample of your behavior and, on the basis of your responses, suggests that you have an IQ that is slightly below average—94, let's say. Two weeks later, you take the same test and are told that your IQ is now 127—nearly in the top 3 percent of the entire population. Something is terribly wrong. We have not yet discussed IQ scores, but surely we recognize that one's IQ—as a measure of intelligence—does not change by 33 points within two weeks.

A test is said to be reliable if it measures something (anything) consistently. Let's say that I have developed a short multiple-choice test that claims to measure the extent of one's extroversion or introversion—the extent to which one values the company of others, social stimulation, and the opportunity to try new and different things (extroversion) or values solitude and generally withdraws from social stimulation (introversion). I give my test to a group of 200 college freshmen. If I administered the same test one month later to the same subjects, I would be surprised if everyone earned exactly the same score on this second administration. I'd expect *some* fluctuation in the scores, but changes on a retest one month later should be small if I have a reliable test. If an instrument does not measure whatever it measures with consistency, it will not be very useful. If a month ago your test scores indicated that you were a very extroverted person and today's test indicates tendencies toward introversion, which test result am I to believe?

The type of reliability with which we are usually concerned is called **test-retest reliability**. As its name suggests, test-retest reliability involves administering a test to the same group of subjects on two different occasions. Scores on the two administrations are then correlated with each other. Correlation will tell us directly if the test in question is reliable. If the correlation coefficient is zero, or near zero, the test may be declared un-

reliability *consistency or dependability; in testing, consistency of test scores*

test-retest reliability *a check of a test's consistency determined by correlating the results of a test taken by the same subjects at two different times*

reliable. Acceptable levels of reliability are indicated by correlation coefficients that approach + 1.00 (where a correlation above + .70 is usually taken as acceptable).

Test-retest reliability makes good sense when we are attempting to measure characteristics that we assume to be consistent and stable, such as one's intelligence or extroversion. Test scores should be consistent because we assume that what we are measuring is itself reliable and consistent over time. What happens if the characteristic we are trying to measure is known or suspected to change over time? Consider developing a test to measure anxiety. If we realize nothing else about it, we recognize that how anxious we are changes from week to week, from day to day, and even from hour to hour.

So if I do write a test to measure anxiety, test-retest reliability will not be a sensible way to evaluate my test. A person may earn a very high score one day, right before midterm exams, and a very low score just a few days later after having learned that she did well on all her exams. In such cases, we do not abandon the notion of reliability altogether, however. There are two alternatives to test-retest reliability.

One thing I might do is make up two forms of my test. They will be very much alike in almost every detail; they will ask the same sorts of questions about the same behaviors, but in slightly different ways. I will then ask you to take both forms of the test. Your score, or your reactions, should be essentially the same on both forms if my test is reliable.

At the very least, we expect any psychological test to have internal reliability. That is, we require that the test be consistent from beginning to end. We may correlate the scores on items from the first half of the test with scores on the second half of the test. We may correlate scores on the odd-numbered items with scores on the even-numbered items. Such a measure would yield a **split-half reliability** score and tell us if there is consistency *within* the test, even if consistency over time is irrelevant.

split-half reliability *a check on the internal consistency of a test found by correlating one part of a test with another part of the same test*

BEFORE YOU GO ON

What is reliability, and how do we measure the reliability of psychological tests?

validity *in testing, the extent to which a test measures what it claims to measure*

Validity. When people worry about the usefulness of a test, their concern is usually with that test's **validity**. Measures of validity tell us the extent to which a test actually measures what it claims to measure. It is the extent to which there is agreement between a test score and the quality the test is believed to measure (Kaplan & Saccuzzo, 1989).

We determine a test's *reliability* by correlating the test with itself (at a later time, with test-retest reliability, or at the same time, with alternate forms or split-half reliability). We determine a test's *validity* by correlating test scores with some other, independent measure, or *criterion*. As it happens, psychologists have devised various types of validity, although there is considerable overlap among the different types (Anastasi, 1986).

One of the most practical types of test validity is **predictive validity** (Jones & Appelbaum, 1990). A test has predictive validity to the extent that it adequately predicts some future behavior. Does this test of extroversion predict which college students are most likely to join clubs or sororities or fraternities? Does this aptitude test predict who will do well in college and who will not? Does this typing test predict who will do well working with a word processor and who will not? Does this assessment procedure predict whether or not this subject is likely to injure himself or others in the future?

predictive validity *the extent to which a test can be used to predict future behaviors*

Determining a test's predictive validity also is a matter of correlation. The test in question is given to a large group of subjects. All subjects are later measured on the independent criterion, and test scores are correlated with criterion scores. Now you find out if, in fact, those who earn high test scores also earn good grades in college courses. You find out, for example, if those who get high scores on your extroversion test do, in fact, tend to join sororities and fraternities. (Note that determining the validity of a test requires that we have a good, reliable, and valid criterion to correlate the test with.)

I should mention in this context a related concern about test quality: *validity generalization* (Glass et al., 1981; Sackett et al., 1985). The issue here is the extent to which predictive validity determined in one situation can be applied in other, different situations. For example, you'll recall that in Topic 1B, I used an example of correlation that demonstrates that reading test scores are good predictors of performance in introductory psychology. Well, just because a reading test has predictive validity for psychology, we have no reason to suspect that it *necessarily* will be useful as a predictor of grades in biology, mathematics, or any other course.

If a psychological test is well correlated with other tests or measures of the same characteristic, the test is said to have **concurrent validity**. If you generate a new technique to measure test anxiety that is not at all correlated with any of the well-established techniques already available that measure test anxiety, your technique probably lacks concurrent validity.

concurrent validity *the extent to which the scores on a test are correlated with other assessments made at about the same time*

Concurrent validity is often a useful concept in the realm of employment testing. On the one hand, we may want a test that enables us to predict if an applicant can do a job at some time in the future (and our concern would be with predictive validity). On the other hand, we may want to know the extent to which an applicant can do a job *now* (or concurrently). We can assess the concurrent validity of an employment test for auto mechanics by giving our test to currently employed mechanics. If efficient, successful mechanics do well on our test and if less able mechanics do poorly, we have demonstrated a degree of concurrent validity for our test.

One additional form of validity ought to be mentioned here because it is relevant for students taking classroom exams. It is **content validity**, which is the extent to which a test adequately samples the behaviors that it claims to be testing. For example, you may be told that you are to be given an exam covering all of learning and memory. The test is to be made up of 50 multiple-choice items. You might be more than a little upset if you were to find that 48 of the 50 items deal only with classical conditioning. You would claim that the test was not fair. It would lack validity because it does not measure what it claims to measure. In this case, it would lack content validity because the content of the test does not cover a broad

content validity *the extent to which a test provides an adequate and fair sample of the behaviors being measured*

range of material on learning and memory. Content validity usually is determined by the judgment of content area experts.

BEFORE YOU GO ON

What are predictive, concurrent, and content validity?
How is each of these measured?

norms *results of a test taken by a large group of subjects whose scores can be used to make comparisons or give meaning to new scores*

Norms. Let's say that you have just filled out an objective, paper-and-pencil questionnaire, designed to measure the extent to which you are extroverted. You know that the test is a reliable and valid instrument. You are told that you scored a 50 on the test. So what? What does a score of 50 mean? It doesn't mean that you answered 50 percent of the items correctly, because on this test there are no correct or incorrect answers. Does a 50 mean that you are extroverted, introverted, neither, or both?

The point is that if you don't have a basis of comparison, any one test score by itself is meaningless. You need to compare your score of 50 with the scores of other people like yourself who have already taken the test. Results of a test taken by a large group of subjects whose scores can be used to make comparisons are called **norms**.

You may discover by checking with the norms that a score of 50 is indeed quite average and indicative of neither extreme extroversion nor extreme introversion. On the other hand, a 50 might be a very high score, indicating extroversion, or a very low score, indicating introversion. An aptitude test score of 134 sounds pretty good until you discover that the average score was 265 and that scores in the norms range from 115 to 360. If the norms tell you that the average score on the aptitude test was only 67 and that scores tend to range between 30 and 140, then your score of 134 would be very good indeed.

The usefulness of a test, then, often depends on the adequacy of the norms that are used to make comparisons or judgments about any one test score. If the extroversion-introversion test you took had been administered to only 40 or 50 grade school students to compile its norms, it would hardly provide an adequate measure of *your* extroversion or introversion. Scores that make up norms should be from subjects similar to those who are going to be tested later—and the more similar, the better.

So writing a good psychological test is not as easy as it may at first appear. Writing a series of questions and deciding on acceptable answers may be relatively simple, but the rest takes considerable time and effort. Now that we have an idea of the types of considerations that need to be made when constructing a psychological test, we can see how psychologists have attempted to measure intelligence. Given the difficulty we've had agreeing on the nature of intelligence in theory, you won't be surprised to find that not all psychologists are pleased with currently available intelligence tests.

BEFORE YOU GO ON

In the context of psychological testing, what are norms, and for what purpose are they used?

PSYCHOLOGICAL TESTS OF INTELLIGENCE

In this section, we'll briefly review some of the psychological tests that are used to measure intelligence. As we do so, there are two major ideas you'll need to keep in mind. You'll need to remember the definition of a test (an objective, standardized measure of a sample of behavior) and the criteria for evaluating psychological tests (reliability, validity, and norms). You'll also have to remember that test scores provide only one measure of intelligence—as we've seen, no one approach or one measure is going to provide a universally satisfactory description of intelligence.

The Stanford-Binet Intelligence Scale

Historians of psychology would refer to the contributions of Alfred Binet (1857—1911) even if he hadn't written the first practical test of general intelligence. He was the leading psychologist in France at the turn of the century. When psychology was first beginning to emerge as a science, Binet worked at the psychology laboratory at the Sorbonne. He studied all sorts of things there: hypnosis, abnormal behaviors, optical illusions, and thinking processes. By far, however, his major concern was with individual differences. This interest was fostered by his observations of his two daughters, who were remarkably different in many ways (Hothersall, 1990). In particular, Binet was curious about how people differed in their abilities to solve problems.

It was not surprising, then, that Binet's expertise was sought on a wide range of educational issues. Of great concern in 1900 were those children in the Paris school system who seemed unable to profit from the educational experiences they were being given. What was the problem? Were they not interested? Did they have some emotional sickness? Or were they intellectually unable to grasp and use the material they were being presented? With a group of collaborators, Binet set out to construct a test to measure the intellectual abilities of children. His most important collaborator was Théodore Simon, who had volunteered to serve as Binet's research assistant. Binet and Simon wanted to identify those students who should be placed in special (largely remedial) classes, where their education could proceed more efficiently than it had in the standard classroom.

Binet's first test appeared in 1905 and was revised and expanded in 1908. The test was an immediate success. It caught the attention of Lewis M. Terman at Stanford University, who supervised a translation and revision

Alfred Binet

Lewis Terman

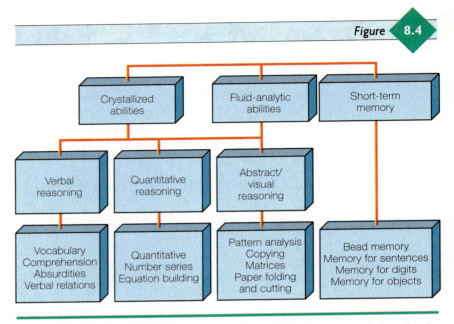

The factors tested by the Stanford-Binet, Fourth Edition, arranged in three levels, including a listing of each subtest. (After Thorndike et al., 1986.)

Pictured here are some of the materials that make up the revised Stanford-Binet test. The fourth edition represents the most significant changes made to the test and its scoring.

g *on an intelligence test, a measure of one's overall, general intellectual abilities, commonly thought of as IQ*

of the test in 1916. (This revision included changing some clearly French questions into items more suitable for American children.) Since then, the test has been referred to as the Stanford-Binet and has undergone a number of subsequent revisions. A 1937 edition provided two alternate forms of the test, labeled Form L and Form M, after Terman's initials. The most recent version of the Stanford-Binet was published in 1986. This edition— the fourth—made several significant changes in the test and in its scoring. So what is this test like?

Although a number of individual items from earlier editions of the Stanford-Binet are still to be found, the 1986 revision of the test is quite different from its predecessors. The test now follows what its authors call a three-level hierarchical model of cognitive ability (Thorndike et al., 1986). As did Binet's original test, the current edition yields an overall test score which reflects **g**, or general intellectual ability (not unlike Spearman's "g"). The test's authors describe this **g**-factor as "what an individual uses when faced with a problem that he or she has not been taught to solve" (1986, p. 3).

Underlying **g** are three second-level factors (see Figure 8.4). *Crystallized abilities* represent those skills needed for acquiring and using information about verbal and quantitative concepts to solve problems. They are influenced by schooling and could be called an academic ability factor. *Fluid-analytic abilities* are typified by skills needed to solve problems that involve figural or nonverbal types of information. The bases of these skills are less tied to formal schooling. Essentially, they involve the ability to see things in new and different ways. The third factor at the second level of the model is *short-term memory*. Items that test one's ability to hold information in memory for relatively short periods of time can be found on Binet's original test.

Figure   **8.5**

THE 15 SUBTESTS OF THE 1986 EDITION OF THE STANFORD-BINET INTELLIGENCE SCALE

1. Vocabulary	For ages 2-6, provide name and definition of picture of object; for older subjects, define words increasing in difficulty
2. Bead memory	String a series of multicolored beads after seeing a picture of the required string
3. Quantitative	Complete a series of arithmetic problems, from simple counting to complex word problems
4. Memory for sentences	Repeat a series of sentences of increasing complexity
5. Pattern analysis	At young ages, match shapes to holes; at older levels, use blocks of different designs to copy patterns of increasing complexity
6. Comprehension	Answer questions like "Why does the government regulate radio and television broadcasts?"
7. Absurdities	Identify what is wrong with picture; for example, a wagon with triangular wheels
8. Memory for digits	Repeat a list of digits of increasing length; forward or backward
9. Copying	Draw (duplicate) a series of geometric line drawings of increasing complexity
10. Memory for objects	Recognize a series of pictures of simple objects presented one at a time from a larger picture displaying many objects
11. Matrices	Shown a series of pictures, determine which of a number of alternatives comes next in the series
12. Number series	Presented with a series of numbers, determine what number comes next in the series
13. Paper folding and cutting	Fold and/or cut sheet of paper according to a prescribed pattern
14. Verbal relations	Given three words that are alike and a fourth that is different, explain why the three are alike and the fourth is different
15. Equation building	Given a series of digits and algebraic signs ($+$, $\times$, $\div$), create a balanced equation

The third level of abilities tested on the new Stanford-Binet provides more specific, content-oriented definitions of the factors from level two. As you can see from Figure 8.4, at this level, crystallized abilities are divided into verbal and quantitative reasoning, fluid analytic abilities are seen as abstract/visual reasoning, and there simply is no ability at this level that corresponds to short-term memory.

At the base of the hierarchy are the 15 subtests that operationally define the structure of the actual Stanford-Binet test. Figure 8.5 lists each subtest and provides an example item.

What all of this means is that the authors of the 1986 revision of the Stanford-Binet acknowledge that a person's measured intelligence should be reflected in more than just one test score. Now, not only can we determine an overall **g** score, but we also can calculate scores for each factor at each of three levels. In addition, we can calculate scores for the 15 subtests by themselves, although it is difficult to say that individual subtest scores are very meaningful. It's also unlikely that an examiner would administer all 15 of the subtests to any one subject.

Within each subtest, items are arranged by difficulty, indicated by appropriate age level. Age levels vary from 2 years old to adult (18 years +), although only six subtests have items appropriate for all age levels. This means that if you were testing an 8-year-old whom you thought had average intellectual abilities, you might start testing for vocabulary, let's say with the items at the 6-year-old level. You would give credit for the easier, lower-age-level items. You would then continue with items of increasing difficulty until your subject failed three out of four questions or problems at any two consecutive age levels. At this point, there would be no reason to continue testing; to do so would only lead to frustration.

The test manual would then provide you with the data that would allow you to convert your subject's earned score—how many vocabulary items were answered correctly, for example—into a score that compared her performance with that of other children of the same age. You would then make comparisons for each of the factors you tested (see Figure 8.4 again), including the **g** score. When your subject's earned scores are compared to those of others of the same age who have taken the test (the test's *norms*, remember), the resulting score is called a **standard age score** or **SAS**. Standard age scores on the Stanford Binet are defined so that an average SAS *always* comes out to be 100. Individuals who do better than average have standard age scores above 100, and those who perform less well than others their age have standard age scores below 100. Figure 8.6 shows the way SASs on the Stanford-Binet are distributed for the general population.

Before we go on, let's take a minute to discuss what has happened to the concept of IQ. **IQ** is an abbreviation for the term *intelligence quotient*. As you know, a quotient is the result you get when you divide one number by another. If one divides 8 by 6, the quotient is 1.33. For the early versions of the Stanford-Binet, the examiner's job was to determine a subject's *mental age* (or *MA*), the age level at which the subject was functioning in terms of intellectual abilities. A subject with the intellectual abilities of an average 8-year-old would have an MA of 8. IQ was then determined by dividing the subject's earned mental age by his or her actual age (called *chronological age*, or *CA*). This quotient was then multiplied by 100 to determine IQ, or IQ = (MA/CA) × 100. If an 8-year-old girl had a mental age of 8, that girl would be average, and her IQ would equal 100 (or (8/8) × 100 = 1 × 100). If the 8-year-old were above average, with the intellectual abilities of an average 10-year-old, then her IQ would be 125 (that's (10/8) × 100, or 1.25 × 100). If she were below average, perhaps with the mental abilities of an average 6-year-old, then her computed IQ would be 75. Many people are used to the term IQ as a measure of one's general intellectual abilities. Because it is a term that is engrained in our vocabulary, *we will continue to use "IQ" as a measure of general intelligence,* even though we now report scores as standard scores and no longer compute MAs or calculate quotients.

The Stanford-Binet test has been in use for a long time. There is much to be said for it. It is a well-recognized measure of those behaviors that we commonly label intelligent—at least in an educational or academic sense—and is in that way, at least, a valid instrument. It is also reliable. Test-retest

standard age score (SAS) *a score on an intelligence test in which one's performance is compared to that of others of the same age; average equals 100*

IQ *the intelligence quotient, found by dividing one's mental age (MA) by one's chronological age (CA), and multiplying by 100, or MA/CA × 100*

Figure 8.6

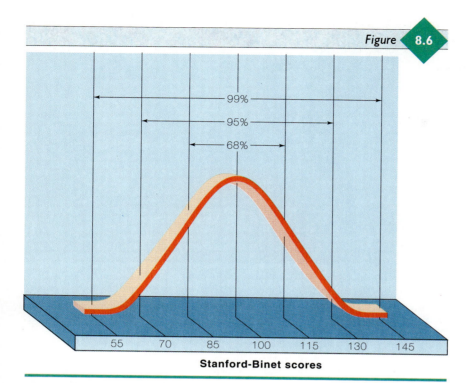

Stanford-Binet scores

An idealized curve that shows the distribution of scores on the Stanford-Binet Intelligence Scale if the test were taken by a very large sample of the general population. The numbers at the top of the curve indicate the percentage of the population expected to score within the indicated range of scores, 68 percent score between 85 and 115; 95 percent score between 70 and 130; and 99 percent score between 55 and 145.

reliability scores (correlation coefficients) are usually around .90 (Matarazzo, 1990). Even so, we can expect a change in standard scores of as much as eight points on repeated administrations (that is, a test score of 100 ought to be thought of as representing a "true" score somewhere between 96 and 104). The Stanford-Binet also has some drawbacks. It is an individual test (one subject and one examiner) and should be administered, scored, and interpreted only by well-trained professionals. The test can take longer than an hour to administer and, hence, is quite expensive.

BEFORE YOU GO ON

Briefly describe the Stanford-Binet Intelligence Scale.

The Wechsler Tests of Intelligence

David Wechsler published his first general intelligence test in 1939. Unlike the version of the Stanford-Binet that existed at the time, it was designed for use with adult populations and to reduce the heavy reliance

The Wechsler tests provide verbal and performance scores that are compared to scores earned by subjects of the same age in the norm group. The Wechsler Intelligence Scale for Children (WISC-R) is a general intelligence test for children between the ages of 6 and 17.

on verbal skills that characterized Binet's tests. With a major revision in 1955, the test became known as the *Wechsler Adult Intelligence Scale (WAIS)*. The latest revision (called the WAIS-R) was published in 1981. The WAIS-R is appropriate for subjects between 16 and 74 years of age and is reported to be the most commonly used of all psychological tests (Lubin et al., 1984).

A natural extension of the WAIS was the *Wechsler Intelligence Scale for Children (WISC)*, originally published 11 years after the WAIS. After a major revision in 1974, it became known as the WISC-R. With updated norms and a number of new items (among other things, designed to minimize bias against any ethnic group or gender), the WISC-III appeared in 1991. The WISC-III is appropriate for testing children between the ages of 6 and 16 (there is some overlap with the WAIS-R). A third test in the Wechsler series is designed for younger children between the ages of 4 and 6½. It is called the *Wechsler Preschool and Primary Scale of Intelligence*, or *WPPSI*. It was published in 1967. It, too, was revised recently—in 1989—and is now the WPPSI-R. There are some subtle differences among the three Wechsler tests, but each is based on the same general logic. Therefore, we'll consider only one, the WAIS-R, in any detail.

The WAIS-R is made up of 11 subtests arranged by the type of ability being tested. The subtests are organized into two categories. Six subtests define the *verbal scale*, and five subtests constitute a *performance scale*. Figure 8.7 lists the different subtests of the WAIS-R and describes some of the sorts of items found on each. With each of the Wechsler tests, we can compute three scores: a verbal score, a performance score, and a total (or full-scale) score. As with the Stanford-Binet, the total score can be taken as an approximation of "g", or general intellectual ability.

To administer the WAIS-R, you present each of the 11 subtests to your subject. The items within each subtest are arranged in order of difficulty. You start with relatively easy items—those you are confident your examinee

Figure **8.7**

THE SUBTESTS OF THE WECHSLER ADULT INTELLIGENCE SCALE-REVISED (WAIS-R)

Verbal scale

Information (29 items) Questions designed to tap one's general knowledge about a variety of topics dealing with one's culture; for example, "Who wrote *Huckleberry Finn?*" or "How many nickels in a quarter?"

Digit span (7 series) Subject is read a series of three to nine digits and is asked to repeat them; then a different series is to be repeated in reverse order.

Comprehension (16 items) A test of judgment, common sense, and practical knowledge; for example, "Why is it good to have prisons?"

Similarities (14 pairs) Subject must indicate the way(s) in which two things are alike; for example, "In what way are an apple and a potato alike?"

Vocabulary (35 words) Subject must provide an acceptable definition for a series of words.

Arithmetic (14 problems) Math problems must be solved without the use of paper and pencil; for example, "How far will a bird travel in 90 minutes if it flies at the rate of 10 miles per hour?"

Performance scale

Picture completion (20 pictures) Subject must identify or name the missing part or object in a drawing; for example, a truck with only three wheels.

Picture arrangement (10 series) A series of cartoonlike pictures must be arranged in an order so that they tell a story.

Block design (9 items) Using blocks whose sides are either all red, all white, or diagonally red and white, subject must copy a designed picture or pattern shown on a card.

Object assembly (4 objects) Free-form jigsaw puzzles must be put together to form familiar objects.

Digit symbol In a key, each of nine digits is paired with a simple symbol. Given a random series of digits, the subject must provide the paired symbol within a time limit.

will respond to correctly—and then you progress to more difficult ones. You stop administering any one subtest when your subject fails a specified number of consecutive items. You alternate between the performance and the verbal subtests. The whole process may take up to an hour and a half.

Each item on each subtest is scored. (Some of the performance items have strict time limits that affect scoring.) You now have 11 scores earned by your subject. As is now the case with the fourth edition of the Stanford-Binet, each subtest score is compared to the score provided with the test's norms. How your subject's score compares to the score earned by subjects in the norm group determines your subject's *standard score* for each of the Wechsler subtests. In addition to one overall score, the Wechsler tests provide verbal and performance scores, which supplies information about a person's particular strengths and weaknesses. The Wechsler tests are every bit as "good" as the Stanford-Binet in terms of reliability, validity, and norms.

For many years, there has been controversy and debate about the use and quality of individually administered intelligence tests such as the Wechsler tests and the Stanford-Binet. The extent to which the tests may be culturally biased, thus favoring one group of subjects over another, whether they truly measure intelligence and not just academic success, and whether test results can be used for political purposes, perhaps as a basis for racial discrimination, are just some of the questions that keep finding their way into the popular press. A survey of over 600 experts in psychological testing (from a number of disciplines, including education and psychology) indicates considerable agreement about the basic value of intelligence (or IQ) tests (Snyderman & Rothman, 1987). Although the experts are willing to allow that the tests may be somewhat biased on racial and socioeconomic grounds, they "believe that such tests adequately measure more important elements of intelligence" (p.143). We will address issues of test bias and group differences in IQ scores in Topic 8B.

BEFORE YOU GO ON

What are the major features of the Wechsler intelligence scales?

Group Tests of Intelligence

There are a number of advantages of individually administered tests such as the Wechsler tests and the Stanford-Binet. Perhaps most important is that the examiner has the opportunity to interact meaningfully with the subject taking the test. The examiner can use the testing session to develop opinions about the examinee and can observe firsthand how the subject goes about responding to test items.

The major disadvantage of the individually administered tests is that they are time consuming and expensive. There are, of course, alternatives. Group IQ tests are generally paper-and-pencil tests that can be administered to many individuals at one time.

When World War I began, Binet's test already had gained wide approval, and the notion of using psychological methods to measure personal abilities had been generally accepted. There was good reason to know the intellectual capabilities of the thousands of recruits who were entering the armed services, but obviously all these men could not be tested individually. A committee of psychologists was charged with the task of creating a group intelligence test. The result, published in 1917, was the *Army Alpha Test*, a paper-and-pencil test that made rough discriminations among examinees on the basis of intelligence. In the same year, the same committee published the *Army Beta Test*. The Beta was designed for illiterates who could not read the Army Alpha. Basically, it was a performance test, the instructions of which were given orally or were acted out to the examinees.

The military continues to be a major publisher and consumer of group intelligence tests. World War II provided the opportunity for a major revision of the Army Alpha and Beta. The revision was so total that the result was a new test: the *Army General Classification Test (AGCT)*. The AGCT was a paper-and-pencil test that was published in four alternate forms. Like today's individual IQ tests, it was scored using standard scores, with the average being equal to 100. It also allowed subscores for verbal ability, arithmetic computation, arithmetic reasoning, and spatial relations. The AGCT has now been replaced by the *Armed Forces Qualification Test (AFQT)*, and anyone who goes through the process of military induction will have firsthand experience with this test.

In addition to the military, the other large-scale consumer of group intelligence tests is the educational establishment. There are literally dozens of group-administered tests designed to provide an assessment of overall intellectual functioning. Let's note just a few of the more commonly used tests.

There has been a long history of group IQ tests associated with Arthur Otis, one of Terman's students at Stanford. The one used most often is the *Otis-Lennon School Ability Test (OLSAT)*, designed for children in kindergarten through high school. It yields an IQ score approximation. Its main advantage is the huge sample of subjects who comprise its norm group.

The *Cognitive Abilities Test*, or *CAT*, is another group test that is popular in many school systems. It is really a series of tests, each appropriate for different age levels from kindergarten through grade 12. One advantage of the CAT is that it provides subtests and norms that allow the calculation of verbal, quantitative, and nonverbal IQs, as well as an overall IQ score.

When psychological tests are used to make predictions about future behaviors, we call them *aptitude tests*. However, many of the aptitude tests used in the context of education are essentially tests of general intellectual ability. In their construction and administration, they are much like any general intelligence test. The difference is in the use to which the score is put: predicting future academic success. The two most commonly used college entrance tests are the *SAT (Scholastic Aptitude Test)*, which yields verbal and mathematics subscores as well as an overall score, and the *ACT (American College Testing Program)*. In the fall of 1990, the College Entrance Examination Board, which publishes the SAT, announced a major revision of the test (to be called the SAT-I, and introduced in the spring of 1994). The new SAT will include math items that are not in the usual multiple-choice format, and the verbal section will put more emphasis on reading comprehension. At the same time, a new, optional SAT-II will be made available. The SAT-II will include a written essay section, language proficiency tests for native speakers of Japanese and Chinese, and tests for non-native English speakers. The College Entrance Examination Board also publishes the *PSAT (Preliminary Scholastic Aptitude Test)*, which is becoming increasingly popular. It is designed for high school juniors who take the test to qualify for certain scholarships or as practice for the SAT.

As their college careers come to a close, students may once again face the task of taking a standardized aptitude test if they wish to go to a graduate or professional school. Each type of professional school—medical school, law school, and so on—has its own type of exam, and the more general *Graduate Record Exam (GRE)* is like an advanced form of the SAT. These tests, too, are essentially paper-and-pencil IQ tests, but they are used for prediction purposes.

What are the advantages of group intelligence tests?
How are paper-and-pencil IQ tests and educational
aptitude tests alike?

Using psychological tests as measuring instruments requires special care. We sometimes have considerable difficulty providing a solid definition of the very characteristic we are attempting to measure. Using a somewhat circular logic, we often fall back to our psychological tests to provide us with operational definitions of concepts that are difficult to define otherwise. Hence, *anxiety* becomes a score on an anxiety test, and *intelligence* becomes a score on an IQ test.

Psychological tests of high quality must demonstrate reliability and validity and have adequate norms. In this topic, we've reviewed some of psychology's better assessment tools—those designed to measure the cognitive processes we associate with intelligence. We know that at a theoretical level, intelligence is a complex concept, one we often have to consider in operational terms. In Topic 8B we'll consider measured intelligence, or IQ, in terms of what it can tell us about individual and group differences.

Provide a theoretical and an operational definition of intelligence.

In theory, we may define intelligence as David Wechsler has: the capacity of an individual to understand the world about him or her and the resourcefulness to cope with its challenges. An operational definition of intelligence would be "that which an intelligence test measures." / *page 343*

Briefly summarize the approaches to intelligence taken by Spearman, Thurstone, Guilford, Vernon, and Sternberg.

Spearman viewed intelligence as composed of one general factor ("g"), and a number of specific abilities ("s"). Thurstone argued that intelligence reflected a combination of seven unique and primary mental abilities. Guilford argued that there are as many as 120 different cognitive skills that constitute one's intelligence. Vernon suggested that intellectual skills or cognitive abilities can be arranged in a hierarchy from very general at the top to very specific at the bottom. Sternberg argues that intelligence should be conceptualized as an organized set of cognitive processes or techniques (components), not as a set of given facts or ideas. / *page 347*

What is a psychological test?

A psychological test is an *objective* (not open to multiple interpretation), *standardized* (administered and scored in the same way) *measure of a sample* (we cannot measure all behaviors at any one time) of *behavior* (because behavior is all we can measure). / *page 349*

What is reliability, and how do we measure the reliability of psychological tests?

Reliability means consistency or de-pendability. We measure the reliability of psychological tests by administering the same test to the same people at different times (test-retest reliability). We check the internal consistency of a test by comparing scores on some items with scores on other items (split-half reliability). / *page 350*

What are predictive, concurrent, and content validity? How is each of these measured?

Predictive validity is a measure of the extent to which a test can be useful in predicting some future behavior. It is measured by correlating test scores with independent measures of behavior made at some time after the test has been taken. Concurrent validity is the extent to which a test is adequately correlated with independent criteria (e.g., other tests) measured at the time of testing (concurrently). Content validity is the extent to which a test is composed of a fair and representative sample of the material or characteristic being tested. Judgments of content validity are commonly made by experts in the field being tested. / *page 352*

In the context of psychological testing, what are norms, and for what purpose are they used?

Test norms are scores on the test earned by a large number of subjects, similar to those for whom the test has been designed. It is against the standard of these scores that an individual's test score can be compared. / *page 353*

Briefly describe the Stanford-Binet Intelligence Scale.

The Stanford-Binet is the oldest of the tests of general intelligence (commonly called IQ tests). The test is individually administered. Its most recent (1986) revision provides an overall score as well as subscores for a number of abilities that are assumed to underlie general intelligence. The test is comprised of 15 subtests, each assessing a specific cognitive task, where items are arranged in order by difficulty. Scores on the test, standard age scores, compare the performance of a subject to that of others of the same age level. / *page 357*

What are the major features of the Wechsler intelligence scales?

The Wechsler scales are individually administered tests of general intelligence. There are three of them; each recently revised, and appropriate for different age groups ranging from ages 3 to 74. Each test is made up of a number of subtests of different content. The subtests are grouped together as verbal or performance subtests. Hence, three scores can be determined: an overall score, a score on the verbal subtests, and a score on the performance subtests. Scores on the Wechsler tests are standard scores that compare one's abilities to those of others of the same age. / *page 360*

What are the advantages of group intelligence tests? How are paper-and-pencil IQ tests and educational aptitude tests alike?

Group intelligence tests may not provide as much information or be as valid as individually administered tests, but they are much less expensive. They are best used as screening devices. Many educational aptitude tests are essentially paper-and-pencil tests of general intellectual abilities that are used to make predictions about future academic performance. / *page 362*

TOPIC 8B

Differences in Measured Intelligence

Why We Care: A Topic Preview

Throughout this text, we have repeatedly made the point that no two people are exactly alike. One of the most important ways in which people differ is in their intellectual abilities and capabilities. In this topic, we'll review some of the psychological literature on group and individual differences in measured intelligence.

There is no other topic for which two of our "themes and threads" from Chapter 1 are more relevant. (1) We have already had occasion to consider the interaction of one's nature and one's nurture. The impact of heredity and environment seems to take on special significance when we discuss measured intelligence, or IQ. (2) We also will be reminded of the observation that for many questions in psychology there are no simple answers.

There are, however, many questions—and they seem simple. Who are smarter, men or women? Do people become less intelligent in their old age? Are there any real differences in intelligence among persons of different races or ethnic backgrounds? Providing complete answers to these sorts of questions scientifically—and honestly—is not possible at present, particularly if one is going to demand simple answers.

So what we'll do in this topic is raise some interesting questions about differences in intelligence and provide the best answers we have at the moment. We'll start with a general discussion of the roles of heredity and the environment in determining intellectual functioning. We'll briefly review some of the data on differences in intelligence as a function of sex and age. We'll also look at some of the data on measured intelligence and academic achievement as a function of race. Finally, we'll consider the individual extremes of intelligence: the mentally gifted and the mentally retarded.

Throughout this topic, we'll be referring to the concept of IQ. Please keep in mind that IQ is simply a convenient abbreviation for "intelligence as it is measured by psychological tests." We should not take IQ to equal one's intelligence. IQ only reflects a particular measure of intelligence. We also need to remember that intelligence tests are scored in such a way that "intelligence quotients"—which is what IQ stands for—are no longer calculated directly.

THE INFLUENCE OF HEREDITY AND ENVIRONMENT ON INTELLIGENCE

Are the differences we observe in intelligence due to heredity or to environmental influences? Heredity and environment, genetics and experience, nature and nurture; yes, we've been over this before. I first introduced the issue back in Topic 1A. We'll encounter it again at some length in the chapter on psychological development (Topic 9A), and we'll allude to it in our discussion of sexuality and gender (Topic 10B). But nowhere is the concern about biological and experiential influence as focused or controversial as it is in the context of intelligence. Indeed, the relative impact of heredity and environment on intelligence is one of the oldest and most enduring concerns in all of psychology. "Although the social, political, and religious contexts have varied across history, and popular definitions and theories of intelligence have changed, the question has remained about the same: To what extent are genes and environments important variables in accounting for the development of individual differences in intelligence?" (Weinberg, 1989, p. 101). By now you realize that, as reasonable as it may sound, the question does not have a reasonable answer. As we'll see, there is evidence that intelligence tends to run in families and is due in part to innate, inherited factors. There are also data (and common sense) that tell us that a person's environment can and does affect intellectual, cognitive functioning.

A Tentative Answer

Before we examine any of the supporting evidence, we can offer a tentative answer to our opening question. We've been over this argument before (pp. 20–21), but given its centrality, it is worth reviewing in this context. Both heredity *and* the environment are critically important in determining intelligence. One's heredity may put limits on what environmental influences can accomplish. Without a nurturing, stimulating environment, even the best of inherited potential may be wasted.

A person does not inherit intelligence. A person inherits genes. These physical entities may very well set limits on the potential of our intellectual development. Some people may be born with the potential, or even the predisposition, to be very intelligent. If the environment does not encourage that predisposition, however, that potential will never be realized. Some individuals may be born with inherited predispositions that severely limit their intellectual growth. Even the most stimulating of environments may be insufficient to raise intellectual functioning significantly. The point is that the two, environment and heredity, interact. Each may limit the other. Both are important.

Another, related point needs to be made. *Inherited* does not mean *unchangeable*. Even if some trait was entirely influenced by one's genetic constitution, we have no evidence that that trait could not or would not change through interaction with the environment. Genes do not fix behavior; they establish a range of possibilities. Even if it were to be found that intelligence is a reflection only of one's inheritance, that would not mean that one's intelligence was unchangeable. (On this issue, see, e.g., Angoff, 1988; Horowitz, 1987; Plomin, 1989; Weinberg, 1989.)

What the Data Suggest: The Study of Twins

Maybe we cannot all agree on precisely what intelligence is, but we *can* use intelligence test scores as an approximation of an operational definition. Perhaps we cannot do the perfectly controlled experiment, but we *can* look at the relationships among the IQs of people with similar and different genetic histories who have been reared in similar and different environments. Such data may be flawed (Mackenzie, 1984; Mackintosh, 1986), but they can give us some helpful insights.

As you might imagine, there have been many studies that have examined the correlations of IQ test scores of persons with varying degrees of genetic similarity and those reared in similar and dissimilar environments. The results of some of the better of these studies are summarized in Figure 8.8. These are oft-cited data, and we ought to be sure that we understand what they mean.

On the left side of the figure, we have a list of the types of subjects whose IQ scores have been correlated. As you can see, as we go down the list, the genetic similarity between the subjects increases, from unrelated individuals reared apart to identical twins reared together. The graph shows the average (in this case the median) correlation for each of the pairs of groups named under "Subjects." These correlations represent average values from many correlational studies. Quite clearly, such data, drawn from a number of studies conducted at different times, with different subjects, and with different intents, need to be interpreted with great caution. Even with the variability reflected in these data, however, a few general conclusions seem reasonable.

As genetic similarities between subjects increase, correlations also increase. Correlations between the IQ scores of people who are unrelated in any biological sense are quite low. Remembering that fraternal twins are just siblings who happen to be born at about the same time, we find that IQs among family members in general are correlated somewhere near .50. When we examine the correlations of IQs of identical twins (whose genetic constitutions are the same, of course), we find very high correlations—as high as those usually reported as reliability coefficients for the IQ tests that were used. It seems quite obvious by inspection that genetic similarity and IQ scores are positively related.

You should also notice another trend in the data presented in Figure 8.8. Regardless of genetic similarity, the correlations for subjects raised together are consistently higher than for subjects raised apart in different environments. We do need to note that children raised apart were not necessarily reared in significantly different environments, and being raised together does not guarantee that environments are identical. But what these trends suggest is that environmental influences also affect IQ scores. As you can see, we are drawn to the conclusion we made earlier. Even though we are looking at grouped data, and even though many factors are uncontrolled, inheritance clearly influences intelligence as measured by IQ test scores, and so does the environment.

Another survey of similar literature (Bouchard & McGue, 1981) came to the same general conclusion. After reviewing 111 studies, the authors concluded that genetic similarity is related to IQ test scores. Identical twins produce IQ score correlations fully 20 points higher, on the average, than that found for fraternal twins. Again, however, we need to caution that

Figure **8.8**

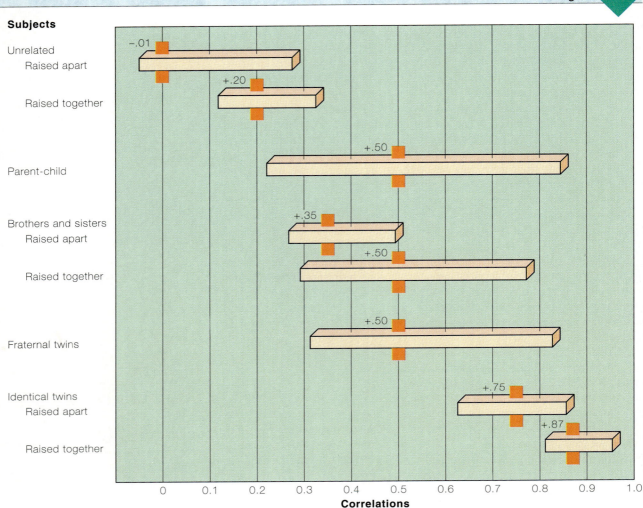

Correlations of IQ test scores as a function of genetic and environmental similarity. Vertical lines indicate average (median) correlations, and horizontal lines indicate the range of correlations from many different studies reviewed by Erlenmeyer-Kimling and Jarvik (1963).

identical twins are often treated in similar ways (are dressed alike, for instance), even more so than are fraternal twins.

Additional insight can be gained by examining the IQs of adopted children. This sort of research also focuses on correlational data. Are the IQs of adopted children more strongly correlated with the IQs of their biological parents (showing a genetic influence) or with the IQs of their foster or adoptive parents (environmental influence)? Once again, the data appear clear-cut, but their interpretation is not. If nothing else, we need to remind ourselves that correlations tell us nothing about cause and effect. When we have large groups of subjects, correlations between the IQs of children and their biological parents are significantly higher (around .48) than when correlations are computed between the IQs of children and their adoptive parents (around .20). One might be tempted to infer that changing environments does not have a significant impact on the relation between the IQs of biological parents and their offspring, but we'd better not make any snap judgments.

Social agencies do not arrange adoption placements in order to satisfy psychologists' needs for adequate experimental control. What we don't know in most of these studies of adopted children is the degree to which the home environments of the adoptive and the biological parents are the same or different. One study (Scarr & Weinberg, 1976) reports very large increases in IQ scores for children from low socioeconomic backgrounds who were placed with families at a higher socioeconomic level. In this study, adoptive parents were of significantly higher educational level than were biological parents. Here, the environment did appear to have a major impact on IQ.

Two years later, the same researchers (Scarr & Weinberg, 1978) reported a study in which socioeconomic status was controlled, at least to some degree. In this study, the researchers concerned themselves only with correlations between the IQs of children and their biological or adoptive parents if the socioeconomic level of both sets of parents was approximately equal. The idea, of course, was to minimize any environmental factors that could be attributed to social-class differences. Under these conditions, with an additional environmental factor controlled, there was a much stronger relationship between a child's IQ and that of its biological parents than that of its adoptive parents. Support once again for the role of inheritance.

So where are we? To review, the perfect experiment, or correlational study, to determine the relative importance of heredity and the environment has not yet been done. In fact, it probably cannot be done. From the data that we have at present, there is ample evidence to justify almost any rationale: that one (heredity) or the other (the environment) or both are important. It seems that, in general, IQ is strongly affected by genetic predispositions. At the same time, it is true that IQ can be influenced or modified by experiences in the environment. The more extreme the differences in environments, the greater the resulting differences in IQ.

The correlation of IQ scores of identical twins is very high (even when the twins are raised apart) due to identical genetic constitutions.

BEFORE YOU GO ON

In general, what has the study of twins and adopted children told us about the importance of heredity and the environment in determining intelligence as measured by IQ tests?

GROUP DIFFERENCES IN IQ

Recognizing that there are individual differences in intelligence, can we make any statements about differences in IQ in general? Here are those easy questions again. Who are smarter, women or men? Do we become more

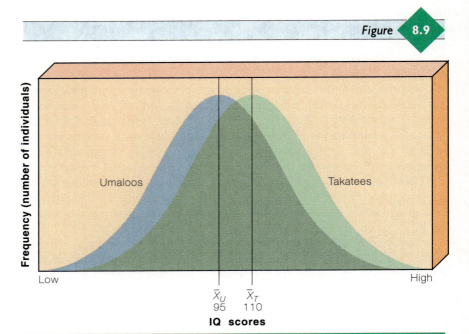

Figure 8.9

Hypothetical distributions of IQ scores for two imaginary groups (Umaloos and Takatees). The average IQ for Takatees (X_T) is higher than that for Umaloos (X_U), but there is considerable overlap in the two distributions. That is, some Umaloos have IQs that are higher than the average for Takatees (110) and some Takatees have IQs lower than the average for Umaloos (95).

or less intelligent with age? Are there differences in intelligence between blacks and whites? As you are aware, simple answers to these questions are often misleading and, if interpreted incorrectly, can be dangerous.

One thing we have to ask ourselves is why we care. What motivates our interest in group differences in IQ? Even the best scientific data can be put to questionable use. Unfortunately, issues of group differences are sometimes raised in order to justify what amounts to social or political ends. Some sexists (male and female), some racists (black and white), and some agists (young and old) like to point to any observed differences in IQ for groups of individuals to make claims of superiority or inferiority. It is in such cases that clear-cut answers can be dangerous.

More commonly, however, reported average differences in intelligence test scores are simply misleading. Let's imagine for a moment that I have tested two large groups of people—1000 Umaloos and 1000 Takatees. On the average, the IQ score (measured general intelligence, remember) for Umaloos is found to be 95; for Takatees, it is 110. Appropriate statistical analyses tell me that this observed difference of 15 points is too large to have been expected by chance. Are Takatees smarter than Umaloos? Yes, *on the average* they are—that's what I just discovered. At the very least, on this test, one group scored higher than the other.

Now look at Figure 8.9. Here we find two curves that represent the distributions of IQ scores from my fictitious study. We clearly can see the difference in the averages (means) of the two groups. However, there *are* Takatees whose IQs are below the average IQ of Umaloos. And there are some Umaloos whose IQs are above the average IQ of Takatees. We may be able to draw some conclusions about average IQ levels, but making definitive statements about individual Takatees and Umaloos is not possible.

Perhaps the most sensible reason for caring about group differences in intelligence (over and above simple curiosity) is the hope that understanding such differences will help us understand the true nature of intelligence and the factors that influence its development (Mackintosh, 1986). Being able to demonstrate a significant difference between the average IQs of two groups of individuals in itself tells us nothing about _why_ those differences exist. Are Takatees genetically superior to Umaloos? Maybe, maybe not. Have Umaloos had equal access to the sorts of things that IQ tests ask about? Maybe, maybe not. Are the tests themselves slanted to provide Takatees with an advantage? Maybe, maybe not. Discovering that two identifiable groups of individuals have different average IQ scores usually raises more questions than it answers. But if we can pursue those questions rigorously, we may learn more about the collection of cognitive processes we call intelligence.

BEFORE YOU GO ON

If group A and group B have different IQ scores on the average, what may be true about two individuals, one from group A and the other from group B, with regard to intelligence?

List some of the factors that might account for group differences in IQ.

Sex Differences and IQ

Here's a question to which we have a reasonably definitive answer: Is there a sex difference in measured IQ? Answer: No. At least there are very few studies that report any differences between men and women on any test of general intelligence of the sort represented by an IQ score (Aiken, 1984; Halpern, 1986; Maccoby & Jacklin, 1974). We have to keep in mind that there may be no measurable differences between the IQs of men and women because our tests are constructed in such a way as to minimize or eliminate any such differences. Usually, if an item on an intelligence test clearly discriminates between women and men, it is dropped from consideration.

When we look beyond the global measure that IQ scores afford, there do seem to be some reliable indications of sex differences on specific intellectual skills (which balance each other out on general IQ tests). For example, it is generally the case that females score (on the average) higher than males on tests of clerical speed and accuracy, verbal fluency, reading ability, and fine dexterity (the ability to manipulate small objects). Males, on the other hand, outscore females on some tests of mathematical reasoning and spatial relations.

Tests of spatial relations require the subject to visualize and mentally manipulate figures and forms. What is curious about this rather specialized

Some psychologists argue that males generally outscore females on tests of math reasoning and spatial relations, because they have been encouraged to enroll in math and science classes. The data may change in the future as females are encouraged to more fully develop this part of their education. Similarly, males are being encouraged to develop their reading and visual arts skills more.

ability is that males seem to perform better than females on such tasks from an early age, widening the gap through the school years, even though this particular ability seems to be only slightly related to any academic course work (McGee, 1979). What this means is that these sex differences cannot be easily attributed to differences in educational opportunity.

On the other hand, educational experiences may have more to do with differences in mathematical ability. Scores on tests of mathematics and arithmetic skills are very well correlated with the number and nature of math classes taken while a student is in high school (Welch et al., 1982). For many reasons, males tend to enroll in advanced math courses at a higher rate than females. It is not surprising, then, that by the time they leave high school, there are significant differences between men and women on some tests of mathematical ability (largely tests of mathematical reasoning and problem solving). We also now have evidence that the differences between males and females on tests of general mathematical abilities have been declining steadily over the past 25 years (Hyde, Fennema, & Lamon, 1990; Jacklin, 1989). On the other hand, some researchers, noting the higher scores that males have earned on the math portion of the SAT over the past 17 years (for example), suspect the possibility of genetic factors at work (Benbow, 1987, 1990). That is, some researchers agree with the assertion that it "seems likely that putting one's faith in boy-versus-girl socialization processes as the only permissible explanation of the sex difference is premature" (Benbow & Stanley, 1980, p. 1264). We'll return to these matters shortly when we discuss gender differences in Chapter 10.

Crystallized intelligence is a function of one's experience and the knowledge acquired through one's lifetime. The skills learned in a college biology lab, for example, may be recalled and serve as a foundation for further skills later on.

BEFORE YOU GO ON

Are there sex differences in IQ?

Age Differences and IQ

In Chapter 9, we'll spend a good deal of time discussing many of the cognitive changes that accompany one's lifelong development. Here we'll simply review a few important observations concerning the relationship between age and IQ.

You know a great deal more now than you did when you were 12 years old. You knew more when you were 12 than you did when you were 10. You learned a lot in fifth and sixth grades. In fact, many 12-year-olds seem to think that they know more than their parents do. Certainly, *what* we know generally changes with age, even *how much* we know changes with age, but neither what nor how much we know is a direct measure of intelligence.

IQ scores are computed in such a way that, by definition, they remain consistent with age. Remember, the IQ score of the average 12-year-old is 100, the same as the IQ of the average 30-year-old and the average 60-year-old. This is true regardless of which test is used to measure general intellectual abilities. But what about the IQ of any one individual? If Kim's IQ is 112 at age 4, will it still be 112 at age 14, or age 40, or age 80? As

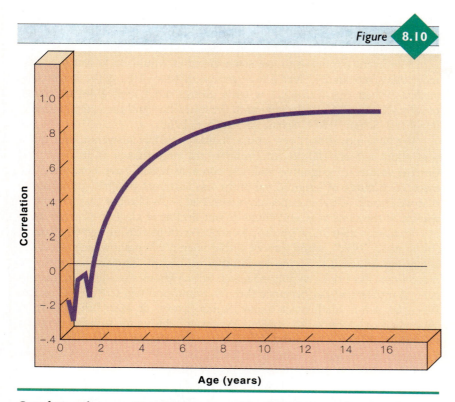

Figure **8.10**

Correlations between IQ test scores earned by males between the ages of 16 and 18 with IQ test scores earned at a younger age by the same subjects. Note that there is no correlation (not even a negative one) between IQ at ages 16 to 18 and IQs determined at ages younger than 3 years. That is, infant and preschool IQ test scores are poor predictors of IQ at older ages. (From Bayley & Schaefer, 1964.)

it happens, the measured IQs of individuals much younger than 7 don't correlate very well with later IQ scores. We cannot put too much stock in IQs earned by 4-year-olds as predictors of adult intellectual abilities (Baumeister, 1987). The data in Figure 8.10 are typical in this regard. They show the correlations between IQ scores earned at ages 16 to 18 with IQ scores at younger ages. Notice that when previous testing was done before the age of 7 or 8 years, the correlations are quite low.

This does not mean that the testing of young children is without purpose. Determining the intellectual abilities of young children is often very useful, particularly if there is some concern about retardation or if there is some thought that the child may be exceptional. The resulting scores may not predict adult intelligence well, but they do help in assessing the development of the child compared to other children. Even when scores are taken as a rough guide or indicator, knowing as early as possible that there may be some intellectual problem with a youngster is useful information.

What about intellectual changes throughout the life span? Does intelligence decrease with old age? You may have anticipated the answer: yes, no, and it depends. Most of the data we have on age differences in IQ scores have been gathered using a *cross-sectional method*. That is, IQ tests are given, at about the same time, to a large number of subjects of different ages.

When this is done, the results seem to indicate that overall, global IQ peaks in the early twenties, stays rather stable for about 20 years, and then declines more sharply (e.g., Schaie, 1983; Wechsler, 1958, 1981).

A different approach to the same question would be to test the same individuals repeatedly, over a long period of time. This is the *longitudinal method*. When this technique is used, things don't look quite the same, usually showing IQ scores rising until the mid-fifties and then very gradually declining (Schaie, 1974; Schaie & Strother, 1968).

We have a qualified "yes" and a qualified "no" as answers to our question about age and IQ so far. Probably the best answer is "it depends." Careful studies of cognitive abilities, some of which have combined the essential features of longitudinal and cross-sectional designs, demonstrate that we should ask about specific intellectual skills because they do not all decline at the same rate, and some do not decline at all. For example, tests of vocabulary often show no drop in scores with increasing age whatsoever (Blum et al., 1970), while tests of verbal fluency often show steep declines beginning at age 30 (Schaie & Strother, 1968). A longitudinal study of more than 300 bright, highly educated adults showed a slight increase in general intellectual performance through adulthood (ages 18 to 54) on the Wechsler Adult Intelligence Scale (Sands, Terry, & Meredith, 1989). A closer look at scores on the various Wechsler subtests for subjects between the ages of 40 and 61 showed significant improvement on the Information, Comprehension, and Vocabulary subtests, but a decline in scores on Digit Symbol and Block Design (see pp. 357–360).

Another "it depends" answer comes to the surface when we consider what is called **fluid intelligence** and **crystallized intelligence** (Horn & Cattell, 1966). It appears that fluid intelligence—abilities that relate to speed, adaptation, flexibility, and abstract reasoning—includes the skills that show the greatest decline with age. On the other hand, crystallized intelligence—abilities that depend on acquired knowledge, accumulated experiences, and general information—includes the skills that remain quite constant or even increase throughout one's lifetime (Horn, 1976; Vernon, 1979). If these concepts sound familiar, you may be reminded of two of the dimensions of intellect that the latest revision of the Stanford-Binet Intelligence Scale attempts to measure (see Topic 8A, p. 354). Put just a bit differently, we can agree with Salthouse who, in his review of age-related cognitive changes, observed that "increased age is assumed to be associated with declines in raw intellectual power or current ability to process information, but little or no declines are expected in measures of the accumulated products of past cognitive activity" (1989, pp. 19–20). This is to say that, with increased age, one's cognitive abilities to acquire new information and to solve new and different sorts of problems may decline, but there is no reason to expect a decline in the intellectual abilities that one already has acquired.

fluid intelligence *those cognitive skills dependent on speed, adaptation, flexibility, and abstract reasoning*

crystallized intelligence *those cognitive skills dependent on knowledge, accumulated experience, and general information*

BEFORE YOU GO ON

Does intelligence decline with age, increase with age, or stay the same?

Racial and Ethnic Differences and IQ

That there are significant differences between the IQ test scores of black and white Americans is not a new discovery. It was one of the conclusions drawn from the testing program for Army recruits during World War I. Since then, many studies have reconfirmed the fact that whites score approximately 15 points higher on tests of general intelligence (IQ) than do blacks. Blacks even seem to earn lower scores on performance tests and on intelligence tests that supposedly minimize the influence of one's culture (called culture-fair tests) (Jensen, 1980). There also are consistent data that tell us that Japanese children between the ages of 6 and 16 score significantly higher on IQ tests—about 11 points *on the average*—than do American children of the same age (e.g., Lynn, 1982). The superiority of Japanese children on mathematics tests is even greater (Stevenson, Lee, & Stigler, 1986). Asian American students have recently been scoring considerably higher on the SAT than have other students, again, particularly in mathematics (e.g., average math scores on the SAT of 525 compared to 476) (College Board, 1989; Hsia, 1988; Sue & Okazaki, 1990). The nagging question, of course, is *why*? Why do these differences appear with such consistency?

The proposed answers have been very controversial and return us to three possibilities we have touched on before in other contexts: (1) The *tests themselves are biased* and unfair. Current IQ tests simply may reflect mainstream life and the experiences of white Americans to a greater extent than they reflect the lives and experiences of blacks or Hispanics. Whether or not such biases occur by intention is not relevant. (2) Differences in IQ scores can be attributed to *environmental and motivational factors*, such as available economic and/or educational opportunities, and the perceived importance of doing well on standardized tests. (3) There are *genetic factors* involved that place some groups at a disadvantage. Now, test bias may account for some of the observed differences in IQ scores, but let's assume for the moment that our available techniques for assessing general intelligence are as valid as possible. What then? Let's first concentrate on black-white differences in IQ.

In the 1950s and 1960s, psychologists generally were confident that most if not all of the difference between the IQ scores of whites and blacks could be explained in environmental terms. There weren't many studies available to support the position, but the logic was compelling and was consistent with prevailing attitudes. Blacks were at a disadvantage on standard tests of general intelligence, the argument went, because they were often denied access to enriching educational opportunities. Their lower socioeconomic status deprived blacks of many of the sorts of experiences that could positively affect IQ scores. The generally poor nutrition and health of blacks also were used to explain why their scores tended to be, on the average, lower.

In 1969, Arthur Jensen shocked the scientific community with a long, thoughtful article in the *Harvard Educational Review*. Quite simply, Jensen argued that there was insufficient evidence to warrant the conclusion that the environment could produce such a large racial difference in IQ scores. The alternative was obvious to Jensen: The differences were attributable to genetic factors. Many readers took Jensen's claim to mean that blacks are genetically inferior to whites. However, Jensen claims that his argument

Measured intelligence (IQ again) may reflect the influences of impoverished environment and a lack of educational opportunity. Nonetheless, such environmental influences can be overcome, as Whoopi Goldberg, among others, has demonstrated.

was meant only as a reasonable hypothesis, intended to provoke scientific efforts to explore such a possibility (Jensen, 1981). It must be kept in mind that Jensen never did offer credible evidence to support an argument for a genetic explanation of these differences. Instead, he accepted the data we have looked at concerning genetic influences on intelligence and tried to discredit the argument that IQ differences are due to environmental factors alone.

Perhaps you can imagine the furor created by Jensen's 1969 article. Researchers took up the challenge and tried to find specific and convincing evidence to demonstrate that the environment *is* the cause of lower black IQ scores. After reviewing the body of literature that has grown from these efforts, Brian Mackenzie (1984) asserted that "what is finally clear from such research, therefore, is that environmental factors have not been identified that are sufficient to account for all or even most of the 15-point mean difference in IQ between blacks and whites in the United States. Jensen's conclusion that half to two-thirds of the gap remains unaccounted for by any proposed combination of environmental influences is still unrefuted" (p. 1217).

Now what does *that* mean? Does it mean that the racial differences in IQ *are* caused by genetic factors? *Are* blacks genetically less able than whites? Of course not; at the very least, there isn't sufficient evidence to support such a conclusion (Mackintosh, 1986). To understand why we have not yet resolved this issue requires that we understand three points: (1) Just because there is evidence to suggest that genetic factors affect differences in intelligence *within* races, that evidence cannot automatically be used as evidence of genetic factors affecting differences in intelligence *between* races. (2) It is improper to assume that the failure to identify any specific environmental causes of racial differences in IQ is sufficient reason to drop the environmental-factors argument. (3) Just because we have not identified the specific environmental factors that can cause racial differences in IQ does not mean that we must then accept genetic explanations. To do so would be to accept what Mackenzie (1984) calls the "hereditarian fallacy." Again, when we consider the impact of heredity and environment the issue is not a matter of either/or. Similar arguments have been proposed by psychologists trying to understand the apparent superiority of Asian American students on standard tests of academic achievement. Some have argued for at least a degree of innate superiority (e.g., Lynn, 1977), while others have pointed to socioeconomic, cultural, and motivational factors (e.g., Stevenson, Lee, & Stigler, 1986).

So where do we stand on the issue of racial-ethnic differences in IQ? We stand in a position of considerable uncertainty. As we have seen, there is a body of research data that underscores the contributions of both genetic and environmental influences on what we call intelligence. Whether any of these data can be used to settle the issue of racial differences in IQ scores is debatable. We would do well to keep in mind the following position, as stated by William Angoff: "The debate over whether intelligence is largely genetically or largely environmentally determined is actually irrelevant in the context of group differences. The real issue is whether intelligence can be changed, an issue that does not at all go hand in hand with the issue of heritability" (1988, p. 713).

Briefly summarize the data on racial differences in IQ scores and arguments about the causes of such differences.

THE EXTREMES OF INTELLIGENCE

When we look at the IQ scores earned by large random samples of individuals, we find that the IQ scores are distributed in a predictable pattern. The most common, or frequently occurring, score is the average IQ score, 100. Most of the other earned scores are relatively close to this average. In fact, virtually 95 percent of all IQ scores fall between scores of 70 and 130 (you might want to review Figure 8.6 on p. 357). In this section, we consider those individuals whose IQ scores place them in the extremes to be in the "tails" of the IQ curve. First we'll look at the upper extreme, then the lower.

The Mentally Gifted

There are many ways in which a person can be gifted. A report of the United States Office of Education (1972) defines giftedness as *a demonstrated achievement or aptitude for excellence* in any one of six areas:

1. *Psychomotor ability:* This is one of the most overlooked areas in which some individuals clearly can excel. We are dealing here with people of outstanding abilities in behaviors or skills that require agility, strength, speed, quickness, coordination, and the like.
2. *Visual and performing arts:* Some people, even as children, demonstrate an unusual talent for art, music, drama, and writing.
3. *Leadership ability:* Leadership skills are valued in most societies, and there seem to be individuals who are particularly gifted in this area. This often is true even with very young children. Youngsters with good leadership skills tend to be intellectually bright, but they are not necessarily the smartest of the group.
4. *Creative or productive thinking:* This aspect of giftedness has received considerable attention over the past 25 years. Here we are talking about individuals who *may* be intellectually or academically above average, but, again, not necessarily so. Indeed, there is ample evidence that scores on measures of creativity are typically *un*related to measures of general intelligence (e.g., Horn, 1976; Kershner & Ledger, 1985). Among other things, people with this type of giftedness are able to generate unique and different, but still useful, solutions to problems. (You might want to review our discussion of creative problem solving in Topic 7B.) I also should mention that persons who demonstrate exceptional creative talents in one area (art, math, or language, for instance) usually show no particular creativity in other areas (e.g., Amabile, 1985; Weisberg, 1986).

mentally gifted *demonstrating outstanding ability or aptitude in a number of possible areas; usually general intelligence where an IQ of 130 is a standard criterion*

Giftedness can be demonstrated in several behaviors, even in childhood. Some children show extraordinary talent in music, others in leadership.

5. *Specific academic aptitude:* In this case, we are talking about people who have a special ability in a particular subject or two. Someone who is a whiz in math, history, or laboratory science, without necessarily being outstanding in other academic areas, would fit this category.

6. *Intellectually gifted:* Inclusion in this group is based on scores earned on a general intelligence test, usually a Wechsler test or the Stanford-Binet Intelligence Scale. It is most likely that when people use the term *mentally gifted,* they are referring to individuals who would fit this category—people of exceptionally high IQ. (IQ scores of 130 or above usually qualify for inclusion in this category. Some prefer to reserve the label for those with IQs above 135. In either case, we are dealing with a very small portion of the population—fewer than 3 percent qualify.)

How can we describe intellectually gifted individuals? The truth is, there have been few large-scale attempts to understand the nature of mental giftedness or to understand the specific cognitive processing of people at the upper end of the IQ distribution (Horowitz & O'Brien, 1985; Reis, 1989). Indeed, a good deal of what we know about the mentally gifted comes directly, or indirectly, from a classic study begun by L. M. Terman in the early 1920s. (This is the same Lewis Terman who revised Binet's IQ test in 1916.) Terman supervised the testing of more than a quarter of a million children throughout California. His research group at Stanford University focused on those children who earned the highest scores—about 1500 in all, each with an IQ above 135.

Lewis Terman died in 1956, but the study of those mentally gifted individuals, who were between the ages of 8 and 12 in 1922, continues. Ever since their inclusion in the original study, and at regular intervals, they have been retested, surveyed, interviewed, and polled by psychologists still at Stanford (Goleman, 1980; Oden, 1968; Sears & Barbee, 1977).

The Terman study has its drawbacks: Choosing a narrow definition of *gifted* in terms of IQ alone is an obvious one. Failing to control for factors such as socioeconomic level or parents' educational level is another. There also is evidence that researchers may have excluded from the sample any children who showed signs of psychological disorders or problems, whether their IQ scores were high enough or not. Nonetheless, the study is an impressive one for having been continued for more than 60 years, if nothing else. What can this longitudinal analysis tell us about people with very high IQs?

Most of Terman's results fly in the face of the common stereotype of the bright child as being skinny, anxious, clumsy, sickly, and almost certainly wearing thick glasses (Sears & Barbee, 1977). The data just do not support that stereotype. In fact, if there is any overall conclusion to be drawn from the Terman-Stanford study, it is that, in general, gifted children experience advantages in virtually everything. They are taller, faster, better coordinated, have better eyesight, fewer emotional problems, and tend to stay married longer than average. These findings have been confirmed by others with different samples of subjects (Holden, 1980). All sorts of obvious things are also true of this sample of bright children, now oldsters. They received much more education, found better, higher-paying jobs, and had brighter children than did people of average intelligence. By now, we know better than to overgeneralize. Every one of Terman's children (sometimes referred to as Termites) did not grow up to be rich and famous and live happily ever after. The truth is that many did, but not all. These conclusions, like so many others, are valid only "in general, on the average."

BEFORE YOU GO ON

List six ways in which individuals can be considered to be gifted.

Summarize the basic findings of the Terman-Stanford study of intellectually gifted youngsters.

The Mentally Retarded

Our understanding of mental retardation has changed considerably over the past 25 years. We have seen changes in approaches to treatment and care, and great strides in prevention. Part of the change in prevention and care is due to the fact that there have been substantial changes in how psychology *defines* mental retardation (Baumeister, 1987; Landesman & Ramey, 1989).

Issues of Definition. Intelligence as measured by IQ tests is often used to confirm suspected cases of **mental retardation**. As is the case for the mentally gifted, however, there is more to retardation than IQ alone. The definition provided by the American Association of Mental Deficiency (AAMD) cites three factors to consider: "subaverage general intellectual functioning which originated during the developmental period and is associated with impairment in adaptive behavior" (Grossman, 1973). Let's look at each of these three points.

mental retardation *a condition indicated by an IQ below 70 that began during the developmental period and is associated with impairment in adaptive functioning*

The IQ cutoff for mental retardation is usually taken to be 70. The AAMD further categorizes mental retardation as follows:

IQ 70–85: *borderline or slow*

IQ 50–69: *mildly mentally retarded*

IQ 35–49: *moderately mentally retarded*

IQ 20–34: *severely mentally retarded*

IQ less than 19: *profoundly mentally retarded.*

As you review this list, you need to keep two things in mind. First, these IQ test scores are suggested limits. Given what we know about IQ tests and their reliability, it is ridiculous to claim after one administration of a test that a person with an IQ of 69 is mentally retarded, while someone else with an IQ of 71 is not. Second, diagnosis of mental retardation is not (should not be) made on the basis of IQ score alone.

To fit the preceding definition of mental retardation, the cause or the symptoms of the below-average intellectual functioning must show up during the usual period of intellectual development (up to age 18). In many circles, the term *developmentally delayed* is coming to replace the narrower term *mentally retarded.* Diagnosis may come only after the administration of an IQ test, but initial suspicions generally come from perceived delays in an individual's normal developmental or adjustive patterns of behavior.

By making "impairment in adaptive behavior" a part of their definition of mental retardation, the AAMD is acknowledging that there is more to getting along in this world than the intellectual and academic sorts of skills that IQ tests emphasize. Being mentally retarded does not necessarily mean being totally helpless, particularly for those who fall into the categories of more moderate levels of retardation. Of major consideration is, or ought to be, the individual's ability to adapt to his or her environment. In this regard, such skills as the ability to dress oneself, to follow directions, to make change, to find one's way home from a distance, and so on become relevant (Coulter & Morrow, 1978). As it happens, there are a number of psychological assessment devices that try to measure these very skills. Three such instruments are the Vineland Adaptive Behavior Scales, the Adaptive Behavior Scale, and the Adaptive Behavior Inventory.

Even without a simple, one-dimensional definition, it is clear that the population of retarded citizens is large. It is difficult to obtain exact figures because many individuals who might fit the criteria and be classified as mildly retarded have never been diagnosed as such. Even so, standard estimates indicate that approximately 3 percent of the population at any one time falls within the IQ range for retardation. Two other relevant estimates are that approximately 900,000 children with mental retardation between the ages of 3 and 21 years are being served in the public schools (Schroeder et al., 1987) and that nearly 200,000 mentally retarded individuals are to be found in community residential facilities, state and county mental hospitals, and nursing homes (Landesman & Butterfield, 1987). Let's now turn to a brief discussion of the causes, treatment, and prevention of mental retardation.

BEFORE
YOU GO
ON

How might we best define mental retardation?

Causes, Treatment, and Prevention. We don't really know what causes *average* intelligence. We have virtually no idea what causes someone to be mentally gifted. We cannot begin to explain the causes of all types of mental retardation, but at least we have some good ideas. In fact, we suspect that there are hundreds of possible causes; at the moment, the list of known or highly suspected causes exceeds 100. The more we learn about the sources of mental retardation, the better able we will be to treat it or to prevent it altogether.

Approximately one-quarter of all cases of mental retardation reflect some problem that developed before, during, or just after birth. Between 15 and 20 percent of those persons referred to as mentally retarded were born prematurely, where prematurity is defined as being born at least three weeks before the due date *or* at a weight below 5 pounds, 8 ounces.

We are coming to appreciate more and more how the health of the mother during pregnancy can affect the health of her child. All sorts of prenatal conditions are thought to cause developmental delays, including hypertension, exposure to X rays, lowered oxygen intake, rubella (German measles), maternal syphilis, and the mother's use of a wide range of drugs, from powerful narcotics to the frequent use of aspirin, alcohol, or nicotine. To greater and lesser degrees, all of these have been linked to mental retardation. In addition, of course, there are those cases that stem from difficulties or injuries during the birth process itself.

As we've seen, the extent to which normal levels of intelligence are inherited is open to debate. Some types of mental retardation, however, are clearly genetic in origin. One of the clearest examples of such a case is the intellectual retardation accompanying **Down's syndrome**, first described in 1866. We don't know exactly why it happens, but occasionally a fetus develops with 47 chromosomes instead of the usual 46, or 23 pairs. (We do know that Down's syndrome becomes more likely as the age of either parent increases.) The clinical signs of Down's syndrome are well known: small round skull, flattened face, large tongue, short broad nose, broad hands, short stubby fingers, and so on. During childhood, behavioral development is noticeably delayed. Down's syndrome children may fall into any of the levels of retardation listed earlier. Many are educable and lead lives of considerable independence, although it is generally true that even as adults, many will require supervision at least some of the time.

Most cases of mental retardation do not have such obvious causes. They are more subtle in their origin. They may be brought on by lack of adequate nutrition in infancy, or even prenatally. As we have already noted, anything approaching extremes of deprivation of any sort may lead to delays in intellectual functioning.

Many Down's syndrome children can benefit greatly from special education programs as well as individualized instruction.

Down's syndrome *a condition of many symptoms, including mental retardation, caused by an extra (forty-seventh) chromosome*

To some degree, our ability to treat mental retardation depends on our ability to specify its causes. Special-education programs have helped. Preparing teachers and mental health professionals to be sensitive to the wide range of behaviors and feelings that mentally retarded persons are capable of has helped. Impressive changes *can* be made in raising the IQs of some mildly retarded and a few moderately retarded children (cf. Landesman & Ramey, 1989). For severely and profoundly retarded persons, the outlook is not bright—certainly not in terms of raising IQ points (cf. Spitz, 1986). But we always need to remind ourselves that quality of life is not necessarily a function of IQ. The emphasis in recent years has been to focus less on overall intellectual growth and more on those specific skills and abilities— social as well as intellectual—that *can* be improved.

There is greater hope in the area of prevention. As we continue to appreciate the influences of the prenatal environment on the development of cognitive abilities, we can educate mothers and fathers about how their behaviors can affect their child even before it is born. Another excellent example of how mental retardation can be prevented concerns a disorder called **phenylketonuria**, or **PKU**. This disorder is genetic in origin, and 50 years ago it was discovered to be a cause of mental retardation. PKU results when a child inherits genes that fail to produce an enzyme that normally breaks down chemicals found in many foods. Although a newborn with PKU usually appears quite normal, a simple blood test has been developed that can detect the disorder soon after birth. Once PKU has been detected, a prescribed diet, which must be maintained for about four years, can reduce or eliminate any of the retardation effects of the disorder. Unfortunately, most cases (about 70 percent) of mental retardation cannot be detected at birth, which means that preventative or therapeutic intervention also has to wait until the child is older (Scott & Carran, 1987).

phenylketonuria (PKU) *a genetically caused disorder that produces mental retardation and that is now detectable and preventable*

BEFORE YOU GO ON

List some of the possible causes of mental retardation.

Our ability to measure one's general intellectual abilities (a measurement we continue to call IQ) is not without limitation. Nonetheless, IQ tests have raised a number of controversial and intriguing questions that psychologists have attempted to answer. We have seen that some of these questions may be of more political importance than scientific importance. We have, in this topic, briefly examined differences in measured intelligence as a function of sex, age, and race. We have also considered those individuals with extreme IQ scores. In each instance, we're confronted with the issue of the extent to which one's intelligence—at least as it is measured by our existing tests—is a function of one's nature or nurture. Beyond saying that both of these influences interact in some way, we must focus on the issue of how one's intelligence can be changed, regardless of the extent to which it reflects either genes or environment.

SUMMARY

In general, what has the study of twins and adopted children told us about the importance of heredity and the environment in determining intelligence as measured by IQ tests?

Although we cannot draw any definite conclusions, it is reasonable to claim that genetic factors can place limits on intellectual potential, but the impact of the environment is needed to exercise such potential. That is, both are influential in determining intelligence as it is measured by IQ tests. This conclusion is justified because we find that correlations of IQ scores increase as the genetic relatedness of subjects increases. On the other hand, when degree of genetic similarity is controlled, we find that correlations of IQ scores are influenced by degree of environmental similarity. / *page 369*

If group A and group B have different IQ scores on the average, what may be true about two individuals, one from group A and the other from group B, with regard to intelligence? List some of the factors that might account for group differences in IQ.

Average (mean) group differences tell us little about individual differences. That is, the two individuals from groups A and B may have the same IQ score, or either may have a score higher than the other. (Review Figure 8.9.) Average group differences in measured intelligence may be accounted for by several factors. On the average, members of one group may be genetically superior to members of the other. Members of one group may have easier access to the sorts of information IQ tests ask about or may be better motivated to perform well on such tests. The tests may be biased in favor of one group over another. / *page 371*

Are there sex differences in IQ?

No and yes. There are no significant differences between men and women on virtually any test that yields a general IQ score. There are some specific skills and abilities that demonstrate sex differences, although the differences are "on the average" and quite small. / *page 372*

Does intelligence decline with age, increase with age, or stay the same?

The evidence suggests that overall intelligence tends to decline slightly as one approaches the age of 50 or 60. There are, however, different skills and abilities that are differentially affected by age. Fluid intelligence, for example, may decline with age, while crystallized intelligence may remain constant or even increase slightly with age. Although with advanced age, one may have a more difficult time assimilating new information, there is little reason to believe that other intellectual skills will be diminished. / *page 374*

Briefly summarize the data on racial differences in IQ scores and arguments about the causes of such differences.

Research evidence suggests that there are reliable differences between the IQs of blacks and whites, most putting the *average* difference at about 15 points, in favor of whites, while Asian American students, *on the average*, perform better on many tests of academic achievement. These data on group differences tell us nothing, however, about their source. Strenuous arguments have been made favoring a genetic cause and environmental causes. Consensus now is that concern should focus on improving IQ scores, not debating their source. / *page 377*

List six ways in which individuals can be considered to be gifted. Summarize the basic findings of the Terman-Stanford study of intellectually gifted youngsters.

Giftedness can mean a number of things in addition to (1) overall intellectual ability as measured by IQ tests (usually taken to be an IQ over 130 points). Other abilities in which individuals may be gifted include: (2) visual and performing arts, (3) psychomotor, (4) leadership, (5) creative, and (6) abilities in specific academic areas. Individuals who are mentally gifted also experience other physical, educational, social, and economic advantages. / *page 379*

How might we best define mental retardation?

Mental retardation is indicated by below-average intellectual functioning (usually IQ scores below 70), originating during the developmental period (within 18 years), and associated with impairment in adaptive behavior (as well as academic behaviors). / *page 381*

List some of the possible causes of mental retardation.

In addition to genetic causes, most of the known causes of mental retardation revolve around the health and care of the mother and fetus during pregnancy, where drugs, lack of oxygen, poor nutrition, and the like have been implicated in mental retardation. In other words, many causes of mental retardation appear to be preventable. / *page 382*

DEVELOPMENTAL PSYCHOLOGY

*T*he Development of Children

Why We Care: A Topic Preview

From conception to death, human beings share certain developmental events that unite us as one species. As we have already noted a number of times, it is also true that each of us is unique and, thus, different from everyone else. Developmental psychologists are interested in the common patterns of our growth and development and in the ways in which we differ as we grow and develop throughout our lives. In many ways, we care about the psychology of human development because of the extent to which it can inform us about how we got to be the person we are today.

We tend to think that a person's development begins at birth. In fact, growth and development begin earlier—at conception, and with the first division of one cell into two. This topic focuses on the factors that influence the development of the human organism from conception through childhood. We'll begin with an examination of the course of development from conception to birth—the prenatal period of development. Then we'll turn our attention to children—development from birth to puberty.

The psychology of child development is particularly important when we realize how many of the general traits, ideas, attitudes, and habits that are formed in this period remain with us well into adulthood. In this topic, we'll consider some of the major landmarks in three areas of development: physical-motor, sensory-perceptual, and cognitive-social. In each case, we will focus attention first on the capabilities of the newborn child. Even though we will be looking at these three areas of development separately, it is important to remember that the divisions are artificial: Each area of development is continually interacting with and influencing the others.

HEREDITY AND ENVIRONMENT: NATURE AND NURTURE

nature-nurture controversy *the debate over which is more important in development, one's genetic, inherited nature, or one's nurture, one's experience through interaction with the environment*

epigenetic model *an interactionist view of development that claims that development emerges based on one's genetic programming and one's experiences*

plasticity *a demonstration of flexibility, or a capacity to be molded and shaped (by the environment) in a wide range of ways*

As we begin our discussion, it is sensible to reflect briefly on an important issue that was introduced earlier. In Topic 1A we noted that at any stage in one's development, a person can be considered to be the unique product of the interaction of both heredity and the environment; genes and experience. As we explore the story of human growth and development, we frequently will be reminded of the age-old search to determine the relative importance of one's heredity and one's environment as they shape the developmental process (see Topic 1A, pp. 20–21).

At any point in the developmental process, we encounter the same question: What determines a particular behavior, our nature or our nurture? How much of a given behavior can be attributed to heredity, and how much can be attributed to the environment? Which is more important, our genes or our experiences? Developmental psychologists now recognize that these are often the wrong questions to be asking. *Both* heredity and the environment shape the course of development; *neither* is sufficient alone.

Today, most psychologists ascribe to what is called the **epigenetic model** of development (Gottlieb, 1970; Lerner, 1978; Plomin, DeFries, & Fulker, 1988; Rowe, 1981). This point of view is an *interactionist* position, claiming that development *emerges* based on one's genetic history *and* one's experiences in the environment. A person's development is influenced by the forces of both nature and nurture, "experienced in an inseparable tangle" (McGraw, 1987, p. 103). To which we can add, with Robert Plomin, "The complex interplay between environment and genes is most apparent in the case of development" (Plomin, 1989, p. 110).

Our genes provide the foundation, or framework, for development, but we have to recognize the extent to which the environment often produces variation within that framework. Developing organisms demonstrate a capacity to be molded and shaped by their experiences with the environment. This capacity is called **plasticity**, and we now recognize that developing organisms are enormously plastic in the sense of being able to express genetic predispositions in a variety of ways (Hall & Oppenheim, 1987). The extent of plasticity may vary at different stages or periods of development (Kolb, 1989) and may vary from species to species, with humans showing the greatest plasticity in development (Gallagher & Ramey, 1987).

As we cover the processes of development in this chapter, you should be ever mindful of the interaction of heredity and the environment, of nature and nurture. This will be particularly true in our discussion of prenatal development.

BEFORE YOU GO ON

What is the epigenetic model of development, and what does it say about the impact of heredity and the environment?

PRENATAL DEVELOPMENT: INFLUENCES BEFORE BIRTH

Human development begins at **conception**, when the father's sperm cell unites with the mother's ovum. At that time, 23 chromosomes from each parent pair off within a single cell, the **zygote**. We have in that one action the complete transmission of all inherited characteristics. (You might want to review the basics of genetics and heredity on pp. 52–56 in Topic 2A.)

Within the next 30 hours or so, that one-celled zygote will divide and become two. In three days, there may be about 10 to 15 cells; after five days, there will be slightly more than 100 (Moore, 1982; Torrey & Feduccia, 1979). No one knows how many cells the average human organism has at birth, and few are willing to even hazard a guess; "more than a trillion" is probably a conservative estimate (Moore, 1982).

The period from conception to birth is called the **prenatal period** of development. Until recently, this period of human development received only minor attention from psychologists. We now recognize that many events that can have lifelong consequences occur during this very sensitive period. In this section, we'll review briefly the physical development of the organism during the prenatal period, and we'll look at some of the environmental factors that might have an impact on that development.

Throughout this discussion we will use *growth* and *development* to mean slightly different things. Growth refers to rather simple enlargement—getting bigger. A child demonstrates growth just by becoming taller and heavier. Development, on the other hand, usually implies a differentiation of structure or function. Something develops when it appears for the first time and remains. Thus, we say that the nervous system "develops" between week 2 and week 8 after conception.

conception *the moment when the father's sperm cell unites with the mother's ovum to produce a zygote*

zygote *the one-cell product of the union of sperm and ovum at conception*

prenatal period *the period of development from conception to birth*

At conception, as pictured here, the egg cell unites with the sperm cell. During this time, the zygote receives all of its inherited characteristics.

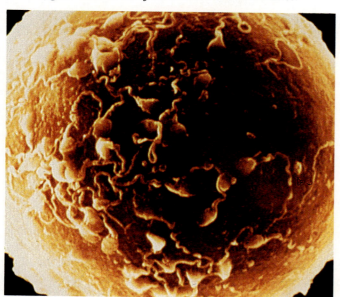

Figure   9.1

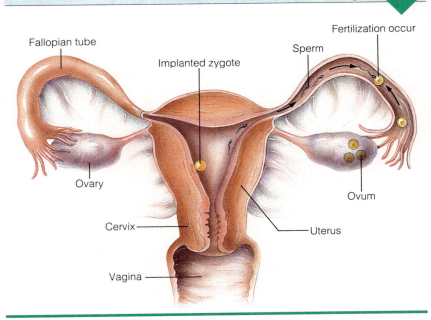

Fallopian tube

Implanted zygote

Sperm

Fertilization occur

Ovary

Ovum

Cervix

Uterus

Vagina

The female reproductive organs, indicating where fertilization and implantation take place.

Physical Aspects of Prenatal Development

Prenatal development is divided into three different stages or periods: the stage of the zygote, the embryo, and the fetus. These stages are not all of the same duration, and each is characterized by its own landmarks of development.

The **stage of the zygote** is the shortest of the prenatal stages of development, lasting from conception until approximately two weeks later, when the zygote becomes implanted in the wall of the uterus. The female's ovum generally is fertilized as it moves along the fallopian tubes from the ovaries, where ova (the plural of ovum) are stored and released, one at a time, at approximately 28-day intervals. It typically takes the zygote about seven days to travel down the fallopian tube to the uterus and another seven days to become firmly attached there (see Figure 9.1). At this point, the zygote has grown to include hundreds of cells, and for the first time, it is clear that not all the cells are exact replicas of each other. That is, there is now clearly some *differentiation* among the cells in the zygote. Some of the cells, for example, develop to form the protective placenta, while others form the umbilical cord that ultimately will supply nourishment to the developing organism.

Once implantation is complete, the stage of the zygote is over, and the organism has entered the **stage of the embryo**. The embryonic stage lasts about six weeks, from week 2 to week 8. During this period, the embryo develops at a rapid rate. At the beginning of this stage, we can differentiate three types of cells: those that will become the nervous system, the sense organs, and the skin; those that will form the internal organs; and those

stage of the zygote *developmental period from conception to the age of 2 weeks*

stage of the embryo *developmental period from 2 to 8 weeks*

that will become the muscles, skeleton, and blood vessels. By the end of this stage, we can identify the face area, eyes, ears, fingers, and toes. That is, not only does the number of cells increase, but the types of cells present also increase.

In other words, it is during this stage—more conservatively, within the first three months—that the unborn is most sensitive to external or environmental influences. It seems that if there are going to be problems (e.g., birth defects), they are most likely to develop during this stage. If the heart, hands, eyes, and ears do not become differentiated and develop during this period, for example, there will be no way to compensate later. Figure 9.2 shows the critical periods during which defects to the developing organism are most likely to occur. Note, for example, that there is little risk of damage to the zygote. It also is clear that the embryonic period is the stage of prenatal development during which the organism is at greatest risk. Note, too, that the central nervous system is at risk throughout prenatal development—particularly in weeks 3 through 6.

Two months after conception, the stage of the embryo draws to a close. The 1-inch-long embryo now has enough of a primitive nervous system to respond to a light touch with a simple reflex movement.

The final stage of prenatal development is also the longest, the **stage of the fetus**. This period includes months 3 through 9. Not only do the organs of the body continue to increase in complexity and size, but they begin to function. The arms and legs move spontaneously by the end of the third month. In two more months, these movements will be substantial enough for the mother to feel them. At the end of the fifth month, the fetus is a full 10 inches long. Internal organs have developed, but not to the point of sustaining life outside the uterus. The brain has developed, but the neurons within it have not formed many synapses.

> **stage of the fetus** *developmental period from week 8 until birth (months 3 through 9)*

Development and growth continue throughout the last few months of pregnancy. The most noticeable change—certainly most noticeable to the mother—is the significant increase in weight and overall movement of the fetus. Sometime during the seventh month, most fetuses have reached the point of **viability**. This means that if they were forced to do so, they could survive, without interference and/or medical intervention, if they were born prematurely. During its last few weeks in the uterus, the fetus grows more slowly. Its movements may be more powerful, but overall activity is also slowed due to the cramped quarters in which the fetus finds itself. After nearly 270 days, the fetus is ready to enter the world as a newborn.

> **viability** *the ability to survive without interference or intervention*

BEFORE YOU GO ON

Briefly summarize the three stages of prenatal development.

Environmental Influences on Prenatal Development

In most cases, the progressive growth and development of the human organism from zygote to embryo to fetus occurs according to the plans of the genes, heredity providing the blueprint for prenatal development. Even

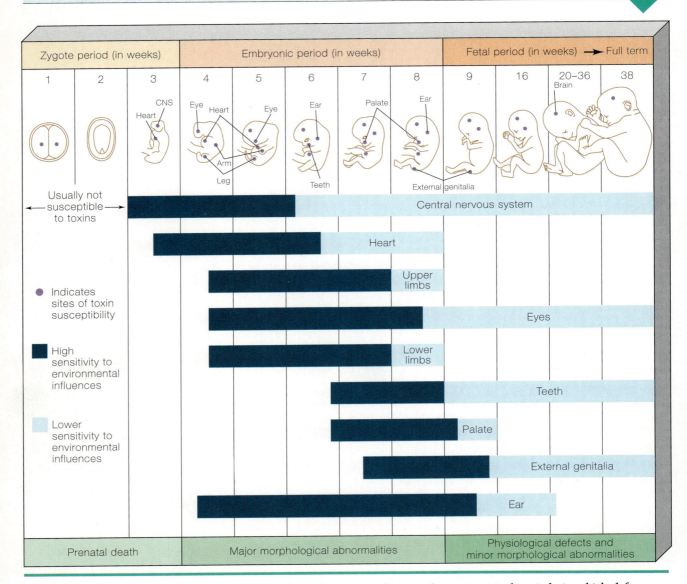

Figure   9.2

Prenatal development, indicating the most critical periods in which defects are likely to occur and which aspect of the developing organism is likely to be affected. (After Moore, 1982.)

as prenatal development takes place, however, the human organism is not immune to environmental influences.

"Until the early 1940s, it was generally accepted that human embryos were protected from environmental agents by their fetal membranes and their mother's abdominal walls and uterus" (Moore, 1982, p. 140). It was then discovered that birth defects often resulted when a pregnant woman contracted rubella (German measles). Twenty years later, it was a well-established fact that many drugs taken by a pregnant woman have measurable effects on the development of the embryo and fetus. It is now common knowledge that during the very rapid period of prenatal development, even small environmental disturbances can have serious and lasting consequences. Most of the external influences on prenatal development that we know about are those that tend to have negative consequences (as we noted in Figure 9.2).

Nourishment. Never meant to be taken literally, the old expression "You are what you eat" does have some truth to it. By the same token, before we are born, we are what our mothers eat. When pregnant women eat poorly, their unborn children may share in the results. Maternal malnutrition often leads to increases in miscarriages, stillbirths, and premature births. At best, the newborn child of a malnourished mother can be expected to be similarly malnourished (e.g., Lozoff, 1989).

It is also the case that deficiencies in specific vitamins and minerals affect the prenatal organism (Bratic, 1982). For example, a mother's calcium deficiencies affect the development of bones and teeth in the fetus. But, as is the case for many nutrients, it may very well be the mother who suffers more. That is, if there are inadequate supplies of calcium in the mother's system, "the fetal need for calcium will be met at the expense of the mother" (Hughes & Noppe, 1985, p. 140).

Drugs and Other Chemicals. There is ample evidence that smoking has harmful effects on the smoker. Research also clearly shows that smoking by pregnant women has harmful effects on their unborn children (Frazier et al., 1961; Fribourg, 1982; Jacobson, 1984). Exactly *how* smoking affects the fetus is not known for certain. It may simply be a matter of reducing the oxygen supply to the fetus. It may be that the tar and nicotine of the smoke act directly as poisons. What we do know is that cigarette smoking is well established as a cause of retarded prenatal growth (Golbus, 1980). Mothers who smoke a pack a day or more double the chances of having a low-weight baby. Smoking mothers have many more miscarriages, stillbirths, and babies who die soon after birth than do mothers who do not smoke (Frazier et al., 1961; Golbus, 1980).

As we indicated earlier, alcohol is perhaps the most commonly abused of all drugs. It is a drug that can be injurious to unborn children. Alcohol is quickly and directly passed through the umbilical cord from the mother to the fetus. The effects are often stunning. In one study, women in their thirty-seventh to thirty-ninth weeks of pregnancy were given a single drink of vodka. Within 3 to 30 minutes after the alcohol was taken, the fetus stopped making breathing movements, many for more than half an hour. Breathing movements began again only as the alcohol level in the mother's bloodstream began to drop (Fox et al., 1978, cited in Clarke-Stewart et al., 1985).

Heavy drinking (3 ounces or more per day) significantly increases the probability of having smaller babies and babies with retarded physical growth, poor coordination, poor muscle tone, intellectual retardation, and other problems, collectively referred to as **fetal alcohol syndrome** (Jones et al., 1973; Mattson, Barron, & Riley, 1988). In the 1970s, it was believed that an occasional social drink or two had no particular lasting effect on prenatal development. The best advice now seems to be total abstinence (Abel, 1981, 1984; Barr et al., 1990).

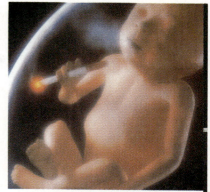

Studies reveal that women who smoke during pregnancy increase significantly their chances of having miscarriages, stillbirths, low-weight babies, and babies who die shortly after birth.

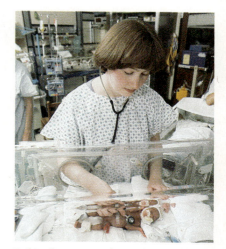

Babies born to mothers who used crack cocaine during their pregnancy enter the world at great risk for numerous physical and psychological disabilities.

fetal alcohol syndrome *a cluster of symptoms (e.g., low birth weight, poor muscle tone, intellectual retardation) associated with a child born to a mother who was a heavy drinker of alcohol during pregnancy*

There is little doubt that mothers who use or abuse psychoactive drugs such as heroine and/or cocaine (or "crack") during pregnancy cause considerable complications for their unborn children. At best, such children enter the world with low birth weights (which puts them at risk for many adverse complications), difficulty regulating their sleep-wake cycles, and many of the symptoms of fetal alcohol syndrome (perhaps because their mothers *also* used or abused alcohol) (Finnegan, 1982). At worst, they are born addicted themselves and must, within days of their birth, suffer the pains of withdrawal (Adler, 1989; Chasnoff et al., 1989; Finnegan, 1982). A question as yet unanswered is what the long-term consequences of maternal drug abuse and addiction during pregnancy will be for the children involved.

Some drugs taken by the mother during her pregnancy seem to have no noticeable effect on the developing child—penicillin, for example (Golbus, 1980). Some have predictable effects that are not life-threatening—the antibiotic tetracycline, for instance, which directly passes to the developing fetus and is deposited in the teeth and bones, coloring them yellow. Other prescription drugs may have devastating effects. One example is the drug thalidomide, routinely prescribed in Europe in the early 1960s as a mild tranquilizer and treatment for nausea associated with pregnancy. Thalidomide children, as they are called, developed shortened, malformed limbs, or no limbs at all, and very often were mentally retarded.

Also in the 1950s and 1960s, many women who had problems during earlier pregnancies were given the drug DES (diethylstilbestrol) to reduce the likelihood of miscarriage. This synthetic hormone is now believed to be related to cervical cancer in the *daughters* of women who took the drug years earlier. Even the sons of women who received DES are now found to have higher than nomal rates of infertility (Stenchever et al., 1981). The bottom-line advice again seems very clear: Pregnant women should use drugs of any sort only with great care, and only after consultation with their physicians.

Maternal Stress. There is a certain logic that tells us that a mother's emotional health can affect her unborn baby. There is even some logic to the physiology of the argument. As we shall see, emotionality is accompanied by many hormonal changes, and these changes may have some influence on the development of the embryo or fetus. It is also the case that when a pregnant mother is under stress, the blood flow in her body is, for a short while at least, diverted from the uterus to other organs in the body, reducing the amount of oxygen available to the prenatal organism (Stechler & Halton, 1982).

BEFORE YOU GO ON

Briefly review the impact of diet, drugs, and stress on prenatal development.

MOTOR DEVELOPMENT

Now we turn our attention to development in *childhood*, the period between birth and adolescence. In this section, we focus on the physical growth of children and note the orderly sequence of the development of their motor responses—their abilities to do things with their bodies. We'll begin by considering some of the abilities of the newborn infant, or neonate.

The Neonate

As recently as 20 years ago, textbooks on child psychology seldom devoted more than a few paragraphs to the behaviors of the **neonate**—the newborn through the first two weeks of life. It seemed as if the neonate did not do much worth writing about. Today, most child psychology texts devote substantially more space to discussing the abilities of newborns. It is unlikely that over the past 20 years neonates have gotten smarter or more able. Psychologists have, though: They have devised new and better ways of assessing the abilities of neonates.

When a baby is first born, it looks like it just can't do a thing. It can cry, and it can dirty a diaper, but mostly it just sleeps. In fact, newborns *do* sleep a lot, about 15 to 17 hours each day. As parents are quick to discover, however, that sleep tends to occur in a series of short naps, seldom lasting for more than a few hours at a time.

A careful examination of babies reveals that they are capable of a wide range of behaviors. Almost all of these behaviors are reflexive—simple, unlearned, involuntary reactions to specific stimuli. Many of the neonate's reflexive responses serve a useful purpose; they mainly help the child in responding to the demands of its environment. Some do not seem to have any particular survival value, but even these are important to know about because they can be used as diagnostic indicators of the quality of the neonate's development, particularly the development of the nervous system. More than a dozen reflexes can be observed and measured (for strength and duration, for example) in the newborn child. Figure 9.3 summarizes some of the major neonatal reflexes.

neonate *the newborn, from birth to age 2 weeks*

Figure ◆ **9.3**

REFLEXES OF THE NEONATE

Name	Stimulus	Response	Age when disappears
Moro	Loud sound, or sudden loss of support	Arms and legs thrown outward; fingers spread; then, with fists clenched arms and legs pulled back	4–6 months
Rooting	Light stroke on cheek	Head turns toward stimulus; mouth opens; sucking begins	3–4 months
Sucking	Object (e.g., nipple) inserted in mouth 3–4 cm.	Rhythmic sucking and mouth movements	variable
Grasping	Rod pressed in palm	Close fist and grasp firmly	3–5 months
Walking/ stepping	With feet just touching surface, baby moved forward	Coordinated rhythmic stepping movements	2–4 months
Babinski	Stroke sole of foot from heel to toes	Small toes spread; big toe raised	9–12 months
Tonic neck	With baby on its back, turn head to one side	Arm and leg on that side thrust outward, while other arm and leg drawn in to body	3–4 months
Swimming	Place infant in water	Rhythmic swimming movements	4–6 months

BEFORE YOU GO ON

What are some of the reflexes that can be observed in neonates?
Why do we care about neonatal reflexes?

Whether a child begins to walk at 10 months or 13 months, he or she will still follow the same sequence of sitting, crawling, and then walking.

The Motor Development of Children

Parents trying to keep their young children in properly fitting clothes know how quickly children can grow. In their first three years, children's height and weight normally increase at a rate never again equaled. Although changes in size and motor skills are rapid, they tend to be orderly and well sequenced, following a prescribed pattern. It is with that pattern that we are concerned here.

As I've said repeatedly, one of psychology's most reliable observations is that individuals differ. No two children are alike. No two children can be expected to grow at exactly the same rate or to develop control over their bodies at the same time. Joanne may walk unaided at the age of 10 months. Bill may not venture forth on his own until he's 13 months old. Differences between children are often as great as their similarities. Children who happen to develop more slowly might benefit from having others appreciate the notion of individual differences in developmental rates. (They might also benefit from the realization that the rate of physical development in infancy and early childhood is largely unrelated to such adult characteristics as intelligence, or even physical coordination.)

Regardless of the *rate* of one's motor development, there are regularities in the *sequence* of motor development. No matter when Joanne does walk, she will first sit, then crawl. It's an old adage, and it's true: We stand before we walk and walk before we run.

A summary of the development of common motor skills is presented in Figure 9.4. There are two important things for you to notice about this figure: First, the sequence of events is very regular, and second, *when* each stage develops includes a wide range of ages that should be considered normal. It is also true that the sequence and timing of the events listed in this figure hold equally for boys and girls. That is, in these basic motor skills there are no significant sex differences.

The regularity of physical growth and development seems to be guided by two different "principles": (1) *Cephalocaudal sequencing* refers to the fact that a child's growth and bodily control proceed from top to bottom, or from head to upper torso to lower body. For example, children's heads and upper torsos develop before their trunks and lower bodies; hands and arms can be manipulated before feet and legs can. (2) *Proximodistal sequencing* refers to the observation that a child's growth and bodily control proceed from the center core to the extremities; from the internal organs to the arms and legs to the hands and feet to the fingers.

Figure **9.4**

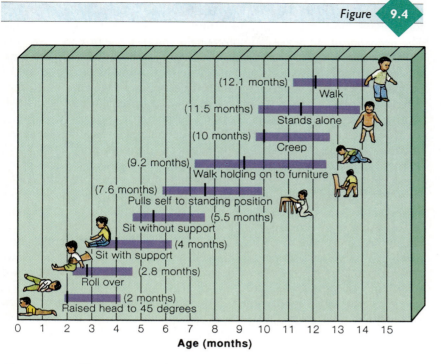

The sequence of human motor development. Each bar represents the age at which 25 percent of children engage in a behavior (left end) to the age at which 90 percent of children engage in that behavior (right end). Also indicated is the age at which 50 percent of children show the behavior. (After Frankenburg & Dodds, 1967.)

BEFORE YOU GO ON

What general observations can we make about physical growth and motor control in childhood?

SENSORY AND PERCEPTUAL DEVELOPMENT

One of the reasons psychologists used to think that newborn children couldn't do much was that it was commonly believed that newborns could not sense or perceive very much. We now understand that neonates can and do respond to a wide range of stimuli in their environments. To some degree, all human senses are functioning at birth, having developed in order: touch, body position, balance, taste, smell, hearing, and finally vision (Gibson, 1987, 1988; Hall & Oppenheim, 1987).

The neonate's ability to sense even subtle changes is quite remarkable. However, there *are* limitations. The ability of the eyes to focus on an object, for example, does not develop fully until the child is about 4 months old. The neonate can focus well on objects held at a distance of 1 to 2 feet, but everything nearer or farther appears blurred or out of focus. This means, however, that even newborns can adequately focus on the facial features of the persons cradling or feeding them. Visual acuity—the ability to discern detail—shows at least a threefold to fourfold improvement during the first year (Aslin & Smith, 1988).

For their first few weeks, babies have difficulty coordinating the movements of their eyes, although within hours after birth they can follow (track) a stimulus object that is swung slowly back and forth in front of them. Newborns can detect differences in brightness and soon develop the ability to detect surfaces, edges, or borders and to differentiate among colors (Cohen et al., 1978; Termine et al., 1987).

An issue that has been of considerable interest to psychologists is just when the perception of depth and distance develops. Apparently, even newborns have some simple reactions to depth. They will close their eyes and squirm away if you rush an object toward their face (a process called "looming") (Bower, Broughton, & Moore, 1971).

In the late 1950s, two Cornell University psychologists, Eleanor Gibson and Richard Walk (1960), constructed an apparatus to test the depth perception of very young children. The *visual cliff*, as it is called, is a deep box covered by a sheet of thick, clear Plexiglas. It is divided into two sides, one shallow, one deep. The deep and shallow sides are separated by a center board (see Figure 9.5).

Gibson and Walk discovered that 6-month-old children would not leave the center board to venture out over the deep side of the box, even to get to their mothers. By crawling age, therefore, the child seems able to perceive depth *and* to make an appropriate response to it.

It seems quite likely that the perception of depth develops before the age of 6 months, and almost certainly before the development of a fear of heights. When neonates (who obviously can't crawl) are placed on the Plexiglas over the deep side of the visual cliff, their heart rates decrease, indicating that at least they notice the change in visual stimulation (Campos et al., 1978). When 7-month-old infants are placed over the deep side of the visual cliff, their heart rates *increase*. The increase in heart rate is taken as indicating fear, a response that develops after the ability to discriminate depth (Bertenthal & Campos, 1989; Campos, 1976). There is also ample evidence that retinal disparity (the discrepancy in images received by the retinas of the two eyes) does not develop until the fourth month after birth (Birch et al., 1983; Fox et al., 1980). So it seems that in some rudimentary form, even a neonate may sense depth, but reacting appropriately to depth may require experiences and learning that come later.

What about the other senses? Newborn infants can hear very well. They certainly can direct their attention to the source of a sound, even a faint one. For example, Wertheimer (1961) reports a study demonstrating sound localization in a newborn between 3 and 10 *minutes* after birth. (The child moved her eyes to the left or right in response to a loud clicking sound.) Sounds probably don't *mean* much to neonates, but they can respond differently to sounds of different pitch and loudness. Even 3-day-old newborns

Figure 9.5

The visual cliff was designed to determine if depth perception is innate or learned. By the time they can move about, most infants will avoid the "deep" side of the apparatus.

are able to discriminate the sound of their mother's voice from other sounds (DeCasper & Fifer, 1980; Kolata, 1987; Martin & Clark, 1982).

Newborns can also respond to differences in taste and smell. They clearly discriminate among the four basic taste qualities of salt, sweet, bitter, and sour. They display a distinct preference for sweet-tasting liquids. Although they are unable to use it then, the sense of smell seems to be established before birth. Right after birth, neonates respond predictably—drawing away and wrinkling their noses—to a variety of strong odors.

In summary, a wide range of sensory and perceptual capabilities appears to be available to the newborn child. The neonate may require some time to learn what to do with the sensory information that it acquires from its environment, but many of its senses are operational. What the newborn makes of the sensations it receives will depend on the development of its mental or cognitive abilities. This is the subject that we turn to now.

BEFORE YOU GO ON

Summarize the basic sensory capacities of the neonate.

COGNITIVE AND SOCIAL DEVELOPMENT

In preceding topics, we have referred to cognitive skills and abilities many times. Cognitive processes are those that enable us to know and understand ourselves and the world around us. In this section, we'll look at how these skills develop throughout childhood, beginning with a summary of the cognitive capacities of the newborn infant. Our major focus will be on the theories of Jean Piaget. Then, we'll consider development from a more social perspective, considering the psychosocial theory of Erik Erikson and Lawrence Kohlberg's theory of moral development. We'll end this topic with a brief section on the development of social attachments. (Remember, we discussed the development of another cognitive skill—language—in Topic 7A, pp. 307–317.)

The Cognitive Abilities of the Neonate

As we have seen, reflex reactions can help neonates survive. For long-term survival, however, neonates must learn to adapt to their environments and profit from their experiences. Neonates have to begin forming memories of their experiences and learn to make discriminations among the many stimuli with which they are presented. Are these cognitive processes possible in a baby just a couple of days or weeks old? In a number of specific ways, the answer seems to be yes.

Friedman (1972) has reported a demonstration of what we might call memory in neonates only 1 to 4 *days* old. Babies were shown a picture of a simple figure, say a checkerboard pattern, for 60 seconds. Experimenters recorded how long the baby looked at the stimulus pattern. After the same pattern was shown over and over again, the baby appeared to be bored and gave it less attention. (You should recognize *this* as "habituation," which we earlier characterized as a simple form of learning (p. 194).) When a different stimulus pattern was introduced, the baby stared at it for almost the full 60 seconds of its exposure.

So what does this have to do with memory? The argument is that for the neonate to stare at the new stimulus, it must have formed some memory of the old one. Otherwise, how would it recognize the new pattern as being new or different? In fact, if the new stimulus pattern was very similar to the old one, the baby would not give it as much attention as it would if it were totally different. It is as if a judgment were being made about the distinctiveness of the new stimulus and the old (remembered) ones.

In talking about recognizing visual patterns, we should mention the research of Robert Fantz (1961, 1963). Fantz presented newborn children with pairs of visual stimuli. In most pairs, one stimulus was more complex than the other. As the babies lay on their backs, looking up at the stimuli, the experimenters could note which one of the two stimuli received more attention from the child. In almost every case, the babies showed a preference for the more complex stimulus pattern.

This in itself is interesting, but difficult to explain. The major finding of these studies is that babies could at least discriminate between the two stimuli. That attention equals "preference" is more of an assumption than a research finding. Fantz also discovered something curious when he found that even newborn infants show a distinct preference for (choose to attend to) drawings of a human face. They chose the face pattern as the focus of their attention no matter what it was paired with. These results have been confirmed by other researchers who have demonstrated that young infants can even discriminate among facial expressions displaying different emotional states, looking more at facial expressions of joy than of anger, for instance (Malatesta & Isard, 1984).

Babies often imitate facial expressions they see, as this 23-day-old newborn is doing.

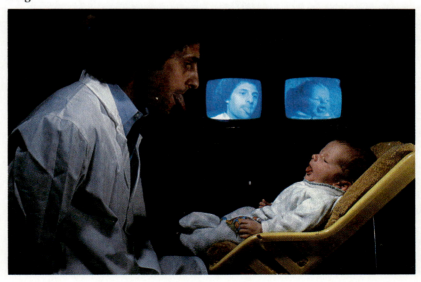

One more step takes us to the research of Meltzoff and Moore (1977), who discovered something in the controlled setting of a laboratory that many parents have discovered by accident. Not only do newborns look at a human face, but they often try to imitate facial expressions. When experimenters stick out their tongues at babies, the babies stick out their tongues. Infants open their mouths to imitate the same facial expression of the experimenter. These attempts at imitation—a cognitive skill indicating an appreciation of the environment—are clearly present by the age of 2 weeks and are often found in neonates only 1 hour old. It is also clear that these attempts at imitation serve a useful social skill, encouraging additional interaction with delighted parents.

BEFORE YOU GO ON

Cite an example of research evidence demonstrating a cognitive reaction in neonates.

Piaget's Theory of Cognitive Development

The physical growth and development of a child is remarkable. Even more impressive are the increases in cognitive and intellectual abilities that occur during childhood. By the time the human reaches adolescence, he or she has acquired an enormous stockpile of information. More than just learning facts, the child comes to appreciate how to learn. Strategies for survival and/or success begin to develop in childhood (Siegler, 1983).

Accounting for *how* children's intellectual capacities and abilities change is a difficult business. It is important to be able to describe the changes that occur, but it is even more important to be able to specify the principles that underlie cognitive development (Siegler, 1989). The theory that has attracted the most attention in this regard is that of the Swiss psychologist Jean Piaget (1896–1980). Although there *are* others, Piaget's theory of cognitive development has been so influential that it will be the focus of our discussion (Piaget, 1948, 1954, 1967).

In Piaget's theory, cognitive development relies on the formation of **schemas**, or organized mental representations of the world. Organizing the world into an interrelated network of schemas is, for Piaget, a process that can be found in all children. For example, children develop a schema for "daddy," for "mommy," for "eating breakfast," and for "bedtime." The function of schemas is to aid the child in adapting to the demands and pressures of the environment. Schemas are formed by experience. (And, indeed, you are correct if it seems to you that *schema* in this context sounds very much like our earlier use of terms like *concepts* and *categories* (pp. 298–306).)

Forming mental representations of the environment involves two basic processes, assimilation and accommodation. **Assimilation** involves taking on new information and fitting it into an existing schema. Children develop

Jean Piaget

schema *one's organized mental representation of the world*

assimilation *the process of adding new material or information to an existing schema*

a rather complex schema for mealtime, for instance. When, for the first time, they are taken to eat out at a fast-food restaurant, new information will have to be added to the mealtime schema. In fact, as you learn about new and different things that psychologists do, we may say that information is being assimilated into your schema for "psychology."

Accommodation involves changing or revising existing schemas— not just adding to them—in the face of new experiences. As children are shifted away from the bottle to strained foods, to chunkier foods, to regular food, they must accommodate their schemas for efficient feeding; what used to work in the past doesn't work any longer. Once the child gets to go out to the fast-food restaurant, not only will new information have to be assimilated, but old ideas about how and where one eats will have to be accommodated. Learning that mommy and daddy won't *always* come running when one cries may require accommodation.

Piaget proposed that as children assimilate new ideas into existing schemas and modify or accommodate old ones, they progress through four stages of development: the sensorimotor stage, the preoperational stage, the concrete operations stage, and the formal operations stage. Now determining precisely when each stage begins or ends is not always possible, since two adjacent stages may overlap and blend for a while. Even so, each stage is characterized by its own schemas, cognitive methods, insights, and abilities.

Sensorimotor Stage. (Ages 0 to 2 years.) For children younger than 2, language is not an effective means of finding out about the world. Children of this age are unable to discover much about their world by asking questions about it or by trying to understand long-winded explanations. Trying to explain to a 10-month-old baby *why* it shouldn't chew on an electrical extension cord is likely to be an unrewarding piece of parental behavior. In this **sensorimotor stage**, children discover by *sensing* (sensori-) and by *doing* (motor). A child may come to appreciate, for example, that a quick pull on a dog's tail (a motor activity) reliably produces a loud yelp (a sensory experience), perhaps followed in turn by parental attention.

One of the most useful schemas to develop in the sensorimotor stage is that of *causality*. Infants gradually come to realize that events sometimes have knowable causes and that some behaviors cause predictable reactions. Pushing a bowl of oatmeal off the high chair causes a mess and gets mommy's attention: If A, then B—a very practical insight.

Another important discovery that occurs during this developmental stage is that objects may exist even when they are not immediately in view. Early in this stage, an object that is out of sight is more than out of mind. The object ceases to exist for the child. By the end of the sensorimotor period, children have learned that objects can exist even if they are not physically present, and children can anticipate their reappearance. This awareness is called **object permanence** (see Figure 9.6).

One of the skills that best characterizes the sensorimotor period of development is that of imitation. So long as it is within the baby's range of abilities, a baby will imitate almost any behavior it sees. A cognitive strategy has developed, one that will be used for a lifetime: trying to imitate the behaviors of a model.

accommodation *the process of altering or revising an existing schema in the light of new information*

sensorimotor stage *in Piaget's theory, from birth to age 2 years, when a child learns by sensing and doing*

object permanence *the appreciation that an object no longer in view can still exist and reappear later*

Figure 9.6

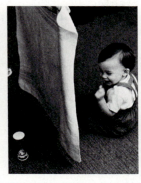

The older infant has developed the concept of object permanence. The infant sees the toy and even when it is blocked from view, he realizes it is still there and crawls under the blanket to get it.

BEFORE YOU GO ON

How are schemas formed during the sensorimotor stage?
What characterizes this stage of development?

Preoperational Stage. (Ages 2 to 6 years.) By the end of the sensorimotor stage, a child has recognized that he or she is a separate, independent person in the world. Throughout most of the preoperational stage, a child's thinking is self-centered, or **egocentric**. According to Piaget, the child has difficulty understanding life from someone else's perspective. In this stage, the world is very much *me*, *mine*, and *I* oriented.

egocentric *to be characterized by self; by "me" and "mine" and "my point of view"*

Perhaps you have seen two preschool children at play. They are right next to each other, one playing with a truck, the other coloring in a coloring book. They are jabbering at each other, taking turns, but each is quite oblivious to what the other is saying:

Jill: *"This sure is a neat truck!"*

Leslie: *"I think I'll paint the sky a kinda purple."*

Jill: *"I'm gonna be a truck driver some day."*

Leslie: *"But if I make the sky a kinda purple, what'll I make the trees?"*

Jill: *"Maybe I'll drive a milk truck. Broooom!"*

Leslie: *"I know, blue."*

Such exchanges, called *collective monologues*, demonstrate the egocentrism of childrens' thinking in this stage.

In the **preoperational stage**, not only do we find egocentric thought, but we also see that children begin to develop and use symbols, usually in

preoperational stage *in Piaget's theory, from age 2 years to age 6 years, when a child begins to develop symbolic representations, but cannot manipulate them; also characterized by egocentricity*

the form of words to represent concepts. But at this stage, children do not appreciate how to manipulate those symbols in a consistent, rule-governed way, which is why it is referred to as *pre*operational. It's not until the end of this period that they can play word games or understand why riddles about rabbits throwing clocks out of windows in order to "see time fly" are funny. It is similarly true that children at this stage of development have great difficulty with many "abstract" concepts, such as those involved with religious beliefs. Manipulating concepts, even abstract concepts, comes in the next stage of development.

BEFORE YOU GO ON

In Piaget's theory, what best characterizes the preoperational stage of development?

concrete operations stage *in Piaget's theory, from age 7 years to age 12 years, when concepts can be manipulated, but not in an abstract fashion*

conservation *in Piaget's theory, an appreciation that changing the physical properties of an object does not necessarily change its essence*

Figure **9.7**

In a demonstration of the concept of "conservation of volume," a child in Piaget's preoperational stage of cognitive development will claim that there is more liquid in the tall beaker than there is in the short one, even when the amounts of liquid are, in fact, equal.

Concrete Operations Stage. (Ages 7 to 12 years.) In the **concrete operations stage**, children begin to develop many concepts *and* show that they can manipulate those concepts. For example, they can organize objects into classes or categories of things. That is to say, they can classify things: balls over here, blocks over there, plastic soldiers in a pile by the door, and so on. Each of these items is recognized as a toy, ultimately to be put away in the toy box and not stored in the closet, which is where clothes are supposed to go. Thus, it is in this period that we may say that rule-governed behavior begins. The concrete, observable objects of the child's world can be classified, ranked, ordered, or separated into more than one category.

A sign of the beginning of the concrete operations stage is an ability to solve conservation problems. **Conservation** involves the cognitive awareness that changing the form or the appearance of something does not necessarily change what it really is. Many experiments convinced Piaget that the ability to demonstrate conservation marked the end of the preoperational stage of development. Figure 9.7 shows a test for conservation of *volume*. We can show the conservation of *size* by giving two equal-sized balls of clay to a 4-year-old. One is then rolled into a long cigar shape, and the child will now assert that it has more clay in it than the ball does. A 7-year-old will seldom hesitate to tell you that each form contains the same amount of clay. The 7-year-old has moved on to the next stage of cognitive development.

During this stage, youngsters enjoy simple games if the rules are easy. Moving pieces around a board to squares that match the color indicated by a spinner is easy; so is moving pieces along a board the same number of spaces as indicated on a pair of dice. Problems arise when choices need to be made that force decisions beyond the (concrete) here and now: "Should I buy this piece of property now or build a house on Boardwalk?" "If I move my piece there, I'll get jumped, but then I can jump two of his pieces." "Should I save sevens, or should I save clubs?"

As its name suggests, in the concrete operations stage, children begin to operate on (use and manipulate) concepts and ideas. Those manipulations are still very concrete, however—very much tied to real objects in the here and now. For example, an 8-year-old can easily be expected to find her way to and from school, even if she throws in a side trip or two along the way. What she will have a hard time doing is *telling* you with any precision just how she gets from one place to another. Drawing a sensible map is very difficult for her. If she actually stands on the corner of Maple Street and Oak Avenue, she knows where to go next to get home. Dealing with the concrete reality, here and now, is fairly easy. Dealing with such knowledge later, in abstract terms, is what is difficult.

BEFORE YOU GO ON

What cognitive skills might we expect from a child in the concrete operations stage of development?

Formal Operations Stage. (Ages over 12 years.) The logical manipulation of abstract, symbolic concepts does not appear until the last of Piaget's stages: **formal operations**. The key to this stage, usually begun at adolescence, is abstract, symbolic reasoning. By the age of 12 years, most children can develop and then mentally test hypotheses—can work through problems in their mind. Many problem-solving strategies of the sort that we discussed in Topic 7B develop at this stage.

It is only at the stage of formal operations that youngsters are able to reason through hypothetical problems: "What if you were the only person in the world who liked rock music?" "If nobody had to go to school, what would happen?" Similarly, children are now able to deal with questions that are literally contrary to fact: "What if John F. Kennedy or Richard Nixon were still president of the United States?"

The stages of Piaget's theory and the cognitive milestones associated with each are summarized in Figure 9.8 on p. 406.

formal operations stage *in Piaget's theory, ages older than 12 years, when one can generate and test abstract hypotheses, and think as an adult, where thinking follows rules*

BEFORE YOU GO ON

What cognitive ability characterizes the stage of formal operations?

Reactions to Piaget

There can be no doubt of the importance of Piaget's influence on the study of the cognitive abilities of children. His observations, insights, and theories about intellectual development spanned decades. On the other hand, there has been a sizable quantity of research that has brought into question some of Piaget's basic ideas. The two major criticisms of Piaget's theory are that (1) the borderlines between his proposed stages are much less clear-cut than his theory suggests, and (2) Piaget significantly under-

---

Figure **9.8**

PIAGET'S STAGES OF COGNITIVE DEVELOPMENT

1. Sensorimotor stage (birth to age 2 years)
"Knows" through active interaction with environment
Becomes aware of cause-effect relationships
Learns that objects exist even when not in view
Imitates crudely the actions of others

2. Preoperational stage (ages 2 to 6 years)
Begins by being very egocentric
Language and mental representations develop
Objects are classified on just one characteristic at a time

3. Concrete operations stage (ages 7 to 12 years)
Develops conservation of volume, length, mass, etc.
Organizes objects into ordered categories
Understands relational terms (e.g., bigger than, above)
Begins using simple logic

4. Formal operations stage (ages over 12)
Thinking becomes abstract and symbolic
Reasoning skills develop
A sense of hypothetical concepts develops

---

estimated the cognitive talents of preschool children (Flavell, 1982, 1985; Gelman, 1978).

For example, the egocentrism said to characterize the preoperational preschool child may not be as flagrant as Piaget would have us believe. In one study (Lempers et al., 1977), children were shown a picture that was pasted inside a box. They were asked to show the picture to someone else. Not only did they do so, but in showing the picture, they turned it so that it would be right side up to the viewer. Every child over 2 years of age indicated such an appreciation of someone else's point of view. Similarly, there is considerable evidence that object permanence may be neither universal nor consistently found in any one child; it depends on how you test for it (Harris, 1983).

Even Piaget's well-researched notion of conservation may not be such an obvious indicator of cognitive development as was once thought. When experimenters pour liquid from a short beaker into a tall one, a 5-year-old probably will say that the taller beaker now holds more liquid—evidence of a failure to conserve in the preoperational stage. If the *child* actually does the pouring from one beaker to the other, as opposed to just watching, even 5-year-olds show definite signs of conservation and recognize that the amount of liquid is the same in both containers (Rose & Blank, 1974).

A further criticism is that Piaget's theory, focusing from the start on a stage approach, gives little attention to the impact of language development. Piaget had little to say about the smooth and gradual increase in the capacity of a child's memory. Indeed, some children may appear to fail at a task designed to measure a cognitive skill simply because they lack the words to describe what they know or because the task puts too great a strain on their abilities to remember (Pines, 1983). Just because a child—of whatever age—*can* demonstrate some cognitive skill is no guarantee that the child normally *does* use that skill in his or her daily activities.

So it seems that a number of Piaget's observations and assumptions have come under attack. This is to be expected in science. In fact, one of the most important contributions of Jean Piaget was that he developed a theory of the cognitive development of children (based on the observations of very few children) that was so rich, so detailed, so thought-provoking, that it will continue to challenge researchers for years to come.

BEFORE YOU GO ON

Cite two criticisms of Piaget's theory of cognitive development.

Erikson's Theory of Psychosocial Development

Erik Erikson (1963, 1965, 1968) is a psychologist who, like Piaget, proposed a stage theory of human development. Unlike Piaget, his theory focuses on much more than cognitive development, although this aspect is included. Erikson's theory is based on his observations of a wide range of different sorts of people of different ages. As we shall see, his theory extends from childhood through adolescence into adulthood. Many of his observations had more of a cross-cultural basis than did Piaget's. Erikson was born in Germany, studied with Anna Freud (Sigmund Freud's daughter) in Vienna, and came to the United States to do his research. Erikson's views of developmental processes were influenced more by Freud than by Piaget. Unlike Freud, Erikson chose to focus on the *social* environment, which is why his theory is referred to as psychosocial.

Erik Erikson

Erikson's theory lists eight stages of development through which an individual passes. These stages are not so much periods of time as they are a series of conflicts, or crises, that need to be resolved. Each of the eight stages can be referenced by a pair of terms that indicates the nature of the conflict that needs to be resolved in this period of development.

As a stage theory, Erikson's implies that we naturally go through the resolution of each conflict or crisis in order and that facing any one type of crisis usually occurs at about the same age for all of us. Figure 9.9 is a summary of each of Erikson's eight stages of development. Also included are very brief descriptions of how each crisis might be resolved.

As you can see, only the first four stages or crises are relevant for children. In fact, one of the major strengths of Erikson's view of development is that it covers the entire life span. While Piaget focused only on the stages of development of children, Erikson extended his views to late adulthood. For now, we'll just describe Erikson's first four crises, but we will return to his theory in Topic 9B.

During one's first year of life, according to Erikson, one's greatest struggle centers around the establishment of a sense of trust. There's just not very much that a newborn can accomplish on its own. If its needs are met in a reasonable fashion, the child will develop a basic sense of safety and

Figure **9.9**

ERIKSON'S EIGHT STAGES OF DEVELOPMENT

Approximate age	Crisis	Adequate resolution	Inadequate resolution
0–1½	Trust vs. mistrust	Basic sense of safety	Insecurity, anxiety
1½–3	Autonomy vs. self-doubt	Perception of self as agent capable of controlling own body and making things happen	Feelings of inadequacy to control events
3–6	Initiative vs. guilt	Confidence in oneself as initiator, creator	Feeling of lack of self-worth
6–puberty	Competence vs. inferiority	Adequacy in basic social and intellectual skills	Lack of self-confidence, feelings of failure
Adolescent	Identity vs. role confusion	Comfortable sense of self as a person	Sense of self as fragmented; shifting, unclear sense of self
Early adult	Intimacy vs. isolation	Capacity for closeness and commitment to another	Feeling of aloneness, separation; denial of need for closeness
Middle adult	Generativity vs. stagnation	Focus on concern beyond oneself to family, society, future generations	Self-indulgent concerns; lack of future orientation
Later adult	Ego-integrity vs. despair	Sense of wholeness, basic satisfaction with life	Feelings of futility, disappointment

After Erikson, 1963.

security, optimistic that the world is a predictable place. If the child's needs aren't adequately met, what develops is a sense of mistrust—feelings of frustration and insecurity.

During the period of *autonomy versus shame and doubt*, what emerges most plainly is what we might call a sense of self-esteem. The child begins to act independently, to dress and feed himself or herself, for example. Physically more able, the child can be seen to strive off on its own, exploring ways of assuming personal responsibility. Frustration at this level of development leads to feelings of inadequacy and doubts of one's self-worth.

From ages 3 years to 6 years we have Erikson's period of *initiative versus guilt*. Now the challenge is to develop as a functioning, contributing member of social groups, particularly the family. If the child is encouraged to do so, he or she should develop a strong sense of initiative, a certain joy of trying new things. How reinforcing it is to a 5-year-old to be asked for an opinion of what the family should do this evening. Without such encouragement, the child is likely to feel guilty, resentful, and lacking in self-esteem.

The final childhood period, *industry versus inferiority*, lasts from about age 6 years to puberty. During this period of choices, the child is challenged to move beyond the safety and comfort of the immediate family unit. Now the major thrust of development is "out there" in the neighborhood and the school. Children have to at least begin to acquire those skills that will enable them to become fully functioning adults in society. If the child's efforts of industry are constantly belittled, criticized, or ignored, the child may develop a sense of inadequacy and inferiority, and remain dependent on others even into adulthood.

BEFORE YOU GO ON

Briefly describe the first four stages, or crises, of development according to Erikson.

Kohlberg's Theory of Moral Development

How children acquire the capacity to judge between right and wrong is a process of development that has received considerable attention, even though psychologists have yet to construct a generally acceptable model of moral reasoning in adults (Darley & Shultz, 1990; Vitz, 1990). Piaget included the study of moral development in his theory, arguing that morality is closely related to one's cognitive awareness (Piaget, 1932). Lawrence Kohlberg has proposed a theory that focuses on moral development (1963, 1969, 1981, 1985). Like Piaget's theory of cognitive development, Kohlberg's is a theory of stages, of progressing from one stage to another in an orderly fashion. Kohlberg's original data base comes from responses made by young boys who were asked a number of questions about stories that involve some moral dilemma. The most commonly cited example of such a story concerns whether or not a man should steal a drug in order to save his wife's life after the pharmacist who invented the drug refuses to sell it to him. Should the man steal the drug; why or why not?

This method led Kohlberg to propose three major levels of moral development, with two stages (or "orientations") at each level. The result is the six stages of moral development, which are briefly summarized in Figure 9.10. A child who says, for example, that the man should not steal the drug to save his wife's life because "he'll get caught and be put in jail" would be at the first, preconventional level of moral reasoning because the prime interest of the child is simply with the punishment that comes from breaking a rule. A child who says that the man should steal the drug because "it will make his wife happy, and probably most people would do it anyway" is reflecting a type of reasoning we can classify at the second level because the judgment is based on a blindly accepted social convention, and social approval matters as much as or more than anything else. The argument that, "no, he shouldn't steal the drug for a basically selfish reason, which in the long run would just promote more stealing in the society in general" is an example of moral reasoning at Kohlberg's third level, reflecting complex, internalized standards.

Research suggests that the basic thrust of Kohlberg's theory has merit (Rest, 1983) and that it has crosscultural application, at least at the lower stages (Edwards, 1977; Snarey, 1987). Problems with the theory also exist, however. For one thing, there is little evidence that many people (including adults) operate at the higher stages of moral reasoning described by the theory (Colby & Kohlberg, 1984). On the other hand, there is evidence that children are quite capable of making involved moral judgments at a much younger age than Kohlberg would predict—perhaps by the age of 3

Figure **9.10**

KOHLBERG'S STAGES OF MORAL DEVELOPMENT

Level 1   **Preconventional morality**

1. Obedience and punishment orientation — Rules are obeyed simply to avoid punishment; "If I take the cookies, I'll get spanked."

2. Naive egotism and instrumental orientation — Rules are obeyed simply to earn rewards; "If I wash my hands, will you let me have two desserts?"

Level 2   **Conventional (conforming) morality**

3. Good boy/girl orientation — Rules are conformed to in order to avoid disapproval and gain approval; "I'm a good boy 'cause I cleaned my room, aren't I?"

4. Authority-maintaining orientation — Social conventions blindly accepted to avoid criticism from those in authority: "You shouldn't steal because it's against the law, and you'll go to jail if the police catch you."

Level 3   **Postconventional morality**

5. Contractual-legalistic orientation — Morality is based on agreement with others to serve the common good and protect the rights of individuals; "I don't like stopping at stop signs, but if we didn't all obey traffic signals, it would be difficult to get anywhere."

6. Universal ethical principle orientation — Morality is a reflection of internalized standards; "I don't care what anybody says, what's right is right."

(Kagan & Lamb, 1987). Another problem is that Kohlberg argued that progress from stage to stage is irreversible, and research suggests that such is not always the case (Darley & Shultz, 1990).

A rather strong argument has been raised against Kohlberg's theory as it applies to women (Ford & Lowery, 1986; Gilligan, 1982). All of Kohlberg's original data came from the responses of young boys, remember. Later, when young girls were tested, some studies seemed to suggest that girls showed slower moral development when compared to boys. Carol Gilligan's argument is that the moral reasoning of females is neither slower nor faster so much as it is *different* from the reasoning of males. Males, concerned with rules, justice, and an individual's rights, simply approach moral dilemma problems differently than do females, who are characteristically more concerned with caring, personal responsibility, and interpersonal relationships (Gilligan, 1982). Gilligan's book has brought a new slant to research on morality and value development in general. The issue is not a judgmental one in the sense of trying to determine if men are more or less moral in their thinking than women. The question is whether or not women and men develop different styles of moral reasoning and/or different types of moral behaviors.

**BEFORE
YOU GO
ON**

*Briefly summarize the stages of Kohlberg's theory
of moral development.*

Developing Social Attachments

Theories of moral development, such as those of Kohlberg and Gilligan, are cognitive in nature to the extent to which they deal with how we come to reason in a certain way. In large measure, because they involve how we come to react to the needs of others, they also address the *social* nature of humans. To a large degree, we adapt and thrive in this world to the extent that we can profit from our interpersonal relationships (e.g., Hartup, 1989). The roots of our social development can be found in early infancy—in the formation of attachment. **Attachment** is defined as a strong, two-way, emotional bond, usually referring to the relationship between a child and its mother or primary care giver (Bowlby, 1982). In this sense, attachment is a product of evolutionary history: a means for keeping the individual near significant others. It has survival advantage "through increasing the chances of an infant being protected by those to whom he or she keeps proximity" (Ainsworth, 1989). Attachment is also associated with more freedom to explore the environment, curiosity, adaptive problem solving, and greater competence when interacting with peers (Collins & Gunnar, 1990).

The place to begin our discussion of human attachment is with Harry Harlow and his research with rhesus monkeys (Harlow, 1959; Harlow et al., 1971). Harlow and his colleagues raised some baby monkeys with their biological mothers and raised others in cages containing "artificial mothers." These "mothers" were models made of a wire mesh and fitted with wooden heads. Small, doll-sized baby bottles within the models provided nourishment to the baby monkeys. One style of artificial mother was covered with a soft, terry-cloth wrap, while the other was left as bare wire (see Figure 9.11).

There was no doubt which model the young monkeys preferred. Whether it provided food or not, baby monkeys clung tightly to the soft, terry-cloth model. It seemed clear to Harlow that mother rhesus monkeys provide more to their young than just food. The opportunity to cling to something soft and cuddly (Harlow called it *contact comfort*) is also important.

What were the long-term implications of raising baby rhesus monkeys under these different conditions? Those raised in isolation, or with bare-wire model mothers, or, to a lesser degree, even with the cloth model mothers, all showed definite signs of abnormal development. As adults, they tended to show inappropriate social behaviors, either withdrawing or acting aggressively. Normal sexual behavior patterns were disrupted. Many never successfully mated. When mating was possible, females turned out to be very poor mothers. For rhesus monkeys, then, forming an early attachment bond is an important step in social development.

As is usually the case, we need to exercise caution when translating data from the animal laboratory to humans. It does seem that a strong bond of attachment is often (though not always) formed between a human child and its primary care giver(s).

Forming an attachment between infant and mother (as an example) involves regular interaction and active give-and-take between the two. Strong attachments are most likely to be formed if the mother is sensitive to the needs of the child, picking up the baby when he or she cries, changing the diaper as soon as it is soiled, feeding on a regular basis, and so on.

attachment *a strong two-way emotional bond, usually between a child and parent, or primary care-giver*

Figure **9.11**

One of Harlow's monkeys and its artificial terry cloth mother. Harlow found that the contact comfort mothers provide is essential for normal social development.

Attachments between parents and their babies are a two-way street, where signs of affection are mutually exchanged. Studies suggest that early father-child attachments are beneficial later on.

Attachment is also promoted by spontaneous hugging, smiling, eye contact, and vocalizing (Stern, 1977). But remember that forming an attachment is a two-way street. The bond will be most secure when baby reciprocates by smiling, cooing, and clinging to mother when attended to (Ainsworth, 1979).

Before we leave this discussion, I need to mention explicitly that infants can and do form attachments with persons other than their mothers. Although it is true that, in general, fathers spend less time with young children than do mothers (fathers' time increases as children get older), father-child attachments are quite common and very helpful for the long-term development of the child (Lamb, 1977, 1979; Lynn, 1974). There is no evidence that fathers are any less sensitive to the needs of their children than are mothers (Parke, 1981).

It may be tentatively concluded that forming secure attachments is important for the later development of the human infant, just as contact comfort is important for the development of the rhesus monkey. Because we have not been able to do the sort of controlled experiment with human infants that Harlow did with monkeys, the data are not as impressive. However, they do suggest that there are long-term benefits (ranging from improved emotional stability to improved problem-solving skills) to be derived from strong attachments formed early in childhood (Ainsworth, 1989; Bowlby, 1982; Etaugh, 1980; Schwartz, 1983).

BEFORE YOU GO ON

In child development, what is meant by attachment?

Human development begins at conception, when the genes from the father's sperm cell unite with genes from the mother's ovum to form the zygote. For the next nine months (or about 270 days), the human organism grows and develops in the mother's uterus. This prenatal period of development has three stages: zygote, embryo, and fetus. During the prenatal period, the organism may be subjected to a variety of environmental factors that can markedly affect the developmental process.

With birth, the neonatal period begins. Although a number of useful reflexes and sensory capacities are available to the newborn, interaction with the environment shapes and modifies the developmental process. Several theories concerning the patterning of cognitive, social, and moral development have stimulated research in child psychology. In this topic, we have reviewed Piaget's theory of cognitive development, Erikson's theory of psychosocial development, and Kohlberg's theory of moral development. We have also examined the lasting importance of the early development of social attachments.

What is the epigenetic model of development, and what does it say about the impact of heredity and the environment?

The epigenetic model is an interactionist position claiming that psychological characteristics are the result of neither heredity nor the environment working alone. Rather, organisms develop through the interaction of one's genetic programming *and* one's experiences in the environment. At most, our nature sets limits on what our nurture may provide through development. The extent to which the environment impacts on genetic predispositions is referred to as plasticity. / *page 388*

Briefly summarize the three stages of prenatal development.

Prenatal development begins at conception and ends at birth. This period is generally divided into three stages: the stage of the zygote (conception to 2 weeks), at which time the zygote becomes implanted in the uterus; the stage of the embryo (week 2 to week 8), during which there is rapid growth and differentiation of developing cells; and the stage of the fetus (month 3 until birth), during which the organs begin to function. / *page 391*

Briefly review the impact of diet, drugs, and stress on prenatal development.

A mother's diet and use of drugs have potentially profound effects on prenatal development. Malnutrition in the mother, or deficiencies of specific vitamins or minerals, are usually shared by the embryo or the fetus. Smoking and alcohol use during pregnancy have well-documented negative effects. The rule of thumb is typically to avoid drugs of any sort unless prescribed by a physician. Research on the effects of stress on prenatal development has not produced clear-cut results. Severe and/or chronic stress may, at least indirectly, produce negative consequences, not only for the mother, but also for her child. / *page 394*

What are some of the reflexes that can be observed in neonates? Why do we care about neonatal reflexes?

Some reflexes have obvious survival value for the neonate; for example, the rooting reflex, in which the newborn turns toward a slight pressure on its cheek, the sucking reflex, or even the grasping reflex. Other reflexes, such as the Moro reflex (thrusting arms to the sides and then quickly bringing them back to the chest in reaction to a sudden noise or loss of support) or the walking reflex, seem to serve no particular function for the neonate but may be used to diagnose developmental delays or confirm normal physical development. / *page 396*

What general observations can we make about physical growth and motor control in childhood?

Although the age at which motor abilities develop varies considerably from child to child, the sequence is quite regular and predictable. Review Figure 9.4 for the ages at which some motor behaviors tend to develop. Growth and development also follow two patterns, (1) cephalocaudal, or from head to torso to feet, and (2) proximodistal, or from center to extremities. / *page 397*

Summarize the basic sensory capacities of the neonate.

The neonate's senses function reasonably well right from birth. The eyes can focus well at arm's length, although they will require a few months to focus over a range of object distances. Rudimentary depth perception seems to be present even in the neonate, but improves considerably within the first year. Hearing and auditory discrimination are quite good, as are the senses of taste, smell, and touch. / *page 399*

Cite an example of research evidence demonstrating a cognitive reaction in neonates.

We have recently come to appreciate that neonates can demonstrate memory. They will attend to a new and different visual pattern after coming to ignore a familiar one, showing an appreciation of the difference between familiar and new. They show definite preferences for complex visual patterns over simple ones and seem most to prefer (attend to) visual representations of the human face. Even babies only one hour old make attempts to imitate the facial expressions of someone in their field of view. / *page 401*

How are schemas formed during the sensorimotor stage? What characterizes this stage of development?

During Piaget's sensorimotor stage of cognitive development, the child learns to develop schemas (assimilating new information and accomodating old concepts) through an active interaction with the environment, by sensing and doing. The baby begins to appreciate cause-and-effect relationships, imitates the actions of others, and by the end of the period, develops a sense of object permanence, which means that he or she understands that just because something is no longer in view does not mean that that something is totally gone, never to return. / *page 403*

In Piaget's theory, what best characterizes the preoperational stage of development?
Egocentrism is a cognitive reaction that occurs during the preoperational stage of development. The child becomes very *me* and *I* oriented, unable to appreciate the world from anyone else's perspective or point of view. In addition, children begin to develop and use symbols, in the form of words to represent concepts. / *page 404*

What cognitive skills might we expect from a child in the concrete operations stage of development?
In the concrete operations stage of cognitive development, a child organizes concepts into classes or categories and begins to use simple logic and to understand relational terms. The cognitive skills of conservation are not acquired until the end of the preoperational stage and mark the beginning of the concrete operations stage. Conservation involves understanding that changing something's form (rolling out a ball of clay, pouring liquid from one type of con-

tainer to another) does not change its essential nature or quality. / *page 405*

What cognitive ability characterizes the stage of formal operations?
The essential nature of the formal operations stage of cognitive development is the ability to think, reason and solve problems symbolically or in abstract rather than concrete, tangible form. / *page 405*

Cite two criticisms of Piaget's theory of cognitive development.
As influential as Piaget's theory of cognitive development has been, it has not escaped criticism. Two of the major criticisms of the theory are that (1) there is little actual evidence that cognitive abilities develop in a series of well-defined, sequential stages (that is, the borders between stages are very poorly defined), and (2) preschool children in particular seem to have more cognitive strengths and abilities than Piaget suggested. / *page 407*

Briefly describe the first four stages, or crises, of development according to Erikson.
Of Erikson's eight stages, or crises, of development, four occur during childhood: (1) trust versus mistrust, whether the child develops a sense of security or anxiety; (2) autonomy versus shame and doubt, whether the child will develop a sense of competence or doubt; (3) initiative versus guilt, whether the child will gain confidence in his or her own ability or develop a sense of inadequacy;

and (4) industry versus inferiority, whether the child develops a sense of confidence in intellectual and social skills or develops a sense of failure and lack of confidence. / *page 409*

Briefly summarize the stages of Kohlberg's theory of moral development.
Kohlberg proposes that one's sense of morality develops through three levels and six stages. First, one decides right from wrong on the basis of avoiding punishment and gaining rewards (preconventional morality), then on the basis of conforming to authority or accepting social convention (conventional morality), and finally on the basis of one's understanding of the common good, individual rights, and the internalization of standards (postconventional morality). Although much of the theory has been supported by research, there is little evidence that many individuals reach the higher levels of moral reasoning, and there may be serious deficiencies in applying the theory equally to both sexes. / *page 410*

In child development, what is meant by attachment?
Attachment is a strong, two-way, emotional bond, formed early in childhood, between the child and primary care giver(s). It has survival value in an evolutionary sense, keeping the child in proximity to those who can best care for it. Harlow first demonstrated a need for what he called *contact comfort* in rhesus monkeys. / *page 412*

Development in Adolescence and Adulthood

Why We Care: A Topic Preview

ADOLESCENCE
Physical Changes During Adolescence
Some Challenges of Adolescence
    Identity Formation
    Adolescent Egocentrism
    Drug Use by Adolescents
    Adolescent Sexuality

ADULTHOOD
Early Adulthood
    Marriage and Family
    Career Choice
Middle Adulthood
Late Adulthood

SUMMARY

Why We Care: A Topic Preview

In this topic, we acknowledge that one's growth and development do not come to a halt when one is no longer a child. We continue to develop throughout our adolescence and adulthood. Most of the changes that reflect our development as adolescents and adults are more gradual and subtle than those that occur in childhood. They may be more difficult to observe, but they are no less significant.

We'll begin our discussion by defining adolescence. We'll review the physical changes that usually occur during this developmental period. Then we'll discuss the mental and social development of adolescents. In this section we'll sample some of the issues that concern developmental psychologists who study adolescents: identity formation, egocentrism, drug use, and adolescent sexuality.

The psychology of adult development is a comparatively recent area of research and theory. We'll arbitrarily divide adulthood into three segments: early adulthood, middle adulthood, and late adulthood, and we'll examine some of the psychologically important milestones related to each of these periods.

ADOLESCENCE

As I was reviewing the literature on the psychology of adolescence for this revision, I was constantly reminded of an observation we made back in Topic 1A: "For many questions in psychology, there are no simple answers." This is true in this context even when the questions appear to be very simple. "How shall we define *adolescence*?" "What are the defining characteristics of the stage of development we call adolescence?"

The period of development that we call adolescence is an exciting one. It is clearly a period of transition—from the dependence of childhood to the independence of adulthood. It is very difficult, however, to specify exactly when adolescence begins or when it ends. There are several choices.

We may choose to define adolescence in biological terms. In that case, adolescence begins with the onset of puberty (with sexual maturity and a readiness to reproduce) and ends with the end of physical growth, usually late in the teen years. An individual's developing sexuality and one's physical growth certainly do have psychological implications that we could address, but there are other ways of defining adolescence.

A more psychological perspective emphasizes the development of the cognitions, feelings, and behaviors that characterize adolescence. This approach views adolescence "as a psychological process occurring within the individual" (Forisha-Kovach, 1983, p. 8). Psychological approaches emphasize the development of problem-solving skills and an increased reliance on the use of symbols, logic, and abstract thinking. Such perspectives stress the importance of identity formation and a developing appreciation of self and self-worth.

We also may consider adolescence from a more social perspective by examining the role of adolescents in society (Kett, 1977). These approaches generally define adolescence in terms of being in between: not yet an adult, but no longer a child (Peterson & Ebata, 1987). In this context, adolescence usually lasts from the early teen years through one's highest educational level, when the individual is thought to enter the adult world. In this case, we can see that the limits of adolescence may presently be changing as more and more youngsters opt to go on to college right after high school, still maintaining contact with and dependence on family and other support groups developed during the teen years.

Actually, whether we accept a biological, psychological, or social view of adolescence, we usually are talking about people who are between the ages of approximately 12 and 20. For the sake of our discussion, we will define **adolescence** as the period of development begun at puberty and lasting through the teen years. This is fairly close to the definition chosen by Anne Peterson for her review of adolescent development. She decided to focus on the second decade of life (Peterson, 1988).

One of the intriguing issues in the psychology of adolescence today is how to characterize the period in a general way. Is adolescence a period of personal growth, independence, and positive change? Or is it a period of stress, turmoil, rebellion, and negativism?

Actually, the view that adolescence should be characterized in terms of turmoil, storm, and stress is the older of the two, attributed to G. Stanley Hall (who wrote the first textbook on adolescence in 1904) and to Anna Freud (who applied Freudian psychoanalytic theory to adolescents (Freud, 1958)). This position claims that normal adolescence involves the experi-

adolescence *the developmental period between childhood and adulthood, often begun at puberty and ending with full physical growth, generally between the ages of 12 and 20*

ence of all sorts of difficulties of adjustment. Anna Freud wrote, "To be normal during the adolescent period is by itself abnormal" (1958, p. 275). Thus, in this view, "Adolescents may be expected to be extremely moody and depressed one day and excitedly 'high' the next. Explosive conflict with family, friends, and authorities is thought of as commonplace" (Powers, Hauser, & Kilner, 1989, p. 200).

Over the past 25 years, psychologists have come to appreciate that such a characterization is inappropriate. Adolescence is not to be considered a period of great emotional distress that, with time, one outgrows. As we'll see shortly, the teen years can present considerable pressure and conflict that require difficult choices. Many teenagers do react to the pressures of their own adolescence in maladaptive ways. Adolescence does require change and adjustment, but those changes and *adjustments are usually made in psychologically healthy ways* (Garbarino, 1985; Manning, 1983; Offer & Offer, 1975; Peterson & Ebata, 1987; Rutter et al., 1976). The picture of the seriously troubled, rebellious, uncooperative adolescent is no doubt based on real experience, but is more often a reflection of a social stereotype.

BEFORE YOU GO ON

How might adolescence be defined from a physical, social, and psychological point of view?

Physical Changes During Adolescence

The onset of adolescence is generally marked by two biological or physical changes. First, there is a marked increase in height and weight, known as a **growth spurt**, and second, there is sexual maturation.

The growth spurt of early adolescence usually occurs in girls at an earlier age than it does in boys. Girls begin their growth spurt as early as 9 or 10 years of age and then slow down at about age 15. Boys generally show their increased rate of growth between the ages of 12 and 17 years. Indeed, males usually don't reach their adult height until their early twenties, whereas girls generally attain their maximum height by their late teens (Roche & Davila, 1972; Tanner, 1981). Figure 9.12 illustrates one way to represent the adolescent growth spurt in graphic form.

At least some of the challenge of early adolescence is a direct result of the growth spurt. It is not uncommon to find increases in weight and height occurring so rapidly that they are accompanied by real, physical growing pains, particularly in the arms and legs. Unfortunately, the spurt of adolescent growth seldom affects all parts of the body uniformly, especially in boys. Thirteen- and 14-year-old boys often appear incredibly clumsy and awkward as they try to coordinate their large hands and feet with the rest of their body. One of the most noticeable areas of growth in boys is that of the larynx and vocal cords. As the vocal cords lengthen, the pitch of the voice is lowered. Much to the embarrassment of many a teenage boy, this transition is seldom a smooth one, and he may suffer through weeks or months of a squeaking, crackling change of pitch right in the middle of a

growth spurt *a marked increase in both height and weight that accompanies the onset of adolescence*

Figure 9.12

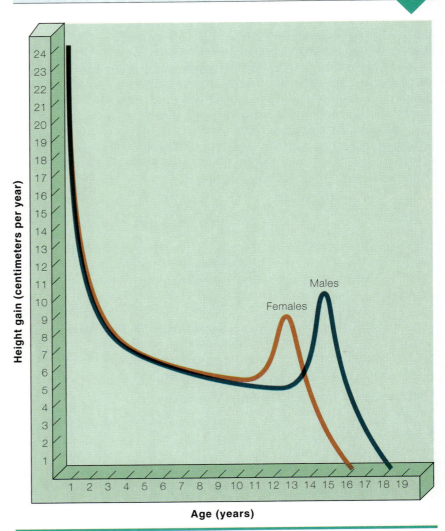

Females begin their main growth spurt around age 10, while the growth spurt in males does not begin until about age 12. In general, males will grow faster and for a longer period of time than females. (After Tanner, Whitehouse, & Takaishi, 1966.)

serious conversation (Adams, 1977; Adams & Gullotta, 1983).

With the onset of **puberty**, there is a significant increase in the production of the sex hormones, primarily androgens in males and estrogens in females. (All of us have both androgens *and* estrogens in our bodies. Males simply have more androgens; females have more estrogens.) Boys seldom know when their own puberty begins. For some time they have experienced penile erections and nocturnal emissions of seminal fluid. Biologically, we say that puberty in males begins with the appearance of live sperm, and most males have no idea when *that* happens; such determinations require a laboratory test.

puberty *the stage of physical development at which one becomes capable of sexual reproduction*

Adolescence can bring with it a number of challenges, including how to deal effectively with acne.

Figure ◆ **9.13**

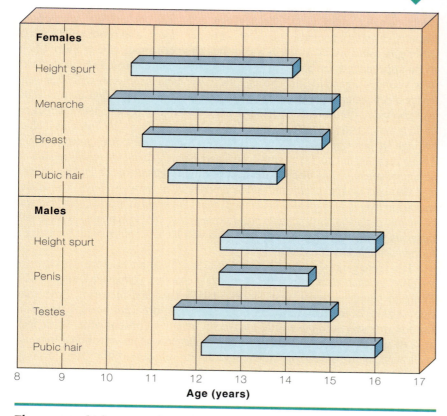

The ages at which certain physical changes occur in the average male and female during puberty. Two figures adapted from "Growing Up" by J. M. Tanner from SCIENTIFIC AMERICAN, September 1973, Volume 229, Number 3. Copyright © 1973 by SCIENTIFIC AMERICAN. All rights reserved. Reprinted by permission.

In females, puberty is quite noticeable. It is most clearly indicated by the first menstrual period, called **menarche**. With puberty, both boys and girls are ready, in a biological sense, to reproduce. Coming to deal with that readiness and making the adjustments that we associate with psychological maturity do not come automatically with sexual maturity. "Perhaps more important than the physical changes themselves are the responses of the self and others to the physical changes" (Peterson, 1988, p. 593).

By now you should realize that the ages we indicate for the beginning and ending of major developmental periods vary considerably from person to person. Such is also the case for puberty. Many boys and girls reach puberty before or after most of their age mates, and are referred to as early or late bloomers. Reaching puberty well before or after others of one's age may have some psychological effects, although few are long-lasting. Let's first get an idea of what early and late puberty means. Figure 9.13 depicts the age ranges during which the major developments associated with puberty may be expected to occur. In some cases, the age range is quite large.

menarche *a female's first menstrual period, often taken as a sure sign of the beginning of adolescence*

I should also mention that many of the ages in this figure are quite subject to change. For example, in the United States 150 years ago, the average age of menarche was 16; now it is closer to $12\frac{1}{2}$ (Hamburg & Takanishi, 1989).

What are the advantages and disadvantages of early maturation? As you might suspect, there are differences for girls and boys. A girl who enters puberty early will probably be taller, stronger, faster, and more athletic than other girls (and many of the boys) in her class at school. She is more likely to be approached for dates, have more early sexual encounters, and marry at a younger age than her peers. She may have problems with her self-image, seeing herself as unattractive, particularly if she puts on extra weight and shows marked breast development (Conger & Peterson, 1984; Crockett & Peterson, 1987). At the same time, she is likely to be *rated* as below average in prestige, popularity, leadership skills, and poise (Jones, 1957). There also seems to be a small but consistent advantage with regard to objective measures of intellectual functioning (Newcombe & Dubas, 1987).

Because of the premium put on physical activity in boys, the early-maturing boy is at a greater advantage than the early-maturing girl. He will have more dating and sexual experiences than his age mates, which will raise his status among his peers. He also will have a better body image and higher self-esteem (Peterson, 1988).

For teenagers of both sexes, being a late bloomer is more negative (*at the time*) in its impact than is being an early bloomer (Gross & Duke, 1980). There is some evidence (e.g., Jones, 1957) that late-maturing boys may carry a sense of inadequacy and poor self-esteem into adulthood. Late maturity for girls seems to have little long-term negative consequence. Some feel, at least in retrospect, that being a late bloomer was an advantage because it allowed them to develop other, broadening interests, rather than becoming "boy-crazy" like so many of their peers in early adolescence (Tobin-Richards et al., 1984).

Summary generalizations are often dangerous, but we may suggest that (1) early maturity is more advantageous than late maturity, at least at the time of one's adolescence, and (2) boys profit from early maturity more than do girls, but may also suffer more from late maturity.

BEFORE YOU GO ON

Briefly describe the physical changes that accompany the beginnings of adolescence.

Some Challenges of Adolescence

Adolescence is a developmental period that is marked by the stage of formal operations in Piaget's theory of cognitive development and by the stage of identity formation in Erikson's psychosocial theory. According to Piaget, in adolescence one is now able to think abstractly and to imagine, to think about what *is*, and to ponder what *might be*. This new, higher level of cognition often gets turned toward self-analysis, toward a contemplation of one's self in a social context (Keating, 1980). In this section, we'll examine a few issues that present specific challenges to the adolescent: identity formation, egocentrism, drug use, and sexuality.

Identity Formation. Adolescents typically give the impression of being great experimenters. They experiment with hairstyles, music, religions, drugs, sexual outlets, fad diets, part-time jobs, part-time relationships, and part-time philosophies of life. In fact, it often appears that most of a teenager's commitments are made on a part-time basis. Teens are busily trying things out, doing things their own way, off on a grand search for Truth.

This perception of adolescents as experimenters is not without foundation. It is consistent with the view that one of the major tasks of adolescence is the resolution of an **identity crisis**—the struggle to define and integrate the sense of who one is, what one is to do in life, and what one's attitudes, beliefs, and values should be. During adolescence, we come to grips with many questions: "Who am I?" "What am I going to do with my life?" "What is the point of it all?" Needless to say, these are not trivial questions. A person's search for his or her identity may lead to conflicts. Some of these conflicts may be resolved very easily, but some continue into adulthood.

As we saw in Topic 9A, the concept of identity formation is associated with the theorist Erik Erikson (1963). For Erikson, the search for identity is the fifth of eight stages of psychosocial development (see Figure 9.9). It is the stage that occurs during the adolescent years. For many young people, adolescence brings very little confusion or conflict in terms of attitudes, beliefs, or values. Many teenagers are able and willing to accept without question the values and sense of self that they began to develop in childhood.

For many teenagers, however, the conflict of identity is quite real. They have a sense of giving up the values of parents and teachers in favor of new ones—their own. On the other hand, physical growth, physiological changes, increased sexuality, and perceived societal pressures to decide what they want to be when they "grow up" may lead to what Erikson calls *role confusion.* Wanting to be independent, to be one's own self, often does not fit in with the values of the past, of childhood. Hence, the teenager tries to experiment with different possibilities in an attempt to see what works out best, occasionally to the dissatisfaction of bewildered parents.

James Marcia (1966, 1980) has expanded on Erikson's basic ideas of identity formation. It is Marcia's view that four states (or degrees) of identity formation can be defined. Each of these states describes a different **identity status**—a combination of crisis and commitment in the search for one's self. In this context, a commitment is a decision, a choice, that leads to a particular set of behaviors. Perhaps this will make better sense if we briefly examine each of Marcia's statuses.

1. *Identity diffusion:* This status is characterized by a lack of commitment, but at the same time no real crisis or conflict exists because the individual has yet to question her or his identity. In this sense, it represents the lowest level or degree of identity formation.
2. *Foreclosure:* There are no real problems or conflicts associated with this status often because the individual simply accepts, without question, the attitudes, goals, and values prescribed by family or society.

One of the challenges of adolescence is identity formation. Who am I? What kind of a person am I to be? What shall be my values? What will I do with my life as I give up my dependence on others?

identity crisis *the struggle to define and integrate one's sense of self and what one's attitudes, beliefs, and values should be*

identity status *one of four states in identity formation, reflecting a sense of conflict and/or a sense of commitment*

3. *Moratorium:* This is the status of real conflict and crisis. Youths at this level suffer more anxiety, in general, than do those at any of the other three statuses. Moratorium is most like Erikson's stage of identity crisis. The search is on, and goals and values are being carefully examined. No commitment has yet been made.

4. *Identity achieved:* This is the fourth status, in which the struggle is over, the conflict resolved, and a satisfying integration of alternatives has been accepted. The individual has a good sense of self, goals, and direction. Notice that this highest level or identity status achieved requires a probing, questioning attitude on the part of the adolescent; that is, one must pass through a moratorium stage before one achieves identity. It is as if identity formation only results from a struggle, at least according to Erikson and Marcia.

Originally, Marcia made no claim that his four identity statuses formed a developmental series of stages through which individuals pass in order. Research does suggest, however, that these statuses may be ordered in time in the same sequence in which they were presented here. Do note, however, that there is no implication in Marcia's theory, or in the data, that every adolescent passes through all four statuses or that everyone completes the fourth level and achieves a full sense of identity (Marcia, 1976, 1980; Meilman, 1979; Super, 1985).

Let's take a look at just one piece of research that will give you some idea of the complications involved in identity formation. It may be that different sorts of identity issues are resolved sooner than others. In a study of junior and senior high school students, Archer (1982) found that many students had already reached the (apparently higher) stages of moratorium and identity achieved in terms of their vocational goals. That is, in terms of their future employment, many teenagers had a good sense of what they wanted to be when they became adults. There was evidence that the students had begun to question their religious beliefs. However, in terms of sex role preference, 132 of the 160 subjects were still at the foreclosure status of development. And of the total sample, 157 had not yet even begun to struggle with their political philosophies, 142 never having considered the question (identity diffusion) and 15 simply accepting parental values (foreclosure). So it seems that when we ask about a teenager's developing identity, we need to specify the domain or area in which we are interested. The cognitive development of a sense of self doesn't just all come together at once.

BEFORE YOU GO ON

Summarize the adolescent's search for identity as described by Erikson and Marcia.

Adolescent Egocentrism. Egocentrism, a focusing on oneself and an inability to take the point of view of others, was used by Piaget to describe part of the cognitive functioning of young children (between the ages of 2 and 6) during the stage of preoperational thought. David Elkind (1967, 1981, 1984) uses the term in a slightly different way. In **adolescent egocentrism**, not only do individuals engage in self-centered thinking, but they also come to believe that virtually everyone else is thinking about them too. Because they can now think abstractly, adolescents begin to think about the thoughts of others and have a tendency to believe that they are usually the focus of others' attention. Needless to say, adolescent egocentrism often leads to a heightened sense of self-consciousness.

Elkind proposes two manifestations of adolescent egocentrism. For one thing, teenagers often feel that they are "on stage," performing. They become quite convinced that when they enter a room, everyone is watching them and making judgments about everything, from what they are wearing to how their hair is styled. Now, in truth, it may be that no one is watching, but the adolescent believes that they are. Elkind calls this the construction of an *imaginary audience*. Coming to think that everyone is watching and analyzing you is explanation enough for the extreme self-consciousness of many young teens (Elkind & Bowen, 1979).

Adolescents often tend to overemphasize their own importance. They are, after all, the focus of their own attention, and given their imaginary audience, they feel they're the focus of everyone else's attention as well. As a result, they tend to develop some rather unrealistic cognitions about themselves, which Elkind calls *personal fables*. These are "stories" about themselves that teenagers generate, often on the basis of irrational beliefs. They come to believe (egocentrically) that no harm can come to *them*. *They* won't become addicted after trying a drug at a party. *They* won't get pregnant. *They* won't get AIDS. *Their* driving won't be affected by alcohol. These sorts of beliefs can be dangerous, of course, and they can trigger considerable parental aggravation. Let's now briefly consider two areas of adolescent experimentation that are often the focus of parental concern: drug use and sexuality.

adolescent egocentrism *self-centered cognitions, plus the belief that one is the center of others' attention*

BEFORE YOU GO ON

What is adolescent egocentrism, and how is it expressed?

Drug Use by Adolescents. There is simply no doubt that many adolescents experiment with using drugs, many use drugs on a regular basis, and many abuse drugs. Smoking (45 percent) and drinking (56 percent) lead the list of drug-related activities that teenagers have tried at least once. And nearly 30 percent have tried illicit, or illegal, drugs (usually marijuana) at least once (National Institute on Drug Abuse, 1987). Very few high school students have ever tried heroin, but in 1987, as many as 15 percent had tried cocaine at least once (Millstein, 1989).

In fact, the use of illicit drugs is on the decline. Both use and abuse figures showed a slow but steady decline throughout the 1980s. The use of cocaine (at least one time), for example, dropped in 1988 from the previous year's 15 percent to 12 percent (Landers, 1989). The use of most

Facing the challenge of drug use is a struggle for many adolescents.

drugs by high school seniors increased between the mid-1970s and the 1981–1982 school year, but since then there has been a (gradual) reduction in drug use (Oetting & Beauvais, 1990). Perhaps more importantly, attitudes about the use of drugs are also becoming more negative among teenagers (Newcomb & Bentler, 1989). It is still the case that the use of licit drugs "remains very high, with 92% of [high school] seniors having had some experience with alcohol, and 66% using it in the past month. Regarding abuse, 5% were daily drinkers and 37.5% reported at least one occasion of heavy drinking (five or more drinks in a row). About one-fifth of seniors were daily cigarette smokers" (Newcomb & Bentler, 1989). (I should mention that even though alcohol and tobacco technically may be classified as licit or legally available drugs, their purchase and/or consumption by minors is illegal in most states.) Surveys also tell us that, among high school students, there are no racial differences in drug use or abuse (Oetting & Beauvais, 1990).

What do all these statistics mean? For one thing, they mean that drug use and abuse among adolescents certainly deserve our strict attention, but at the same time, drug use among teenagers is *not* greater than for any other segment of the population—and it *is* on the decline.

Jonathan Shedler and Jack Block, researchers at the University of California, Berkeley, recently reported on a study of adolescent drug use and psychological health that is bound to affect the way we view drug use among teenagers (1990). The subjects in this investigation were 101 18-year-olds who had been under study since they were 3 years old. Based on reports of their drug use, the subjects were divided into three groups: (1) *abstainers* ($N = 29$), who had never tried any drug; (2) *experimenters* ($N = 36$), who had used marijuana "once or twice, or a few times," and who tried no more than one other drug; and (3) *frequent users* ($N = 20$), who reported using marijuana frequently and tried at least one other drug. (Sixteen subjects could not be placed into any of these three categories.) There were no socioeconomic or IQ differences among the groups.

The major findings of this study had to do with personality characteristics of the 18-year-olds in each group. *Frequent users* were found to be generally maladjusted, alienated, deficient in impulse control, and "manifestly" distressed. The *abstainers* were found to be overly anxious, "emotionally constricted," and lacking in social skills. These same results were apparent when the researchers examined records from when the same subjects were 7 and 11 years old. By and large, then, the *experimenters* were found to be better adjusted and psychologically "healthier" than either of the other two groups. (The investigators also examined the quality of the parenting these teenagers received. We'll look at those findings shortly.)

I feel compelled to echo the concern of the authors of this study that their data may be misinterpreted. Their concern is that these data might be taken to indicate "that drug use might somehow improve an adolescent's psychological health" (p. 628). Clearly, this interpretation would be in error. You will recognize these as correlational data from which no conclusion regarding cause and effect is justified (see Topic 1B, p. 38). Make no mistake. Drug use among adolescents is, and should be, a matter of great concern. A drug-free society is a noble goal. On the other hand, there are data that suggest that we need not get hysterical about infrequent, occasional drug use among teenagers. In a review of substance use and abuse among teenagers, Newcomb and Bentler (1989) put it this way:

Not all drug use is bad and will fry one's brain (as the commercials imply). Such claims as reflected in the national hysteria and depicted in media advertisements for treatment programs, repeat the failed scare tactics of the past. All drug abuse is destructive and can have devastating consequences for individuals, their families, and society. The difference or distinction lies in the use versus abuse of drugs. (p. 247)

To summarize again: Adolescents do use and do abuse drugs, both licit drugs (such as alcohol and tobacco) and illicit drugs (such as marijuana and cocaine). At least the use of illicit drugs does seem to be decreasing, and we can say that drug use is no greater among teenagers than for any other segment of the population. Thus, we cannot point to drug use to support the notion that adolescence is a time of special turmoil and distress. Now let's move from one touchy subject to another: from teenage drug use and abuse to teenage sexuality.

BEFORE YOU GO ON

Briefly summarize the data on drug use and abuse in adolescence.

Adolescent Sexuality. For the adolescent, going through puberty is an intensely personal, private, and potentially confusing process. Under the direction of the hypothalamus and the pituitary gland, large doses of sex hormones enter the bloodstream, stimulating the development of secondary sex characteristics: In males, the neck and shoulders expand, hips narrow, facial and body hair begins to sprout, and the voice crackles then lowers in pitch. In females, the breasts begin to develop, the hips broaden and become more rounded, and the shoulders narrow. All this takes time, of course, but then puberty is more of a process than a single event. It is during this process that sex hormones give rise to sex drives, which are expressed in sexual behaviors. With puberty, sexual behaviors can lead to pregnancy.

As personal and private as his or her sexuality may be for the teenager, discussions of adolescent sexuality often revolve around statistics—impressive and occasionally depressing statistics. What do the statistics tell us about the sexual behaviors of adolescents?

As you might imagine, collecting quality data on the sexual behaviors of adolescents is not easy. Many surveys are biased because sample size is small or not representative of the general population. Truthfulness is a potential problem with any survey data, even if anonymity is assured. This is particularly the case when we are asking young people about an issue as sensitive as their own sexual behaviors. Some respondents stretch reality with tales of numerous sexual exploits, while others, perhaps more anxious or guilt-ridden, tend to minimize reports of their sexual activities. Quality data can be found, however, and they tell us that adolescents are a sexually active group.

One of the first large-scale national studies of teenage sexual practice was that of Sorenson (1973), who found that by the time they are 19 years

Dealing with their emerging sexuality is a difficult challenge for many teenagers.

old, more than half the females (57 percent) and almost three-quarters of the males (72 percent) reported having sexual intercourse. These data are consistent with those found in other large surveys (Coles & Stokes, 1985; Hofferth & Hayes, 1987; Zelnik & Kantner, 1980). A report from the Centers for Disease Control (CDC) released in early 1991 tells us that premarital sexual activity among adolescent females has risen in the last two decades, with a sharp increase since 1985. The survey from the CDC reports that nearly twice as many female teenagers (51.5 percent) had engaged in premarital sex by their late teens in 1988 compared to 1970 (28.6 percent). The largest relative increase occurred among girls 15 years old. When the report was released, the chief of the behavioral studies section of the CDC, Sevgi Aral, was quoted as saying, "This is really important because it happened during a time when we thought we were doing so much in terms of health education and AIDS prevention." Sexual activity is also increasing slightly among boys (Landers, 1990).

Most teens do not "plan" to become sexually active; it just "happens" (Chilman, 1983). One study (Coles & Stokes, 1985), indicates that about 60 percent of the males, but only 23 percent of the females "felt glad" about their first intercourse (34 percent of the males and 61 percent of the females reported feeling "ambivalent"). These data mirror those of Darling and Davidson (1986), who report that 67.4 percent of the males in their survey were "psychologically satisfied after their first sexual experience," while only 28.3 percent of the females in the study shared that satisfaction.

With all this sexual activity among adolescents, it is not surprising that teenage pregnancy has surfaced as a major social problem. What is a bit surprising is that the problem did not gain national recognition until the 1970s, by which time childbearing among teenagers had begun a decline that still continues. There are several ways of looking at the data. We can note that this year more than half a million babies will be born to adolescent mothers (Kisker, 1985). Nearly two-thirds of the white mothers of those babies will be unmarried, and virtually all of the black mothers (97 percent) of those babies will be single (Furstenberg, Brooks-Gunn, & Chase-Lansdale, 1989). Girls in the United States younger than 15 are *five times more likely* to give birth than are young girls from any other developed country for which comparable data are available (Landers, 1987). In 1980, nearly 10,000 babies were born to mothers *age 14 or younger*. Note that so far we are talking about babies, not pregnancies. What of those teenage mothers who have miscarriages or abortions? Hayes (1987) estimates that approximately 400,000 teenage pregnancies end in abortion each year. It is difficult to assess the true number, but estimating teenage pregnancies at over a million a year is probably not far off (Auletta, 1984; Millstein, 1989; Zelnick & Kantner, 1980).

The physical, psychological, and financial costs of teenage pregnancy—to individuals, families, and society—are very high. The child of a teenage mother is certainly a baby at risk. Teenage mothers face innumerable hurdles—among other things, they are much more likely to drop out of school (Hayes, 1987; Hofferth & Hayes, 1987). But remember, most adolescents do not plan to become pregnant. Perhaps more than anything else, teenage pregnancy may reflect a poor understanding of sexuality. For example, a significant number do not believe that they can become pregnant the first time they have intercourse, and teenagers hold negative attitudes about the use of contraceptives (Morrison, 1985).

When adolescents become parents, both the parents and their child face numerous problems.

The statistics reviewed here are, as I said above, both impressive and depressing. Sexually active adolescents number in the millions. Many of these adolescents are woefully ignorant of the consequences of their own sexual behaviors. Those for whom sexual activity results in pregnancy number in the hundreds of thousands. But, again, let's not lose sight of the fact that most teenage females *do not* have unwanted pregnancies. Many adolescents know a lot about sex. Dealing effectively with one's sexuality is never easy, but it is just one of the challenges that we must address as we pass through adolescence.

BEFORE YOU GO ON

What evidence supports the notion that adolescents are a sexually active group?
Briefly sumamrize the data on teenage pregnancy.

ADULTHOOD

The changes that occur during our adult years may not seem as striking or dramatic as those that typify our childhood and adolescence, but they are no less real. Many of the adjustments that we make as adults may go unnoticed as we accommodate physical changes and psychological pressures. As an adult, one's health may become a concern for the first time. Psychological and social adjustments need to be made to marriage, parenthood, career, the death of friends and family, retirement, and ultimately, one's own death.

Our adult lives end with our deaths. Just when adulthood begins is difficult to say. Legally, adult status is often granted by governments, at age 18 for some activities or at age 21 for others. Psychologically speaking, adulthood is marked by two possibilities that at first seem almost contradictory: (1) *independence*, in the sense of taking on responsibility for one's actions and no longer being tied to one's parents, and (2) *interdependence*, in the sense of building new commitments and intimacies in interpersonal relationships.

Following the lead of Erikson (1968) and Levinson (1978, 1986), we'll consider adulthood to be comprised of three overlapping periods, eras, or seasons: early adulthood (roughly ages 18 to 45), middle adulthood (approximately ages 45 to 65), and late adulthood (over 65). Presenting adult development in this way may mislead us, so we must be careful. Although there is support for the notion of developmental stages in adulthood, these stages may be better defined by the individual adult than by the developmental psychologist (Datan et al., 1987). In fact, some psychologists find little evidence for orderly transitions in the life of adults at all (Costa & McCrae, 1980; McCrae & Costa, 1984), while others find significant sex differences in what determines the stage or status of one's adult life (Reinke et al., 1985).

Early Adulthood

If anything marks the transition from adolescence to adulthood, it is choice and commitments independently made. The sense of identity one fashioned during adolescence now needs to be put into action. In fact, the achievement of a strong sense of self by early adulthood is an important predictor of the success of intimate relationships later in adulthood (Kahn et al., 1985). With the attainment of adult status, there are new and often difficult choices to be made. Advice may be sought from elders, parents, teachers, or friends, but as adults, individuals make their own choices. Should I get married? Should I stay single? Perhaps I should live with someone. Who? Should I get a job? Which one? Do I need more education? What sort of education? How? Where? Should we have children? How many? When? Many of these issues are first addressed in adolescence, during identity formation. But for the adult, these questions are no longer abstract. They are very real questions that demand some sort of response.

Levinson (1986) calls early adulthood the "era of greatest energy and abundance and of greatest contradiction and stress" (p. 5). In terms of our physical development, we are at something of a peak during our twenties and thirties, and we're apparently willing to work hard to maintain that physical condition (McCann & Holmes, 1984; Shaffer, 1982). On the one hand, young adulthood is a season for finding our niche, for working through the aspirations of our youth, for raising a family. On the other hand, it is a period of stress, taking on parenthood, finding and maintaining the "right" job, and keeping a balance among self, family, job, and society at large. Let's take a brief look at two important decision-making processes of young adulthood, the choice of mate and family, and the choice of job or career.

Having a baby around requires new parents to make adjustments to their daily lives. As a result, they find themselves staying at home more often.

Marriage and Family. It is Erikson's claim (1963) that early adulthood revolves around the basic choice of *intimacy versus isolation*. A failure to establish close, loving, or intimate relationships may result in loneliness and long periods of social isolation. Marriage is certainly not the only source of interpersonal intimacy, but it is still the first choice for most Americans. More young adults than ever before are postponing marriage plans, but fully 95 percent of us do marry (at least once). In fact, we're more likely to claim that happiness in adulthood depends more on a successful marriage than any other factor, including friendship, community activities, or hobbies (Glenn & Weaver, 1981).

Individuals reach the point of being ready to marry at different ages. Some may decide to marry simply because they perceive that it is "the thing to do." Others choose marriage as an expression of an intimacy that has already developed (Stinnett et al., 1984). In addition to the choices of *when* (and *how*) to marry, of no small consequence is the choice of *who* to marry. If we have learned nothing else about the choice of marriage partners over the last 30 years, it is that mate selection is a complex process.

There are at least three factors that influence the choice of a marriage partner (Newman & Newman, 1984). The first deals with availability. Before we can develop an intimate relationship with someone, we need the opportunity to develop the relationship in the first place. Availability is one thing, eligibility may be another. Here, matters of age, religion, politics, race, and background come into play. Available and eligible, yes; now what

Figure 9.14

CHARACTERISTICS SOUGHT IN MATES

Rank (most important)	Male choices	Female choices
1	Kindness and understanding	Kindness and understanding
2	Intelligence	Intelligence
3	Physical attractiveness	Exciting personality
4	Exciting personality	Good health
5	Good health	Adaptability
6	Adaptability	Physical attractiveness
7	Creativity	Creativity
8	Desire for children	Good earning capacity
9	College graduate	College graduate
10	Good heredity	Desire for children
11	Good earning capacity	Good heredity
12	Good housekeeper	Good housekeeper
13	Religious orientation	Religious orientation

From Buss & Barnes, 1986.

about attractive? To a degree, attractiveness in this context means physical attractiveness, but as we all know, judgments of physical beauty depend on who's doing the judging. "Attractiveness" also involves judgments about psychological characteristics such as understanding, emotional supportiveness, and similarity in values and goals.

Psychologist David Buss has reviewed the available evidence on mate selection with a particular focus on the question of whether or not opposites attract (Buss, 1985). He concluded that, at least in marriage, they do not. He found that "we are likely to marry someone who is similar to us in almost every variable" (Buss, 1985, p. 47). Most important are age, education, race, religion, and ethnic background (in order), followed by attitudes and opinions, mental abilities, socioeconomic status, height, weight, and even eye color. More than that, he found that men and women are in nearly total agreement on those characteristics they commonly seek in a mate (Buss, 1985; Buss & Barnes, 1986). Figure 9.14 presents 13 such characteristics ranked by men and women. There is a significant *difference* in ranking for only two: good earning potential and physical attractiveness.

You should not conclude from this discussion that choosing a marriage partner is always a matter of making sound, rational decisions. Clearly it isn't. Many factors, including romantic love, affect such choices. The fact that approximately 50 percent of all first marriages end in divorce and that, in the United States, 9.4 years is the average life span of a marriage is an unsettling reminder that people don't always make the best choices. Just as men and women agree on what matters in choosing a mate, so do they agree on what matters in maintaining a marriage, listing first such things as liking one's spouse as a friend, agreeing on goals, and a mutual concern for making the marriage work (Lauer & Lauer, 1985). In fact, one of the best predictors of a successful marriage is the extent to which marriage partners were able to maintain close, effective relationships (such as with parents) *before* marriage (Wamboldt & Reiss, 1989).

Beyond establishing an intimate relationship, becoming a parent is generally taken as a sign of adulthood. For many couples, parenthood has become more a matter of choice than ever before because of more available means of contraception and new treatments for infertility. Having one's own family helps foster the process of *generativity* that Erikson associates with middle adulthood. This process reflects a growing concern for family and for one's impact on future generations (Chilman, 1980). Although such concerns may not become central until one is over 40, parenthood usually begins much sooner.

There is no doubt that having a baby around the house significantly changes established routines, often leading to negative consequences (Miller & Sollie, 1980). The freedom for spontaneous trips, intimate outings, and privacy is in large measure given up in trade for the joys of parenthood. As parents, men and women take on the responsibilities of new social roles—that of father and mother. These new roles in adulthood add to the already established roles of being a male or a female, a son or a daughter, a husband or a wife, and so on. There seems to be little doubt that choosing to have children (or at least choosing to have a large number of children) is becoming less and less popular (Schaie & Willis, 1986). Although many people still regard the decision not to have children as basically selfish, irresponsible, and immoral (Skolnick, 1978), there is little evidence that such a decision leads to a decline in well-being or life satisfaction later in life (Beckman & Houser, 1982; Keith, 1983).

Career Choice. By the time a person has become a young adult, it is generally assumed that he or she has chosen a vocation or life's work. With so many possibilities to choose from, this decision is often difficult to make. Selection of a career is driven by many factors; family influence and the potential for earning money are just two. In truth, most young adults are dissatisfied with their initial choice(s) (Rhodes, 1983; Shertzer, 1985).

Jeffrey Turner and Donald Helms (1987) claim that choosing a career path involves seven identifiable stages. Let's review their list:

1. *Exploration:* Here there is a general concern that something needs to be done, a choice needs to be made, but alternatives are poorly defined, and plans for making a choice are not yet developed. This period is what Daniel Levinson (1978) calls "formulating a dream."
2. *Crystallization:* Now some actual alternatives are being weighed, pluses and minuses are associated with each possibility, and although some are eliminated, a choice is not made.
3. *Choice:* For better or worse, a decision is made. Now there is a sense of relief that at least one knows what one wants, and an optimistic feeling develops that everything will work out.
4. *Career clarification:* Now the individual's self-image and career choice are meshed together. Adjustments and accommodations are made. This is largely a matter of fine-tuning one's initial choice: "I know I want to be a teacher; now what do I want to teach, and to whom?"
5. *Induction:* The career decision is implemented. This presents a series of potentially frightening challenges to one's own values and goals.
6. *Reformation:* Here one finds that changes need to be made if one is to fit in with fellow workers and do the job as one is expected to do it.
7. *Integrative:* The job and one's work become part of one's self, and one gives up part of self to the job. This is a period of considerable satisfaction.

Occasionally, a person may make the wrong career decision. This is most likely to happen, of course, in the third stage of choosing a career path, but probably won't be recognized until the fourth or fifth stage. In such cases, there is little to do but begin again and work through the process, seeking the self-satisfaction that comes at the final stage.

BEFORE YOU GO ON

What developments may be said to characterize young adulthood?

Middle Adulthood

As the middle years of adulthood approach, many aspects of one's life become settled. By the time most people reach the age of 40, their place in the framework of society is fairly well set. They have chosen their life-style and grown accustomed to it. They have a family (or have decided not to). They have chosen what is to be their major life work or career. "Most of

By middle adulthood most people have chosen careers and lifestyles and have more time for leisure activities.

us during our 40s and 50s become 'senior members' in our own particular worlds, however grand or modest they may be" (Levinson, 1986, p. 6).

The movement to middle adulthood involves a transition filled with reexamination, at least for men (Levinson et al., 1974). During the middle years, one is forced to contemplate one's own mortality. One's "middle-age spread," loss of muscle tone, facial wrinkles, and graying hair are evident each day in the mirror. At about the age of 40, sensory capacities begin to slowly diminish. Most people in this stage now notice obituaries in the newspaper, where more and more people of the same age (or even younger) are listed every day.

For some people, perhaps for men more than women, the realization that time is running out produces something of a crisis, even approaching panic. But, by and large, the notion of a mid-life crisis is mostly myth (Costa & McCrae, 1980; Farrell & Rosenberg, 1981). *For most, middle age is a time of great satisfaction and true opportunity* (Rossi, 1980). In most cases, children are grown. Careers are in full bloom. Time is available as never before for leisure and commitment to community, perhaps in the form of volunteer work.

Robert Havighurst (1972) says there are seven major tasks that one must face in the middle years:

1. *Accepting and adjusting to the physiological changes of middle age:* Although there certainly are many physical activities that middle-aged persons can engage in, they sometimes must be selective or must modify the vigor with which they attack such activities.
2. *Reaching and maintaining satisfactory performance in one's occupation:* If career satisfaction is not attained, one may attempt a mid-career job change. And, of course, changing jobs in middle age is often more a matter of necessity than choice. In either case, the potential for further growth and development or for crisis and conflict exist.
3. *Adjusting to aging parents:* This can be a major concern, particularly for "women in the middle" (Brody, 1981) who are caring for their own children and parents at the same time. In spite of widespread opinions to the contrary, individual concern and responsibility for the care of the elderly has not deteriorated in recent years (Brody, 1985). In fact, 80 percent of all health care for the elderly is provided by the family.
4. *Assisting teenage children to become happy and responsible adults:* During the middle years of adulthood, parents see their children mature through adolescence. Helping to prepare them for adulthood and independence (leaving the nest) becomes a task viewed with ambivalence. Because adults at this stage may be caring for children and parents alike, they have been referred to as the "sandwich generation" (Neugarten & Neugarten, 1989).
5. *Achieving adult social and civic responsibility:* This task is similar to what Erikson calls the crisis of *generativity versus stagnation*. People shift from thinking about all they have done with their life to considering what they will do with what time is left for them and how they can leave a mark on future generations (Erikson, 1963; Harris, 1983).
6.–7. *Relating to one's spouse as a person and developing leisure-time activities:* Although all seven of these tasks are clearly related and interdependent, this is particularly true of these last two. As children leave home and financial concerns diminish, there is more time for one's spouse and for leisure. Taking advantage of these changes in meaningful ways provides a

challenge for some adults whose whole lives previously have been devoted to children and career.

BEFORE YOU GO ON

What are some of the issues typically faced during the middle years of adulthood?

Late Adulthood

The transition to what we are here calling late adulthood generally occurs in our early to mid-sixties. Perhaps the first thing we need to acknowledge is that persons over the age of 65 comprise a sizable and growing proportion of the population in the United States. More than 30.4 million Americans were in this age bracket in 1988, and the numbers are increasing by an average of 1400 per day (Fowles, 1990; Kermis, 1984; Storandt, 1983). This is an increase of 18 percent since 1980, compared to an increase of 7 percent for the under-65 population. By the year 2020, Americans over 65 will make up nearly 20 percent of the population (Eisdorfer, 1983). Because of the coming of age of the "baby boom" generation, by the year 2030, there will be about *66 million* older persons in the United States (Fowles, 1990).

Agism is the name given to the discriminatory practice or negative stereotypes that are formed solely on the basis of age. Agism is particularly acute in our attitudes about the elderly (Kimmel, 1988). One misconception about the aged is that they live in misery. There may be some miseries that need attention; sensory capacities, for example, are not what they used to be. But as Skinner (1983) suggested, "If you cannot read, listen to book recordings. If you do not hear well, turn up the volume of your phonograph (and wear headphones to protect your neighbors)." Many cognitive abilities suffer with age, but others are developed to compensate for most losses (Salthouse, 1989). Some apparent memory loss may reflect more of a choice of what one wants to remember than an actual loss. There is no doubt that mental speed is reduced, but the accumulated experience of years of living can, and often does, far outweigh any advantages of speed (Meer, 1986). Perhaps you recognize this as another example of plasticity, a concept we introduced in our discussion of early childhood development.

Death does become a reality. As many as 50 percent of the women over the age of 65 in this country are widows, and about one-fifth as many are widowers. But many elderly people (3000 in 1978) choose this time of their lives to marry for the *first time* (Kalish, 1982).

Children have long since left the nest, but they're still in touch, and now there are grandchildren with whom to interact. And the children of the elderly have themselves now reached adulthood and are more able and likely to provide support for aging parents. Most older adults live in a family setting (about 67 percent). In fact, only about 5 percent of Americans over the age of 65 live in nursing homes (Fowles, 1990; Harris, 1975, 1983).

agism *discrimination or negative stereotypes about someone formed solely on the basis of age*

Many people who reach late adulthood use the time very productively. They look forward to visits with their grandchildren and continue to be active in organizations, such as a senior legislature.

Many individuals dread retirement, but most welcome it as a chance to do things they have planned on for years (Haynes et al., 1978). Many people over 65 become *more* physically active after retiring from a job where they sat at a desk all day long.

Although we often assume that old age necessarily brings with it the curse of poor health, in 1987 only 31 percent of the respondents over age 65 claimed poor health to be a serious problem (Fowles, 1990). That may sound like a high percentage, but it compares to 7 percent in the 18 to 54 age range and 18 percent in the 55 to 65 age range. So although health problems *are* more common (in 1987 the 65+ group represented 12 percent of the U.S. population but accounted for 36 percent of health care costs), they are not nearly as widespread or devastating as we might think. (It should also be noted that poor health among the elderly is related to income and educational levels. For example, elderly persons with incomes below $5000 are much more likely to report having serious health problems. Once again reminding ourselves of the nature of correlational data, we may argue that at least some of the elderly may have low incomes because of their poor health, as well as vice versa.)

One scheme that developmental psychologists are finding useful is to divide those over age 65 into two groups: the *young-old* and the *old-old*. This distinction is not made on the basis of one's actual age, but on the basis of psychological, social, and health characteristics (Committee on an Aging Society, 1986; Neugarten & Neugarten, 1986). The distinction reinforces the notion that aging is in itself not some sort of disease. The young-old group is the large majority (80 to 85 percent). They are described as "vigorous and competent men and women who have reduced their time investments in work or homemaking, are relatively comfortable financially and relatively well educated, and are well-integrated members of their families and communities" (Neugarten & Neugarten, 1989).

The concept of "successful aging" is a similar one and has been with us for some time. It is, however, a concept that seldom gets much attention. John Rowe and Robert Kahn (1987) would have us do no less than change the entire focus of our study of human aging, particularly aging late in life.

Most research has focused on *average* age-related losses and deficits. Rowe and Kahn claim that "the role of aging per se in these losses has often been over-stated and that a major component of many age-associated declines can be explained in terms of life style, habits, diet, and an array of psychosocial factors extrinsic to the aging process" (p. 143). What goes unnoticed is the variability in adjustments made by older persons. Simply put, this argument is that the declines, deficits, and losses of the elderly are not the result of advanced age, but of factors over which we all can exercise some degree of control. The major contributors to decline in old age are poor nutrition, smoking, alcohol consumption, inadequate calcium intake, not maintaining a sense of autonomy and control over one's life circumstances, and lack of social support (so long as the support does not erode self-control). Attention to these factors may not significantly lengthen the life span, but should extend what the authors call the "health span, the maintenance of full function as nearly as possible to the end of life" (p. 149). Recent research suggests, for example, that maintaining close family relationships and involvement in effective exercise programs predict successful aging (Clarkson-Smith & Hartley, 1989; Valliant & Valliant, 1990).

Of the two sure things in life, death and taxes, the former is the surer. There are no loopholes. Dealing with the reality of our own death is the last major conflict or crisis that we face in life. As it happens, many people never have to deal with their own death in psychological terms. These are the people who die young or suddenly, from natural or accidental causes. But many individuals do have the time to contemplate their own death, and this usually takes place in late adulthood.

Much attention was focused on the confrontation with death in the popular book *On Death and Dying,* by Elisabeth Kübler-Ross (1969). Her description of the stages that one goes through when facing death was based on hundreds of interviews with terminally ill patients who were aware that they were dying. Kübler-Ross suggests that the process takes place in five stages: (1) *Denial*—a firm, simple avoidance of the evidence; a sort of, "No, this can't be happening to me" reaction. (2) *Anger*—often accompanied by resentment and envy of others, along with a realization of what is truly happening; a sort of "Why me? Why not someone else" reaction. (3) *Bargaining*—a matter of dealing, or barter, usually with God; a search for more time; a sort of "If you'll just grant me a few more weeks, or months, I'll go to church every week; no, every day" reaction. (4) *Depression*—a sense of hopelessness that bargaining won't work, that a great loss is imminent; a period of grief and sorrow over both past mistakes and what will be missed in the future. (5) *Acceptance*—a rather quiet facing of the reality of death, with no great joy or sadness; simply a realization that the time has come.

It turns out that the Kübler-Ross description is an idealized one. Many dying patients do not fit this pattern at all (Butler & Lewis, 1981). Some may show behaviors consistent with one or two of the stages, but seldom all five (Schultz & Alderman, 1974). There is some concern that this pattern of approaching death may be viewed as the "best" or the "right'" way to go about it. The concern here is that caretakers may try to force dying people into and through these stages, instead of letting each face the inevitability of death in his or her own way (Kalish, 1976, 1985).

Although elderly people may have to deal with dying and death, they are generally less morbid about it than are adolescents (Lanetto, 1980). In one study (Kalish, 1976), adults over 60 did more frequently think about and talk about death than did the younger adults surveyed. However, of all the adults in the study, the oldest group expressed the least fear of death, some even saying they were eager for it.

BEFORE YOU GO ON

Briefly summarize some of what we know about the elderly.

If you have read both of the topics in this chapter, you might now be quite impressed with the orderliness and predictability of human development. Ova and sperm cells unite to form zygotes. Zygotes become embryos, fetuses, and, through birth, neonates. Neonates are born with a range of adaptive reflexes and sensory capabilities. Motor development progresses through identifiable stages. Cognitive development appears to progress through four stages, psychosocial development passes through eight stages, and moral development through six. Many of the conflicts of adolescence are quite predictable. Adulthood moves from choice to commitment to preparation for death.

As easy as it is to be impressed with the orderliness of human development, we must always remember not to take all of this too literally. Orderly sequences of development emerge from examining averages and progressions *in general*. Developmental trends and stages are like so many other things: If one looks hard enough, they can be found. But the individual differences that we see around us constantly remind us that for any one individual—child, adolescent, or adult—many of our observations may not hold true. The orderliness of development may very well exist only in the eyes of the observer. It is important to keep in mind that the picture we have drawn in this chapter is one of general conclusions to which there will always be exceptions.

SUMMARY

How might adolescence be defined from a physical, social, and psychological point of view?

Adolescence may be defined in a number of ways. Physically, it begins with puberty (attainment of sexual maturity) and lasts until the end of one's physical growth. Psychologically, it is defined in terms of the cognitions and feelings that characterize the period, searching for identity and abstract thinking. Socially, it is a marginal period of transition, coming between childhood and adulthood, and is defined in terms of how the adolescent is viewed by others. / page 419

Briefly describe the physical changes that accompany the beginnings of adolescence.

Two significant physical developments mark adolescence: a spurt of growth (seen at an earlier age in girls (9 to 15) than in boys (12 to 17)), and the beginning of sexual maturity, a period called *puberty*. That is, as adolescents, individuals are for the first time physically prepared for sexual reproduction and begin to develop secondary sex characteristics. / page 422

Summarize the adolescent's search for identity as described by Erikson and Marcia.

The search for one's identity—a sense of who one is and what one is to do with one's life—is, for Erikson, the major crisis of adolescence. Most teenagers do develop such a sense of identity, while some enter adulthood in a state of role confusion. Marcia has proposed that the search for identity is a process that can be reflected in four states, defined in terms of both sensing that a crisis exists and making a commitment to one's own attitudes, goals, and beliefs. All aspects of self-awareness and commitments to

different domains of life need not be resolved at the same time. / page 424

What is adolescent egocentrism, and how is it expressed?

When youngsters engage in adolescent egocentrism they think mostly about themselves and come to believe that everyone else is thinking about them also. It is demonstrated by the creation of an *imaginary audience* when the adolescent comes to feel that everyone is watching and that they are "on stage," performing for and being noticed by others. This form of egocentrism also leads to the creation of *personal fables* when the individual develops unrealistic, storylike cognitions in which harm can come only to others. / page 425

Briefly summarize the data on drug use and abuse in adolescence.

There is certainly ample cause for concern about drug use and abuse among adolescents. Most teenagers have experimented with drugs (mostly alcohol, tried by 92 percent of high school seniors), and a disturbing number use drugs (again, mostly licit drugs) quite frequently. The use of illicit drugs is clearly on the decline. One recent study demonstrated that among frequent users, experimenters, and abstainers, the experimenters evidenced the fewest psychological problems as 18-year-olds. Drug use and abuse among teenagers is no worse (but not much better) than it is among the adult population. / page 427

What evidence supports the notion that adolescents are a sexually active group? Briefly summarize the data on teenage pregnancy.

By the time they are 19 years old, more than half of all females and nearly three-quarters of all males report having had

sexual intercourse. Sexual activity is on the increase for both males and females. One's first sexual encounter most often just "happens," without planning or forethought. This may help explain the fact that over 1 million teenagers become pregnant each year. Slightly more than half of those pregnancies will result in live births. About two-thirds of white teenage mothers are unmarried, and virtually all black teenage mothers are single. / page 429

What developments may be said to characterize early adulthood?

Early adulthood (roughly ages 18 to 45) is a period characterized by choices and commitments independently made. One assumes new responsibilities and is faced with a series of difficult decisions concerning career, marriage, and family. For Erikson, the period is marked by the conflict between intimacy and social relationships on the one hand and social isolation on the other. Although many marriages fail, most young adults list a good marriage as a major source of happiness in their lives. Psychologists have found that many factors determine one's selection of a mate, but there is little support for the notion that opposites attract. / page 433

What are some of the issues typically faced during the middle years of adulthood?

In many ways, middle adulthood (roughly ages 45 to 65) defines a period first of reexamination and then of settling down to one's life goals. Entering into the period may be troublesome for some, but most find middle age a period of great satisfaction and opportunity. The individual comes to accept his or her own mortality in a number of ways. The tasks or issues of middle age involve one's changing physiology, one's occupation, one's aging parents and growing children, one's social and civic responsibilities, and one's spouse and leisure time. / *page 435*

Briefly summarize some of what we know about the elderly.
There are now more than 30 million Americans over the age of 65, and the number of elderly is growing steadily.

Although there are often sensory, physical, and cognitive limits forced by old age, only 21 percent of elderly people rate health problems as a major concern. Although some elderly are isolated and lonely, fewer than 5 percent live in nursing homes and only 8 percent consider themselves lonely. Older people are naturally concerned about death, but they are neither consumed nor morbid about it. With good nutrition and

diet, with the development of a healthy life-style, with proper social support, and with the maintenance of some degree of autonomy and control over one's life, "successful aging" can become more common than it is today. This is another way of saying that we can increase the already large percentage (now 80 to 85 percent) of those over the age of 65 who have been characterized as young-old, as opposed to old-old. / *page 438*

PERSONALITY

TOPIC 10A   Theories of Personality

TOPIC 10B   Human Sexuality and Gender

TOPIC IOA

Theories of Personality

Why We Care: A Topic Preview

442

Why We Care: A Topic Preview

Most of us think we understand ourselves fairly well. We believe that we have a good sense of who we are, how we tend to think and feel, and what we are likely to do in most situations. To a somewhat lesser extent, we also feel that we understand a few other people we know particularly well, such as very close friends and family members. We have come to believe that knowing someone's personality is required if we are to truly understand that person. We also have come to appreciate that it is not easy to know someone's personality, because a personality is made up of internal, private experiences, often difficult to determine from the outside.

Psychology has valued the concept of personality throughout its history. Over the years, many theories have emerged that have sought to describe the nature of personality. In this topic, we'll examine some of those theories of personality. We care about these theories because each theory can provide us with insights that help us understand and predict a person's behavior. We care about these theories because each, in its own way, has contributed to our contemporary understanding of personality. We'll organize our discussion of specific theories into four basic approaches. Before we do, let's see what we mean by theory and what we mean by personality in this context.

A theory is a series of assumptions; in our particular case, these are assumptions about people and their personalities. The ideas or assumptions that comprise a theory are reasonably and logically related to each other. Further, the ideas of a theory should lead, through reason, to specific, testable hypotheses. In short, a good theory is an organized collection of ultimately testable ideas used to explain a particular subject matter.

What is personality? Few terms have been as difficult to define. In many ways, each of the theoretical approaches we will study in this topic generates its own definition of personality. What we are looking at with personality are the affects, behaviors, and cognitions of people that can characterize them in a number of situations over time. (Here again is our ABC mnemonic from Topic 1A.) We assume that these affects, behaviors, and cognitions help them adapt to their environments. Personality also includes those dimensions we can use to judge people to be different from one another. So we are looking for ways to describe how individuals remain the same over time and circumstances, and that allow us to describe differences that we know exist among people (Baumeister, 1987). Psychologist David Buss (1984) put it this way: "The field of personality psychology is centrally concerned with the traits that characterize our species as well as the major ways in which individuals characteristically differ" (p. 1143).

THE PSYCHOANALYTIC APPROACH

psychoanalytic *the approach to personality associated with Freud and his followers that relies on instincts and the unconscious as explanatory concepts*

We begin our discussion of personality by considering the **psychoanalytic** approach. This approach is associated with Sigmund Freud and his students. We begin with Freud because he was the first to present a truly unified theory of personality.

Freud's theory of personality has been one of the most influential and, at the same time, most controversial in all of science. Although there are many facets to Freud's theory (and those of his students), two premises characterize the psychoanalytic approach: (1) reliance on innate, inborn drives as explanatory concepts for human behavior, and (2) acceptance of the power and influence of unconscious forces to mold and shape our behavior.

Freud's Approach

Freud's ideas about the nature of personality arose largely from observations of his patients, his reading of the works of many philosophers, and from intense self-examination. The context of his private practice provided Freud with the experiences from which he proposed a general theory of personality and developed a technique of therapy called *psychoanalysis*. Freud's approach to psychotherapy is discussed in Topic 13B. For now, let's review some of Freud's basic ideas about the structure and dynamics of human personality.

Levels of Consciousness. Freud thought that only a small portion of one's mental life was readily available to one's awareness at any one time. Ideas, memories, feelings, and motives of which we are actively aware at the moment are said to be *conscious*.

Aspects of our mind that are not conscious at any one moment, but that can be easily brought to awareness, are stored or housed at a *preconscious* level. For example, right now you may not be thinking about what you had for dinner last night or what you might have for dinner tonight. But with little effort, the matter of tonight's or last night's dinner can be brought into your conscious awareness.

Cognitions, feelings, and motives that are not available at the conscious or preconscious level are said to be in the *unconscious*. At this level we keep ideas, memories, and desires of which we are not aware and cannot easily become aware. This is a strange notion: that there are ideas, thoughts, and feelings stored away in our minds of which we are completely unaware. However, the unconscious mind does influence us. Unconscious content passing through the preconscious may show itself in slips of the tongue, humor, neurotic symptoms, and, of course, dreams. There was no doubt in Freud's mind that unconscious forces could be used to explain behavior that otherwise seemed irrational and beyond description.

As we shall see, a good deal of Freudian psychoanalysis as a psychotherapeutic technique is aimed at helping a patient learn about the contents of the unconscious level of the mind. A husband, for instance, who constantly forgets his wedding anniversary and occasionally can't remember his wife's name when he tries to introduce her may be experiencing some unconscious conflict or doubts about being married in the first place. (There *are*, of course, other possibilities.)

What are the three levels of consciousness proposed by Freud?

Basic Instincts. According to Freudian theory, our behaviors, thoughts, and feelings are governed largely by innate biological drives, commonly referred to as *instincts* in this context. These are inborn impulses or forces that rule our personalities. There may be many separate drives or instincts, but they can be grouped into two categories.

On the one hand are **life instincts (eros)**, or impulses for survival, in particular, those that motivate sex, hunger, and thirst. Each instinct has its own energy that compels us into action (drives us). Freud called the energy through which the sexual instincts operate **libido**. On the other hand, and opposed to the life instincts, are **death instincts (thanatos)**. These are largely impulses of destruction. Directed inward, they give rise to feelings of depression or suicide; directed outward, they result in aggression toward other people or their property. In large measure, life (according to Freud) is an attempt to resolve conflicts between these two natural but diametrically opposed instincts.

The "Structure" of Personality. As we have seen, Freud believed that the mind operates on three levels of awareness: conscious, preconscious, and unconscious. Freud also proposed that the human personality is composed of three separate, though interacting, structures or subsystems: the id, ego, and superego. Each of these subsystems has its own job to do and its own principles to follow.

The **id** is the totally inborn or inherited portion of personality. The id resides in the unconscious level of the mind, and it is through the id that one's basic instincts develop. The driving force of the id is libido, or sexual energy, although it may be more fair to Freud to say "sensual" rather than "sexual."

The id seeks satisfaction for instinctual impulses, regardless of the consequences. It operates on what Freud labeled the **pleasure principle**, indicating that the major function of the id is to find satisfaction for basic pleasurable impulses. Although two other divisions of personality develop later, our id remains with us always and is the basic energy source in our lives.

The **ego** is the part of the personality that develops through one's experience with reality. In many ways, it is our self, the rational, reasoning part of our personality. The ego operates on the **reality principle**. One of the ego's main jobs is to try to find satisfaction for the id, but in ways that are reasonable and rational. The ego may have to delay gratification of some libidinal impulse or may need to find an acceptable outlet for some need.

When the ego cannot find acceptable ways to satisfy the drives of the id, conflict and anxiety result. Then ways must be found to deal with the resulting anxiety. It was for this purpose that Freud suggested the notion of ego **defense mechanisms**. Defense mechanisms are *unconsciously* applied techniques that protect the self, or ego, against strong feelings of

life instincts (eros) *inborn impulses, proposed by Freud, that compel one toward survival; include hunger, thirst, and sex*

libido *the energy that activates the life (sexual) instincts (largely of the id)*

death instincts (thanatos) *the inborn impulses, proposed by Freud, that compel one toward destruction; include aggression*

id *the instinctive aspect of personality that seeks immediate gratification of impulses; operates on the pleasure principle*

pleasure principle *the impulse of the id to seek immediate gratification to reduce tensions*

ego *the aspect of personality that encompasses the sense of "self"; in contact with the real world; operates on the reality principle*

reality principle *the force that governs the ego, arbitrating between the demands of the id, the superego, and the real world*

defense mechanisms *unconsciously applied techniques that protect the self (ego) from feelings of anxiety*

Figure 10.1

THE EGO DEFENSE MECHANISMS

Repression: "Motivated forgetting," in which anxiety-producing events are forced from awareness into the unconscious and cannot be remembered. Example: Extremely anxious about an upcoming dentist appointment, you forget all about it and agree to go shopping with a friend.

Denial: Refusal to acknowledge the reality of an anxiety-producing situation. Example: Told by her physician that she has terminal cancer, a patient simply refuses to believe that the diagnosis is accurate.

Rationalization: Generating excuses for one's behaviors rather than facing the real reasons for those behaviors. Example: Having failed a big exam because he did not study, a student blames the instructor, the textbook, and a friend's party instead of facing the truth.

Fantasy: An escape from anxiety through the use of imagination or daydreaming. Example: Particularly after a series of exams, isn't it pleasant to sit back in a comfortable chair and fantasize about graduating from college—with honors?

Projection: Seeing in others those very characteristics or motives that would make one anxious to see them in oneself. Example: Under pressure to do well on an exam, a student who may want to cheat tends to see cheating going on all around the class.

Regression: A return to earlier, childish levels of previously productive behaviors as an escape from anxiety. Example: Used to being the center of attention, a 5-year-old reverts to bed-wetting when a new baby brother comes home from the hospital.

Displacement: Directing one's motives at some substitute person or object rather than expressing them directly. Example: Really, and justifiably, angry at her boss, a woman comes home and yells at her spouse.

anxiety. Figure 10.1 provides a list of some defense mechanisms. Remember as you review this list that using defense mechanisms is a normal, even common, reaction. You shouldn't be alarmed if some of these techniques sound like something you may have done.

The last of the three structures to develop is the **superego**, which we can liken to one's sense of morality or conscience. It reflects our internalization of society's rules. The superego operates on an **idealistic principle**. One problem we have with our superegos is that they, like the id, have no contact with reality and therefore often place unrealistic demands on the individual. The superego demands that we do what it deems to be right and proper, no matter what the circumstances. Failure to do so may lead to guilt and shame. Again, it falls to the ego to try to maintain a realistic balance between the conscience of the superego and the libido of the id.

Now this isn't as complicated as it may sound. Let's suppose a bank teller discovers an extra $20 in her cash drawer at the end of the day. She certainly could use an extra $20. "Go ahead. Nobody will miss it. The bank can afford a few dollars here and there. Think of the fun you can have with an extra $20," is the basic message from her id. "The odds are that you'll get caught if you take this money. If you *are* caught, you may lose your job, then you'll have to find another one," reasons her ego. "But you shouldn't even think about taking that money. Shame on you! It's not yours. It belongs to someone else and should be returned," the superego protests. Clearly, the interaction of the three components of one's personality is not always this simple and straightforward, but this example illustrates the general idea.

superego *the aspect of personality that refers to ethical or moral considerations; operates on the idealistic principle*

idealistic principle *the force that governs the superego; opposed to the id, seeks adherence to standards of ethics and morality*

BEFORE YOU GO ON

According to Freud, what are the three structures of personality, and by what principle does each operate?

The Psychoanalytic Approach After Freud

Sigmund Freud was a persuasive communicator. In person, he was a powerful speaker. In his writings, he was without peer. His ideas were challenging and new, and they attracted many students. Freud founded a psychoanalytic society in Vienna. He had many friends and colleagues who shared his ideas, but some of his colleagues did not entirely agree with his theory. Among other things, they were bothered by the strong emphasis on biological instincts and libido, and what they perceived as a lack of concern for social influences. Some of these psychoanalysts left Freud and proposed theories of their own; they became known as **neo-Freudians**. Because they had their own ideas, they had to part from Freud; he apparently would not tolerate disagreement with his theory. One had to accept all of psycho-analysis—including psychoanalysis as a treatment for mental disorders—or one had to leave Freud's inner circle.

Remembering that a theory consists of a set of logically interrelated, testable assumptions, it is obvious that we cannot do justice to someone's theory of personality in a short paragraph or two. What we can do, perhaps, is sketch the basic idea behind the theories of a few neo-Freudians.

Alfred Adler (1870—1937). At first, as the psychoanalytic movement was beginning to take shape, Adler was one of Freud's closest friends and

neo-Freudians *personality theorists (including Adler, Jung, and Horney) who kept many basic psychoanalytic principles, but differed from a strict Freudian view, adding new concepts of their own*

Alfred Adler

Being "left out" and ignored can foster feelings of inferiority.

associates. However, Adler left Freud and, in 1911, founded his own version of a psychoanalytic approach to personality. Two things seemed most to offend Adler: the negativity of Freud's views (the death instinct, for one) and the idea of sexual libido as the prime impulse in life.

Adler proposed that we are a product of the social influences on our personality. We are motivated not so much by drive and instincts as by goals and incentives. The future and one's hope for what it holds for us is often more important than one's past. For Adler, our major goal is the achievement of success or superiority. This goal is fashioned in childhood when, because we are then weak and vulnerable, we develop an **inferiority complex**. Though we may seem inferior as children, with the help of social influences and our own creativity, we can overcome and succeed.

inferiority complex *the Adlerian notion that as children, in dealing with our environment, we develop a sense of inferiority that needs to be overcome to reach maturity*

Carl Jung (1875–1961). Another student and colleague of Freud, Carl Jung left the inner circle in 1913. Jung was chosen by Freud to be his successor. But disagreements developed, mostly about the role of sexuality and the nature of the unconscious—two central themes in psychoanalysis. Jung was more mystical in his approach to personality and, like Adler, was certainly more positive about one's ability to control one's own destiny. He believed that our major goal in life was to unify all the aspects of our personality, conscious and unconscious, introverted (inwardly directed) and extroverted (outwardly directed). Libido was energy for Jung, but not sexual energy; it was energy for personal growth and development.

Carl Jung

Jung accepted the idea of an unconscious mind, but expanded on it, claiming that there are *two* types of unconscious: the *personal unconscious*, which is very much like Freud's view of the unconscious, and the *collective unconscious*, which contains very basic ideas and notions that go beyond an individual's own personal experiences. These ideas and notions are common to all of humanity and are inherited from all past generations. The contents of our collective unconscious include what Jung called *archetypes*—universal forms and patterns of thought. These are very basic "ideas" that transcend generations and transcend history. They include such notions as the themes that repeatedly show up in myths: motherhood, opposites, good, evil, masculinity, femininity, and the circle as a symbol representing travel from a beginning back to where one started, or the complete, whole self.

Karen Horney (1885–1952). Trained as a psychoanalyst in Germany, Horney came to the United States in 1934. She held onto some Freudian concepts, but changed most of them significantly. Horney believed that the idea of levels of consciousness made sense, as did anxiety and repression. But she theorized that the prime impulses that motivate behavior are not biological and inborn or sexual and aggressive. A major concept for Horney was *basic anxiety*, which grows out of childhood when the child feels alone and isolated in a hostile environment. If proper parental nurturance is forthcoming, basic anxiety can be overcome. If, however, parents are overly punishing, inconsistent, or indifferent, children may develop *basic hostility* and may feel very hostile and aggressive toward their parents. However, young children cannot express hostility toward their parents openly, so the hostility gets repressed (into the unconscious), building even more anxiety.

Karen Horney

So, Horney placed great emphasis on early childhood experiences, but more from a perspective of social interaction and personal growth. Horney claimed that there are three distinct ways in which people tend to interact with each other. In some cases, people *move away from* others, seeking self-sufficiency and independence. The idea here is something like, "If I am on my own and uninvolved, you won't be able to hurt me." On the other hand, some may *move toward* others, tending to be compliant and dependent. This style of interaction protects against anxiety in the sense of, "If I always do what you want me to do, you won't be upset with me." Horney's third interpersonal style involves *moving against* others, where the effort is to be in control, to gain power and dominate: "If I am in control, you'll have to do what I want you to." Now the ideal, of course, is to maintain a balance among these three styles of interpersonal relationships, but Horney argued that many people tend to have one of these three predominate in their dealings with others.

Horney also disagreed with Freud's position regarding the biological necessity of differences between men and women. Freud's theories have been taken to task a number of times for their male chauvinist bias (e.g., Fisher & Greenberg, 1977). Horney was one of the first to do so.

BEFORE YOU GO ON

Briefly summarize the contributions of Adler, Jung, and Horney to the psychoanalytic approach to personality.

THE BEHAVIORAL-LEARNING APPROACH

Many American psychologists in the early twentieth century did not think much of the psychoanalytic approach, regardless of its form or who happened to propose it. From its very beginnings, American psychology was oriented toward the laboratory and theories of learning. Explaining personality in terms of learning and focusing on observable behaviors seemed a reasonable course of action. In this section, we'll briefly review some of the behavioral approaches to personality.

John B. Watson (1878–1958) and his followers in behaviorism argued that psychology should turn away from the study of consciousness and the mind because they are unverifiable and ultimately unscientific. Behaviorists argued that psychologists should study observable behavior. Yet here were the psychoanalysts arguing that *un*conscious and *pre*conscious forces are determiners of behavior. "Nonsense," the behaviorist would say. "We don't even know what we mean by consciousness, and you want to talk about levels of unconscious influence!"

Among other things, Watson and his followers emphasized the role of the environment in shaping one's behaviors. Behaviorists could not accept the Freudian notion of inborn traits or impulses, whether called id or libido or anything else. What mattered was *learning*. A personality theory was not needed. A theory of learning would include all the details about so-called personality that one would ever need to know.

Who we are has been determined by our learning experiences, and early experiences count heavily; on that point Watson and Freud might have agreed. Even our fears are conditioned (remember Watson's Little Albert study). So convinced was Watson that instincts and innate impulses

The third general goal involves the question of whether a measured personality characteristic can be used to predict some other behavior. This concern also is a practical one, particularly in vocational placement. For example, if we know that Joe is, in fact, dominant and extroverted, does that knowledge tell us anything about his leadership potential? Which characteristics are best associated with success as a sales clerk? Which personality traits best describe a successful astronaut, police officer, or secretary?

In brief, personality assessment has three goals: diagnosis, theory building, and/or behavioral prediction. These three goals may interact. A clinical diagnosis, made in the context of some theoretical approach, is often used to predict possible outcomes, such as which therapy technique is most appropriate for a given diagnosis.

BEFORE YOU GO ON

What are the basic goals of personality assessment?

Behavioral Observations

As you and I develop our own impressions of the personalities of our friends and acquaintances, we do so largely by relying on **behavioral observation**. As its name suggests, this approach involves drawing conclusions about an individual's personality on the basis of observations of his or her behaviors. We judge Dan to be bright because he was the only one who knew the answer to a question in class. We feel that Maria is submissive because she always seems to do whatever her husband demands.

As helpful as our observations may be to us, there may be problems with the casual, unstructured observations that you and I normally make. Because we have only observed a small range of behaviors in a small range of settings, we may be overgeneralizing when we assume that those same behaviors will show up in new, different situations. Dan may never again know the answer to a question in class. Maria may give in to her husband only because she knows that we are there. That is, the behaviors we happen to observe may not be typical, or characteristic, at all.

Nonetheless, behavioral observations can be an excellent source of information, particularly when the observations being made are purposeful, careful, and structured, as opposed to the casual observations that you and I usually make. Behavioral observations are commonly a part of any clinical assessment. The clinical psychologist may note any number of behaviors of a client as being potentially significant—style of dress, manner of speaking, gestures, postures, and so on.

Let's consider an example. A small child is reportedly having trouble at school, behaving aggressively and being generally disruptive. One thing a psychologist may do is visit the school and observe the child's behaviors in the natural setting of the classroom. It may be that the child does behave aggressively and engage in fighting behavior, but only when the teacher is

behavioral observation *the personality assessment technique of drawing conclusions about one's personality based on observations of one's behaviors*

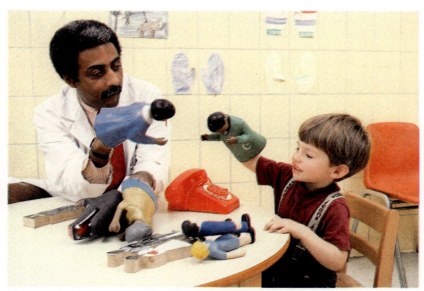

Behavioral observation involves drawing conclusions about an individual's personality on the basis of his or her behaviors. Role-playing is one technique psychologists use to gain insights about a child's behavior.

in the room. Otherwise, the child is quite pleasant. It may be that the child's aggressive behaviors reflect a ploy to get the teacher's attention.

In an attempt to add to her original observations, a psychologist may use *role-playing* as a means to collect more information. Role-playing is a matter of acting out a given life situation. "Let's say that I'm a student, and that you're the teacher, and that it's recess time," the psychologist says to a child. "Let's pretend that somebody takes a toy away from me, and I hit him on the arm. What will you do?"

Some observational techniques are supplemented with some sort of *rating scale* (see Figure 10.5, p. 464). Rating scales provide many advantages over casual observation. For one thing, they focus the attention of the observer on a set of specified behaviors to be observed. Rating scales also yield a more objective measure of a sample of behavior. Using rating scales, one can have behaviors observed by a number of raters. If different raters are involved in the observation of the same behaviors (say, children at play in a nursery school), you can check on the reliability of the observations. That is, if all five of your observers agree that Timothy engaged in "hitting behavior" on the average of five times per hour, the consistency (or reliability) of that assessment adds to its usefulness.

BEFORE YOU GO ON

How are behavioral observations used to assess personality?

Figure 10.5

Poor   **Superior**

Dependability				
Requires prodding and supervision	Needs occasional prodding	Steady; responsible worker	Needs little supervision; uses own judgement	Self-starter; needs no supervision
Personal relations				
Rude; causes trouble	Inconsiderate; unkind	Relations with others usually good	Helpful; kind; polite	Well liked; good social skills
Poise				
Nervous; ill at ease	Easily upset; tense	Average poise and self-assurance	Self-assured	Composed; handles crises well

A graphic rating scale such as this might be used by an employer in evaluating employees or potential employees. It could also be used by psychologists studying behavior.

Interviews

interview *the personality assessment technique involving a conversational interchange between the interviewer and subject to gain information about the subject*

We can learn some things about people by watching them. We also can gain insight about some aspects of their personality by simply asking them about themselves. In fact, the **interview** "remains the most important instrument of clinical assessment" (Korchin & Schuldberg, 1981). It also is "one of the oldest and most widely used, although not always the most accurate, of the methods of personality assessment" (Aiken, 1984, p. 296).

The basic data of the interview are what people say about themselves, rather than what they do. The interview is not, strictly speaking, a measurement technique, because the results of interviews usually are impressionistic and not easily quantifiable (although some interview techniques are clearly more structured and objective than others). The interview is more a technique of discovering generalities than specifics.

A major advantage of the interview is its flexibility. The interviewer may decide to drop a certain line of questioning, if it is producing no useful information, and to pursue some other area of interest. Unfortunately, there is little evidence that unstructured interviews have very much reliability or validity. In discussing interviews used to assess personality characteristics of job applicants, Tenopyr (1981) calls the validity of interviews "dismal." She says that the employment interview, "despite various innovations over the years, has never been consistently shown to improve selection" (p. 1123). (We'll review many of these assessment techniques in the context of employee testing in Topic 15A.)

Although the data derived from casual interviews is seldom very reliable, psychologists can gain useful insights about someone's personality by using formal, structured interviews.

As is the case for observational techniques, there is considerable variety in the degree to which interviews may be unstructured or structured. In the latter type of interview, there are a specific set of questions to be asked in a prescribed order. The structured interview, then, becomes more like a psychological test to the extent that it is objective and standardized, and asks about a particular sample of behavior.

BEFORE YOU GO ON

Cite one advantage and one disadvantage of the interview as a technique of personality assessment.

Paper-and-pencil Tests

Observational and interview techniques barely qualify as psychological tests. They are seldom as standardized or as objective as we would like them to be. (At this point, you might want to review our discussion of the nature of psychological tests in Topic 8A.) In this section, we'll focus on one of the most often used paper-and-pencil personality tests, the **Minnesota Multiphasic Personality Inventory**, or **MMPI** for short. The test is referred to as multiphasic because it measures a number of different personality dimensions with the same set of items.

The MMPI was designed to help in the diagnosis of persons with mental disturbances and, hence, is not a personality test in the sense of identifying

Minnesota Multiphasic Personality Inventory (MMPI-2) *a paper-and-pencil inventory of 567 true-false questions used to assess a number of personality dimensions, some of which may indicate the presence of a psychological disorder*

personality traits. The test is the most researched test in all of psychology and remains one of the most commonly used (Lubin et al., 1984). In August 1989, a revision of the MMPI (called the MMPI-2) was made available. The revision made two major changes and several lesser ones. Anitiquated and offensive items (having to do with religion or sexual practices) were replaced. The norm group for the MMPI-2 was much larger (2600 subjects) than for the MMPI (about 700 subjects). The intent of the authors of the MMPI-2 was to update and improve, but *not change* the basic design or the meaning of test scores. The extent to which the revision has succeeded remains to be seen (e.g., Adler, 1990). Many psychologists had grown very comfortable with the original MMPI, and some were against changing such a well-researched test.

The MMPI-2 is composed of 567 true-false questions that ask about feelings, attitudes, physical symptoms, and past experiences. What makes the MMPI-2 a somewhat unique test is the method used to choose items to include in the inventory and the test's "validity scales."

Potential test items were administered to subjects who already had been diagnosed as belonging to some psychiatric category: schizophrenia, paranoia, or depression, for example. The items also were given to a group of subjects who had no diagnosis of disorder. If an item was answered by both normals and subjects with psychiatric problems in the very same way, the item did not discriminate normals from nonnormals and was dropped. Items were included only if they differentiated among the groups of subjects and patients responding to them.

Because of the way in which it was constructed, the MMPI is called a *criterion-referenced* test, which means that items on the test are referenced to one of the criterion groups—either normals or patients with a particular diagnosis. Some of the items appear quite sensible. "I feel like people are plotting against me," seems like the sort of item that someone with paranoia would call "true," while normals would tend to respond "false." Many items, however, are not so obvious. "I like to visit zoos," is not an MMPI-2 item, but it might have been if subjects of one diagnostic group responded to the item differently from the way other subjects did. What the item looks like is irrelevant. The only thing that matters is if subjects of different groups respond differently to the item. (I also should add that no one will, or can, make even a tentative diagnosis of a psychological disorder on the basis of a subject's response to just a few items. What matters is one's *pattern* of responding to a large number of items.)

The MMPI-2's "validity scales" are collections of items from among the 567 that assess the extent to which the subject is attending to the task at hand or is trying to present herself or himself in a particularly favorable light instead of responding truthfully to the items. For example, responding "true" to a number of statements such as "I always smile at everyone I meet" would lead an examiner to believe to doubt the validity of the subject's responses.

Although the MMPI is the most commonly used personality inventory, it certainly is not the only paper-and-pencil personality test. There are dozens of such tests. The *California Personality Inventory*, or *CPI*, was written using only normal subjects, not people who were diagnosed as having some psychological problem or disorder. The CPI assesses 18 personality traits, including self-acceptance, dominance, responsibility, and sociability. Because it is designed to measure a number of different traits, it can also be referred to as a multiphasic test.

Some multiphasic tests have been designed in conjunction with a particular personality theory. For example, Cattell's trait theory approach investigated a number of potential personality traits. These traits are what are measured with Cattell's *16 PF Questionnaire* (where PF stands for personality factors). Analyses of responses on this test (of statements to which the subject responds yes or no) results in a personality profile. That profile can then be compared with one gathered from a large norm group.

Finally, we should mention that some personality questionnaires or inventories are designed to measure just one trait and thus are not multiphasic. One example is a commonly used test called the *Taylor Manifest Anxiety Scale*. Taylor began with a very large pool of items, many of them from the MMPI, and asked psychologists to choose those items that they thought would best measure anxiety. The 50 items most commonly chosen as indicators of anxiety make up this test, which has gained wide acceptance as an indicator of anxiety.

BEFORE YOU GO ON

What does multiphasic mean?

How was the MMPI constructed?

What can paper-and-pencil tests tell us about personality?

Projective Techniques

A **projective technique** involves asking a subject to respond to ambiguous stimuli. The stimuli can be any number of things, as we shall see, and there are clearly no right or wrong answers. The procedure is reasonably unstructured and open-ended. The basic idea is that because there is, in fact, so little content in the stimulus presented, the subject will *project* some of his or her own self into the response. In many ways, projective techniques are more of an aid to interviewing than they are psychological tests (Korchin & Schuldberg, 1981).

Some projective techniques are very simple. The word association technique, introduced by Galton in 1879 and used in psychoanalysis, is a sort of projective technique (although not a test). "I will say a word, and I want you to say the first thing that pops into your head. Do not think about your response; just say the first thing that comes to mind." There certainly are no right answers in this type of procedure. The idea is that the psychologist can gain some insight, perhaps into the problems of a patient, by using this technique.

A similar technique is the *unfinished sentences* or *sentence completion* test. For example, a sentence is begun, "My greatest fear is. . . . " The subject is asked to complete the sentence. Although there are several published tests available (e.g., the *Rotter Incomplete Sentences Blank*), many clinicians prefer

projective technique *a personality assessment technique requiring a subject to respond to ambiguous stimuli, thus projecting his or her self into the responses*

Figure 10.6

A sample Rorschach-like inkblot. The subject is asked what the inkblot represents or what he or she sees in the inkblot.

Rorschach inkblot test *a projective technique in which the subject is asked to say what he or she sees in a series of inkblots*

Thematic Apperception Test (TAT) *a projective technique in which subjects are asked to tell a story about each of a set of ambiguous pictures*

to make up their own forms. There are no right or wrong responses, and interpreting responses is rather subjective, but a skilled examiner can use these procedures to gain new insights about a subject's personality.

Of all the projective techniques, none is as famous as the **Rorschach inkblot test**. This technique was introduced in 1921 by Hermann Rorschach, who believed that people with different personalities respond differently to inkblot patterns (see Figure 10.6). There are 10 cards in the test: 5 are black on white, 2 are red and gray, and 3 are multicolored. Subjects are asked to tell what they see in the cards or what the inkblot represents.

Scoring of Rorschach test responses has become quite controversial. Standard scoring procedures require attending to a number of factors: what the subject says (content), where the subject focuses attention (location), mention of detail versus global features, reacting to color or open spaces, and how many different responses there are per card. Many psychologists have questioned the efficiency of the Rorschach as a diagnostic instrument. Much of what it can tell an examiner may be gained directly. For example, Rorschach responses that include many references to death, sadness, and dying are probably indicative of a depressed subject. One has to wonder if inkblots are really needed to discover such depression. As a psychological test, the Rorschach seems neither very reliable nor valid, yet it remains a very popular instrument. It is used primarily as an aid to assessment and the development of subjective impressions.

A projective device we'll see again in Chapter 11 (in the context of achievement motivation, Topic 11A), is the **Thematic Apperception Test**, or **TAT**, devised by Henry Murray in 1938. This test is made up of a series of ambiguous pictures about which a subject is asked to tell a story. The subject is asked to describe what is going on, what led up to this situation, and what the outcome is likely to be.

The test is designed to provide a mechanism to discover the subjects' hidden needs, desires, and emotions, which will be projected into their stories. The test is called a *thematic* test because scoring depends largely on the interpretation of the themes of the stories that are told. Although some formal scoring schemes are available, scoring and interpretation are usually quite subjective and impressionistic. It is likely that the TAT remains popular for the same reason as the Rorschach: Psychologists are used to it, comfortable with the insights it provides, and willing to accept any source of additional information they can use to make a reasonable assessment or diagnosis.

BEFORE YOU GO ON

What is the essence of a projective technique, the Rorschach and TAT in particular?

In this topic, we have briefly outlined a number of different approaches to human personality and have examined a sample of specific theories. Which of these various approaches or theories is the right one? Which is best? These are clearly unanswerable questions. Each approach is qualitatively different from the others and emphasizes different aspects of personality. In its own separate way, each has a contribution to make. In its own separate way, each is "right" and the "best one."

We also have explored some of the techniques psychologists use in their efforts to measure or assess personality characteristics of the individual: behavioral observations, interviews, paper-and-pencil tests, and projective techniques. Although none of these, in itself, can provide a full picture of one's personality, each can contribute to our understanding of the complex fabric we call human personality.

One aspect of our "self"—our being, our personality—that often becomes central in the adjustments that we have to make to others and the world around us is our sexuality—our femaleness or our maleness. To discuss personality without addressing issues of sexuality and gender is to present an incomplete discussion. It is to these issues that we turn next.

What are the three levels of consciousness proposed by Freud?

Freud proposed that at any time we are only aware, or *conscious*, of a few things; with a little effort, some ideas or memories can be accessed from our *preconscious*, while others—those in our *unconscious* mind—may be accessed only with great difficulty. / *page 445*

According to Freud, what are the three structures of personality, and by what principle does each operate?

The three structures of personality according to Freud are the inborn, instinctive *id*, operating on the *pleasure principle* and seeking immediate gratification, the *ego*, or sense of self, which operates on the *reality principle*, mediating needs in the context of the real world; and the *superego*, or sense of morality or conscience, which operates on the *idealistic principle*, attempting to direct one to do what is right and proper. When aspects of personality are in conflict, anxiety may result. To fend off feelings of anxiety, the ego may unconsciously employ one of a number of *defense mechanisms*. / *page 447*

Briefly summarize the contributions of Adler, Jung, and Horney to the psychoanalytic approach to personality.

Adler, Jung, and Horney each parted with Freud on theoretical grounds, while remaining basically psychoanalytic in their approaches to personality. For Adler, social influences and inferiority complexes mattered much more than Freud's innate drives. Jung was less biological, more positive, and expanded on Freud's view of the unconscious mind, adding the notion of the collective unconscious. Horney also rejected the notion of instinctual impulses and discussed instead the notion of basic anxiety and how one reacts to it as the sculptor of one's personality. / *page 449*

Specify a contribution to the concept of personality made by Watson, Dollard and Miller, Skinner, and Bandura.

Many psychologists have argued that personality can be approached using basic learning principles and observable behavior. Watson emphasized focusing on behavior and abandoning mental concepts. Dollard and Miller attempted to explain personality development in terms of learning theory and habits. Skinner emphasized the notion of the consequences of one's behavior. Bandura stressed the role of observation and social learning in the formation of personality. / *page 451*

Briefly summarize the humanistic-phenomenological approach to personality as epitomized by Rogers and Maslow.

The theories of Rogers and Maslow are alike in many ways, emphasizing the integrity of the self and the power of personal growth and development. Both deny the negativity and biological bias of psychoanalytic theory and the environmental determinism of behaviorism. / *page 453*

What is a personality trait? What are the major traits that influence personality, according to Allport, Cattell, and Eysenck?

A personality trait is a characteristic and distinctive way in which one individual may differ from others. According to Allport, there are two kinds of traits: *common traits* and *personal dispositions*, the former found in virtually everyone, the latter unique just to some individuals. Cattell also feels that there are two kinds of traits: *surface traits*, which are readily observable, and *source traits*, from which surface traits develop. Eysenck believes that one's personality can be described somewhere among the intersections of three major dimensions: *extroversion-introversion*, *stability-instability*, and *psychoticism*. / *page 456*

What are the Big Five personality dimensions?

Recent research in personality trait theory suggests that from all the traits that have been proposed, five emerge most regularly, although there is as yet no agreement on what to call these dimensions. One position calls them (1) "Extroversion/Introversion," (2) "Agreeableness or Friendliness," (3) "Will or Conscientiousness," (4) "Stability/Instability," and (5) "Intelligence." / *page 457*

What are some of the strengths and weaknesses of each of the four approaches to personality that we have discussed?

The psychoanalytic approach is the most comprehensive and may be credited with focusing our attention on the importance of early childhood experience, biological drives, and sexuality. Unfortunately, many of its insights and ideas are scientifically untestable. Behavioral-learning approaches profit from their strict definitions and experimental bases, but lack comprehensiveness. They put what many feel is too much emphasis on the environment as the determiner of behavior. The humanistic-phenomenological approach is quite positive, emphasizing personal growth and development, but many of its concepts are poorly defined and many of its predictions are difficult to test. Trait approaches are not really theories, but are descriptions, and as such explain very little about personality. Although there may be a growing consensus, there is still no universally accepted vision of which traits are most important, how they develop, or how they are related. / page 459

Briefly summarize the debate concerning personality versus situational influences on behavior.

One of the key issues of interest among psychologists who study personality is the extent to which we can claim that there *are* any internal, individual traits that demonstrate consistency over time and over situations. One's personal characteristics, or traits, should be discernible at least within a range of different situations. The debate over the stability or consistency among personality variables begun in the late 1960s is essentially over. A point of view, called interactionism, has emerged that says that predicting how a person may or may not respond in a certain situation is determined by the interaction of identifiable, stable personality characteristics and that person's perception of the situation at hand. / page 461

What are the basic goals of personality assessment?

Personality assessment (including testing) is used to (1) make a clinical diagnosis about the presence and nature of a psychological disorder, (2) help build theories of personality based on which traits are important and how they are interrelated, and (3) predict what someone may do in the future. / page 462

How are behavioral observations used to assess personality?

Conclusions about an individual's personality can be inferred from the observation of that individual's behaviors. Behaviors should be observed in a large number of settings. Observations should be as objective as possible and may involve the use of behavioral rating scales to check reliability. / page 463

Cite one advantage and one disadvantage of the interview as a technique of personality assessment.

The major advantage of the interview is its flexibility, allowing the interviewer to pursue avenues of interest and abandon lines of questioning that are not informative. Unfortunately, there is little support for the position that interviewing is a valid technique for many purposes. / page 465

What does multiphasic mean? How was the MMPI constructed? What can paper-and-pencil tests tell us about personality?

Multiphasic instruments attempt to measure a number of characteristics or traits with the same set of items. The MMPI was designed (in the early 1940s and revised, as the MMPI-2, in 1989) as an aid to psychological diagnosis. The test includes only those items that discriminate between subjects of different diagnostic categories (including "normal"). The test also includes items to assess the extent to which the subject is doing a thorough and honest job of answering the 567 true-false questions. Paper-and-pencil tests can serve as useful screening devices to indicate which traits or patterns of traits are likely to be found within a given individual. / page 467

What is the essence of a projective technique, the Rorschach and TAT in particular?

With a projective technique, the assumption is that in responding to an ambiguous stimulus (describing what is indicated in a series of inkblots with the Rorschach, or telling short stories about a set of pictures with the TAT), a subject will *project* conscious or unconscious aspects of him- or herself into his or her responses. / page 469

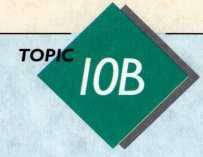

Human Sexuality and Gender

Why We Care: A Topic Preview

You may have wondered why I've included this topic on human sexuality and gender in a chapter on personality. The truth is, some of my colleagues have questioned this decision also. Many of the issues introduced in this topic could have been placed elsewhere. We could have expanded our coverage of sex drives in the chapter on motivation. Many gender-related issues could have been included in the chapter on social psychology. Sexual dysfunctions and sexually transmitted diseases could have been covered in the context of disorders. There are many other possibilities. My rationale is that who we are, what we feel, do, or think—our very personality—is often influenced (if not determined) by our maleness or femaleness, our masculinity or femininity. Whether we are male or female—our sex—and the extent to which we think of ourselves as male or female—our gender—has an impact on virtually every decision we make as adults. This is why we care, and it is one reason you find this topic here.

This topic is divided into two sections, one dealing with sexuality, the other with gender. The differences, if any, between one's sex and one's gender are often subtle. Many writers and psychologists use the terms interchangeably. We'll try to adhere to the following differentiation. When we talk about sex, we will be referring to matters genetic, hormonal, or anatomical. That is, we will take sex to be essentially a biological term. We will use the term gender when we add psychological or social influences to one's basic biology. One researcher in human sexuality refers to gender as "the state of being male or female" (Hyde, 1986, p. 3). In a way then, gender refers to the extent to which an individual feels, behaves, and/or thinks like a male or female (our ABC—affect, behavior, and cognition—again). Thus, terms like masculine and feminine refer to one's gender.

One more point for you to consider: In this topic, we will consider sex and gender to be what social psychologist Kay Deaux (1984) calls "subject variables." This approach considers sex and gender as consistent, stable aspects of one's personality, which is why I have chosen to include this topic in our chapter on personality.

We'll begin by outlining some of the biological determinants of sex. We'll discuss the nature of the human sexual response. Then we'll review what is known about homosexuality, discuss sexual dysfunctions (problems with sexual behaviors), and explore sexually transmitted diseases. Finally, we'll turn our attention to gender identity and gender roles, ending the topic with a brief review of the few ways in which men and women may differ psychologically.

HUMAN SEXUALITY

Our story of human sexuality begins with a brief look at where our sexuality comes from. How is it that some of us are biologically male and some are biologically female? This question, which seems transparently easy, is not easily answered.

The Biological Bases of Human Sexuality

Whether we are biologically male or female depends on the delicate interaction of a number of different factors. Among the most important are genetic and hormonal processes. For the most part, our sex is inherited, but hormones influence the expression of our genetically determined sexuality, and some of the most important hormonal influences occur well before we're born. Let's start with genetics.

Genetic Bases. When a male's sperm cell unites with a female's ovum to form a single-celled zygote, the sex of the offspring has been established. That newly formed cell holds in its nucleus 23 pairs of chromosomes. Just one of those pairs, usually counted as the twenty-third pair, will determine the sex of the person-to-be.

The chromosomes that determine a person's sex are called the **X** and **Y chromosomes**. Neither can do much by itself; these chromosomes have their effect by working in pairs. Being genetically female results from receiving an X chromosome from each parent, forming an XX pair. Being male is determined by having one X chromosome and one Y chromosome, or an XY pair.

Think about that for a minute. Cells in a female's body have, in their nuclei, a pair of X chromosomes. That means that a female's sex cells, or ova, must contain one X chromosome, since a female has no Y chromosomes. Cells in a male's body, on the other hand, contain both X and Y chromosomes, so half of a male's sex cells, or sperm, will contain X chromosomes, and half will contain Y chromosomes. Because the female always contributes an X chromosome, and because the male contributes either an X or a Y, we can say that, genetically, the sex of a child is determined by the father—or at least by the father's chromosomes. As it happens, this observation has, as yet, no practical application.

This rather straightforward chain of events for genetic sex holds true when everything works smoothly. Occasionally, however, chromosomal transfer from female and male to zygote does not go smoothly, resulting in an abnormal pattern of sex chromosomes. One such pattern is referred to as *Klinefelter's syndrome*. In this condition, a Y chromosome-bearing sperm unites with an ovum that carries two X chromosomes, and we have an individual whose sex chromosomes are XXY. The result of this genetic "error" is a person with male genitals, but usually of much smaller size than normal. Perhaps because of the resulting reduction in male sex hormone production, there often is reduced interest in sexual activity. Klinefelter's syndrome males are usually sterile. In adolescence and adulthood, they often develop breasts and may be quite feminine in appearance. Treatment with male sex hormones during adolescence often can offset these side effects.

X and Y chromosomes *the chromosomes that determine one's genetic sex; XX for females, XY for males*

Another, much less common genetic abnormality occurs when one X chromosome unites with two Y chromosomes, yielding an individual with an XYY pattern. Here, the individual will be a male, with normal-appearing sex organs and characteristics. These men are usually tall and of below-average intelligence. For nearly 20 years (in the 1960s and 1970s), it was believed that there might be a causal relationship between the XYY chromosome pattern and crime, particularly violent crime. This hypothesis arose when it was discovered that prison inmates were found to have this genetic abnormality at a rate significantly higher than is found in the general population (Gardner & Neu, 1972). Subsequent research has indicated that if such a relationship does exist, it is a very weak one.

So, the first step to becoming a male is to inherit an XY chromosome combination, and the first step to becoming a female is to inherit an XX chromosome combination, but the story does not end here. Still at the level of our biological sexuality, we must next consider the role of hormones in the shaping of one's sex.

BEFORE YOU GO ON

How is one's sex genetically determined?

Hormonal Bases. In biological terms, human sexuality may be primarily determined by the chromosomes inherited at conception, but the expression of that sexuality requires the action of sex hormones. In fact, for about six or seven weeks after conception, there is *no differentiation* between male and female zygotes. That is, the only way to determine if the zygote is male or female is to examine the sex chromosomes, looking for the XX female pairing or the XY male pairing. At about 7 weeks, physical differentiation of the **gonads**, or sex glands, begins. Which sex glands develop is controlled by the presence of the Y chromosome. When the Y chromosome is present, the **testes**, or male sex glands, develop. When the Y chromosome is not present, the **ovaries**, or female sex glands, develop (Bernstein, 1981; Money, 1987). (See Figure 10.7.)

Once the sex glands begin to develop, they do what they are designed to do: secrete their own variety of sex hormone. In fact, both the ovaries and the testes produce and secrete a number of hormones (collectively, they are called *steroids*). The most important hormones produced by the testes are the **androgens**, and the most important of these is **testosterone**. The most important hormones produced by the ovaries are the **estrogens** (there are more than one) and **progesterone**. Put most simply, the androgens direct the development of male reproductive organs: the penis, testes, and scrotum. The estrogens direct the development of female reproductive organs: the vagina, uterus, and ovaries. But that's put most simply, and the issue is far from simple.

One complication is that both male and female sex hormones are produced by both male and female sex glands. Yes, that's right; even the male testes produce the female estrogens, and the female ovaries produce the

gonads *the sex glands:* **testes** *in males,* **ovaries** *in females*

androgens *the male sex hormones (steroids) produced by the testes*

testosterone *the most important of the male androgens, or sex hormones*

estrogens *the female sex hormones (steroids) produced by the ovaries*

progesterone *one of the most important of the female estrogens, or sex hormones*

Figure 10.7

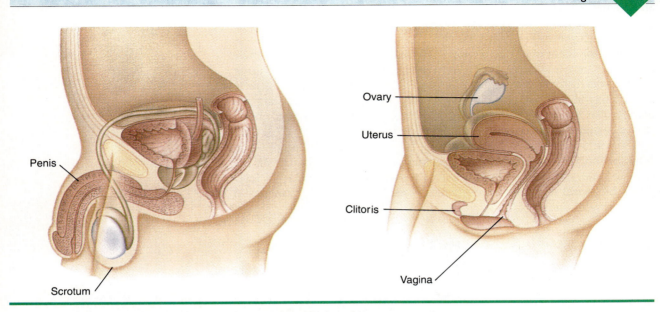

Male and female anatomy.

male androgens. The critical difference, of course, is the *relative amount* of each that is produced. It turns out that the development of the genitals is mostly controlled by the androgens in this way: If sufficient androgen levels are reached, the genitals will be those of a male. If there are insufficient androgen levels, the genitals will be those of a female. And remember, all of this differentiation of genitals goes on prenatally—before birth. (A colleague suggests that one way to express this is to say that we are all basically female, and it takes the addition of androgens to produce male development in some of us.) As you might imagine, occasionally there are "errors." Individuals who are genetically female (XX chromosome pair) and are exposed to well above average amounts of male androgens during this phase of differentiation may show physical signs of the external genitals of a male (perhaps a small penis and/or scrotum) as well as those of a female.

Another complication is that the sex hormones are not produced only in the sex glands. Both estrogens and androgens are produced in the adrenal glands as well. Furthermore, the release of sex hormones is monitored and controlled by complex interactions of the pituitary gland and the hypothalamus.

Once the sex glands and their hormones have set the course of development under way, sex hormone production stabilizes at rather low levels through infancy and childhood. Then, in a huge surge of hormonal activity, the hypothalamus, adrenal glands, and gonads—all working together—bring about that developmental period we call *puberty*. We have defined puberty as the stage of development during which one becomes capable of sexual reproduction, and in Topic 9B we examined some of the psychological "fallout" of this stage of development. Puberty marks a reawakening of the hormonal basis of sexuality.

Now that we have a general idea of why a person is biologically male or female, we can turn our attention to behavior. As it happens, we now have a fairly detailed picture of the specific reactions involved in the human sexual response.

BEFORE YOU GO ON

Summarize the role of hormones in the determination of one's sex.

The Human Sexual Response

Much of what we know about human sexual behaviors we have learned through survey research. As you might imagine, however, obtaining honest and accurate information about intimate sexual behaviors has been notoriously difficult. In 1966, William Masters and Virginia Johnson published *Human Sexual Response*, a landmark book that demonstrated the value of the direct observation of sexual behaviors in a controlled laboratory setting. Masters began making his observations of sexual behaviors in 1954, choosing female prostitutes as his subjects. His belief at the time was that he would be unable to get a sufficient number of volunteers to act as subjects. After all, he wanted people to engage in a wide range of sexual behaviors while being observed by others and while hooked up to a variety of instruments designed to measure their physiological reactions as they engaged in those sexual behaviors.

For a number of reasons, Masters's sample of prostitutes did not provide him with the quality of data he was looking for. Fortunately, he was quite wrong about the willingness of people to volunteer for his studies of sexual responses. As word spread throughout the Washington University (St. Louis) community that subjects were needed for sex research, more than 1273 persons volunteered. From these, 382 women and 312 men were chosen for the studies reported in *Human Sexual Response*. These studies allow us to fashion an accurate picture of the physiological reactions that occur during sexual behaviors. To be sure, the Masters and Johnson sample was not a random one, but there is no evidence, as yet, that the results from their sample differ in any significant way from those that would have been found with a different sample. The Masters and Johnson model of the human sexual response is not the only one available (e.g., Kaplan, 1979; Zilbergeld & Evans, 1980), but it is by far the most widely known and accepted. In this section, we'll review the four stages of the Masters and Johnson model of the human sexual response.

Virginia Johnson and William Masters.

Phase 1: Excitement. The excitement stage of the sexual response is one of arousal, often in anticipation of having a sexual experience. In both sexes there is increased muscle tension and increased blood flow in the genital area. The most noticeable effects include an erection of the penis and an elevation of the scrotum in males and a lubrication of the vagina and an erection of the nipples in females. In both males and females, there is an increase in heart rate and blood pressure, and a "flush" or blotchy reddening (or darkening) of the skin, usually on the abdomen and chest.

erogenous zones *areas of the body that, when stroked, lead to sexual arousal*

The excitement phase may last from a few minutes to several hours, depending on the individual and the situation. What initiates this stage; what stimulates sexual arousal? Sexual arousal normally occurs through some variety or combination of sensory experiences. Sexually arousing sensory experiences vary considerably from person to person, supporting the position that learning and experience are very relevant. What one person finds exciting and arousing someone else may find boring or even repulsive. Of all the senses, touch is the one most commonly associated with sexual arousal. Individuals do indeed have a number of **erogenous zones**, or areas of their bodies which, when they are stroked or touched, lead to sexual arousal. These areas usually include the genitals, the breasts (for both sexes, but more commonly in women), the inner surface of the thighs, the ears (particularly the lobes), and the mouth region.

Arousal may be instigated visually by the viewing of erotic materials or even at the sight of a nude sex partner. It used to be thought that sexual arousal brought about by viewing sexual or erotic materials was much more common in men than in women (e.g., Kinsey et al., 1948, 1953). In fact, sexual arousal brought about in this way is just as common in women as in men, although women are less likely to report verbally (admit to) being sexually aroused by looking at erotic stimuli (Kelley, 1985).

The sense of smell, through the detection of pheromones, is very important in stimulating the sexual responsiveness of nonhumans (see Topic 3B). There is evidence that humans produce pheromonelike chemicals also, although their relationship to sexual arousal is still not firmly established. Before we leave our discussion of sexual arousal to consider the next stage in the human sexual response, I should note that there is no evidence for the existence of a human **aphrodisiac**. An aphrodisiac is a substance that, when ingested, increases one's sexual arousal. For generations, people of many different cultures have believed in the power of certain concoctions (from alcohol to "Spanish fly," to amphetamines and marijuana, to oysters and a powder made from rhinoceros tusks) to stimulate sexual arousal. In fact, none of these work as intended, and most (alcohol in particular) have precisely the opposite effect.

aphrodisiac *a substance that, when drunk or eaten, increases sexual arousal; none are known to exist*

Phase 2: Plateau. It is rather difficult to determine just when the plateau phase begins. The reactions involved in this phase carry the processes begun in the excitement phase to the brink of orgasm. In the male, the erection of the penis becomes complete; the testes enlarge and rise up very close to the body; the penis reddens. In the female, the opening to the vagina reddens; the outer third of the vagina, gorged with blood, enlarges; the clitoris elevates and shortens. In both men and women, blood pressure and heart rate increase, breathing becomes more shallow and rapid, and skin flushing becomes more pronounced. This stage seldom lasts very long, generally a few minutes, although with practice this stage can be extended. Tension has now built to its maximum; the body is now prepared for orgasm.

Phase 3: Orgasm. The orgasm stage of sexual behavior is by far the shortest, lasting only a matter of seconds. Once a male has reached the plateau stage, orgasm is almost sure to follow. In the male, orgasm actually is comprised of two separate substages: "coming," in which one senses, through a series of contractions, that ejaculation is about to happen, and ejaculation itself, in which semen is forced out through the penis. Orgasm in the female, which need not necessarily follow from the plateau stage, also involves a series of short, intense contractions in the genital area.

The experience of orgasm is apparently very much the same (and for most, highly pleasurable) for both men and women. Describing the experience of orgasm, however, seems to be quite difficult for most women. I also should mention that Masters and Johnson have found female orgasms to be of only one type. There is a common belief (which derives from the writings of Freud) that women experience either clitoral or vaginal orgasms, depending on which of these two structures is more stimulated.

Phase 4: Resolution. As its name suggests, in the resolution phase of sexual behavior, the body returns to its unaroused state. If orgasm has been reached, this stage begins immediately. If orgasm has not been reached, stimulation may repeat the entire process. In the resolution phase, we see a major difference between males and females. Once a male has experienced orgasm he enters a **refractory period** during which arousal, erection, and another orgasm are impossible. This period may last for a few minutes, hours, or even days, depending on the person. The length of one's refractory period generally increases with age. Women, on the other hand, do not experience a refractory period and thus may experience multiple orgasms if appropriately stimulated.

The different physiological changes that develop during sexual activity take varying amounts of time to resolve and return to normal. In both males and females, heart rate and blood pressure return to normal very quickly. The coloration of the genital area and skin flushing usually disappear in minutes. The oversupply of blood to the genital region takes a bit longer to return to normal.

Masters and Johnson found these four phases of sexual response in their subjects with such frequency and consistency that they were willing to claim them to be "standard" reactions during sexual behavior. Psychologists are always pleased to find such regularities in behavior of any kind. Years of research on the human sexual response have convinced Masters and Johnson that there are enormous individual differences in the intensity to which each or any of these four phases is felt or experienced. They acknowledge that what best stimulates the excitement phase and thus begins the chain of events we call the human sexual response also varies considerably from one individual to another. But what is most impressive is that, in spite of these individual differences, the basic pattern of human sexual responsiveness is always the same.

refractory period *during the process of the human sexual response, the period following orgasm during which arousal in the male is not possible*

BEFORE YOU GO ON

Briefly describe the changes that occur during the excitement, plateau, orgasm, and resolution phases of the human sexual response.

Homosexuality

The complexities of human sexual responsiveness and behaviors are no more apparent than when we consider persons who are homosexuals. **Homosexuals** are individuals who are sexually attracted to and sexually aroused by members of their own sex, as opposed to heterosexuals, who seek outlets for their sexual drives among members of the opposite sex. Psychologists have argued that homosexuality should be referred to as an orientation (or status), *not* as a matter of sexual preference. "*Sexual preference* is a moral and political term. Conceptually it implies voluntary choice. . . . The concept of voluntary choice is as much in error here as in its application to handedness or to native language. You do not choose your native language, even though you are born without it" (Money, 1987, p. 385).

Psychologists agree that homosexuality and heterosexuality are not mutually exclusive categories, but rather endpoints of a dimension of sexual orientations, and that many combinations are possible. Alfred Kinsey and his colleagues (1948, 1953) first brought the prevalence of homosexuality to the attention of the general public. Kinsey devised a seven-point scale (0 to 6) of sexual orientation with those who are exclusively heterosexual at one end and persons who are exclusively homosexual at the other extreme (see Figure 10.8). Kinsey found that about half of the males who responded to his surveys fell somewhere *between* these two endpoints. Even though homosexuality is now more openly discussed than it was in the 1940s and 1950s (more "out of the closet"), it is still difficult to get accurate estimates of the numbers of persons who are exclusively or predominantly homosexual. Conservative estimates suggest that about 2 percent of North American males are exclusively homosexual in their sexual orientation and that 8 to 10 percent have had more than just an occasional homosexual encounter. Comparable figures indicate that female homosexuality is approximately half as prevalent as male homosexuality. These estimates are much higher in some settings, such as prisons, leading to what is called deprivational homosexuality. In these cases, persons who engage in homosexual behaviors almost always return to heterosexuality when the deprivation situation changes.

In most ways, there is little difference between homosexuals and heterosexuals, including the pattern of their sexual responsiveness. Most homosexuals have experienced heterosexual sex. They simply find same-sex relationships more satisfying. In fact, homosexual couples are often more at ease and comfortable with their sexual relationship than most heterosexual couples (Masters & Johnson, 1979). Contrary to popular opinion, most homosexuals are indistinguishable from heterosexuals in their appearance and mannerisms.

As yet, we have no generally accepted theory of the causes of homosexuality. (Some homosexuals argue that we have no acceptable theory to explain heterosexuality either.) What we do know is that the matter is not a simple one and probably involves some interaction of genetic, hormonal, and environmental factors (Money, 1987). There are now a number of hypotheses along each of these lines. For example, there is evidence that homosexuality tends to "run in families," but the evidence for a direct genetic cause of homosexuality is very weak (Diamond & Karlen, 1980).

homosexuals *persons who are sexually attracted to and aroused by members of their own sex*

Though homosexuals are able to be more open about their sexual orientation, homosexuality is still a controversial issue.

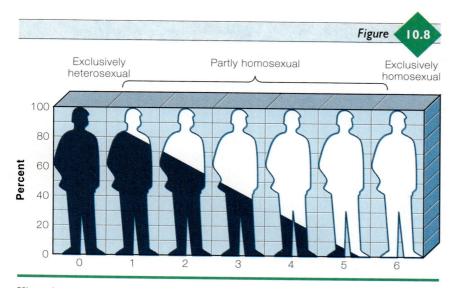

Figure 10.8

Kinsey's seven-point scale of sexual orientation.

Likewise, there is scant evidence of any significant differences in the hormone levels of heterosexuals and homosexuals at adulthood. Providing homosexual males and females with extra amounts of sex hormones may increase overall sex drive and the incidence of sexual behaviors, but it seems to have virtually no effect on sexual orientation. A hypothesis with more research support suggests that *prenatal* hormonal imbalances may affect one's sexual orientation in adulthood (Money, 1987). The claim of this hypothesis is that embryos (genetically male or female) exposed to above-average concentrations of female hormones will develop into adults attracted to persons having masculine characteristics, and vice versa (Ellis & Ames, 1987).

Psychologists remain unwilling to totally disregard hypotheses that emphasize the importance of environmental influences. It is clear, however, that sexual orientation cannot be attributed to any one simple early childhood experience. Most homosexuals themselves claim that their parents had little influence on their adult sexual orientation (Bell et al., 1981). On the other hand, one's sexual orientation does seem to be established before adolescence (Bell et al., 1981). The early family life of homosexuals, when compared to that of heterosexuals, is found to be more "troubled": more one-parent families (Wolff, 1971), more domination of an opposite-sex parent (Saghir & Robins, 1973), more marital problems (Hoffman, 1977), and so on. Some research indicates that early signs of effeminate behavior in boys may predict homosexuality. In particular, an aversion to boys' sports and games, and cross-dressing by boys younger than 10 years old were seen as part of a sequence leading to male homosexuality (Zuger, 1988).

Although we are not yet able to discount them totally, environmental causes of sexual orientation seem to be mostly of theoretical interest, with little research evidence to support them. One major problem with much of our current data on the early experiences of homosexuals is that it most often comes from persons who are in therapy and are distressed with their sexual orientation. We have considerably less data about homosexuals who are comfortable with their sexuality (the clear majority). A reasonable position at the moment would be to hypothesize that genetic and hormonal predispositions may interact with subtle environmental influences in complex ways to form one's adult sexual orientation.

BEFORE YOU GO ON

What is homosexuality?

What causes homosexuality?

Sexual Dysfunctions

Sexual drives and behaviors, which seem so natural and virtually automatic in lower species, are often the source of considerable distress for humans. **Sexual dysfunction** is the name given to any chronic (long-term) problem, disturbance, or inadequacy in sexual functioning. One of the reasons sexual dysfunctions are found almost exclusively in humans is that in most cases, their basic cause is psychological, not physical.

Sexual dysfunctions are much more common than most people believe. As you can imagine, it is difficult to determine the number of persons who experience sexual dysfunctions. Part of the problem is the commonly held belief that everyone else's sex life is perfect and that other couples engage in sexual activities almost constantly. People generally don't like to talk about their sex life if they think they are having problems. Once someone openly admits to having sexual problems, treatment in some form of sex therapy is usually quite successful. Masters and Johnson (1970, 1979) claim a success rate of more than 80 percent, but that seems to hold only for some of the more easily treated dysfunctions (Zilbergeld & Evans, 1980). Those physicians and therapists who ask their patients about sexual problems report many more cases than do those who wait for patients to volunteer such information (Pauly & Goldstein, 1970). In terms of prevalence, most experts agree that about 50 percent of all married couples experience some sexual dysfunction (Masters & Johnson, 1970; McCarthy et al., 1975). That's a lot of people; and when you add in those persons with sexual problems who happen not to be married, the number is even more impressive. In this section, we'll briefly review six of the most commonly reported sexual dysfunctions, three that occur in males and three that occur in females.

Sexual Dysfunctions in Males. *Erectile dysfunction* is the inability to attain or maintain an erection long enough to experience intercourse. It is the preferred term for what is often called impotence. This is the most commonly reported dysfunction among men seeking treatment. Nearly half of all sexually mature men have at some time experienced at least one episode of erectile dysfunction. The dysfunction can be found in males of any age (Kaplan, 1974, 1975). By far, most cases of this dysfunction are

sexual dysfunction *any of a number of chronic difficulties or problems with sexual functioning; usually caused by psychological factors*

classified as secondary, implying that there has been some success at achieving an erection in the past (Masters & Johnson, 1970). Men who have never had an erection are said to have primary erectile dysfunction. An occasional failure, perhaps due to fatigue or alcohol, does not qualify as a dysfunction. Psychological reactions to erectile dysfunction can be severe. Self-esteem is often involved. Embarrassment, depression, fear of future failures, and guilt often accompany this dysfunction. Unfortunately, when left untreated, these very reactions almost ensure that achieving an erection will become less likely in the future.

The other two major dysfunctions of male sexual responsiveness involve the timing of ejaculation during vaginal intercourse (or coitus). *Premature ejaculation* is difficult to define. The implication, of course, is that the male ejaculates too soon. But what determines what is too soon? Is it the time elapsed after penetration? Does prematurity relate to the number of pelvic thrusts or to the timing of the female's orgasm? The most generally accepted definitions have to do with the male's voluntary control over ejaculation, rather than with time per se (Kaplan, 1974). In most cases, prematurity of ejaculation is self-defined by the individual (or his partner) as a condition in which ejaculation chronically occurs too early to provide satisfaction. As is the case with erectile dysfunction, premature ejaculation rarely has a physical basis, and it, in turn, can result in considerable psychological distress. Also, like the failure to attain an erection, the more one worries about ejaculating too soon, the more likely it is to occur.

A related but much less common ejaculatory problem is *retarded ejaculation*. Here the male has difficulty ejaculating at all during coitus, although he may have little difficulty doing so while masturbating or when he is with a new sex partner. When this dysfunction does occur, we tend to find frustration and anxiety on the part of the male and a sense of rejection in his partner. As with all the sexual dysfunctions, retarded ejaculation occurs to varying degrees, with a partial failure to ejaculate more common than total ejaculation failure.

Sexual Dysfunctions in Females. *Female sexual unresponsiveness* is the term that psychiatrist Helen Kaplan (1974, 1975) uses to describe what is commonly referred to by the nontechnical term *frigidity*. It is a condition in which a woman gains little or no pleasure from sexual encounters. In severe forms, an actual fear or loathing of sexual activities may develop. This dysfunction usually is self-diagnosed, because what may be "acceptably responsive," or pleasurable, clearly varies from person to person. What matters most is the extent to which a woman and her partner feel satisfied with the woman's ability to become sexually aroused. As we saw to be true for sexual dysfunctions in males, the causes of female sexual unresponsiveness are almost always psychological, often involving feelings of shame and guilt, accompanied by a belief that sex is somehow "dirty." The dysfunction itself can then cause other related psychological problems such as lack of self-esteem, embarrassment, and depression.

Orgasmic dysfunction is the inability to experience an orgasm. (Again, this is often a matter of degree; in many cases there may be an occasional orgasm, although perhaps not as forceful or timely as may be desired.) This sexual dysfunction is most often mentioned by women seeking therapy for sexual problems. Part of the problem may be the mystique associated with orgasm attained through coitus. Many women who experience orgasm through masturbation, for example, and seldom experience orgasm during intercourse come to believe that they are somehow sexually inadequate, maladjusted, or a disappointment to their sex partners. Sex partners may experience guilt if orgasm is not reached. Although most women (nearly 90 percent) *can* and *do* experience orgasm through one means or another, perhaps fewer than half do so with only the stimulation from vaginal intercourse (Kaplan, 1974; Masters & Johnson, 1970; Wilcox & Hager, 1980).

Vaginismus is the powerful, spasmotic, and occasionally painful contraction of the muscles surrounding the opening to the vagina. In some cases, the contractions are severe enough to prohibit the penis from entering the vagina. This is a relatively rare dysfunction, accounting for fewer than 10 percent of the cases treated by Masters and Johnson. Hypotheses about why women devleop vaginismus usually refer to a reflexlike reaction of the woman against pain—either the anticipated pain of coitus not yet achieved or pain experienced in the past.

There are other difficulties associated with human sexual behaviors, to be sure. This list includes only those most commonly encountered by sex therapists and psychologists. The incidence of sexual dysfunctions is quite high. Many adults will suffer the distress caused by one or more of these dysfunctions during most of their sexually active years. Most sexual dysfunctions are psychological in their basic nature and are amenable to treatment and therapy where the prognosis (likely outcome) is good. We now turn to problems that are clearly more physical or medical in their nature, but which carry with them considerable psychological impact: the sexually transmitted diseases.

BEFORE YOU GO ON

List and briefly describe six sexual dysfunctions.

Sexually Transmitted Diseases

sexually transmitted diseases (STDs) *contagious diseases that are usually transmitted through sexual contact*

Sexually transmitted diseases (STDs) are contagious diseases that are usually, although not exclusively, transmitted through sexual contact. *Sexually transmitted diseases* is a label that has all but replaced the term venereal disease, or VD. In this section, we'll briefly describe a few of the most common STDs. Even though STDs are mainly a medical problem, we've chosen to include them in this topic for two reasons: (1) Sexually transmitted diseases, and the fear of them, often have a profound influence on sexual behaviors, and (2) persons with STDs often suffer as many psychological consequences as medical ones. STDs affect millions of individuals each year, and for each person we know of with an STD, there may be two to five others with the disease, but in a stage that is nonsymptomatic, so the disease is not yet diagnosed.

chlamydia *a very common STD; a bacterial infection of the genital area*

Chlamydia is one of the most common of the STDs in North America. It is usually diagnosed in sexually active persons younger than 35 years old. Its incidence is soaring. Approximately 4 million Americans are stricken, and about 100,000 women become sterile because of the infection in one year. Chlamydia is caused by a bacterial infection (*Chlamydia trachomatis*). Symptoms include burning urination in men and women. Men may experience a penile discharge; women may experience a disruption in their menstrual cycle. Left untreated in women, chlamydia may lead to pelvic inflammatory disease (PID), which, in turn, may cause infertility. When diagnosed (and the disease does *not* show up on routine Pap smear tests), treatment with an antibiotic (mostly erythromycin) usually is effective within one week.

Gonorrhea is also a disease of the young and the sexually active. Of the more than 1.8 million cases that will be diagnosed this year, most will be men between the ages of 20 and 24. It, too, is a bacterial infection that affects the moist tissue areas around the genitals (or any other opening to the body that is used sexually). The bacteria that produce the symptoms of gonorrhea can live for only a few seconds outside of the human body, so the likelihood of contracting the disease from toilet seats, eating utensils, towels, or drinking fountains is very slim.

In many cases, one may be infected with the gonorrhea bacteria and not even know it. This is particularly true for women, most of whom remain relatively free of symptoms. When symptoms do develop, they are much like those experienced with chlamydia: frequent, painful urination; vaginal discharges; and a reddening of the genital area. In men, there is a thin milky discharge from the penis and painful, frequent urination. Left untreated, complications can develop in both males and females. Fortunately, treatment for gonorrhea—penicillin, or tetracycline for those allergic to penicillin—is simple and usually successful.

Syphilis is an STD with a very long and ignoble history. Syphilis is a disease caused by a little bacterium called a spirochete. If left untreated, the disease may run its course through four known stages, from a relatively simple and painless sore, all the way to the infection of other, nonsexual organs, which may lead even to death. As many as 25 percent of those infected by the spirochete bacterium may ultimately die as a result. Just 10 years ago, it was believed that syphilis was becoming a disease of the past. Then, in the fall of 1990, the Centers for Disease Control (CDC) in Atlanta released figures that since 1985, the number of syphilis cases had skyrocketed—rates were up 60 percent (132 percent among blacks) to levels not seen since 1949. Nearly 85,000 new cases can be expected this year. Treatment is quite simple, once diagnosis has been confirmed. Penicillin (or tetracycline) is used, and the prognosis is related to length of infection. As is the case for so many diseases, the sooner treatment begins, the better the prognosis.

Genital herpes (herpes type II) is a skin disease that affects the genital area, producing small sores and blisters. It is not caused by bacteria, but by a virus. Herpes type 1 is a very common viral infection of the skin that almost always occurs above the waist—in the form of cold sores or fever blisters, for example. It is the herpes II virus that infects the genital area and is the true STD. This virus was virtually unknown until the mid-1960s. Now, genital herpes is one of the most common STDs. Some estimates place incidence rates as high as 40 million Americans, with 500,000 new cases diagnosed each year. Herpes has no cure, although some medications can reduce the occasionally painful symptoms of genital herpes. A

gonorrhea *an STD caused by a bacterial infection of moist tissues in the genital area*

syphilis *an STD caused by a bacterial infection, which may pass through four stages, ultimately resulting in death*

genital herpes (herpes type II) *the most common STD; a skin infection in the form of a rash or blisters in the genital area*

acquired immune deficiency syndrome (AIDS) *a deadly disease caused by a virus (the HIV) that destroys the body's natural immune system, and which can be transmitted by sexual behaviors*

person with genital herpes is most infectious when the sores and blisters are active and erupting. There may be long periods during which an infected person remains symptom free, only to have the reddening and sores recur. It also seems that levels of stress in one's life are related to the onset of active herpes symptoms (VanderPlate, Aral, & Magder, 1988.) There are no known life-threatening complications of this disease in males, but genital herpes in females does increase the risk of contracting cervical cancer. Another complication may occur when pregnant women contract genital herpes. The herpes virus may be passed along during childbirth, which can cause considerable damage, even death, to the newborn.

No STD has attracted so much public attention as **acquired immune deficiency syndrome**, or **AIDS**. AIDS was virtually unknown in the United States before 1981. Just 10 years later, over 161,000 cases of the disease and more than 100,000 deaths in the United States had been reported by the Centers for Disease Control. Of the 100,000 deaths, 31,000 were in 1990 alone, leading the chief of the AIDS surveillance branch of the Centers for Disease Control, Dr. Ruth Berkelman, to state unequivocally, "The epidemic is here. We see from these numbers alone that AIDS has already taken an incredibly heavy toll, and there's no letup in sight." Recently, AIDS has risen to be among the most common (fifth) killers of women. In 1982, 18 women died of AIDS; in 1988, 1430 died of the disease. Globally, estimates of the World Health Organization (WHO) suggest that nearly 20 million men and women will be infected by the year 2000. Just what is AIDS?

AIDS is caused by a virus called the *human immunodeficiency virus*, or HIV (of which a new strain, the HIV-B, was discovered in early 1988). The HIV almost always enters the body through sexual contact or through the use of contaminated needles in intravenous (IV) drug use. In infected individuals, concentrations of the virus are highest in the blood and semen. Once infected, a person may experience few symptoms other than those usually associated with a common cold. Then the person enters what is called a carrier state. He or she is infected with the virus and may pass it on to others, but remains free of any noticeable symptoms. What is not clear is just how many persons infected with the HIV will develop the full-blown symptoms of AIDS. Of those with a diagnosis of AIDS (not just the presence of the HIV), virtually all will die within four years.

The HIV directly attacks the body's immune system—the system that naturally fights off infections. With a weakened or nonfunctioning immune system, a person with AIDS does not have the resources to defend against other infections that normally would not be life-threatening. In other words, patients don't die from AIDS directly, but from other diseases or opportunistic infections (often cancer or pneumonia) against which the body cannot defend itself.

AIDS is *not* a highly contagious STD—certainly not when compared to diseases such as chlamydia, gonorrhea, or herpes. It cannot be transmitted by casual contact; there has to be an interchange of bodily fluids—blood or semen. Early in the 1980s, it was believed that AIDS was restricted to homosexual males and intravenous drug users. This is clearly not the case. That the disease first appeared and spread through the gay male population is, as much as anything else, an accident of history. Intercourse, particularly anal intercourse, commonly leads to the transmission of the HIV, and whether or not both sex partners are male seems to matter little.

Whereas other sexually transmitted diseases may cause discomfort and/or pain, AIDS can be fatal. There is no vaccine to prevent it. There is no cure for AIDS, and it is unlikely that one will be discovered soon. At the moment, the only reasonable way to protect against AIDS is through the monitoring of behavior. Totally abstaining from sexual activity, not sharing needles with IV drug users, and donating your own blood prior to surgery would minimize personal risk.

On the assumption that many adolescents and adults won't abstain from sex altogether, many experts counsel "safe" sex; but there is disagreement on just what safe sex *is*. In general, the advice seems sensible. The fewer sexual contacts one has, the less the probability of encountering someone infected with the AIDS virus. The more selective one is in choosing a partner (has your partner been tested for the HIV?), the less the risk. The use of condoms significantly reduces, but does not eliminate, the likelihood of infection. Engaging in sexual behaviors in which there is no exchange of bodily fluids at all (such as mutual masturbation, for example) also constitutes safe sex (Masters et al., 1987).

AIDS is a physical disease. A biological organism, a virus, attacks a physiological system, the immune system, which increases the possibility of further infection, which ultimately can result in death. But AIDS is a physical disease with unprecedented psychological complications. In fact, patients who have been diagnosed as carrying the HIV virus, but who have not yet developed AIDS, tend to be more depressed and disturbed than those who have developed the full-blown and fatal symptoms of the disease (Chuang et al., 1989). AIDS researcher Tom Coates put it this way: "AIDS, as I see it, is primarily a psychological problem. What we're dealing with is a disease that gets in the way of people relating in intimate ways. And it becomes a psychological problem to figure out how we, as people who know something about motivation and know something about behavior, can help people not do something that's natural" (quoted in Landers, 1987, p. 28). Because AIDS is such a frightening disease, AIDS patients often are shunned—by loved ones and even by health care professionals. (In late 1987, the American Medical Association felt it had to issue a statement that it is unethical for a physician to refuse treatment to an AIDS patient.) Because AIDS began in the homosexual community and is still largely concentrated there, gays and lesbians are concerned that they will become the focus of even greater discrimination than they have suffered in the past. The fear, alienation, and stress experienced by AIDS patients, and often their friends and family, are in many ways as painful as the disease itself and require psychological treatment (e.g., Knapp & Vandecreek, 1989).

Here, under the microscope, the AIDS virus (blue) attacks a helper T cell. © Boehringer Ingelheim International GmbH. Photo: Lennart Nilsson.

BEFORE YOU GO ON

Name and briefly describe five sexually transmitted diseases.

GENDER ISSUES

So far in this topic, we have focused on biologically based sexuality. Now, let's direct our attention to the more psychologically and socially

Nationally renown artist Keith Haring is pictured here with students painting a mural. He died on February 16, 1990, from an AIDS-related virus.

based issues of gender. We have defined gender in terms of how one tends to think, feel, and/or behave as a male or a female. First we'll discuss gender identity and gender roles; then we'll examine gender differences.

Gender Identity and Gender Roles

gender identity *a basic sense or self-awareness of one's maleness or femaleness*

Gender identity is a basic sense or self-awareness of one's maleness or femaleness. Gender identity development begins early in life. Most of us began developing a sense of our own gender identity by the time we were 2 or 3 years old (Money, 1972; Paludi & Gullo, 1986). Once gender identity becomes established, it remains quite invulnerable to change (Bem, 1981; Spence, 1985).

gender roles *attitudes and expectations about how a person should act, think, and/or feel solely on the basis of being a female or a male*

Gender identity is related to the concept of **gender roles**. Gender roles are attitudes and expectations about how a person should feel, think, or act solely on the basis of whether that person is male or female. Gender identity then becomes a matter of acquiring one's gender role. Developing gender identity is a matter of learning those feelings, behaviors, and cognitions you are expected to display simply because you are a male or female. When a person has acquired the behaviors that are deemed gender-appropriate, that person has formed his or her gender identity and shows an appreciation of gender roles.

One's sex is biologically determined through the complex interaction of a number of processes, and one's gender is socially and culturally determined through an equally complex interaction of learning experiences. As we have said, gender identity formation begins very early. Indeed, the argument commonly is made that the differentiation of sex-appropriate responses begins in the delivery room with the exclamation, "It's a boy!" or "It's a girl!" It is still a very common practice to surround infant girls in pink and boys in blue. From day one, we are led to believe that there are, and ought to be, significant differences between the sexes (Paludi & Gullo, 1986). Children's toys, clothing, or playmates often are chosen on the basis of an understanding of what is acceptable for them as boys or girls (Schau et al., 1980).

Fortunately, sharp distinctions between male-appropriate and female-appropriate behaviors are softening. Parents are no longer so quick to claim that "big boys don't cry." Girls are not so automatically pushed away from toy cars and trucks toward dolls and frilly things. Boys playing with dolls has become a more common sight.

androgyny *a balanced combination of traits that are both masculine and feminine*

To be sure, movement away from a sharp distinction between gender role behaviors is slow and far from universal. Nonetheless, there seems to be an increased appreciation for a concept psychologists call **androgyny**. Androgyny involves a combination of traits usually associated with males *and* females. Although she did not coin the term, *androgyny* is commonly associated with Sandra Bem (1974, 1975, 1977, 1981). Bem developed a test, called the *Bem Sex Role Inventory (BSRI)*, to measure both masculinity and femininity as if they were personality traits. In Topic 10A, we defined a personality trait as any distinguishable, relatively enduring way in which an individual may differ from others. Initially, androgyny was associated with scores that fell somewhere between the extremes of masculinity and femininity on the BSRI. Now, an androgynous person (who, biologically, may be a male or a female) is one who scores high on *both* masculine and feminine scales. In other words, androgynous men and women exhibit both masculine and feminine behaviors. Being androgynous was thought to lead to flexibility (Bem, 1975). When it was appropriate, one could "act like a man," and when it was appropriate, an androgynous person could just as easily "act like a woman." In the 1970s, androgyny became quite the rage. As Deaux put it, "Not only was androgyny to be a particular conceptual focus, it was also proclaimed as a value. Thus it was good and wise and liberal to be androgynous, and mental health was proposed to be synonymous with androgynous scores" (1984, p. 109).

What Deaux called the "backlash to androgyny" developed in the 1980s. The present argument does not deny the reality of male and female gender roles or claim that femininity and masculinity cannot be measured. It's just that using the concept of androgyny as the combination of high masculinity and high femininity is too simple. Among other things, gender-appropriate personality traits that are stable over a wide range of different situations are difficult to find. Psychologists are now trying to develop models that will adequately describe interactions among gender-related traits, one's own beliefs about gender, and a variety of social contexts or situations (Deaux & Major, 1987; Edwards & Spence, 1987).

BEFORE YOU GO ON

What are gender identity and gender roles, and how are they related to the concept of androgyny?

Differences Between Females and Males

Men and women are clearly and significantly different from each other in many ways. Men tend to be taller than women. On the average, girls mature much faster than do boys. Usually, men weigh more than women and are physically stronger. When they become overweight, women seem to add weight to their hips and thighs, while men develop "pot bellies." We could keep going with this list, but we are listing here only ways in which women and men are *physically* different. Are men and women *psychologically* different?

What do you think about these differences? Do they sound reasonable to you? Boys have higher self-esteem than girls. Girls are more social than boys. Boys are more analytical than girls. Girls are more likely to conform than boys. Boys are better at rote learning, while girls are more creative. Let's stop right here. As sensible as these differences may sound, there is virtually no research evidence to support any of them. That there are, in fact, no gender differences in sociability, analytic skills, rote learning, self-esteem, creativity, or suggestibility was one of the findings of the first major research on sex differences, reported by Eleanor Maccoby and Carol Jacklin in 1974. Maccoby and Jacklin's work certainly was not the first to ask if there are consistent differences between males and females (their study was more of a reanalysis of data that existed at the time than it was a compilation of new data). It did, however, stimulate many others to join in the search for ways in which gender could be used to help us predict how a person might respond in a variety of circumstances.

Probably the most striking aspect of subsequent research on gender differences is the extent to which it continually fails to find significant differences between men and women. The list of ways in which the sexes are psychologically alike is much longer than any list of the ways in which they are psychologically different. And here's an important point to keep in mind: Even when we do find consistent differences between men and women, the variability within each sex is greater than the variability between the two. What does that mean? It means that when differences exist, they tend to be very small; differences exist only "on the average" or "in the long run," and making specific predictions based on gender alone is very difficult. Using the physical measure of height as an example, it is clear that there are millions of women who are taller than the average male, even though men are, generally, taller than women. And one more point to keep in mind: When differences are found, we are hard-pressed even to estimate the extent to which they reflect biologically based differences versus learned gender role differences. Well, in what ways *are* men and women different? There are two categories in which differences have been found: cognitive abilities and social behaviors.

Cognitive Abilities. In terms of cognitive abilities, let me first remind you of a point made in Topic 8B, where we discussed group differences in IQ: There are no sex differences in general intelligence as indicated by IQ test scores. Having said that, we can list three areas in which gender differences have been found:

1. *Verbal skills:* Females generally are found to earn superior scores on tests of verbal skills. This is true whether we use tests of very simple verbal skills, such as vocabulary tests, or more complex skills, such as verbal problem solving. Some researchers have found females to be slightly advanced in language development, but most gender differences on verbal skills are found after puberty (Halpern, 1986; Hyde & Linn, 1988).

2. *Spatial relations skills:* Males tend to outscore females on tests of spatial relations. Here there is evidence that the gender difference is established before puberty and lasts through adulthood (Halpern, 1986; Hyde, 1981; Linn & Peterson, 1985). Spatial relations skills are those we use to mentally represent objects and events in our minds and then manipulate those representations. People who have good spatial abilities can easily find simple figures embedded in more complex figures or can picture what a box would look like if it were opened up and laid flat.

3. *Mathematical skills:* About the only other cognitive area in which gender differences have been found is with general arithmetic or mathematical skills. There are few more hotly debated issues in all of psychology. The basic problem here is that we have contradictory data. Some studies show females to be at an advantage (*on the average*, remember) until puberty or early adolescence. Then, and with consistency, test scores tend to favor males. At least this was true of data from the 1970s and earlier. A forceful argument can be made that females' lower scores have little to do with sex or gender per se, but reflect gender roles and opportunity. As studies were able to control more and more extraneous variables (e.g., the number and

type of math classes taken), it became clear that the difference between men and women in general mathematics was very slim. Some of the confusion in the data may reflect the difference between achievement (where males do score higher than females) and aptitude (where differences, if any, are slight) (Becker & Jacobs, 1983; Benbow & Stanley, 1980; Hogrebe, 1987). In terms of mathematics achievement, we can still say with conviction that males earn higher scores than females. The largest differences are found among those who earn the highest scores: Males are much more likely than females to earn the very top scores on math tests (Feingold, 1988; Holden, 1987; Hyde, Fennema, & Lamon, 1990). Just what these differences mean for society, for psychology, or for individual men and women remains debatable (Benbow, 1990; Hyde, Fennema, & Lamon, 1990).

Social Behaviors. There are two social behaviors that show significant gender differences: aggression and communication style. There is much more agreement on the former than the latter. Maccoby and Jacklin (1974, 1980) found males to be more aggressive than females starting at preschool levels and continuing throughout adulthood (although the differences diminish with age). That males are more aggressive than females seems to be a highly supportable conclusion. This is true even when aggression is measured, or defined, in a number of different ways—as outward physical aggression, as verbal aggression, or as aggression in fantasy (Block, 1984; Hyde, 1984). As consistent as the data on gender differences in aggression may be, there still is debate about the extent to which these differences reflect some true biologically based difference rather than the development of gender roles.

Whether there are other gender differences in social behaviors that consistently occur across situations is also debatable. One possibility that has received some research support is communication style. Men actually are much more talkative (across most situations) than are women, and men are much more likely to interrupt others (Key, 1975). In some situations, females tend to "self-disclose" more than males do (Cozby, 1973). In other words, women are more likely to share ideas and feelings about themselves.

There is some evidence that there are also gender differences in nonverbal communications, or "body language" (Henley, 1977). The data here, however, are weak. Women are thought to be more sensitive at decoding body language than are men (Hall, 1978). Some have tried to argue that one's posture and gestures during communication give messages of dominance and submissiveness, and that males tend to be more dominant in nonverbal social interactions. Although this may be a commonly held belief, there is virtually no evidence to support it (Halberstadt & Saitta, 1987).

When we talk about gender differences in communication style, we clearly are starting to venture onto thin ice. When we treat gender as a subject variable and look for consistent differences among people that we can attribute to their gender, we find very little, indeed. Over and over, we run into the same conclusion: In psychological terms, men and women are much more alike than they are different. Particularly in social settings, gender may not be a viable, useful subject variable. This doesn't mean that gender is not important in social settings. In fact, quite the opposite. It's just that gender may be more of a stimulus variable than a subject variable

(Deaux, 1985; Deaux & Major, 1987). What that means is that one's gender, or one's perception of gender, acts as a cue or stimulus and influences how people behave and how they are expected to behave in a particular situation.

BEFORE YOU GO ON

Summarize what we know about gender differences.

Our biologically based sexuality and our more psychologically based sense of gender are very much a part of who we are. They are very important and often salient aspects of our personalities. In this topic, we have reviewed some of the issues that have attracted the attention of psychologists working in the area of sexuality and gender. We've explored the genetic and hormonal bases of our sexuality, focusing particularly on adolescence, when an individual's sexuality first becomes an important, occasionally central, concern. The pioneering work of Masters and Johnson has given us a fairly complete description of the human sexual response. On the other hand, our understanding of sexual orientation remains somewhat clouded, although the genetic and prenatal bases for homosexuality and heterosexuality are becoming more clear. We have also noted that sexual dysfunctions and sexually transmitted diseases present problems of enormous scope and that interventions for treatment and prevention include a large psychological component. Finally, we discussed gender formation and gender identity, the extent to which one develops a sense of being male or female, and we discovered that there are, in fact, few ways in which sex or gender can be used to explain individual differences in psychological functioning.

How is one's sex genetically determined?

At conception, a zygote receives an X chromosome from the mother's ovum and either an X or a Y chromosome from the father's sperm. If the zygote receives two X chromosomes (XX), it is genetically a female; if it receives one X and one Y chromosome (XY), it is genetically a male. / page 475

Summarize the role of hormones in the determination of one's sex.

As the sex glands develop (beginning about six weeks after conception), they begin secreting sex hormones, androgens from the male sex glands (testes) and estrogens from the female sex glands (ovaries). Androgen and estrogen levels are also controlled by the adrenal gland, which is, in turn, under the control of the pituitary gland and the hypothalamus. Although androgens and estrogens are present in both males and females, the relative amounts of each stimulate the development of the genitals and, hence, determine one's anatomical sex. / page 477

Briefly describe the changes that occur during the excitement, plateau, orgasm, and resolution phases of the human sexual response.

Masters and Johnson have identified four standard phases of human sexual response. In the *excitement phase*, both males and females become sexually aroused; there is increased tension in the genital area. The male attains an erection, and the female's vagina becomes lubricated. There are many stimuli that may evoke this phase. The *plateau phase* carries arousal to the brink of orgasm. Blood pressure levels and heart rates increase for both males and females. The penis becomes fully erect. The vagina enlarges and the clitoris elevates into the body. The *orgasm phase* is the shortest of the four. In the male, there is a series of pelvic contractions

followed by ejaculation. Females also experience a series of short, intense contractions. The *resolution phase* returns the body to its more relaxed, non-aroused state. After orgasm, males experience a refractory period during which they cannot be stimulated to repeat the cycle of phases just described. Females have no refractory period and, hence, may experience multiple orgasms if properly stimulated. / page 479

What is homosexuality? What causes homosexuality?

Homosexuals are individuals who are attracted to and sexually aroused by members of their own sex. There is thought to be a continuum, or gradual dimension, that extends from exclusively homosexual on the one extreme to exclusively heterosexual on the other. Kinsey found that more than half of the males in his sample fell somewhere between these two endpoints. We do not know what "causes" homosexuality, but strongly suspect that three potential factors interact in complex ways: genetic predispositions, prenatal hormonal influences, and early childhood experiences. / page 482

List and briefly describe six sexual dysfunctions.

Sexual dysfunctions are chronic problems in sexual functioning. The most commonly reported by males is *erectile dysfunction*, which is an inability to attain or maintain an erection long enough to experience intercourse. *Premature ejaculation* and *retarded ejaculation* obviously have to do with the timing of ejaculation during intercourse. The former problem is much more common than the latter. In either case, what is "premature" or "retarded" is usually defined by the individual; that is, there are no normal time limits. *Female sexual unresponsiveness* is a condition in which a woman gains little or no pleasure from sexual activities. This dys-

function is usually self-diagnosed. *Orgasmic dysfunction* involves the inability to experience orgasm, at least to one's satisfaction. This is the dysfunction most commonly reported by women. *Vaginismus* is the powerful, spasmodic, painful contraction of the muscles surrounding the entry to the vagina. It makes vaginal intercourse nearly impossible. These sexual dysfunctions (in males or females) usually are caused by psychological, not physical, factors. / page 484

Name and briefly describe five sexually transmitted diseases.

Sexually transmitted diseases (STDs) are very common. Among the most troublesome are the following: (1) *Chlamydia*, a bacterial infection of the genital area that results in painful urination and a fluid discharge, is the most common of the STDs in North America. Left untreated in women, chlamydia may lead to pelvic inflammatory disease (PID) and infertility. (2) *Gonorrhea*, a bacterial infection of the moist tissues around the genitals, is transmitted only by sexual activity. Its symptoms increase in severity when the disease is left untreated. Penicillin is an effective treatment. (3) *Syphilis*, another bacterial infection, passes through four stages as symptoms increase in severity. Left untreated, it may result in death. Penicillin, again, is an effective treatment. (4) *Genital herpes*, a viral infection that affects the skin in the genital area, is the most common STD and has no cure. A person with herpes may go for prolonged periods without any noticeable symptoms. (5) *Acquired immune deficiency syndrome (AIDS)* is perhaps the most frightening of all STDs. AIDS can be transmitted by nonsexual means. It is a viral (HIV) infection that can only be transmitted through the exchange of bodily fluids, as in sexual activity. Once infected, a person remains symptom-free (but capable of infecting others) in a "carrier state" until full-blown symptoms of AIDS develop. Virtually all persons with AIDS symptoms will die within four years. There is, at the moment, no effective vaccine or treatment for AIDS. Prevention of HIV infection through behavioral (sexual practice) change is recommended. / *page 487*

What are gender identity and gender roles, and how are they related to the concept of androgyny?

Gender identity develops as we become aware of our own sense of maleness or femaleness. This process essentially involves learning one's gender roles, or those attitudes and expectations of how a person should feel, think, or behave on the basis of whether that person is a male or female. Androgyny is a concept used to refer to the combination of male and female gender role traits in one person. An androgynous individual (sexually either male or female) would exhibit both masculine and feminine characteristics appropriate to prevailing circumstances. The usefulness of the concept of androgyny is now under debate. / *page 489*

Summarize what we know about gender differences.

Having first said that in most ways males and females are very much alike, and having pointed out that even when differences are found they are very small and that we cannot be sure if they reflect biological predispositions or reflect gender role development, we can say that there are a few psychological differences between males and females that show some consistency. Females generally are better at verbal skills than males, particularly after puberty, whereas males score higher, on the average, on tests of spatial relations. Tests of mathematics achievement seem to favor males (at least after puberty), particularly at high levels, but whether there are any significant differences in aptitudes for mathematics has yet to be settled. In terms of social behaviors, we have perhaps our best indication of gender differences: on the average, males are more aggressive than females, at any age level. There is some evidence of consistent differences in communication style based on gender, but the data are not clear on this issue. / *page 492*

MOTIVATION, EMOTION, AND STRESS

Motivational Issues

Why We Care: A Topic Preview

Why We Care: A Topic Preview

In this topic, we will address some important practical issues. We are going to deal with questions concerning motivation, the processes that arouse, direct, and maintain behavior. For the first time, our focus is on questions that begin with the word why. "Why did she do that (as opposed to doing nothing)?" "Why did she do that (as opposed to something else)?" "Why does she keep doing that (as opposed to stopping)?" "Why did she stop doing what she was doing (as opposed to continuing)?" For that matter, "Why do we care about this topic?" As you can see, the study of motivation deals with the origin of behaviors, the direction or choice of behaviors, the maintenance of behaviors, and of course, the cessation of behaviors. In short, the study of motivation gets us involved with attempts to explain the causes of one's behaviors.

You certainly don't need a psychologist to convince you that motivation is an important concept in your daily life. We already have seen that motivation affects virtually everything we do. Motivation influences our ability to learn, affects our memory, and even has an impact on so basic a process as perception.

We'll get our discussion under way by considering some different ways in which psychologists have approached the study of motivation, and we'll define some basic terms. The theoretical approaches presented here are not always in conflict. They have much in common, and we will be able to find a number of useful ideas within each approach.

Having defined relevant terminology and having summarized a few basic approaches to motivation, the rest of the topic will review what we know about two different sorts of motivating forces: (1) those related to our survival, and rooted in our biology (we'll call these physiologically based drives), and (2) those more clearly learned and/or social in nature (we'll call these psychologically based motives).

APPROACHES TO MOTIVATION

arousal *one's level of activation or excitement; indicative of a motivational state*

An assumption that we make about motivation is that it is comprised of two subprocesses. First, we say that motivation involves **arousal**—one's level of activation or excitement. Here we are using the term *motivation* in the sense of a force that initiates and activates behaviors, that gets an organism going, energized to *do* something. The second subprocess provides *direction* or focus to one's behaviors. In addition to simply being aroused and active, a motivated organism's behavior can be viewed as goal-directed and in some way purposeful. Hence our definition: **motivation** is the process that arouses, directs, and maintains behavior.

motivation *the process of arousing, maintaining, and directing behavior*

From its earliest days, psychology has attempted to find a systematic theory that could summarize and organize what different motivational states have in common. Psychologists have long struggled to describe one general pattern or scheme that could be used to account for *why* organisms tend to do what they do. In this section, we'll review some of these theories in a somewhat chronological order. As you might anticipate, we have no one approach to motivation that satisfactorily answers all our questions. Even though each of the approaches summarized below may have its drawbacks, we should focus our attention on how each contributes to our understanding of behavior and mental processes. Let me also draw your attention to Topic 15A on industrial-organizational psychology, which includes a section on different approaches to motivation, specifically those related to work motivation.

Approaches Based on Instincts

instincts *unlearned, complex patterns of behavior that occur in the presence of particular stimuli*

In the early days of psychology, behaviors often were explained in terms of **instincts**—unlearned, complex patterns of behavior that occur in the presence of certain stimuli. They are inherited, or innate. Why do birds build nests? A nest-building instinct. When conditions are right, birds build nests. Why do salmon swim upstream to mate? Instinct. Swimming upstream at mating season is a built-in part of what it means to be a salmon. These behaviors can be modified somewhat by the organisms' experiences, but the basic driving force behind them is unlearned or instinctive.

That salmon—such as these sockeyes—swim upstream at mating season, can be explained by instinct: Unlearned, complex patterns of behavior that occur in the presence of certain stimuli.

That may explain some of the behavior of birds and salmon, but what about people? William James (1890) reasoned that humans, being more complex organisms, no doubt had many more instincts than did the "lower" animals.

No one expressed the instinctual explanation of human behaviors more forcefully than William McDougall (1908). He suggested that human behaviors were motivated (caused) by 11 basic instincts: repulsion, curiosity, flight, parenting, reproduction, gregariousness, acquisitiveness, construction, self-assertion, self-abasement, and pugnacity. Soon McDougall extended his list to include 18 instincts. As new and different behaviors required explanation, new and different instincts were devised to explain them.

As lists of human instincts got longer and longer, the basic problem with this approach became obvious. Particularly for humans, *explaining* behavior patterns by alluding to instinct simply renamed or relabeled them and didn't explain anything at all. But, lest we simply dispense with this approach totally, the psychologists who argued for instincts did introduce and draw attention to an idea that is still very much with us today: that we may engage in some behaviors for reasons that are basically physiological, and more inherited than learned.

Approaches Based on Needs and Drives

One approach that provided an alternative to explaining behavior in terms of instincts was one that attempted to explain the whys of behavior in terms of needs and drives. This approach, dominant in the 1940s and 1950s, is best associated with the psychologist Clark Hull (e.g., Hull, 1943).

Hull's Theory. In Hull's system, a **need** is a lack or shortage of some biological essential required for survival. A need arises from deprivation. When an organism is kept from food, it develops a need for food. If deprived of water, it develops a need for water. A need then gives rise to a drive. A **drive** is a state of tension, arousal, or activation. When an organism is in a *drive state*, it is motivated. It is aroused and directed to do something to satisfy the drive by reducing or eliminating the underlying need. The implication is that needs produce tensions (drives) that the organism seeks to reduce; hence, this approach is referred to in terms of drive reduction.

This approach *is* less circular than a direct appeal to instincts. For example, having gone without food for some time, one develops a need. The need for food may give rise to a hunger drive. Then what? Then learning and experience come into play. Whereas instincts are directly tied to a specific pattern of behavior, needs and drives are not. They are concepts that can be used to explain why we do what we do, while clearly allowing for the influence of experience and the environment. Doing without food gives rise to a need, which in turn gives rise to a drive, but how that drive is expressed in behavior is influenced by one's experiences and learning history.

need *a lack or shortage of some biological essential resulting from deprivation*

drive *a state of tension resulting from a need that arouses and directs an organism's behavior*

Activities ranging from mountain climbing to exploring around the house, suggest that people often try to reduce primary (biological) or secondary (learned) drives in order to satisfy certain needs.

Some complications do arise with a drive reduction theory of motivation. One concerns the relationship between the strength of a need and the strength of the drive that results from it. In most cases, as needs increase, so do the drives to reduce them. But the relationship between needs and the drives that result from them may not be straightforward. If you've ever been on a strict diet for a while, you may appreciate this point. When you first begin a diet, depriving yourself of food produces a need that results in a hunger drive. At first, you are likely to feel very hungry. After a week or so on your diet, you may notice that you no longer feel quite as hungry as you did during the first few days. Your need for food may now be even greater than it was at first, but the drive state is no longer quite as strong.

A second complication of a drive reduction approach centers on the biological nature of needs. To claim that drives arise only from needs that result from biological deprivations seems unduly restrictive. It seems that not all of the drives that activate a person's behavior are based on biological needs. Humans often engage in behaviors to satisfy *learned* drives. Drives based on one's learning experiences are called *secondary drives*, as opposed to *primary drives*, which are based on unlearned, physiological needs. In fact, most of the drives that arouse and direct our behavior have little to do with our physiology.

You may feel that you need a new car this year. I may convince myself that I need a new set of golf clubs, and we'll both work very hard to save the money to buy what we need. Although we may say that we are "driven" to work for money, it's difficult to imagine how your car or my golf clubs could be satisfying a biological need. A good bit of advertising is directed at trying to convince us that we "need" many products and services that will have very little impact on our survival.

A related complication can be seen when we consider behaviors that organisms engage in even after all their biological needs are met. Think about it. Drives are states of arousal, activation, or tension. This position claims that we behave as we do in order to reduce or eliminate drives. That is, we act in order to reduce tension or arousal. Yet we know that sky divers jump out of airplanes; mountain climbers risk life and limb to scale sheer cliffs of stone; monkeys play with mechanical puzzles even when solving the puzzles leads to no specific reward, and children explore the pots and pans kept in kitchen cabinets even when repeatedly told not to. These actions surely do not appear to be useful in reducing tension, do they? We might suggest, as some psychologists have, that these organisms are attempting to satisfy exploration drives, or manipulation drives, or curiosity drives. But then we run the risk of trying to explain why people behave as they do by generating longer and longer lists of drives—the same sort of problem we have when we try to explain behavior in terms of instinct.

So what do all these complications mean? It seems that people often do behave in order to reduce drives and thereby satisfy needs. Sometimes, drives are produced by biological, tissue, needs; we call these primary drives. At other times, the drives that arouse and direct our behaviors are learned or acquired; we call these secondary drives. How drives are satisfied, or reduced, will reflect the learning history of the organism. Thus, the concept of drive reduction is a useful one and is still very much with us in psychology, but it cannot be accepted as a complete explanation for motivated behaviors. Let's now turn to an approach to motivation that relies

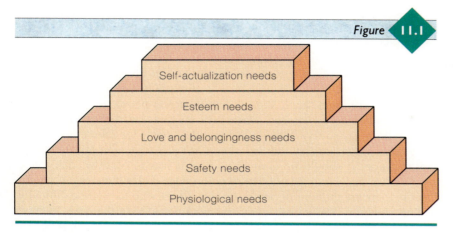

Self-actualization needs

Esteem needs

Love and belongingness needs

Safety needs

Physiological needs

Maslow's hierarchy of needs.

on the concepts of drives and needs and places them in a hierarchy of importance.

Maslow's Hierarchy. Abraham Maslow is one of the names we associate with the humanistic movement in psychology. Humanistic psychologists emphasize the person and his or her psychological growth. Maslow combined his concern for the person with Hull's drive reduction theory and proposed that human behavior does, in fact, respond to needs. Not all of those needs are physiological, however. It was Maslow's belief that the needs that ultimately motivate human action are limited in number and hierarchically arranged (Maslow, 1943, 1970). Figure 11.1 summarizes this hierarchy of needs in pictorial form.

What this means is that Maslow's approach is essentially a stage theory. It proposes that what motivates us first are *physiological needs*. These include the basic needs that are related to survival, for example, the need for food, water, and shelter. Until these needs are met, there is little reason to suspect that an individual will be concerned with anything else. But once physiological needs are under control, a person is still motivated, now by *safety needs*: the need to feel secure, protected from dangers that might arise in the future. We are now motivated to see to it that the cupboard has food for later, that we won't freeze this winter, and that there's enough money saved to protect against sudden calamity. Notice here the hierarchical nature of this scheme. We're surely not going to worry about what we'll be eating tomorrow if there's not enough to eat today; but if today's needs *are* taken care of, we can then focus on the future. Once our safety needs are met, our concern shifts to needs for *love and belongingness*: the need for someone else to care about us, to love us. After these needs are satisfied, then our concern is for *esteem*. Our aim is to be recognized for what we do, our achievements, our efforts. That is, once we have found that others value us for who we are, we focus on our need to be recognized for our accomplishments. These needs are social in nature; they imply that our behaviors are motivated by our awareness of others and our concern for their approval. And the list goes on. One moves higher in the hierarchy only if lower needs

By participating in organized competitions, such as the International Games for the Disabled, individuals strive to be the best that they can be, responding to what Maslov calls a need to self-actualize.

are met. Ultimately, we may get to the highest level of needs in Maslow's hierarchy: *self-actualization needs*. These are the most difficult to achieve. We self-actualize when we become the best that we can be, when we are taking the fullest advantage of our potential as human beings. We are self-actualizing when we strive to be as creative and/or productive as possible.

In many ways, Maslow's arrangement of needs in a hierarchical fashion conforms to common sense. We can hardly expect people to be motivated to grow and achieve "success" when they are concerned about their very survival on a day-to-day basis. When people's needs for safety, belonging, and esteem are reasonably fulfilled, they don't just stop, unmotivated to do anything else. It should be clear to you, as it was to Maslow, that many people never make it to the self-actualization stage of this hierarchy of needs. Clearly, there are millions of people on this planet who have great difficulty dealing with the very lowest levels and who never have the time, energy, and/or opportunity to be concerned with such issues as self-esteem or belongingness, much less self-actualization.

As a comprehensive theory of human motivation, however, Maslow's hierarchy has some serious difficulties. Perhaps the biggest stumbling block is the idea that one can assign ranks to needs and put them in a neat order, regardless of what that order may be. It is quite clear that some persons are motivated in ways that violate the stage approach of this theory. Individuals will, for example, freely give up satisfying basic survival needs for the sake of "higher" principles (as in hunger strikes). For the sake of love, people may very well abandon their own needs for safety and security. The truth of the matter is, there is very little empirical research support for Maslow's approach to ranking needs in a hierarchy. It remains the case, however, that because of its intuitive appeal, Maslow's approach to human motivation has found considerable favor both within and outside of psychology.

Approaches Based on Incentives

One alternative to a drive reduction approach to motivation focuses not on what starts behavior, but on the *end state*, or goal of behavior. According to this approach, external stimuli serve as motivating agents, or **incentives**, for our behavior. Incentives are external events that act to *pull* our behavior, as opposed to drives, which are internal events (somehow "in the person") that *push* our behavior. Incentive theory frees us from relying on biological concepts to explain the whys of one's behaviors.

incentives *external stimuli that an organism may be motivated to approach or avoid*

When a mountain climber says that he or she climbs a mountain "because it is there," the climber is indicating a type of motivation through incentive. After a very large meal, we may order a piece of cherry cheesecake, not because we *need* it in any physiological sense, but because it's there on the dessert cart and *looks* so good (and because previous experience tells us that it is likely to taste very good).

You may be reading this topic because you think that reading it will help you reach your goal of a good grade on your next exam—for some, a very powerful incentive. This is a good place to mention that some of our motivated behavior may occur not so much to enable us to reach positive goals as to escape or avoid negative goals. That is, some students may be motivated to read this topic not to earn an A on their next exam, but to avoid getting an F. The behaviors may be the same, but the incentives—and hence, motivation—involved are clearly different.

Some parents want to know how to motivate their child to clean up his or her room. We can interpret this case in terms of establishing goals or incentives. What those parents *really* want to know is how they can get their child to value, work for, and be reinforced by a clean room. What they want is a clean room, and they would like to have the child clean it. If they want the child "to be motivated" to clean his or her room, the child needs to learn the value or incentive of having a clean room. You can imagine the child's response: "Why should I?" "Because I told you to" becomes the almost reflexive response. *How* to teach a child that a clean room is a thing to be valued is, in fact, another story, probably involving other incentives that the child does value. For now, let's simply acknowledge that establishing a clean room as a valued goal is the major task at hand. Clearly, having a clean room is not an innate, inborn need. The parents have learned to value clean rooms, and there is hope that their child also can learn to be similarly "motivated."

If this discussion of incentives sounds something like our discussion of operant conditioning (Topic 5B), you're right. Remember, the basic tenet of operant conditioning is that one's behaviors are controlled by their consequences. We tend to do (are motivated to do) whatever leads to reinforcement (positive incentives), and we tend *not* to do whatever leads to punishment or failure of reinforcement (negative incentives).

Having children help with household chores may involve motivating them to do so. In such cases, the child must learn to appreciate the incentive value of the task at hand.

BEFORE YOU GO ON

How have the concepts of instinct, drive, and incentive been used to explain motivated behaviors?

Approaches Based on Balance or Equilibrium

A concept that has proven to be very useful in discussions of motivated behaviors is that of balance, or equilibrium. The basic idea here is that we are motivated or driven to maintain a state of balance. What is it that we are motivated to balance? Sometimes equilibrium involves physiological processes that need to be maintained at some level, or restricted range, of activity. Sometimes balance involves our overall level of excitement or arousal. Sometimes balance is required among our thoughts or cognitions. In this section, we'll review three of the approaches to motivation that emphasize a basic, general drive or motive to maintain a state of balance, equilibrium, or optimum level of functioning.

Homeostasis. One of the first references to a need to maintain a balanced state is found in the work of Walter Cannon (1932). Cannon was concerned with our internal physiological reactions, and the term he used to describe a state of balance or equilibrium within those reactions was **homeostasis**. The idea here is that each of our physiological processes has

homeostasis *a state of balance or equilibrium among internal, physiological conditions*

set point *a normal, optimum level (or value) of equilibrium or balance among physiological or psychological reactions*

a balanced, **set point** of operation. One's set point, then, is a level of activity that can be considered "normal" or "most suitable." Whenever anything happens to upset this balance, we become motivated. We are driven to do whatever we can to return to our set point, our optimum, homeostatic level. If we drift only slightly from our set point, our own physiological mechanisms may act to return us to homeostasis without our intention or our awareness. If these automatic involuntary processes are unsuccessful, then we may take action, motivated by the basic drive to maintain homeostasis.

For example, everyone has a normal, set level of body temperature, blood pressure, basal metabolism (the rate at which energy is consumed in normal bodily functions), heart rate, and so on. When any of these are caused to deviate from their set point, homeostatic level, we become motivated to do something that will return us to our state of balance. Cannon's concept of homeostasis was devised to explain physiological processes. As we shall soon see, however, the basic ideas of balance and optimum level of operation have been applied to psychological processes as well.

Arousal. We have already defined arousal in terms of one's overall level of activation or excitement. A person's level of arousal may change from day to day and within the same day. After a good night's sleep and morning shower, your level of arousal may be quite high. (Your level of arousal also may be quite high as your instructor moves through your class handing out exams.) Late at night, after a busy day at school, your level of arousal may be quite low. Your arousal level is probably at its lowest when you are in the deepest stages of sleep.

Arousal theories of motivation (e.g., Berlyne, 1960, 1971; Duffy, 1962; Hebb, 1955) claim that there is an optimal level of arousal (an arousal set point) that organisms are motivated to maintain. Drive reduction approaches, remember, argue that we are motivated to reduce tension or arousal by satisfying the needs that give rise to drives. Arousal theories argue that sometimes we actually seek out arousing, tension-producing activities, motivated to maintain our optimal arousal level. If we find ourselves bored and in a rut, the idea of going to an action-adventure movie may seem like a good one. On the other hand, if we've had a very busy and hectic day, just staying at home doing nothing may sound appealing. This approach is, of course, much like Cannon's idea of homeostasis, but in more general terms than specific physiological processes.

This point of view suggests that for any activity or situation, there is a "best," most efficient level of arousal. To do well on an exam, for example, requires that a student have a certain level of overall arousal. If a student is tired, bored, or just doesn't care one way or the other about the exam, we can expect a poor performance. If, on the other hand, a student is *so* worried, nervous, and anxious that she or he can barely function, we'll also predict a poor exam score. The relationship between arousal and the efficiency of performance is depicted in Figure 11.2.

Arousal theory also takes into account the difficulty or complexity of the task or activity in which a person is engaged. That is, for very easy, simple tasks, a high level of arousal may be optimal, while that same high level of arousal would be disastrous for very difficult, complex tasks (Brehm & Self, 1989). For example, students judged to be poorly, moderately, or highly motivated attempted a series of difficult anagram problems (naming a word whose letters have been scrambled). In fact, the most highly mo-

Figure **11.2**

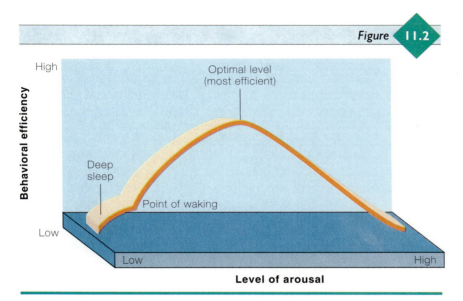

For each task we attempt there is an optimal level of arousal. What that level is will depend on the task. In other words, it is possible to be too aroused (motivated), just as it is possible to be under aroused. (After Hebb, 1955.)

tivated subjects did significantly worse than did the moderately motivated subjects (Ford, Wright, & Haythornthwaite, 1985). The observation that optimum levels of arousal vary with the nature (difficulty) of a task can be traced back to an article published in 1908 by Yerkes and Dodson, even though the concept of "arousal" did not appear in psychology until many decades later (Winton, 1987).

An interesting twist on the theory that we are motivated to maintain a set, optimal level of arousal is the observation that, for some unknown reason, optimum levels of arousal may vary considerably from individual to individual. Some people seem to need and seek particularly high levels of arousal and excitement in their lives. They are what Marvin Zuckerman calls "sensation seekers" (Zuckerman, et al. 1978, 1980). They enjoy sky-diving or mountain climbing and may look forward to the challenge of driving in heavy city traffic. Zuckerman further suggested that sensation seekers would have some sort of disturbance in their noradrenergic system (the hormonal system related to arousal levels). Such a disturbance in the noradrenergic system—also linked to pathological gambling—has been discovered (Roy, DeJong, & Linnoila, 1989).

Cognitive Dissonance. There is also a point of view that we are motivated to maintain a state of balance among our ideas or beliefs (our cognitions) as well as our physiological processes and levels of arousal. This approach claims that we are motivated to maintain what Leon Festinger (1957) calls a *state of consonance* among our cognitions.

Suppose you believe yourself to be a good student. You study very hard for an exam in biology. You think that you're prepared. You judge the exam to be a fairly easy one. But when you get your exam paper back, you discover that you failed the test! Now that's hard to accept. You believe

For many of us, jumping out of an airplane would be overly arousing to say the least. For "sensation seekers," sky diving may provide a near-optimum level of arousal.

cognitive dissonance *a motivating discomfort or tension caused by a lack of balance or consonance among one's cognitions*

you're a good student. You believe that you studied adequately. You believe the test wasn't difficult. But you also know that you failed the test. Here are a number of cognitions that don't fit together very well. They are not consonant; they are not balanced. You are experiencing what Festinger calls **cognitive dissonance**, a state of tension or discomfort that exists when we hold inconsistent, dissonant cognitions. When this occurs, Festinger argues, we are motivated to bring about a change in our system of cognitions. In our example, you may come to believe that you're not such a good student after all. Or you may come to believe that your paper was unfairly graded. Or you may come to believe that you are a poor judge of an exam's difficulty. This theory doesn't predict specifically *what* will happen, but it does predict that cognitive dissonance produces motivation to return to a balanced state of cognitive consonance.

These days, almost all smokers experience cognitive dissonance. They *know* that smoking is a very dangerous habit, and yet they continue to smoke. Smokers usually reduce their dissonance by coming to believe that although smoking is bad for one's health in general, it really isn't bad for them, at least when compared to perceived "benefits." We'll return to Festinger and cognitive dissonance again when we discuss attitude change (see Topic 14A).

BEFORE YOU GO ON

How can the concept of balance or equilibrium be used to help us understand motivated behaviors?
In what way is cognitive dissonance theory based on equilibrium?

PHYSIOLOGICALLY BASED DRIVES

Now that we have reviewed some theoretical approaches to the motives that activate and direct our behaviors, we can turn our attention to a few specific examples. As you can imagine, this discussion could be organized in a number of different ways. As I suggested earlier, we'll use a simple system that refers to just two major types of motivators: those that have a biological basis, which we will call *physiologically based*, and those that are more clearly learned or social in nature, which we'll call *psychologically based*.

There are two points for you to keep in mind as we go through this discussion. First, we are going to treat the terms *drive* and *motive* as if they were synonyms. However, we will follow convention here and use the term *drive* for those activators of behavior that have a known biological or physiological basis (e.g., a hunger drive) and the term *motive* for those that do not (e.g., a power motive). Second, you should note that even drives that are rooted in an organism's physiology often are influenced by psychological processes. Hunger, for example, is clearly a physiologically based drive, but what we eat, when we eat, and how much we eat often are influenced by psychological and social factors.

Temperature Regulation

Most of us seldom give our own body temperature much thought. We all have a fuzzy notion that 98.6°F is a normal, homeostatic body temperature. That body temperature has anything to do with motivation becomes sensible only in the context of homeostasis. Whenever anything happens to raise or lower our body temperature above or below its homeostatic, set point range, we become motivated. We become motivated to return our body temperature to its normal, balanced 98.6°F.

Let's say you are outside on a very cold day, and you are improperly dressed for the low temperature and high wind. Soon your body temperature starts to drop. Automatically, your body starts to respond to do what it can to elevate your temperature back to its normal level: Blood vessels in the hands and feet constrict, forcing blood back to the center of the body to conserve heat (as a result, your lips turn blue); you start to shiver, and the involuntary movements of your muscles create small amounts of heat energy. These are exactly the sorts of physiological reactions that Cannon had in mind when he wrote about homeostasis.

As another example, imagine that you are walking across a desert, fully dressed, at noon on a day in August. Your temperature begins to rise. Automatically, blood is forced toward the body's surface and your face becomes flushed. You perspire, and as the moisture on the surface of the skin evaporates, the skin is cooled, and blood is now near the surface—all in an attempt to return your body's temperature to its homeostatic level.

There are two centers in your brain that together act as a thermostat and instigate these attempts at temperature regulation. Both are located in the **hypothalamus** deep inside the brain (see Figure 11.3). One center is particularly sensitive to elevated body temperatures, the other to lowered temperatures. Together they act to mobilize the internal environment when normal balance is upset.

If these automatic reactions are not successful, you may be motivated to take some voluntary action on your own. You may have to get inside, out of the cold or heat. You may need to turn on the furnace or the air conditioner. In fact, you may very well *anticipate* the lowering or raising of your body temperature and act accordingly—by putting on your coat before going out on a blustery day, for example. Over and above what your brain and body can do automatically, you may have to engage in (learned) voluntary behaviors in order to maintain homeostasis.

BEFORE YOU GO ON

Given the concept of homeostasis, how might temperature regulation be thought of as a physiologically based drive?

Thirst and Drinking Behavior

We need water for survival. If we don't drink, we die. As the need for water increases, it gives rise to a thirst drive. The intriguing issue is not so

When our body temperature is above or below its normal level, we are motivated to return the temperature to its normal 98.6°. Feeling cold may motivate you to put on more clothes before starting the long trek to the bus stop. Feeling hot may motivate you to douse yourself with water after running a long race.

Figure **11.3**

Cerebral cortex

Hypothalamus

Thalamus

Cerebellum

Spinal cord

hypothalamus *a small brain structure involved in many drives, including thirst, hunger, sex, and temperature regulation*

The brain, showing the location of the hypothalamus.

Drinking behaviors may be motivated by any one of several internal or external cues, but basically, they are a response to our need for water.

much that we need to drink, but how we *know* that we're thirsty. What actually causes us to seek liquid and drink it?

Internal, Physiological Cues. For a very long time, we thought that we knew the answer to the question of why we drink: to relieve the discomfort caused by the dryness of our mouths and throats. No doubt, the unpleasantness of a dry mouth and throat *can* cause us to drink. But there must be more to drinking behavior than this.

Animals with no salivary glands, whose mouths and throats are constantly dry, drink no more than normal animals (more frequently, yes, but no more in terms of quantity). Normal bodily processes (urination, exhaling, perspiration, and so on) cause us to lose about 2½ liters of water a day (Levinthal, 1983). That water needs to be replaced, but what motivates us to do so?

About two-thirds of the fluid in our bodies is contained *within* our body's cells (intracellular), and about one-third is held in the spaces *between* cells (extracellular). There seem to be two separate mechanisms sensitive to losses of fluid, one associated with each of these areas. Intercellular loss of fluid is monitored by regions of the hypothalamus. One small center acts to "turn on" the thirst drive when fluid levels are low, and another center "turns off" thirst when fluid levels are adequate. Thirst that stems from extracellular fluid loss is monitored, in a complex chain of events, by the kidneys, which stimulate the production of a hormone that leads to a thirst drive.

External, Psychological Cues. Often our drinking behavior is motivated by a physiological drive that arises from our physiological need for water. Sometimes, however, our drinking behavior may be influenced by external factors, or incentives. The implication here, as we have mentioned earlier, is that we may become motivated to drink, not in response to internal needs, but in response to external stimulation. For example, the aroma of freshly brewed coffee may stimulate us to order a second (unneeded) cup. A frosty glass of iced tea may look too good to refuse. We may drink a cold beer or a soda simply because it tastes good, whether we *need* the fluid they contain or not.

Notice also that once motivated in terms of being aroused, *what* we drink may be strongly influenced by our previous learning experiences. Some people prefer Coke, some prefer Pepsi, while others would choose a different brand. Some people do not like cola drinks at all. Choices and preferences for what we drink are shaped by availability (people in Canada do not regularly drink coconut milk) and past experience. So even with so obvious a physiological drive as thirst, and so obvious a physiological need as our need for water, we see that psychological factors can be very relevant.

BEFORE YOU GO ON

List some of the internal and external factors that influence drinking behavior.

Sex Drives and Sexual Behavior

We had quite a bit to say about human sexuality in Topic 10B. Here, the intent is simply to summarize some of the internal and external factors that directly relate to sexual motivation. First, we need to emphasize that the sex drive is different from other physiologically based drives.

As a *physiologically based* drive, the sex drive is unique in a number of ways. First, the survival of the individual does not depend on its satisfaction. If we don't drink, we die; if we don't regulate our temperature, we die; if we don't eat, we die. If we don't have sex—well, we don't die. The survival of the *species* requires that an adequate number of its members successfully respond to a sex drive, but an individual member can get along without doing so.

Second, most physiologically based drives, including hunger, thirst, and temperature regulation, provide mechanisms that ultimately replenish and/or maintain the body's energy. When satisfied, the sex drive depletes bodily energy. In fact, the sex drive actually motivates the organism to seek tension, as opposed to drives that seek to reduce tension to return to homeostasis.

A third point about the sex drive that makes it different from the rest is that it is not present—at least in the usual sense—at birth, but requires a certain level of maturation (puberty) before it is apparent. The other drives are present, and even most critical, early in life.

A fourth unique quality of the sex drive is the extent to which internal and external influences have different degrees of impact depending on the

The sex drive in humans may have an internal, physiological basis, but its expression in behavior is influenced by many nonphysiological factors, such as cultural, societal, and religious pressures, past experiences, personal preferences, and opportunity.

species involved. The importance of internal, physiological states is much greater in "lower" species than it is in primates and humans. At the level of human sexual behaviors, sex hormones may be necessary, but they are seldom sufficient for the maintenance of sexual responding; and for an experienced human, they may not even be necessary.

Internal, Physiological Cues. With rats, matters of sex are quite simple and straightforward. In the male rat, if adequate supplies of testosterone (the male sex hormone) are present, and if there is the opportunity, the rat will respond to the hormone-induced sex drive and will engage in sexual behaviors. In the female rat, if adequate supplies of estrogen and progesterone (the female sex hormones) are present, and if the opportunity is available, the female rat will also engage in appropriate sexual behaviors. For rats at least, learning and past experience seem to have little to do with sexual behaviors; they are tied closely to physiology, to hormonal levels. It is difficult to tell the difference between the mating behaviors of sexually experienced rats, rats that have mated once or twice, and virgin rats. If the sex hormones of a female rat are removed (by surgically removing the ovaries), there will be a complete and immediate loss of sexual receptivity. If these sex hormones are then replaced by injection, sexual behaviors return to normal (Davidson et al., 1968). Removing the sex hormone from male rats produces a slightly different story. Sexual behaviors do diminish and may disappear, but they take longer to do so. Again, injections of testosterone quickly return the male rat to normal sexual functioning.

Removal of the sex hormones from male dogs or cats ("higher" species than rats) also produces a reduction in sexual behaviors, but much more gradually than for rats. An experienced male primate ("higher" still) may persist in sexual behaviors for the rest of his life, even after his sex hormones have been removed. (The same also seems true of human males, although the data here are sketchy.)

Even in primate females, removal of the sex hormones (by removing the ovaries) results in a rather sudden loss of sex drive and a cessation of sexual behaviors. In female primates (and in dogs, cats, rats, and so on), sexual responsiveness is well predicted by the hormone-driven fertility cycle. The period during which ovulation (the release of the eggs or ova from the ovary) occurs is the time of greatest sexual drive and activity. In the human female, we find a different story. The human female's receptiveness to sexual activity appears not to be related to the fertility, or estrous, cycle (Bennett, 1982). And menopause, the period after which the ovaries no longer produce ova and sex hormones, does *not* bring about an end to sexual interest or sexual behavior for the human female.

So what we find is that the sex drive in "lower" species is tied to its physiological, hormonal base. As the complexity of the organism increases, from rats, to dogs, to primates, to humans, the role of internal cues becomes less certain and less noticeable.

External, Psychological Cues. No one would get far arguing that sex is not an important human drive. However, it is easy to lose sight of the fact that it is basically a *biological* drive. Particularly in societies like ours, where so much learning is involved, one could easily come to believe that sex drives are learned through experience and practice alone. (Considerable unlearning may also be involved here: Satisfying the sex drive may involve unlearning prohibitions and anxieties acquired in childhood and adolescence.) Hormones may provide humans with an arousing force to do something, but *what* to do, *how* to do it, and *when* to do it often seem to require training and practice. Sex manuals of a "how to" nature sell well, and sex therapy has become a standard practice for many clinical psychologists trying to help people cope with the pressures that external factors put on their "natural" sexual motivation.

In addition to the internal forces produced by the sex hormones, sex drives can be stimulated by a wide range of environmental stimuli. Some people engage in sexual behaviors simply to reproduce; others do so for the physical pleasure they experience; others, because they feel it demonstrates a romantic "love" for another; yet others want to display their femininity or masculinity.

Sexual drives in humans are seldom satisfied with "just anybody." Many social (external) and cognitive constraints are often placed on one's choice of a sexual partner. What "turns someone on" sexually varies considerably from person to person. Virtually any of the senses—touch, smell (particularly important in lower mammals and primates), sight, and sound—can stimulate sexual arousal. (Again, see Topic 10B for a discussion of the external cues that arouse sexual behaviors in humans and a discussion of problems related to human sexuality.)

We'll close this discussion of physiologically based drives with hunger, which is based on the clear physiological need for food. Here too, we will see that the physiological basis for a drive is often influenced by factors that are psychological and social in nature.

BEFORE YOU GO ON

In what ways is the sex drive a unique physiologically based drive?

Hunger and Eating Behavior

Our need for food is as obvious as our need for water. If we don't eat, we die. Again, the interesting question is, what gives rise to the hunger drive? As it happens, many factors motivate a person to eat. Some of them are physiological in nature. Some are more psychological and reflect learning experiences. Some involve social pressures.

Internal, Physiological Cues. People and animals with no stomachs still feel hungry periodically and eat amounts of food not unlike those eaten by people with their stomachs intact. Cues from our stomachs, then, don't seem to be very important in producing a hunger drive. The two structures that seem most involved in the hunger drive are the hypothalamus (again) and the liver, which is involved in the production and breakdown of fat.

Theories of hunger that focus on the role of the hypothalamus are referred to as *dual-center* theories. This label is used because such views suggest that there are *two* regions in the hypothalamus that regulate food intake. One is an "eat" center that gives rise to feelings of hunger, while the other is a "no-eat" center that lets us know when we've had enough.

There are two centers (called *nuclei*) in the hypothalamus that have predictable effects on eating behavior when they are electrically stimulated or when they are destroyed. Removing or lesioning the "eat center," for example, leads to starvation, while lesioning the "no-eat center" leads to extreme overeating (Friedman & Stricker, 1976; Keesey & Powley, 1975).

Although the hypothalamus may be involved in eating behaviors, normal eating patterns are not under the influence of artificial electrical stimulation and lesioning procedures. What activates the brain's hunger-regulating centers in a normal organism? Here, we are still at the level of hypothesis and conjecture, not fact.

One long-accepted view was that the body responds to levels of blood sugar, or glucose in our blood, that can be metabolized, or converted into energy, for the body's use. When glucose metabolism levels are low, which they are when we haven't eaten for a while, we are stimulated to eat. When blood sugar levels are adequate, we are stimulated to stop eating. And, it may be that our *liver* is the organ that most closely monitors such blood chemistry for us.

Another view holds that we respond, through a complex chain of events, to levels of fat stored in our bodies. When fat stores are adequately filled, we feel no hunger. When fat supplies are depleted, a hunger drive arises. Once again, it is the *liver* that is involved in the cycle of storing and depleting fat supplies.

Yet another view that emphasizes the role of internal, physiological cues also relies heavily on the concept of set point, or homeostasis. The essence of this position is that a person's overall *body weight*, like one's blood pressure or temperature, is physiologically regulated (Nisbett, 1972). "Being so regulated, weight is normally maintained at a particular level or set-point, not only by the control of food intake, as is often assumed, but also by complementary adjustments in energy utilization and expenditure" (Keesey & Powley, 1986). The implication, of course, is that as body weight decreases significantly, either through dieting, exercise, or both, the organism becomes motivated to return to the set point level. The result may be to abandon the diet, cut down on exercise, or both. Conversely, if one eats too much—more than is necessary to maintain one's homeostatic level of energy consumption and storage—one will become motivated to expend energy to return to set point levels. Still to be determined are the mechanisms involved in establishing one's set point body weight and energy utilization levels to begin with. There is some evidence that these are influenced by both genetic factors (Nisbett, 1972) and feeding behaviors during infancy (Knittle, 1975).

We no doubt receive a number of internal cues that simultaneously inform us of our physiological need for food (Friedman & Stricker, 1976). Many of the cues may be subtle and effective in the long term (e.g., sensitivity to stored fat levels or energy utilization), while others may be more immediate. As we all know, like drinking behavior and sexual behaviors, eating behaviors also may be influenced by factors over and above those from our physiology.

External, Psychological Cues. We often respond to external cues that stimulate us to engage in eating behaviors. Here we'll consider a few of the nonphysiological influences that may motivate us to eat.

Sometimes, just the *stimulus properties* of foods—aroma, taste, or appearance—may be enough to get us to eat. You may not want any dessert after a large meal until the waitress shows you a piece of cheesecake with cherry topping. Ordering and eating that cheesecake has nothing to do with your internal physiological conditions.

Sometimes people eat more from *habit* than from need (Schachter & Gross, 1968). "It's 12 o'clock. It's lunch time; so let's eat." We may fall into habits of eating at certain times, tied more to the clock than to internal cues from our bodies. Some people are virtually unable to watch television without poking food into their mouths, a behavioral pattern motivated more by learning than by physiology.

Occasionally, we find that we eat simply because others around us are eating. Such "socially facilitated" eating has been noted in several species (e.g., Harlow, 1932; Tolman, 1969). For example, if a caged chicken is allowed to eat its fill of grain, it eventually stops eating. When other hungry chickens are placed in the cage and begin to eat, the "full" chicken starts right in eating again. Its behaviors are not noticeably different from those of the chickens just added to the cage.

It may very well be the case that overweight people tend to be less sensitive to internal hunger cues from their bodies and more sensitive to external eating cues from the environment (Schachter, 1971), although there also is research evidence that this logical analysis is not always true (Rodin, 1981). On the other hand, some persons may have a body weight set point that is genetically, or physiologically, higher than average. Persons who are significantly overweight generally have larger *and* greater numbers of fat cells (Nisbett, 1972).

Research evidence suggests that there are powerful genetic forces at work that determine one's overall body size *and* the distribution of fat throughout the body (Stunkard, 1988; Stunkard et al., 1986). One experiment (Bouchard et al., 1990) looked at the effects of forced overeating on 12 pairs of young adult (age 19 to 27) male identical twins. After eating normally for a two-week period, the subjects were required to consume an excess of 1000 calories of food each day for 6 days a week over a 100-day period. In other words, each subject was overfed 84,000 calories during the experiment. Weight gain compared between twin pairs varied considerably by the end of the study. But, significantly, there were virtually *no differences in weight gain within each pair of twins*! Not only that, but where excess was stored in the body (waist or hips, for example) during the overeating varied between pairs of twins, but not within pairs. The researchers concluded that "the most likely explanation for the intrapair similarity in the adaptation to long-term overfeeding and for variations in weight gain and fat distribution among the pairs of twins is that genetic factors are involved. These may govern the tendency to store energy as either fat or lean tissue and the various determinants of the resting expenditure of energy" (p. 1477).

A related correlational study looked at the body weights of identical twins and fraternal twins reared together and reared apart (Stunkard et al.,

Habit is a cue that can motivate us to eat. For many people, watching television and consuming salty snacks go hand in hand.

1990). This study found that regardless of where or how the twins were reared, there was a significant relationship between genetic similarity and body mass. Even early childhood environment had little or no effect. There is some concern that these results might be overinterpreted. "There is a risk that publishing this conclusion may lead the popular media to declare that what goes on in the home really makes no difference. That would be regrettable" (Sims, 1990). All these data suggest is that genetic factors are important in the ultimate determination of body weight and size and the distribution of fat within the body. They do not suggest that the only factors involved are genetic.

For people who are overweight, it would be nice to know that there is some simple, foolproof way to lose weight. Given that there are so many factors that influence eating, such a hope is not likely to be fulfilled in the near future. It seems that no one physiological mechanism has the sole control of our hunger drive (Thompson, 1980). And no one personality trait leads to obesity (Leon & Roth, 1977). Occasionally, a concern about becoming overweight can lead to seriously maladjusted behaviors, called eating disorders. It is to this issue that we turn next.

BEFORE YOU GO ON

List the internal and external factors that influence eating.

Eating Disorders. It is clear that the eating habits of many North Americans are not what they ought to be. Some of us simply eat too much—too much saturated fat in particular. In this section, we focus on two disruptive disorders of eating: anorexia nervosa and bulimia. Although these two disorders are thought of as being independent, there are many cases in which an individual shows the symptoms of both at the same time.

anorexia nervosa *an eating disorder characterized by the reduction of body weight through self-starvation and/or increased activity levels*

Anorexia nervosa is characterized by an inability (or refusal) to maintain one's body weight. It is essentially a condition of self-starvation, accompanied by a fear of becoming fat and a feeling that one is fat despite the fact that the person is considerably *under*weight (usually less than 85 percent of normal weight) (APA, 1987; Yates, 1989). The person with anorexia nervosa maintains a reduced body weight by severely cutting down on food intake and/or by increasing levels of physical activity. The disorder is surprisingly common, particularly among females. Nearly 1 percent of adolescent girls suffer from anorexia. Only about 10 to 15 percent of anorexic patients are males (Yates, 1990).

bulimia *an eating disorder characterized by recurrent episodes of binge eating and then purging to remove the just-eaten food*

Bulimia is a disorder characterized by repeated episodes of binge eating followed by purging—usually self-induced vomiting or the use of laxatives to rapidly rid the body of just-eaten food (APA, 1987; Yates, 1989). The binge eating episodes are usually well planned, anticipated with a great deal of pleasure, and involve rapidly eating large amounts of high-calorie, sweet-tasting food. Like the anorexic patient, the individual with bulimia shows great concern about body weight. Unlike someone with anorexia nervosa, a bulimic patient is typically of normal to slightly below normal weight.

Anorexia nervosa is an eating disorder that can be so devastating patients need to be fed through a stomach tube inserted through their nose.

Again, most bulimic patients are female, and usually from upper socioeconomic classes. Nearly 4 percent of female college freshmen suffer from the disorder, compared to only 0.4 percent of male freshmen. *Fifteen* percent of female medical students develop an eating disorder sometime in their lives (Yates, 1989).

What causes these eating disorders, and can anything be done to treat them effectively? Eating disorders probably have a number of interacting causes, and at present it is impossible to say which might be the most important. The high value that Western culture places on thinness may be one contributor. We constantly are being bombarded with messages that communicate the same theme: "To be thin is good; to be fat is bad." Role models for many young girls include superthin fashion models, dancers, and entertainers. More than 75 percent of all adolescent girls desire to weigh less than they do (Yates, 1989).

When we look for specific behavioral or personality traits that might predict the development of an eating disorder, we find very little. There is a tendency for adolescent girls with eating disorders to have rather strong needs for achievement and approval. There is evidence that patients with eating disorders show relatively high rates of depression. But a reaction such as depression may very well be a response to an eating disorder rather than a cause (Garner et al., 1990).

A number of psychologists have looked at parenting and family "style" as contributors to eating disorders. As it happens, anorexia nervosa patients *do* tend to come from very rigid, rule-governed, overprotecting families. And bulimic patients often experienced inordinate blame and rejection in childhood (Bruch, 1980; Yates, 1990). You know by now not to overinterpret general findings like these; there are many exceptions.

prognosis *the prediction of the outlook or likely course for an illness or a disorder*

Obviously, researchers have considered physiological processes as at least potential causes of eating disorders. One potentially significant line of scientific detective work stems from the often-confirmed observation that bulimic patients do not "feel full" after they eat, even after they binge (Pyle, Mitchell, & Eckert, 1981; Walsh et al., 1989). This may be due to the fact that the hormone *cholecystokinin* (or CCK) is produced in very low levels in bulimic patients. This is significant because CCK is a hormone normally produced in the small intestine that may signal that one is full and need eat no more. When drug treatment elevates CCK levels in bulimic patients, they often (but not always) show fewer symptoms of the disorder.

Evidence on the treatment of eating disorders is sketchy, unclear, and very tentative. In part this reflects the fact that we do not know for sure what causes the disorders. The **prognosis**, or prediction of the future course of a disorder, for anorexia nervosa is particularly poor. Nearly 50 percent of those who *are* released from treatment relapse within one year (Yates, 1990). Approximately 5 percent of patients with anorexia actually die from excessive weight loss (Hsu, 1986). At first, treatment will be medical in response to nourishment needs. Hospitalization may be required. Virtually all forms of psychotherapy (see Topic 13B) have been tried, but with little consistent success. At the moment no one form of therapy seems significantly more effective than any other form. The best predictor of the success of psychotherapy is the extent to which the family of the patient gets involved, which reinforces the notion that parental and family pressures may be part of the cause of eating disorders.

The outlook for bulimia is usually much better. If nothing else, bulimic patients are seldom malnourished and do not require hospitalization for that reason. For persons with bulimia it is also true that the prognosis is much better with family-oriented therapy programs rather than with individual treatment. With bulimic patients there has been some good (but generally short-lived) success with antidepressant medications (Geracioti & Liddle, 1988; Pope et al., 1985; Pope & Hudson, 1986).

The increasingly more common disorders of anorexia nervosa and bulimia serve to remind us how physiological processes and psychological processes can interact to produce complex patterns of behavior. Even a motivator with as obvious a physiological basis as our need for food can be, and often is, influenced by forces that have nothing to do with biological survival. Having seen how experience can impact on physiologically based drives, now we can move on to consider motivators of human behavior for which there is virtually no known physiological basis: the sources of motivation we're calling psychologically based.

BEFORE YOU GO ON

Describe the symptoms of anorexia nervosa and bulimia.
What can we say about their causes and treatment?

PSYCHOLOGICALLY BASED MOTIVATION

From time to time, you may be able to analyze your own behavior in terms of physiologically based needs and drives. For example, that you had breakfast this morning soon after you got up might have reflected your response to a hunger drive. That you got dressed might have been your attempt to do what you could to control your body temperature, which also may have influenced your choice of clothes. Perhaps some sexual motivation affected what you chose to wear today.

Many of our behaviors seem to be aroused and directed (motivated) by forces that are more subtle and less clearly biological in origin. In this section, we'll review some of the motivators that reflect learned or social influences on our behaviors. Remember that we are going to refer to these psychologically based drives as *motives*. Although there are potentially a large number of such motives, we will review four that have generated considerable attention as mechanisms for "explaining" human behavior: achievement, power, affiliation, and competency motivation.

Achievement Motivation

The hypothesis that people are motivated to varying degrees by a need to achieve was introduced to the literature of psychology in 1938 by Henry Murray. The **need to achieve** (**nAch**) is defined as the acquired need to meet or exceed some standard of excellence in one's behaviors. Measuring nAch and determining its sources and implications have been the major work of David McClelland and his associates (e.g., McClelland, 1985; McClelland et al., 1953).

need to achieve (nAch) *the learned need to meet or exceed some standard of excellence in performance*

Although there are short, paper-and-pencil tests for the same purpose, achievement motivation is usually assessed by means of the **Thematic Apperception Test** (**TAT**). This test is a *projective test* (see Topic 10A). Subjects are asked to tell short stories about a series of rather ambiguous pictures depicting people in various settings (see Figure 11.4). Subjects' stories are then interpreted and scored according to a series of objective criteria that note references to attempting difficult tasks, succeeding, being rewarded for one's efforts, setting short- and long-term goals, and so on. Because there are no right or wrong responses to the TAT, judgments are made about the references to achievement that a subject "projects" into the picture.

Thematic Apperception Test (TAT) *a projective personality test requiring a subject to tell a series of short stories about a set of ambiguous pictures*

One of the first things that McClelland and his co-workers found was that there *were* consistent differences in measured levels of nAch among the male subjects they tested. One of the most reliable findings concerning people with high needs for achievement involves the nature of tasks they choose to attempt. When given a choice, they generally try to do tasks in which success is not guaranteed (otherwise, there is no challenge), but in which there still is a reasonable chance of success. Both young children (McClelland, 1958) and college students (Atkinson & Litwin, 1960) who were high in nAch were observed playing a ring-toss game, where the object was to score points by tossing a small ring over a peg from a distance. The farther away from the peg one stood, the more points one could earn with success. High nAch subjects in both studies chose to stand at a moderate

Figure **11.4**

A picture like one of those found in the TAT. What is going on here? What led up to this situation? What is going to happen next? Because the answers to these questions are not immediately obvious, a subject may project some of his or her own feelings, beliefs, and motives into a response to these questions.

distance from the peg. They didn't stand so close as to guarantee success, but they didn't choose to stand so far away that they would almost certainly fail. Subjects with low nAch scores tended to go to either extreme—very close, earning few points for their successes, or so far away they rarely succeeded.

McClelland would argue that you are reading this text at this moment because you are motivated by a need to achieve. You want to do well on your next exam. You want to get a good grade in this course, and you have decided that to do so, you need to study the assigned text material. Some students read assignments not because they are motivated by a need to achieve, but because they are motivated by a *fear of failure* (Atkinson & Feather, 1966). In such a case, the incentive that is relevant is a negative one (avoid an F), which is a different matter than working toward a positive incentive (earn an A). Individuals motivated by a fear of failure tend to take very few risks. They either choose to attempt tasks that they are bound to do well or to attempt tasks that are virtually impossible (if the task is impossible, they can't blame themselves for their failures). There *are* explanations for why people choose tasks of the difficulty they do that do not rely on the notions of achievement or failure. One (e.g., Dweck, 1986) suggests that persons choose tasks of moderate difficulty when they are motivated to learn from their experience and improve themselves, while people choose easy tasks when they are motivated to "show off" and demonstrate superior performance.

In this regard, I should mention the concept of *fear of success*. This concept, introduced in 1969 by Horner, was used to account for the motivation of many women who were said to back off from competition for fear of succeeding and thereby losing popularity and femininity. It turns out that although there may be some merit in the notion of fear of success as an explanatory mechanism, it has not fared well in experimental tests (e.g., Jackaway & Teevan, 1976; Mednick, 1979).

It seems that the need to achieve is learned, usually in childhood. Children who show high levels of achievement motivation are generally those who have been encouraged in a positive way to excel ("Leslie, that grade of B is very good; do you think you could make an A next time?" as opposed to, "What! only a B?"). High nAch children generally are encouraged to work things out for themselves, independently, perhaps with parental support and encouragement ("Here, Leslie, you see if you can do this" as opposed to, "Here, dummy, let me do it; you'll never get it right!"). McClelland is convinced that achievement motivation can be specifically taught and acquired by almost anyone, of any age, and he has developed training programs designed to increase achievement motivation levels (e.g., McClelland & Winter, 1969).

Achievement motivation is one of the most actively researched types of human motivation. No doubt, nAch can be a useful concept to explain the "why" of what motivates many people. But for many others, achievement per se is only part of the answer. Let's now consider some of the alternatives.

BEFORE YOU GO ON

What is achievement motivation, and how is it usually measured?

Power Motivation

Some people are motivated not only to excel, but also to be in control, to be in charge both of the situation and of others. In such cases, we may speak of a **need for power** (McClelland, 1982; Winter & Stewart, 1978). Power needs generally are measured in the same way as achievement needs, through the interpretations of stories generated with the Thematic Apperception Test. Notice that a high need for power is, in itself, neither good nor bad. Power, in itself is neither good nor bad. What matters is the end to which one's power is put.

People with high power needs like to be admired. They prefer to be in situations where they can control the fate of others, usually by manipulating access to information. They present an attitude of, "If you want to get this job done, you'll have to come to me to find out how to do it." People with low power needs tend to avoid situations in which others would have to depend on them. They tend to be rather submissive in interpersonal relationships. Even though the situation is changing ever so slowly, in Western cultures, men are more commonly to be found in positions of power than are women (Darley & Fazio, 1980; Falbo & Peplau, 1980; Mulac, Incontro, & James, 1985). At the same time, there seem to be *no* reliable differences between men and women in measured needs for power (Winter, 1988).

need for power *the learned need to be in control of events or persons, usually at another's expense*

Some people are strongly influenced by a need for power; to be in control of the fate of others, to be "in charge."

Affiliation Motivation

need for affiliation *the need to be with others and to form relationships and associations*

Another psychologically based motivator that has been found to be helpful in explaining the behaviors of some people is the **need for affiliation**. This motive involves a need to be with others, to work with others toward some end, and to form friendships and associations.

One interesting implication of having a high need for affiliation is that it is often at odds with a need for power. Logic suggests that if you are simultaneously motivated to be in control *and* to be with others in a truly supportive way, conflicts may arise. It is more difficult to exercise power over people whose friendship you value than it is to exercise power and control over people whose friendship is of little concern to you. It remains the case, however, that there *are* circumstances in which we find persons who are high on both power and affiliation needs. These are often politicians who certainly enjoy the exercise of power, but who also value being public figures and being surrounded by aides and advisors (e.g., Winter, 1987). It is also the case that affiliation and achievement motives are somewhat independent. Achievement and success can be earned either with others (high affiliation) or on one's own (low affiliation).

Although we might be quite confident that achievement and power motives are learned, we are less confident about the sources of affiliation motivation. There is a reasonable argument that the need to affiliate and be with others is at least partly biologically based. We are basically social animals for whom complete social isolation is quite difficult (particularly when we are young). On the other hand, it seems clear that the extent to which we come to value affiliation relationships can be attributed to our learning experiences. A somewhat different approach to motivation comes to us from the work of Robert White, who claims that often we respond to a simple human need to demonstrate some degree of competence in dealing with the world around us.

Some people are strongly influenced by a need for affiliation; to be with others, socializing, perhaps working together for common goals.

Competency Motivation

need for competence *the need to meet the challenges, large and small, provided by one's environment*

Robert White has proposed that everyone is motivated by a basic **need for competence** (White, 1959, 1974). To be competent does not imply excellence, nor does it suggest success at the expense of others. It simply means managing to cope effectively, on one's own, with the challenges of everyday living.

More general than the needs for achievement, power, or affiliation, the need for competence has been used to account for a wide range of behaviors. Some people develop competence with musical instruments, others in their jobs, others at some hobby or sport. The point is that we are all motivated to find something we can do reasonably well. When you start to help a child who is attempting to do something that you judge he or she cannot do, the child may respond, "I can do it myself!" The child is trying to maintain (or develop) a sense of competence, which you may have challenged simply by offering to help.

As with other types of human motivation, the need for competency varies considerably from person to person. Some people are satisfied with being able to handle a small number of everyday tasks. Others seek to find new and different ways to express their competency or mastery over the environment (Harter, 1978).

Our behaviors are often motivated by a need for competence. We are all motivated to find something we can do well—perhaps some artistic or creative hobby that we can enjoy and master.

The motivational concepts we have briefly introduced in this section might be useful in trying to understand why students decide to attend college. Although there may be many reasons, all operating at once, some become college students to satisfy achievement needs ("I can do college work, and do it well"). Some see college as a means of gaining power ("With a college degree I can be the boss and tell others what to do"). Some see attending college as providing opportunities for meeting new people and establishing relationships. Others try college just because they want to see if they can do it; they appreciate the challenge to demonstrate competency.

BEFORE YOU GO ON

Define the needs for power, affiliation, and competence.

In this topic, we have examined some of the issues related to the psychology of motivation. The study of motivation is directed at trying to explain what arouses and directs an organism's behaviors and/or mental processes. As we have seen, psychologists have generated a number of concepts to explain why organisms do what they do: instinct, need, drive, homeostasis, arousal, and cognitive dissonance, to name just a few. The approaches that these terms represent have each added to our understanding of motivation. We also have seen, by looking at examples, how these concepts can help us explain some common behaviors.

How have the concepts of instinct, drive, and incentive been used to explain motivated behaviors?

In trying to explain why organisms do what they do, three concepts have proven useful. *Instincts* are complex patterns of behavior that occur in the presence of certain stimuli. Instinct approaches take the position that some complex behavioral patterns are unlearned, or innate. The concept of instinct has not proven to be a satisfactory explanation of human behavior. *Needs* are shortages of some biological necessity. Deprivation leads to a need, which gives rise to a drive, which arouses and directs the organism's behavior. The relationship between deprivation, need, drive, and behavior is often not very straightforward; many drives are more learned than biologically based. Maslow has proposed that human needs can be placed in an ordered hierarchy, beginning with basic survival needs and ending with a need to self-actualize. Focusing on *incentives* explains behaviors more in terms of their goals and outcomes than on their internal driving forces. We may say that incentives "pull" behavior, whereas drives "push" behavior. In this sense, we become motivated to reach some desired end state. These three approaches are not mutually exclusive, and each may be used to explain some types of motivated behavior. / *page 503*

How can the concept of balance or equilibrium be used to help us understand motivated behaviors? In what way is cognitive dissonance theory based on equilibrium?

The basic idea here is that organisms are motivated to reach and maintain a state of balance—a set point level of activity. With *homeostasis*, we have a general drive to maintain a state of equilibrium among internal physiological conditions such as blood pressure, metabolism, and heart rate. Others argue for a general drive to maintain a balanced state of *arousal*, with different optimal levels of arousal being best suited for different tasks or situations. Similarly, Festinger claims that we are motivated to maintain consonance or balance among cognitive states, thereby reducing *cognitive dissonance*. / *page 506*

Given the concept of homeostasis, how might temperature regulation be thought of as a physiologically based drive?

Temperature regulation can be viewed as a physiological drive because we clearly have a need (and are driven) to maintain our body temperatures within certain strict (homeostatic) levels. Doing so often involves voluntary as well as involuntary responding. / *page 507*

List some of the internal and external factors that influence drinking behavior.

We are motivated to drink for a number of reasons: to relieve dryness in our mouths and throats and to maintain a homeostatic level of fluid within our bodies (monitored by the hypothalamus). We also engage in drinking behavior in response to external cues (stimulus values), such as taste, aroma, or appearance. What we drink is often influenced by our learning experiences. /*page 509*

In what ways is the sex drive a unique physiologically based drive?

There are four ways in which the sex drive is an unusual physiological drive.

(1) Individual survival does not depend on its satisfaction. (2) The drive involves seeking tension rather than seeking relief from tension. (3) It is not fully present at birth, but matures later. (4) The extent to which it is influenced by learned or external influences varies from species to species. / *page 511*

List the internal and external factors that influence eating.

A number of factors, both internal and external, affect eating behaviors. Internal factors include cues mediated by the hypothalamus, which may be responding to stored fat levels, blood sugar levels, or other indicators that our normal, homeostatic balance has been disrupted. Associated with this view is the position that body weight is maintained at a given set point both by food intake and exercise levels. There is evidence that body size may be largely determined by genetic factors. The stimulus properties of foods may motivate eating, as may habit patterns and social pressures. / *page 514*

Describe the symptoms of anorexia nervosa and bulimia. What can we say about their causes and treatment?

Anorexia nervosa and bulimia are eating disorders, most commonly found in females. The anorexic patient is essentially engaged in self-starvation, reducing body weight significantly. Bulimia involves recurrent episodes of binging and purging of large amounts of sweet, high-calorie foods. We do not know what causes eating disorders, but cultural, family, and hormonal influences have been implicated. Virtually all sorts of psychotherapy have been tried as treatments for eating disorders. The prognosis for anorexia is particularly poor. Family-oriented therapy seems most effective, and antidepressant medication occasionally is effective in the treatment of bulimia, at least for the short term. / *page 516*

What is achievement motivation, and how is it usually measured?

Achievement motivation, based on the need to achieve (nAch), is defined as one's need to attempt and succeed at tasks in such a way as to meet or exceed some standard of excellence. Achievement needs are usually assessed through the interpretation of short stories generated in response to the Thematic Apperception Test, or TAT, in which one looks for themes of striving and achievement. / *page 519*

Define the needs for power, affiliation, and competence.

The need for power is defined as the need to be in charge, to be in control of a situation or of others, usually at the expense of others. Affiliation needs involve being motivated to be with others, to form friendships and interpersonal relationships. A need for competence implies a need to demonstrate the ability to do something, to cope on one's own with the challenges of daily living. / *page 521*

TOPIC IIB

Emotion and Stress

Why We Care: A Topic Preview

Most of us like to think of ourselves as reasonable, rational, intellectual, and logical. We like to talk about our cognitive abilities—perceiving, learning, remembering, and problem solving. But if we were totally honest with each other, we probably would admit that it is our emotions that concern us most. We enjoy reflecting on our pleasant emotions and seek out ways to minimize our unpleasant emotions.

Some emotional reactions are quite unpleasant—fear, rage, jealousy, shame, and so on. Just the same, we would not want to give up our ability to experience emotions. To do so would be to surrender the likes of love, joy, satisfaction, and ecstasy. What causes us to become emotional and how we deal with our emotional reactions are important aspects of our identity, our personality.

We'll begin this topic with a brief discussion of how one might go about studying emotions scientifically, and we'll see that defining and classifying emotional reactions have proven to be difficult tasks. We'll also touch on two areas of research that have proven particularly fruitful: physiological aspects of emotion and how inner emotional states are expressed in behavior.

Once we have laid a foundation for our understanding of emotion in general, we'll turn our attention to the concept of stress. We'll see that stress is very much like an emotion: Stress involves both physiological reactions and unpleasant feelings. Stress also is like a motivator: People who are experiencing stress are motivated to do something to deal with the sources of that stress.

Our discussion of stress, the events that cause it, and the reactions that it motivates will be divided into two major sections. First, we'll enumerate a number of the common stressors, or sources of stress. Then, we'll examine the complex patterns of responses we may make when we are under stress. It will be clear by the end of this topic that psychologists care about emotions and about stress for the same reason that most people do: Stress and emotions are central to our life experiences.

THE NATURE OF EMOTION

Psychology has included emotion as part of its subject matter since its very earliest days in the late 1800s. Psychologists have learned a lot about emotional reactions, but answers to some critical questions have remained elusive. We want psychology to tell us just what emotions are and where they come from. We want to know what we can do to increase the pleasant emotions and eliminate the unpleasant ones. It is in regard to our emotional reactions that we most want simple, easy, and direct answers. These are the very reactions about which we tend to get emotional. As we'll see, however, there are good reasons why psychologists cannot provide direct and simple answers to all our questions about emotions.

Studying Emotion

In a way, one of our problems with the study of emotion involves limits on our methodology. In Chapter 1, I made the case that psychology's best, most useful method is the experiment. I noted that most of what we know in psychology today we have learned through doing experiments. One of the problems we have when studying emotion is that we often find that our best method is difficult or impossible to use, at least with humans. Even when it is possible to do experiments on emotionality, we often are prohibited from doing so by ethical considerations.

For example, we might want to measure the physiological changes that occur in subjects who are very afraid, very angry, and very happy. There is no doubt that we have at our disposal many instruments and techniques for monitoring physiological changes. But ethical considerations, as well as common sense, prohibit us from wiring subjects to measuring devices and scaring them out of their wits, making them very angry, and then making them very happy, just because we want to measure physiological changes. Even if we were not concerned with ethics, how could we ever be sure that our subjects' reactions of fear, anger, and joy were in any way equal in strength or degree? For that matter, how could we produce these emotional reactions in the laboratory in the first place?

Doing experiments is not psychology's only method of investigation. Why not use naturalistic observation? Why not observe emotional behaviors as they occur naturally, outside the laboratory? The problem here, at least with humans, and particularly for adults, is that it is often very difficult to accurately assess someone's emotional state—or the magnitude of someone's emotional state—on the basis of observable behaviors alone.

"Growing up," becoming a mature adult, often involves learning to hide or control one's true feelings and emotions. No matter how sad they may be, children often learn that "big boys don't cry." We learn that, in some circumstances at least, it is inappropriate to display our happiness outwardly in the presence of others. In Western cultures, we are taught that when we are angry, we should count to 10 and try to control our expressions of anger. As a result, it is often very difficult to make accurate observations about a person's emotional state by simple observation.

*Why are emotional responses
particularly difficult to study scientifically?*

Defining Emotion

For the moment, try to recall the last time you experienced an emotional reaction of some significance—perhaps the fear of going to the dentist, the joy of receiving an A on a classroom exam, the sadness at the death of a friend, or the anger at being unable to register for a class you really wanted to take. A careful analysis suggests that there are four components to your emotional reaction, whatever it may be. (1) You will experience a *subjective feeling*, or *affect*, which you may label fear, joy, sadness, anger, or the like. (2) You will have a *cognitive* reaction; you'll recognize, or "know," what has just happened to you. (3) You will have an internal, *physiological* reaction. This reaction will be largely visceral, involving your glands, hormones, and internal organs. (4) And you will probably engage in an overt, observable, *behavioral* reaction. You may tremble as you approach the dentist's office. You may run down the hallway, a broad smile on your face, waving your exam paper over your head. You may cry at the news of your friend's death. You may shake your fist and yell at the registrar when you cannot enroll in the class of your choice.

Emotions have four components: subjective feelings, cognitive interpretations, bodily reactions, and behavioral response. Viewing the Vietnam Veterans War Memorial in Washington D.C. is an emotional experience that causes sadness for many visitors. Graduation brings on a variety of emotions; while being a sad time of leaving friends and favorite school activities, it is also one of the most joyful times.

Notice that when we add an overt, behavioral component to emotions, we most clearly can see how emotions and motivation are related. Emotions are often viewed as being motivational in nature (Greenberg & Safran, 1989; Lang, 1985). As we saw in Topic 11A, to be motivated is to be aroused and directed to action. Emotional experiences often arouse and direct our behavior.

As it happens, there has been considerable debate within psychology concerning the definition of emotion. As one researcher puts it, "There is no consensus about the definition of emotion; one may quarrel endlessly about the word" (Frijda, 1988). The major issues, of course, have been: (1) What are the basic components of an emotional reaction, and (2) in what way or ways are those components related? Different answers to these questions have given rise to what are called theories of emotion, which we'll review next. For now, we need a working definition of emotion. An **emotion** is an experience that includes a subjective feeling, a cognitive interpretation, a physiological reaction, and some behavioral expression.

emotion *a reaction involving subjective feeling, physiological response, cognitive interpretation, and behavioral expression*

BEFORE
YOU GO
ON

What are the four components that define an emotional experience?

Theories of Emotion

Psychologists have long sought an acceptable theoretical model of emotion. Theories of emotion are attempts to state, in a systematic way, just how we become emotional and how the various components of an emotional state interact. In this section, we'll briefly review some of the theories that have had a significant impact on the way we think about emotion. In its own way, each has had a part to play in explaining the nature of emotion.

The James-Lange Approach. In the late 1890s, William James in the United States and Carl Lange in Denmark both arrived at essentially the same view of emotion. Common sense suggested that one perceives an emotion-producing stimulus, experiences some appropriate emotion, and then behaves accordingly. You see a low grade on a term paper, you become angry, and then slam your fist against the desk. Your behavior occurs because you are in an emotional state. James and Lange suggested a different chain of events.

Common sense approach

Stimulus ⟶ experience ⟶ appropriate
of emotion   response

According to James and Lange, you felt angry *because* you slammed your fist on the desk. You saw the low grade, banged the desk, and *then* you felt angry because you noticed what you had done. If you had realized that you were laughing and smiling, you would have interpreted your emotional reaction as joy or happiness.

The James-Lange theory claims that we experience an emotion as we do because of our awareness of the physiological and bodily responses we make to a stimulus situation. As James said (1890), we are sad because we cry, afraid because we tremble, and happy because we smile; not the other way around. If nothing else, the James-Lange theory was the first serious statement about the the relationships among the different components of an emotional reaction.

James-Lange approach

Stimulus ⟶ appropriate ⟶ experience
　　　　　　　response　　　　of emotion

The Cannon-Bard Approach. One of the toughest critics of the James-Lange approach was Walter Cannon (1927). Of prime concern for Cannon was an assumption, made by both James and Lange, that people can differentiate among the physiological changes that accompany an emotional reaction and thereby identify the emotion they are experiencing. We may be able to tell the difference between crying and trembling, but most physiological reactions in emotional situations are much more subtle. Cannon charged that there was no evidence that we can differentiate among internal physiological changes that occur during different emotional states.

It seemed to Cannon that the internal, visceral changes that we were supposed to be responding to were very slow in coming. Often stimulated by hormonal changes, they would be too slow to give rise to identifiable emotional feelings quickly enough. Cannon also knew that the mere presence of physiological reactions like those that occur in emotion does not produce the true experience of an emotional state (aerobic exercise, for example, can produce physiological reactions very much like those that occur when we are emotional). Cannon proposed a theory of his own, which was later expanded upon by Philip Bard (1934), and has come to be called the Cannon-Bard theory.

Cannon and Bard proposed that a lower brain center, the thalamus, receives emotion-producing stimulation and immediately sends messages to the cerebral cortex for interpretation *and* to yet lower brain centers to initiate a physiological reaction. (We now might feel more comfortable replacing the role of the thalamus with that of the limbic system, but the idea is the same in either case.)

Walter Cannon recognized that the physiological reactions that occur when we are emotional can also occur in nonemotional situations. For example, aerobic exercise produces many physiological reactions that are similar to those found in emotional states.

Cannon-Bard approach

　　　　　　　　　　　　　　　　　appropriate
　　　　　　　　　　　　　⟶　　response
Stimulus ⟶ thalamus
　　　　　　　　　　　　　⟶　experience
　　　　　　　　　　　　　　　of emotion

So, for this theory, the perception of an emotion-producing stimulus goes first to a lower brain center, then simultaneously to the cerebral cortex for interpretation and to the sympathetic division of the autonomic nervous system for expression. Although Cannon's focusing on the thalamus may have been misplaced, it did direct attention to lower brain centers, and it did suggest that higher brain centers also become involved early on in an emotional reaction.

Lazarus would say no. Zajonc would say yes. As is the case for many theoretical issues in psychology, the debate continues, and we are reminded of one our themes from Topic 1A: "For many questions in psychology, there are no simple answers."

Let us now turn to one last issue of theory: Are there basic, primary emotions, and if so, what are they?

BEFORE YOU GO ON

What are the major issues involved in theories of emotion? Name four theories of emotion and briefly summarize each.

Classifying Emotions

Although one's cognitions, physiology, and overt behavior are usually involved in an emotional reaction, there seems to be little doubt that a very important aspect is the subjective-feeling component. Perhaps it would help if we had a scheme or plan that described and classified different, specific emotional reactions in a systematic way.

In fact, there are a number of ways to classify emotional responses, and each has its own supporters. Wilhelm Wundt, in that first psychology laboratory in Leipzig, was concerned with emotional reactions. He believed that emotions could be described in terms of three intersecting dimensions: pleasantness-unpleasantness, relaxation-tension, and calm-excitement.

Carroll Izard (1972, 1977) has proposed a classification scheme that calls for nine primary emotions. From these, he claims, all others can be constructed. Izard's nine primary emotions are fear, anger, shame, contempt, disgust, distress, interest, surprise, and joy. (Isn't it sad that six of the nine are "negative" emotions? Only the last three are neutral or pleasant.) Izard calls these emotions primary because they cannot be dissected into simpler, more basic emotions and because each is thought to have its own underlying physiological basis. Other known emotions are then some combination of any two or more of these nine.

Robert Plutchik (1980a), on the other hand, argues for eight basic emotions. What makes these emotions primary, Plutchik argues, is that each can be directly tied to some adaptive pattern of behavior; they are emotions that can be related to survival. Plutchik's eight primary emotions, and their adaptive significance, are listed in Figure 11.5.

Plutchik also believes that emotions in addition to these eight are simply variants of the primary emotions. While rage, for example, may be an extreme emotion, it is viewed as being essentially the same as anger. Anger in a weaker form is annoyance (Plutchik, 1980b). Figure 11.6 is referred to as Plutchik's emotion solid. It shows the basic eight emotions on the top around the top row of the solid, more extreme versions of the same emotion on the top surface and weaker versions of the same experience below them. Notice also that emotions opposite each other on the solid represent opposite feelings. That is, ecstasy is taken to be the opposite of grief in this

Figure **11.15**

PLUTCHIK'S EIGHT PRIMARY EMOTIONS AND HOW THEY RELATE TO ADAPTIVE BEHAVIORS

Emotion, or feeling	Common stimulus	Typical behavior
1. Anger	blocking of goal-directed behavior	destruction of obstacle
2. Fear	a threat or danger	protection
3. Sadnes	loss of something valued	search for help and comfort
4. Disgust	something gruesome or loathsome	rejection; pushing away
5. Surprise	a sudden, novel stimulus	orientation; turning toward
6. Curiosity	a new place or environment	explore and search
7. Acceptance	a member of own group; something of value	sharing; taking in; incorporating
8. Joy	potential mate	reproduction; courting; mating

view. The fact that the solid has a smaller diameter toward the bottom is meant to represent the fact that as emotions become less intense, it is more difficult to tell them apart.

Whether there are eight or nine primary emotions (or more or fewer) and how they might be combined to form different emotions will depend on one's theoretical perspective. A recent review by Ortony and Turner (1990) lists more than a dozen different theoretical versions of basic, or primary, emotions. *None of them is in complete agreement with any other.* About the only issue on which there seems to be some consensus is that emotions are *valenced* states (Ortony, Clore, & Collins, 1988). That means that emotions can be classified as being either positive (relief, happiness, and the like) or negative (fear, anger, shame, and the like). But a related problem is that there isn't even complete agreement on how to distinguish between positive and negative emotions. Fear, for example, seems like a reasonable candidate for a list of negative emotions. Yet it is clear that fear can be *useful* and can serve to protect and guide one's behavior in adaptive ways. On what basis shall we make our judgments of positive and negative?

So where does this leave us? As sensible as it sounds to try to discover or construct a system of basic, primary emotions—particularly if such a system had a strong physiological or evolutionary foundation—the attempt may be somewhat misguided. One problem is that there is less than total agreement on just what *basic* or *primary* means when we're talking about emotions. Ortony and Turner end their summary this way: "Thus, the question 'Which are the basic emotions?' is not only one that probably cannot be answered, it is a misdirected question, as though we asked, 'Which are the basic people?' and hoped to get a reply that would explain human diversity" (1990).

If there is a conclusion regarding emotion with which all theorists seem to agree, it is that part of being emotional is a physiological, visceral response. To put it plainly, being emotional is a gut-level reaction. To be emotional involves more than our thinking, reasoning cerebral cortex. We turn next to discuss briefly the physiological aspects of emotionality.

Figure **11.16**

Plutchik's emotion solid.

Schachter-Singer model of emotion—the notion that how we feel in a given situation depends in large measure on how we cognitively assess, or appraise, that situation. Is that co-worker *really* trying to do you out of a promotion? Do you *really* care if you get invited to that party? *Must* you get an A on the next quiz to pass that course? Are things *really* as bleak as they seem, and so on? Meichenbaum (1977) argues that we can deal with stress by talking to ourselves, replacing negative statements (such as, "Oh, I'm in trouble now; I'm sure to be called on, and I'll embarrass myself in front of the entire class") with coping statements (such as, "I'll just do the best that I can, and in a little while this will all be over"). This cognitive approach does take a good bit of practice, but it can be effective.

Dealing with stress effectively may also entail learning how to relax. Now learning good relaxation techniques may not be as easy as it sounds, and may take some time, but there are a number of systematic ways of learning how to relax. Hypnosis may help. Meditation may help (see our discussion of these issues in Topic 4B). Feeling stressed and being relaxed are not compatible responses. If you can become totally relaxed, the experience of stress will be diminished (e.g., Lehrer & Woolfolk, 1984).

There is a growing body of evidence that physical exercise is a useful agent against stress (Crews & Landers, 1987; McCann & Holmes, 1984). It is sometimes difficult to say if physical exercise combats stress directly, or if it does so indirectly by improving one's physical health, self-esteem, and self-confidence. And, of course, one must be careful. Deciding that tomorrow you'll start running five miles each day, rain or shine, may be a decision that in itself will create more stress than it will reduce. Choose an exercise program that is enjoyable, that is not overly strenuous, and that helps you feel better about yourself.

Finally, I should mention the advantage of social support for persons who are experiencing stress. Stress is a common phenomenon. Perhaps no one else knows precisely how you feel or has experienced exactly the situation in which you find yourself, but all of us have known stress, and we all are aware of what kinds of situations give rise to it and how upsetting it can be. Social support, from friends and relatives if possible, from others if need be, can be very helpful. One should not face stress alone (Gottlieb, 1981; Hobfoll, 1986; Janis, 1983; Lieberman, 1983; Rook, 1987).

Now that we've reviewed some of the steps that one can take to help alleviate the unpleasantness of stress, let's consider some other reactions that stress may produce that are not so adaptive.

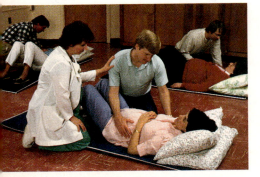

There is little doubt that pregnancy and childbirth are stressful life experiences. Social support in such situations provides an effective coping mechanism.

BEFORE YOU GO ON

What are some adaptive ways of dealing with stress?

Dealing with Stressors Ineffectively

Logic tells us that if one experiences stress and does *not* do any of the things we've just mentioned, then that person is not dealing effectively with the stressors in his or her life. To not change is to *fixate*, to keep accepting the same stress from the same stressor. Fixation is seldom an adequate reaction to stress. Don't get me wrong here. "If at first you don't succeed, try, try, again." Why, of course; this is sound advice. But, again, and again, and again? At some point one must be ready and able to give up a particular course of action to try something else. In a way, procrastination is a form of fixation, isn't it? A student has a term paper due in two weeks and just can't seem to get going on it, deciding to "put if off until this weekend." This weekend may not bring any progress either, but at least the stress of dealing with the paper is momentarily postponed. The catch, of course, is that there's going to be a price to pay. Eventually, the paper will *have* to be done, and then, with very little time before the deadline, the experienced stress probably will be greater than ever before. In addition to not changing one's behavior, or simply not doing anything at all, there are two other relatively common reactions to stressors that are clearly maladaptive: aggression and anxiety.

It is clear that there are many sources and causes of aggression and that one thing that motivates aggressive behavior is stress, stress that results from frustration in particular. At one time, it was proposed that frustration was *the* only cause of aggression, the so-called **frustration-aggression hypothesis** (Dollard et al., 1939). This point of view claimed that frustration could produce a number of reactions, including aggression, but that aggression was always caused by frustration. There *are* other sources of aggression (some view it as innate or instinctive, while others see it as a response learned through reinforcement or modeling that need not be stimulated by frustration). It is true, however, that frustration remains a prime candidate as the cause of a great deal of aggression. It doesn't do much good in the long run, but a flash of aggressive behavior often follows stress (Berkowitz, 1978; 1982, 1989, 1990).

frustration-aggression hypothesis *the view (now discredited) that all aggression stems from frustration*

There you are in the parking lot, trying to get home from class, and your car won't start. Over and over you crank the ignition. Frustrated, you swing open your door, get out, kick the front left fender, throw up the hood, and glower at the engine. Having released a bit of tension, you might feel better for a few seconds, but being angry and kicking at the car (or yelling at someone who offers to assist) won't help you solve your problem.

If stressors cannot be minimized or removed, if stressful experiences linger, the results may become quite debilitating. One of the consequences of stress that may occur is impaired physical health. Stress has been implicated in a number of physical disorders, mostly cardiovascular disease. We'll explore this relationship in some detail in Topic 15B in a section on health psychology.

Acts of aggression are usually unhelpful but are common reactions to frustration.

Another debilitating consequence of stress is *anxiety*—a general feeling of tension, apprehension, and dread that involves predictable physiological changes. Anxiety is a very difficult concept to define precisely, but everyone "knows" what you're talking about when you refer to anxiety. It is a reaction that we all have experienced. Often, it is a reaction that follows or accompanies stress. In many ways we can think of anxiety as an unpleasant emotional component of the stress response. As much as anything else, we want to rid ourselves of stress in order to minimize our anxiety.

Sometimes, the amount of stress and anxiety in one's life becomes more than one can cope with effectively. Feelings of anxiety start to interfere with natural, normal adaptation to the environment and to other people. Feelings of anxiety may become the focus of one's attention. More anxiety follows, and more distress, and more discomfort, and more pain. For many people—perhaps tens of millions of people in the United States and Canada—the anxiety that results from the stress in their lives is so discomforting and so maladaptive that we may say that they are suffering from an anxiety-based psychological disorder. In Chapter 12 we begin our discussion of psychological disorders (sometimes called mental illness), and we start with the anxiety-based disorders. Try to keep in mind when you get to that discussion just how commonplace stress and anxiety are.

BEFORE YOU GO ON

What is the frustration-aggression hypothesis?
What are some maladaptive reactions to stress?

In this topic, we have summarized some of what we know about emotion. Have you noticed the extent to which we have used the ABC model introduced back in Topic 1A? When we discuss emotions, there is little doubt that our primary focus is on the subjective experience or feeling of *a*ffect. But we've also seen that emotionality implies *b*ehavior, in terms of both overt action and phsyiological reaction. Although its precise role in emotionality may be questioned, being emotional also involves the *c*ognitive reactions of perceiving, knowing, and thinking.

We've seen how difficult it is to study emotions scientifically and to classify emotional reactions. We've noted that there is a consistency in how emotion is expressed through facial expressions. We've seen, particularly with stress, how emotional reactions also can serve a motivational function, arousing and directing our behaviors. To some degree, stress is unavoidable. We're faced with many potential stressors, among them frustration, conflict, and changes in our daily lives. Of particular importance is how one reacts to the stress that comes into his or her life. We have reviewed several adaptive and maladaptive reactions. Now we turn to patterns of affect, behavior, and/or cognitions that are clearly maladaptive: the psychological disorders.

Why are emotional responses particularly difficult to study scientifically?

It is difficult to study emotions in humans because (1) our ability to control important variables well and ethical considerations make it difficult to do many experiments, and (2) adults often have learned to hide their emotions from public view, making the use of naturalistic observation questionable. / page 527

What are the four components that define an emotional experience?

There are four possible components of an emotional reaction: the experience of a subjective feeling, or *affective* component; a *cognitive* appraisal or interpretation; an internal, visceral, *physiological* reaction; and an overt *behavioral* response. / page 528

What are the major issues involved in theories of emotion? Name four theories of emotion and briefly summarize each.

Theories of emotion are attempts to specify the components of an emotional experience and show how those components are interrelated. The *James-Lange theory* claims that we perceive an emotion-producing situation that produces a bodily reaction. We then interpret our bodily reaction to identify our emotional state; that is, we are afraid because we tremble, sad because we cry. The *Cannon-Bard theory* proposes that emotion-producing stimuli are processed by lower brain centers that simultaneously inform the cerebral cortex of the nature of the situation and stimulate other lower brain centers to initiate a physiological reaction. The *Schachter-Singer model* theorizes that one's interpretation of an emotional state depends on the interpretation of diffuse physiological arousal in terms of the cognitive appraisal of what is happening in the environment. The *opponent-process theory*

takes a somewhat different approach, suggesting that any felt emotion is accompanied by an opposite reaction that persists after the emotion-producing stimuli are no longer present. In theories of emotion, psychologists continue to try to characterize the relationships among the environment, our perceptions, our feelings, our physiological reactions, and our overt responses. / page 532

Can emotions be classified?

There have been several attempts to categorize emotional reactions, dating back to Wundt in the late 1800s. Izard has a scheme that calls for nine primary emotions. Plutchik argues that there are eight basic emotions and many combinations and degrees of them. Other theorists have proposed as few as two or as many as dozens of primary emotions. The inconsistency among the different theories leads some psychologists to wonder if the attempt to classify basic emotions is misguided. / page 534

Summarize the activities of the sympathetic division of the autonomic nervous system during emotional states.

Among the many changes that take place when we become emotional are those produced by the sympathetic division of the autonomic nervous system. Occurring to varying degrees and dependent on the situation, these reactions include dilation of the pupils, increased heart rate and blood pressure, cessation of digestive processes, deeper and more rapid breathing, increased perspiration, and elevated blood sugar levels. / page 535

What brain centers are involved in emotionality?

The cerebral cortex is involved in the cognitive interpretation of emotional events and also acts as an inhibitory mechanism, exerting some degree of

control over the activity of lower brain centers for emotionality (largely the limbic system and the hypothalamus). Basically, the brain coordinates physiological aspects of emotionality. / page 536

What is the relationship, if any, between facial expression and emotion?

Facial expressions indicate the internal, emotional state of an individual. What leads us to believe that facial expression of emotion is unlearned (and, hence, innate) is that there is such universal reliability in the interpretation of facial expressions, even across widely different cultures. Additionally, there are data indicating that one can actually change one's subjective emotional state by changing one's facial expression. / page 539

What is meant by frustration-induced stress? Define environmental and personal frustration, citing an example of each.

Frustration, a stressor, is the blocking or thwarting of goal-directed behaviors. The specific type of frustration that leads to stress is named according to the source of the blocking. If the source of the blocking is something in the environment, we call the frustration *environmental*. There are many examples: your car won't start; your pen runs out of ink in the middle of an exam; your dog eats your term paper. If the source of frustration is from within, from the person himself or herself, we call it *personal*. Examples include someone who does poorly in a physics course because of a poor math background or someone who agrees to go mountain climbing even though inexperienced and totally out of shape. / page 542

Name four types of motivational conflict and provide an example of each.

Motivational conflicts are stressors. They are situations in which we find that we cannot achieve all of our goals because our own motives and goals are in conflict. In an *approach-approach* motivational conflict, one is faced with two (or more) attractive goals and must choose among them when all are not available. In an *avoidance-avoidance* conflict, a choice must be made among unpleasant, potentially punishing alternatives. In an *approach-avoidance* conflict, there is but one goal under consideration; in some ways that goal is attractive, while in others it is not—it attracts and repels at the same time. Perhaps the most common conflict for humans is the *multiple approach-avoidance* conflict in which one faces a number of alternatives, each with its own strengths and weaknesses. / *page 544*

In what ways might simply being alive in the world produce stress?

Many psychologists argue that life events, particularly changes in one's life situation, act as stressors. The Social Readjustment Rating Scale (SRRS), for example, is an attempt to measure the severity of stress in one's life by having the person note recent life change events. Some events are rated as more stress producing than others. High scores on the SRRS have been correlated with increased incidence of physical illness. Some psychologists argue that little "hassles" in life can be more stress-inducing than large, catastrophic events. A recent view claims that we experience stress whenever we perceive that our psychological and physical resources are being threatened. / *page 546*

What are some adaptive ways of dealing with stress?

The only way to deal with stress effectively, for the long term, is to bring about some relatively permanent change in the situation. That is, one must learn to change one's goal-directed behaviors or learn to modify one's goals. In many cases, stress (and frustration-induced stress in particular) provides experiences and motivation for learning. Specific strategies for dealing with stress in an adaptive way include cognitive reappraisal (rethinking a situation in a more positive way), relaxation techniques, physical exercise, and the seeking of social support. / *page 548*

What is the frustration-aggression hypothesis? What are some maladaptive reactions to stress?

Many of our reactions to stress are maladaptive and unhealthy, in both a physical and psychological sense. Two ineffective reactions are fixation and aggression. The frustration-aggression hypothesis holds that frustration may produce a number of reactions, but aggression can always be traced to frustration. This view is now seen as overly simplistic, although some aggression does stem from frustration. In addition to fixation and aggression, a maladaptive response to stress is anxiety, which, in turn, may lead to further maladaptive responses and ultimately to any one of several physical and psychological disorders. / *page 550*

ABNORMAL PSYCHOLOGY

TOPIC 12A Anxiety-based and Personality Disorders

TOPIC 12B Organic, Mood, and Schizophrenic Disorders

Anxiety-based and Personality Disorders

Why We Care: A Topic Preview

I do not believe that there is any other chapter for which the answer to the question, "Why do we care?" is more obvious or straightforward as it is for this one. In this topic, we begin a discussion of psychological disorders, or mental illness. If we can say nothing else about psychological disorders, we can acknowledge that they are unpleasant, distressful, painful, and often devastating in their effects. We also can acknowledge that psychological disorders have an impact on all of us. I will spare you a lengthy recitation of the statistics on incidence and prevalence here. We'll talk about these data as we discuss specific disorders. For now, we only need to note that best available estimates tell us that as you read this sentence, at least 40 to 50 million men, women, and children in the United States are suffering from a psychological disorder (e.g., National Institute of Mental Health, 1984; Offord et al., 1987). Another commonly accepted claim is that at any point in time, "one in five Americans has mental illness" (e.g., Anderson et al., 1987; Backer & Richardson, 1989, p. 546). In many respects, statistics such as these are both astounding and frightening; they are also impersonal. It is difficult to conceptualize what it really means to say that tens of millions of people are suffering from a mental disorder. What we can say is that it is unlikely that any of us can be exempt from personally experiencing, or having someone close to us experience, the pain and suffering of psychological disorders, and that is why we care.

We'll begin our discussion with matters of definition. We'll review the implications of classification systems for the variety of psychological disorders. Having tackled some large theoretical issues, we'll begin a brief description of some of the more common or typical or bizarre psychological disorders. Simply to describe all of the known, identifiable psychological disorders is well beyond the scope of our needs. The intent in this chapter is to give you an idea of what some of the psychological disorders are like. In this topic, we'll examine some of the disorders for which anxiety is a major concern and we'll cover the personality disorders very briefly; more severe disorders will be covered in Topic 12B.

What is considered abnormal or deviant in one society may be quite normal in another. Cultures vary in many respects, including styles of dress. This Arab woman's layered clothing (top) is a sharp contrast to the way these Bororo tribesmen of West Africa are dressed (bottom).

DEFINITION AND CLASSIFICATION

We all have a basic idea of what we mean by such terms as *abnormal*, *mental illness*, or *psychological disorder*. The more we think about abnormality and what it means, however, the more difficult it becomes to define. In this section, we'll do two things: We'll generate a working definition of *abnormal* from a psychological perspective, and we'll consider the implications that follow from defining psychological disorders in terms of specific symptoms and then classifying and labeling those disorders.

Defining Abnormality

The concept of abnormal as it is used in psychology is not a simple one. Here's the definition we'll use: **Abnormal** means statistically uncommon, maladaptive cognitions, affect, and/or behaviors that are at odds with social expectations and that result in distress or discomfort. That is a lengthy definition, but to be complete, our definiton must include a number of crucial points. Let's now briefly review them one at a time.

One way to think about abnormality is to take a *literal* or statistical approach. Literally, abnormal means "not of the norm" or "not average." Thus, any behaviors or mental processes that are rare should be considered abnormal, and in a literal, statistical sense, of course, they are. The problem with this approach is that it would identify the behaviors of Michael Jordan, Michael Jackson, Albert Schweitzer, Frank Lloyd Wright, Whoopi Goldberg, and Madonna as abnormal. Statistically, they *are* abnormal; there are few others who do what these people do (or did); yet, as far as we know, none of these people has (or had) a psychological disorder. Psychological disorders are not common. They are not average or the norm in a statistical sense, but that in itself is not enough.

The reactions of people who suffer from a psychological disorder are *maladaptive*. This is a critical part of our definition. Thoughts, feelings, and behaviors are such that the individual does not function as well as he or she could without the disorder. To be different, or to be strange, does not in itself mean that someone has a psychological disorder. There must be some degree of impairment. That is, psychological functioning is "abnormal *if* it is maladaptive, that is, *if* it interferes with functioning and growth, if it is self-defeating" (Carson et al., 1988).

Another observation reflected in our definition is that abnormality may show itself at a number of different levels. We have anticipated this earlier. A person with a psychological disorder may experience abnormal *affect* (moods or feelings), engage in abnormal *behaviors*, have abnormal *cognitions* (thoughts, perceptions, and beliefs), or any combination of these. Once again we see our ABCs from Topic 1A.

A definition of psychological abnormality should acknowledge social and/or cultural expectations. What may be clearly abnormal and disordered in one culture may be viewed as quite normal or commonplace in another. In some cultures, loud crying and wailing at the funeral of a total stranger is considered strange or deviant; in others, it is common and expected. In some cultures, to claim that you have been communicating directly with dead ancestors would be taken as a sign of severe disturbance; in others, it would be treated as a great gift. The social context we are talking about here need not be so dramatic. Even in your own culture, behaviors that are appropriate, or at least tolerated, in one situation, say a party, may be judged to be quite inappropriate in another context, say a religious service.

One other issue needs to be addressed when we define psychological abnormality: Psychological disorders involve *distress* or *discomfort*. People who we consider to be abnormal are, in some way, suffering or are the source of suffering in others. Psychological disorders cause emotional distress, and individuals with psychological disorders are often the source of distress and discomfort to others—friends and family who care and worry about them.

So, as complex as it is, I hope that you can see that there is a reason for each of the points in our definition of abnormal: behaviors or mental processes that are statistically uncommon, at odds with social expectations, and result in distress or discomfort.

Now that we have a sense of what the term abnormal means in the context of psychology, let's be sure that we understand a few things that it does *not* mean. (1) Abnormal and normal are not two distinct categories. They may be thought of as endpoints on some dimension that we can use to describe people, but there is a large gray area between the two where distinctions get fuzzy. (2) Abnormal does not mean dangerous. True, some people diagnosed as having a mental disorder *may* do great violence to themselves and/or to others, but most people with psychological disorders are not dangerous at all. (3) Abnormal does not mean bad. People who are diagnosed to have psychological disorders are not necessarily bad people, or weak people, in any evaluative sense. They may do bad things, and bad things may have happened to them, but it is certainly not in psychology's tradition to make moral and ethical judgments about good and bad.

abnormal *statistically uncommon, maladaptive cognitions, affect, and/or behaviors that are at odds with social expectations and that result in distress or discomfort*

In 1979, Ted Bundy, pictured here, was convicted of the murder of two sorority girls in Tallahassee, FL. He confessed to the murder of 16 other women, and he was suspected of killing many others across the country. He was electrocuted on January 24, 1989. His is a fascinating case that illustrates the difficulty of understanding why patterns of behavior develop or what we can do about them even if we can give those behaviors a name.

BEFORE YOU GO ON

How do we define psychological abnormality?

The Classification of Abnormal Reactions

One way of dealing with the broad concept of psychological abnormality is to consider each individual psychological disorder separately, in terms of how that disorder is to be diagnosed. Indeed, **diagnosis** is the act of recognizing a disorder on the basis of the presence of particular symptoms. Once we've described individual disorders, it also would help if they could be organized or classified in a systematic way.

Systems of classification are quite common in science and are not at all new in psychology. In 1883, Emil Kraepelin published the first significant classification scheme for mental disturbances. It was based on the premise that each disorder had its own collection of symptoms (a *syndrome*) and its own cause (in Kraeplin's time each disorder was thought to have a biological cause). Although we now recognize that some of Kraeplin's work is no longer valid, he did demonstrate the value of classifying psychological disorders in a systematic way.

Emil Kraepelin

diagnosis *the act of recognizing a disorder on the basis of the presence of particular symptoms*

An example of the difficulty is as follows: Mary Beth, a third-grader, is referred to the school psychologist because she is very withdrawn, often seems to be on the verge of tears, will not talk about her home life, and is doing poorly in her academic work. Without going into the particulars of how to diagnose Mary Beth's problem, doesn't it seem misguided to focus all of our attention on Mary Beth (disregarding her family or the demands of the school) as we try to identify her problems? Is it acceptable to diagnose and label the individual without attending to the larger social networks of which that person is a part?

On "Insanity." So far I have used terms such as *mental disorder, behavior disorder*, and *psychological disorder* interchangeably. I shall continue to do so because the differences between such terms are of no real consequence. There is one term, however, with which we need to exercise particular care, and that's *insanity*.

insanity *a legal term for diminished capacity and inability to tell right from wrong*

Insanity is not a psychological term. It is a legal term. It relates to problems with psychological functioning, but in a rather restricted sense. Definitions of **insanity** vary from state to state, but to be judged as insane usually requires evidence that a person did not know or fully understand the consequences of his or her actions at a given time (showed diminished capacity), could not discern the difference between right and wrong, and was unable to exercise control over his or her actions.

A related issue has to do with whether or not a person is in enough control of his or her mental and intellectual functions to understand courtroom procedures and aid in his or her own defense. If one is not, one may be ruled "not competent" to stand trial for his or her actions, whatever those actions may have been.

Having discussed in a general way the problems of defining abnormality and classifying psychological disorders, it is time to turn our attention to specific disorders. We will not cover all of the disorders in the *DSM-III-R*. Instead, we'll look at disorders that are among the most common or that are particularly unusual in their symptoms. Remember, when we talk about the psychological disorders, by definition, we are talking about conditions that are not average, not to be accepted as the way things should be. Even though psychological disorders are not to be found in the majority, they are not rare.

BEFORE YOU GO ON

What is the DSM-III-R?
What are some of its advantages and disadvantages?

ANXIETY-BASED DISORDERS

anxiety *a general feeling of apprehension or dread accompanied by predictable physiological changes*

As we've seen, *anxiety* is a term that is difficult to define precisely. Even so, we can be confident in claiming that everyone has experienced anxiety and recognizes it as being unpleasant. We will define **anxiety** as a general feeling of apprehension or dread accompanied by predictable physiological changes: increased muscle tension, shallow rapid breathing, cessation of digestion, increased perspiration, and drying of the mouth. Thus, anxiety involves two levels of reaction: subjective feelings (e.g., dread or fear) and physiological responses (e.g., rapid breathing). Anxiety is the definitional characteristic of all the anxiety-based disorders, even though in some cases the anxiety is not clearly observable. The anxiety-based disorders used to be called *neuroses*. The term *neurosis* is no longer used in the *DSM-III-R*, but it is still in common use, even among mental health professionals.

As a group, anxiety-based disorders are the most common of all the psychological disorders. The National Institute of Mental Health reports high rates: Within a six-month period, from 7 to 15 percent of the population can be diagnosed with "one or more of the several anxiety diagnoses" (Freedman, 1984). Other studies indicate that these may be underestimates; rates in excess of 20 percent of the population, or nearly 50 million people, may be more accurate (Reich, 1986; Weissman, 1988). Anxiety-based disorders are two to three times more common in women than in men (Roth & Argyle, 1988). In any case, percentages of this sort do not convey the enormity of the problem. We need to remember that we're talking about real people here—people like you and me. In this section, we'll consider three subtypes of anxiety-based disorders: the anxiety disorders, somatoform disorders, and dissociative disorders.

Anxiety Disorders

We are beginning our discussion of psychological disorders with those that are anxiety based, and the first set of those disorders we'll cover are called, simply, anxiety disorders. We'll discuss five subtypes of anxiety disorder: phobic disorder, panic disorder, generalized anxiety disorder, obsessive-compulsive disorder, and posttraumatic stress disorder. The major symptom of *anxiety disorders* is experienced anxiety, often coupled with what is called avoidance behavior, or the attempt to resist or avoid the stimulus situation that produces the anxiety reaction.

Phobic Disorder. The essential feature of a **phobic disorder** (or phobia) is a persistent fear of some object, activity, or situation that consistently leads a person to avoid that object, activity, or situation. Implied in this definition is the notion that the fear is intense enough to be disruptive or debilitating. The definition also implies that there is no real or significant threat involved in the stimulus that gives rise to a phobia; that is, the fear is unreasonable, exaggerated, or inappropriate.

Many things in this world are life-threatening and downright frightening. If, for example, you were driving down a rather steep hill and suddenly realized that the brakes on your car were not working properly, you would be likely to feel an intense reaction of anxiety. Such a reaction would not be phobic because it is not irrational.

Similarly, there are few of us who truly enjoy the company of large numbers of bees. Just because we don't like bees and would rather they not be around does not qualify us as having a phobic disorder. What is missing here is *intensity* of response. People who do have a phobic reaction to bees (called mellissaphobia) often will refuse to leave the house in the summer for fear of encountering a bee and become genuinely upset and

phobic disorder *an intense, irrational fear that leads a person to avoid the feared object, activity, or situation*

A SAMPLE OF PHOBIC REACTIONS

Phobia	Is a fear of
Acrophobia	High places
Agoraphobia	Open places
Algophobia	Pain
Astraphobia	Lightning and thunder
Autophobia	One's self
Claustrophobia	Small, closed places
Hematophobia	Blood
Monophobia	Being alone
Mysophobia	Dirt or contamination
Nyctophobia	The dark
Pathophobia	Illness or disease
Pyrophobia	Fire
Thanatophobia	Death and dying
Xenophobia	The unknown
Zoophobia	Animals

Figure **12.2**

prognosis *the prediction of the future course of an illness or disorder*

agoraphobia *a phobic fear of open places, of being alone, or of being in public places from which escape might be difficult*

panic disorder *a disorder in which anxiety attacks suddenly and unpredictably incapacitate; there may be periods free from anxiety*

anxious at the buzzing sound of any insect, fearing it to be a bee. People with this disorder may become uncomfortable simply reading a paragraph, such as this one, about bees.

There are many different types of phobias. Most are named after the object or activity that is feared. Figure 12.2 lists some of the most common phobic reactions. Most phobias involve a fear of animals, although these phobias are not the type for which people most commonly seek treatment (Costello, 1982). In many such cases, the person with a phobic disorder can be successful simply by avoiding the source of the fear and, as a result, never seeks treatment. So long as one's phobia does not impact on one's day-to-day adjustment, treatment or therapy is not necessary. Sometimes, however, avoiding the source of one's phobia is impossible. Fortunately, the **prognosis** (the prediction of the future course of a disorder) is quite good for phobic disorders. That is, therapy for persons with a phobia is likely to be successful. You might want to review our earlier discussion of phobias (in Topic 5A) where we examined possible causes and treatments for simple phobias.

One of the most commonly *treated* varieties of phobia is **agoraphobia**, which means "fear of open places." The fear here is not reserved for those occasions in which one stands in the middle of a large open field, however. The diagnosis is for people who have an exaggerated fear of being alone or of venturing forth into the world where they may be trapped in an unpleasant or embarrassing situation. People with this disorder avoid crowds, streets, stores, and the like. They essentially establish for themselves a safe home base and may, in extreme cases, refuse to leave it altogether.

BEFORE YOU GO ON

What are the essential characteristics of a phobic disorder?

Panic Disorder. In phobic reactions, there is always a specific stimulus that brings about an intense fear response, and we find people taking steps to avoid the stimulus or object of their phobias. For a person suffering from **panic disorder**, the major symptom is recurrent, unpredictable unprovoked attacks of sudden, intense anxiety, or a panic attack (see APA, *DSM-III-R*, 1987, p. 236). These attacks may last for a few seconds or for hours. The subjective experience is similar to the fear of a phobic reaction, except that there is no particular stimulus to bring it on. The panic attack is unexpected. It just happens. And because it just happens, without warning, a complication of this disorder is that the individual soon begins to fear the next attack and the loss of control that it will bring.

At some point in their lives, about 1.5 percent of the adult population experiences panic disorder. (That 1.5 percent doesn't sound very significant until we realize that that's nearly 4 million people!) The age of onset for this disorder is commonly the mid-twenties (Markowitz et al., 1989). Initial panic attack episodes often are associated with stress, particularly the stress that results from the loss of an important relationship (Ballenger, 1989).

You may know from your own experience what such an attack feels like. For a person to be diagnosed with panic disorder, panic attacks must have occurred at a rate of at least four within a four-week period and be accompanied by a number of physiological symptoms (such as chest pain, difficulty breathing, dizziness, hot and cold flashes, sweating, or trembling—and a fear of going crazy). As it happens, most people who are diagnosed as having a panic disorder are also agoraphobic. The reverse is also true: Most cases of agoraphobia are seen as complications of a panic disorder.

Another complication of panic disorder is that it can be accompanied by intermittent feelings of depression (Noyes et. al., 1990). This may be why the rate of suicide and suicide attempts is so high for persons with this diagnosis (20 percent), which is higher, in fact, than for persons diagnosed with depression alone (15 percent) (Johnson, Weissman, & Klerman, 1990; Weissman et al., 1989).

BEFORE YOU GO ON

What is a panic disorder?

A job as a construction worker, laboring high above a city, would be out of the question for an individual afflicted with acrophobia, the fear of high places. Following the idea of avoidance, a person with agoraphobia, the fear of open places, would never participate in a crowd-filled activity, such as Earth Day in Central Park, April 22, 1990.

Generalized Anxiety Disorder. Yet another disorder in which anxiety is the major symptom is the **generalized anxiety disorder**. Here we have unrealistic, excessive, and persistent worry or anxiety. The anxiety may be very intense, but it is also quite diffuse, meaning that it does not seem to be brought on by anything specific in the person's environment. The anxiety just seems to come and go (or come and stay) without reason or warning. This type of anxiety disorder is often complicated by the presence of symptoms of other disorders, such as an occasional panic attack, phobic-like reaction, or depressive episode. People with this disorder are almost always in some state of uneasiness. If they are not experiencing a particularly high level of anxiety at the moment, they may be afraid that they soon will be. The self-reports of persons with generalized anxiety disorder show that their major concerns are with (in order): an inability to relax, tenseness, difficulty concentrating, feeling frightened, being afraid of losing control, and so on (Beck & Emery, 1985). Clearly, this is a distressing and disruptive disorder that brings with it considerable pain. Although people with this disorder can often continue to function in social situations and on the job, they may be particularly prone to drug and alcohol abuse.

What is most difficult for you and me to understand about generalized anxiety disorder (and panic disorder, too) is that people with the disorder usually have no good explanations for their feelings of anxiety. When you and I are anxious, we generally know *why* we're anxious: There's an exam coming up on Wednesday and we're not prepared; the boss wants to see us in his or her office; the dentist recommends having a root canal immediately, and so on. In many cases, persons with anxiety disorders cannot specify with any degree of certainty why it is that they are experiencing their anxiety. That in itself is often enough to make someone even more anxious.

generalized anxiety disorder *persistent, chronic, and distressingly high levels of unattributable anxiety*

posttraumatic stress disorder (PTSD) *an anxiety disorder in which disruptive recollections, distressing dreams, flashbacks, and felt anxiety occur well after the experience of a traumatic event.*

Posttraumatic Stress Disorder (PTSD). Before we move on to other disorders, we should briefly consider an anxiety disorder that has been the subject of much public discussion over the past decade. **Posttraumatic stress disorder** (**PTSD**) involves several distressing symptoms that arise at some time well *after* (usually six months) the experiencing of a traumatic, highly stressful event that is "outside the range of normal human experience" (*DSM-III-R*). The traumatic events that trigger this disorder are many, from natural disasters, to life-threatening situations (such as kidnapping, rape, assault, or combat), to the sudden loss of property. As it happens, most of us associate this disorder with veterans of military conflict, the Vietnam War in particular.

No psychologist will diagnose someone who had just experienced some horrendous event, such as the loss of a friend who died in the patient's arms in the midst of a furious battle, as having a disorder simply because he or she is very emotional and anxious. Indeed, we might be somewhat concerned about a person who showed little or no distress about such an experience. What makes the anxiety of PTSD qualify as a symptom of disorder is that it occurs persistently, in distressing dreams, in recurrent, disruptive recollections of the event, or in sudden feelings that the traumatic event is occurring again (in flashbacks) even well *after* the event itself. We see persons with this disorder trying to avoid any stimulus that would remind them of the trauma they experienced: Vietnam veterans who refuse to visit the memorial in Washington, D.C., are an example. People with PTSD see themselves as special, detached from others who cannot "share their experience." The case history presented in Figure 12.3 is reasonably typical. PTSD is not uncommon. About 1 percent of the population can be expected to experience the disorder in their lifetime. Of those who experience a severe trauma, nearly 15 percent will experience at least some of the symptoms of PTSD (Helzer, Robins, & McEnvoy, 1987). Not surprisingly, PTSD often is associated with other disorders, commonly alcohol and substance abuse or depression. The likelihood of recovery from posttraumatic stress syndrome often is related to the extent to which there are complicating factors (such as alcoholism), the extent to which the patient experienced psychological problems before the traumatic event, and the extent to which social support can be made available.

Posttraumatic stress disorder (PTSD) may be one of the long-term effects of experiencing life-threatening situations such as those that occur in military combat.

BEFORE YOU GO ON

Describe the symptoms of posttraumatic stress disorder.

Somatoform Disorders

somatoform disorders *psychological disorders that reflect imagined physical or bodily symptoms or complaints*

Soma means "body." Hence, all of the **somatoform disorders** in some way or another involve physical, bodily symptoms or complaints. What makes these *psychological* or *mental* disorders is that there is no known medical or biological cause for the symptoms. What makes them anxiety-based is that we can suspect that the individual with these disorders is experiencing a good deal of anxiety, even though that anxiety is not clearly

Figure **12.3**

A CASE HISTORY OF POSTTRAUMATIC STRESS DISORDER

Steve W. is a 40-year-old white male who visited his family doctor in search of narcotic drugs to treat his chronic pain ("I was shot in the war and never really healed up completely") and a tranquilizer for his "shot nerves." He complained of chronic headaches and leg pains, and said that his arms "get paralyzed." His responses to questioning indicated that he was a frequent user of alcohol. He denied drug use or abuse and appeared restless and hostile ("*You* aren't going to help me either"). He reported nightmares, early-morning awakening, and loss of interest in pleasurable activities, but denied having ideas of suicide.

Steve is the son of a successful businessman and a teacher. He was valedictorian of his high school class and married his high school sweetheart. Steve spent four years in Vietnam, was wounded twice, saw heavy combat regularly, and was well decorated. He has been married twice, is now separated, and has three children (one from his first marriage, two from his second). He has lost every job he has held due to his habitual outbursts of anger and has been jailed four times for minor offenses (e.g., being abusive to a police officer). Although he was graduated from the local community college with a degree in computer science, he has not applied his training. He has spent the last two years living alone in the woods.

Steve's physician made a diagnosis of posttraumatic stress disorder and alcohol abuse. He referred Steve to a local veteran's support group and to Alcoholics Anonymous. Steve's wife and children received counseling aimed at educating them to Steve's disorder.

After McGlynn & Metcalf, 1989.

visible as one of the defining symptoms of these disorders. We'll consider just two of the somatoform disorders: one quite common, hypochondriasis, and the other quite rare but very dramatic, conversion disorder.

Hypochondriasis. Hypochondriasis is the appropriate diagnosis for someone preoccupied with the fear of developing or having some serious disease. Persons with this disorder are unusually aware of every ache and pain. They often read popular magazines devoted to health issues, and they usually feel free to diagnose their own ailments. The catch is that they have no medical disorder, illness, or disease. Nonetheless, they constantly seek medical attention and will not be convinced of their good health despite the best of medical opinion and reassurance.

A man with occasional chest pains, for example, may diagnose his own condition as lung cancer. Even after numerous physicians reassure him that his lungs are perfectly fine and that he has no signs of lung cancer, the patient's fears are not put to rest: "They are just trying to make me feel better by not telling me, because they know, as I do, that I have lung cancer and am going to die soon."

It's not too difficult to imagine why someone would develop the symptoms of hypochondriasis. If a person comes to believe that he or she (and the disorder is found equally in men and women) has contracted some serious disease, three possible problems might be solved: (1) The person now has a way to explain otherwise unexplainable anxiety: "Well, my goodness, if you had lung cancer, you'd be anxious too." (Remember, this disorder is one we are calling anxiety-based.) (2) The illness may be used to

hypochondriasis *a mental disorder involving the fear of developing some serious disease or illness* excuse the person from those activities that he or she finds anxiety producing: "As sick as I am, you don't possibly expect me to go to work, do you?" (3) The illness or disease may be used as a way to gain attention or sympathy: "Don't you feel sorry for me, knowing that I have such a terrible disease?"

conversion disorder *the display of a severe physical disorder for which there is no medical explanation; often accompanied by an apparent lack of concern on the part of the patient*

Conversion Disorder. Although **conversion disorder** is now quite rare (accounting for fewer than 5 percent of the anxiety-based disorders), its symptoms are striking. Here we find an individual with a "loss or alteration in physical functioning that suggests a physical disorder, but that instead is apparently an expression of a psychological conflict or need. The symptoms are not intentionally produced and cannot be explained by any physical disorder" (*DSM-III-R*, 1987, p. 257). The loss in physical functioning is typically of great significance: paralysis, blindness, and deafness are classic examples. As difficult as it may be to believe, the symptoms are not fully imaginary; they are quite real in the sense that the person cannot feel, see, or hear. What makes the disorder psychological is that there is no known medical explanation for the symptoms. In some cases, medical explanations even run contrary to the symptoms. For example, one symptom sometimes found in conversion disorder is called *glove anesthesia*, in which the hands lose all feeling and become paralyzed. As it happens, it is physically impossible to have such a paralysis and loss of feeling in the hands alone; normally there would be some paralysis in the forearm, upper arm, and shoulder, as well. Actual paralysis, of course, must follow neural pathways.

One of the most remarkable secondary symptoms of this disorder (which occurs only in some patients) is known as *la belle indifference*—a seemingly inappropriate lack of concern over one's condition. Persons with this disorder seem to feel quite comfortable with and accepting of their infirmity. Here are people who are demonstrably blind, deaf, or paralyzed and who show very little concern over their condition.

Did you notice that at the beginning of this section I indicated that this disorder is *now* quite rare. In fact, during World War I, it was the most commonly diagnosed of all psychological disorders among military personnel. It was also quite common during World War II (Carson, Butcher, & Coleman, 1988). One hypothesis about the declining incidence of this disorder is that people generally have become more sophisticated about medical symptoms and the relationships between physical and psychological functioning.

This particular disorder holds an important position in psychology's history. This was the disorder that most intrigued Sigmund Freud in his clinical practice and ultimately led him to develop a new method of therapy, which we now call *psychoanalysis* (see Topic 13B). The disorder was known to the Greeks, who named it hysteria, a label that is still used occasionally, as in "hysterical blindness." The Greeks believed that the disorder was to be found only in women and reflected a disorder of the uterus, or *hysterium*, hence the name hysteria. The logic was that the disease would leave the uterus, float through the body, and settle in the eyes, hands, or whatever part of the body was affected. Of course, this notion is no longer considered valid, although the potential sexual basis for the disorder was one of the aspects that caught Freud's attention.

BEFORE YOU GO ON

Describe hypochondriasis and conversion disorder.

Dissociative Disorders

To *dissociate* means to become separate from or to escape. The underlying theme of disorders classified as **dissociative disorders** is that in some way a person dissociates or escapes from some aspect of life or personality that is seen as the source of stress, discomfort, or anxiety (which, again, justifies our classifying them as anxiety-based disorders). These mental disorders are statistically quite rare, but they are also quite dramatic and are often the subject of novels, movies, and television shows. We will briefly discuss three dissociative disorders: psychogenic amnesia, psychogenic fugue, and multiple personality.

Psychogenic Amnesia. *Psychogenic* means "psychological in origin," and *amnesia* refers to a loss of memory. Thus, **psychogenic amnesia** is an inability to recall important personal information that is too extensive to be explained by ordinary forgetfulness. It is usually the case that what is forgotten is some traumatic incident and some or all of the experiences that led up to or followed the incident. As you might suspect, there is no medical explanation for the loss of memory. As you also might suspect, there is a large range of the extent of the forgetting associated with psychogenic amnesia. In some cases, a person may "lose" entire days and weeks at a time; in other cases, only specific details cannot be recalled. Not surprisingly, cases of this disorder tend to be more common in wartime, when traumatic experiences are more common.

Psychogenic Fugue. Occasionally, amnesic forgetfulness is accompanied by a physical change of location. That is, the person finds himself or herself in a strange and different place, with no reasonable explanation for how he or she got there. When this dimension is added, we have a disorder known as **psychogenic fugue**. For example, we may find a man wandering around a Florida beach dressed in a three-piece suit. He has no idea of how or why he got there or where he is.

Both psychogenic amnesia and fugue are, in their own way, not unlike some of the somatoform disorders in that they may involve an escape from stressful situations. In conversion disorders, for example, a person may escape from stress by taking on the symptoms of a major physical disorder. Here, escape is more literal. People escape by forgetting altogether, or they avoid conflict and stress by psychologically or physically running away.

Multiple Personality. Perhaps the most important fact to recognize about the disorder called **multiple personality** is that it is listed here as an anxiety-based dissociative disorder and *not* as schizophrenia. I say that because the popular press and media quite consistently give the impression

dissociative disorder *a disorder in which one separates from or dissociates from aspects of one's personality*

psychogenic amnesia *a psychologically caused inability to recall important personal information*

psychogenic fugue *a condition of amnesia accompanied by unexplained travel or change of location*

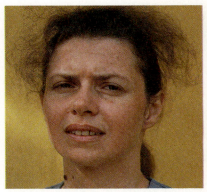

This woman, dubbed "Jane Doe," was found incoherent and near death in Florida in 1980. She was suffering from psychogenic amnesia and was unable to remember her name, her past, and how to read and write. After extensive publicity, a couple from Roselle, Illinois came forward and identified Jane Doe as their daughter who had moved to Florida and had been missing since 1976. Despite the certainty of the couple, Jane Doe was never able to remember her past.

multiple personality *the existence within one individual of two or more distinct personalities, each of which is dominant at a particular time*

that these are one in the same. They are not. Schizophrenia is a psychotic disorder that we will discuss in Topic 12B.

The major symptom of multiple personality is "the existence within the individual of two or more distinct personalities or personality states" (*DSM-III-R*, 1987, p. 269). It is also important to recognize that the disorder is extremely rare, although for unknown reasons its incidence is increasing (Carson, Butcher, & Coleman, 1988).

The very idea of split personality—of two or more personalities inhabiting the same person—is difficult for most of us to imagine. Perhaps it would help to contrast this disorder with a pattern of behavior that is typical of all of us. We all change our behaviors, and in some small way, our personalities change every day, depending on the situation in which we find ourselves. We do not act, think, or feel exactly the same way at school as we do at work, at a party, or at a house of worship. We modify our behaviors to fit the circumstances in which we find ourselves. At a party, you may be carefree, uninhibited, and happy. At work, you may be a different person: reserved, quiet, serious, and concentrating on the task at hand. You and I do not have multiple personalities, however. What's the difference?

The main difference is one of degree. We've seen this before. For a person with a multiple personality disorder, the change in personality is usually dramatic, extreme, and complete. We are not dealing with a person who slightly alters his or her behaviors; we are dealing with two or more distinct personalities—about half the reported cases show more than 10 distinct personalities (*DSM-III-R*, 1987). A second difference is that when you and I change our behaviors, feelings, or thinking, we do so as a response to the context of our environment. That is, we change in reaction to cues in the situation in which we find ourselves. Such is not the case for a person with this dissociative disorder, where changes in personality usually take place without warning. The third major difference has to do with control. When we change our behaviors, we do so consciously and intentionally. Individuals with a multiple personality disorder can neither control nor

Multiple personality disorder is one of the most intriguing disorders to consider. It is difficult to imagine as many as 16 separate personalities, each with their own capabilities, living in one human being. One such woman is Sybil, whose artwork illustrates how distinct one personality is from the other. The piece on the right was done by the more home-loving Mary in contrast to one on the left, done by Peggy, an angry, fearful personality.

predict which of their personalities will be dominant at any one time. Persons diagnosed with multiple personality disorder often report unusually high incidences of child abuse, sexual abuse, and drug abuse (Ross et al., 1989).

BEFORE YOU GO ON

What is the defining symptom of the dissociative disorders?

PERSONALITY DISORDERS

All of the psychological disorders we have reviewed so far, and those we'll consider in Topic 12B, are disorders that seem to afflict people who previously were quite normal and undisturbed. In most cases, we can remember a time when the person did not show the symptoms of his or her disorder. That is much harder to do with the personality disorders because persons with these disorders have a long-standing history of symptoms. **Personality disorders** are "enduring patterns of perceiving, relating to, and thinking about the environment and oneself [that are] inflexible and maladaptive" and cause either impaired functioning or distress (*DSM-III-R*, 1987). The problems associated with personality disorders are usually identifiable by the time an individual is an adolescent.

The *DSM-III-R* lists 11 different personality disorders, organized into three groups or clusters. Group 1 includes disorders in which the person can be characterized as being odd or eccentric in some way. People with disorders from this cluster are often difficult to get along with. Group 2 includes those disorders in which the individual appears overly dramatic, emotional, or erratic, and where behaviors are quite impulsive. Group 3 includes disorders that add the dimension of anxiety or fearfulness to the standard criteria for personality disorder. Notice that it is only for the varieties of disorder classified in Group 3 that we find any reports of fear, anxiety, or depression.

We have already mentioned that there is no clear distinction between behaviors (and affects and cognitions) that can be called normal and those that can be classified as disordered. There is no set of psychological disorders for which this observation is more pertinent than personality disorders. It is often very difficult for a psychologist to diagnose someone as having a personality disorder rather than just being a little strange. Remember that being strange or eccentric in *itself* is an insufficient reason to make a diagnosis of disorder. There need to be symptoms that indicate distress or discomfort and some indication that the person's strangeness or eccentricity is in some way maladaptive and interferes with functioning in the world. Because personality disorders are difficult to diagnose accurately, estimates of their prevalence tend to be very inexact. Another problem in finding accurate estimates of prevalence rates is that many people with these disorders manage to function well enough in the community that there is no reason to make a diagnosis in the first place. Many, if not most, cases

personality disorders *enduring patterns of perceiving, relating to, and thinking about the environment and one's self that are inflexible and maladaptive*

The case of Ferdinand Waldo Demara, Jr., called the "great impostor" in the 1950s illustrates one type of personality disorder. For years, Demara assumed numerous identities including a Navy doctor in Korea, a deputy prison warden, and a Catholic monk. He is now a minister, living at an interfaith monastery in central Missouri.

of personality disorder first come to the attention of mental health professionals on referral from the courts or because of related problems such as child abuse or alcoholism. What we do find is that "while the overall rate of PD [personality disorder] may be between 10% and 20%, the rates of specific disorders are very low" (Zimmerman & Coryell, 1989). One surprising finding of recent studies of the prevalence of personality disorders is that about one-fourth of those with symptoms of PD fit more than one diagnostic category. In other words, specific types of personality disorder may be particularly difficult to find.

The prognosis, or prediction of likely outcome, is usually quite poor for personality disorders. These maladaptive patterns of behavior often have taken a lifetime to develop. Changing them is very difficult. Rather than attempting to deal with all of the personality disorders, I'll list and briefly describe just two examples from each of the three main groups or clusters. Remember that to be classified as a personality disorder, these behaviors or symptoms must be relatively long-standing, generally beginning in childhood or adolescence.

Cluster 1: Disorders of "Odd" or "Eccentric" Reactions

Paranoid personality disorder—an extreme sensitivity, suspiciousness, envy, and mistrust of others. Persons with this personality disorder tend to interpret the actions of other people as deliberately demeaning or threatening, and there is no reason to believe that this suspiciousness is at all justified. Persons with a paranoid personality disorder also tend to show a restricted range of emotional reactions and seem to avoid any intimacy in interpersonal relations. Given their suspiciousness, people with this disorder rarely seek help for it on their own. Examples: a person who continuously and without justification accuses a spouse of infidelity and believes that every wrong number was really a call from some secret lover; or a student who constantly believes that professors are "out to get him," thus justifying poor grades.

Schizoid personality disorder—an inability to form, and a marked indifference to, interpersonal relationships. A person with a schizoid personality disorder shows little involvement in social affairs, appears cold and aloof, and often engages in excessive fantasy or daydreaming. Example: the "loner" who never joins any groups or social clubs or shows any interest in doing so; the person who lives, as he or she has done for years, alone in a one-room flat in a poor part of town, venturing out only to pick up a social security check and to buy a few necessities at the corner store.

Cluster 2: Disorders of Dramatic, Emotional, or Erratic Reactions

Antisocial personality disorder—a history of disregard for the rights and property of others. Early signs of this disorder include lying, truancy, stealing, fighting, resisting authority, and general irresponsibility. Someone with an antisocial personality disorder often has difficulty maintaining a job and demonstrates poor parenting skills. A key symptom is impulsive behavior with little regard for the consequences of that behavior. The person with this disorder is first recognized after involvement with the criminal court system. Examples: the person who first steals a car, then drives it down an alley, knocking over garbage cans "just for the fun of it"; the "successful" worker who embezzles money; the salesman who is well liked by his fellow workers and his employer, but moves on to yet another job without giving notice.

Histrionic personality disorder—a long-term pattern of overly dramatic, reactive, and intensely expressed behaviors. Persons with histrionic personality disorder tend to be very lively and love to draw attention to themselves and be the center of whatever is happening. They tend to overreact to matters of small consequence, seek excitement, and try to avoid the routine and mundane. They actually tend to be dependent on others, but have difficulty forming meaningful interpersonal relationships. Example: a woman with a dramatic or "wild" hairdo, who spends an inordinate amount of time on her appearance, calls almost everyone "Darling," seems to be constantly seeking feedback in ways such as, "Don't you just *love* this new outfit?" and describes virtually all of her experiences as being "wonderful!!" and "vastly outstanding!" even when such an experience is finding detergent on sale at the supermarket; at the same time, minor annoyances are viewed as "terrible, terrible, just awful terrible."

Cluster 3: Disorders Involving Anxiety and Fearfulness

Avoidant personality disorder—as the name suggests, being overly sensitive to the possibility of being rejected by others. Here we have someone who, unlike the schizoid personality, who does not want to be alone, genuinely desires to enter into social relationships, but is so afraid that such relationships will result in total failure that he or she avoids them. Someone with this disorder is devastated by rejection or disapproval. Example: a man with few close friends who almost never dates and only talks to women who are much older and less attractive than he. He has worked at the same position for years, never seeking a job change or promotion; he seldom speaks in public; he occasionally attends meetings and social gatherings, but never participates.

Passive-aggressive personality disorder—being resistive, negative, and indirect. This term sounds virtually contradictory. What we have here is a good deal of aggression, but it is not expressed in violence, hostility, or direct action. Instead, we find procrastination, dawdling, stubbornness, inefficiency, and "forgetfulness." Persons with this disorder tend to be constant whiners, bitchers, moaners, and complainers. Example: the grandmother who, when invited to join the family on a short trip to the store, says, "No, I'll stay here. You go." Then, as the family readies to leave, she says, "Sure, go ahead; go without me. I never get to go anywhere. I just stay here all day and all night staring at these walls." When she is asked once again to join the group, she responds, "No, you go ahead, have a good time; I'll stay here and wax the kitchen floor."

Again, please remember that these descriptions (largely from the DSM-III-R) and accompanying examples are isolated examples. The diagnosis of personality disorder requires a consistent pattern of behaviors that have been evidenced for a long period of time, that essentially reflect the very personality of the individual.

BEFORE YOU GO ON

What are the defining characteristics of the personality disorders?

When most people think about psychology, their first thoughts generally deal with abnormal psychology: psychological disorders and their treatment. As we have seen in this topic, the concept of abnormality in psychology is a very complex, multidimensional one. Even so, we've seen that psychological disorders are much more common than any of us care to think about. Applying labels indicative of abnormality or disorder to a person's reactions can have widespread consequences and should be done only with great care. We've seen that psychologists also take great care making sure that only a person's affect, cognitions, or behaviors—*and not the person*—are labeled as disordered.

In this topic, we have briefly considered two classes, or types, of psychological disorders. In the first type, the anxiety-based disorders, there runs a common thread of anxiety—high levels of discomforting anxiety that impair normal functioning. Within the category of anxiety-based disorders, we discussed a variety of anxiety disorders, the somatoform disorders, and dissociative disorders. We then looked at the personality disorders, which are characterized by lifelong patterns of inflexible and maladaptive behavior. These disorders often are difficult to diagnose and are equally difficult to treat. The pain and suffering caused by anxiety-based and personality disorders alone are widespread, touching the lives of tens of millions of North Americans. Next, we'll discuss disorders that may be considered even more severe than the disorders we reviewed in this topic, as we turn to the mood disorders, the organic mental disorders, and the psychological disorder that may best fit our definition of abnormal: schizophrenia.

How do we define psychological abnormality?

In the context of psychological disorders, we take abnormal to mean statistically uncommon maladaptive behaviors, cognitions, and/or affect that are at odds with social expectations and that result in distress or discomfort. / *page 557*

What is the DSM-III-R? What are some of its advantages and disadvantages?

The *DSM-III-R* is the revised third edition of the *Diagnostic and Statistical Manual of Mental Disorders*, the "standard" classification scheme for psychological disorders as determined by a large committee of psychologists and psychiatrists. The major advantage of this system is that it provides one standard label and cluster of symptoms for each disorder that all mental health practitioners can use; it is an aid in communication. It does have its limitations, however. It includes nearly 250 separate entries, which some believe to be too many. On the other hand, there are deviations from social norms that are not included in the manual. Such schemes should not be used to confuse description with explanation; the *DSM-III-R* does the former, not the latter. / *page 560*

What are the essential characteristics of a phobic disorder?

By definition, a phobic disorder is typified by an intense, persistent fear of some object, activity, or situation that is in no real sense a threat to the individual's well-being; in brief, an intense, irrational fear. / *page 562*

What is a panic disorder?

The defining symptom of a panic disorder is a sudden, often unpredictable attack of intense anxiety, called a panic attack. These attacks may last for seconds or for hours. Unlike phobic reac-

tions, there is no particular stimulus to prompt the attack. / *page 563*

Describe generalized anxiety disorder, and contrast it with panic disorder.

Panic disorders and generalized anxiety disorders are alike in that their major defining characteristic is a high level of anxiety that cannot be attributed to any particular source. The major difference between the two is that for the generalized anxiety disorder, the felt anxiety is chronic, persistent, and diffuse. In the panic disorder, however, there may be periods during which the person is totally free from feelings of anxiety; the anxiety occurs in acute, debilitating attacks. / *page 565*

In the context of anxiety-based psychological disorders, what is an obsession, and what is a compulsion?

Obsessions and compulsions are the main presenting complaint in obsessive-compulsive disorder, or OCD. An obsession is an idea or thought that constantly intrudes on one's awareness. A compulsion, on the other hand, is a repeated and stereotyped behavior or act that constantly intrudes on one's behavior. / *page 565*

Describe the symptoms of posttraumatic stress disorder.

Posttraumatic stress disorder, or PTSD, is an anxiety disorder in which the symptoms of high levels of anxiety, recurrent and disruptive dreams and recollections of a highly traumatic event (e.g., rape, combat, natural disaster, etc.) occur well after the danger of the event has passed. / *page 566*

Describe hypochondriasis and conversion disorder.

By definition, somatoform disorders reflect a physical or bodily symptom or complaint. In each case, however, there is no known biological or medical cause

for the complaint. In hypochondriasis, a person lives in fear and dread of contracting some serious illness or disease, when there is no medical evidence that such fears are well founded. In conversion disorder, there is an actual loss or alteration in physical functioning—often dramatic, such as blindness or deafness—not under voluntary control, suggesting a physical disorder, but without medical basis. / *page 569*

What is the defining symptom of the dissociative disorders?

Dissociative disorders are marked by a retreat or escape from (dissociation with) some aspect of one's personality. It may be a matter of an inability to recall some life event (amnesia), sometimes accompanied by unexplained travel to a different location (fugue state). In some very rare cases, certain aspects of one's personality become so dissociated that we may say that the person suffers from multiple personality disorder, where two or more personalities are found in the same individual. / *page 571*

What are the defining characteristics of the personality disorders?

Personality disorders are enduring patterns of perceiving, relating to, and thinking about the environment and oneself that are inflexible and maladaptive. These are essentially lifelong patterns of maladjustment and may be classified as belonging to one of three groups, or clusters. Group 1 includes those PDs involving odd or eccentric reactions, such as paranoid and schizoid personality disorder. Group 2 includes disorders of dramatic, emotional, or erratic reactions, such as the antisocial or histrionic personality disorder. Group 3 includes disorders involving fear and anxiety, such as the avoidant or passive-aggressive personality disorder. / *page 573*

TOPIC

12B

*O*rganic, Mood, and Schizophrenic Disorders

Why We Care: A Topic Preview

ORGANIC MENTAL DISORDERS
Substance-induced Organic Mental Disorders
Degenerative Dementia of the Alzheimer's Type

MOOD DISORDERS
Depression and Mania
Causes of Depression
>   Biological Factors
>   Psychological Factors

SCHIZOPHRENIA
Types of Schizophrenia
>   Process and Reactive
>   Positive and Negative Symptoms
>   DSM-III-A-Types
Observations on the Causes of Schizophrenia
>   Hereditary Factors
>   Biochemical Factors: The Dopamine Hypothesis
>   Psychological and Social Factors

SUMMARY

Why We Care: A Topic Preview

In this topic, we continue our discussion of psychological disorders. It is probably inappropriate and, in a sense, unfair to classify some disorders as being more or less severe or debilitating than others. To the person who is experiencing the disorder, and to those who care about that person, any psychological disorder can seem severe and debilitating.

It is nonetheless the case that the disorders we'll introduce in this topic do tend to be more disruptive than those we reviewed in Topic 12A. Most forms of the disorders we'll cover in this topic are those that can be classified as psychotic disorders, or psychoses. That is usually taken to mean two things: a gross impairment in functioning (difficulty dealing with the demands of everyday life) and a gross impairment in reality testing (a loss of contact with the real world as the rest of us know it). As a result, persons with these disorders frequently require hospitalization. It hardly needs to be mentioned that we care about these disorders for the same reasons that we care about those we've already discussed: They are hurtful and distressing, and they afflict millions of people.

The label "psychotic disorder" is not a specific term or classification in the Diagnostic and Statistical Manual of Mental Disorders (DSM-III-R) of the American Psychiatric Association (1987). The term is a general one and, like neurosis, has come to mean so many different things that it has lost some of its usefulness. It is still clear, however, that at least most of the symptoms of the disorders we'll examine in this topic qualify as being psychotic: involving a loss of contact with reality and a gross impairment in functioning.

As was the case for the disorders we discussed in Topic 12A, we will again see that psychological disturbances often have an impact on each of three levels of functioning: affect, behavior, and/or cognition. In some cases, it is a disturbance in behavior that is most noteworthy: A person actually does strange and unusual things. In some cases, the most noticeable symptoms are cognitive: A person has strange, unusual, and unreal thoughts or beliefs. In some cases, the most obvious impairment is affective: A person has flattened affect and shows little or no emotional response or responds with inappropriate affect.

We'll begin this topic by taking a brief look at a grouping of disorders often classified as psychotic: organic mental disorders. Our focus here will be on just one of these disorders, Alzheimer's disease. Then we'll discuss two of the major psychoses: mood disorders and schizophrenia.

Observations on the Causes of Schizophrenia

Schizophrenia is obviously a complex set of disorders. There is even some disagreement about how to define schizophrenia. (In one study, a sample of schizophrenics was reduced by more than half when the researchers simply imposed the *DSM-III* criteria rather than those from the *DSM-II* to define their subjects (Winters et al., 1981).) As you might suspect, our bottom-line conclusion on the cause of schizophrenia is going to be tentative and multidimensional. Although we don't know what causes the disorder, we do have a number of interesting ideas to consider.

Hereditary Factors. There is little doubt that schizophrenia tends to run in families (Gottesman & Bertelsen, 1989; Kessler, 1980; Rosenthal, 1970). The data are not as striking as they are for the mood disorders, but it is clear that one is at a higher risk of being diagnosed as schizophrenic if there is a history of the disorder in one's family.

Adult children of schizophrenics are significantly more likely to develop schizophrenia than are adult children of nonschizophrenic parents. If one parent is schizophrenic, his or her child is 10 to 15 times more likely to develop schizophrenia as an adult, and when both parents are schizophrenic, their children are about 40 times more likely to develop this illness (Cornblatt & Erlenmeyer-Kimling, 1985; Erlenmeyer-Kimling, 1968). The risk of becoming schizophrenic is 4 to 5 times greater for an identical twin than it is for a fraternal twin if the other member of the twin pair has the disorder. Remember that the odds of being diagnosed as having schizophrenia are, in the general population, about 1 in 100. For those who are identical twins of persons with schizophrenia, the odds jump to nearly 1 in 2 (Bloom et al., 1985). It is also true that if adopted children develop schizophrenia, it is much more likely that other cases of schizophrenia will be found among members of their biological family than their adoptive family (Bootzin & Acocella, 1984). Some of these data (from Nicol &

The genetic predisposition for schizophrenia is well illustrated by the Genain quadruplets, shown here celebrating their 51st birthday in 1981. All four women experienced a schizophrenic disorder of varying severity, duration, and outcome— facts that may suggest an environmental role in schizophrenia.

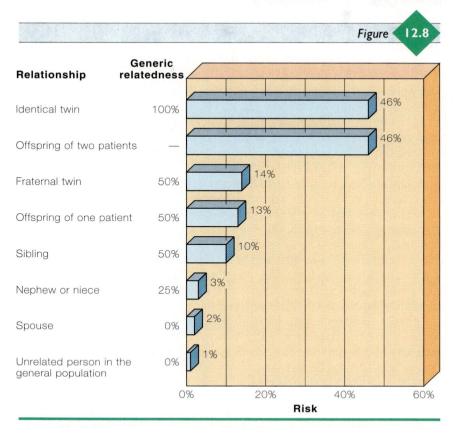

Figure **12.8**

Lifetime risks of developing schizophrenia are largely a function of how closely an individual is genetically related to a schizophrenic and not a function of how much their environment is shared. (Data from Gottesman & Shields, 1982.)

Gottesman, 1983) are presented in Figure 12.8. We need to remember, once again, that such data do not mean that schizophrenia is directly inherited. Notice, for example, that *nearly half of the identical twins of schizophrenics never do develop the disorder*. It is more reasonable to say that one may inherit a predisposition to develop schizophrenia. This distinction is an important one, recalling our earlier discussions about the role of genetics in the development of psychological reactions and not drawing cause-and-effect conclusions from correlational data.

   Biochemical Factors: The Dopamine Hypothesis. Dopamine is a neurotransmitter found in every human brain. The role of this particular neurotransmitter in schizophrenia has come to light from several different lines of research.

   For one thing, we know that the abuse of amphetamines often leads to the development of many symptoms also found in schizophrenia. We also know that amphetamines are chemically very similar to dopamine and may actually cause an increase in dopamine levels in the brain. Logic then leads us to wonder if perhaps schizophrenic symptoms (particularly those we have recognized as positive symptoms) are caused by excess amounts of dopamine.

Additional support for this view comes from examining the workings of various antipsychotic drugs that actually reduce schizophrenic symptoms. Apparently, drugs that alleviate schizophrenic symptoms commonly block receptor sites for dopamine in the brain (Snyder, 1980). If reducing the effectiveness of dopamine by blocking its activity at the synapse can control schizophrenic symptoms, might we not assume that these symptoms are caused by dopamine in the first place (Tandon & Greden, 1989)?

The arguments for this hypothesis appear compelling, but they are far from certain. For one thing, there is little evidence that schizophrenics have elevated levels of dopamine in their brains (Karoum et al., 1987). Even so, there may be a heightened sensitivity in the brains of schizophrenics to what dopamine is present (perhaps more receptor sites for dopamine). In other words, people with schizophrenia may not have excess levels of dopamine; they may be more responsive to what they do have, thus creating psychotic symptoms. Again, this sounds reasonable, but there is little direct evidence to support such a conclusion. For another thing, not all antipsychotic medications have their effects by blocking dopamine receptor sites. It is also troublesome that when drugs *are* effective, their effects generally take a few weeks to show up. If the effect of the drugs on receptor sites is immediate, why isn't the effect on symptoms immediate also?

Finally, we have a "chicken-and-egg" problem with the dopamine hypothesis. Even if dopamine were shown to be related to schizophrenic symptoms, we would still have to ask if there is a direct *causal* relationship. That is, do increased levels of dopamine cause schizophrenic symptoms, or does the disorder of schizophrenia cause elevated dopamine levels? Or does some other factor—say, stress—cause both elevated dopamine levels and schizophrenic symptoms? We can note in passing that we have the same chicken-and-egg problem with some interesting findings concerning brain structure and schizophrenia. For example, the brains of many patients with schizophrenia, mostly those with positive symptoms, have abnormally large ventricles (cavities or openings that contain cerebrospinal fluid) (Andreasen et al., 1982, 1990), and recent evidence suggests a lack of balance between the two hemispheres of the brain (Gur et al., 1987; Reveley et al., 1987). Even if these differences in the brains of schizophrenics and nonschizophrenics are confirmed, we still don't know if we're dealing with causes or effects.

Psychological and Social Factors. Perhaps genetic and/or biochemical factors predispose a person to develop the symptoms of schizophrenia. What sorts of events or situations tend to turn such predispositions into reality? To this question, our answers are very sketchy. One of the standard views (e.g., Lidz, 1973) is that schizophrenia develops as a response to early experiences within the family unit. The early experiences of people who later develop schizophrenic symptoms often seem different from those who do not develop schizophrenia. One factor that has been isolated is inefficient or improper means of communication within the family. That is, there seems to be an inability or unwillingness to share feelings and emotions or to talk openly about problems and conflicts. Early childhood experiences of adults diagnosed with schizophrenia seem filled with conflict, anxiety, doubt, and emotional tension. There also seems to be an unusually high incidence of double messages and double binds being presented to children who later develop the disorder. For example, a mother may tell her child that she becomes upset when everyone forgets about her birthday and then turn around and scold the child for spending lunch money to buy a birthday present. Parents who communicate something like, "We want you to be independent and show responsibility, but so long as you live in this house, you'll do things the way we say, no questions asked," are certainly delivering a double message to their child.

There is also evidence that in some people, the development of the symptoms of schizophrenia may remain dormant, or unexpressed, unless or until the individual is subjected to environmental stressors (e.g., Gottesman & Bertelsen, 1989; Johnson, 1989; Ventura et al., 1989). The theory here is that some people are (genetically) prone to develop the symptoms of schizophrenia when they are exposed to stressors. Other people faced with the very same type or amount of stress might develop ulcers, or might become excessively anxious, or might show no particular symptoms at all.

We will save our discussion of the treatment of the psychological disorders until Chapter 13. Nonetheless, let me note again that one treatment method for schizophrenia involves the use of medication to alleviate the symptoms of the disorder. Largely because of the introduction of these so-called antipsychotic medications, the outlook for patients with schizophrenia is not nearly as dismal as it was just 25 years ago. We estimate now that nearly one-third of all persons diagnosed as schizophrenic will recover (be symptom-free for at least five years). About one-third will be at least partially recovered and may assume, at least to some degree, the normal responsibilities of adaptive living in society. It is still the case, however, that nearly one-third of all patients diagnosed as having schizophrenia will never recover to the point where they will be freed from institutionalization or daily supervision (Bloom et al., 1985).

BEFORE YOU GO ON

Describe some of the factors that have been implicated as possible causes of schizophrenic symptoms.

In this topic, we have reviewed some of the psychological disorders that can be classified as psychotic because they demonstrate symptoms of gross impairment of functioning and a loss of contact with reality. In these disorders, we commonly find delusions and/or hallucinations. Although these disorders may have genetic or biochemical bases, such is necessarily the case for the grouping of disorders referred to as organic mental disorders. It is a distortion of affect, usually extreme depression, that marks the mood disorders. Schizophrenia is actually a set of disorders that to some degree involves impairment of all areas of functioning: affect, cognition, and behavior. The prevalence of these disorders is staggering. Millions of people are, at this moment, suffering from one of the disorders we've discussed in this topic. Now it is time to consider what can be done to help, to alleviate the symptoms, and to provide relief to those who suffer the pain of the psychological disorders.

By what criteria is a disorder classified as psychotic? What are the syndromes associated with organic mental disorders? What gives rise to these symptoms? What is Alzheimer's disease, and what causes it?

To qualify as psychotic, a symptom or disorder should display a gross impairment of functioning and a loss of contact with reality. Impairment and loss of reality may be evidenced in thinking, affect, or behavior. Organic mental disorders involve a number of different syndromes, including delirium, a clouded state of consciousness and lessening of awareness; dementia, a marked loss of intellectual abilities, including judgment, and impulse control; amnestic syndrome, an impairment of memory with no other intellectual deficit; delusions, firmly held but false personal beliefs; hallucinations, perceptions without sensory stimulation; intoxication, the impairment of behavioral and mental processes following the use of a drug; and withdrawal, any of the above symptoms that result when one stops taking a drug. These syndromes arise through some problem with brain function, sometimes due to a problem associated with the aging process, as in Alzheimer's disease, or to the abuse of drugs or chemical substances such as alcohol, sedatives, opiates, cocaine, or amphetamines. Alzheimer's disease, in particular, is a form of degenerative dementia associated with known abnormalities in the brain—among other things, the formation of tangles and plaques. There is a strong likelihood of a genetic basis for the disease. Research also is focusing on the formation of certain brain proteins and the neurotransmitter acetylcholine. / page 581

How are the mood disorders defined? What do we know about their prevalence and their causes?

Although many psychological disorders involve disturbances of affect, in mood disorders, a disturbance in mood or feeling is the prime, and perhaps only, major symptom. Most commonly we find the disorder to be one of depression alone; less commonly we find mania and depression occurring in cycles (bipolar mood disorder). In any case, whether the major symptom be depression, mania, or a combination, there is no rational reason for the observed mood. Depression is a common disorder, affecting as many as 20 percent of all women and 10 percent of all men at some time in their lives. The disorder seems to have a strong hereditary basis. Neurotransmitters (biogenic amines) such as serotonin and dopamine have been implicated in depression. Psychological explanations tend to focus on the learned ineffectiveness of reinforcers and cognitive factors, such as a poor self-image, as models for explaining the causes of depression. / page 585

What are the major symptoms of schizophrenia?

Schizophrenia is a label applied to a number of disorders that all seem to involve varying degrees of cognitive impairment (delusions, hallucinations, disturbances of thought, and the like), social isolation, and disturbances of affect and behavior. / page 587

What characterizes the following varieties of schizophrenia: process versus reactive, positive versus negative, catatonic, disorganized, paranoid, undifferentiated, and residual?

Process schizophrenia is the term used when symptoms tend to develop slowly and gradually, whereas we call those cases in which symptoms arise suddenly reactive schizophrenia. The latter has a better prognosis than the former. We talk about positive symptoms of schizophrenia when a patient has hallucinations, delusions, or bizarre behaviors. Negative symptoms refer to losses: social withdrawal, loss of appropriate affect, apathy, and/or loss of attention. Catatonic schizophrenia is characterized by catatonia (states of physical impassivity) and/or extreme excitement. Disorganized schizophrenia is marked by a more severe disintegration of personality, with emotional distortions, inappropriate laughter, and bizarre behaviors, while paranoid schizophrenia is characterized by delusions, usually absurd and illogical. Undifferentiated schizophrenia involves a variety of psychotic symptoms, none of which dominate, and residual schizophrenia indicates a mild form of the disorder following a schizophrenic episode. / page 589

Describe some of the factors that have been implicated as possible causes of schizophrenic symptoms.

Although we certainly do not know the causes of schizophrenia, three lines of investigation have produced hopeful leads. (1) There seems to be little doubt of at least a genetic predisposition for the disorder. Although schizophrenia is not inherited, it does tend to run in families. (2) Research on biochemical correlates of schizophrenia have localized the neurotransmitter dopamine as being involved in the production of schizophrenia-like symptoms, although dopamine's role in the disorder is now being questioned. (3) It also seems reasonable to hypothesize that early childhood experiences, particularly those involving parent-child interactions and communications, may also predispose one toward schizophrenia. Probably the most reasonable position at the moment is that for some persons, environmental events, such as extreme stress, trigger biochemical and structural changes in the brain that result in the symptoms of schizophrenia. / page 593

TREATMENT AND THERAPY

Background and Biomedical Treatment

Why We Care: A Topic Preview

In Chapter 12, we reviewed a number of psychological disorders. We also noted that, unfortunately, such disorders are far from rare experiences. Tens of millions of Americans are afflicted with psychological disturbances, from minor difficulties in adjusting to stress, to disorders that involve excessive anxiety, to the devastating disorders of schizophrenia and other psychotic reactions. Put in a different way, nearly one-quarter of all the days that Americans spend in the hospital can be accounted for by mental disorders (Kiesler & Sibulkin, 1987). In this chapter, we turn our attention to what can be done to help people suffering from psychological disorders. We care about the subject matter of this chapter simply because of the extent of the distress caused by mental illnesses.

The basic premise that persons with psychological disorders should be treated humanely is remarkably recent in our history. Acceptance of the position that we should actively intervene to improve the quality of life of persons suffering from mental disorders is even more recent. In many ways, we can claim that the systematic, humane treatment of persons with psychological problems is a twentieth-century phenomenon.

To begin this topic, we'll take a brief look at the history of treatment for psychological disorders. We care about this history because it gives us some insight as to why, even today, so many people have such strong negative attitudes about people with psychological disorders.

The bulk of this topic will be devoted to types of treatment that typically fall outside the realm of psychology: treatments that are medical or physical in nature. We will examine psychosurgery and shock therapies, but will concentrate on the use of drugs and chemicals to control and treat the symptoms of mental illness. Psychological approaches—psychotherapy—will be reserved for Topic 13B.

A HISTORICAL PERSPECTIVE

The history of the treatment of psychological disorders is not a pleasant one. By today's standards, therapy—in the sense of active, humane intervention to improve the condition of persons in psychological distress—does not even seem like an appropriate term to describe the way in which most disordered persons were dealt with in the past.

Mental illness is not a new phenomenon. Among the earliest written records from the Babylonians, Egyptians, and ancient Hebrews we can find descriptions of what we now recognize as psychological disorders (Murray, 1983). How individuals with disorders were treated was consistent with the prevailing view of what caused the disorder.

The ancient Greeks and Romans believed that people who were manic, depressed, irrational, or intellectually retarded, or who had hallucinations and delusions, had in some way offended the gods. In some cases, individuals were viewed as being temporarily out of favor with the gods, and it followed that their condition could be improved through prayer and religious ritual. More severely disturbed patients were seen as being physically possessed by evil spirits. These cases were more difficult, often impossible, to cure. The aim of ancients was to exorcise the evil spirits and demons inhabiting the minds and souls of the mentally deranged. Such intervention was seldom successful, and many unfortunate people died as a direct result of their treatment or were killed outright when treatment failed. Treatment was left to the priests, who were, after all, thought to be skilled in the ways and means of spirit manipulation.

There were those in ancient times who had a more reasonable view, by today's standards, of psychological disorders. Among them was Hippocrates (460–377 B.C.), who believed that mental disorders had physical causes, not spiritual ones. He identified epilepsy as being a disorder of the brain, for example. Some of his views were incorrect (e.g., that hysteria is a disorder of the uterus), but at least he tried (without success) to demystify mental illness. Throughout most of history, the impact of enlightened scientists, such as Hippocrates, was slight and short lived.

The Middle Ages (1000–1500) was a period during which the oppression and persecution of the mentally ill were at their peak. During this period, the prevailing view continued to be that psychologically disordered people were "bad people," under the spell of the devil and evil spirits. They had brought on their own grief, and there was no hope for them, except that they save their immortal souls and confess their evil ways.

For hundreds of years, well into the eighteenth century, the attitude toward the mentally ill continued to be that they were in league with the devil or that they were being punished by God for sinful thoughts and deeds. They were witches who could not be cured except by confession and a denunciation of their evilness. When such confessions were not forthcoming, the prescribed treatment was torture. If torture failed to evoke a confession, death was the only recourse; often it was death by being burned at the stake.

A large volume, the *Malleus Maleficarum* (the Witches' Hammer), was written by two priests, Johann Sprenger and Heinrich Kraemer, with the blessing of the pope, in 1487. It described in great detail the symptoms of witches and how witches were to be interrogated so as to ensure a true confession. The techniques described in *Malleus* comprise a catalog of the

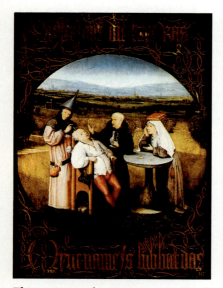

This painting by Hieronymus Bosch depicts one of the measures used on the mentally ill in the Middle Ages. Here, people believing that stones were the cause of this patient's insanity, attempt to remove them by boring a hole in his head.

most horrible of tortures. It has been estimated that between the early fourteenth and mid-seventeenth centuries, nearly 200,000 to 500,000 "witches" were put to death (Ben-Yehuda, 1980). Martin Luther has been quoted as suggesting (in 1540) that a mentally retarded boy be suffocated because he was a captive of the devil and "simply a mass of flesh without a soul" (Tappert, 1967). We must keep in mind that it was not until very recently (around the late 1800s) that a generally accepted distinction was made between persons who suffered from a psychological disorder and persons who were intellectually retarded.

When the insane were not tortured or immediately put to death, they were institutionalized in asylums. The first insane asylum was St. Mary of Bethlehem Hospital in London, which housed "fools" and "lunatics" in 1547. The institution became known as Bedlam (a cockney pronunciation of Bethlehem). It was a terrible place. Inmates were tortured, poorly fed, or starved to death. To remove the "bad blood" from their systems, thought to be a cause of their melancholy or delirium, some patients were regularly led to bleeding chambers, where a small incision was made in a vein in the calf of their legs so that their blood would ooze into leather buckets. There was no professional staff at Bedlam. The keepers, as they were called, could make some extra money by putting their charges on view for the general public. Viewing the lunatics of Bedlam became an established entertainment for the nobility. Those inmates who were able were sent into the streets to beg, wearing a sign that identified them as "fools of Bedlam." Notice that even today we use the word *bedlam* to describe a condition or scene of wild uproar and confusion.

It would be comforting to think that Bedlam was an exception, an aberration. It was not. In the eighteenth and nineteenth centuries, and often well into the twentieth century, institutions like Bedlam were commonplace. Philippe Pinel (1745–1826) was a French physician who, in the midst of the French Revolution (on April 25, 1793), was named director of an asylum for the insane in Paris. Here, in Pinel's own words, is the scene he discovered upon taking over:

> On my entrance to the duties of that hospital, every thing presented to me the appearance of chaos and confusion. Some of my unfortunate patients labored under horrors of a most gloomy and desponding melancholy. Others were furious, and subject to the influence of a perpetual delirium. . . . Symptoms so different, and all comprehended under the general title of insanity. . . . The halls and the passages of the hospital were much confined, so arranged as to render the cold of winter and the heat of summer equally intolerable and injurious. The chambers were exceedingly small and inconvenient. Baths we had none, though I made repeated applications for them; nor had we extensive liberties for walking, gardening or other exercises. So destitute of accommodations, we found it impossible to class our patients according to the varieties and degrees of their respective maladies. (Shipley, 1961)

We know of Pinel today largely because of an act of compassion and courage. The law of the period required that inmates in an asylum be chained and confined. On September 2, 1793, Pinel ordered the chains and shackles removed from about 50 of the inmates of his "hospital." He allowed

Associating mental illnesses with witchcraft was an attitude that flourished during the fifteenth and sixteenth centuries. Goya's painting entitled **The Witches Sabbath** *reflects the popular preoccupation of the times.*

Benjamin Rush

Dorothea Dix

Clifford Beers

them to move freely about the institution and its grounds. This humane gesture produced surprising effects: The conditions of the patients, in many cases, improved markedly. Pinel continued to treat those in his care with kindness and respect, which, in some cases, provided complete cures. Unfortunately, we cannot report that Pinel's humane treatment became the norm in France and the rest of the world. It did not, but the tide did begin to turn late in the 1700s. Pinel's unchaining of the insane and his personal belief in moral treatment for the mentally ill can be viewed as the beginning of a very gradual enlightenment concerning mental illness, even though Pinel's success did not lead to broad, sweeping reforms.

In the United States, three people stand out as pioneers of reform for the treatment of the mentally ill and retarded. The first is Benjamin Rush (1745–1813), who is considered the founder of American psychiatry, having published the first text on the subject of mental disorders in the United States in 1812. Although many of the treatments recommended by Rush may strike us as barbaric today (he was a believer in bleeding), his general attitudes were comparatively humane. For example, he argued vehemently and successfully that the mentally ill should not be put on display simply to satisfy the curiosity of onlookers. He was largely responsible for bringing the moral consideration of the mentally ill to America.

The second pioneer of reform was Dorothea Dix (1802–1887), a nurse. In 1841, she took a position at a women's prison and was appalled at what she saw there. Included among the prisoners, and treated no differently, were hundreds of persons who were clearly mentally retarded and/or mentally ill. Despite her slight stature and her own ill health, she entered upon a crusade of singular vigor. She went from state to state campaigning for reform in prisons, mental hospitals, and asylums. One of the ironic outcomes of Dix's crusade was that many state governments did agree that the mentally ill should not be housed in prisons, and large state-run institutions and insane asylums were built. Although they began operation in the tradition of moral treatment, they often became no more humane or moral in their treatment than Bedlam had been.

In this brief historical sketch, another name deserves mention: Clifford Beers. A graduate of Yale University, Beers had been institutionalized in a series of hospitals or asylums. It seems likely that he was suffering from what we now call a mood disorder. Probably in spite of his treatment, rather than because of it, Beers recovered and was released—in itself an unusual occurrence. He wrote a book about his experience, *A Mind that Found Itself*, in 1908. Both Theodore Roosevelt and psychologist William James were very impressed by Beers and his story. The book became a bestseller, and it is often cited as providing the stimulus for the reform that we identify as the mental health movement.

History suggests that until very recently, the prevailing understanding of the psychologically disturbed was that they were bad people, possessed by demons and devils, unable to control their behaviors and thoughts and unable to be cured. The only recourse was to separate the retarded and mentally ill from everyone else—to "put them away." Since the early 1900s, progress in providing help for the mentally ill has been both slow and unsteady. World War I and the Great Depression reduced the monies available to support state institutions for mental patients. Within the past 50 years, conditions have improved immeasurably, but there is still a long way to go. We continue to fight a prejudice against persons suffering from psychological disorders.

BEFORE YOU GO ON

Briefly trace the history of the treatment of persons with psychological disorders.

BIOMEDICAL TREATMENTS OF PSYCHOLOGICAL DISORDERS

As we have seen, biological and medical approaches can be traced to ancient times. By definition, treatments that are medical in nature are not those that psychologists use. Currently, performing surgery, administering shock treatments, or prescribing medication requires a medical degree. (We'll discuss the different mental health professionals and their specialties in Topic 13B.) Psychologists often are involved in biomedical approaches to treatment, however. Psychologists may recommend medical treatment and refer a client to the care of a physician or psychiatrist (a person with a medical degree who specializes in mental disorders). The treatments that psychologists use, the psychotherapies, will be the subject of Topic 13B.

Here we'll review three types of biomedical intervention: psychosurgery, which was quite common just 50 years ago, but is now quite rare; shock treatment, which is used less frequently now than it was 20 years ago, but is far from uncommon; and drug therapy, the use of psychoactive drugs, which is the newest and one of the most promising developments in the treatment of mental illness.

Psychosurgery

Psychosurgery is the name we give to surgical procedures, usually directed at the brain, designed to affect psychological reactions. Most psychosurgical techniques in use today can be considered somewhat experimental. They are aimed at making rather minimal lesions in the brain (to treat chronic pain, epilepsy, or depression, for example). Small surgical lesions in the limbic system can be effective in reducing or eliminating violent behaviors. Surgical techniques also have been used, albeit infrequently, to reduce extreme anxiety and the symptoms of obsessive-compulsive disorders. Of all the varieties of psychosurgery, none has ever been employed as commonly as a procedure called a prefrontal lobotomy or, simply, **lobotomy** (Valenstein, 1980, 1986). This surgery severs the major neural connections between the prefrontal lobes (the area at the very front of the cerebral cortex) and lower brain centers.

The lobotomy was first performed in 1935 by a Portuguese psychiatrist, Egas Moniz. For developing the procedure, Moniz was awarded the Nobel Prize in 1949. (The next year, in an ironic twist of fate, Moniz was shot by

psychosurgery *a surgical procedure designed to affect one's psychological or behavioral reactions*

lobotomy *a psychosurgical technique in which the prefrontal lobes of the cerebral cortex are severed from lower brain centers*

one of his lobotomized patients. He was rendered paraplegic and was confined to a wheelchair for the rest of his life.) The logic behind a lobotomy was that the frontal lobes of the cerebral cortex influence the more basic emotional centers of the brain. Severely psychotic patients were thought to have difficulty in coordinating these two parts of the brain. It was reasoned that if the parts were separated surgically, the more depressed, agitated, or violent patients could be brought under control.

The operation often appeared to be successful. Used as a measure of last resort, stories of the remarkable changes it produced in chronic mental patients circulated widely. *Time* magazine, in its November 30, 1942, issue, called the procedure "revolutionary," claiming that at that time, "some 300 people in the United States have had their psychoses surgically removed." During the 1940s and 1950s, prefrontal lobotomies were performed with regularity. *Time* reported (on September 15, 1952) that, at that time, neurologist Walter Freeman was performing about 100 lobotomies a week. It is difficult to estimate precisely how many lobotomies were performed just within these two decades, but certainly they numbered in the tens of thousands.

Treating severely disturbed, depressed, and schizophrenic patients had always been difficult. Perhaps we shouldn't be surprised that this relatively simple surgical technique was accepted so widely and uncritically at first. The procedure often was done under local anesthetic in the physician's office and took only 10 minutes. An instrument that looks very much like an ice pick was inserted through the eye socket, on the nasal side, and was pushed up into the brain. A few simple movements of the instrument and the job was done—the lobes were severed. Within hours, the patient would be ready to return to his or her room.

It always was appreciated that the procedure was an irreversible one. What took longer to realize was that it often carried with it terrible side effects. In fact, between 1 and 4 percent of patients receiving prefrontal lobotomies died (Carson et al., 1988). Many of those who survived suffered seizures, memory loss, an inability to plan ahead, and a general listlessness and loss of affect. Many behaved childishly and were difficult to manage within institutions. By the late 1950s, lobotomies had become very rare. Contrary to common belief, it is not an illegal procedure, although the conditions under which it might even be considered are very restrictive. Prefrontal lobotomies are not done anymore for the simple reason that they are no longer needed. There are other means, with fewer side effects, that can produce similar beneficial results more safely and reliably.

BEFORE YOU GO ON

What is a prefrontal lobotomy?
Why was it ever used, and why is it not used today?

Electroconvulsive Therapy

As gruesome as the procedures of psychosurgery can be, many people find the very notion of **electroconvulsive therapy (ECT)**, or shock treatments, even more difficult to appreciate. This technique, first introduced in 1937, involves passing an electric current of between 70 and 150 volts across a patient's head for a fraction of a second. The patient has been given a fast-acting general anesthetic and, thus, is unconscious when the shock is delivered. As soon as the anesthetic is administered, the patient also receives a muscle relaxant to minimize muscular contractions, which were quite common—and potentially dangerous—in the early days of ECT. The shock induces a reaction in the brain that is not unlike an epileptic (grand mal) seizure. The whole procedure takes about five minutes. One of the side effects of ECT is a (rather protective) memory loss for events just preceding the administration of the shock and for the shock itself.

At first, the treatment was used to help calm agitated schizophrenics, but it soon became clear that its most beneficial results were for those patients suffering from deep depression. It often alleviates the symptoms of depression and, in some cases, has beneficial effects on other psychotic symptoms as well. In fact, the subgroup of patients that seems best suited to the ECT procedure are those for whom depression is a major symptom, but for whom other psychotic symptoms (such as hallucinations or delusions) are present also (Joyce & Paykel, 1989).

Virtually all patients (97 percent) receiving ECT give their consent to the procedure, and negative side effects are quite rare. The most commonly reported side effect is memory loss and general mental confusion. In nearly all cases, these effects gradually disappear in a few days or weeks. In one study of 99,425 treatments given to 18,627 patients, only two deaths were reported. The death rate for childbirth in the United States is nearly six times greater (Kramer, 1985). Additionally, once they have experienced the procedure, most ECT patients are far from terrorized by the notion of having an electrical shock delivered to their brain. For example, in one study, 82 percent of 166 patients surveyed rated ECT as no more upsetting than a visit to the dentist (Sackeim, 1985). The beneficial effects of ECT are reasonably long-lasting. After only 10 to 12 treatments, many patients remain free of symptoms for months.

Just why ECT produces the benefits that it does is not fully understood even today. As you might guess, most researchers are now looking at the action of neurotransmitters in the brain for possible explanations. It seems that the effects, if not the actual amounts, of some neurotransmitters—GABA, serotonin, and norepinephrine, in particular—are increased by ECT.

The poor reputation that ECT has among the general population, and among some psychologists and psychiatrists, did not develop without some foundation. There *are* horror stories of the negative side effects that can follow abuse of the procedure. (At first, the seizures of the shock treatment were induced by drugs, not electricity. It was largely from these drug-induced treatments that we have the stories of convulsions so massive as to result in broken bones.) It is now recommended that no more than a dozen treatments be given and that they be administered over an extended period of time. There is little doubt that some patients in the past have received hundreds of ECT treatments. In such cases, there has been evidence of brain damage and permanent memory loss.

Even though we do not understand fully how ECT works, and even though it is a treatment that must be used with extreme care, ECT is still very much in practice today. Although the numbers declined during the late 1970s, nearly 100,000 patients receive shock treatments each year, and

electroconvulsive therapy (ECT) *a treatment, usually for the symptoms of severe depression, in which an electric current passed through a patient's head causes a seizure and loss of consciousness*

numbers again are on the rise (Thompson & Blaine, 1987). For example, in 1986, 88,847 ECT treatments were reimbursed through medicare, while in 1988, 96,276 treatments were reimbursed.

The introduction of psychoactive, antidepressant medications has reduced the need to use ECT. But psychiatrists realize that drug treatment is not always successful, and even when it is, it often takes six to eight weeks for the drugs to produce beneficial results. Researchers also have found that, in many cases, ECT is a more effective treatment than are antidepressant medications (e.g., Small et al., 1988).

Electroconvulsive therapy now is generally reserved for (1) patients for whom drug therapies seem ineffective, (2) patients with acute suicidal tendencies (because drugs take so long to have their full antidepressant effects), and (3) depressed patients who also suffer from delusions (Kalat, 1984). Some researchers have argued that administering a shock to just one side of the brain, called a *unilateral ECT*, is a safer yet equally effective procedure with even fewer side-effects. More success has been found by creating seizures in the right hemisphere of the cerebral cortex (thought to be more associated with emotional reactions) than in the left hemisphere (Squire & Slater, 1978).

BEFORE YOU GO ON

What is ECT?
Why is it still being used?

Drug Therapy

Chemicals that have their effect on a person's cognitions, affect, or behavior are collectively referred to as *psychoactive drugs*. As we have seen, there are many of them, and most are used to produce an altered state of consciousness or awareness. Using chemicals to improve the condition of the mentally disordered is a much more recent development and has been hailed as one of the most significant scientific achievements of the latter half of the twentieth century (Snyder, 1984). In this section, we'll examine the three main types, or classes, of psychoactive drugs used as therapy: the antipsychotic, antidepressant, and antianxiety drugs.

Antipsychotic Drugs. Antipsychotic drugs, as their name suggests, alleviate or eliminate the major symptoms of psychoses. The real breakthrough in the use of antipsychotic medication came with the introduction of *chlorpromazine*. The antipsychotic effects of chlorpromazine were recorded in France in 1950. A neurosurgeon, Henri Laborit, was looking for a drug that would calm his patients before surgery. Just before undergoing surgery, patients often feel nervous and anxious. Laborit wanted to help them relax because he knew that if they did, his patients' postsurgical recovery would be improved. A drug company supplied Laborit with chlorpromazine. It worked even better than anyone had expected, producing

antipsychotic drugs *chemicals, such as chlorpromazine, that are effective in reducing psychotic symptoms*

relaxation and calm in his patients. Laborit convinced some of his colleagues to try the drug on their more agitated patients, some of whom were suffering from mental disorders. The experiments met with great success, and by the late 1950s, the drug was widely used both in North America and in Europe. In its June 14, 1954, issue, *Time* magazine referred to chlorpromazine as "the wonder drug of 1954," claiming that "patients who were formerly violent or withdrawn lie molded to their bed [and] when a doctor enters the room, they sit up and talk sense with him, perhaps for the first time in months." The drug revolution had begun. With this success in hand, the search for other chemicals that could improve the plight of the mentally ill began in earnest. By 1956 more than half a dozen different antipsychotic medications were available in the United States. During the period from 1976 to 1985 the use of antipsychotic medication remained quite stable, overall, with between 19 and 21 million prescriptions being written during the period (Wysowski & Baum, 1989).

Chlorpromazine is just one of many drugs currently being used with success to treat psychotic symptoms. Most antipsychotic drugs are of the same general type as chlorpromazine. Although there now are many varieties of antipsychotic drugs, most work in essentially the same way: by influencing neurotransmitter activity in the brain. Most act by blocking receptor sites for the neurotransmitter dopamine (see p. 64). Antipsychotic drugs are most effective in treating the positive symptoms of psychosis: delusions, hallucinations, and bizarre behaviors (see p. 588). A recently introduced medication, *clozapine* (trade name *Clozaril*), appears to be an exception, because it is effective in reducing negative symptoms as well as positive symptoms. Unfortunately, clozapine carries with it the risk of some very serious side effects, some of which can be fatal. As a result, the use of this drug is very carefully monitored.

Although most antipsychotic drugs are prescribed for patients with schizophrenia, one exception is *lithium*, or lithium salts such as lithium carbonate. Regulating the precise dosage is very difficult, and its side effects are many and often severe. Nonetheless, lithium salts have been found to be very effective in treating some patients with bipolar mood disorders. The drug occasionally alleviates depression, but seems much more useful in controlling the manic cycle of bipolar disorders. There are those individuals for whom the drug has no beneficial effect, and its prolonged use can lead to convulsions, kidney failure, and other serious reactions.

The effects of the antipsychotic drugs are remarkable and impressive, and they have revolutionized the care of psychotic patients. Nonetheless, they are not the ultimate solution for disorders such as schizophrenia and the other psychoses. For one thing, there are patients for whom the drugs either have no effect or have harmful effects. With high dosages or prolonged use, a variety of side effects emerge that are very unpleasant at best, including dry mouth and throat, sore muscles and joints, heavy sedation, sexual impotence, and muscle tremors. Sometimes side effects are even more significant, including seizures and cardiovascular damage. Although the most effective of the antipsychotic drugs do control symptoms, the question is, Are they in any sense curing the disorder? Symptom-free patients, who often are released from institutional care to the outside world, soon stop using their medication only to find that their psychotic symptoms return.

What are antipsychotic drugs, and what are their effects?

antidepressant drugs *chemicals, such as MAO inhibitors and tricyclics, that reduce and/or eliminate the symptoms of depression*

Antidepressant Drugs. Antidepressant drugs elevate the mood of persons who are feeling depressed. The first effective antidepressant was *iproniazid*, which originally was used in the treatment of tuberculosis. One of its side effects was that it made tubercular patients feel cheerful and happy. When tested on depressed patients, it was found to have the same effect. Unfortunately, it soon was discovered that iproniazid causes irreversible liver damage, and its use as an antidepressant was stopped.

The antidepressant medications used today are of two types: *MAO inhibitors* (MAO, or monoamine oxidase, is a chemical found in the brain that reduces levels of two neurotransmitters; MAO inhibitors thus increase levels of these neurotransmitters) and *tricyclics*. No one antidepressant is universally any better than any other. Each seems to be particularly effective for certain kinds of depressive disorders (Cole, 1988). Tricyclics are best suited for uncomplicated, major depression; the MAO inhibitors are most effective for depression accompanied by anxiety or panic symptoms; and, as we have seen, the lithium salts are best suited for bipolar mood disorders (Joyce & Paykel, 1989; Tyrer & Shawcross, 1988). It is also the case that an antidepressant drug that has no effect for one person may produce severe, unpleasant side effects in another person and yet have remarkably beneficial effects for a third person.

Antidepressant drugs would be of little use for anyone who was a bit depressed about receiving a low grade on a history exam. These medications generally require weeks to have their maximum effect and need to be taken on a long-term basis to prevent a recurrence of the depression. Although they can elevate the mood of many truly depressed individuals, they have virtually no effect on people who are not depressed. That is, they do not produce a euphoric high in people who are already in a good mood.

Of the two classes of antidepressants, the tricyclic types (trade names Elavil or Tofranil, for example) are more commonly used. As you might have guessed, the tricyclic drugs do produce unfortunate side effects in some patients, including intellectual confusion, increased perspiration, and weight gain. Some tricyclics have been implicated as a cause of heart disease. A major problem with the MAO inhibitor drugs is that they require adherence to a strict diet and carefully monitored dosages to have their best effect. They also produce a wide range of serious side effects, such as dizziness, sexual impotence, elevated blood pressure, and liver damage, to name just a few.

A relatively new antidepressant, *flouxetine* (trade name *Prozac*) was introduced in December 1987. It is currently the single most prescribed antidepressant; about 650,000 new or renewed prescriptions are written each month. It is chemically unrelated to either the tricyclics or the MAO inhibitors, although it, too, affects a brain neurotransmitter: serotonin. Often a very effective medication, its major advantage is that it seems to produce fewer negative side effects—skin rashes, agitation, and weight loss among them. Nonetheless, occasionally these side effects are so unpleasant that patients stop using it. In clinical trials (before it was openly marketed) 15 percent of the patients receiving Prozac discontinued treatment because of adverse side effects. Since it has been available for a relatively short time, long-term effects of its use are as yet unknown.

Unlike antipsychotic drugs, there is evidence that when antidepressant drugs *are* effective, they may actually bring about long-term cures rather than symptom suppression. In other words, the changes in mood caused by the drugs may outlast use of the drug itself. The hope and plan, in fact, is to gradually reduce the dosage of the drug over time. For persons with mood disorders who do not respond to the medications presently available, other varieties are being tested, and for such patients, electroconvulsive therapy may be indicated.

BEFORE YOU GO ON

What are three types of antidepressant drugs, and what are they meant to do?

Antianxiety Drugs. Antianxiety drugs (or tranquilizers) help reduce the felt aspect of anxiety. They are the most commonly prescribed of all drugs. Some antianxiety drugs, the *meprobamates* (trade names Miltown or Equanil, for example), are basically muscle relaxers. When muscular tension is reduced, the patient often reports feeling calm and at ease.

The other major variety of antianxiety drug is the group of chemicals called *benzodiazepines* (trade names Librium or Valium, for example). These drugs act directly on the central nervous system, and their impact is obvious and significant. They help anxious people feel less anxious. At first, the only side effects appear to be a slight drowsiness, blurred vision, and a slight impairment of coordination. Unfortunately, the tranquilizing effects of the drugs are not long-lasting. Patients can fall into a pattern of relying on the drugs to alleviate even the slightest of fears and worries. Soon a dependency and addiction can develop from which withdrawal can be difficult. In fact, a danger of the antianxiety medications is the very fact that they *are* so effective. So long as one can avoid the unpleasant feelings of anxiety simply by taking a pill, there is little to motivate one to seek and deal with the actual cause of one's anxiety.

antianxiety drugs *chemicals, such as the meprobamates and benzodiazepines, that alleviate the symptoms of anxiety*

BEFORE YOU GO ON

What are the common antianxiety drugs, and what are the dangers inherent in their use?

DEINSTITUTIONALIZATION: A MIXED BLESSING

As I have mentioned, the first institution expressly for the mentally ill was St. Mary of Bethlehem Hospital, or Bedlam, so designated in 1547. Despite reform and well-intentioned efforts to promote mental health (rather than merely housing the disordered), not much changed for nearly 400 years. By the middle of the twentieth century, large state-supported institutions were the commonplace residences of the chronically mentally retarded and mentally ill. Lack of public support, leading to a lack of adequate funding for staff and facilities, resulted in what amounted to a national disgrace.

Mental institutions became overcrowded and unmanageable. Individual therapy and/or personal care for patients was all but unknown in many such institutions. Privacy was unheard of, food was inedible, and filth and squalor prevailed—not in all institutions, of course, but in most. Within the last 30 years, there has been a truly revolutionary shift in mental health care. For a number of seemingly sound and sensible reasons, many patients have experienced **deinstitutionalization**. They have been released from the large mental institutions to return to family and community. The drop in institutional patient population has been dramatic (see Figure 13.1). Compared to 1955, the number of patients in state and county mental hospitals has dropped nearly 75 percent. What has brought about this great change, and has it been a change for the better or the worse?

There are several reasons for deinstitutionalization that we might list. We've already alluded to some of them. Let's consider just three.

deinstitutionalization *the practice, begun in the mid-1950s, of releasing patients from mental institutions and returning them to their home communities*

Community mental health centers help account for the deinstitutionalization that has taken place during the last 30 years. In addition to providing outpatient care, many offer other services such as educational programs and short-term in-patient care.

1. *A concern for the rights of the patient arose.* The overcrowded and virtually inhumane conditions that existed in many institutions simply became more than society was willing to bear. The courts entered the picture, ordering that either patients receive adequate and proper treatment or be released. The landmark decision was set down in 1971 in the *Wyatt v. Stickney* case in Alabama. Ricky Wyatt was a patient in a state hospital who felt that he (and the fellow patients who joined in his suit) was not being fairly or adequately treated. He filed suit against the Alabama mental health commissioner, Stonewall Stickney. Not only did the judge find in favor of Wyatt, but he also set down a list of conditions that state institutions must meet to ensure the "adequate treatment" of all patients. He further specified that if significant changes were not made in a timely fashion, the patients were to be released.

2. *Symptoms can be managed through chemical means.* We've already touched on this matter. In the mid-1950s, the introduction of effective drugs that at least suppressed or masked psychotic symptoms made it all the more reasonable that patients no longer displaying unusual or bizarre behaviors could be released from institutional care.

3. *Community mental health centers were to be established.* In 1963, Congress passed the Community Mental Health Act. This law included a provision for the establishment of a large number of mental health centers to be located in local communities rather than centralized in one or two state institutions. The plan was for there to be one easily accessible mental health center for every 50,000 people in the country. These centers would accommodate people on an outpatient basis and could provide care for those

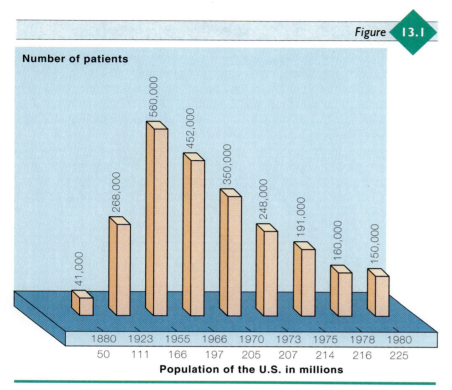

Figure 13.1

Number of patients

41,000 — 1880 — 50
268,000 — 1923 — 111
560,000 — 1955 — 166
452,000 — 1966 — 197
350,000 — 1970 — 205
248,000 — 1973 — 207
191,000 — 1975 — 214
160,000 — 1978 — 216
150,000 — 1980 — 225

Population of the U.S. in millions

The number of patients institutionalized in county and state mental hospitals. Also indicated is the approximate U.S. population. Remember that it was in the mid- and late 1950s that antipsychotic medications became widely used. (Adapted from NIMH, 1984.)

recently discharged from large residential mental hospitals. These community mental health centers were to provide many other services, including short-term inpatient care, as well as consultation, education, and prevention programs.

Has the system of deinstitutionalization worked? On this question, the house is divided. There are those who applaud the change (Braun et al., 1981) and argue that, within limits, "continued optimism about community care seems warranted" (Shadish, 1984). On the other hand, many see deinstitutionalization as trading one set of problems for a host of others. Many of the patients released from mental hospitals are, quite literally, "dumped" back into their home communities. There, resources for their assistance often are minimal. For example, there is seldom adequate housing for those who have been released. (Frequently, negative attitudes seem to be involved, as in, "We don't want housing for 'those people' in *our* neighborhood.") Many released patients become street people, particularly in large cities. Recent estimates from the National Institute of Mental Health place the percentage of homeless with psychological disorders at 30 to 35 percent. Many require the support of the welfare system. And no matter how capable a community mental health center may be (assuming there is one nearby), if patients do not seek its support, it will do them little good. Inadequate funding for community mental health centers has become a chronic con-

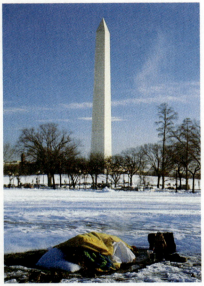

Although cities may be trying, many fall short and are unable to provide adequate assistance for patients newly released from mental hospitals. Consequently, many will live on the streets. On the positive side, successful programs do exist and meet patients' needs often by staying in contact with the patient.

dition. As we have noted, most of the antipsychotic medication that patients require does not have lasting effects. When patients stop taking their medication (perhaps because of its expense or its side effects), symptoms return, and they will likely need to return once again to the institution. In fact, since deinstitutionalization has become a matter of policy, admissions to mental hospitals have actually increased, although the average length of stay in such institutions has decreased (Kiesler, 1982). Those who work in community mental health centers often refer to this phenomenon as the revolving-door consequence of deinstitutionalization.

It appears that the trend to reduce the population of patients in mental institutions is likely to continue. Effective community programs and more resources are needed to assist those released from these institutions to ensure that discharge is appropriate for them and for the community to which they return.

BEFORE YOU GO ON

What is deinstitutionalization, why did it come about, and has it been successful?

In summary, we can say that there is great hope that biochemical techniques can be found to suppress, if not eliminate, many severe symptoms associated with psychological disorders. At the moment, however, we should probably remain somewhat cautious. Remember that only 35 years ago it was widely held that prefrontal lobotomies and other forms of psychosurgery would be the ultimate long-term answer to the question of how to treat persons with psychological disorders. However, scientists continue to learn about the chemistry of the nervous system and the delicate balance between brain and behavior. If we remain ever mindful of the harsh and inhumane treatment of the mentally ill that characterized our not-too-distant past, we can now be more cautiously optimistic than ever before.

SUMMARY

Briefly trace the history of the treatment of persons with psychological disorders.

In ancient times, and throughout the Middle Ages, the prevailing view of the mentally ill was that they were possessed by evil spirits. As a result, treatment was often harsh, involving torture and placement in dungeonlike asylums for the insane, which in many ways were worse than prisons. It was not uncommon for the mentally ill, who were often viewed as witches, to be put to death for their unusual behaviors. Throughout history, there have been attempts by compassionate persons to provide humane treatment to the disordered. It wasn't until the twentieth century that what we now call the mental health movement began with an aim of treating the mentally ill in the most humane way possible. / page 601

What is a prefrontal lobotomy? Why was it ever used, and why is it not used today?

A prefrontal lobotomy is a psychosurgical technique that severs the connections between the prefrontal lobes of the cerebral cortex and lower brain centers. It was first used in the mid-1930s and was a common treatment in the 1940s and 1950s. It was used as a last resort because it was often successful in alleviating the worst of psychotic symptoms. It also produced many mild to severe side effects, including death. Because of its inherent danger, and because safer, reversible treatments such as drug therapy are available today, it is no longer used. / page 602

What is ECT? Why is it still being used?

ECT stands for electroconvulsive therapy, commonly called shock therapy. In this treatment, a brain seizure is produced by passing an electric current across the patient's head. Upon regaining consciousness, the patient has no memory of the procedure. Although there may be negative side effects, particularly with prolonged or repeated use, the technique is demonstrably useful for most patients as a means of reducing or even eliminating severe depression and some other psychotic symptoms. / page 604

What are antipsychotic drugs, and what are their effects?

Chlorpromazine was the first antipsychotic drug. Introduced in 1950, it was commonly used by the mid-1950s to suppress symptoms associated with psychosis: hallucinations, delusions, disordered thought, inappropriate effect, and the like. Antipsychotic drugs have their effect by altering the action of neurotransmitters in the brain. Lithium salts have been found to be useful in treating bipolar mood disorders, mania in particular. Although these drugs definitely reduce the psychotic symptoms in many patients, it is not correct to say that they cure the disorder, because symptoms often return when the drugs are discontinued. / page 606

What are three types of antidepressant drugs, and what are they meant to do?

Two major types of antidepressant drugs are the MAO inhibitors and the tricyclics. A relatively new antidepressant, flouxetine, produces fewer side effects while maintaining effectiveness. Unlike the antipsychotic drugs, these often have long-term beneficial effects (alleviating feelings of depression), even after the patient stops taking them. They often take weeks to produce their effects, and they do not work for all patients. Long-term use of the drugs may produce a number of potentially harmful or unpleasant side effects. / page 607

What are the common antianxiety drugs, and what are the dangers inherent in their use?

The most common anxiety-alleviating drugs, or tranquilizers, are the meprobamates and the benzodiazepines, including Valium and Librium, which are two of the most commonly prescribed of all drugs in the world. These drugs are effective in reducing felt levels of anxiety. Unfortunately, there is evidence that some patients who use antianxiety drugs develop addictions to them. Like many psychoactive drugs, they suppress symptoms; they do not cure the underlying anxiety, and even small overdoses can lead to severe complications. / page 607

What is deinstitutionalization, why did it come about, and has it been successful?

Deinstitutionalization refers to the policy of taking measures to release patients from publicly supported mental institutions. As national policy, deinstitutionalization is a response to pressures that became apparent in the mid-1950s: (1) Conditions in mental hospitals generally were very bad, (2) antipsychotic medications significantly reduced many troublesome psychotic symptoms, and (3) community-based mental health centers were going to be created to care for patients (as outpatients) after they were released back to the community. The data are not yet in to allow us to render final judgment on deinstitutionalization. The blessing is mixed, to be sure. Many patients are infinitely better off living at home and visiting their community mental health centers as the need arises. Others are much less fortunate. They have no nearby mental health facility and soon stop taking their medication, so psychotic symptoms return. / page 610

The Psychotherapies

Why We Care: A Topic Preview

All varieties of psychotherapy are techniques "designed to influence the patient's behavior by psychological means, that is, they seek to persuade the patient to think, feel, or act differently" (Strupp, 1986, p. 128). Because there are so many different varieties of psychotherapy—literally hundreds— this topic is titled "The Psychotherapies." In this topic, we will examine some of the major forms of psychotherapy.

Although the overriding goal of psychotherapy may be to persuade the patient to think, feel, or act differently, different types of therapy often have different specific goals, or subgoals: Some attempt to help a person gain insight about the true nature of his or her disorder and its underlying cause or causes; Some attempt to help a person develop a stronger sense of self-identity and self-esteem; others focus on bringing about lasting and measurable changes in overt behavior. As we shall soon see, some varieties of psychotherapy focus primarily on one's affect or feelings; some focus on one's cognitions or beliefs; some focus on overt behaviors. Once again we see that we can use our simple ABC mnemonic.

We care about the psychotherapies reviewed in this topic for many reasons, including the observation that seeking psychotherapy is becoming more and more common. Just 30 years ago, only 13 percent of the population sought psychotherapy at any time in their life (Meredith, 1986). Now we find that almost 30 percent will have some experience in psychotherapy at some point in their lifetime. In 1987 alone, "15 million of us [made] roughly 120 million visits to mental health professionals—nearly twice as many visits as to internists" (Hunt, 1987, p. 28).

We will begin our discussion with a brief section on the types of professionals that typically provide psychotherapy. With this introduction aside, we'll divide our discussion of the major varieties of psychotherapy into four main parts: psychoanalytic (or Freudian) techniques, humanistic techniques, behavioral techniques, and cognitive techniques. We will also examine group approaches to psychotherapy. Having reviewed some major forms of therapy, we will then examine the issue of evaluating it. Does it work? Under what circumstances?

psychotherapy *the treatment of mental disorders through psychological means, effecting change in cognitions, affect, and/or behavior*

CHOOSING A THERAPIST

Throughout the last three topics, I repeatedly have mentioned the reality that psychological disorders affect many people. As you read these words, tens of *millions* of North Americans are in need of treatment for psychological distress. What if *you* were such a person? What if you were to realize that you were showing the symptoms of a psychological disorder and that therapy would help? Where would you turn; how would you begin?

Who Provides Psychotherapy?

Perhaps the first thing that you should realize in this hypothetical situation is that many professionals are equipped to provide psychotherapy. Let's begin, then, by listing the most common types of mental health providers, as they are sometimes called. Please remember that this is a list of generalities; our descriptions will not hold true for everyone within a given category. Remember also that because of their experience and/or training, some professionals develop specialties within their fields. That is, some therapists specialize in the disorders of children and adolescents; some work primarily with adults; some prefer to work with families; some devote their efforts to people with substance and alcohol abuse problems. Finally, it is important to understand that a psychotherapist can and will use several of the techniques of therapy outlined in this topic. In other words, few therapists take any one approach to treatment and none other. As many as 40 percent of therapists in the United States claim to have no particularly dominant approach to their psychotherapy (Norcross, 1986). The following may be considered psychotherapists:

1. The *clinical psychologist* usually has earned a Ph.D. in psychology that provides practical, applied experience, as well as an emphasis on research. The Ph.D. clinician spends a year on internship, usually at a mental health center or psychiatric hospital. The clinical psychologist has extensive training in psychological testing (in general, *psychodiagnostics*). Some clinical psychologists have a Psy.D. (pronounced sigh-dee), which is a Doctor of Psychology, rather than the more common Doctor of Philosophy degree. Generally, Psy.D. programs take as long to complete as Ph.D. programs, but emphasize more practical, clinical work and less research.

2. Psychiatry is a specialty area in medicine. In addition to the course work required for an M.D., the *psychiatrist* spends an internship (usually one year) and a residency (usually three years) in a mental hospital, specializing in the care of psychologically disturbed patients. At least at the moment, the psychiatrist is the only kind of psychotherapist permitted to use the biomedical treatments we reviewed in Topic 13A. (There is a campaign under way to get some medical privileges for Ph.D. psychologists.)

3. The *counseling psychologist* usually has a Ph.D. in psychology. The focus of study (and the required one-year internship), however, is generally on patients with less severe psychological problems. For instance, rather than spending one's internship in a psychiatric hospital, a counseling psychologist would more likely spend time at a university counseling center.

Psychoanalysts, like the one pictured above, are trained and certified in the methods of Freudian psychoanalysis. A number of professionals, including social workers and licensed counselors are involved in family and group therapy. The picture on the right shows a counselor working with family members of AIDS victims.

4. A *licensed professional counselor* will have a degree in counselor education and will have met state requirements for a license to do psychotherapy. Counselors can be found in school settings, but also work in mental health settings, specializing in family counseling and drug abuse.
5. *Psychoanalyst* is a special label given either to a clinical psychologist or a psychiatrist who has also received intensive training (and certification) in the particular methods of (Freudian) psychoanalysis.
6. The terminal degree for *clinical social workers* is generally the master's degree, although Ph.D.s in social work are becoming more common. Social workers can and do engage in a variety of psychotherapies, but their traditional role has been involvement in family and group therapy.

Psychotherapy may be offered by a number of other professionals and paraprofessionals. Some people practice therapy or counseling with a master's degree in psychology (although because of licensing or certification laws in many states, they may not advertise themselves as psychologists). *Occupational therapists* usually have a master's degree (or, less frequently, a bachelor's degree) in occupational therapy, which includes many psychology classes and internship training in aiding the psychologically and physically handicapped. *Psychiatric nurses* often work in mental hospitals and clinics. In addition to their R.N. degrees, psychiatric nurses have special training in the care of mentally ill patients. *Pastoral counseling* is a specialty of many with a religious background and a master's degree in either psychology or educational counseling. The *mental health technician* usually has an associate degree in mental health technology (MHT). MHT graduates are seldom allowed to provide unsupervised psychotherapy, although they may be involved in the delivery of many mental health services.

How Do I Choose the Right Therapist?

Realizing that many different professionals offer psychotherapy, how does one go about choosing one? Many people and agencies can serve as a good resource at this point. Do you have any family or friends who have been in therapy or counseling? What (or whom) do they recommend? If you get no useful information from friends or family, there are many other people you could ask (assuming that your symptoms are not acute and that time is not critical). You might check with your psychology instructor. He or she may not be a psychotherapist, but almost certainly will be familiar with the mental health resources of your community. You also might see if your college or university maintains a clinic or counseling center service for students (this is often an inexpensive route to take). Check with your family physician. Among other things, a complete physical exam may turn up some leads about the nature of your problem. You might talk with your rabbi, priest, or minister. Members of the clergy commonly deal with people in distress and, again, are usually familiar with community resources. You also could call the local mental health center or mental health association. If you think that you have a problem, the most important thing is not to give up. Find help. It is available.

Now let's assume that a therapist has been recommended to you. You have scheduled an appointment. How will you know if you've made a wise choice? To be sure, only you can be the judge of that. Three cautions are appropriate here: (1) Not everyone who advertises that he or she is skilled in psychotherapy has either the training or the experience to do so effectively. Unfortunately, there are those who advertise themselves as being therapists with very little to recommend them to the task. Therefore, it is appropriate for you to ask about a therapist's credentials. What sort of training has he or she had? How much experience? If your state requires it, is the therapist licensed or certified? (2) Give the therapy and the therapist a chance. By now, surely you recognize that psychological problems are seldom simple and easily solved. (In fact, you should be leery of a therapist who suggests that your problem can be easily solved.) It may take three or four sessions before your therapist has learned what the exact and real nature of your problem *is*. Most psychological problems develop over a long period of time. An hour or two per week for a week or two cannot be expected to automatically make everything right again, as if by magic. You should expect progress, and you might expect some sessions to be more helpful than others. To expect a miracle cure is to be unreasonable. In this context, I should mention that the course of your therapy will depend a great deal on *you* and the extent to which you are motivated to do what your therapist asks of you and to make the changes your therapist recommends. (3) At some point, you may feel that you have given your therapy every opportunity to succeed. If you have been truly open and honest with your therapist and feel that you are not profiting from your sessions, then say so. Express your displeasure and disappointment. After careful consideration, be prepared to change therapists. Starting over again with someone new may involve costs in time and effort, but occasionally it is the only reasonable option.

With this general introduction in mind, and an awareness that few therapists follow just one and only one approach to treatment, we now can review the major varieties of psychotherapy that have evolved over the years. Because it was the first systematic approach, we will start with Freudian psychoanalysis.

Who may offer psychotherapy?
How does one find an effective psychotherapist?

PSYCHOANALYTIC TECHNIQUES

We begin our review of the psychotherapies with **psychoanalysis**. Psychoanalysis began with Sigmund Freud toward the end of the nineteenth century. Psychoanalysis did not really evolve from Freudian personality theory (see Topic 10A). If anything, the reverse is true. Freud was a therapist first, a personality theorist second. But his techniques of therapy and theory of personality sprang forth from the same mind, and they are very interrelated.

Psychoanalysis is based on a number of assumptions, most of them having to do with the nature of conflict and the unconscious mind. For Freud, one's life is often a struggle to resolve conflicts between naturally opposing forces: instincts for life and instincts for death. The biological, sexual, and aggressive strivings of the id are often in conflict with the superego, which is associated with guilt and overcautiousness. The strivings of the id are also often in conflict with the rational, reality-based ego, which is often called upon to mediate between the id and the superego. Anxiety-producing conflicts that go unresolved are repressed; that is, they are forced out of awareness into the unconscious levels of the mind. Conflicts and anxiety-producing traumas of childhood can be expected to produce symptoms of psychological disturbance later on in life.

According to Freud, the best way to rid oneself of anxiety is to enter the unconscious, identify the nature of the repressed, anxiety-producing conflict, bring it out into the open, and then resolve it as well as possible. The first step is to gain insight into the nature of one's problems; only then can problem solving begin. Thus, the goals of Freudian psychoanalysis are insight and resolution of repressed conflict.

Sigmund Freud died in 1939, but his approach to psychotherapy did not die with him. It has been modified (as Freud himself modified it over the years), but it remains true to the basic thrust of Freudian psychoanalysis. Before we consider how it has changed, let's examine Freudian analysis as Freud practiced it.

Freudian Psychoanalysis

Psychoanalysis with Sigmund Freud was a time-consuming (up to five days per week for six to ten years), often tedious process of self-examination and introspection. The major task for the patient was to talk openly and honestly about all aspects of his or her life, from early childhood memories to the dreams of the present. The major task of the therapist, or analyst,

psychoanalysis *the form of psychotherapy associated with Freud, aimed at helping the patient gain insight into unconscious conflicts*

To help his patients relax, Freud had them lie on this couch while he sat out of view.

was to interpret what was being expressed by the patient, always on the lookout for clues to possible repressed conflict. Once identified, the patient and analyst together could try to resolve the conflict(s) that brought the patient to analysis in the first place. Several procedures and processes were used in the search for repressed conflicts. We'll list some of the most important ones.

Free Association. In 1881, Freud graduated from the University of Vienna Medical School. From the start, he was interested in the treatment of what were then called nervous disorders. He went to France to study the technique of hypnosis, which many were claiming to be a worthwhile treatment for mental disorders. Freud wasn't totally convinced, but when he returned to Vienna, he and a colleague, Josef Breuer, tried hypnosis as a treatment for neurotic disorders, conversion reaction (hysteria) in particular. They both became convinced that hypnosis itself was of little benefit. What mattered more, they believed, was to have the patient talk—talk about anything and everything. In fact, Freud and Breuer's method became known as the "talking cure."

free association *the procedure in psychoanalysis in which the patient is to express whatever comes to mind without editing responses*

Soon, the method of **free association** became a central procedure of psychoanalysis. Patients were told to say out loud whatever came into their minds. Sometimes the analyst would provide a stimulus word to get a chain of freely flowing associations going. To free-associate the way Freud would have wanted you to is not an easy task. It often required many sessions for patients to learn the technique. Patients were not to edit their associations. They were to say *whatever* they thought of, and that is not always an easy thing to do. Many people are uncomfortable, at least initially, sharing their private, innermost thoughts and desires with anyone, much less a stranger. Here is where the "Freudian couch" came in. To help his patients relax, Freud would have them lie down, be comfortable, and avoid eye contact with him. The job of the analyst through all this was to try to interpret the apparently free-flowing and random verbal responses, always looking for expressions of unconscious desires and conflicts.

Resistance. During the course of psychoanalysis, and particularly during periods of free association, the psychoanalyst listens very carefully to what the patient is saying. The analyst also carefully listens for what the patient is not saying. Freud believed that **resistance**, the unwillingness or inability to freely discuss some aspect of one's life, was a significant process in analysis. Resistance can show itself in many ways, from simply avoiding the mention of some topic, to joking about matters as being inconsequential, to disrupting a session when a particular topic came up for discussion, to missing appointments altogether.

resistance *in psychoanalysis, the inability or unwillingness to freely discuss some aspect of one's life*

Let's say, for example, that over the last six months in psychoanalysis you have talked freely about a wide variety of subjects, including your early childhood memories and all the members of your family— all, that is, except your older brother. You have talked about all sorts of private experiences, some of them sexual, some of them pleasant, some unpleasant. But after six months of talking, you have not had anything to say about your older brother. Your analyst, noting this possible resistance, suggests that during your next visit, she would like to hear more about your brother. Then, for the first time since analysis began, you miss your next appointment. You come to the following appointment, but you're 10 minutes late.

Your analyst may now suspect that there is some problem with your relationship with your older brother, a problem that may have begun in childhood and has been repressed ever since. Of course, *there may be no problem here at all*, but for analysis to be successful, resistances need to be broken down and investigated.

Dream Interpretation. We should not be surprised to discover that analyzing a patient's dreams is an important part of psychoanalysis. Freud referred to dreams as the "royal road" to the unconscious level of the mind. Freud often trained his patients to recall and record their dreams in great detail. Then he would have them share the content of their dreams with him. He analyzed dreams at two levels: *manifest content*, the dream as recalled and reported by the patient; and *latent content*, the dream as a symbolic representation of the contents of the unconscious. Symbolism hidden in the latent content of reported dreams has been one of the most controversial of Freud's beliefs. The basic idea was that true motives, desires, and feelings might be camouflaged in a dream. For example, someone who reports a dream about suffocating under a huge pile of pillows *may* be expressing negative feelings about parental overprotectiveness. Someone who dreams of driving into an endless tunnel and becoming lost there *may* be expressing fears or concerns of a sexual nature. The job for the analyst, Freud argued, was to interpret dreams in terms of whatever insights and information they could provide about the true nature of the patient's unconscious mind.

Transference. One of the most controversial aspects of Freudian psychoanalysis is his concept of transference. **Transference** occurs when the patient unconsciously comes to view and feel about the analyst in much the same way he or she feels about some other important person in his or her life, usually a parent. As therapy continues over a long period of time, the relationship between analyst and patient does become a complex and often emotional one. If feelings that were once directed toward someone else of significance are now directed toward the analyst, they are more accessible, more easily observed by the analyst, and more readily interpreted and dealt with. Therapists have to guard against doing the same thing themselves—letting their own feelings and past experiences interfere with their neutral and objective interactions with their patients. Failure to do so is called *countertransference*.

transference *in psychoanalysis, the situation in which the patient comes to feel about the analyst in the same way he or she once felt about some other important person*

Post-Freudian Psychoanalysis. Early in the twentieth century, Freudian psychoanalysis was the only form of psychotherapy. In the 1940s and 1950s, it was *the* psychotherapy of choice. "Psychoanalytic theory was the dominant force in psychiatry in the postwar period and was embraced by a large number of clinical psychologists. To a certain extent, and for all practical purposes, there was no rival orientation" (Garfield, 1981, p. 176). Recently, psychoanalysis has become a much less common form of therapy, and strict, Freudian-style psychoanalysis has become very rare indeed. Let's see how the Freudian notion of therapy has been changed, but first we should note what hasn't changed.

To still qualify as a psychoanalytic approach, the basic aim of therapy must be the uncovering of deep-seated, unconscious conflict, usually caused by early childhood experiences. This broad statement is about all that unites psychoanalytic approaches to therapy today.

Probably the most significant change since Freud's time is the concern for shortening the length of analysis (e.g., Strupp & Binder, 1984). Today we talk about time-limited and short-form psychoanalysis. Today's analyst will also take a more active role than did Freud. The couch as a requirement is usually gone; the comfort of the patient is what matters, and some patients feel more comfortable pacing or sitting than they do lying on a couch. A major shift in emphasis is that modern psychoanalysts, although not insensitive to the effects of early childhood experiences, tend to spend more time exploring the present, the here and now. For example, a patient may come for analysis complaining of feelings of depression and anger to the point where the analyst believes there is a real and present danger that the patient might harm himself or herself, or even commit suicide. The thrust of therapy is going to be in the here and now, dealing with the patient's current anger and depression until the analyst is quite convinced that the patient has his or her anger under control.

BEFORE YOU GO ON

Describe the essential nature of Freudian psychoanalysis, defining some of its major features.

How is psychoanalysis different today from when it was practiced by Freud?

HUMANISTIC TECHNIQUES

There are many different brands of humanistic psychotherapy and their closely allied cousins, the *existential therapies*. What they have in common is a concern for self-examination, personal growth, and development. The goal of these therapies is not to uncover any deep-seated conflicts, but to foster psychological growth, to help the person take fullest advantage of life's opportunities. Based on the premise that we all can take charge of ourselves and our futures, and grow and change, therapy is devised to assist us with that process.

client-centered therapy *the humanistic psychotherapy associated with Rogers, aimed at helping the client grow and change from within*

Client-centered therapy, sometimes called Rogerian therapy after its founder, Carl Rogers, is the therapy that best typifies the humanistic approach. As its name suggests, the client is the center of the therapeutic interaction. (Rogers never used the term *patient*, and before his death in 1987 began using the term *person-centered* rather than *client-centered* to describe his approach to therapy.) For Rogers, therapy provides a special opportunity for a person to engage in self-discovery.

What are the characteristics of client-centered therapy? Again, there are many variants, but the following ideas generally characterize a client-centered approach. The focus is on the present, not one's past or childhood. The focus is on one's feelings or affect, not beliefs or cognitions; that is, you are more likely to hear, "How do you feel about that?" than "What do you think about that?" The therapist will attempt to reflect or mirror, not interpret, how a client is feeling (using statements such as, "You seem angry about that," or "Does that make you feel sad?"). I should point out that assessing the true nature of a client's feelings is not necessarily easy to do. To do so accurately requires that the therapist be an active listener and **empathic**, or able to understand and share the essence of another's feelings.

Throughout each session, the therapist will express what is called *unconditional positive regard*. This is the expression of being accepting and noncritical. "I will not be critical. If that is the way you feel, that is the way you feel. Anything you say in here is okay." The exchange between client and therapist presented in Figure 13.2 (p. 622) is rather typical.

A friend of mine, a Rogerian psychotherapist, was once elated about how well a session with an undergraduate student had gone. When I asked him why he thought it had gone so well, he said that when the student came into his office and sat down, he asked her how she was feeling and what she'd like to talk about. She said that she didn't want to talk about anything. So my friend said, "If you don't want to talk, that's okay. If you change your mind, I'm right here, and I'm willing to listen." For the next 50 minutes, the two of them sat there, neither doing or saying anything. At the end of their hour, the therapist said, "Well, our time's up. I'll see you next week." The student replied, "Right, see you then." It was my friend's point of view that the value of this quiet session was that his client had learned something. She had learned that if she did not want to talk about anything, she didn't have to. That acceptance may then lead her to the realization that if she *did* want to talk about anything, no matter what, that would be okay too.

BEFORE YOU GO ON

What are the essential characteristics of client-centered therapy?

BEHAVIORAL TECHNIQUES

In a literal sense, there is no one behavior therapy. **Behavior therapy** is a collection of many specific techniques. What unites them is that they are "methods of psychotherapeutic change founded on principles of learning established in the psychological laboratory" (Wolpe, 1981, p. 159). There are many different principles of learning and many psychological disorders to which such methods and principles can be applied. Reflecting this observation, we already have discussed two varieties of behavior therapy in Chapter 5 (see pp. 204 and 221). In this section, we will list some of the more prominent applications that have become part of behavior therapy.

Systematic desensitization, the application of classical conditioning procedures to alleviate extreme feelings of anxiety, is one of the first applications of learning principles to have met with success, and it has experienced lasting acceptance. It was formally introduced by Joseph Wolpe

empathic *able to understand and share the essence of another's feelings, or to view from another's perspective*

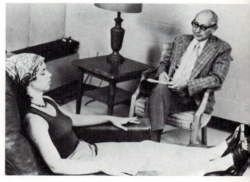

Joseph Wolpe is shown here conducting systematic desensitization therapy to reduce a client's anxiety. The client, in a relaxed state, is told to imagine the weakest anxiety on her list. If she feels anxious, she is instructed to stop and relax again.

behavior therapy *techniques of psychotherapy founded on principles of learning established in the psychological laboratory*

systematic desensitization *the application of classical conditioning procedures to alleviate extreme anxiety in which anxiety-producing stimuli are presented while the subject is in a relaxed state*

Figure **13.2**

AN INTERCHANGE BETWEEN A CLIENT-CENTERED THERAPIST AND A CLIENT.

Barbara is an 18-year-old freshman at City Community College. Still living at home with her parents and two younger brothers, she is having difficulty dealing with the demands on her time. She has a full-time job at a restaurant and is trying to manage four classes at college. The pressures of home, school, and work seem to be making Barbara uncharacteristically anxious and depressed. She is falling behind in her school work, performing poorly at her job, and finding life at home almost unbearable. On the recommendation of her psychology instructor, Barbara has been seeing a counselor at the Student Services Center. She has had six visits there.

Psychotherapist: Good morning, Barbara; how do you feel today?

Barbara: [snapping back quietly] Good lord, can't you ever say anything but "how do you feel today?" I feel fine, just fine.

P. You sound angry.

B. [in a sarcastically mocking tone] "You sound angry."

P. [silence]

B. Well I'm not angry, so there.

P. Um. Hmm.

B. Well, maybe a little angry.

P. So you feel "a little angry"?

B. Yeah, so I'm angry. So big deal! So what of it? Is there something wrong with being angry?

P. Of course not.

B. You'd be angry too.

P. Oh?

B. My old man threatened to throw me out of the house last night.

P. He threatened you?

B. He said that if I didn't get my act together and shape up, he'd send me packing. God knows where I'd go, but if he pulls that crap on me one more time I'll show him. I will leave.

P. Would you like to leave?

B. Yes! No! No, I don't really want to. It's just that nobody cares about me around there. They don't know how hard it is trying to work and go to school and everything, ya' know?

P. [nods]

B. *They* never went to college. What do *they* know? They don't know what it's like.

P. You feel that your parents can't appreciate your problems?

B. Damn right! What do they know? They've never tried to work and go to college at the same time.

P. They don't know what it's like.

B. Right! Of course I suppose it's not all their fault. They've never been in this situation. I suppose I could try to explain it to them better.

P. You mean it would be helpful to share with them how you feel about this, about how hard it is for you, and maybe they'll understand?

B. Yeah! That's a good idea! I'll do that. At least I'll try. I don't want to just whine and complain all the time, but maybe I can get them to understand what it's like. Boy that would help—just to have somebody besides you understand and maybe be on my side once in awhile instead of on my case all the time. That's a real good idea. Thanks.

in the late 1950s (Wolpe, 1958, 1982), although others had used similar procedures earlier. The therapy is designed to alleviate extreme anxieties, particularly of the sort we find in phobic disorders. You'll recall from our discussion back in Topic 5A that systematic desensitization is basically a matter of teaching a patient first to relax totally and then to remain relaxed as he or she thinks about or is exposed to a range of stimuli that produce anxiety at ever-increasing levels. If the patient can remain calm and relaxed, that response can be conditioned to replace the anxious or fear response that was previously associated with a particular stimulus.

Flooding is another behavioral procedure aimed at eliminating fears or anxieties associated with specific stimuli. Bootzin and Acocella describe flooding as "a cold-turkey extinction therapy" (1984, p. 505). Flooding is an in vivo, or in real life, procedure. In this approach, the subject, accompanied by the therapist, actually is placed in his or her most fear-arousing situation and is prohibited from escaping. For example, someone afraid of heights might be taken to the top of a tall building or to a very high bridge. Someone afraid of water might be taken out on a large lake or to a nearby swimming pool. There, with the therapist close at hand providing encouragement and support, the individual comes face to face with his or her fear, survives the situation (although the session may be terrifying for some), and thus comes to learn that the fear is irrational.

Implosive therapy is based on the same premise, but involves the use of imagination rather than real-life situations. In implosive therapy, you don't slowly work your way up any anxiety hierarchy. You are forced to come to imagine your worst fears, all at once, here and now. The therapist does not try to get the subject to relax. On the contrary, the idea is to experience the full force of anxiety while in the ultimately safe surroundings of the therapist's office. Repeated trials of fear paired with the safety of the office often lead to the extinction of the maladaptive fear response.

Although flooding and implosive therapy do sound a bit bizarre, and are definitely not for everyone (some therapists have difficulty dealing with such focused anxiety), they are demonstrably effective and usually require less time than does systematic desensitization.

You should recognize **aversion therapy** as another example of learning applied to solving psychological problems. In aversion therapy, a stimulus that may be harmful, but that produces a pleasant response, is paired with an aversive, painful stimulus until the original stimulus is avoided. Every time you put a cigarette in your mouth, I deliver a painful shock to your lip. Every time you take a drink of alcohol, you get violently sick to your stomach. Every time a child molester is shown a picture of a young child, he receives a shock.

None of these situations sounds like the sort of thing that anyone would agree to voluntarily. Many people do, however. They volunteer for such treatments for two reasons: (1) aversion therapy is very effective at suppressing a specific behavior, at least for a while, and (2) it is seen as the lesser of two evils—shocks and nausea-producing drugs are not much fun, but subjects see the continuation of their inappropriate behaviors as even more dangerous in the long run.

It is probably aversion therapy more than any other technique that has given behavior therapy a bad reputation among the general public, which often equates behavior therapy with cruel and unusual punishment and mind control. There are a couple of things that we need to recognize here.

flooding *a technique of behavior therapy in which a subject is confronted (in vivo) with the object of his or her phobic fear while accompanied by the therapist*

implosive therapy *a behavior therapy in which one imagines one's worst fears, experiencing extreme anxiety in the safe surroundings of the therapist's office*

aversion therapy *a technique of behavior therapy in which an aversive stimulus, such as a shock, is paired with an undesired behavior*

Aversion therapy, though not a commonly used technique, is one way to help smokers stop smoking. For a series of sessions, shocks are administered to the smoker. Eventually smoking becomes less desirable and the person will quit his or her habit—at least for a short while.

One is that aversion therapy, in any form, is not commonly practiced. A second reality is that, at best, it tends to suppress behaviors for a relatively short time. During that time, other techniques may be used in an attempt to bring about a more lasting change in behavior. That is, the techniques of aversion therapy are seldom effective when used alone; they are used in conjunction with some other form(s) of therapy.

Contingency management and contingency contracting borrow heavily from the learning principles of operant conditioning. The basic idea, of course, is to have an individual come to appreciate the consequences of his or her behaviors. Appropriate behaviors lead to rewards and opportunities to do valued things; inappropriate behaviors do not lead to reinforcement and provide fewer opportunities.

In many cases, these basic procedures work very well. Their ultimate effectiveness is, as operant conditioning would predict, a function of the extent to which the therapist has control over the situation. If the therapist can control rewards and punishments, called **contingency management**, he or she stands a good chance of modifying the client's behavior. The therapist modifies behavior by managing contingencies. If a patient (say, a severely disturbed, hospitalized schizophrenic) engages in the appropriate response (leaving her room to go to dinner), *then* the patient will get something she really wants (an after-dinner cigarette).

contingency management *bringing about changes in one's behaviors by controlling rewards and punishments*

Contingency contracting amounts to establishing a token economy of secondary reinforcers. What that means is that the patient is first taught that some token—a checker, a poker chip, or just a check mark on a pad—can be saved. When enough tokens are accumulated, they are cashed in for something of value to the patient. With contracting, the value of a token for a specific behavior is spelled out ahead of time. Because control over the environment of the patient/learner is most complete in such circumstances, this technique is particularly effective in institutions and with young children. (Again, we went through examples of token economies in Topic 5B, p. 221.)

contingency contracting *establishing a token economy of secondary reinforcers to reward appropriate behaviors*

We realize that learning cannot always be explained readily in terms of classical or operant conditioning. It should be no surprise that some types of behavior therapy use learning principles other than those from simple conditioning. **Modeling**, a term introduced by Albert Bandura, involves the acquisition of a new, appropriate response through the imitation of a model. As we saw in Topic 5B, modeling can be an effective means of learning.

modeling *the acquisition of new responses through the imitation of another who responds appropriately*

In a therapy situation, modeling often amounts to having or letting patients watch someone else perform a certain appropriate behavior, perhaps earning a reward for it (called vicarious reinforcement, you'll recall). Some phobias, particularly those in children, can be overcome through modeling. A child who is afraid of dogs, for example, may profit from watching another child (which would be more effective than using an adult) playing with a dog. Assertiveness training involves helping individuals stand up for their rights and come to the realization that *their* feelings and opinions matter and should be expressed. Such training involves many processes, including direct instruction, group discussion, role-playing, and contingency management, and often relies on modeling to help someone learn appropriate ways to express how they feel and what they think in social situations.

Bandura uses modeling to help people overcome phobias. By watching other people handle snakes without fear, people can overcome their fears and handle the snakes themselves.

BEFORE YOU GO ON

Briefly describe some of the techniques used in behavior therapy, including systematic desensitization, flooding, implosive therapy, aversion therapy, contingency management and contracting, and modeling.

COGNITIVE TECHNIQUES

Psychotherapists who use cognitive techniques do not deny the importance of a person's behaviors (these therapies are often called *cognitive-behavioral*). Rather, they believe that what matters most in the therapeutic session is the client's set of thoughts, perceptions, attitudes, and beliefs about himself or herself and the environment. The principle here is that to change how one feels and acts, therapy should first be directed at changing how one thinks. As we have seen with other approaches to psychotherapy, there is not just one type of cognitive-behavioral therapy; there are many. A recent survey identified nearly two dozen distinct varieties (Dobson, 1988). We'll examine just two: rational-emotive therapy and cognitive restructuring therapy.

Rational-Emotive Therapy

Rational-emotive therapy (RET) is associated with Albert Ellis (1970, 1973, 1991). Its basic premise is that psychological problems arise when a person tries to interpret (a cognitive activity) what happens in the world on the basis of irrational beliefs. Ellis puts it this way, "Rational-emotive therapy (RET) hypothesizes that people largely disturb themselves by thinking in a self-defeating, illogical, and unrealistic manner—especially by escalating their natural preferences and desires into absolutistic, dog-

rational-emotive therapy (RET) *a form of cognitive therapy, associated with Ellis, aimed at changing the subject's irrational beliefs or maladaptive cognitions*

Albert Ellis

matic musts and commands on themselves, others, and their environmental conditions" (1987, p. 364). In other words, disturbed behaviors and feelings arise from maladaptive cognitions, which in most cases are unrealistic beliefs about oneself and one's environment.

When compared to client-centered techniques, RET is quite directive. In fact, Ellis takes exception with techniques of psychotherapy that are designed to help a person *feel* better without providing useful strategies by which the person can *get* better (Ellis, 1991). In RET, the therapist takes an active role in interpreting the rationality of a client's system of beliefs and encourages active change. Therapists often act as role models and make homework assignments for clients that help them bring their expectations and perceptions in line with reality.

To give a very simplified example, refer back to Figure 13.2, the dialogue between Barbara and her client-centered therapist. A cognitive therapist might see a number of irrational beliefs operating in this scene, including two that Ellis (1970) claims are very common: (1) a person should always be loved for everything they do, and (2) it's better to avoid problems than to face them. These, claims Ellis, are exactly the sort of cognitions that create psychological difficulties (others are listed in Figure 13.3). Rather than waiting for self-discovery, which might never come, a rational-emotive therapist would point out to Barbara that the fact that her parents never went to college and don't understand what it is like to work and go to school at the same time is *their* problem, not hers. Rather than agonizing over the fact that her parents don't seem to appreciate her efforts, she needs to either set them straight (pleasantly, of course, which might constitute a homework assignment for Barbara) or move out (there are a number of other possibilities, of course).

Figure **13.3**

SOME OF THE IRRATIONAL BELIEFS THAT LEAD TO MALADJUSTMENT AND DISORDER. THE MORE RATIONAL ALTERNATIVE TO THESE BELIEFS SHOULD BE OBVIOUS.

1. One should be loved by everyone for everything one does.
2. Because I strongly desire to perform important tasks competently and successfully, I absolutely must perform them well at all times.
3. Because I strongly desire to be approved of by people I find significant, I absolutely must always have their approval.
4. Certain acts are wicked and people who perform them should be severely punished no matter what.
5. It is horrible when things are not the way we want them to be.
6. It is better to avoid life's problems, if possible, than to face them.
7. One needs something stronger or more powerful than oneself to rely on.
8. One must have perfect and certain self-control.
9. Because I very strongly desire people to treat me considerably and fairly, they must absolutely do so.
10. Because something once affected one's life, it will always affect it.

From Ellis, 1970, 1987.

Cognitive Restructuring Therapy

Similar to rational-emotive therapy is **cognitive restructuring therapy**, associated with Aaron Beck (1976). Although the basic ideas and goals are similar, restructuring therapy is much less confrontational and direct than RET.

Beck's assumption is that considerable psychological distress stems from a few simple, but misguided beliefs (cognitions, again). According to Beck, people with psychological disorders share certain characteristics. For example:

1. They tend to have very negative self-images. They do not value themselves or what they do.
2. They tend to take a very negative view of life experiences.
3. They overgeneralize. For example, having failed one test, a person comes to believe that there is no way he or she can do college work and withdraws from school and looks for work, even though he or she believes there's little chance that anyone would offer a job to someone who is such a failure and a college dropout.
4. They actually seek out experiences that reinforce their negative expectations. The student in the above example may apply for a job as a law clerk or as a stockbroker. Lacking even minimal experience, he or she will not be offered either job and, thus, will confirm his or her own worthlessness.
5. They tend to hold a rather dismal outlook for the future.
6. They tend to avoid seeing the bright side of any experience.

In cognitive restructuring therapy, the patient is given opportunities to test or demonstrate his or her beliefs. The patient and therapist make up a list of hypotheses based on the patient's assumptions and beliefs and then actually go out and test these hypotheses. Obviously, the therapist tries to exercise enough control over the situation so that the experiments do not confirm the patient's beliefs about himself or herself, but will lead instead to positive outcomes. (For example, given the hypothesis, "Nobody cares about me," the therapist need only find one person who does care to refute it.) This approach, of leading a person to the self-discovery that negative attitudes directed toward oneself are inappropriate, has proven very successful in the treatment of depression, although it has been extended to cover a wide range of psychological disorders (Beck, 1985).

cognitive restructuring therapy *a form of cognitive therapy, associated with Beck, in which patients are led to overcome negative self-images and pessimistic views of the future*

**BEFORE
YOU GO
ON**

Briefly summarize the logic behind rational-emotive therapy and cognitive restructuring therapy.

GROUP APPROACHES

Many patients profit from some variety of *group therapy*. Group therapy is a label applied to a variety of situations in which a number of people are involved in a therapeutic setting at the same time. If nothing else, group therapy provides an economic advantage over individual psychotherapy: One therapist can interact with several people in the same time frame.

In standard forms of group therapy, clients are brought together at the same time, under the guidance of a therapist, to share their feelings and experiences. Most groups are quite informal, and no particular form of psychotherapy is dominant. In other words, meeting with people in groups is something that a psychotherapist with any sort of training or background may do from time to time.

There are a number of possible benefits from this procedure, including an awareness that "I'm not the only one with problems." The sense of support that one can get from someone else with problems occasionally may be even greater than that afforded by a therapist alone—a sort of "she really knows from her own experience the hell that I'm going through" logic. And there is truth in the basic idea that getting involved in helping someone else with a problem is, in itself, a therapeutic process. Yet another advantage of group therapy situations is that the person may learn new and more effective ways of "presenting" himself or herself to others.

A group approach that has become quite popular is **family therapy**, which focuses on the roles, interdependence, and communication skills of family members. Family therapy is often implemented after one member of a family enters psychotherapy. After discussing the person's problems for a while, other members of the family are invited to join in the therapy sessions. There is evidence that getting the family unit involved in therapy has benefit for patients with a wide range of disorders, from alcoholism and agoraphobia to depression and schizophrenia (Goldfried, Greenberg, & Marmar, 1990).

Two related assumptions underlie a family therapy approach. One is that each individual family member is a part of a *system* (the family unit), and his or her feelings, thoughts, and behaviors necessarily impact on other family members (e.g., Minuchin & Fishman, 1981). Bringing about a change (even a therapeutic one) in one member of the family system without involving the other members of the system will not last for long without the support of the others. This is particularly true when the initial problem appears to be with a child or adolescent. I say "appears to be" because we can be confident that other family members have at least contributed to the troublesome symptoms of the child or adolescent's behavior. A therapist is going to have a very difficult time bringing about significant and lasting change in a child whose parents refuse to become involved in therapy.

A second assumption that is often relevant in family therapy sessions is that difficulties arise from improper methods of family *communication* (e.g., Satir, 1967). Quite often, individuals develop false beliefs about the feelings and/or needs of family members. The goal of therapy in such situations, then, is to meet with the family in a group setting to foster and encourage open expressions of feelings and desires. It may be very helpful for an adolescent to learn that her parents are upset and anxious about work-related stress and financial affairs. The adolescent has assumed all along that her parents yelled at her and each other because of something *she* was doing (remember how egocentric adolescents can be). And the parents didn't want to share their concerns over money with the adolescent for fear that it would upset her.

Family therapy may be used as an alternative to individual therapy or as a continuation of it. By meeting together, families are given an opportunity to express their feelings and resolve their problems under a therapist's guidance.

family therapy *a variety of group therapy focusing on the roles, interdependence, and communication skills of family members*

Evaluating group therapy techniques is particularly difficult, and few good reviews of outcome studies are available. In general, there seems to be support for the sorts of group approaches we have briefly outlined here, and there is some indication that family therapy is a better approach for many problems than is individual treatment (Gurman et al., 1986).

BEFORE YOU GO ON

What are some advantages of group therapy?
Describe two assumptions underlying family therapy.

EVALUATING PSYCHOTHERAPY

Evaluating psychotherapy has proven to be a difficult task. Is psychotherapy effective? Compared to what? Is any type of psychotherapy better than any other? These are obviously important questions, but the best we can do is offer partial, tentative answers. Yes, psychotherapy is effective. Compared to what? Compared to doing nothing. "By about 1980 a consensus of sorts was reached that psychotherapy, as a generic treatment process, was demonstrably more effective than no treatment" (VandenBos, 1986, p. 111; also Gelso & Fassinger, 1990; Goldfried, Greenberg, & Marmar, 1990). What's more, more treatment appears to be better than less treatment (Howard et al., 1986) (see Figure 13.4). Research also confirms the logical assertion that the sooner one begins therapy, the better the prognosis (e.g., Kupfer, Frank, & Perel, 1989). There is evidence that some therapists are more effective than others, regardless of what type of therapy is practiced (Beutler, Crago, & Arizmendi, 1986; Lafferty, Beutler, & Crago, 1989).

Before we go on, let's mention just a few of the problems encountered when doing research on the effectiveness of psychotherapy. First, we have little quality data on how people might have responded without treatment. In other words, we often do not have a good baseline for comparison. We know that sometimes there is a spontaneous remission of symptoms. Sometimes people "get better" without the formal intervention of a therapist. To say that people get better on their own is not literally accurate. There are many factors that may contribute to improve one's mental health, even if one is not officially in psychotherapy (Erwin, 1980). You can imagine many such factors (which in an experiment we would call extraneous variables (Topic 1B)). Perhaps the source of one's stress is removed; a nagging parent moves out of state; an aggravating boss gets transferred. Perhaps an interpersonal relationship is begun that provides needed support.

Second, we can't seem to agree on what we mean by recovery. For some, it is simply the absence of observable symptoms for a specified period of time. For others, however, the goal of therapy is something different: the self-report of "feeling better," personal growth, a relatively permanent

Figure   **13.4**

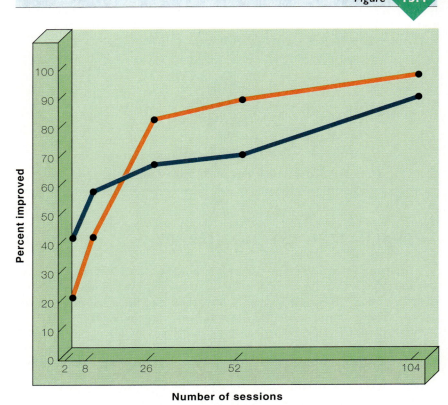

Number of sessions

The relationship between the number of sessions of psychotherapy and the percentage of patients improved. Objective ratings made by professionals are indicated by the blue line, subjective ratings of well-being made by the patients themselves are indicated by the orange line. In other words, most improvement in psychotherapy is made early on, but improvement continues as therapy continues.

change in behavior, a restructuring of cognitions, or insight into deep-seated motivational conflicts.

Finally, even when we can agree on criteria for recovery there is often concern about how to measure or assess therapy outcomes. It hardly seems realistic to expect unbiased responses from therapists *or* their patients if we were to ask them to report if therapy had been a helpful experience.

These are three of the most commonly cited general problems with designing studies to evaluate the outcome of psychotherapy. Even so, a number of quality studies have been done. Most have focused on just one technique at a time, and in most cases, the results have been very positive (Erwin, 1980; Eysenck, 1952; Greenberg & Safran, 1987; Kazden et al., 1987; Marziali, 1984; Miller & Berman, 1983; Wolpe, 1981). Several studies also have indicated that even when the the primary treatment option is medical (say, an antidepressant drug), psychotherapy and medication together provide the best prognosis (e.g., Frank et al., 1990; Free & Oei, 1989; Klerman, 1990).

Figure **13.5**

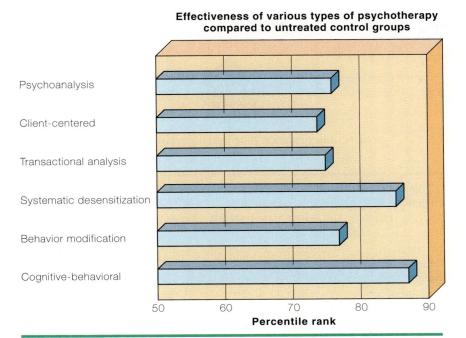

**Effectiveness of various types of psychotherapy
compared to untreated control groups**

Psychoanalysis

Client-centered

Transactional analysis

Systematic desensitization

Behavior modification

Cognitive-behavioral

50   60   70   80   90

Percentile rank

A summary of the results of 475 studies that assessed the effectiveness of psychotherapy. These data reflect the percentage of clients treated with various forms of therapy who scored higher, or more favorably, on a number of outcome measures compared to similar clients who were not treated. That is, the average subject of behavior modification scored higher on outcome measures than did 75 percent of subjects not treated.

A meta-analysis by Smith, Glass, and Miller (1980) showed positive results for psychotherapy and has become a commonly cited study of its effectiveness. Smith and her colleagues found that a variety of techniques produce results that are significantly better than what might be expected through spontaneous remission. As Figure 13.5 shows us, an average patient in psychotherapy scored better on a number of outcome variables than did 75 percent of control subjects who received no treatment. Remember the nature of a meta-analysis (from our discussion in Topic 1B). Smith, Glass, and Miller did not go out and collect new data for their report; they carefully reviewed and statistically analyzed 475 published studies on the effectiveness of psychotherapy.

What about comparing psychotherapy methods? Here the answer is also quite clear: *In general*, there are no differences. There is virtually no evidence that any one type of therapy is significantly better than any other (Stiles et al., 1986). This conclusion is based on a broad generality. There *is* evidence that some types of therapy may be better suited for some types of psychological problems than are other types of therapy. Behavioral methods, such as systematic desensitization, are demonstrably useful for phobic disorders, whereas cognitive therapies seem best suited to patients with depression (although even this differentiation may be questionable (Mervis, 1986)).

Which therapy is best suited for which particular disorder is just one of the questions to which we do not have a definitive answer, and it is one of the most active areas of research in psychotherapy today (Deffenbacher, 1988; Goldfried, Greenberg, & Marmar, 1990).

BEFORE YOU GO ON

Is there any evidence that psychotherapy is effective?
Is any one type of psychotherapy better than the others?

In general, psychotherapy is an attempt, using psychological means, to bring about a change in the way a person thinks or feels or acts. There are literally hundreds of varieties of such techniques, and in this topic we have briefly reviewed only a few of the more traditional or classic approaches. Research tells us that psychotherapy—be it psychoanalytic, behavioral, cognitive, humanistic, or some combination—can be effective in helping people who are suffering from psychological distress and discomfort. We cannot say that one form of therapy is any more effective than any other for any particular disorder or any particular person. To quote Stiles and his colleagues (1986) on this issue, "Although we know that psychotherapy works, we do not clearly understand how it works. Differently labeled therapies have demonstrably different behavioral contents, yet appear to have equivalent outcomes."

Who may offer psychotherapy? How does one find an effective psychotherapist?

Many different mental health professionals can provide psychotherapy. These include clinical psychologists, Ph.D.s or Psy.D.s in psychology with a one-year internship; psychiatrists, M.D.s with an internship and residency in a mental hospital; counseling psychologists, Ph.D.s in psychology specializing in less severe disorders and with an internship in a counseling setting; licensed counselors, often with degrees in education; psychoanalysts, who specialize in Freudian therapy; clinical social workers, usually with a master's degree; and others, including pastoral counselors and mental health technicians. Finding a therapist involves questioning local resources, such as family doctors, members of the clergy, psychology instructors, or friends who have been in therapy. One can also check the yellow pages or contact a local mental health center or mental health association. / *page 617*

Describe the essential nature of Freudian psychoanalysis, defining some of its major features. How is psychoanalysis different today from when it was practiced by Freud?

Freudian psychoanalysis is a psychotherapeutic approach aimed at uncovering repressed conflicts (perhaps developed in early childhood) so they can be successfully resolved. Among other things, the process involves: (1) free association, in which the patient is to say anything and everything that comes to mind, without editing; (2) resistance, in which a patient seems unable or unwilling to discuss some aspect of his or her life, which suggests that the resisted experiences may be anxiety producing; (3) dream interpretation, in which one analyzes both the manifest and latent content for insights into the nature of the

patient's unconscious mind; and (4) transference, in which feelings that once were directed at some significant person in the patient's life become directed toward the analyst. Although the basis of psychoanalysis has remained unchanged since Freud's day, some changes have evolved. For example, there is now more effort to shorten the duration of analysis; there is less emphasis on childhood experiences and more concern with the here and now. Present-day analysis is also more directive than it was in Freud's day. / *page 620*

What are the essential characteristics of client-centered therapy?

Client-centered therapy, which we associate with Carl Rogers, is based on the belief that people can control their lives and solve their own problems if they can be helped to understand the true nature of their feelings. It promotes self-discovery and personal growth. The therapist reflects or mirrors the client's feelings, focuses on the here and now, and tries to be empathic, relating to the patient's feelings. Throughout therapy sessions, the therapist provides unconditional positive regard for the client. / *page 621*

Briefly describe some of the techniques used in behavior therapy, including systematic desensitization, flooding, implosive therapy, aversion therapy, contingency management and contracting, and modeling.

Behavior therapies have evolved from the learning laboratory. Systematic desensitization is a behavior therapy technique particularly well suited for the treatment of phobic reactions. A subject is first taught to relax. An anxiety hierarchy is made, listing stimuli in order of their capacity to evoke fear or anxiety. Desensitization is accomplished by gradually presenting more anxiety-

producing stimuli from the hierarchy while the subject remains in a relaxed state, learning to be relaxed in the presence of stimuli that previously elicited anxiety. Flooding and implosive therapy are two rather dramatic forms of behavior therapy that are particularly useful in the treatment of phobias. In flooding, the subject is confronted with the object of her or his fear in person (in vivo), accompanied by the therapist. Implosive therapy requires the subject to imagine his or her fears in the most vivid possible way in an effort to increase anxiety to very high levels in the safety and security of the therapist's office. Unlike systematic desensitization, neither procedure is gradual, and neither encourages the subject to remain relaxed; indeed, both require the subject to become anxious in order to face and deal with that anxiety.

Aversion therapy pairs an unwanted behavior with a strongly negative stimulus, such as shock or a nausea-producing drug. It is an effective means of reducing unwanted behaviors, at least temporarily, but should only be thought of as therapy when subjects voluntarily agree to undergo the treatment after recognizing the long-term benefit of submitting to the aversive stimuli.

Contingency management, contingency contracting, and modeling are three specific applications of accepted learning principles that are used as therapy to increase the likelihood of appropriate behaviors and/or decrease the likelihood of inappropriate behaviors. Contingency management amounts to exercising control over the pattern of rewards that a patient or subject may receive. Contracting usually involves a token economy system in which a subject agrees (by contract) to engage in certain behaviors in order to earn specified rewards. Modeling comes from Bandura's theory and suggests that persons can acquire appropriate behaviors through the imitation of models, particularly when the model's behavior is reinforced. / *page 625*

Briefly summarize the logic behind rational-emotive therapy and cognitive restructuring therapy.

Cognitive therapies are designed to alter the way a person perceives and thinks about himself or herself and the environment. Rational-emotive therapy (RET) takes the premise that people with psychological problems are operating on a series of irrational assumptions about the world and themselves. RET is quite directive in its attempts to change people's cognitions. Cognitive restructuring therapy is somewhat less directive, but is based on the same sort of idea as RET. The underlying premise here is that people with psychological

disorders have developed negative self-images and negative views (cognitions) about the future. The therapist then provides opportunities for the patient to test those negative cognitions and discover that everything is not as bad as it may seem. / *page 627*

What are some advantages of group therapy? Describe two assumptions underlying family therapy.

There are a number of potential advantages to group therapy. (1) The basic problem may be an interpersonal one and, thus, will be better understood and dealt with in an interpersonal situation. (2) There is value in realizing that one is not the only person in the world with a problem and that there are others who may have even more difficult problems. (3) There is therapeutic value in providing support for someone else. (4) The dynamics of intragroup communication can be analyzed and changed in a group setting. Family therapy is based on the assumptions that (1) family members can be seen as a part of a system in which one member (and one member's problem) affects all the others, and that (2) many psychological problems arise because of faulty communication, and that this is particularly critical within a family. / *page 629*

Is there any evidence that psychotherapy is effective? Is any one type of psychotherapy better than the others?

Scientifically evaluating the appropriateness and effectiveness of psychotherapy has proven to be very difficult. There have been conflicting research studies. Nonetheless, it is safe to take as a tentative conclusion that, in general, psychotherapy is effective. It is significantly better than leaving disorders untreated. There are data that suggest that some therapies may be better suited to some clients and to some disorders than they are to others. There is evidence that psychotherapy provides an advantage when offered along with appropriate drug therapy. On the other hand, there is no evidence that, in general, any one type of therapy is better than any other. / *page 632*

CHAPTER 14

SOCIAL PSYCHOLOGY

Social Cognition

Why We Care: A Topic Preview

Social psychology is the field of psychology concerned with how others influence the thoughts, feelings, and behaviors of the individual. We care about the material in this chapter because, in a real sense, social psychology deals with us as we live: in a social world, interacting with, influencing, and being influenced by others. Social psychologists focus on the person or individual, not on the group per se (which is more likely to be the concern of sociologists).

As we have seen many times, other areas of psychology are interested in reactions that are social in nature also. Developmental psychologists, for example, are interested in how styles of cooperative and competitive play change and develop through the early years of life. Personality psychologists are interested in individual characteristics that affect interpersonal behavior, such as friendliness and aggression. Learning theorists are interested in how the perception of someone else being rewarded (vicarious reinforcement) affects behavior change. Clinical psychologists recognize that social relationships can play an important role in the development of psychological disorders and their treatment.

In this chapter, we'll consider two major content areas in social psychology: (1) social cognition, or the perception and evaluation of oneself and other people in social situations, and (2) in Topic 14B, social influence, or how other people affect the psychological reactions of the individual.

A basic premise of this topic is that we do not view our social environment solely on the basis of the stimulus information that it presents to us (Higgins & Bargh, 1987). Instead, the argument goes, we have developed a number of cognitive structures and processes (attitudes, schemas, prejudices, and the like) that shape and influence our interpretation of the world around us. Put another way, a focus on social cognition involves two related questions: What information about the social nature of our world do we have stored in memory, and how does that stored information influence future social judgments, choices, and behaviors (Sherman, Judd, & Park, 1989)?

To provide the proper context, we begin with a discussion of the perspective from which social psychologists study behavior and mental processes. Then, we'll spend the bulk of this topic dealing with attitudes. We'll see how social psychologists define attitudes, and we'll study how attitudes are formed and how they may be changed. We'll look at some of the factors that determine how we process information about ourselves and others in social situations, which is to say, how we attribute behaviors to different causes. We'll close this topic with a review of interpersonal (or social) attraction and consider some of the factors that influence how and why people are attracted to others.

The results of the experiment third-grade teacher Jane Elliot conducted with her students were visible in the children's drawings, as well as their behavior in class and their performance on tests. When children were in the "superior" group for a day, their drawings conveyed confidence and happiness such as the top one. When the same children were in the less-favored group their drawings reflected feelings of inferiority and anger, such as the drawing on the bottom by the same student.

THE SOCIAL-PSYCHOLOGICAL PERSPECTIVE

Since we are all social organisms, we are familiar, each in our own way, with many of the concerns of social psychology. Getting along with other people is considered to be an asset, and those of us who are able to do so easily may be demonstrating an appreciation of social psychology in the sense that we are skilled in predicting the behaviors of others and understanding how they affect us. All of us seem to put a great deal of effort into trying to understand social behavior.

To claim that we are familiar with the concerns of social psychology has certain implications. On the one hand, it means that social psychology tends to be perceived as interesting and relevant because it deals with everyday situations that affect us all. On the other hand, it means that often we are willing to accept common sense, personal experience, and even folklore as the basis for our explanations and assumptions about social behavior. Although common sense often may be valid, it is not an acceptable basis for a scientific approach to understanding social behavior. Social psychology relies on experimentation and other scientific methods as sources of knowledge about social behavior, even if the results of applying these methods are contrary to intuition. As we shall see in this chapter, some of the most influential discoveries in social psychology have been unexpected and counterintuitive. During the last 20 years, social psychology has, like many other areas of psychology, taken on a clearly *cognitive* flavor. That is, social psychologists are attempting more and more to understand social behavior by examining the mental structures and processes that are reflected in such behavior.

To give you an appreciation for this approach, and to provide an example we can return to later, let's review a classic classroom project undertaken more than 20 years ago. In the late 1960s, a third-grade teacher in a small elementary school in Riceville, Iowa, wanted to give her pupils a firsthand experience of prejudice. Jane Elliott announced to her students that she had evidence that blue-eyed children clearly were superior in all regards to children with brown eyes. As a result, children with brown eyes were declared second-class citizens. They were forced to sit in the back of the classroom. They had to stand at the end of the lunch line, allowing the blue-eyed children first choice; they were not allowed second helpings of food. They were not allowed to use the drinking fountain. The "superior" blue-eyed children were given special privileges, including extra recess time. To make them more visible, brown-eyed children were forced to wear paper collars that identified their lowly status from a distance.

It wasn't long before the students in Ms. Elliott's third-grade class became active participants in her demonstration. The classroom behaviors of the brown-eyed children deteriorated; they performed below their usual levels on a number of academic tasks. The blue-eyed children did better than usual. They voluntarily avoided contact with their "inferior" brown-eyed classmates. Fights and arguments broke out. The behavior of the blue-eyed children became aggressive, contemptuous, and occasionally vicious—all in one day.

The next school day, Ms. Elliott informed the class that she had made a terrible mistake: She had gotten the evidence reversed. It was blue-eyed children who were inferior; the best people were those with brown eyes! With displays of great joy and enthusiasm, the brown-eyed children tore off their offensive collars and helped fit the blue-eyed pupils with paper collars that identified *them* as inadequate and inferior. Even after their experience of the previous day, the behaviors of the children in the class were exactly the same, only the roles were reversed. Those who just the day before were the objects of prejudice now sat in the front of the class, performed well on classroom tests, rushed to be the first in line at lunch time, and treated their blue-eyed classmates very badly.

On the third day, Ms. Elliott shared her original intent with her pupils and told them that none of what she had said the last two days was, in fact, true. The effects of this classroom demonstration were not long-lived. The children soon returned to their normal classroom routine. The artificially induced prejudice disappeared almost as quickly as it had been created. This exercise was not a carefully controlled experiment, and given current concern about the ethics involved in such manipulations, it is unlikely to be replicated. Nonetheless, the experience was a meaningful one for those Iowa third-graders and a significant one for us, too. It tells us a great deal about the irrationality of prejudice based solely on physical characteristics (Elliott, 1977; Leonard, 1970; Peters, 1971).

Now let's review this demonstration as a social psychologist might. On the first day, children with blue eyes developed unfavorable ideas about brown-eyed classmates. Pupils with brown eyes were thought of as inferior, lazy, and irresponsible. These cognitions developed without any real test. On the basis of very little actual evidence or data, blue-eyed children were willing to think of all brown-eyed children as inferior. They were willing to ignore their previous experiences with their brown-eyed classmates. They formed a **stereotype**—a generalized set of cognitions about members of a group that is based on limited experience and that does not allow for individual differences.

Although this particular example of a stereotype has negative implications because it is based on erroneous information, stereotypes are not necessarily bad. When they are based on accurate information they are useful tools that help us simplify and deal more efficiently with a complex world (Jussim et al., 1987). All of us have formed many stereotypes. Some of those stereotypes are based on accurate, reliable appraisals; some are based on false information. For instance, assume that you have a stereotype of law enforcement officers that includes the belief (cognition) that they will arrest you for speeding. If you are out on the highway and see a law enforcement vehicle in your rear-view mirror, you'll make sure that you are not exceeding the posted speed limit, regardless of whether you see that vehicle as belonging to a state trooper, a city police officer, or a county sheriff. You won't pause to wonder what that officer is doing out there on the highway until after you have checked your speed. Because you have formed a stereotype, your behavior has become predictable and virtually automatic.

Notice also that once the pupils in Jane Elliott's class developed the idea of superiority and inferiority on the basis of eye color, their behaviors changed accordingly. The students had rather strong notions about how one deals with or reacts to classmates who are "inferior." They are to sit at the back of the class, they are to stand at the end of lunch lines, and they are not to be spoken to in a friendly manner, *because* they are inferior.

We all develop a complex set of rules or expectations about how to behave that guides and directs our social actions. In other words, we have

stereotype *a generalized mental (cognitive) representation of someone that minimizes individual differences and is based on limited experience*

come to know what we are supposed to do in different social situations. Perhaps you recall our discussion of discrimination learning back in Topic 5B, where we found that we often learn to make discriminations about which behaviors are acceptable in a given social situation and which behaviors are unacceptable. Shared expectations about how the members of a group *ought to behave* are called social **norms** (Levine & Moreland, 1990). Clearly, norms have a cognitive basis if we are to use them consistently. Like stereotypes, they are cognitions that we may use to help simplify our social world. Because we have developed social norms, we know how we are to act in a wide variety of social situations. Note how uncomfortable you feel when you find yourself in a new and different situation—perhaps a foreign country, a strange religious ceremony, a country club, or a ghetto. Our feelings of discomfort reflect the fact that we do not know what is expected of us; we don't know the rules of behavior; we have not learned the appropriate norms. Now that we have a sense of what we mean by social cognition, let's explore some areas of social psychology in which this concept has been useful.

norms *rules or expectations that guide our behavior in certain social situations by prescribing how we ought to behave*

BEFORE YOU GO ON

What are stereotypes and norms, and in what way are they cognitive?

ATTITUDES

Since the 1920s, a central concern in social psychology has been the nature of attitudes (McGuire, 1985). We'll define **attitude** as a relatively stable and general evaluative disposition directed toward some object; it consists of beliefs, feelings, and behaviors. One component of an attitude, according to this rather traditional definition, is cognitive (beliefs); so in at least one respect, social psychology has nearly always been characterized by a cognitive orientation.

The concept of *evaluative* in this definition refers to a dimension of attitudes that includes such notions as being for or against, pro or con, and positive or negative. By *disposition* we mean a tendency or a preparedness to respond to the object of the attitude (actual responding is not necessary). Also notice that, by definition, attitudes have objects. We have attitudes *toward* or *about* something. We don't just have attitudes, good or bad, in general; we have attitudes about some object. I recognize that the word *attitude* is often used differently in common speech. We hear that someone has a "bad attitude" or just "an attitude" in general, as in, "Boy, does *he* have an attitude!" In psychology, however, an attitude—as a technical term—requires an object.

Anything can be the object of an attitude, whether it be a person, a thing, or an idea (Petty & Cacioppo, 1986). You may have attitudes about

Attitudes consist of beliefs, feelings, and behaviors. Thus, if we believe that our water supply is being damaged by unauthorized dumping of waste, we may show our feelings and beliefs by participating in a demonstration.

this course, the car you drive, your father, the president, or the corner fast-food restaurant where you occasionally eat lunch. Some of our attitudes are more important than others, of course, but the fact that we have attitudes toward so many things is precisely the reason why the study of attitudes is so central in social psychology.

attitude *a relatively stable and general evaluative disposition directed toward some object, consisting of feelings, behaviors, and beliefs*

The Structure of Attitudes

Although many different definitions of attitude have been proposed over the years, most of them suggest that an attitude consists of three components (Chaiken & Stangor, 1987). When we use the term *attitude* in everyday conversation, we most likely are referring to the *affective* component, which consists of our feeling or emotions about the attitudinal object. The *behavioral* component consists of our response or action tendencies toward the object of our attitude. This component includes our actual behaviors and/or our intentions to act should the opportunity arise. The *cognitive* component includes our beliefs or thoughts about the attitudinal object. By now, this notion of three components of affect, behavior, and cognition, or ABC, ought to be quite familiar to you.

Our attitudes and behaviors may not always be consistent, especially in social settings where we may be friendly and congenial toward someone we have negative feelings about.

Notice that all three components are required to fit our definition (Breckler, 1984). If you believe that brown-eyed children are lazy, you have a belief, not an attitude. If you hate brown-eyed children, you have an emotional reaction, not an attitude. If you make fun of brown-eyed children, you are engaging in behavior, but you do not necessarily have an attitude toward them. Strictly speaking, to say that you have an attitude toward brown-eyed children would require evidence of all three components.

In many cases, the cognitive, affective, and behavioral components of our attitudes are consistent. We think that classical music is relaxing and like to listen to it, so we buy classical music recordings. Regardless of your major, you believe that knowledge of psychology will be an asset in your career, you are enjoying your introductory psychology class, and you plan to take more psychology classes in the future. However, there are occasions when our behaviors are not consistent with, or do not demonstrate, our true beliefs and feelings (Ajzen & Fishbein, 1980).

Because our actual behaviors may not reflect our feelings or our beliefs, some social psychologists (e.g., Fazio, 1989; Fishbein & Ajzen, 1975) prefer to exclude this component; they reserve the term *attitude* to refer only to the fundamental like or dislike for the attitudinal object. Other psychologists argue that attitude is a two-dimensional concept, involving both affect and cognition but not behavior per se (Bagozzi & Burnkrant, 1979; Zajonc & Markus, 1982).

Fishbein and Ajzen, for example, maintain that attitudes *may* lead to actual behaviors, but in many social situations they do not. The situation may "overpower" the affective and cognitive components of our attitudes. For example, we may have strong, unfavorable, stereotyped beliefs and negative feelings about someone, yet when we encounter that person at a social gathering, we smile, extend our hand, and say something pleasant. So, when we study the relationship between attitudes and behavior, we should not overlook the circumstances in which those attitudes may be expressed.

BEFORE YOU GO ON

What is an attitude, and what are its three components?

The Usefulness of Attitudes

Attitudes are important for a variety of reasons that are readily apparent in everyday life. For example, attitudes may serve as shorthand summaries for a number of our beliefs. They are stored evaluations that allow us to make appraisals of new situations and objects (Tesser & Shaffer, 1990). Have you ever noticed how quick people are to evaluate the unfamiliar? If a friend tells you that she just bought a new book, saw a new movie, or tried a new restaurant, one of the first things you probably will want to know is if she liked it or not. Further questioning probably will be required for you to go beyond a general evaluative comment (such as "I didn't like it") to explore the reasons behind the initial reaction. Such probing may reveal that your friend believes the book to be too difficult to understand, the movie to be too corny, or the service in the restaurant to be too slow. In short, we can see that our "attitudes serve as convenient summaries of our beliefs" (Petty & Cacioppo, 1981, p. 8).

Attitudes are also useful when they serve a **social identification function** (Greenwald & Breckler, 1984). The attitudes of other people provide useful information about who they are, and similarly, our attitudes tell others about us. Having information about someone's attitudes allows us to predict that person's behaviors more accurately than we could without such information. (At least, having information about the attitudes of others allows us to *think* that we can predict their behaviors better than we could without it.) It is no accident that people in the process of getting to know one another devote a good bit of time to exchanging information about attitudes. You probably have experienced this process yourself, perhaps when going on a date with someone for the first or second time. In this situation, don't you usually spend some time discussing the music you like, political preferences, what you enjoy doing in your spare time, and even where you like to go on dates? Many social evaluations are based on likes and dislikes, particularly if they are extreme. Such discussions about attitudes produce information that people use to get to know each other, a process of social identification.

Most people, of course, are aware that providing social information of this sort does influence what others may think of them. As a result, people often tend to select carefully what information they choose to offer about their own attitudes. Sometimes they may choose to misrepresent their true attitudes completely. In such cases, we say that attitudes can serve an **impression management function** (Chaiken & Stangor, 1987; Edinger & Patterson, 1983; Goffman, 1959; Snyder, 1974). The truth is, we sometimes engage in what amounts to impression management by "putting our best foot forward," but without any particular conscious or manipulative intent in mind. Obviously, managing someone else's impression of you by

social identification function *the observation that attitudes communicate information useful in social evaluation*

impression management function *the selective presentation or misrepresentation of one's attitudes in an attempt to present oneself in a particular way*

providing misleading information about your attitudes will only work for a limited amount of time.

BEFORE YOU GO ON

What are some of the functions served by attitudes?

Attitude Formation

Given the usefulness of attitudes and the fact that we have attitudes toward so many things, we now need to consider their origin. Most experts agree that simple conditioning processes go a long way toward explaining the formation of attitudes. In other words, attitudes appear to be learned. The question is *how* they are learned, and there may be several viable answers to this question.

Classical Conditioning. Some attitudes are no doubt acquired through the simple associative process of classical conditioning. As depicted in Figure 14.1, pleasant events (unconditioned stimuli) are paired with an attitudinal object (conditioned stimulus). As a result of this association, the attitudinal object comes to elicit the same good feeling (a positive evaluative response) that was originally produced by the unconditioned stimulus. The good feeling, originally an unconditioned response elicited by some pleasant event, now becomes a conditioned response elicited by the attitudinal object. Of course, negative attitudes can be acquired in the same way.

Some advertising attempts to work in just such a way by taking an originally neutral object (the product) and trying to create positive associations to it. For instance, a soft drink advertisement may depict young, attractive people having a great time playing volleyball, dancing, or enjoying a concert while drinking a particular soft drink. The obvious intent is that you and I will associate the product with good times and having fun. That sports figures often wear brand name logos and trademarks on their uniforms also may suggest that manufacturers want us to learn to associate their product with the skills of the athlete we're watching. Advertising with sexual connotations (see Figure 14.2) operates along the same lines.

Operant Conditioning. Attitudes also can be formed as a result of the direct reinforcement of behaviors consistent with some attitudinal position. Several studies have shown that verbal reinforcement (saying "good," "fine," or "that's right") when subjects agree with attitudinal statements leads those subjects to develop attitudes consistent with the position expressed in those statements (Insko, 1965). The blue-eyed children in Ms. Elliott's third-grade class in Iowa no doubt received considerable reinforcement and social support from their peers for acting in negative and derogatory ways toward their "inferior" brown-eyed classmates. And it is no small matter that simply having others (perhaps of a different race or ethnic origin) to

Figure **14.1**

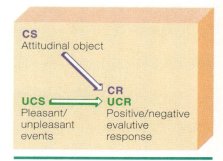

The classical conditioning of attitudes.

Figure **14.2**

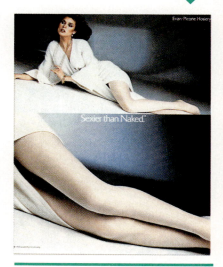

Advertisers often bring sexual connotations to everyday products, illustrating classical conditioning.

Figure **14.3**

"With St. Ives Swiss Formula,
my skin feels soft, silky and...healthy!"

Elizabeth Tricot
Courbevoie, France

St Ives

Collagen-Elastin
Essential Moisturizer
*Balanced Swiss replenishing complex
helps improve skin's texture and softness.*

"I thrive on the outdoors,
so my skin can suffer terrible abuse,
Collagen-Elastin has been my life saver.
It protects so well. But, it feels natural...not heavy.
(P.S. My mother, who's 60, loves it too!)"

Discover what women around the world know about St. Ives Swiss Formula botanical products.   St Ives

Observational learning is demonstrated in advertising that uses satisfied customers to promote the product or service.

view as inferior is in itself somewhat reinforcing. People can feel much better about themselves if they come to believe that they are somehow above, or better than, others.

Observational Learning. As we discussed in Topic 5B, people often tend to imitate behaviors that they have seen reinforced in others (called vicarious reinforcement). To the extent that we perceive that others are gaining reinforcers for having and expressing some attitude, we are likely to adopt that attitude ourselves.

Advertising that relies on testimonials from satisfied customers is basically appealing to a sort of observational learning (see Figure 14.3). The potential consumer is shown that someone has used a certain product with success (has received reinforcement), and the advertiser hopes that this exposure will lead the potential buyer to develop a favorable evaluation of the product. Obviously, the advertiser is going to show us only those people who are happy with their product or service. We seldom stop to think about how many people may have used the product or service and are unhappy with it.

BEFORE YOU GO ON

Briefly describe three ways in which attitudes might be acquired.

Attitude Change and Persuasion

Much of the social-psychological research on attitudes has been concerned with the very practical questions of when and how attitudes change. This research has dealt largely with conscious, planned attempts to change someone's attitude(s), a process called **persuasion**. In this section, we will examine some of the conditions that lead to attitude change, beginning with one of those unexpected and counterintuitive findings to which we referred earlier.

persuasion *the process of intentionally attempting to change an attitude*

Cognitive Dissonance Theory. Common sense would seem to suggest that the affective and cognitive components of an attitude will produce behaviors consistent with those feelings and beliefs. In other words, behavior should follow from attitudes, and attitude change should lead to behavior change. In 1957, Leon Festinger proposed just the reverse: that attitudes may follow behavior. Festinger's theory refers to a state of affairs he called **cognitive dissonance**. We know what cognitions are: thoughts, beliefs, perceptions, and the like. Dissonance means discord, discomfort, or distress that is due to things being out of balance or not fitting together well. When cognitions are dissonant, one possibility is that attitudes will change in order to reduce the unpleasantness of the dissonance. (You may remember that the concept of cognitive dissonance was introduced back in Topic 11A on motivation.)

cognitive dissonance *the state of tension or discomfort that exists when we hold inconsistent cognitions; we are motivated to reduce dissonance*

One example of how this might work that you may be familiar with occurs on the showroom floor of a new car dealer. You have heard all sorts of bad things about the new model Gazelle X-100s. You have not liked other cars this company has produced, and you've developed a negative attitude toward the new X-100. But there you are on the showroom floor. (You're there because the dealer has offered an incentive—perhaps an AM/FM radio—for taking a test drive of the new Gazelle X-100.) You soon find yourself under a great deal of pressure to "Give that ol' X-100 a test drive." It does look pretty sharp, and you take it for a test drive. When you return, you tell the salesperson that you did enjoy the ride and that you were impressed with the car's performance. You've taken an action; you have done something contrary to your original attitude, and cognitive dissonance has been created. ("I thought this car was lousy" and "I did enjoy that ride" are two ideas that both exist at the same time and clearly don't lead to the same conclusion.) Getting you to *do* something may have been the first step in getting you to change your attitude about the new Gazelle X-100. When dissonance is created, we can predict that some cognitions will change to reduce that dissonance. You eventually may convince yourself that your one ride in the X-100 was a fluke and that cars made by this company still aren't very good. Or you may change your attitude about the car maker and the Gazelle X-100, perhaps to the point that you would actually buy the car.

Cognitive dissonance is occurring when you find yourself test-driving and considering a new car that you have previously been against.

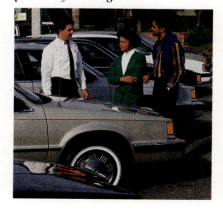

You should be able to generate many additional examples of cognitive dissonance influencing attitude change. A student who supports a military intervention in a Middle East conflict is invited by a friend to attend a peace rally. Accepting the invitation might produce dissonance: "I favor military intervention, but there I was at a peace rally." These two cognitions are dissonant. What will happen next? We can't say exactly, but we can predict that something is likely to change in order to reduce dissonance; perhaps it will be the student's initial attitude. As another example, consider the number of students who have changed their attitude about a course, or a discipline, because they were required to take a course in that discipline. I know that as a chemistry major at the time, my attitudes about psychology and psychology classes changed considerably because of the dissonance created when I was required to take a class in introductory psychology.

BEFORE YOU GO ON

What is cognitive dissonance, and how does it operate?

Figure **14.4**

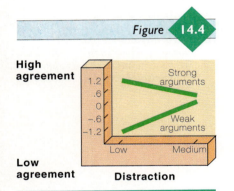

High agreement

1.2
.6
0
–.6
–1.2

Strong arguments

Weak arguments

Low   Medium

Low agreement

Distraction

The extent to which an audience agrees with either strong arguments or weak arguments presented under conditions of low and medium distraction. Note that distraction lowered agreement when strong arguments were used, but raised agreement when weak arguments were used. (After Petty, Wells, & Brock, 1976).

Cognitive Response Theory. A theory of attitude change that is somewhat more recent than Festinger's, but that is still cognitive in its orientation, is called *cognitive response theory* (Petty et al., 1981). This theory proposes that the recipient of a persuasive communication is not at all passive, but is an active information processor who generates *cognitive responses* or ideas about the message being received. These cognitive responses can agree with and be supportive of the message, or they can be unfavorable, disagreeing and counterarguing with the message. This line of reasoning has led researchers to examine variables that may affect persuasion and the cognitive responses that persuasive messages produce. Two interesting variables that have been under study are *message quality* and *distraction*. Let's see what is involved in this sort of research.

In one study, message quality was either high or low. That is, a persuasive speech contained either strong or weak arguments about an attitudinal object (Petty, Wells, & Brock, 1976). Subjects heard one of these two messages under conditions involving either low or moderate distraction. When the message consisted of strong arguments, agreement with the message was reduced (slightly) as distraction was increased (see Figure 14.4). This occurred, the argument goes, because the distraction interfered with the listener's ability to generate cognitive responses that were in favor of the persuasive message. Increasing distraction had the opposite effect when weak arguments were presented, presumably because the distraction interfered with the listener's ability to think of good counterarguments against the message.

Let's look at an example. Imagine that you are headed for a career in medical research and that you believe strongly that research with animals is well justified because of its ultimate benefit for humankind. You hear that an animal rights group is holding a rally on campus and, out of curiosity, you decide to attend. Cognitive response theory says that you will generate counterarguments (cognitions that disagree with those being made) as you listen to the speeches at the rally. Further assume that there is some very loud construction going on nearby. The noise generated by the construction may interfere with your ability to produce good counterarguments, and you will be less able to resist the persuasive speeches than you would be without all that background noise. On the other hand, a person who went to the rally already supporting the animal rights group will generate his or her own arguments that agree with the speeches being made. For this person, the construction noise may cause the speeches to be less influential than they would have been otherwise.

Research suggests that cognitive response theory may also be usefully applied to advertising. Advertisers frequently make strong claims about their products, and they do not want potential consumers in the audience to question the validity of their claims. Since distractions can interfere with the production of counterarguments, distractions leave the consumer more vulnerable to the persuasive message of the advertiser. Loud music, humor, and novelty are commonly used as ways of creating distraction and, thus, enhancing the effectiveness of the advertising.

An additional aspect of cognitive response theory is that the ultimate reaction to persuasive messages depends more on the recipient's *evaluative appraisal* of what was communicated than on the actual content or nature of the argument presented. What that means, of course, is that you're more likely to change your attitude in my direction if what I've said "sounds good to you," whether you fully understand all the implications of what I've said or not. There is a growing body of evidence that supports this position (e.g., Cacioppo & Petty, 1989; DeBono & Harnish, 1988).

The Source of Persuasive Communication. A recent general theory of attitude change claims that there are two factors, or routes, involved in changing one's attitudes (Petty & Cacioppo, 1986). One factor of concern is the *central route*: the nature and quality of the persuasive message itself. The other factor is the *peripheral route*: issues above and beyond the content of the message, arguing that the effectiveness of a persuasive communication is almost always influenced by its source. The peripheral route obviously will be of greater concern when one has a relatively weak message to convey. What the research tells us is that, in general, a highly credible (believable) source will be more persuasive than will a less credible source. There are probably several factors involved in source credibility, but two that seem especially important are expertise and trustworthiness.

A number of studies (Aronson et al., 1963; Hovland & Weiss, 1951) have indicated that the greater the perceived expertise of the communicator, the greater the amount of persuasion that occurs. People who are convinced that they are listening to an expert are more likely to be persuaded than they would be if they thought that the speaker knew little about the subject matter—even if the message were exactly the same. For example, I am much more likely to be persuaded by Michael Jackson if he were trying to influence my attitudes about a stereo system than I would be if he were trying to sell me a certain brand of toaster oven or aftershave. (Celebrities *are* used to promote products even without any apparent expertise on the basis of the following logic: First, you'll recognize them and attend to what they say, and second, their credibility and expertise in some other area, which has brought about their celebrity or fame, will transfer to the product they are selling.)

We are more likely to be persuaded by communicators we perceive as having expertise and trustworthiness. Often cited as an example is Jessie Jackson, who as a communicator, conveys a high degree of credibility for many people. Here Spike Lee is directing Jackson in an anti-drug campaign.

A second factor likely to enhance a communicator's credibility is a high degree of trustworthiness (Cooper & Croyle, 1984). Studies by Walster and Festinger (1962) demonstrated that more attitude change resulted when subjects overheard a persuasive communication than when they believed that the communication was directed at them. Trustworthiness and credibility apparently were enhanced by the perceived lack of intent to persuade ("Why should they lie; they don't even know we can hear them?").

Cognitive response theory also addresses the issue of source credibility. Haas (1981) maintains that persuasive information will be examined (mentally or cognitively) in an attempt to assess its validity, or its truth value. People are less likely to question and argue with information they get from a source they rate as credible; they simply expect it to be accurate.

BEFORE YOU GO ON

*What is cognitive response theory,
and how does it explain attitude change?*

*What communicator characteristics
are known to have an impact on attitude change?*

ATTRIBUTION THEORY

Another facet of the cognitive orientation that we find in social psychology is the study of what is called attribution theory. Social psychologists working with **attribution** theory are interested in understanding the cognitions we use in trying to explain behavior, both our own and that of others. The question here is, "Do we tend to attribute behaviors or events we observe in the world around us to internal or external sources—to personal dispositions or to environmental situations?" You may recognize this question as related to issues we raised in the topic on personality (Topic 10A, pp. 444–451) when we discussed the extent to which one's behaviors are determined by internal, personality (dispositional) factors or external, environmental (situational) factors.

The distinction comes down to believing whether behavior is caused by the person or by the environment. **Internal attributions** explain the source of behavior in terms of some characteristic of the person, often a personality trait or disposition, and for this reason internal attributions are sometimes called *dispositional attributions*. **External attributions**, on the other hand, explain the sources of behavior in terms of the situation or social context outside the individual; they are referred to as *situational attributions*.

The evidence indicates that people tend to rely on different types of information when making judgments about the sources of behavior. Imagine, for example, that your best friend shows his temper only when he is with his girlfriend. That information is useful because of its *distinctiveness* (his bad temper only shows up when he's with his girlfriend). As a result, you may take it as a signal of a troubled relationship.

Imagine that you have just received an A on a test in your history class. In this case, you could (and probably would) use information about how well everyone else did on the test before you decide about your own superiority; this kind of information is concerned with *consensus*. If you discover that everyone else also received an A, your explanation of your own behavior (and theirs) might be different from a situation in which you discover that yours is the only A in the class. But before you got too grandiose about your own accomplishment, you might wait for some sign of *consistency* over time lest this one exam be just a fluke. Using information about distinctiveness, consensus, and consistency is the basis of one major theory about attributions we make about behavior (e.g., Kelley, 1967, 1973; Kelley & Michela, 1980). Figure 14.5 shows a few of the ways in which information about distinctiveness, consensus, and consistency may lead one to attribute behavior to internal or external sources.

An active area of research in social psychology deals with errors we tend to make in our social thinking. One well-documented example of a bias in the attribution process is called the **fundamental attribution error** (Jones, 1979; Ross, 1977). This bias has to do with the basic tendency to favor internal, personal attributions for behavior rather than external, situational explanations. We see a man pick up a wallet that has been dropped on the pavement and race half a block to return it to its true owner. We say to ourselves, "Now there's an honest man." (And we'll probably predict that that person will act honestly in a variety of different situations.) The truth is, however, that the fellow returned the wallet only because he knew that we (and many others) saw him pick it up from the pavement. It may

attribution *the cognitions we generate when we attempt to explain the sources of behavior*

internal attribution *an explanation of behavior in terms of something (a trait) within the person; a dispositional attribution*

external attribution *an explanation of behavior in terms of something outside the person; a situational attribution*

fundamental attribution error *the tendency to overuse internal attributions when explaining behavior*

Figure 14.5

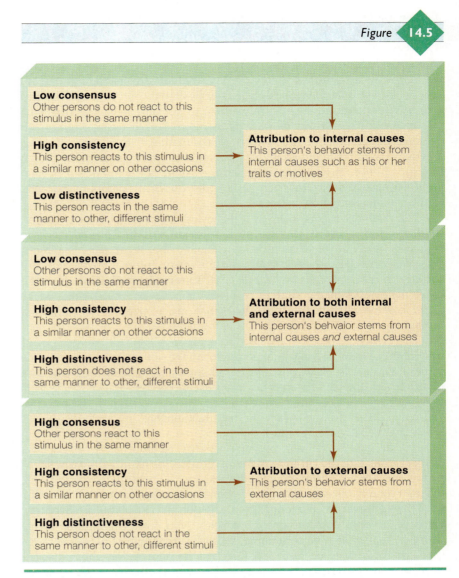

Attributing behavior: some important considerations and possible outcomes. From SOCIAL PSYCHOLOGY: UNDERSTANDING HUMAN INTERACTION, fourth edition by Robert A. Baron and Donn Byrne, page 59. Copyright © 1984, 1981, 1977, 1974 by Allyn and Bacon, Inc. Reprinted by permission.

very well be that if no one else were around, the wallet would not have been returned. The fundamental attribution error, then, is the tendency to disregard, or overly discount, situational factors in favor of internal, dispositional factors when we make inferences about the causes of behaviors. I should also mention that there is some evidence that biases such as the fundamental attribution error may be particular to Western cultures. Subjects from India, for example, particularly adults, make many fewer dispositional attributions than do American subjects (Miller, 1984). They are much more likely than Americans to explain behavior in terms of the situation or the environment than in terms of personality traits, abilities, or inabilities.

As you might imagine, there are a number of other biases that may lead us to make incorrect attributions about ourselves or others. One is called the **just world hypothesis**, in which people take on the belief that we live in a just world where good things happen to good people and bad things happen to bad people (Lerner, 1965, 1980). It's a sort of "everybody ultimately gets what they deserve" mentality. We see this bias (we might say fallacy) when we see people claim that victims of rape often "ask for it by the way they dress and act." In fact, even the victims of rape sometimes engage in self-blame in an attempt to explain why in the world *they* were singled out for what was in fact a crime in which they were the victim quite by chance (Janoff-Bulman, 1979).

just world hypothesis *the belief that the world is just and that people get what they deserve*

Another bias that affects our attributions is one with which we are all familiar. It is called the **self-serving bias** (Harvey & Weary, 1984; Miller & Ross, 1975). It occurs when we attribute positive or successful outcomes to personal, internal sources and failures or negative outcomes to situational, external sources. We tend to think that when we do well it is because we're talented and work hard, whereas when we do poorly it is the fault of someone or something else. "Boy, didn't I do a great job of painting that room" versus "The room looks so shoddy because the paint was cheap and the brush was old" would be an example. (Perhaps you'll recall from our discussion of depression in Topic 12B that some cognitive theorists argue that at least some depression can be explained as a failure to apply the self-serving bias. That is, some people may get into the habit of blaming themselves for failures and negative outcomes regardless of where the real blame resides or regardless of whether there *is* any blame to attribute.)

self-serving bias *the tendency to attribute our successes to our own effort and abilities, and our failures to situational, external sources*

Yet another attribution error is the so-called **actor-observer bias** (Jones & Nisbett, 1971; Monson & Snyder, 1977). What we find here is a basic discrepancy between the way we explain our behavior (as actor) and the way we explain someone else's (as observer). What usually happens is that we use external attributions when we talk about why we do things. The basis of our explanation has to do with something about the situation or the environment. "I took that class because the instructor is entertaining." "I date Bill because he's so caring and considerate." "I went there because the rates were lower than anyplace else." When we explain someone else's behaviors we tend to use internal attributions and refer to characteristics of the person whose behaviors we have been observing. "Oh, he took that class because he's so lazy." "I know that she's dating him only because she wants to be seen with an athlete." "He went there because he wanted to show off." That we explain our own behaviors in ways that are different from the ways in which we account for the behaviors of others should not be surprising. For one thing, we have much more information about ourselves and our own past experiences than we do about anyone else. In fact, the more information we have about someone else, the less likely we are to use internal attributions to explain their behaviors. Also, in any situation, the actor gets quite a different view of what is happening than does the observer. In other words, the actor and the observer both attempt to attribute the cause of behavior on the basis of different information.

actor-observer bias *the overuse of internal attributions to explain the behaviors of others and external attributions to explain our own behaviors*

What are the two basic types of attribution?
Explain the ways in which attributions can be distorted or biased.

INTERPERSONAL ATTRACTION

Interpersonal attraction can be seen as an attitude toward another person—a favorable and powerful attitude at that. Interpersonal attraction reflects the extent to which a person has formed positive feelings and beliefs about another person and is prepared to act on those affects and cognitions. In this section, we'll review some of the processes that influence how these attitudes are formed.

Theories of Interpersonal Attraction

Social psychologists have put forth several theoretical models to explain the bases of interpersonal attraction. Let's briefly review four such theories.

Probably the simplest and most straightforward theory is one we can call the *reinforcement model* (Clore & Byrne, 1974; Lott & Lott, 1974). This model claims that we are attracted to people we associate with rewards. In other words, we learn to like people and become attracted to them through conditioning, by associating them with rewards or reinforcers that are present when they are. We are thus attracted to (have positive attitudes toward) those people we associate with rewarding experiences. It also follows that we'll tend not to be attracted to those we associate with punishment—a sort of "blame the messenger who brings bad news" attitude. One implication of this point of view is that you're going to like your instructor more, and seek him or her out for other classes in the future, if you get (or better, earn) a high grade in his or her class than you will if you get a low grade.

Another popular theory of interpersonal attraction is not quite so direct. It is called the *social exchange model* (Kelley & Thibault, 1978; Thibault & Kelley, 1959). According to this model, what matters most is a comparison of the costs as well as the benefits of establishing and/or maintaining a relationship. For example, Leslie may judge that John is very physically attractive, but that entering into an intimate relationship with him is not worth the grief that she would get from friends and family, who believe John to be lazy and shiftless. On the other hand, if Leslie had just gone through a series of failed relationships with other men who were not physically attractive, she might take a chance on John, judging (in her frustration) that he was "worth it." What this theory takes into account, then, are a number of comparative judgments that people make in social situations. Being attracted to someone else is not just a matter of, "Is this a good thing?" It's more a matter of, "Is the reward that I might get from this relationship worth the cost, *and* what other alternatives exist at the moment?"

A third theoretical approach to interpersonal attraction is called the *equity model*, and it is more an extension of social exchange theory than a departure from it (Greenberg & Cohen, 1982; Walster et al., 1978). Social exchange theory added the notion of cost to that of reward. Equity theory adds the appraisal of rewards and costs of *both* members of a social relationship. That is, you may feel that a certain relationship is worth the effort you've been putting into it, but if your partner in that relationship does not feel likewise, the relationship is in danger. What matters, then, is that both (or all) members of a relationship feel that they are getting a fair deal (equity). Notice two things about this model: (1) Both members of a relationship do not have to share rewards *equally*. What matters is that the ratio of costs to rewards be equitable for both members. (2) If one person were to feel that he or she was getting more from a relationship than was deserved (on the basis of costs and compared to the other's rewards), the relationship would not be equitable and would be jeopardized. The best relationships are those in which all members receive an equal ratio of rewards to costs.

Before we leave the realm of theory, I should mention another, more recent approach to understanding close interpersonal relationships that is based more on feelings and affect than on cognitions. This model is usually referred to as *attachment theory* (Feeney & Noller, 1990; Hazan & Shaver, 1987). It suggests that interpersonal relationships can be classified into one of three types depending on the attitudes that one has about such relationships (descriptions from Shaver, Hazan, & Bradshaw, 1988, p. 80):

Secure: "I find it relatively easy to get close to others and am comfortable depending on them and having them depend on me. I don't often worry about being abandoned or about someone getting too close to me."

Avoidant: "I am somewhat uncomfortable being close to others; I find it difficult to trust them completely, difficult to allow myself to depend on them. I am nervous when anyone gets too close, and often, love partners want me to be more intimate than I feel comfortable being."

Anxious/ambivalent: "I find that others are reluctant to get as close as I would like. I often worry that my partner doesn't really love me or won't stay with me. I want to merge completely with another person, and this desire sometimes scares people away."

One of the things that makes attachment theory particularly appealing is the evidence that suggests that one's "style" of forming attachments with others is remarkably stable throughout the life span. I'm sure that you recall that we first encountered the notion of "attachment" back in Topic 9A when we were discussing infant development. It may very well be that the kinds of interpersonal relationships we form as adults are influenced by the kinds of attachments we developed as very young children.

Finally, before we go on, I should point out that few people enter into relationships having carefully considered all of the factors that these models imply. That is, assessments of reinforcement, or exchange, or equity value are seldom made at a conscious level; nor do we purposively seek out relationships that mirror those we had in childhood.

BEFORE
YOU GO
ON

*Briefly summarize four theoretical models
that account for interpersonal attractions.*

Factors Affecting Interpersonal Attraction

We've reviewed four general models of interpersonal attraction. Now let's look at some empirical evidence related to attraction. What determines whom you will be attracted to? What factors tend to provide the rewards, or the positive reward/cost ratios, that serve as the basis for strong relationships? Here we'll describe four common principles related to interpersonal attraction.

Reciprocity. Our first principle is perhaps the most obvious one. Not surprisingly, we tend to value and like people who like and value us (Backman & Secord, 1959; Curtis & Miller, 1986). Remember that we've already noted, in our discussion of operant conditioning (Topic 5B), that the attention of others often can be a powerful reinforcer. This is particularly true if the attention is positive, supportive, and affectionate. Research indicates that the value of someone else caring for us is particularly powerful when that someone initially seemed to have neutral or even negative attitudes toward us (Aronson & Linder, 1965). That is, we are most attracted to people who like us now, but who didn't originally. The logic here is related to attribution. If someone we meet for the first time expresses nothing but positive feelings and attitudes toward us, we are likely to attribute their reaction internally to the way the person is—rather shallow and the sort who just likes everybody. But if someone at first were to express neutral, or even slightly negative, feelings toward us and then were to become more and more positive, we might have a different, more positive view of their ability to judge others.

Proximity leads to liking, which is why teenagers who go to the same school are likely to form friendships.

Proximity. Our second principle suggests that physical closeness, or proximity, tends to produce attraction. Sociologists, as well as your own personal experience, will tell you that people tend to establish friendships (and romances) with others with whom they have grown up, worked, or gone to school. Similarly, social-psychological studies consistently have found that residents of apartments or dormitories tend to become friends with those other residents living closest to them (Festinger et al., 1950). Being around others gives us the opportunity to discover just who can provide those interpersonal rewards we seek in friendship.

There may be another social-psychological phenomenon at work here called the **mere exposure phenomenon**. Research, pioneered by Robert Zajonc (1968), has shown with a variety of stimuli that liking tends to increase with repeated exposure to stimuli. Examples of this phenomenon are abundant in everyday life. Have you ever bought a record album that you have not heard previously, assuming that you will like it because you have liked all the other albums made by this performer? The first time you

mere exposure phenomenon *the tendency to increase our liking of people and things the more we see of them*

listen to your new album, however, your reaction may be lukewarm at best, and you may be disappointed in your purchase. Not wanting to feel that you've wasted your money, you play the album a few more times over the next several days. What often happens is that you soon realize that you like this album after all. The mere exposure effect has occurred, and this commonly happens in our formation of attitudes about other people as well. (If this sounds a bit like our earlier discussion of cognitive dissonance, you're right. We can't imagine having repeated contacts with someone we don't particularly like—that would be dissonant—so we find that we like them after all.) Apparently, familiarity is apt to breed attraction, not contempt. I also have to add that although there seems to be ample evidence that the mere exposure phenomenon is real, there remains considerable disagreement about *why* familiarity and repeated interactions breed attraction (e.g., Birnbaum & Mellers, 1979; Kunst-Wilson & Zajonc, 1980).

Physical Attractiveness. Our physical appearance is one personal characteristic that we cannot easily hide. It is always on display in social situations, and it communicates something about us. People are aware of the role of appearance in nonverbal, interpersonal communication and may spend many hours each week doing whatever can be done to improve the way they look.

The power of physical attractiveness in the context of dating has been demonstrated experimentally in a classic study directed by Elaine Walster (Walster et al., 1966). University of Minnesota freshmen completed a number of psychological tests as part of an orientation program. The students were then randomly matched for dates to an orientation dance, during which they took a break and evaluated their assigned partners. This study allowed researchers the possibility of uncovering intricate, complex, and subtle facts about interpersonal attraction, such as which personality traits might tend to mesh in such a way as to produce attraction. As it turned out, none of these complex factors, so carefully controlled for, was important. The effect of physical attractiveness was so powerful that it wiped out all other effects. For both men and women, the more physically attractive their date, the more they liked the person and the more they wanted to go out again with that individual.

Numerous studies of physical attractiveness followed this one. Some of these studies simply gave subjects a chance to pick a date from a group of several potential partners (usually using descriptions and pictures). Not surprisingly, subjects almost invariably selected the most attractive person available to be their date (Reis et al., 1980).

You may have noticed, however, that in real life we seldom have the opportunity to request a date without at least the possibility of being turned down. When experimental studies began to build in the possibility of rejection, an interesting effect emerged: Subjects stopped picking the most attractive candidate and started selecting partners whose level of physical attractiveness was more similar to their own. This behavior has been called the **matching phenomenon**, and it is an effect that has been verified by naturalistic observation studies (Walster & Walster, 1969).

The positive effects of physical attractiveness can be found in many social situations. Studies (e.g., Dion et al., 1972; Hatfield & Sprecher, 1986; Vaughn & Langlois, 1983) suggest that attractive persons are assumed to

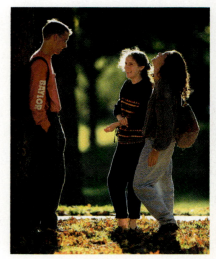

Physical attractiveness is a powerful influence in interpersonal relationships. Numerous studies have found that physical attractiveness is at least at first, the single most important factor in selecting friends and dates.

matching phenomenon *the tendency to select partners whose level of physical attractiveness matches our own*

have other desirable characteristics as well. Attractive persons—both men and women—are routinely judged to be more intelligent, to have happier marriages, to be more successful in their careers and social lives, and so on. This effect of overgeneralizing is referred to as the *physical attractiveness stereotype*.

Some research has indicated that there may be serious implications involved in the application of this stereotype. For instance, Anderson and Nida (1978) have shown that the same piece of work (in this case an essay) will be evaluated more favorably when a physically attractive person is thought to have produced it. Similarly, a study by Clifford and Hatfield (1973) found fifth-grade teachers to judge attractive children as more intelligent. Another study (Dion, 1972) found that women who were asked to recommend punishment for a child who had misbehaved were more lenient when the child was judged to be physically attractive.

The more similar another person is to you, the more you will tend to be like that person. Our friends tend to be people who share our attitudes and who like to do the things we like to do.

Similarity. There is a large body of research on the relationship between similarity and attraction, but the findings are consistent, and we can summarize them briefly. (Remember too, that we introduced many of these issues in Topic 9B when we discussed marriage and mate selection.) Much of this research has been done by Donn Byrne and his colleagues (e.g., Byrne, 1971). It indicates that there is a strong positive relationship between attraction and the proportion of attitudes held in common. Simply put, the more similar another person is to you, the more you will tend to like that person (Buss, 1985; Davis, 1985; Rubin, 1973). Sensibly, we also tend to be repelled, or put off, by persons we believe to be dissimilar to us (Rosenbaum, 1986).

Perhaps you know a happily married couple for whom this sweeping conclusion does not seem to fit. At least some of their behaviors seem to be quite dissimilar, almost opposite. Perhaps the wife appears to be the one who makes most of the decisions while the husband simply seems to follow orders. It may very well be the case, however, that this apparent lack of similarity in behavior exists only on the surface. There may be an important similarity that makes for a successful marriage here: Both have the same idea of what a marriage should be like—wives decide and husbands obey. In such a case, the observed differences in behavior are reflecting a powerful similarity in the view of the roles of married couples.

That similarity enhances interpersonal attraction makes sense in light of the reinforcement theory of attraction we described earlier. Among other things, agreement with our attitudinal positions is reinforcing; it confirms that we were right all along. And, by definition, people who are similar to us tend to agree with us. In Ms. Elliott's third-grade class, brown-eyed pupils made friends with other brown-eyed pupils, if only for a short time, and regardless of whether they thought of themselves as favored or unfavored. Similarity is probably the glue that, over the long haul, holds together romances and friendships.

BEFORE YOU GO ON

What are four determinants of interpersonal attraction?

In this topic, we've addressed some of the important issues related to social cognition: perception and evaluation in a social context. We've spent most of our time on attitudes, which appear largely cognitive in nature, but which also involve affect and action tendencies directed toward some object or event. We've seen that attitudes provide adaptive functions for us, helping us to judge others and to present ourselves to others as we would like to be judged. We've also reviewed the ways in which we theorize, or develop cognitions, about the sources of the behaviors we see around us. In many instances, we make erroneous attributions. We ended this topic with a discussion of interpersonal attraction, trying to find explanations (attributions again) for why some people get along so well with each other and some do not. Although the impact of group influence could be found in each of the issues we covered in this topic, social influence and group processes are the major focuses of Topic 14B.

SUMMARY

What are stereotypes and norms, and in what way are they cognitive?

Both stereotypes and norms are sets of ideas or beliefs (i.e., cognitions) that we form about our social world. Stereotypes are generalized mental representations that we have of other people and are often based on very little information. Norms are learned expectations or rules that guide and influence our behaviors in social situations. They are beliefs about how one ought to behave in social situations. / *page 640*

What is an attitude, and what are its three components?

An attitude is an evaluative disposition (positive or negative) directed toward some object. An attitude consists of feelings (affects), behaviors, and beliefs (cognitions). Although the affective and cognitive components of attitudes are often consistent with each other, behavior—influenced by so many variables—may be inconsistent with the other two major components. / *page 642*

What are some of the functions served by attitudes?

Attitudes can guide our behaviors and summarize the beliefs we hold. They also serve a social identification function; that is, they tell others about us, and the attitudes of others give us useful information about them. When we carefully select the attitudinal information we make available to others, we say that an impression management function is being served. / *page 643*

Briefly describe three ways in which attitudes might be acquired.

Attitudes may be acquired through clas-sical conditioning: After positive or negative experiences are associated with an attitudinal object, the object by itself comes to produce a positive or negative evaluation. Attitudinal behaviors may also be directly reinforced (operant conditioning), or they may be reinforced vicariously (observational learning). / *page 645*

What is cognitive dissonance, and how does it operate?

Cognitive dissonance is an unpleasant state of tension between or among cognitions that may occur when we behave in a fashion inconsistent with our attitudes. Because we are motivated to reduce dissonance, we may do so by changing our attitudes so that they become consistent with the way we behave. / *page 646*

What is cognitive response theory, and how does it explain attitude change? What communicator characteristics are known to have an impact on attitude change?

Cognitive response theory tells us that persons receiving a persuasive message actively form cognitions in response to that message. Further, the quality of the arguments involved in a persuasive communication and one's ability to form supportive or counterarguments are likely to influence the degree of persuasion that the communication produces—the central route to attitude change. Concern with the communicator characteristics and other situational variables reflects a focus on more peripheral routes to attitude change. Those communicators perceived as being expert or trustworthy are seen as credible sources of information and, hence, are more persuasive. / *page 648*

What are the two basic types of attribution? Explain the ways in which attributions can be distorted or biased.
Attributions are cognitions we use to explain the sources of the behaviors we see in our social worlds: The two basic types of attribution are internal and external. An internal attribution identifies the source of behavior as within the person and is sometimes called a dispositional attribution. An external attribution finds the source of behavior to be outside the person and is sometimes called a situational attribution.

The *fundamental attribution error* leads us to overuse internal or personal attributions when explaining behaviors. Those persons who hold to the *just world hypothesis* are likely to believe that good things only happen to good people and bad things only happen to bad people who in some way deserve their misfortune. The *self-serving bias* has us tend to attribute successes to our own efforts and actions and our failures to other, external factors. The *actor-observer* bias refers to the tendency to use external attributions to explain our own (as actor) behaviors, while using internal attributions to explain the behaviors of others (as observer).
/ *page 652*

Briefly summarize four theoretical models that account for interpersonal attractions.
The *reinforcement model* claims simply that we tend to be attracted to those persons we associate with rewards or reinforcers. The *social exchange model* adds the notion of cost to the equation, claiming that what matters in interpersonal relationships is the ratio of the benefits received to the costs invested in that relationship. The *equity model* suggests that both or all members of a relationship assess a benefit/cost ratio, and the best, most stable relationships are those in which the ratio is nearly the same (equitable) for both or all parties, no matter what the value of the benefits for any one member of the relationship. *Attachment theory* tells us that there are only a few relationship styles, and that people are consistent over their lifetime in the style they use when relating to others. / *page 654*

What are four determinants of interpersonal attraction?
The principle of *reciprocity* states that we tend to like people who like us back. This is the most straightforward example of interpersonal attraction being based on a system of rewards. *Proximity* promotes attraction by means of the mere exposure phenomenon: Being near another person on a frequent basis gives us the opportunity to see what that other person has to offer. We also tend to be attracted to people whom we judge to be *physically attractive*. Finally, the principle of *similarity* suggests that we tend to be attracted to others whom we believe are similar to ourselves. / *page 656*

TOPIC 14B

Social Influence

Why We Care: A Topic Preview

Our perception of the world around us is often unclear and ambiguous. When it is, we tend to rely on others for assistance. In other words, our affects, cognitions, and behaviors are often influenced by others, and this, of course, is why we care about the issues raised in this topic. In truth, we are so accustomed to the pressures of social influence that much of the time it escapes our awareness. You probably didn't consider just why you happened to walk on the right side of the sidewalk the last time you were downtown shopping, or why you quietly took a place at the very end of the line the last time you bought tickets for a movie, or why you applauded and cheered at the last concert you attended. Nevertheless, each of these behaviors was shaped by social influence.

In Topic 14A, we focused primarily on how social forces affect our cognitions, perceptions, and judgments in social situations. Here we're going to stress how social forces influence our behaviors. Of course, it is somewhat artificial to separate thinking from acting since, as we have seen repeatedly, the two processes are intertwined. In this topic, however, we'll focus on overt, directly observable forms of socially influenced behavior. Although they have much in common, we'll consider the processes of influence by conformity and influence through obedience separately. We'll consider the phenomena of bystander apathy and intervention and list some of the factors that determine how, or if, someone will intervene on behalf of someone else. We'll end our discussion by reviewing a number of situations in which social influence is a potent force in our lives. In each case, the theme will be the same: how the actions of others influence the behavior of the individual.

CONFORMITY

One of the most obvious and direct forms of social influence occurs whenever we modify our behavior, under perceived pressure to do so, so that it is consistent with the behavior of others, a process referred to as **conformity**. Often this means that we follow some norm or standard that prescribes how we should act in a given situation. Although we tend to think of conformity in a negative way, to conform is natural and often desirable. Conformity helps to make social behaviors efficient and, at least to some degree, predictable.

conformity *the changing of one's behavior, under perceived pressure, so that it is consistent with the behavior of others*

Norm Formation and Conformity

Some of the earliest research to demonstrate the power of conformity was performed by Muzafer Sherif (1936). Sherif used the perceptual phenomenon called the *autokinetic effect* to show how social norms can develop and induce conformity in an ambiguous situation. We described the autokinetic effect in Topic 4A in our discussion of illusions of motion. If a person in a completely darkened room is presented with a small stationary spot of light, within a few moments that light will appear to move. This compelling, illusory movement is not at all regular—the light seems to dart from place to place. When asked to estimate how far the light moves, people vary widely in their judgments, which may range from a few inches to several feet (remember that the light is actually stationary). Sherif first asked people who were alone in the testing room to make independent judgments about the apparent movement of the light. Then, in each of several sessions that took place on different days, Sherif asked his subjects to make their judgments with other subjects present in the room. The other subjects were also asked to estimate how far the light moved.

As a result of the group experience, each participant adjusted his or her judgments to match the estimates of others. That is, over the course of the study, the judgments by members of a group of subjects converged, and the end result was agreement within the group as to how far the light had moved. A norm had emerged to guide behavior in this ambiguous situation, and the individuals in the study conformed to it.

The Asch Studies

The results of the demonstrations by Sherif may not be all that surprising. After all, the situation was completely ambiguous. The subjects had no prior experience with the autokinetic effect, and there were no cues to guide their judgments, at least until the other subjects entered the picture. How might people respond to group pressure when the reality of the situation is much clearer?

Solomon Asch (1951, 1956) initially believed that people are not very susceptible to social pressure when the social situation is clear-cut and unambiguous. Asch hypothesized that subjects would behave independently of group pressure when there was little question that their own judgments were accurate, and he developed an interesting technique for testing his hypothesis.

A subject in Asch's procedure would join a group seated around a table. In his original study, the group consisted of seven people. Unknown to the

After consistently disagreeing with the other subjects in Asch's study, the lone dissenter begins to doubt his judgment and looks again at the card, even though the correct answer is obvious.

subject, however, six individuals were confederates of the experimenter; that is, they were "in on" the experiment. The subjects were led to believe that the study dealt with the ability to make perceptual judgments. The participants had to do nothing more than to decide which of three lines was the same length as a standard line (see Figure 14.6). The experimenter showed each set of lines to the group and then collected responses, one by one, from each member of the group. There were 18 sets of lines to judge, and the only real subject was always the last one to respond.

It is important to note that each of the 18 judgments the subjects made involved unambiguous stimuli. The correct answer was always obvious. However, on 12 of the 18 trials, the confederates gave a unanimous but *incorrect* answer. Now what would the subjects do? How would they resolve this conflict? Their own perceptual experience was telling them what the right answer was, but the group was saying something else. Should they trust the judgments of the others, or should they trust their own ability?

The results of his initial study surprised Asch, because they did not confirm his original hypothesis. Across all of the critical trials (when confederates gave "wrong" answers), conformity occurred 37 percent of the time. That is, subjects responded with an incorrect answer that agreed with the majority on more than one-third of the critical trials. Moreover, three-quarters of Asch's subjects conformed to the group pressure at least once.

In subsequent studies, Asch tried several variations of his original procedure. In one experiment, he varied the size of the unanimous, incorrect majority. As you might now expect, the level of conformity increased as the size of the majority increased (leveling off at about three or four people) (Asch, 1956; Knowles, 1983). Subjects gave an erroneous judgment only 4 percent of the time when only one incorrect judgment preceded their own. In another study, Asch found that subjects gave an erroneous judgment

Figure 14.6

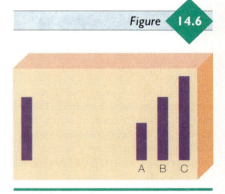

The type of stimuli used in Asch's conformity experiment. Subjects are to say which of the three lines on the right (A, B, or C) equal the line on the left. Associates of the experimenter will occasionally make incorrect choices.

only 10 percent of the time when there was one dissenter among the six confederates who voiced an accurate judgment before the subjects gave theirs. In short, when the subjects had at least some social support for what their eyes had told them, they tended to trust their own judgment. Recent experiments have demonstrated that the minority opinion (say one dissenter in an Asch-type procedure) can have particularly significant effects on conformity if that minority position is maintained consistently (e.g., Moscovici et al., 1969, 1985; Nemeth, 1986).

Conformity involves yielding to the perceived pressure of a group. In most circumstances, it is assumed that group members are peers, or at least similar to the conformer. When one yields to the pressure of a perceived authority, the result is obedience. It is to the issue of obedience that we turn next.

BEFORE YOU GO ON

Briefly describe the methodology and the basic findings of the Sherif and Asch conformity studies.

OBEDIENCE TO AUTHORITY

Although the subjects in Asch's studies took the procedure seriously, the consequences of either conforming or maintaining independence were rather trivial. At worst, Asch's subjects might have experienced some discomfort as a result of voicing their independent judgments. There were no external rewards or punishments for their behavior, and there was no one telling them how to respond. Stanley Milgram (1933–1984), a social psychologist at Yale University, went beyond Asch's procedure. Milgram's research has become among the most famous and controversial in all of psychology. His experiments pressured subjects to comply with the demand of an authority figure—a demand that was both unreasonable and troubling (Milgram, 1963, 1965, 1974).

The original impetus for Milgram's research was his interest in the obedience to Nazi authority displayed by many German military personnel during World War II. Milgram wondered whether mass executions and other forms of cruelty perpetrated by the Nazis might reflect something about the German character. The original goal of his research was to determine if people of different nationalities differ in the degree to which they will obey a request to inflict pain on another person. Milgram's research procedure was designed to serve as a basis for making such comparisons.

All of the studies carried out in this series involved the same basic procedure. Subjects arrived at the laboratory to find that they would be participating with a second person (once again, a confederate of the experimenter). The experimenter explained that the research dealt with the effects of punishment on learning and that one subject would serve as a teacher while the other would act as learner. The two roles were assigned by a rigged drawing in which the actual subject was always assigned the role of

Extreme, unquestioning obedience to authority can have negative consequences. Consider concentration camp commander Franz Hoessler, whose blind obedience to Hitler's decrees led to the brutal murder of millions of innocent people.

teacher, while the confederate was always the learner. The subject watched as the learner was taken into the next room and wired to electrodes that would be used for delivering punishment in the form of electric shocks.

The teacher then received his instructions. First, he was to read to the learner a list of four pairs of words. Then the teacher would read the first word of one of the pairs, and the learner was to supply the second word. The teacher sat in front of a rather imposing electric "shock generator" (see Figure 14.7) that had 30 switches, each with its voltage level labeled. From left to right, the switches increased by increments of 15 volts, ranging from 15 volts to 450 volts. Labels were also printed under the switches on the face of the generator. These ranged from "Slight" to "Moderate" to "Extreme Intensity" to "Danger: Severe Shock." The label at the 450-volt end simply read "XXX."

As the task proceeded, the learner periodically made errors according to a prearranged schedule. The teacher had been instructed to deliver an electric shock for each incorrect answer. With each error, the teacher was to move up the scale of shocks on the generator, giving the learner a more potent shock with each new mistake. (The learner, remember, was part of the act, and no one was actually receiving any shocks.)

Whenever the teacher hesitated or questioned whether he should continue, the experimenter was ready with one of several verbal prods, such as "Please continue," or "The experiment requires that you continue." If the subject protested, the experimenter would become more assertive and offer an alternative prod: "You have no choice; you must go on," he might say. The degree of obedience—the behavior of interest to Milgram—was determined by the level of shock at which the teacher refused to go further.

Milgram was astonished by the results of his first study, and the results continue to amaze students of psychology more than 25 years later. Twenty-six of Milgram's 40 subjects—65 percent—obeyed the demands of the experimenter and went all the way to the highest shock value and closed all the switches. In fact, *no subject* stopped prior to the 300-volt level, the point at which the learner pounded on the wall in protest. One later variation of this study added vocal responses from the learner, who delivered an increasingly stronger series of demands to be let out of the experiment. The level of obedience in this study was still unbelievably high, as 25 of 40 subjects, or 62.5 percent, continued to administer shocks to the 450-volt level.

It is important to note that the behavior of Milgram's subjects did not indicate that they were unconcerned about the learner. All of the subjects experienced genuine and extreme stress in this situation. Some fidgeted, some trembled, many perspired profusely. A number of subjects giggled nervously. In short, the people caught up in this unusual situation showed obvious signs of conflict and anxiety. Nevertheless, they continued to obey the orders of the authoritative experimenter even though they had good reason to believe that they might well be harming the learner.

Milgram's first study was performed with male subjects ranging in age from 20 to 50. A later replication with adult women produced precisely the same results: 65 percent obeyed fully. Other variations of the basic procedure, however, uncovered that several factors could reduce the amount of obedience. Putting the learner and teacher in the same room, or having the experimenter deliver his orders over the telephone, for example, reduced obedience markedly. Another variation produced an interesting

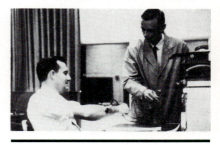

A shock generator apparatus of the sort the teacher would use to punish the learner in Stanley Milgram's research on obedience. In the photo on the bottom, the subject is given a sample shock.

parallel to one of the Asch studies we discussed: When the shocks were delivered by a team consisting of the subject and two disobedient confederates, full-scale obedience dropped to only 10 percent.

Attribution Errors and a Word of Caution

When one first hears about these rather distressing results, there is a tendency for many people to think that Milgram's obedient subjects were cold, callous, unfeeling, unusual, or even downright cruel and sadistic people (Safer, 1980). Nothing could be further from the truth. As I have already mentioned, the participants in this research were truly troubled by what was happening. If you thought that Milgram's subjects must be strange or different, perhaps you were a victim of what we identified in our last topic as an *attribution error*. That is, you were willing to attribute the subjects' behavior to (internal) personality characteristics instead of recognizing the powerful situational forces at work.

Attributing negative personality characteristics to the "teachers" is particularly understandable in light of the unexpected nature of the results. A number of psychologists in commenting on this research have suggested, in fact, that the most significant aspect of Milgram's findings is that they *are* so surprising to us. As part of his research, Milgram asked people, including a group of psychiatrists and a group of ministers, to predict what they would do under these circumstances, and he also asked them to predict how far others would go before refusing the authority. Needless to say, respondents in both cases predicted very little obedience, expecting practically no one to proceed all the way to the final switch on the shock generator.

We have already suggested that people tend to rely on others for help in determining social reality when ambiguity is present. The experimental procedures of Asch and Milgram created conflict for those subjects who tried to define the situations in which they found themselves. Asch created a discrepancy between what the subject perceived as true and what others said was true. In the same way, Milgram created a discrepancy between what the subject felt was the right and proper thing to do and what an authority figure said must be done. The situation was probably made even more difficult for Milgram's subjects by the tendency that we have to accept perceived authority without questioning it. From very early in life, we are conditioned to obey our parents, teachers, police officers, and the like. We often tend to trust others when faced with tasks of resolving conflicts such as those presented in these two classic studies.

A Reminder on Ethics in Research

In reading about Milgram's research, it should have occurred to you that putting subjects in such a stressful experience might be considered morally and ethically objectionable. Milgram himself was quite concerned with the welfare of his subjects. He took great care to *debrief* them fully after each session had been completed. He informed them that they had not really administered any shocks and explained why deception had been necessary. It is, of course, standard practice in psychological experiments to conclude the session by disclosing the true purpose of the study and alleviating any anxiety that might have arisen.

Milgram reported that the people in his studies generally were not upset over having been deceived and that their principal reaction was one of relief when they learned that no electric shock had, in fact, been used. Milgram also indicated that a follow-up study performed a year later with some of the same subjects showed that no long-term adverse effects had been created by his procedure.

Despite these precautions, Milgram was severely criticized for placing people in such an extremely stressful situation. Indeed, one of the effects of his research was to establish in the scientific community a higher level of awareness of the need to protect the well-being of human research subjects. It is probably safe to say that because of the nature of Milgram's experience, no one would be allowed to perform such experiments today.

BEFORE YOU GO ON

Briefly describe Stanley Milgram's experimental demonstrations of obedience.

BYSTANDER INTERVENTION

In March 1964, a New York City cocktail waitress named Kitty Genovese was brutally murdered in front of her apartment building as she returned from work at approximately 3:30 A.M. Although murders may have become somewhat commonplace in our large urban centers, there were some unusual and particularly disturbing circumstances surrounding this incident:

> For more than half an hour, thirty-eight respectable law-abiding citizens in Queens watched a killer stalk and stab a woman in three separate attacks in Kew Gardens.
>
> Twice the sound of their voices and the sudden glow of their bedroom lights interrupted him and frightened him off. Each time he returned, sought her out and stabbed her again. Not one person telephoned the police during the assault; one witness called after the woman was dead. (*The New York Times*, March 27, 1964)

This tragic event stimulated public concern and sparked a good deal of commentary in the media. People wondered how the witnesses could have shown such a lack of concern for a fellow human being. Apathy and alienation were terms often used in describing what had happened. One positive outcome of this unfortunate incident was that a program of research was begun that helped to establish a basic understanding of the social factors that can influence people to intervene or not to intervene in such a situation.

Bibb Latané and John Darley, two social psychologists who at the time were at universities in New York City, were not satisfied that terms such as *bystander apathy* or *alienation* adequately explained what happened in the Genovese case. They were not willing to attribute people's failure to help

Researchers have found that there are many reasons why people should not be expected to get involved in an emergency, including risk of physical injury and legal consequences. Nevertheless, some bystanders will choose to intervene as was the case with the heart attack victim pictured here.

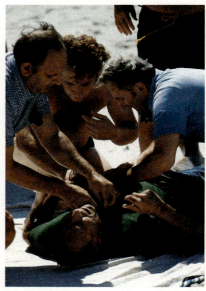

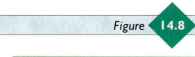

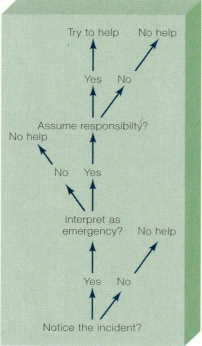

Some of the decisions and outcomes involved as a bystander considers intervening. (After Latané & Darley, 1968.)

to internal, dispositional, or personality characteristics. They were convinced that situational factors make such events possible.

Latané and Darley (1970) pointed out that there are several logical reasons why people should *not* be expected to offer help in an emergency. Emergencies tend to happen quickly and without advance warning. Except for medical technicians, fire fighters, and a few other select categories of individuals, people generally are not prepared to deal with emergencies when they do arise. In fact, one good predictor of who will intervene in an emergency turns out to be previous experience with similar emergency situations (Huston et al., 1981). By their nature, emergencies are not commonplace occurrences for most of us. It also goes without saying that the risk of physical injury, as was clearly present in the Genovese case, is an understandable deterrent to helping. Finally, people may fail to help because they genuinely want to avoid the legal consequences that might follow. They simply do not want to get involved.

A Cognitive Model of Bystander Intervention

Latané and Darley (1968) suggest that a series of cognitive events must occur before a bystander can intervene in an emergency (Figure 14.8). First, the bystander must *notice* what is going on. A person who is window shopping and thus fails to see someone collapse on the opposite side of the street cannot be expected to rush over and offer assistance. If the bystander does notice something happen, he or she still must *interpret* the situation as an emergency; perhaps the person who has collapsed is simply drunk or tired and not really having a stroke or a heart attack. The third step involves the decision that it is the bystander's (and not someone else's) *responsibility* to do something.

Even if the bystander has noticed something occurring, has interpreted the situation as one calling for quick action, and has assumed responsibility for helping, he or she still faces the decision of what form of assistance to offer. Should he or she attempt to administer first aid? Should he or she try to find the nearest telephone? Or should he or she simply start shouting for help? As a final step in the process, the person ultimately must decide how to implement his or her decision to act. What is the appropriate first aid under these circumstances? Just where can a phone be found? We can see that intervening on behalf of someone else in a social situation involves a series of cognitive choices.

A negative outcome at any of these cognitive steps of decision making will lead a bystander to decide not to offer assistance. When one considers the cognitive events necessary for actually helping, along with the many potential costs associated with intervention, it becomes apparent that the deck is stacked against the victim in an emergency. As Latané and Darley have suggested, perhaps we should be surprised that bystanders *ever* offer help.

Although tragedies such as the Kitty Genovese murder do not happen every day, hundreds of media reports involving the same sort of scenario have appeared in the more than 25 years since that event. Rather ironically, it is the very presence of others that leads to this disturbing social-psychological phenomenon (Cunningham, 1984; Shotland, 1985). There seem to be several psychological processes that account for what we might call the *social inhibition of helping*, or *bystander effect*. Let's just review three such processes (Latané & Darley, 1970; Latané & Nida, 1981).

Audience Inhibition. Audience inhibition refers to our tendency to be hesitant to do things in front of others, especially when the others are strangers. We tend to be concerned about how others will evaluate us (a point we will return to later). In public, no one wants to do anything that might appear to be silly, incompetent, or improper. The bystander who intervenes risks embarrassment if he or she blunders. That risk increases as the number of people present increases.

audience inhibition *reluctance to intervene and offer assistance in front of others*

Pluralistic Ignorance. Emergencies tend to be ambiguous: Is the raggedly dressed man who has collapsed on the street ill or drunk? Is the commotion in a neighboring apartment an assault or a family quarrel that's just a little out of hand? As we have already seen, when social reality is unclear, we turn to others for clues.

While a person is in the process of getting information from others, he or she will probably try to remain calm and collected, behaving as if there is no emergency. Everyone else, of course, is doing the very same thing, showing no outward sign of concern. The result is that each person is led by the others to think that the situation is really not an emergency after all, a psychological state called **pluralistic ignorance** (Miller & McFarland, 1987). What pluralistic ignorance amounts to is the belief on the part of the individual that only she or he is confused and doesn't know what to do in an emergency, while everyone else is standing around doing nothing for some good reason. The group is paralyzed, in a sense, and the phenomenon can be interpreted as a type of conformity—conformity to the inaction of others.

pluralistic ignorance *a condition in which the inaction of others leads each individual in a group to interpret a situation as a nonemergency, thus leading to general inactivity*

This process was demonstrated clearly in a classic experiment by Latané and Darley (1968, 1970). Columbia University students reported to a campus building to participate in an interview. They were sent to a waiting room and were asked to complete some preliminary forms. While they did so, white smoke began to billow through a vent in the wall. After six minutes (the point at which the procedure was terminated if the "emergency" had not been reported), there was enough smoke in the room to interfere with breathing and prevent seeing across the room.

When subjects were alone in the waiting room, 75 percent of them emerged to report the smoke. However, when two passive confederates were in the room with the subject, only 10 percent responded. Those people who reported the smoke did so quickly. Those from the groups who failed to do so generated all sorts of explanations for the smoke: steam, vapors from the air conditioner, smog introduced to simulate an urban environment, and even "truth gas." In short, the subjects who remained unresponsive had been led by the inaction of their peers to conclude just about anything other than the obvious—that something was wrong.

Diffusion of Responsibility. In the Kitty Genovese murder, it was terribly clear that an emergency was in progress; there was very little ambiguity about what was happening. Furthermore, the 38 witnesses were not in a face-to-face group that would allow social influence processes such as pluralistic ignorance to operate. Latané and Darley suggested that a third

diffusion of responsibility *the tendency to allow others to share in the obligation to intervene*

important process is necessary to complete the explanation of bystander behavior.

A single bystander in an emergency situation must bear the full responsibility for offering assistance, but the witness who is part of a group shares that responsibility with other onlookers. The greater the number of other people present, the smaller is each individual's perceived obligation to intervene, a process referred to as **diffusion of responsibility**.

Latané and Darley devised a clever demonstration of this phenomenon. In this study, college students arrived at a laboratory to take part in a group discussion of some of the personal problems they experienced as college students in an urban environment. To reduce the embarrassment of talking about such matters in public, each group member was isolated in his or her own cubicle and could communicate with the others through an intercom system. Actually there were no other group members, only tape-recorded voices. Thus, there was only one subject in each group, and the perceived size of the group could be easily manipulated to see whether diffusion of responsibility would occur.

The first person to speak mentioned that he was prone to seizures when under pressure, such as when studying for an exam. The others, including the actual subject, then took turns talking for about 10 minutes about their problems. A second round of discussion then began with the seizure-prone student who, shortly after he started talking, began to suffer one of his seizures.

Just as in the Genovese incident, it was obvious that something was wrong. As the "victim" began stammering, choking, and pleading for help, the typical subject became quite nervous—some trembled, some had sweaty palms. This study had another feature in common with the Genovese episode: Subjects could not be sure if any other bystanders (members of the group) had taken any action. (In fact, remember, there were no others.)

As expected, the likelihood of helping decreased as the perceived size of the group increased. Eighty-five percent of those in two-person groups (subject and victim) left the cubicle to report the emergency. When the subject thought that he or she was in a three-person group, 62 percent responded. Only 31 percent of the participants who believed that they were in a six-person group took any step to intervene. The responsibility for reporting the seizure was clearly divided (diffused) among those thought to be present.

Incidentally, diffusion of responsibility does come in forms that are less serious in their implications. Those of you with a few siblings can probably recall times at home when the telephone has rung five or six times before anyone has made a move to answer it, even though the entire family was there at the time. And some of you have probably been at parties where the doorbell went unanswered with everyone thinking that someone else would get it.

The Bystander Effect: A Conclusion

The situational determinants of helping behavior continued to be a popular research topic for social psychologists throughout the 1970s. Many of these studies included a manipulation of the size of the group witnessing the event that created the need for help in the first place. Latané and Nida (1981) reviewed some 50 studies involving nearly 100 different helping–not-helping situations. Although these experiments involved a wide range of settings, procedures, and participants, the social inhibition of help- ing (the bystander effect) occurred in *almost every instance*. Latané and Nida combined the data from all of these studies into a single statistical analysis (a meta-analysis of the sort introduced in Topic 1B). Their conclusion: There is very little doubt that a person is more likely to help when he or she is alone rather than in a group. In other words, the bystander effect is a remarkably consistent phenomenon, perhaps as predictable as any phe- nomenon in social psychology.

BEFORE YOU GO ON

What effect does the presence of others have on a person's willingness to help in an emergency?

How do audience inhibition, pluralistic ignorance, and diffusion of responsibility account for the lack of bystander intervention?

OTHER EXAMPLES OF SOCIAL INFLUENCE

We have just reviewed how being a part of a group can alter one's behavior. Since a great deal of our behavior occurs in groups, group influ- ence is an important topic in social psychology. In this section, we'll briefly survey a few additional examples of behavioral phenomena that occur in groups.

Social Impact Theory

Latané has gone on from his studies of bystander behavior to suggest that other social behaviors can be predicted from data about the size and nature of a group (Latané, 1981; Latané & Nida, 1980). In fact, this idea has become a major cornerstone of Latané's theory of social impact.

Latané has proposed a **psychosocial law** that seems to predict the extent to which group size influences the actions of people in that group. Fundamentally, this law specifies that each person added to a group has less impact on a target individual than the previous person to join the group. In terms of helping in an emergency, for example, this means that adding one other bystander besides yourself to the situation should decrease sig- nificantly your likelihood of responding. If, however, you are in a group of 49 bystanders, a fiftieth person would have little effect on the chances of your helping. This law can be usefully applied to almost all of the phenom- ena of social influence we have reviewed so far.

The data from a typical experiment in diffusion of responsibility also support this logic. An idealized graph of the relationship between group size and the likelihood of individual intervention is presented in Figure 14.9. For example, tipping in restaurants follows such a pattern. Freeman and his colleagues (1975) found that tipping declined systematically with

psychosocial law *the view that each per- son who joins a social situation adds less influence than did the previous person to join the group*

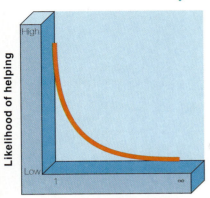

The psychosocial law applied to helping. This theoretical curve predicts the likelihood that someone will help in an emergency. As the number of fellow bystanders increases, the likelihood of helping behavior drops rapidly. (After Latané, 1981.)

social loafing *the tendency for a person to work less hard when part of a group in which everyone's efforts are pooled*

increases in the size of the dining party. On the average, people eating alone left about a 19 percent tip, while those dining in groups left only about 13 percent of the total check.

As you might guess, Latané's theory also takes into account factors beyond the mere size of the group. Your perception of the status of others in a group will influence your behaviors. Imagine, for example, that you are in an Asch-type conformity situation, asked to judge the length of lines. Might you not feel more pressure to state an incorrect judgment if everyone else in the group was in error, and everyone else in the group was an architect, or a draftsman who worked with lines all day long? Not only will the status of group members be likely to affect your behavior, but so will the immediacy of their influence. If you're standing in a group, watching a fire in a downtown office building, you're not likely to engage spontaneously in any other behavior as you stand at a distance, admiring the coordinated efforts of the fire fighters. But, what if a fireman came up to you and asked you to do something—help hold onto a hose, for example? Then, under that immediate pressure, particularly from a person of status, are you not likely to pitch in and help as best you can?

Social Loafing

In a similar vein, Latané, Williams, and Harkins (1979) have identified an effect they call **social loafing**, which refers to the tendency to work less (decrease one's individual effort) as the size of the group in which one is working becomes larger. Their studies had participants shout or clap as loud as possible, either in groups or alone. If individuals were led to believe that their performance could not be identified, they invested less and less effort in the task as group size increased. Other studies (e.g., Petty et al., 1977; Weldon & Gargano, 1988) have used more cognitive tasks, such as evaluating poetry. The results tend to be consistent: When people can hide in the crowd, their effort (and hence their productivity) declines. Notice that although social loafing is a widespread phenomenon, it is not always predicted when one works in a group setting. Social loafing can be virtually eliminated if group members believe that their effort is special and required for the group's success, or if group members believe that their performance can be identified and evaluated individually (Harkins, 1987; Harkins & Petty, 1982; Williams et al., 1981, 1989). Indeed, there are situations in which social influence actually facilitates behavior.

Social Facilitation

Many years ago, a psychologist by the name of Norman Triplett (1898) was struck by his observation that bicycle riders competing against other cyclists outperformed those racing against a clock. He then performed what is considered to be the first laboratory experiment in social psychology. Triplett had children wind a fishing reel as rapidly as possible. They engaged in this task either alone or with another child alongside doing the same thing. Just as he had noticed in his records of bicycle races, Triplett found that the children worked faster when another child was present. We now know that such an effect sometimes occurs not only with coactors (others engaged in the same task), but also if a person performs in front of an audience. When the presence of others improves an individual's performance on some task, we have evidence of what is called **social facilitation**.

Numerous studies of these phenomena were performed early in the twentieth century, but with a puzzling inconsistency in their results. Sometimes social facilitation would occur, but on other occasions, just the opposite would occur. Sometimes people actually performed more poorly in the presence of others than they did alone, an effect social psychologists call **social interference**. The inconsistency in these findings was so bewildering that psychologists for the most part eventually gave up investigating social facilitation.

In 1965, Robert Zajonc resurrected the topic of social facilitation by providing a plausible interpretation for the lack of consistency in social facilitation effects. In his examination of the research, Zajonc noticed that social facilitation occurred whenever the behavior under study was simple, routine, or very well learned (such as bicycle riding or winding a fishing reel). Social interference, on the other hand, tended to occur whenever the behavior involved was complex or not well practiced. Zajonc suggested that the presence of others creates increased *arousal*, which in turn energizes the dominant (most likely) response under the circumstances. When the dominant response is correct, as with a simple, well-practiced task, facilitation occurs. When the dominant response is incorrect, as with a complex task or one with which we have had little practice, the result is interference.

You may have experienced this effect yourself if you have ever tried to acquire a skill at a sport that is totally new to you. Whereas skilled athletes tend to perform better in front of audiences, the novice tends to do better

social facilitation *improved performance due to the presence of others*

social interference *impaired performance due to the presence of others*

Because of social facilitation, we perform better when we are in the presence of others. Bicycle racers ride faster when racing against other riders than when racing against the clock.

when alone. (There is evidence that skilled athletes don't always perform better in front of audiences, sometimes "choking" in front of home crowds during important games (Baumeister, 1985).) You may have experienced (as a novice, that is) the frustration of finding it difficult even to hit a golf ball or tennis ball when there are others standing nearby watching you.

As an overall conclusion, we may safely assume that social interference and social loafing are more common phenomena than is social facilitation. Although there are occasions in which co-workers or an audience may enhance the individual's performance, the presence of others is more likely to inhibit it.

BEFORE YOU GO ON

What can we conclude concerning the effects of social influence on the quality of an individual's performance?

Decision Making in Groups

Many of the decisions that we face in our daily lives are the sort that must be made in groups. Committees, boards, family groups, and group projects for a class are only a few of many possible examples. There is logic in the belief that group efforts to solve problems should be superior to the efforts of individuals. One might reason that problem solving ought to be more effective in a group because individuals can pool resources. Having more people available should necessarily mean having more talent and knowledge available. It also seems logical that the cohesiveness of the group might contribute to a more productive effort (and for some groups and some problems, this is exactly the case). But by now we know better than to assume that simply because a conclusion is logical it is necessarily true. In this section, we'll look briefly at two curious phenomena that can occur in the process of group decision making.

When he was an MIT graduate student in industrial management, James Stoner gave subjects in his research a series of dilemmas to grapple with (Stoner, 1961). The result of each decision was to be a statement of how much risk the fictitious character in the dilemma should take. Much to his surprise, Stoner found that the decisions rendered by groups generally were much riskier than those that the individual group members had made prior to the group decision. Stoner called this move away from conservative solutions a *risky shift*. For example, a number of doctors, if they were asked individually, might express the opinion that a patient's present problem (whatever it might be) could be handled with medication and a change in diet. If these very same doctors were to get together to discuss the patient's situation, they might very well end up concluding that what was called for here was a new and potentially dangerous (risky) surgical procedure.

Several hundred studies later, we now know that this effect can occur in the opposite direction as well (Levine & Moreland, 1990; Moscovici et al., 1985). In other words, the risky shift is simply a specific case of a more general **group polarization** phenomenon. The process of group discussion

Many of the decisions we face daily are the sort that are best made in groups, whether committees, boards, or family groups.

group polarization *the tendency for members of a group to give more extreme judgments following a discussion than they gave initially* usually leads to an enhancement of the beliefs and attitudes of the group members that existed before the discussion began. The group process tends to push members further in the direction in which they leaned initially. One explanation for group polarization suggests that open discussion gives group members an opportunity to hear persuasive arguments they have not previously considered, leading to a strengthening of their original attitudes (Isenberg, 1986). Another possibility is that after comparing attitudinal positions with one another, some group members feel pressure to catch up with other group members who have more extreme attitudes (Hinsz & Davis, 1984).

Irving Janis (1972, 1983) has described a related phenomenon of social influence he calls **groupthink**, an excessive concern for reaching a consensus in group decision making to the extent that critical evaluations of input are withheld. Janis maintains that this style of thinking emerges when group members are so interested in maintaining harmony within the group that differences of opinion are suppressed. Groupthink is especially likely to occur in cohesive groups. Alternative courses of action are not considered realistically, and the frequent result is a poor decision. Janis has analyzed several key historical events, including the Pearl Harbor and the Bay of Pigs invasions and the escalation of the Vietnam War, in terms of the operation of groupthink. Janis argues that each of these situations involved a cohesive decision-making group that was relatively isolated from outside judgments, a directive leader who supplied pressure to conform to his position, and an illusion of unanimity.

Before you conclude that decision making in a group or social situation always leads to negative consequences, let me point out that there are circumstances in which groups *are* more efficient than individuals working alone. As we implied above, groups are useful when problems are complex and require skills and abilities that are more likely to be found in a number of different individuals working together. Group decision making can also serve to identify errors that individuals might not identify.

groupthink *a style of thinking of cohesive groups concerned with maintaining agreement to the extent that independent ideas are discouraged*

BEFORE YOU GO ON

How does social influence affect decision making in groups?

We are social animals. Our behaviors as well as our feelings and cognitions are often influenced by those around us in our social environments. In this topic, we have discussed some of the results of group influence, and many of them have been unfavorable, leading people to avoid helping someone else in need, to exert less effort, to perform poorly, to think inefficiently, or to act aggressively. At the same time, groups are a major part of social life, and some goals simply cannot be reached alone, without group membership. It is important to realize that effective group performance can be fostered by good morale, healthy communication, sound leadership, and teamwork that is accomplished through the appropriate division of responsibility. Hopefully, an awareness of the possible negative consequences of group activity and the conditions that produce them will enable us to counter obstacles to group productivity and satisfaction.

SUMMARY

Briefly describe the methodology and the basic findings of the Sherif and Asch conformity studies.

Sherif used the autokinetic effect (an ambiguous situation) to explore the emergence of norms (expectations of how one ought to behave) in groups. Over several days of judging how far a light moved, subjects adjusted their own estimates in the direction of estimates made by others. In the Asch studies, people made simple judgments about unambiguous perceptual stimuli: the length of lines. On some trials, confederates gave clearly incorrect judgments before the actual subject had a chance to respond. Although there were situations in which yielding to perceived group pressure could be lessened, many of Asch's subjects followed suit and conformed. / page 664

Briefly describe Stanley Milgram's experimental demonstrations of obedience.

Subjects in Milgram's experiments were led to believe that they were administering more and more potent shocks to another subject in a learning task. Whenever they hesitated to deliver shocks, an authority figure, the experimenter, prodded them to continue. All subjects obeyed to some degree, and nearly two-thirds delivered what they thought was the most intense shock, even over the

protests of the learner. The individuals who obeyed in Milgram's experiments were neither cruel nor inhumane. Rather, the experimenter created a powerful social situation that made it very difficult to refuse the authority figure's orders. / page 667

What effect does the presence of others have on a person's willingness to help in an emergency? How do audience inhibition, pluralistic ignorance, and diffusion of responsibility account for the lack of bystander intervention?

Research data tell us that the likelihood that someone will intervene on behalf of another in an emergency situation is lessened as a function of how many others (bystanders) are present at the time. A number of factors have been proposed to account for this phenomenon. *Audience inhibition* is the term used to describe the hesitancy to intervene in front of others, perhaps for fear of embarrassing oneself. *Pluralistic ignorance* occurs when other bystanders lead one to think (by their inactivity) that nothing is really wrong in an ambiguous emergency situation. *Diffusion of responsibility* causes a member of a group to feel less obligated to intervene (less responsible) than if he or she were alone. Each of these processes tends to discourage helping and is more likely to operate as the number of persons present increases. / page 671

What can we conclude concerning the effects of social influence on the quality of an individual's performance?

The data suggest that as group size increases, social loafing increases. That is, one is less likely to invest full effort and energy in the task at hand as a member of a group than he or she would if working alone. It is also the case that the quality of one's performance tends to suffer when one works in a group, a phenomenon called social interference. On the other hand, when tasks are simple or well rehearsed, performance may be enhanced, a process called social facilitation. / page 674

How does social influence affect decision making in groups?

There are some advantages to problem solving in a group setting. With proper leadership and communication, the combined expertise present in a group may provide better solutions and provide a better check on errors than we might find if individuals worked independently. On the other hand, *group polarization*, the tendency of group discussion to solidify and enhance preexisting attitudes, and *groupthink*, the unwillingness to promote an unpopular view in front of others in a group, operate to detract from group decision making. / page 675

CHAPTER

15

APPLIED PSYCHOLOGY

TOPIC 15A Industrial-Organizational Psychology

TOPIC 15B Health, Environmental, and Sport Psychology

TOPIC

15A

Industrial-Organizational Psychology

Why We Care: A Topic Preview

FITTING THE PERSON TO THE JOB
Defining "Good Work"—The Job Analysis
Selecting People Who Can Do Good Work
    Application Forms
    Interviews
    Psychological Tests
    Assessment Centers
Training People to Do Good Work
    Assessing Training Needs
    Specific Training Techniques
    Measuring Training Effectiveness
Motivating People to Do Good Work
    Values and Expectations
    Fair Rewards
    Goal Setting

FITTING THE JOB TO THE PERSON
Job Satisfaction
Job Satisfaction and Work Behaviors
Worker Safety

SUMMARY

Why We Care: A Topic Preview

We have noted repeatedly throughout this text that psychology has many practical applications in everyday life. Indeed, this is one of the major themes introduced back in Topic 1A. The principles of psychology can be brought to bear on many of the problems we face from day to day, and this is why we care. In this chapter, we will focus even more directly on the application of psychological principles to real-world events and issues.

We begin with a brief examination of industrial-organizational (I/O) psychology. Industrial-organizational psychologists specialize in the study of affect, behavior, and cognition in work settings. Often, psychologists in this field are concerned with applying psychological principles in order to improve the effectiveness and efficiency of business and/or industrial organizations. That does not mean, of course, that I/O psychologists are "company people," concerned only with the best interests of management. The I/O psychologist cares about the workplace in general, and that includes a consideration of workers' needs as well as management's needs.

Industrial-organizational psychology is one of the fastest growing of psychology's specialty areas. More than 2500 members of the American Psychological Association belong to its Division for Industrial and Organizational Psychology (Zedeck, 1987). We will examine two of the major thrusts of I/O psychology. First, we'll discuss how best to fit the right person to a given job. This will entail a brief discussion of what we mean by "doing a good job," followed by a consideration of how we can select, train, and/or motivate an individual to do that job well. Then, we'll examine how best to fit the job to the person, which will involve examining such matters as the quality of work life, job satisfaction, and safety in the workplace. Each of the issues raised here is relevant and meaningful to anyone who has ever entered the world of work.

FITTING THE PERSON TO THE JOB

It is generally to everyone's advantage to have the best available person assigned to any particular job. Employers benefit from having workers who are well qualified and well motivated to do their work. Employees also benefit from being assigned tasks that they enjoy and that are within the scope of their talents and abilities. When I was a college student, a summer job required that I fill in for another employee and drive a large truck loaded with milk from a dairy in upstate New York to various locations in New York City. That I ever got that milk delivered had more to do with good luck and youthful enthusiasm than anything else. It no doubt took me twice as long as the regular driver to make the deliveries, and, to say the least, I did not enjoy spending most of a summer's day being lost in New York City with a truck filled with milk. I was clearly not the best worker for the task.

What is involved in getting the best person to do a job? The relevant issues from the perspective of the I/O psychologist are personnel selection, training, and motivation. That is, one way to get a person to do good work is to *select* and hire a person who already has the ability and the motivation to do that work. On the other hand, we may choose to *train* people to do good work. We may also have to face the task of *motivating* people with ability to do good work. These are the processes we examine in this section. However, before we can begin selecting, training, or motivating someone for a job, we need to understand the nature of the job itself. We have to define what we mean by "a good job" before we can fit a person to it.

Defining "Good Work"—The Job Analysis

Assume that you are an industrial-organizational psychologist hired by a company to help select a manager for one of its retail stores in a local shopping center. You could not begin to tell your employers what sort of person they were looking for until you had a full description of the job this new manager was to do. In general terms, you would have to know the duties and responsibilities of a store manager in this company. Then, you could translate that job description into a set of measurable characteristics that a successful store manager should possess. In other words, you would begin your selection efforts by doing a **job analysis**, "the systematic study of the tasks, duties, and responsibilities of a job and the knowledge, skills, and abilities needed to perform it" (Riggio, 1990, p. 59).

job analysis *a complete and specific description of a job, including the qualities required to do it well*

Typically, writing a complete job analysis is a two-step process. The first step involves compiling a complete description of what a person in that job is expected to do. There are many sources of information that one might use to generate such a description. Most companies have job descriptions for their employees, but these are usually stated in very general terms, such as "supervise workers in the store; maintain acceptable levels of sales; prepare payrolls; monitor inventory; schedule work loads," and the like.

To be useful, a job analysis must be more specific in describing the actual *behaviors* engaged in by someone in a given position. Does a store manager have to know how to operate the cash register and inventory control devices? Does the manager deal with the sales staff on a one-to-one basis or in groups? Are interactions with employees informal and random, or are there regularly scheduled, formal meetings that need to be organized?

One of the most important roles of the industrial-organizational psychologists is to help employers make the best possible personnel selections. The first step is doing a job analysis to get a complete description of a job and the personal qualities required to do it well.

To what extent is the store manager responsible for employee training and development? Will he or she be involved in labor negotiations? Clearly this list of questions can be a long one. The underlying concern at this level of analysis is, "On a daily basis, just what does a store manager do?"

Valuable information can be gained through careful observation. It is always advisable for the job analyst to spend some time watching a person actually performing the job being analyzed. In addition, one can get a good deal of information from questionnaires and interviews with other store managers or with supervisors of store managers. There are many standardized instruments (such as surveys) available to help at this level of analysis.

Once duties and responsibilities have been specified, the second step requires that these be translated into terms of measurable personal characteristics. That is, one determines the **performance criteria** required to do a job well. The goal is to generate a list of characteristics that a person in a given position should have in order to do that job as well as possible.

A number of different areas might be explored at this point. P. C. Smith (1976), for example, distinguishes between what she calls "hard" criteria and "soft" criteria. These criteria are commonly referred to as "objective" and "subjective," respectively. The former come from available data and are objective: salary, number of units sold, number of days absent, and the like. Soft criteria require some degree of subjective judgment: sense of humor, congeniality, creativity, and so on. Let's use an academic example. Suppose your psychology department wants to give an award to its "outstanding senior." Some of the criteria that determine which student has done a good job and is worthy of the award may be hard—senior standing, a certain grade point average, a minimum number of psychology classes, and so on. But other criteria may be subjective, or "soft." The department

performance criteria *specific behaviors or characteristics that a person should have in order to do a job as well as possible*

may want to give this award to a student only if he or she is well known to many members of the faculty, has impressive communication skills, or has been active in the Psychology Club. These criteria require the judgment of those making the award. Indeed, most job analyses involve consideration of both hard, objective and soft, subjective criteria.

Remember that the basic task here is to find the best available person to do a job as well as possible. If we are not fully aware of the demands of a job and have not translated those demands into specific performance criteria, we'll have difficulty determining if we have found the right person. In other words, we need to build in procedures early on by which our selection, training, or motivation program can be evaluated (Dunnette & Borman, 1979). Once a job analysis has been completed—once we know what an applicant will be expected to do on the job *and* once we have translated those tasks into measurable criteria—we are ready to begin designing an assessment process.

BEFORE YOU GO ON

What is involved in doing a job analysis?

Selecting People Who Can Do Good Work

As you can imagine, a wide variety of techniques and sources of information are available to the employer for screening and evaluating applicants for any given position. Personnel selection not only involves devising procedures to help one decide which of many applicants to hire, but it also involves decisions relating to retention, promotion, and termination (Guion & Gibson, 1988). If the job analysis has been done properly, the I/O psychologist has a complete list of those duties and characteristics in which the employer is interested. The task now is to find the person who has those characteristics. In this section, we'll briefly examine some specific selection techniques.

Application Forms. Some useful information can be gleaned from a well-constructed *job application form*. An application form can serve three useful functions. (1) It can be used as a rough screening device. Some applicants may be denied simply because they do not meet some basic requirement for the job, such as a minimal educational level or specified job experience. (2) It can supplement and/or provide cues for interviewing. Bits of data from application forms can be pursued later during in-depth interviews. (3) It provides biographical data (called *biodata*), including educational and work history, that may be useful in making direct predictions about a candidate's potential for success. Some I/O psychologists list biographical information of the sort that can be uncovered on job application forms as the best source of data for predicting success on the job (Baley, 1985; Drakeley, Herriot, & Jones, 1988; Muchinsky, 1987; Reilly & Chao, 1982).

Interviews. An integral part of many personnel selection procedures is the *employment interview*. We have already commented (Topic 10B) on the dangers of relying too heavily on information gained through interviews. Unstructured interviews in particular are subject to error. Nonetheless, the interview is the most widely used employee selection procedure in the United States (Arvey & Campion, 1982; Thayer, 1983). This is true in spite of the fact that results of validity studies for interviews are "dismal" and that "despite various innovations over the years, [the interview] has never been consistently shown to improve selection" (Tenopyr, 1981, p. 1123). For one thing, interviews, by their very nature, involve the interaction of two people: the interviewer and the person being interviewed. As a result, the biases of the interviewer, conscious or unconscious, may influence the results of an interview (Cash & Kilcullen, 1985).

There is evidence of considerable individual differences in interviewer skill. That is, some interviewers consistently obtain more useful (or valid) information than do others (e.g., Thayer 1983; Zedeck et al., 1983). Training interviewers to be sensitive to personal biases can improve the validity of the technique, but such training is expensive. According to Cronbach, "In employment practice, interviews have several functions and will continue to be used. The best general advice is to make sure that interviewer judgments are not given excessive weight in selection" (1984, p. 406).

Within the last few years, the outlook for the use of the interview has become a bit more positive and optimistic. In large measure, this is because of the increased use of the structured interview. As the name implies, structured interviews consist of a carefully prescribed series of questions that is asked of all applicants in the same order. Structured interviews may take away some of the interviewer's latitude and freedom to explore different issues, but they are demonstrably more valid than are unstructured interviews (Arvey et al., 1987; Schmitt & Robertson, 1990; Wiesner & Cronshaw, 1988).

Psychological Tests. Beyond the application form and the interview, personnel selection often involves the administration and interpretation of *psychological tests* (see Topic 8A). Many tests are designed to assess only one specific characteristic of the applicant (finger dexterity, for example, which a job analysis may indicate to be very relevant for an assembly line worker in an electronics plant). Other tests are more general, assessing a number of different skills and abilities. Tests of intelligence and/or certain personality characteristics may be called for, particularly when evaluating candidates for managerial or supervisory positions. There are literally hundreds of published paper-and-pencil tests designed to measure a variety of characteristics, from typing skills, to mechanical aptitude, to leadership style, to motivation for sales work, to critical thinking skills. Some popular tests of general traits or abilities are being modified to focus more sharply on work-related applications (e.g., Gough, 1985). In general, the data suggest that the most useful of all psychological tests are those that assess some sort of cognitive function, such as ability or achievement tests (Guion & Gibson, 1988). An I/O psychologist involved in personnel decisions will know about these tests and recommend specific instruments for specific selection tasks.

From time to time, it is necessary to construct one's own test to assess some unique or special ability not measured by available instruments. A form of testing found in employment settings is called *situational testing*, in which applicants are given the opportunity to role-play the task they may be hired to do (e.g., Weekley & Gier, 1987). If you were going to hire someone to work at the counter of your dry cleaning business, for instance, you might ask an applicant how he or she would respond to an irate customer whose suit was damaged in cleaning. Actually role-playing the part of an angry customer while the applicant plays the part of employee might provide very useful information.

A very important consideration when using psychological tests for personnel decisions is the demonstrated validity of such tests. You'll recall from our earlier discussion of testing (Topic 8A, pp. 350–352) that there are several types of validity. What is particularly crucial in employee testing is that the employer be able to demonstrate that performance on a test used for selection is actually related to performance on the job.

assessment center *a personnel selection procedure in which persons are tested, interviewed, and observed in a number of stressful situations by a team of evaluators*

Assessment Centers. Some large corporations use what is called an **assessment center** approach to select management personnel (both for initial hiring and promotion decisions). This approach gives evaluators opportunities to observe applicants in various social situations and under stress. The assessment center was first introduced during World War II as a device for selecting candidates for the Office of Strategic Services, now known as the CIA. The first nongovernmental application was by AT&T in the mid-1950s, but it wasn't until the 1960s that this approach was widely used for selecting and promoting executives in business and industry (Bray et al., 1974).

The assessment center involves an intensive period of evaluation, usually lasting three or four days. A number of applicants (usually 6 to 12) are brought together with executives of the company and a team of psychologists. In addition to batteries of standard paper-and-pencil tests and interviews, the applicants are given situational tests in which their behaviors in situations similar to those they might encounter on the job can be observed. One assessment center method is called the **in-basket technique**. Here, applicants are provided with a variety of tasks, memos, and assignments of the sort they might encounter in a typical day at the office (as previously determined through a job analysis). They can then be observed as they attempt to sort out and deal with the imaginary issues they find in the in-basket.

in-basket technique *an assessment technique requiring applicants to respond to a variety of situations that might be encountered in a typical workday*

Assessment centers are now very popular, and their usefulness is virtually taken for granted (Gaugler et al., 1987; Hinrichs, 1976; Saal & Knight, 1988). On the other hand, while the technique can be useful for predicting such general outcomes as who gets promoted or who gets larger salaries, it is not very useful in making specific predictions with regard to specific behaviors (e.g., Hunter & Hunter, 1984; Zedeck & Cascio, 1984). "The research question seems not to be whether to use assessment centers but how to understand what goes on in them, how to evaluate the results, and how to make them better" (Guion & Gibson, 1988).

It may not always be practical or possible to find people who have the abilities and motivation for doing the kind of work we are looking for. It may be that major personnel issues facing an organization involve training and motivating existing workers to do good (or better) work. Let's first look at training.

*What are some of the sources of information
that can be used in making personnel decisions?*

*What is the rationale for using assessment centers
in selecting and promoting employees?*

Training People to Do Good Work

The training of employees is one of the major concerns of business, industry, and government. The cost of such training runs into billions of dollars every year. Training or retraining present employees will become even more critical in the years ahead as the number of people entering the work force decreases (Offermann & Gowing, 1990).

In the context of industrial/organizational psychology, **training** is taken to mean "a systematic intentional process of altering behavior of organizational members in a direction which contributes to organizational effectiveness" (Hinrichs, 1976). This definition implies that training is an activity intended to increase the skills or abilities of employees to do their job. Training implies a systematic intervention, as opposed to a hit-or-miss approach to instruction.

New York University psychologists Raymond Katzell and Richard Guzzo (1983) reviewed more than 200 research studies that dealt with approaches to improving productivity and concluded, "Training and instruction activities represent the most frequently reported approach to productivity improvement during 1971–1981" (p. 469). Typically, training programs have been found to be successful in a variety of organizational settings, with various types of personnel, and as indicated by a number of productivity criteria, including quantity and quality of work, cost reduction, turnover, accident reduction, and absenteeism (Katzell & Guzzo, 1983).

Developing a successful training program is a complex, multifaceted enterprise. Let's review some of the steps involved in designing and implementing a training program. Our discussion is based on the system proposed by Goldstein (1980, 1986) and is summarized in Figure 15.1. You might want to follow along in this diagram of the major aspects of designing a training program.

Assessing Training Needs. Training programs usually are designed to address some need within the organization. So, one of the first things you will have to do is a complete assessment of instructional needs. In many ways, a needs assessment in this context is very much like a job analysis in personnel selection. A number of questions must be raised and answered at this critical stage. Just what is the problem that training is supposed to solve? Is production down? Is there a new product that salespeople need to know about? Is the accident rate getting too high? The first stage of assessing instructional needs will be to state the general goals of your training program. At this point, a very difficult question to face is

The interview remains an integral part of the employees selection process, though studies reveal that biases on the part of the interviewer may influence the results.

training *a systematic and intentional process of altering the behaviors of employees to increase organizational effectiveness*

Retraining employees to learn new skills and procedures will help keep worker motivation high and will also help industries stay abreast of new technologies.

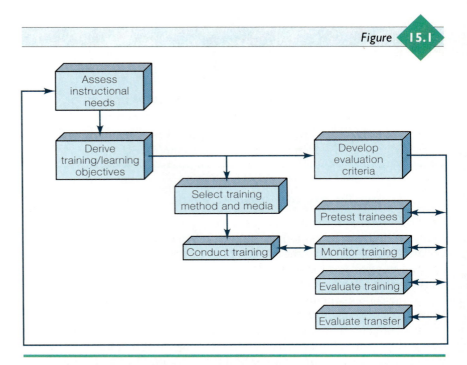

Figure 15.1

A flowchart of the steps involved in planning and conducting a training program. (After Goldstein, 1986.)

whether or not a training program is the best solution for a given problem. In fact, the most crucial decision to be made about training is if it is really needed (Latham, 1988).

The second step requires translating these general goals into actual training objectives. At this stage, general statements of outcomes will no longer suffice. Now you need *specific* statements of what you expect the training program to accomplish. Just precisely what do you want trainees to know (or be able to do) at the end of the training session that they do not know (or do not do) now? Your training program usually will be evaluated in terms of these specific learning or behavioral objectives.

With your objectives in mind, but before you begin actual training, you will want to specify criteria by which your training can be evaluated when it is over. Clearly, your criteria for evaluating your program will be closely related to the needs and objectives of the program. For your program evaluation to be effective, it is important to list now—before training begins—how you will evaluate outcomes (Latham, 1988). There are many factors you might want to consider here. Did the trainees develop the skills and acquire the information you intended? How did the trainees feel about the program? Did the training program have an impact on the organizational needs that prompted the training in the first place? To aid in this process, you might want to consider designing a pretest procedure to assess your trainees in terms of their present skill or information level. Such pretesting may provide a means of determining the impact of your program.

In this context I also can mention that training objectives or outcomes need to be evaluated repeatedly. The evaluation of training programs is commonly an ongoing process. What are the immediate effects of training, if any? Is the training still having the desired impact a month later? Has the training been responsible for any year-end increases in profits? In short, a training-program evaluation should not be thought of as a one-shot intervention.

Specific Training Techniques. After you have determined the criteria for assessing outcomes, you now have to decide how you will go about the actual training. Given what you know about your needs and objectives and what you know about your employees, what will be the most efficient type of training mechanism you can use to reach your specified goals?

There are many different methods that might be used in a training program. In some cases, bringing workers together for what amounts to classroom instruction works well. On the other hand, there are situations in which assembling large numbers of workers would be unrealistic. Automobile manufacturers, for example, can hardly be expected to have all car salespeople report to the home office for instruction on improvements in the new models of cars they will be selling. Occasionally, training has to go to the worker—in the form of printed material, audiocassettes, videotaped programs, or live presentations by a trainer—rather than having the worker go to the training.

In any case, as designer of a training program, you will have many decisions to make about the methods you will use in your program. Should you use "live" instructors, or should information be presented in the form of some media: print, audiotapes, videotapes, videodisks, and the like? Should training be formalized and time-limited, or can trainees be allowed to work individually, at their own pace? Will there need to be hands-on experience? Will training be in groups, or will it be individually oriented? Will on-the-job training be efficient or disruptive? Can the job be simply simulated for the purposes of training (called *vestibule training*)? As you can

Motivation to do quality work can reach creative proportions as in this television assembly plant. Here, signs of encouragement were posted by workers themselves.

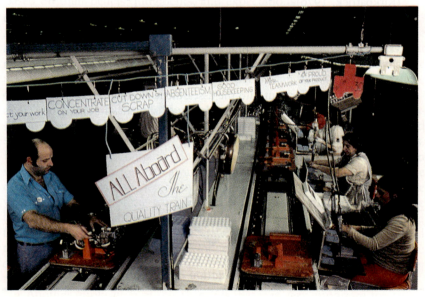

expect will happen if they behave in a certain way. Which behaviors lead to positive outcomes, and which lead to negative outcomes? Why should an employee work very hard, put in overtime, and take work home on the weekend if he or she has little or no reason to believe that such behaviors will lead to valued rewards? Indeed, one reality is that fewer than one-third of workers believe that their compensation is based on their work performance (Plawin & Suied, 1988). You may recognize these issues as being directly related to our earlier discussion of basic learning principles (particularly those in Topic 5B, which covered operant conditioning).

equity theory *the view that workers are motivated to match their inputs and outcomes with those of fellow workers in similar positions*

Fair Rewards. Another approach to work motivation that has received support is called **equity theory**, and it is associated with J. Stacy Adams (1965). Equity theory is also cognitive in nature, claiming that what matters most to workers is their perception of the extent to which they are being treated fairly compared to fellow workers in similar work situations.

In Adams's view, workers make a number of social comparisons (or cognitive judgments). First, they judge how much they are getting from the organization compared to what they are putting into it. That is, the worker judges the extent to which effort, skill, education, experience, and so on (inputs) are being rewarded by salary, fringe benefits, praise, awards, and the like (outcomes). Then, this ratio of inputs and outcomes is compared with a ratio from some other, similarly placed employee. If the relationship is perceived as being approximately the same, or equitable, the worker will not be motivated to change. If, however, there is a perceived inequity when compared to the inputs and outcomes of a fellow worker, then changes can be predicted. The worker may increase or decrease inputs (work longer or shorter hours; take fewer or more breaks) or try to effect a change in outcomes. Notice that what matters most here is not the absolute value of what a worker gains for his or her efforts. What matters is the *perception* of equity—what he or she gains in comparison to others. (Remember our theme from Topic 1A: Things are not always as they seem?) A worker will be much more willing to maintain effort (input) and take a cut in pay (outcome) if that worker believes that everyone else in the company is taking a similar cut in pay (Locke, 1976; Middlemist & Peterson, 1976; Mowday, 1983).

Goal Setting. Attention to establishing goals has been the centerpiece of a number of approaches to worker motivation, particularly that of Edwin Locke (1968; Locke & Latham, 1984). This approach, too, has a cognitive basis, assuming that workers are best motivated to perform a task for which goals are clearly and specifically detailed. In order for goal setting to have a positive influence on a worker's behavior on a task, two things are necessary. First, the goal must be clear. The employee must be clearly *aware* of just what he or she is working for. Second, the employee must *accept* the goal as something worth the effort.

The mechanisms of goal setting in motivating workers have received considerable research interest. Here are some general conclusions. (1) Difficult but achievable goals tend to increase productivity more than easy goals. The issue here seems to hinge on the acceptance of goals as being worthwhile. Goals that are too easy to reach may simply fail to require any change in performance. At the same time, goals that are perceived as being *too* difficult and beyond the abilities of workers are not likely to be very useful (Erez & Zidon, 1984). (2) Specific goals are better than general ones. Simply telling workers to "do better" or "do your best" provides little information about what behaviors are expected. (3) Feedback that informs workers of their progress toward established goals is important in maintaining motivated behaviors. Feedback delivered soon after an appropriate response is made is more effective than delayed feedback (e.g., Geller, Bruff, & Nimmer, 1985; Geller et al., 1987). (4) Although it may seem reasonable to predict that goals set by employers and employees working together are more effective than goals established by employers alone, the evidence suggests that this is not necessarily the case. Again, what matters most is that the employee be aware of specific goals and accept those goals as reasonable (Locke et al., 1981).

As you can well imagine, there are many other approaches to work motivation. Some refer directly to motivational concepts we introduced back in Topic 11A when we discussed motivation in general. That is, some approaches stress the importance of workers' needs (as in Maslow's theory about a hierarchy from basic physiological needs to needs to self-actualize). Some approaches stress the importance of principles of behavior change through operant conditioning procedures and attention to the consequences of behavior, reinforcers, and punishers (an approach called organizational behavior management when applied in work environments).

Here's a brief summary of our discussion. Workers will tend to be well motivated to do a good job if:

1. Clear and specific goals are established and accepted.
2. The goals that employers set match workers' expectations and needs.
3. Workers see clearly the relationship between their work performance and accepted outcomes.
4. Workers judge the outcomes that follow from their efforts as being in line with those earned by fellow workers making similar efforts.
5. Workers are given feedback about the nature of their work. (Katzell & Thompson, 1990)

Now let's shift our emphasis slightly from a concern about finding and fitting the person to the job to the issue of fitting the job to the person. In large measure, our interest here is with what we call job satisfaction. What can be done to make jobs more satisfying? What is the result of doing so?

BEFORE YOU GO ON

Briefly summarize some of the factors
that affect the motivation of workers to do a good job.

FITTING THE JOB TO THE PERSON

To this point, we have considered what an employer can do to find the best person for a given task. For the remainder of this topic, we'll change our perspective just a bit and focus on some of the issues that are relevant to the person on the job in the workplace. There are two major issues here. The first has to do with job satisfaction. We'll define the concept, and then we'll see if job satisfaction is correlated with job performance measures. The second issue has to do with the design of work and the workplace. How can jobs be designed to maximize such factors as employee safety and health?

Job Satisfaction

job satisfaction *an attitude; a collection of positive feelings about one's job or job experiences*

Job satisfaction refers to the attitude that one holds toward one's work: "a pleasurable or positive emotional state resulting from the appraisal of one's job or job experiences" (Locke, 1976). Although we may talk about job satisfaction in general terms (what Riggio (1990) calls a "global approach"), it is clear that an employee's degree of satisfaction can vary considerably for different aspects of the job itself (a "facet approach"). As you know from your own work experience, you might be reasonably happy with your physical working conditions, very unhappy with base salary, pleased with your fringe benefits, satisfied with the level of challenge provided by the job, very dissatisfied with relationships with co-workers, and so on. In fact, there may be as many facets of job satisfaction and/or dissatisfaction as there are aspects to the job.

A great deal of research has looked for relationships between job satisfaction and personal characteristics of workers. Let's summarize some of that research very briefly. (1) There is a positive correlation between overall satisfaction and age. Younger workers tend to be most dissatisfied with their jobs (Rhodes, 1983). (2) Data on sex differences in job satisfaction tend to be inconsistent. By and large, however, sex differences are quite small (Sauser & York, 1978) and virtually nonexistent when pay, tenure, and education are controlled (Hulin & Smith, 1964). (3) Racial differences in job satisfaction consistently have been shown to be small, with whites having more positive attitudes about their jobs than nonwhites (Weaver, 1980). (4) Satisfaction is positively related to the perceived level or status of one's job or occupation, where those of lowest rank tend to be filled by least satisfied workers (King et al., 1982). Of course, the real issue here for I/O psychologists is to determine *why* or *why not* these differences in job satisfaction occur. All we have listed here are results of correlational studies and we need to keep in mind that correlational studies tell us nothing about cause and effect.

Although it seems logical that job satisfaction should be a predictor of productivity, the relationship between quality of work life and job productivity is tenuous at best.

quality of work life (QWL) *a group of factors concerning one's work that influence one's attitude toward one's job*

Recently, I/O psychologists have become interested in a concept somewhat broader than job satisfaction called **quality of work life**, or **QWL**. QWL is a difficult concept to define concisely, but may be taken to include such factors as (1) a sense of respect from supervisors; (2) employee security (the future of the job); (3) income adequacy and equity (present and future); (4) a sense of self-esteem, challenge, and independence; (5) opportunities for social interaction; (6) a sense of making a real contribution; (7) a relationship between life on the job and life off the job; and (8) active participation in decision making (from Davis & Cherns, 1975; Levine, Taylor, & Davis, 1984; Stein, 1983). The major concern of I/O psychology in this area has been to develop strategies to improve the quality of work life within an organization (Beer & Walton, 1987; Lawler, 1982; Tuttle, 1983).

It is sometimes difficult to remember that concerns about the welfare of workers, much less their satisfaction with any part of their job, is relatively new in the history of work. Concern for the quality of work life first began to take hold only about 55 years ago (Hoppock, 1935; Mayo, 1933). Before then, workers were often viewed by the organizations that hired them not so much as people, but as pieces of machinery—chosen, hired, and minimally trained to do a particular, often narrowly defined, task (Latham, 1988). The examples are numerous and often shameful—from assembly line work, to mining, to construction, to railroading, to textile mills, and on and on. As I mentioned earlier, until quite recently there has been little evidence of a concern for employee safety, much less a concern for the quality of work life. Many companies now employ industrial-organizational psychologists whose main charge is to recommend changes in organizational structure that will best facilitate worker satisfaction and improve the quality of work life. Is this recent emphasis on the well-being of workers motivated only by humane considerations? Or is there research support for the hypothesis that increased worker satisfaction leads to increased productivity and increased profitability?

BEFORE YOU GO ON

What are meant by job satisfaction and quality of work life?

Job Satisfaction and Work Behaviors

It may seem reasonable to assert that "the happy worker is a productive worker"—that increased job satisfaction necessarily will be reflected in increased worker productivity. For the last 50 years, many managers and executives have assumed, without question, a causal relationship between satisfaction and productivity. In many ways, satisfaction and productivity *may* be related, but the relationship is not a simple one and is at best a weak one (Iaffaldano & Muchinsky, 1985). In fact, research on job satisfaction often refutes the contention that increased performance *necessarily* results from increased satisfaction (Howell & Dipboye, 1982). Over and over, we find contradictory evidence, which among other things reflects the difficulties involved in agreeing on good operational definitions for both quality of work life and worker productivity (Hartman et al., 1986). The only conclusion we can safely draw about these two variables is that in some instances they may be correlated. Cause-and-effect statements are out of the question.

The lack of a strong, consistent relationship between satisfaction and productivity may not be that difficult to explain. Some workers may hate their present jobs, but work very hard at them so that they can be promoted to another position that they believe they will prefer. Some individuals may be very satisfied with their present positions simply because expectations for productivity are very low; if demands for productivity increase, satisfaction may decrease, at least in this situation. *Increasing productivity may have the effect of increasing satisfaction*, rather than vice versa. A well-motivated employee, who wants to do her very best at her job, will be pleased to enter a training program to improve her on-the-job efficiency. Doing the job better leads to pride and an overall increase in satisfaction for this worker; for another, the same training program may be viewed as a ploy on management's part to make his or her life miserable.

I shouldn't give the impression that job satisfaction is not consistently or meaningfully related to *any* work behavior. There is evidence that job satisfaction measures can be used to aid the prediction of which workers are likely to be absent from work and which are likely to quit (what Saal and Knight (1988) call "withdrawal behaviors"). As it happens, job satisfaction is not the best predictor of absenteeism—marital status, age, and size of one's work group are better (Watson, 1981)—but the correlations are at least reasonably consistent (Porter & Steers, 1973). The relationship between dissatisfaction with one's job and turnover seems to be even stronger, although the relationship may not be direct. That is, dissatisfaction may be an important contributing factor, but it is only one of a number of variables that can be used to explain why one leaves a job. (Many times people are forced to quit their jobs for reasons that have nothing to do with the job or the employer—illness and family concerns, for example.) Nonetheless, the logic that persons who are most unhappy with their work are the ones most likely to leave it does have research support (Mobley, 1977; Muchinsky & Tuttle, 1979).

BEFORE YOU GO ON

Briefly summarize the relationship between job satisfaction and job productivity.

Worker Safety

In this final section, we'll review one of the oldest concerns of industrial-organizational psychologists: safety in the workplace. The statistics on industrial accidents are impressive. One compelling example is provided by Schultz and Schultz (1986, p. 445), who claim that during the peak years of the Vietnam War (1966–1970), more Americans were killed in industrial accidents than in combat. Looked at from a different perspective, accidents in the workplace cost the United States well over $50 billion a year in lost wages, insurance and medical expenses, and property loss (DeReamer, 1980). The challenge is clear: Increase the safety of the workplace. But how? Here we list three approaches that I/O psychologists have explored (after Landy, 1989).

1. *The engineering approach:* This approach attempts to reduce accidents through the design and implementation of safe equipment and procedures. Of the three approaches, this one has been most successful in a wide range of applications. Examples abound. All automobiles now sold in this country

are required to have a (third) stop light positioned at eye level. This requirement evolved from a safety study done with taxicabs in San Francisco in a successful attempt to reduce rear-end collisions (Voevodsky, 1974). Complex control panels are engineered with safety in mind, so that the most critically important dials, meters, buttons, and switches are in clear view and easy to read and interpret. Work areas are designed so that there is adequate illumination and sufficient space to move about, and so that scrap materials and trash can be readily removed. Heavy equipment is designed so that it can only be operated in a reasonably safe way. (I once had a job using a large paper cutter that could easily cut through hundreds of sheets of paper with one thrust of a huge, very sharp blade. It took two hands to activate that blade; one moved a lever from right to left, while the other hand moved a second lever downward. There was no way that I could lower the blade through a stack of paper and cut my finger at the same time.)

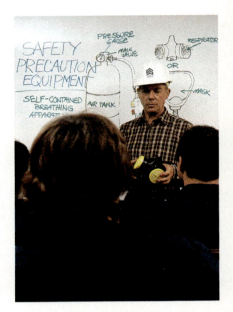

Engineering approaches to accident prevention may involve the scheduling of work time as well as the design of machinery and equipment. There is ample evidence of a positive relationship between fatigue and accidents. Scheduling work time (reducing overtime work, for example) to minimize fatigue seems to improve safety (Dunham, 1979).

2. *The personnel approach:* This approach is based on the popular notion that some people are more "accident prone" than others, or that at least there are some personality traits that are consistently related to high incidences of accidents. If this were true, then safety could be improved by not hiring those applicants who are prone to accidents. The problem is that the basic notion is not true. After many years of trying to identify characteristics of persons likely to behave in dangerous ways, psychologists are about to give up the search. There just don't seem to be people who are, in general, any more accident prone than anyone else. (Which, of course, may reflect our inability to adequately assess such a trait.) There still is some obvious sense to this approach that relates to a number of points we raised in the first section of this topic. The less well qualified a person is for a job, the less well trained, or the less well motivated, the more likely that person will have an accident—particularly if the job is a dangerous one. You wouldn't want to send an employee with poor coordination and balance to work high above the ground on scaffolding, for example.

Training employees to work safely involves telling the worker what constitutes safe behaviors and that the employer values safe work.

3. *The industrial-social approach:* This point of view takes the rather strange-sounding position that workers often need to be motivated to work safely. At first you might think that anyone in his or her right mind would want to work safely and avoid being in an accident. And you might be right. But does the worker know *specifically* what constitutes safe behaviors? Does the worker know that the employer *values* safe work and that safe work will be rewarded? If such is not the case, workers may take shortcuts and cut corners, working too quickly—and too dangerously—if they believe that the only rewards are for amount of work or size of output. This approach suggests that employers must make sure that workers are trained in safe ways to do their job (Levine, 1983) and that they realize that safe behaviors are valued (Zohar, 1980). What matters most, as we have seen before, is clearly establishing safety goals, providing feedback to workers, and reinforcing those behaviors that lead to attaining stated goals.

**BEFORE
YOU GO
ON**

*What are three approaches to improving safety,
and is there any evidence that they are effective?*

In this topic, we have been able only to scratch the surface of what industrial-organizational psychologists do in their attempt to apply basic principles of psychology to the world of work. We have focused on just two interrelated issues. First, we considered how employers can best fit a person to a given job. This process involves several subprocesses, such as doing a complete job analysis, specifying performance criteria by which personnel can be evaluated for a given job, using a number of techniques to select the best person for a job, and training or motivating a person to best do the job. Then we turned our attention to the worker in an organization, looking at such issues as job satisfaction and the quality of work life and how these are related to productivity. We also reviewed some of the approaches that I/O psychologists have taken to improve the safety of the workplace. In Topic 15B, we'll look at a few other areas of applied psychology: health psychology, environmental psychology, and sport psychology.

What is involved in doing a job analysis?

Doing a proper job analysis involves two stages: (1) constructing a complete and specific description of the activities performed by someone in a given position, that is, a listing of the characteristics required to do the job, and (2) developing a means of evaluating the performance of a person in that job (performance criteria). This information is accumulated through an inspection of official documents, interviews, questionnaires, and the direct observation of job activities. / *page 682*

What are some of the sources of information that can be used in making personnel decisions? What is the rationale for using assessment centers in selecting and promoting employees?

Once a job analysis has been completed, personnel selection involves using assessment tools to measure the relevant characteristics of applicants. Many such tools are available, including application forms, interviews, psychological tests, situational tests, and assessment center approaches. Of these, interviews seem to be of the least value. The assessment center is one location where many applicants (or present employees) can be brought together for a period of intense evaluation. In most instances, assessment centers can simulate actual job situations and give evaluators a sense of how someone will perform on the job, in social situations, and under stress. Although assessment centers are popular, their specific role in personnel decision making has been questioned. / *page 685*

List some of the factors that need to be considered in the design, implementation, and evaluation of a training program.

Several factors need to be considered in

the design and implementation of an employee training program. These include an assessment of the organization's instructional needs (what training, if any, is required?), the development of specific training objectives, the means by which training will be evaluated, and the selection of appropriate methods and media for the actual training. Once training has begun, it should be monitored constantly to see if objectives are being met. After training has been completed, the program itself should be evaluated in the short and long term, as should the transfer of information and skills from training to actual on-the-job performance. / *page 688*

Briefly summarize some of the factors that affect the motivation of workers to do a good job.

Even workers with ability may not do a good job unless they are motivated to do so. There are many theories to describe what motivates workers. We looked at three approaches. Vroom's *expectancy theory* says that workers develop expectations concerning the relationship between their work behaviors and the likelihood of certain outcomes. They also assign values to different outcomes. They will be most highly motivated to behave in ways that earn valued rewards. Adams's *equity theory* says that what matters most is the perception of fairness or equal reward for equal effort when one's work behaviors are compared with those of a significant other. Locke's *goal-setting* approach says that what matters most is that workers be clearly aware of just what they are working for and that they accept that goal as worth the effort. / *page 691*

What are meant by job satisfaction and the quality of work life?

Job satisfaction and quality of work life are complex concepts, usually inferred

from interview and questionnaire data. In the broadest sense, job satisfaction is an attitude, a measure of an employee's evaluation of his or her position in an organization. Quality of work life (QWL) involves many factors, such as feelings about employment conditions, job security, compensation, autonomy, opportunities for social interaction, self-esteem, and participation in the decision-making process. / *page 693*

Briefly summarize the relationship between job satisfaction and job productivity.

Although job satisfaction and productivity may be related, there is little evidence to suggest that the relationship is a strong one and no evidence to suggest that one causes the other. Interventions designed to increase job satisfaction do sometimes have a positive impact on productivity, but interventions designed to improve productivity may also increase job satisfaction. Job satisfaction seems most closely related to employee turnover and somewhat less related to absenteeism. / *page 694*

What are three approaches to improving safety, and is there any evidence that they are effective?

I/O psychologists have long been interested in making the workplace as accident-free as possible. We looked at three ways of approaching work safety. (1) *Engineering* the job and equipment to be as safe as possible has generally been an effective process. (2) Looking at *personnel* to identify accident-prone individuals or characteristics has not proven to be very worthwhile. (3) *Motivating* workers to work more safely by providing training in specific, safe behaviors and convincing them that safety is valued in the organization has been a successful approach. / *page 696*

Health, Environmental, and Sport Psychology

Why We Care: A Topic Preview

PSYCHOLOGY AND HEALTH
Psychological Factors that Influence Physical Health
Psychological Interventions and Physical Health

PSYCHOLOGY AND THE ENVIRONMENT
Space and Territory
Life in the City: An Example
Noise, Temperature, and Environmental Toxins
    Noise
    Temperature
    Environmental Toxins
Changing Behaviors that Impact on the Environment

PSYCHOLOGY AND SPORT

SUMMARY

Why We Care: A Topic Preview

We have noted right from the start that one of the major goals of psychology is to apply what we have learned about our subject matter in the real world (see Topic 1A, pp. 23–25). Generally, we first think of applying psychology in the context of diagnosis and therapy for psychological disorders. We also think about applying principles of learning and memory to improve education and to make child rearing easier and more effective. In Topic 15A, we saw how our understanding of affect, behavior, and cognition can be applied in the workplace. In this topic, we'll briefly examine three more areas in which psychological principles are being applied.

First, we'll look at an emerging field of psychology that attempts to understand the relationships among psychological variables and physical health. There are several related issues we could explore here. We'll choose two: (1) Is there a relationship between our behaviors, thoughts, and feelings and our state of physical health? (2) What role can psychologists play in improving the physical health of individuals?

Second, we'll sample some of the work of psychologists who are concerned about the interactions between the physical environment and one's psychological state of well-being. We'll examine the notions of space and territory, using life in a big city as an example. We'll review some of the evidence concerning psychological reactions to environmental pollutants: noise, temperature, and toxins. We'll see how applied psychologists can help people change their behaviors in such a way as to have a positive impact on the environment. Finally, we'll look at a few ways in which psychology can be applied to the world of sports and athletics.

On the surface, there appears to be little justification for combining issues of physical health, environmental concerns, and athletic performance in one topic. In terms of actual content, they have little in common. They are brought together in this final topic only to serve as additional examples of areas in which we find the direct, purposeful application of psychological principles. We care about the material presented in this topic not only because of the specific benefits that can be derived from these applications, but also because they can act as examples for the larger issue of applying psychological principles in general to a range of real-world problems.

PSYCHOLOGY AND HEALTH

Health psychology is a field of applied psychology that is just over 20 years old, although the issues involved have been of general concern for a very long time. Health psychology became a division of the American Psychological Association in 1978 and currently has approximately 3000 members (Taylor, 1990). **Health psychology** is the study of psychological or behavioral factors affecting physical health and illness. The involvement of psychologists in the medical realm of physical health and well-being is based on at least four assumptions:

health psychology *the field of applied psychology that studies psychological factors affecting physical health and illness*

1. Certain behaviors increase the risk of certain chronic diseases.
2. Changes in behaviors can reduce the risk of certain diseases.
3. Changing behaviors is often easier and safer than treating many diseases.
4. Behavioral interventions are comparatively cost-effective (Kaplan, 1984).

In this section, we'll look at the role of psychologists in the understanding, treatment, and prevention of physical disease.

Psychological Factors that Influence Physical Health

Is there a relationship between aspects of one's personality and that person's state of physical health? Can psychological evaluations of an individual be used to predict physical as well as psychological disorders? Is there such a thing as a disease-prone personality? Our response is very tentative, and the data are not all supportive, but for the moment we can say yes, there does seem to be a positive correlation between some personality variables and physical health.

One recent meta-analysis of 101 previously published research articles looked for relationships between personality and physical disease (coronary heart disease, asthma, ulcers, arthritis, headaches). The strongest associations were those that predicted coronary heart disease, although depression, anxiety, and anger/hostility were each associated to some degree with all of the physical components studied (Friedman & Booth-Kewley, 1987). On the basis of their analysis, the authors argued that there are sufficient (albeit weak) data linking some personality variables to some physical diseases to "argue for a key role for psychological research on the prevention and treatment of disease" (p. 539).

Type A behavior pattern (TABP) *a collection of behaviors (competitive, achievement-oriented, impatient, easily aroused, often hostile or angry) often associated with coronary heart disease*

When we talk about relating personality variables to physical diseases, what commonly comes to mind is the **Type A behavior pattern (TABP)** and its relationship to coronary heart disease. As it originally was defined, TABP refers to a competitive, achievement-oriented, impatient individual who generally is working at many tasks at the same time, is easily aroused, and is generally hostile or angry (Friedman & Rosenman, 1959; Rosenman et al., 1964). Coronary heart disease (CHD) is a general label given to a number of physical symptoms, including chest pains and heart attacks, caused by a buildup of substances, such as cholesterol, that block the supply of blood to the heart. For nearly 20 years—from the early 1960s to the early 1980s—study after study seemed to show a clear, positive relationship between CHD and behaviors typical of the Type A personality (Jenkins,

1976; Rosenman et al., 1975; Wood, 1986). A review panel of the National Institute of Health declared the Type A behavior pattern an independent risk factor for heart disease (National Institutes of Health Panel, 1981). It all seemed quite clear. Find people who have the Type A behavior pattern, intervene to change their behaviors, and see how coronary heart disease rates decline. By now you know to be suspicious when complex problems seem to have such simple solutions.

Beginning in the early 1980s, data began to surface that failed to show a clear relationship between TABP and CHD (Fishman, 1987; Krantz & Glass, 1984; Matthews, 1982, 1988; Shekelle et al., 1985; Wright, 1988). Perhaps Type A people were no more at risk for heart disease than anyone else. Perhaps studies that failed to find a relationship between TABP and CHD were seriously flawed. In fact, both of these alternative hypotheses have some evidence to support them. For one thing, the Type A behavioral pattern is, by its nature, quite complex and difficult to diagnose. It seems likely that simple paper-and-pencil inventories—of the sort that have been used in many studies—fail to identify correctly a large number of people with the TABP.

It also may be that the TABP, as presently defined, is simply too global a pattern of behaviors (Dembroski & Costa, 1987). Perhaps there is a subset of behaviors within the constellation of Type A behaviors that does predict coronary disease. This is a hypothesis now under investigation by psychologist Logan Wright, a self-confessed Type A personality, who was required to undergo bypass surgery to relieve blockage of a coronary artery. As Wright puts it, ". . . if certain so-called active ingredients, or subcomponents of the TABP are what is really responsible for coronary-prone risk, one would expect to find them to correlate more highly with CHD than does the global Type A pattern itself" (1988, p. 3).

What are Wright's candidates for the most likely active ingredients of the Type A personality? (1) *Time urgency*: concern over wasting precious, small bits of time; shifting lanes while in traffic to gain a car length; (2) *chronic activation*: the tendency to stay alert and aroused and ready all the time; being "fired up" for everything, no matter how mundane; and (3) *multiphasia*: the tendency to have several projects all going at once, having many irons in the fire; doing homework and eating while watching TV. There is research evidence to suggest that these components may be predictors of coronary heart disease, but the evidence is not conclusive. More work needs to be done. We need more research on adequate diagnosis for Type A behavior patterns and on the mechanisms that underlie whatever relationships there may be between TABP and CHD. We also need research on how to bring about psychological changes in individuals that would reduce the likelihood of their contracting any physical disease. In many ways, the so-called active ingredients of the Type A personality are precisely the characteristics that many people in our society learn to value and to imitate in their quest to get ahead. But, as Wright says, "although much Type A functioning may be productive, one *must* still learn to glide" (1988, p. 12). How can psychologists best intervene to help people glide? How can psychologists intervene to help people change those behaviors that directly and indirectly impact on their state of health? It is to matters of intervention that we now turn.

People who exhibit the Type A behavior pattern are usually impatient, easily angered, and highly competitive. While many studies support the idea that there is a link between Type A behavior and coronary heart disease, the Type A behavior pattern remains difficult to diagnose.

Psychological Interventions and Physical Health

At the very least, it is possible that some personality characteristics have an impact on the state of one's physical health. The specific traits involved and the nature of that impact are the subject of debate and ongoing research. There is no debate and no doubt, however, that certain behaviors put people at risk for certain physical ailments. Today, the leading causes of death in this country are cardiovascular disorders and cancers. These diseases are caused and maintained by the interaction of a number of factors, including biological, social, environmental, and behavioral influences. Among the behavioral influences, such variables as cigarette smoking, nutrition, obesity, and stress have been identified as important risk factors (Krantz et al., 1985). What this means is that for millions of people, factors we may collectively call life-style are deadly. (Clearly, a deadly life-style may involve behaviors that lead to death quite directly, such as failing to wear safety belts or knowingly engaging in other unsafe behaviors at work or play. Recall that we covered the relationship between psychological factors and AIDS in Topic 10B.)

One role of the health psychologist is to intervene to bring about changes in potentially dangerous behaviors (Kirscht, 1983; Matarazzo, 1980; Miller, 1983). In fact, "7 of the 10 leading causes of death in the United States are in large part behaviorally determined. We believe these unhealthy behaviors can be significantly reduced with help from psychologists" (Heffernan & Albee, 1985, p. 202). Interventions designed to prevent health problems from arising in the first place have been applied to a wide range of behaviors, including smoking, misuse of alcohol, nutrition, physical fitness and exercise, control of stress, control of high blood pressure, family planning, immunization, and sexually transmitted diseases (Jeffery, 1989; McGinnis, 1985; Rodin & Salovey, 1989). Psychologists also use behavioral techniques in attempts to promote healthy and safe behaviors such as the wearing of car safety belts (Geller et al., 1987).

Although efforts to effect attitudinal and behavioral change have been moving forward on all these fronts, few have received as much attention as efforts to discourage young people from smoking. Part of the reason for special efforts in this area is that smoking is so deadly, accounting for about one-third of all cancer deaths (Doll & Peto, 1981). Another way to put it is to say that there would be nearly 100,000 *fewer* deaths in any one year if no one smoked (Jeffery, 1989). In the 1990s concern has included the impact of "secondhand smoke," and we see emerging evidence that children of parents who smoke are significantly at risk for lung cancer even if they,

Anti-smoking ads such as this one from the American Cancer Society are aimed directly at young people. Studies reveal that quitting on one's own is much more effective in the long-run than specialized programs.

as adults, have never smoked. Yet another reason for concern among health psychologists is that the success rates of programs to persuade smokers to quit smoking have been less than encouraging: Nearly 80 percent of "quitters" relapse within a year (e.g., Cohen et al., 1989; Glasgow & Lichtenstein, 1987; Leventhal & Cleary, 1980). (In fact, most smokers who quit permanently do so without any special program of intervention.) Approaches that use role models and peers to teach specific skills to be used to resist pressures to begin smoking in the first place have been quite successful (e.g., Murray et al., 1984).

Health psychologists also intervene to help in the actual treatment of physical illness and disease (Meichenbaum & Turk, 1987; Rodin & Salovey, 1989). As an example of this sort of work, consider efforts to help patients comply with the orders of physicians. Even the best of medical advice will be useless if it is not followed. One estimate (Ley, 1977) suggests that as many as 50 percent of patients fail to follow doctors' orders with regard to taking prescribed medicines. This will be particularly true when the illness produces no immediate discomfort or apparent risk (Rodin & Salovey, 1989). There are many reasons why patients fail to comply with doctors' orders, including lack of communication between patient and doctor, the financial burden imposed by expensive medications, the extent of disruption of daily routine required to follow the regimen of daily medication, and the lack of clear vision of the advantage of doing so.

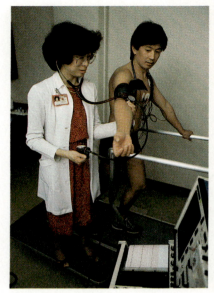

Health psychologists continue to search for relationships between psychological variables and coronary heart disease.

Psychologists can assist in improving patient-physician communication concerning medication and can assist patients in monitoring their daily medications. For example, many diabetics find it difficult to maintain their daily treatment regimens. A number of strategies have proven useful for this purpose, including:

1. *Specific assignments* that unambiguously define what is to be done
2. *Skill training* to develop new behaviors relevant to treatment
3. *Cuing* of specific behaviors with salient stimuli
4. *Tailoring* of the regimen to meet the schedule and particular needs of the patient
5. *Contracts* between patient, therapist, and significant others for prescribed behavior change
6. *Shaping* of successive approximations of the desired treatment regimen
7. *Self-monitoring* of behaviors relevant to treatment
8. *Reinforcement* of new behaviors (Surwit et al., 1983, p. 260)

Psychologists involved in health psychology, then, are involved in a wide range of activities. Some are investigating the relationships between psychological variables and the incidence of disease; some look for ways to use psychological methods to help ease the symptoms of physical illness; some seek ways to help people change their attitudes and behaviors in order to become healthier and to prevent health problems; some assist patients in complying with prescribed treatment plans; and still others fill a more traditional role, dealing directly with the psychological and emotional distress that often accompanies the knowledge that one has a serious or life-threatening disorder.

BEFORE YOU GO ON

What are some of the ways health psychologists intervene to promote physical health?

PSYCHOLOGY AND THE ENVIRONMENT

environmental psychology *the field of applied psychology that studies the effect of the general environment on organisms within it*

Environmental psychology is the subfield that studies how the general environment (as opposed to specific stimuli) affects the behavior and mental processes of organisms living in it. Environmental psychologists are also concerned with how people, in turn, affect their environments. This field tends to be an interdisciplinary endeavor (Saegert & Winkel, 1990). Environmental psychologists often work with urban planners, economists, clinical psychologists, sociologists, interior decorators, architects, landscape architects, builders, and others.

The range of specific interests within environmental psychology is quite large. Some psychologists are interested in such factors as how color and lighting, for example, might affect workers' productivity, students' learning, or nursing home patients' mental and physical health. Some are concerned with behavioral and psychological reactions to the poisons, or toxins, that are present in our environments. Some are interested in the design and construction of physical space that maximizes the functions for which that space is constructed. Some seek efficient means of changing behaviors in order to influence the natural environment in positive ways, through anti-littering campaigns, for example. Others focus on the impact of crowding, territoriality, and adjustment to the demands of city living. Of course, many of these issues are interrelated.

Consistent with a theme we first discussed in Topic 1A, environmental psychologists recognize that what may influence behavior most is one's *perception* of the environment. A room with 10 persons in it can appear to be terribly small and crowded if it is perceived as an office. The same room can seem quite large and uncrowded if the room is perceived as a waiting area. In fact, two rooms of exactly the same area, one square and one rectangular, will not be perceived as being the same size; the square room will appear smaller than the rectangular room (Sadalla & Oxley, 1984). Let's begin our introduction to environmental psychology by considering some of the issues involved in the perception of space and distance.

BEFORE YOU GO ON

Define environmental psychology, and list some of the issues that environmental psychologists study.

Space and Territory

Imagine that you are seated in the library, studying at a large table. There is no one else at your table. Then another student enters the room and sits right next to you. Although there are seven other chairs at your table, she chooses to sit in the one just to your left. Or imagine that you are in the process of buying a car. While you are examining a new sports car, a salesman approaches you, stands right in front of you (not more than 8 inches away), and begins to tell you about all the positive features of the car you are looking at. Or imagine that in your psychology class you always sit in the same seat. The semester is about over, and you have gotten to know some of the people who habitually sit near you. Then, the next time you go to class, you find that there is someone else in "your seat." Or imagine that you are a suburban homeowner. You have spent years getting your backyard to look just the way you want it to. Then, neighborhood children discover that going through your rose garden makes a great short-cut for them on their way to school.

In each of these scenarios, and in hundreds of others we might easily imagine, you will probably feel a sense of discomfort. Your personal space or your territory has been invaded without invitation. The study of the effects of invading personal space and territory has been an active research area for environmental psychologists.

Personal space is mobile. It goes with you wherever you go. It is an imaginary "bubble" of space that surrounds you and into which others may enter comfortably by invitation only. The extent of your personal space depends on the situation as well as on other factors, including your age (Aiello & Aiello, 1974), gender (Evans & Howard, 1973), and who the "intruder" happens to be. You will be much more likely to allow an invasion of your personal space by someone you know well, by someone about your age, or by an attractive member of the opposite sex (Hayduk, 1983). The anthropologist Edward Hall (1966) claimed that the extent of one's personal space is also determined in part by one's culture. Westerners, for example, are said to require a larger personal space than either Arabs or Japanese.

personal space *the mobile "bubble" of space around you reserved for intimate relationships into which others may enter only by invitation*

Personal distance is reserved for day-to-day interactions with acquaintances and friends as illustrated in the far left picture. Social distance, as in the middle photo, involves a space of 4 to 12 feet between the people and is appropriate for people who do not know each other well. Public distance is used in formal situations, such as a lecture, performance on stage, or address to business associates as in the far-right picture.

This cultural stereotype may be somewhat overgeneralized. The evidence that supports such cultural differences in personal space is not that compelling (Hayduk, 1983).

Hall (1966) also claimed that personal space can be subdivided into four different distances, each relevant for different types of social interaction. First, *intimate distance* is defined as being between actual contact and about 18 inches. This space tends to be reserved for very special, intimate communications: displays of affection by lovers, offerings of comfort, and the like. This space is usually reserved only for people whom you know very well and care about, and you will feel uncomfortable if someone else is in it.

Second, *personal distance*, according to Hall, is reserved for day-to-day interactions with acquaintances and friends. It extends from about 18 inches to approximately 4 feet, or just beyond arm's length. This space can be seen clearly in social gatherings, where small clusters of persons gather around to share in conversation. Actual physical contact in this sort of situation is unusual and generally unwelcomed. We typically keep our bubble of personal space adjusted to this size.

Third, Hall refers to the distance of 4 to 12 feet as *social distance*. This distance is appropriate for social interactions with persons we do not know well. It commonly includes some sort of physical barrier, such as a desk or table, between us and others around us. Within this space, communication can continue, but there is an implied message of lack of intimacy. This is the distance used when conducting business or at formal meetings.

Fourth, there is *public distance*, in which personal contact is minimized, though communication remains possible. This distance is defined as being between 12 and 25 feet. Formal lectures in large classrooms, performances from a stage, and after-dinner talks presented from behind the head table are examples. Because of the distances involved, communication in these settings tends to flow in only one direction.

The point of this discussion is that we will tend to feel pressured, stressed, or discomforted whenever these distances are violated. When that perfect stranger sits right next to you in the library, she is violating your personal space. The salesman with his nose almost touching yours is violating your intimate space. When a lecturer leaves the podium and begins to wander through the audience, we may feel strange because our defined public space is being invaded.

territoriality *the setting off and marking of a piece of territory (a location) as one's own*

Territoriality is also related to an individual's use of space in the environment. It involves the setting off and marking of a piece of territory (a geographical location) as one's own. It is the tendency to want to declare that "this space is mine; it's my turf and someone else can enter here only at my request or with my permission."

Territoriality was first studied extensively in nonhumans (e.g., Lorenz, 1969). Many species of animals have been observed to establish, mark, and defend geographical areas that they use either for finding and hunting food or for mating and rearing their young. These territories are often defended vigorously—most commonly with ritualistic posturing and threats of aggression, but only occasionally with actual combat.

It seems clear that people, too, establish territories as their own, not to be entered without invitation. Reviewing the evidence for territoriality in humans, Altman (1975) noted that like personal space, our territories vary

Primary territory, shown at left, is space defined and marked as one's own, such as a child's room at home. Public territory, center, is space we occupy for only a short time, such as on public transportation. Secondary territory, right, is set aside for social gatherings such as the "turf" of an inner city gang.

in their value to us. Some are *primary* territories, defined by us as ours and no one else's. "This is my room, and you'd better stay out of it." We often invest heavily in our primary territories. We decorate our homes, yards, dormitory rooms, or apartments to put our mark on our space. Primary territories will be claimed for the long term, well marked, and defended. By controlling our primary territory, we maintain a sense of privacy and a sense of identity. Evidence of such a territoriality among humans is all around us, perhaps most obvious in any teenager's room.

Altman also suggests that we are sensitive to two other types of territory: *secondary* and *public*. Secondary territories are more flexible and less well defined. They are areas we set aside for social gatherings, not so much for personal privacy. Teenage gang members who stake out a portion of a city park as being "their turf" may have established a secondary territory. It's where they meet and interact with their peers. They make it quite clear (often in threatening ways) that outsiders are unwelcome. Members of the faculty may stake out a room in a college building as a faculty lounge and may be quite unnerved to discover students using it, even if they are using it to study. Secondary territories are not "owned" by those who use them and tend not to be used for expressing personal identity. That is, there may be a sign on the door that says "Faculty Lounge," but the area *can* be used for other functions, and occasional intrusions by nonfaculty may be tolerated.

Public territories are those we tend to occupy for only a short time. They are not ours in any literal sense, and we will not feel much distress if these territories are violated. While waiting for your plane, you sit in a seat in the airport terminal and place your luggage at your feet. You get up for a minute to buy a newspaper, and when you return, you discover that someone has claimed your seat. In such a situation, you may be momentarily annoyed, but you will have less difficulty in finding another seat than in starting a major confrontation.

Personal space and territories that we claim as our own serve many functions. They provide a sense of structure and continuity in what otherwise may seem to be a complex and ever-changing environment. They help us claim some sense of identity. They help us set ourselves apart from others. They regulate and reinforce needs for privacy. When space and territory are violated, we can predict negative outcomes: anxiety, distress, and sometimes even aggressive attempts of reclamation.

BEFORE YOU GO ON

Define the concepts of personal space and territoriality.

Life in the City: An Example

In 1962, John B. Calhoun published the results of his studies of the overcrowding of rats. The data were impressive and intriguing. Calhoun raised colonies of rats in a number of different environments. In some environments, population density was allowed, even encouraged, to increase to the point where the overcrowding began to affect the behavior of the rats within the colony. Male rats became aggressive, newborn rats were often cannibalized or ignored and left to die; female rats became unreceptive to sexual advances from male rats; and when mating did occur, litter size decreased, apparently in response to the pressures of colony overpopulation. As you might imagine, it did not take long for some psychologists to look for parallels between Calhoun's rat studies and life in modern cities. Indeed, early investigations found several correlations between population density and negative behavioral consequences, such as mental illness, crime, stress, and delinquency (Altman, 1975; Freedman, 1975).

As psychologists began to look more closely at the lives of people in urban environments, it became clear that the translation of the data from Calhoun's rats to residents of our metropolitan centers was not all that straightforward. The first thing we need to do is distinguish between two easily confused terms (Stokols, 1972). The first is **population density**, which refers to the number of persons (or animals) per unit of area. Density is an objective, descriptive measure. **Crowding**, on the other hand, is a psychological concept. It is a *subjective feeling* of discomfort or distress produced by a perceived lack of space. Crowding may be quite independent of the number of persons involved. That is, you might feel very crowded and uncomfortable if you have to sit in the back seat of a small car with just two other people and not at all crowded when you all get to the stadium and are jammed together with 60,000 others to watch a football game (Freedman, 1975).

Crowding is a negative condition, one that leads to discomfort and stress. As such, it tends to produce a number of negative consequences. But it is incorrect to conclude that living in a densely populated city *necessarily* produces negative consequences. Other potential stressors, such as noise, pollution, and the threat of crime, that we commonly associate with city life may be more than offset by better medical care, better sanitation, and systems for handling emergencies of all kinds (Creekmore, 1985). One's perception of control also matters. Someone who believes that he or she can leave the city whenever he or she so chooses will have more positive

population density *a quantitative measure of the number of persons (or animals) per unit of area*

crowding *the subjective feeling of discomfort caused by a sense of lack of space*

attitudes about living in that city than will someone who feels "trapped" there.

Indeed, there is increasing evidence to support the claim that living in the city can be healthier, in a variety of physical and psychological ways, than living in the country (Creekmore, 1985; Krupat, 1985; Milgram, 1970, 1977). Many of the advantages of city living are unavailable to residents of smaller communities. Few cities with populations of less than 50,000 can support large symphony orchestras, opera companies, museums, and art galleries—or fully staffed emergency rooms or trauma centers such as those found in much larger urban areas. Nor can small communities afford stadiums and arenas for professional sports (Barker, 1968). The challenge for environmental psychologists is to help urban planners and architects design living spaces in areas of high population density that minimize the subjective experience of crowding, that maintain privacy, and that allow for expressions of individual territoriality.

BEFORE YOU GO ON

What is the difference between population density and crowding?
What are some of the positive and negative aspects of city living?

Noise, Temperature, and Environmental Toxins

In this section, we'll review some of the evidence that suggests that three types of environmental variables can have a profound effect on behavior. We'll consider noise, temperature, and environmental toxins (poisons) and how they affect human performance.

Noise. Noise is defined as any intrusive, unwanted, or excessive experience of sound. Almost any environment will be filled with some level of background noise, and noise per se need not be disruptive or stressful. In fact, the total absence of sound can induce stress. Noise becomes most stressful when it is loud, high-pitched, and unpredictable (Glass & Singer, 1972). Continued exposure to high-intensity sound can produce lasting deafness (Scharf, 1978; Taylor et al., 1965), although prolonged exposure to high levels of noise seem to produce few other serious physical problems directly (Matlin, 1983). However, there is ample evidence that prolonged exposure to noise increases levels of stress and anxiety and also increases levels of aggressive behaviors (Bell et al., 1978).

Noise levels have predictable effects on the performance of cognitive tasks. S. Cohen and his associates (1980, 1986), for example, have shown that children who attended schools near the busy Los Angeles airport tended to have higher blood pressure and were more easily distracted from their work than children who attended schools in quieter neighborhoods. In fact, there is evidence that persistently high levels of noise can have a negative impact on all sorts of everyday behaviors (e.g., Smith & Stansfield, 1986). On the other hand, Glass and Singer (1972) suggest that absolute levels of background noise may not be the major determiner of disruption. What

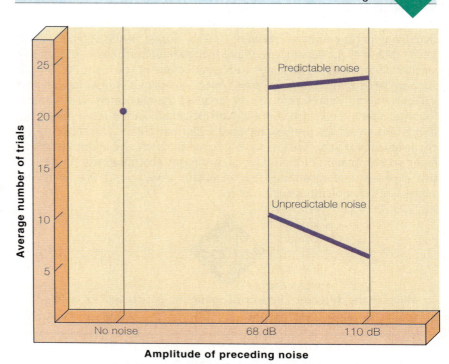

The effects of the predictability of noise as a distractor during a cognitive task. When stimulus noise occurred unpredictably, subjects spent fewer trials attempting to solve insolvable puzzles. (After Glass, Singer & Friedman, 1969.)

may matter more in the disruption of performance is the *predictability* of the noise and the degree of one's control over that noise. The results of one experiment that demonstrated this phenomenon are presented in Figure 15.2 (Glass, Singer, & Friedman, 1969).

Subjects were given the task of trying to solve problems that, in fact, had no solution. Subjects worked on these puzzles under three levels of background noise. In one condition, there was no noise; in a second, a relatively soft (68-decibel) noise was presented; in the third, a loud (110-decibel) noise was introduced. In the conditions using background noise, the predictability of the noise was also manipulated. That is, in one condition, the onset of the noise was regular and predictable; in the other, the noise was introduced on a random schedule. The introduction of predictable noise did not significantly alter the subjects' persistence in working on the problems. Unpredictable noise, however, significantly reduced the number of trials that the subjects were willing to invest in the problem task. Glass and Singer (1972) also report that when subjects are able to control the occurrence of noise, their problem-solving tasks are also unaffected. When noise is uncontrollable, performance levels drop, and they often remain poor even after the stimulus noise has been removed.

Temperature. It is clear that extremes of temperature can have adverse effects on behavior. Probably any task can be accomplished most effectively within a range of moderate environmental temperatures (Baron, 1977). It is no doubt important, for example, to try to keep the temperature of a workplace within reasonable limits. If temperatures become excessively high or low, performance will deteriorate, although the effects of temperature on performance depend in large measure on the type of task being performed.

Environmental psychologists have also been concerned with the effects that extremely high temperatures have on social interactions, particularly on aggression. There is a common perception that riots and other more common displays of violent behaviors are more frequent during the long, hot days of summer. This observation is largely supported by research evidence (Anderson, 1989; Anderson & Anderson, 1984; Rotton & Frey, 1985). Anderson, for example, reported on a series of studies (1987, 1989) that show that violent crimes are more prevalent in hotter quarters of the year and in hotter years, although nonviolent crimes were less affected. Anderson also concluded that differences in crime rates between cities is better predicted by temperature than by social, demographic (age, race, education), and economic variables. Baron and Ransberger (1978) point out that riots are most likely to occur when the outside temperature is only moderately high, between about 75° and 90° Fahrenheit. But when temperatures get much above 90°, energy (even for aggression) becomes rapidly depleted, and rioting is less likely to occur.

Environmental Toxins. As societies become more heavily invested in technological advancement, an accompanying side effect is an increased level of environmental toxins or pollutants. Psychologists concerned with issues of the quality of life are becoming increasingly involved in issues concerning the quality of the natural environment (Daniel, 1990; Fischhoff, 1990; Kaplan, 1987; Stokols, 1990).

Of the nearly 100,000 chemicals in use in this country's industries, more than 600 have been declared dangerous in large doses by the federal

Environmental neurotoxin pollution can pose a serious threat not only to people's health, but also to their entire way of life. Imagine this tranquil setting as the site of illegal chemical dumping, and you can imagine the quality of life for the people who live here would be changed.

neurotoxins *chemicals (poisons) that affect psychological processes through the nervous system*

government (Anderson, 1982). Many of the chemicals that poison the natural environment are called **neurotoxins** because they have their poisonous effects on the human nervous system. Even in small doses, they can cause detectable behavioral and emotional changes in individuals.

Environmental psychologists are involved in research on neurotoxins at several different levels. On the one hand, there is education: Workers and consumers need to know about the short-term and long-term effects of contact with chemical toxins and how to deal with such materials. Because many of the effects of pollutants are psychological in nature, and particularly because these chemicals may affect the behaviors of young children (and the unborn), it is becoming more common to find psychologists involved in the actual diagnosis of the effects of toxins (Fein et al., 1983). Exposure to neurotoxins may be more readily diagnosed through behavioral and/or psychological means than through medical diagnosis.

Just to give you an idea of the extent of the effects that neurotoxins may have on behavior, refer to Figure 15.3, in which you'll find some of the more common neurotoxins and the effects they are likely to have through prolonged exposure.

BEFORE YOU GO ON

What are some of the effects that noise, extreme temperature, and neurotoxins have on behavior?

Changing Behaviors that Impact on the Environment

In 1962, Rachel Carson published *Silent Spring*. This powerful and poignant best-seller helped to raise public consciousness about environmental issues as no book had ever done before. It spoke eloquently about the fragility of earth's natural environment, the limits of earth's resources, and the interrelationships among the inhabitants of the planet. In particular, it made clear the dangers inherent in the continued use of DDT and other harmful pesticides. After *Silent Spring* was published, the word *environmentalist* took on new meaning and significance. A movement had begun; a broad-based coalition of people from all walks of life became concerned with the quality of the environment and the limited nature of its resources. The agenda of the environmentalist is to conserve and restore: to conserve those resources that are still available and, whenever possible, to restore the environment to its clean and natural state. DDT use is now banned in the United States, although it is still manufactured and exported to other countries. In the late spring of 1988, a few chemical companies suspended the production of products that contained chlorofluorocarbons (or CFCs, used in refrigeration and in the manufacture of Styrofoam products) because of undeniable evidence that these chemicals, once in the atmosphere, were destroying the earth's protective ozone layer.

Psychologists have long been active in helping to establish programs aimed at changing the behaviors of large numbers of people in such a way as to benefit the environment. In this context, finding solutions to real-

Figure **15.3**

WORKERS AT RISK FROM NEUROTOXINS.

Neurotoxins used in industry that most commonly affect people, the symptoms associated with them, and the numbers of workers chronically exposed according to government estimates. Chemicals in capital letters pose the greatest risk.

Substance	Industry	Year of First Report of Neurotoxicity	Effect	Number of Workers Potentially at Risk
TOLUENE	Paints, explosives	1961	Tremors; vertigo; lack of coordination; bizarre behavior; emotional instability	4.8 million
TRICHLOROETHYLENE	Degreasing, dry cleaning	1915	Loss of facial sensation; impaired memory and concentration; tremors	3.6 million
METHYLENE CLORIDE	Solvent—multiple uses	1967	Delusions; hallucinations	2.2 million
CARBON TETRACHLORIDE	Dry cleaning	1909	Visual-field constriction	2 million
Cadmium	Metalworking	1930	Loss or impairment of sense of smell	1.4 million
Thalium	Glass making	1862	Nerve damage in lower limbs; damage to optic nerves and eye	853,000
N-HEXANE	Gluing, shoemaking	1960	Nerve damage in lower limbs	764,000
LEAD, INORGANIC	Smelters	Before Christ	Disorientation; blindness; nerve damage to hands and feet	649,000
STYRENE	Plastics, manufacturing	1963	Short-term memory loss; nerve damage in hands and feet	329,000
METHYL BROMIDE	Fumigation	1899	Nerve damage in hands and feet	105,000

Data from the National Institute for Occupational Safety and Health. Figure "Workers at Risk from Neurotoxins" by Alan Anderson. Reprinted with permission from PSYCHOLOGY TODAY MAGAZINE. Copyright © 1982 by Sussex Publishers, Inc.

world human environment problems is one of the major goals of what is called **applied behavior analysis (ABA)**. The specific techniques of applied behavior analysis derive from the work of B. F. Skinner and the procedures of operant conditioning (see Topic 5B). In simple terms, ABA attempts to operationally define some target behavior that one wishes to modify (for example, the conservation of energy or water or the reduction of roadside litter), determine the antecedent environmental conditions that set the occasion for (or signal) the behavior, and determine the consequences that serve to increase, decrease, or maintain the targeted behavior (Geller, 1986; Geller & Nimmer, 1985). Programs of this sort have been implemented successfully to impact on a number of environmentally sensitive issues, such as natural gas energy conservation (Shippee & Gregory, 1982), home-based energy conservation (Winett et al., 1985), home weatherization projects (Pavlovich & Greene, 1984), gasoline conservation (Hake & Foxx, 1978), and paper recycling (Witmer & Geller, 1976).

Let's look at one example of how this approach works: motivating waste management behavior (Geller, 1985; Geller & Lehman, 1986). First, we recognize that solid waste management *is* a major problem. Millions of tons of solid waste are disposed of daily, often in ways that directly threaten environmental quality.

Throughout this text, we have used the notation ABC to refer to the three levels of psychological functioning: affect, behavior, and cognition.

applied behavior analysis (ABA) *an approach, based on operant conditioning, that attempts to find solutions to human environment problems in the real world*

Geller and his associates use the ABC model in a different way, to represent the three stages of using applied behavior analysis to motivate appropriate behaviors: *antecedent-behavior-consequences*. The first step is to develop a precise definition of so-called target behaviors. Just what behaviors does one want to change? Do you want to increase the use of trash receptacles? Do you want to have litter removed from roadsides? Do you want to increase the use of solid waste recycling? What waste materials do you want to emphasize?

Once you have decided which behavior is to be modified, attention shifts to antecedent strategies, or prompting procedures. Here you have to let the people know just what it is that you want done. This is essentially an educational component of the program. Prompts may be general ("Please dispose of properly!") or specific ("Leave your old newspapers here"). Prompts may also communicate possible consequences of one's actions ("Fine for Littering: $50" or "Bring your own container and receive a 5% discount"). Securing a behavioral commitment to a waste management program has proven to be an effective means of prompting, or priming, participation. For example, people who sign pledges or engage in a discussion of the benefits of community waste management are more likely to follow through.

As we have learned through the study of operant conditioning in the laboratory, behaviors will change and be maintained to the extent that those behaviors produce certain consequences (the *C* of this ABC model). An important point for the success of large-scale programs designed to modify behavior that impacts on the environment is that consequences be tied to a person's *response*, not to some potentially *long-term outcome*. For example, scouts who volunteer to remove trash from the area surrounding a highway should be immediately rewarded with a few cents for each bag of litter they collect rather than given an award (or reward) for providing the community with a litter-free stretch of roadway. Positive consequences for desired actions (thanking someone for picking up loose trash) are generally more effective than negative consequences (fining someone for leaving a soda can on a public beach). Intervention programs that are successful and have a positive impact on the environment should be designed so that they can be maintained by some supporting agency or institution within the community.

We have come a long way since the publication of Carson's *Silent Spring*. There is still a very long way to go. Scattered and uncoordinated attempts to recycle solid waste materials, or preserve wildlife habitat, or control the pollution of industrial emissions only begin to take us in the right direction. At least there is some hope that the 1990s *can* be the decade of the environment and that significant improvements can be made. If such is to be the case, applied psychologists will have much work to do.

BEFORE YOU GO ON

How can environmental psychologists help to have a positive impact on the environment?

PSYCHOLOGY AND SPORT

Sport psychology is another new and exciting area of applied psychology. Although it has had a long history in Europe, sport psychology has become an organized focus of attention in this country only within the last 15 to 20 years. **Sport psychology** is "the application of psychological principles to sport and physical activity at all levels of skill development" (Browne & Mahoney, 1984, p. 605). Although there are many potential applications of psychology to sports and athletes, we'll briefly review just two: analyzing the psychological characteristics of athletes and maximizing athletic performance.

Psychology's history is filled with research on the measurement of individual differences. Wouldn't it be useful to be able to predict who might become a world-class athlete on the basis of psychological testing? It is certainly the case that there are physiological differences between athletes and nonathletes—amount of muscle, muscle type, height, weight, lung capacity, and so on. Are there any differences between athletes and nonathletes on personality measures?

Generally, research in this area has been less than satisfactory, and results often tend to confirm the obvious. Although differences tend to be small, athletes usually score higher than nonathletes on tests of assertion, dominance, aggression, and need for achievement; they score lower on anxiety level, depression, and fatigue (Browne & Mahoney, 1984; Cox, 1990; Morgan, 1980). This is particularly true when the athletes are at a high skill level. Athletes in some sports, such as hockey and football, are more tolerant of pain than are athletes in other sports, such as golf and bowling (e.g., Ryan & Kovacic, 1966). Tolerance of pain, however, may be more of an outcome (or result of their activity) for some athletes than a determinant of success. And this last point raises a problem that has plagued research on the personality of the athlete: Just how shall we define *athlete*? Given the differences that are likely to occur among hockey players, golfers, long-distance runners, billiards players, cowboys, rock climbers, bowlers, gymnasts, and the like, it is a bit surprising that we can find any research that finds significant differences between athletes and nonathletes. In fact, when general trends are sought, they are often not found (e.g., Fisher, 1977).

Of practical importance to coaches and athletes (and psychologists) is the performance of the athlete in competition, and what can be done to maximize that performance. One area of interest focuses on manipulating the arousal level of the athlete. Clearly the athlete in competition needs to be fully aroused and motivated to perform—"psyched up" to his or her best. Psychologists also know that too much arousal can interfere with athletic performance. (If this argument sounds familiar, it's because we addressed this issue of arousal in general terms back in the topic on motivation, Topic 11A.) Psychologists can help athletes be sensitive to maintaining high levels of arousal while still maintaining appropriate levels of concentration on the task at hand. This often involves training athletes to monitor and control arousal levels (Harris, 1973; Landers, 1982).

In a similar vein, sport psychologists now claim that the so-called home field advantage (Varca, 1980) often may be exaggerated, particularly in important games (Baumeister, 1985; Baumeister & Steinhilber, 1984). The argument is that the frenzied, yelling, screaming hometown fans may raise arousal levels of the home team *beyond* the point of maximum efficiency.

sport psychology *the application of psychological principles to sport and physical activity at all levels of skill development*

The negative effect of fans' reactions seems more potent when teams are on offense than when they are playing defense, and it is clearly more potent in end-of-season playoff and championship games.

One psychologist who researches sports and athletes, Michael Mahoney, commenting on Olympic athletes, has said, "At this level of competition, the difference between two athletes is 20 percent physical and 80 percent mental" (quoted in Kiester, 1984a, pp. 20–21). To the extent that this observation is accurate, psychologists have tried to help athletes to do their best—to give what is called their *peak performance*. Mental practice, or "imagery," combined, of course, with physical practice, has proven to be quite beneficial (e.g., Smith, 1987). In addition to manipulating acceptable levels of arousal, mental practice is useful in:

1. Mentally rehearsing a particular behavioral pattern. (Think about and mentally picture that golf swing and the flight of the ball before you step up to the tee.)
2. Reducing negative thoughts that may interfere with performance. (Forget about an earlier error and focus on positive experiences, perhaps past victories.)
3. Rehearsing one's role in a team sport. (Mentally practice what you are supposed to do and when you are supposed to do it in different game situations.)
4. Setting realistic goals. (Don't get tense worrying about a competitor in this race, simply try to better your last performance; e.g., Creekmore, 1984; Fenker & Lambiotte, 1987; Kiester, 1984a, 1984b; Ogilvie & Howe, 1984; Scott & Pelliccioni, 1982; Smith, 1987; Suinn, 1980.)

Obviously, using mental imagery is not the only way in which athletes can improve their performance. It's just one technique with which sports psychologists can help.

BEFORE YOU GO ON

What are some of the ways in which psychologists may become involved in sports and athletics?

In this topic, we have briefly reviewed three general areas in which psychological understanding can be applied to real-life situations. We have seen how personality and behavioral factors may be related to physical disease and illness; how the physical environment can have sweeping effects on our affect, cognitions, and behavior; and how even sports and athletics can benefit from our knowledge of human behavior.

Our sampling of examples in this topic was just that—a sampling, not a complete listing of psychological applications. There are many other applied fields of psychology that we might have included in this topic, such as psychology and the law, consumer psychology, the psychology of advertising and marketing, engineering psychology, military psychology, and political psychology. Psychology is a science, and it is an academic discipline. It is also a field ready and able to be a powerful force of change in the real world.

Briefly summarize the relationship between the Type A behavioral pattern and coronary heart disease.

Many health psychologists believe that there is a relationship between personality variables and physical health, that is, that some psychological traits put one at risk for disease. Beginning in the late 1950s, evidence accumulated that seemed to show a positive relationship between the Type A behavioral pattern, or TABP (typified by a person who is competitive, achievement-oriented, impatient, easily aroused, often angry or hostile, and who tends to have many projects all going on at once) and coronary heart disease (blockage of major arteries). More recent evidence suggests that perhaps only some of the characteristics of TABP (time urgency, chronic activation, and multiphasia) are adequate predictors of coronary heart disease. / page 702

What are some of the ways health psychologists intervene to promote physical health?

Reacting to the observation that 70 percent of the leading causes of death in the United States are in large part determined by life-style behaviors that put an individual at risk, many health psychologists intervene to try to bring about changes in what might be called unhealthy behaviors, such as smoking, overeating, and not exercising. Health psychologists also intervene to assist in the actual treatment of physical disease, helping patients to understand and comply with physicians' orders, for example. / page 704

Define environmental psychology, and list some of the issues that environmental psychologists study.

Environmental psychology is the study of how the environment affects the behavior and mental processes of persons living within it, and vice versa. Environmental psychologists study such issues as personal space, crowding, privacy, interior design, territoriality, environmental pollutants and neurotoxins, and the effects of weather and noise. / page 704

Define the concepts of personal space and territoriality.

Personal space is the imaginary bubble of area around a person into which others enter only by invitation or in specified situations. It is mobile and goes with the person. There may be different types of personal space—acceptable distances—defined for different situations. Territoriality, on the other hand, is one's claim to certain areas (territories) in the environment. Territories may be defended against intrusion and are often used as statements of self-expression. Intrusion into one's personal space or territory leads to tension, stress, and even aggression. / page 708

What is the difference between population density and crowding? What are some of the positive and negative aspects of city living?

Population density is simply a quantitative measure of the number of units (people, for example) occupying a given geographic area. Crowding, on the other hand, is a psychological reaction of distress that occurs when individuals feel that their space or privacy has been invaded. City living increases the probability of living with crowding, noise, and other pollutants, but these stressors may be offset by the advantages of a wide range of opportunities not found outside large population centers, such as health care, police protection, and access to the arts. / page 709

What are some of the effects that noise, extreme temperature, and neurotoxins have on behavior?

Noise, extreme temperatures, and neurotoxins may all be viewed as environmental pollutants and harmful to physical and psychological well-being. Noise per se is less stressful than is unexpected, unpredictable, or uncontrollable noise. High temperatures may lead to aggressive, violent reactions, but extremely high (and low) temperatures tend to decrease all levels of behavior. Many chemicals commonly found in the environment have negative consequences for behavior and mental activities; those that directly affect the nervous system are called neurotoxins. / page 712

How can environmental psychologists help to have a positive impact on the environment?

Environmentalists work to conserve natural resources and to restore the environment to its natural and unspoiled state. Environmental psychologists can help in this effort by designing large-scale intervention programs. Such programs target specific behaviors, identify antecedent conditions that prompt those behaviors, and attempt to control consequences of relevant target behaviors to increase the rate of appropriate responses. / page 714

What are some of the ways in which psychologists may become involved in sports and athletics?

Psychologists have become involved in sports and athletics in many ways, including trying to discover how athletes are different from nonathletes, attempting to improve an athlete's peak performance, studying the effects of audience reactions on athletic performance, and investigating the effects of participation on the athlete. / page 716

STATISTICAL APPENDIX

Statistical Appendix

Why We Care: A Topic Preview

Doing research in psychology, or applying psychology, often involves the measurement of some aspect of behavior and/or mental processes. When we measure the affect, cognitions, or behaviors of organisms, the result of our measurement is a set of numbers. Assuming that we have adequately measured what we are interested in, now we have to deal with the numbers we have accumulated. That's where statistics come in.

It's one thing to be able to measure some psychological characteristic and something else again to make sense out of those measurements once they've been made. This is particularly true when we have a very large number of measurements, either made repeatedly on the same individual or on many different subjects. After making our measurements and generating a large number of numbers, we need to be able to summarize and describe our data. We may also want to make decisions on the basis of the numbers we have collected. Statistics help us to summarize, describe, and make judgments about measurements. How they do so will be the principle subject of this appendix.

Before we go on, I would like to insert a word of caution. In this topic, we are going to be dealing with numbers and a few simple formulas. Please don't let the numbers make you anxious. Some students find dealing with numbers difficult and think that statistics are not relevant for psychology students. Keep in mind that statistics are tools, necessary tools, to help us understand our subject matter. I have long argued that (at this level at least) you don't need to be mathematically sophisticated to appreciate statistics. What is required is a positive attitude and a few arithmetic skills, such as addition, subtraction, multiplication, and division. If you haven't had much math background, just go slowly and think about the issues involved in our discussion.

AN EXAMPLE TO WORK WITH

Statistics involve numbers; when we measure something, we assign it a numerical value, and statistics help us to analyze and understand measurements once we have made them. So that we'll have some numbers to work with, let's consider the following problem.

You and your best friend are both enrolled in the same introductory psychology class this semester. You have just taken your first exam, a 50-item multiple-choice test. Concerned about the possibility of cheating, your instructor provided two forms of your first exam, form A and form B. They both covered the same material, of course, but the questions were different on the two forms. By chance, you took form A of the test, and your friend took form B. You had studied together, and you thought that you both knew the material equally well. But your score on the test was eight points lower than your friend's. You suspect that perhaps the two forms of your first test were not equally difficult. You believe that your test (form A) was harder than your friend's (form B). You ask your instructor for all the grades on the test for both forms. Because of confidentiality, your instructor cannot provide you with names, but does supply you with all the grades from the exam.

There are 100 students in your class who took the first exam. Fifty took form A and 50 took form B. When you get the scores from your instructor, you find that they are arranged as follows:

FORM A:					FORM B:				
98	86	100	60	94	82	100	90	80	60
72	80	78	66	86	72	86	82	88	80
92	62	86	96	62	82	76	84	74	84
82	86	78	88	84	86	74	78	78	78
64	86	68	76	80	78	74	84	80	80
86	96	76	72	80	90	84	68	78	86
80	82	82	64	78	80	80	80	84	80
68	74	98	98	84	76	76	80	82	82
66	64	70	90	86	86	74	70	78	76
96	92	82	68	92	82	82	80	76	80

What a mess. Just looking at all these numbers doesn't tell you much at all. Arranged as they are, it's difficult to see if either form of the exam yielded higher or lower scores. To answer your original question (was there a difference in performance on the two forms of the exam?), you're going to have to manipulate these numbers somehow. Such manipulations involve statistics. As we'll repeat throughout this appendix, statistics are tools that we use to help us make sense out of data we have collected. They will be very helpful in analyzing these data. Statistical manipulations are more useful (even necessary) when we have collected many more than 100 numbers.

ORGANIZING DATA

Let's assume that we have collected the measurements, or data, in which we are interested. Now the task before us is to make some decisions based on those data. The first thing we need to do is to assemble our data, our numbers, in some sensible way so that we can quickly and easily get some idea of what they mean. At the very least, we should put our data into the form of a frequency distribution. We might then consider some graphic representation of our data.

Frequency Distributions

Once we have collected a large number of numbers, we seek ways to organize and summarize them to make them useful and meaningful. One of the easiest things to do with our numbers is to arrange them in a **frequency distribution.** As its name suggests, a frequency distribution lists, in order, all of the numbers or scores that we have collected and indicates the frequency with which each occurs.

Figure A.1 shows two types of frequency distributions for the scores earned on form A and form B of the exam we introduced as an example in the last section. One type of frequency distribution indicates the frequency of each score with a hash mark (/), while the other type simply indicates the frequency of each score with a number. In this figure, we've placed the two frequency distributions side by side. You can easily see, just by inspection of these distributions, that there is a difference between the scores earned on form A and form B of our imaginary classroom exam.

frequency distribution *an ordered listing of all X-values, indicating the frequency with which each occurs*

Figure ◢ **A.1**

FREQUENCY DISTRIBUTIONS FOR OUR SAMPLE DATA OF TWO FORMS (A AND B) OF A CLASSROOM EXAM.
Scores, or measurements, are listed in order in the left column, and the frequency with which each occurs is indicated with either a hash mark (/) or a number.

Score	Form A Frequency		Form B Frequency	
100	/	1	/	1
98	/ /	2		0
96	/ / /	3		0
94	/	1		0
92	/ / /	3		0
90	/	1	/ /	2
88	/	1	/	1
86	/ / / / / / /	7	/ / / /	4
84	/ /	2	/ / / / /	5
82	/ / / /	4	/ / / / / / /	7
80	/ / / /	4	/ / / / / / / / / / /	11
78	/ / /	3	/ / / / / / /	6
76	/ /	2	/ / / / /	5
74	/	1	/ / / /	4
72	/ /	2	/	1
70	/	1	/	1
68	/ / /	3	/	1
66	/ /	2		0
64	/ / / /	4		0
62	/ /	2		0
60	/	1	/	1
		$N = 50$		$N = 50$

Graphic Representations

It is often helpful to go one step beyond the simple frequency distribution and draw a graph of our data. A number of different graphs have been used throughout this text. Graphs of frequencies of scores are among the most common types of graphs in psychology. For such a graph, our scores (in general referred to as *X-scores*) are plotted on the horizontal (*x*) axis of the graph, and frequencies (*f*) are plotted on the vertical (*y*) axis of our graph.

histogram *a bar graph; a graphical representation of a frequency distribution*

Figure A.2 shows one way to graph frequencies. This sort of bar graph is called a **histogram.** The frequency of each *X-score* is indicated by the height of the bar above that score. When we have few *X-scores*, and when frequencies are not too large, histograms provide clear depictions of our data. The differences between form A and form B of the classroom exam are more clearly seen in the two histograms of Figure A.2 than in a simple frequency distribution.

Figure A.3 shows the same data in a simple line graph. The advantage of this sort of graph is obvious: We can easily show both distributions of test scores on the same axes. As is the case with histograms, scores are plotted on the *x*-axis and frequencies are indicated on the *y*-axis. With line graphs, it is important to provide a key indicating which line represents each group of scores.

BEFORE YOU GO ON

*What is a frequency distribution, and what is a histogram?
What are they used for?*

Histograms showing the frequency with which scores were earned on form A and form B of the classroom exam.

Figure **A.2**

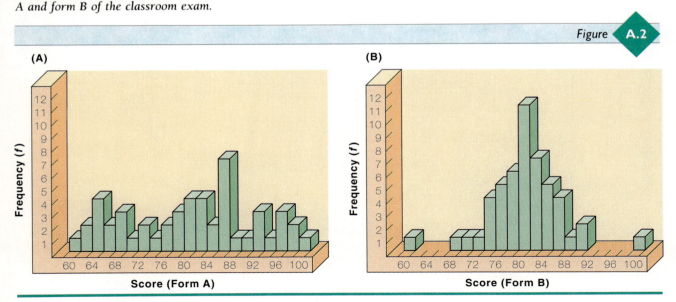

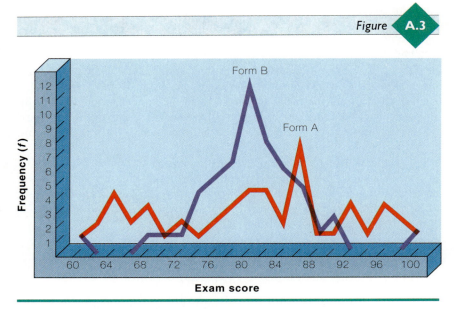

Figure **A.3**

A line graph showing the frequency of scores earned on classroom exams for both form A and form B.

DESCRIPTIVE STATISTICS

Let's continue working with our opening problem. We began with two sets of 50 numbers, scores earned on form A and form B of a classroom exam. Our basic question was whether or not these two forms of the same test were really equally difficult. To get started, we put the scores into frequency distributions and then constructed graphs that represented our data. That helped, but there is much more that we can do.

When describing collections or distributions of data, our two major concerns are usually with measures of central tendency and variability. Measures of **central tendency** are statistics that tell us where our scores tend to center. In general terms, measures of central tendency are called *averages*. If we want to know if performance on form A was better or worse *on the average* than performance on form B, we would have to compute a measure of central tendency for both distributions of scores. Measures of **variability** are statistics that tell us about the extent of dispersion, or the spread of scores within a distribution. Are scores clustered closely around the average, or are they more variable, deviating considerably from the average? First we'll deal with measures of central tendency, then with variability.

central tendency *a measure of the middle, or average, score in a set*

variability *the extent of spread or dispersion in a set or distribution of scores*

Measures of Central Tendency

There are three statistics that we can use to represent the central tendency of a distribution of numbers. The most commonly used is the mean. The median and mode are also measures of central tendency, but they are used less frequently.

mean (X̄), *the sum of all X-scores* (ΣX) *divided by N, the number of X-scores*

The Mean. When we think about computing the average of a distribution of scores we are usually thinking about computing the **mean**. The mean of a set of scores is their total divided by the number of scores in the set. For example, if Max is 6 feet tall and Ruth is 4 feet tall, their mean height is 5 feet. Four inches of snow yesterday and 2 inches today yields a mean snowfall of 3 inches for the two days (4″ + 2″ = 6″ ÷ 2 = 3″).

So, to compute the mean scores for form A of our example we add up all the scores and divide by 50 because there are 50 scores in the set. We'd do the very same thing for the scores earned on form B—add them up and divide by 50.

The mean of a set of numbers is symbolized by X̄, read *X bar*. The uppercase Greek letter sigma, Σ, stands for "take the sum of whatever follows." We use the symbol X to represent an individual score from a set of scores and N for the number of scores in the set. So the formula for computing a mean looks like this:

$$\overline{X} = \frac{\Sigma X}{N}$$

This is just a fancy shorthand way of expressing what you already know: To find the mean of a set of scores (X̄), add the scores (X) together and then divide by the number of scores (N). When we do this for form A and form B of our classroom exam example, we find that the mean for both sets of scores is 80. That is, ΣX = 4000 and N = 50 in each case, so ΣX ÷ N = 80 for both forms of the exam. In terms of average score (as indicated by the mean), there is clearly no difference between the two forms of the test.

The Median. Although the mean is generally the central-tendency measure of choice, there are occasions when it may not be appropriate. These occasions occur when a distribution includes a few extreme scores. For a simple example, the mean of the numbers, 2, 3, 3, 5, 7 is 4 (ΣX = 20; N = 5; so X̄ = 4). Even on inspection, 4 looks right; it is a value near the middle or center of the set. Now consider the numbers 2, 3, 3, 5, 37. What is their mean? The sum of these 5 numbers is 40, so their mean equals 10. Here it seems by inspection that the extreme score of 37 is adding too much weight to our measure of central tendency. For a real-life example, imagine computing the average income of a small, working-class community that happened to include two millionaires. The *mean* income of this community would be unduly influenced by just two persons with unusually high incomes.

median *the score of an ordered set above which and below which fall half the scores*

In such cases, we might prefer to use the **median** as our measure of central tendency. The median is the value of a set of numbers that divides it exactly in half. There are as many scores above the median as below it. Perhaps you recognize that the median is the same as the fiftieth percentage of a distribution—50 percent of the scores are higher; 50 percent are lower.

Don't fall for this trick: "What is the median of these test scores: 42, 58, 37, 62, 55?" There is a tendency to want to say "37" because it is in the middle of the list with two scores to the left and two scores to the right. But "37" certainly isn't at the center of these scores; it's the lowest of the five! Before you choose the median, the scores must first be placed in order: 37, 42, 55, 58, 62. *Now* the score in the middle, 55, is the median score, the one that divides the set in half. Whenever we have an even number of scores, there will be no one number in the middle, will there? What is the median of these numberes: 3, 6, 8, 10, 14, 18? What we do here is calcuate the mean of the two numbers in the middle (here 8 and 10). So, the median of these six numbers is 9. When we have a large number of scores to deal with, the computation of the median becomes slightly more complicated. We can't always just put our scores in order and identify the median by inspection. But in such cases, the logic is the same, and we have formulas that tell what steps to take to calculate the median. For the two distributions of our example, the median for form A of the exam is 80; for form B it is 79.

The Mode. No doubt the easiest measure of central tendency to calculate is the **mode.** The mode is simply the most frequently occurring value in a set or distribution of scores. If you have already constructed a frequency distribution, finding the mode is particularly easy. Just locate the *X*-value with the greatest frequency and you've found the mode. For many psychological characteristics measured for large numbers of subjects, the mode *does* tend to fall at or near the center of the distribution of scores. For our example problem, the mode of scores earned on form A is 86 and on form B the mode is 80.

mode *the most frequently occurring X-value in a set*

As it happens, the mode is seldom used as a measure of central tendency. For one thing, computing the mode disregards all of the other values in the distribution. For another, there is no guarantee that the most frequently occurring number will be at (or even near) the middle. Notice also that it is quite possible for a collection of numbers to have two modes (be "bimodal") or three modes, or more.

BEFORE YOU GO ON

Name and define three measures of central tendency.

Variability

If we know how two sets of scores, or distributions, differ "on the average," we know a lot. We know, for instance, that there is no apparent difference in central tendency for the two sets of scores we have been using as an example. There is, however, a second descriptive characteristic of distributions of numbers that may be of interest: their spread, or dispersion, or *variability*.

It is quite possible to have two sets of scores that have identical means but that, at the same time, are clearly different from each other. This sort of difference can be seen in Figure A.3 and is even more clearly obvious in Figure A.4. In this figure, we can see that most of the scores of distribution A are packed, or clustered, around the mean of the distribution. The scores of distribution B are much more spread out, or variable, even though the mean of this set of scores equals the mean of distribution A.

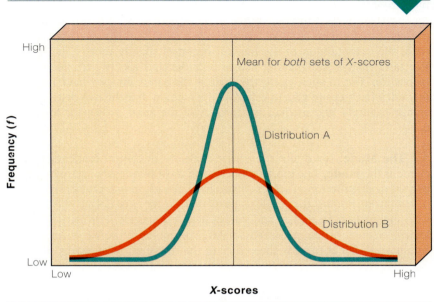

Two distributions of X-scores (A and B) that have identical means, but clearly different variability.

Imagine for a moment that the two graphs in Figure A.4 represent grades earned by two very large classes. Further imagine that the mean grade for each class is a C. If this is the case, then these graphs tell us that almost everyone in class A received a C, a C+, or a C−. Some may have received a B− or a D+, but most grades were near the average C. In class B, on the other hand, there were obviously many more A's, B's, D's, and F's than were earned by the other class, even though the mean grade for the two classes was a C. So knowing about a distribution's variability is to have some useful information. How shall we represent variability statistically?

One way to measure the spread of scores in a distribution is to use a statistic called the **range**. Range is one of the easiest statistics to calculate. It is found by subtracting the lowest score from the highest. Unfortunately, range (as a measure of variability) simply disregards all the other scores between the highest and lowest. Even when most scores are bunched tightly around the mean, if there are just a couple of extreme scores, the range will be large. The range would be an inappropriate measure of variability for our example. Scores on both form A and form B of the classroom exam range from a high score of 100 to a low score of 60. Thus, the range for both sets of scores is 40 points. An inspection of our Figure A.3, however, indicates that scores on form A are generally more variable than scores on form B.

A measure of variability that does take into account all of the scores of a distribution is **standard deviation.** Standard deviation is usually symbolized by **SD**. What it amounts to is a kind of average of the extent to which all the scores in a distribution are different from (deviate from) their mean. Let's go through the procedures that reflect this definition of standard deviation.

range *the highest score in a distribution, minus the lowest*

standard deviation (SD) *a type of average of the deviations of each X-score from the mean of the distribution:*

$$SD = \sqrt{\frac{\Sigma(X - \bar{X})^2}{N}}$$

The first thing that we need to know is the mean of our distribution ($\overline{X}$). Then we find the difference between each score (X, remember) and the mean ($\overline{X}$). This is a simple process of subtraction, yielding a collection of ($X - \overline{X}$) scores. Because means are, by definition, in the middle of distributions, some X-scores will be above the mean (so $X - \overline{X}$ will be a positive number), and some X-scores will be below the mean (so $X - \overline{X}$ will be a negative number). If we then simply add up all of our deviations, $\Sigma(X - \overline{X})$, we will always have a sum of zero. What we do to deal with this complication is simply square each deviation score, so that we have a set of ($X - \overline{X}$)^2 scores. Any real number, even a negative one, that is squared, or multiplied by itself, will yield a positive number. *Now* we add together our squared deviations, $\Sigma(X - \overline{X})^2$. We then find an average by dividing this total by N, the number of scores we are dealing with. In formula form, what we have so far is: $\Sigma(X - \overline{X})^2/N$. This statistic is called *variance*.

In our calculations, we introduced a squaring operation just to get rid of negative numbers. We now reverse that operation by taking the square root of our result (variance). What we end up with then is our formula for standard deviation, and it looks like this.

$$SD = \sqrt{\frac{\Sigma(X - \overline{X})^2}{N}}$$

You may never be called upon to actually compute a standard deviation using this formula. For one thing, even simple hand-held calculators often come with a button that yields a standard deviation value once you've punched in all the X-scores. For another, there are simpler computational formulas that provide the same result in fewer, easier steps. But you should appreciate what standard deviations do. They tell us the extent to which

---

Figure **A.5**

THE COMPUTATION OF THE STANDARD DEVIATION FOR A SMALL DISTRIBUTION OF X-SCORES.

X-scores	$X - \overline{X}$	$(X - \overline{X})^2$
12	6.5	42.25
10	4.5	20.25
7	1.5	2.25
6	.5	.25
5	−.5	.25
5	−.5	.25
4	−1.5	2.25
4	−1.5	2.25
1	−4.5	20.25
1	−4.5	20.25
		110.50 $= \Sigma(X - \overline{X})^2$

$\Sigma X = 55$
$N = 10$
$\overline{X} = \Sigma X \div N = 5.5$

$$SD = \sqrt{\frac{\Sigma(X - \overline{X})^2}{N}} = \sqrt{\frac{110.50}{10}} = \sqrt{11.05} = \underline{3.32}$$

scores in a distribution deviate, or are spread from the distribution's mean. We use them often in psychology.

To reinforce our discussion, Figure A.5 depicts the computation of a standard deviation for some simple data. When the procedure is applied to our example data we find that the standard deviation for form A of the exam is 11.29; for form B, *SD* = 6.18. This result conforms to our observation that the scores on form A of the test are more variable than those earned on form B.

BEFORE YOU GO ON

What is the formula for standard deviation, and of what is it a measure?

INFERENTIAL STATISTICS

We have already seen that statistics can be used to summarize and describe some of the essential characteristics of large collections of data. Statistics can also be used to guide our decision making concerning the data we have collected. That is, statistics can allow us to make inferences about our data. **Inferential statistics** tell us about the *significance* of the results of our experimental or correlational studies. In general, they tell us the likelihood that the data we have collected might have occurred by chance. Let's use another example, again dealing with means.

For this example, let's say that our concern is with the effects of background music on studying. You want to do an experiment to determine if background music affects study skills. To keep matters simple, let's assume that you have two groups of volunteer subjects. Each group is to try to learn 50 words in a five-minute study session. One group will practice in silence (your control group); the other will have classical music playing in the background (the experimental group). We'll call the first group, group S and the second, group C. Let's say there are 40 subjects in each group, or *N* = 40. After each group studies their word lists for five minutes, you test to see how many words have been learned. Then you construct a frequency distribution of your data and compute the means and standard deviations for each set of data. What you discover is that group S has a mean number of words learned equal to 26.0 and group C's mean is 28.5. Now what? There's no doubt that 28.5 is larger than 26.0, but the difference is not very large. Is the difference large enough for you to claim that the background music had an effect? We need to backtrack just a little.

Imagine that we had two groups of subjects in a similar experiment, but that both groups received exactly the same treatment. That is, both groups performed the same task under the same conditions. Some dependent variable is measured for both groups (perhaps the number of words that were learned in a five-minute study session). Even though both groups

inferential statistics *statistical tests that tell us about the significance of the results of experimental or correlational studies*

were treated exactly the same, would we expect the mean scores for the two groups to be *exactly* equal? Wouldn't we expect *some* chance variation in scores between the two groups? If we did this same experiment again tomorrow, or next week, would we expect (again) to get exactly the same mean scores, even though experimental conditions remain the same? No. We generally anticipate that simply because of chance factors alone there will be some difference between the scores earned by two different groups of subjects—even if they are doing the same thing under the same conditions. So if mean scores for our two groups turn out to be somewhat different, we aren't surprised; we can attribute the difference to chance. But what if the groups are treated differently? What if the differences in measured responses are large? Can these differences also be attributed to chance? Or do they reflect real, significant differences between the two groups? This is where inferential statistics come in.

Inferential statistics allow us to make probability statements. They help us to determine the likelihood that observed differences in our descriptive statistics (such as means) are differences due to chance and random factors or reflect some true difference between the groups we have measured. Differences that are not likely to have occurred by chance are called **statistically significant differences.** If the difference between two calculated means is found to be statistically significant, that difference may or may not be *important* or *meaningful,* but we can claim that the difference is not likely to be due to chance.

One way to think about statistical significance is in terms of replication. If, for example, two means are found to be significantly different, it is likely that if the measurements were taken over and over again, the same difference in the same direction would show up most of the time. Inferential statistics can be used to judge the statistical significance of any statistic. They can be used to tell us about the probability with which means, or medians, or standard deviations, or proportions, or correlation coefficients are truly different or, rather, are different by chance alone.

Significance is usually stated as a proportion. We talk about means being different at the "0.05 level," for instance. What this means is that the likelihood of our finding a mean difference as large as we did by chance alone is less than 5 in 100. The "0.01 level of significance" is even more conservative. It implies that the difference that we have observed would have occurred by chance—if in fact no real differences exist—less than 1 time in 100.

Let's return now to the example with which we are working in this section and add a small insight to this business of statistical significance. We have reported that the results of an experiment provide us with two mean scores: 26.0 for the group that studied in silence and 28.5 for subjects who studied with classical music in the background. Our interest now is in determining the extent to which these means are statistically different or due to chance factors. As we have implied, there is a statistical test of significance that can be applied to our data to this very question. The statistical test is called a *t-test.*

There are *three* factors that influence a test of significance such as the one that would be applied to our data for this example. One, of course, is the size of the mean difference itself. *Everything else being equal,* the larger the measured difference, the more likely that the difference reflects a real

statistically significant differences *differences between descriptive statistics not likely to have occurred by chance if the descriptive statistics were describing the same group*

have IQs above 115.

fall between 1 standard deviation below the mean and 1 standard deviation above the mean (see Figure A.7). It is also the case that 95 percent of the cases fall between ± 2 standard deviations around the mean. Almost all the cases (about 99 percent) in a normal distribution fall between − 3 and + 3 standard deviations around the mean. What good is this sort of information? Let's look at an example problem.

When many people are measured, IQ scores tend to fall in distributions that we may consider to be normal distributions. Figure A.8 depicts a theoretical IQ distribution where, by definition, the mean equals 100 and the standard deviation is equal to 15 IQ points. We might want to know, for instance, what percentage of the population has an IQ score above 100. Well, that's an easy one. Because the mean equals 100, and because the mean divides the distribution exactly in half, 50 percent of the cases fall above 100 and 50 percent of the cases fall below an IQ of 100, so the answer is 50 percent.

What percentage of the population has an IQ score above 115? This takes a little more effort, and following along with Figure A.8 might help. We might work backward. If we know the percentage of cases in the shaded portion of the curve (up to IQ = 115) then the difference between that percentage and 100 will be the percentage who have IQs above 115. We can't determine the shaded percentage by inspection, but we can do so in a few easy steps. Up to the mean fall one-half, or 50 percent, of the cases (this we've already established). Now what about that segment between 100 and 115? What we do know (check on Figure A.7 again) is that 68 percent of the cases fall between − 1 standard deviation and + 1 standard deviation. In a normal distribution, the mean divides this segment exactly in half, so that between the mean and 1 standard deviation above the mean are in-

The percentage of cases in a normal distribution falling between ± 1 SD around the mean (68%), ± 2 SD (95%), and ± 3 SD (99%). Note that the curve is symmetrical and the mean divides it exactly in half, and that virtually all scores fall between 3 standard deviations below the mean and 3 standard deviations above the mean.

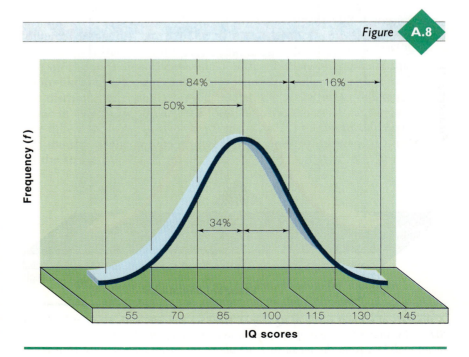

Figure **A.8**

cluded 34 percent of the cases. (Note that IQ = 115 *is* 1 SD above the mean.) So now we have 50 percent to the mean of 100, and 34 percent from the mean to 115. We add the two together and determine that 84 percent of the cases fall *below* an IQ of 115, so 16 percent must fall above it. Using the same logic, we can convert any score to a percentage or proportion, if we are dealing with a normal curve. To do so for scores that do not fall precisely on standard deviation units above or below the mean involves a slight complication, but the general method is the same as we have indicated here. What percentage of the population (in accord with our Figures A.7 and A.8) have earned IQ scores above 130? (The answer is 2.5 percent. Can you see where that comes from?)

BEFORE YOU GO ON

What is a normal curve? ·

In a normal curve, what percentage of the cases fall between ±1, ±2, and ±3 standard deviations around the mean?

SUMMARY

What is a frequency distribution and what is a histogram? What are they used for?

As its name suggests, a frequency distribution is a way of organizing collected data by listing all scores (X-values) in order and indicating the frequency with which each occurs. A histogram is a bar graph that represents the frequency with which X-values occur by the height of a bar over each X-value. Both histograms and frequency distributions help us to summarize data so that we may make some determinations about its nature by visual inspection. / *page 724*

Name and define three measures of central tendency.

There are three measures of central tendency, or average: (1) the *mean* ($\overline{X}$), the sum of X-scores divided by the number of scores, that is, $\overline{X} = \Sigma X/N$; (2) the *median*, the score above which and below which fall 50 percent of the scores; and (3) the *mode*, the most fre-

quently occurring score in the distribution. / *page 727*

What is the formula for standard deviation, and of what is it a measure?

The standard deviation (SD) is a measure of the spread, or dispersion, of the scores in a distribution. It is, essentially, the average of the extent to which each score in the distribution deviates from its mean. The formula for standard deviation is:

$$SD = \sqrt{\frac{\Sigma(X - \overline{X})^2}{N}}$$

/ *page 730*

What is meant by "test of statistical significance"? What does it mean to say that two means, for example, are statistically significant at the 0.01 level?

A test of statistical significance tells us about the likelihood that an observed descriptive statistical difference might have occurred by chance. For example,

to say that the difference between the two means is "statistically significant at the 0.01 level" means that if there were no real difference between the groups from which the means came, the likelihood of discovering a mean difference as large as the one observed is less than 1 in 100. / *page 732*

What is a normal curve? In a normal curve, what percentage of the cases fall between ±1, ±2, and ±3 standard deviations around the mean?

The normal curve depicts data often encountered in psychology when large numbers of measurements are made. It is a graph of frequencies of scores that is symmetrical and bell-shaped. Within 1 standard deviation above the mean and 1 standard deviation below the mean fall 68 percent of all the cases measured. Between ±2 SDs around the mean fall 95 percent of all cases, and 99 percent of all cases fall between −3 SD and +3 SDs around the mean. / *page 735*

GLOSSARY

ACT theory a network model of LTM (both episodic and semantic) that suggests that we store meaningful and related propositions that can be judged as true or false (p. 263)

abnormal statistically uncommon, maladaptive cognitions, affect, and/or behaviors that are at odds with social expectations and that result in distress or discomfort (p. 557)

absolute threshold the physical intensity of a stimulus that one can detect 50 percent of the time (p. 98)

accommodation in vision, the process in which the shape of the lens is changed by the ciliary muscles to focus an image on the retina (p. 53)

accommodation in Piaget's theory, the process of altering or revising an existing schema in the light of new information (p. 402)

acquired immune deficiency syndrome (AIDS) a deadly disease caused by a virus (the HIV) that destroys the body's natural immune system, and which can be transmitted by sexual behaviors (p. 486)

acquisition the process in classical conditioning in which the strength of the CR increases with repeated pairings of the CS and UCS (p. 196)

acquisition the process in operant conditioning in which the rate of a reinforced response increases (p. 217)

action potential the short-lived burst of a change in the difference in electrical charge between the inside and the outside of a neuron when it fires (+40 mV) (p. 60)

actor-observer bias the overuse of internal attributions to explain the behaviors of others and external attributions to explain our own behaviors (p. 651)

addiction an extreme dependency, usually accompanied by symptoms of tolerance and painful withdrawal (p. 179)

adolescence the developmental period between childhood and adulthood, often begun at puberty and ending with full physical growth, generally between the ages of 12 and 20 (p. 418)

adolescent egocentrism self-centered cognitions, plus the belief that one is the center of others' attention (p. 425)

affect the feelings or mood that accompany an emotional reaction (p. 6)

agism discrimination or negative sterotypes about someone formed solely on the basis of age (p. 435)

agoraphobia a phobic fear of open places, of being alone, or of being in public places from which escape might be difficult (p. 562)

algorithm a problem-solving strategy in which all possible solutions are generated and tested and an acceptable solution is guaranteed (p. 326)

all-or-none principle the fact that a neuron will either fire and generate a full impulse (an action potential), or it will not fire at all (p. 60)

alpha activity an EEG pattern associated with quiet relaxation and characterized by slow wave cycles of 8 to 12 per second (p. 167)

androgens the male sex hormones (steroids) produced by the testes (p. 475)

androgyny a balanced combination of traits that are both masculine and feminine (p. 488)

anorexia nervosa an eating disorder characterized by the reduction of body weight through self-starvation and/or increased activity levels (p. 514)

antianxiety drugs chemicals, such as the meprobamates and benzodiazepines, that alleviate the symptoms of anxiety (p. 607)

antidepressant drugs chemicals, such as MAO inhibitors and tricyclics, that reduce and/or eliminate the symptoms of depression (p. 606)

antipsychotic drugs chemicals, such as chlorpromazine, that are effective in reducing psychotic symptoms (p. 604)

anxiety a general feeling of apprehension or dread accompanied by predictable physiological changes (p. 560)

aphrodisiac a substance that, when drunk or eaten, increases sexual arousal; none are known to exist (p. 478)

applied behavior analysis (ABA) an approach, based on operant conditioning, that attempts to find solutions to human environment problems in the real world (p. 713)

aqueous humor watery fluid found in the space between the cornea and the lens that nourishes the front of the eye (p. 109)

arousal one's level of activation or excitement; indicative of a motivational state (p. 498)

assessment center a personnel selection procedure in which persons are tested, interviewed, and observed in a number of stressful situations by a team of evaluators (p. 684)

assimilation the process of adding new material or information to an existing schema (p. 401)

association areas those areas of the frontal, parietal, and temporal lobes in which higher mental processing occurs (p. 87)

atonia muscular immobility, associated with REM sleep, caused by the total relaxation of the muscles (p. 171)

attachment a strong two-way emotional bond, usually between a child and parent, or primary care-giver (p. 411)

attitude a relatively stable and general evaluative disposition directed toward some object, consisting of feelings, behaviors, and beliefs (p. 641)

attribution the cognitions we generate when we attempt to explain the sources of behavior (p. 649)

audience inhibition reluctance to intervene and offer assistance in front of others (p. 669)

autokinetic effect the visual illusion of apparent motion in which a stationary pinpoint of light in an otherwise dark environment appears to move (p. 156)

autonomic nervous system (ANS) those neurons of the PNS that activate the smooth muscles and glands (p. 65)

availability heuristic the rule of thumb that suggests that whatever is more available in our memory is also more common or probable (p. 332)

aversion therapy a technique of behavior therapy in which an aversive stimulus, such as a shock, is paired with an undesired behavior (p. 623)

axon the long, taillike extension of a neuron that carries an impulse away from the cell body toward the synapse (p. 57)

axon terminals the series of branching end points of an axon where one neuron communicates with the next in a series (p. 58)

babbling speech sounds produced in rhythmic, repetitive patterns (p. 313)

basal ganglia a collection of structures in front of the limbic system that produce and depend on dopamine to control large, slow bodily movements (p. 82)

baseline design a method in which subjects' performance with an experimental treatment is compared with performance without that treatment (the baseline) (p. 43)

basilar membrane a structure within the cochlea that vibrates and thus stimulates the hair cells of the inner ear (p. 128)

behavior what an organism does; an action of an organism that can be observed and measured (p. 6)

behavioral observation the personality assessment technique of drawing conclusions about one's personality based on observations of one's behaviors (p. 462)

behaviorism an approach to psychology emphasizing the overt, observable, measurable behavior of organisms (p. 13)

behavior therapy techniques of psychotherapy founded on principles of learning established in the psychological laboratory (p. 621)

blind spot the small region of the retina, containing no photoreceptors, where the optic nerve leaves the eye (p. 111)

brain stem the lowest part of the brain, just above the spinal cord, comprised of the medulla and the pons (p. 79)

brightness the psychological experience associated with a light's intensity or wave amplitude (p. 103)

British empiricists philosophers (including Locke) who claimed, among other things, that the contents of mind come from experience (p. 9)

bulimia an eating disorder characterized by recurrent episodes of binge eating and then purging to remove the just-eaten food (p. 514)

CAT scan (computerized axial tomography) a method of imaging brain structures through the computer enhancement of X-ray pictures (p. 71)

case history an intensive, retrospective, and detailed study of some aspects of one (or a few) individual(s) (p. 34)

category clustering at recall, grouping words together into categories even if they are presented in a random order (p. 261)

cell body the largest mass of a neuron, containing the cell's nucleus, and which may receive neural impulses (p. 57)

central nervous system (CNS) those neurons in the brain and spinal cord (p. 65)

central tendency a measure of the middle, or average, score in a set (p. 725)

cerebellum a spherical structure at the lower rear of the brain involved in the coordination of bodily movements (p. 80)

cerebral cortex (or cerebrum) the large, convoluted outer covering of the brain that is the seat of cognitive functioning and voluntary action (p. 84)

cerebral hemispheres the two halves of the cerebral cortex, separated by a deep fissure running from front to back (p. 85)

chlamydia a very common STD; a bacterial infection of the genital area (p. 484)

chromosome literally, "colored body"; that tiny, threadlike structure found in 23 pairs in human cells that carry genes (p. 52)

chunk a somewhat imprecise concept referring to a meaningful unit of information as represented in memory (p. 253)

ciliary muscles small muscles attached to the lens that control its shape and focusing capability (p. 109)

classical conditioning learning in which an originally neutral stimulus comes to elicit a new response after having been paired with a stimulus that reflexively elicits that same response (p. 194)

client-centered therapy the humanistic psychotherapy associated with Rogers, aimed at helping the client grow and change from within (p. 620)

closure the Gestalt principle of organization claiming that we tend to perceive incomplete figures as whole and complete (p. 149)

cochlea part of the inner ear where sound waves become neural impulses (p. 128)

cognitions the mental processes of knowing, perceiving, thinking, remembering, and the like (p. 6)

cognitive dissonance a motivating discomfort or tension caused by a lack of balance or consonance among one's cognitions (p. 506)

cognitive map a mental representation of the learning situation or physical environment (p. 234)

cognitive reappraisal a rethinking of a stressful situation to consider it in a more positive light, for example, determining if a stressor is real or imagined (p. 547)

cognitive restructuring therapy a form of cognitive therapy, associated with Beck, in which patients are led to overcome negative self-images and pessimistic views of the future (p. 627)

common fate the Gestalt principle of organization claiming that we group together into the same figure elements of a scene that move together in the same direction at the same speed (p. 149)

compulsions constantly intruding, stereotyped, and essentially involuntary acts or behaviors (p. 565)

concept a mental representation of a category or class of events or objects (p. 298)

conception the moment when the father's sperm cell unites with the mother's ovum to produce a zygote (p. 389)

concrete operations stage in Piaget's theory, from age 7 years to age 12 years, when concepts can be manipulated, but not in an abstract fashion (p. 404)

concurrent validity the extent to which the scores on a test are correlated with other assessments made at about the same time (p. 351)

conditioned response (CR) in classical conditioning, the learned response (for example, salivation) evoked by the CS after conditioning (p. 195)

conditioned stimulus (CS) in classical conditioning, an originally neutral stimulus (for example, a tone) that, when paired with a UCS, comes to evoke a new response (a CR) (p. 195)

cones photosensitive cells of the retina that operate best at high levels of illumination and are responsible for color vision (p. 109)

conflict a stressor in which some goals can be satisfied only at the expense of others (p. 542)

conformity the changing of one's behavior, under perceived pressure, so that it is consistent with the behavior of others (p. 662)

consciousness our awareness or perception of the environment and of our own mental processes (p. 166)

conservation in Piaget's theory, an appreciation that changing the physical properties of an object does not necessarily change its essence (p. 404)

content validity the extent to which a test provides an adequate and fair sample of the behaviors being measured (p. 351)

contingency contracting establishing a token economy of secondary reinforcers to reward appropriate behaviors (p. 624)

contingency management bringing about changes in one's behaviors by controlling rewards and punishments (p. 624)

continuity the Gestalt principle of organization claiming that a stimulus or a movement will be perceived as continuing in the same smooth direction as first established (p. 149)

continuous reinforcement schedule (CRF) a reinforcement schedule in which each and every response is followed by a reinforcer (p. 222)

contrast the extent to which a stimulus is in some physical way different from other surrounding stimuli (p. 142)

control group those participants in an experiment who do not receive any experimental treatment or manipulation (p. 42)

convergence the tendency of the eyes to move toward each other as we focus on objects up close (p. 150)

convergent thinking the reduction or focusing of many different ideas into one possible problem solution (p. 333)

conversion disorder the display of a severe physical disorder for which there is no medical explanation; often accompanied by an apparent lack of concern on the part of the patient (p. 568)

cornea the outermost structure of the eye that protects the eye and begins to focus light waves (p. 108)

corpus callosum a network of nerve fibers that interconnect the two hemispheres of the cerebrum (p. 88)

correlation a largely statistical technique used to determine the nature and extent of the relationship between two measured responses (p. 35)

correlation coefficient a number that indicates the nature (+ or −) and the strength (0.00 to +1.00 or −1.00) of the relationship between measured responses (p. 36)

cross laterality the process of nerve fibers crossing over at the brain stem so that the left side of the body sends impulses to and receives impulses from the right side of the brain and vice versa (p. 80)

crowding the subjective feeling of discomfort caused by a sense of lack of space (p. 708)

crystallized intelligence those cognitive skills dependent on knowledge, accumulated experience, and general information (p. 374)

dark adaptation the process by which our eyes become more sensitive to light as we spend time in the dark (p. 103)

death instincts (thanatos) the inborn impulses, proposed by Freud, that compel one toward destruction; include aggression (p. 445)

debrief to fully inform a subject about the intent and/or hypotheses of one's research once data have been collected (p. 46)

decibel scale a scale of our experience of loudness in which 0 represents the absolute threshold and 140 is sensed as pain (p. 124)

defense mechanisms unconsciously applied techniques that protect the self (ego) from feelings of anxiety (p. 445)

degenerative dementia a marked loss of intellectual and cognitive abilities that worsens with age (p. 579)

deinstitutionalization the practice, begun in the mid-1950s, of releasing patients from mental institutions and returning them to their home communities (p. 608)

dendrites branchlike extensions from a neuron's cell body where most neural impulses are received (p. 57)

dependence a state in which drug use is either necessary or believed to be necessary to maintain functioning at some desired level (p. 179)

dependent variables those responses measured in an experiment whose values are hypothesized to depend upon manipulations of the independent variable (p. 39)

depressants drugs (such as alcohol, opiates, heroin, and barbiturates) that slow or reduce nervous system activity (p. 182)

diagnosis the act of recognizing a disorder on the basis of the presence of particular symptoms (p. 557)

difference threshold the minimal difference in some stimulus attribute, such as intensity, that one can detect 50 percent of the time (p. 100)

diffusion of responsibility the tendency to allow others to share in the obligation to intervene (p. 670)

discrimination the phenomenon in classical conditioning in which an organism learns to make a CR in response to only one CS but not to other stimuli (p. 198)

discrimination the process of differential reinforcement wherein one stimulus is reinforced while another stimulus is not (p. 228)

dissociative disorder a disorder in which one separates from or dissociates from aspects of one's personality (p. 569)

divergent thinking the creation of many ideas or potential problem solutions from one idea (p. 333)

dominant gene a gene that carries a trait that will be expressed regardless of the gene it is paired with (p. 52)

double-blind technique a protection against bias in which both the subjects and the data collecter/analyzer are kept from knowing the hypothesis of an experiment (p. 44)

Down's syndrome a condition of many symptoms, including mental retardation, caused by an extra (forty-seventh) chromosome (p. 381)

drive a state of tension resulting from a need that arouses and directs an organism's behavior (p. 499)

drug abuse a lack of control, a disruption of interpersonal relationships or difficulties at work, and a history of maladaptive use for at least one month (p. 179)

eardrum the outermost membrane of the ear; is set in motion by the vibrations of a sound; transmits vibrations to the ossicles (p. 128)

ego the aspect of personality that encompasses the sense of "self"; in contact with the real world; operates on the reality principle (p. 445)

egocentric to be characterized by self; by "me" and "mine" and "my point of view" (p. 403)

elaborative rehearsal a mechanism for processing information into LTM that involves the meaningful manipulation of the information to be remembered (p. 258)

electroconvulsive therapy (ECT) a treatment, usually for the symptoms of severe depression, in which an electric current passed through a patient's head causes a seizure and loss of consciousness (p. 603)

electrode a fine wire used to either stimulate or record the electrical activity of neural tissue (p. 69)

electroencephalogram (EEG) an instrument used to measure and record the electrical activity of the brain (p. 167)

electromyogram (EMG) an instrument used to measure and record muscle tension/relaxation (p. 167)

emotion a reaction involving subjective feeling, physiological response, cognitive interpretation, and behavioral expression (p. 528)

empathic able to understand and share the essence of another's feelings, or to view from another's perspective (p. 621)

encoding the active process of representing, or putting information into memory (p. 246)

encoding specificity principle the hypothesis that we can only retrieve what we have stored and that retrieval is enhanced to the extent that retrieval cues match encoding cues (p. 276)

endocrine system a network of glands that secrete hormones directly into the bloodstream (p. 66)

environmental psychology the field of applied psychology that studies the effect of the general environment on organisms within it (p. 704)

epigenetic model an interactionist view of development that claims that development emerges based on one's genetic programming and one's experiences (p. 388)

episodic memory in LTM, where life events and experiences are stored (p. 261)

equity theory the view that workers are motivated to match their inputs and outcomes with those of fellow workers in similar positions (p. 690)

erogenous zones areas of the body that, when stroked, lead to sexual arousal (p. 478)

estrogens the female sex hormones (steroids) produced by the ovaries (p. 475)

etiology the cause or predisposing factors of a disturbance or disorder (p. 559)

expectancy theory the view that workers make logical choices to do what they believe will result in their attaining outcomes of highest value (p. 689)

experiment a series of operations used to investigate relationships between manipulated events (independent variables) and measured events (dependent variables), while other events (extraneous variables) are eliminated (p. 39)

experimental group those participants in an experiment who receive some treatment or manipulation—there may be more than one in an experiment (p. 42)

external attribution an explanation of behavior in terms of something outside the person; a situational attribution (p. 649)

extinction the process in operant conditioning in which the rate of a response decreases as reinforcers are withheld (p. 217)

extinction the process in classical conditioning in which the strength of the CR decreases with repeated presentations of the CS alone (without the UCS) (p. 197)

extraneous variables those factors in an experiment that need to be minimized or eliminated so as not to affect the dependent variable (p. 39)

family therapy a variety of group therapy focusing on the roles, interdependence, and communication skills of family members (p. 628)

fetal alcohol syndrome a cluster of symptoms (e.g., low birth weight, poor muscle tone, intellectual retardation), associated with a child born to a mother who was a heavy drinker of alcohol during pregnancy (p. 393)

figure-ground relationship the Gestalt psychology principle that stimuli are selected and perceived as figures against a ground or background (p. 147)

flashbulb memories particularly clear, and vivid memories that are easily retrieved but not necessarily accurate in all detail (p. 277)

flooding a technique of behavior therapy in which a subject is confronted (in vivo) with the object of his or her phobic fear while accompanied by the therapist (p. 623)

fluid intelligence those cognitive skills dependent on speed, adaptation, flexibility, and abstract reasoning (p. 374)

formal concepts concepts with relatively few, well-defined attribute values and clearly defined rules to relate them (p. 299)

formal operations stage in Piaget's theory, ages older than 12 years, when one can generate and test abstract hypotheses, and think as an adult, where thinking follows rules (p. 405)

fovea the region at the center of the retina, comprised solely of cones, where acuity is best in daylight (p. 111)

free association the procedure in psychoanalysis in which the patient is to express whatever comes to mind without editing responses (p. 618)

frequency distribution an ordered listing of all X-values, indicating the frequency with which each occurs (p. 723)

frontal lobes the largest of the cerebral lobes, located in front of the central fissure and above the lateral fissure (p. 85)

frustration a stressor; the blocking or thwarting of goal-directed behavior (p. 541)

frustration-aggression hypothesis the view (now discredited) that all aggression stems from frustration (p. 549)

functionalism an approach to psychology emphasizing the study of the mind and consciousness as they help the organism adapt to the environment (p. 12)

functional fixedness the phenomenon in which one is unable to see a new use or function for an object because of experience using the object in some other function (p. 330)

fundamental attribution error the tendency to overuse internal attributions when explaining behavior (p. 649)

g on an intelligence test, a measure of one's overall, general intellectual abilities, commonly thought of as IQ (p. 354)

gate-control theory the theory of pain sensation that argues that there are brain centers that regulate the passage of pain messages from different parts of the body to the brain (p. 135)

gender identity a basic sense or self-awareness of one's maleness or femaleness (p. 488)

gender roles attitudes and expectations about how a person should act, think, and/or feel solely on the basis of being a female or a male (p. 488)

gene the basic mechanism of hereditary transmission; that which gets passed from one generation to the next (p. 52)

generalization the phenomenon in classical conditioning in which a CR is elicited by stimuli different from, but similar to, the CS (p. 198)

generalization the phenomenon in operant conditioning in which a response that was reinforced in the presence of one stimulus appears in response to other similar stimuli (p. 228)

generalized anxiety disorder persistent, chronic, and distressingly high levels of unattributable anxiety (p. 563)

genetics the science that studies the transmission of traits or characteristics from one generation to the next (p. 52)

genital herpes (herpes type II) the most common STD; a skin infection in the form of a rash or blisters in the genital area (p. 485)

gestalt whole, totality, configuration; where the whole (gestalt) is seen as more than the sum of its parts (pp. 16, 147)

g-factor in Spearman's model, a general, overall intellectual skill (p. 343)

gonads the sex glands: **testes** in males, **ovaries** in females (p. 475)

gonorrhea an STD caused by a bacterial infection of moist tissues in the genital area (p. 485)

group polarization the tendency for members of a group to give more extreme judgments following a discussion than they gave initially (p. 674)

groupthink a style of thinking of cohesive groups concerned with maintaining agreement to the extent that independent ideas are discouraged (p. 675)

growth spurt a marked increase in both height and weight that accompanies the onset of adolescence (p. 419)

habituation in classical conditioning, a simple form of learning in which an organism comes to ignore a stimulus of no consequence (p. 194)

hair cells the receptor cells for hearing, located in the cochlea, stimulated by the vibrating basilar membrane; they send neural impulses to the temporal lobe of the brain (p. 128)

hallucinations perceptual experiences without sensory input; that is, perceiving that which is not there or not perceiving that which is there (p. 176)

hallucinogens drugs (such as LSD) whose major effect is the alteration of perceptual experience and mood (p. 184)

health psychology the field of applied psychology that studies psychological factors affecting physical health and illness (p. 700)

hertz (Hz) the standard measure of sound wave frequency that is the number of wave cycles per second (p. 124)

heuristic a problem-solving strategy in which hypotheses about problem solutions are generated and tested in a time-saving and systematic way, but that does not guarantee an acceptable solution (p. 327)

histogram a bar/graph; a graphical representation of a frequency distribution (p. 724)

holophrastic speech the use of one word to communicate a number of different meanings (p. 314)

homeostasis a state of balance or equilibrium among internal, physiological conditions (p. 503)

homosexuals persons who are sexually attracted to and aroused by members of their own sex (p. 480)

hormones a variety of chemical compounds, secreted by the glands of the endocrine system, many of which have effects on behavior or mental states (p. 66)

hue the psychological experience associated with a light's wavelength (p. 104)

humanistic psychology an approach to psychology emphasizing the person or self as a central matter of concern (p. 15)

hypnosis an altered state of consciousness characterized by an increase in suggestibility, attention, and imagination (p. 175)

hypochondriasis a mental disorder involving the fear of developing some serious disease or illness (p. 567)

hypothalamus a small structure near the limbic system in the center of the brain, associated with feeding, drinking, sex, and aggression (p. 82)

hypothesis a tentative proposition or explanation that can be tested and confirmed or rejected (p. 5)

IQ the intelligence quotient, found by dividing one's mental age (MA) by one's chronological age (CA), and multiplying by 100, or MA/CA × 100 (p. 356)

id the instinctive aspect of personality that seeks immediate gratification of impulses; operates on the pleasure principle (p. 445)

idealistic principle the force that governs the superego; opposed to the id, seeks adherence to standards of ethics and morality (p. 446)

identity crisis the struggle to define and integrate one's sense of self and what one's attitudes, beliefs, and values should be (p. 423)

identity status one of four states in identity formation, reflecting a sense of conflict and/or a sense of commitment (p. 423)

illusion a perception that is at odds with (different from) what we know as physical reality (p. 156)

implosive therapy a behavior therapy in which one imagines one's worst fears, experiencing extreme anxiety in the safe surroundings of the therapist's office (p. 623)

impression management function the selective presentation or misrepresentation of one's attitudes in an attempt to present oneself in a particular way (p. 642)

in-basket technique an assessment technique requiring applicants to respond to a variety of situations that might be encountered in a typical workday (p. 684)

incentives external stimuli that an organism may be motivated to approach or avoid (p. 502)

independent variables those events in an experiment that are manipulated by the experimenter that are hypothesized to produce changes in responses (p. 39)

inferential statistics statistical tests that tell us about the significance of the results of experimental or correlational studies (p. 730)

inferiority complex the Adlerian notion that as children, in dealing with our environment, we develop a sense of inferiority that needs to be overcome to reach maturity (p. 447)

insanity a legal term for diminished capacity and inability to tell right from wrong (p. 560)

insomnia the chronic inability to get to sleep and to get an adequate amount of sleep (p. 167)

instinctive drift the tendency of behaviors that have been conditioned to eventually revert to more natural, instinctive behaviors (p. 231)

instincts unlearned, complex patterns of behavior that occur in the presence of particular stimuli (p. 498)

intelligence the capacity to understand the world and the resourcefulness to cope with its challenges; that which an intelligence test measures (p. 342)

interactive dualism Descartes's position that a separate body and mind influence each other and are thus knowable (p. 9)

intermittent reinforcement schedules reinforcement schedules in which responses are not reinforced every time they occur (p. 223)

internal attribution an explanation of behavior in terms of something (a trait) within the person; a dispositional attribution (p. 649)

interview the personality assessment technique involving a conversational interchange between the interviewer and subject to gain information about the subject (p. 464)

introspection a technique in which one examines one's own mental experiences and reports them in the most fundamental, basic way (p. 11)

ion an electrically charged (either + or −) chemical particle (p. 59)

iris the colored structure of the eye that reflexively opens or constricts the pupils (p. 108)

job analysis a complete and specific description of a job, including the qualities required to do it well (p. 680)

job satisfaction an attitude; a collection of positive feelings about one's job or job experiences (p. 692)

just noticeable difference (j.n.d.) the minimal change in some stimulus attribute, such as intensity, that can be detected (p. 101)

just world hypothesis the belief that the world is just and that people get what they deserve (p. 651)

kinesthetic sense the position sense that tells us the position of different parts of our bodies and what our muscles and joints are doing (p. 133)

language a large collection of arbitrary symbols that have significance for a language-using community and that follow certain rules of combination (p. 307)

latent learning hidden learning that is not demonstrated in performance until that performance is reinforced (p. 234)

law of effect (Thorndike's) the observation that responses that lead to "satisfying states of affairs" tend to be repeated, while those that do not are not (p. 215)

learning demonstration of a relatively permanent change in behavior that occurs as the result of practice or experience (p. 192)

learning set an acquired strategy for learning or problem solving; learning to learn (p. 232)

lens the structure behind the iris that changes shape to focus visual images in the eye (p. 108)

lesion a cut or incision that destroys specific areas of tissue (p. 69)

levels of processing models of memory the view that there is only one memory, but that information can be processed within that memory at different degrees, levels, or depths (p. 247)

libido the energy that activates the life (sexual) instincts (largely of the id) (p. 445)

life instincts (eros) inborn impulses, proposed by Freud, that compel one toward survival; include hunger, thirst, and sex (p. 445)

light a radiant energy that can be represented in wave form with wavelengths between 380 and 760 nanometers (p. 103)

lightness constancy the tendency to see objects as the same regardless of the intensity of light reflected from them (p. 159)

limbic system a collection of structures, including the amygdala and septum, which are involved in emotionality; and the hippocampus, involved in forming long-term memories (p. 82)

linguistic intuitions judgments or decisions about the syntactic acceptability of utterances without the ability to specify why (p. 311)

lobotomy a psychosurgical technique in which the prefrontal lobes of the cerebral cortex are severed from lower brain centers (p. 601)

long-term memory (LTM) a type of memory with virtually unlimited capacity and very long, if not limitless, duration (p. 255)

loudness the psychological experience correlated with the intensity, or amplitude, of a sound wave (p. 124)

MRI (magnetic resonance imaging) a process that provides clear, detailed pictures of the brain by recording energy from cells when the brain has been placed in a magnetic field (p. 71)

maintenance rehearsal a process of rote repetition (reattending) to keep information in STM (p. 252)

malleus, incus, and stapes (collectively, *ossicles*) three small bones that transmit and intensify sound vibrations from the eardrum to the oval window (p. 128)

matching phenomenon the tendency to select partners whose level of physical attractiveness matches our own (p. 655)

mean ($\overline{X}$), the sum of all X-scores (ΣX) divided by N, the number of X-scores (p. 726)

meaningfulness the extent to which information evokes associations with information already in memory (p. 279)

median the score of an ordered set above which and below which fall half the scores (p. 726)

meditation the focusing of awareness in order to arrive at an altered state of consciousness and relaxation (p. 177)

medulla an area of the brain stem that monitors breathing and heart rate, and where most cross laterality occurs (p. 79)

memory the cognitive ability to encode, store, and retrieve information (p. 246)

menarche a female's first menstrual period, often taken as a sure sign of the beginning of adolescence (p. 421)

mentally gifted demonstrating outstanding ability or aptitude in a number of possible areas; usually general intelligence where an IQ of 130 is a standard criterion (p. 377)

mental processes internal activities of consciousness, including cognitions and affect (p. 6)

mental retardation a condition indicated by an IQ below 70 that began during the developmental period and is associated with impairment in adaptive functioning (p. 379)

mental set a predisposed (set) way to perceive something; an expectation (p. 145)

mere exposure phenomenon the tendency to increase our liking of people and things the more we see of them (p. 654)

meta-analysis a statistical procedure of combining the results of several studies to see more clearly any relationships among observations that may be present (p. 44)

metamemory in LTM, our stored knowledge of how our own memory systems work (p. 261)

method of loci the mnemonic device that mentally places information to be retrieved at a series of familiar locations (loci) (p. 282)

microsleeps very brief episodes of sleep discernible only by examination of an EEG record (p. 173)

Minnesota Multiphasic Personality Inventory (MMPI-2) a paper-and-pencil inventory of 567 true-false questions used to assess a number of personality dimensions, some of which may indicate the presence of a psychological disorder (p. 465)

mnemonic devices strategies for improving retrieval that take advantage of existing memories in order to make new material more meaningful (p. 279)

mode the most frequently occuring X-value in a set (p. 727)

modeling the acquisition of new responses through the imitation of another who responds appropriately (p. 624)

monochromatic literally *one-colored*; a pure light made up of light waves all of the same wavelength (p. 106)

mood disorders disorders of affect or feeling; usually depression; less frequently mania and depression occurring in cycles (p. 581)

morpheme the smallest unit of meaning in a language (p. 310)

motivation the process of arousing, maintaining, and directing behavior (p. 498)

motor areas the strips at the back of the frontal lobes that control voluntary movement (p. 86)

multiple personality the existence within one individual of two or more distinct personalities, each of which is dominant at a particular time (p. 569)

multistore models of memory descriptions of memory that propose a number of separate and distinct types (or stores) of memory, each with its own manner of processing information (p. 247)

myelin a white, fatty covering found on some axons that serves to insulate and protect them, while increasing the speed of impulses (p. 58)

nanometer (nm) one millionth of a millimeter—the unit of measurement for the wavelength of light (p. 104)

narrative chaining the mnemonic device of relating words together in a story, thus organizing them in a meaningful way (p. 279)

natural concepts the potentially "fuzzy" sorts of concepts that occur in real life, with ill-defined attributes and/or rules (p. 301)

naturalistic observation the method of observing and noting behaviors as they occur naturally (p. 32)

nature-nurture controversy the debate over which is more important in development, one's genetic, inherited nature, or one's nurture, one's experience through interaction with the environment (p. 388)

need a lack or shortage of some biological essential resulting from deprivation (p. 499)

need for affiliation the need to be with others and to form relationships and associations (p. 520)

need for competence the need to meet the challenges, large and small, provided by one's environment (p. 520)

need for power the learned need to be in control of events or persons, usually at another's expense (p. 519)

need to achieve (nAch) the learned need to meet or exceed some standard of excellence in performance (p. 517)

negative reinforcer a stimulus that increases the rate of a response when that stimulus is removed after the response is made (p. 220)

neo-Freudians personality theorists (including Adler, Jung, and Horney) who kept many basic psychoanalytic principles, but differed from a strict Freudian view, adding new concepts of their own (p. 447)

neonate the newborn, from birth to age 2 weeks (p. 395)

network models organizational schemes that describe the relationships among meaningful units stored in semantic memory (p. 262)

neural impulse a sudden and reversible change in the electrical charges within and outside the membrane of a neuron, which travels from the dendrite to the axon end of a neuron (p. 59)

neural threshold the minimum amount of stimulation required to produce an impulse within a neuron (p. 60)

neuron a nerve cell, the basic building block of the nervous system that transmits neural impulses (p. 56)

neurotoxins chemicals (poisons) that affect psychological processes through the nervous system (p. 712)

neurotransmitters chemical molecules released at the synapse that will, in general, either excite or inhibit neural impulse transmission (p. 62)

normal curve a commonly found symmetrical, bell-shaped frequency distribution (p. 733)

norms in the context of psychological testing results of a test taken by a large group of subjects whose scores can be used to make comparisons or give meaning to new scores (p. 352)

norms in the context of social psychology rules or expectations that guide our behavior in certain social situations by prescribing how we ought to behave (p. 640)

nuclei small collections or bundles of neural cell bodies (p. 80)

object permanence the appreciation that an object no longer in view can still exist and reappear later (p. 402)

observer bias when one's own motives, expectations, and past experiences interfere with the objectivity of one's observations (p. 32)

obsessions ideas or thoughts that involuntarily and persistently intrude into awareness (p. 564)

occipital lobes the cerebral lobes at the very back of the brain (p. 85)

operant referring to behavior(s) used by an organism to operate on its environment (p. 214)

operant conditioning changing the rate of a response on the basis of the consequences that result from that response (p. 214)

operational definition a definition of a concept given in terms of the methods (or operations) used to measure that concept (p. 7)

optic chiasma the location in the brain where impulses from light in the left visual field cross to the right side of the brain and light from the right visual field cross to the left side of the brain (p. 112)

optic nerve the fiber composed of many neurons that leaves the eye and carries impulses to the occipital lobe of the brain (p. 110)

organic mental disorders disorders characterized by any of the organic mental syndromes *and* a known organic cause of the syndrome (p. 578)

orienting reflex the simple, unlearned response of orienting toward, or attending to, a new or unusual stimulus (p. 194)

overlearning the practice or rehearsal of material over and above what is needed to learn it (p. 285)

overregularization the excessive application of an acquired language rule (e.g., for plurals or past tense) in a situation where it is not appropriate (p. 316)

PET scan (positron emission transaxial tomography) a method of imaging the brain and its activity by locating small amounts of radioactive chemical injected into the brain (p. 72)

panic disorder a disorder in which anxiety attacks suddenly and unpredictably incapacitate; there may be periods free from anxiety (p. 562)

parasympathetic division (of the ANS) those neurons involved in the maintenance of states of calm and relaxation (p. 65)

parietal lobes the lobes of the cerebrum found behind the frontal lobes, in front of the occipital lobes, and above the temporal lobes (p. 85)

Parkinson's disease a disorder of movement caused by damage to tissues in the basal ganglia (p. 83)

peg word method the mnemonic device of forming interactive visual images of materials to be learned and items previously associated with numbers (p. 281)

perception the cognitive process of selecting, organizing, and interpreting stimuli (p. 142)

performance criteria specific behaviors or characteristics that a person should have in order to do a job as well as possible (p. 681)

peripheral nervous system (PNS) those neurons not found in the brain or spinal cord, but in the periphery of the body (p. 65)

personality disorders enduring patterns of perceiving, relating to, and thinking about the environment and one's self that are inflexible and maladaptive (p. 571)

personal space the mobile "bubble" of space around you reserved for intimate relationships into which others may enter only by invitation (p. 705)

persuasion the process of intentionally attempting to change an attitude (p. 645)

phenomenological relating to an approach that emphasizes one's perception and awareness of events as being more important than the events themselves (p. 451)

phenomenology the study of events as they are experienced by the individual; that experience is reality (p. 21)

phenylketonuria (PKU) a genetically caused disorder that produces mental retardation and that is now detectable and preventable (p. 382)

pheromones chemicals that produce an odor used as a method of communication between organisms (p. 130)

phi phenomenon the visual illusion of the apparent motion of stationary lights flashing on and off in sequence (p. 156)

phobic disorder an intense, irrational fear that leads a person to avoid the feared object, activity, or situation (p. 204)

phoneme the smallest unit of sound in the spoken form of a language (p. 310)

photoreceptors light-sensitive cells (cones and rods) of the retina that convert light energy into neural energy (p. 109)

pinna the outer ear, which collects and funnels sound waves into the auditory canal toward the eardrum (p. 128)

pitch the psychological experience that corresponds to sound wave frequency and gives rise to high (treble) or low (bass) sounds (p. 124)

placebo an inactive substance that has its effect because a person has come to believe that it will be effective (p. 136)

plasticity a demonstration of flexibility, or a capacity to be molded and shaped (by the environment) in a wide range of ways (p. 388)

pleasure principle the impulse of the id to seek immediate gratification to reduce tensions (p. 445)

pluralistic ignorance a condition in which the inaction of others leads each individual in a group to interpret a situation as a nonemergency, thus leading to general inactivity (p. 669)

pons a brain stem structure forming a bridge between the brain and the spinal cord that monitors the sleep-wake cycle (p. 80)

population density a quantitative measure of the number of persons (or animals) per unit of area (p. 708)

positive reinforcer a stimulus that increases the rate of a response when it is presented after the response is made (p. 219)

positive test strategy the heuristic of sticking with an acceptable decision or solution, even if a better one might exist (p. 332)

posttraumatic stress disorder (PTSD) an anxiety disorder in which disruptive recollections, distressing dreams, flashbacks, and felt anxiety occur well after the experience of a traumatic event (p. 566)

pragmatics The study of how social context affects the meaning of linguistic events (p. 312)

predictive validity the extent to which a test can be used to predict future behaviors (p. 351)

prenatal period the period of development from conception to birth (p. 389)

preoperational stage In Piaget's theory, from age 2 years to age 6 years, when a child begins to develop symbolic representations, but cannot manipulate them; also characterized by egocentricity (p. 403)

primary hues red, green, and blue; those colors of light from which all others can be produced (p. 116)

primary mental abilities in Thurstone's model, the seven unique abilities taken to comprise intelligence (p. 344)

primary reinforcers stimuli (usually biologically or physiologically based) that increase the rate of a response with no previous experience required (p. 221)

proactive interference the inhibition of retrieval of recently learned material caused by material learned earlier (p. 290)

problem a situation in which there is a discrepancy between one's current state and one's desired, or goal, state, with no clear way of getting from one to the other (p. 322)

procedural memory in LTM, where stimulus-response associations and skilled patterns of responses are stored (p. 259)

process schizophrenia schizophrenia in which the onset of the symptoms is comparatively slow and gradual (p. 588)

progesterone one of the most important of the female estrogens, or sex hormones (p. 475)

prognosis the prediction of the future course of an illness or disorder (p. 516)

projective technique a personality assessment technique requiring a subject to respond to ambiguous stimuli, thus projecting his or her self into the responses (p. 467)

prototype the member of a concept or category that best typifies or represents that concept or category (p. 302)

proximity the Gestalt principle of organization claiming that stimuli will be perceived as belonging together if they occur together in space or time (p. 148)

psychoactive drug a chemical that affects psychological processes and consciousness (p. 179)

psychoanalysis the form of psychotherapy associated with Freud, aimed at helping the patient gain insight into unconscious conflicts (p. 15)

psychoanalytic the approach to personality associated with Freud and his followers that relies on instincts and the unconscious as explanatory concepts (p. 444)

psychogenic amnesia a psychologically caused inability to recall important personal information (p. 569)

psychogenic fugue a condition of amnesia accompanied by unexplained travel or change of location (p. 569)

psycholinguistics the science that studies the cognitive processes involved in the use and acquisition of language (p. 307)

psychological test an objective, standardized measure of a sample of behavior (p. 347)

psychology the scientific study of behavior and mental processes (p. 4)

psychophysics the study of the relationship between physical attributes of stimuli and the psychological experiences they produce (p. 96)

psychosocial law the view that each person who joins a social situation adds less influence than did the previous person to join the group (p. 671)

psychosurgery a surgical procedure designed to affect one's psychological or behavioral reactions (p. 601)

psychotherapy the treatment of mental disorders through psycho-logical means, effecting change in cognitions, affect, and/or behavior (p. 613)

puberty the stage of physical development at which one becomes capable of sexual reproduction (p. 420)

publicly verifiable the agreement (verifiability) of observers (public) that an event did or did not take place (p. 6)

punishment the administration of a punisher, which is a stimulus that decreases the rate or probability of a response that precedes it (p. 226)

pupil the opening in the iris that changes size in relation to the amount of light available and emotional factors (p. 108)

quality of work life (QWL) a group of factors concerning one's work that influence one's attitude toward one's job (p. 692)

REM sleep rapid eye movement sleep during which vivid dreaming occurs, as do heightened levels of physiological functioning (p. 169)

random assignment the selection of members of a population in such a way that each has an equal opportunity to be assigned to any one group (p. 43)

range the highest score in a distribution minus the lowest (p. 728)

rational-emotive therapy (RET) a form of cognitive therapy, associated with Ellis, aimed at changing the subject's irrational beliefs or maladaptive cognitions (p. 625)

reactive schizophrenia schizophrenia in which the onset of the symptoms is comparatively sudden (p. 588)

reality principle the force that governs the ego, arbitrating between the demands of the id, the superego, and the real world (p. 445)

recall a measure of retrieval in which an individual is given the fewest possible cues to aid retrieval (p. 272)

recessive gene a gene that carries a trait that will be expressed only if it is paired with another similar recessive gene (p. 52)

recognition a measure of retrieval in which an individual is required to identify material previously learned as being familiar (p. 272)

reflex an unlearned, automatic response that occurs in the presence of specific stimuli (p. 194)

refractory period during the process of the human sexual response, the period following orgasm during which arousal in the male is not possible (p. 479)

reinforcement a process that increases the rate or probability of the response that it follows (p. 218)

reinforcers stimuli that increase the rate or probability of the responses they follow (p. 219)

relearning a measure of memory in which one notes the improvement in performance when learning material for a second time (p. 274)

reliability consistency or dependability; in testing, consistency of test scores (p. 349)

representativeness heuristic the rule of thumb that suggests that judgments made about a prototypic member of a category will hold for all members of the category (p. 332)

resistance in psychoanalysis, the inability or unwillingness to freely discuss some aspect of one's life (p. 618)

resting potential the difference in electrical charge between the inside of a neuron and the outside when it is at rest (-70 mV) (p. 60)

reticular activating system (RAS) a network of nerve fibers extending from the brain stem to the cerebrum that is involved in maintaining levels of arousal (p. 81)

retina layers of cells at the back of the eye that contain the photosensitive rod and cone cells (p. 109)

retinal disparity the phenomenon in which each retina receives a different (disparate) view of the same three-dimensional object (p. 153)

retrieval the process of locating, removing, and using information that is stored in memory (p. 246)

retroactive interference the inhibition of retrieval of previously learned material caused by material learned later (p. 289)

rods photosensitive cells of the retina that are most active in low levels of illumination and do not respond differentially to different wavelengths of light (p. 109)

Rorschach inkblot test a projective technique in which the subject is asked to say what he or she sees in a series of inkblots (p. 468)

sample the portion of a larger population chosen for study (p. 34)

saturation the psychological experience associated with the purity of a light wave, where the most saturated lights are monochromatic and the least saturated are white light (p. 106)

schema a system of organized, general knowledge, stored in long-term memory, that guides the encoding and retrieval of information (p. 283)

schizophrenia complex psychotic disorders characterized by impairment of cognitive functioning, delusions and hallucinations, social withdrawal, and inappropriate affect (p. 585)

science an organized body of knowledge gained through application of scientific methods (p. 4)

scientific law a statement about one's subject matter thought to be true, based on evidence (p. 30)

scientific methods systematic procedures of discovery that include observation, description, control, and replication (p. 5)

secondary reinforcers stimuli that increase the rate of a response because of their having been associated with other reinforcers; also called conditioned, or learned, reinforcers (p. 221)

self-serving bias the tendency to attribute our successes to our own effort and abilities, and our failures to situational, external sources (p. 651)

semantics the study of the meaning of words and sentences (p. 310)

semantic memory in LTM, where vocabulary, facts, simple concepts, rules, and the like are stored (p. 259)

sensation the process of receiving information from the environment and changing that input into nervous system activity (p. 96)

sensorimotor stage in Piaget's theory, from birth to age 2 years, when a child learns by sensing and doing (p. 402)

sensory adaptation (in most cases) the process in which our sensory experience tends to decrease or diminish with continued exposure to a stimulus (p. 102)

sensory areas those areas of the cerebral cortex that receive impulses from our sense receptors (p. 86)

sensory memory the type of memory that holds large amounts of information registered at the senses for very brief periods of time (p. 247)

set point a normal, optimum level (or value) of equilibrium or balance among physiological or psychological reactions (p. 504)

sexual dysfunction any of a number of chronic difficulties or problems with sexual functioning; usually caused by psychological factors (p. 482)

sexually transmitted diseases (STDs) contagious diseases that are usually transmitted through sexual contact (p. 484)

s-factors in Spearman's model, those specific cognitive abilities that together with "g" constitute intelligence (p. 343)

shape constancy the tendency to see objects as being of constant shape regardless of the shape of the retinal image (p. 158)

shaping a procedure of reinforcing successive approximations of a desired response until that desired response is made (p. 217)

short-term memory (STM) a type of memory with limited capacity (7 ± 2 bits of information) and limited duration (15–20 seconds) (p. 249)

signal detection theory the view that stimulus detection is a matter of decision making, of separating a signal from background noise (p. 101)

similarity the Gestalt principle of organization claiming that stimuli will be perceived together if they share some common characteristic(s) (p. 148)

single-blind technique a protection against bias in which subjects are kept from knowing the hypothesis of an experiment (p. 43)

size constancy the tendency to see objects as being of constant size regardless of the size of the retinal image (p. 158)

social facilitation improved performance due to the presence of others (p. 673)

social identification function the observation that attitudes communicate information useful in social evaluation (p. 642)

social interference impaired performance due to the presence of others (p. 673)

social learning theory the theory that learning takes place through observation and imitation of models (p. 236)

social loafing the tendency for a person to work less hard when part of a group in which everyone's efforts are pooled (p. 672)

somatic nervous system sensory and motor neurons outside the CNS that serve the sense receptors and the skeletal muscles (p. 65)

somatoform disorders psychological disorders that reflect imagined physical or bodily symptoms or complaints (p. 566)

spinal cord a mass of interconnected neurons within the spine that conveys impulses to and from the brain and is involved in some reflex behaviors (p. 76)

spinal reflex an automatic, involuntary response to a stimulus that involves sensory neurons carrying impulses to the spinal cord, interneurons within the spinal cord, and motor neurons carrying impulses to muscles (p. 77)

split-brain procedure a surgical technique of severing the corpus callosum, allowing the two hemispheres to operate independently (p. 88)

split-half reliability a check on the internal consistency of a test found by correlating one part of a test with another part of the same test (p. 350)

spontaneous recovery the phenomenon in operant conditioning in which a previously extinguished response returns after a rest interval (p. 197)

spontaneous recovery the phenomenon in classical conditioning in which a previously extinguished CR returns after a rest interval (p. 218)

sport psychology the application of psychological principles to sport and physical activity at all levels of skill development (p. 715)

stage of the embryo developmental period from 2 to 8 weeks (p. 390)

stage of the fetus developmental period from week 8 until birth (months 3 through 9) (p. 391)

stage of the zygote developmental period from conception to the age of 2 weeks (p. 390)

standard age score (SAS) a score on an intelligence test in which one's performance is compared to that of others of the same age; average equals 100 (p. 356)

standard deviation (SD) a type of average of the deviations of each X-score from the mean of the distribution (p. 728)

state-dependent memory the hypothesis that retrieval can be enhanced by the extent to which one's state of mind at retrieval matches one's state of mind at encoding (p. 277)

statistically significant differences differences between descriptive statistics not likely to have occurred by chance if the descriptive statistics were describing the same group (p. 731)

stereotype a generalized mental (cognitive) representation of someone that minimizes individual differences and is based on limited experience (p. 639)

stimulants drugs (such as caffeine, cocaine, and amphetamines) that increase nervous system activity (p. 180)

storage the process of holding encoded information in memory (p. 246)

strategy in problem solving, a systematic plan for generating possible solutions that can be tested to see if they are correct (p. 326)

stress a complex pattern of reactions to real or perceived threats to one's sense of well-being that motivates adjustment (p. 540)

stressors real or perceived threats to one's sense of well-being; sources of stress (p. 540)

subjective contours the perception of a contour (a line or plane) that is not there, but is suggested by other aspects of a scene (p. 150)

subjective organization the tendency of subjects to impose some order on their recall of randomly presented events or items (p. 261)

subliminal perception the process of responding to, or perceiving, stimuli that are presented at levels below one's absolute threshold (p. 99)

superego the aspect of personality that refers to ethical or moral considerations; operates on the idealistic principle (p. 446)

survey a means of collecting observations from a large number of subjects, usually by interview or questionnaire (p. 34)

sympathetic division (of the ANS) those neurons involved in states of emotionality (p. 65)

synapse the general location where an impulse is relayed from one neuron to another by means of neurotransmitters (p. 62)

synaptic cleft the space between the membrane of an axon terminal and the membrane of the next neuron in a sequence (p. 62)

syndrome a collection of psychological symptoms used to describe a disorder (p. 578)

syntax the rules that govern how the morphemes of a language may be combined to form meaningful utterances (p. 311)

syphilis an STD caused by a bacterial infection, which may pass through four stages, ultimately resulting in death (p. 485)

systematic desensitization the application of classical conditioning procedures to alleviate anxiety in which anxiety-producing stimuli are paired with a state of relaxation (p. 204)

Thematic Apperception Test (TAT) a projective personality test requiring a subject to tell a series of short stories about a set of ambiguous pictures (p. 468)

taste buds the receptors for taste located in the tongue (p. 129)

temporal lobes the lobes of the cerebrum, located at the temples (p. 85)

territoriality the setting off and marking of a piece of territory (a location) as one's own (p. 706)

testosterone the most important of the male androgens, or sex hormones (p. 475)

test-retest reliability a check of a test's consistency determined by correlating the results of a test taken by the same subjects at two different times (p. 349)

thalamus the last sensory relay station; it sends impulses to the appropriate area of the cerebral cortex (p. 83)

timbre the psychological experience related to wave purity by which

we differentiate the sharpness, clearness, or quality of a tone (p. 126)

tolerance in using a drug, a state in which more and more of the drug is required to produce the same desired effect (p. 179)

training a systematic and intentional process of altering the behaviors of employees to increase organizational effectiveness (p. 685)

traits distinguishable, relatively enduring ways in which individuals may differ (p. 454)

transducer a mechanism that converts energy from one form to another—a basic process common to all our senses (p. 96)

transference in psychoanalysis, the situation in which the patient comes to feel about the analyst in the same way he or she once felt about some other important person (p. 619)

tremors involuntary, trembling, jerky movements (p. 81)

type A behavior pattern (TABP) a collection of behaviors (competitive, achievement-oriented, impatient, easily aroused, often hostile or angry) often associated with coronary heart disease (p. 700)

unconditioned response (UCR) in classical conditioning, a response (for example, salivation) reliably and reflexively evoked by a stimulus (the UCS) (p. 194)

unconditioned stimulus (UCS) in classical conditioning, a stimulus (for example, food powder) that reflexively and reliably evokes a response (the UCR) (p. 194)

validity in testing, the extent to which a test measures what it claims to measure (p. 350)

variability the extent of spread or dispersion in a set or distribution of scores (p. 725)

vesicles the small containers, concentrated in axon terminals, that hold neurotransmitter molecules (p. 62)

vestibular sense the position sense that tells us about balance, where we are in relation to gravity, and acceleration or deceleration (p. 133)

viability the ability to survive without interference or intervention (p. 391)

vicarious reinforcement (or punishment) increasing the rate (with reinforcement) or decreasing the rate (with punishment) of responses due to observing the consequences of someone else's behaviors (p. 237)

vitreous humor the thick fluid behind the lens of the eye that helps keep the eyeball spherical (p. 109)

wave amplitude a characteristic of wave forms (the height of the wave) that indicates intensity (p. 103)

wavelength a characteristic of wave forms that indicates the distance between any point on a wave and the corresponding point on the next cycle of the wave (p. 104)

white light a light of the lowest possible saturation, containing a mixture of all visible wavelengths (p. 107)

white noise a sound composed of a random assortment of all wave frequencies from the audible spectrum (p. 126)

withdrawal a negative, painful reaction that may occur when one stops taking a drug (p. 179)

X and Y chromosomes the chromosomes that determine one's genetic sex; XX for females, XY for males (p. 474)

zygote the one-cell product of the union of sperm and ovum at conception (p. 389)

REFERENCES

A

Abel, E. L. (1981). Behavioral teratology. *Psychological Bulletin, 90*, 564–581.

Abel, E. L. (1984). *Fetal alcohol syndrome and fetal alcohol effects*. New York: Plenum.

Adams, G. R. (1977). Physical attractiveness, personality, and social reactions to peer pressure. *Journal of Psychology, 96*, 287–296.

Adams, G. R., & Gullotta, T. (1983). *Adolescent life experiences*. Monterey, CA: Brooks/Cole.

Adams, J. A. (1980). *Learning and memory: An introduction*. Homewood, IL: Dorsey Press.

Adams, J. L. (1974). *Conceptual blockbusting*. Stanford, CA: Stanford Alumni Association. Cited in A. L. Glass, K. J. Holyoak, & J. L. Santa (1979). *Cognition*. Reading, MA: Addison-Wesley.

Adams, J. S. (1965). Inequity in social exchange. In L. Berkowitz (Ed.), *Advances in experimental social psychology*. New York: Academic Press.

Adelmann, P. K., & Zajonc, R. B. (1989). Facial efference and the experience of emotion. *Annual Review of Psychology, 40*, 249–280.

Adelson, B. (1984). When novices surpass experts: The difficulty of a task may interfere with expertise. *Journal of Experimental Psychology, 10*, 483–495.

Adler, T. (1989). Cocaine babies face behavior deficits. *APA Monitor, 20*, 14.

Adler, T. (1990a). Does the "new" MMPI beat the "classic"? *APA Monitor, 21*, 18–19.

Adler, T. (1990b). MEG scan's future is now in the making. *Psychological Monitor, 21*, 5.

Agnew, H. W., Webb, W. W., & Williams, R. L. (1964). The effects of stage 4 sleep deprivation. *Electroencephalography and Clinical Neurophysiology, 17*, 68–70.

Aiello, J. R., & Aiello, T. D. (1974). The development of personal space: Proxemic behavior of children 6 through 16. *Human Ecology, 2*, 177–189.

Aiken, L. R. (1984). *Psychological testing and assessment* (4th ed.). Boston: Allyn & Bacon.

Ainsworth, M. D. S. (1979). Infant-mother attachment. *American Psychologist, 34*, 932–937.

Ainsworth, M. D. S. (1989). Attachments beyond infancy. *American Psychologist, 44*, 709–716.

Ajzen, I., & Fishbein, M. (1980). *Understanding attitudes and predicting social behavior*. Englewood Cliffs, NJ: Prentice-Hall.

Alba, J. W., & Hasher, L. (1983). Is memory schematic? *Psychological Bulletin, 93*, 201–231.

Allen, M. G. (1976). Twin studies of affective illness. *Archives of General Psychiatry, 33*, 1476–1478.

Altman, I. (1975). *The environment and social behavior*. Monterey, CA: Brooks/Cole.

Amabile, T. M. (1985). Motivation and creativity. *Journal of Personality and Social Psychology, 48*, 393–399.

American Psychiatric Association. (1987). *Diagnostic and statistical manual of mental disorders* (3rd rev. ed.). Washington, DC: American Psychiatric Association.

American Psychological Association. (1990). Ethical principles of psychologists. *American Psychologist, 45*, 390–395.

Amoore, J. E. (1970). *Molecular basis of odor*. Springfield, IL: Thomas.

Anastasi, A. (1982). *Psychological testing* (5th ed.). New York: Macmillan.

Anastasi, A. (1986). Evolving concepts of test validation. *Annual Review of Psychology, 37*, 1–15.

Anderson, A. (1982). Neurotoxic follies. *Psychology Today, 16*, 30–42.

Anderson, C. A. (1987). Temperature and aggression: Effects on quarterly, yearly, and city rates of violent and nonviolent crime. *Journal of Personality and Social Psychology, 52*, 1161–1173.

Anderson, C. A. (1989). Temperature and aggression: Ubiquitous effects of heat on occurrence of human violence. *Psychological Bulletin, 106*, 74–96.

Anderson, C. A., & Anderson, D. C. (1984). Ambient temperature and violent crime: Tests of the linear and curvilinear hypotheses. *Journal of Personality and Social Psychology, 46*, 91–97.

Anderson, R. & Nida, S. A. (1978). Effect of physical attractiveness on opposite- and same-sex evaluations. *Journal of Personality, 46*, 401–413.

Anderson, J. C., Williams, S., McGee, R., & Silva, P. A. (1987). DSM-III disorders in preadolescent children. *Archives of General Psychiatry, 44*, 69–76.

Anderson, J. R. (1976). *Language, memory, and thought*. Hillsdale, NJ: Erlbaum.

Anderson, J. R. (1980a). *Cognitive psychology and its implications*. San Francisco: Freeman.

Anderson, J. R. (1980b). On the merits of ACT and information-processing psychology: A response to Wexler's review. *Cognition, 8*, 73–88.

Anderson, J. R. (1983a). *The architecture of cognition*. Cambridge, MA: Harvard University Press.

Anderson, J. R. (1983b). A spreading activation theory of memory. *Journal of Verbal Learning and Verbal Behavior, 22*, 261–295.

Anderson, J. R. (1986). Knowledge compilation: The general learning mechanism. In R. Michalski, J. Carbonnell, & T. Mitchell (Eds.), *Machine learning II*. Palo Alto, CA: Tioga Press.

Anderson, J. R. (1987). Skill acquisition: Compilation of weak-method problem solutions. *Psychological Review, 94*, 192–210.

Anderson, R. C., & Pichert, J. W. (1978). Recall of previously unrecallable information following a shift in perspective. *Journal of Verbal Learning and Verbal Behavior, 17*, 1–12.

Andreasen, N. C. (1982). Negative versus positive schizophrenia: Definition and validation. *Archives of General Psychiatry, 39*, 789–794.

Andreasen, N. C., Ehrhardt, J. C., Swayze, V. W., Alliger, R. J., Yuh, W. T. C., Cohen, G., & Ziebell, S. (1990). Magnetic resonance imaging of the brain in schizophrenia. *Archives of General Psychiatry, 47*, 35–44.

Andreasen, N. C., Flaum, M., Swayze, V. W., Tyrrell, G., & Arndt, S. (1990). Positive and negative symptoms in schizophrenia. *Archives of General Psychiatry, 47*, 615–621.

Andreasen, N. C., Olsen, S. A., Dennert, J. W., & Smith, M. R. (1982). Ventricular enlargement in schizophrenia: Definition and prevalence. *American Journal of Psychiatry, 139,* 292–296.

Andrews, R. J. (1963). Evolution of facial expression. *Science, 142,* 1034–1041.

Angoff, W. H. (1988). The nature-nurture debate, aptitudes, and group differences. *American Psychologist, 43,* 713–720.

Anisfeld, M. (1984). *Language development from birth to three.* Hillsdale, NJ: Erlbaum.

Anisman, H., & Zacharko, R. M. (1982). Depression: The predisposing influence of stress. *The Behavioral and Brain Sciences, 5,* 89–137.

APA. (1987). *Diagnostic and statistical manual of mental disorders* (3rd rev. ed.). Washington, DC: American Psychiatric Association.

Archer, S. L. (1982). The lower age boundaries of identity development. *Child Development, 53,* 1551–1556.

Aronson, E., & Linder, D. (1965). Gain and loss of esteem as determinants of interpersonal attractiveness. *Journal of Personality and Social Psychology, 1,* 156–171.

Aronson, E., Turner, J. A., & Carlsmith, J. M. (1963). Communicator credibility and communication discrepancy as a determinant of opinion change. *Journal of Abnormal and Social Psychology, 67,* 31–36.

Arvey, R. D., & Campion, J. E. (1982). The employee interview: A summary and review of recent research. *Personnel Psychology, 35,* 281–322.

Arvey, R. D., Miller, H. E., Gould, R., & Burch, P. (1987). Interview validity for selecting sales clerks. *Personnel Psychology, 40,* 1–12.

Asch, S. E. (1951). The effects of group pressure upon the modification and distortion of judgment. In H. Guetzkow (Ed.), *Groups, leadership, and men.* Pittsburgh: Carnegie Press.

Asch, S. E. (1956). Studies of independence and conformity: I. A minority of one against a unanimous majority. *Psychological Monographs: General and Applied, 70* (Whole No. 416), 1–70.

Aserinsky, E., & Kleitman, N. (1953). Regularly occurring periods of eye mobility and concomitant phenomena during sleep. *Science, 118,* 273–274.

Aslin, R. N., & Smith, L. B. (1988). Perceptual development. *Annual Review of Psychology, 39,* 435–473.

Atkinson, J. W., & Feather, N. T. (1966). *A theory of achievement motivation.* New York: Wiley.

Atkinson, J. W., & Litwin, G. H. (1960). Achievement motive and test anxiety conceived as motive to approach success and motive to avoid failure. *Journal of Abnormal and Social Psychology, 60,* 27–36.

Atkinson, R. C. (1975). Mnemotechnics in second-language learning. *American Psychologist, 30,* 821–828.

Atkinson, R. C., & Shiffrin, R. M. (1968). Human memory: A proposed system and its control processes. In K. W. Spence & J. T. Spence (Eds.), *The psychology of learning and motivation: Advances in research and theory.* New York: Academic Press.

Atwood, M. E., & Polson, P. G. (1976). A process model for water jug problems. *Cognitive Psychology, 8,* 191–216.

Auletta, K. (1984). Children of children. *Parade Magazine, 17,* 4–7.

Axelrod, S., & Apsche, J. (1983).*The effects of punishment on human behavior.* New York: Academic Press.

Azrin, N. H., & Holz, W. C. (1966). Punishment. In W. K. Honig (Ed.), *Operant behavior: Areas of research and application.* Englewood Cliffs, NJ: Prentice-Hall.

B

Babor, T. F., Berglas, S., Mendelson, J. H., Ellinboe, J., & Miller, K. (1983). Alcohol, effect and the disinhibition of behavior. *Psychopharmacology, 80,* 53–60.

Backer, T. E., & Richardson, D. (1989). Building bridges: Psychologists and families of the mentally ill. *American Psychologist, 44,* 546–550.

Backman, C. W., & Secord, P. F. (1959). The effect of perceived liking on interpersonal attraction. *Human Relations, 12,* 379–384.

Baddeley, A. D. (1966). Short-term memory for word sequences as a function of acoustic, semantic and formal similarity. *Quarterly Journal of Experimental Psychology, 18,* 362–365.

Baddeley, A. D. (1982). Domains of recollection. *Psychological Review, 89,* 708–729.

Bagozzi, R. P., & Burnkrant, R. E. (1979). Attitude organization and the attitude-behavior relationship. *Journal of Personality and Social Psychology, 37,* 913–929.

Bahrick, H. P. (1984). Semantic memory content in permastore. *Journal of Experimental Psychology: General, 113,* 1–29.

Balay, J., & Shevrin, H. (1988). The subliminal psychodynamic activation method: A critical review. *American Psychologist, 43,* 161–174.

Baley, S. (1985). The legalities of hiring in the 80s. *Personnel Journal, 64,* 112–115.

Ballenger, J. C. (1989). Toward an integrated model of panic disorder. *American Journal of Orthopsychiatry, 59,* 284–293.

Bandura, A. (1965). Influence of models' reinforcement contingencies on the acquisition of imitative responses. *Journal of Personality and Social Psychology, 1,* 589–595.

Bandura, A. (1973). *Aggression; A social learning analysis.* Englewood Cliffs, NJ: Prentice-Hall.

Bandura, A. (1974). Behavior theory and the models of man. *American Psychologist, 29,* 859–869.

Bandura, A. (1976). Modeling theory: Some traditions, trends and disputes. In W. S. Sahakian (Ed.), *Learning: Systems, models, and theories.* Skokie, IL: Rand McNally.

Bandura, A. (1977). *Social learning theory.* Englewood Cliffs, NJ: Prentice-Hall.

Bandura, A. (1978). The self-system in reciprocal determinism. *American Psychologist, 33,* 344–358.

Bandura, A. (1982). Self-efficacy mechanism in human agency. *American Psychologist, 37,* 122–147.

Bandura, A., Ross, D., & Ross, S. A. (1963). Imitation of film-mediated aggressive models. *Journal of Abnormal and Social Psychology, 66,* 3–11.

Barber, T. F. X. (1972). Suggested (hypnotic) behavior: The trace paradigm vs. an alternative paradigm. In E. Fromm & R. E. Shorr (Eds.), *Hypnosis: Research developments and perspectives.* Chicago: Aldine-Atherton.

Bard, P. (1934). The neurohormonal basis of emotional reactions. In C. A. Murchison (Ed.), *Handbook of general experimental psychology.* Worcester, MA: Clark University Press.

Barker, R. (1968). *Ecological psychology.* Stanford, CA: Stanford University Press.

Baron, R. A. (1977). *Human aggression.* New York: Plenum Press.

Baron, R. P. & Byrne, D. (1984). *Social psychology: Understanding human behavior* (4th ed.) Boston: Allyn and Bacon.

Baron, R. A., & Ransberger, V. M. (1978). Ambient temperature and the occurrence of collective violence: The "long hot summer" revisited. *Journal of Personality and Social Psychology, 36,* 351–360.

Barr, H. M., Streissguth, A. P., Darby, B. L., & Sampson, P. D. (1990). Prenatal exposure to alcohol, caffeine, tobacco, and aspirin: Effects on fine and gross motor performance in 4-year-old children. *Developmental Psychology, 26,* 339–348.

Barron, F., & Harrington, D. M. (1981). Creativity, intelligence, and personality. *Annual Review of Psychology, 32,* 439–476.

Barsalou, L. S. (1983). Ad hoc categories. *Memory and Cognition, 11,* 211–227.

Barsalou, L. W. (1989). Intra-concept similarity and its implications for inter-concept similarity. In S. Vosniadou & A. Ortony (Eds.), *Similarity and analogical reasoning.* New York: Cambridge University Press.

Bartus, R. T., Dean, R. L., Beer, B., & Lippa, A. S. (1982). The cholinergic hypothesis of geriatric memory dysfunction. *Science, 217,* 408–417.

Baumeister, A. A. (1987). Mental retardation: Some conceptions and dilemmas. *American Psychologist, 42,* 796–800.

Baumeister, R. F. (1985). The championship choke. *Psychology Today, 19,* 48–52.

Baumeister, R. F. (1987). How the self became a problem: A psychological review of historical research. *Journal of Personality and Social Psychology, 52,* 163–176.

Baumeister, R. F., & Steinhilber, A. (1984). Paradoxical effects of supportive audiences on performance under pressure: The home field disadvantage in sports championships. *Journal of Personality and Social Psychology, 47,* 85–93.

Bayley, N. & Schaefer, E. S. (1964). Correlations of maternal and child behaviors with the development of mental abilities: Data from the Berkeley Growth Study. *Monographs of the Society for Research in Child Development, 29,* 1–80.

Beck, A. T. (1967). *Depression: Clinical, experimental, and theoretical aspects.* New York: Harper Collins.

Beck, A. T. (1976). *Cognitive therapy and the emotional disorders.* New York: International University Press.

Beck, A. T. (1985). Theoretical perspectives in clinical anxiety. In A. H. Tuma & J. D. Master (Eds.), *Anxiety and the anxiety disorders.* Hillsdale, NJ: Erlbaum.

Beck, A. T., & Emery, G. (1985). *Anxiety disorders and phobias: A cognitive perspective.* New York: Basic Books.

Becker, J. R., & Jacobs, J. E. (1983). Sex: Is it an issue in mathematics? *Educational Horizons, 61,* 60–67.

Beckman, L. J., & Houser, B. B. (1982). The consequences of childlessness on the social-psychological well-being of older women. *Journal of Gerontology, 37,* 243–250.

Beecroft, R. (1966). *Classical conditioning.* Goleta, CA: Psychonomic Press.

Beer, M., & Walton, A. E. (1987). Organization change and development. *Annual Review of Psychology, 38,* 339–367.

Begg, I., & Paivio, A. (1969). Concreteness and imagery in sentence meaning. *Journal of Verbal Learning and Verbal Behavior, 8,* 821–817.

Bell, A. P., Weinberg, M. S., & Hammersmith, S. K. (1981). *Sexual preference: Its development in men and women.* Bloomington: Indiana University Press.

Bell, P. A., Fisher, J. D., & Loomis, R. J. (1978). *Environmental psychology.* Philadelphia: Saunders.

Bem, S. (1974). The measurement of psychological androgyny. *Journal of Consulting and Clinical Psychology, 42,* 155–162.

Bem, S. (1975). Sex role adaptability. One consequence of psychological adrogeny. *Journal of Personality and Social Psychology, 31,* 634–643.

Bem, S. (1977). On the utility of alternative procedures for assessing psychological adrogeny. *Journal of Consulting and Counseling Psychology, 45,* 196–205.

Bem, S. (1981). Gender schema theory: A cognitive account of sex typing. *Psychological Review, 88,* 354–364.

Bemis, K. M. (1978). Current approaches to the etiology and treatment of anorexia nervosa. *Psychological Bulletin, 85,* 593–617.

Ben-Yehuda, N. (1980). The European witch craze. *American Journal of Sociology, 86,* 1–31.

Benbow, C. P. (1987). Possible biological correlates of precocious mathematical reasoning ability. *Trends in Neuroscience, 10,* 17–20.

Benbow, C. P. (1990). Gender differences: Searching for facts. *American Psychologist, 45,* 988.

Benbow, C. P., & Stanley, J. C. (1980). Sex differences in mathematical ability: Fact or artifact? *Science, 210,* 1262–1264.

Benedict, H. (1979). Early lexical development: Comprehension and production. *Journal of Child Language, 6,* 183–200.

Benjamin, L. T. (1984). Staying with initial answers on objective tests: Is it a myth? *Teaching of Psychology, 11,* 133–141.

Bennett, T. L. (1982). *Introduction to physiological psychology.* Monterey, CA: Brooks/Cole.

Bennett, W. (1980). The cigarette century. *Science, 80,* 36–43.

Benson, H. (1975). *The relaxation response.* New York: Morrow.

Berkowitz, L. (1978). What ever happened to the frustration-aggression hypothesis? *American Behavioral Scientist, 21,* 691–708.

Berkowitz, L. (1982). Aversive conditions as stimuli to aggression. *Advances in Experimental Social Psychology, 15,* 249–288.

Berkowitz, L. (1989). Frustration-aggression hypothesis: Examination and reformulation. *Psychological Bulletin, 106,* 59–73.

Berkowitz, L. (1990). On the formation and regulation of anger and aggression. *American Psychologist, 45,* 494–503.

Berlyne, D. E. (1960). *Conflict, arousal, and curiosity.* New York: McGraw-Hill.

Berlyne, D. E. (1971). *Aesthetics and psychobiology.* Englewood Cliffs, NJ: Prentice-Hall.

Bernstein, I. (1978). Learned taste aversion in children receiving chemotherapy. *Science, 200,* 1302–1303.

Bernstein, R. (1981). The Y chromosome and primary sexual differentiation. *Journal of the American Medical Association, 245,* 1953–1956.

Berrettini, W. H., Golden, L. R., Gelernter, J., Gejman, P. V., Gershon, E. S., & Datera-Wadleigh, S. (1990). X-chromosome markers and manic-depressive illness. *Archives of General Psychiatry, 47,* 366–374.

Bertenthal, B. I., & Campos, J. J. (1989). A systems approach to the organizing effects of self-produced locomotion during infancy. In C. Rovee-Collier & L. P. Lipsett (Eds.), *Advances in infancy research.* Norwood, NJ: Ablex.

Beutler, L. E., Crago, M., & Arizmendi, T. G. (1986). Therapist variables in psychotherapy process and outcome. In S. L. Garfield & A. E. Bergin (Eds.), *Handbook of psychotherapy and behavior change* (3rd ed.), New York: Wiley.

Birch, E. E., Gwiazda, J., & Held, R. (1983). The development of vergence does not account for the onset of stereopsis. *Perception, 12,* 331–336.

Birdwhistell, R. L. (1952). *Introduction to kinesics.* Louisville, KY: University of Louisville Press.

Birnbaum, M. H., & Mellers, B. A. (1979). Stimulus recognition may mediate exposure effects. *Journal of Personality and Social Psychology, 37,* 391–394.

Blanchard, D. C., & Blanchard, R. J. (1988). Ethoexperimental approaches to the biology of emotion. *Annual Review of Psychology, 39,* 43–68.

Block, J. (1965). *The challenge of response sets.* Englewood Cliffs, NJ: Prentice-Hall.

Block, J. (1984). *Sex-role identity and ego development.* San Francisco: Jossey-Bass.

Bloom, F. E., Lazerson, A., & Hotstadter, L. (1985). *Brain, mind, and behavior.* San Francisco: Freeman

Blum, J. E., Jarvik, L. F., & Clark, E. T. (1970). Rate of change on selective tests of intelligence: A twenty-year longitudinal study. *Journal of Gerontology, 25,* 171–176.

Bolles, R. C. (1970). Species-specific defense reactions and avoidance learning. *Psychological Review, 71,* 32–48.

Bolles, R. C. (1972). Reinforcement, expectancy, and learning. *Psychological Review, 79,* 394–409.

Bolles, R. C. (1975). Learning, motivation, and cognition. In W. K. Estes (Ed.), *Handbook of learning and cognitive processes* (Vol. 1). Hillsdale, NJ: Erlbaum.

Bootzin, R. R., & Acocella, J. R. (1984). *Abnormal psychology: Current perspectives* (4th ed.). New York: Random House.

Borbely, A. (1986). *Secrets of sleep*. New York: Basic Books.

Boring, E. G. (1930). A new ambiguous figure. *American Journal of Psychology, 42,* 109–116.

Bouchard, C., Tremblay, A., Després, J., et al. (1990). The response to long-term overfeeding in identical twins. *The New England Journal of Medicine, 322,* 1477–1482.

Bouchard, T. J., & McGue, M. (1981). Familial studies of intelligence: A review. *Science, 212,* 1055–1059.

Bourne, L. E., Dominowski, R. L., & Loftus, E. F. (1983). *Cognitive process*. Englewood Cliffs, NJ: Prentice-Hall.

Bousfield, W. A. (1953). The occurrence of clustering in the free recall of randomly arranged associates. *Journal of General Psychology, 49,* 229–240.

Bower, G. H. (1970). Imagery as a relational organizer in associative learning. *Journal of Verbal Learning and Verbal Behavior, 9,* 529–533.

Bower, G. H. (1972). Mental imagery and associative learning. In L. W. Gregg (Ed.), *Cognition in learning and memory*. New York: Wiley.

Bower, G. H. (1981). Mood and memory. *American Psychologist, 36,* 129–148.

Bower, G. H., & Clark, M. C. (1969). Narrative stories as mediators for serial learning. *Psychonomic Science, 14,* 181–182.

Bower, G. H., Monteiro, K. P., & Gilligan, S. G. (1978). Emotional mood as a context for learning and recall. *Journal of Verbal Learning and Verbal Behavior, 17,* 573–587.

Bower, G. H., & Springston, F. (1970). Pauses as recoding points in letter series. *Journal of Experimental Psychology, 83,* 421–430.

Bower, T. G. R., Broughton, J. M., & Moore, M. K. (1971). Infant responses to approaching objects: An indicator of response to distal variables. *Perception and Psychophysics, 9,* 193–196.

Bowlby, J. (1982). *Attachment and loss: Vol. 1. Attachment* (2nd ed.). New York: Basic Books.

Bradley, D. R., & Dumais, S. T. (1975). Ambiguous cognitive contours. *Nature, 257,* 582–584.

Bradshaw, J. L., & Nettleton, N. C. (1983). *Human cerebral asymmetry*. Englewood Cliffs, NJ: Prentice-Hall.

Braine, M. D. S. (1976). Children's first word combinations. *Monographs for the Society for Research in Child Development, 41* (Serial No. 164).

Bransford, J. D., & Johnson, M. K. (1972). Contextual prerequisites for understanding: Some investigations of comprehension and recall. *Journal of Verbal Learning and Verbal Behavior, 11,* 717–720.

Bratic, E. B. (1982). Healthy mothers, healthy babies coalition. *Prevention, 97,* 503–509.

Braun, P., Kochansky, G., Shapiro, R., Greenberg, S., Gudeman, J. E., Johnson, S., & Shore, M. (1981). Overview: Deinstitutionalization of psychiatric patients, a critical review of outcome studies. *American Journal of Psychiatry, 138,* 736–749.

Bray, D. W., Campbell, R. J., & Grant, D. L. (1974). *Formative years in business: A long-term AT&T study of managerial lives.* New York: Wiley.

Breckler, S. J. (1984). Empirical validation of affect, behavior, and cognition as distinct components of attitude. *Journal of Personality and Social Psychology, 47,* 1191–1205.

Brehm, J. W., & Self, E. A. (1989). The intensity of motivation. *Annual Review of Psychology, 40,* 109–131.

Breland, K., & Breland, M. (1961). This misbehavior of organisms. *American Psychologist, 16,* 681–684.

Brewer, W. F., & Nakamura, G. V. (1984). The nature and function of schemas. In R. S. Wyler & T. K. Sroll (Eds.), *Handbook of social cognition.* Hillsdale, NJ: Erlbaum.

Brody, E. M. (1981). Women in the middle and family help to older people. *Gerontologist, 21,* 471–480.

Brody, E. M. (1985). Parent care as a normative family stress. *Gerontologist, 25,* 19–29.

Brooks-Gunn, J., & Furstenberg, F. F. (1989). Adolescent sexual behavior. *American Psychologist, 44,* 249–257.

Brown, J. (1958). Some tests of the decay theory of immediate memory. *Quarterly Journal of Experimental Psychology, 10,* 12–21.

Brown, J. (1976). An analysis of recognition and recall and of problems in their comparison. In J. Brown (Ed.), *Recall and recognition.* New York: Wiley.

Brown, J. S. (1948). Gradients of approach and avoidances responses and their relation to motivation. *Journal of Comparative and Physiological Psychology, 41,* 450–465.

Brown, L., Durning, A., & Flavin, C. (1990). *State of the world.* New York: Norton.

Brown, R. (1973). *A first language: The early stages.* Cambridge, MA: Harvard University Press.

Brown, R., Cazden, C. B., & Bellugi, U. (1969). The child's grammar from 1 to 3. *Symposia on child language* (Vol. 2). Minneapolis: University of Minnesota Press.

Brown, R., & Kulik, J. (1977). Flashbulb memories. *Cognition, 5,* 73–99.

Browne, M. A., & Mahoney, M. J. (1984). Sport psychology. *Annual Review of Psychology, 35,* 605–626.

Bruch, H. (1980). Preconditions for the development of anorexia nervosa. *American Journal of Psychoanalysis, 40,* 169–172.

Bruner, J. S., & Goodman, C. C. (1947). Value and need as organizing factors in perception. *Journal of Abnormal and Social Psychology, 42,* 33–44.

Bruner, J. S., Goodnow, J. J., & Austin, G. A. (1956). *A study of thinking.* New York: Wiley.

Buck, R. (1980). Nonverbal behavior and the theory of emotion: The facial feedback hypothesis. *Journal of Personality and Social Psychology, 38,* 811–824.

Buck, R. (1985). Prime theory: An integrated view of motivation and emotion. *Psychological Review, 92,* 389–413.

Buckhout, R. (1975). Nearly 2000 witnesses can be wrong. *Social Action and the Law, 2,* 7.

Burisch, M. (1984). Approaches to personality inventory construction. *American Psychologist, 39,* 214–227.

Buss, D. (1985). Human mate selection. *American Scientist, 73,* 47–51.

Buss, D., & Barnes, M. (1986). Preferences in human mate selection. *Journal of Personality and Social Psychology, 50,* 559–570.

Buss, D. M. (1984). Evolutionary biology and personality psychology. *American Psychologist, 39,* 1135–1147.

Buss, D. M. (1985). Human mate selection. *American Scientist, 73,* 47–51.

Buss, D. M. (1989). Personality as traits. *American Psychologist, 44,* 1378–1388.

Butler, R., & Lewis, M. (1981). *Aging and mental health.* St. Louis: Mosby.

Butler, R., N. & Emr, M. (1982). SDAT research: Current trends. *Generations, 7,* 14–18.

Byrne, D. (1971). *The attraction paradigm.* New York: Academic Press.

Byrne, D., & Clore, G. L. (1970). A reinforcement model of evaluative responses. *Personality: An International Journal, 1,* 103–128.

C

Cacioppo, J. T., & Petty, R. E. (1989). Effects of message repetition on argument processing, recall, and persuasion. *Basic Applied Social Psychology, 10,* 3–12.

Calhoun, J. B. (1962). Population density and social pathology. *Scientific American, 206,* 139–148.

Campos, J. J. (1976). Heart rates: A sensitive tool for the study of emotional development. In L. Lipsett (Ed.), *Developmental psychobiology: The significance of infancy.* Hillsdale, NJ: Erlbaum.

Campos, J. J., Hiatt, S., Ramsey, D., Henderson, C., & Svejda, M. (1978). The emergence of fear on the visual cliff. In M. Lewis & L. A. Rosenbaum (Eds.), *The development of affect.* New York: Plenum.

Cannon, T. D., Mednick, S. A., & Parnas, J. (1990). Antecedents of predominantly negative- and predominantly positive-symptom schizophrenia in a high-risk population. *Archives of General Psychiatry, 47,* 622–632.

Cannon, W. B. (1927). The James-Lange theory of emotions: A critical examination and an alternative theory. *American Journal of Psychology, 39,* 106–124.

Cannon, W. B. (1932). *The wisdom of the body.* New York: Norton.

Carey, S. (1978). The child as word learner. In M. Halle, J. Bresnan, & G. A. Miller (Eds.), *Linguistic theory and psychological reality.* Cambridge, MA: MIT Press.

Carson, R., Butcher, J. N., & Coleman, J. C. (1988). *Abnormal psychology and modern life* (8th ed.). Glenview: IL: Scott, Foresman.

Carson, R. C. (1989). Personality. *Annual review of psychology, 40,* 227–248.

Carson, R. L. (1962). *Silent Spring.* Boston: Houghton Mifflin.

Carson, T. P., & Carson, R. C. (1984). The affective disorders. In H. E. Adams & P. B. Sutker (Eds.)., *Comprehensive handbook of psychopathology.* New York: Plenum.

Cash, T. F., & Kilcullen, R. N. (1985). The eye of the beholder: Susceptibility to sexism and beautyism in the evaluation of managerial applicants. *Journal of Applied Social Psychology, 15,* 591–605.

Centers for Disease Control. (1985). *Suicide surveillance 1970–1980.* Atlanta: U.S. Department of Health and Human Resources.

Cermack, L. S., & Craik, F. I. M. (Eds.). (1979). *Levels of processing in human memory.* Hillsdale, NJ: Erlbaum.

Chaiken, S., & Stangor, C. (1987). Attitudes and attitude change. *Annual Review of Psychology, 38,* 575–630.

Chase, M. H., & Morales, F. R. (1990). The atonia and myoclonia of active (REM) sleep. *Annual Review of Psychology, 41,* 557–584.

Chase, W. G., & Simon, H.A. (1973). The mind's eye in chess. In W. G. Chase (Ed.), *Visual information processing.* New York: Academic Press.

Chasnoff, I. J., Griffith, D. R., MacGregor, S., Dirkes, K., & Burns, K. (1989). Temporal patterns of cocaine use in pregnancy. *Journal of the American Medical Association, 261,* 1741–1744.

Cheesman, J., & Merikle, P. M. (1984). Priming with and without awareness. *Perception and Psychophysics, 36,* 387–395.

Chi, M. T. H. (1978) Knowledge structures and memory development. In R. Siegler (Ed.), *Children's thinking: What develops?* Hillsdale, NJ: Erlbaum.

Chi, M. T. H., & Glaser, R. (1985). Problem solving ability. In R. J. Sternberg (Ed.), *Advances in the psychology of human intelligence.* San Francisco: Freeman.

Chilman, C. S. (1980). Parent satisfactions, concerns, and goals for their children. *Family Relations, 29,* 339–346.

Chilman, C. S. (1983). *Adolescent sexuality in a changing American society: Social and psychological perspectives for the human services profession* (2nd ed.). New York: Wiley.

Chomsky, N. (1957). *Syntactic structures.* The Hague: Mouton.

Chomsky, N. (1965). *Aspects of a theory of syntax.* Cambridge, MA: Harvard University Press.

Chomsky, N. (1975). *Reflections on language.* New York: Pantheon Books.

Chuang, H. T., Devins, G. M., Hunsley, J., & Gill, M. J. (1989). Psychosocial distress and well-being among gay and bisexual men with immunodeficiency virus infection. *American Journal of Psychiatry, 146,* 876–880.

Clark, D. M, & Teasdale, J. D. (1985). Constraints on the effects of mood on memory. *Journal of Personality and Social Psychology, 48,* 1595–1608.

Clarke-Stewart, A., Friedman, S., & Koch, J. (1985) *Child development: A topical approach.* New York: Wiley.

Clarkson-Smith, L., & Hartley, A. A. (1989). Relationships between physical exercise and cognitive abilities in older adults. *Psychology and Aging, 4,* 183–189.

Clifford, B. R., & Lloyd-Bostock, S. (Eds.). (1983). *Evaluating witness evidence: Recent psychological research and new perspectives.* Norwood, NJ: Ablex.

Clifford, M. M., & Hatfield, E. (1973). The effect of physical attractiveness on teacher expectation. *Sociology of Education, 46,* 248–258.

Clore, G. L., & Byrne, D. (1974). A reinforcement-affect model of attraction. In T. L. Huston (Ed.), *Foundations of interpersonal attraction.* New York: Academic Press.

Cohen, G. D. (1980). *Fact sheet: Senile dementia (Alzheimer's disease).* [No. ADM 80-929]. Washington, DC: Center for Studies of the Mental Health of the Aging.

Cohen, L. R., DeLoach, J., & Strauss, M. (1978). Infant visual perception. In J. Osofky (Ed.), *The handbook of infant development.* New York: Wiley.

Cohen, S., Evans, G. W., Krantz, D.S., Stokols, D., & Kelly, S. (1980). Aircraft noise and children: Longitudinal and cross-sectional evidence on the adaptation to noise and the effectiveness of noise abatement. *Journal of Personality and Social Psychology, 40,* 331–345.

Cohen, S., Evans, G. W., Stokols, D., & Krantz, D.S. (1986). *Behavior, health, and environmental stress.* New York: Plenum.

Cohen, S., Lichtenstein, E., Prochaska, J. O., Rossi, J. S., Gritz, E. R., Carr, C. R., et al. (1989). Debunking myths about self-quitting: Evidence from 10 prospective studies of persons who attempt to quit smoking by themselves. *American Psychologist, 44,* 1355–1365.

Colby, A., & Kohlberg, L. (1984). Invariant sequence and internal consistency in moral judgment stages. In W. M. Kurtines & J. L. Gewitz (Eds.), *Morality, moral behavior, and moral development.* New York: Wiley.

Cole, J. O. (1988). Where are those new antidepressants we were promised? *Archives of General Psychiatry, 45,* 193–194.

Coles, R., & Stokes, G. (1985). *Sex and the American teenager.* New York: HarperCollins.

College Board. (1989). *College-bound seniors: 1989 SAT profile.* New York: College Entrance Examination Board.

Collins, A. M., & Loftus, E. F. (1975). A spreading activation theory of semantic processing. *Psychological Review, 82,* 407–428.

Collins, A. M., & Quillian, M. R. (1969). Retrieval time from semantic memory. *Journal of Verbal Learning and Verbal Behavior, 8,* 240–247.

Collins, W. A., & Gunnar, M. R. (1990). Social and personality development. *Annual Review of Psychology, 41,* 387–416.

Committee on an Aging Society. (1986). *America's aging: Productive roles in an older society.* Washington, DC: National Academy Press.

Conger, J. J., & Peterson, A. C. (1984). *Adolescence and youth: Psychological development in a changing world.* New York; HarperCollins.

Conrad, R. (1963). Acoustic confusions and memory span for words. *Nature, 197,* 1029–1030.

Conrad, R. (1964). Acoustic confusions in immediate memory. *British Journal of Psychology, 55,* 75–84.

Cooper, J., & Croyle, R. T. (1984). Attitudes and attitude change. *Annual Review of Psychology, 35,* 395–426.

Cooper, L. A., & Shepard, R. N. (1973). Chronometric studies of the rotation of mental images. In W. G. Chase (Ed.), *Visual information processing.* New York: Academic Press.

Coren, S. (1972). Subjective contours and apparent depth. *Psychological Review, 79,* 359–367.

Coren, S., & Girgus, J. S. (1978). *Seeing is deceiving: The psychology of visual illusions.* Hillsdale, NJ: Erlbaum.

Corkin, S. (1984). Lasting consequences of bilateral medial temporal lobectomy: Clinical course and experimental findings in H. M. *Seminars in Neurology, 4,* 249–259.

Cornblatt, B. A., & Erlenmeyer-Kimling, L. (1985). Global attention deviance as a marker of risk for schizophrenia: Specificity and predictive validity. *Journal of Abnormal Psychology, 94,* 470–486.

Costa, P. T., & McCrae, R. R. (1980). Still stable after all these years: Personality as a key to some issues in adulthood and old age. In P. B. Baltes & O. G. Brim, Jr. (Eds.), *Life-span development and behavior.* New York: Academic Press.

Costello, C. G. (1982). Fears and phobias in women: A community study. *Journal of Abnormal Psychology, 91,* 280–286.

Coulter, W. A., & Morrow, H. W. (Eds.). (1978). *Adaptive behavior: Concepts and measurements.* New York: Grune & Stratton.

Cowan, W. M. (1979). The development of the brain. In *The brain* (pp. 56–69). San Francisco: Freeman.

Cowen, N. (1984). On short and long auditory stores. *Psychological Bulletin, 96,* 341–370.

Cox, R. H. (1990). *Sport psychology: concepts and applications.* Dubuque, IA: Brown.

Coyle, J. T., Price, D. L., & DeLong, M. H. (1983). Alzheimer's disease: A disorder of central cholinergic innervation. *Science, 219,* 1184–1189.

Cozby, P. C. (1973). Self-disclosure: A literature review. *Psychological Bulletin, 79,* 73–91.

Craik, F. I. M. (1970). The fate of primary memory items in free recall. *Journal of Verbal Learning and Verbal Behavior, 9,* 143–148.

Craik, F. I. M., & Lockhart, R. S. (1972). Levels of processing: A framework for memory research. *Journal of Verbal Learning and Verbal Behavior, 11,* 671–684.

Craik, F. I. M., & Tulving, E. (1975). Depth of processing and the retention of words in episodic memory. *Journal of Experimental Psychology: General, 104,* 268–294.

Creekmore, C. R. (1984). Games athletes play. *Psychology Today, 19,* 40–44.

Creekmore, C. R. (1985). Cities won't drive you crazy. *Psychology Today, 19,* 46–53.

Crews, D. J., & Landers, D. M. (1987). A meta-analytic review of aerobic fitness and reactivity to psychosocial stressors. *Medicine and Science in Sport and Exercise, 19,* 114–120.

Crockett, L. J., & Peterson, A. C. (1987). Pubetal status and psychosocial development: Findings from the Early Adolescence Study. In R. M. Lerner & T. T. Foch (Eds.), *Biological-psychosocial interactions in early adolescence: A life-span approach.* Hillsdale, NJ: Erlbaum.

Cronbach, L. J. (1984). *Essentials of psychological testing* (4th ed.). Cambridge, MA: HarperCollins.

Crooks, R., & Bauer, K. (1987). *Our sexuality* (3rd ed.). Menlo Park, CA: Benjamin/Cummings.

Crow, T. J. (1980). Molecular pathology of schizophrenia: More than one disease process? *The British Medical Journal, 280,* 66–68.

Cunningham, S. (1984). Genovese: 20 years later, few heed stranger's cries. *APA Monitor, 15,* 30.

Curtis, R. C., & Miller, K. (1986). Believing another likes or dislikes you: Behaviors making the beliefs come true. *Journal of Personality and Social Psychology, 51,* 284–290.

Cutler, W. B., Preti, G., Krieger, A., Huggins, G. R., Ramon Garcia, C., & Lawley, H. J. (1986). Human axillary secretions influence women's menstrual cycles: The role of donor extract from men. *Hormones and Behavior, 20,* 463–473.

D

Daniel, T. C. (1990). Measuring the quality of the natural environment: A psychophysical approach. *American Psychologist, 45,* 633–637.

Darley, J. M., & Fazio, R. H. (1980). Expectancy confirmation processes arising in the interaction sequence. *American Psychologist, 35,* 861–866.

Darley, J. M., & Schultz, T. R. (1990). Moral rules: Their content and acquisition. *Annuual Review of Psychology, 41,* 525–556.

Darling, C. A., & Davidson, J. K. (1986). Coitally active university students: Sexual behaviors, concerns, and challenges. *Adolescence, 21,* 403–419.

Darwin, C. (1959). *The origin of species.* London: John Murray.

Darwin, C. (1872). *The expression of emotion in man and animals.* New York: Philosophical Library [reprinted in 1955 and 1965 by the University of Chicago Press, Chicago].

Darwin, C. T., Turvey, M. T., & Crowder, R. G. (1972). An auditory analogue of the Sperling partial report procedure: Evidence for brief auditory storage. *Cognitive Psychology, 3,* 255–267.

Datan, N., Rodeheaver, D., & Hughes, F. (1987). Adult development and aging. *Annual Review of Psychology, 38,* 153–180.

Davidson, J. M., Smith, E. R., Rodgers, C. H., & Bloch, G. J. (1968). Relative thresholds of behavioral and somatic responses to estrogen. *Physiology and Behavior, 3,* 227–229.

Davis, K. (1985). Near and dear: Friendship and love compared. *Psychology Today, 19,* 22–30.

Davis, L. E., & Cherns, A. B. (1975). *The quality of working life: Vol. I. Problems, prospects and the state of the art.* New York: Free Press.

DeAngelis, T. (1989). Behavior is included in report on smoking. *APA Monitor, 20,* 3–4.

Deaux, K. (1984). From individual differences to social categories: Analysis of a decade's research on gender. *American Psychologist, 39,* 105–116.

Deaux, K. (1985). Sex and gender. *Annual Review of Psychology, 36,* 49–81.

Deaux, K., & Major, B. (1987). Putting gender into context: An interactive model of gender-related behavior. *Psychological Review, 94,* 369–389.

DeBono, K. G., & Harnish, R. J. (1988). Source expertise, source attractiveness, and the processing of persuasive information: A functional approach. *Journal of Personality and Social Psychology, 55,* 541–546.

DeCasper, A. J., & Fifer, W. P. (1980). Of human bonding: Newborns prefer their mother's voice. *Science, 208,* 1174–1176.

deCuevas, J. (1990, September/October). "No, she held them loosely." *Harvard Magazine,* pp. 60–67.

Deffenbacher, J. L. (1988). Some recommendations and directions. *Counseling Psychology, 35,* 234–236.

DeGroot, A. D. (1965). *Thought and chance in chess.* The Hague: Mouton Press.

DeGroot, A. D. (1966). Perception and memory versus thought: Some old ideas and recent findings. In B. Kleinmuntz (Ed.), *Problem solving*. New York: Wiley.

Dembroski, T. M., & Costa, P. T., Jr. (1987). Coronary prone behavior: Components of the Type A pattern and hostility. *Journal of Personality, 55*, 211–235.

Dement, W. C. (1960). The effect of dream deprivation. *Science, 135*, 1705–1707.

Dement, W. C. (1974). *Some must watch while some must sleep*. San Francisco: Freeman.

Dement, W. C., & Kleitman, N. (1957). The relation of eye movements during sleep to dream activity: An objective method for the study of dreaming. *Journal of Experimental Psychology, 53*, 339–346.

DeReamer, R. (1980). *Modern safety and health technology*. New York: Wiley.

Deutsch, J. A. (1973). The cholinergic synapse and the site of memory. In J. A. Deutsch (Ed.), *The physiological basis of memory*. New York: Academic Press.

deVilliers, J. G., & deVilliers, P. A. (1978). *Language acquisition*. Cambridge, MA: Harvard University Press.

Diamond, M., & Karlen, A. (1980). *Sexual decisions*. Boston: Little, Brown.

Digman, J. M. (1990). Personality structure: Emergence of the five-factor model. *Annual Review of Psychology, 41*, 417–440.

Dion, K. K. (1972). Physical attractiveness and evaluation of children's transgressions. *Journal of Personality and Social Psychology, 24*, 207–213.

Dion, K. K., Berscheid, E., & Walster (Hatfield), E. (1972). What is beautiful is good. *Journal of Personality and Social Psychology, 24*, 285–290.

Dirkes, M. A. (1978). The role of divergent production in the learning process. *American Psychologist, 33*, 815–820.

Dixon, N. F. (1971). *Subliminal perception: The nature of a controversy*. New York: McGraw-Hill.

Dixon, N. F. (1981). *Preconscious processing*. New York: Wiley.

Dobson, K. S. (1988). *Handbook of cognitive-behavioral therapies*. New York: Guilford.

Doll, R., & Peto, R. (1981). *The causes of cancer*. New York: Oxford University Press.

Dollard, J., Doob, L., Miller, N., Mowrer, O. H., & Sears, R. R. (1939). *Frustration and aggression*. New Haven, CT: Yale University Press.

Domjan, M. (1987). Animal learning comes of age. *American Psychologist, 42*, 556–564.

Doty, R. Y. (1986). Gender and endocrine-related influences on human olfactory perception. In H. Meiselman & R. S. Rivlin (Eds.), *Clinical measurement of taste and smell*. New York: Macmillan.

Drakeley, R. J., Herriot, P., & Jones, A. (1988). Biographical data, training success and turnover. *Journal of Occupational Psychology, 61*, 145–152.

Duffy, E. (1962). *Activation and behavior*. New York: Wiley.

Duncan, J. (1985). Two techniques for investigating perception without awareness. *Perception and Psychophysics, 38*, 296–298.

Duncker, K. (1945). On problem solving. *Psychological Monographs, 58* (Whole No. 270).

Dunham, R. B. (1979). Job design and redesign. In S. Kerr (Ed.), *Organizational behavior*. Columbus, OH: Grid.

Dunnette, M. D., & Borman, W. C. (1979). Personnel selection and classification systems. *Annual Review of Psychology, 30*, 477–525.

Dweck, C. S. (1986). Motivational processes affecting learning. *American Psychologist, 41*, 1040–1048.

E

Ebbinghaus, H. E. (1885/1964). *Memory: A contribution to experimental psychology*. New York: Dover.

Edinger, J. A., & Patterson, M. L. (1983). Nonverbal involvement and social control. *Psychological Bulletin, 93*, 30–56.

Edwards, C. P. (1977). The comparative study of the development of moral judgment and reasoning. In R. L. Munroe, R. Munroe, & B. B. Whiting (Eds.), *Handbook of cross-cultural human development*. New York: Garland.

Edwards, V. J., & Spence, J. T. (1987). Gender-related traits, stereotypes, and schemata. *Journal of Personality and Social Psychology, 53*, 146–154.

Egeland, J. A., Gerhard, D. S., Pauls, D. L., Suddex, J. N., Kidd, K. K., Allen, C. R., Hostetter, A. M., & Housman, D. E. (1987). Bipolar affective disorders linked to DNA markers on chromosome 11. *Nature, 325*, 783–787.

Eich, J. E., Weingartner, H., Stillman, R. C., & Gillan, J. C. (1975). State-dependent accessibility of retrieval cues in the retention of a categorized list. *Journal of Verbal Learning and Verbal Behavior, 14*, 408–417.

Eisdorfer, C. (1983). Conceptual models of aging. *American Psychologist, 38*, 197–202.

Ekman, P. (1972). Universals and cultural differences in facial expression of emotion. In J. K. Cole (Ed.), *Nebraska symposium on motivation*. Lincoln: University of Nebraska Press.

Ekman, P. (1973). Cross-cultural studies in facial expression. In P. Ekman (Ed.), *Darwin and facial expressions: A century of research in review*. New York: Academic Press.

Ekman, P., Friesen, W. V., O'Sullivan, M., Diacoyanni-Tarlatzis, I., Krause, R., et al. (1987). Universals and cultural differences in the judgment of facial expressions of emotion. *Journal of Personality and Social Psychology, 53*, 712–717.

Ekman, P., Levenson, R. W., & Friesen, W. V. (1983). Autonomic nervous system activity distinguishes among emotions. *Science, 221*, 1208–1210.

Elkind, D. (1967). Egocentrism in adolescence. *Child Development, 38*, 1025–1034.

Elkind, D. (1981). *Children and adolescents: Interpretive essays on Jean Piaget*. New York: Oxford University Press.

Elkind, D. (1984). *All grown up and no place to go*. Reading, MA: Addison-Wesley.

Elkind, D., & Bowen, R. (1979). Imaginary audience behavior in children and adolescents. *Developmental Psychology, 15*, 38–44.

Elliot, G. R., & Eisdorfer, C. (1982). *Stress and human health*. New York: Springer.

Elliott, J. (1977). The power and pathology of prejudice. In P. G. Zimbardo & F. L. Ruch, *Psychology and life* (9th ed., Diamond Printing). Glenview, IL: Scott, Foresman.

Ellis, A. (1970). *Reason and emotion in psychotherapy*. Secaucus, NJ: Stuart.

Ellis, A. (1973). *Humanistic psychotherapy: The rational-emotive approach*. New York: McGraw-Hill.

Ellis, A. (1987). The impossibility of achieving consistently good mental health. *American Psychologist, 42*, 364–375.

Ellis, A. (1991). How can psychological treatment aim to be briefer and better? The rational-emotive approach to brief therapy. In K. N. Anchor (Ed.), *Handbook of medical psychotherapy*. Toronto: Hogrefe & Huber.

Ellis, L., & Ames, M. A. (1987). Neurohormonal functioning and sexual orientation: A theory of homosexuality-heterosexuality. *Psychological Bulletin, 101*, 233–258.

Epstein, S. (1979). The stability of behavior: On predicting most of the people much of the time. *Journal of Personality and Social Psychology, 37*, 1097–1126.

Epstein, S. M. (1967). Toward a unified theory of anxiety. In B. A.

Gilligan, C. (1982). *In a different voice.* Cambridge, MA: Harvard University Press.

Glaser, R. (1984). Education and thinking. *American Psychologist, 39,* 93–104.

Glasgow, R. E., & Lichtenstein, E. (1987). Long term effects of behavioral smoking cessation interventions. *Behavior Therapy, 18,* 297–324.

Glass, A. L., Holyoak, K. J., & Santa, J. L. (1979). *Cognition.* Reading, MA: Addison-Wesley.

Glass, D. C., & Singer, J. E. (1972). *Urban stress.* Hillsdale, NJ: Erlbaum.

Glass, D. C., Singer, J. E., & Friedman, L. N. (1969). Psychic cost of adaptation to an environmental stressor. *Journal of Personality and Social Psychology, 12,* 200–210.

Glass, G. V., McGaw, B., & Smith, M. L. (1981). *Meta-analysis in social research.* Beverly Hills, CA: Sage.

Glenn, N. D., & Weaver, C. N. (1981). The contribution of marital happiness to global happiness. *Journal of Marriage and the Family, 43,* 161–168.

Glucksberg, S., & Danks, J. H. (1968). Effects of discriminative labels and of nonsense labels upon the availability of novel function. *Journal of Verbal Learning and Verbal Behavior, 7,* 72–76.

Goffman, M. S. (1959). *The presentation of self in everyday life.* Garden City, NY: Doubleday.

Golbus, M. S. (1980). Teratology for the obstetrician: Current status. *American Journal of Obstetrics and Gynecology, 55,* 269.

Gold, P. E. (1987). Sweet memories. *American Scientist, 75,* 151–155.

Goldfried, M. R., Greenberg, L. S., & Marmar, C. (1990). Individual psychotherapy: Process and outcome. *Annual Review of Psychology, 41,* 659–688.

Goldstein, I. L. (1980). Training in work organizations. *Annual Review of Psychology, 31,* 229–272.

Goldstein, I. L. (1986). *Training in organizations.* Monterey, CA: Brooks/Cole.

Goleman, O. (1980). 1,528 little geniuses and how they grew. *Psychology Today, 14,* 28–53.

Goodwin, D. W. (1985). Alcoholism and genetics. *Archives of General Psychiatry, 42,* 171–174.

Goodwin, D. W., Powell, B., Bremer, D., Hoine, H., & Stein, J. (1969). Alcohol and recall: State-dependent effects in man. *Science, 163,* 1358–1360.

Gorenstein, E. E. (1984). Debating mental illness. *American Psychologist, 39,* 50–56.

Gormezano, I. (1972). Investigations of defense and reward conditioning in the rabbit. In A. H. Black & W. F. Prokasy (Eds.), *Classical conditioning II: Current theory and research.* Englewood Cliffs, NJ: Prentice-Hall.

Gottesman, I. I., & Bertelsen, A. (1989). Confirming unexpressed genotypes for schizophrenia. *Archives of General Psychiatry, 46,* 867–872.

Gottlieb, B. H. (1981). *Social networks and social support.* Beverly Hills, CA: Sage.

Gottlieb, G. (1970). Conceptions of prenatal development. In L. R. Aronson, E. Tobach, D. S. Lehrman, & J. S. Rosenblatt (Eds.), *Development and evolution of behavior.* San Francisco: Freeman.

Gough, H. G. (1985). A work orientation scale for the California Psychological Inventory. *Journal of Applied Psychology, 70,* 505–513.

Graf, P., & Schacter, D. A. (1985). Implicit and explicit memory for new associations in normal and amnesic subjects. *Journal of Experimental Psychology: Learning, Memory, and Cognition, 11,* 501–518.

Green, D. M., & Swets, J. A. (1966). *Signal detection theory and psychophysics.* New York: Wiley.

Greenberg, J., & Cohen, R. L. (1982). *Equity and justice in social behavior.* New York: Academic Press.

Greenberg, L. S., & Safran, J. D. (1987). *Emotion in psychotherapy.* New York: Guilford.

Greenberg, L. S., & Safran, J. D. (1989). Emotion in psychotherapy. *American Psychologist, 44,* 19–29.

Greeno, J. G. (1978). Natures of problem-solving abilities. In W. K. Estes (Ed.), *Handbook of learning and cognitive processes* (Vol. 5). Hillsdale, NJ: Erlbaum.

Greeno, J. G. (1989). A perspective on thinking. *American Psychologist, 44,* 134–141.

Greenough, W. T. (1984). Structural correlates of information storage in mammalian brain. *Trends in Neurosciences, 7,* 229–233.

Greenwald, A. G., & Breckler, S. J. (1984). To whom is the self presented? In B. R. Schlenker (Ed.), *The self and social life.* New York: McGraw-Hill.

Gregory, R. L. (1977). *Eye and brain: The psychology of seeing* (3rd ed.). New York: New World Library.

Grinspoon, L. (1977). *Marihuana reconsidered* (2nd ed.). Cambridge, MA: Harvard University Press.

Gross, R. T., & Duke, P. M. (1980). The effect of early and late maturation on adolescent behavior. *The Pediatric Clinics of North America, 27,* 71–77.

Grossman, H. J. (Ed.). (1973). *Manual on terminology and classification in mental retardation.* Washington, DC: American Association on Mental Deficiency.

Guilford, J. P. (1959a). *Personality.* New York: McGraw-Hill.

Guilford, J. P. (1959b). Traits of creativity. In H. H. Anderson (Ed.), *Creativity and its cultivation.* New York: HarperCollins.

Guilford, J. P. (1967). *The nature of human intelligence.* New York: McGraw-Hill.

Guilford, J. P. (1988). Some changes in the structure-of-intellect model. *Educational and Psychological Measurement, 48,* 1–4.

Guion, R. M., & Gibson, W. M. (1988). Personnel selection and placement. *Annual Review of Psychology, 39,* 349–374.

Gur, R. E., Resnick, S. M., Alavi, A., Gur, R. C., Caroff, S., Dann, R., et al. (1987). Regional brain function in schizophrenia. *Archives of General Psychiatry, 44,* 119–125.

Gurman, A. S., Kniskern, D. P., & Pinsof, W. M. (1986). Research on the process and outcome of marital and family therapy. In S. L. Garfield & A. E. Bergin (Eds.), *Handbook of psychotherapy and behavior change* (3rd ed.). New York: Wiley.

H

Haas, R. G. (1981). Effects of source characteristics on cognitive responses and persuasion. In R. E. Petty, T. M. Ostrom, & T. C. Brock (Eds.), *Cognitive responses in persuasion.* Hillsdale, NJ: Erlbaum.

Hake, D. F., & Foxx, R. M. (1978). Promoting gasoline conservation: The effects of reinforcement schedules, a leader, and self-recording. *Behavior Modification, 2,* 339–369.

Halberstadt, A. G., & Saitta, M. B. (1987). Gender, nonverbal behavior, and perceived dominance: A test of the theory. *Journal of Personality and Social Psychology, 53,* 257–272.

Hall, E. T. (1966). *The hidden dimension.* Garden City, NY: Doubleday.

Hall, G. S. (1904). *Adolescence.* Englewood Cliffs, NJ: Prentice-Hall.

Hall, J. A. (1978). Gender effects in decoding nonverbal cues. *Psychological Bulletin, 85,* 845–857.

Hall, W. G., & Oppenheim, R. W. (1987). Developmental psychology. *Annual Review of Psychology, 38,* 91–128.

Halpern, D. F. (1986). *Sex differences in cognitive abilities.* Hillsdale, NJ: Erlbaum.

Hamburg, D. A., & Takanishi, R. (1989). Preparing for life: The critical transition of adolescence. *American Psychologist, 44,* 825–827.

Hammen, C., Burge, D., Burney, E., & Adrian, C. (1990). Longitudinal study of diagnoses in children of women with unipolar and bipolar affective disorder. *Archives of General Psychiatry, 47,* 1112–1117.

Harding, C. M. (1988). Course types in schizophrenia: An analysis of European and American studies. *Schizophrenia Bulletin, 14,* 633–642.

Harkins, S. (1987). Social loafing and social facilitation. *Journal of Experimental Socialpsychology, 23,* 1–18.

Harkins, S., & Petty, R. E. (1981). Effects of source magnification of cognitive effort in attitudes: An information-processing view. *Journal of Personality and Social Psychology, 40,* 401–413.

Harkins, S. G. & Petty, R. E. (1982). Effects of task difficulty and task uniqueness on social loafing. *Journal of Personality and Social Psychology, 43,* 1214–1229.

Harlow, H. F. (1932). Social facilitation of feeding in the albino rat. *Journal of Genetic Psychology, 41,* 211–221.

Harlow, H. F. (1949). The formation of learning sets. *Psychological Review, 56,* 51–65.

Harlow, H. F. (1959). Love in infant monkeys. *Scientific American, 200,* 68–74.

Harlow, H. F., Harlow, M. K., & Suomi, S. J. (1971). From thought to therapy: Lessons from a private library. *American Scientist, 59,* 536–549.

Harris, B. (1979). What ever happened to Little Albert? *American Psychologist, 34,* 151–160.

Harris, D. V. (1973). *Involvement in sport: A somatopsychic rationale for physical activity.* Philadelphia: Lea & Febiger.

Harris, L., & Associates. (1975, 1981, 1983). *The myth and reality of aging in America.* Washington, DC: The National Council on Aging.

Harris, P. L. (1983). Infant cognition. In P. H. Mussen (Ed.), *Handbook of child psychology* (Vol. 2). New York: Wiley.

Harrow, M., Goldberg, J. F., Grossman, L. S., & Meltzer, H. Y. (1990). Outcome in manic disorders. *Archives of General Psychiatry, 47,* 665–671.

Harter, S. (1978). Effectance motivation reconsidered: Toward a developmental model. *Human Development, 21,* 34–64.

Hartman, E. L. (1973). *The functions of sleep.* New Haven, CT: Yale University Press.

Hartman, S., Grigsby, D. W., Crino, M. D., & Chhokar, J. (1986). The measurement of job satisfaction by action tendencies. *Educational and Psychological Measurement, 46,* 317–329.

Hartup, W. W. (1989). Social relationships and their developmental significance. *American Psychologist, 44,* 120–126.

Harvey, J. H., & Weary, G. (1984). Current issues in attribution theory. *Annual Review of Psychology, 35,* 427–459.

Hastorf, A. H., & Cantril, H. (1954). They saw a game: A case study. *Journal of Abnormal and Social Psychology, 49,* 129–134.

Hatfield, E., & Sprecher, S. (1986). *Mirror, mirror . . . The importance of looks in everyday life.* Albany: State University of New York Press.

Havighurst, R. J. (1972). *Developmental tasks and education* (3rd ed.). New York: McKay.

Hayduk, L. A. (1983). Personal space: Where we now stand. *Psychological Bulletin, 94,* 293–335.

Hayes, C. D. (Ed.). (1987). *Risking the future* (Vol. 1). Washington, DC: National Academy Press.

Hayes, S. C., Nelson, R. O., & Jarrett, R. B. (1987). The treatment utility of assessment: A functional approach to evaluating assessment quality. *American Psychologist, 42,* 963–974.

Haynes, S. G., McMichael, A. J., & Tyroler, H. A. (1978). Survival after early and normal retirement. *Journal of Gerontology, 33,* 872–883.

Hazan, C., & Shaver, P. (1987). Romantic love conceptualized as an attachment process. *Journal of Personality and Social Psychology, 52,* 511–524.

Hebb, D. O. (1955). Drives and the C.N.S. (conceptual nervous system). *Psychological Review, 62,* 243–254.

Heffernan, J. A., & Albee, G. W. (1985). Prevention perspectives. *American Psychologist, 40,* 202–204.

Heidbreder, E. (1946). The attainment of concepts. *Journal of General Psychology, 24,* 93–108.

Hellige, J. B. (1990). Hemispheric asymmetry. *Annual Review of Psychology, 41,* 55–80.

Hellige, J. B. (Ed.). (1983). *Cerebral hemisphere asymmetry: Method, theory, and application.* New York: Praeger.

Helzer, J. E., Robins, L. N., & McEnvoy, L. (1987). Post-traumatic stress disorder in the general population. *New England Journal of Medicine, 317,* 1630–1634.

Henley, N. M. (1977). *Body politics: Power, sex, and nonverbal communication.* Englewood Cliffs, NJ: Prentice-Hall.

Henley, T. B., Johnson, M. G., Jones, E. M., & Herzog, H. A. (1989). Definitions of psychology. *The Psychological Record, 39,* 143–152.

Higgins, E. T., & Bargh, J. A. (1987). Social cognition and social perception. *Annual Review of Psychology, 38,* 369–426.

Hilgard, E. R. (1975). Hypnosis. *Annual Review of Psychology, 26,* 19–44.

Hilgard, E. R. (1978, January). Hypnosis and consciousness. *Human Nature,* pp. 42–49.

Hilgard, E. R., & Hilgard, J. R. (1975). *Hypnosis in the relief of pain.* Los Altos, CA: W. Kaufman.

Hilgard, J. R. (1970). *Personality and hypnosis: A study of imaginative involvement.* Chicago: University of Chicago Press.

Hinrichs, J. R. (1976). Personnel training. In M. Dunnette (Ed.), *Handbook of industrial and organizational psychology.* Skokie, IL: Rand McNally.

Hinsz, V. B., & Davis, J. H. (1984). Persuasive arguments theory, group polarization, and choice shifts. *Personality and Social Psychology Bulletin, 10,* 260–268.

Hobfoll, S. E. (1986). *Stress, social support, and women.* Washington, DC: Hemisphere.

Hobfoll, S. E. (1988). *The ecology of stress.* Washington, DC: Hemisphere.

Hobfoll, S. E. (1989). Conservation of resources: A new attempt at conceptualizing stress. *American Psychologist, 44,* 513–524.

Hobson, J. A. (1977). The reciprocal interaction model of sleep cycle control: Implications for PGO wave generation and dream amnesia. In R. R. Drucker-Colin & J. L. McGaugh (Eds.), *Neurobiology of sleep and memory.* New York: Academic Press.

Hobson, J. A., & McCarley, R. W. (1977). The brain as a dream state generator: An activation-synthesis hypothesis of the dream process. *American Journal of Psychiatry, 134,* 1335–1348.

Hofferth, S. L., & Hayes, C. D. (Eds.). (1987). *Risking the future: Adolescent sexuality, pregnancy, and childbearing.* Washington, DC: National Academy Press.

Hoffman, D. D. (1983). The interpretation of visual illusions. *Scientific American, 245,* 154–162.

Hoffman, M. (1977). Homosexuality. In F. A. Beach (Ed.), *Human sexuality in four perspectives.* Baltimore: Johns Hopkins University Press.

Hogan, R., & Nicholson, R. A. (1988). The meaning of personality test scores. *American Psychologist, 43,* 621–626.

Hogrebe, M. C. (1987). Gender differences in mathematics. *American Psychologist, 42,* 265–266.

Holden, C. (1980). A new visibility for gifted children. *Science, 210*, 879–882.

Holden, C. (1987). Female math anxiety on the wane. *Science, 236*, 660–661.

Holman, B. L., & Tumeh, S. S. (1990). Single-photon emission computed tomography (SPECT): Applications and potential. *Journal of the American Medical Association, 263*, 561–564.

Holmes, D. S. (1984). Meditation and somatic arousal reduction: A review of the experimental evidence. *American Psychologist, 39*, 1–10.

Holmes, D. S. (1985). To meditate or simply rest, that is the question: A response to the comments of Shapiro. *American Psychologist, 40*, 722–725.

Holmes, T. H., & Rahe, R. H. (1967). The social readjustment rating scale. *Journal of Psychosomatic Research, 11*, 213–218.

Holmes, T. S., & Holmes, T. H. (1970). Short-term intrusions into the life-style routine. *Journal of Psychosomatic Research, 14*, 121–132.

Hoppock, R. (1935). *Job satisfaction.* New York: HarperCollins.

Horn, J. L. (1976). Human abilities: A review of research and theories in the early 1970s. *Annual Review of Psychology, 27*, 437–485.

Horn, J. L., & Cattell, R. B. (1966). Refinement and test of the theory of fluid and crystallized intelligence. *Journal of Educational Psychology, 57*, 253–276.

Horne, J. A., & Minard, A. (1985). Sleep and sleepiness following a behaviorally "active" day. *Ergonomics, 28*, 567–575.

Horner, M. S. (1969). Women's will to fail. *Psychology Today, 3*, 36.

Horowitz, F. D. (1987). *Exploring developmental theories: Toward a structural/behavioral model of development.* Hillsdale, NJ: Erlbaum.

Horowitz, F. D., & O'Brien, M. (Eds.). (1985). *The gifted and talented: Developmental perspectives.* Washington, DC: American Psychological Association.

Hostetler, A. J. (1987). Alzheimer's trials hinge on early diagnosis. *APA Monitor, 18*, 14–15.

Hothersall, D. (1990). *History of psychology* (2nd ed.). New York: McGraw-Hill.

Houston, J. P. (1986). *Fundamentals of learning and memory* (3rd ed.). New York: Harcourt Brace Jovanovich.

Hovland, C. I., & Weiss, W. (1951). The influence of source credibility on communication effectiveness. *Public Opinion Quarterly, 15*, 635–650.

Howard, D. V. (1983). *Cognitive psychology.* New York: Macmillan.

Howard, K. I., Kopata, S. M., Krause, M. S., & Orlinsky, D. E. (1986). The dose-effect relationship in psychotherapy. *American Psychologist, 41*, 159–164.

Howell, W. C., & Dipboye, R. L. (1982). *Essentials of industrial and organizational psychology.* Homewood, IL: Dorsey Press.

Hörmann, H. (1986). *Meaning and context.* New York: Plenum.

Hsia, J. (1988). Limits on affirmative action: Asian American access to higher education. *Educational Policy, 2*, 117–136.

Hsu, L. K. G. (1986). The treatment of anorexia nervosa. *American Journal of Psychiatry, 143*, 573–581.

Hubel, D. H. (1979). The brain. *Scientific American, 241*, 45–53.

Hubel, D. H., & Wiesel, T. N. (1979). Brain mechanisms of vision. *Scientific American, 241*, 150–162.

Huesmann, L. R., & Malamuth, N. M. (1986). Media violence and antisocial behavior. *Journal of Social Issues*, all.

Hughes, F. P., & Noppe, L. D. (1985). *Human development.* St. Paul, MN: West.

Hughes, J., Smith, T. W., Kosterlitz, H. W., Fothergill, L. A., Morgan, G. A., & Morris, H. R. (1975). Identification of two related peptides from the brain with potent opiate agonist activity. *Nature, 258*, 577–579.

Hulin, C. L., & Smith, P. C. (1964). Sex differences in job satisfaction. *Journal of Applied Psychology, 48*, 88–92.

Hull, C. L. (1943). *Principles of behavior.* Englewood Cliffs, NJ: Prentice-Hall.

Hunt, E. (1989). Cognitive science: Definition, status, and questions. *Annual Review of Psychology, 40*, 603–629.

Hunt, M. (1987, August 30). Navigating the therapy maze. *The New York Times Magazine*, pp. 28–31, 37, 44, 46, 49.

Hunter, J. E., & Hunter, R. F. (1984). Validity and utility of alternative predictors of job performance. *Psychological Bulletin, 96*, 72–98.

Huston, T. L., Ruggiero, M., Conner, R., & Geis, G. (1981). Bystander intervention into crime: A study based on naturally occurring episodes. *Social Psychology Quarterly, 44*, 14–23.

Hyde, J. S. (1981). How large are cognitive gender differences? A meta-analysis using omega squared and d. *American Psychologist, 36*, 892–901.

Hyde, J. S. (1984). How large are gender differences in aggression? A developmental meta-analysis. *Developmental Psychology, 20*, 697–706.

Hyde, J. S. (1986). *Understanding human sexuality* (3rd ed.). New York: McGraw-Hill.

Hyde, J. S., Fennema, E., & Lamon, S. J. (1990). Gender differences in mathematics performance: A meta-analysis. *Psychological Bulletin, 107*, 139–155.

Hyde, J. S., & Linn, M. C. (1988). Gender differences in verbal ability: A meta-analysis. *Psychological Bulletin, 104*, 53–69.

I

Iaffaldano, M. T., & Muchinsky, P. M. (1985). Job satisfaction and job performance: A meta-analysis. *Psychological Bulletin, 97*, 251–273.

Ilgen, D. R., & Klein, H. J. (1989). Organizational behavior. *Annual Review of Psychology, 40*, 327–351.

Insko, C. A. (1965). Verbal reinforcement of attitude. *Journal of Personality and Social Psychology, 2*, 621–623.

Isenberg, D. J. (1986). Group polarization: A critical review and meta-analysis. *Journal of Personality and Social Psychology, 50*, 1141–1151.

Izard, C. E. (1971). *The face of emotion.* Englewood Cliffs, NJ: Prentice-Hall.

Izard, C. E. (1972). *Patterns of emotion: A new analysis of anxiety and aggression.* New York: Academic Press.

Izard, C. E. (1977). *Human emotions.* New York: Plenum.

Izard, C. E. (1984). Emotion-cognition relationships and human development. In C. E. Izard, J. Kagan, & R. B. Zajonc (Eds.), *Emotions, cognition and behavior.* New York: Cambridge University Press.

Izard, C. E., Huebner, R. R., Risser, D., McGuinnes, G. C., & Dougherty, L. M. (1980). The young infant's ability to produce discrete emotional expressions. *Developmental Psychology, 16*, 132–141.

Izard, C. E., & Malatesa, C. Z. (1987). Perspectives on emotional development I: Differential emotions theory of early emotional development. In J. D. Ofsofsky (Ed.), *Handbook of infant development* (2nd ed.). New York: Wiley.

J

Jackaway, R., & Teevan, R. (1976). Fear of failure and fear of success: Two dimensions of the same motive. *Sex Roles, 2*, 283–294.

Jacklin, C. N. (1989). Female and male: Issues of gender. *American Psychologist, 44*, 127–133.

Jacobs, B. L. (1987). How hallucinogenic drugs work. *American Scientist, 75*, 386–392.

Jacobs, B. L., & Trulson, M. E. (1979). Mechanisms of action of LSD. *American Scientist, 67,* 396–404.

Jacobson, D. S. (1984). Neonatal correlates of prenatal exposure to smoking, caffeine, and alcohol. *Infant Behavior and Development, 7,* 253–265.

James, W. (1890). *Principles of psychology.* New York: Holt, Rinehart and Winston.

James, W. (1892). *Psychology: Briefer course.* New York: Holt, Rinehart and Winston.

James, W. (1904). Does consciousness exist? *Journal of Philosophy, 1,* 477–491.

Janis, I. L. (1972). *Victims of groupthink.* Boston: Houghton Mifflin.

Janis, I. L. (1983a). *Groupthink: Psychological studies of policy decisions and fiascos* (2nd ed.). Boston: Houghton Mifflin.

Janis, I. L. (1983b). The role of social support in adherence to stressful decisions. *American Psychologist, 38,* 143–160.

Janoff-Bulman, R. (1979). Characterological versus behavioral self-blame: Inquiries into depression and rape. *Journal of Personality and Social Psychology, 37,* 1798–1809.

Jeffery, R. W. (1989). Risk behaviors and health: Contrasting individual and population perspectives. *American Psychologist, 44,* 1194–1202.

Jenkins, C. D. (1976). Recent evidence supporting psychological and social risk factors for coronary disease. *New England Journal of Medicine, 294,* 1033–1038.

Jenkins, J. G. & Dallenbach, K. M. (1924). Oblivescence during sleep and waking. *American Journal of Psychology, 35,* 605–612.

Jensen, A. R. (1969). How much can we boost IQ and scholastic achievement? *Harvard Educational Review, 39,* 1–123.

Jensen, A. R. (1973). *Educability and group differences.* London: Methuen.

Jensen, A. R. (1980). *Bias in mental testing.* New York: Free Press.

Jensen, A. R. (1981). *Straight talk about mental tests.* London: Methuen.

Johnson, D. L. (1989). Schizophrenia as a brain disease. *American Psychologist, 44,* 553–555.

Johnson, E. H. (1978). Validation of concept-learning strategies. *Journal of Experimental Psychology, 107,* 237–265.

Johnson, J., Weissman, M. M., & Klerman, G. L. (1990). Panic disorder, comorbidity, and suicide attempts. *Archives of General Psychiatry, 47,* 805–808.

Johnson, M. K., & Hasher, L. (1987). Human learning and memory. *Annual Review of Psychology, 38,* 631–668.

Jones, E. E. (1979). The rocky road from acts to dispositions. *American Psychologist, 34,* 107–117.

Jones, E. E., & Nisbett, R. E. (1971). *The actor and the observer: Divergent perceptions of behavior.* Morristown, NJ: General Learning Press.

Jones, K. L., Smith, D. W., Ulleland, C. N., & Streissgoth, A. P. (1973). Patterns of malformation in offspring of chronic alcoholic mothers. *Lancet, 3,* 1267–1271.

Jones, L. V., & Appelbaum, M. I. (1990). Psychometric methods. *Annual Review of Psychology, 40,* 23–43.

Jones, M. C. (1957). The careers of boys who were early or late maturing. *Child Development, 28,* 113–128.

Joyce, P. R., & Paykel, E. S. (1989). Predictors of drug response in depression. *Archives of General Psychiatry, 46,* 89–99.

Julien, R. M. (1985). *A primer of drug action* (4th ed.). San Francisco: Freeman.

Jussim, L., Coleman, L. M., & Lerch, L. (1987). The nature of stereotypes: A comparison and integration of three theories. *Journal of Personality and Social Psychology, 52,* 536–546.

K

Kagan, J. (1988). The meanings of personality predicates. *American Psychologist, 43,* 614–620.

Kagan, J. (1989). Temperamental contributions to social behavior. *American Psychologist, 44,* 668–674.

Kagan, J., & Lamb, S. (1987). *The emergence of morality in young children.* Chicago: University of Chicago Press.

Kagan, J., Reznick, J., & Snidman, N. (1988). Biological bases of childhood shyness. *Science, 240,* 167–171.

Kahn, S., Zimmerman, G., Csikzentmihalyi, M., & Getzels, J. W. (1985). Relations between identity in young adulthood and intimacy at midlife. *Journal of Personality and Social Psychology, 49,* 1316–1322.

Kahneman, D., & Tversky, A. (1973). On the psychology of prediction. *Psychological Review, 80,* 237–251.

Kahneman, D., & Tversky, A. (1979). On the interpretation of intuitive probability: A reply to Jonathan Cohen. *Cognition, 7,* 409–411.

Kahneman, D., & Tversky, A. (1984). Choices, values, and frames. *American Psychologist, 39,* 341–350.

Kail, R., & Nippold, M. A. (1984). Unrestrained retrieval from semantic memory. *Child Development, 55,* 944–951.

Kalat, J. W. (1984). *Biological psychology* (2nd ed.). Belmont, CA: Wadsworth.

Kalish, R. A. (1976). Death and dying in a social context. In R. H. Binstock & E. Shanas (Eds.), *Handbook of aging and the social sciences.* New York: Van Nostrand Reinhold.

Kalish, R. A. (1982). *Late adulthood: Perspectives on human development.* Monterey, CA: Brooks/Cole.

Kalish, R. A. (1985). *Death, grief, and caring relationships.* Monterey, CA: Brooks/Cole.

Kamin, L. (1968). Attention-like processes in classical conditioning. In M. Jones (Ed.), *Miami symposium on the prediction of behavior: Aversive stimulation.* Miami: University of Miami Press.

Kamin, L. (1969). Predictability, surprise, attention, and conditioning. In R. Church & B. Campbell (Eds.), *Punishment and aversive behaviors.* Englewood Cliffs, NJ: Prentice-Hall.

Kandel, E. R. & Schwartz, J. H. (1982). Molecular biology of learning: Modulation of transmitter release. *Science, 218,* 433–443.

Kanizsa, G. (1976). Subjective contours. *Scientific American, 234,* 48–52.

Kaplan, H. S. (1974). *The new sex therapy: Active treatment of sexual dysfunction.* New York: Quadrangle.

Kaplan, H. S. (1975). *The illustrated manual of sex therapy.* New York: Quadrangle.

Kaplan, H. S. (1979). *Disorders of sexual desire.* New York: Simon & Schuster.

Kaplan, R. M. (1984). The connection between clinical health promotion and health status. *American Psychologist, 39,* 755–765.

Kaplan, R. M., & Saccuzzo, D. P. (1989). *Psychological testing* (2nd ed.). Monterey, CA: Brooks/Cole.

Kaplan, S. (1987). Aesthetics, affect and cognition: Environmental preference from an evolutionary perspective. *Environment and Behavior, 19,* 3–32.

Karniol, R. (1978). Children's use of intention cues in evaluating behavior. *Psychological Bulletin, 85,* 76–85.

Karniol, R. (1980). A conceptual analysis of immanent justice responses in children. *Child Development, 51,* 118–130.

Karoum, F., Karson, C. N., Bigelow, L. B., Lawson, W. B., & Wyatt, R. J. (1987). Preliminary evidence of reduced combined output of dopamine and its metabolites in chronic schizophrenia. *Archives of General Psychiatry, 44,* 604–607.

Kassin, S. M., Ellsworth, P. C., & Smith, V. L. (1989). The "general acceptance" of psychological research on eyewitness testimony: A survey of experts. *American Psychologist, 44,* 1089–1098.

Katzell, R. A., & Guzzo, R. A. (1983). Psychological approaches to productivity improvement. *American Psychologist, 38,* 468–472.

Katzell, R. A., & Thompson, D. E. (1990). Work motivation: Theory and practice. *American Psychologist, 45,* 144–153.

Kay, S. R., & Singh, M. M. (1989). The positive-negative distinction in drug-free schizophrenic patients. *Archives of General Psychiatry, 46,* 711–717.

Kazdin, A. E., Esveldt-Dawson, K., French, N. H., & Unis, A. S. (1987). Problem-solving skills training and relationship therapy in the treatment of antisocial child behavior. *Journal of Consulting and Clinical Psychology, 55,* 76–85.

Keating, D. P. (1980). Thinking processes in adolescents. In J. Adelson (Ed.) *Handbook of adolescent psychology.* New York: Wiley.

Keesey, R. E., & Powley, T. L. (1975). Hypothalamic regulation of body weight. *American Scientist, 63,* 558–565.

Keesey, R. E., & Powley, T. L. (1986). The regulation of body weight. *Annual Review of Psychology, 37,* 109–133.

Keith, P. M. (1983). A comparison of the resources of parents and childless men and women in very old age. *Family Relations, 32,* 403–409.

Kelly, H. H. (1967). Attribution theory in social psychology. In D. Levine (Ed.), *Nebraska symposium on motivation.* Lincoln: University of Nebraska Press.

Kelley, H. H. (1973). The process of causal attribution. *American Psychologist, 28,* 107–128.

Kelley, H. H., & Michela, J. L. (1980). Attribution theory and research. *Annual Review of Psychology, 31,* 457–501.

Kelley, H. H., & Thibault, J. W. (1978). *Interpersonal relations: A theory of interdependence.* New York: Wiley.

Kelley, K. (1985). Sex, sex guilt, and authoritarianism: Differences in responses to explicit heterosexual and masturbatory slides. *The Journal of Sex Research, 21,* 68–85.

Kelsoe, J. R., Ginns, E. I., Egeland, J. A., Gerhard, D. S., Goldstein, A. M., Bale, S. J., Pauls, D. L., Long, R. T., Kidd, K. K., Conte, G., Housman, D. E., & Paul, S. M. (1989). Reevaluation of the linkage relationship between chromosome 11p loci and the gene for bipolar affective disorder in the Old Order Amish. *Nature, 342,* 238–243.

Kempler, D., & Van Lanker, D. (1987). The right turn of phrase. *Psychology Today, 21,* 20–22.

Kendrick, D. T., & Funder, D. C. (1988). Profiting from controversy: Lessons from the person-situation debate. *American Psychologist, 43,* 23–34.

Kermis, M. D. (1984). *The psychology of human aging.* Boston: Allyn & Bacon.

Kershner, J. R., & Ledger, G. (1985). Effect of sex, intelligence, and style of thinking on creativity: A comparison of gifted and average IQ children. *Journal of Personality and Social Psychology, 48,* 1033–1040.

Kessler, S. (1980). The genetics of schizophrenia: A review. In S. J. Keith & L. R. Mosher (Eds.), *Special report: Schizophrenia.* Washington, DC: U.S. Government Printing Office.

Kett, J. F. (1977). *Rites of passage: Adolescence in America from 1790 to the present.* New York: Basic Books.

Key, M. R. (1975). *Male/female language.* Metuchen, NJ: Scarecrow Press.

Kientzle, M. J. (1946). Properties of learning curves under varied distributions of practice. *Journal of Experimental Psychology, 36,* 187–211.

Kiesler, C. A. (1982). Mental hospitals and alternative care. *American Psychologist, 37,* 349–360.

Kiesler, C. A., & Sibulkin, A. (1987). *Mental hospitalization: Myths and facts about a national crisis.* Beverly Hills, CA: Sage.

Kiester, E. (1984a). The playing fields of the mind. *Psychology Today, 18,* 18–24.

Kiester, E. (1984b). The uses of anger. *Psychology Today, 18,* 26.

Kiester, E., Jr. (1980). Images of the night: The physiological roots of dreaming. *Science 80, 1,* 36–43.

Kiger, J. I., & Glass, A. L. (1983). The facilitation of lexical decisions by a prime occurring after the target. *Memory and Cognition, 11,* 356–365.

Kimble, G. A. (1981). Biological and cognitive constraints on learning. In L. Benjamin (Ed.), *The G. Stanley Hall Lecture Series* (Vol. 1). Washington, DC: American Psychological Association.

Kimble, G. A. (1989). Psychologist from the standpoint of a generalist. *American Psychologist, 44,* 491–499.

Kimmel, D. C. (1988). Ageism, psychology, and public policy. *American Psychologist, 43,* 175–178.

King, M., Murray, M. A., & Atkinson, T. (1982). Background, personality, job characteristics, and satisfaction with work in a national sample. *Human Relations, 35,* 119–133.

Kinsbourne, M. (1982). Hemispheric specialization and the growth of human understanding. *American Psychologist, 37,* 411–420.

Kinsey, A. C., Pomeroy, W. B., & Martin, C. E. (1948). *Sexual behavior in the human male.* Philadelphia: Saunders.

Kinsey, A. C., Pomeroy, W. B., Martin, C. E., & Gebhard, P. H. (1953). *Sexual behavior in the human female.* Philadelphia: Saunders.

Kirkpatrick, D. L. (1976). Evaluation of training. In R. L. Craig (Ed.), *Training and development handbook* (2nd ed.) New York: McGraw-Hill.

Kirscht, J. P. (1983). Preventive health behavior: A review of research and issues. *Health Psychology, 2,* 277–301.

Kisker, E. (1985). Teenagers talk about sex, pregnancy, and contraception. *Family Planning Perspectives, 17,* 83–90.

Klayman, J., & Ha, Y-W. (1987). Confirmation, disconfirmation, and information in hypothesis testing. *Psychological Review, 94,* 211–228.

Kleitman, N. (1963a). Patterns of dreaming. *Scientific American, 203,* 82–88.

Kleitman, N. (1963b). *Sleep and wakefulness.* Chicago: University of Chicago Press.

Klerman, G. L. (1990). Treatment of recurrent unipolar major depressive disorder. *Archives of General Psychiatry, 47,* 1158–1162.

Knapp, S., & VandeCreek, L. (1989). What psychologists need to know about AIDS. *The Journal of Training and Practice in Professional Psychology, 3,* 3–16.

Knittle, J. L. (1975). Early influences on development of adipose tissue. In G. A. Bray (Ed.), *Obesity in perspective.* Washington, DC: U.S. Government Printing Office.

Knowles, E. S. (1983). Social physics and the effects of others: Tests of the effects of audience size and distance on social judgments and behavior. *Journal of Personality and Social Psychology, 45,* 1263–1279.

Kohlberg, L. (1963). Moral development and identification. In H. W. Stevenson (Ed.), *Child psychology.* Chicago: University of Chicago Press.

Kohlberg, L. (1969). *Stages in the development of moral thought and action.* New York: Holt, Rinehart and Winston.

Kohlberg, L. (1981). *Philosophy of moral development.* New York: HarperCollins.

Kohlberg, L. (1985). *The psychology of moral development.* New York: HarperCollins.

Kohler, W. (1969). *The task of Gestalt psychology.* Princeton, NJ: Princeton University Press.

Kohut, H. (1977). *The restoration of self.* New York: International Universities Press.

Kolata, G. (1987). What babies know, and noises parents make. *Science, 237,* 726.

Kolb, B. (1989). Brain development, plasticity, and behavior. *American Psychologist, 44,* 1203–1212.

Korchin, S. J., & Scheldberg, D. (1981). The future of clinical assessment. *American Psychologist, 36,* 1147–1158.

Kosslyn, S. M. (1987). Seeing and imagining in the cerebral hemispheres: A computational approach. *Psychological Review, 94,* 148–175.

Kraeplin, E. (1883). *Compendium der psychiatrie.* Leipzig: Abel.

Kraeplin, E. (1919). *Dementia praecox and paraphrenia.* Edinburgh, Scotland: E & S Livingstone.

Kramer, B. A. (1985). The use of ECT in California, 1977–1983. *The American Journal of Psychiatry, 142,* 1190–1192.

Krantz, D. S., & Glass, D. C. (1984). Personality, behavior patterns, and physical illness: Conceptual and methodological issues. In W. D. Gentry (Ed.), *Handbook of behavioral medicine.* New York: Guilford.

Krantz, D. S., Grunberg, N. E., & Braum, A. (1985). Health psychology. *Annual Review of Psychology, 36,* 349–383.

Krueger, W. C. F. (1929). The effect of overlearning on retention. *Journal of Experimental Psychology, 12,* 71–78.

Krupat, E. (1985). *People in cities: The urban environment and its effects.* New York: Cambridge University Press.

Kübler-Ross, E. (1969). *On death and dying.* New York: Macmillan.

Kübler-Ross, E. (1981). *Living with death and dying.* New York: Macmillan.

Kunst-Wilson, W. R., & Zajonc, R. B. (1980). Affective discrimination that cannot be recognized. *Science, 207,* 557–558.

Kupfer, D. J., Frank, E., & Perel, J. M. (1989). The advantage of early treatment intervention in recurrent depression. *Archives of General Psychiatry, 46,* 771–775.

L

Labov, W. (1973). The boundaries of words and their meaning. In C. J. N. Bailey & R. W. Shuy (Eds.), *New ways of analyzing variations in English.* Washington, DC: Georgetown University Press.

Lafferty, P., Beutler, L. E., & Crago, M. (1989). Differences between more and less effective psychotherapists: A study of select therapist variables. *Journal of Consulting and Clinical Psychology, 57,* 76–80.

Laird, J. (1984). The real role of facial response in the experience of emotion: A reply to Tourangeau and Ellsworth, and others. *Journal of Personality and Social Psychology, 47,* 909–917.

Lamb, M. E. (1977). Father-infant and mother-infant interaction in the first year of life. *Child Development, 48,* 167–181.

Lamb, M. E. (1979). Paternal influences and the father's role: A personal perspective. *American Psychologist, 34,* 938–943.

Landers, D. M. (1982). Arousal, attention, and skilled performance: Further considerations. *Quest, 33,* 271–283.

Landers, S. (1987a). AIDS: Behavior change yes, test no. *APA Monitor, 18,* 28–29.

Landers, S. (1987b). Panel urges teen contraception. *APA Monitor, 18,* 6.

Landers, S. (1989). High school seniors' illicit drug use down. *APA Monitor, 20,* 33.

Landers, S. (1990). Sex, condom use up among teenage boys. *APA Monitor, 21,* 25.

Landesman, S., & Butterfield, E. C. (1987). Normalization and deinstitutionalization of mentally retarded individuals. *American Psychologist, 42,* 809–816.

Landesman, S., & Ramey, C. (1989). Developmental psychology and mental retardation: Integrating scientific principles with treatment practices. *American Psychologist, 44,* 409–415.

Landy, F. J. (1989). *Psychology of work behavior* (2nd ed.). Homewood, IL: Dorsey Press.

Lanetto, R. (1980). *Children's conceptions of death.* New York: Springer.

Lang, P. J. (1985). The cognitive psychophysiology of emotion: Fear and anxiety. In A. H. Tuma & J. D. Maser (Eds.), *Anxiety and the anxiety disorders.* Hillsdale, NJ: Erlbaum.

Langer, S. K. (1951). *Philosophy in a new key.* New York: New American Library.

Lashley, K. S. (1950). In search of the engram. *Symposia of the Society for Experimental Biology, 4,* 454–482.

Lasky, R. E., & Kallio, K. D. (1978). Transformation rules in concept learning. *Memory and Cognition, 6,* 491–495.

Latané, B. (1981). The psychology of social impact. *American Psychologist, 36,* 343–356.

Latané, B., & Darley, J. M. (1968). Group inhibition of bystander intervention in emergencies. *Journal of Personality and Social Psychology, 10,* 215–221.

Latané, B., & Darley, J. M. (1970). *The unresponsive bystander: Why doesn't he help?* Englewood Cliffs, NJ: Prentice-Hall.

Latané, B., & Nida, S. (1980). Social impact theory and group influence: A social engineering perspective. In P. L. Paulus (Ed.), *Psychology and group influence.* Hillsdale, NJ: Erlbaum.

Latané, B., & Nida, S. (1981). Ten years of research on group size and helping. *Psychological Bulletin, 89,* 308–324.

Latané, B., Williams, K., & Harkins, S. (1979). Many hands make light work: The causes and consequences of social loafing. *Journal of Personality and Social Psychology, 37,* 822–832.

Latham, G. P. (1988). Human resource training and development. *Annual Review of Psychology, 39,* 545–582.

Lauer, J., & Lauer, R. (1985). Marriages made to last. *Psychology Today, 19,* 22–26.

Lawler, E. E. (1982). Strategies for improving the quality of work life. *American Psychologist, 37,* 486–493.

Lazarus, R. S. (1981). Little hassles can be hazardous to your health. *Psychology Today, 15,* 58–62.

Lazarus, R. S. (1982). Thoughts on the relations between emotion and cognition. *American Psychologist, 37,* 1019–1024.

Lazarus, R. S. (1984). On the primacy of cognition. *American Psychologist, 39,* 124–129.

Lazarus, R. S., & Folkman, S. (1984). *Stress, appraisal, and coping.* New York: Springer.

Leahey, T. H., & Harris, R. J. (1989). *Human learning* (2nd ed.). Englewood Cliffs, NJ: Prentice-Hall.

Lehrer, P. M., & Woolfolk, R. L. (1984). Are stress reduction techniques interchangeable, or do they have specific effects? A review of the comparative empirical literature. In L. Woolfolk & P. M. Lehrer (Eds.), *Principles and practice of stress management.* New York: Guilford.

Lempers, J. D., Flavell, E. R., & Flavell, J. H. (1977). The development in very young children of tactile knowledge concerning visual perception. *Genetic Psychology Monographs, 95,* 3–53.

Lenneberg, E. H. (1967). *Biological foundations of language.* New York: Wiley.

Lenneberg, E. H., Rebelsky, F. G., & Nichols, I. A. (1965). The vocalizations of infants born to deaf and hearing parents. *Human Development, 8,* 23–27.

Lenzenweger, M. F., Dworkin, R. H., & Wethington, E. (1989). Models of positive and negative symptoms in schizophrenia: An empirical evaluation of latent structures. *Journal of Abnormal Psychology, 98,* 62–70.

Leon G. R., & Roth, L. (1977). Obesity: Psychological causes, correlations and speculations. *Psychological Bulletin, 84,* 117–139.

Leonard, J. (1970, May 8), Ghetto for blue eyes in the classroom. *Life,* p. 16.

Leonard, J. M., & Whitten, A. (1983). Information stored when expecting recall or recognition. *Journal of Experimental Psychology: Learning, Memory, and Cognition, 9,* 440–455.

Lerner, M. J. (1965). The effect of responsibility and choice on a partner's attractiveness following failure. *Journal of Personality, 33,* 178–187.

Lerner, M. J. (1980). *The belief in a just world.* New York: Plenum.

Lerner, R. M. (1978). Nature, nurture, and dynamic interactionism. *Human Development, 21,* 1–20.

Lerner, R. M., & Foch, T. T. (1987). *Biological-psychosocial interactions in early adolescence: A life-span approach.* Hillsdale, NJ: Erlbaum.

Leventhal, H., & Cleary, P. D. (1980). The smoking problem: A review of the research and theory in behavioral risk modification. *Psychological Bulletin, 88,* 370–405.

Levine, H. Z. (1983). Safety and health programs. *Personnel, 3,* 4–9.

Levine, J. D., Gordon, N. C., & Fields, H. L. (1979). Naloxone dose dependently produces analgesia and hyperalgesia in postoperative pain. *Nature, 278,* 740–741.

Levine, J. M., & Moreland, R. L. (1990). Progress in small group research. *Annual Review of Psychology, 41,* 585–634.

Levine, M. F., Taylor, J. C., & Davis, L. E. (1984). Defining quality of work life. *Human Relations, 37,* 81–104.

Levinson, D. J. (1978). *The seasons of a man's life.* New York: Ballantine Books.

Levinson, D. J. (1986). A conception of adult development. *American Psychologist, 41,* 3–13.

Levinson, D. J., Darrow, C. M., Klein, E. B., Levinson, M. H., & McKee, B. (1974). *The seasons of a man's life.* New York: Knopf.

Levinthal, C. F. (1983). *Introduction to physiological psychology* (2nd ed.). Englewood Cliffs, NJ: Prentice-Hall.

Lewinsohn, P. M., Zeiss, A. M., & Duncan, E. M. (1989). Probability of relapse after recovery from an episode of depression. *Journal of Abnormal Psychology, 98,* 107–116.

Ley, P. (1977). Psychological studies of doctor-patient communication. In S. Rachman (Ed.), *Contributions to medical psychology* (Vol. 1). Elmsford, NY: Pergamon Press.

Lidz, T. (1973). *The origin and treatment of schizophrenic disorders.* New York: Basic Books.

Lieberman, M. A. (1983). The effects of social support on response to stress. In L. Goldbert & D. S. Breznitz (Eds.), *Handbook of stress management.* New York: Free Press.

Liebert, R. M. (1986). Effects of television on children and adolescence. *Developmental and Behavioral Pediatrics, 7,* 43–48.

Lindsley, D. B., Bowden, J., & Magoun, H. W. (1949). Effect upon EEG of acute injury to the brain stem activating system. *Electroencephalography and Clinical Neurophysiology, 1,* 475–486.

Linn, M. C., & Peterson, A. C. (1985). Emergence and characterization of sex differences in spatial ability: A meta-analysis. *Child Development, 56,* 1479–1498.

Linz, D., Donnerstein, E., & Penrod, S. (1984). The effects of long-term exposure to violence against women. *Journal of Communication, 34,* 130–147.

Litt, M. D. (1988). Self-efficacy and perceived control: Cognitive mediators of pain tolerance. *Journal of Personality and Social Psychology, 54,* 149–160.

Locke, E. A. (1968). Toward a theory of task motivation and incentives. *Organizational Behavior and Human Performance, 3,* 157–189.

Locke, E. A. (1976). The nature and causes of job satisfaction. In M. D. Dunnette (Ed.), *Handbook of industrial and organizational psychology.* Skokie, IL: Rand McNally.

Locke, E. A., & Latham, G. P. (1984). *Goal setting: A motivational technique that works.* Englewood Cliffs, NJ: Prentice-Hall.

Locke, E. A., Shaw, K. N., Saari, L. M., & Latham, G. (1981). Goal-setting and task performance: 1969–1980. *Psychological Bulletin, 90,* 124–152.

Locke, J. (1690/1964). *An essay concerning human understanding.* New York: New American Library (Meridian Books).

Loftus, E. F. (1984). The eyewitness on trial. In B. D. Sales & A. Alwork (Eds.), *With liberty and justice for all.* Englewood Cliffs, NJ: Prentice-Hall.

Loftus, E. F., & Loftus, G. R. (1980). On the permanence of stored information in the human brain. *American Psychologist, 35,* 409–420.

Long, P. (1986). Medical mesmerism. *Psychology Today, 20*(1), 28–29.

Lord, C. G. (1980). Schemas and images as memory aids. *Journal of Personality and Social Psychology, 38,* 257–269.

Lorenz, K. (1969). *On aggression.* New York: Bantam Books.

Lott, A. J., & Lott, B. E. (1974). The role of reward in the formation of positive interpersonal attitudes. In T. L. Huston (Ed.), *Foundations of interpersonal attraction.* New York: Academic Press.

Lozoff, B. (1989). Nutrition and behavior. *American Psychologist, 44,* 231–236.

Lubin, B., Larsen, R. M., & Matarazzo, J. D. (1984). Patterns of psychological test usage in the United States: 1935–1982. *American Psychologist, 39,* 451–454.

Lugaresi, E., Medori, R., Montagna, P., Baruzzi, A., Cortelli, P., Lugaresi, A., Tinuper, P., Zucconi, M., & Gambetti, P. (1986). Fatal familial insomnia and dyautonomia with selective degeneration of the thalamic nuclei. *New England Journal of Medicine, 315,* 997–1003.

Luh, C. W. (1922). The conditions of retention. *Psychological Monographs,* Whole No. 142.

Luxenberg, J. S., Swedo, S. E., Flament, M. F., Friedland, R. P., Rapoport, J. L., & Rapoport, S. I. (1988). Neuroanatomic abnormalities in obsessive-compulsive disorder detected with quantitative x-ray computed tomography. *American Journal of Psychiatry, 145,* 1089–1094.

Lynch, G., & Baudry, M. (1984). The biochemistry of memory: A new and specific hypothesis. *Science, 224,* 1057–1063.

Lynn, D. (1974). *The father: His role in child development.* Monterey, CA: Brooks/Cole.

Lynn, R. (1977). The intelligence of the Japanese. *Bulletin of the British Psychological Society, 30,* 69–72.

Lynn, R. (1982). IQ in Japan and the United States shows a greater disparity. *Nature, 297,* 222–223.

Lynn, S. J., & Rhue, J. W. (1986). The fantasy-prone person: Hypnosis, imagination, and creativity. *Journal of Personality and Social Psychology, 51,* 404–408.

M

Macarthy, B. W., Ryan, M., & Johnson, F. (1975). *Sexual awareness.* San Francisco: Boyd & Fraser.

Maccoby, E. E., & Jacklin, C. N. (1974). *The psychology of sex differences.* Stanford, CA: Stanford University Press.

Maccoby, E. E., & Jacklin, C. N. (1980). Sex differences in aggression: A rejoinder and reprise. *Child Development, 51,* 964–980.

Mace, N. L., & Rabins, P. V. (1981). *The 36-hour day.* Baltimore: Johns Hopkins University Press.

Mackenzie, B. (1984). Explaining race differences in IQ: The logic, the methodology, and the evidence. *American Psychologist, 39,* 1214–1233.

Mackintosh, N. J. (1975). A theory of attention: Variations in the associability of stimuli with reinforcement. *Psychological Review, 82,* 276–298.

Mackintosh, N. J. (1983). *Conditioning and associative learning.* New York: Oxford University Press.

Mackintosh, N. J. (1986). The biology of intelligence? *British Journal of Psychology, 77,* 1–18.

MacLeod, M. D., & Ellis, H. D. (1986). Modes of presentation in eyewitness testimony research. *Human Learning Journal of Practical Research and Applications, 5,* 39–44.

Magnusson, D., & Edler, N. S. (Eds.). (1977). *Personality at the crossroads: An international perspective.* Hillsdale, NJ: Erlbaum.

Maharishi, Mahesh Yogi. (1963). *The science of living and art of being.* London: Unwin.

Mahowald, M. W., & Schenck, C. H. (1989). REM sleep behavior disorder. In M. H. Krygr, T. Roth, & W. C. Dement (Eds.), *Principles and practice of sleep medicine.* Philadelphia: Saunders.

Maier, N. R. F. (1931). Reasoning in humans II: The solution of a problem and its appearance in consciousness. *Journal of Experimental Psychology, 105,* 181–194.

Maki, R. H., & Swett, S. (1987). Metamemory for narrative text. *Memory and Cognition, 15,* 72–83.

Malatesta, C. A., & Isard, C. E. (1984). The ontogenesis of human social signals: From biological imperative to symbol utilization. In N. A. Fox & R. J. Davidson (Eds.), *The psychobiology of affective development.* Hillsdale, NJ: Erlbaum.

Mandler, G. (1980). Recognizing: The judgment of previous occurrence. *Psychological Review, 87,* 252–271.

Manning, M. L. (1983). Three myths concerning adolescence. *Adolescence, 18,* 823–829.

Marcia, J. (1966). Development and validation of ego-identity status. *Journal of Personality and Social Psychology, 3,* 551–558.

Marcia, J. (1976). Identity six years after: A follow-up study. *Journal of Youth and Adolescence, 5,* 145–160.

Marcia, J. (1980). Identity in adolescence. In J. Adelson (Ed.), *Handbook of adolescent psychology.* New York: Wiley.

Marengo, J. T., & Harrow, M. (1987). Schizophrenic thought disorder at follow-up. *Archives of General Psychiatry, 44,* 651–659.

Markowitz, J. S., Weissman, M. M., Ouellete, R., Lish, J. D., & Klerman, G. L. (1989). Quality of life in panic disorder. *Archives of General Psychiatry, 46,* 984–992.

Marks, I. M. (1986). Epidemiology of anxiety. *Social Psychiatry, 21,* 167–171.

Marks, M. L. (1986). The question of quality circles. *Psychology Today, 20,* 36–38, 42–46.

Marschark, M., Richmond, C. L., Yuille, J. C., & Hunt, R. R. (1987). The role of imagery in memory: On shared and distinctive information. *Psychological Bulletin, 102,* 28–41.

Marshall, G. D., & Zimbardo, P. G. (1979). Affective consequences of inadequately explained physiological arousal. *Journal of Personality and Social Psychology, 37,* 970–988.

Martin, B. J. (1986). Sleep deprivation and exercise. In K. B. Pandolf (Ed.), *Exercise and sport sciences review.* (pp. 213–229). New York: Macmillan.

Martin, G. B., & Clark, R. D. (1982). Distress crying in neonates: Species and peer specificity. *Developmental Psychology, 18,* 3–9.

Martindale, C. (1981). *Cognition and consciousness.* Homewood. IL: Dorsey Press.

Marx, J. (1990). Alzheimer's pathology explored. *Science, 249,* 984–986.

Marziali, E. (1984). Prediction of outcome of brief psychotherapy from therapist interpretive interactions. *Archives of General Psychiatry, 41,* 301–304.

Maslach, C. (1979). The emotional consequences of arousal without reason. In C. E. Izard (Ed.), *Emotions in personality and psychopathology.* New York: Plenum.

Maslow, A. H. (1943). A theory of human motivation. *Psychological Review, 50,* 370–396.

Maslow, A. (1954). *Motivation and personality.* New York: Harper.

Maslow, A. H. (1970). *Motivation and personality* (2nd ed.). New York: HarperCollins.

Massaro, D. W. (1975). *Experimental psychology and information processing.* Skokie, IL: Rand McNally.

Masters, W., & Johnson, V. (1966). *Human sexual response.* Boston: Little, Brown.

Masters, W., & Johnson, V. (1970). *Human sexual inadequacy.* Boston: Little, Brown.

Masters, W., & Johnson, V. (1979). *Homosexuality in perspective.* Boston: Little, Brown.

Masters, W., Johnson, V., & Kolodny, R. C. (1987). *Human sexuality* (3rd ed.). Glenview, IL: Scott, Foresman/Little, Brown.

Matarazzo, J. D. (1980). Behavioral health and behavioral medicine: Frontiers for a new health psychology. *American Psychologist, 35,* 807–817.

Matarazzo, J. D. (1990). Psychological assessment versus psychological testing: Validation from Binet to the school, clinic, and courtroom. *American Psychologist, 45,* 999–1017.

Matlin, M. W. (1983). *Perception.* Boston: Allyn & Bacon.

Matsumoto, D. (1987). The role of facial response in the experience of emotion: More methodological problems and a meta-analysis. *Journal of Personality and Social Psychology, 52,* 769–774.

Matthews, K. A. (1982). Psychological perspectives on the Type A behavior pattern. *Psychological Bulletin, 91,* 293–323.

Matthews, K. A. (1988). Coronary heart disease and Type A behavior: Update on an alternative to the Booth-Kewley and Friedman (1987) quantitative review. *Psychological Bulletin, 104,* 373–380.

Matthies, H. (1989). Neurobiological aspects of learning and memory. *Annual Review of Psychology, 40,* 381–404.

Mattson, S. N., Barron, S., & Riley, E. P. (1988). The behavioral effects of prenatal alcohol exposure. In K. Kuriyama, A. Takada, & H. Ishii (Eds.), *Biomedical and social aspects of alcohol and alcoholism.* Tokyo: Elsevier.

Mayer, R. E. (1983). *Thinking, problem solving, cognition.* San Francisco: Freeman.

Mayer, W. (1983). Alcohol abuse and alcoholism. *American Psychologist, 38,* 1116–1121.

Mayo, E. (1933). *The human problems of an industrial civilization.* Cambridge, MA: Harvard University Press.

McCann, I. L., & Holmes, D. S. (1984). Influence of aerobic exercise on depression. *Journal of Personality and Social Psychology, 46,* 1142–1147.

McCarley, R. W., & Hoffmann, E. (1981). REM sleep, dreams, and the activation-synthesis hypothesis. *American Journal of Psychiatry, 138,* 904–912.

McCarthy, B. W., Ryan, M., & Johnson, F. (1975). *Sexual awareness.* San Francisco: Boyd & Fraser.

McClelland, D. C. (1958). Risk-taking in children with high and low need for achievement. In J. W. Atkinson (Ed.), *Motives in fantasy, action, and society.* New York: Van Nostrand Reinhold.

McClelland, D. C. (1982). The need for power, sympathetic activation, and illness. *Motivation and Emotion, 6,* 31–41.

McClelland, D. C. (1985). *Human motivation.* Glenview, IL: Scott, Foresman.

McClelland, D. C., Atkinson, J. W., Clark, R. A., & Lowell, E. L. (1953). *The achievement motive.* Englewood Cliffs, NJ: Prentice-Hall.

McClelland, D. C., & Winter, D. G. (1969). *Motivating economic development.* New York: Free Press.

McClintock, M. K. (1971). Menstrual synchrony and suppression. *Nature, 229,* 244–245.

McClintock, M. K. (1979). Estrous synchrony and its mediation by airborne chemical communication. *Hormones and Behavior, 10,* 264.

McCloskey, M., & Egeth, H. (1983). Eyewitness identification: What can a psychologist tell a jury? *American Psychologist, 38,* 550–563.

McCloskey, M., & Glucksberg, S. (1979). Decision processes in verifying category membership statements: Implications for the models of semantic memory. *Cognitive Psychology, 11,* 1–37.

McCloskey, M., Wible, C., & Cohen, N. J. (1988). Is there a special flashbulb-memory mechanism? *Journal of Experimental Psychology: General, 117,* 171–181.

McCloskey, M., & Zaragoza, M. (1985). Misleading postevent information and memory for events: Arguments and evidence against memory impairment hypotheses. *Journal of Experimental Psychology: General, 114,* 1–16.

McConnell, P. S., Boerr, G. J., Romijn, H. J., van de Poll, N. E., & Carner, M. A. (Eds.). *Adaptive capabilities of the nervous system.* New York: Elsevier.

McCormick, D. A., Clark, G. A., Lavond, D. G., & Thompson, R. F. (1982). Initial localization of the memory trace for a basic form of learning. *Proceeding, National Academy of Sciences, 79,* 2731–2735.

McCrae R. R., & Costa, P. T. (1984). *Emerging lives, enduring dispositions: Personality in adulthood.* Boston: Little, Brown.

McCrae, R. R., & Costa, P. T. (1986). Clinical assessment can benefit from recent advances in personality psychology. *American Psychologist, 41,* 1001–1002.

McCrae, R. R., & Costa, P.T. (1987). Validation of the five-factor model of personality across instruments and observers. *Journal of Personality and Social Psychology, 52,* 81–90.

McDougall, W. (1908). *An introduction to social psychology.* London: Methuen.

McGaugh, J. L. (1983). Hormonal influences on memory. *Annual Review of Psychology, 34,* 297–323.

McGee, M. G. (1979). Human spatial abilities: Psychometric studies and environmental, genetic, hormonal, and neurological influences. *Psychological Bulletin, 86,* 889–918.

McGinnis, J. M. (1985). Recent history of federal initiatives in prevention policy. *American Psychologist, 40,* 205–212.

McGlynn, T. J. & Metcalf, H. L. (1989). Diagnosis and treatment of anxiety disorders: A physician's handbook. *American Psychiatric Press,* 80.

McGraw, K. O. (1987). *Developmental psychology.* San Diego: Harcourt Brace Jovanovich.

McGuire, W. J. (1985). Attitudes and attitude change. In G. Lindzey & E. Aronson (Eds.), *Handbook of social psychology.* New York: Random House.

McKim, W. A. (1986). *Drugs and behavior.* Englewood Cliffs, NJ: Prentice-Hall.

McNaughton, B. L., & Morris, R. G. M. (1987). Hippocampal synaptic enhancement and information storage within a distributed memory system. *Trends in Neuroscience, 10,* 408–415.

McNeil, D. (1970). *The acquisition of language: The study of developmental psycholinguistics.* New York: HarperCollins.

Medin, D. L. (1989). Concepts and concept structure. *American Psychologist, 44,* 1469–1481.

Mednick, M. T. S. (1979). The new psychology of women: A feminist analysis. In J. E. Gullahorn (Ed.), *Psychology and women: In transition.* New York: Wiley.

Meer, J. (1986). The reason of age. *Psychology Today, 20,* 60–64.

Meichenbaum, D. (1977). *Cognitive-behavior modification: An integrative approach.* New York: Plenum.

Meichenbaum, D., & Turk, D. C. (1987). *Facilitating treatment adherence.* New York: Plenum.

Meilman, P. W. (1979). Cross-sectional age changes in ego identity status during adolescence. *Developmental Psychology, 15,* 230–231.

Meltzoff, A. N., & Moore, M. K. (1977). Imitation of facial and manual gestures by human neonates. *Science, 198,* 75–78.

Melzack, R. (1973). *The puzzle of pain.* Baltimore: Penguin Books.

Melzack, R., & Wall, P. D. (1965). Pain mechanisms: A new theory. *Science, 150,* 971–979.

Meredith, N. (1986). Testing the talking cure. *Science 86, 7(5),* 30–37.

Merikangas, K. R., Spence, A., & Kupfer, D. J. (1989). Linkage studies of bipolar disorder: Methodological and analytic issues. *Archives of General Psychiatry, 46,* 1137–1141.

Mervis, J. (1986). NIMH data points the way to effective treatment. *APA Monitor, 17,* 1, 13.

Metcalfe, J., & Wiebe, D. (1987). Intuition and insight and non-insight problem solving. *Memory and Cognition, 15,* 238–246.

Michael, J. L. (1985) Behavior analysis: A radical perspective. In B. L. Hammonds, (Ed.), *Psychology and learning.* Washington, DC: American Psychological Association.

Middlemist, R. D., & Peterson, R. B. (1976). Test of equity theory by controlling for comparison of workers' efforts. *Organizational Behavior and Human Performance, 15,* 335–354.

Milgram, S. (1963). Behavioral studies of obedience. *Journal of Abnormal and Social Psychology, 67,* 371–378.

Milgram, S. (1965). Some conditions of obedience and disobedience to authority. *Human Relations, 18,* 57–76.

Milgram, S. (1970). The experience of living in cities. *Science, 167,* 1461–1468.

Milgram, S. (1974). *Obedience to authority.* New York: HarperCollins.

Milgram, S. (1977). *The individual in a social world.* Reading, MA: Addison-Wesley.

Miller, B. C., & Sollie, D. L. (1980). Normal stress during the transition to parenthood. *Family Relations, 29,* 459–465.

Miller, D. T., & McFarland, C. (1987). Pluralistic ignorance: When similarity is interpreted as dissimilarity. *Journal of Personality and Social Psychology, 53,* 298–305.

Miller, D. T., & Ross, M. (1975). Self-serving biases in the attribution of causality: Fact or fiction? *Psychological Bulletin, 82,* 213–225.

Miller, G. A. (1956). The magical number seven plus or minus two: Some limits on our capacity for processing information. *Psychological Review, 63,* 81–96.

Miller, G. A., Galanter, E., & Pribram, K. H. (1960). *Plans and the structure of behavior.* New York: Holt, Rinehart and Winston.

Miller, J. G. (1984). Culture and the development of everyday social explanation. *Journal of Personality and Social Psychology, 46,* 961–978.

Miller, N. E. (1944). Experimental studies of conflict. In J. M. Hunt (Ed.), *Personality and the behavior disorders.* New York: Ronald Press.

Miller, N. E. (1959). Liberalization of basic S-R concepts: Extensions to conflict behavior, motivation, and social learning. In S. Koch (Ed.), *Psychology: A study of a science* (Vol. 2.). New York: McGraw-Hill.

Miller, N. E. (1983). Behavioral medicine: Symbiosis between laboratory and clinic. *Annual Review of Psychology, 34,* 1–31.

Miller, R. C., & Berman, J. S. (1983). The efficacy of cognitive behavior therapies: A quantitative review of the research evidence. *Psychological Bulletin, 94,* 39–53.

Miller, R. R., & Spear, N. E. (Eds.). (1985). *Information processing in animals: Conditioned inhibition*. Hillsdale, NJ: Erlbaum.

Millstein, S. G. (1989). Adolescent health: Challenges for behavioral scientists. *American Psychologist, 44,* 837–842.

Milner, B. (1959). The memory deficit in bilateral hippocampal lesions. *Psychiatric Research Reports, 11,* 43–52.

Milner, B. (1965). Memory disturbances after bilateral hippocampal lesions. In B. Milner & S. Glickman (Eds.), *Cognitive processes and the brain*. New York: Van Nostrand Reinhold.

Milner, B., Corkin, S., & Teuber, H. L. (1968). Further analysis of the hippocampal amnesic syndrome: 14-year follow-up study of H. M. *Neuropsychologica, 6,* 215–234.

Minami, H., & Dallenbach, K. M. (1946). The effect of activity upon learning and retention in the cockroach. *American Journal of Psychology, 59,* 682–697.

Minuchin, S., & Fishman, H. C. (1981). *Family therapy techniques*. Cambridge, MA: Harvard University Press.

Mischel, W. (1968). *Personality and assessment*. New York: Wiley.

Mischel, W. (1979). On the interface of cognition and personality. *American Psychologist, 34,* 740–754.

Mischel, W. (1981). *Introduction to personality* (3rd ed.). New York: Holt, Rinehart and Winston.

Mischel, W., & Peake, P. K. (1982). Beyond déja vu in the search for cross-situational consistency. *Psychological Review, 89,* 730–755.

Mishkin, M., & Appenzeller, T. (1987). The anatomy of memory. *Scientific American, 256,* 80–89.

Mobley, W. H. (1977). Intermediate linkages in the relationship between job satisfaction and employee turnover. *Journal of Applied Psychology, 62,* 237–240.

Money, J. (1972). *Man woman/Boy girl*. Baltimore: Johns Hopkins University Press.

Money, J. (1987). Sin, sickness, or status? Homosexual gender identity and psychoneuroendocrinology. *American Psychologist, 42,* 384–399.

Monson, T. C., & Snyder, M. (1977). Actors, observers, and the attribution process. *Journal of Experimental Social Psychology, 13,* 89–111.

Moore, K. L. (1982). *The developing human* (3rd ed.). Philadelphia: Saunders.

Morgan, W. P. (1980). The trait psychology controversy. *Research Quarterly for Exercise and Sport, 51,* 50–76.

Morris, C. W. (1946). *Signs, language, and behavior*. Englewood Cliffs, NJ: Prentice-Hall.

Morrison, D. M. (1985). Adolescent contraceptive behavior: A review. *Psychological Bulletin, 98,* 538–568.

Moruzzi, G. (1975). The sleep-wake cycle. *Reviews of Psychology, 64,* 1–165.

Moruzzi, G., & Magoun, H. W. (1949). Brain stem reticular formation and activation of the EEG. *Electroencephalography and Clinical Neurophysiology, 1,* 455–473.

Moscovici, S., Lage, E., & Naffrechoux, M. (1969). Influences of a consistent minority on the response of a majority in a color perception task. *Sociometry, 32,* 365–380.

Moscovici, S., Mugny, G., & Van Avermaet, E. (1985). *Perspectives on minority influence*. New York: Cambridge University Press.

Mowday, R. T. (1983). Equity theory prediction of behavior in organizations. In R. M. Steers & L. W. Porter (Eds.), *Motivation and work behavior* (3rd ed.). New York: McGraw-Hill.

Muchinsky, P. M. (1987). *Psychology applied to work* (2nd ed.). Homewood, IL: Dorsey Press.

Muchinsky, P. M., & Tuttle, M. L. (1979). Employee turnover: An empirical and methodological assessment. *Journal of Vocational Behavior, 14,* 43–77.

Mulac, A., Incontro, C. R., & James, M. R. (1985). Comparison of gender-linked language effect and sex role stereotypes. *Journal of Personality and Social Psychology, 49,* 1098–1109.

Murdock, B. B. (1974). *Human memory: Theory and data*. New York: Wiley.

Murray, D. J. (1983). *A history of western psychology*. Englewood Cliffs, NJ: Prentice-Hall.

Murray, D. M., Johnson, C. A., Leupker, R. F., & Mittlemark, M. B. (1984). The prevention of cigarette smoking in children: A comparison of four strategies. *Journal of Applied Social Psychology, 14,* 274–288.

Murray, H. A. (1938). *Explorations in personality*. New York: Oxford University Press.

N

Nakazima, S. (1962). A comparative study of the speech developments of Japanese and American English in children. *Studies in Phonology, 2,* 27–39.

Nash, M. (1987). What, if anything, is regressed about hypnotic age regression? *Psychological Bulletin, 102,* 42–52.

Nathan, P. E. (1983). Failures in prevention: Why we can't prevent the devastating effect of alcoholism and drug abuse. *American Psychologist, 38,* 459–467.

National Council on Alcoholism. (1979). *Facts on alcoholism*. New York: Author.

National Institute on Drug Abuse. (1987). *National household survey on drug abuse: Population estimates 1985*. Rockville, MD: Author.

National Institute of Mental Health. (1984). The NIMH epidemiologic catchment area program. *Archives of General Psychiatry, 41,* 931–1011.

National Institutes of Health, Review Panel on Coronary Prone Behavior and Coronary Heart Disease. (1981). Coronary-prone behavior and coronary heart disease: A critical review. *Circulation, 63,* 1199–1215.

Neely, J. H. (1977). Semantic priming and retrieval from lexical memory: Rules of inhibitionless spreading activation and limited capacity attention. *Journal of Experimental Psychology: General, 106,* 226–254.

Nemeth, C. (1986). Differential contributions of majority and minority influence. *Psychological Review, 93,* 23–32.

Neugarten, B. L., & Neugarten, D. A. (1986). Changing meanings of age in the aging society. In A. Piter & L. Bronte (Eds.), *Our aging society: Paradox and promise*. New York: Norton.

Neugarten, B. L., & Neugarten, D. A. (1989). Policy issues in an aging society. In M. Storandt & G. R. VandenBos (Eds.), *The adult years: Continuity and change*. Washington, DC: American Psychological Association.

Newby, R. W. (1987). Contextual areas in item recognition following verbal discrimination learning. *Journal of General Psychology, 114,* 281–287.

Newcomb, M. D., & Bentler, P. M. (1989). Substance abuse among children and teenagers. *American Psychologist, 44,* 242–248.

Newcomb, N., & Dubas, J. S. (1987). Individual differences in cognitive ability: Are they related to timing of puberty? In R. M. Lerner & T. T. Foch (Eds.), *Biological-psychosocial interactions in early adolescence: A life-span approach*. Hillsdale, NJ: Erlbaum.

Newell, A., Shaw, J. C., & Simon, H. A. (1962). The process of creative thinking. In H. E. Gruber, G. Terrell, & M. Wertheimer (Eds.), *Contemporary approaches to creative thinking*. New York: Atherton Press.

Newell, A., & Simon, H. A. (1972). *Human problem solving*. Englewood Cliffs, NJ: Prentice-Hall.

Newman, B. M. & Newman, P. R. (1984). *Development through life: A psychosocial approach*. Homewood, IL: Dorsey Press.

Nickerson, R. S., & Adams, M. J. (1979). Long-term memory for a common object. *Cognitive Psychology, 11,* 287–307.

Nicol, S. E., & Gottesman, I. I. (1983). Clues to the genetics and neurobiology of schizophrenia. *American Scientist, 71,* 398–404.

Nisbett, R. E. (1972). Hunger, obesity, and the ventromedial hypothalamus. *Psychological Review, 79,* 433–453.

Norcross, J. C. (1986). *Handbook of eclectic psychotherapy.* New York: Brunner/Mazel.

Norman, G. R., Brooks, L. R., & Allen, S. W. (1989). Recall by expert medical practitioners and novices as a record of processing attention. *Journal of Experimental Psychology: Learning, Memory, and Cognition, 15,* 1166–1174.

Noyes, R., Reich, J., Christiansen, J., Suelzer, M., Pfohl, B., & Coryell, W. A. (1990). Outcome of panic disorder. *Archives of General Psychiatry, 47,* 809–818.

O

Oden, G. C. (1987). Concept, knowledge, and thought. *Annual Review of Psychology, 38,* 203–227.

Oden, M. H. (1968). The fulfillment of promise: 40-year follow-up of the Terman gifted group. *Genetic Psychology Monographs, 77*(1), 3–93.

Oetting, E. R., & Beauvais, F. (1990). Adolescent drug use: Findings of national and local surveys. *Journal of Consulting and Clinical Psychology, 58,* 385–394.

Offer, D., & Offer, J. (1975). *From teenage to young manhood: A psychological study.* New York: Basic Books.

Offermann, L. R., & Gowing, M. K. (1990). Organizations of the future: Changes and challenges. *American Psychologist, 45,* 95–108.

Offord, D. R., Boyle, M. H., Szatmari, P., Rae-Grant, N. I., Links, P. S., et al. (1987). Ontario child health study. *Archives of General Psychiatry, 44,* 832–836.

Ogilvie, B. C., & Howe, M. A. (1984). Beating slumps at their game. *Psychology Today, 18,* 28–32.

Oller, D. K. (1981). Infant vocalization. In R. E. Stark (Ed.), *Language behavior in infancy and early childhood.* New York: Elsevier.

Olton, D. S. (1978). Characteristics of spatial memory. In S. H. Hule, H. F. Fowler, & W. K. Honig (Eds.), *Cognitive processes in animal behavior.* Hillsdale, NJ: Erlbaum.

Olton, D. S. (1979). Mazes, maps, and memory. *American Psychologist, 34,* 583–596.

Olton, D. S., & Samuelson, R. J. (1976) Remembrance of places passed: Spatial memory in rats. *Journal of Experimental Psychology: Animal Behavior Processes, 2,* 96–116.

Orne, M. (1969). Demand characteristics and the concept of quasi-controls. In R. Rosenthal & R. Rosnow (Eds.), *Artifact in behavioral research.* New York: Academic Press.

Ortony, A. (1987). Is guilt an emotion? *Cognition and Emotion, 1,* 283–298.

Ortony, A., Clore, G. L., & Collins, A. (1988). *The cognitive structure of emotions.* New York: Cambridge University Press.

Ortony, A., & Turner, T. J. (1990). What's basic about basic emotions? *Psychological Review, 97,* 315–331.

Oswald, I. (1980). Sleep as a restorative process: Human clues. In P. S. McConnell, G. J. Boer, H. J. Romjin, N. E. van de Poll, & M. A. Carner (Eds.), *Adaptive capabilities of the nervous system.* New York: Elsevier.

P

Paivio, A. (1971). *Imagery and verbal processes.* New York: Holt, Rinehart and Winston.

Paivio, A. (1986). *Mental representations: A dual coding approach.* New York: Oxford University Press.

Paludi, M. A., & Gullo, D. F. (1986). The effect of sex labels on adults' knowledge of infant development. *Sex Roles, 16,* 19–30.

Parke, R. D. (1981). *Fathers.* Cambridge, MA: Harvard University Press.

Parker, E. S., Birnbaum, I. M., & Noble, E. P. (1976) Alcohol and memory: Storage and state dependency. *Journal of Verbal Learning and Verbal Behavior, 15,* 691–702.

Pauly, I. B., & Goldstein, S. G. (1970, November). Prevalence of significant sexual problems in medical practice. *Medical Aspects of Human Sexuality,* pp. 48–63.

Pavlov, I. (1927). *Conditioned reflexes.* New York: Oxford University Press.

Pavlov, I. (1928). *Lectures on conditioned reflexes: The higher nervous activity of animals* (Vol. I) (H. Gantt, Trans.). London: Lawrence and Wishart.

Pavlovich, M., & Greene, B. F. (1984). A self-instructional manual for installing low-cost/no-cost weatherization material: Experimental validation with scouts. *Journal of Applied Behavior Analysis, 17,* 105–109.

Pearce, J. M., & Hall, G. (1980). A model for Pavlovian conditioning: Variations in the effectiveness of conditioned but not of unconditioned stimuli. *Psychological Review, 87,* 532–552.

Penfield, W. (1975). *The mystery of the mind.* Princeton, NJ: Princeton University Press.

Penfield, W., & Rasmussen, T. (1950). *The cerebral cortex of man.* New York: Macmillan.

Peters, W. A. (1971). *A class divided.* Garden City, NY: Doubleday.

Peterson, A. C. (1988). Adolescent development. *Annual Review of Psychology, 39,* 583–607.

Peterson, A. C., & Ebata, A. T. (1987). Developmental transitions and adolescent problem behavior: Implications for prevention and intervention. In K. Hurrelmann (Ed.), *Social prevention and intervention,* New York: de Gruyter.

Peterson, L. R., & Peterson, M. J. (1959). Short-term retention of individual verbal items. *Journal of Experimental Psychology, 58,* 193–198.

Petty, R. E., & Cacioppo, J. T. (1981). *Attitudes and persuasion: Classic and contemporary approaches.* Dubuque, IA: Brown.

Petty, R. E., & Cacioppo, J. T. (1986). The elaboration likelihood model of persuasion. *Advances in Experimental Social Psychology, 19,* 123–205.

Petty, R. E., Harkins, S. G., Williams, K. D., & Latané, B. (1977). The effects of group size on cognitive effort and evaluation. *Personality and Social Psychology Bulletin, 3,* 579–582.

Petty, R. E., Ostrow, T. M., & Brock, T. C. (1981). *Cognitive responses in persuasive communications: A text in attitude change.* Hillsdale, NJ: Erlbaum.

Petty, R. E., Wells, G. L., & Brock, T. C. (1976). Distraction can enhance or reduce yielding to propaganda: Thought disruption versus effort justification. *Journal of Personality and Social Psychology, 34,* 874–884.

Piaget, J. (1932/1948). *The moral judgment of the child.* New York: Free Press.

Piaget, J. (1954). *The construction of reality in the child.* New York: Basic Books.

Piaget, J. (1967). *Six psychological studies.* New York: Random House.

Pinel, J. P. J. (1990). *Biopsychology.* Boston: Allyn & Bacon.

Piner, K. E., & Kahle, L. R. (1984). Adapting to the stigmatizing label of mental illness: Foregone but not forgotten. *Journal of Personality and Social Psychology, 47,* 805–811.

Pines, M. (1983, November). Can a rock walk? *Psychology Today,* pp. 46–54.

Pittman, T. S., & Heller, J. F. (1987). Social motivation. *Annual Review of Psychology, 38,* 461–489.

Plawin, P., & Suied, M. (1988, December). Can't get no satisfaction. *Changing Times*, p. 106.

Plomin, R. (1989). Environment and genes: Determinants of behavior. *American Psychologist, 44,* 105–111.

Plomin, R. (1990). The role of inheritance in behavior. *Science, 248,* 183–188.

Plomin, R., DeFries, J. C., & Fulker, D. W. (1988). *Nature and nurture during infancy and early childhood.* New York: Cambridge University Press.

Plutchik, R. (1980a). *Emotion: A psychoevolutionary synthesis.* New York: HarperCollins.

Plutchik, R. (1980b, February). A language for the emotions. *Psychology Today,* pp. 68–78.

Pola, J., & Martin, L. (1977). Eye movements following autokinesis. *Bulletin of the Psychonomic Society, 10,* 397–398.

Pollio, H. R. (1974). *The psychology of symbolic activity.* Reading, MA: Addison-Wesley.

Pope, H. G., & Hudson, J. I. (1986). Antidepressant therapy for bulimia: Current status: *Journal of Clinical Psychiatry, 47,* 339–345.

Pope, H. G., Hudson, J. I., Jonas, J. M., & Yurgelun-Todd, D. (1985). Antidepressant treatment of bulimia: A two-year follow-up study. *Journal of Clinical Psychopharmacology, 5,* 320–327.

Porter, L. W., & Steers, R. M. (1973). Organizational, work, and personal factors in employee turnover and absenteeism. *Psychological Bulletin, 80,* 151–176.

Posner, M. I. (1973). *Cognition: An introduction.* Glenview, IL: Scott, Foresman and Company.

Posner, M. I., & Keele, S. W. (1968). On the genesis of abstract ideas. *Journal of Experimental Psychology, 83,* 304–308.

Posner, M. I. & Keele, S. W. (1970). Retention of abstract ideas. *Journal of Experimental Psychology, 83,* 304–308.

Post, R.B., & Leibowitz, H. W. (1985). A revised analysis of the role of efference in motion perception. *Perception, 14,* 631–643.

Powers, S. I., Hauser, S. T., & Kilner, L. A. (1989). Adolescent mental health. *American Psychologist, 44,* 200–208.

Pressley, M., Levin, J. R., & Delaney, H. D. (1982). The mnemonic keyword method. *Review of Educational Research, 52,* 61–91.

Pyle, R. L., Mitchell, J. E., & Eckert, E. D. (1981). Bulimia: Report of 34 cases. *Journal of Clinical Psychiatry, 42,* 60–64.

Q

Quayle, D. (1983). American productivity: The devastating effect of alcoholism and drug abuse. *American Psychologist, 38,* 454–458.

R

Rachlin, H. C., & Green, L. (1972). Commitment, choice, and self-control. *Journal of the Experimental Analysis of Behavior, 17,* 15–22.

Rafaeli, A. (1985). Quality circles and employee attitudes. *Personnel Psychology, 38,* 603–615.

Rahe, R. H., & Arthur, R. J. (1978). Life changes and illness reports. In K. E. Gunderson & R. H. Rahe (Eds.), *Life stress and illness.* Springfield, IL: Thomas.

Rappaport, D. (1951). The autonomy of the ego. *Bulletin of the Menninger Clinic, 15,* 113–123.

Rechtschaffen, A. (1971). The control of sleep. In W. A. Hunt (Ed.), *Human behavior and its control.* Cambridge, MA: Schenkman.

Reich, J. (1986). The epidemiology of anxiety. *The Journal of Nervous and Mental Disease, 174,* 129–136.

Reilly, R. R., & Chao, G. T. (1982). Validity and fairness of some alternative employee selection procedures. *Personnel Psychology, 35,* 1–62.

Reinke, B. J., Ellicott, A. M., Harris, R. L., & Hancock, E. (1985). Timing of psychological changes in women's lives. *Human Development, 28,* 259–280.

Reis, H. T., Nezlek, J., & Wheeler, L. (1980). Physical attractiveness in social interaction. *Journal of Personality and Social Psychology, 38,* 604–617.

Reis, S. M. (1989). Reflections on policy affecting the education of gifted and talented students: Past and future perspectives. *American Psychologist, 44,* 399–408.

Rescorla, R. A. (1968). Probability of shock in the presence and absence of CS in fear conditioning. *Journal of Comparative and Physiological Psychology, 66,* 1–5.

Rescorla, R. A. (1987). A Pavlovian analysis of goal-directed behavior. *American Psychologist, 42,* 119–129.

Rescorla, R. A. (1988). Pavlovian conditioning: It's not what you think it is. *American Psychologist, 43,* 151–160.

Rescorla, R. A., & Wagner, A. R. (1972). A theory of Pavlovian conditioning: Variations in the effectiveness of reinforcement and nonreinforcement. In A. H. Black & W. F. Prokasy (Eds.), *Classical conditioning II: Current research and theory.* Englewood Cliffs, NJ: Prentice-Hall.

Resnick, L. B. (1987). *Education and learning to think.* Washington, DC: National Academy Press.

Rest, J. R. (1983). Morality. In J. Flavell & E. Markman (Eds.), *Handbook of child development: Cognitive development.* New York: Wiley.

Reveley, M. A., Reveley, A. M., & Baldy, R. (1987). Left cerebral hemisphere hypodensity in discordant schizophrenic twins. *Archives of General Psychiatry, 44,* 624–632.

Revelle, W. (1987). Personality and motivation: Sources of inefficiency in cognitive performance. *Journal of Reseach in Personality, 21,* 436–452.

Revulsky, S. H. (1985). The general process approach to animal learning. In T. D. Johnston & A. T. Petrewicz (Eds.), *Issues in the ecological study of learning.* Hillsdale, NJ: Erlbaum.

Revulsky, S. H., & Garcia, J. (1970). Learned associations over long delays. In G. H. Bower & J. T. Spence (Eds.), *The psychology of learning and motivation* (Vol. 4). New York: Academic Press.

Reynolds, A. G., & Flagg, P. W. (1983). *Cognitive psychology.* Boston: Little, Brown.

Rhodes, S. R. (1983). Age-related differences in work attitudes and behaviors: A review and conceptual analysis. *Psychological bulletin, 93,* 328–367.

Rice, B. (1984). Square holes for quality circles. *Psychology Today, 18,* 17.

Rice, M. L. (1989). Children's language acquisition. *American Psychologist, 44,* 149–156.

Richardson-Klavehn, A., & Bjork, R. A. (1988). Measures of memory. *Annual Review of Psychology, 39,* 475–543.

Riggio, R. E. (1990). *Introduction to industrial/organizational psychology.* Glenview, IL: Scott, Foresman.

Robins, L. N., Helzer, J. E., Weissman, M. M., Orvaschel, H., Guenberg, E., Burke, J. D., & Regier, D. A. (1984). Lifetime prevalence of specific psychiatric disorders in three sites. *Archives of General Psychiatry, 41,* 949–958.

Roche, A. F., & Davila, G. H. (1972). Late adolescent growth in stature. *Pediatrics, 50,* 874–880.

Rock, I. (1986). The description and analysis of object and event perception. In K. R. Boff, L. Kaufman, & J. P. Thomas (Eds.), *Handbook of perception and human performance: Vol. 2. Cognitive processes and performance.* New York: Wiley.

Rodin, J. (1981). Current status of the internal-external hypothesis of obesity: What went wrong? *American Psychologist, 36,* 361–372.

Rodin, J., & Salovey, P. (1989). Health psychology. *Annual Review of Psychology, 40,* 533–579.

Roediger, H. L. (1990). Implicit memory: Retention without remembering. *American Psychologist, 45,* 1043–1056.

Rook, K. S. (1987). Social support versus companionship: Effects of life stress, loneliness, and evaluation by others. *Journal of Personality and Social Psychology, 52,* 1132–1147.

Rosch, E. (1973). Natural categories. *Cognitive Psychology, 4,* 328–350.

Rosch, E. (1975). Cognitive representations of semantic categories. *Journal of Experimental Psychology: General, 104,* 192–253.

Rosch, E. (1978). Principles of categorization. In E. Rosch & B. B. Lloyd (Eds.), *Cognition and categorization.* Hillsdale, NJ: Erlbaum.

Rosch, E., & Mervis, C. B. (1975). Family resemblances: Studies in the internal structure of categories. *Cognitive Psychology, 7,* 573–605.

Rose, A. S., & Blank, M. (1974). The potency of context in children's cognition: An illustration through conservation. *Child Development, 45,* 499–502.

Rosenbaum, M. E. (1986). The repulsion hypothesis: On the nondevelopment of relationships. *Journal of Personality and Social Psychology, 51,* 1156–1166.

Rosenman, R. H., Brand, R. J., Jenkins, C. D., Friedman, M., Strauss, R., & Wurm, M. (1975). Coronary heart disease in the Western Collaborative Group Study: Final follow-up experience of 8½ years. *Journal of the American Medical Association, 233,* 872–877.

Rosenman, R. H., Friedman, M., Strauss, R., Wurm, M., Kositcheck, R., Hahn, W., & Werthessen, N. T. (1964). A predictive study of coronary heart disease. *Journal of the American Medical Association, 189,* 15–22.

Rosenthal, D. (1970). *Genetics of psychopathology.* New York: McGraw-Hill.

Rosenzweig, M. R., Bennett, E. L., & Diamond, M. C. (1972). Brain changes in response to experiences. *Scientific American, 226,* 22–29.

Ross, C. A., Heber, S., Norton, G. R., & Anderson, G. (1989). Differences between multiple personality disorder and other diagnostic groups on structured interview. *Journal of Nervous and Mental Disorders, 177,* 487–491.

Ross, L. D. (1977). The intuitive psychologist and his shortcomings: Distortions in the attributional process. In L. Berkowitz (Ed.), *Advances in experimental social psychology* (Vol. 10). New York: Academic Press.

Rossi, A. S. (1980). Aging and parenthood in the middle years. In P. B. Baltes & O. G. Brim, Jr. (Eds.), *Lifespan development and behavior* (Vol. III). New York: Academic Press.

Roth, E. M., & Shoben, E. J. (1983). The effect of context on the structure of categories. *Cognitive Psychology, 15,* 346–378.

Roth M., & Argyle, N. Anxiety, panic and phobic disorders: An overview, *Journal of Psychiatric Research, 22,* (Suppl. 1), 33–54.

Rotter, J. B. (1982). *The development and application of social learning theory: Selected papers.* New York: Praeger.

Rotter, J. B. (1990). Internal versus external control of reinforcement. *American Psychologist, 45,* 489–493.

Rotton, J., & Frey, J. (1985). Air pollution, weather, and violent crimes: Concomitant analysis of archival data. *Journal of Personality and Social Psychology, 49,* 1207–1220.

Rowe, D. C. (1981). Environmental and genetic influences on dimensions of perceived parenting: A twin study. *Developmental Psychology, 17,* 203–208.

Rowe, D. C. (1987). Resolving the person-situation debate. *American Psychologist, 42,* 218–227.

Rowe, J. W., & Kahn, R. L. (1987). Human aging: Usual and successful. *Science, 237,* 143–149.

Roy, A., DeJong, J., & Linnoila, M. (1989). Extraversion in pathological gamblers. *Archives of General Psychiatry, 46,* 679–684.

Rubin, Z. (1973). *Liking and loving: An invitation to social psychology.* New York: Holt, Rinehard and Winston.

Rutter, M., Graham, P., Chadwick, O., & Yule, W. (1976). Adolescent turmoil: Fact or fiction? *Journal of Child Psychology and Psychiatry, 17,* 35–56.

Ryan, E. D., & Kovacic, C. R. (1966). Pain tolerance and athletic participation. *Journal of Personality and Social Psychology, 22,* 383–390.

S

Saal, F. E., & Knight, P. A. (1988). *Industrial/organizational psychology.* Monterey, CA: Brooks/Cole.

Sackeim, H. A. (1985). The case for ECT. *Psychology Today, 19,* 36–40.

Sackett, P. R., Schmitt, N., Tenopyr, M. L., Kehoe, J., & Zedeck, S. (1985). Commentary on forty questions about validity generalization and meta-analysis. *Personnel Psychology, 38,* 697–798.

Sadalla, E. K., & Oxley, D. (1984). The perception of room size: The rectangularity illusion. *Environment and Behavior, 16,* 394–405.

Saegert, S., & Winkel, G. H. (1990). Environmental psychology. *Annual Review of Psychology, 41,* 441–477.

Safer, M. (1980). Attributing evil to the subject, not the situation: Student reactions to Milgram's film on obedience. *Personality and Social Psychology Bulletin, 6,* 205–209.

Saghir, M. T., & Robins, E. (1973). *Male and female homosexuality: A comprehensive investigation.* Baltimore: Johns Hopkins University Press.

Salthouse, T. A. (1989). Age-related changes in basic cognitive processes. In M. Storandt & G. R. VandenBos (Eds.), *The adult years: Continuity and change.* Washington, DC: American Psychological Association.

Samuelson, F. J. B. (1980). Watson's Little Albert, Cyril Burt's twins, and the need for a critical science. *American Psychologist, 35,* 619–625.

Sands, L. P., Terry, H., & Meredith, W. (1989). Change and stability in adult intellectual functioning assessed by Wechsler item responses. *Psychology and Aging, 4,* 79–87.

Satir, V. (1967). *Conjoint family therapy.* Palo Also, CA: Science and Behavior Books.

Sauser, W. J., & York, C. M. (1978). Sex differences in job satisfaction: A reexamination. *Personnel Psychology, 31,* 537–547.

Scarr, S., & Weinberg, R. A. (1976). IQ test performance of black children adopted by white families. *American Psychologist, 31,* 726–739.

Scarr, S., & Weinberg, R. A. (1978, April). Attitudes, interests, and IQ. *Human Nature,* pp. 29–36.

Schacter, D. L. (1987). Implicit memory: History and current status. *Journal of Experimental Psychology: Learning, Memory, and Cognition. 13,* 501–518.

Schacter, S. (1971). Some extraordinary facts about obese humans and rats. *American Psychologist, 26,* 129–144.

Schacter, S., & Gross, L. P. (1968). Manipulated time and eating behavior. *Journal of Personality and Social Psychology, 10,* 98–106.

Schacter, S., & Singer, J. (1962). Cognitive, social, and physiological determinants of emotional states. *Psychological Review, 69,* 379–399.

Schacter, S., & Singer, J. (1979). Comments on the Maslach and Marshall-Zimbardo experiments. *Journal of Personality and Social Psychology, 37,* 989–995.

Schaie, K. W. (1974). Translations in gerontology—from lab to life: Intellectual functioning. *American Psychologist, 29,* 802–807.

Schaie, K. W. (1983). The Seattle Longitudinal Study: A 21-year exploration of psychometric intelligence in adulthood. In K. W. Schaie (Ed.), *Longitudinal studies of adult psychological development.* New York: Guilford.

Schaie, K. W., & Strother, C. R. (1968) A cross-sequential study of age changes in cognitive behavior. *Psychological Bulletin, 70,* 671–680.

Schaie, K. W., & Willis, S. L. (1986). *Adult development and aging* (2nd ed.). Boston: Little, Brown.

Scharf, B. (1978). Loudness, In E. C. Carterette & M. P. Friedman (Eds.), *Handbook of perception.* New York: Academic Press.

Schau, C. G., Kahn, L., Diepold, J. H., & Cherry, F. (1980). The relationships of parental expectations and preschool children's verbal sex typing to their sex-typed toy play behavior. *Child Development, 51,* 266–270.

Scheerer, M. (1963). Problem solving. *Scientific American, 208,* 118–128.

Schiffman, H. R. (1990). *Sensation and perception: An integrated approach.* New York: Wiley.

Schmitt, N., & Robertson, I. (1990). Personnel selection. *Annual Review of Psychology, 41,* 289–319.

Schneider, A. M., & Tarshis, B. (1986). *Physiological Psychology.* New York: Random House.

Schroeder, S. R., Schroeder, C. S., & Landesman, S. (1987). Psychological services in educational settings to persons with mental retardation. *American Psychologist, 42,* 805–808.

Schultz, D. P., & Schultz, S. E. (1990). *Psychology and industry today.* New York: Macmillan.

Schultz, R., & Alderman, D. (1974). Clinical research on the "stages of dying." *Omega, 5,* 137–144.

Schultz, R., & Decker, S. (1985). Long-term adjustment to physical disability: The role of social support, perceived control and self-blame. *Journal of Personality and Social Psychology, 48,* 1162–1172.

Schwartz, B. (1984). *Psychology of learning and behavior* (2nd ed.). New York: Norton.

Schwartz, P. (1983). Length of day-care attendance and attachment behavior in eighteen-month-old infants. *Child Development, 54,* 1073–1078.

Scott, K. G., & Carran, D. T. (1987). The epidemiology and prevention of mental retardation. *American Psychologist, 42,* 801–804.

Scott, M. D., & Pelliccioni, L., Jr. (1982). *Don't choke: How athletes become winners.* Englewood Cliffs, NJ: Prentice-Hall.

Sears, P. S., & Barbee, A. H. (1977). Career and life satisfaction among Terman's gifted women. In J. Stanley et al. (Eds.), *The gifted and the creative: Fifty year perspective.* Baltimore: Johns Hopkins University Press.

Seligman, M. E. P. (1975). *Helplessness: On depression development and death.* San Francisco: Freeman.

Selkoe, D. J. (1990). Deciphering Alzheimer's disease: The amyloid precursor protein yields new clues. *Science, 248,* 1058.

Selye, H. (1976). *The stress of life.* New York: McGraw-Hill.

Shadish, W. R. (1984). Policy research: Lessons from the implementation of deinstitutionalization. *American Psychologist, 39,* 725–738.

Shaffer, M. (1982). *Life after stress.* New York: Knopf.

Shapiro, D. H., Jr. (1985). Clinical use of meditation as a self-regulation strategy: Comment on Holmes's conclusions and implications. *American Psychologist, 40,* 719–722.

Shaver, P., Hazan, C., & Bradshaw, D. (1988). Love as attachment: The integration of three behavioral systems. In R. J. Sternberg & M. L. Barnes (Eds.), *The psychology of love.* New Haven, CT: Yale University Press.

Shedler, J., & Block, J. (1990). Adolescent drug use and psychological health: A longitudinal study. *American Psychologist, 45,* 612–630.

Sheer, D. E. (Ed.). 1961. *Electrical stimulation of the brain.* Austin: University of Texas Press.

Shekelle, B., Hulley, S. B., Neaton, J. D., Billings, J. H., Borhani, N. O., et al. (1985). The MRFIT behavior pattern study II: Type A behavior and the incidence of coronary heart disease. *American Journal of Epidemiology, 122,* 559–570.

Sherif, M. (1936). *The psychology of social norms.* New York: HarperCollins.

Sherman, S. J., Judd, C. M., & Park, B. (1989). Social cognition. *Annual Review of Psychology, 40,* 281–326.

Shertzer, B. (1985). *Career planning* (3rd ed.). Boston: Houghton Mifflin.

Shimamura, A. P. (1986). Priming effects in amnesia: Evidence for a dissociable memory function. *Quarterly Journal of Experimental Psychology, 38A,* 619–644.

Shipley, T. (1961). *Classics in psychology.* New York: Philosophical Library.

Shippee, G., & Gregory, W. L. (1982). Public commitment and energy conservation. *American Journal of Community Psychology, 10,* 81–93.

Shotland, R. L. (1985). When bystanders just stand by. *Psychology Today, 19,* 50–55.

Shulman, H. G. (1971). Similarity effects in short-term memory. *Psychological Bulletin, 75,* 399–415.

Shulman, H. G. (1972). Semantic confusion errors in short-term memory. *Journal of Verbal Learning and Verbal Behavior, 11,* 221–227.

Siegler, R. S. (1983). Five generalizations about cognitive development. *American Psychologist, 38,* 263–277.

Siegler, R. S. (1989). Mechanisms of cognitive development. *Annual Review of Psychology, 40,* 353–379.

Silverman, L. H. (1976). Psychoanalytic theory. "The reports of my death are greatly exaggerated." *American Psychologist, 31,* 621–637.

Simon, H. A. (1990), Invariants of human behavior. *Annual Review of Psychology, 41,* 1–19.

Sims, E. A. H. (1990). Destiny rides again as twins overeat. *New England Journal of Medicine, 322,* 1522–1523.

Singer, J. L., & Singer, D. G. (1981). *Television; imagination; and aggression: A study of preschoolers.* Hillsdale, NJ: Erlbaum.

Skinner, B. F. (1938). *The behavior of organisms: A behavioral analysis.* Englewood Cliffs, NJ: Prentice-Hall.

Skinner, B. F. (1956). A case history in the scientific method. *American Psychologist, 11,* 221–233.

Skinner, B. F. (1957). *Verbal behavior.* Englewood Cliffs, NJ: Prentice-Hall.

Skinner, B. F. (1983). Intellectual self-management in old age. *American Psychologist, 38,* 239–244.

Skinner, B. F. (1984). *A matter of consequence.* New York: Knopf.

Skinner, B. F. (1987). What ever happened to psychology as the science of behavior? *American Psychologist, 42,* 780–786.

Skinner, B. F. (1989). The origins of cognitive thought. *American Psychologist, 44,* 13–18.

Skinner, B. F. (1990). Can psychology be a science of mind? *American Psychologist, 45,* 1206–1210.

Skolnick, A. (1979). *The intimate environment* (2nd ed.). Boston: Little, Brown.

Slobin, D. I. (1979). *Psycholinguistics.* Glenview, IL: Scott, Foresman.

Small, J. G., Klapper, M. H., Kellams, J. J., Miller, M. J., Milstein, V., Sharpley, P. H., & Small, I. F. (1988). Electroconvulsive treatment compared with lithium in the management of manic states. *Archives of General Psychiatry, 45,* 727–732.

Smith, A., & Stansfield, S. (1986). Aircraft noise exposure, noise sensitivity, and everyday errors. *Environment and Behavior, 18,* 214–226.

Smith, D. (1987). Conditions that facilitate the development of sport imagery training. *The Sport Psychologist, 1,* 237–247.

Smith, M. L., Glass, G. V., & Miller, T. I. (1980). *The benefits of psychotherapy.* Baltimore: Johns Hopkins University Press.

Smith, P. C. (1976). Behavior, results, and organizational effectiveness: The problem of criteria. In M. D. Dunnette (Ed.), *Handbook of industrial and organizational psychology.* Skokie, IL: Rand McNally.

Smith, S. (1979). Remembering in and out of context. *Journal of Experimental Psychology: Human Learning and Memory, 5,* 460–471.

Snarey, J. (1987). A question of morality. *Psychology Today, 21,* 6–8.

Snyder, M. (1974). The self-monitoring of expressive behavior. *Journal of Personality and Social Psychology, 30,* 526–537.

Snyder, S. H. (1980). *Biological aspects of mental disorder.* New York: Oxford University Press.

Snyder, S. H. (1984, November). Medicated minds. *Science 84,* pp. 141–142.

Snyderman, M., & Rothman, S. (1987). Survey of expert opinion on intelligence and aptitude testing. *American Psychologist, 42,* 137–144.

Solomon, R. L. (1980). The opponent-process theory of acquired motivation: The costs of pleasure and the benefits of pain. *American Psychologist, 35,* 691–712.

Solomon, R. L., & Corbit, J. D. (1974). An opponent-process theory of motivation. I. Temporal dynamics of affect. *Psychological Review, 81,* 119–145.

Sorenson, R. C. (1973). *Adolescent sexuality in contemporary America.* New York: Abrams.

Spanos, N. P., & Barber, T. F. X. (1974). Toward convergence in hypnosis research. *American Psychologist, 29,* 500–511.

Spear, N. E., Miller, J. S., & Jagielo, J. A. (1990). Animal learning and memory. *Annual Review of Psychology, 41,* 169–211.

Spearman, C. (1904). "General intelligence" objectively determined and measured. *American Journal of Psychology, 15,* 201–293.

Spence, J. T. (1985). Gender identity and its implications for concepts of masculinity and femininity. In T. Sondregger (Ed.), *Nebraska symposium on motivation* (pp. 59–95). Lincoln: University of Nebraska Press.

Sperling, G. (1960). The information available in brief visual presentation. *Psychological Monographs, 74,* (Whole No. 498).

Sperling, G. (1963). A model for visual memory tasks. *Human Factors, 5,* 19–31.

Sperry, R. (1968). Hemispheric disconnection and unity in conscious awareness. *American Psychologist, 23,* 723–733.

Sperry, R. (1982). Some effects of disconnecting the cerebral hemispheres. *Science, 217,* 1223–1226.

Spitz, H. (1986). *The raising of intelligence: A selected history of attempts to raise retarded intelligence.* Hillsdale, NJ: Erlbaum.

Springer, J. P., & Deutsch, G. (1981). *Left brain, right brain.* San Francisco: Freeman.

Squire, L. R. (1982). The neuropsychology of human memory. *Annual Review of Neuroscience, 5,* 241–273.

Squire, L. R. (1986). Mechanisms of memory. *Science, 232,* 1612–1619.

Squire, L. R. (1987). *Memory and the brain.* New York: Oxford University Press.

Squire, L. R., & Slater, P. C. (1978). Bilateral and unilateral ECT: Effects on verbal and nonverbal memory. *American Journal of Psychiatry, 135,* 1316–1320.

Standing, L. (1973). Learning 10,000 pictures. *Quarterly Journal of Experimental Psychology, 25,* 207–222.

Standing, L., Canezio, J., & Haber, R. N. (1970). Perception and memory for pictures: Single-trial learning 2500 visual stimuli. *Psychonomic Science, 19,* 73–74.

Stapp, J., & Fulcher, R. (1983). The employment of APA members: 1982. *American Psychologist, 38,* 1298–1320.

Stechler, G., & Halton, A. (1982). Prenatal influences on human development. In B. B. Woolman (Ed.), *Handbook of developmental psychology.* Englewood Cliffs, NJ: Prentice-Hall.

Stein, B. A. (1983). *Quality of work life in action: Managing for effectiveness.* New York: American Management Association.

Stenchever, M. A., Williamson, R. A., Leonard, J. Karp, L. E., Ley, B., Shy, K., & Smith, D. (1981). Possible relationship between in utero diethylstibestrol exposure and male infertility. *American Journal of Obstetrics and Gynecology, 140,* 186–193.

Stern, D. (1977). *The first relationship.* Cambridge, MA: Harvard University Press.

Stern, L. (1985). *The structures and strategies of human memory.* Homewood, IL: Dorsey Press.

Sternberg, R. J. (1979). The nature of mental abilities. *American Psychologist, 34,* 214–230.

Sternberg, R. J. (1981). Testing and cognitive psychology. *American Psychologist, 36,* 1181–1189.

Sternberg, R. J. (1985). *Beyond IQ.* New York: Cambridge University Press.

Sternberg, R. J. (1988). *The triarchic mind.* New York: Viking Press.

Stevenson, H. W., Lee, S. Y., & Stigler, J. W. (1986). Mathematics achievement of Chinese, Japanese, and American children. *Science, 231,* 693–696.

Stiles, W. B., Shapiro, D. A., & Elliot, R. (1986). "Are all psychotherapies equivalent?" *American Psychologist, 41,* 165–180.

Stinnett, N., Walters, J., & Kaye, E. (1984). *Relationships in marriage and family* (2nd ed.). New York: Macmillan.

Stokols, D. (1972). On the distinction between density and crowding: Some implications for future research. *Psychological Review, 79,* 275–277.

Stokols, D. (1990). Instrumental and spiritual views of people-environment relations. *American Psychologist, 45,* 641–646.

Stoner, J. A. F. (1961). *A comparison of individual and group decisions involving risk.* Unpublished master's thesis, Massachusetts Institute of Technology, Cambridge, MA.

Storandt, M. (1983). Psychology's response to the graying of America. *American Psychologist, 38,* 323–326.

Strupp, H. H. (1986). Psychotherapy: Research, practice, and public policy (How to avoid dead ends). *American Psychologist, 41,* 120–130.

Strupp, H. H., & Binder, J. L. (1984). *Psychotherapy in a new key.* New York: Guilford.

Stunkard, A. J. (1988). Some perspectives on human obesity: Its causes. *Bulletin of the New York Academy of Medicine, 64,* 902–923.

Stunkard, A. J., Harris, J. R., Pederson, N. L., & McClearn, G. E. (1900). The body-mass index of twins who have been reared apart. *New England Journal of Medicine, 322,* 1483–1487.

Stunkard, A. J., Sørensen, T. I. A., Hanis, C., et al. (1986). An adoption study of human obesity. *New England Journal of Medicine, 314,* 193–198.

Sue, S., & Okazaki, S. (1990). Asian-American educational achievements: A phenomenon in search of an explanation. *American Psychologist 45,* 913–920.

Suinn, R. M. (1980). *Psychology in sports: Methods and applications.* Minneapolis: Burgess.

Suler, J. R. (1985). Meditation and somatic arousal: A comment on Holmes's review. *American Psychologist, 40,* 717.

Suomi, S. J. (1989). Uptight and laid-back monkeys: Continuities and changes during biobehavioral development. Invited Address: American Psychological Society Convention, Alexandria, VA.

Super, D. E. (1985). Coming of age in Middletown. *American Psychologist, 40,* 405–414.

Surwit, R. S., Feinglos, M. N., & Scovern, A. W. (1983). Diabetes and behavior. *American Psychologist, 38,* 255–262.

Swaim, R. C., Oetting, E. R., Edwards, R. W., & Beauvais, F. (1989). Links from emotional distress to adolescent drug use: A path model. *Journal of Consulting and Clinical Psychology, 57,* 227–231.

Swedo, S. E., Rapoport, J. L., Leonard, H., Lenane, M., & Cheslow, D. (1989a). Obsessive-compulsive disorder in children and adolescence. *Archives of General Psychiatry, 46,* 335–341.

Swedo, S. E., Schapiro, M. B., Grady, C. L., Cheslow, D. L., et al. (1989b). Cerebral glucose metabolism in childhood-onset obsessive-compulsive disorder. *Archives of General Psychiatry, 46,* 518–523.

Szasz, T. S. (1960). *The myth of mental illness.* New York: HarperCollins.

Szasz, T. S. (1982). The psychiatric will: A new mechanism for protecting persons against "psychosis" and psychiatry. *American Psychologist 37,* 762–770.

T

Tandon, R., & Greden, J. F. (1989). Cholinergic hyperactivity and negative schizophrenic symptoms. *Archives of General Psychiatry 46,* 745–753.

Tanner, J. M. (1973). Growing up. *Scientific America, 135,* 34–43.

Tanner, J. M. (1981). Growth and maturation during adolescence. *Nutrition Review, 39,* 43–55.

Tanner, J. M., Whitehouse, R. H., & Takaishi, M. (1966). Standards from birth to maturity for height, weight, height velocity, and weight velocity: British children, 1965. *Archives of Diseases in Childhood, 41,* 457–471, 613–635.

Tappert, H. T. (1967). *Luther's work: Vol. 54. Table talk.* Philadelphia: Fortress Press.

Taylor, S. E. (1990). Health psychology: The science and the field. *American Psychologist, 45,* 40–50.

Taylor, W., Pearson, J., Mair, A., & Burns, W. (1965). Study of noise and hearing in jute weaving. *Journal of the Acoustical Society of American, 4,* 144–152.

Tenopyr, M. L. (1981). The realities of employment testing. *American Psychologist, 36,* 1120–1127.

Terenius, L. (1982). Endorphins and modulation of pain. *Advances in Neurology, 33,* 59–64.

Termine, N., Hrynick, T., Kestenbaum, R., Gleitman, H., & Spelke, E. S. (1987). Perceptual completion of surfaces in infancy. *Journal of Experimental Psychology: Perception and Performance, 13,* 524–532.

Tesser, A., & Shaffer, D. R. (1990). Attitudes and attitude change. *Annual Review of Psychology, 41,* 479–523.

Thayer, W. P. (1983). Industrial/organizational psychology: Science and application. In C. J. Scheirer & A. M. Rogers (Eds.), *The G. Stanley Hall lecture series (Vol. 3).* Washington, DC: American Psychological Association.

Thibault, J. W., & Kelley, H. H. (1959). *The social psychology of groups.* New York: Wiley.

Thompson, C. I. (1980). *Controls of eating.* Jamaica, NY: Spectrum.

Thompson, C. P. (1982). Memory for unique personal events: The roommate study. *Memory and Cognition, 10,* 324–332.

Thompson, J. W., & Blaine, J. D. (1987). Use of ECT in the United States in 1975 and 1980. *American Journal of Psychiatry, 144,* 557–562.

Thompson, R. (1969). Localization of the "visual memory system" in the white rat. *Journal of Comparative and Physiological Psychology, 2,* 1–17.

Thompson, R. (1981). Rapid forgetting of spatial habit in rats with hippocampal lesions. *Science, 212,* 959–960.

Thompson, R. (1986). The neurobiology of learning and memory. *Science, 233,* 941–947.

Thorndike, A. L., Hagen, E. P., & Sattler, J. M. (1986). *The Stanford-Binet Intelligence scale, Fourth edition: Technical manual.* Chicago: Riverside.

Thorndike, E. L. (1911). *Animal intelligence.* New York: Macmillan.

Thornton, G. C., III, & Cleveland, J. N. (1990). Developing managerial talent through simulation. *American Psychologist, 45,* 190–199.

Thurstone, L. L. (1938). Primary mental abilities. *Psychometric Monographs* (No. 1).

Tilley, A. J., & Empson, J. A. C. (1978). REM sleep and memory consolidation. *Biological Psychology, 6,* 293–300.

Tobin-Richards, M., Boxer, A., & Peterson, A. C. (1984). The psychological impact of pubertal change: Sex differences in perceptions of self during early adolescence. In J. Brooks-Gunn & A. C. Peterson (Eds.), *Girls at puberty: Biological, psychological, and social perspectives.* New York: Plenum.

Tohen, M., Waternaux, C. M., & Tsuang, M. T. (1990). Outcome in mania. *Archives of General Psychiatry, 47,* 1106–1111.

Tolman, C. W. (1969) Social feeding in domestic chicks: Effects of food deprivation of non-feeding companions. *Psychonomic Science, 15,* 234.

Tolman, E. C. (1932). *Purposive behaviorism in animals and men.* Englewood Cliffs, NJ: Prentice-Hall.

Tolman, E. C., & Honzik, C. H. (1930). Introduction and removal of reward and maze performance in rats. *University of California Publication in Psychology, 4,* 257–275.

Tomkins, S. S. (1962). *Affect, imagery, consciousness: Vol. I. The positive affects.* New York: Springer.

Torrey, T. W., & Feduccia, A. (1979). *Morphogenesis of the vertebrates.* New York: Wiley.

Triplett, N. (1898). The dynamogenic factors in pacemaking and competition. *American Journal of Psychology, 9,* 507–533.

Tucker, D. M. (1981). Lateral brain function, emotion, and conceptualization. *Psychological Bulletin, 89,* 19–46.

Tulving, E. (1962). Subjective organization in free recall of "unrelated" words. *Psychological Review, 69,* 344–354.

Tulving, E. (1972). Episodic and semantic memory. In E. Tulving & W. Donaldson (Eds.), *Organization of memory.* New York: Academic Press.

Tulving, E. (1985). How many memory systems are there? *American Psychologist, 40,* 385–398.

Tulving, E. (1986). What kind of a hypothesis is the distinction between episodic and semantic memory? *Journal of Experimental Psychology: Learning, Memory, and Cognition, 12,* 307–311.

Tulving, E., & Thompson, D. M. (1973). Encoding specificity and retrieval processes in episodic memory. *Journal of Experimental Psychology: Learning, Memory, and Cognition, 8,* 336–342.

Turkington, C. (1985). Computer unlocks secrets in folds, functions of brain. *APA Monitor, 16,* 12–13.

Turner, J. S., & Helms, D. B. (1987). *Contemporary adulthood.* New York: Holt, Rinehart, and Winston.

Tuttle, T. C. (1983). Organizational productivity: A challenge for psychologists. *American Psychologist, 38,* 479–486.

Tversky, A., & Kahneman, D. (1974). Judgment under uncertainty: Heuristics and biases. *Science, 125,* 1124–1131.

Tyrer, P., & Shawcross, C. (1988). Monoamine oxidase inhibitors in anxiety disorders. *Journal of Psychiatric Research, 22* (Suppl. 1), 87–98.

U

Underwood, B. J. (1957). Interference and forgetting. *Psychological Review, 64,* 49–60.

V

Valenstein, E. S. (1980). *The psychosurgery debate: Scientific, legal, and ethical perspectives.* San Francisco: Freeman.

Valenstein, E. S. (1986). *Great and desperate cures.* New York: Basic Books.

Valliant, G. E., & Valliant, C. O. (1990). Natural history of male psychological health, XII: A 45-year study of predictors of successful aging at age 65. *American Journal of Psychiatry, 147,* 31–37.

VandenBos, G. R. (1986). Psychotherapy research: A special issue. *American Psychologist, 41,* 111–112.

VanderPlate, C., Aral, S. O., & Magder, L. (1988). The relationship among genital herpes simplex virus, stress, and social support. *Health Psychology, 7,* 159–168.

Varca, P. E. (1980). An analysis of home and away game performance of male college basketball teams. *Journal of Sport Psychology, 2,* 245–257.

Vaughn, B. E., & Langlois, J. H. (1983). Physical attractiveness as a correlate of peer status and social competence in preschool children. *Developmental Psychology, 19,* 561–567.

Ventura, J., Nuechterlein, K. H., Lukoff, D., & Hardesty, J. P. (1989). A prospective study of stressful life events and schizophrenic relapse. *Journal of Abnormal Psychology, 98,* 407–411.

Verillo, R. T. (1975). Cutaneous sensation. In B. Scharf (Ed.), *Experimental sensory psychology.* Glenview, IL: Scott, Foresman.

Vernon, P. E. (1960). *The structure of human abilities* (rev. ed.). London: Methuen.

Vernon, P. E. (1979). *Intelligence: Heredity and environment.* San Fransisco: Freeman.

Vinacke, W. E. (1974). *The psychology of thinking* (2nd ed.). New York: McGraw-Hill.

Vitz, P. C. (1990). The use of stories in moral development. *American Psychologist, 45,* 709–720.

Voevodsky, J. (1974). Evaluations of a deceleration warning light for reducing rear-end automobile collisions. *Journal of Applied Psychology, 59,* 270–273.

Vokey, J. R., & Read, J. D. (1985). Subliminal messages: Between the devil and the media. *American Psychologist, 40,* 1231–1239.

Vroom, V. (1964). *Work and motivation.* New York: Wiley.

W

Wallace, P. (1977). Individual discrimination of humans by odor. *Physiology and Behavior, 19,* 577–579.

Wallace, R. K., & Benson, H. (1972). The physiology of meditation. *Scientific American, 226,* 85–90.

Wallach, H. (1987). Perceiving a stable environment when one moves. *Annual Review of Psychology, 38,* 1–28.

Wallas, G. (1926). *The art of thought.* New York: Harcourt Brace Jovanovich.

Walsh, B. T., Kissileff, H. R., Cassidy, S. M., & Dantzic, S. (1989). Eating behavior of women with bulimia. *Archives of General Psychiatry, 46,* 54–58.

Walster, E., Aronson, V., Abrahams, D., & Rottman, L. (1966). Importance of physical attractivness in dating behavior. *Journal of Personality and Social Psychology, 4,* 508–516.

Walster, E., & Festinger, L. (1962). The effectiveness of "over-heard" and persuasive communications. *Journal of Abnormal and Social Psychology, 65,* 395–402.

Walster, E., & Walster, G. W. (1969). The matching hypothesis. *Journal of Personality and Social Psychology, 6,* 248–253.

Walster, E., Walster, G. W., & Berschied, E. (1978). *Equity: Theory and research.* Boston: Allyn & Bacon.

Walters, G. C., & Grusec, J. E. (1977). *Punishment.* San Francisco: Freeman.

Wamboldt, F. S., & Reiss, D. (1989). Defining a family heritage and a new relationship identity: Two central tasks in the making of a marriage. *Family Process, 28,* 317–335.

Warrington, E. K., & Weiskrantz, L. (1968). New method of testing long-term retention with special reference to amnesic patients. *Nature, 217,* 972–974.

Warrington, E. K., & Weiskrantz, L. (1970). Amnesic syndrome: Consolidation or retrieval? *Nature, 228,* 629–630.

Watkins, L. R., & Mayer, D. J. (1982). Organization of endogenous opiate and nonopiate pain control systems. *Science, 216,* 1185–1192.

Watkins, M. J. (1990). Mediationism and the obfuscation of memory. *American Psychologist, 45,* 328–335.

Watson, C. J. (1981). An evaluation of some aspects of the Steers and Rhodes model of employee attendance. *Journal of Applied Psychology, 66,* 385–389.

Watson, J. B. (1919). *Psychology from the standpoint of a behaviorist.* Philadelphia: Lippincott.

Watson, J. B. (1925). *Behaviorism.* New York: Norton.

Watson, J. B. (1926). What is behaviorism? *Harper's Monthly Magazine, 152,* 723–729.

Watson, J. B., & Raynor, R. (1920). Conditioned emotional reactions. *Journal of Experimental Psychology, 3,* 1–14.

Watson, M. W., & Amgott-Kwan, T. (1984). Development of family-role concepts in school-age children. *Developmental Psychology, 20,* 953–959.

Waugh, N. C., & Norman, D. A. (1965). Primary memory. *Psychological Review, 72,* 89–104.

Weaver, C. N. (1980). Job satisfaction in the United States in the 1970s. *Journal of Applied Psychology, 65,* 364–367.

Webb, W. B. (1974). Sleep as an adaptive process. *Perceptual and Motor Skills, 38,* 1023–1027.

Webb, W. B. (1975). *Sleep, the gentle tyrant.* Englewood Cliffs, NJ: Prentice-Hall.

Webb, W. B. (1981). The return of consciousness. In L. T. Benjamin (Ed.), *The G. Stanley Hall Lecture Series* (Vol. I). Washington, DC: American Psychological Association.

Webb, W. B., & Cartwright, R. D. (1978). Sleep and dreams. *Annual Review of Psychology, 29,* 223–252.

Wechsler, D. (1958). *The measurement and appraisal of adult intelligence* (4th ed.). Baltimore: Williams & Wilkins.

Wechsler, D. (1975). Intelligence defined and undefined: A relativistic reappraisal. *American Psychologist, 30,* 135–139.

Wechsler, D. (1981). *Manual for the Wechsler Adult Intelligence Scale—Revised.* New York: The Psychological Corporation.

Weekley, J. A., & Gier, J. A. (1987). Reliability and validity of the situational interview for a sales position. *Jornal of Applied Psychology, 72,* 484–487.

Weil, A. T., Zinberg, N., & Nelson, J. M. (1968). Clinical and psychological effects of marijuana in man. *Science, 162,* 1234–1242.

Weinberg, R. R. (1989). Intelligence and IQ: Landmark issues and great debates. *American Psychologist, 44,* 98–104.

Weiner, B. (1985). An attributional theory of achievement motivation and emotion. *Psychological Review, 92,* 548–573.

Weisberg, R. W. (1986). *Creativity: Genius and other myths.* San Francisco: Freeman.

Weissman, M. M. (1988). The epidemiology of anxiety disorders: Rates, risks and familial patterns. *Journal of Psychiatric Research, 22,* (Suppl. 1), 99–114.

Weissman, M. M., Klerman, G. L., Markowitz, J. S., & Ouellette, R. (1989). Suicidal ideation and suicide attempts in panic disorders and attacks. *The New England Journal of Medicine, 321,* 1209–1214.

Welch, W. W., Anderson, R. E., & Harris, L. J. (1982). The effects of schooling on mathematics achievement. *American Educational Research Journal, 19,* 145–153.

Weldon, E., & Gargano, G. M. (1988). Cognitive loading: The effects of accountability and shared responsibility on cognitive effort. *Personality and Social Psychology Bulletin, 14,* 159–171.

Wender, P. H., Rosenthal, D., Kety, S. S., Schulsinger, F., & Welner, J. (1974). Crossfostering: A research strategy for clarifying the role of genetic and experiential factors in the etiology of schizophrenia. *Archives of General Psychiatry, 30,* 121–128.

Werner, H., & Kaplan, E. (1950). Development of word meaning through verbal context: An experimental study. *Journal of Psychology, 29,* 251–257.

Wertheimer, M. (1961). Psychomotor coordination of auditory and visual space at birth. *Science, 134,* 1692.

West, M. A. (1985). Meditation and somatic arousal reduction. *American Psychologist, 40,* 717–719.

White, R. W. (1959). Motivation reconsidered: The concept of competence. *Psychological Review, 66,* 297–333.

White, R. W. (1974). Strategies of adaptation: An attempt at a systematic description. In G. V. Coelheo, D. A. Hamburg, & J. E. Adams (Eds.), *Coping and adaptation.* New York: Basic Books.

Whitehurst, G. (1982). Language development. In B. Wolman (Ed.), *Handbook of developmental psychology.* Englewood Cliffs, NJ: Prentice-Hall.

Wickens, D. D. (1973). Some characteristics of word encoding. *Memory and Cognition, 1,* 485–490.

Wiesner, W. H., & Cronshaw, S. F. (1988). A meta-analytic investigation of the impact of interview format and degree of structure on the validity of the employment interview. *Occupational Psychology, 61,* 275–290.

Wilcox, D., & Hager, R. (1980). Toward realistic expectations for orgasmic response in women. *Journal of Sex Research, 16,* 162–179.

Wilkes, J. (1986). Conversation with Ernest R. Hilgard: A study in hypnosis. *Psychology Today, 20*(1), 23–27.

Williams, K., Harkins, S., & Latané, B. (1981). Identifiability as a deterrent to social loafing: Two cheering experiments. *Journal of Personality and Social Psychology, 40,* 303–311.

Williams, K., Nida, S. A., Baca, L. D., & Latané, B. (1989). Social loafing and swimming: Effects of identifiability of individual and relay performance of intercollegiate swimmers. *Basic and Applied Social Psychology, 10,* 73–82.

Wilson, G. T. (1982). Adult disorders. In G. T. Wilson & C. M. Franks (Eds.), *Contemporary behavior therapy: Conceptual and empirical foundations.* New York: Guilford Press.

Wimer, R. E., & Wimer, C. C. (1985). Animal behavior genetics: A search for the biological foundations of behavior. *Annual Review of Psychology, 36,* 171–218.

Winett, R. A., Leckliter, I. N., Chinn, D. E., Stahl, B., & Love, S. Q. (1985). Effects of television modeling on residential energy conservation. *Journal of Applied Behavior Analysis, 18,* 33–44.

Winter, D. G. (1987). Leader appeal, leader performance, and the motive profiles of leaders and followers: A study of American presidents and elections. *Journal of Personality and Social Psychology, 52,* 196–202.

Winter, D. G. (1988). The power motive in women—and men. *Journal of Personality and Social Psychology, 54,* 510–519.

Winter, D. G., & Stewart, A. J. (1978). The power motive. In H. London & J. E. Exner (Eds.), *Dimensions of personality.* New York: Wiley.

Winters, K. C., Weintraub, S., & Neale, J. M. (1981). Validity of MMPI code types in identifying DSM-III schizophrenics. *Journal of Consulting and Clinical Psychology, 49,* 486–487.

Winton, W. M. (1987). Do introductory textbooks present the Yerkes-Dodson Law correctly? *American Psychologist, 42,* 202–203.

Witmer, J. F., & Geller, E. S. (1976). Facilitating paper recycling: Effects of prompts, raffles, and contests. *Journal of Applied Behavior Analysis, 9,* 315–322.

Wolff, D. (1971). *Love between women.* New York: HarperCollins.

Wollen, K. A., Weber, A., & Lowry, D. H. (1972). Bizarreness versus interaction of mental images as determinants of learning. *Cognitive Psychology, 3,* 518–523.

Wolpe, J. (1958). *Psychotherapy by reciprocal inhibition.* Stanford, CA: Stanford University Press.

Wolpe, J. (1969). Basic principles and practices of behavior therapy of neuroses. *American Journal of Psychiatry, 125,* 1242–1247.

Wolpe, J. (1981). Behavior therapy versus psychoanalysis. *American Psychologist, 36,* 159–164.

Wolpe, J. (1982). *The practice of behavior therapy* (3rd ed.). New York: Pergamon Press.

Wood, C. (1986). The hostile heart. *Psychology Today, 20,* 10–12.

Woodworth, R. S., & Schlosberg, H. (1954). *Experimental Psychology.* New York: Holt, Rinehart and Winston.

Wright, L. (1988). The Type A behavior pattern and coronary artery disease. *American Psychologist, 43,* 2–14.

Wurtman, R. J. (1985). Alzheimer's disease. *Scientific American, 247,* 62–74.

Wysowski, D. K., & Baum, C. (1989). Antipsychotic drug use in the United States, 1976–1985. *Archives of General Psychiatry, 46,* 929–932.

Y

Yager, E. G. (1981). The QC explosion. *Training and Development Journal, 35,* 98–105.

Yaniv, I., & Meyer, D. E. (1987). Activation and metacognition of inaccessible stored information: Potential basis for incubation effects in problem solving. *Journal of Experimental Psychology: Learning, Memory, and Cognition, 13,* 187–205.

Yates, A. (1989). Current perspectives on the eating disorders: 1 History, psychological and biological aspects. *Journal of the American Academy of Child and Adolescent Psychiatry, 28,* 813–828.

Yates, A. (1990). Current perspectives on eating disorders: II Treatment, outcome, and research directions. *Journal of the American Academy of Child and Adolescent Psychiatry, 29,* 1–9.

Yates, F. A. (1966). *The art of memory.* Chicago: University of Chicago Press.

Yerkes, R. M., & Dodson, J. D. (1908). The relation of strength of stimulus to rapidity of habit-formation. *Journal of Comparative Neurology and Psychology, 18,* 459–482.

Z

Zadeh, L. (1965), Fuzzy sets. *Information and Control, 8,* 338–353.

Zajonc, R. B. (1965). Social facilitation. *Science, 149,* 269–274.

Zajonc, R. B. (1968). Attitudinal effects of mere exposure. *Journal of Personality and Social Psychology,* Monograph Suppl. *9,* 1–27.

Zajonc, R. B. (1980). Feeling and thinking: Preferences need no inferences. *American Psychologist, 35,* 151–175.

NAME INDEX

SUBJECT INDEX

Abnormal psychology, 555–593; anxiety disorders, 561–566; classification in, 557–561; defining abnormality and, 556–557, 575; dissociative disorders, 569–571, 575; mood disorders, 581–585, 594; organic mental disorders, 578–581, 594; personality disorders, 571–574, 575; schizophrenia, 23, 55, 585–593, 594; somatoform disorders, 566–568, 575; treatment in. See Treatment
Abortion, 428
Absolute threshold, 97–98, 114–116, 120, 124
Acceptance, of dying, 437
Accommodation, 109, 153–154, 163, 402
Acetylcholine (ACh), 64, 73, 267, 581
Achievement motivation (nAch), 517–519, 523
Acquired immune deficiency syndrome (AIDS), 486–487, 494
Acquisition, in conditioning, 196, 211, 217, 223–226, 240
ACT (American College Testing Program), 361
Action potential, 60, 73
Actor-observer bias, 651, 659
ACT theory, 263–264, 269
Acupuncture, 137
Adaptive Behavior Inventory, 380
Adaptive Behavior Scale, 380
Addiction, drug, 179, 394
Adolescence, 405, 418–429, 434; defined, 418–419, 439; drug use in, 425–427, 439; eating disorders in, 515–516; egocentrism of, 424–425, 439; family therapy and, 628; identity formation in, 423–424, 439; physical changes during, 419–422, 439; puberty, 418, 420–422, 427, 439, 476, 509; sexuality in, 422, 427–429, 439
Adoption studies, 55, 73, 368–369, 383
Adrenal glands, 476
Adulthood, 429–438
Advertising, 201, 500, 643, 644, 647
Advised consent, 46, 48
Affect, 6
Affective disorders. See Mood disorders
Affiliation motivation, 520, 523
Affirmation rules, 300, 318
Age: IQ and, 356, 372–374, 383; of puberty, 421–422
Aggression, 549, 552, 711; gender differences in, 491; social learning theory and, 236–237
Agism, 435
Agoraphobia, 562, 563
AIDS. See Acquired immune deficiency syndrome
Alcohol, 182–183, 393, 425–427, 478, 566, 578–579
Algorithms, 326–327, 338
All-or-none principle, 60–61, 73
Alpha activity, 167–168
Alzheimer's disease, 579–581, 594

Ambiguous figure, 152
Ambiguous stimuli, 467–469
American Association of Mental Deficiency (AAMD), 379–380
American Psychiatric Association, 180, 558–559
American Psychological Association (APA), 18, 44–45, 679
Amnesia, 266, 269, 274–275, 293; psychogenic, 569, 575
Amnestic syndrome, 579
Amphetamines, 181, 578–579, 591–592
Amygdala, 82, 91
Analgesics, 183
Androgens, 475–476, 493
Androgyny, 488–489, 494
Anger, at dying, 437
Anorexia nervosa, 514–516, 523
Antianxiety drugs, 607, 611
Antidepressant drugs, 606–607, 611
Antidepressant medications, 604
Antipsychotic drugs, 604–605, 611
Antisocial personality disorder, 572
Anxiety, 448–449, 549–550, 560–561
Anxiety disorders, 561–566; antianxiety drugs and, 607, 611; generalized, 563, 575; obsessive-compulsive, 564–565, 575; panic, 562–563, 575; phobic, 204–205, 211, 561–562, 575; posttraumatic stress disorder (PTSD), 566, 567, 575
Aphrodisiac, 478
Apparent motion, 156–157
Applied behavior analysis (ABA), 713–714
Applied psychology: environment and, 24–25, 704–714, 717; health and, 19, 24, 27, 701–704, 717; industrial-organizational (I/O), 19, 27, 679–696, 697; sports and, 715–716, 717
Approach-approach conflicts, 542–543, 552
Approach-avoidance conflicts, 543–544, 552
Aptitude tests, 361, 363
Aqueous humor, 109, 120
Armed Forces Qualification Test (AFQT), 361
Army Alpha Test, 360
Army Beta Test, 360
Army General Classification Test (AGCT), 361
Arousal, 504–505, 522, 673; athletes and, 715–716; motivation and, 499–501, 504–505; sexual, 477–478
Assessment centers, 684, 697
Assimilation, 401–402
Association: in conditioning, 208–209; meaningfulness and, 278–279, 293
Association areas, of brain, 85, 87–88
Athletes, and psychology, 715–716, 717
Atonia, 171–172
Attachment, 411–412, 415, 653, 659
Attitudes, 640–648, 658; changing, 645–648; forming, 643–644, 658; structure of, 641; usefulness of, 642–643, 658
Attractiveness, 655–656, 659

Attribution error, 666
Attribution theory, 649–651, 659
Audience inhibition, 669, 676
Audition. See Hearing
Authority, obedience to, 664–667, 676
Autokinetic effect, 157, 163, 662
Autonomic nervous system (ANS), 65–68, 73, 534–535, 551
Autonomy versus shame and doubt, 408, 415
Availability heuristic, 332, 338
Aversion therapy, 623–624, 633
Avoidance-avoidance conflicts, 543, 552
Avoidant personality disorder, 573
Axons, 57–59, 62, 73
Axon terminals, 58, 62, 73

Babbling, 313–314, 319
Barbiturates, 184
Bargaining, and death, 437
Basal ganglia, 82–83, 91
Baseline design, 43, 48
Base rate of responding, 216–218
Basilar membrane, 128, 138
Behavior, 6
Behavioral-learning approach, 449–451, 458, 470, 471
Behavioral observations, 462–463, 471
Behaviorism, 13–14, 26, 449–451, 458
Behavior of Organisms, The (Skinner), 230
Behavior therapy, 621–625, 633
Bem Sex Role Inventory (BSRI), 488–489
Benzodiazepines, 607, 611
Bias, 43–44; in attribution theory, 649–651
Binet-Simon test, 17
Bipolar cells, 109–110, 120
Bipolar mood disorders, 583–585, 602, 603, 605, 606–607
Blind spot, 111
Blocking, 207
Body language, 491, 537
Brain. See also Central nervous system: Alzheimer's disease and, 580, 594; cerebral cortex, 84–90, 265, 529, 536, 551; damage to, 68–69, 73, 81, 82, 265–266; electrical stimulation of, 69–70, 73, 602–604, 611; emotions and, 529, 535–536, 551; hemispheres, 85, 88–90, 91; lobes, 84–88, 91; lower centers of, 79–84, 265–266; observation of, 70–72; recording electrical activity of, 70, 167–174, 187; schizophrenia and, 592; surgery and, 69, 73, 265–266, 601–602, 611
Brain activity, 70, 167–174, 187
Brain stem, 79–80, 91
Brightness, 103–104, 120
British empiricists, 9–10
Bulimia, 514–516, 523
Bystander intervention, 667–671, 676

Caffeine, 180, 578–579
California Personality Inventory (CPI), 466–467